lonely planet

Ireland

THIS EDITION WRITTEN AND RESEARCHED BY

Fionn Davenport, Damian Harper, Catherine Le Nevez, Ryan Ver Berkmoes, Neil Wilson

PLAN YOUR TRIP

DESIGN PICS/THE IRISH IMAGE COLLECTION/GETTY IMAGES ©
COUNTY KILKENNY P192

GARETH MCCORMACK/GETTY IMAGES ©
CONNEMARA P382

ON THE ROAD

Contents

ON THE ROAD

Contents

UNDERSTAND

SURVIVAL GUIDE

SPECIAL FEATURES

Welcome to Ireland

A small country with a big reputation, helped along by a breathtaking ancient landscape and fascinating, friendly people, whose lyrical nature is expressed in the warmth of their welcome.

A Scenic Wonderland

Don't think the Ireland of postcards is just a two-dimensional fiction: it very much exists. You'll find it along the peninsulas of the southwest, in the brooding loneliness of Connemara and the dramatic wildness of County Donegal. It can be uncovered in the lakelands of Counties Leitrim and Roscommon and the undulating hills of the sunny southeast ('sunny' of course being a relative term). Brave the raging Atlantic on a crossing to Skellig Michael or spend a summer's evening in the yard of a thatched-cottage pub and you'll experience an Ireland that has changed little in generations.

A Rich Historical Heritage

History presents itself everywhere: from the breathtaking monuments of prehistoric Ireland at Brú na Bóinne, Slea Head in Kerry and Carrowmore in Sligo, to the fabulous ruins of Ireland's rich monastic past at Glendalough and Clonmacnoise. More recent history is visible in the *Titanic* museum in Cobh and the forbidding Kilmainham Gaol in Dublin. And there's history so young that it's still considered the present, best experienced on a black-taxi tour of West Belfast or an examination of Derry's colourful political murals.

A Cultural Well

You will be overwhelmed by the cultural choices on offer in Ireland – see a play by one of the theatrical greats in Dublin, experience a traditional music 'session' in a west Ireland pub or attend a rock gig in a Limerick saloon. The Irish summer is awash with festivals celebrating everything from flowers in bloom to high literature.

A Warm Welcome

On the plane and along your travels you might hear it said: *tá fáilte romhat* (taw fall-cha row-at) – 'You're very welcome'. Or, more famously, *céad míle fáilte* – a hundred thousand welcomes. Irish friendliness is a tired cliché, an over-simplification of a character that is infinitely complex, but the Irish are nonetheless warm and welcoming. Wherever you meet them there's a good chance a conversation will begin, pleasantries will be exchanged and, should you be a stranger in town, the offer of a helping hand extended. But, lest you think this is merely an act of unfettered altruism, rest assured that the comfort they seek is actually their own, for the Irish cannot be at ease in the company of those who aren't. A hundred thousand welcomes. It seems excessive, but in Ireland, excess is encouraged, so long as it's practised in moderation.

Why I Love Ireland

By Fionn Davenport, Writer

There's an unvarnished informality about Ireland that I cherish, based on an implied assumption that life is a tangled, confusing struggle that all of us – irrespective of who we are and how we worship – have to negotiate to the best of our abilities. We're all in this together, come hell or high water, so we may as well be civil and share a moment when we can.

For more about our writers, see page 704

Above: Connemara (p382), County Galway

Ireland

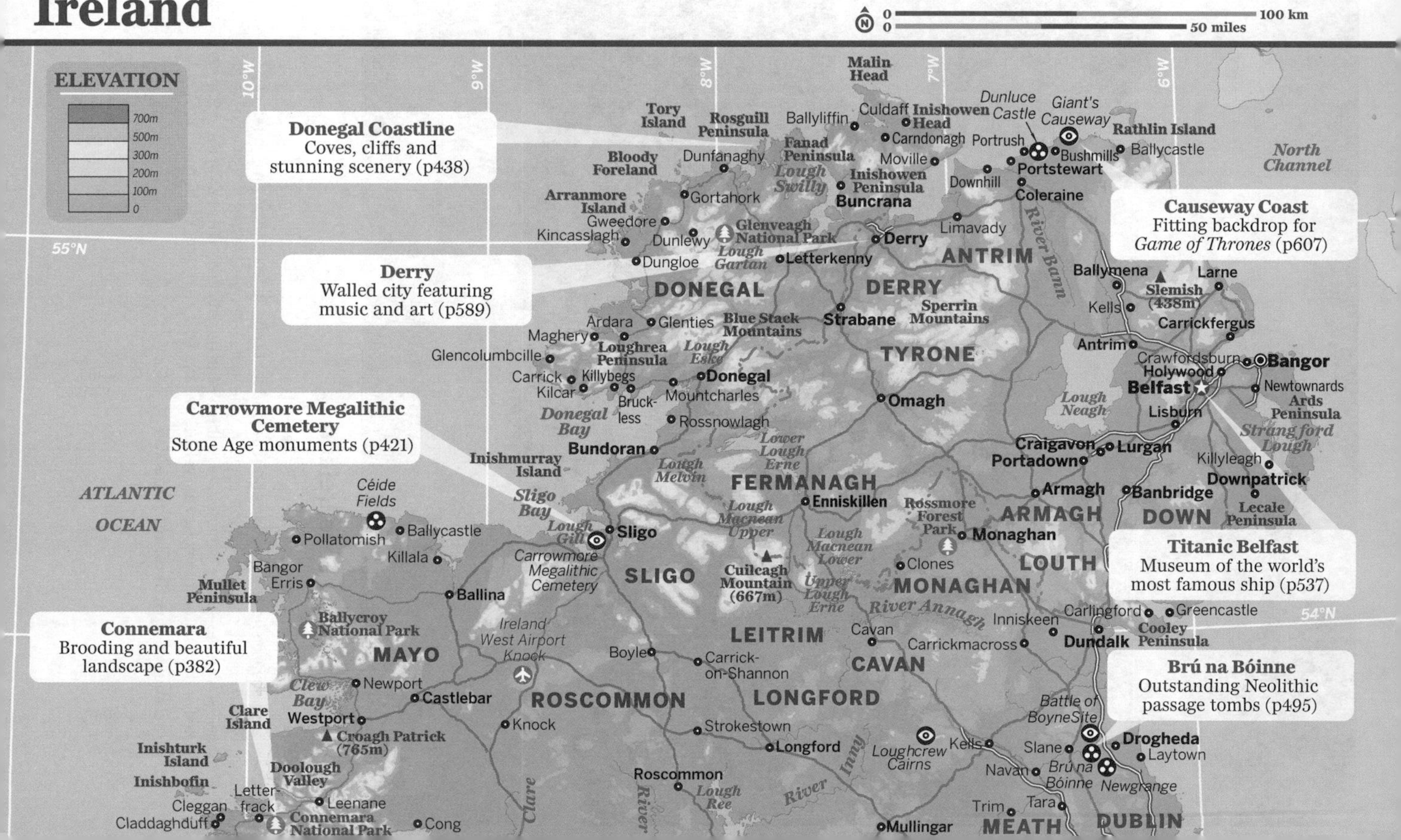
0 100 km
0 50 miles
ELEVATION
700m
500m
300m
200m
100m
0
10°W
9°W
8°W
7°W
6°W
55°N
54°N
Donegal Coastline
Coves, cliffs and stunning scenery (p438)
Derry
Walled city featuring music and art (p589)
Carrowmore Megalithic Cemetery
Stone Age monuments (p421)
Connemara
Brooding and beautiful landscape (p382)
Causeway Coast
Fitting backdrop for Game of Thrones (p607)
Titanic Belfast
Museum of the world's most famous ship (p537)
Brú na Bóinne
Outstanding Neolithic passage tombs (p495)
ATLANTIC OCEAN
North Channel
Malin Head
Tory Island
Rosguill Peninsula
Ballyliffin
Culdaff
Inishowen Head
Dunluce Castle
Giant's Causeway
Rathlin Island
Bloody Foreland
Dunfanaghy
Fanad Peninsula
Carndonagh
Portrush
Bushmills
Ballycastle
Lough Swilly
Moville
Portstewart
Arranmore Island
Gortahork
Inishowen Peninsula
Downhill
Buncrana
Coleraine
Gweedore
Glenveagh National Park
Limavady
Kincasslagh
Dunlewy
Derry
Lough Gartan
River Bann
Dungloe
Letterkenny
ANTRIM
DONEGAL
DERRY
Ballymena
Larne
Slemish (438m)
Kells
Strabane
Sperrin Mountains
Ardara
Glenties
Blue Stack Mountains
Carrickfergus
Maghery
Loughrea Peninsula
Lough Eske
TYRONE
Antrim
Glencolumbcille
Crawfordsburn
Bangor
Holywood
Carrick
Killybegs
Donegal
Belfast
Newtownards
Kilcar
Bruck-less
Mountcharles
Omagh
Lough Neagh
Ards Peninsula
Donegal Bay
Rossnowlagh
Lisburn
Strangford Lough
Bundoran
Lower Lough Erne
Craigavon
Lurgan
Inishmurray Island
Lough Melvin
Portadown
Killyleagh
FERMANAGH
Downpatrick
Céide Fields
Armagh
Banbridge
Sligo Bay
Enniskillen
Rossmore Forest Park
Lecale Peninsula
Lough Macnean Upper
ARMAGH
DOWN
Ballycastle
Lough Gill
Sligo
Monaghan
Pollatomish
Carrowmore Megalithic Cemetery
Killala
Lough Macnean Lower
Clones
LOUTH
Bangor Erris
Culleagh Mountain (667m)
SLIGO
Upper Lough Erne
MONAGHAN
Mullet Peninsula
Ballina
River Annagh
Carlingford
Greencastle
Ireland West Airport Knock
Inniskeen
Cooley Peninsula
Ballycroy National Park
LEITRIM
Cavan
Dundalk
MAYO
Boyle
Carrick-on-Shannon
Carrickmacross
CAVAN
Clew Bay
Newport
Castlebar
ROSCOMMON
LONGFORD
Battle of Boyne Site
Clare Island
Westport
Knock
Strokestown
Drogheda
Croagh Patrick (765m)
Longford
Loughcrew Cairns
Kells
Slane
Laytown
Inishturk Island
Inny
Doolough Valley
Roscommon
Brú na Bóinne
Inishbofin
Navan
Newgrange
Letterfrack
Leenane
Lough Ree
River
Tara
Cleggan
Trim
Claddaghduff
Connemara National Park
Cong
Clare
River
Mullingar
MEATH
DUBLIN

Galway Festivals
City that epitomises Irish hedonism (p368)
Clare Coast
Iconic cliffs and surf beaches (p331)
Dingle Town
Beautiful, Irish-speaking fishing town (p281)
Ring of Kerry
Ireland's most famous panoramic loop (p267)
Cork
Superb restaurants in Ireland's second city (p210)
Rock of Cashel
Breathtaking ancient fortress atop rock (p310)
Kilkenny
A regal medieval city (p193)
Glendalough
Ancient monastic site in stunning setting (p140)
Dublin
Pulsating and manageable capital city (p60)
GALWAY
WESTMEATH
KILDARE
OFFALY
LAOIS
CARLOW
KILKENNY
WICKLOW
WEXFORD
TIPPERARY
CLARE
LIMERICK
KERRY
CORK
WATERFORD
DUBLIN
Howth
Dalkey
Maynooth
Straffan
Newbridge
Kildare
Wicklow
Mizen Head
Glendalough
Wicklow Mountains
River Avoca
Castledermot
Donnelly's Hollow
Rock of Dunamaise
Portarlington
Mountmellick
Timahoe
Abbeyleix
Carlow
Ballon
Durrow
Kilkenny
Borris
Mt Leinster (796m)
River Barrow
Ferns
Enniscorthy
Wexford Bay
Curracloe Beach
Wexford
New Ross
St Mullins
Dungarvan
Kells
Rosslare Strand
Rosslare Harbour
Kilmore Quay
Saltee Islands
Hook Peninsula
Waterford
Tramore
Dunmore East
Curraghmore Estate
Carrick-on-Suir
River Suir
Clonmel
Fethard
Ballingarry
Cashel
Donaghmore
Roscrea
Kinnitty
Slieve Bloom Mountains
Birr
Banagher
Tullamore
Durrow Abbey
Kilbeggan
Clonmacnoise
Shannonbridge
Athlone
Ballinasloe
Suck
Athenry
Galway
River
Lough Corrib
Oughterard
Lough Inagh
Cashel
Roundstone
Clifden
Omey Island
Mace Head
Aran Islands
Inishmór
Inishmaan
Inisheer
Black Head
Ballyvaughan
Clarinbridge
Kilcolgan
Loughrea
Kinvara
Fanore
Burren
Gort
Portumna
Doolin
Lisdoonvarna
Kilfenora
Corofin
Cliffs of Moher
Hag's Head
Liscannor
Ennistymon
Mountshannon
Nenagh
Miltown Malbay
Ennis
Ballina
Killaloe
Bunratty
Shannon Airport
Limerick
Kilkee
Kilrush
Scattery Island
Loop Head
Tarbert
Mouth of the Shannon
Ballybunion
Adare
Ballingarry
Tipperary
Glen of Aherlow
Cahir
Galtee Mountains
Newcastle
Mitchelstown Caves
River Blackwater
Lismore
Cappoquin
Dungarvan
Ring Peninsula
Ardmore
Youghal
Youghal Bay
Fota Wildlife Park
Cork
Cobh
Kinsale
Clonakilty
Mallow
Listowel
Tralee
Castlemaine
Killorglin
Killarney
Killarney National Park
Kerry Bog Village Museum
Connor Pass
Dingle Peninsula
Annascaul
Dingle
Inch
Rossbeigh Strand
Kells
Caherciveen
Ring of Kerry
Valentia Island
Portmagee
Skellig Ring
Skellig Islands
Waterville
Caherdaniel
Sneem
Kenmare
Gougane Barra Forest Park
Glengarriff
Beara Peninsula
Bantry
Sheep's Head Peninsula
Dursey Island
Mizen Head Peninsula
Schull
Skibbereen
Castletownshend
Baltimore
Clear Island
St George's Channel
53°N
52°N
9°W
8°W
7°W
6°W

Ireland's Top 21

1

Dublin

1 Ireland's capital and largest city by some stretch is the main gateway into the country, and it has enough distractions to keep visitors engaged for at least a few days. From world-class museums and entertainment, superb dining and top-grade hotels, Dublin (p60) has all the baubles of a major international metropolis. But the real clinchers are Dubliners themselves, who are friendlier, more easy-going and welcoming than the burghers of virtually any other European capital. And it's the home of Guinness.

O'Connell Bridge (p87)

Connemara, County Galway

2 A filigreed coast of tiny coves and beaches forms the beautiful border between the Connemara Peninsula (p382) and the wild waters of the Atlantic. Wandering characterful roads bring you from one village to another, each with trad pubs and restaurants serving seafood chowder cooked from recipes that are family secrets. Inland, the scenic drama is even greater. In fantastically desolate valleys, green hills, yellow wildflowers and wild streams reflecting the blue sky provide elemental beauty. Rambles take you far from others, back to a simpler time.

Lough Inagh (p386)

RICHARD I'ANSON/GETTY IMAGES ©

2

CHRIS HILL/GETTY IMAGES ©

The Pub

3 Every town and hamlet has at least one: no matter where you go, you'll find that the social heart of the country beats loudest in the pub, still the best place to discover what makes the country tick. In suitable surroundings – whether a quiet traditional pub with flagstone floors and a large peat fire or a more modern bar with flashing lights and music – take a moment or an evening to listen for that beating heart...and drink some decent beer in the process. Kehoe's (p114)

Traditional Music

4 Western Europe's most vibrant folk music is Irish traditional music, which may have earned worldwide fame thanks to the likes of *Riverdance* but is best expressed in a more sedate setting, usually an old-fashioned pub. The west of Ireland is particularly musical: from Donegal down to Kerry there are centres of musical excellence, none more so than Doolin (p347) in County Clare, the unofficial capital of Irish music. It's unlikely you'll be asked to join in, but there's nothing stopping your foot from tapping and your hands from clapping. Dungeon Bar, Kinnitty Castle Hotel (p485)

3

MARTIN GOOD/GETTY IMAGES ©

4

HOLGER LEUE/LOOK-FOTO/GETTY IMAGES ©

Galway City

5 One word to describe Galway City (p359)? Craic! Ireland's liveliest city literally hums through the night at music-filled pubs where you can hear three old guys playing spoons and fiddles, or a hot young band. Join the locals as they bounce from place to place, never knowing what fun lies ahead but certain of the possibility. Add in local bounty such as the famous oysters and nearby adventure in the Connemara Peninsula and the Aran Islands and the fun never ends.

Dingle, County Kerry

6 Dingle is the name of both the picturesque peninsula (p279) jutting into the Atlantic from County Kerry, strewn with ancient ruins, and its delightful main town (p281), the peninsula's beating heart. Fishing boats unload fish and shellfish that couldn't be any fresher if you caught it yourself, many pubs are untouched since their earlier incarnations as old-fashioned shops, artists sell their creations (including beautiful jewellery with Irish designs) at intriguing boutiques, and toe-tapping trad sessions take place around roaring pub fires.

Glendalough, County Wicklow

7 St Kevin knew a thing or two about magical locations. When he chose a remote cave on a glacial lake nestled at the base of a forested valley as his monastic retreat (p140), he inadvertently founded a settlement that would later prove to be one of Ireland's most dynamic universities and, in our time, one of the country's most beautiful ruined sites. The remains of the settlement (including an intact round tower), coupled with the stunning scenery, are unforgettable.

St Kevin's Kitchen (p144)

8

DANITA DELIMONT/GETTY IMAGES ©

9

IIC/ AXIOM/GETTY IMAGES ©

10

PETER ZOELLER/DESIGN PICS/GETTY IMAGES ©

Rock of Cashel, County Tipperary

8 Soaring up from the green Tipperary pastures, this ancient fortress (p310) takes your breath away at first sight. The seat of kings and churchmen who ruled over the region for more than a thousand years, it rivalled Tara as a centre of power in Ireland for 400 years. Entered through the 15th-century Hall of the Vicars Choral, its impervious walls guard an awesome enclosure with a complete round tower, a 13th-century Gothic cathedral and the most magnificent 12th-century Romanesque chapel in Ireland.

Links Golf

9 If Scotland is the home of golf (p40), then Ireland is where golf goes on holiday. And the best vacation spots are along the sea, where the country's collection of seaside links are dotted in a steady string along virtually the entire Irish coastline, each more revealed than carved in the undulating, marram-grass-covered landscapes. Some of the world's best-known courses share spectacular scenery with lesser-known gems, and each offers the golfer the opportunity to test their skills against the raw materials provided by Mother Nature.

Cork City

10 The Republic's second city is second only in terms of size – in many other respects it will bear little competition. A tidy, compact city centre is home to an enticing collection of art galleries, museums and – most especially – places to eat. From cheap cafes to top-end gourmet restaurants, Cork city (p210) excels, although it's hardly a surprise given the county's exceptional foodie reputation. At the heart of it is the wonderful English Market, a covered produce market that is an attraction unto itself.

Walking & Hiking

11 Yes, you can visit the country easily enough by car, but Ireland is best explored on foot (p37), whether you opt for a gentle afternoon stroll along a canal towpath or take on the challenge of any of the 31 waymarked long-distance routes. There are coastal walks and mountain hikes; you can explore towns and villages along the way or steer clear of civilisation by traipsing along lonely moorland and across barren bogs. All you'll need is a decent pair of boots and, inevitably, a rain jacket. Diamond Hill, Connemara National Park (p391)

Brú na Bóinne, County Meath

12 Looking at once ancient and yet eerily futuristic, Newgrange's immense, round, white stone walls topped by a grass dome is one of the most extraordinary sights you'll ever see. Part of the vast Neolithic necropolis Brú na Bóinne (p495; the Boyne Palace), it contains Ireland's finest Stone Age passage tomb, predating the Pyramids by some six centuries. Most extraordinary of all is the tomb's precise alignment with the sun at the time of the winter solstice. Newgrange (p495)

11

12

Ring of Kerry

13 Driving around the Ring of Kerry (p267) is an unforgettable experience, but you don't need to limit yourself to the main route. Along this 179km loop around the Iveragh Peninsula there are countless opportunities for detours. Near Killorglin, it's a short hop up to the beautiful, little-known Cromane Peninsula. Between Portmagee and Waterville, you can explore the Skellig Ring. The peninsula's interior offers mesmerising mountain views. And that's just for starters. Wherever your travels take you, remember to charge your camera!

Causeway Coast

14 County Antrim's Causeway Coast is an especially dramatic backdrop for *Game of Thrones* filming locations. Put on your walking boots by the swaying Carrick-a-Rede rope bridge, then follow the rugged coastline for 16.5 spectacular kilometres, passing Ballintoy Harbour (aka the Iron Islands' Lordsports Harbour) and the geological wonder of the outsized basalt columns of the Giant's Causeway (p606), as well as cliffs and islands, sandy beaches and ruined castles, before finishing with a dram at the Old Bushmills Distillery.

Carrick-a-Rede Rope Bridge (p609)

13

PETER UNGER/GETTY IMAGES ©

14

CHRIS HILL/GETTY IMAGES ©

JOHN ELK/GETTY IMAGES ©

M.V. PHOTOGRAPHY/SHUTTERSTOCK ©

Carrowmore Megalithic Cemetery, County Sligo

15 The collection of stone circles, passage tombs and dolmens at Carrowmore (p421) is rich in superlatives: the oldest Stone Age monument in Ireland, one of the largest cemeteries of its kind in Europe. But what makes a visit here truly fascinating is the ongoing process of discovery, as archaeologists continue to excavate new monuments and piece together clues as to the site's deeper meaning, including its mathematical relationship with the rising and setting of the sun at Halloween.

Kilkenny City

16 From its regal castle to its soaring medieval cathedral, Kilkenny (p193) exudes a permanence and culture that have made it an unmissable stop on journeys to the south and west. Its namesake county boasts scores of artisans and craftspeople and you can browse their wares at Kilkenny's classy shops and boutiques. Chefs eschew Dublin in order to be close to the source of Kilkenny's wonderful produce and you can enjoy the local brewery's brews at scores of delightful pubs.

Titanic Belfast

17 The construction of the world's most famous ocean liner is celebrated in high-tech, multimedia glory at this wonderful museum (p537). Not only can you explore virtually every detail of the construction of the *Titanic* – including a simulated 'fly-through' of the ship from keel to bridge – but you can place yourself in the middle of the industrial bustle that was Belfast's shipyards at the turn of the 20th century. The experience is heightened by the use of photography, audio and – perhaps most poignantly – the only footage of the actual *Titanic* still in existence.

Donegal Coastline

18 Depending on what direction you travel in, the craggy, crenellated Donegal coastline is either the wildly dramatic finale of the Wild Atlantic Way (p49) or its breathtaking beginning. Ireland's northwestern corner is an untamed collection of soaring cliffs (the tallest in Europe), lonely, sheep-speckled headlands and, between them, secluded coves and long stretches of white, powdery sand: among them is Rossnowlagh in the southwest of the county, one of Europe's premier surf beaches and a mecca for big-wave surfers.

17

18

WADE EAKLE/GETTY IMAGES ©

IIC/AXIOM/GETTY IMAGES ©

ROBERT RIDDELL/GETTY IMAGES ©

A Gaelic Football or Hurling Match

19 It depends on whether you're in a football or hurling stronghold (some places, like County Cork, are both) but attending a match of the county's chosen sport (p666) is not just a unique Irish experience but also a key to unlocking local passions and understanding one of the cultural pillars of Ireland. Whether you attend a club football match in County Galway or an intercounty hurling battle between old foes like Kilkenny and Tipperary, you cannot but be swept up in the emotion of it all. Women's hurling match

Derry

20 History runs deep in Derry (p589). The symbols of the country's sectarian past are evident, from the 17th-century city walls built to protect Protestant settlers, to the latter forcing the adoption of its Loyalist name, Londonderry. But the new bridge that spans the River Foyle provides another symbol, of an attempt to bridge that divide and to look to the future as a city filled with a restless creative energy, expressed in its powerful murals, vibrant music scene and numerous art galleries – not to mention the guarantee of a good night out. *Hands Across the Divide* by Maurice Harron

Clare Coast

21 Bathed in the golden glow of the late afternoon sun, the iconic Cliffs of Moher (p344) are but one of the splendours of County Clare. From a boat bobbing below, the towering stone faces have a jaw-dropping dramatic beauty that's enlivened by scores of seabirds, including cute little puffins. Down south in Loop Head, pillars of rock towering above the sea have abandoned stone cottages whose very existence is inexplicable. All along the coast are cute little villages like trad-session-filled Ennistymon and the surfer mecca of Lahinch. Cliffs of Moher

Need to Know

For more information, see Survival Guide (p669)

Currency

Republic of Ireland: euro (€); Northern Ireland: pound sterling (£)

Language

English, Irish

Visas

Not required by most citizens of Europe, Australia, New Zealand, USA and Canada.

Money

Although notes issued by Northern Irish banks are legal tender throughout the UK, many businesses outside of Northern Ireland refuse to accept them and you'll have to swap them in British banks.

Mobile Phones

Phones from most other countries work in Ireland but attract roaming charges. Local SIM cards cost from €10; SIM and basic handsets around €40.

Time

Western European Time (UTC/GMT November to March; plus one hour April to October).

When to Go

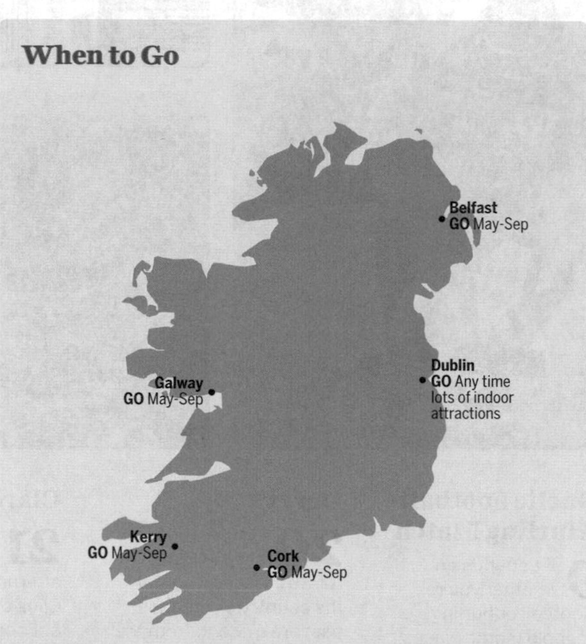

High Season
(Jun–mid-Sep)

➡ Weather at its best.

➡ Accommodation rates at their highest (especially in August).

➡ Tourist peak in Dublin, Kerry, southern and western coasts.

Shoulder
(Easter–May, mid-Sep–Oct)

➡ Weather often good: sun and rain in May; 'Indian summers' and often warm in September.

➡ Summer crowds and accommodation rates drop off.

Low Season
(Nov–Feb)

➡ Reduced opening hours from October to Easter; some destinations close.

➡ Cold and wet weather throughout the country; fog can reduce visibility.

➡ Big city attractions operate as normal.

Useful Websites

Entertainment Ireland (www.entertainment.ie) Country-wide listings for every kind of entertainment.

Failte Ireland (www.discoverireland.ie) Official tourist-board website – practical info and a huge accommodation database.

Lonely Planet (lonelyplanet.com/ireland) Destination information, hotel bookings, traveller forums and more.

Northern Ireland Tourist Board (www.nitb.com) Official tourist site.

Important Numbers

Include area codes only when dialling from outside the area or from a mobile phone. Drop the initial 0 when dialling from abroad.

Country code	☎353 Republic of Ireland; ☎44 Northern Ireland
International access code	☎00
Emergency (police, fire, ambulance)	☎999

Exchange Rates

Australia	A$1	€0.66	£0.47
Canada	C$1	€0.70	£0.50
Japan	¥100	€0.75	£0.54
New Zealand	NZ$1	€0.61	£0.43
UK	UK£1	€1.41	£1
USA	US$1	€0.91	£0.65

For current exchange rates see www.xe.com

Daily Costs

Budget: Less than €60

- Dorm bed: €12–20
- Cheap meal in cafe or pub: €6–12
- Inter-city bus travel (200km trip): €12–25
- Pint: €4.50–5 (more expensive in cities)

Midrange: €60–120

- Double room in hotel or B&B (more expensive in Dublin): €80–180
- Main course in midrange restaurant: €12–25
- Car rental (per day): from €25–45
- Three-hour train journey: €65

Top End: More than €120

- Four-star hotel stay: from €150
- Three-course meal in good restaurant: around €50
- Top round of golf (midweek): from €90

Opening Hours

Banks 10am–4pm Monday to Friday (to 5pm Thursday)

Pubs 10.30am–11.30pm Monday to Thursday, 10.30am–12.30am Friday and Saturday, noon–11pm Sunday (30 minutes 'drinking up' time allowed); closed Christmas Day and Good Friday

Restaurants noon–10.30pm; many close one day of the week

Shops 9.30am–6pm Monday to Saturday (until 8pm Thursday in cities), noon–6pm Sunday

Arriving in Ireland

Dublin Airport Private coaches run every 10 to 15 minutes to the city centre (€7). Taxis take 30 to 45 minutes and cost €20 to €25.

Dun Laoghaire Ferry Port Public bus takes around 45 minutes to the centre of Dublin; DART (suburban rail) takes about 25 minutes.

Dublin Port Terminal Buses are timed to coincide with arrivals and departures; costs €3 to the city centre.

Belfast International Airport/ George Best Belfast City Airport A bus runs to the centre every 15 to 20 minutes from both airports; a taxi from the international airport costs around £30, or £10 from George Best City Airport.

Getting Around

Transport in Ireland is efficient and reasonably priced to and from major urban centres; smaller towns and villages along those routes are well served. Service to destinations not on major routes is less frequent and often impractical.

Train A limited network links Dublin to all major urban centres, including Belfast in Northern Ireland. Expensive if you're on a budget.

Car The most convenient way to explore Ireland's every nook and cranny. Cars can be hired in major towns and cities; drive on the left.

Bus An extensive network of public and private buses makes them the most cost-effective way to get around; there's service to and from most inhabited areas.

Bike Dublin operates a bike-share scheme with over 100 stations spread throughout the city.

For much more on **getting around**, see p678

First Time Ireland

For more information, see Survival Guide (p669)

Checklist

- ➡ Make sure your passport is valid for at least six months past your arrival date
- ➡ Make all necessary bookings (accommodation, events and travel)
- ➡ Check the airline baggage restrictions
- ➡ Inform your debit/credit-card company
- ➡ Arrange appropriate travel insurance
- ➡ Check if you can use your mobile phone

What to Pack

- ➡ Good walking shoes, as Ireland is best appreciated on foot
- ➡ Raincoat – you will undoubtedly need it
- ➡ UK/Ireland electrical adapter
- ➡ Finely honed sense of humour
- ➡ A hollow leg – all that beer has to go somewhere
- ➡ Irish-themed MP3 or Spotify playlist

Top Tips for Your Trip

- ➡ Quality rather than quantity should be your goal: instead of a hair-raising race to see everything, pick a handful of destinations and give yourself time to linger. The most memorable experiences in Ireland are often the ones where you're doing very little at all.
- ➡ If you're driving, get off the main roads when you can: some of Ireland's most stunning scenery is best enjoyed on secondary or tertiary roads that wind their narrow way through standout photo ops.
- ➡ Make the effort to greet the locals: the best experiences can be had courtesy of the Irish themselves, whose helpfulness, friendliness and fun has not been overexaggerated.

What to Wear

You can wear pretty much whatever you want: smart casual is the most you'll need for fancy dinners, the theatre or the concert hall. Irish summers are warm but rarely hot, so you'll want something extra when the temperatures cool, especially in the evening. Ultimately, the ever-changeable weather will determine your outfits, but a light waterproof jacket should never be beyond reach for the almost inevitable rain.

Sleeping

From basic hostel to five-star hotel, you'll find every range of accommodation in Ireland. Advance bookings are generally recommended and an absolute necessity during the busy holiday period.

- ➡ **Hotels** From chain hotels with comfortable digs to Norman castles with rainfall shower rooms and wi-fi – with prices to match.
- ➡ **B&Bs** From a bedroom in a private home to a luxurious Georgian town house, the ubiquitous B&B is the bedrock of Irish accommodation.
- ➡ **Hostels** Every major town and city has a selection of hostels, with clean dorms and wi-fi – some have laundry and kitchen facilities.

Money

ATMs are found pretty much everywhere. They're all linked to the main international money systems, allowing you to withdraw money with your own card – but be sure to check with your bank before you travel.

Credit and debit cards can be used almost everywhere except for some rural B&Bs that only accept cash. Make sure bars or restaurants will accept cards before you order. The most popular are Visa and MasterCard; American Express is only accepted by the major chains, and virtually no one will accept Diners or JCB. Chip-and-PIN is the norm for card transactions – only a few places will accept a signature.

If you don't want to rely on plastic, banks, post offices and some of the larger hotels will change cash and travellers cheques.

For more information, see p674.

Bargaining

Ireland doesn't do bargaining – unless you're buying a horse.

Tipping

➡ **Hotels** €1/£1 per bag is standard; gratuity for cleaning staff at your discretion.

➡ **Pubs** Not expected unless table service is provided, then €1/£1 for a round of drinks.

➡ **Restaurants** For decent service 10%; up to 15% in more expensive places.

➡ **Taxis** Tip 10% or round up fare to nearest euro/pound.

➡ **Toilet Attendants** Loose change; no more than 50c/50p.

RICHARD I'ANSON/GETTY IMAGES ©

Guinness at the Guinness Storehouse's Gravity Bar (p83)

Etiquette

Although largely informal in their everyday dealings, the Irish do observe some (unspoken) rules of etiquette.

➡ **Greetings** Shake hands with men, women and children when meeting for the first time and when saying goodbye. The Irish expect a firm handshake with eye contact. Female friends are greeted with a single (air) kiss.

➡ **Conversation** Generally friendly but often reserved, the Irish avoid conversations that might embarrass. They are deeply mistrustful of 'oversharers'.

➡ **Round System** The Irish generally take it in turns to buy a 'round' of drinks for the whole group and everyone is expected to take part. The next round should always be bought before the previous round is finished.

Eating

Booking ahead is recommended in cities and larger towns; same-day reservations are usually fine except for top-end restaurants – book those two weeks in advance.

➡ **Restaurants** From cheap cafes to Michelin-starred feasts, covering every imaginable cuisine.

➡ **Cafes** Open during the daytime (rarely at night), cafes are good for all-day breakfasts, sandwiches and basic dishes.

➡ **Pubs** Pub grub ranges from toasted sandwiches to carefully crafted dishes as good as any you'll find in a restaurant.

➡ **Hotels** All hotel restaurants take non-guests. They're a popular option in the countryside.

What's New

Wild Atlantic Way

The single biggest development in Irish tourism in the last couple of decades is this 2500km-long coastal touring route, the longest in the world. (p49)

Teeling Distillery, Dublin

The first new distillery in Dublin for 125 years opened in 2015, but it'll be a few years yet before what they make is actually whiskey; in the meantime, the visitor centre explains how it's made. (p47)

Lusitania Museum, Kinsale

A 200-year-old signal tower on the Old Head of Kinsale has been converted into a museum dedicated to the sinking of the RMS *Lusitania* by a German U-boat in 1915. (p229)

Cavan Burren Park, County Cavan

This otherworldly megalithic site within the Cuilcagh Mountain Park was formally established in late 2014. A promontory fort from 500 BC and a wedgetomb from 2500 BC are highlights. (p523)

Tayto Park, Meath

Europe's biggest inverted roller coaster opened in 2015 in this amusement park sponsored by the country's best-loved potato-crisp manufacturer. Also new are a 5D cinema and other high-tech rides. (p505)

Tullamore Dew Visitor Centre, Tullamore

Late 2014 saw the return of this distillery to its namesake town; you can visit its new home in a 19th-century canalside warehouse and taste some of its produce. (p489)

Malin Head Viewing Area, Donegal

There's a new viewing area (with free telescopes!) at Banba's Crown, at the very tip of the head, with stunning views of the Donegal coastline and beyond – on crisp, winter nights you might even spot the Northern Lights. (p463)

For more recommendations and reviews, see lonelyplanet.com/ireland

If You Like...

Tracing Your Roots

Roughly 80 million people worldwide can claim to be part of, or descended from, the Irish diaspora, with about 41 million of those in the US alone. Most major towns have a heritage centre with a genealogical service.

Genealogy Advisory Service Based in the National Library in Dublin, this is the place to start your search for your Irish ancestors. (p75)

PRONI (Public Record Office of Northern Ireland) Belfast's purpose-built centre is the place to go to track down your Ulster family history. (p530)

The Queenstown Story Cobh's superb heritage museum houses a genealogy centre. (p223)

Dún na Sí Heritage Park A folk park 16km east of Athlone with an associated genealogical centre attached. (p477)

Ulster American Folk Park Ulster's rich links with the US are explored in one of Northern Ireland's best museums. (p634)

Rothe House & Garden An excellent genealogical service is housed in this 16th-century merchant's house in Kilkenny city. (p195)

Great Views

Irish scenery is among the most spectacular in Europe, with breathtaking views and stunning landscapes throughout the country. There are the famous spots, of course, but they're not alone.

Binevenagh Lake Spectacular views over Lough Foyle, Donegal and the Sperrin Mountains from the clifftop at the height of the Bishop's Road. (p601)

Kilkee Cliffs Jaw-dropping views of soaring cliffs that aren't the Cliffs of Moher. (p339)

Poisoned Glen The views down this Donegal valley are breathtaking; the final touch is the ruined church at the foot of the glen. (p456)

Priest's Leap A scenic clifftop on the north side of the Beara Peninsula with sensational views of Bantry Bay and the eponymous town. (p248)

Sky Road Astonishing views over the sea from this dramatic coastal road just outside Clifden in Connemara. (p387)

Horn Head Some of the Wild Atlantic Way's most glorious scenery, with impressive cliffs topped with bog and heather. (p449)

Traditional Music

Western Europe's most vibrant folk music is kept alive by musicians who ply their craft (and are plied with drink) in impromptu and organised sessions in pubs and music houses throughout the country; even the 'strictly for tourists' stuff will feature excellent performances.

An Droichead Excellent music sessions at a Belfast arts centre dedicated to Irish culture. (p557)

Matt Molloy's The Chieftain's fife player owns this Westport pub where the live *céilidh* (session of traditional music and dancing) kicks off at 9pm nightly. (p408

Miltown Malbay Every pub in this County Clare town features outstanding Irish trad sessions. (p341)

Tig Cóilí Galway's best trad sessions are held in a pub whose name means 'house of music'. (p367)

Marine Bar Wonderful music nightly during summer months at this 200-year-old pub on the Ring Peninsula. (p183)

Cobblestone The nightly sessions in this Smithfield pub are the best in the capital. (p119)

Literary Corners

Four Nobel laureates for literature are just the highlight of a rich literary tradition. Ireland is one of the English-speaking world's most notable heavyweights of the written word, a tradition that continues to thrive through contemporary writers and literary festivals.

Cape Clear Island International Storytelling Festival The storytelling tradition is kept alive by tales tall and long from all over the world. (p240)

Cúirt International Festival of Literature Galway attracts writers from far and wide to its April literary showcase. (p369)

Dublin Literary Tours No city of comparable size has been more written about, or has produced as many great authors as the capital, so take one of its many literary tours to find out more. (p97)

Listowel Writers' Week The Irish literary festival, held in June in the hometown of John B Keane. (p296)

Traditional Pubs

Everybody's got their favourite, so picking the best ones is a futile exercise. What can be done, however, is to select a handful that won't disappoint you, especially if you're looking for a traditional pub in the classic mould.

Blake's of the Hollow Ulster's best pint of Guinness in a Victorian classic. (p625)

John Benny's Stone slab floor, memorabilia on the walls and rocking trad sessions in this Dingle pub most nights. (p285)

Top: Cross of the Scriptures (King Flann's Cross; p487), Clonmacnoise

Bottom: Kilkee cliffs (p339)

McCarthy's A pub, restaurant and undertakers, all in one, in Fethard. (p320)

Séhán Ua Neáchtain In Galway, one of Ireland's best-known traditional pubs. (p367)

John Mulligan's The most famous of the capital's traditional pubs and a star of film and TV – where it usually plays itself. (p114)

Vaughan's Pub Superb bar in Kilfenora with outstanding reputation for traditional music. (p351)

Golf

If Scotland is the home of golf, then Ireland is where golf goes on holidays. There are over 400 courses spread throughout the island, but for a proper Irish golfing experience, tee it up on a links course by the sea.

Ballybunion Golf Club A perennial favourite with visiting celebrities and professionals – the course is as tough as the views are beautiful. (p296)

County Sligo Golf Course Stunning links on a peninsula in the shadow of Benbulben. (p421)

Lahinch Golf Club One of Ireland's most beloved links was laid out by Scottish soldiers in 1892. (p342)

Royal County Down Hallowed links designed by Old Tom Morris, often rated as the best course in Ireland. (p574)

Royal Portrush A stunner that hosted the Open Championship in 1951 and will do so again in 2019. (p604)

Waterville Golf Links A world-class links with views to match. (p275)

Family Days Out

There are plenty of family-friendly activities throughout the country, from heritage museums to ziplines across a forest canopy.

Lough Key Forest Park A 142-hectare adventure playland for the whole family, including a 300m-long canopy walk and an outdoor adventure playground. (p475)

Great Western Greenway Flat and popular bike path from Westport to Achill with plenty of castles and sites to see along the way. (p408)

Fota Wildlife Park Huge outdoor zoo just outside Cork city with ne'er a cage or fence in sight. The cheetah run is especially popular. (p222)

Tralee Bay Wetlands Centre When you're done learning about the habitats of this 300-hectare reserve, you can hop aboard a boat for the 15-minute safari ride. (p293)

Ancient Ruins

Thanks to the pre-Celts, Celts and early Christians, ancient and monastic sites are a feature of the Irish landscape. Thanks to the Vikings and Henry VIII, many of these are ruins, but no less impressive.

Athassel Priory Sublime and haunting ecclesiastical ruin. (p314)

Athenry A magnificent castle, Dominican priory, an original market cross and lengthy sections of town walls. (p394)

Brú na Bóinne Europe's most impressive Neolithic burial site. (p495)

Carrowkeel Megalithic cemetery and majestic views. (p423)

Clonmacnoise Ireland's finest monastic site. (p486)

Devenish Island Ruins of an Augustinian monastery and near-perfect round tower on the biggest island in Lough Erne. (p629)

Dún Aengus Stunning Stone Age fort perched perilously on Inishmór's cliffs. (p373)

Glendalough Ruins of a once-powerful monastic city in stunning surroundings. (p140)

Month by Month

TOP EVENTS

St Patrick's Day, March

Galway Arts Festival, July

Willie Clancy Summer School, July

Féile An Phobail, August

All-Ireland Finals, September

February

Bad weather makes February the perfect month for indoor activities. Some museums launch new exhibits, and it's a good time to visit the major towns and cities.

☆ Six Nations Rugby

Ireland, winners of the 2015 championship, play their three home matches at the Aviva Stadium in the Dublin suburb of Ballsbridge. The season runs from February to April (www.rbs6nations.com).

Jameson Dublin International Film Festival

Most of Dublin's cinemas participate in the country's biggest film festival (www.jdiff.com), a two-week showcase for new films by Irish and international directors. It features local flicks, arty international films and advance releases of mainstream movies.

March

Spring is in the air, and the whole country is getting ready for arguably the world's most famous parade. Dublin's is the biggest, but every town in Ireland holds one.

St Patrick's Day

Ireland erupts into one giant celebration on 17 March (www.stpatricksday.ie), but Dublin throws a four-day party around the parade (attended by 600,000), with gigs and festivities that leave the city with a giant hangover.

April

The weather is improving, the flowers are beginning to bloom and the festival season begins anew. Seasonal attractions start to open around the middle of the month or at Easter.

☆ Circuit of Ireland International Rally

Northern Ireland's most prestigious rally race – known locally as 'the Circuit' (www.circuitofireland.net) – sees over 130 competitors throttle and turn through some 550km of Northern Ireland and parts of the Republic over two days at Easter.

☆ Irish Grand National

Ireland loves horse racing, and the race that's loved the most is the Grand National (www.fairyhouse.ie), the showcase of the national hunt season that takes place at Fairyhouse in County Meath on Easter Monday.

☆ World Irish Dancing Championships

There's far more to Irish dancing than *Riverdance*. Every April, some 4500 competitors from all over the world gather to test their steps and skills against the very best. The location varies from year to year; see www.irishdancingorg.com.

May

The May Bank Holiday (on the first Monday) sees the first of the busy summer weekends as the Irish take to the roads to enjoy the budding good weather.

Cork International Choral Festival

One of Europe's premier choral festivals (www.corkchoral.ie), with the winners going on to the Fleischmann International Trophy Competition; held over four days at the beginning of May.

Cathedral Quarter Arts Festival

Belfast's Cathedral Quarter hosts a multidisciplinary arts festival (www.cqaf.com) including drama, music, poetry and street theatre over 10 days at the beginning of the month.

North West 200

Ireland's most famous road race (www.northwest200.org) is also the country's biggest outdoor sporting event; 150,000-plus people line the triangular route to cheer on some of the biggest names in motorcycle racing. Held in mid-May.

Fleadh Nua

The third week of May sees the cream of the traditional music crop come to Ennis, County Clare, for one of the country's most important festivals (www.fleadhnua.com).

Listowel Writers' Week

Well-known writers engaged in readings, seminars and storytelling are the attraction at the country's premier festival for bibliophiles (www.writersweek.ie), which runs over five days in the County Kerry town of Listowel at the end of the month. There's also poetry, music and drama.

June

The bank holiday at the beginning of the month sees the country spoilt for choice as to what to do. Weekend traffic gets busier as the weather gets better.

The Cat Laughs Comedy Festival

Kilkenny gets very, very funny in early June with the country's premier comedy festival (www.thecatlaughs.com), which draws comedians both known and unknown from the four corners of the globe.

Irish Derby

Wallets are packed and fancy hats donned for the best flat-race festival in the country (www.curragh.ie), run during the first week of the month.

Bloomsday

Edwardian dress and breakfast of 'the inner organs of beast and fowl' are but two of the elements of the Dublin festival celebrating 16 June, the day on which James Joyce's *Ulysses* takes place; the real highlight is retracing Leopold Bloom's steps.

Mourne International Walking Festival

The last weekend of the month plays host to a walking festival (www.mournewalking.co.uk) in the Mourne Mountains of County Down, designated an Area of Outstanding Natural Beauty.

July

There isn't a weekend in July when a major festival doesn't take place, while visitors to Galway will find that the city is in full swing for the entire month.

Willie Clancy Summer School

Inaugurated to celebrate the memory of a famed local piper, this exceptional festival of traditional music (www.scoilsamhraidhwillieclancy.com) sees the world's best players show up for gigs, pub sessions and workshops over nine days in Miltown Malbay, County Clare.

Galway Film Fleadh

Irish and international releases make up the program at one of the country's premier film festivals (www.galwayfilmfleadh.com), held in early July.

Galway Arts Festival

Music, drama and a host of artistic endeavours are on the menu at the most important arts festival (www.galwayartsfestival.com) in the country, which sees Galway go merriment-mad for the last two weeks of the month.

Longitude

A mini-Glastonbury in Dublin's Marlay Park, Longitude (www.longitude.ie) packs them in over three days in mid-July for a feast of electronic dance music, nu-folk, rock and pop. In 2015 Hozier and the Chemical Brothers were the big headliners.

Folkfest Killarney

Late July, 2015 saw the debut edition of a festival (http://folkfestkillarney.com) devoted to all things folk, featuring music, beards and flannel from all over Ireland and abroad, including performers from Britain, the USA and Mali.

August

Schools are closed, the sun is shining (or not!) and Ireland is in holiday mood. Seaside towns and tourist centres are at their busiest as the country looks to make the most of its time off.

Galway Race Week

The biggest horse-racing festival (www.galwayraces.com) west of the Shannon is not just about the horses, it's also a celebration of Irish culture, sporting gambles and elaborate hats.

Mary From Dungloe

Ireland's second-most important beauty pageant (www.maryfromdungloe.com) takes place in Dungloe, County Donegal, at the beginning of the month. Although it's an excuse for a giant party, the young women really do want to be crowned the year's 'Mary'.

Féile An Phobail

The name translates simply as the 'people's festival' and it is just that: Europe's largest community arts festival (www.feilebelfast.com) takes place on the Falls Rd in West Belfast over two weeks.

Top: Street performer, Grafton St (p65), Dublin

Bottom: Punters at Galway Race Week (p369)

Fleadh Cheoil na hÉireann

The mother of all Irish music festivals (www.comhaltas.ie), usually held at the end of the month, attracts in excess of 250,000 music lovers and revellers to whichever town is playing host – there's some great music amid the drinking.

Puck Fair

Ireland's oldest festival (www.puckfair.ie) is also its quirkiest: crown a goat king and celebrate for three days. Strange idea, brilliant festival that takes place in Killorglin, County Kerry, in mid-August.

Rose of Tralee

The Irish beauty pageant sees wannabe Roses plucked from Irish communities throughout the world competing for the ultimate prize. For everyone else, it's a big party (www.roseoftralee.ie).

September

Summer may be over but September weather can be surprisingly good, so it's often the ideal time to enjoy the last vestiges of the sun as the crowds dwindle.

Galway International Oyster & Seafood Festival

Over the last weekend of the month Galway kicks off its oyster season with a festival (www.galwayoysterfest.com) celebrating the local catch. Music and beer have been the accompaniment since its inception in 1953.

Dublin Fringe Festival

Upwards of 100 different performances take the stage, the street, the bar and the car in the fringe festival (www.fringefest.com) that is unquestionably more innovative than the main theatre festival that follows it.

All-Ireland Finals

The second and fourth Sundays of the month see the finals of the hurling and Gaelic football championships respectively, with 80,000-plus crowds thronging into Dublin's Croke Park for the biggest sporting days of the year.

October

The weather starts to turn cold, so it's time to move the fun indoors again. The calendar is still packed with activities and distractions, especially over the last weekend of the month.

Dublin Theatre Festival

The most prestigious theatre festival in the country (www.dublintheatrefestival.com) sees new work and new versions of old work staged in theatres and venues throughout the capital.

Belfast Festival at Queen's

Northern Ireland's top arts festival (www.belfastfestival.com) attracts performers from all over the world for the second half of the month; on offer is everything from visual arts to dance.

Wexford Opera Festival

Opera fans gather in the Wexford Opera House, the country's only theatre built for opera, to enjoy Ireland's premier lyric festival (www.wexfordopera.com), which tends to eschew the big hits in favour of lesser-known works.

Guinness Cork Jazz Festival

Ireland's best-known jazz festival (www.guinnessjazzfestival.com) sees Cork taken over by more than a thousand musicians and their multitude of fans during the last weekend of the month.

December

Christmas dominates the calendar as the country prepares for the feast with frenzied shopping and after-work drinks with friends and family arrived home from abroad. On Christmas Day nothing is open.

Christmas

This is a quiet affair in the countryside, though on 26 December (St Stephen's Day) the ancient custom of Wren Boys is re-enacted, most notably in Dingle, County Kerry, when groups of children dress up and go about singing hymns.

Christmas Dip

A traditional Christmas Day swim at the Forty Foot Pool in the Dublin suburb of Sandycove sees a group of very brave swimmers go for a 20m swim to the rocks and back.

Itineraries

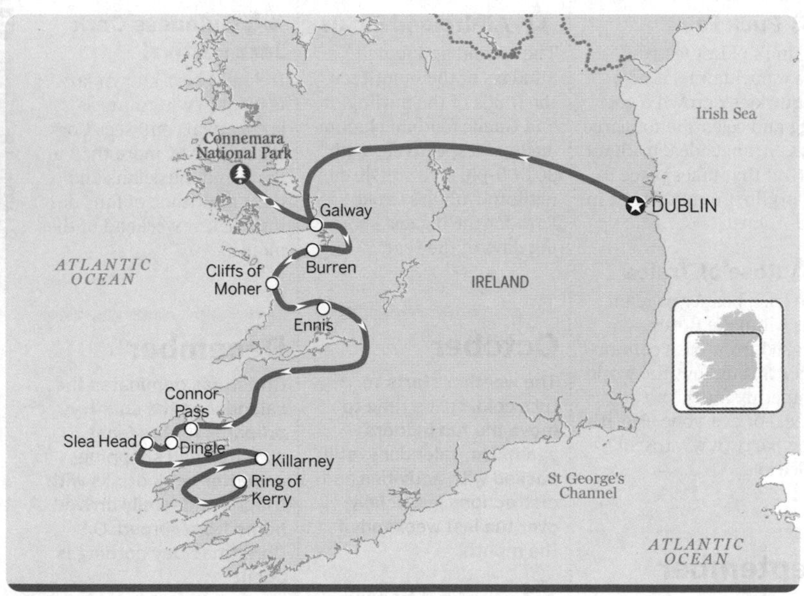

Ireland Highlights

This 300km-tourist trail takes you past some of Ireland's most famous attractions and through spectacular countryside. Start with a whistle-stop tour of **Dublin**, including visits to Trinity College and the *Book of Kells* as well as a sample of Guinness in its hometown. The next day, head west to **Galway**, from where you should take a drive through stunning, brooding **Connemara National Park** (which can be driven in a nice loop) before heading south through the moonlike landscape of the **Burren**. Take a detour to the **Cliffs of Moher**, then head to **Ennis**, a good spot to enjoy a bit of traditional Irish music. Keep going south through the **Connor Pass** into County Kerry, stopping for a half-day in **Dingle** before setting out to visit its peninsula, taking in the views and prehistoric monuments of **Slea Head**. Via the ferry, continue on to **Killarney**, the perfect base from which to explore the famous **Ring of Kerry**, a much-trafficked 179km loop around the Iveragh Peninsula.

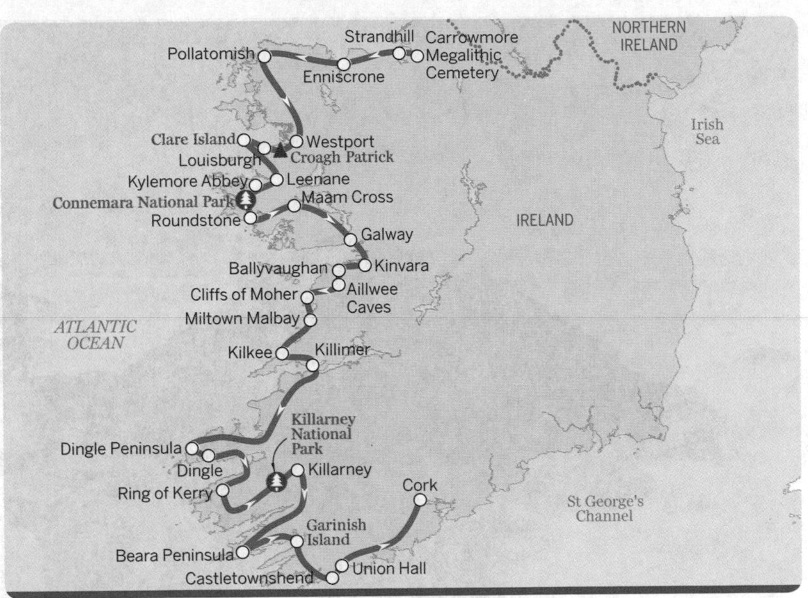

Best of the West

The west of Ireland is rightly at the top of most people's must-visit lists. Start in County Sligo, where prehistory and panorama combine to wonderful effect at **Carrowmore Megalithic Cemetery**. Wind your way south along the coast, stopping at some of Ireland's best surf beaches like **Strandhill** and **Enniscrone**, to the pretty village of **Pollatomish**. Continue south to the pub-packed heritage town of **Westport**. Southwest of here is magnificent **Croagh Patrick**, which is worth a climb if only to feast your eyes on island-studded Clew Bay. Go west to **Louisburgh**, from where you can head offshore to craggy **Clare Island** (home of the pirate queen Grace O'Malley), before turning south along the beautiful Doolough Valley to **Leenane**, situated on Ireland's only fjord. This is the northern gateway to **Connemara National Park**, which you can explore via the beautiful coastal route, passing **Kylemore Abbey**, venturing onto Clifden's scenic Sky Road and then winding your way around the coast through pretty **Roundstone**. Alternatively, you could savour the stunning wilderness of the inland route through **Maam Cross** to **Galway**, where you should devote at least a day to exploring the colourful streets and wonderful pubs.

South of Galway, the fishing villages of **Kinvara** and **Ballyvaughan** are at the edge of the strange, karst landscape of the Burren, home to all manner of flora and fauna, as well as big-ticket attractions like the ancient **Aillwee Caves** and the **Cliffs of Moher**. Going south, be sure to sample some of Ireland's exquisite traditional music by attending a session in one of the pubs of **Miltown Malbay**; beach lovers should also opt for a stop in **Kilkee**, a favourite with surfers.

The easiest way to cross into County Kerry is via the ferry at **Killimer**. Take a day to explore the **Dingle Peninsula**, with its rich menu of ancient sites and stunning views, before overnighting in **Dingle** – one of the prettiest towns along the entire west coast. Take another day to explore the world-famous **Ring of Kerry**, ending in **Killarney National Park**, right on the edge of **Killarney** itself. Take the scenic route across the middle of the **Beara Peninsula** and make your way to the Italianate **Garinish Island**, with its exotic flowers. Then follow the coast through **Castletownshend** and the fishing village of **Union Hall** to the city of **Cork**.

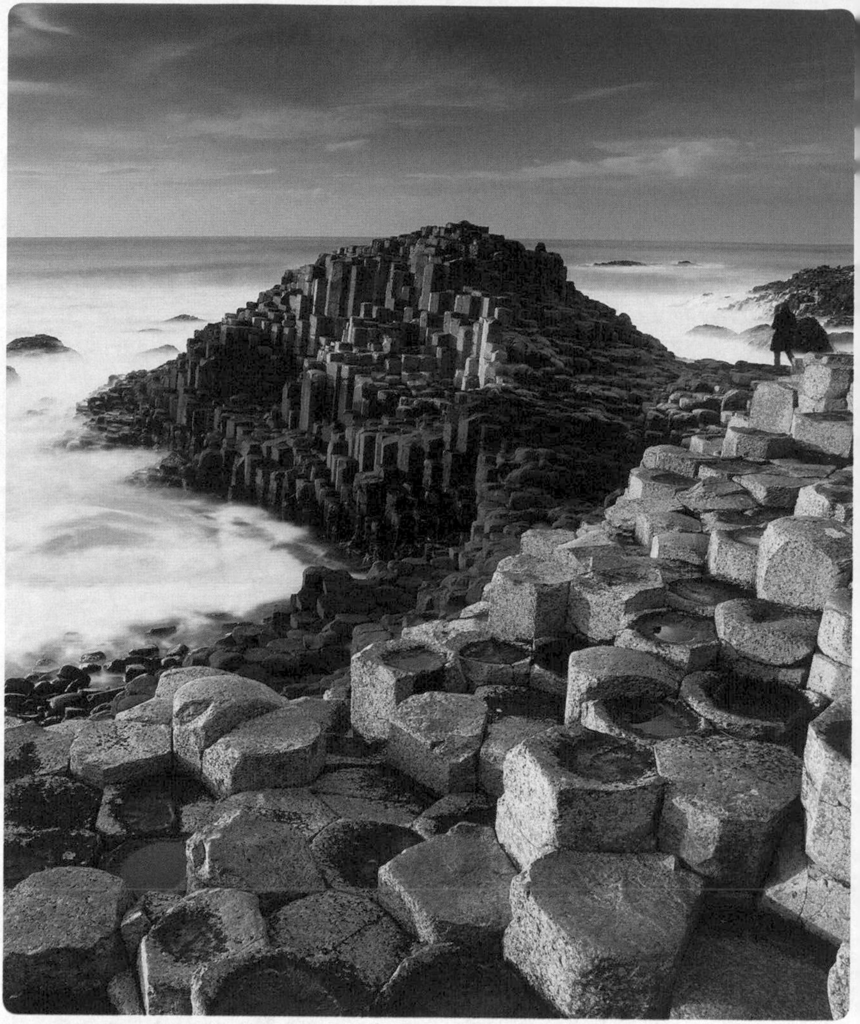

DAVID EPPERSON/GETTY IMAGES ©

Top: Giant's Causeway (p606), County Antrim

Bottom: Stone circle, Beara Peninsula (p247)

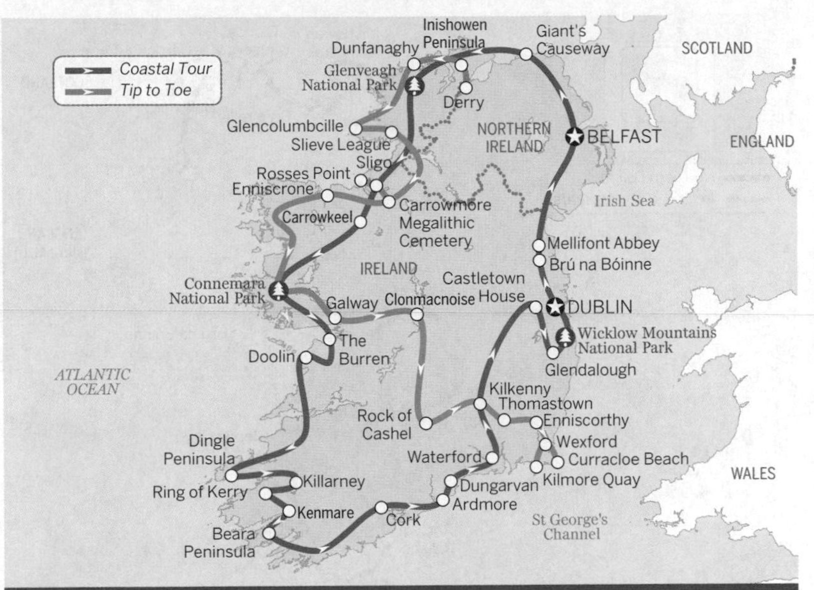

3 WEEKS Coastal Tour

Start in **Dublin**, then head north to the Neolithic necropolis at **Brú na Bóinne**. Continue on to **Mellifont Abbey** before crossing the border into Northern Ireland and heading to **Belfast**. Go northwest along the Antrim coast to the **Giant's Causeway**. Continue around the coastline of north Donegal, stopping at **Glenveagh National Park**. Head south into **Sligo** and climb the Stone Age passage grave at **Carrowkeel** for views of Lough Arrow. Make your way to the southwest via **Connemara National Park**. Wonder at the **Burren** and check out traditional music in **Doolin** before crossing into County Kerry and exploring the **Dingle Peninsula**. Go through **Killarney** on your way round the **Ring of Kerry**. Camp in **Kenmare** and explore the **Beara Peninsula**, then Ireland's second city, **Cork**. Explore County Waterford from seaside **Ardmore**. Visit **Dungarvan** and its castle, and the museums in **Waterford**. Go north through Thomastown to St Canice's Cathedral in **Kilkenny** before exploring the city's medieval core. Visit **Castletown House** in County Kildare, then cut east to **Glendalough** in the **Wicklow Mountains National Park**. Finally, head back to Dublin.

2 WEEKS Tip to Toe

Begin in Northern Ireland's second city, **Derry**, walking the city walls and exploring the Bogside district. Then cross into County Donegal and explore the **Inishowen Peninsula** before overnighting in **Dunfanaghy**. As you move down Donegal's coastline, check out the monastic ruins of **Glencolumbcille** and the sea cliffs at **Slieve League**. Cross into County Sligo and visit the **Carrowmore Megalithic Cemetery** before checking in to your **Sligo Town** hotel. The next day, treat yourself to a round of golf at the County Sligo Golf Course at **Rosses Point** or a seaweed bath in **Enniscrone**. You'll skirt the eastern edge of **Connemara National Park** as you travel south to **Galway**, from where you should strike out for **Clonmacnoise**. From here, move through the heart of the Midlands to another monastic gem, the **Rock of Cashel**. Medieval **Kilkenny** is only an hour away – visit its stunning castle before exploring nearby **Thomastown** and Jerpoint Abbey. Using **Wexford** as a base, explore **Curracloe Beach** and visit **Enniscorthy** and the excellent National 1798 Rebellion Centre. Or you could chill out and watch the fishermen draw in their lines in **Kilmore Quay**.

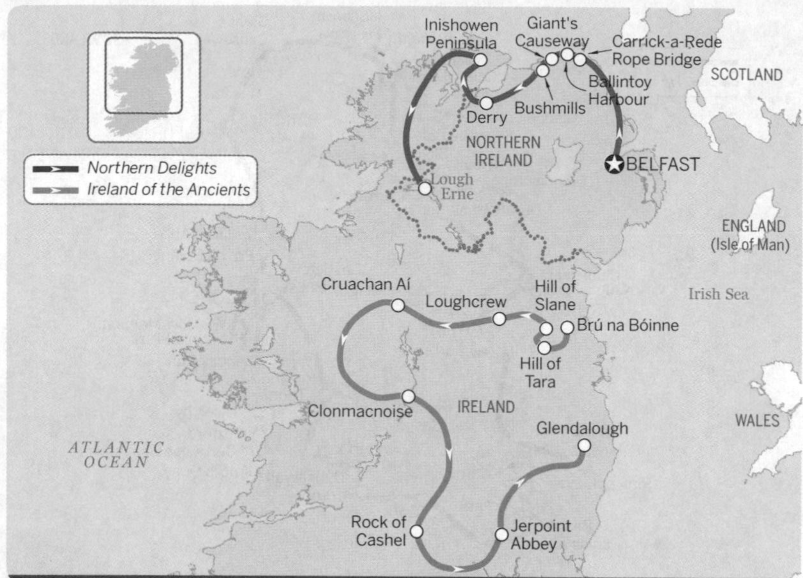

Northern Delights

Start in **Belfast**, where you should visit the Titanic Experience and take a black-taxi tour, before heading north toward the Antrim coast and the **Carrick-a-Rede Rope Bridge**. Head west toward the Unesco World Heritage–listed **Giant's Causeway**, a highlight of any trip to Northern Ireland; along the way, Game of Thrones fans can check out **Ballintoy Harbour**, which stood in for the Iron Islands' Lordsport Harbour in the TV series. The causeway coast finishes in the the fascinating village of **Bushmills**, home to the famous distillery. **Derry** is worth a day – walk the city's walls and explore its more recent past in the Bogside district, and then cross the invisible border into the Republic by visiting the **Inishowen Peninsula** in County Donegal. Back in the North, finish your visit in **Lough Erne**, taking in both White Island and the carved stones of Devenish Island.

Ireland of the Ancients

Begin at the stunning Neolithic tombs of Newgrange and Knowth in County Meath, in the heart of **Brú na Bóinne**. Nearby, stand at the top of the celebrated **Hill of Tara**, a site of immense folkloric significance and seat of the high kings of Ireland until the 11th century. Across the plain is the **Hill of Slane**, where St Patrick lit a fire in 433 to proclaim Christianity throughout the land. To the west is the Neolithic monument of **Loughcrew** – a quieter alternative to Brú na Bóinne. Keep going west to County Roscommon. Just outside Tulsk village is **Cruachan Aí**, the most important Celtic site in Europe. Head south to **Clonmacnoise**, the 6th-century monastic site in County Offaly, then continue through the heart of the country to the impressive **Rock of Cashel** in County Tipperary. Turn east and head through County Kilkenny, stopping at the Cistercian **Jerpoint Abbey**, at the pretty village of Thomastown. From here, travel north-east to Wicklow and magnificent **Glendalough**, where the substantial remains of a monastic settlement linger by two beautiful lakes.

Plan Your Trip

The Great Outdoors

There is no better way of experiencing this wildly beautiful country than by exploring its varied landscapes – and the rewards can be spectacular. From majestic craggy mountains to lush lakeside woods, from broad sandy beaches to blankets of wild bog stretching as far as the eye can see, Ireland's great outdoors will never disappoint.

Walking

Gentle hills, rocky ridges, wild moorlands, spectacular sea cliffs, remote islands, warm hospitality, and the gloriously unpredictable weather – all are part of the wonderful experience of exploring Ireland on foot. There is something for everyone, from post-prandial strolls to challenging 1000m peaks.

What to Bring

For short walks on waymarked trails, all you will need is comfortable footwear, a rain jacket and some food and water.

Hikers venturing further into Ireland's hills and bogs should be properly equipped and cautious, as the weather can become vicious at any time of year.

➡ After rain, peaty soil can become boggy, so always wear stout shoes or boots and carry good waterproofs and extra food and drink.

➡ Always take a map and compass (and know how to use them). Don't depend on mobile phones (although carrying one with you is a good idea).

➡ Leave a note with your route and expected time of return with a trusted person (either at your accommodation, or via email or text to a friend or family member), and let them know when you have returned safely.

Top Outdoor Tips

Best Time to Go

May, June and September are the best months for hiking and biking – best chance of dry weather and less chance of midges.

Best Outdoor Experiences

Hike the Wicklow Way (Wicklow), climb Carrauntoohil (Kerry), cycle the Great Western Greenway (Mayo), mountain bike at Davagh Forest (Tyrone), tee off at Royal Portrush (Antrim), sea kayak in Lough Hyne (Cork) and canoe the Lough Erne Canoe Trail (Fermanagh).

Essential Hill Walking Gear

Good waterproofs, spare warm clothing, map and compass, mobile phone (but don't rely on it), first-aid kit, head torch, whistle (for emergencies), spare food and drink.

Safety Checklist

Check the weather forecast first, let someone know your plans, set pace and objective to suit slowest member of party, don't be afraid to turn back if it's too difficult.

Walking Guides & Maps

There are several good hiking guidebooks that cover Ireland, notably the Collins Press (www.collinspress.ie) series of walking guides.

The **Ordnance Survey of Ireland** (www.ose.ie) and the **Ordnance Survey of Northern Ireland** (www.nidirect.gov.uk/ordnance-survey-of-northern-ireland) cover the entire island with their 1:50,000 *Discovery/Discoverer* series (€8.99/£6.50 per sheet). There are also more detailed 1:25,000 *Adventure/Activity* maps (€12.99/£7.80) covering popular areas such as MacGillicuddy's Reeks & Killarney National Park, the Wicklow Mountains, the Mournes, and the Causeway Coast.

Maps produced specifically for walkers:

Harveys Superwalker (www.harveymaps.co.uk) Waterproof 1:30,000 hill-walking maps covering Connemara, the Mournes, the Wicklow Mountains and MacGillicuddy's Reeks.

EastWest Mapping (www.eastwestmapping.ie) Walkers' maps of the Wicklow Mountains, the Wicklow Way and the Blackstairs Mountains & Barrow Valley.

TOP FIVE IRISH HILL WALKS

Ireland's mountain ranges aren't as magnificent as the Alps, but they do offer some superb hill-walking opportunities.

Carrauntoohil (1040m; MacGillycuddy's Reeks, Kerry, p267) The ascent of Ireland's highest summit involves scrambling and challenging navigation; inexperienced hill walkers should hire a guide.

Slieve Donard (853m; Mourne Mountains, Down; p574) Northern Ireland's highest hill is a straightforward climb; its near-neighbour Slieve Binnian is more interesting.

Errigal Mountain (752m; Donegal; p457) This pyramidal quartzite peak is one of Ireland's shapeliest hills.

Twelve Bens (729m; Connemara, Galway) Though small in stature, Connemara's craggy hills offer some of Ireland's toughest terrain. The Glencoaghan Horseshoe is often cited as the country's finest hill walk.

Mt Brandon (951m; Kerry; p289) The highest peak on the Dingle Peninsula has rugged trails that yield jaw-droppingly spectacular views.

Access to the Countryside

Unlike Scotland, England and Wales (and most other European countries) where there are public rights of way and/or a public right of access to most areas of uncultivated land, walkers and cyclists in Ireland have no rights of access to privately owned land, not even on wild moorland and mountains (unless it is part of a national park).

The absence of a legal framework has led to a rather fraught situation in recent years as the popularity of walking, mountaineering and off-road biking has increased, and numerous disputes have blown up across the country, forcing the closure or rerouting of some traditional walking routes.

Access has been negotiated with landowners for all of the national trails and waymarked walks listed in this guidebook (disputes over access is why many of these trails follow public roads for long distances). However, you will occasionally come across locked gates, barbed wire fences or 'no walkers allowed' signs.

For more information on access rights and responsible walking see:

Keep Ireland Open (www.keepirelandopen.org) Voluntary body campaigning for rights of access to the countryside.

Leave No Trace (www.leavenotraceireland.org) Educational charity promoting responsible use of the outdoors.

Mountaineering Ireland (www.mountaineering.ie) Good information and advice on their Access Policy page.

Where to Walk

For a small country, Ireland is packed with choice – from seaside ambles to long-distance treks through the mountains. Tourist offices stock maps and leaflets with details of local walks. Online resources:

Discover Ireland (www.discoverireland.ie/walking) Downloadable PDF maps and guides to more than 600 walks in the Republic of Ireland.

Irish Trails (www.irishtrails.ie) Details of more than 40 (mostly long-distance) waymarked trails in the Republic of Ireland.

Walk Northern Ireland (www.walkni.com) Descriptions and PDF downloads of more than 400 walks in Northern Ireland, from a 400m stroll to the 1000km Ulster Way.

Pilgrim Paths (www.pilgrimpath.ie) Waymarked walking trails that follow ancient Christian pilgrimage routes.

Coillte Outdoors (www.coillteoutdoors.ie) Ireland's state forestry service has hundreds of walking trails on its properties.

Day Walks

You can take a leisurely day hike in just about any part of Ireland. Some suggestions:

➡ **Barrow Towpath** Along the River Barrow in Counties Carlow and Kilkenny, pleasant walks can be had along the towpath from Borris to Graiguenamanagh and on to St Mullins. (p155)

➡ **Glendalough** The wooded trails around this ancient monastic site in County Wicklow lure many a traveller from nearby Dublin for a few hours' rambling. (p144)

➡ **Lough Key Forest Park** The woods around this lake in County Roscommon have a wonderful canopied trail. (p475)

➡ **Sky Road** In County Galway, Clifden's Sky Road yields views of the Connemara coast; it's suitable for walking or cycling. (p387)

➡ **South Leinster Way** The prettiest section of this waymarked way is a 13km hike between the charming villages of Graiguenamanagh and Inistioge in County Kilkenny. (p204)

➡ **Brandon Way** Not to be confused with Mt Brandon in County Kerry, the smaller Brandon Hill (516m) in County Kilkenny has a path that wends up to the summit from woodlands and moorlands along the River Barrow. (p204)

➡ **Killarney National Park** Superb short walks on the shores of Lough Leane in County Kerry, plus the slightly longer Muckross Lake Loop. (p260)

➡ **Killary Harbour** Scenic walks along the shore of this long, fjord-like inlet of the sea in County Galway. (p392)

➡ **Glen of Aherlow** Fine walking amid lush woodland and low hills in County Tipperary with grand views towards the high Galtee Mountains. (p310)

➡ **Fair Head** Easy paths lead to the top of huge basalt sea cliffs in county Antrim, with a panorama that takes in Rathlin Island and the Scottish coast. (p614)

MIDGES

Midges are tiny, 2mm-long blood-sucking flies that appear in huge swarms in summer, and can completely ruin a holiday if you're not prepared to deal with them.

They proliferate from late May to mid-September, but especially mid-June to mid-August – which unfortunately coincides with the main tourist season – and are most common in the western and northern parts of Ireland, especially in boggy areas like Connemara and Donegal.

Midges are at their worst during the twilight hours, and on still, overcast days – strong winds and bright sunshine tend to discourage them. The only way to combat them is to cover up, particularly in the evening. Wear long-sleeved, light-coloured clothing (midges are attracted to dark colours) and, most importantly, use a reliable insect repellent.

Coastal Trails

Ireland's coastlines are naturally conducive to long and reflective walks with or without shoes on. Here are five to get you started:

➡ **Arranmore Way** (County Donegal) This 14km trail makes a circuit of the wild seacliff scenery of this rocky island off the Donegal coast. (p446)

➡ **Causeway Coast Way** (County Antrim) A waymarked trail that follows Antrim's north coast. Particularly spectacular is the final 16.5km of this waymarked way, from Carrick-a-Rede to the Giant's Causeway. (p607)

➡ **Wexford Coastal Walk** (County Wexford) Following 221km of trails overlooking vast sandy beaches, bird-haunted backwaters and the bones of old shipwrecks.

➡ **Sheep's Head Lighthouse** (County Cork) A superb short walk leads from the road-end to one of the country's most spectacularly sited lighthouses. (p244)

➡ **Tory Way** (County Donegal) A 12km looped trail around the rocky coast of Tory Island. (p448)

Waymarked Trails

The opening of the 1000km Ulster Way in the 1970s followed by the Wicklow Way in 1982 prompted the establishment of a network of more than 40 long-distance walking trails that total over 5000km in length. Though many of these would take several days, or even weeks, to complete, you can easily walk shorter sections of each trail as you see fit.

Our top 10 of Ireland's long-distance trails:

➡ **Barrow Way** A 114km wander through some of Ireland's loveliest riverside scenery between Lowtown in County Kildare and St Mullins in County Carlow. (p191)

➡ **Beara Way** A moderately easy loop of 196km that follows historic routes and tracks on a stunning peninsula in West Cork. (p249)

➡ **Burren Way** This 123km walk takes in County Clare's unique rocky landscape, the Cliffs of Moher and the musical town of Doolin. (p346)

➡ **Cavan Way** Impressive topographic variety is packed into this short (26km) route, taking in bogs, Stone Age monuments and the source of the River Shannon. (p524)

➡ **Dingle Way** A popular 168km route in County Kerry that loops around one of Ireland's most beautiful peninsulas. (p279)

➡ **East Munster Way** Starting in County Tipperary and ending up in County Waterford, a 70km walk through forest and open moorland, and along the towpath of the River Suir. (p321)

➡ **Kerry Way** A 214km route that takes in Killarney National park, the spectacular Macgillycuddy's Reeks and the Ring of Kerry coast. (p258)

➡ **Sheep's Head Way** Sweeping seascapes and splendid isolation mark out this 88km off-the-beaten-track peninsular circuit. (p244)

➡ **Ulster Way** A route totalling 1000km, making a circuit around the six counties of Northern Ireland and Donegal. It can easily be broken down into smaller sections. (p628)

➡ **Wicklow Way** Ireland's most popular walking trail is this 132km route, which starts in southern Dublin and ends in Clonegal in County Carlow.(p145)

Golfing

With over 400 courses dotted around the island, golf is one of Ireland's most popular pastimes. There are plenty of parkland courses, but the more memorable golf experience is to be had on a seaside links – the Irish coastline is home to 30% of the world's links courses.

Most golf courses are privately owned, but all welcome nonmember bookings and walk-ins: to avoid disappointment, book the better-known courses in advance. For the top courses, expect to pay €80 to €100 or more per round; lesser-known courses charge as little as €25, depending on when you play. Some courses will insist that you have a registered handicap from your home country. Most courses will also rent clubs, but they're not usually very good.

A great option is to rent a customised set of clubs at Dublin or Cork airport through www.clubstohire.com, which you can drop back at the airport when you leave.

Our favourite courses:

Ballybunion Golf Club, County Kerry (p296)

Royal Portrush Golf Club, County Londonderry (p604)

County Sligo Golf Course, County Sligo (p421)

Waterville Golf Links, County Kerry (p275)

Mount Juliet, County Kilkenny (p201)

For more information, check out **Golf Ireland** (www.golf.discoverireland.ie), or the **Golfing Union of Ireland** (www.golfnet.ie), both of which offer booking services.

There are specials and discounted green fees available throughout the year: a good online resource is www.teetimes.ie, where you can book heavily discounted green fees at dozens of courses throughout the country.

Cycling

Ireland has a lot to offer the cycle tourist, not least in the huge network of minor roads that criss-cross even the wildest parts of the island. Take along a good map and a spirit of adventure (and decent waterproofs, of course), and you can clock up hundreds of miles of happy exploration.

Several operators offer guided and self-guided cycling tours in Ireland, including:

Iron Donkey (www.irondonkey.com)

Ireland by Bike (www.irelandbybike.com)

Where to Cycle

➡ **Great Western Greenway** This 42km-long, mostly off-road cycleway stretches from Westport to Achill Island in County Mayo. (p408)

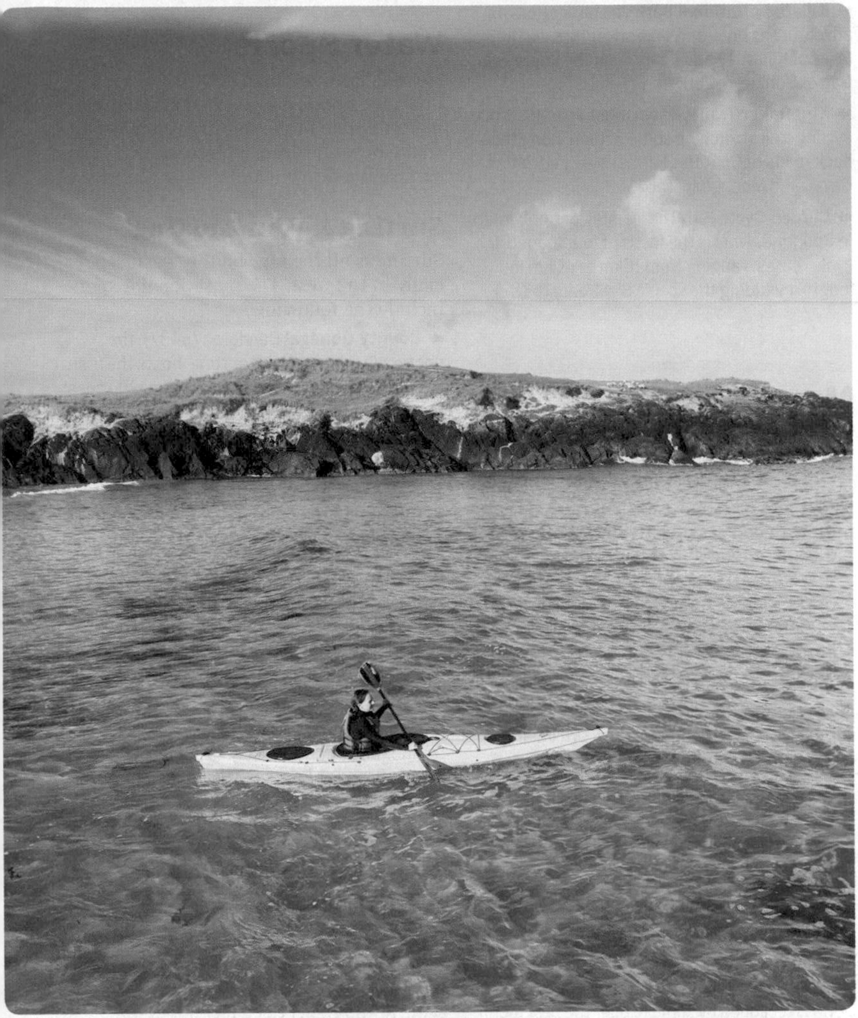

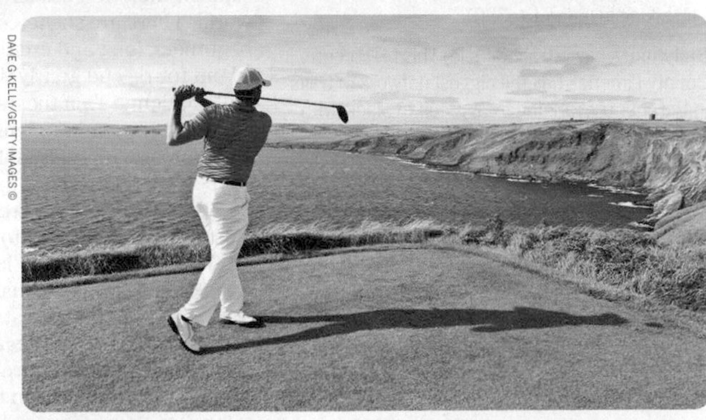

Top: Sea kayaking, Connemara (p382)

Bottom: Golfing, County Cork (p207)

DAVE G KELLY/GETTY IMAGES ©

➡ **Killarney National Park** The park offers an adventurous boat-and-bike adventure via the lakes of Killarney and up through the impressive Gap of Dunloe. (p260)

➡ **Kingfisher Trail** A waymarked, long-distance cycling trail stretching some 370km along the back roads of Counties Fermanagh, Leitrim, Cavan and Monaghan. (p621)

➡ **Clifden Cycle Hub** The 'capital' of Connemara in County Galway is the focus of four looped cycle routes, ranging from 16km to 40km in length, including the scenic Sky Road. (p387)

Mountain Biking

The lack of a legal right of access to private land has meant that off-road biking in Ireland lags behind the rest of the UK. That said, there are some excellent purpose-built trail centres, mostly in state forest parks on both sides of the border.

In many areas, local riders quietly work away at their own network of self-built trails; the local bike shop is a great source of information on these.

For more details, check out:

Mountain Bike NI (www.mountainbikeni.com) Full details of MTB centres in Northern Ireland.

TrailBadger (www.trailbadger.com) Useful database of mountain bike trails in Ireland.

Top MTB Trail Centres

Davagh Forest Forest trails for beginners, rock slabs and drop-offs for experts, in the heart of County Tyrone. (p635)

Rostrevor With a thigh-crunching 27km red trail and a terrifying 19km black, Rostrevor in County Down is reckoned by some to offer the best mountain biking in Ireland. (p580)

Ballyhoura (www.trailriders.ie) This MTB centre in County Limerick has the biggest network of trails in the country, ranging from green to black, with the longest at more than 50km.

Ballinastoe (www.coillteoutdoors.ie) This trail centre on the edge of the Wicklow Mountains south of Dublin has a superbly flowing, 14km blue trail. There are plenty more trails to explore in the nearby hills.

Bike Park Ireland (http://bikeparkireland.ie) This purpose-built centre in County Tipperary has an uplift service to the top of the hill, and downhill trails for all levels of rider.

Water Sports

Ireland has more than 3000km of coastline and countless rivers and lakes, so no matter where in the country you may be, you're never far from a place to surf, windsurf, scuba dive or canoe.

Surfing & Windsurfing

Surfing is all the rage on the coast, especially in the west. The most popular spots include the following:

➡ **County Donegal** Bundoran (p437), the unofficial capital of Irish surfing, hosts the Irish national championships in April. Along the coast there are at least half a dozen top-rated spots for beginners and advanced surfers. Windsurfing and kitesurfing are equally popular around Port-na-Blagh (p449).

➡ **County Sligo** Easkey (p426) and Strandhill (p422) are famous for their year-round surf, and have facilities for travellers who seek room and board (with the room being optional).

➡ **County Clare** Nice breaks at Kilkee (p337), Lahinch (p341) and Fanore (p353).

➡ **County Waterford** Tramore Beach (p180) is home to Ireland's largest surf school.

➡ **County Kerry** Surfers flock to massive Inch Strand (p280) for its nicely sized, well-paced waves. Brandon Bay and Ballybunion (p296) are also top spots.

➡ **County Antrim** The beaches around Portrush (p603) afford good surfing and body-surfing. The swells are highest and the water warmest in September and October.

Canoeing & Sea Kayaking

Ireland's long, indented coastline provides some of the finest sea kayaking in the world. There are sheltered inlets ideal for beginners, long and exciting coastal and island tours, and gnarly tidal passages that will challenge even the most expert paddler, all amid spectacular scenery and wildlife – encounters with seals, dolphins and even whales are relatively common. The **Irish Sea Kayaking Association** (www.iska.ie) lists providers of kayak tours and courses.

The country's inland lakes and waterways offer excellent Canadian canoeing. Northern Ireland has established a network of official **canoe trails** (www.canoeni.com), with infrastructure that includes access points, information boards, toilets and campsites. South of the border, waterways like the Shannon, Barrow and Grand Canal (see www.waterwaysireland.org) all offer long-distance canoe touring possibilities.

Scuba Diving

Ireland's west coast has some of the best scuba diving in Europe. The best period for diving is roughly March to October when visibility averages more than 12m, but can increase to 30m on good days.

Top dive locations include Kilkee (Mayo), Baltimore (Cork), Castlegregory (Kerry) and Arranmore Island and Rosguill (Donegal).

For more details about diving, contact Comhairle Fó-Thuinn (CFT), also known as the **Irish Underwater Council** (www.diving.ie); it publishes the dive magazine *SubSea* (available online).

Coasteering

If sometimes a simple clifftop walk doesn't cut the mustard, then coasteering might appeal. It's like mountaineering, but instead of going up a mountain, you go sideways along a coast – a steep and rocky coast – with waves breaking around your feet. And if the rock gets too steep, no problem – you jump in and start swimming. Coasteering centres provide wetsuits, helmets and buoyancy aids; you provide an old pair of training shoes and a sense of adventure.

Providers include:

Coasteering Ireland (www.coasteering-ireland.com) Operates mostly in the Beara Peninsula (Cork) and the Ring of Kerry.

Coasteering NI (www.coasteeringni.co.uk) Operates in County Antrim near the Giant's Causeway, and at Glencolumbcille in Donegal.

Fishing

Fishing – whether in sea, lough or river – is one of Ireland's most popular pastimes. Ireland is justly famous for its salmon, sea trout and brown trout fishing, and for its superb sea angling.

Top Irish angling experiences include:

➡ Fly fishing for brown trout on the big limestone loughs of Corrib and Mask (County Galway); the annual mayfly hatch here attracts thousands of anglers from all over the world.

➡ Sea trout fishing on Lough Currane in County Kerry, one of the best sea trout fisheries in all of Britain and Ireland.

➡ Fishing for salmon on the Blackwater (Cork), Laune (Kerry) or Roe (Londonderry), three of Ireland's top salmon rivers.

➡ Shore fishing for sea bass in the southwest, or boat fishing for blue shark out of Kinsale – Ireland has some of Europe's finest sea angling.

The books *Rivers of Ireland* and *Loughs of Ireland* by Peter O'Reilly provide a comprehensive guide to fishing for trout and salmon in both Northern Ireland and the Republic of Ireland.

Permits & Rod Licences

Neither a permit nor a licence is needed for sea angling.

Permits Fishing for brown trout in many of Ireland's most famous loughs, including Corrib, Mask and the Killarney lakes, is free. However, most loughs and rivers require a permit (ask at the local hotel or tackle shop). Day ticket prices range from €3 to €20.

Rod Licences In addition to a permit, a rod licence is required for all freshwater fishing in Northern Ireland (three days/14 days £3.50/9). In the republic, a rod licence is needed only for salmon and sea trout fishing (one day/three weeks €20/40). You can buy them from local tackle shops and from some tourist offices.

For more information, see www.fishinginireland.info.

Rock Climbing

Ireland's mountain ranges aren't high – Mt Carrauntoohil in Kerry's Macgillycuddy's Reeks is the highest peak in Ireland at only 1040m – but they offer some excellent rock climbing, notably in the Mournes, the Reeks and around Glendalough in the Wicklow Mountains.

However, the cream of the country's climbing is on its superb sea cliffs – from Malin Beg in Donegal and the cliffs of Achill Island, to the soaring basalt columns of Fair Head and perfect limestone crags of the Burren. *Rock Climbing in Ireland* (€25) by David Flanagan covers 400 of the country's best routes.

Plan Your Trip

Eat & Drink Like a Local

In the last decade Ireland has 'rediscovered' its own native cuisine. A host of chefs and producers have led a foodie revolution that, at its heart, is about bringing to the table the kind of meals that have long been taken for granted on well-run Irish farms. Coupled with the growing sophistication of the Irish palate – by now well used to the varied flavours of worldwide cuisines – it's relatively easy to eat well on all budgets. This has been a boon to the tourist industry, which no longer has to explain why so many Irish meals are so memorable – for all the wrong reasons.

Finding the Best of Irish Food & Drink

www.bestofbridgestone.com Extensive coverage of artisan producers and the best restaurants serving their produce.

www.bordbia.ie Irish Food Board website, with a few local producers listed, as well as a comprehensive list of farmers markets.

www.irishcheese.ie The Association of Irish Farmhouse Cheesemakers, with every small dairy covered.

www.slowfoodireland.com Organisation supporting small producers, with social events across Ireland.

The Year in Food

January–March

The coldest time of the year is perfect for the fry – a cooked Irish breakfast.

April–June

The budding of spring sees freshly picked fruit and vegetables, such as asparagus and rhubarb, make an appearance. Food festivals include the following:

- **West Waterford Festival of Food** (p182) Three days of local produce and fine food in Dungarvan, including a seaside BBQ and a craft beer garden.
- **Só Sligo Festival** (www.sosligo.ie; ⌚mid-Jun) Professional chefs from around the globe compete in the World Irish Stew Championship (there's also an amateur category open to all).
- **Taste of Dublin** (p98) The capital's best restaurants combine to serve up sample platters of their best dishes amid music and other entertainment.

July–September

In July, the first of the season's new potatoes appear, along with jams and berry pies with gooseberries, blackberries and loganberries. Culinary celebrations take place all over the country, and include the following:

➡ **Carlingford Oyster Festival** (p519) Oysters come early in this County Louth town and the season is marked with a small festival.

➡ **Clarenbridge Oyster Festival** (p393) A long-established festival in the South Galway town.

➡ **Hillsborough Oyster Festival** (p582) Some 12,000 people from all over the world gather over the first weekend of September to sample the region's best and to take part in the World Oyster Eating Championships.

➡ **Taste of West Cork Food Festival** (p237) Skibbereen brings together its best producers to put on this weeklong festival.

➡ **Waterford Harvest Food Festival** (www.waterfordharvestfestival.ie; ⏲mid-Sep) A 10-day festival with food markets, taste workshops, celebrity-chef clinics and open-air picnics.

➡ **Galway International Oyster & Seafood Festival** (p369)Last weekend in September sees plenty of oysters, washed down with lashings of Guinness.

October–December

October is apple-picking month, and the main potato crop is dug up. It's the end of the food-festival season, but it goes out with a bang:

➡ **Kinsale Gourmet Festival** (www.kinsalerestaurants.com; ⏲early Oct) The unofficial gourmet capital of Ireland struts its culinary stuff over three days.

Food Experiences

Meals of a Lifetime

➡ **Restaurant Patrick Guilbaud** (p110), Dublin

➡ **Finn's Table** (p231), Kinsale, Country Cork

➡ **Castle Murray** (p438), Dunkineely, County Donegal

➡ **Jacks Coastguard Restaurant** (p270), Cromane Peninsula, County Kerry

➡ **Restaurant 1826 Adare** (p308), County Limerick

Dare to Try

Ironically, while the Irish palate has become more adventurous, it is the old-fashioned Irish menu that features some fairly challenging dishes. Dare to try the following:

➡ **Black pudding** Made from congealed pork blood, suet and other fillings; a ubiquitous part of an Irish cooked breakfast.

➡ **Boxty** A Northern Irish starchy potato cake made with a half-and-half mix of cooked mashed potatoes and grated, strained raw potato.

➡ **Carrageen** The typical Irish seaweed that can be found in dishes as diverse as salad and ice cream.

➡ **Corned beef tongue** Usually accompanied by cabbage, this dish is still found on a traditional Irish menu.

➡ **Lough Neagh eel** A speciality of Northern Ireland, typically eaten around Halloween; it's usually served in chunks with a white onion sauce.

➡ **Poitín** It's rare enough to be offered a drop of the 'cratur', as illegally distilled whiskey (made from malted grain or potatoes) is called here. Still, there are pockets of the country with secret stills – in Donegal, Connemara and West Cork.

Local Specialities

To Eat

➡ **Potatoes** Still a staple of most traditional meals and presented in a variety of forms. The mashed potato dishes colcannon and champ

THE BEST IRISH CHEESES

➡ **Ardrahan** Flavoursome farmhouse creation with a rich, nutty taste.

➡ **Corleggy** Subtle, pasteurised goats cheese.

➡ **Durrus** A creamy, fruity cheese, beloved of fine-food fans (p244).

➡ **Cashel Blue** Creamy blue cheese from Tipperary.

➡ **Cooleeney** Award-winning Camembert-style cheese.

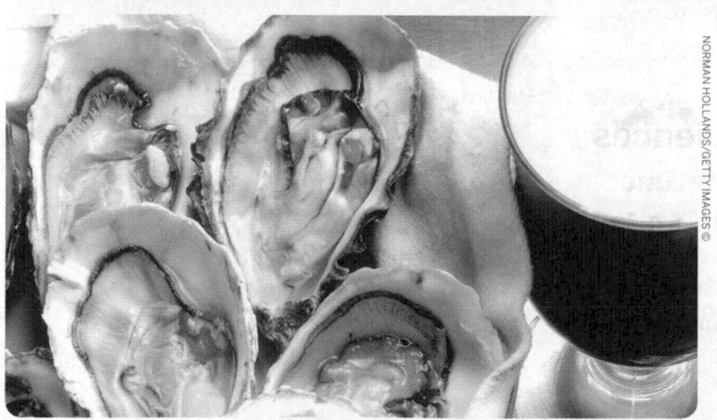

NORMAN HOLLANDS/GETTY IMAGES ©

Top: A pub meal at the Crown Liquor Saloon (p554), Belfast

Bottom: Oysters and stout

(with cabbage and spring onion, respectively) are two of the tastiest recipes in the country.

➡ **Meat and seafood** Beef, lamb and pork are common options. Seafood is widely available in restaurants and is often excellent, especially in the west. Oysters, trout and salmon are delicious, particularly if they're direct from the sea or a river rather than a fish farm.

➡ **Soda bread** The most famous Irish bread is made with bicarbonate of soda, to make up for soft Irish flour that traditionally didn't take well to yeast. Combined with buttermilk, it makes a superbly tasty bread, and is often on the breakfast menus at B&Bs.

➡ **The fry** Who can say no to a plate of fried bacon, sausages, black pudding, white pudding, eggs and tomatoes? For the famous Ulster fry, common throughout the North, simply add fadge (potato bread).

To Drink

➡ **Stout** While Guinness has become synonymous with stout the world over, few outside Ireland realise that there are two other major producers competing for the favour of the Irish drinker: Murphy's and Beamish & Crawford, both based in Cork city.

➡ **Tea** The Irish drink more tea, per capita, than any other nation in the world and you'll be offered a cup as soon as you cross the threshold of any Irish home. Taken with milk (and sugar, if you want) rather than lemon, preferred blends are very strong, and nothing like the namby-pamby versions that pass for Irish breakfast tea elsewhere.

➡ **Whiskey** At last count, there were almost 100 different types of Irish whiskey, brewed by only three distilleries – Jameson's, Bushmills and Cooley's. A visit to Ireland reveals a depth of excellence that will make the connoisseur's palate spin while winning over many new friends to what the Irish call *uisce beatha* (water of life).

Craft Distilleries

A handful of independently owned distilleries have opened in the last few years, producing whiskies (and, in some cases, other spirits) that have added a fine bit of diversity to the range of Irish spirits.

➡ **Blackwater Distillery** (www.blackwaterdistillery.ie; Unit 3, Cappoquin Enterprise Park) A distillery in Cappoquin, County Waterford that produces around 50 casks of whisky (without the 'e' in accordance with Munster tradition) a year.

➡ **Dingle Whiskey Distillery** (www.dingledistillery.ie; Milltown Rd) Whisky, a quintuple-distilled vodka and a London dry gin made on the edge of town.

➡ **West Cork Distillers** (www.westcorkdistillers.com; Market Street) Blended, pot still and single-malt whiskies, as well as liqueurs and vodka.

➡ **Teeling Distillery** (Map p70; www.teelingwhiskey.com; 17 Newmarket; ⌚9am-6pm Mon-Fri) Dublin's first new distillery in 125 years was opened in 2015 by the same family who own the Cooley Distillery in County Louth.

How to Eat & Drink

When to Eat

Irish eating habits have changed over the last couple of decades, and there are differences between urban and rural practices.

➡ **Breakfast** Usually eaten before 9am (although hotels and B&Bs will serve until 11am Monday to Friday, to noon at weekends in urban areas), as most people rush off to work. Weekend brunch is popular in bigger towns and cities.

➡ **Lunch** Urban workers eat on the run between 12.30pm and 2pm (most restaurants don't begin to serve lunch until at least midday). At weekends, especially Sunday, the midday lunch is skipped in favour of a substantial mid-afternoon meal (called dinner), usually between 2pm and 4pm.

VEGETARIANS & VEGANS

Ireland has come a long, long way since the days when vegetarians were looked upon as odd creatures; nowadays, even the most militant vegan will barely cause a ruffle in all but the most basic of kitchens. Which isn't to say that travellers with plant-based diets are going to find the most imaginative range of options on menus outside the bigger towns and cities – or in the plethora of modern restaurants that have opened in the last few years – but you can rest assured that the overall quality of the home-grown vegetable is top-notch and most places will have at least one dish that you can tuck into comfortably. For info on dining in Dublin, see p105.

IRELAND'S CRAFT BEERS

Although mainstream lagers such as Heineken, Carlsberg and Coors Lite are most pubs' best-selling beers, the craft beer revolution has resulted in dozens of microbreweries springing up all over the island, so that artisan beers are served in more than 600 of Ireland's pubs and bars. Here's a small selection to whet the tastebuds:

➡ **Devil's Backbone** (4.9% ABV) Rich amber ale from Donegal brewer Kinnegar.

➡ **The Full Irish** (6% ABV) Pale ale by Eight Degrees Brewery outside Mitchelstown, County Cork voted Irish beer of the year in 2015.

➡ **O'Hara's Leann Folláin** (6% ABV) Dry stout with vaguely chocolate notes produced by Carlow Brewing Company.

➡ **Metalman Pale Ale** (4.3% ABV) American-style pale ale by the much-respected Metalman Brewing Company in Waterford – now available in cans.

➡ **Puck Pilsner** (4.5% ABV) A light lager brewed by Jack Cody's Brewery in Drogheda.

➡ **Twisted Hop** (4.7% ABV) Blond ale produced by Hilden just outside Lisburn, Ireland's oldest independent brewery.

➡ **Tea** Not the drink, but the evening meal – also confusingly called dinner – is the main meal of the day for urbanites, usually eaten around 6.30pm. Rural communities eat at the same time but with a more traditional tea of bread, cold cuts and, yes, tea. Restaurants follow international habits, with most diners not eating until at least 7.30pm.

➡ **Supper** A before-bed snack of tea and toast or sandwiches, still enjoyed by many Irish, although urbanites increasingly eschew it for health reasons. Not a practice in restaurants.

Where to Eat

➡ **Restaurants** From cheap 'n' cheerful to Michelin-starred, Ireland has something for every palate and budget.

➡ **Cafes** Ireland is awash with cafes of every description, many of which are perfect for a quick, tasty bite.

➡ **Hotels** Even if you're not a guest, most hotel restaurants cater to outside diners. Top hotels usually feature good restaurants with prices to match.

➡ **Pubs** Pub grub is ubiquitous, mostly of the toasted-sandwich variety. However, a large number also have full menu service, with some of them being as good as any top restaurant.

Dining Etiquette

The Irish aren't big on restrictive etiquette, preferring friendly informality to any kind of stuffy to-dos. Still, the following are a few tips to dining with the Irish:

➡ **Children** All restaurants welcome kids up to 7pm, but pubs and some smarter restaurants don't allow them in the evening. Family restaurants have children's menus, others have reduced portions of regular menu items.

➡ **Returning a dish** If the food is not to your satisfaction, it's best to politely explain what's wrong with it as soon as you can; any respectable restaurant will endeavour to replace the dish immediately.

➡ **Paying the bill** If you insist on paying the bill for everyone, be prepared for a first, second and even third refusal to countenance such an exorbitant act of generosity. But don't be fooled: the Irish will refuse something several times even if they're delighted with it. Insist gently but firmly and you'll get your way!

Plan Your Trip

Wild Atlantic Way

Ireland's western edge is one of the world's most stunning stretches of coastline, a 2500km-long necklace of jagged cliffs, crescent strands and latticed fields strung out from West Cork to northeastern Donegal. It's been there since time immemorial, but it wasn't until 2013 that the Irish tourist board officially launched the Wild Atlantic Way, the world's longest coastal driving route, richly decorated with the panoramic pit stops you probably came to Ireland to experience.

Cork & Kerry

Ireland's southwestern corner is packed with scenic highlights along its 463km coastline, skirting around the best-known (and explored) peninsulas in the country.

Highlights

➡ **Mizen Head** (Cork; p241) The spectacular views from the rugged clifftop – cross the Mizen footbridge to get right to the edge – include the Fastnet Lighthouse, perched on a rock known as Ireland's Teardrop, for this was the last sight of the country for emigrants who embarked for America during the Famine.

➡ **Slea Head Drive** (Kerry; p288) Only 50km long, this circular route around the tip of the peninsula is one of Ireland's best scenic drives. The main distraction from the stunning scenery is the heavy concentration of prehistoric sites dotted throughout the hills.

Worth Discovering

Dursey Island (Cork; p250) At the tip of the remote Beara Peninsula is a quiet island, blissfully free of shops, pubs and restaurants but

Need to Know

The Route

Split into five connected sections spread across nine counties: Cork, Kerry, Clare, Limerick, Galway, Mayo, Sligo, Leitrim and Donegal.

Clearly marked by nearly 4000 signposts featuring an aquamarine-coloured wave and punctuated by 157 'Discovery Points' where you can stop and learn about must-sees and the lesser-known diversions of each area.

Direction

Car Do the route in either direction, but to stay closest to the sea – with the best views – drive south to north.

Bicycle Prevailing wind is southerly, so north to south is easier (even if the wind can't be relied upon to cooperate).

Information

For up-to-date information on everything to do with the Wild Atlantic Way, check out Failte Ireland's designated website at www.wildatlanticway.com or download the terrific app, which is available for Android and iPhone.

Wild Atlantic Way

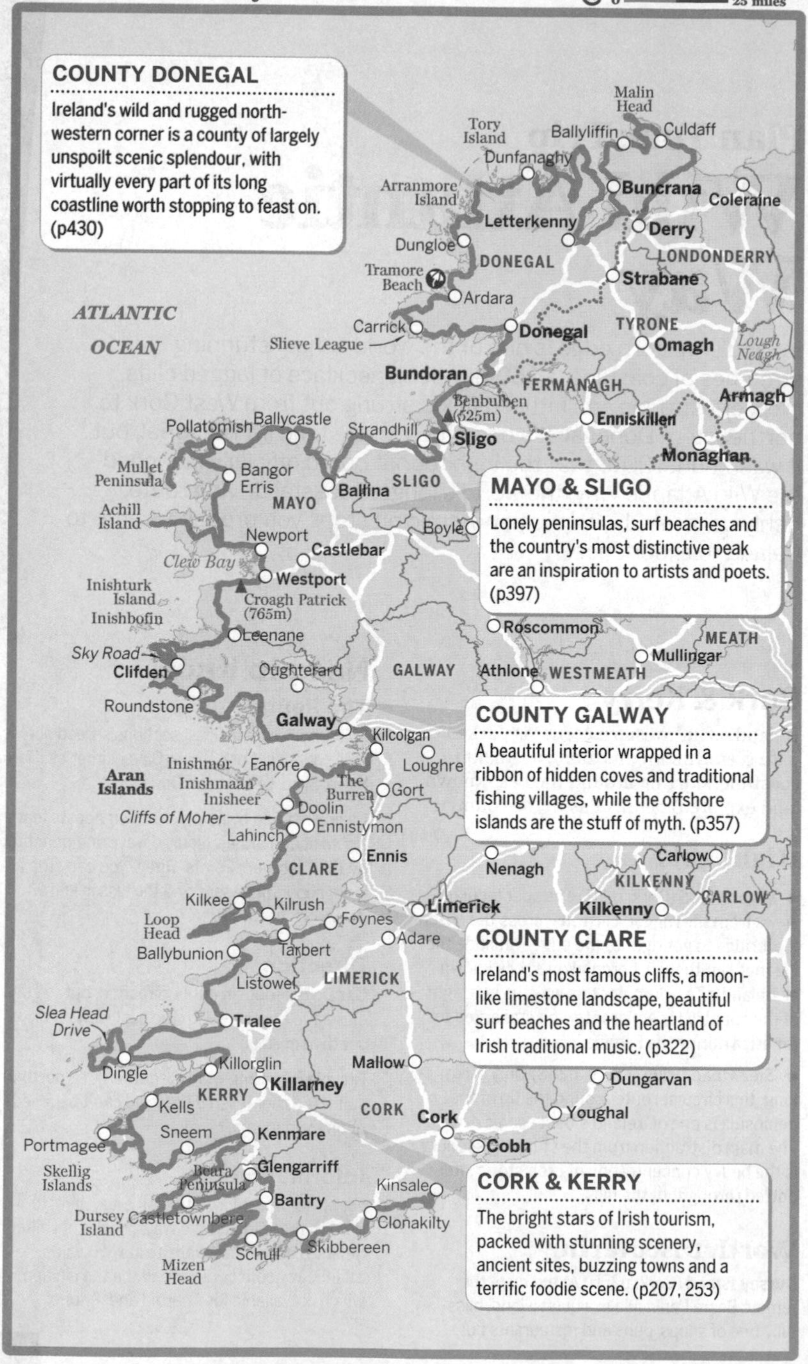

0 — 50 km
0 — 25 miles

COUNTY DONEGAL

Ireland's wild and rugged northwestern corner is a county of largely unspoilt scenic splendour, with virtually every part of its long coastline worth stopping to feast on. (p430)

MAYO & SLIGO

Lonely peninsulas, surf beaches and the country's most distinctive peak are an inspiration to artists and poets. (p397)

COUNTY GALWAY

A beautiful interior wrapped in a ribbon of hidden coves and traditional fishing villages, while the offshore islands are the stuff of myth. (p357)

COUNTY CLARE

Ireland's most famous cliffs, a moonlike limestone landscape, beautiful surf beaches and the heartland of Irish traditional music. (p322)

CORK & KERRY

The bright stars of Irish tourism, packed with stunning scenery, ancient sites, buzzing towns and a terrific foodie scene. (p207, 253)

ATLANTIC OCEAN
Malin Head
Tory Island
Ballyliffin
Culdaff
Dunfanaghy
Arranmore Island
Buncrana
Coleraine
Letterkenny
Derry
Dungloe
DONEGAL
LONDONDERRY
Tramore Beach
Strabane
Ardara
Carrick
Slieve League
Donegal
TYRONE
Omagh
Lough Neagh
Bundoran
FERMANAGH
Benbulben (525m)
Armagh
Pollatomish
Ballycastle
Strandhill
Enniskillen
Sligo
Monaghan
Mullet Peninsula
Bangor Erris
Ballina
SLIGO
MAYO
Achill Island
Boyle
Newport
Castlebar
Clew Bay
Westport
Inishturk Island
Croagh Patrick (765m)
Inishbofin
Roscommon
Leenane
MEATH
Sky Road
Clifden
Mullingar
Oughterard
GALWAY
Athlone
WESTMEATH
Roundstone
Galway
Kilcolgan
Aran Islands
Inishmór
Fanore
Loughrea
Inishmaan
Inisheer
The Burren
Gort
Cliffs of Moher
Doolin
Lahinch
Ennistymon
Ennis
CLARE
Nenagh
Carlow
KILKENNY
CARLOW
Kilkee
Kilrush
Limerick
Kilkenny
Loop Head
Foynes
Adare
Ballybunion
Tarbert
Listowel
LIMERICK
Slea Head Drive
Tralee
Dingle
Killorglin
Mallow
Killarney
KERRY
Dungarvan
Kells
CORK
Cork
Youghal
Portmagee
Sneem
Kenmare
Cobh
Skellig Islands
Beara Peninsula
Glengarriff
Kinsale
Bantry
Dursey Island
Castletownbere
Clonakilty
Schull
Skibbereen
Mizen Head

SIGNATURE EXPERIENCES

The Wild Atlantic Way is interspersed with a series of 'signature experiences' designed to enhance your visit. They include the following:

➡ **Cork & Kerry** Visit Skellig Michael (p276), a rocky crag with the beehive huts of 8th-century monks; it was described by George Bernard Shaw as 'part of our dream world'.

➡ **Clare** Take a guided tour (p346) of the Burren, as the local guides will give you a remarkable insight into 'Europe's largest rock garden' – an area rich in flora and home to Neolithic monuments that predate the Egyptian pyramids.

➡ **Clare/Galway** Explore Inisheer, the smallest of the Aran Islands, by pony and trap. If it suits, catch the ferry (p373) to Doolin, in County Clare: if you time it right, you'll go by the Cliffs of Moher just as the sun is going down.

➡ **Sligo** Take an oily soak in hand-harvested Atlantic seaweed and briny water, the traditional organic cure for stress and other ailments due to the high concentration of iodine in the seaweed. Voya Seaweed Baths (p422) in Strandhill is renowned.

➡ **Donegal** Take the ferry out to the remote island of Tory, where nearly everybody is a painter in the native art style developed in the 1950s; you'll most likely be met at the dock by the 'King' of the island, Patsy Dan...who happens to be a painter too.

worth visiting for its lighthouse, castle ruins and standing stones. Get here via a 10-minute ride on the cable car, but remember that the handful of residents take precedence over tourists!

County Clare

Clare's coastline is justifiably renowned throughout Europe for its dramatic cliffs, shaped over aeons by the crashing waves of the relentless Atlantic.

Highlights

➡ **Loop Head** (p339) This narrow shelf of headland, surrounded on both sides by the sea, has a long hiking trail between the tip and Kilkee. The views – of the Dingle Peninsula to the south and Galway and the Aran Islands to the north – are mesmerising.

➡ **Cliffs of Moher** (p344) Ireland's most famous cliffs rise vertically from the sea to 203m and their majesty entirely justifies the busloads of visitors that come, gawp and leave in wonder. For the best views, head south for about 5km along the southerly trail to Hag's Head.

Worth Discovering

Lahinch (p341) The Blue Flag beach at Lahinch is a surfer's paradise thanks to its flooding tide. Nearby is one of the best golf courses in Ireland, and, a little further afield, Ennistymon is a fine spot for traditional music.

County Galway

Wildness abounds in Galway, even beyond the crazy nights in its namesake city. Connemara is a stunning wilderness of bog, mountain and glacial lakes while the Aran Islands' dramatic desolation is at the heart of their beguiling beauty.

Highlights

➡ **Sky Road** (p387) A 12km circular route from Clifden, Connemara's 'capital': the scenery is staggering, especially northward toward remote Inishbofin and the islands of Clew Bay in Mayo. It's also a popular cycling route; you can rent bikes in Clifden.

➡ **Aran Islands** (p371) Forty minutes by ferry (or 10 by plane) and you're in another century: take your pick of three islands, each with their distinctive features (Inishmór the most visited,

Inisheer the smallest, Inishmaan the most isolated) but each giving the feeling of living at the edge of the world.

Worth Discovering

Dog's Bay/Gurteen Bay (p387) About 3km from Roundstone, the twin beaches of Dog's Bay and Gurteen are among Ireland's most beautiful: two back-to-back crescents of brilliant white sand made entirely of tiny bits of seashells rather than the crushed limestone common in other beaches.

Mayo to Sligo

Less visited than their southern counterparts, Mayo and Sligo adorn the Wild Atlantic crown with some truly stunning and desolate landscapes, beautiful islands and a handful of superb beaches that are surfers' favourites.

Highlights

➡ **Achill Island** (Mayo; p409) Ireland's largest offshore island is easily reached by causeway from the mainland. Once there, you'll have soaring cliffs and sandy beaches to explore as well as blanket bogs and even a mountain range.

➡ **Benbulben** (Sligo; p427) On a clear day, you won't miss the distinctive peak of Sligo's most famous mountain, which is like a table covered in a pleated tablecloth. Its beguiling look inspired WB Yeats.

Worth Discovering

Mullet Peninsula (Mayo; p413) Few spots in Ireland are as unspoilt and as unpopulated as this beautiful peninsula, which juts out into the Atlantic for about 30km. The eastern shores are lined with pristine beaches and the tiny population speaks Irish.

County Donegal

Wild, remote in parts but beautiful throughout, Donegal is the fitting end (or start) to the Wild Atlantic Way. Its jagged coastline of sheer cliffs, hidden coves and long stretches of golden sand are the stuff of myth and postcard – and an easy rival to any other county in the natural beauty stakes.

Highlights

➡ **Slieve League** (p440) These spectacular, monochrome cliffs in southwestern Donegal get far less press than their southern equivalent, but they're taller, at 600m, and every bit as dramatic.

➡ **Malin Head** (p463) Ireland's northernmost point is a rocky, weather-battered promontory topped by an early 19th-century Martello tower called Banba's Crown.

Worth Discovering

Tramore Beach (p443) An exhilarating 2km hike from the pretty village of Dunfanaghy takes you through some impressive dunes to a beautiful, usually empty strand; at the far end a path leads to Pollaguill Bay.

Regions at a Glance

The historic counties of Antrim, Armagh, Down, Fermanagh, Londonderry and Tyrone form Northern Ireland, which is part of the United Kingdom and (despite the lack of border controls) separate from the Republic of Ireland.

Dublin

Museums
Entertainment
History

Cultural Exhibits

The capital is the nation's primary repository of archaeological artefacts, artistic treasures and other cultural treasures. The National Museum's three Dublin branches are the place to start, while the city's multitude of galleries have art on their walls from the Renaissance to the current day.

Pubs & Nightlife

With a thousand-odd pubs to choose from, there is plenty of choice when deciding where to enjoy a pint of Dublin's most celebrated produce. But beyond Guinness and pub chatter there is theatre old and new, all manner of gigs and a host of sporting distractions.

History & Heritage

Virtually every Dublin street is lined with monuments to its storied history, from the cobbled grounds of Trinity College to the bloodied walls of Kilmainham Gaol. Its finest buildings and most elegant streets belong to its golden Georgian age, when Dublin was the second city of the empire. But even the most innocuous alley and unassuming house have a story to tell.

p60

Counties Wicklow & Kildare

Scenery
Monastic Ruins
Activities

Mountain Views

There are splendid views pretty much everywhere in the Wicklow Mountains, especially at the top of the passes that cut through the range; on a clear day you can see five counties. In Kildare, the fecund Bog of Allen offers another classic Irish landscape.

Ancient Monasteries

Not only are the ruins of Glendalough utterly absorbing, but their location, at the bottom of a glacial valley by two lakes, is absolutely enchanting and well worth the visit alone.

Walking Routes

Ireland's most popular walking trail, the Wicklow Way, cuts through the county north to south. Kildare is horse-breeding country, where the walking paths are a little bit gentler but no less enjoyable.

p134

Counties Wexford, Waterford, Carlow & Kilkenny

Scenery
History
Food

Seaside Vistas

Iconic emerald-green fields above ragged ebony cliffs that end in a cerulean sea: you will never tire of the vista. Should you need a break, perfect pockets of sand dot the coast, while Wexford's beaches stretch beyond the horizon. Inland, rural Ireland includes wild rivers and bucolic farms.

Viking Trails

You half expect to encounter a Viking as you wander the streets of Waterford and Wexford, where traces of the Middle Ages are all around you. Kilkenny's medieval past is impossible to miss, from its soaring cathedral to its great castle.

Local Produce

Head to Dungarvan to enjoy Irish cooking at its best, and enjoy the region's wonderful produce in all towns, big and small.

p158

County Cork

Food
Scenery
History

Gourmet Treats

County Cork is the unofficial gourmet heartland of Ireland, from the fabulous eateries of Cork city to the wealth of local producers and foodie artisans of West Cork, where you can buy directly at source and eat like a lord.

Peninsular Panoramas

The county's three western peninsulas – Mizen Head, Sheep's Head and Beara – have it all: mountain passes, lonely windswept hills, beautiful beaches and views that will stay with you long after you've left for home.

Story of Rebellion

The Rebel County wears its history with pride, even the sorrowful kind. You can explore it all, from Famine memorials and scenes of 17th-century battles to the powerful tribute to its more recent fallen heroes.

p207

County Kerry

Scenery
Seafood
Traditional Music

An Irish Postcard

County Kerry is the very definition of scenic Ireland – the Connor Pass, the Dingle Peninsula and, particularly, the Ring of Kerry are the gold standard by which Irish landscapes are judged.

Fresh from the Sea

Kerry's intimate relationship with the sea means that the fresh catch of the day is exactly that: throughout the Dingle Peninsula you can eat fish fresh off the boat you've just watched dock.

Traditional Sound

No Kerry town or village is complete without at least one pub featuring traditional music, played by musicians schooled in the respective styles of their region. It's the proper accompaniment to a visit to the county.

p253

Counties Limerick & Tipperary

Walking
History
Scenery

Heritage Trails

It's a long way to Tipperary, but keep going once you get there, tramping through the chequered Glen of Aherlow and along the more challenging Tipperary Heritage Trail, a 56km walk through beautiful river valleys dotted with ancient ruins.

Castles & Monasteries

From the mighty monastic city of Cashel in County Tipperary to the impressive fortifications of King John's Castle in Limerick city, the varied fortunes of the region's history are easily discernible throughout the two counties.

Atmospheric Ruins

At its broadest point, the mighty River Shannon makes for some beautiful vistas, while the rolling hills and farmland of County Tipperary, peppered with ancient ruins, offer the kind of views for which Ireland is renowned for.

p297

County Clare

Scenery
Music
Pubs

Dramatic Cliffs

Rising from the stormy Atlantic in all their sheer dramatic glory, the Cliffs of Moher are an arresting sight not to be missed. Elsewhere on the Clare coast are similar levels of drama and beauty, especially at Loop Head and the coastal roads leading to and from its spectacular views of the restless Atlantic.

Traditional Sessions

Clare plays Ireland's most traditional music, with few modern influences. At festivals, in pubs or even just around any corner, you can hear brilliant trad sessions by the county's surfeit of musicians.

Old-Style Drinking

There is *no* town in Clare that doesn't have at least one wonderful old pub where the Guinness is ready, the peat is lit and the craic never ends.

p322

County Galway

Scenery
Food
Culture

Islands & Mountains

Hundreds of years of ceaseless toil have brought green accents to the otherwise barren rocks of the Aran Islands. The results are gorgeous, and a walk around these windswept and intriguing islands is one of Ireland's highlights. In spring, when the gorse blooms in brilliant yellow, the Connemara Peninsula's beauty astounds.

Fresh Oysters

Even as you read this, millions of succulent oysters are growing to the perfect size out in the tidal waters of Galway Bay. Local chefs excel at creating taste treats with the water's bounty.

Gigs Everywhere

On any given night, Galway city's pubs and clubs hum with trad sessions, brilliant rock and tomorrow's next big band. It's a feast for the ears.

p357

Counties Mayo & Sligo

Islands
Megalithic Remains
Yeats Country

Scenery

There are reputed to be 365 islands in Clew Bay, including one once owned by John Lennon. There's also Craggy Island, which isn't the island of Father Ted fame but rather the home of the notorious pirate queen, Grace O'Malley (or Granuaile).

Ancient Ruins

From the world's most extensive Stone Age monument at Céide Fields to the megalithic cemeteries at Carrowmore and Carrowkeel, the environs of Ballycastle are a step back into prehistory.

Poetic Inspiration

County Sligo is Yeats country: he's buried in the church at Drumcliff, in the shadow of Benbulben; and throughout the county you'll find tributes to him in museums and heritage centres, while the landscapes are reflected in his poetry.

p397

County Donegal

Wild Landscapes
Pristine Beaches
Surfing

Mountains & Cliffs

Untamed and almost impossibly wild, Donegal is the ultimate frontier country, from the wave- and wind-lashed cliffs and beaches of the coast to the mountainous interior, as brooding as it is beautiful.

Pristine Coastlines

The county with the second-longest coastline has the country's best beaches, including surf-friendly Rossnowlagh, unspoilt Tramore and the red-tinged sands of Malinbeg. The multitude of coves hides an astonishing number of sandy hideaways.

Sea Activities

In Donegal you can learn to surf as well as take on some of the world's toughest breaks – the county is arguably the best place in the country to ride the waves due to its great mix of beaches and abundance of surf centres.

p430

The Midlands

Traditional Pubs
Shannon Cruise
Ecclesiastical Remains

Authentic Atmosphere

Spread almost innocuously across the Midlands are some of the most atmospheric pubs in the country, including Morrissey's of Abbeyleix, perhaps the most perfect pub in Ireland.

The Mighty River

What better way to explore the length and breadth of the country's belly than by cruiser along Ireland's longest river? See the sights and stop off along the way to eat in the riverbank restaurants that have sprouted for that purpose.

Saints & Scholars

The top monastic site in Ireland is Clonmacnoise, perched on the edge of the Shannon in County Offaly. Within its walled enclosure you'll find early churches, high crosses, round towers and graves in astonishingly good condition.

p466

Counties Meath, Louth, Cavan & Monaghan

History
Fishing
Scenery

Chieftains & Conflict

Irish history was lived and written across these counties, at the Hill of Tara, the Neolithic monuments of Brú na Bóinne and Loughcrew, in the magnificent abbeys of Mellifont and Monasterboice, and in towns like Drogheda.

Angling & Coarse Fishing

County Cavan's myriad lakes are famed for coarse fishing. County Monaghan isn't far behind, and if you fancy a little sea angling, towns like Clogherhead and Carlingford in County Louth are the places to go.

Lakelands & Hills

These counties offer all kinds of scenery, from the lakelands of Cavan and Monaghan to the fecund hills of County Meath. There are beautiful seaside views too, along the Louth coast as far up as scenic Carlingford.

p494

Belfast

History
Pubs
Music

Titanic Belfast

Belfast's shipbuilding heritage has been salvaged and transformed into Northern Ireland's most visited museum – a fabulous multimedia experience centred on the construction of the world's most famous shipwreck, which you can explore in virtual detail.

Victorian Gems

The Victorian classics of the city centre are Belfast's most beloved treasure – the Crown might be the most famous pub, but equally beautiful are the John Hewitt and the Garrick, while older taverns like White's and Kelly's have even more atmosphere.

Banging Tunes

From DJs spinning tunes in the Eglantine to sell-out gigs at the Odyssey, Belfast's music scene is top-notch. Best of the lot is probably the Belfast Empire, which features new bands and established acts nightly.

p528

Counties Down & Armagh

Activities
Wildlife
Food

Walking Festivals

With an impressive calendar of events including bird-watching meets, walking festivals and more-strenuous activities such as rock climbing and canoeing, there's enough here to keep you busy every day of the year.

Birds & Seals

The bird-filled mudflats of Castle Espie in County Down are home to a wildfowl and wetlands centre that will entice even the most indifferent of ornithologists, while large colonies of grey seals are but the most obvious of visitors to Strangford Lough in County Armagh.

Gastro-Goodness

You'll find first-rate dining in the restaurants and gastropubs of Hillsborough, Bangor and Warrenpoint, all in County Down, plus wonderful spots in the unlikeliest of places, such as the marvellous bistro at the back of Ireland's oldest pub in Donaghadee, on the Ards Peninsula.

p562

Counties Londonderry & Antrim

History
Scenery
Pop Culture

A Walled City

Derry, Ireland's only walled city, has a rich historical past, poignantly told along the walls that withstood a siege in 1688–89, in its storied museums and, most tellingly, in the political murals of the Bogside district, where history was played out on its very streets.

Giant's Footsteps

Virtually the entire length of the Antrim coast is scenic gold, but the real stars are the southern section around Carnlough Bay and the North's most outstanding tourist attraction, the surreal geological formations of the Giant's Causeway.

Game of Thrones

Game of Thrones fans will recognise Antrim's Dark Hedges as the Kingsroad; Mussenden Temple on the Causeway Coast as Dragonstone; Cushenden Caves as the spot where Melisandre gave birth to the shadow baby in Season 2; and Ballintoy Harbour as the Iron Islands' Lordsports Harbour.

p588

Counties Fermanagh & Tyrone

Activities
Scenery
History

Walking & Fishing

Need something to do? How about fishing in the waters of County Fermanagh, or taking part in the Ulster American Folk Park's annual Appalachian and bluegrass festival? Or, for something more spiritual, why not climb to the summit of Mullaghcarn along with other pilgrims?

From a Height

Whether you're boating on Lough Erne, staring out the top of the round tower on Devenish Island, or hiking across the broad range of the Sperrin Mountains, the scenery is beguiling, especially if you have any kind of decent weather.

Conflict & Connections

The towns of Omagh and Enniskillen speak volumes about the atrocities of violence, but Northern Ireland's history isn't just one of conflict: the Ulster American Folk Park expertly tells the story of the province's strong links with the USA.

p620

On the Road

County Donegal p430
Counties Londonderry & Antrim p588
Belfast p528
Counties Fermanagh & Tyrone p620
Counties Down & Armagh p562
Counties Mayo & Sligo p397
Counties Meath, Louth, Cavan & Monaghan p494
The Midlands p466
Dublin p60
County Galway p357
Counties Wicklow & Kildare p134
County Clare p322
Counties Limerick & Tipperary p297
Counties Wexford, Waterford, Carlow & Kilkenny p158
County Kerry p253
County Cork p207

Dublin

POP 1.27 MILLION / AREA 921 SQ KM

Includes ➡

Best Places to Eat

- ➡ Chapter One (p112)
- ➡ Da Mimmo's (p111)
- ➡ Restaurant Patrick Guilbaud (p110)
- ➡ Musashi Noodles & Sushi Bar (p112)
- ➡ Fumbally Cafe (p111)

Best Places to Stay

- ➡ Aberdeen Lodge (p103)
- ➡ Isaacs Hostel (p102)
- ➡ Merrion (p101)
- ➡ Number 31 (p101)
- ➡ Radisson Blu Royal Hotel (p100)

Why Go?

Sultry rather than sexy, Dublin exudes personality as only those who've managed to turn careworn into carefree can. The city has seen its fair share of triumph and disaster in recent years, but it treats both as imposters and continues to grind out the good times, which have finally become that bit easier after the crash and burn of the recession. They do so through their music, their art and their literature – things which Dubs often take for granted but which, once brought to mind, generate immense pride.

There are fascinating museums, mouth-watering restaurants and the best range of entertainment available anywhere in Ireland – and that's not including the pub, the ubiquitous centre of the city's social life and an absolute must for any visitor. And should you wish to get away from it all, the city has a handful of seaside towns at its edges that make for wonderful day trips.

When to Go

➡ March brings the marvellous mayhem of St Patrick's Festival, with 600,000 parade viewers.

➡ The Taste of Dublin and Forbidden Fruit festivals are in June, featuring the best of food and music.

➡ The last two weeks of September host the Dublin Fringe Festival, which is followed by the main theatre festival in October.

➡ Although impossible to predict, the best weather is often in September, to make up for a regularly disappointing August!

History

Dublin's been making noise since around 500 BC, when a bunch of intrepid Celts camped at a ford over the River Liffey, which is the provenance of the city's tough-to-pronounce Irish name, Baile Átha Cliath (*Bawl*-ya Aw-ha *Klee*-ya; Town of the Hurdle Ford). The Celts went about their merry way for a thousand years or so, but it wasn't until the Vikings showed up that Dublin was urbanised in any significant way. By the 9th century raids from the north had become a fact of Irish life, and some of the fierce Danes chose to stay rather than simply rape, pillage and depart. They intermarried with the Irish and established a vigorous trading port at the point where the River Poddle joined the Liffey in a *dubh linn* (black pool). Today there's little trace of the Poddle, which has been channelled underground and flows under St Patrick's Cathedral to dribble into the Liffey by the Capel St (Grattan) Bridge.

The Normans arrived in the 12th century, and so began the slow process of subjugating Ireland to Anglo-Norman (then British) rule, during which Dublin generally played the role of Anglo-Norman, later British, bandleader. By the beginning of the 18th century, the squalid city packed with poor Catholics hardly reflected the imperial pretensions of its Anglophile burghers. The great and the good – aka the Protestant ascendancy – wanted big improvements, and they set about transforming what was in essence still a medieval town into a modern, Anglo-Irish metropolis. Roads were widened, landscaped squares laid out and new town houses built, all in a proto-Palladian style that soon became known as Georgian after the kings then on the English throne. For a time, Dublin was the second-largest city in the British Empire and all was very, very good – unless you were part of the poor, mostly Catholic masses living in the city's ever-developing slums.

The Georgian boom came to a sudden and dramatic halt after the Act of Union (1801), when Ireland was formally united with Britain and its separate parliament closed down. Dublin went from being the belle of the imperial ball to the annoying

EASTER RISING CENTENARY

Amid the tumult of Dublin's WWI centenary commemorations, the marking of the centenary of the Easter Rising in 1916 is undoubtedly the most important, and the most fraught with social and political tensions.

In Easter week 1916, rebels took over landmark buildings in the city centre and declared an independent Irish republic, only to be defeated by British troops; the leaders of the rebellion were then executed. The events were not just a defining moment in Ireland's struggle for freedom; their significance and interpretation remain the subject of contentious debate today.

As Dublin geared up to mark the centenary with a year-long program of events, there was plenty of discussion as to how best to pay tribute, what it all meant and – most controversially – who should be commemorated. There were contentious calls to invite members of the British royal family so as to acknowledge both Britain's role in the events and, more importantly, Ireland's positive relationship with its nearest neighbour today. Despite an immensely popular and successful visit by Prince Charles in 2015, the government decided not to extend an official invitation to the events.

Less controversial was the call to make it an all-inclusive event, which meant commemorating not just the rebels of 1916 but all those Irish men and women who died during this time, whether fighting against British rule or for the British in the fields of France and Flanders; in excess of 350,000 Irish enlisted to fight for Britain in WWI, and more than 30,000 died. Ireland's war dead have largely been ignored since independence – it's long been an uncomfortable historical incongruity that so many Irish gave their lives for Britain while at the same time others sacrificed theirs for independence from her. Most Irish schoolchildren learned about the sacrifices of Pádraig Pearse, James Connolly and other leaders of the rising, while never learning that Ireland suffered three times as many fatalities during the exact same period on the battlefields of WWI.

Both the government and the Sinn Féin political party planned a series of events throughout 2016; see www.ireland.ie and www.sinnfein.ie for more information.

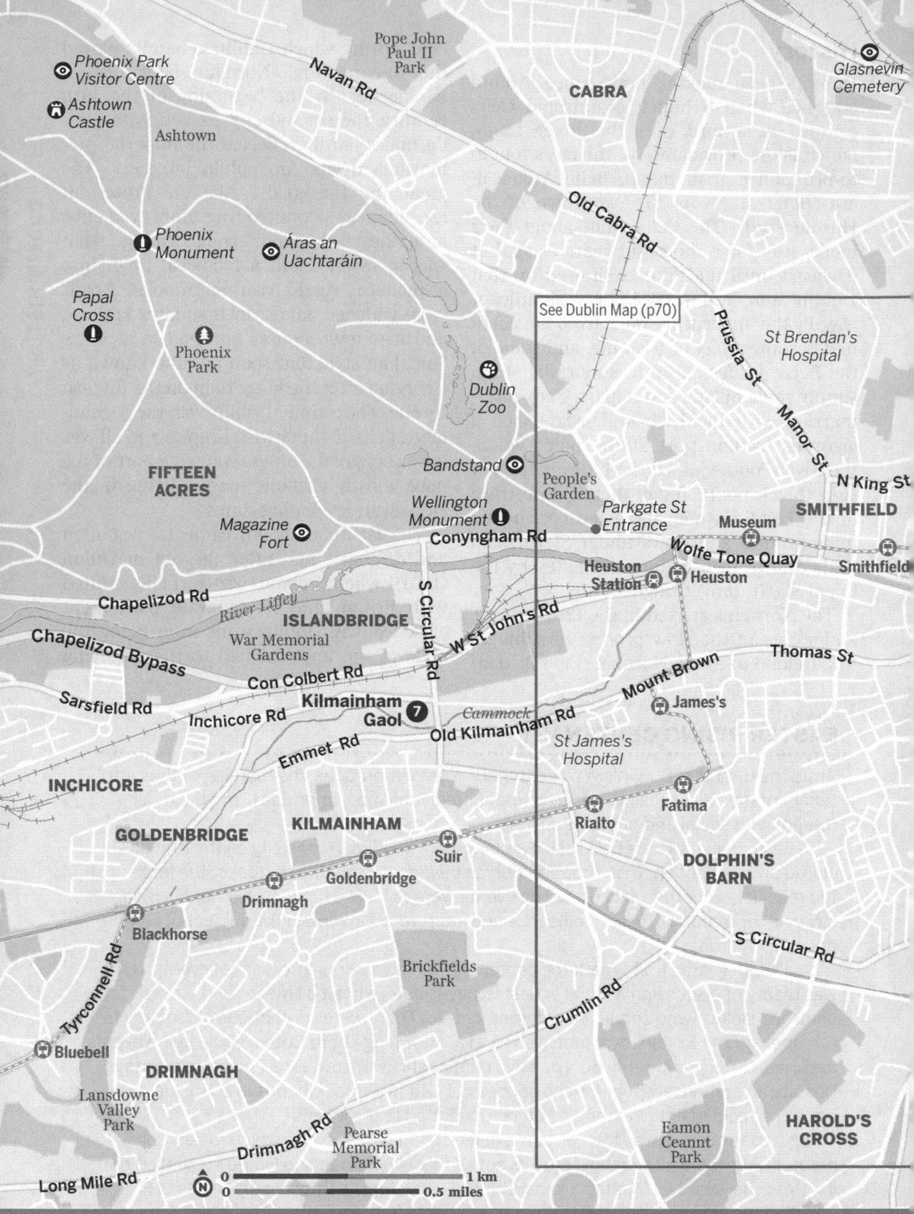

Dublin Highlights

❶ Stroll the Elizabethan grounds of **Trinity College** (p66).

❷ Pore over ancient books and treasures in the **Chester Beatty Library** (p73).

❸ Explore your thespian side by taking in a play at one of Dublin's theatres, such as the **Abbey** (p125) or the **Gate** (p124).

❹ Get to grips with Ireland's historic treasures and ancient past with a visit to the **National Museum of Ireland – Archaeology** (p78).

5 Tap into your inner Victorian botanist (and watch the kids go 'wow') with a visit to the 'dead zoo', the **Museum of Natural History** (p79).

6 Enjoy Georgian gems surrounding the landscaped **Merrion Square** (p78) and **St Stephen's Green** (p75).

7 See the past up close at **Kilmainham Gaol** (p86).

8 Quaff a pint or five in one of Dublin's many pubs – our favourite is **John Mulligan's** (p114).

cousin who just wouldn't take the hint, and slid quickly into economic turmoil and social unrest. During the Potato Famine (1845–51), the city's population was swollen by the arrival of tens of thousands of starving refugees from the west, who joined the ranks of an already downtrodden working class. As Dublin entered the 20th century, it was a dispirited place plagued by poverty, disease and more social problems than anyone cared to mention. It's hardly surprising that the majority of Dublin's citizenry were disgruntled and eager for change.

County Dublin

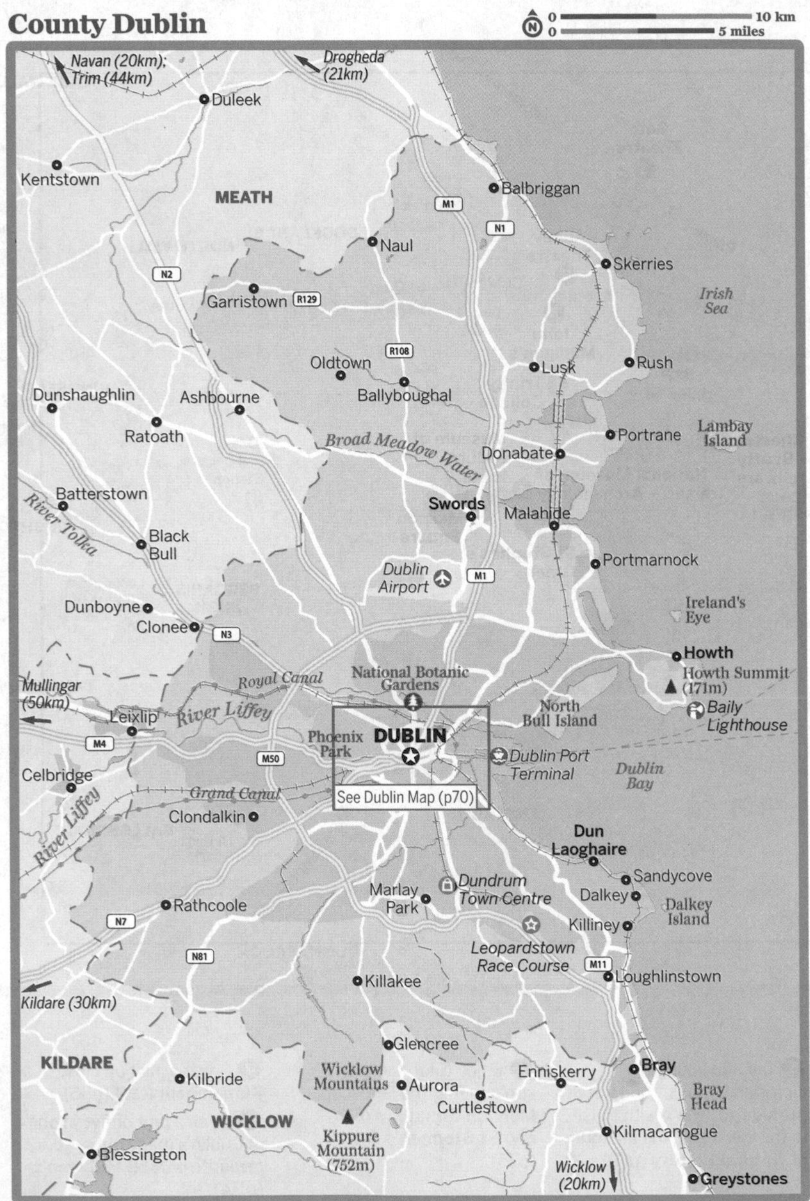

The first fusillade of transformation came during the Easter Rising of 1916, which caused considerable damage to the city centre. At first, Dubliners weren't too enamoured of the rebels, who caused more chaos and disruption than most locals were willing to put up with, but they soon changed their tune when the leaders were executed – Dubliners being natural defenders of the underdog.

As the whole country lurched radically towards full-scale war with Britain, Dublin was, surprisingly, not part of the main theatre of events. In fact, although there was an increased military presence, the odd shooting and the blowing up of some notable buildings – such as the Custom House in 1921 – in the capital it was business as usual for much of the War of Independence.

A year later, Ireland – minus its northern bit – was independent, but it then tumbled into the Civil War, which led to the burning of more notable buildings, including the Four Courts in 1922. Ironically, the war among the Irish was more brutal than the struggle for independence – O'Connell St became 'sniper row' and the violence left deep scars that took most of the 20th century to heal.

When the new state finally started doing business, Dublin was an exhausted capital. Despite slow and steady improvements, the city – like the rest of Ireland – continued to be plagued by rising unemployment, high emigration rates and a general stagnation that hung about like an impenetrable cloud. Dubliners made the most of the little they had, but times were tough.

The city has been in and out of recession for decades, but the dramatic dip that followed the sky-high good times of the Celtic Tiger was especially severe: Dublin is recovering more than the rest of the country, but recuperation has been slow.

Sights

Grafton Street & Around

The bustling heart of the city centre revolves around pedestrianised Grafton St and the warren of streets around it. Within this neighbourhood's easily walkable confines is where most of the action takes place, where you'll find the biggest range of pubs and restaurants, and where most Dubliners come to blow off some retail steam. Many of the

DUBLIN IN...

Two Days

If you've only got two days (whatever is taking you away better be worth it!), start with **Trinity College** (p66) and the **Book of Kells** before venturing into the Georgian heartland – amble through **St Stephen's Green** (p75) and **Merrion Square** (p78), and be sure to visit both the **National Museum of Ireland – Archaeology** (p78) and the **National Gallery** (p79). In the evening, try an authentic Dublin pub – **Kehoe's** (p114) off Grafton St will do nicely. The next day go west, stopping at the **Chester Beatty Library** (p73) on your way to the **Guinness Storehouse** (p83); if you still have the legs for it, the **Irish Museum of Modern Art** (p86) and **Kilmainham Gaol** (p86) will round off your day perfectly. Take in a traditional Irish music session at the **Cobblestone** (p119).

Four Days

Follow the two-day itinerary, but stretch it out with refuelling stops at some of the city's better pubs. Visit **Glasnevin Cemetery** (p96) and the **Dublin City Gallery – The Hugh Lane** (p87). Become a whiskey expert at the **Old Jameson Distillery** (p92) and a literary (or beer) one with a **Dublin Literary Pub Crawl** (p97). Explore the north side's blossoming foodie scene – there's terrific Japanese at **Musashi Noodles & Sushi Bar** (p112) and superb Italian at **Da Mimmo's** (p111). Oh, and don't forget **Temple Bar**, where there are distractions for every taste.

One Week

Follow the four-day itinerary, and add: a day for the seaside village of **Howth** (p132; be sure to eat in one of the **fish restaurants** along its pier); a visit to **Phoenix Park** (p94); and exploration of the **Docklands** (p93). There might even be someone you'd love to see performing at the **Bord Gáis Energy Theatre** (p121). Alternatively, attend a play at either the **Abbey** (p125) or the **Gate** (p124).

Trinity College

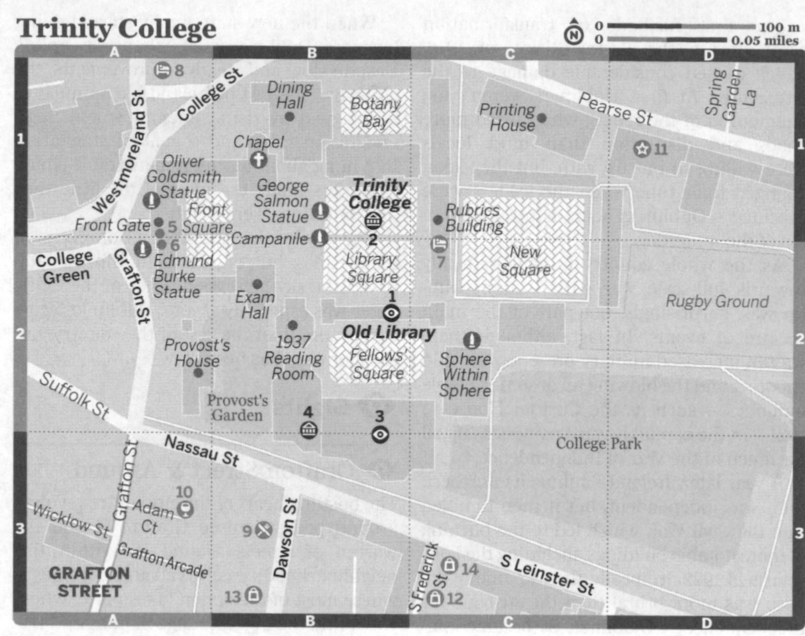

city's most important sights and museums are here, as is Dublin's best-loved city park, St Stephen's Green.

★Trinity College HISTORIC BUILDING

(Map p66; ☎01-896 1000; www.tcd.ie; College Green; ⏰8am-10pm; 🚌all city centre) FREE This calm and cordial retreat from the bustle of contemporary Dublin is not just Ireland's most prestigious university; it's also a throwback to those far-off days when a university education was the preserve of a very small elite who spoke passionately of the importance of philosophy and the need for empire. The student body has diversified since then, but Trinity's bucolic charms persist and on a summer evening it's one of the city's most delightful places to be.

The college was established by Elizabeth I in 1592 on land confiscated from an Augustinian priory in an effort to stop the brain drain of young Protestant Dubliners, who were skipping across to continental Europe for an education and becoming 'infected with popery'. Trinity went on to become one of Europe's most outstanding universities, producing a host of notable graduates – how about Jonathan Swift, Oscar Wilde and Samuel Beckett at the same alumni dinner?

It remained completely Protestant until 1793, but even when the university relented and began to admit Catholics, the Catholic Church held firm; until 1970, any Catholic who enrolled here could consider themselves excommunicated.

The campus is a masterpiece of architecture and landscaping beautifully preserved in Georgian aspic. Most of the buildings and statues date from the 18th and 19th centuries, each elegantly laid out on a cobbled or grassy square. The newer bits include the 1978 **Arts & Social Science Building** (Map p66; all city centre), which backs on to Nassau St and forms the alternative entrance to the college. Like the college's Berkeley Library, it was designed by Paul Koralek; it houses the **Douglas Hyde Gallery of Modern Art** (Map p66; www.douglashydegallery.com; 11am-6pm Mon-Wed & Fri, to 7pm Thu, to 4.45pm Sat; all city centre) FREE.

A great way to see the grounds is on a **walking tour** (Authenticity Tours; Map p66; www.tcd.ie/Library/bookofkells/trinity-tours; per person €5, incl Book of Kells €12; 10.15am-3.40pm Mon-Sat, to 3.15pm Sun May-Sep, fewer midweek tours Oct-Apr), which depart from the **Regent House entrance** on College Green.

★Old Library

(Map p66; Library Sq; 9.30am-5pm Mon-Sat year-round, noon-4.30pm Sun Oct-Apr, 9.30am-4.30pm Sun May-Sep) To the south of Library Sq is the Old Library, built in a severe style by Thomas Burgh between 1712 and 1732. It is one of five copyright libraries across Ireland and the UK, which means it's entitled to a copy of every book published in these islands – around five million books, of which only a fraction are stored here. You can visit the library as part of a tour of the Long Room, home of the famous *Book of Kells*.

The remainder of the library's constantly growing collection – they need about 1km of additional shelving every year – is stored in facilities throughout the city: students requiring a title fill out a docket and the relevant title is brought to the college within a day.

Long Room

(Map p66; www.tcd.ie/visitors/book-of-kells; East Pavilion, Library Colonnades; adult/student/child €10/9/free; 9.30am-5pm Mon-Sat year-round, noon-4.30pm Sun Oct-Apr, 9.30am-4.30pm Sun May-Sep) Trinity's greatest treasures are kept in the Old Library's stunning 65m Long Room, which houses about 200,000 of the

THE PAGE OF KELLS

More than half a million visitors stop into the **Long Room** each year to see Trinity College's top treasure, the world-famous **Book of Kells**. This illuminated manuscript, dating from around AD 800 and therefore one of the oldest books in the world, was probably produced by monks at St Colmcille's Monastery on the remote island of Iona, off the west coast of Scotland. Repeated looting by marauding Vikings forced the monks to flee to the temporary safety of Kells, County Meath, in AD 806, along with their masterpiece. Around 850 years later, the book was brought to the college for safekeeping and has remained here since.

The *Book of Kells* contains the four Gospels of the New Testament, written in Latin on vellum (prepared calfskin). If it were merely words, the *Book of Kells* would simply be a very old book – it's the extensive and amazingly complex illustrations that make it so wonderful. The superbly decorated opening initials are only part of the story, for the book has smaller illustrations between the lines.

And here the problems begin. Of the 680 pages, only two are on display – one showing an illumination, the other showing text – which has led to it being dubbed the *page* of Kells. No getting around that one, though: you can hardly expect the right to thumb through a priceless treasure at random. No, the real problem is its immense popularity, which makes viewing it a rather unsatisfactory pleasure. Punters are herded through the specially constructed viewing room at near lightning pace, making for a there-you-see-it, there-you-don't kind of experience.

To really appreciate the book, you can buy your own reproduction copy for a mere €22,000. Failing that, the library bookshop stocks a plethora of souvenirs and other memorabilia, including Otto Simm's excellent *Exploring the Book of Kells* (€12.95), a thorough guide with attractive colour plates. The book is also now part of Trinity's Digital Collection (digitalcollections.tcd.ie) and is the theme of an elegant app for tablet devices.

Trinity College, Dublin

STEP INTO THE PAST

Ireland's most prestigious university, founded on the order of Queen Elizabeth I in 1592, is an architectural masterpiece, a cordial retreat from the bustle of modern life in the middle of the city. Step through its main entrance and you step back in time, the cobbled stones transporting you to another era, when the elite discussed philosophy and argued passionately in favour of empire.

Standing in Front Square, the 30m-high **Campanile** ❶ is directly in front of you with the **Dining Hall** ❷ to your left. On the far side of the square is the Old Library building, the centrepiece of which is the magnificent **Long Room** ❸, which was the inspiration for the computer-generated imagery of the Jedi Archive in *Star Wars Episode II: Attack of the Clones*. Here you'll find the university's greatest treasure, the **Book of Kells** ❹. You'll probably have to queue to see this masterpiece, and then only for a brief visit, but it's very much worth it.

Just beyond the Old Library is the very modern **Berkeley Library** ❺, which nevertheless fits perfectly into the campus' overall aesthetic: directly in front of it is the distinctive **Sphere Within a Sphere** ❻, the most elegant of the university's sculptures.

DON'T MISS

» Douglas Hyde Gallery, the campus' designated modern-art museum.

» cricket match on pitch, the most elegant of pastimes.

» pint in the Pavilion Bar, preferably while watching the cricket.

» visit to the Science Gallery, where science is made completely relevant.

FIONN DAVENPORT ©

Campanile
Trinity College's most iconic bit of masonry was designed in the mid-19th century by Sir Charles Lanyon; the attached sculptures were created by Thomas Kirk.

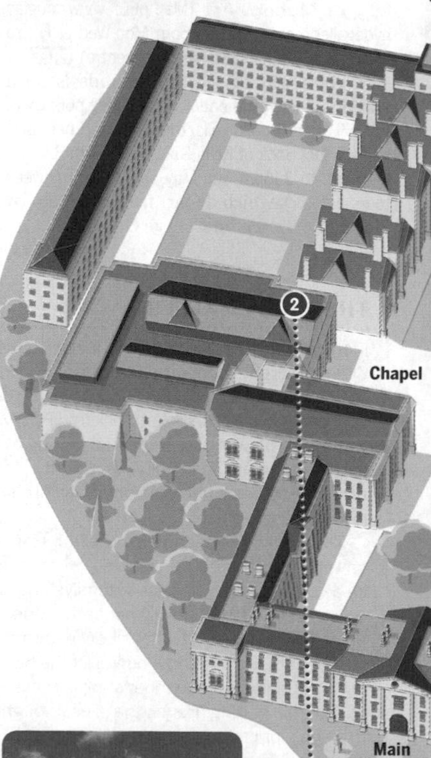

FIONN DAVENPORT ©

Dining Hall
Richard Cassels' original building was designed to mirror the Examination Hall directly opposite on Front Square: the hall collapsed twice and was rebuilt from scratch in 1761.

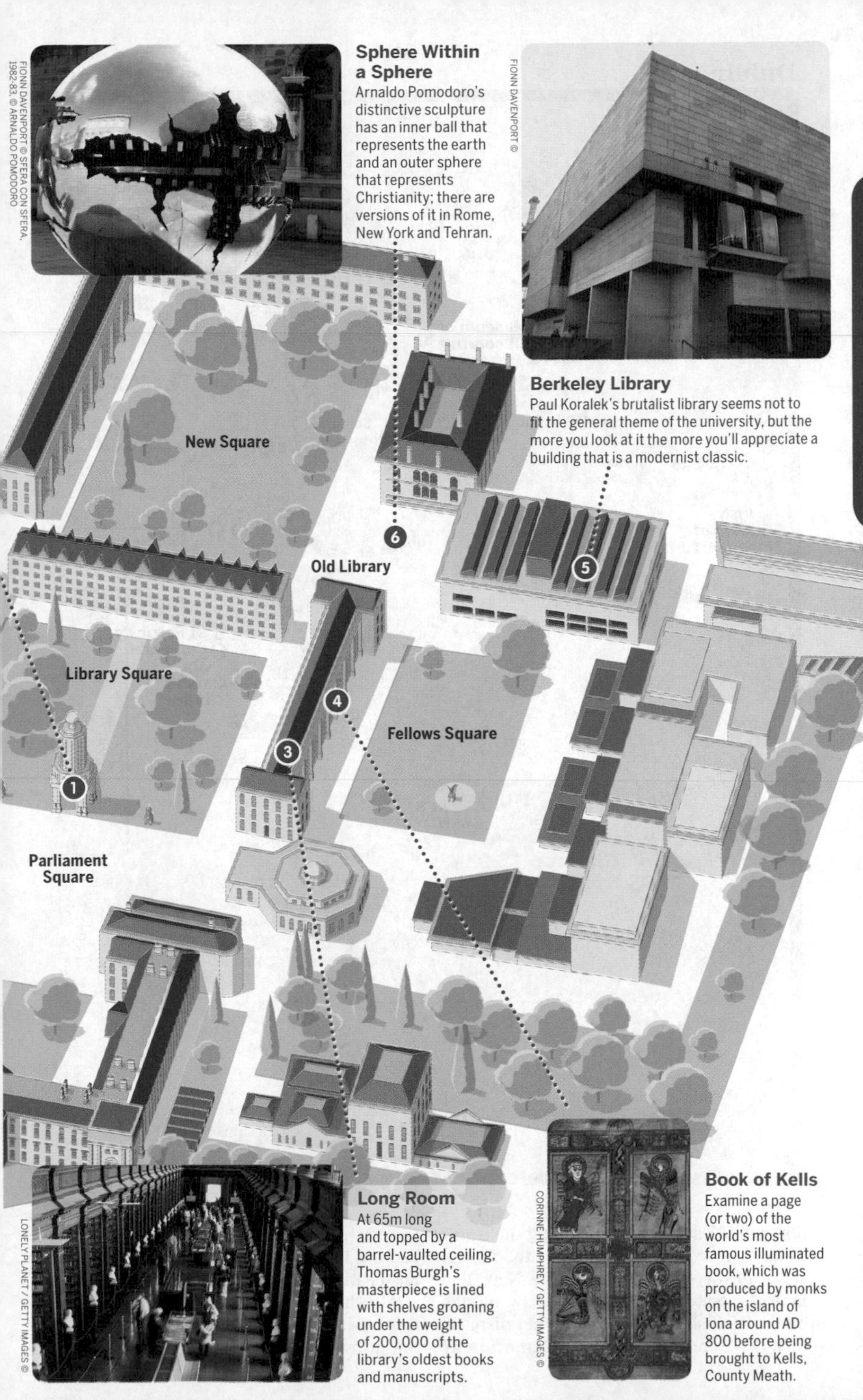

Sphere Within a Sphere
Arnaldo Pomodoro's distinctive sculpture has an inner ball that represents the earth and an outer sphere that represents Christianity; there are versions of it in Rome, New York and Tehran.
FIONN DAVENPORT © SFERA CON SFERA, 1982-83, © ARNALDO POMODORO
FIONN DAVENPORT ©
Berkeley Library
Paul Koralek's brutalist library seems not to fit the general theme of the university, but the more you look at it the more you'll appreciate a building that is a modernist classic.
New Square
6
Old Library
5
Library Square
4
Fellows Square
3
1
Parliament Square
Long Room
At 65m long and topped by a barrel-vaulted ceiling, Thomas Burgh's masterpiece is lined with shelves groaning under the weight of 200,000 of the library's oldest books and manuscripts.
LONELY PLANET / GETTY IMAGES ©
CORINNE HUMPHREY / GETTY IMAGES ©
Book of Kells
Examine a page (or two) of the world's most famous illuminated book, which was produced by monks on the island of Iona around AD 800 before being brought to Kells, County Meath.

Dublin

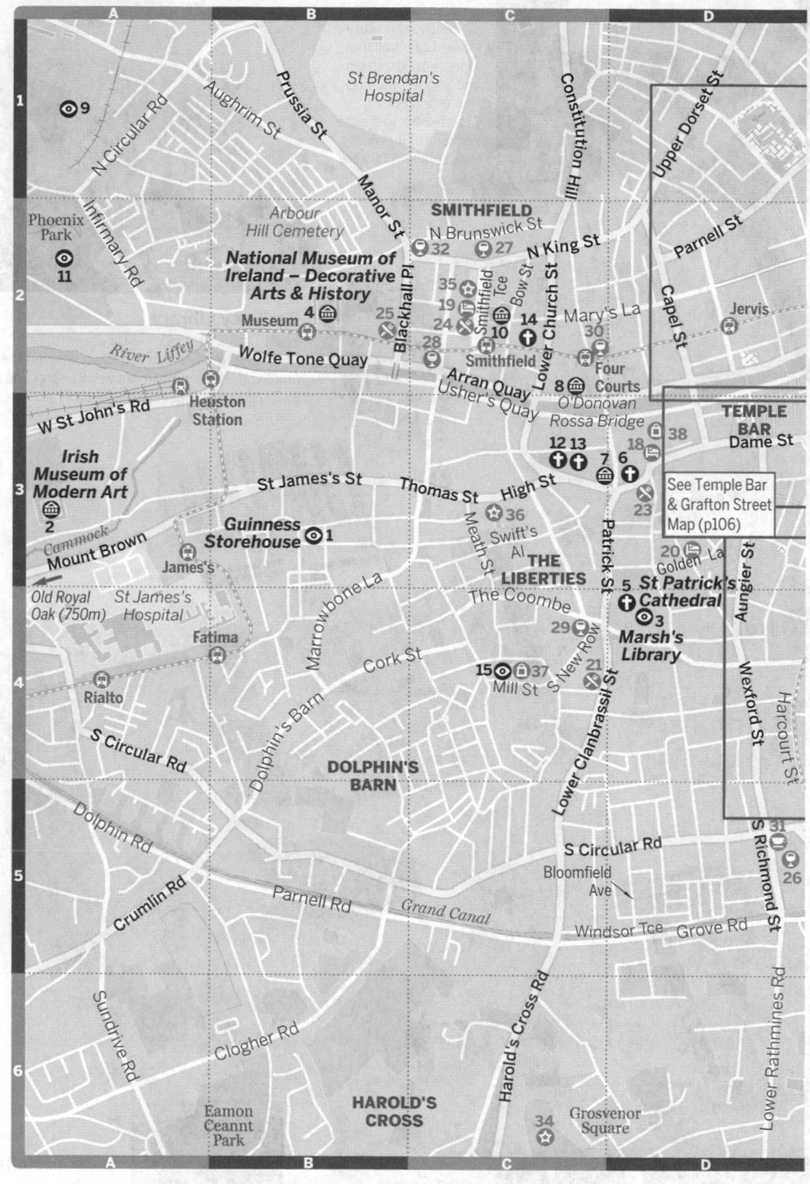

library's oldest volumes, including the **Book of Kells**, a breathtaking, illuminated manuscript of the four Gospels of the New Testament, created around AD 800 by monks on the Scottish island of Iona. Other displays include a rare copy of the **Proclamation of the Irish Republic**, which was read out by Pádraig Pearse at the beginning of the 1916 Easter Rising.

Also here is the so-called harp of **Brian Ború**, which was definitely not in use when the army of this early Irish hero defeated

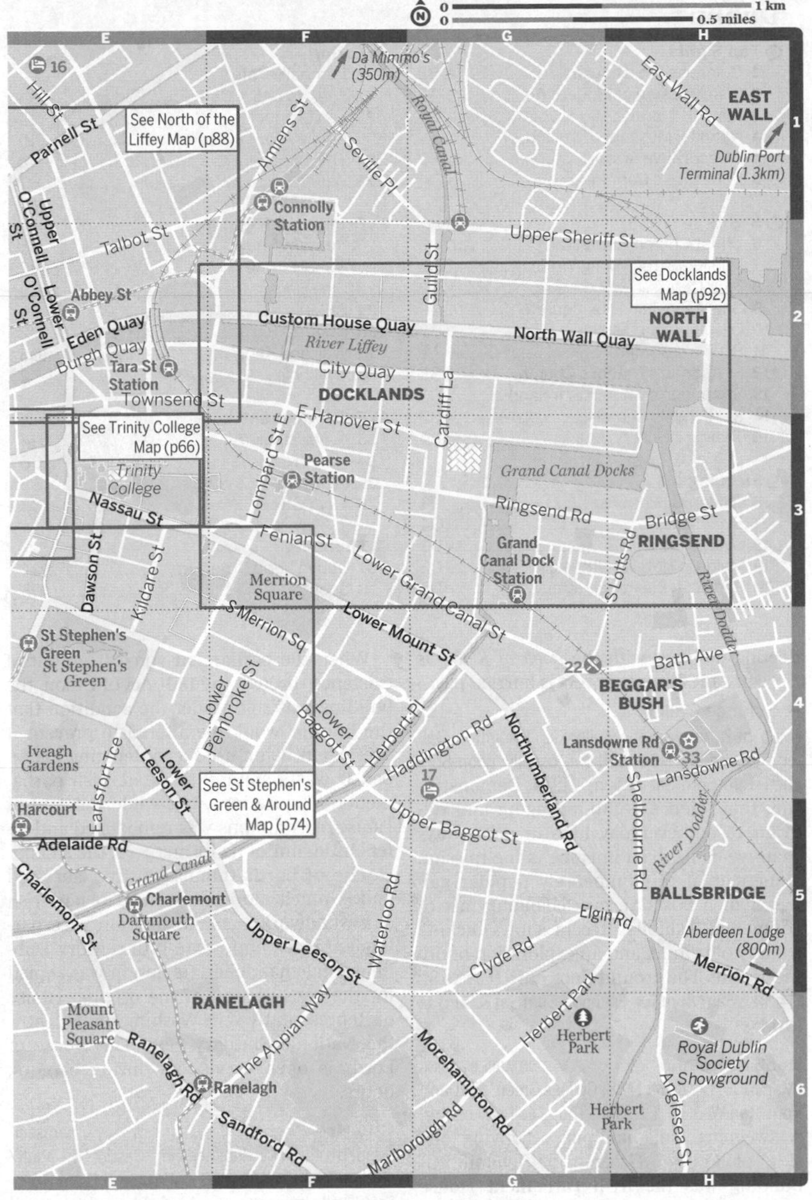

the Danes at the Battle of Clontarf in 1014. It does, however, date from around 1400, making it one of the oldest harps in Ireland. Your entry ticket also includes admission to temporary exhibitions on display in the East Pavilion.

The Long Room gets very busy during the summer months, so it's recommended to go online and buy a fast-track ticket (adult/student/family €13/11/26), which gives timed admission to the exhibition and allows visitors to skip the queue. You'll still get only a

Dublin

Top Sights
1 Guinness Storehouse B3
2 Irish Museum of Modern Art A3
3 Marsh's Library D4
4 National Museum of Ireland – Decorative Arts & History B2
5 St Patrick's Cathedral D4

Sights
6 Christ Church Cathedral D3
7 Dublinia & the Viking World C3
8 Four Courts C2
9 Garda Síochána Headquarters A1
10 Old Jameson Distillery C2
11 People's Garden A2
12 St Audoen's Catholic Church C3
13 St Audoen's Church of Ireland C3
14 St Michan's Church C2
15 Teeling Distillery C4

Sleeping
16 Clifden Guesthouse E1
17 Dylan G4
18 Kinlay House D3
19 Maldron Hotel Smithfield C2
20 Radisson Blu Royal Hotel D3

Eating
21 Fumbally Cafe C4
22 Juniors Deli & Cafe G4
23 Leo Burdock's D3
Paulie's Pizza .... (see 22)
24 Third Space C2
25 Wuff B2

Drinking & Nightlife
26 Bernard Shaw D5
27 Cobblestone C2
28 Dice Bar C2
29 Fallon's C4
30 Hughes' Bar C2
31 Wall and Keogh D5
32 Walshe's C2

Entertainment
33 Aviva Stadium H4
34 Harold's Cross Park C6
35 Lighthouse Cinema C2
36 Vicar Street C3

Shopping
37 Dublin Food Co-op C4
38 Scout D3

fleeting moment with the *Book of Kells*, as the constant flow of viewers is hurried past.

➡ **Science Gallery**
(Map p92; www.sciencegallery.ie; Naughton Gallery, Pearse St; ⏲exhibitions usually noon-8pm Tue-Fri, to 6pm Sat & Sun) FREE Demonstrating that science is fun, engaging and relevant to our everyday lives in more ways than we could even imagine is the mission statement of this immensely popular gallery, which hosts an ever-changing mix of compelling exhibits. Recent shows include a study of trauma and an exploration of domestic life. The ground-floor **cafe** (Pearse St; €4-8; ⏲8am-8pm Tue-Fri, noon-6pm Sat & Sun) is lovely.

Bank of Ireland NOTABLE BUILDING
(Map p106; ☎01-671 1488; College Green; ⏲10am-4pm Mon-Wed & Fri, to 5pm Thu; 🚌all city centre) A sweeping Palladian pile occupying one side of College Green, this magnificent building was the Irish Parliament House until 1801 and is the first purpose-built parliament building in the world. The original building – the central colonnaded section that distinguishes the present-day structure – was designed by Sir Edward Lovett Pearce in 1729 and completed by James Gandon in 1733.

When the parliament voted itself out of existence through the 1801 Act of Union, the building was sold under the condition that the interior would be altered to prevent it ever again being used as a debating chamber. It was a spiteful strike at Irish parliamentary aspirations, but while the central House of Commons was remodelled and offers little hint of its former role, the smaller **House of Lords** (admission free) survived and is much more interesting. It has Irish oak woodwork, a mahogany longcase parliament clock and a late-18th-century Dublin crystal chandelier. Its design was copied for the construction of the original House of Representatives in Washington, DC, now the National Statuary Hall. The House of Lords is open to visitors during banking hours.

City Hall MUSEUM
(Map p106; www.dublincity.ie; Castle St; adult/student/child €4/2/1.50; ⏲10am-5.15pm Mon-Sat; 🚌all city centre) One of the architectural triumphs of the Dublin boom was the magnificent restoration of City Hall (in 2000). It was originally built by Thomas Cooley as the Royal Exchange between 1769 and 1779, and botched in the mid-19th century when it became the offices of the local government.

Thankfully, the more recent renovation has restored it to its gleaming Georgian best.

The rotunda and its ambulatory form a breathtaking interior, bathed in natural light from enormous windows to the east. A vast marble statue of former mayor and Catholic emancipator Daniel O'Connell stands here as a reminder of the building's links with Irish nationalism (the funerals of both Charles Stewart Parnell and Michael Collins were held here). Dublin City Council still meets here on the first Monday of the month, gathering to discuss the city's business in the Council Chamber, which was the original building's coffee room.

There was a sordid precursor to City Hall on this spot in the shape of the Lucas Coffee House and the adjoining Eagle Tavern, in which the notorious Hellfire Club was founded by Richard Parsons, Earl of Rosse, in 1735. Although the city abounded with gentlemen's clubs, this particular one gained a reputation for messing about in the arenas of sex and Satan, two topics that were guaranteed to fire the lurid imaginings of the city's gossipmongers.

The striking vaulted basement hosts a multimedia exhibition, the **Story of the Capital**, which traces the history of the city from its earliest beginnings to its hoped-for future – with ne'er a mention of sex and Satan. More's the pity, as the info is quite overwhelming and the exhibits are a little text-heavy. Still, it's a pretty slick museum with informative audiovisual displays.

★Chester Beatty Library MUSEUM

(Map p106; ☎01-407 0750; www.cbl.ie; Dublin Castle; ⌚10am-5pm Mon-Fri, 11am-5pm Sat, 1-5pm Sun year-round, closed Mon Nov-Feb, free tours 1pm Wed, 3pm & 4pm Sun; 🚌50, 51B, 77, 78A or 123) FREE This world-famous library, in the grounds of Dublin Castle, houses the collection of mining engineer Sir Alfred Chester Beatty (1875–1968), bequeathed to the Irish state on his death. And we're immensely grateful for Chester's patronage: spread over two floors, the breathtaking collection includes more than 20,000 manuscripts, rare books, miniature paintings, clay tablets, costumes and other objects of artistic, historical and aesthetic importance.

The **Artistic Traditions Gallery** on the 1st floor begins with memorabilia from Beatty's life, before embarking on an exploration of the art of Mogul India, Persia, the Ottoman Empire, Japan and China. Here you'll find intricately designed little medicine boxes and perhaps the finest collection of Chinese jade books in the world. The illuminated European texts are also worth examining.

The **Sacred Traditions Gallery** on the 2nd floor gives a fascinating insight into the rituals and rites of passage of the major world religions – Judaism, Christianity, Islam, Buddhism and Hinduism. There are audiovisual explorations of the lives of Christ and the Buddha, and of the Muslim pilgrimage to Mecca.

Head for the collection of Qu'rans from the 9th to the 19th centuries, considered to be among the best illuminated Islamic texts. You'll also find ancient Egyptian papyrus texts (including Egyptian love poems from around 1100 BC), scrolls and exquisite artwork from Burma, Indonesia and Tibet – as well as the second-oldest biblical fragment ever found (after the Dead Sea Scrolls).

The comprehensive **Reference Library**, complete with a finely lacquered ceiling that Beatty himself had installed in his London home, is a great resource for artists or students.

The library regularly holds specialist workshops, exhibitions and talks on everything from origami to calligraphy. It's easy to escape from the rigours of Western life in the serene Japanese rooftop garden or at the **Silk Road Café** (Map p106; Chester Beatty Library, Dublin Castle; mains €11; ⌚11am-4pm Mon-Fri, closed Mon Nov-Feb; 🚌50, 51B, 77, 78A or 123) on the ground floor, which serves delicious Middle Eastern cuisine.

Dublin Castle HISTORIC BUILDING

(Map p106; ☎01-677 7129; www.dublincastle.ie; Dame St; adult/child €8.50/6.50; ⌚9.45am-4.45pm Mon-Sat, noon-4.45pm Sun; 🚌all city centre) If you're looking for a turreted castle straight out of central casting you'll be disappointed; the stronghold of British power in Ireland for 700 years is principally an 18th-century creation that is more hotchpotch palace than medieval castle. Only the Record Tower, completed in 1258, survives from the original Anglo-Norman fortress commissioned by King John from 1204.

The castle is now used by the Irish government for meetings and functions, and can be visited only on a guided tour of the State Apartments and of the excavations of the former Powder Tower.

It was officially handed over to Michael Collins, representing the Irish Free State, in 1922, when the British viceroy is reported to

St Stephen's Green & Around

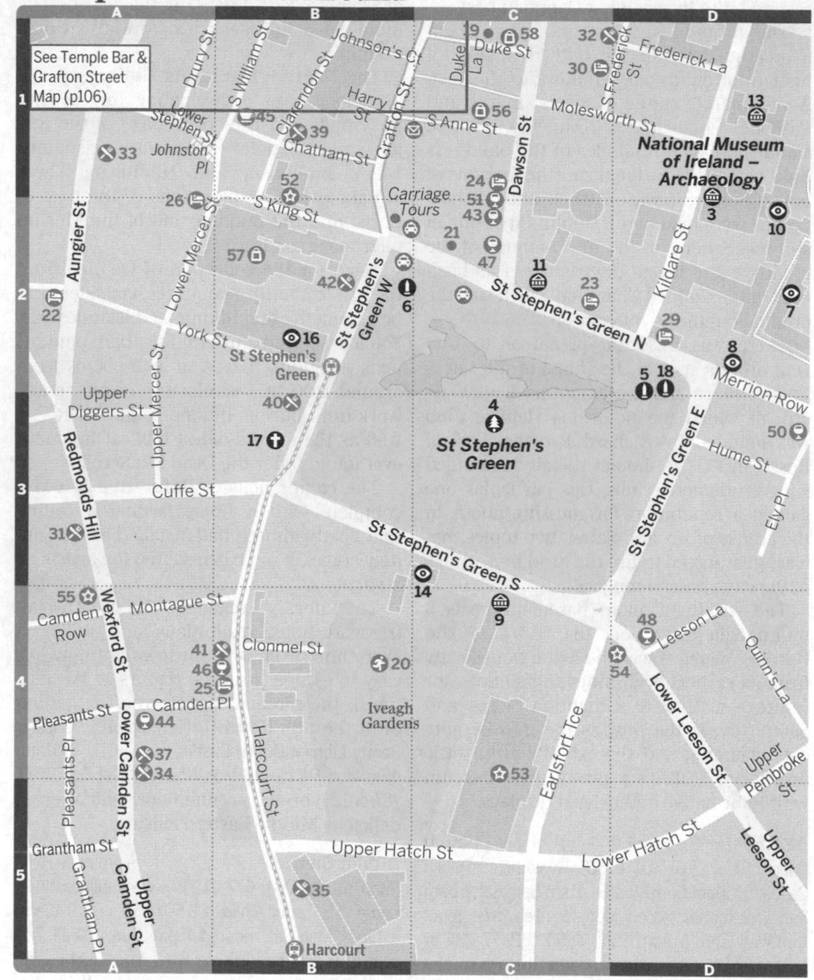

have rebuked Collins on being seven minutes late. Collins replied, 'We've been waiting 700 years, you can wait seven minutes.'

As you walk into the grounds from the main Dame St entrance, there's a good example of the evolution of Irish architecture. On your left is the Victorian **Chapel Royal** (occasionally part of the Dublin Castle tours), decorated with more than 90 heads of various Irish personages and saints carved out of Tullamore limestone. Beside this is the Norman **Record Tower** with its 5m-thick walls. It's currently closed to the public pending a long-awaited revamp. On your right is the Georgian **Treasury Building**, the oldest office block in Dublin, and behind you, yikes, is the uglier-than-sin Revenue Commissioners Building of 1960.

Heading away from that eyesore, you ascend to the Upper Yard. On your right is a figure of Justice with her back turned to the city, an appropriate symbol for British justice, reckoned Dubliners. Next to it is the 18th-century **Bedford Tower**, from which the Irish Crown Jewels were stolen in 1907 and never recovered. Opposite is the entrance for the tours.

The 45-minute **guided tours** (departing every 20 to 30 minutes, depending on numbers) are pretty dry, but you get to visit the **State Apartments**, many of which are decorated in dubious taste. You will also see **St Patrick's Hall**, where Irish presidents are inaugurated and foreign dignitaries toasted, and the room in which the wounded James Connolly was tied to a chair while convalescing after the 1916 Easter Rising, so that he could be executed by firing squad.

The highlight is a visit to the **medieval undercroft** of the old castle, discovered by accident in 1986. It includes foundations built by the Vikings (whose long-lasting mortar was made of ox blood, eggshells and horse hair), the hand-polished exterior of the castle walls that prevented attackers from climbing them, the steps leading down to the moat and the trickle of the historic River Poddle, which once filled the moat on its way to join the Liffey.

There's a self-guided tour option, but that only includes the State Apartments.

National Library HISTORIC BUILDING

(Map p74; www.nli.ie; Kildare St; 9.30am-7.45pm Mon-Wed, to 4.45pm Thu & Fri, 10am-12.45pm Sat; all city centre) FREE Suitably sedate and elegant, the National Library was built from 1884 to 1890 by Sir Thomas Newenham Deane, at the same time and to a similar design as the National Museum of Ireland – Archaeology. Its extensive collection has many valuable early manuscripts, first editions and maps.

Parts of the library are open to the public, including the domed reading room where Stephen Dedalus expounded his views on Shakespeare in James Joyce's *Ulysses*.

There's a **Genealogy Advisory Service** on the 2nd floor, where you can obtain free information on how best to trace your Irish roots.

For those prints that are worth a thousand words, you'll have to head down to Temple Bar to the National Photographic Archive (p82) extension of the library.

★ St Stephen's Green PARK

(Map p74; dawn-dusk; all city centre, St Stephen's Green) FREE As you watch the assorted groups of friends, lovers and individuals splaying themselves across the nine elegantly landscaped hectares of St Stephen's Green, Dublin's most popular green lung, consider that those same hectares once formed a common for public whippings, burnings and hangings. These days, the harshest treatment you'll get is the warden chucking you off the grass for playing football or Frisbee.

The buildings around the square date mainly from the mid-18th century, when the green was landscaped and became the centrepiece of Georgian Dublin. The northern side was known as the Beaux Walk and it's still one of the city's most esteemed stretches, home to Dublin's original society hotel, the Shelbourne (p101). Nearby is the tiny **Huguenot Cemetery**, established in 1693 by French Protestant refugees.

St Stephen's Green & Around

Top Sights
1 Museum of Natural History ... E2
2 National Gallery ... E1
3 National Museum of Ireland – Archaeology ... D1
4 St Stephen's Green ... C3

Sights
5 Famine Victims Memorial ... D2
6 Fusiliers' Arch ... B2
7 Government Buildings ... D2
8 Huguenot Cemetery ... D2
9 Iveagh House ... C4
10 Leinster House ... D2
11 Little Museum of Dublin ... C2
12 Merrion Square ... F2
13 National Library ... D1
14 Newman House ... C3
15 Oscar Wilde Statue ... E1
16 Royal College of Surgeons ... B2
17 Unitarian Church ... B3
18 Wolfe Tone Monument ... D2

Activities, Courses & Tours
19 Dublin Literary Pub Crawl ... C1
Guided Tour of Oireachtas ... (see 10)
20 Taste of Dublin ... B4
21 Viking Splash Tours ... C2

Sleeping
22 Avalon House ... A2
23 Cliff Townhouse ... C2
24 Dawson ... C1
25 Dean Hotel ... B4
26 Mercer Court Campus Accommodation ... A2
27 Merrion ... E2
28 Number 31 ... E5
29 Shelbourne ... D2
30 Trinity Lodge ... C1

Eating
31 Bunsen ... A3
Cliff Townhouse ... (see 23)
32 Dunne & Crescenzi ... C1
33 Govinda's ... A1
34 Green Nineteen ... A4
35 Harcourt Street Food Market ... B5
36 L'Ecrivain ... F3
37 Neon ... A4
38 Restaurant Patrick Guilbaud ... E2
39 Saba ... B1
40 Shanahan's on the Green ... B3
41 Sophie's @ The Dean ... B4
42 Thornton's ... B2

Drinking & Nightlife
43 37 Dawson St ... C2
44 Anseo ... A4
45 Clement & Pekoe ... B1
46 Copper Face Jacks ... B4
47 Dawson Lounge ... C2
48 Hartigan's ... D4
49 James Toner's ... E3
50 O'Donoghue's ... D3
51 Sam's Bar ... C1

Entertainment
52 Gaiety Theatre ... B1
53 National Concert Hall ... C4
54 Sugar Club ... D4
55 Whelan's ... A4

Shopping
56 Sheridan's Cheesemongers ... C1
57 St Stephen's Green Shopping Centre ... B2
58 Ulysses Rare Books ... C1

Railings and locked gates were erected in 1814, when an annual fee of one guinea was charged to use the green. This private use continued until 1877 when Sir Arthur Edward Guinness pushed an act through parliament opening the green to the public once again. He also financed the central park's gardens and ponds, which date from 1880.

The main entrance to the green today is beneath **Fusiliers' Arch**, at the top of Grafton St. Modelled to look like a smaller version of the Arch of Titus in Rome, the arch commemorates the 212 soldiers of the Royal Dublin Fusiliers who were killed fighting for the British in the Boer War (1899–1902).

Spread across the green's lawns and walkways are some notable artworks; the most imposing of these is a **monument to Wolfe Tone**, the leader of the abortive 1798 rebellion. Occupying the northeastern corner of the green, the vertical slabs serving as a backdrop to the statue have been dubbed 'Tonehenge'. At this entrance is a **memorial** to all those who died in the Potato Famine (1845–51).

On the eastern side of the green is a **children's playground** and to the south there's a fine old **bandstand**, erected to celebrate Queen Victoria's jubilee in 1887. Musical performances often take place here in summer. Near the bandstand is a **bust of James Joyce**.

Little Museum of Dublin MUSEUM

(Map p74; ☎01-661 1000; www.littlemuseum.ie; 15 St Stephen's Green N; adult/student €7/4.50, guided tours €12; ⏰9.30am-5pm Mon-Fri, to 8pm Thu; 🚌all city centre, 🚊St Stephen's Green) The idea is ingeniously simple: a museum, spread across two rooms of an elegant Georgian building, devoted to the history of Dublin in the 20th century, made up of memorabilia contributed by the general public. You don't need to know anything about Irish history or Dublin to appreciate it: visits are by guided tour and everyone is presented with a handsome booklet on the history of the city.

Since opening in 2011, the contributions have been impressive. Amid the nostalgic posters, time-worn bric-a-brac and wonderful photographs of personages and cityscapes of yesteryear are some extraordinary finds, including a lectern used by John F Kennedy on his 1963 visit to Ireland and an original copy of the fateful letter given to the Irish envoys to the treaty negotiations of 1921, whose contradictory instructions were at the heart of the split that resulted in the Civil War.

Unitarian Church CHURCH

(Map p74; www.dublinunitarianchurch.org; 112 St Stephen's Green W; ⏰worship 7am-5pm; 🚌all city centre, 🚊St Stephen's Green) FREE The Unitarian Church was built in 1863 to house two Unitarian congregations. Although nominally rooted in Presbyterianism, the church is a favourite with Dubliners looking to marry in accordance with a range of personal beliefs, including agnostics and nonbelievers who still want a little pizzazz in their ceremony.

Royal College of Surgeons UNIVERSITY

(Map p74; www.rcsi.ie; 123 St Stephen's Green W; 🚌all city centre) This early-19th-century building has one of the finest facades on St Stephen's Green. During the 1916 Easter Rising, the building was occupied by rebel forces led by the colourful Countess Markievicz (1868–1927), an Irish Nationalist married to a supposed Polish count. The columns are scarred from the bullet holes. Today it continues to produce doctors, and is especially popular with students from overseas.

Newman House NOTABLE BUILDING

(Map p74; ☎01-477 9810; www.ucd.ie; 85-86 St Stephen's Green S; adult €7; ⏰tours 2pm Tue, also by arrangement; 🚌10, 11, 13, 14 or 15A, 🚊St Stephen's Green) Among the finest examples of Georgian architecture open to the public in Dublin are these two town houses, founded by Cardinal Newman as the Catholic University of Ireland in 1865, along with an adjoining Victorian hall. The college was founded as an alternative to the Protestant hegemony of Trinity College, which was then the only option available to those seeking third-level education in Ireland. The alma mater of James Joyce, Pádraig Pearse and Eamon de Valera can be visited by guided tour.

Iveagh House HISTORIC BUILDING

(Map p74; www.dfa.ie; 80 St Stephen's Green S; 🚌10, 11, 13, 14 or 15A, 🚊St Stephen's Green) The headquarters of the Department of Foreign Affairs occupies two splendid Georgian houses that were joined together by Benjamin Guinness when he bought them in 1862 as his city residence. No 80 – the house on the left as you look at the building – was designed by Richard Cassels in 1736. The house was given to the Irish state in 1939 by Benjamin's grandson Rupert. It is not open to the public.

Government Buildings NOTABLE BUILDING

(Map p74; www.taoiseach.gov.ie; Upper Merrion St; ⏰tours hourly 10.30am-1.30pm Sat; 🚌7 & 44 from city centre) FREE This gleaming Edwardian pile was the last building (almost) completed by the British before they were evicted; it opened as the Royal College of Science in 1911. When the college vacated in 1989, the then-Taoiseach (prime minister) Charles Haughey and his government moved in and spent a fortune refurbishing the complex.

Free 40-minute tours visit the Taoiseach's office, the Cabinet Room, the ceremonial staircase with a stunning stained-glass window – designed by Evie Hone (1894–1955) for the 1939 New York Trade Fair – and many fine examples of modern Irish arts and crafts.

Merrion Square & Around

Genteel, sophisticated and elegant, the exquisite Georgian architecture spread around handsome Merrion Sq is a near-perfect mix of imposing public buildings, museums, and private offices and residences. It is round these parts that much of moneyed Dublin works and plays, amid the neoclassical beauties thrown up during Dublin's 18th-century prime. These include the home of the Irish parliament at Leinster House and, immediately surrounding it, the National Gallery, the main branch of the National Museum of Ireland and the Natural History Museum.

★ National Museum of Ireland – Archaeology

MUSEUM

(Map p74; www.museum.ie; Kildare St; 10am-5pm Tue-Sat, 2-5pm Sun; all city centre) FREE Ireland's most important cultural institution was established in 1877 as the primary repository of the nation's archaeological treasures. These include the most famous of Ireland's crafted artefacts, the **Ardagh Chalice** and the **Tara Brooch**, dating from the 12th and 8th century respectively. They are part of the **Treasury**, itself part of Europe's finest collection of Bronze and Iron Age gold artefacts, and the most complete assemblage of medieval Celtic metalwork in the world.

Also part of the Treasury is the exhibition **Ór-Ireland's Gold**, featuring stunning jewellery and decorative objects created by Celtic artisans in the Bronze and Iron Ages. Among them are the **Broighter Hoard**, which includes a 1st-century-BC large gold collar, unsurpassed anywhere in Europe, and an extraordinarily delicate gold boat. There's also the wonderful Loughnashade bronze war trumpet, which dates from the 1st century BC.

The other showstopper is the collection of Iron Age 'bog bodies' in the **Kingship and Sacrifice** exhibit – four figures in varying states of preservation dug out of the midland bogs. The bodies' various eerily preserved details – a distinctive tangle of hair, sinewy legs, and fingers with fingernails intact – are memorable, but it's the accompanying detail that will make you pause: scholars now believe that all of these bodies were victims of the most horrendous ritualistic torture and sacrifice – the cost of being notable figures in the Celtic world.

Upstairs are **Medieval Ireland 1150–1550**, **Viking Ireland** – which features exhibits from the excavations at Wood Quay, the area between Christ Church Cathedral and the river – and **Ancient Egypt**, featuring items acquired from excavations conducted between 1890 and 1930.

The museum has three sister museums throughout the country: the stuffed beasts of the Museum of Natural History, the decorative arts section at Collins Barracks (p92), and a **country life museum** (p416) in County Mayo, on Ireland's west coast.

Merrion Square

PARK

(Map p74; dawn-dusk; 7 & 44 from city centre) FREE Arguably the most elegant of Dublin's Georgian squares, Merrion Sq is also the most prestigious. It's well-kept lawns and beautifully tended flower beds are flanked on three sides by gorgeous Georgian houses with colourful doors, peacock fanlights, ornate door knockers and, occasionally, foot-scrapers, used to remove mud from shoes before venturing indoors. Over the last two centuries they've been used by some notable residents.

The square, laid out in 1762, is bordered on its fourth side by the National Gallery and Leinster House – all of which, apparently, isn't enough for some. One former resident, WB Yeats (1865–1939), was less than impressed and described the architecture as 'grey 18th century'; there's just no pleasing some people.

Just inside the northwestern corner of the square is a flamboyant **statue of Oscar Wilde**, who grew up across the street at No 1 (now used exclusively by the American University Dublin); Wilde wears his customary smoking jacket and reclines on a rock. Atop one of the plinths, daubed with witty one-liners and Wildean throwaways, is a small green statue of Oscar's pregnant mother.

LITERARY ADDRESSES

Merrion Sq has long been the favoured address of Dublin's affluent intelligentsia. Playwright Oscar Wilde (1854–1900) spent much of his youth at 1 North Merrion Sq. Poet WB Yeats (1865–1939) lived at 52 East Merrion Sq and later, between 1922 and 1928, at 82 South Merrion Sq. George ('AE') Russell (1867–1935), the self-proclaimed 'poet, mystic, painter and cooperator', worked at No 84. Political leader Daniel O'Connell (1775–1847) was a resident of No 58 in his later years. The Austrian Erwin Schrödinger (1887–1961), co-winner of the 1933 Nobel Prize for Physics, lived at No 65 between 1940 and 1956. Dublin also seems to attract writers of horror stories: Joseph Sheridan Le Fanu (1814–73), who penned the vampire classic *Carmilla*, was a resident of No 70.

★National Gallery MUSEUM

(Map p74; www.nationalgallery.ie; West Merrion Sq; ⌚9.30am-5.30pm Mon-Wed, Fri & Sat, to 8.30pm Thu, noon-5.30pm Sun; 🚌7 & 44 from city centre) FREE A magnificent Caravaggio and a breathtaking collection of works by Jack B Yeats – William Butler's younger brother – are the main reasons to visit the National Gallery, but not the only ones. Its excellent collection is strong in Irish art, and there are also high-quality collections of every major European school of painting. The gallery is open but it's in the middle of a major renovation, so until at least 2016 the entrance is on Clare St.

Spread about its four wings you'll find: works by Rembrandt and his circle; a Spanish collection with paintings by El Greco, Goya and Picasso; and a well-represented display of Italian works dating from the early Renaissance to the 18th century. Fra Angelico, Titian and Tintoretto are among the artists represented, but the highlight is undoubtedly Caravaggio's *Taking of Christ* (1602), which lay for over 60 years in a Jesuit house in Leeson St and was accidentally discovered by chief curator Sergio Benedetti.

The ground floor displays the gallery's fine Irish collection, plus a smaller British collection, with works by Reynolds, Hogarth, Gainsborough, Landseer and Turner. Absolutely unmissable is the **Yeats Collection** at the back of the gallery, displaying more than 30 works by Irish impressionist Jack B Yeats (1871–1957), Ireland's most important 20th-century painter.

With its light-filled, modern design, the **Millennium Wing** can also be entered from Clare St. It houses a small collection of 20th-century Irish art, high-profile visiting collections (for which there are admission charges), an art reference library, a lecture theatre, a good bookshop and Fitzer's Café.

There are free tours at 12.30pm on Saturdays and at 11.30am, 12.30pm and 1.30pm on Sundays. The gallery has also launched a free Masterpieces app (available for both Android and iPhone) featuring 80% of its collection.

★Museum of Natural History MUSEUM

(National Museum of Ireland – Natural History; Map p74; www.museum.ie; Upper Merrion St; ⌚10am-5pm Tue-Sat, 2-5pm Sun; 🚌7 & 44 from city centre) FREE Dusty, weird and utterly compelling, this window into Victorian times has barely changed since Scottish explorer Dr David Livingstone opened it in 1857 – before disappearing into the African jungle for a meeting with Henry Stanley. It is a beautifully preserved example of Victorian charm and scientific wonderment, and its enormous collection is a testament to the rich diversity of the natural world and the skill of taxidermy.

The **Irish Room** on the ground floor is filled with mammals, sea creatures, birds and some butterflies all found in Ireland at some point, including the skeletons of three 10,000-year-old Irish elk that greet you as you enter. The **World Animals Collection**, spread across three levels, has as its centrepiece the skeleton of a 20m-long fin whale found beached in County Sligo. Evolutionists will love the line-up of orangutan, chimpanzee, gorilla and human skeletons on the 1st floor. A new addition here is the **Discovery Zone**, where visitors can do some first-hand exploring of their own, handling taxidermy specimens and opening drawers. Other notables include the Tasmanian tiger (an extinct Australian marsupial, mislabelled as a Tasmanian wolf), a giant panda from China, and several African and Asian rhinoceros. The wonderful **Blaschka Collection** comprises finely detailed glass models of marine creatures whose zoological accuracy is incomparable.

Leinster House NOTABLE BUILDING

(Oireachtas Éireann; Map p74; ☎01-618 3271; www.oireachtas.ie; Kildare St; ⌚observation galleries 2.30-8.30pm Tue, 10.30am-8.30pm Wed, 10.30am-5.30pm Thu Nov-May, tours 10.30am, 11.30am, 2.30pm & 3.30pm Mon-Fri; 🚌all city centre) All the big decisions are made at the Oireachtas (parliament). This magnificent Palladian mansion was built as a city residence for James Fitzgerald, the Duke of Leinster and Earl of Kildare, by Richard Cassels between 1745 and 1748 – hence its name.

Free, pre-arranged **guided tours** are available when parliament is in session (but not sitting). You can get an entry ticket to the lower- or upper-house observation galleries from the Kildare St entrance on production of photo identification.

The Kildare St facade looks like a town house (which inspired Irish architect James Hoban's design for the US White House), whereas the Merrion Sq frontage resembles a country mansion. The obelisk in front of the building is dedicated to Arthur Griffith, Michael Collins and Kevin O'Higgins, the architects of independent Ireland.

WAYNE WALTON/GETTY IMAGES ©

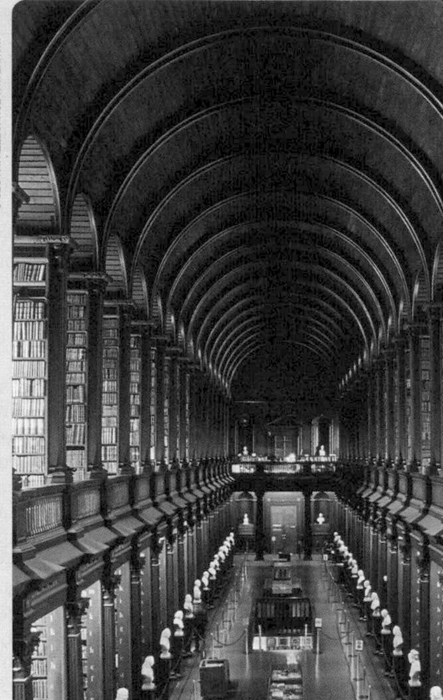

1. Oscar Wilde statue by Danny Osborne (p78) **2.** Long Room (p67), Trinity College Library **3.** Samuel Beckett Bridge
4. James Joyce statue by Marjorie Fitzgibbon (p87)

2

BRUNO BARBIER/GETTY IMAGES ©

4

Literary Dublin

Is there a city of comparable size anywhere in the world that can hold a candle to Dublin as a literary heavyweight? It's not just the Nobel Prize winners – it's the host of other scribes, writing in every conceivable genre, for every conceivable taste.

Marsh's Library

Dublin's oldest working library is an early-18th-century classic, packed with ancient books and manuscripts including some of the world's rarest.

Samuel Beckett

Like his great mentor Joyce, Beckett left Dublin for Paris, where he produced his finest work, including the watershed *Waiting For Godot,* a modernist classic. A memorial bridge dedicated to Beckett, designed by architect Santiago Calatrava, was opened in Dublin in 2009.

James Joyce

Ireland's most famous literary export, Joyce devoted virtually his entire career to writing about one subject: Dublin. His book of short stories, *Dubliners,* remains one of the must-reads on the capital.

Dublin Writers Museum

A collection of memorabilia associated with Dublin's rich literary past, including Brendan Behan's union card and Samuel Beckett's phone.

Trinity College Library

Two super-highlights: the breathtaking 65m Long Room, the most beautiful library in Ireland; and the *Book of Kells*, the most famous illustrated gospels in the world.

Oscar Wilde

Outstanding playwright, thoughtful poet, writer of children's literature and famous wit, Oscar Wilde is one of Dublin's most beloved literary progeny.

The first government of the Irish Free State moved in from 1922, and both the Dáil (lower house) and Seanad (senate, or upper house) still meet here to discuss the affairs of the nation and gossip at the exclusive members bar. The 60-member Seanad meets for fairly low-key sessions in the north-wing saloon, while there are usually more sparks and tantrums when the 166-member Dáil bangs heads in a less-interesting room, formerly a lecture theatre, which was added to the original building in 1897. Parliament sits for 90 days a year.

Temple Bar

Virtually all visitors to Dublin find their way to the cobbled streets of Temple Bar, Dublin's so-called 'cultural quarter,' a maze of streets and alleys sandwiched between Dame St and the River Liffey, and running from Trinity College west to Christ Church Cathedral.

You can visit all of Temple Bar's attractions in less than half a day, but that's not really the point: this neighbourhood is really more about ambience than attractions. If you visit during the day, the district's bohemian bent is on display. You can browse for vintage clothes, get your nipples pierced, nibble on Mongolian barbecue, buy organic food, pick up the latest musical releases and buy books on every conceivable subject. You can check out the latest art installations, watch an outdoor movie or join in a pulsating drum circle. By night – or at the weekend – it's a different story altogether, as the area's bars are packed to the rafters with revellers looking to tap into their inner Bacchus: it's loud, raucous and usually a lot of fun. Temple Bar is also Dublin's official 'cultural quarter', so you shouldn't ignore its more high-minded offerings such as the progressive Project Arts Centre (p125) and the Irish Film Institute (p124).

At the western end of Temple Bar, in the shadow of Christ Church Cathedral, is **Fishamble Street**, the oldest street in Dublin. It dates back to Viking times – not that you'd know that to see it now.

To the east, buildings on interesting Eustace St include the 1715 Presbyterian Meeting House, now the Ark (p85), an excellent children's cultural centre. The Dublin branch of the Society of United Irishmen, who sought Parliamentary reform and equality for Catholics, was first convened in 1791 in the Eagle Tavern, now the **Friends' Meeting House** (Map p106; Eustace St; all city centre). (This shouldn't be confused with the other Eagle Tavern, which is on Cork St.)

Meeting House Square is one of the real success stories of Temple Bar. It's fronted by two museums and on Saturdays it hosts a popular food market (p128).

Merchant's Arch leads to the **Ha'penny Bridge**, the city's most cherished bridge and named after the ha'penny (half-penny) toll once needed to cross.

Gallery of Photography GALLERY

(Map p106; www.galleryofphotography.ie; Meeting House Sq; 11am-6pm Mon-Sat; all city centre) FREE This small gallery devoted to photography is set in an airy three-level space overlooking Meeting House Sq. It features a constantly changing menu of local and international work, and while it's a little too small to be considered a really good gallery, the downstairs shop is well stocked with all manner of photographic tomes and manuals.

National Photographic Archive MUSEUM

(Map p106; Meeting House Sq; 10am-4.45pm Mon-Sat, noon-4.45pm Sun; all city centre) FREE What should be a wonderful resource putting a face on all facets of Irish history is actually a sadly disappointing archive of photographs taken from the 19th century onwards. Its visitor-friendly catalogue is computer accessible and the eager staff are always willing to help with queries, but the available material is not nearly as extensive as we'd hoped.

Sunlight Chambers NOTABLE BUILDING

(Map p106; Parliament St; all city centre) On the southern banks of the Liffey, Sunlight Chambers, designed by Liverpool architect Edward Ould (designer of England's Port Sunlight village), stands out among the Georgian and modern architecture for its romantic Italianate style and beautiful art nouveau friezework by German sculptor Conrad Dressler. Sunlight was a brand of soap made by Lever Brothers. The frieze shows the Lever Brothers' view of the world: men make clothes dirty, women wash them.

The Liberties & Kilmainham

For the first 500 years of its official existence, Dublin didn't spread far beyond a hill just west of Dublin Castle. Here, firmly within the old city walls, is the most impressive monument of the medieval city: Christ Church Cathedral. Outside the perimeter walls to the south was built that other great place of worship, St Patrick's – although you'd hardly notice anything today save a few buildings and the stretch of an elegant garden. West of both is the Liberties, Dublin's oldest surviving neighbourhood, and just at its western edge is the imposing Guinness plant, which is the city's single biggest tourist attraction. Beyond that is Kilmainham, home to the old prison that was central to the struggle for Irish independence (now a city highlight) and an ancient soldiers' hospital, now the country's most important modern-art museum.

★ Guinness Storehouse — BREWERY, MUSEUM

(Map p70; www.guinness-storehouse.com; St James's Gate, South Market St; adult/student/child €16.20/14.50/6.50, connoisseur experience €46.20; 9.30am-5pm Sep-Jun, to 7pm Jul & Aug; ; 21A, 51B, 78, 78A or 123 from Fleet St, St James's) The most popular visit in town is this multimedia homage to Guinness, one of Ireland's most enduring symbols. A converted grain storehouse is the only part of the 26-hectare brewery that is open to the public, but it's a suitable cathedral in which to worship the black gold. Across its seven floors you'll discover everything about Guinness before getting to taste it in the top-floor **Gravity Bar**, with its panoramic views. Pre-booking your tickets online will save you money.

Since Arthur Guinness (1725–1803) founded the brewery in 1759, the operation has expanded down to the Liffey and across both sides of the street; at one point, it had its own railway and there was a giant gate stretching across St James's St, hence the brewery's proper name, St James's Gate Brewery. At its apogee in the 1930s, it employed over 5000 workers, making it the largest employer in the city. Increased automation has reduced the workforce to around 600, but it still produces 2.5 million pints of stout every day.

You'll get to drink one of those pints at the end of your tour, but not before you have walked through the extravaganza that is the Guinness floor show, spread across 1.6 hectares and involving an array of audiovisual, interactive displays that cover pretty much all aspects of the brewery's history and the brewing process. It's slick and sophisticated, but you can't ignore the man behind the curtain: the extensive exhibit on the company's incredibly successful history of advertising is a reminder that for all the talk of mysticism and magic, it's all really about marketing and manipulation.

DUBLIN PASS

For heavy-duty sightseeing, the **Dublin Pass** (www.dublinpass.com; adult/child one-day pass €39/21, three-day pass €71/42) will save you a packet. It provides free entry to 33 attractions (including the Guinness Storehouse), discounts at 20 others and guaranteed fast-track entry to some of the busiest attractions. To avail yourself of the free Aircoach transfer to and from the airport, order the card online so you have it when you land. Otherwise, it's available from any Dublin Discover Ireland Centres.

The point is made deliciously moot when you finally get a pint in your hand and let the cream pass your lips in the vertiginous heights of the Gravity Bar. It's the best pint of Guinness in the world, claim the cognoscenti, and die-hards can opt for the Connoisseur Experience, where a designated barkeeper goes through the histories of the four variants of Guinness – Draught, Original, Foreign Extra Stout and Black Lager – and provides delicious samples of each.

Around the corner at **1 Thomas Street** a plaque marks the house where Arthur Guinness lived. In a yard across the road stands **St Patrick's Tower**, Europe's tallest smock windmill (with a revolving top), which was built around 1757.

★ St Patrick's Cathedral — CHURCH

(Map p70; www.stpatrickscathedral.ie; St Patrick's Close; adult/student/child €6/5/free; 9.30am-5pm Mon-Fri, 9am-6pm Sat, 9-10.30am & 12.30-2.30pm Sun; 50, 50A or 56A from Aston Quay, 54 or 54A from Burgh Quay) Ireland's largest church is St Patrick's Cathedral, built between 1191 and 1270 on the site of an earlier church that had stood here since the 5th century. It was here that St Patrick himself reputedly baptised the local Celtic chieftains, making this bit of ground some fairly sacred turf: the well in question is in the adjacent **St Patrick's Park**, which was once a slum but is now a lovely spot to sit and take a load off.

Like Christ Church Cathedral, the building has suffered a rather dramatic history of storm and fire damage and has been altered several times (most questionably in

EVENSONG AT THE CATHEDRALS

In a rare coming together, the choirs of St Patrick's Cathedral and Christ Church Cathedral both participated in the first-ever performance of Handel's *Messiah,* conducted by the great composer himself in nearby Fishamble St in 1742. Both houses of worship carry on their proud choral traditions, and visits to the cathedrals during evensong will provide enchanting and atmospheric memories. The choir performs evensong in St Patrick's at 5.45pm Monday to Friday (not on Wednesday in July and August), while the Christ Church choir competes at 5.30pm on Sunday, 6pm on Wednesday and Thursday, and 5pm Saturday. If you're going to be in Dublin around Christmas, do not miss the carols at St Patrick's; call ahead for the hard-to-get tickets on ☎01-453 9472.

1864 when the flying buttresses were added, thanks to the neo-Gothic craze that swept the nation). Oliver Cromwell, during his 1649 visit to Ireland, converted St Patrick's to a stable for his army's horses, an indignity to which he also subjected numerous other Irish churches. Jonathan Swift, author of *Gulliver's Travels,* was the dean of the cathedral from 1713 to 1745, but after his tenure the cathedral was very neglected until its restoration in the 1860s. Also like Christ Church, St Patrick's is a Church of Ireland cathedral – which means that overwhelmingly Catholic Dublin has two Anglican cathedrals!

Entering the cathedral from the southwestern porch you come almost immediately, on your right, to the **graves of Swift and his long-time companion Esther Johnson**, aka Stella. On the wall nearby are Swift's own (self-praising) Latin epitaphs to the two of them, and a bust of Swift.

The huge, dusty **Boyle Monument** to the left was erected in 1632 by Richard Boyle, Earl of Cork, and is decorated with numerous painted figures of members of his family. The figure in the centre on the bottom level is the earl's five-year-old son Robert Boyle (1627–91), who grew up to become a noted scientist. His contributions to physics include Boyle's Law, which relates the pressure and volume of gases.

★**Marsh's Library** LIBRARY

(Map p70; www.marshlibrary.ie; St Patrick's Close; adult/child €3/free; ⏲9.30am-5pm Mon & Wed-Fri, 10am-5pm Sat; 🚌50, 50A or 56A from Aston Quay, 54 or 54A from Burgh Quay) This magnificently preserved scholars' library, virtually unchanged in three centuries, is one of Dublin's most beautiful open secrets, and an absolute highlight of any visit. Atop its ancient stairs are beautiful, dark-oak bookcases, each topped with elaborately carved and gilded gables, and crammed with books, manuscripts and maps.

Founded in 1701 by Archbishop Narcissus Marsh (1638–1713) and opened in 1707, the library was designed by Sir William Robinson, the man also responsible for the Royal Hospital Kilmainham (now the Irish Museum of Modern Art, p86). It's the oldest public library in the country, and contains 25,000 books dating from the 16th to the early 18th century, as well as maps, manuscripts (including one in Latin dating back to 1400) and a collection of incunabula (books printed before 1500).

Christ Church Cathedral CHURCH

(Church of the Holy Trinity; Map p70; www.christchurchcathedral.ie; Christ Church Pl; adult/student/child €6/4.50/2; ⏲9.00am-5pm Mon-Sat & 12.30-2.30pm Sun year-round, longer hours Jun-Aug; 🚌50, 50A or 56A from Aston Quay, 54 or 54A from Burgh Quay) Its hilltop location and eye-catching flying buttresses make this the most photogenic of Dublin's cathedrals. It was founded in 1030 and rebuilt from 1172, mostly under the impetus of Richard de Clare, Earl of Pembroke (better known as Strongbow), the Anglo-Norman noble who invaded Ireland in 1170 and whose monument has pride of place inside.

Guided tours (adult/family €4/10; ⏲11.30am & 1.15pm Sat, 1.15pm Sun) include the belfry, where a campanologist explains the art of bell-ringing and you can even have a go.

Once the original wooden church was replaced by the building you see today, the cathedral vied for supremacy with nearby St Patrick's Cathedral, but like its sister church it also fell on hard times in the 18th and 19th centuries – the nave had been used as a market and the crypt had housed taverns – and was virtually derelict by the time restoration took place. Today, both Church of Ireland cathedrals are outsiders in a largely Catholic nation.

From the southeastern entrance to the churchyard, walk past ruins of the **chapter house**, which dates from 1230. The entrance to the cathedral is at the southwestern corner and as you enter you face the northern wall. This survived the collapse of its southern counterpart but has also suffered from subsiding foundations.

The monument to Strongbow is in the southern aisle. The armoured figure on the tomb is unlikely to be Strongbow (it's more probably the Earl of Drogheda), but his internal organs may have been buried here. A popular legend relates that the half-figure beside the tomb is Strongbow's son, who was cut in two by his father when his bravery in battle was suspect.

The southern transept contains the superb baroque **tomb** of the 19th Earl of Kildare (died 1734). His grandson, Lord Edward Fitzgerald, was a member of the United Irishmen and died in the abortive 1798 Rising.

An entrance just by the southern transept descends to the unusually large arched **crypt**, which dates back to the original Viking church. Curiosities in the crypt include a glass display case housing a mummified cat chasing a mummified rat (known as Tom and Jerry), which were trapped inside an organ pipe in the 1860s! From the main entrance, a bridge, part of the 1871–78 restoration, leads to Dublinia.

Dublinia & Viking World MUSEUM
(Map p70; ☎01-679 4611; www.dublinia.ie; Christ Church Pl; adult/student/child €8.50/7.50/5.50; ⏲10am-5.30pm Mar-Sep, to 4.30pm Oct-Feb; 🚌50, 50A or 56A from Aston Quay, 54 or 54A from Burgh Quay) A must for the kids, the old Synod Hall, added to Christ Church Cathedral during its late-19th-century restoration, is home to the seemingly perennial Dublinia, a lively and kitschy attempt to bring medieval Dublin to life. Models, streetscapes and somewhat old-fashioned interactive displays do a fairly decent job of it, at least for kids. Your ticket gets you into Christ Church Cathedral free, via the link bridge.

The model of a medieval quayside and a cobbler's shop are both excellent, as is the scale model of the medieval city. Up one floor is **Viking World**, which has a large selection of objects recovered from Wood Quay, the world's largest Viking archaeological site. Interactive exhibits tell the story of Dublin's 9th- and 10th-century Scandinavian invaders, but the real treat is exploring life aboard the recreated longboat.

Finally, you can climb neighbouring **St Michael's Tower** (Map p106; Christ Church Pl;

DUBLIN FOR CHILDREN

Kid-friendly? You bet. Dubliners love little 'uns, and will enthusiastically ooh and aah at the cuteness of your progeny. But alas, such admiration hasn't fully translated into child services such as widespread and accessible baby-changing facilities. Nevertheless, the city has plenty to keep kids entertained.

If your kids are aged between three and 14, spend an afternoon at **Ark Children's Cultural Centre** (Map p106; www.ark.ie; 11a Eustace St; 🚌all city centre), which runs activities aimed at stimulating participants' interests in science, the environment and the arts – be sure to book well in advance.

There are loads of ways to discover Dublin's Viking past; **Dublinia**, the city's Viking and medieval museum, has interactive exhibits that are specifically designed to appeal to younger visitors. Kids of all ages will love a **Viking Splash Tour** (p98), where you board an amphibious vehicle, put on a plastic Viking hat and roar at passers-by as you do a tour of the city, before landing in the water at the Grand Canal basin.

A perennial favourite is **Dublin Zoo** (p95), while the **National Leprechaun Museum** (p91) lets the kids' imaginations run wild among the optical illusions and oversized furniture. On the 2nd floor of the Powerscourt Townhouse Shopping Centre is the **Dolls Store** (Map p106; www.dollstore.ie; ⏲10am-6pm Mon-Sat; 🚌all city centre), which sells all kinds of dolls and doll's houses; should your little one's doll or teddy get 'ill', this is also the home of Ireland's only doll and teddy-bear hospital.

All but a few hotels will provide cots (cribs), and most top-range hotels have babysitting services (€8 to €15 per hour). Restaurants are generally accommodating until 7pm, after which things can get difficult, especially for babies: check while making a booking.

50, 50A or 56A from Aston Quay, 54 or 54A from Burgh Quay) and peek through its grubby windows for views over the city to the Dublin hills. There is also a pleasant cafe and the inevitable souvenir shop.

★**Kilmainham Gaol** MUSEUM

(www.heritageireland.com; Inchicore Rd; adult/child €7/3; 9.30am-6pm Apr-Sep, 9.30am-5.30pm Mon-Sat, 10am-6pm Sun Oct-Mar; 23, 25, 25A, 26, 68 or 69 from city centre) If you have *any* desire to understand Irish history – especially the juicy bits about resistance to British rule – then a visit to this former prison is an absolute must. This threatening grey building, built between 1792 and 1795, played a role in virtually every act of Ireland's painful path to independence and even today, despite closing in 1924, it still has the power to chill.

The uprisings of 1798, 1803, 1848, 1867 and 1916 ended with the leaders' confinement here. Robert Emmet, Thomas Francis Meagher, Charles Stewart Parnell and the 1916 Easter Rising leaders were all visitors, but it was the executions in 1916 that most deeply etched the jail's name into the Irish consciousness. Of the 15 executions that took place between 3 May and 12 May after the revolt, 14 were conducted here. As a finale, prisoners from the Civil War were held here from 1922.

An excellent audiovisual introduction to the building is followed by a thought-provoking tour of the eerie prison, the largest unoccupied building of its kind in Europe. Sitting incongruously outside in the yard is the *Asgard*, the ship that successfully ran the British blockade to deliver arms to Nationalist forces in 1914. The tour finishes in the gloomy yard where the 1916 executions took place.

★**Irish Museum of Modern Art** MUSEUM

(IMMA; Map p70; www.imma.ie; Military Rd; 11.30am-5.30pm Tue-Fri, 10am-5.30pm Sat, noon-5.30pm Sun, tours 1.15pm Wed & 2.30pm Sat & Sun; Heuston) FREE Ireland's most important collection of modern and contemporary Irish and international art is housed in the elegant, airy expanse of the Royal Hospital Kilmainham, designed by Sir William Robinson and built between 1684 and 1687 as a retirement home for soldiers. It fulfilled this role until 1928, after which it languished for nearly 50 years until a 1980s restoration saw it come back to life as this wonderful repository of art.

The building, which was inspired by Les Invalides in Paris, is a marvellous example of the Anglo-Dutch style that preceded the Georgian age; at the time of its construction there were mutterings that it was altogether too fine a place for its residents.

Following Irish independence it was briefly considered as a potential home for the new Irish parliament, but it ended up as a storage facility for the National Museum of Ireland. Restorations began on the occasion of its 300th birthday in 1984 and it opened in 1991. A major restoration in 2012–13 gave it an extra bit of sparkle.

The blend of old and new works wonderfully, and you'll find such contemporary Irish artists as Louis Le Brocquy, Sean Scully, Barry Flanagan, Kathy Prendergast and Dorothy Cross featured here, as well as a film installation by Neil Jordan. The permanent exhibition also features paintings from heavy hitters Pablo Picasso and Joan Miró, and is topped up by regular temporary exhibitions. There's a good cafe and bookshop on the grounds.

There are free **guided tours** of the museum's exhibits throughout the year, and we strongly recommend the free seasonal heritage tours (50 minutes) of the building itself, which run from July to September.

St Audoen's Church of Ireland CHURCH

(Map p70; www.heritageireland.ie; Corn Market, High St; 9.30am-4.45pm May-Oct; 50, 50A or 56A from Aston Quay, 54 or 54A from Burgh Quay) FREE Two churches, side by side, each bear the same name, a tribute to St Audoen, the 7th-century bishop of Rouen (aka Ouen) and patron saint of the Normans. They built the older of the two, the Church of Ireland, between 1181 and 1212, and today it is the only medieval church in Dublin still in use. A free 30-minute guided tour departs every 30 minutes from 9.30am to 4.45pm. Attached to it is the newer, bigger, 19th-century **Catholic St Audoen's**.

Through the Norman church's heavily moulded Romanesque door you can touch the 9th-century 'lucky stone' that was believed to bring good luck to business, and check out the 9th-century slab in the porch that suggests it was built on an even older church. As part of the tour you can explore the ruins as well as the present church, which has funerary monuments that were beheaded by Cromwell's purists. Its tower and door date from the 12th century and the aisle from the 15th century, but the church today is mainly a product of a 19th-century restoration.

St Anne's Chapel, the visitor centre, houses a number of tombstones of leading members of Dublin society from the 16th to the 18th centuries. At the top of the chapel is the tower, which holds the three oldest bells in Ireland, dating from 1423. Although the church's exhibits are hardly spectacular, the building itself is beautiful and a genuine slice of medieval Dublin.

The church is entered from the south off High St through **St Audoen's Arch**, which was built in 1240 and is the only surviving reminder of the city gates. The adjoining park is pretty but attracts many unsavoury characters, particularly at night.

War Memorial Gardens PARK

(www.heritageireland.ie; South Circular Rd, Islandbridge; 8am-dusk Mon-Fri, 10am-dusk Sat & Sun; 25, 25A, 26, 68 or 69 from city centre) FREE Hardly anyone ever ventures this far west, but they're missing a lovely bit of landscaping in the shape of the War Memorial Gardens – by our reckoning as pleasant a patch of greenery as any you'll find in the heart of the Georgian centre. Designed by Sir Edwin Lutyens, the memorial commemorates the 49,400 Irish soldiers who died during WWI – their names are inscribed in the two huge granite bookrooms that stand at one end.

North of the Liffey

Grittier than their more genteel southside counterparts, the neighbourhoods immediately north of the River Liffey offer a fascinating mix of 18th-century grandeur, traditional city life and the multicultural melting pot that is contemporary Dublin. Radiating off its widest boulevard you'll find art galleries and whiskey museums, as well as some of the coolest cafes and restaurants in town.

Dublin City Gallery – The Hugh Lane GALLERY

(Map p88; 01-222 5550; www.hughlane.ie; 22 North Parnell Sq; 10am-6pm Tue-Thu, to 5pm Fri & Sat, 11am-5pm Sun; 3, 7, 10, 11, 13, 16, 19, 46A, 123) FREE Whatever reputation Dublin has as a repository of world-class art has a lot to do with the simply stunning collection at this exquisite gallery, housed in the equally impressive Charlemont House, designed by William Chambers in 1763. Within its walls you'll find the best of contemporary Irish art, a handful of impressionist classics

O'CONNELL STREET STATUARY

O'Connell St is lined with statues of Irish history's good and great. The big daddy of them all is the 'Liberator' himself, **Daniel O'Connell** (Map p88; Lower O'Connell St; all city centre, Abbey), whose massive bronze bulk soars high above the street at the bridge end. The four winged figures at his feet represent O'Connell's supposed virtues: patriotism, courage, fidelity and eloquence.

O'Connell is rivalled for drama by the spread-armed figure of trade-union leader **Jim Larkin** (1876–1947; Map p88; Lower O'Connell St; all city centre, Abbey), just south of the General Post Office; you can almost hear the eloquent tirade.

Looking on with a bemused air from the corner of pedestrianised North Earl St is a small statue of **James Joyce** (Map p88; North Earl St; all city centre, Abbey), whom wagsters like to refer to as 'the Prick with the Stick'. Joyce would have loved the vulgar rhyme.

Further north is the statue of **Father Theobald Mathew** (1790–1856; Map p88; Upper O'Connell St; all city centre, Abbey), the 'Apostle of Temperance' – a hopeless role in Ireland. This quixotic task, however, also resulted in a Liffey bridge bearing his name. The northern end of the street is completed by the imposing statue of **Charles Stewart Parnell** (1846–91; Map p88; Upper O'Connell St; all city centre, Abbey), Home Rule advocate and victim of Irish morality.

Finally, a word about the street's most dominant bit of decoration – the **Spire** (Map p88; O'Connell St; all city centre, Abbey). The brainchild of London-based architect Ian Ritchie, this 120m-high steel 'needle' is apparently the tallest sculpture in the world; whatever the case it has become the city's most recognisable symbol since its erection in 2001.

North of the Liffey

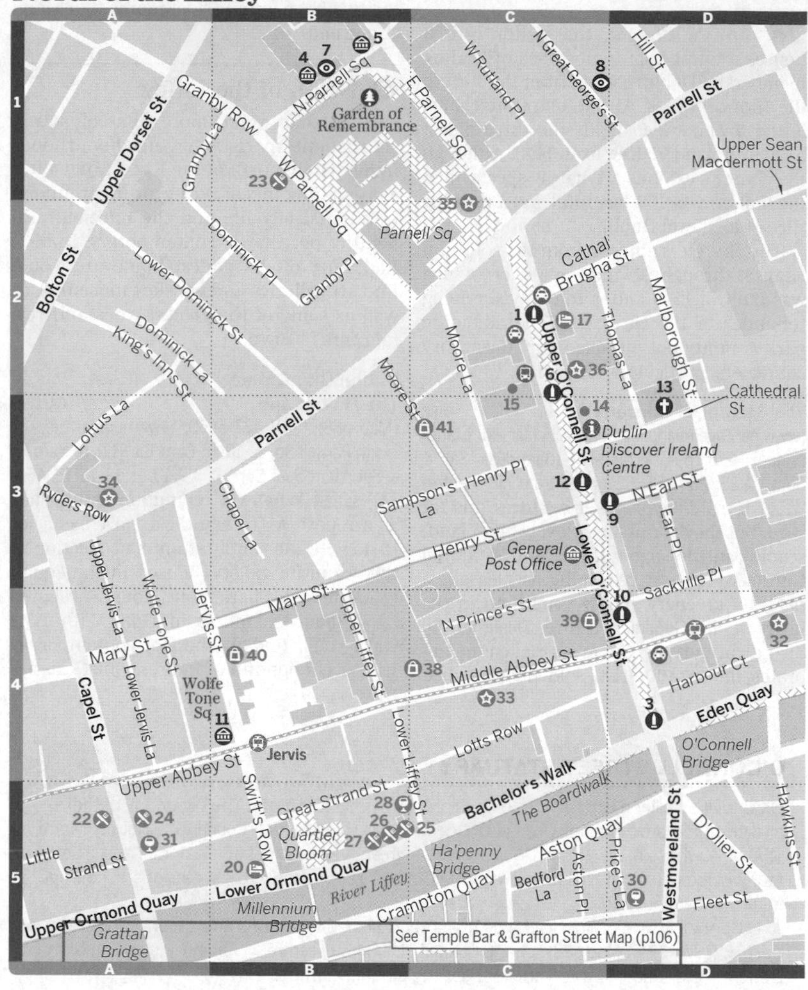

and the complete reconstruction of Francis Bacon's studio.

The gallery owes its origins to one Sir Hugh Lane (1875–1915). Born in County Cork, Lane worked in London art galleries before setting up his own gallery in Dublin in 1908. He had a connoisseur's eye and a good nose for the directions of the market, which enabled him to build up a superb collection, particularly strong in impressionists.

Unfortunately for Ireland, neither his talents nor his collection were much appreciated. Irish rejection led him to rewrite his will and bequeath some of the finest works in his collection to the National Gallery in London. Later he relented and added a rider to his will leaving the collection to Dublin but failed to have it witnessed, thus causing a long legal squabble over which gallery had rightful ownership.

The collection of eight paintings (known as the **Hugh Lane Bequest 1917**) was split in two in a 1959 settlement that sees half of them moving back and forth every six years. From 2015, the gallery has *Les Parapluies* by Auguste Renoir, *Portrait of Eva Gonzales* by Edouard Manet, *Jour d'Ete* by

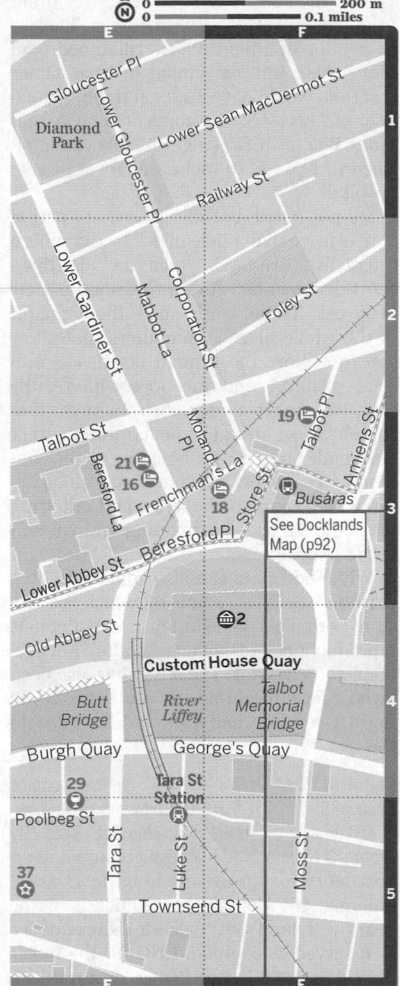

Berthe Morisot and *View of Louveciennes* by Camille Pissarro.

Impressionist masterpieces notwithstanding, the gallery's most popular exhibit is the **Francis Bacon Studio**, which was painstakingly moved, in all its shambolic mess, from 7 Reece Mews, South Kensington, London, where the Dublin-born artist (1909–92) lived for 31 years. The display features some 80,000 items madly strewn about the place, including slashed canvases and the last painting Bacon was working on.

The gallery is also home to a permanent collection of seven abstract paintings by

North of the Liffey

Sights

1 Charles Stewart Parnell Statue C2
2 Custom House F4
Custom House Visitor Centre .... (see 2)
3 Daniel O'Connell Statue D4
4 Dublin City Gallery – The Hugh Lane B1
5 Dublin Writers Museum B1
6 Father Theobald Mathew Statue C2
7 Irish Writers Centre B1
8 James Joyce Cultural Centre C1
9 James Joyce Statue D3
10 Jim Larkin Statue D4
11 National Leprechaun Museum B4
12 Spire C3
13 St Mary's Pro-Cathedral D3

Activities, Courses & Tours

14 City Sightseeing C3
15 Dublin Bus Tours C2
James Joyce Walking Tour .... (see 8)

Sleeping

16 Anchor House E3
17 Gresham Hotel C2
18 Isaacs Hostel F3
19 Jacob's Inn F3
20 Morrison Hotel B5
21 Townhouse Hotel E3

Eating

22 Brother Hubbard A5
Chapter One .... (see 5)
23 Hot Stove B1
Morrison Grill .... (see 20)
24 Musashi Noodles & Sushi Bar A5
25 Winding Stair B5
26 Woollen Mills B5
27 Yamamori Sushi B5

Drinking & Nightlife

28 Grand Social B5
29 John Mulligan's E5
30 Palace Bar D5
31 Pantibar A5

Entertainment

32 Abbey Theatre D4
33 Academy C4
34 Cineworld Multiplex A3
35 Gate Theatre C2
36 Savoy C2
37 Screen E5

Shopping

38 Arnott's C4
39 Eason's C4
40 Jervis St Centre B4
41 Moore Street Market C3

Irish-born, New York–based Sean Scully, probably Ireland's most famous living painter.

At noon on Sundays from September to June, the art gallery hosts up to 30 concerts of contemporary classical music.

Dublin Writers Museum MUSEUM

(Map p88; www.writersmuseum.com; 18 North Parnell Sq; adult/child €8/5; ⏲10am-5pm Mon-Sat, 11am-5pm Sun; 🚌3, 7, 10, 11, 13, 16, 19, 46A, 123) Memorabilia aplenty and lots of literary ephemera line the walls and display cabinets of this elegant museum devoted to preserving the city's rich literary tradition up to 1970. The building, comprising two 18th-century houses, is worth exploring on its own; Dublin stuccodore Michael Stapleton decorated the upstairs gallery.

However, the curious decision to omit living writers limits its appeal, and no account at all is given to contemporary writers, who would arguably be more popular with today's readers.

Although the busts and portraits of the greats in the gallery upstairs warrant more than a cursory peek, the real draws are the ground-floor displays, which include Samuel Beckett's phone (with a button for excluding incoming calls, of course), a letter from the 'tenement aristocrat' Brendan Behan to his brother, and a first edition of Bram Stoker's *Dracula*.

The **Gorham Library** next door is worth a visit, and there's also a calming Zen garden. The museum cafe is a pleasant place to linger, while the basement restaurant, Chapter One (p112), is one of the city's best.

While the museum focuses on the dearly departed, the **Irish Writers Centre** (Map p88; ☎01-872 1302; irishwriterscentre.ie; 19 North Parnell Sq; ⏲10am-10pm; 🚌3, 7, 10, 11, 13, 16, 19, 46A, 123) next door provides a meeting and working place for their living successors.

James Joyce Cultural Centre CULTURAL CENTRE

(Map p88; www.jamesjoyce.ie; 35 North Great George's St; adult/student/child €5/4/free; ⏲10am-5pm Tue-Sat; 🚌3, 10, 11, 11A, 13, 16, 16A, 19, 19A, 22 from city centre) Denis Maginni, the exuberant, flamboyant dance instructor and 'confirmed bachelor' immortalised by James Joyce in *Ulysses,* taught the finer points of dance out of this beautifully restored Georgian house, now a centre devoted to promoting and preserving the Joycean heritage.

Inside are a handful of exhibits that will pique the interest of a Joyce enthusiast. These include some of the furniture from Joyce's Paris apartment; a life-size re-creation of a typical Edwardian bedroom (not Joyce's, but one similar to what James and Nora would have used); and the original door of 7 Eccles St, the home of Leopold and Molly Bloom in *Ulysses,* which was demolished in real life to make way for a private hospital.

It's not much, but the absence of period stuff is more than made up for by the superb interactive displays, which include three short documentary films on various aspects of Joyce's life and work, and – the highlight of the whole place – computers that allow you to explore the content of *Ulysses* episode by episode and trace Joyce's life year by year. It's enough to demolish the myth that Joyce's works are an impenetrable mystery and render him as he should be to the contemporary reader: a writer of enormous talent who sought to challenge and entertain his audience with his breathtaking wit and use of language.

While here, you can also admire the fine plastered ceilings, some of which are restored originals while others are meticulous reproductions of Dublin stuccodore Michael Stapleton's designs. The street has also been given a facelift and now boasts some of the finest Georgian doorways and fanlights in the city.

General Post Office HISTORIC BUILDING

(Map p88; ☎01-705 7000; www.anpost.ie; Lower O'Connell St; ⏲8am-8pm Mon-Sat; 🚌all city centre, 🚋Abbey) Not just the country's main post office, or an eye-catching neoclassical building: the General Post Office is at the heart of Ireland's struggle for independence as it served as command HQ for the rebels during the 1916 Easter Rising. As a result, it has become the focal point for all kinds of protests, parades and remembrances.

The building – a neoclassical masterpiece designed by Francis Johnston in 1818 – was burnt out in the siege that resulted from the rising, but that wasn't the end of it. There was bitter fighting in and around the building during the Civil War of 1922; you can still see the pockmarks of the struggle in the Doric columns. Since its reopening in 1929 it has lived through quieter times, although its role in Irish history is commemorated inside with a series of communist noble-worker-style paintings depicting scenes from the Easter Rising.

St Mary's Pro-Cathedral CHURCH

(Map p88; Marlborough St; 8am-6.30pm; all city centre, Abbey) FREE Dublin's most important Catholic church is not quite the showcase you'd expect. It's in the wrong place for starters. The large neoclassical building, built between 1816 to 1825, was intended to stand where the General Post Office is, but Protestant objections resulted in its location on a cramped street that was then at the heart of Monto, the red-light district.

In fact, it's so cramped for space around here that you'd hardly notice the church's six Doric columns, which were modelled on the Temple of Theseus in Athens, much less be able to admire them. The interior is fairly functional, and its few highlights include a carved altar by Peter Turnerelli and the high relief representation of the Ascension by John Smyth. The best time to visit is 11am on Sunday when the Latin Mass is sung by the Palestrina Choir, with whom Ireland's most celebrated tenor, John McCormack, began his career in 1904.

National Leprechaun Museum MUSEUM

(Map p88; www.leprechaunmuseum.ie; Twilfit House, Jervis St; adult/child €12/8; 9.30am-6.30pm Mon-Sat, 10.30am-6.30pm Sun; all city centre, Jervis) Ostensibly designed as a child-friendly museum of Irish folklore, this is really a romper-room for kids sprinkled with bits of fairy tale. Which is no bad thing, even if the picture of the leprechaun painted here is more Lucky Charms and Walt Disney than sinister creature of pre-Celtic mythology.

There's the optical illusion tunnel (which makes you appear smaller to those at the other end), the room full of oversized furniture, the wishing wells and, inevitably, the pot of gold; all of which is strictly for the kids. But if Walt Disney himself went on a leprechaun hunt when visiting Ireland during the filming of *Darby O'Gill and the Little People* in 1948, what the hell do we know?

Four Courts HISTORIC BUILDING

(Map p70; Inns Quay; 9am-5pm Mon-Fri; 25, 66, 67 or 90 from city centre, Four Courts) FREE This masterpiece of James Gandon (1743–1823) is a mammoth complex stretching 130m along Inns Quay, as fine an example of Georgian public architecture as there is in Dublin. Despite the construction of a brand new criminal courts building further west along the Liffey, the Four Courts is still the enduring symbol of Irish law going about its daily business.

Visitors are allowed to wander through the building, but not to enter courts or other restricted areas.

The Corinthian-columned central block, connected to flanking wings with enclosed quadrangles, was begun in 1786 and not completed until 1802. The original four courts (Exchequer, Common Pleas, King's Bench and Chancery) all branch off from the central rotunda. In the lobby of the central rotunda you'll see bewigged barristers conferring and police officers handcuffed to their charges.

St Michan's Church CHURCH

(Map p70; www.stmichans.com; Lower Church St; adult/child/student €5/3.50/4; 10am-12.45pm & 2-4.45pm Mon-Fri, 10am-12.45pm Sat; Smithfield) Macabre remains are the main attraction at this church, which was founded by the Danes in 1095 and named after one of their saints. Among the 'attractions' is an 800-year-old Norman crusader who was so tall that his feet were lopped off so he could fit in a coffin. Visits are by guided tour only.

The oldest architectural feature is the 15th-century battlement tower; otherwise the church was rebuilt in the late 17th century, considerably restored in the early 19th century and again after the Civil War. The interior of the church, which feels more like a courtroom, is worth a quick look as you wait for your guide. It contains an organ from 1724, which Handel may have played for the first-ever performance of his *Messiah*. The organ case is distinguished by the fine oak carving of 17 entwined musical instruments on its front. A skull on the floor on one side of the altar is said to represent Oliver Cromwell. On the opposite side is the Stool of Repentance, where 'open and notoriously naughty livers' did public penance.

The tours of the **underground vaults** are the real draw, however. The bodies within are aged between 400 and 800 years, and have been preserved by a combination of methane gas coming from rotting vegetation beneath the church, the magnesium limestone of the masonry (which absorbs moisture from the air), and the perfectly constant temperature. The corpses have been exposed because the coffins in the vaults were stacked on top of one another and some toppled over and opened when the wood rotted. The guide sounds like he's been delivering the same, albeit fascinating,

Docklands

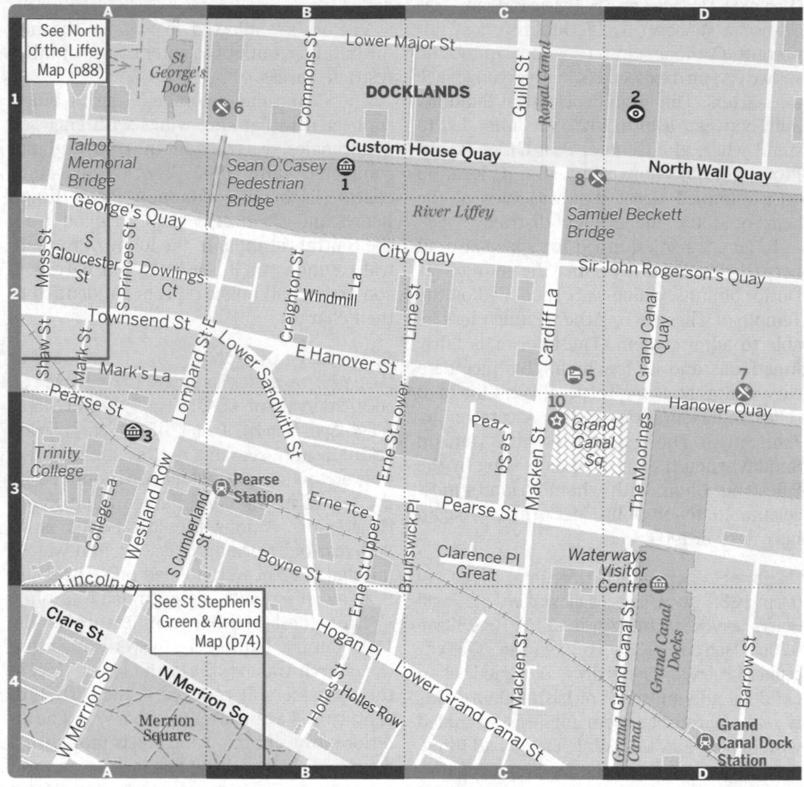

spiel for too long, but you'll definitely be glad you're not alone down there.

Old Jameson Distillery MUSEUM

(Map p70; www.jamesonwhiskey.com; Bow St; adult/student/child €15/12/8; 9am-6pm Mon-Sat, 10am-6pm Sun; 25, 66, 67 or 90 from city centre, Smithfield) Smithfield's biggest draw is devoted to *uisce beatha* (ish-kuh ba-ha, 'the water of life'); that's Irish for whiskey. To its more serious devotees, that is precisely what whiskey is, although they may be put off by the slickness of the museum (occupying part of the old distillery that stopped production in 1971), which shepherds visitors through a compulsory tour of the re-created factory (the tasting at the end is a lot of fun) and into the ubiquitous gift shop.

If you're buying whiskey, go for the stuff you can't buy at home, such as the excellent Red Breast or the superexclusive Midleton, a very limited reserve that is appropriately expensive.

★National Museum of Ireland – Decorative Arts & History MUSEUM

(Map p70; www.museum.ie; Benburb St; 10am-5pm Tue-Sat, 2-5pm Sun; 25, 66, 67 or 90 from city centre, Smithfield) FREE Once the world's largest military barracks, this splendid early-neoclassical grey-stone building on the Liffey's northern banks was completed in 1704 according to the design of Thomas Burgh, whose CV also includes the Old Library in Trinity College and St Michan's Church. It is now home to the Decorative Arts & History collection of the National Museum of Ireland.

The building's central square held six entire regiments and is a truly awesome space, surrounded by arcaded colonnades and blocks linked by walking bridges. Following the handover to the new Irish government in 1922, the barracks was renamed to honour Michael Collins, a hero of the struggle for independence, who was killed that year

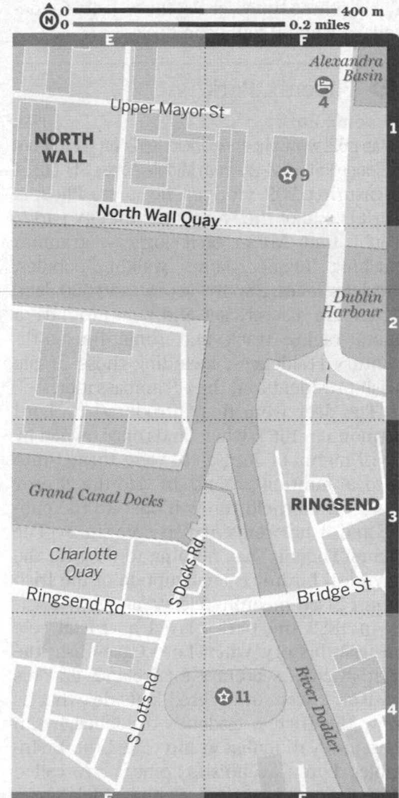

Docklands

Sights

1	Jeanie Johnston	B1
2	National Convention Centre	D1
3	Science Gallery	A3

Sleeping

4	Gibson Hotel	F1
5	Marker	C2

Eating

6	Ely Bar & Brasserie	B1
7	Herbstreet	D2
8	Quay 16	C1

Entertainment

9	3 Arena	F1
10	Bord Gáis Energy Theatre	C3
11	Shelbourne Park Greyhound Stadium	F4

in the Civil War; to this day most Dubliners refer to the museum as the **Collins Barracks**. Indeed, the army coat Collins wore on the day of his death (there's still mud on the sleeve) is part of the **Soldiers and Chiefs** exhibit, which covers the history of Irish soldiery at home and abroad from 1550 to the 21st century.

The museum's exhibits include a treasure trove of artefacts ranging from silver, ceramics and glassware to weaponry, furniture and folk-life displays – and an exquisite exhibition dedicated to iconic Irish designer **Eileen Gray** (1878–1976). The fascinating **Way We Wore** exhibit displays Irish clothing and jewellery from the past 250 years. An intriguing sociocultural study, it highlights the symbolism jewellery and clothing had in bestowing messages of mourning, love and identity. An exhibition chronicling Ireland's **1916 Easter Rising** is on the ground floor. Visceral memorabilia, such as first-hand accounts of the violence of the Black and Tans and post-Rising hunger strikes, the handwritten death certificates of the Republican prisoners and their postcards from Holloway prison, bring to life this poignant period of Irish history. Some of the best pieces are gathered in the **Curator's Choice** exhibition, which is a collection of 25 objects hand-picked by different curators, and displayed alongside an account of why they were chosen.

Docklands

It's a cardinal rule of any program of urban development: if your city is at the mouth of the sea, you cannot modernise without giving the docklands a revamp. And so it was with Dublin: the eastern banks north and south of the Liffey – aka 'Canary Dwarf' – have been given a major makeover and now sport an impressive array of contemporary office blocks, fancy apartments and snazzy public buildings, including Kevin Roche's angled, tubelike **National Convention Centre** (Map p92; Spencer Dock, North Wall Quay; Spencer Dock) and Daniel Libeskind's marvellous Bord Gáis Energy Theatre (p121).

Custom House MUSEUM

(Map p88; Custom House Quay; 10am-5pm Mon-Fri, 2-5pm Sat & Sun; all city centre) Georgian genius James Gandon (1743–1823) announced his arrival on the Dublin scene with this magnificent building (built 1781–91), constructed just past Eden Quay at a wide stretch in the River Liffey. It's a

WORTH A TRIP

SOUTH WALL WALK

One of the city's most rewarding walks is a stroll along the south wall to the Poolbeg Lighthouse (that red tower visible in the middle of Dublin Bay). To get there, you'll have to make your own way from Ringsend (which is reachable by buses 1, 2 or 3 from the city centre), past the power station to the start of the wall (it's about 1km). It's not an especially long walk – about 800m or so – and it will give you a stunning view of the bay and the city behind you, a view best enjoyed just before sunset.

colossal, neoclassical pile that stretches for 114m topped by a copper dome, beneath which the **visitor centre** (Map p88; Custom House Quay; admission €1.50; ⏲10am-12.30pm Mon-Fri, 2-5pm Sat & Sun mid-Mar–Oct, closed Mon, Tue & Sat Nov–mid-Mar; 🚌 all city centre) features a small museum on Gandon and the history of the building.

It's best appreciated from the south side of the Liffey, but its fine detail deserves closer inspection. Below the frieze are heads representing the gods of Ireland's 13 principal rivers; the sole female head, above the main door, represents the River Liffey. The cattle heads honour Dublin's beef trade, and the statues behind the building represent Africa, America, Asia and Europe. Set into the dome are four clocks and, above that, a 5m-high statue of Hope.

Jeanie Johnston MUSEUM, SHIP

(Map p92; www.jeaniejohnston.ie; Custom House Quay; adult/child €9/5; ⏲ tours hourly 10am-noon & 2-4pm; 🚌 all city centre) One of the city's most original tourist attractions is an exact working replica of a 19th-century coffin ship, as the sailing boats that transported starving emigrants away from Ireland during the Famine were gruesomely known. A small on-board museum details the harrowing plight of a typical journey, which usually took around 47 days.

This particular ship, a three-masted barque originally built in Quebec in 1847, made 16 transatlantic voyages, carrying more than 2500 people, and never suffered a single death. The ship also operates as a Sail Training vessel, with journeys taking place from May to September. If you are visiting during these times, check the website for details of when it will be in dock.

Phoenix Park

Phoenix Park PARK

(Map p62; www.phoenixpark.ie; ⏲24hr; 🚌10 from O'Connell St, 25 & 26 from Middle Abbey St) FREE Measuring 709 glorious hectares, Phoenix Park is one of the world's largest city parks; you'll find MP3-rigged joggers, grannies pushing buggies, ladies walking poodles, gardens, lakes, a sporting oval, and 300 deer. There are also cricket and polo grounds, a motor-racing track and some fine 18th-century residences, including those of the Irish president and the US ambassador.

The deer were first introduced by Lord Ormond in 1662, when lands once owned by the Knights of Jerusalem were turned into a royal hunting ground. In 1745 the viceroy Lord Chesterfield threw it open to the public and it has remained so ever since. (The name 'Phoenix' has nothing to do with the mythical bird; it is a corruption of the Irish *fionn uisce*, meaning 'clear water'.)

In 1882 the park played a crucial role in Irish history, when Lord Cavendish, the British chief secretary for Ireland, and his assistant were murdered outside what is now the Irish president's residence by an obscure Nationalist group called the Invincibles. Lord Cavendish's home is now called Deerfield and is used as the official residence of the US ambassador.

➡ **Wellington Monument**

Near the Parkgate St entrance to the park is the 63m-high Wellington Monument. This took from 1817 to 1861 to build, mainly because the Duke of Wellington fell from public favour during its construction. Nearby is the **People's Garden** (Map p70), dating from 1864, and the **bandstand** in the Hollow.

➡ **Garda Síochána Headquarters**

(Map p70) The large Victorian building behind Dublin Zoo, on the edge of the park, is the 19th-century Garda Síochána (Irish police force) Headquarters, designed by Benjamin Woodward (also author of the Old Library in Trinity College).

➡ **Papal Cross**

In the centre of Phoenix Park, the Papal Cross marks the site where Pope John Paul II preached to 1.25 million people in 1979.

➡ **Phoenix Monument**

The Phoenix Monument, a Corinthian column topped by a very un-phoenix-like bird, was erected by Lord Chesterfield in 1747, and is often referred to as the Eagle Monument. In the early years of the 20th century it was removed to facilitate motor racing in the park, but returned to its original spot in the 1990s.

➡ **Magazine Fort**

Towards Phoenix Park's Parkgate entrance is Magazine Fort on Thomas' Hill. Built at a snail's pace between 1734 and 1801, the fort has served as an occasional arms depot for the British and, later, the Irish armies. It was a target during the 1916 Easter Rising and again in 1940, when the IRA made off with the entire ammunitions reserve of the Irish army (they retrieved it after a few weeks).

Dublin Zoo ZOO

(www.dublinzoo.ie; Phoenix Park; adult/child/family €16.80/12/47; ⏲9.30am-6pm Mar-Sep, to dusk Oct-Feb; 🚌10 from O'Connell St, 25 & 26 from Middle Abbey St) Established in 1831, the 28-hectare Dublin Zoo just north of the Hollow is one of the oldest in the world. It is well known for its lion-breeding program, which dates back to 1857, and includes among its offspring the lion that roars at the start of MGM films. You'll see these tough mucats, from a distance, on the 'African Savannah', just one of several habitats created in the last few years.

The zoo is home to roughly 400 animals from 100 different species, and you can visit all of them across the eight different habitats that range from an Asian jungle to a family farm, where kids get to meet the inhabitants up close and milk a (model) cow. There are restaurants, cafes and even a train to get you round.

Áras an Uachtaráin HISTORIC BUILDING

(www.president.ie; Phoenix Park; ⏲guided tours hourly 10am-4pm Sat; 🚌10 from O'Connell St, 25 & 26 from Middle Abbey St) **FREE** The residence of the Irish president is a Palladian lodge that was built in 1751 and enlarged a couple of times since, most recently in 1816. Tickets for the free one-hour tours can be collected from the **Phoenix Park Visitor Centre** (Phoenix Park; admission free; ⏲9.30am-5pm; 🚌10 from O'Connell St, 25 & 26 from Middle Abbey St) **FREE**, the converted former stables of the papal nunciate (embassy), where you'll see a 10-minute introductory video before being shuttled to the Áras itself to inspect five staterooms and the president's study.

The residence was home to the British viceroys from 1782 to 1922, and then to the governors general until Ireland cut ties with the British Crown and created the office of president in 1937. Queen Victoria stayed here during her visit in 1849, when she appeared not to even notice the Famine. The candle burning in the window is an old Irish tradition, to guide 'the Irish diaspora' home.

Next door is the restored four-storey **Ashtown Castle** (Phoenix Park; 🚌10 from O'Connell St, 25 & 26 from Middle Abbey St), a 17th-century tower house 'discovered' inside the 18th-century nuncio's mansion when the latter was demolished in 1986 due to dry rot. You can visit the castle only on a guided tour from the visitor centre.

Beyond the Royal Canal

Beyond the Royal Canal lie the suburbs and an authentic slice of north-city life. There are also some beautiful gardens, the country's biggest stadium, a historic cemetery and one of the most interesting buildings in all of Dublin.

Croke Park Experience MUSEUM

(www.crokepark.ie; Clonliffe Rd, New Stand, Croke Park; adult/child/student museum €6/4/5, museum & tour €12.50/8.50/9.50; ⏲9.30am-6pm Mon-Sat, to 5pm Sun Jun-Aug, 9.30am-5pm Mon-Sat, 10.30am-5pm Sun Sep-May; 🚌3, 11, 11A, 16, 16A or 123 from O'Connell St) The Gaelic Athletic Association (GAA) considers itself not just the governing body of a bunch of Irish games but also the stout defender of a cultural identity that is ingrained in Ireland's sense of self. To get an idea of how important the GAA is, a visit is a must, though it will help if you're a sporting enthusiast.

The twice-daily tours (except match days) of the impressive Croke Park stadium are excellent, and well worth the extra cost. Admission to the tour includes a museum visit.

The stadium's newest attraction is the **Skyline** (www.skylinecrokepark.ie; Croke Park; adult/student/children €20/18/12; ⏲11.30am & 2.30pm Mon-Fri May-Sep, hourly 10.30am-2.30pm Sat & 11.30am-2.30pm Sun; 🚌3, 11, 11A, 16, 16A or 123 from O'Connell St), a guided tour around the stadium roof, with stops at five different viewing platforms that have bird's-eye views of the city. The most thrilling stop is on the platform that extends right out on-to the pitch.

Glasnevin Cemetery CEMETERY

(Prospect Cemetery; www.glasnevintrust.ie; Finglas Rd; 40, 40A or 40B from Parnell St) FREE The tombstones at Ireland's largest and most historically important burial site read like a 'who's who' of Irish history, as most of the leading names of the last 150 years are buried here, including Daniel O'Connell and Charles Stewart Parnell. It was established in 1832 by O'Connell as a burial ground for people of all faiths – a high-minded response to Protestant cemeteries' refusal to bury Catholics.

A modern replica of a round tower acts as a handy landmark for locating the tomb of O'Connell, who died in 1847 and was re-interred here in 1869 when the tower was completed. Charles Stewart Parnell's tomb is topped with a large granite rock, on which only his name is inscribed – a remarkably simple tribute to a figure of such historical importance. Other notable people buried here include Sir Roger Casement, executed for treason by the British in 1916; the Republican leader Michael Collins, who died in the Civil War; the docker and trade unionist Jim Larkin, a prime force in the 1913 general strike; and the poet Gerard Manley Hopkins.

The history of the cemetery is told in wonderful, award-winning detail in the **museum** (www.glasnevintrust.ie; Finglas Rd; museum €6, museum & tour €8; 10am-5pm Mon-Fri, 11am-6pm Sat & Sun; 40, 40A or 40B from Parnell St), which tells the social and political story of Ireland through the lives of the people, known and unknown, that are buried in the cemetery. The City of the Dead covers the burial practice and religious beliefs of the roughly 1½ million people whose final resting place this is, while the Milestone Gallery features a 10m-long digitally interactive timeline outlining the lives of the cemetery's most famous residents.

The best way to visit the cemetery is to take one of the daily **tours** (11.30am and 2.30pm year-round, also 1pm June to August) that will (ahem) bring to life the rich and important stories of those buried in what is jokingly referred to by Dubs as 'Croak Park'.

National Botanic Gardens GARDENS

(Botanic Rd; 9am-6pm Mon-Sat, 11am-6pm Sun Apr-Oct, 10am-4.30pm Mon-Sat, 11am-4.30pm Sun Nov-Mar; 13, 13A or 19 from O'Connell St, or bus 34 or 34A from Middle Abbey St) FREE Founded in 1795, the 19.5-hectare botanic gardens are home to a series of curvilinear glasshouses, dating from 1843 to 1869, created by Richard Turner, who was also responsible for the glasshouse at Belfast Botanic Gardens and the Palm House in London's Kew Gardens. Within these Victorian masterpieces you will find the latest in botanical technology, including a series of computer-controlled climates reproducing environments of different parts of the world.

Casino at Marino MUSEUM

(www.heritageireland.ie; Malahide Rd; adult/child/senior €4/2/3; 10am-5pm May-Sep; 20A, 20B, 27, 27B, 42, 42C or 123 from city centre) It's not the roulette-wheel kind of casino but the original Italian kind, the one that means 'summer home' (it literally means 'small house'), and this particular casino is one of the most enchanting constructions in all of Ireland. Entrance is by guided tour only; the last tour is 45 minutes before closing.

It was built in the mid-18th century for the Earl of Charlemont, who returned from his grand tour of Europe with more art than he could store in his own home, Marino House, which was on the same grounds but was demolished in the 1920s. He also came home with a big love of the Palladian style – hence the architecture of this wonderful folly.

The exterior of the building, with a huge entrance doorway, and 12 Tuscan columns forming a templelike facade, creates the expectation that its interior will be a simple single open space. But instead it is an extravagant convoluted maze: flights of fancy include chimneys for the central heating that are disguised as roof urns, downpipes hidden in columns, carved draperies, ornate fireplaces, beautiful parquet floors constructed of rare woods, and a spacious wine cellar. A variety of statuary adorns the outside but it's the amusing fakes that are most enjoyable. The towering front door is a sham – a much smaller panel opens to reveal the secret interior. The windows have blacked-out panels to hide the fact that the interior is a complex of rooms, not a single chamber.

Tours

There are all kinds of walking, cycling and – if you opt for a booze-focused option – crawling tours, covering a variety of themes from architecture and history to music and literature. Some companies combine a city tour with trips further afield. You'll save a few euro booking online.

> **A WORD IN YOUR EAR**
>
> If you fancy a go-it-alone guided walk, why not download one of Pat Liddy's excellent **iWalks** (www.visitdublin.com/iwalks), which you can play on your MP3 player. You can download them from the website or subscribe to them via iTunes. The 12 walks range from tours of the city's different districts to walks tailored to historical, architectural and activity themes.

★Historical Walking Tour WALKING TOUR
(Map p66; ☎01-878 0227; www.historicalinsights.ie; Trinity College Gate; adult/child €12/free; ⊙11am & 3pm May-Sep, 11am Apr & Oct, 11am Fri-Sun Nov-Mar; all city centre) Trinity College history graduates lead this 'seminar on the street' that explores the Potato Famine, Easter Rising, Civil War and Partition. Sights include Trinity, City Hall, Dublin Castle and Four Courts. In summer, themed tours on architecture, women in Irish history, and the birth of the Irish state are also held. Tours depart from the College Green entrance.

City Sightseeing BUS TOUR
(Map p88; www.citysightseeingdublin.ie; 14 Upper O'Connell St; adult/student €19/17; all city centre, Abbey) A typical hop-on-hop-off tour should last around 1½ hours and lead you up and down O'Connell St, past Trinity College and St Stephen's Green, before heading up to the Guinness Storehouse and back around the north quays, via the main entrance to Phoenix Park. Tours run every eight to 15 minutes, from 9am to 6pm.

Dublin Bus Tours BUS TOUR
(Map p88; www.dublinsightseeing.ie; 59 Upper O'Connell St; tours €22-27; ⊙tours daily; all city centre, Abbey) Offers a variety of tours, including the hop-on-hop-off Dublin City Tour, Ghost Bus Tour, Coast and Castles Tour, and South Coast and Gardens Tour.

See Dublin by Bike CYCLING TOUR
(Map p106; ☎01-280 1899; www.seedublinbybike.ie; Fade St; tours €25-30; all city centre) Three-hour themed tours that start outside Cafe Rothar on Fade St and take in the city's highlights and not-so-obvious sights. The Taste of Dublin is the main tour, but you can also take a U2's Dublin tour and a literary Dublin tour. Bikes, helmets and high-vis vests included.

1916 Rebellion Walking Tour WALKING TOUR
(Map p106; ☎086 858 3847; www.1916rising.com; 23 Wicklow St; per person €12; ⊙11.30am Mon-Sat, 1pm Sun Mar-Oct; 7 & 44 from city centre) Superb two-hour tour starting in the International Bar (p117), Wicklow St. Lots of information, humour and irreverence to boot. The guides – all Trinity graduates – are uniformly excellent and will not say no to the offer of a pint back in the International at tour's end.

Dublin Literary Pub Crawl WALKING TOUR
(Map p74; ☎01-670 5602; www.dublinpubcrawl.com; 9 Duke St; adult/student €12/10; ⊙7.30pm daily Apr-Oct, 7.30pm Thu-Sun Nov-Mar; all city centre) A tour of pubs associated with famous Dublin writers is a sure-fire recipe for success, and this 2½-hour tour/performance by two actors – which includes them acting out the funny bits – is a riotous laugh. There's plenty of drink taken, which makes it all the more popular. It leaves from the Duke on Duke St; get there by 7pm to reserve a spot for the evening tour.

Dublin Musical Pub Crawl WALKING TOUR
(Map p106; ☎01-478 0193; www.discoverdublin.ie; 58-59 Fleet St; adult/student €12/10; ⊙7.30pm daily Apr-Oct, 7.30pm Thu-Sat Nov-Mar; all city centre) The story of Irish traditional music and its influence on contemporary styles is explained and demonstrated by two expert musicians in a number of Temple Bar pubs over 2½ hours. Tours meet upstairs in the Oliver St John Gogarty (p114) pub and are highly recommended.

James Joyce Walking Tour WALKING TOURS
(Map p88; ☎01-878 8547; www.jamesjoyce.ie; 35 North Great George's St; adult/student €10/8; ⊙2pm Tue, Thu & Sat; 3, 10, 11, 11A, 13, 16, 16A, 19, 19A, 22 from city centre) Joyce lived, schooled and lost his virginity on the north side – and he put it all down on paper with cartographic precision from his self-imposed continental exile. You can explore all of the north-side attractions associated

with the bespectacled one on a 1¼-hour tour run by the James Joyce Cultural Centre (p90).

Pat Liddy Walking Tours WALKING TOURS
(Map p106; ☎01-831 1109; www.walkingtours.ie; Discover Dublin Tourism Centre, St Andrew's Church, 2 Suffolk St; tours €8-12; all city centre) Dublin's best-known tour guide is local historian Pat Liddy, who leads a variety of guided walks including Dublin Highlights and The Best of Dublin – The Complete Heritage Walking Tour. He is also available for private guided walks. Check the website for timings. He also has a bunch of **podcast walks** (www.visitdublin.com/iwalks) available for download.

Sandeman's New Dublin Tour WALKING TOURS
(Map p106; ☎01-878 8547; www.newdublintours.com; City Hall, Castle St; 11am & 2pm; all city centre) FREE A high-energy and thoroughly enjoyable three-hour walking tour of the city's greatest hits for free: tip only if you enjoyed the tour (they make sure you do). Spanish-language tours are also available.

Dublin Discovered Boat Tours BOAT TOUR
(☎01-473 4082; www.dublindiscovered.ie; Bachelor's Walk; adult/student/child €14/12/8; 9am-5.30pm Mar-Oct; all city centre, Abbey) 'See the sights without the traffic' is the pitch; you get to hear the history of Dublin from a watery point of view aboard an (all-important) all-weather cruiser.

Viking Splash Tours BUS TOUR, BOAT TOUR
(Map p74; ☎01-707 6000; www.vikingsplash.ie; St Stephen's Green N; adult/child €22/12; every 30-90min 10am-3pm; all city centre, St Stephen's Green) Go on, what's the big deal? You stick a plastic Viking's helmet on your head and yell 'yay' at the urging of your guide, but the upshot is you'll get a 1¼-hour semi-amphibious tour that ends up in the Grand Canal Dock. 'Strictly for tourists' seems so… superfluous.

DISCOVER DUBLIN APP

The tourist office has put together an app called Dublin Discovery Trails, with four themed walking tours covering the city's history over the last 200 years. Each walk takes approximately two hours; the app is available for both iPhone and Android.

Festivals & Events

Temple Bar Trad Festival MUSIC
(www.templebartrad.com) Traditional music festival in the bars of the cultural quarter over the last weekend in January.

St Patrick's Festival PARADE
(www.stpatricksfestival.ie) The mother of all festivals; 600,000-odd gather to 'honour' St Patrick over four days around 17 March on city streets and in venues.

Jameson Dublin International Film Festival FILM
(www.jdiff.com) Local flicks, arty international films and advance releases of mainstream movies make up the menu of the city's film festival, which runs over two weeks in mid-March.

International Literature Festival Dublin LITERATURE
(ilfdublin.com) Four-day literature festival in the third week of May that attracts Irish and international writers to its readings, performances and talks.

Forbidden Fruit MUSIC
(www.forbiddenfruit.ie) A two-day alternative music festival over the first weekend in June in the grounds of the Irish Museum of Modern Art.

Taste of Dublin FOOD
(Map p74; www.tasteofdublin.ie; Iveagh Gardens) The capital's best restaurants combine to serve up sample platters of their finest dishes amid music and other entertainment over three food-filled days in June.

Longitude MUSIC
(www.longitude.ie; Marlay Park) A three-day alt-music festival in mid-July featuring old and new acts, art installations and food stalls.

Street Performance World Championships CARNIVAL
(www.cityspectacular.com) The world's best street performers test their skills over two July weekends in Merrion Sq – from jugglers to sword-swallowers.

Dublin Fringe Festival THEATRE
(www.fringefest.com) Initially a festival for those shows too 'out-there' or insignificant to be considered for the main Dublin Theatre Festival, this is now a three-week extravaganza in its own right, with more than 100 events and over 700 performances held in September.

BLOOMSDAY

The yearly paean to James Joyce's *Ulysses* takes place every 16 June, when committed Bloomsdayers don Edwardian garb and move about the city tracing the itinerant route followed by the fictional Leopold Bloom on 16 June 1904. The date was significant to Joyce because it was the day he first 'stepped out' with Nora Barnacle, the woman he had met six days earlier and with whom he would spend the rest of his life. (When James' father heard about this new love he commented that with a name like that she would surely stick to him.)

Although Ireland treated Joyce like a literary pornographer while he was alive, Dublin celebrates him like a favourite son these days, even if Bloomsday is strictly for Joyce fanatics and tourists.

In general, events are designed to follow Bloom's progress around town, and in recent years festivities have expanded to continue over four days around 16 June. The best source of information about what's on in any particular year is likely to be the **James Joyce Cultural Centre** (p90), close to the date.

On Bloomsday proper you can kick things off with breakfast at the James Joyce Cultural Centre, where the 'inner organs of beast and fowl' come accompanied by celebratory readings.

Guided tours of Joycean sites usually stop for lunch at **Davy Byrne's** (Map p106; 01-677 5217; www.davybyrnes.com; 21 Duke St; all city centre), Joyce's 'moral pub', where Bloom paused to dine on a glass of burgundy and a slice of Gorgonzola. Street entertainers are likely to keep you amused through the afternoon as you take guided walks and watch animated readings from *Ulysses* and Joyce's other books.

Dublin Theatre Festival THEATRE
(www.dublintheatrefestival.com) For two weeks in October, most of the city's theatres participate in this festival, originally founded in 1957 and today a glittering parade of quality productions and elaborate shows.

Sleeping

Beds in Dublin are the most expensive in the country. As the capital is virtually a year-round destination, booking well in advance is highly recommended whatever time of year you visit, especially if you want to secure a bed in the city centre.

Location dictates value for money, in both price and quality. For around €70 you can find a roomy B&B in the north-side suburbs, but the owners of a small, mediocre guesthouse within walking distance of St Stephen's Green won't blink when asking €120 for a room the size of a shoebox. A quality guesthouse or midrange hotel can cost anything from €80 to €150, while rates at the city's top digs usually start at around €150 – even allowing for the fact that in this climate you'd be mad not to check around for deals, or not to call the hotel directly and make polite enquiries along the lines of 'is that the best price you can offer me?'.

The bedrock of cheap accommodation remains the hostel, and in Dublin the standards are generally good – beds will cost anything from €18 to €34 (note that hostel rates generally don't include breakfast).

Grafton Street & Around

You can't get more central than the relatively small patch of real estate just south of the Liffey, which has a good mix of options ranging from backpacker hostels to the fanciest hotels. Bear in mind that the location comes with a price.

Dublin Citi Hotel HOTEL €
(Map p106; 01-679 4455; www.dublincitihotel.com; 46-49 Dame St; d from €59; @; all city centre) An unusual turreted 19th-century building right next to the Central Bank is home to this midrange hotel. Rooms aren't huge, are simply furnished and have fresh white quilts. It's only a stagger (literally) from the heart of Temple Bar, hic.

Avalon House HOSTEL €
(Map p74; 01-475 0001; www.avalon-house.ie; 55 Aungier St; dm/s/d from €10/34/54; @; all city centre, St Stephen's Green) One of the city's most popular hostels, welcoming Avalon House has pine floors, high ceilings and

UNIVERSITY ACCOMMODATION

From mid-June to late September, you can stay in accommodation provided by the city's universities. Be sure to book well in advance.

Trinity College (Map p66; ☎01-896 1177; www.tcd.ie; Accommodations Office, Trinity College; s/d from €62/82; @ 📶; 🚌all cross-city) The closest thing to living like a student at this stunningly beautiful university is crashing in their rooms when they're on holidays. Rooms and two-bed apartments in the newer block have their own bathrooms; those in the older blocks share facilities, though there are private basins. Breakfast is included.

Mercer Court Campus Accommodation (Map p74; ☎01-478 2179; www.rcsi.ie; Lower Mercer St; s/d 85/130; @ 📶; 🚌all city centre) Owned and run by the Royal College of Surgeons, this is the most luxurious student-accommodation option in the city. It's close to Grafton St and St Stephen's Green. The rooms are modern and up to hotel standard.

large, open fireplaces that create the ambience for a good spot of meet-the-backpacker lounging. Some of the cleverly designed rooms have mezzanine levels, which are great for families. Book well in advance.

Barnacles HOSTEL €
(Map p106; ☎01-671 6277; www.barnacles.ie; 19 Lower Temple Lane; dm/tw from €17.50/55; 📶; 🚌all city centre) If you're here for a good time, not a long time, then this bustling Temple Bar hostel is the ideal spot to meet fellow revellers, and tap up the helpful and knowledgeable staff for the best places to cause mischief. Rooms are quieter at the back.

Kinlay House HOSTEL €
(Map p70; ☎01-679 6644; www.kinlaydublin.ie; 2-12 Lord Edward St; dm/d from €15/50; 📶; 🚌all city centre) This former boarding house for boys has massive, mixed dormitories (for up to 20), and smaller rooms, including doubles. It's in Temple Bar, so it's occasionally raucous. Staff are friendly, and there are cooking facilities and a cafe. Breakfast is included.

★Trinity Lodge GUESTHOUSE €€
(Map p74; ☎01-617 0900; www.trinitylodge.com; 12 South Frederick St; r from €150; 📶; 🚌all city centre, 🚊St Stephen's Green) Martin Sheen's grin greets you upon entering this award-winning guesthouse, which he declared his favourite spot for an Irish stay. Marty's not the only one: this place is so popular they've added a second town house across the road, which has also been kitted out to the highest standards. Room 2 of the original house has a lovely bay window.

Radisson Blu Royal Hotel HOTEL €€
(Map p70; ☎01-898 2900; www.radissonblu.ie/royalhotel-dublin; Golden Lane; r from €160; ❄ @ 📶; 🚌all city centre, 🚊St Stephen's Green) A business hotel that is an excellent example of how sleek lines and muted colours combine beautifully with luxury, ensuring a memorable night's stay. From hugely impressive public areas to sophisticated bedrooms (each with a flat-screen digital TV embedded in the wall to go along with all the other little touches), this hotel will not disappoint.

Cliff Townhouse GUESTHOUSE €€
(Map p74; ☎01-638 3939; www.theclifftownhouse.com; 22 St Stephen's Green N; r from €150; @ 📶; 🚌all city centre, 🚊St Stephen's Green) As pieds-à-terre go, this is a doozy: there are 10 exquisitely appointed bedrooms spread across a wonderful Georgian property whose best views overlook St Stephen's Green. Downstairs is Sean Smith's superb restaurant Cliff Townhouse (p111).

Grafton House B&B €€
(Map p106; ☎01-648 0010; www.graftonguesthouse.com; 26-27 South Great George's St; s/d from €90/140; @ 📶; 🚌all city centre, 🚊St Stephen's Green) This slightly offbeat guesthouse in a Gothic-style building gets the nod in all three key categories: location, price and style. Just next to George's St Arcade, the Grafton offers the traditional friendly features of a B&B (including a terrific breakfast), coupled with a funky design – check out the psychedelic wallpaper. Hard to beat at this price.

Central Hotel HOTEL €€
(Map p106; ☎01-679 7302; www.centralhoteldublin.com; 1-5 Exchequer St; s/d from €90/140; 📶; 🚌all city centre, 🚊St Stephen's Green) The rooms are a modern – if miniaturised – version of Edwardian luxury. Heavy velvet curtains and custom-made Irish furnishings

(including beds with draped backboards) fit a little too snugly into the space afforded them, but they do lend a touch of class. Note that street-facing rooms can get a little noisy. Location-wise, the name says it all.

Paramount Hotel HOTEL €€

(Map p106; 01-417 9900; www.paramounthotel.ie; cnr Parliament St & Essex Gate; s/d €85/150; ; all city centre) Behind the Victorian facade, the lobby is a faithful re-creation of a 1930s hotel, complete with dark-wood floors, deep-red leather Chesterfield couches and heavy velvet drapes. The 70-odd rooms don't quite bring *The Maltese Falcon* to mind, but they're handsomely furnished and very comfortable. Downstairs is the **Turk's Head** (Map p106; 01-679 9701; 27-30 Parliament St), one of the area's most popular bars.

Dawson HOTEL €€

(Map p74; 01-612 7900; www.thedawson.ie; 35 Dawson St; r from €125; ; all city centre, St Stephen's Green) A boutique hotel with a range of elegant rooms designed in a variety of styles, from classical French to more exotic Moroccan. Crisp white sheets throughout, and Gilchrist & Soames amenities in the bathrooms. There's also a fancy spa and the trendy Sam's Bar (p117) below.

★**Number 31** GUESTHOUSE €€€

(Map p74; 01-676 5011; www.number31.ie; 31 Leeson Close; s/d/tr incl breakfast €200/240/340; ; all city centre) The city's most distinctive property is the former home of modernist architect Sam Stephenson, who successfully fused '60s style with 18th-century grace. Its 21 bedrooms are split between the retro coach house, with its coolly modern rooms, and the more elegant Georgian house, where rooms are individually furnished with tasteful French antiques and big comfortable beds.

Gourmet breakfasts with kippers, homemade breads and granola are served in the conservatory.

Irish Landmark Trust SELF-CATERING €€€

(Map p106; 01-670 4733; www.irishlandmark.com; 25 Eustace St; 2 nights for 7 people €635; all city centre) This 18th-century heritage house has been gloriously restored to the highest standard by the Irish Landmark Trust. Furnished with tasteful antiques and authentic furniture and fittings (including a grand piano in the drawing room), it sleeps up to seven in its three bedrooms, which must be booked for a minimum of two nights.

Merrion HOTEL €€€

(Map p74; 01-603 0600; www.merrionhotel.com; Upper Merrion St; r/ste from €295/715; ; all city centre) This resplendent five-star hotel, in a terrace of beautifully restored Georgian town houses, opened in 1988 but looks like it's been around a lot longer. Try to get a room in the old house (with the largest private art collection in the city), rather than the newer wing, to sample its truly elegant comforts.

Located opposite Government Buildings, its marble corridors are patronised by politicos, visiting dignitaries and the odd celeb. Even if you don't stay, book a table for the superb afternoon tea (€38), with endless cups of tea served out of silver pots by a raging fire.

Westbury Hotel HOTEL €€€

(Map p106; 01-679 1122; www.doylecollection.com; Grafton St; r/ste from €240/360; ; all city centre) Tucked away just off Grafton St is one of the most elegant hotels in town, although you'll need to upgrade to a suite to really feel the luxury. The standard rooms are perfectly comfortable but not really of the same theme as the luxurious public space – the upstairs lobby is a great spot for afternoon tea or a drink.

Westin Dublin HOTEL €€€

(Map p66; 01-645 1000; www.thewestindublin.com; Westmoreland St; r from €185; ; all city centre) Once a fancy bank branch, now a fancier hotel: rooms decorated in elegant mahogany and soft colours that are reminiscent of the USA's finest. You will sleep on 10 layers of the Westin's own trademark Heavenly Bed, which is damn comfortable indeed. The old bank vault is now the basement bar.

Shelbourne HOTEL €€€

(Map p74; 01-676 6471; www.theshelbourne.ie; 27 St Stephen's Green N; r from €440; ; all city centre, St Stephen's Green) Dublin's most famous hotel was founded in 1824 and has been the preferred halting post of the powerful and wealthy ever since. Several owners and refurbs later it is now part of Marriott's Renaissance portfolio, and while not quite Dublin's best any more, it is still very luxurious.

Guests are staying in a slice of history: it was here that the Irish Constitution was drafted in 1921, and this is the hotel in Elizabeth Bowen's eponymous novel. Afternoon tea in the refurbished Lord Mayor's Lounge remains one of the best experiences in town.

Dean Hotel HOTEL €€€
(Map p74; ☎01-607 8110; www.deanhoteldublin.ie; 33 Harcourt St; r/ste from €170/400; 🚌10, 11, 13, 14 or 15A, 🚊St Stephen's Green) Dublin's newest hotel is terribly hip: instead of 'rooms' you have a choice of Mod Pods (single bed on a couch) and Punk Bunks (yup, bunk-beds) – as well as as deluxe doubles (Hi-Fis) and suites. The more expensive rooms come with Netflix and a turntable; all rooms have earplugs and Berocca (you'll need them).

The hotel deliberately advertises as an upmarket party hotel: sandwiched between two of the most popular nightclubs in town, the rooms can get very noisy indeed. The top floor is home to Sophie's (p110), a brasserie that turns into a popular bar after 11pm.

Clarence Hotel HOTEL €€€
(Map p106; ☎01-407 0800; www.theclarence.ie; 6-8 Wellington Quay; r/ste from €170/390; @📶; 🚌all city centre) Bono and the Edge's discreet little bolthole is no longer the hottest bedroom in town, which is a good thing because the reality never lived up to the hype. Instead, what's left is a handsome boutique hotel designed to reflect the aesthetic of a 1930s gentlemen's club, complete with an excellent bar and a fine restaurant.

North of the Liffey

There is a scattering of good midrange options between O'Connell St and Smithfield. Gardiner St, to the east of O'Connell St, is the traditional B&B district of town; you're best off sticking to the southern end of the street where the properties are better and the street is safer.

★ **Isaacs Hostel** HOSTEL €
(Map p88; ☎01-855 6215; www.isaacs.ie; 2-5 Frenchman's Lane; dm/tw from €10/54; @📶; 🚌all city centre, 🚊Connolly) The north side's best hostel – hell, for atmosphere alone it's the best in town – is in a 200-year-old wine vault just around the corner from the main bus station. With summer barbecues, live music in the lounge, internet access and colourful dorms, this terrific place generates consistently good reviews from backpackers and other travellers.

Jacob's Inn HOSTEL €
(Map p88; ☎01-855 5660; www.jacobsinn.com; 21-28 Talbot Pl; dm/d from €12/70; 📶; 🚊Connolly) Sister hostel to Isaacs around the corner, this clean and modern hostel offers spacious accommodation with private bathrooms and outstanding facilities, including some wheelchair-accessible rooms, a money exchange bureau, bike storage and a self-catering kitchen.

Anchor House B&B €€
(Map p88; ☎01-878 6913; www.anchorhousedublin.com; 49 Lower Gardiner St; s/d from €100/115; 📶; 🚌all city centre, 🚊Connolly) While most B&Bs round these parts offer pretty much the same stuff – TV, half-decent shower, clean linen and tea- and coffee-making facilities – the Anchor does all of that, and also has an elegance you won't find in many of the others.

Clifden Guesthouse GUESTHOUSE €€
(☎01-874 6364; www.clifdenhouse.com; 32 Gardiner Pl; r from €109; 🚌36 or 36A) The Clifden is a very nicely refurbished Georgian house with 14 tastefully decorated rooms. They all come with bathroom, and are immaculately clean and extremely comfortable. A nice touch is the free parking, even after you've checked out!

Townhouse Hotel INN €€
(Map p88; ☎01-878 8808; www.townhouseofdublin.com; 47-48 Lower Gardiner St; r from €120; 🚌36 or 36A, 🚊Connolly) The ghostly writing of Irish-Japanese author Lafcadio Hearn may have influenced the Gothic-style interior of his former home. A dark-walled, gilt-framed foyer with jingling chandelier leads into 82 individually designed, comfy (but cramped) rooms.

Maldron Hotel Smithfield HOTEL €€
(Map p70; ☎01-485 0900; www.maldronhotels.com; Smithfield Village; r from €90; 📶; 🚌25, 25a, 25b, 66, 66a, 66b, 67, 90, 151 to Upper Ormond Quay, 🚊Smithfield) With big bedrooms and plenty of earth tones to soften the contemporary edges, this functionally modern hotel is your best bet in this part of town. We love the floor-to-ceiling windows: great for checking out what's going on below in the square.

Morrison Hotel HOTEL €€€
(Map p88; ☎01-887 2400; www.morrisonhotel.ie; Lower Ormond Quay; r from €250; @📶; 🚌all city centre, 🚊Jervis) Space-age funky design is the template at this hip hotel, recently taken over by the Hilton Doubletree group. King-size beds (with Serta mattresses), 40-inch LCD TVs, free wi-fi and Crabtree & Evelyn

toiletries are just some of the hotel's offerings – easily the north side's most luxurious address.

Gresham Hotel HOTEL €€€
(Map p88; ☎01-874 6881; www.gresham-hotels.com; Upper O'Connell St; r from €185; ❄@📶; 🚌all cross-city) A landmark hotel with a bright, modern appearance and a fabulous open-plan foyer, all of which pleases its loyal clientele – elderly groups on shopping breaks to the capital and well-heeled Americans. Rooms are spacious and well serviced.

Docklands

You'll be relying on public transport or a taxi to get you in and out of town for things to do.

Marker HOTEL €€€
(Map p92; ☎01-687 5100; www.themarkerhoteldublin.com; Grand Canal Sq; r from €280; @📶; 🚌56a & 77A, 🚆Grand Canal Dock) Behind the eye-catching chequerboard facade created by Manuel Aires Mateus are 187 swanky rooms and suites decked out in a wintry palette (washed-out citruses and cobalts) and starkly elegant furnishings, which give them an atmosphere of cool sophistication. The public areas are a little wilder and the rooftop bar is a summer favourite with the 'in' crowd.

Gibson Hotel HOTEL €€€
(Map p92; ☎01-618 5000; www.thegibsonhotel.ie; Point Village; r from €180; @📶; 🚌151 from city centre, 🚆Grand Canal Dock) Built for business travellers and out-of-towners taking in a gig at the 3 Arena (p121) next door, the Gibson is impressive: 250-odd ultramodern rooms decked out in Respa beds, flat-screen TVs and internet work stations. You might catch last night's star act having breakfast the next morning in the snazzy restaurant area.

Beyond the Grand Canal

You'll get more for your euro in the largely stylish digs dotted throughout the southern suburb of Ballsbridge, 3km south of the city centre. You'll be rubbing shoulders with the jet set and embassy crowd.

Aberdeen Lodge GUESTHOUSE €€
(☎01-283 8155; www.aberdeen-lodge.com; 53-55 Park Ave; s/d/tr €99/149/179; @📶; 🚌2, 3, 🚆DART Sydney Parade) Not only is this absolutely one of Dublin's best guesthouses, but it's also a carefully guarded secret, known only to those who dare stay a short train ride from the city centre. Their reward is a luxurious house with a level of personalised service as good you'll find in one of the city's top hotels.

Most of the stunning rooms have either a four-poster, a half-tester or a brass bed to complement the authentic Edwardian furniture and tasteful art on the walls. The suites even have fully working Adams fireplaces. As there is one member of staff for every two rooms, the service is exceptional, not to mention totally hands-on and very courteous.

Dylan HOTEL €€€
(Map p70; ☎01-660 3001; www.dylan.ie; Eastmoreland Pl; r from €200; ❄@📶; 🚌5, 7, 7A, 8, 18, 27X or 44 from city centre) The Dylan's baroque-meets-Scandinavian-sleek designer look was a big hit when it opened – a reflection of a time when too much was barely enough for the glitterati who signed contracts over cocktails, before retiring to crisp Frette linen sheets in the wonderfully appointed rooms upstairs.

BOOKING SERVICES

The Dublin Tourism office offers a useful computerised booking system. Alternatively, check out one of these competitive internet booking sites:

Lonely Planet (www.lonelyplanet.com/hotels)

All Dublin Hotels (www.irelandhotels.com/hotels/dublin)

Dublin City Centre Hotels (http://dublin-city-centre-hotels.com)

Dublin Hotels (www.dublinhotels.com)

Go Ireland (www.goireland.com)

Hostel Dublin (www.hosteldublin.com)

Eating

In the last two decades Dubliners have embraced foodie culture with the desperate fervour of a people denied decent cuisine for far too long. Today, the city offers every conceivable type of dining spread across a multitude of cuisines and a range of prices, from wild boar casseroles washed down with organic beer to exquisite creations adorned with Michelin stars.

The area surrounding Grafton St is full of food joints of every hue and flavour, from funky cafes to the fanciest restaurants, with the latter clustered around Merrion Sq and Fitzwilliam Sq. Scattered among the panoply of overpriced and underwhelming eateries in Temple Bar are some excellent spots that will suit a variety of tastes and pocket depths.

The north side has been the biggest beneficiary of the foodie revolution, with lots of hipster restaurants and cafes sharing space with a plethora of ethnic spots, especially on Capel St, which runs parallel to O'Connell St.

For many restaurants, particularly those in the centre, it's worth booking for Friday or Saturday nights to ensure a table.

Grafton Street & Around

If you spend your whole time in this area you'll eat pretty well; the south city centre is the hub of the city's best offerings.

Honest to Goodness PIZZA €

(Map p106; www.honesttogoodness.ie; 12 Dame Court; mains €6-15; all city centre) By day, the downstairs cafe serves wholesome sandwiches, tasty soups and a near-legendary sloppy joe. By night, the upstairs restaurant serves what might be the best pizza in town – authentic enough to earn a Neapolitan's approval. Terrific staff, wonderful atmosphere.

Pepperpot CAFE €

(Map p106; www.thepepperpot.ie; Powerscourt Townhouse Shopping Centre; mains €5-9; 10am-6pm Mon-Wed & Fri, to 8pm Thu, 9am-6pm Sat & noon-6pm Sun; all city centre) Everything is baked and made daily at the lovely cafe on the 1st-floor balcony of the Powerscourt Townhouse Shopping Centre. The salads with homemade brown bread are delicious but the real treat is the soup of the day (€4.50) – the ideal liquid lunch.

Bunsen AMERICAN €

(Map p106; www.bunsen.ie; 22 Essex St E; burgers €7-10; noon-9.30pm Mon-Wed, noon-10.30pm Thu-Sat, 1-9.30pm Sun; all city centre) Burgers like Dublin has never seen before: succulent lumps of prime beef cooked to perfection and served between two halves of a homemade bap. Want fries? You've a choice between skinny, chunky or sweet potato. Order the double at your peril. There's another **branch** (Map p74; www.bunsen.ie; 36 Wexford St; burgers €7-10; noon-9.30pm Mon-Wed, noon-10.30pm Thu-Sat, 1-9.30pm Sun; all city centre) on Wexford St.

Fallon & Byrne DELI €

(Map p106; www.fallonandbyrne.com; Exchequer St; mains €5-10; 8am-9pm Mon-Wed, 8am-10pm Thu & Fri, 9am-9pm Sat, 11am-7pm Sun; all city centre) Dublin's answer to the American Dean & DeLuca chain is this upmarket food hall and wine cellar, which is where discerning Dubliners come to buy their favourite cheeses and imported delicacies, as well as to get a superb lunch-to-go from the deli counter.

Upstairs is an elegant **brasserie** (Map p106; 01-472 1000; mains €5-10; noon-3pm & 6-9pm; all city centre) that serves Irish-influenced Mediterranean cuisine.

Green Nineteen IRISH €

(Map p74; 01-478 9626; www.green19.ie; 19 Lower Camden St; mains €10-19; 8.30am-11pm; ; all city centre) A firm favourite on Camden St's corridor of cool is this sleek restaurant that specialises in locally sourced, organic grub – without the fancy price tag. Braised lamb chump, corned beef, pot roast chicken and the ubiquitous burger are but the meaty part of the menu, which also includes salads and veggie options.

Neon ASIAN €

(Map p74; 01-405 2222; www.neon17.ie; 17 Lower Camden St; mains €10-12; noon-11pm; all city centre) A brilliant spot that specialises in authentic Asian street food from Thailand and Vietnam, served in takeaway boxes, which you can eat at home or in the canteen-style dining room. Hardened palates can jump right into the super-spicy *pad ki mow* noodles; more delicate taste buds can live with a delicious massaman curry. They also deliver (from 5pm).

Bottega Toffoli ITALIAN €

(Map p106; 34 Castle St; sandwiches & salads €9-14; 8am-4pm Tue-Wed, 8am-9pm Thu-Fri, 11am-8pm Sat, 1-8pm Sun; all city centre) Tucked away on a side street that runs alongside Dublin Castle is this superb Italian cafe, the loving creation of its Irish-Italian owners. Terrific sandwiches (beautifully cut prosciutto, baby tomatoes and rocket salad drizzled with imported olive oil on homemade *piadina*, a type of rustic bread), and the pizzas are as good as any you'd get out of a Neapolitan oven.

Lemon CREPERIE €

(Map p106; 66 South William St; pancakes from €5; ⌚9am-7pm Mon-Sat, 10am-6pm Sun; 🚌all city centre) Dublin's best pancake joint has branches on both sides of Grafton St, one on South William and the other on **Dawson Street** (Map p66; 61 Dawson St; pancakes from €5; ⌚9am-7pm Mon-Sat, 10am-6pm Sun). Each serves up a wide range of sweet and savoury crêpes – those paper-thin ones stuffed with a variety of goodies and smothered in toppings – along with super coffee in a buzzy atmosphere.

Simon's Place CAFE €

(Map p106; George's St Arcade, South Great George's St; sandwiches €5; ⌚8.30am-5pm Mon-Sat; 🌿; 🚌all city centre) Simon's soup-and-sandwich joint is a city stalwart, impervious to the fluctuating fortunes of the world around it mostly because its doorstep sandwiches and wholesome vegetarian soups are delicious and affordable. As trustworthy cafes go, this is the real deal.

Queen of Tarts CAFE €

(Map p106; www.queenoftarts.ie; 4 Cork Hill; mains €5-10; ⌚8am-7pm Mon-Fri, 9am-7pm Sat & Sun; 🚌all city centre) This cute little cake shop does a fine line in tarts, meringues, crumbles, cookies and brownies, not to mention a decent breakfast: the smoked bacon and leek-potato cakes with eggs and cherry tomatoes are excellent. There's another, bigger, branch around the corner on **Cow's Lane** (Map p106; www.queenoftarts.ie; 3-4 Cow's Lane; mains €5-10; ⌚8am-7pm Mon-Fri, 9am-7pm Sat & Sun; 🚌all cross-city).

Fade Street Social MODERN IRISH €€

(Map p106; ☎01-604 0066; www.fadestreetsocial.com; Fade St; mains €19-32, tapas €5-12; ⌚12.30-2.30pm Mon-Fri, 5-10.30pm daily; 📶; 🚌all city centre) 🍃 Two eateries in one, courtesy of renowned chef Dylan McGrath: at the front, the buzzy tapas bar, which serves up gourmet bites from a beautiful open kitchen. At the back, the more muted restaurant specialises in Irish cuts of meat – from veal to rabbit – served with homegrown, organic vegetables. There's a bar upstairs too. Reservations suggested.

Söder + Ko ASIAN, FUSION €€

(Map p106; www.soderandko.ie; 64 South Great George's St; plates €6-10; 🚌all city centre, 🚊St Stephen's Green) This new restaurant was introduced in 2015 as a fusion of Scandinavian style and Asian food, and while the former is largely inconspicuous, the food, by ex-Cliff Townhouse chef Kwanghi Chan, is unmistakably Asian. The menu has a range of sharing platters and tapas-style dishes divided into Raw, Dim Sum and Hot. Generous portions of excellent cuisine.

VEGGIE BITES

Vegetarians are having it increasingly easier in Dublin as the capital veers away from the belief that food isn't food until your incisors have had to rip flesh from bone, and towards an understanding that healthy eating leads to, well, longer lives. Most contemporary places, including **Yamamori** (p108) and **Chameleon** (Map p106; ☎01-671 0362; www.chameleonrestaurant.com; 1 Lower Fownes St; mains €16.50-19.50; ⌚5-11pm Mon-Sat, to 10pm Sun; 🌿; 🚌all city centre), pay more than just lip service to vegetarians, with options a little more exciting than a token dish of mixed greens and pulses.

Blazing Salads (Map p106; 42 Drury St; salads €4-9; ⌚10am-6pm Mon-Sat, to 8pm Thu; 🌿; 🚌all city centre) Organic breads (including many special diet varieties), Californian-style salads from a serve-yourself salad bar, smoothies and pizza slices can all be taken away from this delicious deli.

Cornucopia (Map p106; www.cornucopia.ie; 19 Wicklow St; mains €10-13; ⌚8.30am-9pm Mon & Tue, 8.30am-10.15pm Wed-Sat, noon-9pm Sun; 🌿) Dublin's best-known vegetarian restaurant is this terrific eatery that serves wholesome salads, sandwiches and a selection of hot main courses from a daily changing menu. It's so popular they've recently expanded onto the 2nd floor.

Govinda's (Map p74; www.govindas.ie; 4 Aungier St; mains €7-10; ⌚noon-9pm Mon-Sat; 🌿) An authentic beans-and-pulses place run by the Hare Krishna, with three branches in the city centre. Its cheap, wholesome mix of salads and Indian-influenced hot daily specials is filling and tasty.

Temple Bar & Grafton Street

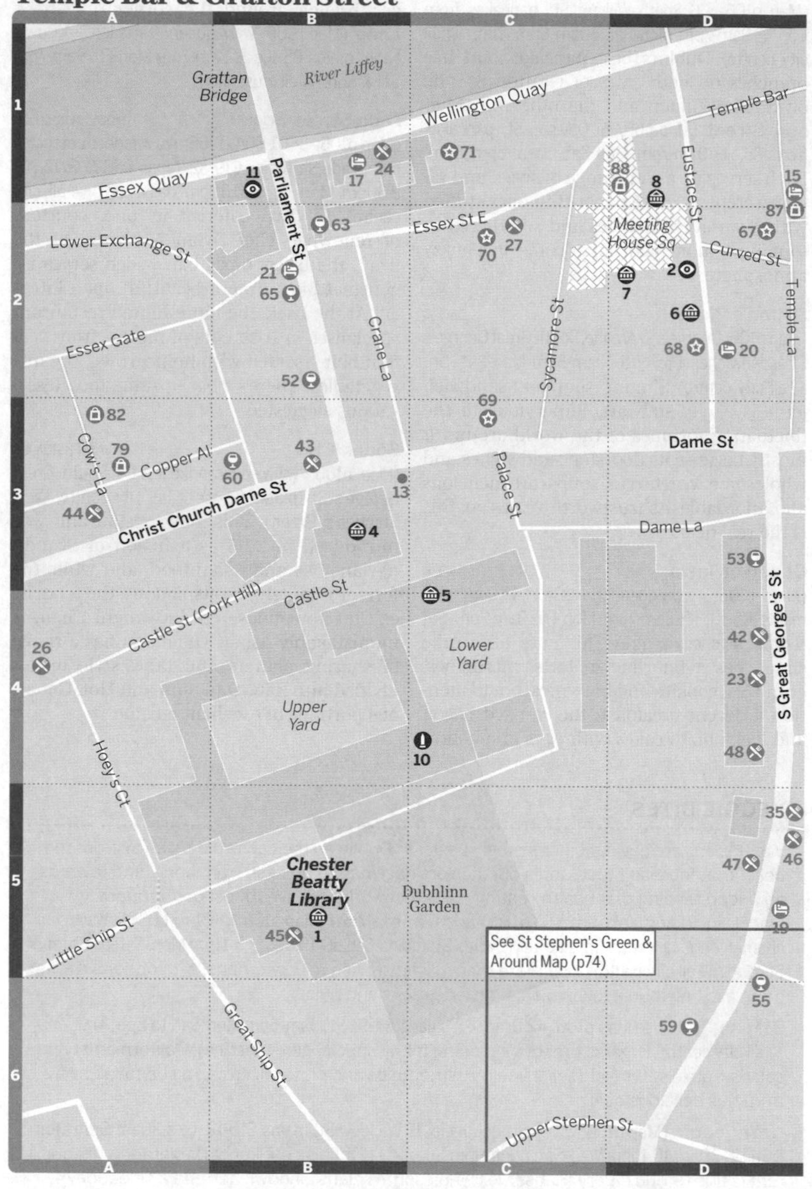

Bison Bar & BBQ BARBECUE €€
(Map p106; 086 056 3144; www.bisonbar.ie; 11 Wellington Quay; mains €14; all city centre) Beer, whiskey sours and finger-lickingly good Texas-style barbecue – served on throwaway plates along with tasty sides such as slaw or mac and cheese – is the fare at this boisterous restaurant. The cowboy theme is taken to the limit with the saddle chairs (yes, actual saddles); this is a place to eat, drink and be merry.

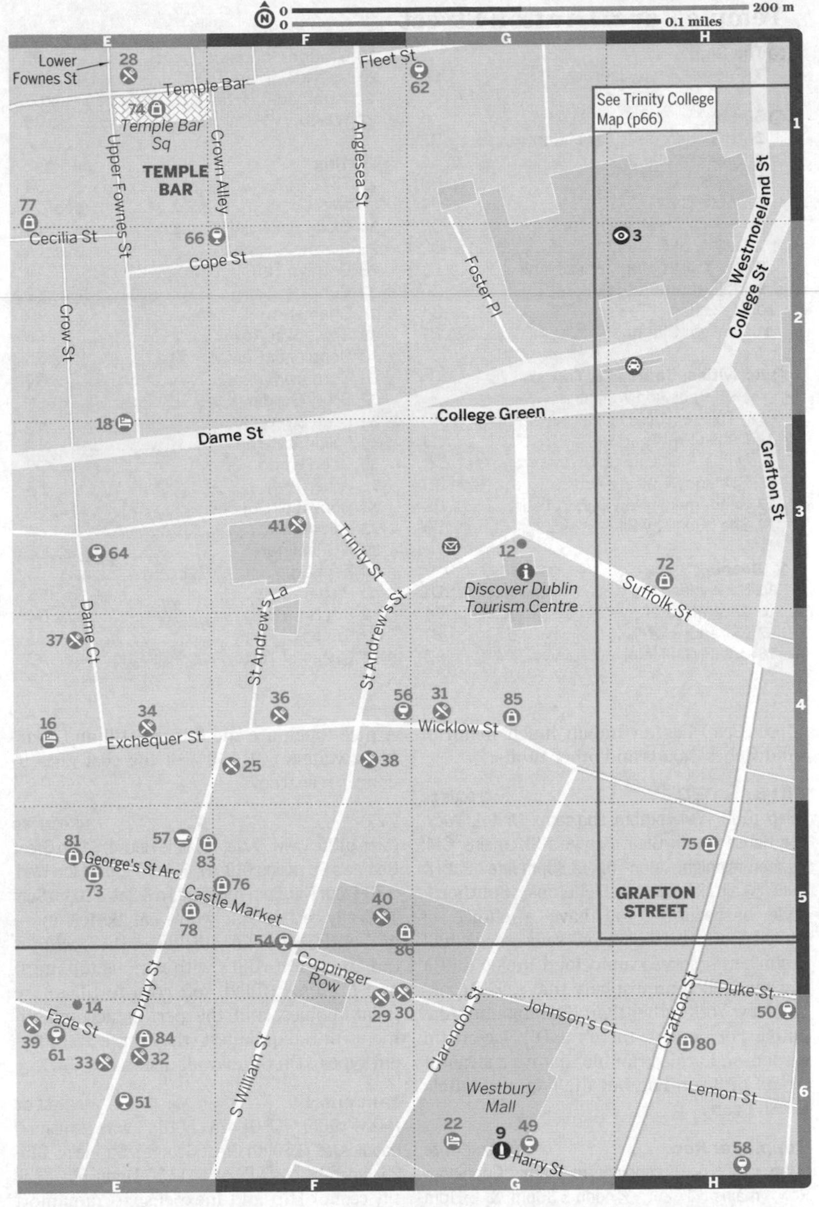

Drury Buildings ITALIAN €€

(Map p106; ☎01-960 2095; drurybuildings.com; 52-55 Drury St; mains €17.50-32; ⏰5-10.30pm daily & noon-3pm Sat & Sun; 🚌all city centre) An elegant, 1st-floor restaurant in a converted rag-trade warehouse...sounds like New York's SoHo, and that's exactly what it's trying to emulate. The food – Italian dishes made with local produce and infused with an international twist – is excellent. The ground-floor **cocktail bar** (Map p106; www.drurybuildings.com; 52-55 Drury St; mains €10;

Temple Bar & Grafton Street

Top Sights
1 Chester Beatty Library ... B5

Sights
2 Ark Children's Cultural Centre ... D2
3 Bank of Ireland ... H2
4 City Hall ... B3
5 Dublin Castle ... C4
6 Friends' Meeting House ... D2
7 Gallery of Photography ... D2
8 National Photographic Archive ... D1
9 Phil Lynott Statue ... G6
10 St Michael's Tower ... C4
11 Sunlight Chambers ... B1

Activities, Courses & Tours
1916 Rebellion Walking Tour ... (see 56)
12 Dublin Bus Tours ... G3
Dublin Musical Pub Crawl ... (see 62)
Pat Liddy Walking Tours ... (see 12)
13 Sandeman's New Dublin Tour ... B3
14 See Dublin by Bike ... E6

Sleeping
15 Barnacles ... D1
16 Central Hotel ... E4
17 Clarence Hotel ... B1
18 Dublin Citi Hotel ... E3
19 Grafton House ... D5
20 Irish Landmark Trust ... D2
21 Paramount Hotel ... B2
22 Westbury Hotel ... G6

Eating
23 777 ... D4
Avoca ... (see 72)
24 Bison Bar & BBQ ... B1
25 Blazing Salads ... F4
26 Bottega Toffoli ... A4
27 Bunsen ... C2
28 Chameleon ... E1
29 Coppinger Row ... F6
30 Coppinger Row Market ... F5
31 Cornucopia ... G4
32 Drury Buildings ... E6
33 Fade Street Social ... E6
34 Fallon & Byrne ... E4
35 Good World ... D5
36 Green Hen ... F4
37 Honest to Goodness ... E4
38 Lemon ... F4
39 L'Gueuleton ... E6
40 Pepperpot ... F5
41 Pichet ... F3
42 Pitt Bros BBQ ... D4
43 Queen of Tarts ... B3
44 Queen of Tarts ... A3

noon-3pm) has an Italian lunch menu of sandwiches, salads and other titbits.

Pitt Bros BBQ BARBECUE €€
(Map p106; www.pittbrosbbq.com; Unit 1, Wicklow House, South Great George's St; mains €14; noon-midnight Mon-Fri, 12.30pm-late Sat & Sun; all city centre) Delicious, Southern-style barbecue – you have a choice of pulled pork, brisket, ribs, sausage or half a chicken – served amid loud music and a hipster-fuelled atmosphere that says Brooklyn, New York rather than Birmingham, Alabama. For dessert, there's a DIY ice-cream dispenser. Locals grumble that it's a straight rip-off of Bison Bar, but the happy clientele doesn't care.

Coppinger Row MEDITERRANEAN €€
(Map p106; www.coppingerrow.com; Coppinger Row; mains €17-26; noon-5.30pm & 6-11pm Mon-Sat, 12.30-4pm & 6-9pm Sun; all city centre) Virtually all of the Mediterranean basin is represented on the ever-changing, imaginative menu here. Choices include the likes of pan-fried sea bass with roast baby fennel, tomato and olives; or rump of lamb with spiced aubergine and dried apricots. A nice touch are the filtered still and sparkling waters (€1): 50% of the cost goes to cancer research.

777 MEXICAN €€
(Map p106; www.777.ie; 7 Castle House, South Great George's St; mains €19-36; 5.30-10pm Mon-Wed, 5.30-11pm Thu, 5pm-midnight Fri & Sat, 2-10pm Sun; all city centre) You won't eat better, more authentic Mexican cuisine – the *tostados* (crispy corn tortillas with various toppings) and *taquitos* (filled, soft corn tortillas) are great nibbles, and the perfect accompaniment for a tequila fest (they serve 22 different types). On Sunday all dishes are €7.77.

Yamamori JAPANESE €€
(Map p106; 01-475 5001; www.yamamorinoodles.ie; 71 South Great George's St; mains €16-25, lunch bentos €9.95; 12.30-11pm; ; all city centre) Hip and inexpensive, Yamamori rarely disappoints with its bubbly service and vivacious cooking that swoops from sushi and sashimi to whopping great plates of noodles, with plenty in between. The lunch bento is one of the best deals in town. There's another branch (p112) north of the river.

Good World CHINESE €€

(Map p106; 18 South Great George's St; dim sum €4-6, mains €12-20; 12.30pm-2.30am; all city centre) The hands-down winner of our best-Chinese-restaurant competition. To appreciate just how good it is, ignore the green Western-style menu and stick to the black-covered one, which is packed with dishes and delicacies that have made it a favourite with Dublin's Chinese community for two decades.

L'Gueuleton FRENCH €€

(Map p106; www.lgueuleton.com; 1 Fade St; mains €22-26; 12.30-3.30pm & 5.30-10pm Mon-Sat, noon-3.30pm & 5.30-9pm Sun; all city centre) Despite the tongue-twister name (it means 'gluttonous feast' in French), L'Gueuleton is a firm favourite with locals for its robust (meaty, filling) take on French rustic cuisine – it does a mean onion soup and the steak frites is a big crowd-pleaser. It has a no-reservations, leave-your-name-at-the-door policy; just go for a drink and wait for the call.

Dunne & Crescenzi ITALIAN €€

(Map p74; www.dunneandcrescenzi.com; 14-16 South Frederick St; 3-course evening menu €35; 8am-11pm Mon-Sat, 9.30am-11pm Sun; all city centre) This exceptional Italian eatery delights its regulars with a basic menu of rustic pleasures, such as panini, a single pasta dish and a superb plate of mixed antipasto drizzled in olive oil. It's always full, and the tables are just that little bit too close to one another, but the coffee is perfect and the desserts are sinfully good.

Green Hen FRENCH €€

(Map p106; 01-670 7238; www.greenhen.ie; 33 Exchequer St; mains €18-26; noon-3pm daily, 5-11pm Mon-Thu & Sun, 5pm-1am Fri & Sat; all city centre) New York's Soho meets Parisian brasserie at this stylish eatery, where elegance and economy live side by side. If you don't fancy gorging on oysters or tucking into a divine Irish Hereford rib-eye, you can opt for the *plat du jour* or avail yourself of the early-bird menus; watch out for their killer cocktails. Reservations recommended for dinner.

Saba ASIAN, FUSION €€

(Map p74; 01-679 2000; www.sabadublin.com; 26-28 Clarendon St; mains €13-19; noon-11pm; all city centre) The name means 'happy meeting place' and this Thai-Vietnamese fusion restaurant is just that. It's a very popular eatery with Dubliners, who tuck into a wide selection of Southeast Asian dishes and test the limits of the cocktail menu. The atmosphere is all designer cool, the fare a tad shy of being truly authentic, but it's a good night out.

Pichet FRENCH **€€**

(Map p106; ☎01-677 1060; www.pichetrestaurant.ie; 14-15 Trinity St; mains €17-26; ⊙noon-3pm & 5-10pm Mon-Sat, 11am-4pm & 5-9pm Sun; 🚌all city centre) Head chef Stephen Gibson (formerly of L'Ecrivain) delivers his version of modern French cuisine to this elongated dining room replete with blue leather chairs and lots of windows to stare out of. The result is pretty good indeed, the food excellent – we expected nothing less – and the service impeccable. Sit in the back for atmosphere.

Sophie's @ The Dean ITALIAN **€€**

(Map p74; www.sophies.ie; 33 Harcourt St; mains €15-28; ⊙11am-3am; 🚌10, 11, 13, 14 or 15A, 🚋St Stephen's Green) In 2015 this rooftop brasserie was the place to be seen, even if the friendly service was sketchy and the food – New York–style Italian given a contemporary twist – not as good as its high-flying location and prices suggest it should be. But the owners are nothing if not eager, so expect vast improvements by the time you visit.

★Restaurant Patrick Guilbaud FRENCH **€€€**

(Map p74; ☎01-676 4192; www.restaurantpatrickguilbaud.ie; 21 Upper Merrion St; 2-/3-course set lunch €45/55, dinner menus €90-185; ⊙12.30-2.30pm & 7.30-10.30pm Tue-Sat; 🚌7 & 44 from the city centre) Ireland's only Michelin two-star is understandably considered the best in the country by its devotees, who proclaim Guillaume Lebrun's French haute cuisine the most exalted expression of the culinary arts. If you like formal dining, this is as good as it gets: the lunch menu is an absolute steal, at least in this stratosphere. The food is innovative without being fiddly, beautifully cooked and superbly presented.

The room itself is all contemporary elegance and the service expertly formal yet surprisingly friendly – the staff are meticulously trained and are as skilled at answering queries and addressing individual requests as they are at making sure not one breadcrumb lingers too long on the immaculate tablecloths. Owner Patrick Guilbaud usually does the rounds of the tables himself in the evening to salute regular customers and charm first-timers into returning. Reservations are absolutely necessary.

L'Ecrivain FRENCH **€€€**

(Map p74; ☎01-661 1919; www.lecrivain.com; 109a Lower Baggot St; 3-course lunch menus €40, 8-course tasting menus €75, mains €40-47; ⊙12.30-2pm Thu & Fri, 6.30-10pm Mon-Sat; 🚌38

FARMERS & ORGANIC MARKETS

Dublin Food Co-op (Map p70; www.dublinfoodcoop.com; 12 Newmarket; ⊙noon-8pm Thu-Fri, 9.30am-4.30pm Sat & 11am-5pm Sun; 🚌49, 54a & 77x from city centre) From dog food to detergent, everything in this market hall is organic and/or ecofriendly. Thursday has a limited selection of local and imported fair-trade products, but Saturday is when it's all on display – Dubliners from all over drop in for their responsible weekly shop. There's an on-the-premises baker and even baby-changing facilities.

Coppinger Row Market (Map p106; Coppinger Row; ⊙9am-7pm Thu; 🚌all city centre) It's small – only a handful of stalls – but packs a proper organic punch, attracting punters with the waft of freshly baked breads, delicious hummus and other goodies.

Harcourt Street Food Market (Map p74; www.irishfarmersmarkets.ie; Park Pl, Station Bldgs, Upper Hatch St; ⊙10am-4pm Thu; 🚌all city centre) Organic veggies, cheeses, olives and meats made into dishes from all over the world.

Temple Bar Farmers Market (Map p106; Meeting House Sq; ⊙9am-4.30pm Sat; 🚌all city centre) This little market is a fabulous place to while away a Saturday morning, sampling the organic gourmet goodies. The market is bound by one rule: local producers only. From cured meats to wild flowers, you could fill an entire pantry with its selection of delights.

For details of local markets, check out www.irishfarmersmarkets.ie, www.irishvillagemarkets.com or local county council sites such as www.dlrcoco.ie/markets.

& 39 from city centre) Head chef Derry Clarke is considered a gourmet god for the exquisite simplicity of his creations, which put the emphasis on flavour and the best local ingredients – all given the French once-over and turned into something that approaches divine dining. The Michelin people like it too and awarded it one of their stars.

Thornton's FRENCH €€€
(Map p74; ☎01-478 7000; www.thorntonsrestaurant.com; 128 St Stephen's Green W; 2/3-course lunch €35/45, dinner tasting menus €75-85; ⏰12.30-2pm & 7-10pm Tue-Sat; 🚌all city centre) Chef Kevin Thornton's culinary genius is to take new French cuisine and give it a theatrical, Irish revamp: the result is a Michelin-starred, wonderful mix of succulent seafood dishes and meatier fare like noisette of milk-fed Wicklow lamb. A nice touch is when Kevin himself comes out to greet his guests and explain his creations. Reservations are essential.

Shanahan's on the Green STEAK €€€
(Map p74; ☎01-407 0939; www.shanahans.ie; 119 St Stephen's Green W; mains €35-49; ⏰from 6pm Mon-Thu, Sat & Sun, from noon Fri; 🚌all city centre) You could order seafood or a plate of vegetables, but you'd be missing the point of this supremely elegant steakhouse: the finest cuts of juicy and tender Irish Angus beef you'll find anywhere. The ambience is upscale Americana – the bar downstairs is called the Oval Office and pride of place goes to a rocking chair owned by JFK.

Cliff Townhouse IRISH €€€
(Map p74; ☎01-638 3939; www.thecliffTownhouse.com; 22 St Stephen's Green N; mains €19-35; ⏰noon-2.30pm & 6-11pm Mon-Sat, noon-4pm & 6-10pm Sun; 🚌all city centre) Sean Smith's menu is a confident expression of the very best of Irish cuisine – Warrenpoint fish pie, organic fillet of pork and a loin of venison share the menu with a masterful fish and chips. The dining room is supremely elegant – lots of white linen, beautiful art on the wall and deep-blue leather booths.

The Liberties & Kilmainham

Among this area's fast-food outlets and greasy-spoon diners you'll find a superb cafe and Dublin's most famous fish-and-chip shop.

★ **Fumbally Cafe** CAFE €
(Map p70; Fumbally Lane; mains €5-8; ⏰8am-5pm Mon-Sat; 🚌49, 54a & 77x from city centre) The unofficial home of Dublin's hipster crowd is this warehouse cafe drenched in daylight from the floor-to-ceiling windows, where couples in skinny jeans and worn-in high-tops pore over a laptop, working out the finer details of their start-up pitch, their energy fuelled by excellent coffee and delicious sandwiches.

Leo Burdock's FISH & CHIPS €
(Map p70; 2 Werburgh St; cod & chips €10; ⏰noon-midnight Mon-Sat, 4pm-midnight Sun; 🚌all city centre) It's Dublin's most famous fish-and-chip shop, but these days it's living off the deep-fried fumes of its reputation rather than the quality of its fish – which isn't bad, but it's no better than what you'd get at any decent fish-and-chip shop throughout the city. Still, reputation counts for something, judging from the longish queues.

North of the Liffey

Dublin's foodie revolution has done wonders for the north side's dining options, which now include a fine selection of cafes and midrange restaurants, plus a broad range of ethnic cuisines.

Third Space CAFE €
(Map p70; www.thirdspace.ie; Unit 14, Block C, Smithfield Market; sandwiches €6; ⏰8am-7pm Mon, Tue & Fri, 8am-9.30pm Wed & Thu, 9.30am-5pm Sat; 🚊Smithfield) One of the most welcoming cafes in town is this wonderful spot in Smithfield, which serves gorgeous sandwiches, wraps and baps, as well as a tart of the day and wines by the glass. Sit in the window, take out a book and just relax. The staff are fabulous.

Brother Hubbard CAFE €
(Map p88; 153 Capel St; dishes €7-10; ⏰8am-5.30pm Mon-Fri, 10am-5pm Sat; 🚌all city centre, 🚊Jervis) Anchored by its excellent baristas (beans by coffee experts 3FE), this cafe with a small garden at the back also does a nice menu of sandwiches, flatbreads (very trendy in 2015) and salads. A lovely place to hang out.

Da Mimmo's ITALIAN €
(www.damimmo.ie; 148 North Strand Rd; 2-course lunch €8.50, dinner mains €9-13; ⏰10.30am-11pm; 🚌53 from Talbot St) Da Mimmo's was a traditional fish-and-chip shop until the son of the original owners converted it into a sit-down restaurant; it now serves arguably the best Italian food in the city. Everything here –

from the bresaola-and-Parmesan starter to the lasagne – is as authentic as if you were dining in Tino's home town of Casalattico (between Naples and Rome).

★Musashi Noodles & Sushi Bar JAPANESE €€

(Map p88; 01-532 8057; www.musashidublin.com; 15 Capel St; mains €13-17; noon-10pm; all city centre, Jervis) A lovely, low-lit room, this is the most authentic Japanese restaurant in the city, serving up freshly crafted sushi to a city once starved of it. The lunch bento deals are a steal, and if you don't fancy raw fish they also do a wide range of other Japanese specialities. It's BYOB (corkage charged). Evening bookings recommended.

Woollen Mills MODERN IRISH €€

(Map p88; www.thewoollenmills.com; 42 Lower Ormond Quay; sandwiches €10-11, mains €15-26; 9am-11pm Mon-Fri, 9am-4pm & 5-11pm Sat, noon-4pm & 5-10.30pm Sun; all city centre) Styling itself as a modern Irish brasserie, this newish restaurant spread over two floors serves a spruced-up version of Irish farmhouse cooking, from tasty sandwiches to dishes such as smoked pork belly. For over a century the building was a much-loved knitwear shop (James Joyce worked here for a time), so you're dining in a piece of local history.

Wuff INTERNATIONAL €€

(Map p70; 23 Benburb St; mains €18-22; 7.30am-4pm Mon-Wed, 7.30am-10pm Thu & Fri, 10am-10pm Sat, 10am-4pm Sun; 25, 25A, 66, 67 from city centre, Museum) This neighbourhood bistro does excellent breakfasts and brunches – the truffle-infused poached eggs with Gruyère on toast is divine – as well as fine dinner mains that feature fish, duck, beef and a couple of veggie options.

Yamamori Sushi JAPANESE €€

(Map p88; www.yamamorinoodles.ie; 38-39 Lower Ormond Quay; sushi €4-4.50, mains €17-35; noon-10.30pm; all city centre) A sibling of the long-established Yamamori on South Great George's St (p108), this large restaurant – spread across two converted Georgian houses and including a bamboo garden – does Japanese with great aplomb, serving up all kinds of favourites from steaming bowls of ramen to a delicious *nami moriawase* (sushi platter).

Hot Stove MODERN IRISH €€

(Map p88; www.thehotstoverestaurant.com; 38-39 Parnell Sq W; mains €22-30; noon-2.30pm & 5-9.30pm Tue-Fri, 5.30-10pm Sat; 3, 10, 11, 13, 16, 19 or 22 from city centre) This elegant restaurant serves locally sourced, beautifully prepared Irish dishes including pork belly, a changing selection of fish dishes and the ubiquitous steak. The wine list is excellent and the service is right on point.

★Chapter One MODERN IRISH €€€

(Map p88; 01-873 2266; www.chapteronerestaurant.com; 18 North Parnell Sq; 2-course lunch €50, 4-course dinner €85; 12.30-2pm Tue-Fri, 7.30-10.30pm Tue-Sat; 3, 10, 11, 13, 16, 19 or 22 from city centre) Flawless haute cuisine and a relaxed, welcoming atmosphere make this Michelin-starred restaurant in the basement of the Dublin Writers Museum our choice for best dinner experience in town. The food is French-inspired contemporary Irish, the menus change regularly and the service is top-notch. The three-course pretheatre menu (€37.50) is great if you're going to the Gate (p124) around the corner.

Winding Stair MODERN IRISH €€€

(Map p88; 01-873 7320; www.winding-stair.com; 40 Lower Ormond Quay; 2-course lunch €20, mains €21-28; noon-5pm & 5.30-10.30pm; all city centre) In a beautiful Georgian building that once housed the city's most beloved bookshop (the ground floor still is one), the Winding Stair's conversion to elegant restaurant has been faultless. The wonderful Irish menu – creamy fish pie, bacon and organic cabbage, steamed mussels, and Irish farmyard cheeses – coupled with an excellent wine list makes for a memorable meal.

Morrison Grill INTERNATIONAL €€€

(Map p88; 01-878 2999; www.morrisonhotel.ie; Morrison Hotel, Lower Ormond Quay; mains €18-31; noon-10pm; all city centre) The main eatery of the newly refurbished Morrison Hotel is really a very fancy grill whose specialities are meats cooked in Ireland's only Josper indoor barbecue oven. If you don't fancy steaks, burgers or grilled fish, there's a selection of other main courses, but the real treat here is food cooked at over 500°F.

Docklands

Although the crash has put paid to some of the grander plans for restaurant openings in the Docklands, there are a couple of good options that reflect the best of new dining in the city.

Ely Bar & Brasserie FUSION €€

(Map p92; www.elywinebar.ie; Custom House Quay; mains €14-29; noon-3pm & 6-10pm Mon-Fri, 1-4pm & 6-10pm Sat; Grand Canal Dock) Scrummy homemade burgers, bangers and mash, and wild smoked salmon salad are some of the meals served in this converted tobacco warehouse in the International Financial Services Centre (IFSC). Dishes are prepared with organic and free-range produce from the owner's family farm in County Clare, so you can be assured of the quality.

Herbstreet FUSION €€

(Map p92; www.herbstreet.ie; Hanover Quay; mains €13-19; 8.30am-10pm Mon-Fri, 10am-4pm Sat & Sun; Grand Canal Dock) Low-power hand dryers, one-watt LED bulbs, secondhand furniture and strictly European wines: this eatery is taking its green responsibilities seriously. Most of the food is sourced locally, but what really makes this place a hit is the terrific brunch menu – pancakes, Irish breakfasts, Mexican-style eggs...it's all good.

Quay 16 FUSION €€€

(Map p92; 01-817 8760; www.mvcillairne.com; MV Cill Airne, North Wall Quay; bar food €4-12, mains €19-32; noon-3pm Mon-Fri, 6-10pm Mon-Sat; Grand Canal Dock) The MV *Cill Airne*, commissioned in 1961 as a passenger liner tender, is now permanently docked along the north quays, where it serves the public as a bar, bistro and a fine restaurant. Dishes such as Himalayan salt–aged fillet steak and pan-roasted sea bass are expertly prepared and are served alongside an excellent variety of wines.

Beyond the Grand Canal

There are some excellent restaurants in the fancy suburbs south and southeast of the city centre.

Paulie's Pizza ITALIAN €€

(Map p70; www.juniors.ie; 58 Upper Grand Canal St; pizzas €12-17; 6-10pm; ; 3 from city centre, Grand Canal Dock) At the heart of this lovely, occasionally boisterous restaurant is a Neapolitan pizza oven, used to create some of the best pizzas in town. Margheritas, *biancas* (no tomato sauce), calzoni and other Neapolitan specialities are the real treat, but there's also room for a classic New York slice and a few local creations.

Juniors Deli & Cafe ITALIAN €€

(Map p70; 01-664 3648; www.juniors.ie; 2 Bath Ave; mains €17-26; 8.30am-2.30pm & 5.30-10pm Mon-Fri, 11am-3pm & 5.30-10.30pm Sat, 11am-3.30pm Sun; 3 from city centre, Grand Canal Dock) Cramped and easily mistaken for any old cafe, Juniors is anything but ordinary. Designed to imitate a New York deli, the food (Italian-influenced, all locally sourced produce) is delicious, the atmosphere always buzzing (it's often hard to get a table) and the ethos top-notch, which is down to the two brothers who run the place.

Drinking & Nightlife

The alpha and omega of most social life in Dublin is the pub, although its form has evolved since the days of the traditional boozer populated by flat-capped locals quietly sipping a pint of Guinness (although you'll find those too). Whatever your taste you'll find it here, and we suspect that exploring a variety of Dublin's legendary pubs and bars ranks pretty high on the list of reasons you're here.

Last orders are at 11.30pm Monday to Thursday, 12.30am Friday and Saturday, and 11pm on Sunday, with 30 minutes' drinking-up time each night. However, many central pubs have licences to serve until 1.30am or 2.30am.

CAFE CULTURE & BEST COFFEES

Dublin's coffee junkies are everywhere, looking for that perfect barista fix that will kill the hunger (until it's time for the next one). You can top-up at any of the chains – including that one from Seattle – but we reckon your caffeine craving will get the best fix at an individual, Dublin locale.

Clement & Pekoe (Map p74; www.clementandpekoe.com; 50 South William St; 8am-7pm Mon-Fri, 10am-6pm Sat, noon-6pm Sun; all city centre)

Brother Hubbard (p111)

Wall and Keogh (Map p70; www.wallandkeogh.ie; 45 South Richmond St; 8.30am-8.30pm Mon-Fri, 11am-7pm Sat & Sun; all city centre)

Kaph (Map p106; 31 Drury St; 9am-6pm Mon-Sat, noon-6pm Sun; all city centre)

With so many bars now staying open until late and not charging for the privilege, the day of the pay-at-the-door club in Dublin is in its twilight hour. Still, there are a handful of nightclubs that still pack a crowd, even if all but a few DJs play it pretty safe.

The busiest nights for clubbing are Thursday to Saturday, and most places are free if you arrive before 11pm. After that, you'll pay between €6 and €10.

Grafton Street & Around

★John Mulligan's PUB

(Map p88; 8 Poolbeg St; 10.30am-11.30pm Mon-Thu, to 12.30am Fri & Sat, noon-11pm Sun; all city centre) This brilliant old boozer has barely changed since its establishment in 1782. It has one of the finest pints of Guinness in Dublin and a colourful crew of regulars. It's just off Fleet St, outside the eastern boundary of Temple Bar.

★Stag's Head PUB

(Map p106; www.louisfitzgerald.com/stagshead; 1 Dame Ct; 10.30am-1am Mon-Sat, to midnight Sun; all city centre) The Stag's Head was built in 1770, remodelled in 1895 and thankfully not changed a bit since then. It's a superb pub: so picturesque that it often appears in films, and also featured in a postage-stamp series on Irish bars. A bloody great pub, no doubt.

★Mother CLUB

(Map p106; twitter.com/motherdublin; Copper Alley, Exchange St; admission €10; 11pm-3.30am Sat; all city centre) The best club night in the city is ostensibly a gay night but does not discriminate: clubbers of every sexual orientation come for the sensational DJs who throw down a mixed bag of disco, modern synth-pop and other danceable styles.

Kehoe's PUB

(Map p106; 9 South Anne St; 10.30am-11.30pm Mon-Thu, to 12.30am Fri & Sat, noon-11pm Sun; all city centre) This is one of the most atmospheric pubs in the city centre and a favourite with all kinds of Dubliners. It has a beautiful Victorian bar, a wonderful snug, and plenty of other little nooks and crannies. Upstairs, drinks are served in what was once the publican's living room – and looks it!

Long Hall PUB

(Map p106; 51 South Great George's St; 10.30am-11.30pm Mon-Thu, to 12.30am Fri & Sat, noon-11pm Sun; all city centre) Luxuriating in full Victorian splendour, this is one of the city's most beautiful and best-loved pubs. Check out the ornate carvings in the woodwork behind the bar, and the elegant chandeliers. The bartenders are experts at their craft, an increasingly rare attribute in Dublin these days.

37 Dawson St BAR

(Map p74; 01-902 2908; www.37dawsonstreet.ie; 37 Dawson St; 10.30am-11.30pm Mon-Thu, to 12.30am Fri & Sat, noon-11pm Sun; all city centre) Antiques, eye-catching art and elegant bric-a-brac adorn this bar that quickly established itself as a favourite with the trendy crowd. At the back is a Whiskey Bar, a '50s-style bar that Don Draper & co would feel comfortable sipping a fine scotch at; upstairs is an elegant restaurant that serves a terrific brunch.

Anseo BAR

(Map p74; 18 Lower Camden St; 10.30am-11.30pm Mon-Thu, to 12.30am Fri & Sat, 11am-11pm Sun; all city centre) Unpretentious, unaffected and incredibly popular, this cosy alternative bar – which is pronounced 'an-*shuh*', the Irish for 'here' – is a favourite with those who live by the credo that to try too hard is far worse than not trying at all. The pub's soundtrack is an eclectic mix; you're as likely to hear Peggy Lee as Lee Perry.

No Name Bar BAR

(Map p106; 3 Fade St; to 1.30am Tue-Sat; all city centre) A low-key entrance just next to the trendy French restaurant L'Gueuleton leads upstairs to one of the nicest bar spaces in town, consisting of three huge rooms in a restored Victorian town house plus a sizeable heated patio area for smokers. There's no sign or a name – folks just refer to it as the No Name Bar or, if you're a real insider, Number 3.

Oliver St John Gogarty PUB

(Map p106; 58-59 Fleet St; 10.30am-11.30pm Mon-Thu, to 12.30am Fri & Sat, noon-11pm Sun; all city centre) You won't see too many Dubs ordering drinks in this bar, which is almost entirely given over to tourists who come for the carefully manufactured slice of authentic traditionalism…and the toe-tappin' sessions that run throughout the day. The kitchen serves up dishes that most Irish cooks have consigned to the culinary dustbin.

Grogan's Castle Lounge PUB

(Map p106; www.grogranspub.ie; 15 South William St; 10.30am-11.30pm Mon-Thu, to 12.30am Fri & Sat, 12.30-11pm Sun) This place is known simply

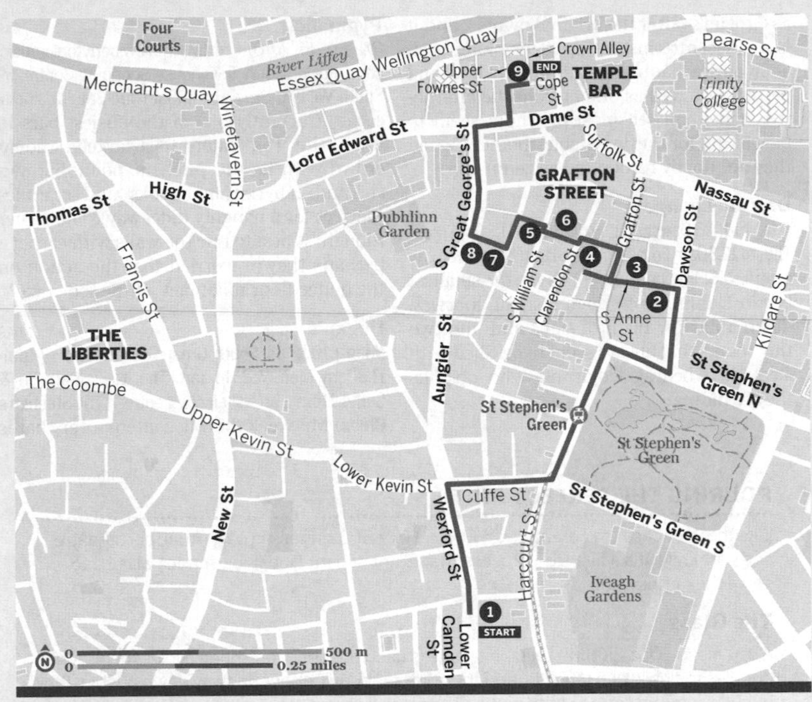

City Walk
Dublin Crawl

START LOWER CAMDEN ST
FINISH CROWN ALLEY
LENGTH 2KM; ONE HOUR TO TWO DAYS

Dubliners of old would assure their 'bitter halves' that they were 'going to see a man about a dog' before retreating to the nearest watering hole. Visiting barflies need no excuse to enjoy the social and cultural education – ahem – of a tour of Dublin's finest, most charming and most hard-core bars.

Start in the always excellent 1 **Anseo** (p114), where hipsters rub shoulders with the hoi polloi and everyone toe-taps to the great bag of DJ tunes. Head deep into the city centre and rub shoulders with the beautiful people at 2 **Sam's Bar** (p117). Go old school by sinking a pint of plain in the snug at South Anne St's 3 **Kehoe's** (p114), one of the city centre's most atmospheric bars. Find a spot out front of 4 **Bruxelles** (p117): the bronze statue of Thin Lizzy's Phil Lynott outside is testament to the bar's reputation as a great spot for rock music, even if it's just on the stereo. Discuss the merits of that unwritten masterpiece with a clutch of frustrated writers and artists in 5 **Grogan's Castle Lounge** (p114), a traditional haunt that admirably refuses to modernise. Directly across the street in the basement of the Powerscourt Townhouse Shopping Centre is 6 **Pygmalion** (p116), which is all about now. A couple of streets away, on Fade St, a couple of bars vie for hipster euros: the upstairs 7 **No Name Bar** (p114) is elegant and discreet, while 8 **Hogan's** (p116), at the corner with South Great George's St, has been one of the most popular watering holes in the city for longer than its clientele have been alive.

Finally, make your way into Temple Bar and ring the doorbell to access the 9 **Vintage Cocktail Club** (p117), upstairs behind a plain steel door on Crown Alley, where the in-crowd sips cocktails and eats delicious titbits in a speakeasy atmosphere. If you've followed the tour correctly, it's unlikely that you'd now be referring to this guide. How many fingers?

as Grogan's (after the original owner), and it is a city-centre institution. It has long been a favourite haunt of Dublin's writers and painters, as well as others from the alternative bohemian set, most of whom seem to be waiting for the 'inevitable' moment when they are finally recognised as geniuses.

Dawson Lounge PUB

(Map p74; 25 Dawson St; ⏲10.30am-11.30pm Mon-Thu, to 12.30am Fri & Sat, noon-11pm Sun; 🚌all city centre, 🚊St Stephen's Green) To see *the* smallest bar in Dublin, go through a small doorway, down a narrow flight of steps and into two tiny rooms that always seem to be filled with a couple of bedraggled drunks who look like they're hiding.

Pygmalion BAR

(Map p106; ☎01-674 6712; www.bodytonicmusic.com; Powerscourt Townhouse Shopping Centre, 59 South William St; ⏲to 1.30am Tue-Sat; 🚌all city centre) Currently one of the busiest bars in town, the 'Pyg' caters to a largely student crowd with its €10 pitchers, pounding music and labyrinthine nooks and crannies (perfect for a naughty hideaway). The owner thought it best to line the walls with carpet – perhaps they're worried that the action on the dance floor might get a little too crazy?

Hogan's BAR

(Map p106; 35 South Great George's St; ⏲1pm-11.30am Mon-Wed, to 1am Thu, to 2.30am Fri & Sat, 4-11pm Sun; 🚌all city centre, 🚊St Stephen's Green) Midweek this big contemporary bar is

POURING THE PERFECT PINT

Like the Japanese tea ceremony, pouring a pint of Guinness is part ritual, part theatre and part logic. It's a five-step process that every decent Dublin bartender will use to serve the perfect pint.

The Glass

A dry, clean 20oz (568ml) tulip pint glass is used because the shape allows the nitrogen bubbles to flow down the side, and the contour 'bump' about halfway down pushes the bubbles into the centre of the pint on their way back up.

The Angle

The glass is held beneath the tap at a 45-degree angle – and the tap shouldn't touch the sides of the glass.

The Pour

A smooth pour should fill the glass to about three-quarters full, after which it is put on the counter 'to settle'.

The Head

As the beer flows into the glass its passes through a restrictor plate at high speed that creates nitrogen bubbles. In the glass, the agitated bubbles flow down the sides of the glass and – thanks to the contour bump – back up through the middle, settling at the top in a nice, creamy head. This should take a couple of minutes to complete.

The Top-Off

Once the pint is 'settled', the bartender will top it off, creating a domed effect across the top of the glass with the head sitting comfortably just above the rim. Now it's the perfect pint.

Where to Find It?

Now that you know what you're looking for, it's time to find it. The pint in Gravity Bar (p83) is good, but it's missing one key ingredient: atmosphere, the kind found only in a traditional pub.

Kehoe's (p114) Stalwart popular with locals and tourists.

John Mulligan's (p114) Perfect setting for a perfect pint.

Grogan's Castle Lounge (p114) Great because the locals demand it!

Fallon's (p119) Centuries of experience.

a relaxing hang-out for young professionals, and restaurant and bar workers on a night off. But come the weekend the sweat bin downstairs pulls them in for some serious music courtesy of the usually excellent DJs.

Vintage Cocktail Club BAR
(Map p106; Crown Alley; ⏲5pm-1.30am Mon-Fri, from 12.30pm Sat & Sun; 🚌all city centre) Behind the inconspicuous, unlit doorway initialled with the letters 'VCC' is one of the coolest bars in Dublin, a '60s-style London members' club or Vegas Rat Pack hang-out. The emphasis is on expertly made cocktails served in a super-stylish setting: the 2nd-floor smoking lounge is easily the most elegant place in town in which to light up. All-round class.

Bruxelles PUB
(Map p106; 7-8 Harry St; ⏲9.30am-1.30am; 🚌all city centre) Bruxelles is a raucous music bar split across different areas. It's comparatively trendy on the ground floor, while downstairs is a great, loud and dingy rock bar with live music each weekend. Just outside, a **bronze Phil Lynott** is there to remind us of Bruxelles' impeccable rock credentials.

Sam's Bar BAR
(Map p74; 36 Dawson St; ⏲4pm-2am Mon-Thu, 1pm-2.30am Fri-Sun; 🚌all city centre, 🚊St Stephen's Green) A posh Dawson St drinking spot, Sam's decor is Middle Eastern (a hangover of its previous incarnation as an Asian-themed bar) meets art-college graffiti. None of which seems to bother the young professional clientele, who come to share tales of success over fancy cocktails.

James Toner's PUB
(Map p74; 139 Lower Baggot St; ⏲10.30am-11.30pm Mon-Thu, to 12.30am Fri & Sat, noon-11pm Sun; 🚌7 & 44 from city centre) Toner's, with its stone floors and antique snugs, has changed little over the years and is the closest thing you'll get to a country pub in the heart of the city. The shelves and drawers are reminders that it once doubled as a grocery shop.

Hartigan's PUB
(Map p74; 100 Lower Leeson St; ⏲10.30am-11.30pm Mon-Thu, to 12.30am Fri & Sat, noon-11pm Sun; 🚌all city centre) This is about as spartan a bar as you'll find in the city, and is the daytime home of some serious drinkers, who appreciate the quiet, no-frills surroundings. In the evening it's popular with students from the medical faculty of University College Dublin (UCD).

O'Donoghue's PUB
(Map p74; 15 Merrion Row; ⏲10.30am-11.30pm Mon-Thu, to 12.30am Fri & Sat, noon-11pm Sun; 🚌all city centre) Once the most renowned traditional music bar in all Dublin, this is where the world-famous folk group the Dubliners refined their raspish brand of trad in the 1960s. On summer evenings a young, international crowd spills out into the courtyard beside the pub. It's also a famous rugby pub and the Dublin HQ for many Irish and visiting fans.

International Bar PUB
(Map p106; 23 Wicklow St; ⏲10.30am-11.30pm Mon-Thu, to 12.30am Fri & Sat, noon-11pm Sun; 🚌7 & 44 from city centre) This tiny pub with a huge personality is a top spot for an afternoon pint. It has a long bar, stained-glass windows, red-velour seating and a convivial atmosphere. Some of Ireland's most celebrated comedians stuttered through their first set in the **Comedy Cellar**, which is, of course, upstairs.

Porterhouse BAR
(Map p106; 16-18 Parliament St; ⏲to 1.30am Tue-Sat; 🚌all city centre) The second-biggest brewery in Dublin, the Porterhouse looks like a cross between a Wild West bar and a Hieronymus Bosch painting. It has lots of its own delicious brews, including its Plain Porter (some say it's the best stout in town) as well as unfamiliar imported beers.

Bernard Shaw BAR
(Map p70; www.bodytonicmusic.com; 11-12 South Richmond St; ⏲to 1.30am Tue-Sat; 🚌7 & 44 from city centre) This deliberately ramshackle boozer is probably the coolest bar in town for its marvellous mix of music (courtesy of its owners, the Bodytonic production crew) and diverse menu of events such as afternoon car-boot sales, storytelling nights and fun competitions like having a 'tag-off' between a bunch of graffiti artists.

Palace Bar PUB
(Map p88; 21 Fleet St; ⏲10.30am-11.30pm Mon-Thu, to 12.30am Fri & Sat, noon-11pm Sun; 🚌all city centre) With its mirrors and wooden niches, the Palace (established in 1823) is one of Dublin's great Victorian pubs and a stubborn stalwart against the modernising influences of the last half-century. Writers Patrick Kavanagh and Flann O'Brien were once regulars and it was for a long time the unofficial head office of the *Irish Times*.

Lost Society CLUB
(Bassment; Map p106; ☎01-677 0014; www.lostsociety.ie; Powerscourt Townhouse Shopping Centre, South William St; admission €6-10; ⏲10pm-3am; 🚌all city centre) Part of the magnificent 18th-century Powerscourt complex, Lost Society (Twitter: @lostsocdublin) offers two distinct nightlife experiences for the price

GAY & LESBIAN DUBLIN

Dublin voted overwhelmingly in favour of the marriage equality referendum in 2015, proof that the capital has become one of Europe's most inclusive cities. Although the occasional harassment of LGBT people remains a sad fact of life, for the most part the city is a perfectly safe place to be out and proud.

Festivals & Events

International Dublin Gay Theatre Festival (www.gaytheatre.ie) The only event of its kind anywhere in the world, with more than 30 gay- and lesbian-themed productions over two weeks in May.

Gaze International LGBT Film Festival (www.gaze.ie) An international film and documentary festival held at the Irish Film Institute (p124) in August.

Drinking

George (Map p106; www.thegeorge.ie; 89 South Great George's St; ⏲2-11.30pm Mon, 2pm-2.30am Tue-Fri, 12.30pm-2.30am Sat, 12.30pm-1.30am Sun; 🚌all city centre) The purple mother of Dublin's gay bars is a long-standing institution, having lived through the years when it was the only place in town where the gay crowd could, well, be gay. Shirley's legendary Sunday-night bingo is as popular as ever, while Wednesday's Space N Veda is a terrific night of cabaret and drag.

Front Lounge (Map p106; 33 Parliament St; ⏲10.30am-11.30pm Mon-Thu, to 12.30am Fri & Sat, noon-11pm Sun; 🚌all city centre) The unofficially gay 'Flounge' is a sophisticated and friendly bar that stands out from other gay joints in that it is quieter, more demure and popular with a mixed crowd. Here, sexual orientation is strictly secondary to having a drink and a laugh with friends, even though the 'Back Lounge', toward the back of the bar, is traditionally predominantly gay.

Pantibar (Map p88; www.pantibar.com; 7-8 Capel St; ⏲5-11.30pm Mon, Wed & Sun, to 2am Tue, to 2.30am Thu-Sat; 🚌all city centre) In 2014 Pantibar's owner Rory O'Neill (better known as drag queen Panti) made international headlines when his Noble Call speech, delivered with articulate grace from the Abbey Theatre stage, went viral on YouTube. As a result, Pantibar went from being just a raucous, fun gay bar to a place of pilgrimage for LGBT people from all over the world.

Information

Gay & Lesbian Garda Liaison Officer (☎01-666 9000) If you encounter any sort of trouble on the streets, don't hesitate to call. (For sexual assaults, contact the Sexual Assault Unit.)

Gay Community News (www.gcn.ie) A useful, nationwide news- and issues-based monthly paper. The glossy *Q-Life* and *Free!* are entertainment guides that can be found in Temple Bar businesses and the Irish Film Institute.

Gay Switchboard Dublin (☎01-872 1055; www.gayswitchboard.ie) A friendly and useful voluntary service that provides information on matters such as legal issues and where to find accommodation for gay travellers.

Outhouse (☎01-873 4932; www.outhouse.ie; 105 Capel St; 🚌all city centre) Top gay, lesbian and bisexual resource centre. Great stop-off point to see what's on, check noticeboards and meet people. It publishes the free *Pink Pages*, a directory of gay-centric services, which is also accessible on the website.

Sexual Assault Unit (☎01-666 6000) Call, or visit the Garda (Police) Station on Pearse St.

of one ticket. Upstairs, spread across three levels and a host of rooms, the music is eclectic and the crowd beautifully self-aware. Downstairs is the Bassment, where the music is thumping and the dancing is hot and sweaty.

Copper Face Jacks CLUB

(Map p74; www.copperfacejacks.ie; 29-30 Harcourt St, Jackson Court Hotel; admission free–€10; ⏲10.30pm-3am; 🚌10, 11, 13, 14 or 15A, 🚊St Stephen's Green) In rural Ireland you don't go clubbing; you go to 'the disco' for a drink, a dance and – hopefully – 'the shift', a particularly Irish way of describing making out. Coppers (Twitter: @CopperFaceJacks) is a slice of country clubbing in the middle of the capital, and it's all the more popular for it.

Lillie's Bordello CLUB

(Map p66; ☎01-679 9204; www.lilliesbordello.ie; Adam Ct; admission €10-20; ⏲11pm-3am) The most upmarket club (Twitter: @lilliesdublin) in Dublin makes sure to attract whatever Cristal-swilling superstar is in town. Not that you'll rub shoulders with them, as they'll be safely ensconced in the ultra-VIP Jersey Lil's private members' bar. The hoi polloi make do with bland music and, from 2015, Lillie's Lab, where they can distil their own gin.

The Liberties & Kilmainham

Fallon's PUB

(Map p70; ☎01-454 2801; 129 The Coombe; ⏲10.30am-11.30pm Mon-Thu, to 12.30am Fri & Sat, noon-11pm Sun; 🚌123, 206 or 51B from city centre) Just west of the city centre, in the heart of medieval Dublin, this is a fabulously old-fashioned bar that has been serving a great pint of Guinness since the end of the 17th century. Prize fighter Dan Donnelly, the only boxer ever to be knighted, was head bartender here in 1818. It's a genuine Irish bar filled with Dubs.

Old Royal Oak PUB

(11 Kilmainham Lane; ⏲10.30am-11.30pm Mon-Thu, to 12.30am Fri & Sat, noon-11pm Sun; 🚌68, 69 & 79 from city centre) Locals are fiercely protective of this gorgeous traditional pub, which opened in 1845 to serve the patrons and staff of the Royal Hospital (now the Irish Museum of Modern Art). The clientele has changed, but everything else has remained the same, which makes this one of the nicest pubs in the city in which to enjoy a few pints.

North of the Liffey

Cobblestone PUB

(Map p70; North King St; ⏲10.30am-11.30pm Mon-Thu, to 12.30am Fri & Sat, noon-11pm Sun; 🚊Smithfield) This pub in the heart of Smithfield has a great atmosphere in its cosy upstairs bar, where there are superb nightly music sessions performed by traditional musicians (especially Thursday) and up-and-coming folk acts.

Walshe's PUB

(Map p70; 6 Stoneybatter; ⏲10.30am-11.30pm Mon-Thu, to 12.30am Fri & Sat, noon-11pm Sun; 🚌25, 25A, 66, 67 from city centre, 🚊Museum) If the snug is free, a drink in Walshe's is about as pure a traditional experience as you'll have in any pub in the city; if it isn't, you'll have to make do with the old-fashioned bar, where the friendly staff and brilliant clientele (a mix of locals and hipster imports) are a treat. A proper Dublin pub.

Grand Social BAR

(Map p88; ☎01-874 0076; www.thegrandsocial.ie; 35 Lower Liffey St; ⏲to 1.30am Tue-Sat; 🚌all city centre, 🚊Jervis) This multipurpose venue hosts club nights, comedy and live-music gigs, and is a decent bar for a drink. It's spread across three floors, each of which has a different theme: The Parlour downstairs is a cosy, old-fashioned bar; the midlevel Ballroom is where the dancing is; the upstairs Loft hosts a variety of events.

Dice Bar BAR

(Map p70; ☎01-674 6710; www.thatsitdublin.com; 79 Queen St; ⏲3pm-midnight Mon-Thu, to 1am Fri & Sat, to 11.30pm Sun; 🚌25, 25A, 66, 67 from city centre, 🚊Museum) Co-owned by Huey from the Fun Lovin' Criminals, the Dice Bar looks like something you might find on New York's Lower East Side. Its dodgy locale, black-and-red painted interior, dripping candles and stressed seating, combined with rocking DJs most nights, make it a magnet for Dublin hipsters. It has Guinness and local microbrews.

Hughes' Bar PUB

(Map p70; 19 Chancery St; ⏲10.30am-11.30pm Mon-Thu, to 12.30am Fri & Sat, noon-11pm Sun; 🚌25, 66, 67 or 90 from city centre, 🚊Four Courts) Traditional purists love the nightly music sessions at this pub, which by day caters to barristers, solicitors and their clients from the nearby Four Courts – all of whom probably need a pint, but for different reasons!

DUBLIN BY SONG

Dublin is one of the most musical cities in Europe, so it stands to reason that there are a few worthwhile songs that sing its praises – and its faults. Here's our pick of tracks to download to your MP3 to enrich your Dublin saunter:

Running to Stand Still (U2) A poignant portrayal of the 1980s heroin epidemic; the 'seven towers' of the song refer to a (now demolished) notorious flat complex in the north-city suburb of Ballymun.

Old Town (Philip Lynott) If you want to see what Dublin looked like at the end of '80s, check out the video for this fabulous tune.

Summer in Dublin (Bagatelle) A nostalgic, singalong pop tune that was Bagatelle's biggest hit and is the city's favourite song about itself.

City of Screams (Paranoid Visions) Dublin in the 1980s, envisioned in all its anger and ugliness by the city's foremost '80s punk band.

Phil Lynott (Jape) Captures the essence of the city today – without naming any locations.

The city's most famous folk band, the Dubliners, have a bunch of songs about the capital – these are our favourites:

Auld Triangle Taken from Brendan Behan's play *The Quare Fellow*, this poignant tune is about being imprisoned in Mountjoy Prison.

Raglan Road Patrick Kavanagh's poem given music, life and profound meaning by Luke Kelly.

Rocky Road to Dublin A traditional 19th-century tune about a difficult journey to Dublin.

Take Her up to Monto A charming traditional ditty about taking a girl up to the city's one-time notorious red-light district.

Although the playing is very good, the atmosphere is a little lacking and the sessions can be a bit dead.

☆ Entertainment

There is life in Dublin beyond the pub – or more accurately, around it. There are comedy clubs and classical concerts, recitals and readings, marionettes and music – lots and lots of music, both live and recorded. The theatre has an important place in the entertainment firmament, with plays both popular and serious usually on the bill.

Theatre, comedy and classical concerts are usually booked directly through the venue. Tickets for touring international bands and big-name local talent are either sold at the venue or through a booking agency such as **Ticketmaster** (www.ticketmaster.ie), which sells tickets to every genre of big- and medium-sized show – but be aware that it charges between 9% and 12.5% service charge per ticket.

Friday's *Irish Times* has a pull-out entertainment section called the *Ticket*, which has comprehensive listings of clubs and gigs; the *Irish Independent*'s version, also out on Friday, is called *Day & Night*. Online resources include:

Entertainment.ie (www.entertainment.ie) For all events.

MCD (www.mcd.ie) Biggest promoter in Ireland.

Nialler9 (www.nialler9.com) Excellent indie blog with listings.

Sweebe (www.sweebe.com) Over 200 venues listed.

Totally Dublin (totallydublin.ie) Comprehensive listings and reviews.

What's On In (www.whatsonin.ie) From markets to gigs and club nights.

Rock & Pop

Dublin's love affair with popular music has made it one of the preferred touring stops for all kinds of musicians, who seem to relish the unfettered manner in which audiences embrace their favourite artists.

Workman's Club LIVE MUSIC
(Map p106; ☎01-670 6692; www.theworkmansclub.com; 10 Wellington Quay; 🚌all city centre) A 300-capacity venue and bar in the former

workingmen's club of Dublin, this new spot puts the emphasis on keeping away from the mainstream, which means a broad range of performers, from singer-songwriters to electronic cabaret. When the live music at the Workman's Club (Twitter: @Workmans-Clubs) is over, DJs take to the stage, playing everything from rockabilly to hip hop and indie to house.

Academy LIVE MUSIC
(Map p88; ☎01-877 9999; www.theacademydublin.com; 57 Middle Abbey St; all city centre, Abbey) A terrific midsized venue, the Academy's stage has been graced by an impressive list of performers, from Nick Cave's Bad Seeds to '80s superstar Nik Kershaw. It's also the place to hear those unknown names who stand a better-than-evens chance of making it somewhere.

Button Factory LIVE MUSIC
(Map p106; ☎01-670 0533; www.buttonfactory.ie; Curved St; all city centre) A multipurpose venue where one night you might be shaking your glow light to a thumping live set by a top DJ, and the next you'll be shifting from foot to foot as an esoteric Finnish band drag their violin bows over their electric guitar strings.

Vicar Street LIVE MUSIC
(Map p70; ☎01-454 5533; www.vicarstreet.com; 58-59 Thomas St; 13, 49, 54a, 56a from city centre) Smaller performances take place at this intimate venue near Christ Church Cathedral. It has a capacity of 1000, between its table-serviced group seating downstairs and theatre-style balcony. Vicar Street offers a varied program of performers, with a strong emphasis on soul, folk, jazz and foreign music.

3 Arena LIVE MUSIC
(Map p92; ☎01-819 8888; www.3arena.ie; East Link Bridge, North Wall Quay; Point Village) The premier indoor venue in the city has a capacity of 23,000 and plays host to the brightest touring stars in the firmament. Fleetwood Mac, The Who, Neil Diamond and Taylor Swift performed here in 2015.

Whelan's LIVE MUSIC
(Map p74; ☎01-478 0766; www.whelanslive.com; 25 Wexford St; 16, 122 from city centre) Perhaps the city's most beloved live venue is this midsized room attached to a traditional bar. This is the singer-songwriter's spiritual home: when they're done pouring out the contents of their hearts on stage, you can find them filling up in the bar along with their fans.

Sugar Club LIVE MUSIC
(Map p74; ☎01-678 7188; www.thesugarclub.com; 8 Lower Leeson St; St Stephen's Green) There's live jazz, cabaret and soul music at weekends in this comfortable theatre-style venue on the corner of St Stephen's Green.

Classical

Classical music concerts and opera take place in a number of city-centre venues. There are also occasional performances in churches; check the press for details.

Bord Gáis Energy Theatre THEATRE
(Map p92; ☎01-677 7999; www.grandcanaltheatre.ie; Grand Canal Sq; Grand Canal Dock) Forget the uninviting sponsored name: Daniel Libeskind's masterful design is a three-tiered, 2000-capacity auditorium where you're as likely to be entertained by the Bolshoi or a touring state opera as you are to see Disney on Ice or Barbara Streisand. It's a magnificent venue – designed for classical, paid for by the classics.

National Concert Hall LIVE MUSIC
(Map p74; ☎01-417 0000; www.nch.ie; Earlsfort Tce; all city centre) Ireland's premier orchestral hall hosts a variety of concerts year-round, including a series of lunchtime concerts from 1.05pm to 2pm on Tuesdays, June to August.

HANDEL WITH CARE

In 1742 the nearly broke GF Handel conducted the very first performance of his epic work *Messiah* in the since-demolished Dublin Music Hall, on the city's oldest street, Fishamble St. Jonathan Swift – author of *Gulliver's Travels* and dean of St Patrick's Cathedral – had suggested that his own and Christ Church's choirs take part, but revoked his invitation when he discovered that the sacred music would be performed in a common music hall rather than in the more appropriate setting of a church, and vowed to punish vicars who let their choirs take part. The concert went ahead nonetheless, and the celebrated work is performed at the original spot in Dublin annually – now a hotel that bears the composer's name.

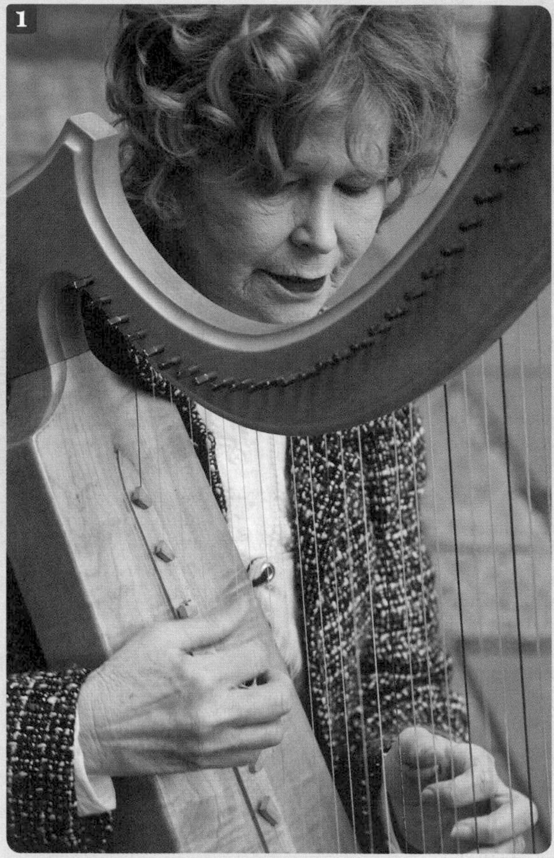
1

CARLOS SANCHEZ PEREYRA/GETTY IMAGES ©

2

4

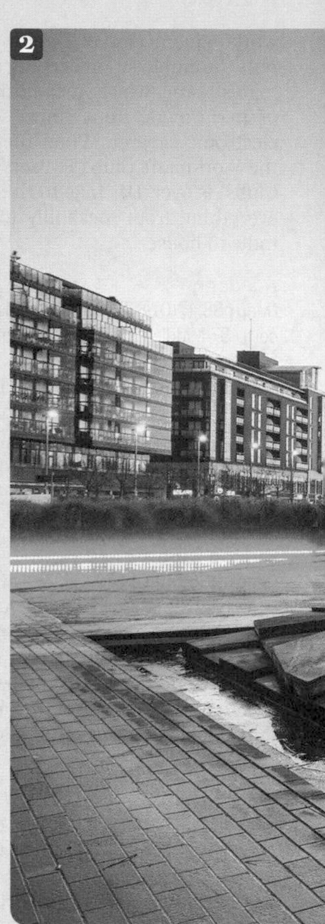

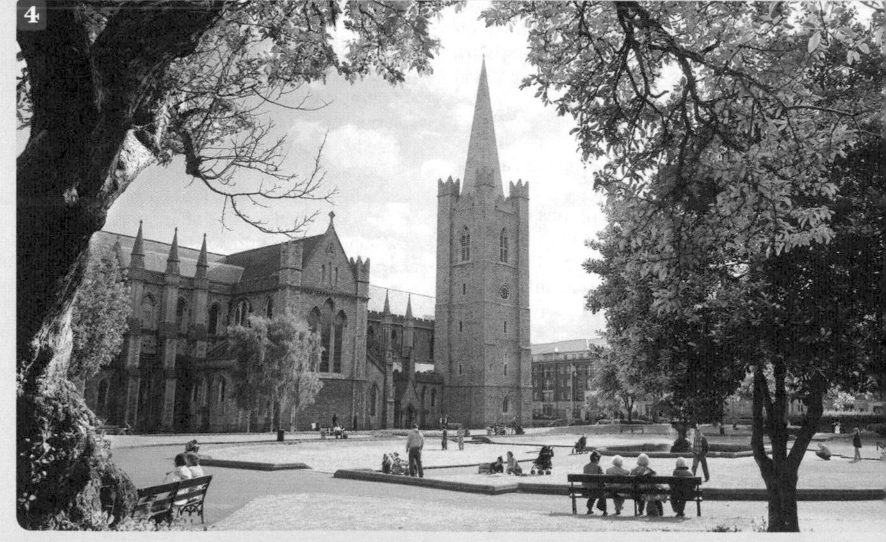

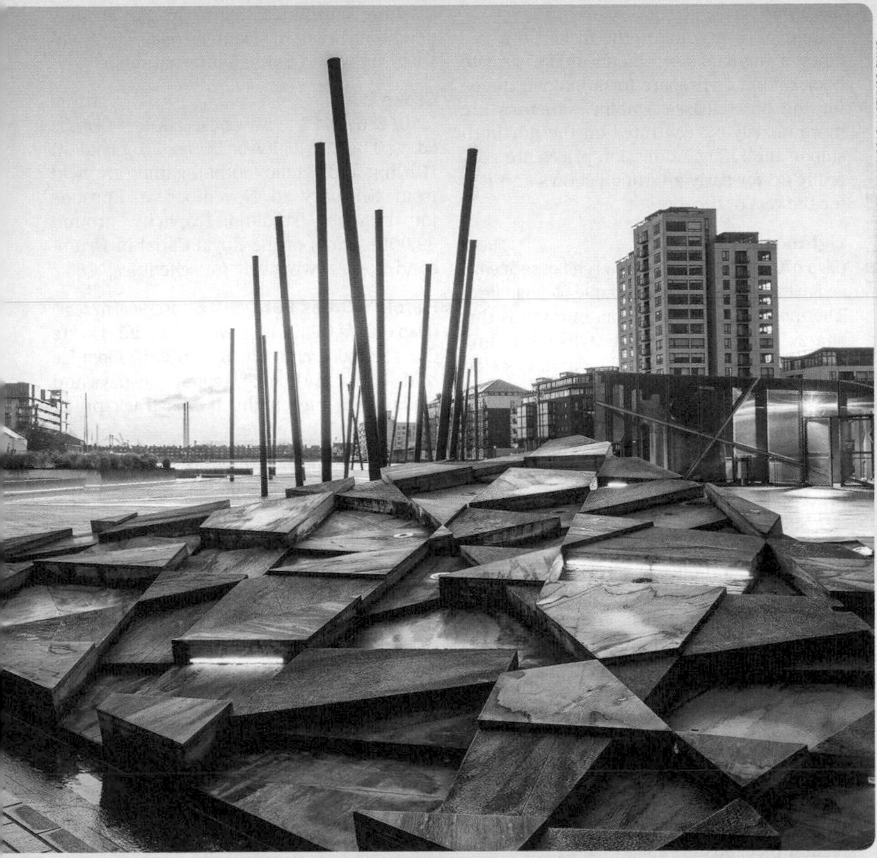

DAVID SOANES PHOTOGRAPHY/GETTY IMAGES ©

1. Live Music (p120)
From street musicians to trad-music sessions, Dublin has plenty of music on offer.

2. Docklands (p93)
The revamped Docklands precinct sports an impressive array of contemporary architecture, including Grand Canal Square, designed by Martha Schwartz Partners.

3. Howth (p132)
Howth's beautiful coastal scenery is easily accessible from Dublin.

4. St Patrick's Park (p83)
The park adjacent to St Patrick's Cathedral is the perfect place to sit and take it all in.

MARKUS GANN/SHUTTERSTOCK ©

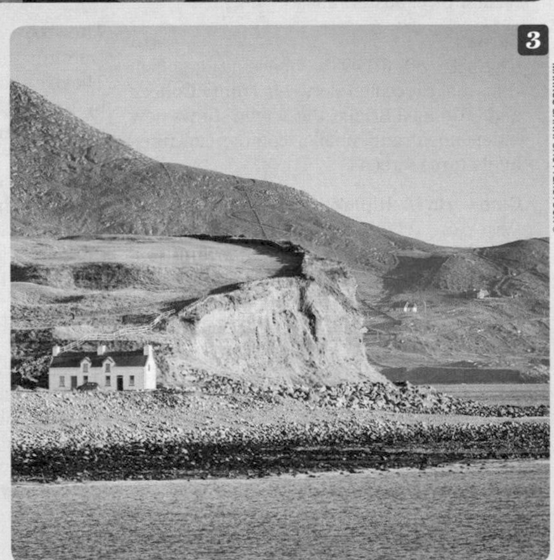

Cinemas

Dubliners love 'going to the flicks', so if you fancy a night at the cinema make sure to book online or prepare for a longish queue for the big releases. Dublin's cinemas are more heavily concentrated on the northern side of the Liffey. Admission prices are generally €6 for early afternoon shows and €10 for the rest of the day.

Lighthouse Cinema CINEMA
(Map p70; ☎01-879 7601; www.lighthousecinema.ie; Smithfield Plaza; 🚌all city centre, 🚊Smithfield) The most impressive cinema in town is this snazzy four-screener in a stylish building just off Smithfield Plaza. The menu is strictly art-house, and the cafe-bar on the ground floor is perfect for discussing the merits of German Expressionism.

Irish Film Institute CINEMA
(IFI; Map p106; ☎01-679 5744; www.ifi.ie; 6 Eustace St; 🚌all city centre) The IFI has a couple of screens and shows classics and new art-house films, although we question some of their selections: weird and controversial can also be a little tedious. The complex also has a bar, a cafe and a bookshop.

Savoy CINEMA
(Map p88; ☎01-874 6000; Upper O'Connell St; ⏱from 2pm; 🚌all city centre) The Savoy is a five-screen, first-run cinema, and has late-night shows at weekends. Savoy Cinema 1 is the largest in the country and its enormous screen is the perfect way to view really spectacular blockbuster movies.

Screen CINEMA
(Map p88; ☎01-671 4988; 2 Townsend St; ⏱from 2pm; 🚌all city centre) Between Trinity College and O'Connell Bridge, the Screen shows new independent and smaller commercial films on its three screens.

Cineworld Multiplex CINEMA
(Map p88; ☎0818 304 204; www.cineworld.ie; Parnell Centre, Parnell St; 🚌all city centre) This 17-screen cinema shows only commercial releases. The seats are comfy, the concession stand is huge and the selection of pick 'n' mix could induce a sugar seizure. It lacks the charm of the older-style cinemas, but we like it anyway.

Sport

Aviva Stadium STADIUM
(Map p70; ☎01-238 2300; www.avivastadium.ie; 11-12 Lansdowne Rd; 🚆Lansdowne Rd) Gleaming 50,000-capacity ground with an eye-catching curvilinear stand in the swanky neighbourhood of Donnybrook. Home to Irish rugby and football internationals.

Croke Park STADIUM
(☎01-836 3222; www.crokepark.ie; Clonliffe Rd; 🚌3, 11, 11A, 16, 16A or 123 from O'Connell St) Hurling and Gaelic football games are held from February to November at Europe's fourth-largest stadium (capacity around 82,000), north of the Royal Canal in Drumcondra; see www.gaa.ie for schedules.

Harold's Cross Park GREYHOUND RACING
(Map p70; ☎01-497 1081; www.igb.ie; 151 Harold's Cross Rd; adult/child €10/6; ⏱6.30-10.30pm Tue & Fri; 🚌16 or 16A from city centre) Tuesdays and Fridays are race night at this track pretty close to the city centre.

Leopardstown Race Course HORSE RACING
(☎01-289 3607; www.leopardstown.com; 🚌special from Eden Quay) The Irish love of horse racing can be observed about 10km south of the city centre in Foxrock. Special buses depart from the city centre on race days; call the racecourse for details.

Shelbourne Park Greyhound Stadium GREYHOUND RACING
(Map p92; ☎01-668 3502, on race nights 01-202 6601; www.igb.ie; Bridge Town Rd, Ringsend; adult/child €10/6; ⏱7-10.30pm Wed-Sat; 🚌3, 7, 7A, 8, 45 or 84 from city centre) A top-class dog track with terrific vantage points from the glassed-in restaurant, where you can eat, bet and watch without leaving your seat.

Theatre

Dublin's theatre scene is small but busy. Theatre bookings can usually be made by quoting a credit-card number over the phone; you can collect your tickets just before the performance. Expect to pay anything between €12 and €25 for most shows, with some costing as much as €30. Most plays begin between 8pm and 8.30pm. Check www.irishtheatreonline.com to see what's playing.

Gate Theatre THEATRE
(Map p88; ☎01-874 4045; www.gatetheatre.ie; 1 Cavendish Row; 🚌all city centre) The city's most elegant theatre, housed in a late-18th-century building, features a generally unflappable repertoire of classic American and European plays. Orson Welles and James Mason played here early in their careers. Even today it is the only theatre in town where you might see established interna-

DUBLIN THEATRE TODAY

Here are six names to look out for in contemporary Irish theatre:

Marina Carr Internationally recognised playwright – her latest play *Hecuba* was performed by the Royal Shakespeare Company in 2015.

Marie Jones Belfast-born playwright whose most recent play is *Fly Me to the Moon* (2012).

Conor McPherson A well-respected talent whose most famous play is *The Seafarer* (2006). His most recent play is *The Night Alive* (2013).

Tom Murphy One of Ireland's leading dramatists; his latest play is *Brigit* (2014).

Mark O'Rowe The writer of *Howie the Rookie* (1999) and *Made in China* (2001) works primarily in film these days but does get back to theatre from time to time – he came back to the stage in 2014 with *Our Few and Evil Days*.

Enda Walsh The writer of *Disco Pigs* (1996; made into a film) was a big hit in 2014 with *Ballyturk*, starring his favourite actor, Cillian Murphy.

tional movie stars work on their credibility with a theatre run.

Abbey Theatre THEATRE
(Map p88; ☎01-878 7222; www.abbeytheatre.ie; Lower Abbey St; 🚌all city centre, 🚋Abbey) Ireland's national theatre was founded by WB Yeats in 1904 and was a central player in the development of a consciously native cultural identity. Its relevance has waned dramatically in recent decades but it still provides a mix of Irish classics (Synge, O'Casey etc), established international names (Shepard, Mamet) and contemporary talent (O'Rowe, Carr et al).

Gaiety Theatre THEATRE
(Map p74; ☎01-677 1717; www.gaietytheatre.com; South King St; 🚌all city centre) The Gaiety's program of plays is strictly of the fun-for-all-the-family type: West End hits, musicals, Christmas pantos and classic Irish plays keep the more serious-minded away, leaving more room for those simply looking to be entertained.

Olympia Theatre THEATRE
(Map p106; ☎01-677 7744; www.olympia.ie; 72 Dame St; 🚌all city centre) This theatre specialises in light plays and, at Christmastime, pantomimes.

Players' Theatre THEATRE
(Map p66; ☎01-677 2941, ext 1239; Regent House, Pearse St; 🚌all city centre) The Trinity College Players' Theatre hosts student productions throughout the academic year, as well as the most prestigious plays from the Dublin Theatre Festival (p99) in October.

Project Arts Centre THEATRE
(Map p106; ☎1850 260 027; www.projectartscentre.ie; 39 Essex St E; 🚌all city centre) The city's most interesting venue for challenging new work – be it drama, dance, live art or film. Three separate spaces allow for maximum versatility. You never know what to expect, which makes it all that more fun: we've seen some awful rubbish here, but we've also seen some of the best shows in town.

Shopping

If it's made in Ireland – or pretty much anywhere else – you can find it in Dublin. Grafton St is home to a range of largely British-owned high-street chain stores; you'll find the best local boutiques in the surrounding streets, selling everything from cheese to Irish designer clothing and streetwear. On the north side, pedestrianised Henry St has international chain stores, as well as Dublin's best department store, Arnott's.

Traditional Irish products such as crystal and knitwear remain popular choices, and increasingly you can find innovative, modern takes on the classics. But steer clear of the mass-produced junk whose joke value isn't worth the hassle of carting it home on the plane: trust us, there's no such thing as a genuine *shillelagh* (Irish fighting stick) for sale anywhere in town.

Citizens of non-EU countries can reclaim the VAT paid on purchases made at stores that display a cash-back sticker; ask for details.

BEST GUARANTEED IRISH

Avoca Handweavers Our favourite department store in the city has myriad homemade gift ideas.

Ulysses Rare Books For that priceless first edition or a beautiful, leather-bound copy of Joyce's *Dubliners*.

Louis Copeland (Map p106; ☎01-872 1600; www.louiscopeland.com; 18-19 Wicklow St; ⏰9am-5.30pm Mon-Wed, Fri & Sat, to 7.30pm Thu; 🚌all city centre) Dublin's very own top tailor, with made-to-measure suits.

Barry Doyle Design Jewellers (Map p106; ☎01-671 2838; 30 George's St Arcade; ⏰10am-6pm Mon-Wed, Fri & Sat, to 7pm Thu; 🚌all city centre) Exquisite handcrafted jewellery with unique contemporary designs.

Most shops open 9.30am to 6pm Monday to Saturday, with later hours – usually to 8pm – on Thursday. Many also open on Sunday, usually from noon to 6pm.

Grafton Street & Around

Avoca Handweavers HANDICRAFTS
(Map p106; ☎01-677 4215; www.avoca.ie; 11-13 Suffolk St; ⏰9.30am-6pm Mon-Wed & Sat, to 7pm Thu & Fri, 11am-6pm Sun; 🚌all city centre) Combining clothing, homewares, a basement food hall and an excellent top-floor **cafe** (mains €11-14; ⏰9.30am-6pm Mon-Wed & Sat, to 7pm Thu & Fri, 11am-6pm Sun), Avoca promotes a stylish but homey brand of modern Irish life – and is one of the best places to find an original present. Many of the garments are woven, knitted and naturally dyed at its Wicklow factory. There's a terrific kids' section.

Kilkenny Shop HANDICRAFTS
(Map p66; ☎01-677 7066; www.kilkennyshop.com; 6 Nassau St; ⏰8.30am-7pm Mon-Wed & Fri, to 8pm Thu, to 6pm Sat, 10am-6pm Sun; 🚌all city centre) A large, long-running repository for contemporary, innovative Irish crafts, including multicoloured, modern Irish knits, designer clothing, Orla Kiely bags and lovely silver jewellery. The glassware and pottery is beautiful and sourced from workshops around the country. A great source for presents.

Siopaella Design Exchange VINTAGE
(Map p106; www.siopaella.com; 25 Temple Lane South; 🚌all city centre) A secondhand shop like no other in Dublin, where you're as likely to find a vintage Chanel bag priced at €3000 as you are a beautiful preloved shirt for €5. You can exchange clothes for cash, or clothes for other clothes. One of the best shopping experiences in town.

DESIGNYARD HANDICRAFTS
(Map p66; ☎01-474 1011; www.designyard.ie; 25 South Frederick St; ⏰10am-5.30pm Mon-Wed & Fri, to 8pm Thu, to 6pm Sat; 🚌all city centre) A high-end, craft-as-art shop where everything you see – glass, batik, sculpture, painting – is one-off and handmade in Ireland. It also showcases contemporary jewellery stock from young international designers. Perfect for that bespoke engagement ring or a very special present.

Ulysses Rare Books BOOKS
(Map p74; ☎01-671 8676; www.rarebooks.ie; 10 Duke St; ⏰9.30am-5.45pm Mon-Sat; 🚌all city centre) Our favourite bookshop in the city stocks a rich and remarkable collection of Irish-interest books, with a particular emphasis on 20th-century literature and a large selection of first editions, including rare ones by the big guns: Joyce, Yeats, Beckett and Wilde.

Gutter Bookshop BOOKS
(Map p106; ☎01-679 9206; www.gutterbookshop.com; Cow's Lane; ⏰10am-6.30pm Mon-Wed, Fri & Sat, 10am-7pm Thu, 11am-6pm Sun; 🚌all city centre) Taking its name from Oscar Wilde's famous line from *Lady Windermere's Fan,* 'we are all in the gutter, but some of us are looking at the stars', this fabulous place is flying the flag for the downtrodden independent bookshop, stocking a mix of new novels, children's books, travel literature and other assorted titles.

Industry HOMEWARES
(Map p106; www.industrydesign.ie; 41 Drury St; ⏰10am-6pm Mon-Sat, noon-6pm Sun; 🚌all city centre) 'Curated vintage' is the tag line at this super-cool, independently owned design shop, where you can pick up everything from kids' booties to a birch veneer desk.

Castle & Drury CLOTHING
(Map p106; www.castledrury.ie; 6 Castle Market; ⏰10am-6pm Mon-Sat, noon-6pm Sun; 🚌all city centre) Contemporary fashions for men, including items by YMC, Soulland and Wood

Wood – with a few Scandinavian designers (Han Kjobenhavn and Mads Norgaard) thrown in for good measure.

Sheridan's Cheesemongers FOOD

(Map p74; ☎01-679 3143; www.sheridanscheesemongers.com; 11 South Anne St; ⏰10am-6pm Mon-Fri, 9.30am-6pm Sat; 🚌all city centre) If heaven were a cheese shop, this would be it. Wooden shelves are laden with rounds of farmhouse cheeses, sourced from around the country by Kevin and Seamus Sheridan, who have almost single-handedly revived cheese-making in Ireland.

Scout CLOTHING

(Map p70; www.scoutdublin.com; 5 Smock Alley Ct, Essex St W; ⏰10.30am-6pm Mon-Wed, Fri & Sat, to 7pm Thu, noon-5pm Sun; 🚌all city centre) Owner Wendy carefully selects every item of vintage clothing, and Irish and international labels including Armor Lux and Manley, plus accessories by Baggu and footwear by Grenson.

Brown Thomas DEPARTMENT STORE

(Map p106; ☎01-605 6666; www.brownthomas.com; 92 Grafton St; ⏰9.30am-8pm Mon, Wed & Fri, 10am-8pm Tue, 9.30am-9pm Thu, 9am-8pm Sat, 11am-7pm Sun; 🚌all city centre) Soak up the Jo Malone–laden rarefied atmosphere of Dublin's most exclusive shop, where presentation is virtually artistic. Here you'll find fantastic cosmetics, shoes to die for, exotic homewares and a host of Irish and international fashion labels such as Balenciaga, Stella McCartney, Lainey Keogh and Philip Treacy. The 3rd-floor Bottom Drawer outlet stocks the finest Irish linen you'll find anywhere.

Costume CLOTHING

(Map p106; ☎01-679 5200; www.costumedublin.ie; 10 Castle Market; ⏰10am-6pm Mon-Wed, Fri & Sat, to 7pm Thu; 🚌all city centre) Costume is considered a genuine pacesetter by Dublin's fashionistas; it has exclusive contracts with innovative designers such as Isabel Marant and Anna Sui. It also has the city's best range of Tempereley and American Retro.

SHOPPING CENTRES

Dublin offers a handful of 'under-the-one-roof' shopping experiences.

Powerscourt Townhouse Shopping Centre (Map p106; ☎01-679 4144; 59 South William St; ⏰10am-6pm Mon-Wed & Fri, to 8pm Thu, 9am-6pm Sat, noon-6pm Sun; 🚌all city centre) This absolutely gorgeous and stylish centre is in a carefully refurbished Georgian town house, built between 1741 and 1744. These days it's best known for its cafes and restaurants but it also does a top-end, selective trade in high fashion, art, exquisite handicrafts and other chichi sundries.

George's Street Arcade (Map p106; www.georgesstreetarcade.ie; btwn South Great George's St & Drury St; ⏰9am-6.30pm Mon-Wed, Fri & Sat, 9am-8pm Thu, noon-6pm Sun; 🚌all city centre) Dublin's best nonfood market is sheltered within an elegant Victorian Gothic arcade. Apart from shops and stalls selling new and old clothes, secondhand books, hats, posters, jewellery and records, there's a fortune teller, some gourmet nibbles, and a fish-and-chipper that does a roaring trade.

Jervis Street Centre (Map p88; ☎01-878 1323; Jervis St; ⏰9am-6.30pm Mon-Wed, Fri & Sat, to 7pm Thu, 11am-6.30pm Sun; 🚌all city centre) This modern, domed mall is a veritable shrine to the British chain store. Boots, Topshop, Debenhams, Argos, Dixons, M&S and Miss Selfridge all get a look-in.

St Stephen's Green Shopping Centre (Map p74; ☎01-478 0888; St Stephen's Green W; ⏰9am-7pm Mon-Wed, Fri & Sat, 9am-9pm Thu, 11am-6pm Sun; 🚌all city centre) A 1980s version of a 19th-century shopping arcade – the dramatic, balconied interior and central courtyard are a bit too grand for the nondescript chain stores within. There's Boots, Benetton and a large Dunnes Store with supermarket, as well as last-season designer warehouse TK Maxx.

Dundrum Town Centre (☎01-299 1700; www.dundrum.ie; Sandyford Rd; ⏰9am-9pm Mon-Fri, 8.30am-7pm Sat, 10am-7pm Sun; 🚌17, 44C, 48A or 75 from city centre, 🚊Ballaly) Modern Ireland's grandest retail cathedral is this huge shopping and entertainment complex in the southern suburb of Dundrum. Over 100 retail outlets are represented.

DUBLIN MARKETS

In recent years Dublin has gone gaga for markets. Which is kind of ironic, considering the city's traditional markets, like Moore St, were ignored for so long by those same folks who now can't get enough of the homemade hummus on sale at the new gourmet spots. It's all so...continental.

Book Fair (Map p106; Temple Bar Sq; ⏲10am-5pm Sat; 🚌all city centre) Rummage through secondhand books.

Cow's Lane Designer Mart (Map p106; Cow's Lane; ⏲10am-5pm Sat Jun-Sep; 🚌all city centre) A real market for hipsters, bringing together over 60 of the best clothing, accessory and craft stalls.

Temple Bar Food Market (Map p106; www.templebar.ie; Meeting House Sq; ⏲10am-4.30pm Sat; 🚌all cross-city) The city's best open-air food market.

Moore Street Market (Map p88; Moore St; ⏲8am-4pm Mon-Sat; 🚌all city centre) Open-air, steadfastly 'Old Dublin' market, with fruit, fish and flowers.

Hodges Figgis BOOKS
(Map p66; ☎01-677 4754; 56-58 Dawson St; ⏲9am-7pm Mon-Wed & Fri, to 8pm Thu, to 6pm Sat, noon-6pm Sun; 🚌all city centre) The mother of all Dublin bookshops has books on every conceivable subject for every kind of reader spread across three huge floors, including a substantial Irish section on the ground floor.

Jenny Vander CLOTHING
(Map p106; ☎01-677 0406; 50 Drury St; ⏲10am-6pm Mon-Sat, noon-6pm Sun; 🚌all city centre) This secondhand shop oozes elegance and sophistication. Discerning fashionistas and film stylists snap up the exquisite beaded handbags, fur-trimmed coats, richly patterned dresses, and costume jewellery priced as if it were the real thing.

Claddagh Records MUSIC
(Map p106; ☎01-677 0262; 2 Cecilia St; ⏲10am-6pm Mon-Sat, noon-6pm Sun; 🚌all city centre) An excellent collection of good-quality traditional and folk music is the mainstay at this centrally located record shop. The profoundly knowledgeable staff should be able to locate even the most elusive recording for you.

Dubray Books BOOKS
(Map p106; ☎01-677 5568; 36 Grafton St; ⏲9am-7pm Mon-Wed & Sat, 9am-9pm Thu & Fri, 11am-6pm Sun; 🚌all city centre) Three roomy floors devoted to bestsellers, recent releases, coffee-table books and a huge travel section make this one of the better bookshops in town. It can't compete with its larger, British-owned rivals on price, but it holds its own with helpful staff and a lovely atmosphere that encourages you to linger.

North of the Liffey

Arnott's DEPARTMENT STORE
(Map p88; ☎01-805 0400; 12 Henry St; ⏲10am-6pm Mon-Wed, Fri & Sat, to 7pm Thu, noon-6pm Sun; 🚌all city centre) Occupying a huge block with entrances on Henry, Liffey and Abbey Sts, this is our favourite of Dublin's department stores. It stocks virtually everything, from garden furniture to high fashion, and it's all relatively affordable.

Eason's BOOKS
(Map p88; ☎01-873 3811; www.easons.ie; 40 Lower O'Connell St; ⏲10am-6pm Mon-Wed, Fri & Sat, to 7pm Thu, noon-6pm Sun; 🚌all city centre) The biggest selection of magazines and foreign newspapers in the whole country can be found on the ground floor of this huge bookshop near the GPO, along with literally dozens of browsers leafing through mags with ne'er a thought of purchasing one.

Information

DANGERS & ANNOYANCES

Dublin is a safe city by almost any standard. Basically, act as you would at home. However, certain parts of the city are pretty dodgy due to the presence of drug addicts and other questionable types, including north and northeast of Gardiner St and along parts of Dorset St, on the north side, and west along Thomas St, on the south side.

EMERGENCY

Drugs Advisory & Treatment Centre
(☎01-677 1122; www.addictionireland.ie; Trinity Ct, 30-31 Pearse St; ⏲24hr; 🚌all city centre)

Police, Fire & Ambulance (999)

Rape Crisis Centre (1800 778 888, 01-661 4911; www.drcc.ie; 70 Lower Leeson St; 24hr; all city centre)

INTERNET ACCESS

Wi-fi and 3G/4G networks are making internet cafes largely redundant (except to gamers); the few that are left will charge around €5 per hour. Most accommodation has wi-fi service, either free or for a daily charge (up to €10 per day). The most central option is the 1st-floor **Central Internet Café** (01-677 8298; 6 Grafton St; 20min €1.50; 9am-10pm Mon-Sat, 10am-8pm Sun; all city centre).

MEDICAL SERVICES

Should you experience an immediate health problem, contact the A&E (accident and emergency) department of the nearest public hospital; in an emergency, call an ambulance (999). There are no 24-hour pharmacies in Dublin; the latest any stay open is 10pm.

Baggot Street Hospital (01-668 1577; 18 Upper Baggot St; 7.30am-4.30pm Mon-Fri; 5, 7, 7A, 8, 18, 27X or 44 from city centre) South-side city centre.

Caredoc (1850 334 999; www.caredoc.ie; 24hr) Doctors on call; available only out of regular surgery hours.

City Pharmacy (01-670 4523; 14 Dame St; 9am-10pm; all city centre)

Dental Hospital (01-612 7200; 20 Lincoln Pl; 9am-5pm Mon-Fri; 7 & 44 from city centre) If you don't have an appointment, head in after noon.

Grafton Medical Centre (01-671 2122; www.graftonmedical.ie; 34 Grafton St; 8.30am-6pm Mon-Fri, 11am-2pm Sat; all city centre) One-stop shop with male and female doctors and physiotherapists.

Health Service Executive (01-679 0700, 1800 520 520; www.hse.ie; Dr Steevens' Hospital, Steeven's Lane; 9.30am-5.30pm Mon-Fri) Central health authority with Choice of Doctor Scheme, which can advise you on a suitable GP from 9am to 5pm Monday to Friday. Also has information services for those with physical and mental disabilities.

Mater Misericordiae Hospital (01-830 1122; Eccles St) North-side city centre, off Lower Dorset St.

O'Connell's Pharmacy Branches at Grafton St (01-679 0467; 21 Grafton St; 9am-10pm) and Upper O'Connell St (01-873 0427; 55-56 Upper O'Connell St; 9am-10pm)

St James's Hospital (01-410 3000; www.stjames.ie; James's St; St James) Dublin's main 24-hour accident and emergency department.

MONEY

You'll get the best exchange rates at banks, although bureaux de change and other exchange facilities are usually open longer hours. There are currency-exchange counters at Dublin airport in the baggage-collection area, and on the arrival and departure floors; they're open 5.30am to 11pm. There's a cluster of banks located around College Green, opposite Trinity College – all have exchange facilities.

POST

The most convenient post offices in the city centre are the General Post Office (p90) on the north side and **An Post** (Map p106; 01-705 8206; www.anpost.ie; St Andrew's St; 8.30am-5pm Mon-Fri; all city centre) on the south side.

TOURIST INFORMATION

You'll find everything you need to kick-start your visit at the **Dublin Discover Ireland Centre** (Map p106; www.visitdublin.com; 25 Suffolk St; 9am-5.30pm Mon-Sat, 10.30am-3pm Sun; all city centre). Besides general visitor information on Dublin and Ireland, it also has a free accommodation-booking service, a concert-booking agent, local and national bus information, rail information, and tour information and bookings. There are also branches at Dublin Airport and **O'Connell St** (Map p88; 14 Upper O'Connell St; 9am-5pm Mon-Sat; all city centre).

USEFUL WEBSITES

Dublin City Council (www.dublincity.ie)
Dublin Tourism (www.visitdublin.com)
Entertainment.ie (www.entertainment.ie)
Lovin Dublin (www.lovindublin.com)
Totally Dublin (www.totallydublin.ie)

Getting There & Away

AIR

Dublin Airport (01-814 1111; www.dublinairport.com), 13km north of the centre, is Ireland's major international gateway airport. It has two terminals: most international flights (including all US flights) use the newer Terminal 2; Ryanair and select others use Terminal 1. Both terminals have the usual selection of pubs, restaurants, shops, ATMs and car-hire desks.

BOAT

Dublin has two ferry ports: the **Dun Laoghaire ferry terminal** (01-280 1905; Dun Laoghaire; 7, 7A or 8 from Burgh Quay, 46A from Trinity College, Dun Laoghaire), 13km east of the city, serves Holyhead in Wales; and the **Dublin Port terminal** (01-855 2222; Alexandra Rd), 3km northeast of the city centre, serves Holyhead and Liverpool.

For Dublin Port terminal, buses from Busáras are timed to coincide with arrivals and departures: for the 9.45am ferry departure from Dublin Port, buses leave Busáras at 8.30am. For the 9.45pm departure, buses depart from Busáras at 8.30pm. For the 1am sailing to Liverpool, the bus departs from Busáras at 11.45pm. All bus trips cost adult/child €3/1.50.

BUS

Busáras (Map p88; ☎ 01-836 6111; www.buseireann.ie; Store St; Ⓡ Connolly), the main bus station, is just north of the river behind Custom House. It serves as the main city stop for **Bus Éireann** (www.buseireann.ie), which has a countrywide network.

CAR & MOTORCYCLE

The main rental agencies also have offices at the airport.

Avis Rent-a-Car (☎ 01-605 7500; www.avis.ie; 35 Old Kilmainham Rd; 🚌 23, 25, 25A, 26, 68 or 69 from city centre)

Budget Rent-a-Car (☎ 01-837 9611; www.budget.ie; 151 Lower Drumcondra Rd; 🚌 41 from O'Connell St)

Europcar (☎ 01-648 5900; www.europcar.com; 1 Mark St; 🚌 all city centre)

Hertz Rent-a-Car (☎ 01-709 3060; www.hertz.com; 151 South Circular Rd; 🚌 9, 16, 77 & 79 from city centre)

Thrifty (☎ 01-844 1944; www.thrifty.ie; 26 Lombard St E; 🚌 all city centre)

TRAIN

Dublin has two main train stations: **Heuston Station** (☎ 01-836 5421; 🚊 Heuston Station), on the western side of town near the Liffey, which serves the southern half of the country; and **Connolly Station** (☎ 01-836 3333; 🚊 Connolly Station, Ⓡ Connolly Station), a short walk northeast of Busáras, behind the Custom House, which covers the west and north.

> **DUBLIN BY BIKE**
>
> One of the most popular ways to get around the city is with the blue bikes of **Dublinbikes** (www.dublinbikes.ie), a pay-as-you-go service similar to the Parisian Vélib system. Cyclists purchase a €10 smartcard (and pay a credit-card deposit of €150) – either online or at any of the 40 stations throughout the city centre – before 'freeing' a bike for use. Use of the bicycle is free of charge for the first 30 minutes, and €0.50 for each half-hour thereafter.

Getting Around

TO/FROM THE AIRPORT

There is no train service to/from the airport, but there are bus and taxi options.

Bus

Aircoach (www.aircoach.ie) Private coach service with two routes from the airport to 18 destinations throughout the city, including the main streets of the city centre. Coaches run every 10 to 15 minutes between 6am and midnight, then hourly from midnight until 6am.

Airlink Express Coach (☎ 01-873 4222; www.dublinbus.ie; one way/return €6/3) Bus 747 runs every 10 to 20 minutes from 5.45am to 11.30pm between the airport, the central bus station (Busáras) and the Dublin Bus office on Upper O'Connell St. Bus 748 runs every 15 to 30 minutes from 6.50am to 10.05pm between the airport, and Heuston and Connolly train stations.

Dublin Bus A number of buses serve the airport from various points in Dublin, including buses 16A (Rathfarnham), 746 (Dun Laoghaire) and 230 (Portmarnock); all cross the city centre on their way to the airport.

Taxi

There is a taxi rank directly outside the arrivals concourse. A taxi should cost about €25 from the airport to the city centre, including a supplementary charge of €2.50 (not applied when going to the airport). Make sure the meter is switched on.

BICYCLE

Despite the intermittent presence of rust-red cycle lanes throughout the city centre, getting around by bike can be something of an obstacle course as cyclists have to share roads with buses and indifferent motorists. Bike theft is a major problem, so be sure to park on busier streets, preferably at one of the myriad U-shaped parking bars, and lock your bike securely. Never leave your bike on the street overnight or it may just be gone in the morning. **Dublin City Cycling** (www.cycledublin.ie) is an excellent online resource.

Bikes are only allowed on suburban trains (not the DART), either stowed in the guard's van or in a special compartment at the opposite end of the train from the engine. There's a flat €5 charge for transporting a bicycle up to 56km. Bicycle helmets are not compulsory.

CAR & MOTORCYCLE

Traffic in Dublin is a nightmare and parking an expensive headache. There are no free spots to park anywhere in the city centre during business hours (7am to 7pm Monday to Saturday), but there are plenty of parking meters, 'pay & display' spots (€3 to €6 per hour) and over a dozen sheltered and supervised car parks (around €5 per hour).

Clamping of illegally parked cars is thoroughly enforced, and there is an €80 charge for removal. Parking is free after 7pm Monday to Saturday, and all day Sunday, in most metered spots and on single yellow lines.

Car theft and break-ins are a problem, and the police advise visitors to park in a supervised car park. Cars with foreign number plates are prime targets; never leave your valuables behind. When you're booking accommodation, check on parking facilities.

The **Automobile Association of Ireland** (AA; ☎01-617 9999, breakdown 1800 667 788; www.aaireland.ie; 56 Drury St; all city centre) is located in the city centre.

PUBLIC TRANSPORT

Bus

The office of **Dublin Bus** (Map p88; ☎01-873 4222; www.dublinbus.ie; 59 Upper O'Connell St; 9am-5.30pm Mon-Fri, to 2pm Sat; all city centre) has free single-route timetables of all its services.

Buses run from around 6am (some start at 5.30am) to 11.30pm. Fares are calculated according to stages:

- one to three stages: €1.95
- four to seven stages: €2.55
- eight to 13 stages: €2.80
- over 13 stages: €3.30

If you're travelling within the designated bus corridor zone (roughly between Parnell Sq to the north and St Stephen's Green to the south) you can use the €0.75 special City Centre fare. You must tender exact change when boarding; anything more and you will be given a receipt for reimbursement, only possible at the Dublin Bus main office. Avoid this by getting a **Leap Card** (www.leapcard.ie), a plastic smartcard available in most newsagents. Once you register it online, you can top it up with whatever amount you need. When you board a bus, Luas or suburban train, just swipe your card and the fare – usually 20% less than a cash fare – is automatically deducted.

Luas

The **Luas light-rail system** (www.luas.ie) has two lines: the green line (running every five to 15 minutes) connects St Stephen's Green with Sandyford in south Dublin via Ranelagh and Dundrum; the red line (every 20 minutes) runs from Lower Abbey St to Tallaght via the north quays and Heuston Station. There are ticket machines at every stop or you can buy a ticket from newsagents in the city centre; a typical short-hop fare (around four stops) is €2.30. Services run from 5.30am to 12.30am Monday to Friday, from 6.30am to 12.30am Saturday and from 7am to 11.30pm Sunday. You can also use a Leap Card.

FARE-SAVER PASSES

A range of fare-saver passes are available.

10 Journey Travel 90 (adult €29.50) Valid for 10 90-minute journeys on all Dublin Bus and Airlink services, except Nitelink.

Freedom Ticket (adult/child €30/14) Three-day unlimited travel on all bus services, including Airlink and Dublin Bus hop-on, hop-off tours.

Rambler Pass (five/30 days €29.50/132) Valid for unlimited travel on all Dublin Bus and Airlink services, except Nitelink.

Nitelink

Nitelink late-night buses run from the College, Westmoreland and D'Olier Sts triangle. On Fridays and Saturdays, departures are at 12.30am, then every 20 minutes until 4.30am on the more popular routes, and until 3.30am on the less frequented ones; there are no services Sunday to Thursday. Fares are €6.50. See www.dublinbus.ie for route details.

Train

The **Dublin Area Rapid Transport** (DART; ☎01-836 6222; www.irishrail.ie) provides quick train access to the coast as far north as Howth (about 30 minutes) and as far south as Greystones in County Wicklow. Pearse Station is convenient for central Dublin south of the Liffey, and Connolly Station for north of the Liffey. There are services every 10 to 20 minutes, sometimes even more frequently, from around 6.30am to midnight Monday to Saturday; services are less frequent on Sunday. Dublin to Dun Laoghaire takes about 15 to 20 minutes. A one-way DART ticket from Dublin to Dun Laoghaire or Howth costs €3.15; to Bray it's €3.70.

There are also suburban rail services north as far as Dundalk, inland to Mullingar and south past Bray to Arklow.

Taxi

All taxi fares begin with a flag-fall fare of €3.60 (€4 from 8pm to 8am), followed by €1.10 per km thereafter from 8am to 10pm (€1.40 per km from 8pm to 8am). In addition to these there are a number of extra charges – €1 for each extra passenger and €2 for telephone bookings. There is no charge for luggage.

Taxis can be hailed on the street and found at taxi ranks around the city, including on the corner of **Abbey and O'Connell Sts** (Map p88); **College Green** (Map p106), in front of Trinity

College; and St Stephen's Green at the end of Grafton St. There are numerous taxi companies that will dispatch taxis by radio. Some options:

City Cabs (☎01-872 2688)

National Radio Cabs (☎01-677 2222; www.radiocabs.ie)

Phone the **Garda Carriage Office** (☎01-475 5888) if you have any complaints about taxis or queries regarding lost property.

Uber & Hailo

Although Uber is available in Dublin, it's not nearly as effective as **Hailo** (www.hailoapp.com), which works virtually the same as Uber but is largely supported by the taxi industry (many members of which have signed up to the service).

AROUND DUBLIN

Without even the smallest hint of irony, Dubliners will tell you that one of the city's best features is how easy it is to get out of – and they do, whenever they can. But they don't go especially far: for many the destination is one of the small seaside villages that surround the capital. To the north are the lovely villages of Howth and Malahide – slowly and reluctantly being sucked into the Dublin conglomeration – while to the south is Dalkey, which has long since given up the fight but still manages to retain that village vibe.

Howth

Tidily positioned at the foot of a bulbous peninsula, the pretty port village of Howth (the name rhymes with 'both') is a major fishing centre, yachting harbour and one of the most sought-after addresses in town, with the best properties discreetly spread atop the gorse-rich hill that dominates the peninsula – spectacular views of Dublin Bay are standard. Dubliners who can't afford to live here make do with a weekend excursion – there are beautiful walks around Howth Head and a popular farmers market at the seafront.

Sights

Howth Castle CASTLE

Most of the town backs onto the extensive grounds of Howth Castle, built in 1564 but much changed over the years, most recently in 1910 when Sir Edwin Lutyens gave it a modernist makeover. Today the castle is divided into four very posh and private residences, although the grounds are open to the public). The **castle gardens** (⏲24hr) FREE are worth visiting, as they're noted for their rhododendrons (which bloom in May and June), azaleas and a long, 10m-high beech hedge planted in 1710.

The original estate was acquired in 1177 by the Norman noble Sir Almeric Tristram,

WORTH A TRIP

SANDYCOVE & THE JAMES JOYCE MUSEUM

About 1km north of Dalkey is Sandycove, with a pretty little beach and a Martello tower – built by British forces as a lookout for signs of a Napoleonic invasion – now home to the James Joyce Museum. To get here, take the DART to Sandycove.

James Joyce Tower & Museum (☎01-280 9265; www.joycetower.ie; Joyce Tower, Sandycove; ⏲10am-6pm Apr-Sep, to 4pm Oct-Mar) This tower is where the action begins in Joyce's epic novel *Ulysses*. The museum was opened in 1962 by Sylvia Beach, the Paris-based publisher who first dared to put *Ulysses* into print, and has photographs, letters, documents, various editions of Joyce's work, and two death masks of Joyce on display.

Forty Foot Pool (Sandycove) Below the Martello tower is the Forty Foot Pool, an open-air, sea-water bathing pool that took its name from the army regiment, the Fortieth Foot, that was stationed at the tower until the regiment was disbanded in 1904. At the close of the first chapter of *Ulysses*, Buck Mulligan heads off to the Forty Foot Pool for a morning swim. A morning wake-up here is still a local tradition, in summer and winter: the Christmas Day Dip is one of Dublin's most enduring traditions.

Pressure from female bathers eventually opened this public stretch of water – originally nudist and for men only – to both sexes, despite strong opposition from the 'forty foot gentlemen'. They eventually compromised with the ruling that a 'Togs Must Be Worn' sign would apply after 9am. Prior to that time nudity prevails and swimmers are still predominantly male.

WORTH A TRIP

IRELAND'S EYE

A short distance offshore from Howth is **Ireland's Eye** (01-831 4200), a rocky seabird sanctuary with the ruins of a 6th-century monastery. There's a Martello tower at the northwestern end of the island, where boats from Howth land, while a spectacularly sheer rock face plummets into the sea at the eastern end. As well as the seabirds overhead, you can see young birds on the ground during the nesting season. Seals can also be spotted around the island.

Doyle & Sons (01-831 4200; www.howth-boats.com; return €14) takes boats out to the island from the East Pier of Howth Harbour during the summer, usually on weekend afternoons. Don't wear shorts if you're planning to visit the monastery ruins because they're surrounded by a thicket of stinging nettles. And bring your rubbish back with you – far too many island visitors don't.

Further north from Ireland's Eye is **Lambay Island**, an important seabird sanctuary that cannot be visited.

who changed his surname to St Lawrence after winning a battle at the behest (or so he believed) of his favourite saint. The family has owned the land ever since, though the unbroken chain of male succession came to an end in 1909.

On the grounds are the ruins of the 16th-century Corr Castle and an ancient dolmen (tomb chamber or portal tomb made of vertical stones topped by a huge capstone) known as Aideen's Grave. Legend has it that Aideen died of a broken heart after her husband was killed at the Battle of Gavra near Tara in AD 184, but the legend is rubbish because the dolmen is at least 300 years older than that.

Also within the grounds are the ruins of **St Mary's Abbey** (Abbey St) FREE, originally founded in 1042 by the Viking King Sitric, who also founded the original church on the site of Christ Church Cathedral. The abbey was amalgamated with the monastery on Ireland's Eye in 1235. Some parts of the ruins date from that time, but most are from the 15th and 16th centuries. The tomb of Christopher St Lawrence (Lord Howth), in the southeastern corner, dates from around 1470. See the caretaker or read the instructions on the gate for opening times.

Howth Summit VIEWPOINT

Howth Summit (171m) has excellent views across Dublin Bay right down to County Wicklow. From the top of Howth hill you can walk to the top of the Ben of Howth, a headland, which has a cairn said to mark a 2000-year-old Celtic **royal grave**. The 1814 **Baily Lighthouse**, at the southeastern corner, is on the site of an old stone fort and can be reached by a dramatic clifftop **walk**.

Eating

Howth Market MARKET €

(01-839 4141; www.howthmarket.ie; 3 Harbour Rd, Howth Harbour; 9am-6pm Sat, Sun & bank holidays) One of the best in greater Dublin, this is the place to come not only for fresh fish (obviously) but also for organic meat and veg, and homemade everything else, including jams, cakes and breads. A great option for Sunday lunch.

House IRISH €€

(01-839 6388; www.thehouse-howth.ie; 4 Main St; mains €17-23; 8.45am-4pm Mon, to 9.30pm Tue-Fri, 10am-10pm Sat & Sun) Wonderful spot on the main street leading away from the harbour where you can feast on dishes such as crunchy Bellingham blue-cheese polenta or wild Wicklow venison stew, as well as a fine selection of fish.

Oar House SEAFOOD €€

(01-839 4562; www.oarhouse.ie; 8 West Pier; mains €16-24; 12.30-10pm) A feast-o-fish is what the menu is all about at this restaurant – particularly the locally caught variety. Par for the course in a fishing village, but this place stands out both for the way the fish is prepared and because you can get everything on the menu in smaller, tapas-style portions as well as mains.

Getting There & Away

The easiest and quickest way to get to Howth from Dublin is on the DART, which whisks you there in just over 20 minutes for a fare of €2.50. For the same fare, buses 32 and 32A, from Lower Abbey St in Dublin city centre, run as far as the Howth Summit, 5km to the southeast of Howth.

Counties Wicklow & Kildare

Includes ➡

Best Places to Eat

➡ Ballyknocken House (p149)

➡ Strawberry Tree (p151)

➡ Tinakilly Country House & Restaurant (p148)

➡ Grangecon Café (p148)

➡ Byrne & Woods (p140)

Best Places to Stay

➡ Brook Lodge & Wells Spa (p151)

➡ Hunter's Hotel (p149)

➡ Powerscourt Hotel & Spa (p139)

➡ Martinstown House (p156)

Why Go?

Wicklow and Kildare may be neighbours and have a boundary with Dublin in common, but that's where the similarities end.

Immediately south of the capital is wild, scenic Wicklow. Its most dramatic natural feature is a gorse-and-bracken mountain spine that is the east coast's most stunning landscape, complete with deep glacial valleys, isolated mountain passes and, dotted throughout, some important historic treasures, including one of Ireland's most important early-Christian sites and a couple of 18th-century Palladian estate houses.

To the west is flat, fecund Kildare, which also has a handful of elegant Palladian piles but is best known as horse country – of the thoroughbred kind. Some of the world's most lucrative stud farms are here, many with links to the horse-breeding centre of Kentucky in the US. Kildare is also home to some of the best golf courses in Ireland and, in recent years, the country's largest outlet mall.

When to Go

➡ Summer – June to September – is the best time to visit Wicklow, especially if you're going to walk the Wicklow Way or do a little green-thumb exploring.

➡ Running from Easter to late August is the Wicklow Gardens Festival.

➡ The Irish Derby – the most prestigious flat race in the Irish racing calendar – is held in June at the Curragh in County Kildare; meets continue right up to October.

COUNTY WICKLOW

POP 136,000 / AREA 2027 SQ KM

Just south of Dublin, Wicklow (Cill Mhantáin) is the capital's favourite playground, a wild pleasure garden of coastline, woodland and a daunting mountain range, home to the country's most popular walking trail.

Stretching 132km from Dublin's southern suburbs to the rolling fields of County Carlow, the **Wicklow Way** leads walkers along disused military supply lines, old bog roads and nature trails. Along the way you can explore monastic ruins, handsome gardens and some magnificent 18th-century mansions.

National Parks

Wicklow Mountains National Park covers just over 200 sq km of mountainous blanket bogs and woodland. Within the boundaries of the protected area are two nature reserves, owned and managed by the Heritage Service and legally protected by the Wildlife Act 1976. The larger reserve, west of the Glendalough Visitor Centre, conserves the extensive heath and bog of the Glendalough Valley plus the Upper Lake and valley slopes on either side. The second, Glendalough Wood Nature Reserve, conserves oak woods stretching from the Upper Lake as far as the Rathdrum road to the east.

Most of Ireland's native mammal species can be found within the confines of the park. Large herds of deer roam on the open hill areas, though these were introduced in the 20th century as the native red-deer population became extinct during the first half of the 18th century. The uplands are the preserve of foxes, badgers and hares. Red squirrels are usually found in the pine woodlands - look out for them around the Upper Lake.

The bird population of the park is plentiful. Birds of prey abound, the most common being peregrine falcons, merlins, kestrels, hawks and sparrowhawks. Hen harriers are a rarer sight, though they too live in the park. Moorland birds found in the area include meadow pipits and skylarks. Less common birds such as whinchats, ring ouzels and dippers can be spotted, as can red grouse, whose numbers are quickly disappearing in other parts of Ireland.

Information

For information about Wicklow Mountains National Park, call in at or contact the **National Park Information Office** (☎0404-45425; www.wicklowmountainsnationalpark.ie; Miners' Rd, Bolger's Cottage, Upper Lake, Glendalough; ⏲10am-5.30pm May-Sep, to dusk Sat & Sun Oct-Apr), off the Green Rd that runs by the Upper Lake, about 2km from the Glendalough Visitor Centre. There's usually someone on hand to help; if you find it closed the staff may be out running guided walks. *Exploring the Glendalough Valley* (Heritage Service; €2) is a good booklet on the trails in the area.

Getting There & Away

Wicklow is relatively easy to get around.

CAR

The main routes are the N11 (M11), which runs north–south through the county from Dublin to Wexford, and the N81, which runs down the western spine of the Wicklow Mountains through Blessington into County Carlow.

BUS

St Kevin's Bus runs twice daily from Dublin and Bray to Roundwood and Glendalough. Dublin Bus 65 runs regularly as far as Blessington.

TRAIN

The Dublin Area Rapid Transport (DART) suburban rail line runs southward from Dublin as far as Bray, and there are regular train and bus connections from the capital to Wicklow town and Arklow.

Wicklow Mountains

As you leave Dublin and cross into Wicklow, the landscape changes dramatically. From Killakee, still in Dublin, the Military Rd begins a 30km southward journey across vast sweeps of gorse-, bracken- and heather-clad moors, bogs and mountains dotted with small corrie lakes.

The numbers and statistics aren't all that impressive. The highest peak in the range, Lugnaquilla (924m), is really more of a very large hill, but that hardly matters here. This vast granite intrusion, a welling-up of hot igneous rock that solidified some 400 million years ago, was shaped during the Ice Ages into the schist-capped mountains visible today. The peaks are marvellously desolate and as raw as only nature can be. Between the mountains are a number of deep glacial valleys, most notably Glenmacnass, Glenmalure and Glendalough - while corrie lakes such as Lough Bray Upper and Lower, gouged by ice at the head of the glaciers, complete the wild topography.

The narrow Military Rd winds its way through the most remote parts of the mountains, offering some extraordinary views of the surrounding countryside. The best place

Counties Wicklow & Kildare Highlights

❶ Go back in time at the evocative ruins and the marvellous slopes and forests of gorgeous **Glendalough** (p140).

❷ Explore County Kildare's huge tracts of fecund land at the **Bog of Allen** (p154).

❸ Walk at least part of Ireland's most popular hiking trail, the **Wicklow Way** (p145).

❹ Examine the art and atmosphere of magnificent **Russborough House** (p147).

❺ Admire the gorgeous Italianate gardens and impressive waterfall at **Powerscourt Estate** (p138), near Enniskerry.

❻ Take the tour at Ireland's most impressive Palladian mansion, **Castletown House** (p152), near Celbridge, once owned by the country's richest man.

❼ Contemplate your spiritual health with an overnight stay in one of the **Glendalough Hermitages** (p146).

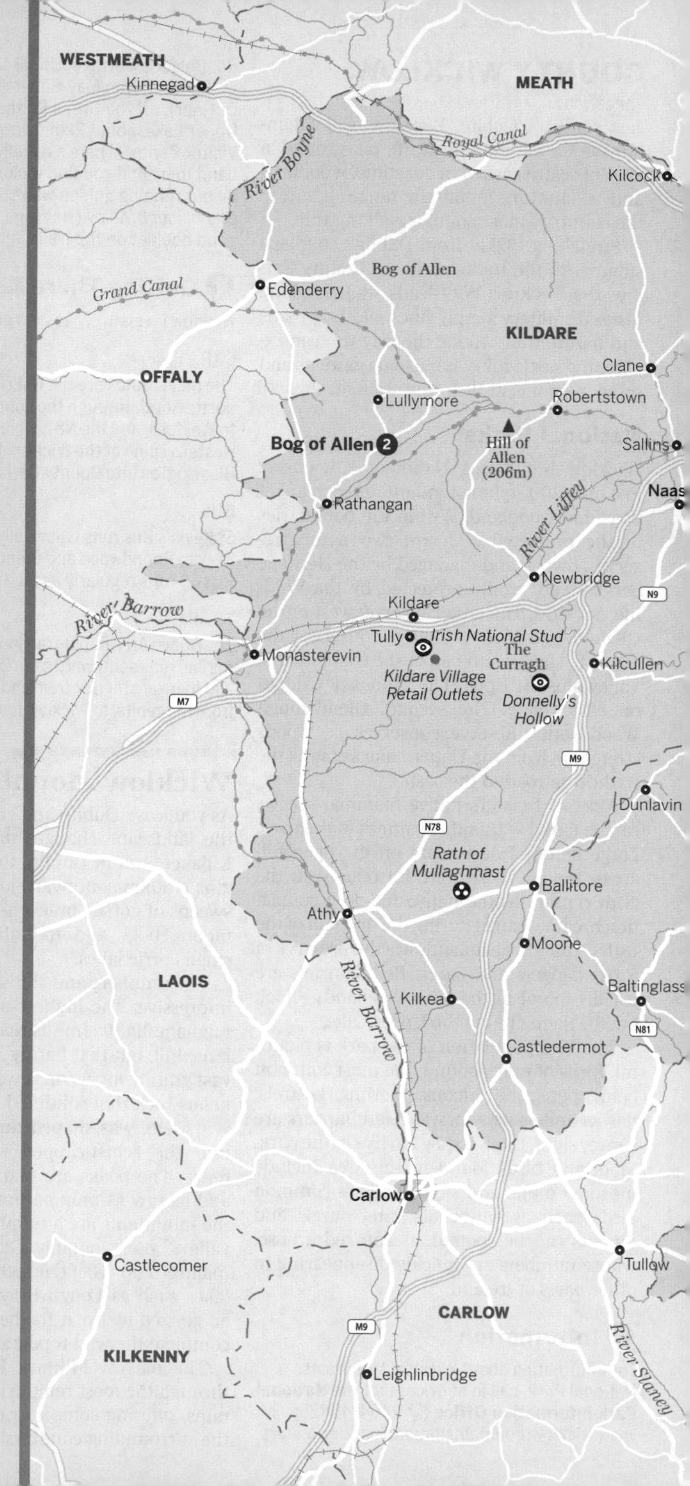

Swords
Howth
North Bull Island
Howth Peninsula
Irish Sea
Maynooth
M4
Leixlip
River Liffey
DUBLIN
Dublin Bay
6 Castletown House
Celbridge
Straffan
Dun Laoghaire
Sandycove
Dalkey
Dalkey Island
Killiney
Rathcoole
Grand Canal
M7
Kill
Loughlinstown
Glencree
R117
Kippure Mountain (752m)
Enniskerry
Bray
Bray Head
Powerscourt Estate 5
Kilbride
N81
R759
Kilmacanogue
Powerscourt Waterfall
Blessington
River Liffey
Great Sugarloaf Mountain (503m)
Greystones
Ballymore Eustace
4 Russborough House
Sally Gap
M11
Poulaphouca Reservoir
Mt Mullaghcleevaun (848m)
Military Rd
Kilpedder
Valleymount
Lough Tay
Kilcoole
River Glenmacnass
Wicklow Mountains
Sraghmore
Hollywood
Lough Dan
Roundwood
Vartry Reservoir
Mt Tonelagee (816m)
Table Mountain (700m)
Wicklow Gap
Devil's Glen
N11
Annamoe
7
Camaderry Mountain (700m)
1 Glendalough
Donard
Ashford
Lugduff (652m)
Laragh
Rathnew
Turlough Hill
Spink Mountain (550m)
Ballinclea
River Avonmore
WICKLOW
Wicklow
Knockanarrigan
Glenmalure
Wicklow Head
Mullacor (657m)
Lugnaquilla Mountain (924m)
Glenealy
River Avonbeg
Drumgoff
Glen of Imaal
Derrynamuck
Vale of Clara
Silver Strand
Rathdrum
Slieve Maan (550m)
Greenane
Ardmore Point
Rathdangan
Avondale House
R754
Aghavannagh
Carrickashane Mtn (508m)
Meeting of the Waters
Redcross
Brittas Bay
Vale of Avoca
3 Wicklow Way
River Ow
Mizen Head
Avoca
Maheramore
Aughrim
Woodenbridge
Clogga Beach
ATLANTIC OCEAN
River Avoca
Arklow
Tinahely
River Bann
N11
Shillelagh
Kilmichael Point
WEXFORD
Carnew
M11
0 10 km
0 5 miles

to join it is at Glencree (from Enniskerry). It then runs south through the Sally Gap, Glenmacnass Valley and Laragh, then on to Glenmalure Valley and Aghavannagh.

On the trip south you can divert east at the Sally Gap to look at Lough Tay and Lough Dan. Further south you pass the great waterfall at Glenmacnass before dropping down into Laragh, with the magnificent monastic ruins of Glendalough nearby. Continue south through the valley of Glenmalure and, if you're fit enough, climb Lugnaquilla.

Enniskerry & Powerscourt Estate

POP 2672

At the top of the '21 Bends', as the winding R117 from Dublin is known, the handsome village of Enniskerry is home to art galleries and the kind of all-organic gourmet cafes that would treat you as a criminal if you admitted to eating battery eggs. Such preening self-regard is a far cry from the village's origins, when Richard Wingfield, earl of nearby Powerscourt, commissioned a row of terraced cottages for his labourers in 1760. These days, you'd want to have laboured pretty successfully to get your hands on one of them.

Sights

Powerscourt Estate HOUSE, GARDENS

(www.powerscourt.ie; near Enniskerry; admission to house free, gardens adult/child €8.50/5; ⌚9.30am-5.30pm Mar-Oct, to dusk Nov-Feb) Wicklow's most visited attraction is this magnificent 64-sq-km estate, whose main entrance is 500m south of Enniskerry town. At the heart of it is a 68-room Palladian mansion, but the real draw are the formal gardens and the stunning views that accompany them. The upper floors of the house are closed, but there's a fine cafe and craft shop on the ground floor, while the grounds are home to two golf courses and the best hotel in Wicklow.

The estate has existed more or less since 1300, when the LePoer (later anglicised to Power) family built themselves a castle here. The property changed Anglo-Norman hands a few times before coming into the possession of Richard Wingfield, newly appointed Marshall of Ireland, in 1603. His descendants were to live here for the next 350 years. In 1730 the Georgian wunderkind Richard Cassels (or Castle) was given the job of building a 68-room Palladian-style mansion around the core of the old castle. He finished the job in 1741, but an extra storey was added in 1787 and other alterations were made in the 19th century.

The Wingfields left during the 1950s, after which the house had a massive restoration. Then, on the eve of its opening to the public in 1974, a fire gutted the whole building. The estate was eventually bought by the Slazenger sporting-goods family who have overseen a second restoration as well as the addition of all the amenities the estate now has to offer, including the two golf courses and the fabulous hotel, now part of Marriott's Autograph collection.

The star of the show is the 20-hectare **garden**, originally laid out in the 1740s but redesigned in the 19th century by gardener Daniel Robinson. Robinson was one of the foremost horticulturalists of his day, and his passion for growing things was matched only by his love of booze: the story goes that by a certain point in the day he was too drunk to stand and so insisted on being wheeled around the estate in a barrow.

Perhaps this influenced his largely informal style, which resulted in a magnificent blend of landscaped gardens, sweeping terraces, statuary, ornamental lakes, secret hollows, rambling walks and walled enclosures replete with more than 200 types of trees and shrubs, all beneath the stunning natural backdrop of the Great Sugarloaf Mountain to the southeast. Tickets come with a map laying out 40-minute and hour-long tours of the gardens. Don't miss the exquisite Japanese Gardens or the Pepperpot Tower, modelled on a three-inch actual pepper pot owned by Lady Wingfield. Our own favourite, however, is the animal cemetery, final resting place of the Wingfield pets and even some of the family's favourite milking cows. Some of the epitaphs are astonishingly personal.

The house itself is every bit as grand, but the ongoing renovation means there's not much to see beyond the bustle of the ground-floor Avoca cafe and craft shop. The sole exception is the **Museum of Childhood** (Tara's Palace; www.taraspalace.ie; adult/child/family €5/3/12; ⌚10am-5pm Mon-Sat, noon-5pm Sun), full of period miniature dolls and dolls'

DON'T MISS

TOP GARDENS IN WICKLOW

- Powerscourt Estate (p138)
- Mt Usher Gardens (p149)
- Kilruddery House & Gardens (p149)
- National Botanic Gardens (p150)

houses, including Tara's Palace, a 22-room house designed to one-twelfth scale and inspired by the Palladian piles of Castletown House, Leinster House and Carton House. Each of the rooms is decorated in exquisite, hand-crafted miniatures.

A 7km walk to a separate part of the estate takes you to the 130m **Powerscourt Waterfall** (adult/child €5.50/3.50; 9.30am-7pm May-Aug, 10.30am-5.30pm Mar-Apr & Sep-Oct, to 4.30pm Nov-Jan). It's the highest waterfall in the British Isles, and is most impressive after heavy rain. You can also get to the falls by road, following the signs from the estate. A nature trail has been laid out around the base of the waterfall, taking you past giant redwoods, ancient oaks, beech, birch and rowan trees. There are plenty of birds in the vicinity, including the chaffinch, cuckoo, chiffchaff, raven and willow warbler.

OFF THE BEATEN TRACK

GLENMACNASS

Desolate and utterly deserted, the Glenmacnass Valley, a stretch of wild bogland between the Sally Gap crossroads and Laragh, is one of the most beautiful parts of the mountains, although the sense of isolation is quite dramatic.

The highest mountain to the west is Mt Mullaghcleevaun (848m), and River Glenmacnass flows south and tumbles over the edge of the mountain plateau in a great foaming cascade. There's a car park near the top of the waterfall. Be careful when walking on rocks near **Glenmacnass Waterfall** as a few people have slipped to their deaths. There are fine walks up Mt Mullaghcleevaun or in the hills to the east of the car park.

Tours

All Powerscourt tours start in Dublin.

Bus Éireann BUS
(01-836 6111; www.buseireann.ie; Busáras; adult/child/student €27.50/19/25.50; 10am mid-Mar–Oct) A whole-day tour that takes in Powerscourt and Glendalough (all admissions included), departing from Busáras. Buy online for discounts.

Dublin Bus Tours BUS
(Map p106; 01-872 0000; www.dublinsightseeing.ie; adult/child €27/12; 11am) A visit to Powerscourt is included in the four-hour South Coast & Gardens tour, which takes in the stretch of coastline between Dun Laoghaire and Killiney before turning inland to Wicklow and on to Enniskerry. Admission to the gardens is included.

Activities

Powerscourt Golf Club GOLF
(www.powerscourtgolfclub.com; Powerscourt Estate, Enniskerry; green fees €75 Apr-Oct, €55 Nov-Mar) You have your choice of two stunning courses: the West Course was designed by David McLay Kidd (who also designed Bandon Dunes in Oregon) and is a shade tougher than the East Course, which is arguably the more scenic.

Sleeping & Eating

Summerhill House Hotel HOTEL €€
(01-286 7928; www.summerhillhousehotel.com; r from €75;) This truly superb country mansion about 700m south of town just off the N11 is the best place around to lay your head; on soft cotton pillows surrounded by delicate antiques and pastoral views in oils. Everything about the place – including the top-notch breakfast – is memorable.

Coolakay House B&B €€
(01-286 2423; www.coolakayhouse.ie; Waterfall Rd, Coolakay; r €70-80;) A modern working farm about 3km south of Enniskerry (signposted along the road), this is a great option for walkers along the Wicklow Way. The four bedrooms are all well-appointed and comfortable, the views are terrific and the breakfast is sensational.

★ **Powerscourt Hotel & Spa** HOTEL €€€
(01-274 8888; www.powerscourthotel.com; Powerscourt Estate, Enniskerry; r from €170) Wicklow's most luxurious hotel is this 200-room stunner on the grounds of the Powerscourt Estate. Inside this Marriott-managed property all is OTT luxury, and the decor is a thoroughly contemporary version of the estate's Georgian style. The rooms are massive. Downstairs there's a decent restaurant and a superb spa.

Kennedy's CAFE €
(Church Hill; mains €3-7; 8.30am-5pm) A lovely craft shop and cafe, this is the place to get excellent homemade soups and sandwiches – they also sell excellent bread made by the Bretzel Bakery in Dublin.

Johnnie Fox SEAFOOD €€
(01-295 5647; www.jfp.ie; Glencullen; mains €12-20; noon-10pm) Busloads of tourists fill

this place nightly throughout the summer, mostly for the knees-up, faux-Irish Hooley Show of music and dancing. But there's nothing contrived about the seafood, which is so damn good we'd happily sit through yet another chorus of 'Danny Boy' and even consider joining in the jig. The pub is 3km northwest of Enniskerry in Glencullen.

Getting There & Away

Enniskerry is 18km south of Dublin, just 3km west of the M11 along the R117. From here, getting to Powerscourt House on foot is not a problem (it's 500m from the town), but getting to the waterfall is a longer hike.

Dublin Bus (☎01-872 0000, 01-873 4222; www.dublinbus.ie) service 44 (€3.30, hourly) takes about 1¼ hours to get to Enniskerry from Hawkins St in Dublin.

Roundwood

POP 589

Roundwood's greatest boast is that it's the highest village in Ireland – hardly impressive at 238m – but it's a handy staging post for a meal and a rest for walkers on the Wicklow Way, which runs past the town 3km to the west.

Sleeping & Eating

Roundwood Caravan & Camping Park CAMPGROUND €
(☎01-281 8163; www.dublinwicklowcamping.com; campsites per adult/child €8/4; ⏲Apr-Sep;) Top-notch facilities, including a kitchen, dining area and TV lounge, make this one of the best camping grounds in all of Wicklow. It is about 500m south of the village and is served by the daily St Kevin's Bus service between Dublin and Glendalough.

Byrne & Woods MODERN IRISH €€
(☎01-281 7078; www.byrneandwoods.com; Main St; mains €16-24; ⏲noon-9.30pm Mon-Sat, to 8pm Sun) Everything that is admirable about contemporary Irish cuisine – a focus on locally sourced produce, inventive reinterpretations of classic dishes and beautiful presentation – is on hand at this superb restaurant housed in an old cottage. Excellent service and a fine collection of wines round out a most satisfying night out.

Coach House INTERNATIONAL €€
(Main St; mains around €13) A black-and-white timbered coach house, this is a terrific spot to take a load off and refuel. The fare on offer is pretty standard – burgers, salads, fish and chips and a nice steak sandwich – but everything is perfectly made and tastes delicious.

Getting There & Away

St Kevin's Bus (☎01-281 8119; www.glendaloughbus.com) passes through Roundwood on its twice-daily jaunt between Dublin and Glendalough (one way €8, 1¼ hours; return €14).

Glendalough

POP 280

If you've come to Wicklow, chances are that a visit to Glendalough (Gleann dá Loch, 'Valley of the Two Lakes') is one of your main reasons for being here. And you're not wrong, for this is one of the most beautiful corners of the whole country and the epitome of the kind of rugged, romantic Ireland that probably drew you to the island in the first place.

The substantial remains of this important monastic settlement are certainly impressive, but the real draw is the splendid setting: two dark and mysterious lakes tucked into a deep valley covered in forest. It is, despite its immense popularity, a deeply tranquil and spiritual place, and you will have little difficulty in understanding why those solitude-seeking monks came here so long ago.

History

In AD 498 a young monk named Kevin arrived in the valley looking for somewhere to kick back, meditate and be at one with nature. He pitched up in what had been a Bronze Age tomb on the southern side of the Upper Lake, and for the next seven years slept on stones, wore animal skins, maintained a near-starvation diet and – according to the legend – became bosom buddies with the birds and animals. Kevin's ecofriendly lifestyle soon attracted a bunch of disciples, all seemingly unaware of the irony that they were flocking to hang out with a hermit who wanted to live as far away from other people as possible. Over the next couple of centuries his one-man operation mushroomed into a proper settlement and by the 9th century Glendalough rivalled Clonmacnoise as the island's premier monastic city. Thousands of students studied and lived in a thriving community that was spread over a considerable area.

Inevitably, Glendalough's success made it a key target for Viking raiders, who sacked the monastery at least four times between 775 and 1071. The final blow came in 1398,

Glendalough

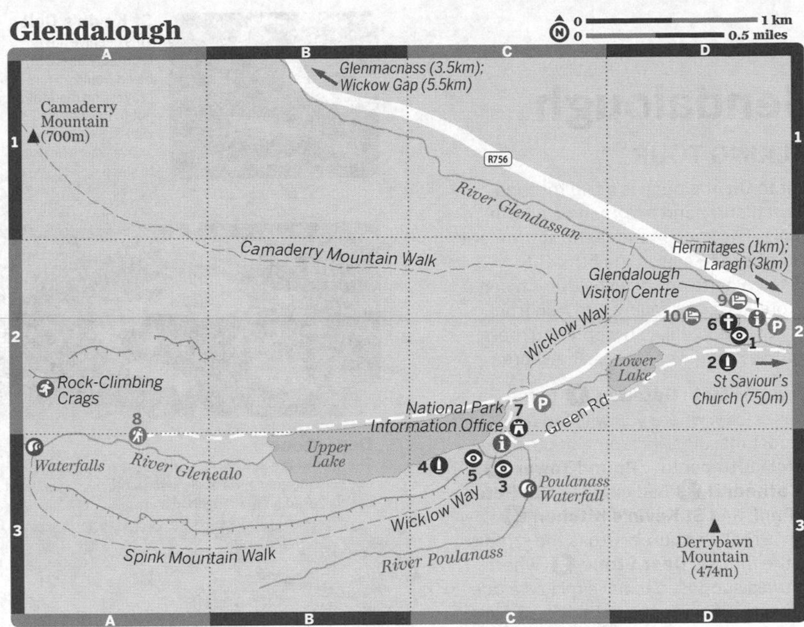

when English forces from Dublin almost destroyed it. Efforts were made to rebuild and some life lingered on here as late as the 17th century when, under renewed repression, the monastery finally died.

Sights

UPPER LAKE

Teampall na Skellig RELIGIOUS SITE

The original site of St Kevin's settlement, Teampall na Skellig, is at the base of the cliffs towering over the southern side of the Upper Lake and accessible only by boat; unfortunately, there's no boat service to the site so you'll have to settle for looking at it across the lake. The terraced shelf has the reconstructed ruins of a church and early graveyard. Rough wattle huts once stood on the raised ground nearby. Scattered around are some early grave slabs and simple stone crosses.

St Kevin's Bed MONUMENT

Just east of Teampall na Skellig, and 10m above the lake's waters, is the 2m-deep artificial cave called St Kevin's Bed, said to be where Kevin lived. The earliest human habitation of the cave was long before St Kevin's era – there's evidence that people lived in the valley for thousands of years before the monks arrived.

Glendalough

Sights

1 Cathedral of St Peter and St Paul.......D2
2 Deer Stone.......D2
Priest's House.......(see 1)
3 Reefert Church.......C3
Round Tower.......(see 1)
4 St Kevin's Bed.......C3
5 St Kevin's Cell.......C3
6 St Kevin's Kitchen.......D2
St Kieran's Church.......(see 1)
St Mary's Church.......(see 1)
7 Stone Fort.......C2
Teampall na Skellig.......(see 4)

Activities, Courses & Tours

8 Mine Workings Walk.......A3

Sleeping

9 Glendalough Hotel.......D2
10 Glendalough International Hostel.......D2

Stone Fort FORT

In the green area just south of the Upper Lake car park is a large circular wall thought to be the remains of an early Christian stone fort *(caher)*.

Reefert Church RELIGIOUS SITE

Follow the Upper Lake lakeshore path southwest of the car park until you come to

Glendalough

WALKING TOUR

A visit to Glendalough is a trip through ancient history and a refreshing hike in the hills. The ancient monastic settlement founded by St Kevin in the 5th century grew to be quite powerful by the 9th century, but it started falling into ruin from 1398 onwards. Still, you won't find more evocative clumps of stones anywhere.

Start at the **Main Gateway** ❶ to the monastic city, where you will find a cluster of important ruins, including the (nearly perfect) 10th-century **Round Tower** ❷, the **Cathedral** ❸ dedicated to **Sts Peter and Paul**, and **St Kevin's Kitchen** ❹ , which is really a church. Cross the stream past the famous **Deer Stone** ❺, where Kevin was supposed to have milked a doe, and turn west along the path. It's a 1.5km walk to the **Upper Lake** ❻. On the lake's southern shore is another cluster of sites, including the **Reefert Church** ❼ , a plain 11th-century Romanesque church where the powerful O'Toole family buried their kin, and **St Kevin's Cell** ❽, the remains of a beehive hut where Kevin is said to have lived.

ST KEVIN

St Kevin came to the valley as a young monk in AD 498, in search of a peaceful retreat. He was reportedly led by an angel to a Bronze Age tomb now known as St Kevin's Bed. For seven years he slept on stones, wore animal skins, survived on nettles and herbs and – according to legend – developed an affinity with the birds and animals. One legend has it that, when Kevin needed milk for two orphaned babies, a doe stood waiting at the Deer Stone to be milked.

Kevin soon attracted a group of disciples and the monastic settlement grew, until by the 9th century Glendalough rivalled Clonmacnoise as Ireland's premier monastic city. According to legend, Kevin lived to the age of 120. He was canonised in 1903.

FIONN DAVENPORT ©

St Kevin's Cell
This beehive hut is reputedly where St Kevin would go for prayer and meditation; not to be confused with St Kevin's Bed, a cave where he used to sleep.

FIONN DAVENPORT ©

Deer Stone
The spot where St Kevin is said to have truly become one with the animals is really just a large mortar called a *bullaun*, used for grinding food and medicine.

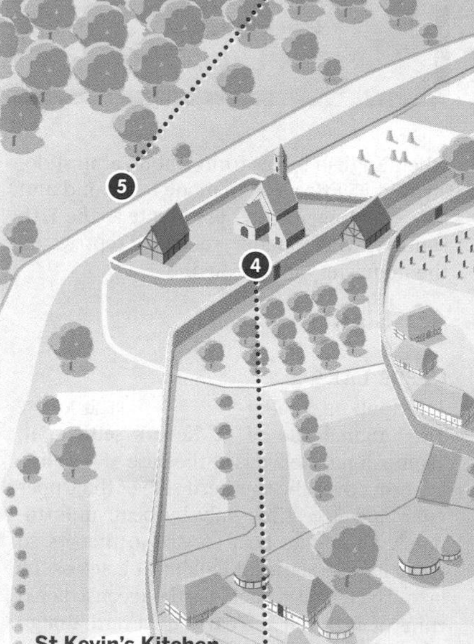

St Kevin's Kitchen
This small church is unusual in that it has a round tower sticking out of the roof – it looks like a chimney, hence the church's nickname.

FIONN DAVENPORT ©

Reefert Church

Its name derives from the Irish *righ fearta*, which means 'burial place of the kings'. Seven princes of the powerful O'Toole family are buried in this simple structure.

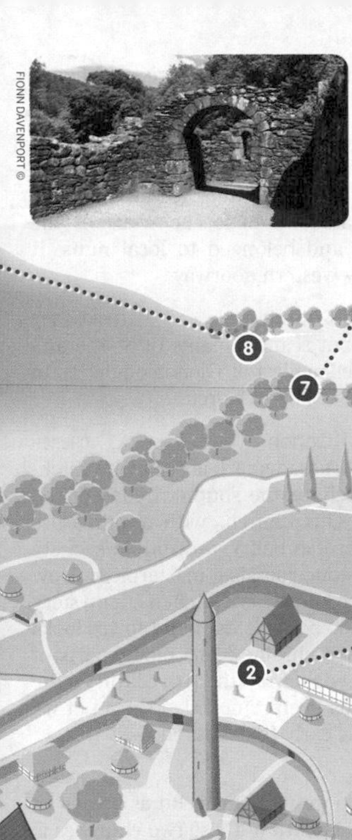

Upper Lake

The site of St Kevin's original settlement is on the banks of the Upper Lake, one of the two lakes that gives Glendalough its name – the 'Valley of the Lakes'.

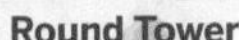

Round Tower

Glendalough's most famous landmark is the 33m-high Round Tower, which is exactly as it was when it was built a thousand years ago except for the roof; this was replaced in 1876 after a lightning strike.

INFORMATION

At the eastern end of the Upper Lake is the National Park Information Point, which has leaflets and maps on the site, local walks, etc. The grassy spot in front of the office is a popular picnic spot in summer.

Cathedral of Sts Peter & Paul

The largest of Glendalough's seven churches, the cathedral was built gradually between the 10th and 13th centuries. The earliest part is the nave, where you can still see the *antae* (slightly projecting column at the end of the wall) used for supporting a wooden roof.

Main Gateway

The only surviving entrance to the ecclesiastical settlement is a double-arch; notice that the inner arch rises higher than the outer one in order to compensate for the upward slope of the causeway.

the considerable remains of Reefert Church above the tiny River Poulanass. It's a small, plain, 11th-century Romanesque nave-and-chancel church with some reassembled arches and walls. Traditionally, Reefert (literally 'Royal Burial Place') was the burial site of the chiefs of the local O'Toole family. The surrounding graveyard contains a number of rough stone crosses and slabs, most made of shiny mica schist.

St Kevin's Cell RELIGIOUS SITE

Climb the steps at the back of the Reefert Churchyard and follow the path to the west and you'll find, at the top of a rise overlooking the lake, the scant remains of St Kevin's Cell, a small beehive hut.

LOWER LAKE

While the Upper Lake has the best scenery, the most fascinating buildings lie in the lower part of the valley east of the Lower Lake, huddled together in the heart of the ancient monastic site.

The road heading away to the east leads to **St Saviour's Church**, with its detailed Romanesque carvings. To the west, a nice woodland trail leads up the valley past the Lower Lake to the Upper Lake.

Monastery Gatehouse GATE

Just round the bend from the Glendalough Hotel is the stone arch of the monastery gatehouse, the only surviving example of a monastic entranceway in the country. Just inside the entrance is a large slab with an incised cross.

Round Tower TOWER

The graveyard, which is still in use, lies beyond the monastery gatehouse. The 10th-century Round Tower here is 33m tall and 16m in circumference at the base. The upper storeys and conical roof were reconstructed in 1876.

Cathedral of St Peter & St Paul RELIGIOUS SITE

The Cathedral of St Peter and St Paul, just southeast of the Round Tower, has a 10th-century nave; the chancel and sacristy date from the 12th century.

Priest's House ARCHITECTURE

At the centre of Glendalough's graveyard, to the south of the Round Tower, is the Priest's House. This odd building dates from 1170 but has been heavily reconstructed. It may have been the location of shrines of St Kevin. Later, during penal times, it became a burial site for local priests – hence the name.

St Mary's Church RELIGIOUS SITE

The 10th-century St Mary's Church, 140m southwest of the Round Tower, probably originally stood outside the walls of the monastery and belonged to local nuns. It has a lovely western doorway.

St Kieran's Church RELIGIOUS SITE

There are but scant remains of St Kieran's Church, the smallest at Glendalough. It's to the east of St Mary's Church.

St Kevin's Kitchen CHURCH

Glendalough's trademark is St Kevin's Kitchen or Church, at the southern edge of the enclosure. This church, with a miniature round-tower-like belfry, protruding sacristy and steep stone roof, is a masterpiece. How it came to be known as a kitchen is a mystery but it may be because its round tower looks like a kitchen chimney. The oldest parts of the building date from the 11th century – the structure has been remodelled since but it's still a classic early Irish church.

Deer Stone MONUMENT

At the junction with Green Rd as you cross the river just south of these two churches is the Deer Stone, in the middle of a group of rocks. Legend claims that, when St Kevin needed milk for two orphaned babies, a doe stood here waiting to be milked. The stone is actually a *bullaun* (a stone used as a mortar for grinding medicines or food).

Many such stones are thought to be prehistoric, and they were widely regarded as having supernatural properties: women who bathed their faces with water from the hollow were supposed to keep their looks forever. The early churchmen brought the stones into their monasteries, perhaps hoping to inherit some of their powers.

Activities

The Glendalough Valley is all about **walking** and clambering. There are nine marked ways in the valley, the longest of which is about 10km, or about four hours' walking. Before you set off, drop by the National Park Information Office (p135) and pick up the relevant leaflet and trail map (all around €1) and, if you're solo, arrange for walking partners. The information office also has a number of excellent guides for sale – you won't go far wrong with Joss Lynam's *Easy Walks Near Dublin* (€9.99) or Helen Fairbairn's *Dublin & Wicklow: A Walking Guide* (€14.99). A word of warning: don't be fooled by the relative gentleness of the surrounding countryside or the fact that the Wicklow Mountains are really no taller than big hills. The weather can be merciless here, so be sure to take the usual precautions, have the right equipment and tell someone where you're going and when you should be back. For Mountain Rescue call ☎999.

The easiest and most popular walk is the gentle hike along the northern shore of the Upper Lake to the lead and zinc **mine workings**, which date from 1800. The better route is along the lakeshore rather than on the road (which runs 30m in from the shore), a distance of about 2.5km one way from the

WALK: THE WICKLOW WAY – GLENDALOUGH TO AUGHRIM

The Wicklow Way (www.wicklowway.com) is one of Ireland's most popular long-distance walks because of its remarkable scenery and its relatively fluid and accessible starting and finishing points – there are plenty of half- and full-day options along the way.

This section is 40km long and takes you through some of the more remote parts of the Wicklow Mountains and down into the southeastern foothills. There's relatively little road walking; the greater part of the day is through conifer plantations. The walk should take between 7½ and eight hours, with an ascent of 1035m.

From the **National Park Information Office** (p135) on the southern side of the Upper Lake, turn left and ascend beside Lugduff Brook and **Poulanass Waterfall**. Veer left when you meet a forest track, then left again at a junction and cross two bridges. The Way leads northeast for about 600m then, from a tight right bend, heads almost directly southwards (via a series of clearly marked junctions), up through the conifer plantations, across Lugduff Brook again and beside a tributary, to open ground on the saddle between **Mullacor** (657m) and **Lugduff** (652m; 1¾ hours from Glendalough). From here on a good day, massive Lugnaquilla sprawls across the view to the southwest; in the opposite direction is Camaderry's long ridge above Glendalough, framed against the bulk of Tonelagee. Follow the raised boardwalk down, contour above a plantation and drop into it where a steep muddy and rocky path descends to a forest road; turn left.

If you're planning to stay at **Glenmalure Hostel** (p147), rather than go all the way to the crossroads in Glenmalure, follow the Way from the left turn for about 1km southwards. At an oblique junction where the Way turns southeast, bear left in a westerly direction and descend steeply to the road in Glenmalure. The hostel is about 2km northwest.

To continue straight on along the Way from the left turn, follow forest roads south then southeast for 1.6km to a wide zigzag above open ground, then contour the steep slope, swing northeast and drop down to a minor road beside two bridges. Continue down to an intersection and Glenmalure; it's about 1¼ hours from the saddle.

The Way presses straight on (south) through the crossroads for 500m, across the River Avonbeg and past silent **Drumgoff Barracks**, built in 1803 but long since derelict, then right along a forest track. Keep left past a ruined cottage and start to gain height in two fairly long reaches; go through two left turns then it's down and across a stream. About 800m further on, turn right along a path to start the long ascent almost to the top of **Slieve Maan** (550m) via four track junctions, maintaining a southwesterly to south-southwesterly direction. Back on a forest track, the Way turns left (southeast) close to unforested ground to the west. With a few more convoluted turns, you're out of the trees and on a path between the plantation and the road (mapped as the Military Rd). The Way eventually meets the latter beside a small tributary of the River Aghavannagh (two hours from Glenmalure).

Walk down the road for about 250m, then turn off left along a forest track, shortly bearing left to gain height steadily on a wide path over **Carrickashane Mountain** (508m). Descend steeply to a wide forest road and continue down for about 1km. Bear right to reach a minor road and turn right. Leave the road 500m further on and drop down to another road – Iron Bridge is just to the right (an hour from Military Rd).

Walk 150m up to a road and turn left; follow this road down the valley of the River Ow for 7.5km to a junction – Aughrim is to the left, another 500m. Buses along the Dublin to Wexford line stop here.

Glendalough Visitor Centre. Continue on up the head of the valley if you wish.

Alternatively, you can walk up the **Spink** (from the Irish for 'pointed hill'; 380m), the steep ridge with vertical cliffs running along the southern flanks of the Upper Lake. You can go part of the way and turn back, or complete a circuit of the Upper Lake by following the top of the cliff, eventually coming down by the mine workings and going back along the northern shore. The circuit is about 6km long and takes about three hours.

The third option is a hike up **Camaderry Mountain** (700m), hidden behind the hills that flank the northern side of the valley. The walk starts on the road just 50m back towards Glendalough from the entrance to the Upper Lake car park. Head straight up the steep hill to the north and you come out on open mountains with sweeping views in all directions. You can then continue up Camaderry to the northwest or just follow the ridge west looking over the Upper Lake. To the top of Camaderry and back is about 7.5km and takes about four hours.

Tours

A couple of bus tours depart Dublin if you don't want to explore Glendalough under your own steam.

Bus Éireann BUS
(01-836 6111; www.buseireann.ie; Busáras; adult/child/student €27.55/19/25.65; departs 10am mid-Mar–Oct) Admission to the Glendalough Visitor Centre and a visit to Powerscourt Estate are included in this whole-day tour, which returns to Dublin at about 5.45pm. The guides are good but impersonal.

Wild Wicklow Tour BUS
(01-280 1899; www.wildwicklow.ie; adult €28, student & child €25; departs 9am) Award-winning tours of Glendalough, Avoca and the Sally Gap that never fail to generate rave reviews for atmosphere and all-round fun. The first pick-up is at the Shelbourne and then the tourist office (p129), but there are a variety of pick-up points throughout Dublin; check the point nearest you when booking. The tour returns to Dublin about 5.30pm.

Sleeping & Eating

Most B&Bs are in or around Laragh, a village 3km east of Glendalough, or on the way there from Glendalough.

Glendalough International Hostel HOSTEL €
(0404-45342; www.anoige.ie; The Lodge; dm/d €16/50; @ 🛜) Conveniently, this modern hostel is situated near Glendalough's ancient Round Tower, set within the deeply wooded glacial area that makes up the Glendalough Valley. All dorms have private bathrooms and there's a decent cafeteria on the premises.

Glendalough Hermitages COTTAGE €
(0404-45571; www.glendaloughhermitage.ie; St Kevin's Parish Church; s/d €50/80; Glendalough) Five hermitages (really just plain one- and two-bed bungalows) are rented out by St Kevin's Parish Church to anyone looking for a little spiritual R&R. Facilities are pretty basic but comfortable: there's a bathroom, a small kitchen and an open fire supplemented by a storage heater. The church is 1km east of Glendalough on the R756 to Laragh.

Visitors are welcome to join in morning and evening prayer, but the venture is not exclusively Catholic and all creeds and denominations are welcome.

Glendalough Hotel HOTEL €€
(0404-45135; www.glendaloughhotel.com; s/d from €65/120; @ 🛜 👪) There's no mistaking Glendalough's best hotel, conveniently located next door to the visitor centre. There is also no shortage of takers for its 44 fairly luxurious bedrooms.

Wicklow Heather INTERNATIONAL €€
(0404-45157; www.wicklowheather.ie; Glendalough Rd, Laragh; mains €15-28; noon-8.30pm) This is the best place for anything substantial to eat. The menu offers Wicklow lamb, wild venison, Irish beef and fresh fish (the trout is excellent) – most of it sourced locally and all of it traceable from farm to fork. Next door is **Heather House** (www.heatherhouse.ie; Glendalough Rd, Laragh; r from €70), the owners' B&B, where there are five well-appointed rooms, all with private bathroom.

Information

The **Glendalough Visitor Centre** (www.heritageireland.ie; adult/child €3/1; 9.30am-6pm mid-Mar–mid-Oct, to 5pm mid-Oct–mid-Mar) is at the valley entrance, before the Glendalough Hotel. It has a high-quality 17-minute audiovisual presentation called *Ireland of the Monasteries*, which does exactly what it says on the tin.

Getting There & Away

St Kevin's Bus (☎01-281 8119; www.glendaloughbus.com) departs from outside the Mansion House on Dawson St in Dublin at 11.30am and 6pm Monday to Saturday, and 11.30am and 7pm Sunday (one way/return €13/20, 1½ hours). It also stops at the Town Hall in Bray. Departures from Glendalough are at 7.15am and 4.30pm Monday to Saturday.

During the week in July and August the later bus runs at 5.30pm, and there is an additional service at 9.45am.

Glenmalure

As you head deeper into the mountains southwest of Glendalough, near the southern end of the Military Rd everything gets a bit wilder and more remote. Beneath the western slopes of Wicklow's highest peak, Lugnaquilla, is Glenmalure, a dark and sombre blind valley flanked by scree slopes of loose boulders.

Sights & Activities

After coming over the mountains into Glenmalure, turn northwest at the Drumgoff bridge. From there it's about 6km up the road beside the River Avonbeg to a car park where trails lead off in various directions.

Near Drumgoff is Dwyer's or **Cullen's Rock**, which commemorates both the Glenmalure battle and Michael Dwyer, a member of the United Irishmen who fought unsuccessfully against the English in the Rising of 1798 and holed up here. Men were hanged from the rock during the Rising.

You can walk up Lugnaquilla mountain or head up the hidden Fraughan Rock Glen east of the car park. Alternatively, you can go straight up Glenmalure Valley passing the small, seasonal An Óige Glenmalure Hostel, after which the trail divides – heading northeast, the trail takes you over the hills to Glendalough, while going northwest brings you into the Glen of Imaal.

The head of Glenmalure and parts of the neighbouring Glen of Imaal are off-limits. It's military land, well posted with warning signs.

Sleeping

Glenmalure Hostel HOSTEL €
(☎01-830 4555; www.anoige.ie; Greenane; dm €15; ⏲Jun-Aug, Sat only Sep-May) No telephone, no electricity (lighting is by gas), just a rustic two-storey former hunting lodge with 19 beds and running water. This place has a couple of heavyweight literary links: it was the setting for JM Synge's play *Shadow of a Gunman* – at the time it was owned by Maud Gonne, the unrequited love of WB Yeats. It's isolated, but is beautifully situated beneath Lugnaquilla.

Western Wicklow

As you go west through the county, the landscape gets less rugged and more rural, especially towards the borders of Kildare and Carlow. The wild terrain gives way to rich pastures; east of Blessington the countryside is dotted with private stud farms where some of the world's most expensive horses are trained in jealously guarded secrecy.

The main attraction in this part of Wicklow is the magnificent Palladian pile at Russborough House, just outside Blessington, but if it's wild scenery you're after, you'll find it around Kilbride and the upper reaches of the River Liffey, as well as further south in the Glen of Imaal.

Blessington

POP 4018

Lined with pubs, shops and 17th- and 18th-century town houses, Blessington makes a convenient base when exploring the surrounding area. The main attraction is Russborough House.

Sights

Russborough House HISTORIC BUILDING
(☎045-865 239; www.russboroughhouse.ie; Blessington; adult/child guided tours €12/9; ⏲10am-6pm daily 17 Mar–Dec) Magnificent Russborough House is one of Ireland's finest stately homes, a Palladian palace built for Joseph Leeson (1705–83), later the first Earl of Milltown and, later still, Lord Russborough. Since 1952 the house has been owned by the Beit family, who founded the DeBeers diamond-mining company and stocked the mansion with a remarkable art collection, including masterpieces by Velázquez, Vermeer, Goya, Rubens and others.

The admission price includes a 45-minute tour of the house, and begins with a 3D exhibition on the life of Sir Alfred Beit (1903–94), who bought the house.

The house was built between 1741 and 1751 to the design of Richard Castle, who was at the height of his fame as an architect. Poor old Richard didn't live to see it finished, but the job was well executed by Francis

WORTH A TRIP

TINAKILLY COUNTRY HOUSE

A magnificent Victorian Italianate house just outside Rathnew, **Tinakilly Country House & Restaurant** (☎0404-69274; www.tinakilly.ie; Rathnew; r €130-200) is one of the most elegant country homes in Wicklow. You have a choice between a period room in the west wing (original antiques, four-poster and half-tester canopy beds) and a sumptuous suite with a view in the east wing. The restaurant takes country-house cuisine to a whole new level of sophistication (dinner mains €20 to €24).

Bindon. The house remained in the Leeson family until 1931, but it was only after the Beits bought the pile that the drama began.

In 1974 the IRA stole 16 of the paintings, all of which were later recovered. In 1984 Loyalist paramilitaries followed suit, hiring Dublin criminal Martin Cahill to mastermind the heist. Although most of that haul was also recovered, some pieces were damaged beyond repair. In 1988 Beit donated the most valuable works to the National Gallery, but that didn't stop two more break-ins in 2001 and 2002: one of the stolen paintings was a Gainsborough that had already been taken – and recovered – twice before. Thankfully, all of the paintings were recovered after both attempts, but where a succession of thieves couldn't succeed, the cost of the upkeep did: in 2015 the owners announced they were going to auction off 10 of the paintings, a decision that caused much consternation as the family had always maintained that the collection was to be held in trust for the Irish people.

On the tour of the house, which is decorated in typical Georgian style, you'll see all the (remaining) important paintings, which, given the history, is a monumental exercise in staying positive.

Sleeping & Eating

Rathsallagh House & Country Club HOTEL €€€
(☎045-403 112; www.rathsallagh.com; Dunlavin; r from €165) About 20km south of Blessington, this fabulous country manor, converted from Queen Anne stables in 1798, is more than just a fancy hotel. Luxury is par for the course here, from the splendidly appointed rooms to the exquisite country-house dining (mains €15 to €27) and the highly rated golf course that surrounds the estate.

Grangecon Café INTERNATIONAL €€
(☎045-857 892; Tullow Rd; mains €12-18; ⏲10am-5pm Tue-Sat) Salads, home-baked dishes and a full menu of Irish cheeses are the staples at this tiny, terrific cafe in a converted schoolhouse. Everything here – from the pasta to the delicious apple juice – is made on the premises, and many of the ingredients are organic. A short but solid menu represents the best of Irish cooking.

Information

The **Tourist Office** (☎045-865 850; Unit 5, Blessington Craft Centre, Main St; ⏲9.30am-4pm Mon-Fri year-round, 10am-2pm Sat & Sun Jul & Aug) is across the road from the Downshire House Hotel.

Getting There & Away

Blessington is 35km southwest of Dublin on the N81. There are regular daily services by **Dublin Bus** (☎01-873 4222, 01-872 0000); catch bus 65 from Eden Quay in Dublin (€3.30, 1½ hours, every 1½ hours). **Bus Éireann** (www.buseireann.ie) operates express bus 005 to and from Waterford, with stops in Blessington two or three times daily; from Dublin it's pick-up only and from Waterford drop-off only.

The Coast

Wicklow's coastline plays second fiddle to its mountains in terms of dramatic scenery, and its largely unassuming towns and small coastal resorts have a subtle charm that quickly disappears under a menacing sky. Highlights include the fine beaches at Brittas Bay, a wide lazy arc of coastline immediately south of Wicklow town.

Kilmacanogue & the Great Sugarloaf

POP 839

At 503m, it's not even Wicklow's highest mountain, but the Great Sugarloaf is one of the most distinctive peaks in Ireland, its conical tip visible for many miles around. The mountain towers over the small village of Kilmacanogue, on the N11 about 4km south of Bray, which would barely merit a passing nod were it not for the presence of the mother of all Irish craft shops just across the road from the village.

Shopping

Avoca Handweavers ARTS & CRAFTS
(☎01-286 7466; www.avoca.ie; Main St; ⌚9am-6pm Mon-Fri, 9.30am-6pm Sat & Sun) This is one hell of an operation, with seven branches nationwide and an even more widespread reputation for adding elegance and style to traditional rural handicrafts. Operational HQ is in a 19th-century arboretum, and its showroom will leave you in no doubt as to the company's incredible success. The attached **restaurant** (mains €12 to €18) is excellent and you can bring a little of it home with you by purchasing one (or all) of its cookbooks.

Getting There & Away

Bus Éireann (☎01-836 6111; www.buseireann.ie) operates bus 133 from Dublin to Arklow. It stops in Kilmacanogue (one way/return €4.50/7.60, 45 minutes, 10 daily).

Greystones to Wicklow

The resort of Greystones, 8km south of Bray, was once a charming fishing village, and the seafront around the little harbour is idyllic. In summer the bay is dotted with dinghies and windsurfers. Sadly, the surrounding countryside is vanishing beneath housing developments.

Sights

★**Kilruddery House & Gardens** HOUSE
(www.killruddery.com; Southern Cross, Bray; adult/child €6.50/5.50; ⌚9.30am-6pm May-Sep, weekends only Apr & Oct) A stunning mansion in the Elizabethan Revival style, Killruddery has been home to the Brabazon family (earls of Meath) since 1618 and has one of the oldest gardens in Ireland. The house is impressive, but the prizewinner here is the magnificent **orangery**, built in 1852 and chock-full of statuary and plant life. If you like fancy glasshouses, this is the one for you. It's 6km north of Greystones just off the R761 coast road.

The house was designed by trendy 19th-century architects Richard Morrisson and his son William in 1820, and it was reduced to its present-day huge proportions by the 14th earl in 1953; he was obviously looking for something a little more bijou. There are guided tours of the house during the summer (hourly from 1pm to 4pm, July to September), as well as a Thursday-night supper club, where dinner is served in the garden by the tea room. There's also an excellent farmers market every Saturday.

Mt Usher Gardens GARDENS
(☎0404-40116; www.mountushergardens.ie; adult/child/student €7.50/3.50/6.50; ⌚10.30am-6pm Mar-Oct) Wicklow's nickname, 'the Garden of Ireland', is justified by green idylls such as the 8-hectare Mt Usher Gardens, just outside the unremarkable town of Ashford, about 10km south of Greystones on the N11. Trees, shrubs and herbaceous plants from around the world are laid out in Robinsonian style – ie according to the naturalist principles of famous Irish gardener William Robinson (1838–1935) – rather than in the formalist style of preceding gardens.

There's also an Avoca cafe on the premises, as well as a 'shopping courtyard' where you can buy freshly baked goods, plants, furniture and clothing, as well as ice cream and photographs.

Sleeping & Eating

★**Hunter's Hotel** HOTEL €€
(☎0404-40106; www.hunters.ie; Newrath Bridge, Rathnew; r from €130; 📶) This exquisite property just outside Rathnew on the R761 is an absolute find, with 16 stunning rooms, each decorated with unerringly good taste. The house, one of Ireland's oldest coaching inns, is surrounded by an award-winning garden that is part of the Wicklow Gardens Festival. The attached fine-dining restaurant (two-course dinner €29.50, three courses €36.50) is also excellent.

Three Q's INTERNATIONAL €€
(☎01-287 5477; Church Rd; mains €19; ⌚9am-10pm Tue-Fri, to 3pm Sat & Sun) You'll find a smart menu at this elegant, award-winning

WORTH A TRIP

BALLYKNOCKEN HOUSE

Ballyknocken House & Cookery School (☎0404-44627; www.ballyknocken.com; Glenealy, Ashford; s/d from €90/160, 4-course tasting menus €49) is a beautiful ivy-clad Victorian home, where each of the seven carefully appointed bedrooms has original furnishings, and some come with original, stencilled claw-foot bathtubs. Besides the home itself, the big draw is Catherine Fulvio's cooking classes (€125), which run throughout the year; check the website for details. It's 5km south of Ashford on the R752 to Glenealy.

restaurant, with superb dishes such as grilled fillet of sea bass with a roasted red pepper and tomato risotto, purple basil and pesto, as well as the usual chicken and steak dishes.

Hungry Monk IRISH €€€
(☎01-287 5759; Church Rd; mains €19-29; ⏲7-11pm Wed-Sat, 12.30-9pm Sun; 👪) An excellent 1st-floor restaurant on Greystones' main street. The blackboard specials are the real treat, with dishes such as suckling pig with prune and apricot stuffing to complement the fixed menu's classic choices – fresh seafood, Wicklow rack of lamb, bangers and mash and so forth. This is one of the better places to get a bite along the whole of the Wicklow coast.

Getting There & Away

Bus Éireann (☎01-836 6111; www.buseireann.ie) operates bus 133 from Dublin to Wicklow town and Arklow. It stops outside Ashford House, in Ashford (one way/return €7.90/11.40, one hour, 10 daily).

Southern Wicklow

Southern Wicklow is softer than its coastal northern half; the landscape is one of rolling hills and valleys cut through by rustling rivers and dotted with lovely little hamlets, including the especially beautiful Vale of Avoca, once favoured by both song and busloads of tourists.

WICKLOW GARDENS FESTIVAL

If you want unfettered access to more than 40 of Wicklow's famed public and private gardens, visit during the yearly **Wicklow Gardens Festival** (www.wicklowgardens.com) which runs from Easter roughly to the end of August. The obvious advantage for green thumbs and other garden enthusiasts is access to beautiful gardens that would ordinarily be closed to the public.

Some of the larger gardens are open throughout the festival, while other smaller ones open only at specific times; call or check the website for details of entrants, openings and special events, including all manner of horticultural courses.

Rathdrum

POP 2123

The quiet village of Rathdrum at the foot of the Vale of Clara comprises little more than a few old houses and shops, but in the late 19th century it had a healthy flannel industry and a poorhouse. It's not what's in the town that's of interest to visitors, however, but what's just outside it.

Sights

Avondale House HOUSE
(☎0404-46111; adult/student/child €7/6.50/4.50; ⏲11am-6pm Easter-Oct) This fine Palladian mansion surrounded by a marvellous 209-hectare estate was the birthplace and Irish headquarters of Charles Stewart Parnell (1846–91), the 'uncrowned king of Ireland' and unquestionably one of the key figures in the Irish independence movement. Designed by James Wyatt in 1779, the house's many highlights include a stunning vermilion-hued library and the American Room, dedicated to Parnell's American grandfather, admiral of the USS *Constitution* during the War of 1812. Tours are self-guided.

From 1880 to 1890 Avondale was synonymous with the fight for Home Rule, which was brilliantly led by Parnell until 1890, when a member of his own Irish Parliamentary Party, Captain William O'Shea, sued his wife Kitty for divorce and named Parnell as co-respondent. Parnell's affair with Kitty O'Shea scandalised this 'priest-ridden' nation, and the ultraconservative clergy declared that Parnell was 'unfit to lead' – despite the fact that as soon as the divorce was granted the two lovers were quickly married. Parnell resigned as leader of the party and withdrew in despair to Avondale, where he died the following year.

The magnificent estate that surrounds the house is managed by the Irish Forestry Service, **Coillte** (www.coillteoutdoors.ie), and there are a number of orienteering trails; download the maps from the website.

National Botanic Gardens GARDENS
(www.botanicgardens.ie; Kilmacurragh, Rathdrum; admission free; ⏲9am-6pm mid-Feb-Oct, to 4.30pm Nov–mid-Feb) Surrounding the ruins of a Queen Anne house are 52 acres of wild gardens originally laid out in 1712 but then replanted under the instruction of the Director of the Botanic Gardens in Dublin in the 19th century to reflect the wilder, anti-formal style of gardener William Robinson

WORTH A TRIP

WICKLOW'S HISTORIC GAOL

The infamous **Wicklow's Historic Gaol** (☎0404-61599; www.wicklowshistoricgaol.com; Kilmantin Hill; adult/child/student incl tour €7.90/5/6.70, adults-only tours €15; ⏲10.30am-4.30pm) was renowned throughout Ireland for the brutality of its keepers and the harsh conditions suffered by its inmates. The smells, vicious beatings, shocking food and disease-ridden air have long since gone, but adults and children alike can experience a sanitised version of what the prison was like – and stimulate the secret sadist buried deep within – on the highly entertaining tour of the prison, now one of Wicklow's most popular tourist attractions.

The prison was opened in 1702 to house inmates sentenced under the repressive Penal Laws and continued in the role until 1877, when it was reduced to the status of a remand prison (bridewell), before closing in 1924. The building fell into ruin before finally being restored in the 1990s in recognition of its historic significance.

Actors play the roles of the various jailers and prisoners, adding to the sense of drama already heightened by the various exhibits on show, including a life-size treadmill that prisoners would have to turn for hours on end as punishment, and the gruesome dungeon.

The prison also has a **genealogical library**, where you can scour Irish digital databases for details of Irish ancestry.

Tours are every 10 minutes except between 1pm and 2pm; on the last Friday of every month there are adults-only tours of the prison, complete with ghouls, finger food and a glass of wine.

(1838–1935). The gardens are 3km east of Rathdrum toward the N11.

Sleeping & Eating

Brook Lodge & Wells Spa HOTEL €€
(☎0402-36444; www.brooklodge.com; Macreddin; r/ste from €120/200; 📶) A luxurious country-house hotel with 86 beautifully appointed rooms ranging from standard rooms to mezzanine suites that wouldn't seem out of place in a New York penthouse. It's 3km west of Rathdrum in the village of Macreddin.

The accommodation is pure luxury, and the other big selling points are the sumptuous spa – one of Ireland's best – and the superb **Strawberry Tree** (☎0402-36444; www.brooklodge.com; dinner menu €65; ⏲7pm-midnight Tue-Sat) restaurant, renowned for its locally sourced, organic cuisine.

Bates Inn PUB FOOD €€
(☎0404-29988; www.batesrestaurant.com; 3 Market Sq, Rathdrum; mains €17-25; ⏲6-9.30pm Tue-Sat, 12.30-8pm Sun) Housed in a coaching inn that first opened its doors in 1785, this outstanding restaurant puts a premium on exquisitely prepared meat dishes (the chargrilled beef options are particularly good). One of the better options in southern Wicklow. Bookings recommended for weekend evenings.

Information

The small **Tourist Office** (☎0404-46262; 29 Main St; ⏲9am-5.30pm Mon-Fri) has leaflets and information on the town and surrounding area, including the Wicklow Way.

Getting There & Away

Iarnród Éireann (www.irishrail.ie) trains serve Rathdrum from Dublin on the main Dublin to Rosslare Harbour line (one way/return €16/20, 1½ hours, five daily).

Bus Éireann (☎01-836 6111; www.buseireann.ie) operates service 133, which goes to Rathdrum from Dublin (one way/return €14/19, 2¼ hours, 10 daily) on its way to Arklow.

Vale of Avoca

One of the most scenic spots in the county is the Vale of Avoca, a darkly wooded valley that begins where the Rivers Avonbeg and Avonmore come together to form the River Avoca. Bearing the literal name the 'Meeting of the Waters', this watery junction was made famous by Thomas Moore's 1808 poem of the same name. Buses to Avoca from Dublin stop at the Meetings pub, or you can walk from Avoca, 3km south of here.

Drinking & Nightlife

Meetings PUB
(☎0402-35226; www.themeetings.ie; ⏲noon-9pm) The Meeting of the Waters is marked by a pub, which serves food (mains €10) and has music at weekends year-round. There are *céilidh* (traditional music and dancing sessions) between 4pm and 6pm Sunday,

April to October. There's also a guesthouse attached (known as Robin's Nest) with decent, clean rooms (single rooms are €50, doubles €80).

Avoca

POP 570

Tiny Avoca (Abhóca) is a pleasant-enough village, best-known as the birthplace of the superstar of all Irish cottage industries, Avoca Handweavers.

Sleeping

★ **River Valley Park** CAMPGROUND €

(☎0402-41647; www.rivervalleypark.com; campsites €12, campsites €12-24, microlodges €60-80;) With six different kinds of camping options, this is probably the best-equipped campground in the county. Besides the family campsites, there are self-catering chalets, mobile homes, glamping microlodges and an adults-only section. It's about 1km south of the village of Redcross, 7km northeast of Avoca on the R754 country road.

Shopping

Avoca Handweavers ARTS & CRAFTS

(☎0402-35105; www.avoca.ie; Main St, Old Mill; ⏲9am-6pm May-Sep, 9.30am-5.30pm Oct-Apr) Housed in Ireland's oldest working mill, Avoca Handweavers has been turning out linens, wools and other fabrics since 1723, and a lot of Avoca's much-admired line is produced here. You are free to wander in and out of the weaving sheds.

Information

Just in case you might want some local info, the **Tourist Office** (☎0402-35022; Old Courthouse; ⏲10am-5pm Mon-Sat) is in a small bungalow called the Courthouse.

WORTH A TRIP

CASTLETOWN HOUSE

The magnificent **Castletown House** (☎01-628 8252; www.castletown.ie; Celbridge; adult/child €7/3; ⏲10am-6pm mid-Mar–Oct) simply has no peer. It is Ireland's largest and most imposing Georgian estate, and a testament to the vast wealth enjoyed by the Anglo-Irish gentry during the 18th century. The hour-long guided tour gives you an insight into how the 1% made out in the 18th century, what furniture they liked, and how they enjoyed a fine oil painting.

Buses 120 and 123 run from Dublin to Celbridge (€3.50; 30 minutes; every half-hour Monday to Friday, hourly Saturday, six buses Sunday).

The house was built between the years 1722 and 1732 for William Conolly (1662–1729), speaker of the Irish House of Commons and, at the time, Ireland's richest man. Born into relatively humble circumstances in Ballyshannon, County Donegal, Conolly made his fortune through land transactions in the uncertain aftermath of the Battle of the Boyne (1690).

The job of building a palace fit for a prince was entrusted to Sir Edward Lovett Pearce (1699–1733) – hence the colonnades and terminating pavilions. Lovett's design was an extension of a preexisting 16th-century Italian palazzo-style building, created by Italian architect Alessandro Galilei (1691–1737) in 1718, but Conolly wanted something even grander, hence Lovett's appearance on the job in 1724. A highlight of the opulent interior is the Long Gallery, replete with family portraits and exquisite stucco work by the Francini brothers.

Conolly didn't live to see the completion of his wonder-palace. His widow, Katherine, continued to live at the unfinished house after his death in 1729, and instigated many improvements. Her main architectural contribution was the curious 42.6m obelisk, known locally as the Conolly Folly. Her other offering is the Heath Robinson–esque (or Rube Goldberg–esque, if you prefer) **Wonderful Barn** (☎01-624 5448; Leixlip; ⏲closed to the public), six teetering storeys wrapped by an exterior spiral staircase, on private property just outside Leixlip.

Castletown House remained in the family's hands until 1965, when it was purchased by Desmond Guinness, who restored the house to its original splendour. His investment was continued from 1979 by the Castletown Foundation. In 1994 Castletown House was transferred to state care and today it is managed by the Heritage Service.

Getting There & Away

Bus Éireann (☎01-836 6111; www.buseireann.ie) operates bus 133 from Dublin. It serves Avoca (one way/return €13.70/22, two hours, 10 daily) on its way to Arklow.

COUNTY KILDARE

POP 210,000 / AREA 1691 SQ KM

Some of Ireland's best grazing farmland has made County Kildare (Cill Dara) prime agricultural real estate, especially for the horse industry: the county is dotted with stud farms where champion racehorses are reared and trained as a matter of course. In recent decades it has had to contend with Dublin's ever-expanding commuter belt, which has swallowed up many of its towns and villages.

The county isn't especially stuffed with must-see attractions, but there are enough diversions to justify a day trip from the capital or a stop on your way out west.

Maynooth

POP 10,715

Bustling Maynooth (Maigh Nuad) is dominated by the local campus of National University of Ireland (NUIM), whose students make up two-thirds of the inhabitants and bring a bit of life to this otherwise demure country town lined with stone-fronted houses and shops. Main St and Leinster St join and run east–west, while Parson St runs south to the canal and the train station (accessed via a couple of footbridges), and Straffan Rd runs south to the M4.

Sights & Activities

St Patrick's College UNIVERSITY

(☎01-628 5222; www.maynoothcollege.ie; Main St; guided tours adult/child/student €8/4/6) Turning out Catholic priests since 1795, St Patrick's College & Seminary is Ireland's second-oldest university (after Trinity College, Dublin). The college buildings are impressive – Gothic architect Augustus Pugin had a hand in designing them – and well worth an hour's ramble. The college grounds contain a number of lofty Georgian and neo-Gothic buildings, gardens and squares, and it's worth taking the **guided tour** (2.30pm Friday to Sunday, June to September) too see the **College Chapel**, the world's largest choir chapel with stalls for more than 450 choristers.

The college was founded so that aspiring priests didn't have to skip off to seminary school in France – and so get infected with strains of republicanism and revolution. In 1898 it was made a Pontifical College (which meant that its curriculum was determined and controlled by the Holy See) and in 1910 it became part of the recently established National University of Ireland. The college's student body remained exclusively clerical until 1966 when lay students were finally admitted, but even today, despite being part of the bigger university, it remains largely autonomous and its 80-odd male seminarians are distinct from the university's 8500 other students.

Maynooth Castle CASTLE

(☎01-628 6744; ⏲10am-6pm Mon-Fri, 1-6pm Sat & Sun Jun-Sep, 1-5pm Sun Oct) FREE Near the entrance to St Patrick's College you can see the ruined gatehouse, keep and great hall of this 13th-century castle, once home of the Fitzgerald family. The castle was dismantled in Cromwellian times, when the Fitzgeralds moved to Kilkea Castle (now closed). Entry is by a 45-minute tour only; there's a small exhibition on the castle's history in the keep.

Carton House GOLF

(www.cartonhousegolf.com; Carton House; green fees weekday/weekends €50/65) Two outstanding courses make Carton House one of eastern Ireland's premier golfing destinations. The Mark O'Meara course has broad fairways and strategically placed greens; the Colin Montgomerie course is more challenging, with bunkers positioned to swallow all but the best-hit shots.

Sleeping

NUI Maynooth UNIVERSITY €€

(☎01-708 6200; www.maynoothcampus.com; s/d from €32/82;) The university campus can accommodate 1000 guests in seven types of room, ranging from a traditional college room to doubles in an apartment in the purpose-built university village. Most are in the mid-1970s North Campus, but rooms are better in the South Campus, where the accommodation office is. These are strewn around the courts and gardens of atmospheric St Patrick's College. Availability is best in the summer months.

Carton House HOTEL €€€

(☎01-505 2000; www.cartonhouse.com; r from €140; @) The former country manor of the Fitzgeralds, the earls of Kildare (their city pile was Leinster House, now the Irish

Parliament), is now an exquisite luxury hotel. Rooms are split between the grander suites of the Richard Castle-designed original house (dating from 1739) and the neat, business-style accommodation in the modern extension. To reach the hotel, follow the R148 east towards Leixlip along the Royal Canal.

Eating

Gatehouse INTERNATIONAL €€

(Main St; mains €10-23; 8.30am-10pm Mon-Sat, 10am-9pm Sun) Its catch-all menu – pizzas, pastas, plus interesting choices such as wild venison and roast confit of duck – is a crowd-pleaser, but what makes this spot stand out is the quality of the ingredients. Everything is fresh and, wherever possible, locally sourced.

Getting There & Away

Dublin Bus (01-873 4222; www.dublinbus.ie) runs a service to Maynooth (€3.30, one hour) leaving several times an hour from Pearse St in Dublin.

Straffan

Teeny Straffan has a few small attractions for the young (or at least the young at heart), and another for the golfer.

Sights & Activities

Steam Museum & Lodge Park Walled Garden MUSEUM

(01-627 3155; www.steam-museum.com; adult/concession €7.50/5; 2-6pm Fri-Sun Jun-Aug, weekends only May & Sep) The history of steam power and its role in the development of industry is told at the Steam Museum, located in an old church. The Power Hall has six 19th-century steam engines, from breweries, distilleries, factories and ships; regular demonstrations of how they worked are held. Next door, the 18th-century walled garden has traditional fruits, flowers and formal plantings.

Straffan Butterfly Farm WILDLIFE

(01-627 1109; www.straffanbutterflyfarm.com; Ovidstown; adult/child/student €8/5/6; 11am-5.30pm) At the Straffan Butterfly Farm, you can wander through a tropical greenhouse full of enormous butterflies, or commune with critters such as Larry, the leopard gecko.

K Club GOLF

(Kildare Hotel & Country Club; 01-601 7200; www.kclub.ie; Straffan; green fees €150-240;) The K Club estate is home to two championship golf courses and a fine hotel. The original Straffan House, established by the Barton wine family in the 19th century, has 92 well-appointed rooms (from €250) and some opulent public spaces. Of the two golf courses, the best known is the Palmer, designed by Arnold and host of the 2006 Ryder Cup.

Getting There & Away

Bus Éireann (01-836 6111; www.buseireann.ie) runs buses from Dublin (one way/return €4/5.90, 30 minutes, every half-hour, six buses Sunday).

BOG OF ALLEN

Stretching like a brown, moist desert through nine counties, including Kildare, Laois and Offaly, the Bog of Allen is Ireland's best-known raised bog, and once covered much of the midlands. Unfortunately, in a pattern repeated across Ireland, the peat is rapidly being turned into potting compost and fuel. Once Ireland had almost 17% of its land covered in bogs; today it's less than 2%. Bogs are home to a wide range of plants and animals, including cranberries, insect-eating sundew plants, and all manner of frogs and butterflies. For more information on ways to discover this rich land, enquire at the **Bog of Allen Nature Centre** found right along the Grand Canal.

Along the Grand Canal

Heading west from Straffan, there are some interesting sites as you follow the banks of the Grand Canal, which flows gently from Dublin to tiny, tranquil **Robertstown**, just past Clane and well worth a detour. This picturesque village has remained largely untouched and is dominated by the now-dilapidated Grand Canal Hotel, built in 1801. It's a good place to start a canal walk.

Just southwest of Robertstown and at the centre of the Kildare flatlands, the **Hill of Allen** (206m) was a strategic spot through the centuries due to its 360-degree view. Today the top is marked by a 19th-century folly and the ruins of some Iron Age fortifications said to mark the home of Fionn McCumhaill (or Finn McCool, mythical hunter-warrior).

Sights & Activities

Bog of Allen Nature Centre NATURE CENTRE

(045-860 133; www.ipcc.ie; R414, Lullymore; adult/child €5/free; 9am-5pm Mon-Fri) The wonderfully interpretive Bog of Allen Nature

Centre is a fascinating institution run by the nonprofit Irish Peatland Conservation Council. It traces the history of bogs and peat production, and has the largest carnivorous plant collection in Ireland, including sundews, butterwort and other bog-native protein-eaters. A nearby boardwalk extends into the Bog of Allen.

Lullymore Heritage & Discovery Park NATURE RESERVE
(045-870 238; www.lullymoreheritagepark.com; Lullymore; adult/family €9/28; 10am-6pm Apr-Sep) A rather mangy rabbit mascot greets visitors to the cheerful Lullymore Heritage & Discovery Park, about 1km north of the Bog of Allen Nature Centre. It's aimed right at kids; a woodland trail leads you past various dwellings (including Neolithic huts, a not-so-festive Famine-era house and an enchanting fairy village). There's also crazy golf and a road train. Should the unthinkable happen and it rains, the Funky Forest is a vast indoor playground.

Newbridge & the Curragh

POP 17,042

Unremarkable Newbridge (Droichead Nua), near the junction of the M7 and M9, is best known for its silverware and as the gateway to the Curragh, one of the country's largest pieces of unfenced fertile land and the centre of the Irish horse industry. The name derives from the Irish for 'place of the running horse,' and they've been doing just that on this plain since the 1700s, although there are tales of chariot races as far back as the 13th century. If you get up early or pass by in the late evening, you'll see the thoroughbreds exercising on the wide-open spaces surrounding the racecourse.

Activities

Curragh Racecourse HORSE RACING
(045-441 205; www.curragh.ie; admission €15-40; mid-Apr–Oct) The Curragh Racecourse is the oldest and most prestigious in the country. The complex is in the midst of a substantial spruce-up, and even if you're not a horsey type it's well worth experiencing the passion and atmosphere of a day at the races.

Shopping

Newbridge Silverware Visitor Centre HANDICRAFTS
(045-431 301; www.newbridgesilverware.com; 9am-6pm Mon-Sat, 11am-6pm Sun) The Newbridge Silverware Showroom is a purely commercial venture that trades on the area's metalwork heritage as it peddles vast quantities of silver-plated spoons, forks and whatnots. At the back of the showroom is the totally out-of-place **Museum of Style Icons** (admission free), which displays an ever-changing range of star-studded memorabilia, including a jacket once worn by Michael Jackson, a dress that belonged to Princess Diana, and dresses that belonged to Audrey Hepburn.

WALKING THE TOWPATH

The Grand Canal towpath is ideal for leisurely walkers and there are numerous access points, none better than Robertstown if you fancy a long-distance ramble. The village is the hub of the Kildare Way and River Barrow towpath trails, the latter stretching all the way to St Mullin's, 95km south in County Carlow. From there it's possible to connect with the South Leinster Way at Graiguenamanagh, or the southern end of the Wicklow Way at Clonegal, north of Mt Leinster.

A variety of leaflets detailing the paths can be picked up at most regional tourist offices. **Waterways Ireland** (www.waterwaysireland.org) is also a good source.

Getting There & Away

The M7 runs through the Curragh (exit 12) and Newbridge from Dublin. There is frequent Bus Éireann (www.buseireann.ie) service between Dublin's Busáras bus station and Newbridge (one way/return €10.60/17, 90 minutes). From Newbridge, buses continue to the Curragh Racecourse (€2.20, 10 minutes) and Kildare town. There are extra buses on race days.

The Dublin–Kildare **train** (01-836 6222) runs from Heuston Station, Dublin, and stops in Newbridge (€14.80, 30 minutes, hourly). Check the timetable for trains that stop at the racecourse.

Kildare Town

POP 7538

Built around a compact, triangular square fronting its impressive cathedral, Kildare is a busy enough place, even if there aren't a lot of attractions within the town itself. It is closely associated with Ireland's second-most important saint, Brigid.

Sights

St Brigid's Cathedral CATHEDRAL
(045-521 229; Market Sq; cathedral admission by donation, round tower admission €7; 10am-1pm & 2-5pm Mon-Sat, 2-5pm Sun May-Sep) The solid presence of 13th-century St Brigid's Cathedral looms over Market Sq. Look out for a fine stained-glass window inside that depicts the three main saints of Ireland: Patrick, Brigid and Colmcille. The church also contains the restored tomb of Walter Wellesley, Bishop of Kildare, which disappeared soon after his death in 1539 and was found in 1971. One of its carved figures has been variously interpreted as an acrobat or a sheila-na-gig (a carved female figure with exaggerated genitalia).

The 10th-century **round tower** in the grounds is Ireland's second-highest at 32.9m, and one of the few that you can climb, provided the guardian is around. Its original conical roof has been replaced with an unusual Norman battlement. Near the tower is a **wishing stone** – put your arm through the hole and touch your shoulder and your wish will be granted. On the north side of the cathedral are the heavily restored foundations of an ancient **fire temple**.

Irish National Stud & Gardens GARDENS
(045-521 617; www.irishnationalstud.ie; Tully; adult/student/child €12.50/9.50/7; 9am-6pm mid-Feb–Dec, last admission 5pm) With highlights such as the 'Teasing Shed', the Irish National Stud, about 3km south of town, is the big attraction in the locality – horse-mad Queen Elizabeth II dropped in during her historic 2011 visit. This immaculately kept centre is owned and managed by the Irish government. It breeds high-quality stallions to mate with mares from all over the world. You can wander the stalls and go eye-to-eye with famous stallions or take a (usually excellent) guided tour.

The stud was founded by Colonel Hall Walker (of Johnnie Walker whisky fame) in 1900. He was remarkably successful with his horses, but his eccentric breeding technique relied heavily on astrology: the fate of a foal was decided by its horoscope and the roofs of the stallion boxes opened on auspicious occasions to reveal the heavens and duly influence the horses' fortunes.

The guided tours take place every hour on the hour, with access to the intensive-care unit for newborn foals. If you visit between February and June, you might even see a foal being born.

Alternatively, the foaling unit shows a 10-minute video with all the action. Given that most of those foals are now geldings, they probably have dim memories of their time in the aforementioned Teasing Shed, the place where stallions are stimulated for mating, while dozens look on. The cost: tens of thousands of euros for a top horse.

After the thrill of seeing such prized stallions up close, the revamped **Irish Horse Museum** is quite disappointing; its celebration of championship horses and the history of horse racing is one step above what you'd expect to see from a really good school project.

Also disappointing are the much-vaunted **Japanese Gardens** (part of the complex), considered to be the best of their kind in Europe – which doesn't say much for other contenders. Created between 1906 and 1910, they trace the journey from birth to death through 20 landmarks, including the Tunnel of Ignorance, the Hill of Ambition and the Chair of Old Age. When in bloom the flowers are beautiful, but the gardens are too small and bitty to really impress.

Sleeping & Eating

★**Martinstown House** HOTEL €€€
(045-441 269; www.martinstownhouse.com; The Curragh; r from €175-210; mid-Jan–mid-Dec) This beautiful 18th-century country manor is built in the frilly Strawberry Hill Gothic style and set in a 170-acre estate and farm surrounded by trees. The house has four rooms filled with antiques; children are banned – darn. You can arrange for memorable dinners in advance (€49.50); ingredients are drawn from the kitchen garden.

Agape CAFE €
(045-533 711; Station Rd; meals €6-12; 9am-6pm Mon-Sat) Just off Market Sq, this trendy little cafe has a fine range of homemade food. There's a full coffee bar and a menu of salads, soups, sandwiches and tasty hot specials.

Shopping

Kildare Village SHOPPING CENTRE
(www.kildarevillage.com; Nurney Road; 10am-7pm Mon-Wed, Sat & Sun, to 8pm Thu & Fri) They come from all over the country to buy discounted versions of their favourite brands at this American-style outlet mall about 1km south of town (just off exit 13 on the M7 motorway). More than a hundred high-street brands are represented and the bargains can be substantial.

Information

The **Tourist Office & Heritage Centre** (045-521 240; www.kildare.ie; Market Sq, Market House; 9.30am-1pm & 2-5.30pm Mon-Sat May-Sep) has a free exhibition outlining Kildare's history. There's also local art for sale.

Getting There & Away

There is frequent Bus Éireann (www.buseireann.ie) service between Dublin Busáras and Kildare (one way/return €13/20, 1¾ hours). Some Dublin buses also service the National Stud.

The Dublin–Kildare **train** (01-836 6222) runs from Heuston Station and stops in Kildare (€16.60, 35 minutes, one to four per hour). This is a major junction and trains continue to numerous places including Ballina, Galway, Limerick and Waterford.

Donnelly's Hollow to Castledermot

This 25km stretch south towards Carlow contains some interesting detours to tiny towns bypassed by the speedy but unlovely N9.

Donnelly's Hollow

Dan Donnelly (1788–1820) is revered as Ireland's greatest bare-knuckle fighter of the 19th century. He's also the stuff of legend – his arms were so long he could supposedly tie his shoelaces without having to bend down. This spot, 4km west of Kilcullen on the R413, was his favourite battleground, and the obelisk at the centre of the hollow details his glorious career.

Ballitore

POP 338

Low-key Ballitore is the only planned and permanent Quaker settlement in Ireland. It was founded by incomers from Yorkshire in 1726. A small **Quaker Museum** (059-862 3344; Main St, Mary Leadbeater House; admission by donation; noon-5pm Tue-Sat year-round, 2-6pm Sun Jun-Sep), in a tiny restored Meeting House attached to the library, documents the lives of the community (including the former owner Mary Leadbeater, who was known for her aversion to war). There's also a Quaker cemetery, and a modern **Shaker Store** (059-862 3372; www.shakerstore.ie; Main St; 10am-6pm Mon-Fri, from 2pm Sat & Sun), which sells delightfully humble wooden toys and furniture. It also has a tearoom.

About 2km west is **Rath of Mullaghmast**, an Iron Age hill fort and standing stone where Daniel O'Connell, champion of Catholic emancipation, held one of his 'monster rallies' in 1843.

Moone

POP 380

Just south of Ballitore, the unassuming village of Moone is home to one of Ireland's most magnificent high crosses. The unusually tall and slender **Moone High Cross** is an 8th- or 9th-century masterpiece, which displays its carved biblical scenes with the confidence and exuberance of a comic strip. The cross can be found 1km west of Moone village and the N9 in an atmospheric early Christian churchyard. Old stone ruins add to the mood of the drive.

Sleeping & Eating

Moone High Cross Inn INN €€

(059-862 4112; www.moonehighcrossinn.com; Bolton Hill; s/d from €60/85) The solid, stone 18th-century Moone High Cross Inn, 2km south of Moone, has five rooms decorated in quaint country-house style. The delightful bar downstairs serves good pub lunches and there's a proper **restaurant** (mains €12 to €19; serving 6pm to 8.30pm), which uses local and organic ingredients. The inn revolves around a Celtic theme, celebrating pagan festivals and hoarding healing stones, lucky charms and even a 'love stone' in the outside courtyards.

Castledermot

POP 1160

Castledermot was once home to a vast ecclesiastical settlement, but all that remains of St Diarmuid's 9th-century **monastery** is a 20m round tower topped with a medieval battlement. Nearby are two well-preserved, carved, 10th-century granite high crosses; a 12th-century Romanesque doorway; and a medieval Scandinavian 'hogback' gravestone, the only one in Ireland. Reach the ruins by entering the rusty gate on all-too-busy Main St (N9), then walking up the tree-lined avenue to St James' Church. At the southern end of town, the ruins of an early-14th-century **Franciscan friary** can be seen alongside the road.

Counties Wexford, Waterford, Carlow & Kilkenny

Includes ➡

Best Historic Buildings

- Hook Lighthouse (p169)
- Kilkenny Castle (p193)
- Ardmore Cathedral (p184)
- Jerpoint Abbey (p201)
- Kells Priory (p200)
- Tintern Abbey (p168)

Best Gardens

- Johnstown Castle Gardens (p159)
- Lismore Castle Gardens (p186)
- Altamont Gardens (p189)
- Woodstock Gardens (p204)
- Huntington Castle Gardens (p192)

Why Go?

Counties Wexford, Waterford, Carlow and Kilkenny are (along with the southern chunk of Tipperary) referred to collectively as the 'sunny southeast'. This being Ireland the term is, of course, relative. But it *is* the country's warmest, driest region. A tiara of golden-sand beaches adorns the counties of Wexford and Waterford, and there are plenty more eye-catching gems, including picturesque thatched cottages, elegant seaside towns and dramatic windswept peninsulas.

If you're looking for real sparkle, check out the world-acclaimed Waterford crystal. Deeper inland, the verdant valley of the River Barrow separates the riverside villages and arts and crafts studios of County Kilkenny from the country houses and flower-filled gardens of County Carlow. Kilkenny city is the urban star with its imposing castle, cathedral, medieval lanes and cracking pubs and restaurants. And thanks to that 'sunny southeast' climate, these four counties offer some of Ireland's best outdoor pursuits.

When to Go

- June to September is the best time for enjoying the superb beaches, seafront cafes and restaurants.
- April to October is good for hiking and walking, although be sure to pack waterproof gear and warm clothing.
- October to early November is great for music lovers with Wexford's world-acclaimed opera festival, while country and trad music fans should head for Kilkenny's Celtic Festival, also held at this time of year.
- Spring and autumn are the best months to visit if you are economising as prices (and tourist numbers) dip when compared to midsummer.

COUNTY WEXFORD

POP 145,300 / AREA 2367 SQ KM

County Wexford's navigable rivers and fertile farmland have long lured invaders and privateers. The Vikings founded Ireland's first major town on the wide, easy-flowing River Slaney, which cuts through the middle of the county. Today the Viking city of Wexford is a centre for opera and art, complementing a beach-fringed coastline and a rural hinterland dotted with cute villages and thatched cottages.

Wexford Town & Around

POP 20,100

A fine example of the contrasts conjured up by the economic boom and bust of the last few decades, Wexford's claustrophobic maze of medieval streets is lined with a mixture of old-time pubs, posh boutiques, boarded-up buildings and modern steel-and-glass facades. The town's rich and bloody history includes being founded by the Vikings, and nearly obliterated by Oliver Cromwell.

It's an arty town, with plenty of craft shops and galleries – and good restaurants – but the big cultural attraction is the world-famous Wexford Opera Festival, a 12-day autumn extravaganza that presents rarely performed works to packed audiences in the town's shiny modern opera house.

History

The Vikings named it Waesfjord (meaning 'harbour of mudflats') and its handy location near the mouth of the River Slaney encouraged landings as early as AD 850. The town was captured by the Normans in 1169; traces of their fort can still be seen in the grounds of the Irish National Heritage Park.

Cromwell included Wexford in his destructive Irish tour of 1649–50. Around 1500 of the town's then 2000 inhabitants were killed, including all the Franciscan friars. During the 1798 Rising, rebels made a determined, bloody stand here before being defeated.

Sights

Wexford doesn't have any don't-miss museums, but you can get a feeling for its long history on a one-hour stroll.

Selskar Abbey RUIN

(Westgate, Spawell Rd; per person €3; tours 3pm Mon-Sat Mar-Oct) After Henry II murdered his former ally Thomas Becket, he did penance at Selskar Abbey, founded in 1190. Basilia, the sister of Richard Fitz Gilbert de Clare (better known as Strongbow), is thought to have married one of Henry II's lieutenants in the abbey. Its present ruinous state is a result of Cromwell's visit in 1649. Admission is by guided tour only – gather at the Westgate, off Spawell Rd.

St Iberius' Church CHURCH

(North Main St; 10am-5pm May-Sep, to 3pm Oct-Apr) FREE St Iberius' Church was built in 1760. The Renaissance-style frontage is worth a look, but the real treat is the Georgian interior with its finely crafted altar rails and 18th-century monuments in the gallery. Oscar Wilde's forebears were rectors here. The church is also famed for its superb acoustics, and is an occasional venue for concerts.

Bull Ring HISTORIC SITE

The Bull Ring is a small, open square in the city centre that gets its name from having been used as a venue for bull baiting in medieval times. The **Lone Pikeman statue** commemorates the rebels of the 1798 Rising, who used the place as an open-air armaments factory. These days the Bull Ring is the site of the city's weekly market (p164).

Westgate LANDMARK

The only survivor of the six original town gates is the 14th-century Westgate. It was originally a toll gate, and the recesses used by the toll collectors are still intact, as is the lock-up used to incarcerate 'runagates' – those who tried to avoid paying.

★ **Johnstown Castle Gardens** GARDENS

(www.irishagrimuseum.ie; Johnstown Castle Estate; adult/child €3/1, incl museum €8/6; 9am-5.30pm Apr-May & Sep, to 7pm Jun-Aug, to 4.30pm Oct-Mar) Parading peacocks guard the splendid 19th-century Johnstown Castle, the former home of the once-mighty Fitzgerald and Esmonde families (the estate was gifted to the nation in 1945). The empty castle (not open to the public) is surrounded by 20 hectares of beautiful wooded gardens complete with ornamental lake, a sunken Italian garden, statues and waterfalls. The castle is 7km southwest of Wexford town.

The outbuildings of the castle house the **Irish Agricultural Museum** (9am-5pm Mon-Fri, 11am-5pm Sat & Sun Apr-May & Sep-Oct, to 6.30pm Jun-Aug, to 4pm Nov-Mar), a fascinating collection of early Ferguson tractors, farm machinery, Irish country furniture and

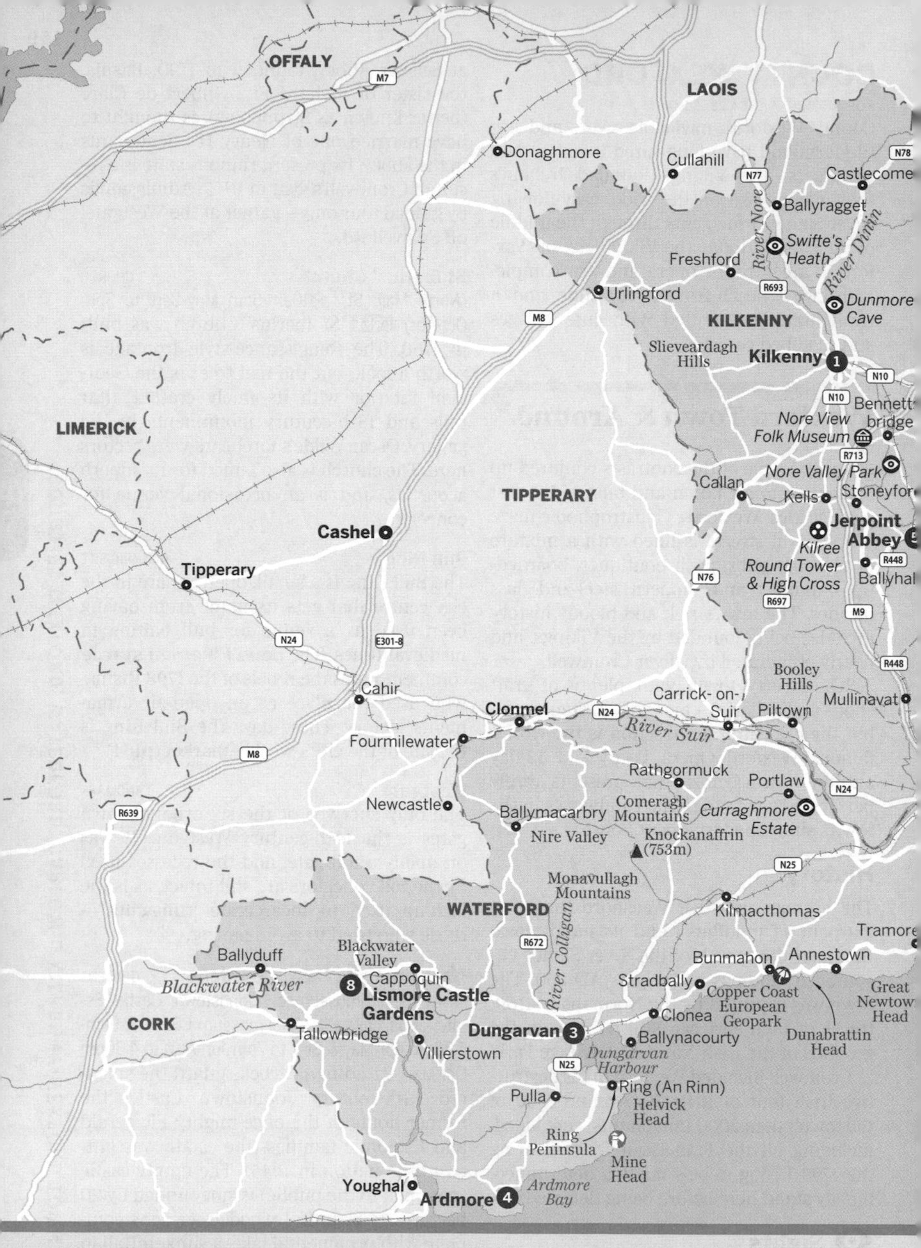

Counties Wexford, Waterford, Carlow & Kilkenny Highlights

1. Revel in the urban pleasures of **Kilkenny** (p193), one of Ireland's most vibrant cities.
2. Learn about Ireland's poignant history aboard the **Dunbrody Famine Ship** (p169) in New Ross.
3. Savour a slice of foodie heaven at **Dungarvan** (p181), home of top chefs.
4. Immerse yourself in County Waterford's coastal beauty around **Ardmore** (p184).
5. Check out the evocative ruins of **Jerpoint Abbey** (p201) in County Kilkenny

6 Walk to the end of **Curracloe Beach** (p165), near Wexford: a seemingly endless vision of white powder.

7 Relive the days of the Vikings and Normans in the excellent museums of **Waterford city** (p173).

8 Tiptoe through the tulips – and azaleas, and roses, and geraniums – in beautiful **Lismore Castle Gardens** (p186).

9 Cycle along the verdant **Barrow Way** (p191) towpath between Graiguenamanagh and St Mullins.

re-created farmhouse kitchens. The exhibition on the Great Famine is one of the best explanations of this national tragedy anywhere in Ireland.

Irish National Heritage Park MUSEUM
(www.inhp.com; Ferrycarrig; adult/child €9.50/4.50; ⌚9.30am-6.30pm May-Aug, to 5.30pm Sep-Apr) Over 9000 years of Irish history are squeezed together at this open-air museum. After a

Wexford Town

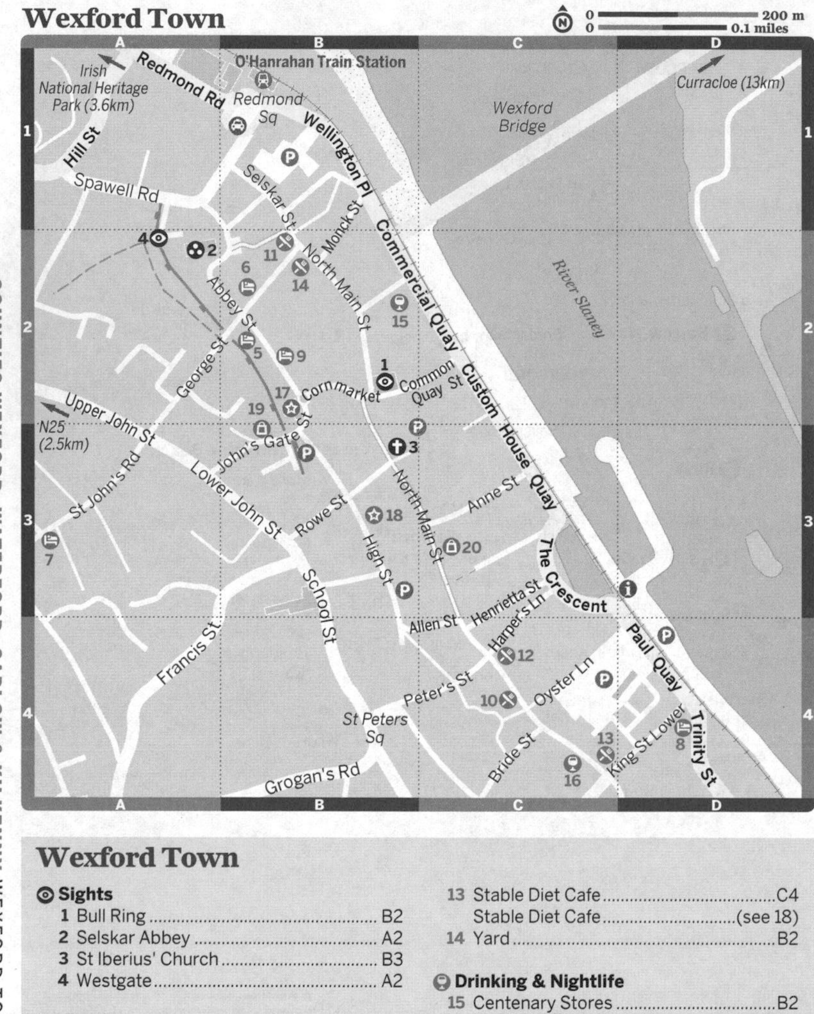

Wexford Town

Sights
1 Bull Ring ... B2
2 Selskar Abbey ... A2
3 St Iberius' Church ... B3
4 Westgate ... A2

Sleeping
5 Abbey B&B ... B2
6 Blue Door ... B2
7 Cuasnog ... A3
8 Talbot Hotel ... D4
9 Whites of Wexford ... B2

Eating
10 Cistín Eile ... C4
11 Greenacres ... B2
12 Simon Lambert & Sons ... C4
13 Stable Diet Cafe ... C4
Stable Diet Cafe ... (see 18)
14 Yard ... B2

Drinking & Nightlife
15 Centenary Stores ... B2
16 Sky & the Ground ... C4

Entertainment
17 Wexford Arts Centre ... B2
18 Wexford Opera House ... B3

Shopping
19 Blue Egg Gallery ... B3
Bull Ring Market ... (see 1)
20 Wexford Book Centre ... C3

short audiovisual presentation, choose a guided or audio self-guided tour, taking in re-creations of a Neolithic farmstead, stone circle, ring fort, monastery, *crannóg* (artificial island), Viking shipyard and Norman castle (on the site of original Norman fort remains). Activities include archery and an adventure playground. The museum is off the N25 on the western edge of Wexford town.

Wexford Wildfowl Reserve NATURE RESERVE
(☎076-100 2660; www.wexfordwildfowlreserve.ie; North Slob; guided tours on request; ⏰9am-5pm) FREE The North Slob (from the Irish *slab,* meaning 'mud or mire') is a large area of reclaimed land to the north of Wexford harbour, drained by ditches and protected by Dutch-style dikes. It's prime birdwatching territory – each winter, it's home to 35% of the world's population of Greenland white-fronted geese – some 10,000 in total. There's an an observation tower, assorted hides and a visitor centre with detailed exhibits. It's signposted 3km north of Wexford on the R741.

Tours

Wexford Walking Tours WALKING TOUR
(www.wexfordwalkingtours.net; per person €5; ⏰11am Mon-Sat Mar-Oct) A guided walking tour is the best way to understand Wexford's complicated past. These 90-minute walks depart from the tourist office.

Festivals & Events

Wexford Opera Festival OPERA
(www.wexfordopera.com; tickets €60-140) This 12-day festival in late October is the country's premier opera event, with rarely performed operas and shows playing to packed audiences. Fringe street theatre, poetry readings and exhibitions give the town a fiesta atmosphere, and many local bars run amateur singing competitions. Book tickets in advance.

Sleeping

Wexford's proximity to Dublin attracts weekenders, and accommodation is scarce during the Wexford Opera Festival. Otherwise there is plenty of choice.

★ **Cuasnog** B&B €€
(☎053-912 3637; www.cuasnog.com; St John's Rd; s/d €60/100; 📶👪) Hosts Caitriona and Theo not only extend a warm welcome – they treat you to a pot of tea with smoked salmon and soda bread on arrival. The compact rooms have a comfortable feel with rustic furniture and fireplaces; breakfast includes homemade scones and local organic produce. Located a few minutes' walk from the centre on a sleepy residential street.

Blue Door B&B €€
(☎053-912 1047; www.bluedoor.ie; 18 Lower George St; s/d from €50/70; 📶) Behind the eponymous cobalt-blue door of this 200-year-old Georgian town house, homey bedrooms with a period feel are brightened by tall windows, and are quiet despite the central location.

Abbey B&B B&B €€
(☎053-912 4408; www.abbeyhouse.ie; 34-36 Abbey St; s/d €45/80; 📶) This cute, black-and-white B&B blazes with window boxes trailing red blooms in summer. Its seven rooms vary considerably in size, but all have private bathrooms with walk-in showers. Breakfast is served in a cheery floral-themed dining room.

Talbot Hotel HOTEL €€
(☎053-912 2566; www.talbotwexford.ie; Trinity St; s/d from €70/110; @📶🏊) A landmark on Wexford's waterfront, this modern hotel has water views from many of its revamped rooms. Facilities include a steam room, sauna, gym and indoor pool. The stylish, high-ceilinged Ballast Bank bar and grill dishes up traditional pub grub along with regular live music.

Whites of Wexford HOTEL €€
(☎053-912 2311; www.whitesofwexford.ie; Abbey St; s/d from €95/145; @📶🏊) Whites is not only a contemporary colossus, it's super cool with its high-tech spa speciality: cryotherapy (extreme cold therapy). Warm up at one of the welcoming bars, enjoy a choice of restaurants or just retreat to your room. Pay €20 more for a slickly decorated executive room with an estuary view, all metal right-angles, tech touches and sparkling glass.

Eating

Stable Diet Cafe CAFE €
(www.stablediet.com; 100 South Main St; mains €8-12; ⏰8.30am-5pm; 👪) 🌿 This bright and busy cafe is famous for its home-baked breads, scones and cakes; the lunch menu consists of freshly made soups and sandwiches, while breakfast choices include French toast with bacon and maple syrup. There's another **branch** (Wexford Opera House, High St; mains €9-13; ⏰10am-4pm Mon-Sat; 📶) on the top floor of the Opera House, where harbour views complement the great cakes and coffee.

Simon Lambert & Sons PUB FOOD €
(Simon's Place; ☎053-918 0041; 37 South Main St; mains €6-10; ⏰9.30am-noon & 12.30-4pm; 📶)

This atmospheric, low-ceilinged pub serves good food during the day, with breakfast offerings that run from scrambled eggs and toast to the full Irish fry-up, complete with excellent coffee. The lunch menu includes tasty and inventive sandwiches, gourmet burgers and pulled-pork rolls, and a grand selection of craft beers to wash it all down.

★Cistín Eile MODERN IRISH €€
(☎053-912 1616; www.cistineilewexford.com; 80 South Main St; lunch mains €7-15, 3-course dinners €29; ⊙noon-3pm Mon-Fri, 12.30-3pm Sat, 6-9pm Wed-Sat;) Bring a hearty appetite when you visit this always-busy restaurant – as the motto on the wall says, *Is maith an t-anlann an t-ocras* (hunger makes a great sauce). Expect the daily menu of locally sourced produce to include slow-cooked beef, bacon and cabbage, mashed potatoes, foraged salad leaves, intense flavours and generous helpings.

★Greenacres BISTRO, DELI €€
(☎053-912 2975; www.greenacres.ie; 7 Selskar St; mains €17-23, 3-course set menus €30; ⊙bistro 9am-10pm Mon-Sat, noon-8pm Sun;) Irish cheeses and local produce are beautifully displayed in the food hall, the wine selection is the best south of Dublin, and the gourmet bistro gets star rating for ingredients such as wild pigeon, rock oysters and smoked rabbit. The upper floors house an excellent art gallery.

Yard MODERN IRISH €€
(☎053-914 4083; www.theyard.ie; 3 Lower George St; mains €10-30; ⊙noon-3pm & 6pm-late) This intimate, low-lit restaurant opens onto an elegant courtyard beneath a canopy of fairy lights. Adventurous contemporary cuisine changes with the season, with an emphasis on fresh and unfussy; think wild mushroom risotto, potato and herb fishcakes, and similar. Best to book at weekends.

THE GUINNESS BOOK OF RECORDS

During a wildfowling trip to the Slobs near Wexford in 1951, the chairman of Guinness Brewery, Sir Hugh Beaver, shot at but missed a golden plover. This provoked a spirited debate over whether it, or the red grouse, was Europe's fastest game bird. Sir Hugh realised that similar debates regularly cropped up all over the world, and that publishing definitive answers could prove profitable.

He was right about that – the first *Guinness Book of Records* was an immediate bestseller when it was published in 1955, and today it is itself a record-holder, as the world's biggest-selling copyrighted book – but wrong about Europe's fastest game bird (it's actually the spur-wing goose).

Drinking & Nightlife

Wexford is a regional centre for frivolity and pubs abound, especially on Monck St and Cornmarket.

Centenary Stores PUB, CLUB
(www.thestores.ie; Charlotte St; ⊙pub 10am-11pm, nightclub 9pm-2am Thu-Sun) One of Wexford's livelier spots, this former warehouse is a mix of old and new with a downstairs darkwood pub with basic food and a crusty local clientele, contrasted with a pulsating modern designer nightclub, The Backroom, that attracts a spirited youthful crowd at weekends. Sunday lunchtime trad music sessions in summer.

Sky & the Ground PUB
(112-113 South Main St; ⊙2-11.30pm Mon-Thu, 1pm-12.30am Fri & Sat, to 11pm Sun) A long-standing favourite, the Sky & the Ground has classic decor, with a roaring fire and walls covered in old enamel signs. Trad music sessions often take place on weeknights, and during the summer there's an outdoor deck upstairs.

Entertainment

Wexford Opera House OPERA
(www.wexfordoperahouse.ie; High St; tickets €20-40;) Opened in 2008, Wexford's gleaming Opera House packs more architectural punch inside than out. In addition to opera, it stages theatre productions and concerts. Hosts the opera festival in autumn.

Wexford Arts Centre DANCE
(☎053-912 3764; www.wexfordartscentre.ie; Cornmarket; tickets €10-20;) Housed in the 18th-century market hall, this centre hosts exhibitions, theatre (including occasional productions in Irish), dance and music, and has a good cafe.

Shopping

Bull Ring Market CRAFTS
(Bull Ring; ⊙9am-2pm Fri & Sat) There is a lively weekly market at the Bull Ring with crafts, vintage clothes, antiques, jewellery, homewares, toys and accessories.

WORTH A TRIP

CURRACLOE BEACH

Soft white sand, gentle surf and lack of development are the most appealing features of the 11km-long, Blue Flag–rated **Curracloe Beach**. On sunny days families flock to the beach, but due to its vast size you can easily find a half-acre to call your own. The beach is 13km northeast of Wexford, signposted at various points along the R741 and R742 road.

The strand doubled for Omaha Beach in the famous D-Day opening scenes of the movie *Saving Private Ryan* (1998), and one of the landing craft used in the film can still be seen in the grounds of Curracloe Holiday Villas at Ballinesker.

There are good walking trails through the pine forests and sand dunes of **Raven Nature Reserve** at the south end, and it's possible to cycle to the beach from Wexford town (waymarked cycle route 2 – ask for a map at the tourist office).

Blue Egg Gallery ARTS & CRAFTS
(John's Gate St; ⏲11am-5.30pm Tue-Sat) One of several commercial galleries and craft shops in town (ask the tourist office for a full list), the Blue Egg concentrates on contemporary Irish crafts in a range of materials, including ceramics, metal and glass.

Wexford Book Centre BOOKS
(5 South Main St; ⏲9am-6pm Mon-Sat, 1-5pm Sun) Lots of worthwhile Irish titles plus local guides and maps.

ℹ Information

Wexford Tourist Office (www.visitwexford.ie; Quay Front; ⏲9.15am-5.15pm Mon-Sat Apr-Oct, shorter hours Nov-Mar; 📶) has maps and leaflets showing local walks and cycling routes.

ℹ Getting There & Around

BUS

Buses depart from the train station.

Dublin €19.50, 2¾ hours, hourly
Enniscorthy €7.80, 20 minutes, hourly
Rosslare Harbour €6, 30 minutes, six daily
Waterford €11.50, one hour, seven daily

Wexford Bus (www.wexfordbus.com) operates to/from Dublin Airport (€20, 2¾ hours, hourly) via Enniscorthy, Ferns and Dublin city centre.

TAXI

Wexford Cabs (☎053-912 3123; 24hr) has services to Rosslare Harbour and Dublin Airport.

TRAIN

Trains from **O'Hanrahan Station** (☎053-912 2522; Redmond Sq) service Dublin Connolly Station (€27, 2½ hours) and Rosslare Harbour (€5.85, four daily, 25 minutes).

Rosslare Harbour

POP 1550

Busy, functional Rosslare Harbour has connections to Wales and France from the **Europort ferry terminal**, home also to **Rosslare Europort train station**. The road leading uphill from the harbour is the N25. The only reason to stay here is if you have to catch an early ferry.

🛏 Sleeping

St Martin's Rd (signposted Rosslare Harbour Village, on the right approaching from Wexford) is lined with B&Bs that cater for ferry passengers, and there are plenty of pubs serving standard fare.

★**O'Leary's Farm B&B** B&B **€€**
(☎053-913 3134; www.olearysfarm.com; Killilane, Kilrane; s/d from €40/76; 📶) A 10-minute drive from Rosslare ferry terminal, this working organic farm offers four homey guest rooms, three with sea views. The delightful sitting room has a fireplace, a piano and plenty of books. Breakfast includes vegan, vegetarian and coeliac options, the farm's produce, and homemade bread. Follow the N25 to Kilrane and turn off at the Kilrane Inn, then follow signs.

ℹ Getting There & Away

Buses and trains depart from the Rosslare Europort station, located beside the ferry terminal.

BOAT

Rosslare ferries link Ireland to Wales and France (note that the frequency of sailings may be reduced in winter). Routes include the following:

Rosslare to Pembroke (Wales) Irish Ferries (www.irishferries.com) offer two crossings daily (foot passenger €35, car and driver from €89, four hours).

Rosslare to Fishguard (Wales) Stena Line (www.stenaline.ie) runs a faster route to Wales (foot passenger €40, car and driver from €99, 3¼ hours, twice daily).

Rosslare to Cherbourg (France) Both Stena Line and Irish Ferries sail this route, with three or four crossings a week between them (foot passenger €85, car and driver from €200, 19 hours).

Rosslare to Roscoff (France) Irish Ferries run this route once or twice a week from May to September only (foot passenger €109, car and driver from €200, 17½ hours).

BUS

Bus Éireann (053-912 2522; www.buseireann.ie) runs services to numerous Irish towns and cities, including Dublin (€23, three hours, seven daily), changing at Wexford (€6, 30 minutes), and Cork (€28.50, 4½ hours, six daily) via Waterford (€20.20, 1½ hours).

TRAIN

Irish Rail runs four trains daily on the Rosslare Europort–Dublin Connolly Station route (€28.65, 2¾ hours) via Wexford (€5.85, 25 minutes).

South of Rosslare Harbour

A maze of minor roads meanders among the flatlands and tidal lagoons that spread from Rosslare Harbour to Kilmore Quay. Traditional Wexford **thatched cottages**, with mud walls, half-hipped roofs and trademark small, square porches, brighten the roadsides, and a sandy beach is never far away.

Sights

Lady's Island Lake LAKE

This lake's brackish waters, separated from the sea by a barrier beach, are an important breeding ground for rare roseate terns. The lake encloses **Our Lady's Island** (www.ourladysisland.ie), site of an early Augustinian priory and still the focus of an annual pilgrimage in August/September. Fervent pilgrims make nine circuits of the island, many of them barefoot (in olden times they used to crawl). Outside of pilgrimage season the pilgrim path makes for a lovely walk (2km); don't miss the picturesque priory graveyard, awash with wild garlic in spring.

Tacumshane Windmill HISTORIC BUILDING

(www.millhousebar.ie; Tacumshane) FREE Tacumshane Windmill is a rare survivor of the mills that once dotted this landscape, and the only complete windmill in the Republic of Ireland. Built in the 19th century using timber washed up on local beaches, it sports a cute thatched cap. It's on a minor road, a few kilometres west of Our Lady's Island; ask for the key at the neighbouring Millhouse pub.

Eating

Meyler's Millhouse Bar & Restaurant PUB FOOD €€

(053-913 1700; www.millhousebar.ie; Tacumshane; mains €12-19; food served 5-9pm Fri-Sat, 12.30-8pm Sun;) This country pub has a good beer garden overlooked by Tacumshane Windmill, and serves fish and chips, homemade burgers and other pub grub (kids menu available). It's 5km southwest of Rosslare Harbour, and a bit hard to find; look out for the pub's own signposts.

Kilmore Quay

POP 400

Kilmore Quay is part commercial fishing port, part picturesque village lined with thatched cottages, where the cry of gulls and smell of the ocean provide the appropriate atmosphere for sampling the local seafood. The harbour is the jumping-off point for Ireland's largest bird sanctuary, the Saltee Islands.

Sights & Activities

The beach and sand dunes of **Ballyteigue Burrow Nature Reserve** stretch for 9km northwest from Kilmore Quay, and are the summer home of chattering terns and serenading skylarks. The salt marsh and mudflats behind the dunes are an important habitat for birds such as golden plover, black-tailed godwit, and pale-bellied brent geese.

Sea anglers can fish for sea bass, plaice and flounder from the shore, or charter one of half a dozen boats from the harbour (details at www.visitkilmorequay.com) for wreck and reef fishing.

Ballycross Apple Farm FARM

(053-913 5160; www.ballycross.com; Bridgetown; adult/child €3.50/2.50; noon-6pm Sat & Sun Apr-Oct) This farm gets top marks from the kids for its pedal-powered tractors and go-karts, animal-feeding sessions and signposted walking trails that run via riverbanks, woodland and orchards. The shop sells apples, apple juice, chutneys and jams, and the cafe serves delicious homemade waffles and pancakes. It's about 9km north of Kilmore Quay, on a minor road 2km southwest of Bridgetown.

Saltee Islands ISLAND

(www.salteeislands.info; 11.30am-4pm) Once the haunt of privateers, smugglers and 'dyvers pyrates', the Saltee Islands now have a peaceful existence as one of Europe's most important bird sanctuaries. More than 220 species have been recorded here, most of them passing migrants; the main breeding populations include chough, gannet, guillemot, razorbill, kittiwake, puffin and Manx shearwater. Boats make the 4km trip from Kilmore Quay harbour, but landing is weather-dependent. Book through **Declan Bates** (053-912 9684, 087 252 9736; Kilmore Quay Harbour; day trips €25).

The 90-hectare Great Saltee and the 40-hectare Little Saltee (closed to visits) were inhabited as long ago as 3500 to 2000 BC. From the 13th century until the dissolution of the monasteries, they were the property of Tintern Abbey, after which various owners were granted the land. The islands are now privately owned.

The best time to visit is the spring and early-summer nesting season. The birds leave once the chicks can fly; by early August it's eerily quiet. There are no toilets or other facilities on the islands.

Festivals & Events

Seafood Festival FOOD
(www.kilmorequayseafoodfestival.com) A four-day festival of music, exhibitions, guided nature walks, kayak races and, of course, local seafood. Held in July.

Sleeping & Eating

Mill Road Farm B&B €
(053-912 9633; www.millroadfarm.com; R739; s/d €45/70; closed late Dec;) About 2km northeast of Kilmore Quay, this dairy farm has four daintily decorated guest rooms with lots of floral fabrics (three with sea views beyond the paddock); the owner breeds horses for racing. The sitting room has plenty of games and books for wet days. Breakfast includes homemade bread and free-range eggs.

Crazy Crab SEAFOOD €€
(www.crazycrab.ie; Harbour Rd; mains €10-20; 5-8pm Thu, noon-8pm Fri-Sun Apr-Oct) Nab a table on the sea-view patio at this unpretentious eatery with a nautical-themed blue-and-white frontage and porthole-style windows. All manner of fresh local seafood is on offer, from classic fish and chips to classy pan-fried scallops.

Silver Fox Seafood Restaurant SEAFOOD €€€
(053-912 9888; www.thesilverfox.ie; Kilmore Quay; mains €16-35; noon-10pm daily Apr-Oct, 5-10pm Fri, noon-10pm Sat & Sun Nov-Mar, closed mid-Jan–mid-Feb;) The Silver Fox's fresh-from-the-ocean offerings include locally landed plaice, langoustines, crab and mussels, plus daily specials depending on what arrives at the quay. The dining room exudes white-tableclothed elegance; don't arrive in flip-flops. Booking advised at weekends.

Getting There & Away

Wexford Bus (www.wexfordbus.com) runs to/from Wexford four times daily except Sunday (€8, 30 minutes).

Hook Peninsula

The road that leads around the long, tapering finger of the Hook Peninsula is signposted as the **Ring of Hook coastal drive**. Around every other bend is a quiet beach, a crumbling fortress, a stately abbey or a seafood restaurant, and the world's oldest working lighthouse stands tall at the peninsula's tip.

Strongbow passed here on his way to capturing Waterford in 1170, reputedly instructing his men to land 'by Hook or by Crooke' (the latter referring to the nearby settlement of Crooke) – the origin of the popular phrase.

Getting There & Away

There is limited public transport as far as Fethard; beyond that you'll need a car or bike.

Duncannon & Around

POP 330

The small, dusty holiday town of Duncannon slopes down to a sandy beach that's transformed into a surrealist canvas during August's **Duncannon Sand Sculpting Festival**.

About 4km northwest of Duncannon is pretty **Ballyhack**, where a car ferry (p178) makes the short crossing to Passage East in County Waterford. It's dominated by the 15th-century **Ballyhack Castle** (www.heritageireland.ie; Ballyhack; 10.30am-5pm mid-May–late Aug) FREE, a Knights Hospitallers tower house, containing a small exhibition on the Crusades.

Sights

Duncannon Fort FORT
(www.duncannonfort.com; Duncannon; adult/child €5/3; 10am-5.30pm daily Jun–mid-Sep, to 4.30pm Mon-Fri mid-Sep–May) Star-shaped Duncannon Fort, just west of Duncannon village, was built in 1588 to stave off a feared attack by the Spanish Armada, and later

DON'T MISS

TINTERN ABBEY

Named after its Welsh counterpart, from where its first monks hailed, the atmospheric remains of **Tintern Abbey** (www.heritageireland.ie; Saltmills; adult/child €4/2; ⏲10am-5pm Apr-Oct) enjoy a lovely setting amid 40 hectares of woodland. Unusually for an abbey, it has a long history as a private residence. Following the dissolution of the monasteries in the early 16th century, Tintern was granted to Staffordshire nobleman Anthony Colclough, and his descendants continued to live here until 1959. The abbey is signposted off the R734, 5km north of Fethard.

William Marshal, Earl of Pembroke, founded the Cistercian abbey in the early 13th century after he nearly perished at sea and swore to establish a church if he made it ashore. The cloister walls, nave, crossing tower, chancel and south transept still stand tall, along with the conversions made by generations of Colcloughs to create a country residence out of a ruined abbey.

Walking trails wind into the surrounding woods, past lakes and streams and more crumbling ruins, including a small single-cell church, to the beautiful, 200-year-old **Colclough Walled Garden** (www.colcloughwalledgarden.com; Saltmills; adult/child €3/2; ⏲10am-6pm May-Sep, to 4pm Oct-Apr), which has been replanted and restored to its former glory.

used by the Irish army as a WWI training base (most buildings here date from this period). There's a small military and maritime museum, plus a cafe, a dry moat and an art gallery. At the time of research, the fort was closed for renovation works.

Dunbrody Abbey HISTORIC BUILDING
(www.dunbrodyabbey.com; Campile; adult/child €3/1; ⏲11am-6pm mid-May–mid-Sep) Beside the R733, 9km north of Duncannon, ruined Dunbrody Abbey is a remarkably intact Cistercian abbey founded by Strongbow in 1170 and completed in 1220. A combined ticket (adult/child €6/3) includes a museum with a huge doll's house, minigolf, and an entertaining yew-hedge maze made up of over 1500 trees. There are tea rooms and a craft shop.

Sleeping & Eating

The Duncannon area is home to some magnificent country-house accommodation in addition to simple beachside B&Bs.

★**Glendine Country House** GUESTHOUSE €€
(☎051-389 500; www.glendinehouse.com; Arthurstown; r €110; 📶) Staying at this 19th-century country house is like staying with friends with impeccable taste. Bay windows overlook grounds populated by deer, cattle and sheep, and paintings by local artists adorn the walls. The rooms typically have hardwood floors, chandeliers and antiques; request room 9 with its princely proportions and king-sized bed. The house is 5km north of Duncannon.

Aldridge Lodge Restaurant & Guesthouse INN €€
(☎051-389 116; www.aldridgelodge.com; Duncannon; s/d from €50/90; 📶) In a windblown spot on open fields above Duncannon, Aldridge takes a bit of finding, but it's worth it for the elegant, contemporary guest rooms and fresh local seafood such as Hook Head crab claws or Kilmore cod (dinner €40; served 7pm till late Wednesday to Sunday). Two caveats: book your table in advance, and children under seven aren't allowed.

Dunbrody Country House Hotel HOTEL €€€
(☎051-389 600; www.dunbrodyhouse.com; Arthurstown; s/d €145/255; 📶) Chef Kevin Dundon is a familiar face on Irish TV and author of several cookbooks, and he even has his own line of cookware. His spa hotel, in a period-decorated 1830s Georgian manor in 120-hectare grounds, is the stuff of foodies' fantasies, with a gourmet **restaurant** (dinner around €55 to €65 per person) and **cookery school** (one-day courses from €175).

Sqigl Restaurant & Roche's Bar MODERN IRISH €€
(☎051-389 188; www.sqiglrestaurant.com; Quay Rd, Duncannon; restaurant mains €20-25, bar mains €7-13; ⏲restaurant 6-9pm Wed-Sat, bar noon-9pm daily; 📶) Local produce is the mainstay of Sqigl, where dishes range from spring lamb to local seafood (bookings essential). Roche's Bar adjoins and has excellent bar food – try the seafood chowder – and an inviting atmosphere with vintage advertising posters. Trad music sessions on Fridays.

Hook Head & Around

The journey from Fethard to Hook Head takes in a hypnotic stretch of horizon, with few houses between the flat, open fields of the tapering peninsula. Views extend across Waterford Harbour and, on a clear day, to the Comeragh and Galtee Mountains.

This is prime day-trip country, from Wexford or Waterford. Villages such as **Slade**, where most of the activity is in the swirl of seagulls above the ruined castle and harbour, beguile. Beaches include the wonderfully secluded **Dollar Bay** and **Booley Bay** just beyond Templetown en route to Duncannon.

Sights

★Hook Lighthouse LIGHTHOUSE

(www.hookheritage.ie; Hook Head; adult/child €6/3.50; 9.30am-5pm;) On its southern tip, Hook Head is capped by the world's oldest working lighthouse, a modern light flashing atop a 13th-century tower. Access is by half-hour guided tour, which includes a climb up the 115 steps for great views. The visitor centre has a good cafe while the grassy grounds and surrounding shore are popular for picnics and walks.

It's said that monks first lit a beacon on the head in the 5th century, and that the first Viking invaders were so happy to have a guiding light that they left them alone. In the early 13th century William Marshal erected a more permanent structure, which is still standing today beneath the lighthouse's neat, black-and-white exterior.

Loftus Hall HISTORIC BUILDING

(051-397 728; www.loftushall.ie; Hook Peninsula; adult/child daytime €10/5, night €15; noon-5pm & 7-10pm Jul-Aug, weekends only Apr-Jun, school hols Sep-Mar) About 3.5km northeast of Hook Head, this crumbling manor house gazes over to Dunmore East across the mouth of Waterford Harbour. Dating from the 1600s and rebuilt in the 1870s, Loftus Hall is reputed to be one of the most haunted houses in Ireland. Daytime tours are historical, while evening tours are 'scary' – for adults only – and comprise an hour-long interactive visit where the guide recounts the ghostly history of the building. Check the website for special events.

Activities

There are brilliant, blustery **walks** on both sides of Hook Head. Poke around the tide pools while watching for surprise showers from blowholes on the western side of the peninsula. The rocks here are Carboniferous limestone, rich in **fossils**. Search carefully and you may find 350-million-year-old brachiopod shells, lacy bryozoans and tiny disc-like pieces of crinoids, an ancient relative of the sea urchin. The slabs beneath the seaward side of Hook Lighthouse are a good place to look.

At low tide, there's a good walk between Grange and Carnivan beaches, past caves, rock pools and **Baginbun Head** which, surmounted by a 19th-century Martello tower, is where the Normans first landed in 1169 to begin their conquest of Ireland. It's a good vantage point for **birdwatching**: more than 200 species have been recorded passing through. You might even spot dolphins or whales in the estuary.

New Ross

POP 8150

The big attraction at New Ross (Rhos Mhic Triúin) is the opportunity to board a 19th-century Famine ship. But New Ross' historical links stretch back much further – to the 12th century, when it developed as a Norman port on the River Barrow. A group of rebels tried to seize the town during the 1798 Rising. They were repelled by the defending garrison, leaving 3000 dead and much of the place in tatters.

Today it's not a pretty town, but the eastern bank retains some intriguingly steep and narrow streets, and the remains of a medieval abbey. Ask at the tourist office for a map of the town's **history trail** (allow 1½ hours).

Sights & Activities

★Dunbrody Famine Ship MUSEUM

(051-425 239; www.dunbrody.com; The Quay; adult/child €8.50/5; 9am-6pm Apr-Sep, to 5pm Oct-Mar) Called 'coffin ships' due to their fatality rate, the leaky, smelly boats that hauled a generation of Irish emigrants to America are re-imagined on board this replica ship on the New Ross waterfront. The emigrants' sorrowful yet often inspiring stories are brought to life by costumed guides during 45-minute tours. A 10-minute introductory film provides historical background about the mid-19th-century Ireland they were leaving.

Galley River Cruising Restaurant BOAT TOUR

(www.rivercruises.ie; North Quay; lunch/afternoon/dinner €15/25/40; Apr-Oct) This floating

WORTH A TRIP

WEXFORD & THE KENNEDYS

In 1848 Patrick Kennedy escaped famine-stricken County Wexford aboard an emigrant ship similar to the Dunbrody Famine Ship in New Ross. Hoping to find better prospects in America, he succeeded beyond his wildest dreams: his descendants included rum-runners, senators and a US president. The family's Irish roots are remembered at two sites near New Ross.

Kennedy Homestead (051-388 264; www.kennedyhomestead.ie; Dunganstown; adult/student/family €7.50/5/20; 10am-5pm Jul & Aug, 11.30am-4.30pm Mon-Fri Feb-Jun & Sep-Nov, closed Dec-Jan) The birthplace of Patrick Kennedy, great-grandfather of John F Kennedy, is a farm that still looks much as it must have 160 years ago. When JFK visited the farm in 1963 and hugged the current owner's grandmother, it was his first public display of affection, according to his sister Jean. A small museum examines the Kennedy dynasty's history on both sides of the Atlantic. It's on a minor road 7km south of New Ross, signposted from R733.

John F Kennedy Arboretum (www.heritageireland.ie; Ballysop; adult/child €4/2; 10am-8pm May-Aug, to 6.30pm Apr & Sep, to 5pm Oct-Mar) This beautiful woodland park, dedicated to the memory of JFK, has 4500 species of trees and shrubs spread across 252 hectares of woods and gardens. Walking trails lead to Slieve Coillte (270m) where, on a clear day, you can gaze out over six counties. The park has a small visitor centre, a tea room (May to September) and a picnic area; a miniature train tootles around in the summer months. It's 12km south of New Ross, signposted off the R733.

restaurant offers scenic cruises along the 'Three Sisters' rivers – the Suir, Nore and Barrow – heading upstream to Inistioge or St Mullins or downstream towards Waterford, depending on the tide. Two-hour lunch cruises depart at 12.30pm, 1½-hour afternoon tea cruises set off at 3pm, and three-hour dinner cruises leave at 6pm.

Sleeping & Eating

MacMurrough Farm Cottages COTTAGE €€
(051-421 383; www.macmurrough.com; MacMurrough; 2-person cottages from €60; mid-Mar–Oct;) A strutting rooster serves as an alarm clock at Brian and Jenny's remote hilltop farm. These well-priced self-catering cottages are located in the former stables and pleasantly furnished with good facilities. Follow the hand-painted signs up a series of tracks 3.5km northeast of New Ross. A cosy old pub and a market are close by.

Brandon House Hotel HOTEL €€
(051-421 703; www.brandonhousehotel.ie; r from €88; @) This sympathetically extended Victorian red-brick manor certainly lives up to its reputation as family friendly, with kids happily bounding around the place. Winning elements include river views, open log fires, a library bar and large rooms, as well as a spa. It's signposted off the N25 ring road on the southern edge of New Ross.

★**Cafe Nutshell** CAFE €
(8 South St; mains €6-16; 9am-6pm Mon-Sat;) Scones, breads and buns are all baked on the premises, inventive hot lunch specials utilise local produce, and there's a great range of smoothies, juices and organic wines. Mains come with an array of fresh salads. The adjacent health-food shop and deli are perfect for picnic provisions.

Information

New Ross Tourist Office (051-425 239; www.experiencenewross.com; The Quay; 9am-6pm Apr-Sep, to 5pm Oct-Mar) Located in the same building as the Dunbrody Famine Ship ticket office.

Getting There & Away

Buses depart from The Quay and travel to Waterford (€9.40, 30 minutes, eight to 12 daily), Wexford (€9.50, 45 minutes, three to four daily) and Dublin (€17.50, three hours, at least four daily).

Enniscorthy

POP 10,900

County Wexford's second-largest town, Enniscorthy (Inis Coirthaidh) has a warren of steep streets descending from Augustus Pugin's cathedral to the Norman castle and the River Slaney. The town is inextricably linked to some of the fiercest fighting of the 1798 Rising, when rebels captured the town and set up camp at Vinegar Hill.

Sights

National 1798 Rebellion Centre MUSEUM
(www.1798centre.ie; Parnell Rd; adult/child €7/3, incl Enniscorthy Castle €10/5; 9.30am-5pm Mon-Fri, noon-5pm Sat Apr-Sep, 10am-4pm Mon-Fri, noon-5pm Sat Oct-Mar;) This exhibition does a fine job of explaining the background to one of Ireland's pivotal historical events. It covers the French and American revolutions, which helped spark Wexford's abortive uprising against British rule in Ireland, before chronicling the Battle of Vinegar Hill. One of the most bloodthirsty battles of the 1798 Rising and a turning point in the struggle, it took place just outside Enniscorthy. A visit here provides context for a walk up Vinegar Hill itself.

Vinegar Hill HISTORIC SITE
(www.vinegarhill.ie) Scene of one of the most important battles of Ireland's 1798 rebellion against British rule, this hill just outside Enniscorthy is topped with a memorial to the uprising, and dotted with explanatory signs about the battlefield. A battle re-enactment takes place each year on the first weekend in August. Access is from a car park on the east side of the hill, reached via Drumgoold Rd; it's about 2km east of Enniscorthy Castle, a 30-minute walk.

Enniscorthy Castle CASTLE
(www.enniscorthycastle.ie; Castle Hill; adult/child €4/2, incl 1798 Centre €10/5; 9.30am-5pm Mon-Fri Apr-Sep, 10am-4pm Mon-Fri Oct-Mar, noon-5pm Sat & Sun year-round) This stout, four-towered keep was originally built by the Normans; like much else in these parts, it was surrendered to Cromwell in 1649. During the 1798 Rising, rebels used this castle as a prison, and from 1901 to 1953 it was the family home of local businessman and landowner Henry J Roche. It now houses a museum about the history of both town and castle, and has a rooftop deck with spectacular views.

St Aidan's Cathedral CATHEDRAL
(www.staidanscathedral.ie; Church St; 8.30am-6pm) FREE Restored to its original glory (check out the star-spangled roof), this dazzling Roman Catholic cathedral (1846) was designed by Augustus Pugin, the architect behind the Houses of Parliament in London.

Festivals & Events

Strawberry Festival FOOD
(www.strawberryfest.ie) Celebrating the favourite crop of Ireland's sunny southeast, this eclectic event in late June includes an agricultural show, a farmers market, cookery demonstrations, live music, children's events and the crowing of the Strawberry Queen. Pubs extend their hours, bands are booked, and strawberries and cream is on sale everywhere.

Sleeping

Salville House B&B €€
(053-923 5252; www.salvillehouse.com; Salville; s/d €75/110;) The views across the great lawn to the River Slaney are reason enough to stay at this Georgian country house, with bedrooms appropriately furnished in period style. There are three rooms with private bathroom in the main house, and another two in a self-contained apartment. Dinner (per person €40) features four courses of seasonal, organic fare. It's signposted off the N11, 2km south of town.

Clone House B&B €€
(053-936 6113; www.clonehouse.ie; Clone; s/d from €50/90;) Stepping into this ivy-clad Georgian farmhouse is like stepping back in time, with the smell of beeswax polish wafting from glowing mahogany furniture, and light sparkling from antique gilt mirrors and hand-cut Irish crystal; bedrooms have all mod cons, though. It's set in beautiful gardens beside the River Bann, on a quiet back road 9km north of Enniscorthy.

Riverside Park HOTEL €€
(053-923 7900; www.riversideparkhotel.com; The Promenade; r from €89;) Enjoy strolls along the grassy banks of the river from this superbly positioned hotel. A dramatic lobby in a circular tower sets the scene. Comfortable rooms are decorated in neutral creams, browns and beige, and most have balconies and river views. This is a popular hotel for weddings so Saturdays may be booked up and/or noisy!

Woodbrook House GUESTHOUSE €€€
(053-925 5114; www.woodbrookhouse.ie; Killanne; s/d from €100/160; Easter-Jun & Aug-Sep;) Rebuilt after sustaining damage in the 1798 Rising, this glorious Georgian country house has a superb setting beneath the Blackstairs Mountains. The lobby features a gravity-defying spiral staircase that amazes

now just as it did over 200 years ago. Green practices are used throughout and you can make arrangements for dinner (€50; organic, of course). It is 13km west of Enniscorthy.

Eating & Drinking

Farmers Market MARKET €
(Abbey Sq; 9am-2pm Sat) Enniscorthy's farmers market sells local and organic goods and prepared foods. Look for Carrigbyrne cheese.

★ **Cotton Tree Cafe** CAFE €
(053-923 4641; Slaney Pl; mains €5-9; 8am-5.30pm Mon-Sat, 11am-5.30pm Sun;) A pleasantly informal cafe charmingly decorated with homey and historic artwork. The menu includes gourmet soups and sandwiches with ingredients such as roast Irish beef and hummus. There's also a choice of imaginative salads and daily lunch specials such as fish pie, Asian pork burger and Indonesian curry.

Toffee & Thyme CAFE €
(24 Rafter St; mains €6-12; 8am-5pm Mon-Sat;) This stylish cafe dishes up tasty light meals created from regional produce. Choose from sandwiches, salads, savoury soups and hot meals. If you're dropping in for a coffee, try the homemade scones.

Galo Chargrill Restaurant PORTUGUESE €€
(19 Main St; mains €10-20; noon-3pm & 7-10pm Tue-Sun) This small Portuguese restaurant has a big reputation. On balmy days the front opens up like the lid on a can of anchovies, and even on dull days the spicy chargrills – such as double chicken fillets with chilli – provide a burst of sunshine.

Bailey IRISH €€
(www.thebailey.ie; Barrack St; mains €10-25; food served 12.30-8.30pm;) The interior of this converted riverside grain store may look a tad dated with its leatherette banquettes, however Baileys remains one of the most popular summertime haunts in town with its regular live gigs, ranging from rock and roll to blues. There's a spacious terrace out front and the pub grub is filling.

Antique Tavern PUB
(14 Slaney St; 5-11.30pm Mon-Fri, 11am-midnight Sat & Sun) Slanted on the side of a steep street sloping up from the river, this creaky black-and-white pub dates from 1790 and is somewhere between twee and rustic. It attracts a rousing crowd of locals, and has an upstairs glassed-in terrace for warm-weather tippling accompanied by great river views.

Information

Tourist Office (053-923 4699; www.enniscorthytourism.com; Castle Hill; 10am-5pm Mon-Fri, noon-5pm Sat & Sun Apr-Sep, 9.30am-4pm Mon-Fri Oct-Mar) Inside Enniscorthy Castle.

Getting There & Away

BUS

Bus Éireann buses run to Dublin (€17.50, 2½ hours, hourly) and Wexford (€7.80, 20 minutes, hourly).

TRAIN

The train station is on the eastern bank of the river. Trains run to Dublin Connolly (€26, 2¼ hours, four daily) and Wexford (€8.05, 20 minutes, five daily).

Ferns

POP 1360

It's hard to believe that the workaday village of Ferns was once the powerhouse of the kings of Leinster, in particular Dermot MacMurrough (1110–71), who is forever associated with bringing the Normans to Ireland. The Normans left behind a cathedral, an abbey and a doughty castle, later smashed to pieces by Cromwell.

Sights

Ferns Castle RUIN
(www.heritageireland.ie; 10am-5pm mid-May–Sep) FREE Ferns Castle was built around 1220, but parliamentarians destroyed the castle and executed most of the local population during Cromwell's rampage through Ireland in 1649. The ruins are thought to stand on the site of Dermot MacMurrough's old fortress. A couple of walls and part of the moat survive incongruously in the middle of town; you can climb to the top of the one complete tower. The visitor centre holds regular exhibitions relating to the history of the town.

St Edan's Cathedral CATHEDRAL
(varies) FREE Built in early Gothic style in 1817, Ferns' 'modern' cathedral is thought to be the smallest in Europe. Its graveyard contains a high cross, said to mark the resting place of Dermot MacMurrough. In the field behind the cathedral stand two medieval

ruins sitting in lonely isolation surrounded by grazing cattle: the Norman-built **Ferns Cathedral** and **St Mary's Abbey**. Dermot MacMurrough founded the abbey in 1158, inviting Augustinian monks to run a monastery here.

Getting There & Away

Ferns is an easy 12km drive northeast of Enniscorthy on the N11. Buses between Dublin and Wexford all stop here.

COUNTY WATERFORD

POP 113,800 / AREA 1855 SQ KM

Diverse County Waterford harbours: seaside resorts of all flavours along its sandy coastline; historic churches, cathedrals and castles; a warren of walking trails in the beautiful Nire Valley, concealed among the Comeragh and Monavullagh Mountains; and lively Waterford city, with its maze of medieval lanes and well-preserved Georgian architecture.

Waterford City

POP 51,500

Waterford (Port Láirge) is Ireland's oldest city – it celebrated its 1100th anniversary in 2014 – with a history that dates back to Viking times. Taking its name from the Old Norse *vedrarfjord* ('winter haven' or 'windy harbour' are just two of several possible translations), it remains a busy port city on a tidal reach of the River Suir, famous as the home of Waterford crystal.

Although the city has been extensively redeveloped, notably along the waterfront, it retains vestiges of its Viking and Norman past in the narrow streets and town walls of the so-called Viking Triangle, where three excellent museums tell the story of Ireland's Middle Ages better than in any other city in the country.

History

The city was established as a Viking port around 914, and its original city walls were extended by King John in 1210 to make it Ireland's most powerful city. In the 15th century it resisted the forces of two pretenders to the English Crown, Lambert Simnel and Perkin Warbeck, and subsequently, in 1649, defied Cromwell. In 1650 his forces returned and Waterford surrendered. Although the city escaped the customary slaughter, Catholics were either exiled to the west or shipped as slaves to the Caribbean, and the population dramatically declined.

Sights

The wedge of ancient streets northwest of the Mall – the so-called **Viking Triangle** (www.waterfordvikingtriangle.com) – is home to three excellent museums (collectively called **Waterford Treasures**) which cover 1000 years of local history. If you only have time to visit one attraction here, make it the Medieval Museum.

★**Medieval Museum** MUSEUM
(www.waterfordtreasures.com; Greyfriars St; adult/child €7/free, incl Bishop's Palace €10/free; 9.15am-5pm Mon-Fri, 10am-5pm Sat, 11am-5pm Sun, longer hours Jun-Aug;) Housed in a stunning modern building which incorporates several medieval buildings and part of the city wall in its basement (all on display), this museum documents Waterford's medieval history in glowing detail. The highlights of the collection are the extraordinary 15th-century **cloth-of-gold church vestments**, made from silk woven in Florence and embroidered in Bruges around 1460. Hidden beneath Christ Church Cathedral and forgotten for 123 years, they are a rare survival and one of the great treasures of medieval Europe.

Other outstanding exhibits include the **Great Parchment Book of Waterford**, an original document which records in fascinating detail what medieval life was like, including cases of petty crime and the impact of the plague, and a **ceremonial sword** and two maces gifted to the city by England's Edward IV in 1462.

Bishop's Palace MUSEUM
(www.waterfordtreasures.com; The Mall; adult/child €7/free, incl Medieval Museum €10/free; 9.15am-5pm Mon-Fri, 10am-5pm Sat, 11am-5pm Sun, longer hours Jun-Aug) The Bishop's Palace, a Georgian mansion dating from 1741, covers Waterford's history from 1700 to 1970 and displays a wide-ranging selection of treasures from the city's coffers, from period furniture, oil paintings and Georgian silverware to old photos recording the 1960s heyday of Irish showbands. Most interesting is the original dining room set with period tableware including the world's oldest surviving piece of Waterford crystal, a decanter dating from 1789.

Waterford

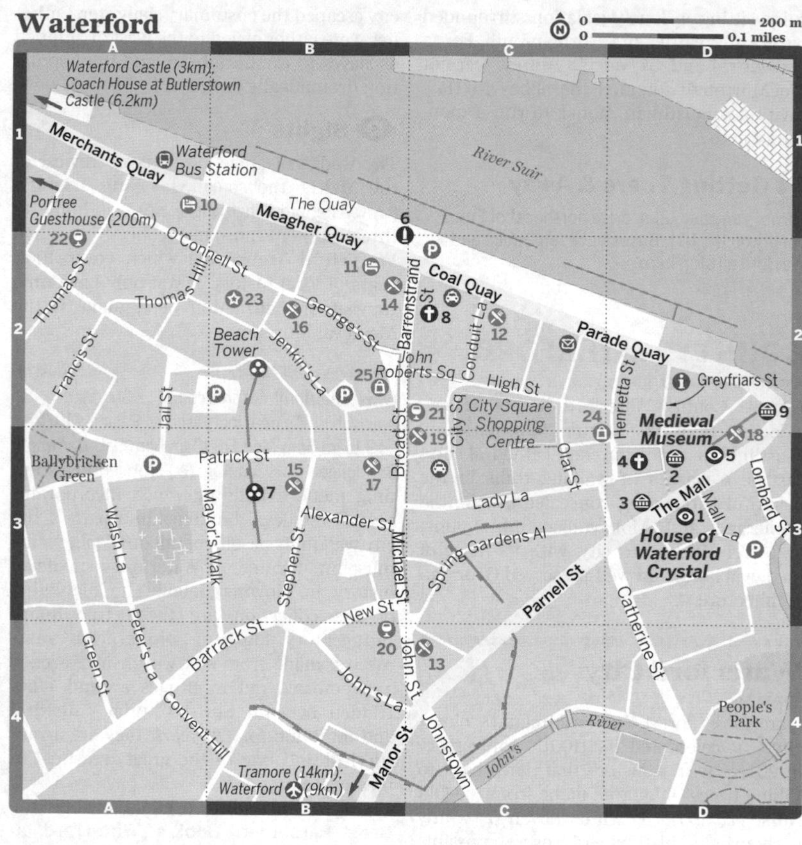

COUNTIES WEXFORD, WATERFORD, CARLOW & KILKENNY WATERFORD CITY

Waterford

Top Sights
1 House of Waterford Crystal D3
2 Medieval Museum D3

Sights
3 Bishop's Palace D3
4 Christ Church Cathedral D3
5 City Hall D3
6 Clock Tower B2
7 Half Moon Tower B3
8 Holy Trinity Cathedral C2
9 Reginald's Tower D2

Sleeping
10 Dooley's Hotel A1
11 Granville Hotel B2

Eating
12 Berfranks C2
13 Bodega! C4
14 Carter's Chocolate Cafe B2
15 Harlequin B3
16 La Bohème B2
17 Momo B3
18 Munster Bar D3
19 Saturday Market C3

Drinking & Nightlife
20 Geoff's B4
21 Gingerman Bar C2
22 Henry Downes Bar A2

Entertainment
23 Garter Lane Arts Centre B2
Theatre Royal .... (see 2)

Shopping
24 Kite Design Studios C3
25 Waterford Book Centre B2

Reginald's Tower MUSEUM
(www.waterfordtreasures.com; The Quay; adult/child €4/2; ⏰9.30am-5.30pm late Mar–Dec, to 5pm Jan–late Mar, closed 24 Dec–6 Jan) The oldest complete building in Ireland and the first to use mortar, 13th-century Reginald's Tower is an outstanding example of medieval architecture. The city's key fortification, its 3m- to 4m-thick walls were built on the site of a Viking wooden tower. Over the years the building served as an arsenal, a prison and a mint; it now houses a museum recording the city's Viking and early medieval history. The sparse exhibits include the tiny but exquisite **Waterford Kite Brooch**, made around 1100.

★**House of Waterford Crystal** CRYSTAL
(www.waterfordvisitorcentre.com; The Mall; adult/student €13/5; ⏰9am-6pm Mon-Sat, 9.30am-6pm Sun Apr-Oct, shorter hours Nov-Mar; 📶) This large modern complex combines a retail shop and cafe with a factory offering a tour that shows how world-famous Waterford crystal is produced. The highlight is the blowing room where you can watch skilled artisans transform blobs of red-hot molten glass into delicate crystalware. The tour ends, inevitably, in the shop, where you can wonder at the twinkling displays which range from a €30 bottle coaster to a €30,000 crystal version of Cinderella's carriage.

The first Waterford glass factory was established at the western end of the riverside quays in 1783. Centuries later, after the boom of the 1980s and 1990s, the company fell on hard times and in 2009 was purchased by an American investment firm. Today around 60,000 pieces are made annually in Ireland, around 55% of the total output; the remainder is manufactured in Europe to strict Waterford standards.

Christ Church Cathedral CATHEDRAL
(www.christchurchwaterford.com; Cathedral Sq; ⏰10am-5pm Mon-Sat Easter-Oct, noon-3pm Mon-Sat Nov-Easter) FREE Christ Church Cathedral is Ireland's only neoclassical Georgian cathedral. Designed by local architect John Roberts, it was built on the site of an 11th-century Viking church, also the site where the 12th-century marriage of Strongbow and Aiofe took place. The rather grim highlight is the 15th-century **tomb of James Rice**, seven times Lord Mayor of Waterford: sculpted worms and frogs crawl over the effigy of his decaying corpse.

Holy Trinity Cathedral CATHEDRAL
(www.waterford-cathedral.com; Barronstrand St; ⏰varies) FREE The sumptuous interior of the city's Roman Catholic cathedral boasts a carved-oak baroque pulpit, painted pillars with Corinthian capitals and 10 Waterford crystal chandeliers. It was built between 1792 and 1796 by John Roberts, who also designed Christ Church Cathedral, making Waterford the only city where both the Catholic and Protestant cathedrals were designed by the same architect.

Historic Buildings

The Mall, a wide 18th-century street, is built on reclaimed land that was once a tidal inlet. Its stateliest buildings are John Roberts' **City Hall** (1788) and the beautifully refurbished Theatre Royal (p177), arguably Ireland's most intact 18th-century theatre. In the middle of the waterfront stands the 1860s **clock tower**, a famous local landmark.

Crumbling fragments of the old city wall include **Beach Tower** at the top of Jenkin's Lane and **Half Moon Tower** (just off Patrick St).

Tours

★**Jack Burtchaell's Guided Walking Tour** WALKING TOUR
(☎051-873 711; www.jackswalkingtours.com; tours adult/child €7/free; ⏰11.45am & 1.45pm mid-Mar–mid-Oct; 👪) Jack's 'gift of the gab' brings Waterford's nooks and crannies to life, effortlessly squeezing 1000 years of history into one hour. Tours leave from near the tourist office (confirm the exact location there), picking up walkers from various hotels en route.

Sleeping

★**Granville Hotel** HOTEL €€
(☎051-305 555; www.granville-hotel.ie; Meagher Quay; s/d from €79/109; 📶) The floodlit 18th-century building overlooking the waterfront is the Granville, one of Ireland's oldest hotels. Brocaded bedrooms maintain a touch of Georgian elegance, as do the public areas with their showstopping stained glass, historic prints and antiques. Star turns at breakfast are the organic porridge with Baileys and a perfect eggs Benedict.

Portree Guesthouse B&B €€
(☎051-874 574; www.portreeguesthouse.ie; Mary St; s/d from €49/79; 📶) This large, 24-room Georgian B&B is on a quiet street, but close

to the city centre. It is well run by a couple of Londoners, and the rooms are spick and span, if not particularly memorable. There's a cosy sitting room with plenty of tourist information and brochures, plus 24-hour coffee and tea on offer. Popular with groups.

Dooley's Hotel HOTEL €€
(051-873 531; www.dooleys-hotel.ie; Merchants Quay; s/d from €109/119;) Family-owned and run like clockwork, Dooley's rooms are large and repro Regency, with brocade fabrics and a dark red-and-gold colour scheme. The breakfast is a belt-notch up from most hotel buffets and includes organic porridge, fresh fruit compote and cooked options. The on-site Thai Therapy Centre offers various treatments.

Coach House at Butlerstown Castle B&B €€
(051-384 656; www.butlerstowncastle.com; Butlerstown; r from €99; Apr-Oct;) This 19th-century stone-built B&B is as appealing inside as it is out, with deep, studded leather armchairs to sink into, toasty open fires to warm up by, canopied beds to drift off in, and pancakes to wake up to. It's a 10-minute drive from Waterford, 6km west of town off the N25.

★ **Waterford Castle** HERITAGE HOTEL €€€
(051-878 203; www.waterfordcastle.com; The Island, Ballinakill; r from €129, cottages from €199;) Getting away from it all is an understatement at this turreted mid-19th-century castle set on its own private island (a free car ferry provides round-the-clock access). All 19 castle rooms have claw-foot baths, and some have four-poster beds. There are also 48 contemporary self-catering cottages on the island.

Both guests and nonguests can dine on organic fare in chef Michael Quinn's sublime oak-panelled restaurant (three-course dinner €49), or play a round of golf (green fees €30 to €40) on the hotel's own course.

Eating

Waterford has a great selection of restaurants and a lively **food market** (John Roberts Sq; 9am-3pm Sat).

Carter's Chocolate Cafe CAFE €
(Georges Court Shopping Centre; mains €4-6; 8am-6.30pm Mon-Sat, 11am-6pm Sun;) The mint-chocolate colour scheme here is lip-smackingly apt for this shop and cafe selling not just Ireland's famous Lily O'Brien's chocolate (six chocs for €2), but also such sweet treats as berry crumble, macaroons and slices of rich dark carrot cake. Savoury snacks include gourmet sandwiches.

Berfranks CAFE, DELI €
(86 The Quay; meals €8-11; 8.30am-5pm Mon-Sat) Irish artisan foods line the shelves in the deli section, while mouth-watering creations adorn the menu on the cafe side, with its cosy back room with bookcases and sofas. This is an ideal place for a pit stop while you unravel Waterford's medieval past.

★ **Momo** BISTRO €€
(051-581 509; www.momorestaurant.ie; 47 Patrick St; mains €9-17; noon-9pm Tue-Thu, to 10pm Fri & Sat, 1-8pm Sun;) This buzzing new bistro is so popular you might struggle to find a table. The big draw is freshly made, flavoursome food based on quality local produce, with a menu that takes in braised lamb shanks, Asian barbecue ribs and crisp fish burgers with salsa, plus a tempting range of vegetarian dishes.

★ **La Bohème** FRENCH €€
(051-875 645; www.labohemerestaurant.ie; 2 George's St; mains €20-25; 5.30pm-late Tue-Sat) This dress-for-dinner kind of place combines French flair with fresh Irish produce. Set in the kitchen basement of a Georgian town house, the dining rooms are intimate spaces with barrel-vault roofs and arches; the wine cellar is more extensive than most. The early-bird menu (available all night Tuesday to Thursday, until 7pm Friday) offers three courses for €29.

Harlequin ITALIAN €€
(051-877 552; 37 Stephen St; mains €9-15; 8.30am-8.30pm Mon-Wed, to 10.30pm Thu-Sat;) Italian-run, this authentic little trattoria morphs through the day from a coffee and pastry breakfast stop, to a busy lunch venue, to a candlelit wine bar. House speciality antipasti platters are laden with cheeses, marinated vegetables and finely sliced cured meats. The menu extends to pasta dishes, but not pizza.

Bodega! MODERN IRISH €€
(051-844 177; www.bodegawaterford.com; 54 John St; mains lunch €14-18, 3-course dinners €25; noon-10pm Mon-Sat) Although the ochre walls and Gaudí-style tile floor seem Spanish, the latest Bodega! incarnation is contemporary Irish with an emphasis on local produce. The menu has a healthy mix of fish

and meat dishes, as well as some lighter fare, such as goat's-cheese tartlets and innovative salads. Keeping it local is a long list of Irish craft brews.

Munster Bar PUB FOOD €€

(www.themunsterbar.com; Bailey's New St; mains €10-14; food served noon-9pm;) Set in a building dating from 1822, this historic pub and restaurant has a snug complete with roaring fire and a spacious pub in the former coach house. Enjoy upscale pub food, such as beef and Guinness pie, and melted Brie and chutney sandwiches. It's the perfect casual end to a long day touring.

Drinking & Nightlife

There are superb pubs around town, and several places where you can hear live music.

★Henry Downes Bar PUB

(Thomas St; 5pm-late;) For a change from stout, drop into Downes, which has been blending its own No 9 Irish whiskey for over two centuries. Have a dram in one of a series of character-filled rooms, or buy a bottle to take away (€45). This place is a real one-off – they even have a squash court out back, as well as a full-sized billiard table.

Geoff's PUB

(9 John St; 11.30am-12.30pm) Geoff's pub is full of character with wood-panelled nooks and crannies, heavy wooden furniture and lofty ceilings (head for the atmospheric so-called 'church bar' out back). Decent food also served.

Gingerman Bar PUB

(6/7 Arundel Lane; 10am-11.30pm Mon-Fri, to 12.30pm Sat, noon-11pm Sun) A dark wood-clad pub on a narrow lane right in the centre, with plenty of blarney atmosphere and a good range of ales on tap, plus meals. Live trad music on Sunday (5pm).

Entertainment

Theatre Royal THEATRE

(www.theatreroyal.ie; The Mall) A beautifully refurbished Georgian building, Waterford's flagship theatre stages plays, musicals and dance.

Garter Lane Arts Centre THEATRE

(www.garterlane.ie; 22a O'Connell St) This excellent theatre stages art-house films, music, dance and plays in an atmospheric 18th-century building set in a courtyard off O'Connell St.

FINDING WATERFORD'S ARTISANS

Crystal aside, Waterford has a wealth of local craftspeople creating textiles, paintings, jewellery, pottery, papier mâché, candles, and furniture built from recycled materials. The website www.waterforddesignermakers.com maintains an up-to-date list.

Shopping

Barronstrand St, the main shopping drag, runs directly south from the Suir.

Kite Design Studios ARTS & CRAFTS

(www.kitedesignstudios.ie; 11 Henrietta St; 9.30am-5pm Mon-Sat) This combination studio and shop provides a workshop and display space for some of Waterford's best artists and craftspeople. As well as watching the artisans at work, you can shop for locally made glassware, textiles, jewellery and more.

Waterford Book Centre BOOKS

(www.thebookcentre.ie; 25 John Roberts Sq; 9am-6pm Mon-Sat, 1-5pm Sun) Three floors of books – with an excellent selection of Irish classics – and a cafe.

Information

The **Tourist Office** (051-875 823; www.discoverwaterfordcity.ie; 120 Parade Quay; 9.15am-5.30pm Mon-Sat) is the best source of info in Counties Waterford and Wexford.

Getting There & Away

AIR

Waterford Airport (051-846 600; www.flywaterford.com; Killowen) is 9km south of the city centre, offering limited flights to London Luton and Birmingham. There is no public transport to the airport; a taxi costs around €20.

BUS

There are frequent Bus Éireann services to Tramore (€3.70, 45 minutes, twice hourly), Dublin (€14.75, 2½ hours, every two hours) and Wexford (€11.50, one hour, six daily).

Suirway (www.suirway.com) buses to Dunmore East (€4, 25 minutes; at least seven daily Monday to Saturday year-round, plus five Sunday late June to August) depart from the bus stop on Merchants Quay, outside the **main bus station** (051-879 000; www.buseireann.ie; Merchants Quay).

WATERFORD–WEXFORD FERRY

If you're driving or cycling between Wexford and Waterford along the coast, the **Passage East Ferry** (www.passageferry.ie; one-way bicycle/car €2/8; 7am-10pm Mon-Sat, 9.30am-10pm Sun Apr-Sep, 7am-8pm Mon-Sat, 9.30am-8pm Oct-Mar) from Ballyhack to Passage East saves a long detour via New Ross. The crossing takes five minutes, with several departures per hour.

TRAIN

Waterford's Plunkett train station is across the river from the city centre. Direct trains:

Carlow €17.35, 1¼ hours, seven daily
Dublin Heuston €31, 2¼ hours, seven daily
Kilkenny €13.85, 35 minutes, six daily
Tipperary €17.35, 1½ hours, two daily

Curraghmore Estate

The 1000-hectare **Curraghmore Estate** (www.curraghmorehouse.ie; Portlaw; house €10, shell house & gardens €5; 10am-4pm Tue-Thu, plus 1st & 3rd Sun of month, mid-Mar–mid-Oct) has belonged to the family of Lord and Lady Waterford since the 12th century. Its lavish gardens incorporate the whimsical **shell house** built in 1754 by Catherine Countess of Tyrone, who arranged for local sea captains to bring her seashells from distant shores. There are 90-minute guided tours of the Georgian main house and shell house at 11am and 2pm. Curraghmore is 14km northwest of Waterford town, off the R680 near the pretty village of Portlaw.

Southeast County Waterford

This hidden corner of the county makes an easy day trip from Waterford city, its winding back roads best explored by bike.

Less than 14km east of Waterford is the estuary village of **Passage East**, from where car ferries shuttle back and forth to Ballyhack in County Wexford. It's a pretty little fishing village with cottages set around a square near the harbour.

A little-travelled 11km-long minor road wiggles south between Passage East and Dunmore East. At times single-vehicle-width and steep, it offers occasional glimpses across undulating fields to the estuary, and passes **Woodstown Beach**, a perfect sandy strand ideal for family picnics, sandcastle building and seashell collecting.

Dunmore East

POP 1560

Some 19km southeast of Waterford, Dunmore East (Dún Mór) is strung out above a coastline of red sandstone cliffs scalloped with concealed coves full of screaming kittiwakes. There are two parts, separated by the town park – the **Upper Village** is poised above the fishing harbour to the south, while the **Lower Village** clusters in a hollow behind Lawlors Strand to the north.

In the 19th century, the town was a port of call for the steam packets that carried mail between England and the south of Ireland. Legacies include picturesque thatched cottages along the main street and an unusual Doric **lighthouse** (1825) overlooking the commercial fishing harbour.

Activities

The town slumbers through the winter months but comes alive in summer when bathers congregate at a series of half a dozen tiny cove beaches beneath the cliffs. Among them, **Lawlors Strand** (the largest) and neighbouring **Councillor's Strand** at the north end of town are close to pubs and cafes while the smaller **Mens Cove** and **Ladies Cove** – at either end of the town's central park – speak of earlier, more prudish times (no segregation today, though). They offer safe swimming, and good snorkelling along the rocks between the coves.

Going west, the 16.5km **scenic drive** to the seaside frivolities of Tramore is packed with enough natural thrills (rolling green hills, soaring coastal vistas, herds of cattle crossing the road…) to more than match the resort's carnival appeal.

Dunmore East Adventure Centre ADVENTURE SPORTS
(www.dunmoreadventure.com; Stoney Cove; 2hr sessions per person €40;) Set in the first cove north of the fishing harbour, this place hires out equipment for kayaking, surfing and snorkelling. It also runs sailing, kayaking, canoeing and windsurfing courses for children and adults, plus land-based activities such as archery and rock climbing.

Festivals & Events

Bluegrass Festival MUSIC
(www.discoverdunmore.com) In August the air thrums with the midsummer beat of banjos as local pubs provide the stage for one of Ireland's liveliest music festivals.

Sleeping

Avon Lodge B&B B&B €
(☎051-385 775; www.avonlodgebandb.com; s/d €35/70; 📶) Although the exterior of this suburban-style house looks perfectly ordinary, it's run by traditional musician Richie Roberts, who is a font of knowledge about the local area. The homey rooms are clean, comfortable and brightened by punchy colour schemes with coordinated fabrics. It's on the Waterford road, a five-minute walk west of Lawlors Strand.

Haven Hotel HOTEL €€
(☎051-383 150; www.thehavenhotel.com; s/d from €50/100; ⏰Mar-Oct; 📶) Built in the 1860s as a summer house for the Malcolmson family, whose coat of arms can still be seen on the fireplaces, the Haven is now run by the Kelly family and remains an elegant retreat with wood-panelled bathrooms and, in two rooms, four-poster beds. Local produce underpins dishes in the casual restaurant (open 5.30pm to 10pm Monday to Saturday, 10am to 3pm Sunday, March to October) and the low-lit crimson-toned bar.

Eating & Drinking

Bay Cafe CAFE €
(Dock Rd, Upper Village; mains €7-11; ⏰9am-5pm) With harbour views so good there's a whale-watching guide stuck to the window, this arty cafe serves interesting twists on casual cafe fare. The open-faced seafood sandwiches come highly recommended, while the guacamole-stuffed bagel is a novelty in these parts.

★ **Lemon Tree Cafe** IRISH €€
(www.lemontreecatering.ie; Coxtown; mains €8-17; ⏰10am-6pm Tue-Sat, 9.30am-4pm Sun year-round, open daily longer hours Jun-Aug; 👪) Come here for organic coffees, delectable baked goods and a deli counter (and freezer) with takeaway dishes ranging from nut and lentil loaf to seafood pie. There's plenty of seating, inside and out, and a menu of dishes with an emphasis on seafood. There's also a play section for children. It's on the southern edge of town.

Spinnaker Bar SEAFOOD €€
(www.thespinnakerbar.com; Glenville Tce, Lower Village; mains €16-29; ⏰food served noon-9pm) Eat at pavement tables watching beachgoers pass by on their way to nearby Lawlors Strand, inside amid nautical knick-knacks, or out back in the sheltered beer garden. Wherever you choose to sit, you'll enjoy top-notch casual seafood fare. Chowders, fish and chips, salads and fresh specials are expertly prepared. There's live music on summer weekends.

Power's Bar PUB
(Dock Rd, Upper Village; ⏰noon-11.30pm Mon-Thu, to 12.30am Fri & Sat, 11.30am-11.30pm Sun) Toe-tapping trad sessions take place on Tuesday nights year-round at this butter-yellow corner pub. It's nicknamed 'the Butcher's' after its former incarnation as a meat and grocery store.

Getting There & Away

Suirway (www.suirway.com) buses connect Waterford with Dunmore East (€4, 30 minutes, seven daily Monday to Saturday year-round, five on Sunday July and August).

Tramore

POP 10,300

In summer the seafront that stretches below the steep town of Tramore (Trá Mhór in Irish, meaning 'big beach') is a whirl of fairground rides, amusement arcades, candyfloss stalls and all the other tack of an old-style seaside resort. In winter, it's considerably quieter.

Sights

Tramore Bay is hemmed in by **Great Newtown Head** to the west and **Brownstown Head** to the east. Their 20m-high concrete pillars (three on Great Newtown and two on Brownstown) were erected by Lloyd's of London in 1816 after a shipping tragedy: 363 lives were lost when the *Seahorse* mistook Tramore Bay for Waterford Harbour and was wrecked.

Atop the central pillar on Great Newtown Head stands the **Metal Man**, a 3.7m-tall sailor made of iron, added in 1819. In white breeches and blue jacket, he points dramatically seawards as a warning to approaching ships. Legend has it that if a girl hops around the base of the statue three times on one leg, she will be married within a year (and no, it doesn't work in reverse for divorce!).

Activities

Tramore's broad, 5km-long **beach** is backed by 30m-high sand dunes at the eastern end, and is one of Ireland's premier **surfing** spots, suitable for all levels of experience thanks to slow-forming waves. The town has year-round surf schools which also offer **eco-walks** around the Back Strand, one of Europe's largest intertidal lagoons, and various other activities.

Two-hour surfing lessons cost around €45 per person for a group class and €85 for one-on-one tuition. Equipment hire is about €25 for a full day including wetsuits and (much-needed) boots, gloves and hoods during winter.

There's a delightful, sheltered swimming spot at **Guillamene Cove** on the west side of the bay. Access is from Newtown Glen Rd (signposted Newtown & Guillamene Swimming Club); there's a car park, toilets and picnic tables.

T-Bay Surf & Eco Centre SURFING
(051-391 297; www.tbaysurf.com; The Prom;) Ireland's largest surf school, which organises a wide range of courses aimed at all levels, including summer surfing camps for children.

Oceanics SURFING
(051-390 944; www.oceanics.ie; Red Cottage, Old Crobally Rd;) Besides providing lessons and courses, Oceanics organises surf parties and summer camps for teens and younger children.

Freedom Surf School SURFING
(086 391 4908; www.freedomsurfschool.com; The Gap, Old Crobally Rd;) As well as surfing courses, this school runs lessons in 'blo-karting' (mini land yachting).

Lake Tour Stable HORSE RIDING
(051-381 958; www.laketourstables.ie; Carrigavantry; treks adult/child from €25/20;) Tramore's pony trekking and riding centre offers a daily trek to a nearby lake, and a weekly canter (on Sundays) along Tramore Beach. About 1.5km west of Tramore, off the R682.

Tramore Golf Club GOLF
(051-386 170; www.tramoregolfclub.com; Newtown Hill; green fees €30-40) One of Ireland's oldest courses, established in 1894, with a new nine-hole (to add to the previous 18-hole) course. Home to several championships, including the Irish Close Championship on four occasions, most recently in 2015.

Festivals & Events

Waterford & Tramore Racecourse HORSE RACING
(www.tramore-racecourse.com; Graun Hill) The first European horse-racing event of the year takes place on 1 January at Tramore Racecourse, one of many race meetings throughout the year.

Sleeping

★ **Beach Haven House** HOSTEL, B&B €
(051-390 208; www.beachhavenhouse.com; Waterford Rd; hostel dm €20, B&B s/d €70/80, 2-person apt from €80; B&B & apts all year, hostel Mar-Nov;) American Avery and his Irish wife Niamh have all budgets covered with their B&B, hostel and apartments (three-night minimum stay for the latter). The B&B and apartments are tastefuly decorated with light wood and earth colours, while the hostel is basic but has excellent facilities, including a comfortable sitting room. In true Californian fashion, Avery fires up the barbecue during the summer months.

O'Shea's Hotel HOTEL €€
(051-381 246; www.osheas-hotel.com; Strand St; s/d from €50/80;) O'Shea's rooms are not quite as classy as the flower-emblazoned, black-and-white exterior suggests. Still, this family-run hotel offers good value and a desirable location close to the beach; several of the rooms have sea views.

Eating & Drinking

If it's deep-fried, you'll find it on a menu in Tramore. At weekends the pubs pull in raucous crowds, especially on long summer evenings. Good pubs for live music include **Martha's** (25 Queen's St) and **The Vic** (Victoria House; 12 Queen's St).

Vee Bistro INTERNATIONAL €€
(051-386 144; www.veebistro.com; 1 Lower Main St; mains €10-25; 8.45am-4pm Mon, to 9pm Tue-Thu, to 9.30pm Fri & Sat, 10am-9pm Sun;) In a port-wine-coloured building with tribal art and abstract canvases on the walls, the Vee dishes up casual bistro-style fare such as chicken stir-fry and chorizo salad, plus some superb bakery goodies and daily specials.

Banyan THAI €€
(051-330 707; Upper Branch Rd; mains €12-15; 5-10pm Tue-Thu, 4-10pm Fri & Sat, 1-9pm Sun;) Come here for delicious Thai food in the elegant surroundings of a historic town house. Dishes such as tom yam soup, massa-

man curry and satay chicken are delicately spiced with just enough heat. As usual the kitchen has to cater to Irish taste buds with a choice of rice, noodles – or chips – to accompany the main dishes.

Getting There & Away

Bus Éireann runs buses between Waterford and Tramore (€3.70, 45 minutes, twice hourly).

Copper Coast

On a sunny day, the azure waters, impossibly green hills and grey-green, rust-red and yellow-ochre seacliffs create a vibrant palette of colour along the beautiful **Copper Coast**, as the R675 winds its way from one stunning vista to another between Tramore and Dungarvan.

There are lots of little coves and beaches to discover – **Stradbally Cove** is a hidden gem – and, just before you reach Dungarvan, there is the beautiful, pristine stretch of sand that is **Clonea Strand**, near Ballynacourty.

Sights & Activities

Copper Coast European Geopark NATURE RESERVE
(www.coppercoastgeopark.com) This 20km stretch of rugged coastline, centred on the village of Bunmahon, takes its name from the copper-mining industry that flourished here in the 19th century. You'll find a Geological Garden on the eastern edge of Bunmahon and, up the hill from here, the **Copper Coast Geopark Centre** (Knockmahon Church, Bunmahon; adult/child €5/3; noon-6pm Tue-Sun;), housing an exhibition about the history and geology of copper mining. You can pick up information on the self-guided Copper Coast Trail, as well as trail cards describing walks in the area.

The area's 460-million-year-old mudstones, sandstones and lavas were contorted by an ancient continental collision, and invaded by hot, metal-rich fluids, which cooled to form quartz veins rich in copper minerals. The most visible legacy of the area's mining industry is the Cornish-style winding-engine house at Tankardstown, 1km east of Bunmahon.

Sea Paddling KAYAKING
(051-393 314; www.seapaddling.com; half-/full-day tours €45/85;) Leads guided kayak tours of the Copper Coast, exploring remote seacliffs, coves, caves and arches, plus half-day beginners' courses.

Dungarvan

POP 9430

Brightly painted buildings ring Dungarvan's picturesque harbour where the River Colligan meets the sea. This famously foodie town is home to some outstanding restaurants, a renowned cookery school and the annual Waterford Festival of Food.

St Garvan founded a monastery here in the 7th century, but most of the centre dates from the early 19th century when the Duke of Devonshire rebuilt the streets around Grattan Sq. Overlooking the bay are a dramatic ruined castle and an Augustinian abbey.

Sights

Dungarvan Castle CASTLE
(www.heritageireland.ie; Castle St; 10am-6pm late May–late Sep) FREE Ongoing renovation is helping to restore this stone fortress to its former Norman glory. Once inhabited by King John's constable Thomas Fitz Anthony, the oldest part of the castle is the unusual 12th-century shell keep, built to defend the mouth of the river. The 18th-century British army barracks house a visitor centre with various exhibits. Admission is by (free) guided tour only.

Waterford County Museum MUSEUM
(www.waterfordcountymuseum.org; St Augustine St; 10am-5pm Mon-Fri, 2-5pm Sat Jun-Sep) FREE This small, well-presented museum covers maritime heritage (with relics from shipwrecks), Famine history, local personalities and various other titbits, all displayed in an 18th-century grain store.

TRIANGLE OF GOLF

There are three championship golf courses within five minutes' drive of Dungarvan: **West Waterford Golf & Country Club** (www.westwaterfordgolf.com); **Dungarvan Golf Club** (www.dungarvangolfclub.com) and the **Gold Coast Golf Club** (www.goldcoastgolfclub.com). All three are part of the Dungarvan Golf Triangle initiative, whereby keen golfers can play three courses for the price of two (€69). Check the website www.golftriangle.com for more information, including directions and maps.

Old Market House Arts Centre GALLERY
(Lower Main St; ⌚11am-12.30pm & 1.30-5pm Tue-Fri, 1-5pm Sat) FREE Housed in a handsome building dating from the 17th century, these light, airy galleries showcase contemporary art by local artists.

Courses

★Tannery Cookery School COOKING COURSE
(☎058-45420; www.tannery.ie; 6 Church St; courses from €55; 📶) Looking like a futuristic kitchen showroom (you can see it through the huge windows on the side street), this school is run by bestselling author and chef Paul Flynn. Courses range from the four-hour 'Cooking for Friends' (€55) to the popular three-day 'Masterclass' (€550), while others cover bread making, seafood, Italian cuisine, and cooking on an Aga stove.

Festivals & Events

★West Waterford Festival of Food FOOD
(www.waterfordfestivaloffood.com) The area's abundant fresh produce is celebrated at this hugely popular festival in mid-April that features cooking workshops and demonstrations, talks by local producers, farmers markets, guided walks and a craft-brew beer garden.

Dungarvan TradFest MUSIC
(www.comeraghs.com/tradfest; ⌚Jun bank holiday weekend) A lively festival of traditional music and dance staged in local pubs and hotels, and on a public stage in Grattan Sq. Famous for its annual bucket singing competition. (Google it!)

Sleeping

In keeping with Dungarvan's foodie credentials, breakfasts at B&Bs are often minor culinary masterpieces prepared using foods sourced from the owner's gardens.

★Cairbre House B&B €€
(☎058-42338; www.cairbrehouse.com; Strandside North; s/d €45/86; ⌚closed mid-Dec–mid-Jan; 📶) Blazing with colourful flowers in summer, this four-room B&B is set on a half-hectare of riverside gardens. The gardens come into their own at breakfast, providing many of the ingredients including fragrant herbs; a small terrace and conservatory overlook the water. It's 1km north of the town centre, on the east side of the river.

Tannery Townhouse GUESTHOUSE €€
(☎058-45420; www.tannery.ie; 2 Church St; s/d from €70/110; 📶) Under the same management as the Tannery restaurant, this boutique guesthouse spans two buildings in the town centre. Its 14 rooms are modern and stylish, and have fridges stacked with juices, fruit and muffins so you can enjoy a continental breakfast in your own time (freshly baked pastries are left outside your door in the morning).

Park Hotel HOTEL €€
(☎058-42899; www.flynnhotels.com; Shandon Rd; s/d from €89/140; 📶🏊👪) This smart, modern hotel sprawls along the west bank of the River Colligan just north of the town centre. Rooms are bright and spacious, service is polite and attentive, and guests can make use of the attached leisure centre. It's a major venue for the Dungarvan TradFest, so book well ahead if you plan on attending the festival.

Eating

Dungarvan Farmers Market MARKET €
(www.dungarvanfarmersmarket.com; Grattan Sq; ⌚9.30am-2pm Thu) As you'd expect, Dungarvan farmers market is a good one: a minor festival of artisan breads, cheeses, bacon, farm vegetables and hot food.

★Meades CAFE €
(☎087 411 6714; www.meadescafe.com; 22 Grattan Sq; mains €5-9; ⌚8am-6pm Mon-Sat, 11am-5pm Sun; 📶👪) Enjoying an ace position on the town's main square, this cafe has a cheerful vibe with a kids' corner, sofas to lounge on, papers to read and a menu of scrumptious baked goods, as well as savoury tartlets, homemade soups, salads and cottage pie. Breakfast special is a *blaa* (local floury bread roll) with crispy bacon, black pudding and country relish.

Nude Food MODERN IRISH €€
(www.nudefood.ie; 86 O'Connell St; mains €10-17; ⌚9.15am-6pm Mon-Thu, to 9.30pm Fri & Sat; 🌿👪) 🍃 The only things naked here are the plates after diners finish. From carefully crafted coffees to a beautiful selection of deli items, this cafe stands out. Lunch and dinner menus feature top local ingredients in sandwiches, salads, starters and hot mains that are hearty, honest and flavourful. Regularly hosts fringe events, such as poetry readings.

Merry's Gastro Pub PUB FOOD €€
(☎058-24488; merrysgastropub.com; Lower Main St; mains €10-17; ⌚food served noon-9.30pm; 👪)

Lots of polished, dark wood and gleaming brass and copper reflected in antique mirrors create a pleasantly old-fashioned atmosphere in this traditional pub gone gastro – the menu runs from barbecue ribs and fish and chips, to pork belly with cumin and fennel braised in local ale. Speaking of which, there's a fine selection of craft beers too.

★Tannery MODERN IRISH €€€
(☎058-45420; www.tannery.ie; 10 Quay St; mains €26-29; ⊙12.30-2.30pm Fri, to 3.30pm Sun, 5.30-9.30pm Tue-Sat) An old tannery building houses this innovative and much-lauded restaurant, where Paul Flynn creates seasonally changing dishes that focus on just a few flavours, and celebrates them through preparations that are at once comforting yet surprising. There's intimate seating downstairs and in the buzzing, loftlike room upstairs. Service is excellent. Book ahead.

Drinking & Nightlife

Look for Dungarvan Brewing's locally produced craft beers in the pubs here, including the crisp and hoppy Helvick Gold Blonde Ale.

Moorings PUB
(www.mooringsdungarvan.com; Davitt's Quay; ⊙11am-midnight) Beautiful original wood panelling and a snug are the main features of the creaky period interior at this waterfront bar. Outside there's a vast beer garden beneath the walls of Dungarvan Castle where you can enjoy local beers on tap and a DJ at weekends. Also offers solid traditional food and B&B accommodation (double room €90).

Kiely's PUB
(O'Connell St; ⊙5-11.30pm Mon-Thu, to 12.30am Fri & Sat, to 11pm Sun) A neighbourhood pub in the town centre, half-timbered Kiely's has frequent trad sessions that have the entire bar joining in.

Information

A helpful **Tourist Office** (☎058-41741; www.dungarvantourism.com; Main/Parnell St; ⊙9.30am-5pm Mon-Fri year-round, plus 10am-5pm Sat Apr-Sep) has stacks of informative brochures; the inconspicuous entrance is next to SuperValu supermarket.

Getting There & Away

Buses pick up and drop off on Davitt's Quay on the way to and from Waterford (€13.90, 50 minutes, hourly) and Cork (€20, 1½ hours, hourly).

Ring Peninsula

POP 500

Just 15 minutes' drive from Dungarvan, the Ring Peninsula (An Rinn, meaning 'the headland') is one of Ireland's best-known Gaeltacht (Irish-speaking) areas. En route, views across Dungarvan Bay to the Monavullagh Mountains and the cliffs of the Copper Coast drift away to the northeast. You could easily spend a day exploring quiet country lanes here, with the promise of a hidden beach or fine old pub around the next corner, or hiking out to enjoy the panorama from Helvick Head.

Ex-Waterford crystal worker Eamonn Terry returned home to the peninsula to set up his own workshop, **Criostal na Rinne** (☎058-46174; www.criostal.com; Baillinagoul, Ring; ⊙9.30am-5.30pm Mon-Fri, 10am-5pm Sat), where you can buy deep-prismatic-cut, full-lead crystal vases, bowls, clocks, jewellery and even chandeliers. The shop is signposted off the main road in Ring (An Rinn) village.

Sleeping & Eating

Dún Ard B&B €€
(☎058-46782; www.ringbedandbreakfast.ie; Na Céithre Gaotha, Ring; r €100;) Perched high above Dungarvan Bay on the western edge of Ring village, the plain exterior of this B&B, set in an upmarket development, is deceiving. Rates may seem high, but the four rooms here really do equal the quality, spaciousness and finish you find in a top-end hotel. Breakfasts are superb, and there's a movie library for the use of guests.

Seaview B&B €€
(☎058-41583; www.seaviewdungarvan.com; Pulla; s/d from €35/70;) This light-filled, pink-hued guesthouse has eight comfy rooms and sweeping views across Dungarvan Bay to the Monavullagh Mountains. Good walks begin at the front door. It's on the N25, 8km southwest of Dungarvan.

★Marine Bar PUB FOOD €€
(www.marinebar.com; Pulla; mains €10-20; ⊙food served noon-9pm) Sure, there's good traditional food at this two-centuries-old pub, but the real reason to stop by is the craic. Year-round, traditional sessions rock the place on Mondays, Fridays and Saturdays (nightly except Wednesday in summer), while locals contest the traditional Irish card game '45' on Wednesday evenings (anyone can join in). Just off the N25, 8km southwest of Dungarvan.

An Seanachaí PUB FOOD €€
(058-46755; www.seanachai.ie; Pulla; mains €12-23; food served 11am-9pm Mon-Sat, 12.30-9pm Sun;) The rough-hewn walls of the 'Old Storyteller' could certainly tell a few stories of their own. Parts of this thatched-roof pub date back to its earliest incarnation as an 18th-century farm. It's an atmospheric spot for a pint, a meal (try the house-speciality fish pie), regular live music, or their fortnightly storytelling sessions (9pm Saturday). Just off the N25, 8km southwest of Dungarvan.

Getting There & Around

Pubs, accommodation and shops are scattered about the peninsula; you'll need your own wheels to get around.

Ardmore

POP 435

The appealing seaside village of Ardmore may look unassuming these days, but it was once one of the most important Christian settlements in Ireland. St Declan is thought to have introduced Christianity to southeast Ireland in the 5th century, well before St Patrick arrived, establishing his monastery on the hill above the harbour. The cathedral that was built here in the 12th century is among Ireland's most remarkable examples of Romanesque architecture.

Today's visitors come mainly to enjoy the local beaches (as well as the town strand, there's secluded Ballyquin Beach, 4km north), water sports, bracing coastal walks and one of the country's best small luxury hotels.

Sights & Activities

★**St Declan's Monastery** RUIN
(Tower Hill; 24hr) FREE The ruins of Ireland's oldest Christian settlement occupy a striking setting on a hill above the town, strewn with gravestones both ancient and new. The most prominent landmark is the 30m-high **round tower**, one of the best examples in Ireland. But the most remarkable is the roofless shell of **Ardmore Cathedral**, in particular the Romanesque arcading on the west gable, decorated with worn but still wonderful 12th-century stone carvings of biblical scenes – very unusual in Ireland.

Inside the cathedral are two **Ogham stones** featuring the earliest form of writing in Ireland (one with the longest such inscription in the country), and a number of medieval grave slabs. The oldest building on the site is the 8th-century **Oratory of St Declan**, which was restored in 1716; the saint is said to be buried beneath a hollow in its southeast corner.

Ardmore Cliff Walk WALKING
An excellent, 5km loop walk leads from St Declan's Monastery (follow 'cliff walk' signs) to the 19th-century lookout tower on Ardmore Head, from where a clifftop path leads back into town along the coast. The footpath passes the wreck of the *Samson,* a crane barge that was blown ashore in 1987, wedged at the foot of the cliffs, and **St Declan's Well**, a sacred spring set within a ruined chapel.

Ardmore Adventures ADVENTURE SPORTS
(083 374 3889; www.ardmoreadventures.ie; Main St; half-day tours €45;) Operates half-day kayak tours around Ardmore Head, as well as surfing, coasteering, canyoning, climbing and more.

Sleeping & Eating

Newtown Farm Guesthouse B&B €€
(024-94143; www.newtownfarm.com; Grange; s/d from €45/72;) Homemade scones, local cheeses and smoked salmon are on the breakfast menu at this stylish and peaceful B&B on a dairy farm 9km northwest of Ardmore, with views over gardens, fields and the distant sea. Coming from Dungarvan on the N25, go *past* the Ardmore turn-off and take the next left (signposted An Rinn); it's 100m along the side road.

★**Cliff House Hotel** LUXURY HOTEL €€€
(024-87800; www.thecliffhousehotel.com; Cliff Rd; r €190-320, ste €290-500;) All bedrooms at this cutting-edge hotel, built into the hillside, overlook Ardmore Bay. Some suites even have two-person floor-to-ceiling glass showers so you don't miss those sea views. There are more sea views from the indoor swimming pool, the outdoor Jacuzzi and spa, the bar and the much-lauded modern Irish restaurant (menu from €65), which has a Michelin star to its name.

Ardmore Gallery & Tearoom CAFE €
(www.ardmoregalleryandtearoom.ie; Main St; dishes €5-12; 9.30am-6pm daily Apr-Sep, 1-5pm Sat & Sun only Oct-Mar) Always a winning combination, the gallery displays local art, while the tea shop sells delicious cakes, plus soup and savoury treats during the summer months. Jewellery, hand-painted silk scarves and knitwear are also for sale.

White Horses SEAFOOD €€€
(☎024-94040; Main St; mains lunch €9-15, dinner €25-35; ⏰12.30-3.30pm & 6-10pm Tue-Sun) Energetically run by three sisters, this bistro set in a former grocery shop concentrates on fresh local seafood. Push the boat out and try the Dublin Bay prawns, served on plates handmade in the village. Enjoy a drink on the bench out front, or a meal at a sunny lawn table out back.

Shopping

Ardmore Pottery & Gallery CERAMICS
(www.ardmorepottery.com; Cliff Rd; ⏰10am-6pm Mon-Sat, 2-6pm Sun Mar-Nov) This cosy little house above the harbour sells beautiful pottery, much of it in lovely shades of blue and cream. Other locally produced goods include warm hand-knitted socks.

Getting There & Away

Bus Éireann operates one to three buses daily to Youghal (€5.20 20 minutes) and Cork (€17, 1½ hours); there are no connections east to Dungarvan except via Youghal.

Cappoquin & Around

POP 760

Slinking up a steep hillside, the small market town of Cappoquin sits at the foot of the rounded, heathery Knockmealdown Mountains. To the west lies the picturesque valley of the **Blackwater River**, one of Ireland's most famous and prolific salmon fisheries.

Sights & Activities

Cappoquin House & Gardens HISTORIC BUILDING
(www.cappoquinhouseandgardens.com; garden €5, house & garden €10; ⏰garden 10am-4pm Mon-Sat) This magnificent 1779 Georgian mansion with formal gardens overlooking the Blackwater River is the private residence of the Keane family, who have lived here for 200 years. The best time to visit is May and June, when the gardens are ablaze with colourful rhododendron, azalea and oleander blossoms. The house is open at limited times – check the website. The entrance to the estate is just north of Cappoquin, at a set of huge black iron gates.

Dromana Gate HISTORIC BUILDING
(Dromana Estate) The Dromana Drive from Cappoquin to Villierstown, 9km to the south, follows the Blackwater Valley through the Dromana Estate. At a bridge over the River Finisk stands this remarkable Hindu-Gothic gate, inspired by the Brighton Pavilion in England. A temporary version was erected here in 1826 to welcome home the estate's owner, Henry Villiers-Stuart, and his wife after their honeymoon (part of which was spent in Brighton). He liked it so much, he had a permanent version built in 1830.

Blackwater River FISHING
(www.cappoquinsalmonandtroutanglers.com; day tickets €12-40) The Blackwater is one of Ireland's finest salmon rivers, and the 6km stretch around Cappoquin offers good value and easy access. You can get advice, permits, licences and fishing tackle from **Titelines** (☎058-54152; Main St; ⏰9am-1pm & 2-5.30pm Mon-Sat).

Sleeping & Eating

Richmond House GUESTHOUSE €€
(☎058-54278; www.richmondhouse.net; Carigeen; s/d from €70/120; 📶) Dating from 1704, Richmond House is set in 6 hectares of parkland. All the same, its nine guest rooms – furnished with countrified plaids, prints and mahogany – are cosy rather than imposing, and service is genuinely friendly. Nonguests are welcome at its **restaurant** (per person €55; serving 6pm to 9pm), where local produce includes West Waterford lamb and Helvick harbour monkfish.

Barron's Bakery BAKERY €
(www.barronsbakery.ie; The Square; mains €4-9; ⏰8.30am-5.30pm Mon-Sat) This famous local bakery has used the same Scotch brick ovens since 1887. Sandwiches, light meals and a mouth-watering selection of cakes and buns baked on the premises are available in the cafe, while its handmade breads are famed throughout the area.

Getting There & Away

Bus Éireann service 366 runs from Waterford to Cappoquin (€6, 1½ hours, once daily Sundays only) en route to Lismore.

Lismore

POP 1370

The quiet, elegant town of Lismore on the Blackwater River was once the location of a great monastic university founded in the 7th century, frequented by statesmen and luminaries from all over Europe. Prince John of England built the first castle here in 1182, and in the 17th century the estate belonged for a while to the family of Robert Boyle, the father of modern chemistry, before passing through marriage to the dukes of Devonshire.

Present-day **Lismore Castle** – more of a vast, battlemented mansion, spreading along a steep slope above the river – dates mostly from the 19th century, and is still the family home of the 12th Duke of Devonshire. Adele Astaire, sister of dance legend Fred, married the son of the 9th duke and lived in Lismore Castle from 1932 to 1944. The castle is not open to the public, but the gardens are one of the most popular attractions in County Waterford.

Sights & Activities

★Lismore Castle Gardens GARDENS
(www.lismorecastlegardens.com; adult/child €8/5; 10.30am-5.30pm Apr-Sep) Although Lismore Castle itself is not open to the public, the 3 hectares of ornate and manicured gardens are well worth a visit. Thought to be the oldest landscaped gardens in Ireland, they are divided into the walled Jacobean upper garden and the less formal lower garden, the latter dotted with **modern sculpture** including two chunks of the Berlin Wall. Highlights include a splendid **yew walk** where Edmund Spenser is said to have written *The Faerie Queene*.

There's a contemporary **art gallery** beside the upper garden, and the castle stables and gardens are used as an opera venue during the annual **Lismore Music Festival** (www.lismoremusicfestival.com) in June.

St Carthage's Cathedral CATHEDRAL
(North Mall; 9am-6pm Apr-Sep, to 4pm Oct-Mar) FREE 'One of the neatest and prettiest edifices I have seen', commented William Thackeray in 1842 after visiting Lismore's 17th-century cathedral. And that was before the addition of the Edward Burne-Jones **stained-glass window**, which features all the Pre-Raphaelite hallmarks: an effeminate knight and a pensive maiden against a sensuous background of deep-blue velvet and intertwined flowers. There are some noteworthy 16th-century **tombs**, including the elaborately engraved MacGrath family crypt dating from 1557, with the 12 apostles carved around the sides.

Lismore Heritage Centre MUSEUM
(www.discoverlismore.com; Main St; adult/child €5/3.50; 9.30am-5.30pm Mon-Fri year-round, 10am-5pm Sat & noon-5pm Sun Apr-Nov) Features a 30-minute audiovisual presentation taking you from the arrival of St Carthage in AD 636 to the present day, via the discovery of the *Book of Lismore* behind a wall in the castle in 1814 and John F Kennedy's visit in 1947. There's also the Family Fun Experience, which is part nature trail, part treasure hunt, and takes you around town. The information 'pack' costs €10; the kids will love it.

Lismore Cycling Holidays CYCLING
(087 935 6610; www.cyclingholidays.ie; rental per day €18;) This outfit will deliver rental bikes to your accommodation, and can arrange cycling tours based around Lismore.

Sleeping & Eating

Lismore House Hotel HOTEL €€
(058-72966; www.lismorehousehotel.com; Main St; s/d from €59/99;) Ireland's oldest purpose-built hotel was built in 1797 by the Duke of Devonshire. He'd still recognise the exterior, but the rooms within have had a contemporary makeover with sleek dark-timber furniture and cream-and-gold fabrics.

★Lismore Farmers Market MARKET €
(Castle Ave; 10am-4pm Sun) The upscale surrounds on the approach to the castle attract a fab collection of vendors to this market, including Naked Lunch – from Dungarvan's Nude Food (p182) deli – whose tasty sandwiches you can enjoy in the park or at tables set up on the gravel path.

Foley's IRISH €€
(www.foleysonthemall.ie; Main St; mains €12-28; food served 12.30-8.30pm) This inviting Victorian pub, complete with decorative wallpaper, leather-backed benches, an open fire, and a beer garden out back, serves good steaks, fish and chips, and bangers and mash.

Information

The **Tourist Office** (www.discoverlismore.com; Main St; 9.30am-5.30pm Mon-Fri year-round, 10am-5pm Sat & noon-5pm Sun Apr-Nov) is inside the Lismore Heritage Centre; pick up the info-packed *Lismore Walking Tour Guide* (€3).

Getting There & Away

Bus Éireann service 366 runs from Lismore to Cappoquin (€3.20, 10 minutes) and Waterford (€18.50, 1¾ hours) once daily on Sundays only.

Northern County Waterford

Some of the most scenic parts of County Waterford are in the north around Ballymacarbry. The **Nire Valley Drive** (signposted from Ballymacarbry) leads deep into the Comeragh and Monavullagh Mountains; the last few miles of narrow, twisting road ends at a car park where there are several waymarked walks into the hills (see www.walkingwaterford.com).

The **Sgilloge Lakes** walk is an easy two-hour round trip to a pair of tiny glacial lakes in one of the dramatic corries, or *coums* (glacial hollows), that give the Comeragh hills their name. The views west to the Galtee Mountains are dramatic, especially towards sunset.

Activities

Clonanav Fly-Fishing Centre FISHING
(☎052-36765; www.flyfishingireland.com; Clonanav, Ballymacarbry; ⌚9am-5pm Tue-Sat, 10am-4pm Sun) From March to September, the Rivers Nire, Tar and Suir offer superb trout fishing. Permits (€30 per day) can be arranged through this centre, which also has a fly-fishing school and guesthouse, and leads guided trips.

Festivals

Nire Valley Walking Festival WALKING
(www.nirevalley.com; ⌚mid-Oct) Keen hikers will want to visit the Nire Valley in time for the Nire Valley Walking Festival, which takes place on the second weekend in October, with guided walks for all and traditional music in the pubs.

Sleeping

★ **Hanora's Cottage** GUESTHOUSE €€
(☎052-36134; www.hanorascottage.com; Nire Valley Dr, Ballymacarbry; s/d from €65/120; 📶) This gorgeous 19th-century cottage sits between the bubbling River Nire and a picturesque church. The rooms are plush and luxurious with Jacuzzi baths for that soothing post-hike soak, and there's an outdoor deck overlooking the river. Everything in the gourmet **restaurant** (three-course dinner €39; 6.30pm to 8.30pm Monday to Saturday) is made on the premises. It's signposted 6.5km east of Ballymacarbry.

Glasha Farmhouse B&B B&B €€
(☎052-36108; www.glashafarmhouse.com; Ballymacarbry; s/d from €60/100; 📶) Olive O'Gorman takes meticulous pride in maintaining the Regency-style bedrooms at her luxury farmhouse overlooking the Comeragh and Knockmealdown Mountains. Some wonderful walks fan out around the farm (including one that takes in the local pub!); afterwards, reward yourself with dinner served by candlelight (€35 to €45) in the conservatory. The farm is signposted 2km northwest of Ballymacarbry.

Getting There & Away

There is no public transport; this region is best explored by car or bike.

COUNTY CARLOW

POP 54,600 / AREA 899 SQ KM

The focus of Ireland's second-smallest county is the River Barrow, Ireland's second-longest river, which flows south from Carlow town through picturesque villages to the monastic hamlet of St Mullins, its towpath followed by the lovely **Barrow Way** walking trail. The Blackstairs Mountains dominate the southeast, their rounded ridges forming the backdrop to many a view, and their underlying granite cropping up everywhere as building stone – most notably as the capstone for Europe's largest prehistoric dolmen.

The county is patchworked with old aristocratic estates, grand country houses both ruined and renovated, and some of Ireland's finest flower-filled gardens – green-fingered visitors should pick up or download a copy of the **Carlow Garden Trail** (www.carlowgardentrail.com).

Carlow Town

POP 23,000

Carlow's compact town centre stretches along the main drag of Tullow St, from the ruins of the castle on the banks of the River Barrow to the cathedral.

Sights

Carlow County Museum MUSEUM
(www.carlowcountymuseum.ie; cnr College & Tullow Sts; ⌚10am-5pm Mon-Sat, 2-4.30pm Sun Jun-Aug, 10am-4.30pm Mon-Sat Sep-May) FREE This thoroughly engaging museum focuses on the lives of local people through the ages. There are some real one-offs, such as the trapdoor from the county gallows, dating from the early 1800s, and a 6m-high exquisitely carved pulpit from Carlow Cathedral,

which the bishop apparently decided to replace with a more modern version (to the chagrin of many locals). The museum is housed in an atmospheric former convent with original stained-glass windows.

Visual Centre for Contemporary Art GALLERY
(www.visualcarlow.ie; Old Dublin Rd; ⏲11am-5.30pm Tue-Sat, 2-5pm Sun; 📶) FREE British architect Terry Pawson was behind the factory-inspired industrial design of this concrete, steel and glass cultural centre which, some consider, sits in uneasy alliance with the historic cathedral across the way. The Main Gallery is the largest single exhibition space in Ireland; changing exhibits highlight local and international artists. The complex also houses the **George Bernard Shaw Theatre**.

Carlow Castle RUIN
(Castle Hill) Built by William Marshal on the site of an earlier Norman motte-and-bailey fort, this 13th-century castle survived Cromwell's attentions. It later succumbed to the grand plans of a certain Dr Middleton, who decided to convert it into a lunatic asylum and demolished much of the the fortress in 1814 in order to 'remodel' it. The evocative portion that survives is part of the keep flanked by two towers.

Carlow Cathedral CATHEDRAL
(Cathedral of the Assumption; www.carlowcathedral.ie; College St; ⏲varies) FREE This elegant Regency Gothic cathedral dating from 1833 was the brainchild of Bishop James Doyle, a staunch supporter of Catholic emancipation. On the right of the nave a statue of the bishop is flanked by a crowned, kneeling woman said to represent Ireland in an attitude of hope. The church also has an elaborate pulpit and some fine stained-glass windows.

Festivals & Events

Éigse Carlow Arts Festival ART
(www.eigsecarlow.ie) Musicians, writers, actors and street performers take over town in May/June.

Carlow Garden Festival GARDENS
(www.carlowgardentrail.com/FFT) Talks and tours by Irish gardening personalities in late August.

Sleeping

Accommodation choices in town are somewhat limited; there are better options in the surrounding countryside.

Red Setter Guest House B&B €€
(☎059-914 1848; www.redsetterguesthouse.ie; 14 Dublin St; s/d from €40/70; 📶) Great attention to detail, simply furnished but comfortable rooms, and extra touches such as fresh flowers make this otherwise humble B&B the town centre's winning choice.

Barrowville Townhouse B&B €€
(☎059-914 3324; www.barrowville.com; Kilkenny Rd; per person €40-49; 📶) This 18th-century town house has been meticulously converted into a classy B&B with elegant rooms. Enjoy local free-range eggs for breakfast in the airy conservatory overlooking the semi-formal gardens.

Eating & Drinking

The town is a nightlife hub with a squadron of large pubs at the east end of Tullow St. Look for local beers brewed by O'Hara, including a fine India Pale Ale.

BeaNice Cafe CAFE €
(17 Dublin St; mains €5-11; ⏲8am-4pm Mon-Sat) Describing itself as an 'artisan food and drink emporium', this cute cafe serves delicious breakfasts, homemade soups, deli sandwiches, cupcakes and more.

Farmers Market MARKET €
(www.carlowfarmersmarket.com; ⏲9am-2pm Sat) Fittingly held at the old Potato Market; look out for Elizabeth Bradley's cheese, homemade pesto at the olive stall, plus handcrafted chocolates, organic vegetables, ready prepared meals, and more.

★**Lennons** MODERN IRISH €€
(☎059-917 9245; www.lennons.ie; Visual Centre for Contemporary Art, Old Dublin Rd; mains lunch €7-14, dinner €17-27; ⏲10.30am-5pm Mon-Sat, 6-9.30pm Thu-Sat, noon-4pm Sun; 📶) Carlow's best dining is found amid the arty surrounds of the Visual Centre for Contemporary Art. It's a sleek and stylish space with a patio bordering the grassy grounds of St Patrick's College. Lunch features creative sandwiches, salads and hot specials, while dinner is more refined with a seasonal menu that showcases local artisan produce. Book a table at weekends.

Teach Dolmain PUB
(76 Tullow St; ⏲9.30am-11.30pm Mon-Thu & Sun, to 1.30am Fri & Sat) Set on a strip of lively pubs, this friendly local has live trad music on Thursdays at 10pm, while Sunday is more of a mix, ranging from jazz to blues (7pm). Good food also served.

Information

Carlow Tourist Office (☎059-913 0411; www.carlowtourism.com; cnr Tullow & College Sts; ⏱9.30am-5.30pm Mon-Sat) is a useful source of county-wide information.

There is a **Post Office** on the corner of Kennedy Ave and Dublin St.

Getting There & Around

BUS

Buses run to Dublin (€14, 1½ hours, every two hours), Kilkenny (€10.10, 35 minutes, three daily) and Waterford (€14, 1½ hours, seven daily).

TAXI

Carlow Cabs (☎059-914 0000; www.carlowcabs.com)

TRAIN

The train station is on Station Rd, northeast of the town centre. Trains run to Dublin Heuston (€17.35, one hour), Waterford (€17.35, 1¼ hours) and Kilkenny (€10.35, 30 minutes), with seven to 10 departures daily.

Around Carlow Town

Although the entire county could be a day trip from Carlow town, the following sights are quite close.

Sights

Delta Sensory Gardens GARDENS
(www.deltasensorygardens.com; Cannery Rd, Strawhall Industrial Estate; adult/child €5/free; ⏱9am-5pm Mon-Fri Sep-May, to 6pm Jun-Aug, 11am-5.30pm Sat & Sun Mar-Oct & Dec, closed weekends Nov & Jan-Feb) A dozen or so interconnecting, themed gardens span the five senses – from sculpture garden to formal rose garden, water and woodland garden, willow garden and even a musical garden with mechanical fountains. Admission proceeds benefit the adjoining Delta Centre, which provides services and respite for adults with learning disabilities. The gardens are hidden in an industrial estate on the northern edge of Carlow town.

Duckett's Grove GARDENS
(www.duckettsgrove.ie; ⏱gardens dawn-dusk, tea room noon-6pm Sat & Sun May-Aug, Sun only Sep-Oct) FREE Dominated by the jackdaw-haunted ruins of a Gothic fantasy of a country house, the former seat of the Duckett family (the house burned down in 1933) was taken over by Carlow County Council in 2005. The walled gardens have been restored as a public park, filled with the scents of lavender and fruit blossom in early summer, while the outbuildings house craft workshops and a tea room. The gardens are 12.5km northeast of Carlow, signposted off the R726 and R418.

Browne's Hill Dolmen HISTORIC SITE
(⏱24hr) This 5000-year-old granite portal dolmen (tomb chamber) is one of Ireland's most famous prehistoric monuments, sporting the largest capstone in Europe (it weighs more than 100 tonnes). It's signposted 3km east of Carlow on the R726.

Killeshin Church RUIN
One of the tallest round towers in Ireland once dominated this former monastery, but was destroyed early in the 18th century by a farmer worried that it might collapse and kill his cows. The ruins of a 12th-century church remain, including a beautifully decorated Romanesque doorway; look for the bearded face on the capstone. The church is 5km west of Carlow on the R430.

★ **Altamont Gardens** GARDENS
(www.heritageireland.ie; Kilbride, near Ballon; ⏱9am-6.30pm Apr-Sep, to 5pm Mar & Oct, to 4.30pm Feb & Nov, to 4pm Dec-Jan) FREE One of Ireland's most magnificent landscaped gardens, Altamont covers 16 hectares on the banks of the River Slaney, with carefully selected plantings arranged in naturalistic settings where peacocks, swans, squirrels and wild hare abound, surrounding an ornamental water-lily lake. The gardens are off the N80 at Kilbride Cross, 24km southeast of Carlow town.

Walkways meander among flower beds, shrubberies, mature trees (some more than 250 years old), rhododendrons and azaleas, before finally leading down a flight of 100 granite steps to a gorgeous bluebell wood beside the river – a great spot for a picnic.

First laid out in the 18th century, the present gardens are largely the work of plant collector Fielding Lecky Watson, who bought the estate in 1924, and his daughter Corona North, who bequeathed them to the nation after her death in 1999. There are plans to open the rather neglected Altamount House to the public once it has been restored.

Sleeping & Eating

★ **Sherwood Park House** GUESTHOUSE €€
(☎059-915 9117; www.sherwoodparkhouse.ie; Kilbride Cross, near Ballon; s/d from €60/100) This greystone Georgian manor dates from 1730.

The five guest rooms are huge with period niceties such as satin- and velvet-adorned four-poster beds. You can make arrangements for dinner (€40 per person); breakfast is included. The house is on the minor road leading to Altamont Gardens, which are just 600m away.

Forge Restaurant IRISH €
(www.theforgekilbride.ie; Kilbride Cross, near Ballon; mains €5-10; 9.30am-5.30pm Mon-Sat, 10.30am-6pm Sun;) Mary Jordan cooks up delicious healthy soups and hot lunch specials using local produce at this former blacksmith's forge near Altamont Gardens. There are baked goods to take away plus deli items and crafts for sale.

Borris & Around

POP 650

This Georgian village has a charming main street running uphill from the Black River, lined on one side with pastel-painted Georgian cottages and on the other by the grounds of Borris House, ancestral home of the High Kings of Leinster.

Sights & Activities

Borris House HISTORIC BUILDING
(www.borrishouse.com; Borris; adult/child €12/2; tours 3pm Mon-Fri May-Sep) This impressive Tudor Gothic mansion, the ancestral home of the McMorrough Kavanghs, High Kings of Leinster, was modelled in 1810–20 around the earlier shells of an 18th-century house and a 15th-century castle. The highlight of the interior is the ornate stucco plasterwork by Michael Stapleton, whose work can also be seen in Trinity College and Powerscourt House in Dublin. Visits are by guided tour only, which must be booked online in advance.

Kilgraney House Herb Gardens GARDENS
(www.kilgraneyhouse.com; Bagenalstown; admission €3; 2-5pm Thu-Sun May-Sep) These delightful gardens are home to a heady cocktail of medicinal and kitchen herbs growing in orderly profusion; the recreated medieval monastic herb garden is a favourite. The herbs are used in the kitchens of the inn and restaurant here, and admission includes a complimentary herbal tea in the cafe. Kilgraney House is signposted off the R705 halfway between Borris and Bagenalstown.

MT LEINSTER HERITAGE DRIVE

Borris is the starting point for the Mt Leinster Heritage Drive, a signposted 75km scenic loop through south Carlow taking in the villages of Bunclody (just over the border in Wexford), Clonegal, Kildavin, Myshall, Fenagh and Bagenalstown; pick up a free leaflet at any tourist office.

The route climbs across the Blackstairs Mountains, where the **Nine Stones viewpoint** offers a breathtaking panorama that takes in eight counties – on a clear day even the coast of Wales can be seen far to the east. Nine Stones is also a popular hang-gliding and paragliding site, and is the starting point for the easiest walking route to the top of **Mt Leinster** (796m), along a road that leads to the telecommunications mast on the summit (5km round trip, allow 1½ hours).

Sleeping & Eating

Forge B&B €
(059-972 5740; www.ullardforgeaccommodation.eu; Ullard, Milltown; per person €35; mid-Feb–Oct;) This modern, purpose-built guesthouse offers great-value accommodation in a quiet rural location near the River Barrow. It's just across the border in County Kilkenny, a 10-minute drive from Borris along a single-track road off the R705 towards Graiguenamanagh.

★ **Step House Hotel** HOTEL €€€
(059-977 3209; www.stephousehotel.ie; 66 Main St, Borris; s/d from €85/150;) This handsome hotel has elegant rooms decorated in shades of pastel green and gold; the more expensive bedrooms have balconies with views of Mt Leinster. Tables in the Cellar Restaurant are tucked in romantic corners beneath vaulted ceilings, while the rustic-style bar is the perfect place for a relaxing drink after a day's hiking or sightseeing.

Lorum Old Rectory B&B €€€
(059-977 5282; www.lorum.com; Kilgraney, Bagenalstown; s/d from €95/150; Feb-Nov;) Halfway between Borris and Bagenalstown off the R705, this historic manor house, dating from the 1800s, sits on a prominent knoll to the east of the road. The gardens provide peaceful views from each of the four rooms, some of which have four-poster beds. The largely organic cooking here is renowned; confirm your four-course dinner when you book (€45 per person).

THE BARROW WAY

The River Barrow, Ireland's second-longest river (after the Shannon), flows for 192km from the Slieve Bloom hills of Laois to meet the tide at St Mullins, and flow on into the sea at Waterford harbour. Made navigable in the 18th century, and linked to Dublin's Grand Canal via the Barrow Line canal, its towpath is followed by the **Barrow Way** (www.irishtrails.ie).

This national waymarked trail leads for 114km from Lowtown (near Robertstown) in County Kildare to St Mullins, with more than half of its length in County Carlow. It passes through a bucolic landscape of riverside villages, Victorian lock-keepers cottages, old stone bridges and boat-crowded quays, offering the chance of spotting wildlife such as otter, heron, little egret and kingfisher.

It would take four days to hike the whole way, but shorter sections make for a great half-day hike or bike route, notably the lovely 7.5km stretch between St Mullins and Tinnahinch (across the river from Graiguenamanagh in County Kilkenny; allow 1½ hours walking, 30 minutes cycling each way).

M O'Shea PUB FOOD €
(Main St, Borris; mains €8-12; ⊙noon-late) Surprises abound in this tidy warren of rooms which combines a general store, a modern grocery shop, and an old-fashioned pub where spare parts and bits of machinery hang from the ceiling. Decent food and occasional live music sessions.

Getting There & Away

Borris is on the east–west R702 road, which links the M9 with the N11 in County Wexford. **Kilbride Coaches** (www.kilbridecoaches.com) runs twice daily Monday to Saturday from Kilkenny to Borris (€6, 40 minutes) and on to Graiguenamanagh (€3.50, 15 minutes).

Trains run between Carlow town and Bagenalstown (€5.85, 12 minutes, seven to 10 daily) en route to Kilkenny.

St Mullins

POP 100

The tranquil hamlet of St Mullins, just a few houses and a pub scattered around a hummocky village green, gives no indication of its illustrious past. Founded by St Moling (St Mullin) in the 7th century, near the holy waters of **St Moling's Well** (signposted from the village car park), this was once an important monastic site.

In the 12th and 13th centuries it became a major Anglo-Norman settlement (those hummocks on the green are the remains of a motte-and-bailey castle) but for some reason the village never grew into a town. Today it's a beautiful and peaceful place, a centre for angling, canoeing, and walks and bike rides along the river.

The village hosts **St James Pattern Day**, an annual pilgrimage and Mass held on the Sunday preceding (or falling on) 25 July.

Sights

St Mullins Monastery RUIN
(⊙24hr) FREE This important monastic site, founded in the 7th century by St Moling, was the legendary burial place of the Kings of Leinster. The remains include four church buildings dating from the 10th to the 15th centuries, the stump of a round tower, and a 9th-century high cross. Nearby is the grave of General Thomas Cloney, a hero of the 1798 Rising, and a monument raised by 'St Mullins exiles in New York' marking the tomb of Art, King of Leinster (1357–1416).

St Mullins Heritage Centre MUSEUM
(www.stmullinsheritagecentre.com; adult/child €3/free; ⊙9.30am-4.30pm Mon-Wed, 2.30-6.30pm Sun May-Sep) The former Church of Ireland in the heart of the St Mullins monastic site houses an exhibition on the life of St Moling, and on the history of the monastery and the village.

Sleeping & Eating

Mulvarra House B&B €€
(☎051-424 936; www.mulvarra.com; St Mullins; s/d from €40/70; 🛜) Most of the bedrooms in this modern, comfortable B&B have balconies with glorious views over the River Barrow. Dinner (€30) is available by arrangement, and you can also indulge in body treatments such as hot stone massages. It's just east of the village on the road towards New Ross.

Old Grainstore COTTAGE €€

(☎051-424 440; www.oldgrainstorecottages.ie; The Quay; 2-bed cottages per week €450;) Martin and Emer O'Brien have eschewed corporate life to convert this former grain warehouse on the River Barrow into three self-catering cottages sleeping two to five people. The interiors are stylish yet homey, with shelves of books and wood-burning stoves. Shorter stays are sometimes possible on request, and guests can borrow bikes and kayaks free of charge.

Mullicháin Café CAFE €

(The Quay; mains €5-12; ⏱11am-6pm Tue-Sun Mar-Oct;) Fabulous riverside cafe serving home-baked bread and cakes, soups, deli platters and lunch specials such as prawn and crab salad.

Clonegal

POP 245

The picturesque village of Clonegal has a tiny green beside an 18th-century stone bridge over the River Derry, whose crystal-clear, limestone-fed waters are thick with waving ribbons of green ranunculus and plump brown trout.

It is the southern terminus of Ireland's inaugural long-distance walking trail, the **Wicklow Way**, and is home to Huntington Castle, the atmospheric setting for Stanley Kubrick's 1975 movie *Barry Lyndon*.

Sights

Huntington Castle CASTLE

(www.huntingtoncastle.com; Clonegal; castle tours adult/child €9/4, gardens only €5/2.50; ⏱house 2-6pm daily Jun-Aug, Sat & Sun only May & Sep, gardens daily 10am-6pm May-Sep) The core of Huntington Castle is a spooky, dusty old tower house built in 1625 by Sir Laurence Esmonde, now surrounded by Georgian terraces and flamboyantly castellated Victorian extensions. Related to the Esmondes by marriage, the Durdin-Robertson family still live here today and offer 45-minute guided tours of the castle's Jacobean hall, Victorian kitchens and living quarters, complete with entertaining ghost stories.

The oddest part of the tour is the **Temple of Isis** in the basement, the idiosyncratic headquarters of the Fellowship of Isis, an order dedicated to the worship of the 'divine feminine' founded by family member Olivia Robertson in 1976.

The **gardens** combine the formal with rural fantasy and include a fabulous 500-year-old Yew Walk, an avenue of lime trees planted in 1680, and a 17th-century fish pond. Facilities include an adventure playground, a tea room and a gift shop.

Eating & Drinking

Sha-Roe Bistro MODERN IRISH €€

(☎053-937 5636; Main St, Clonegal; mains €18-25; ⏱7-8.30pm Wed & Thu, 7-9.30pm Fri & Sat, 12.30-2.30pm Sun, closed Jan) Tucked inside an 18th-century building and run by award-winning chef Henry Stone, this is one of Carlow's top restaurants. A huge open fireplace and a pretty courtyard at the back provide a rustic setting for standout contemporary cuisine based on local produce fresh from the surrounding orchards and farms. Book at least two weeks ahead.

Osborne's PUB

(Main St, Clonegal; ⏱noon-11pm Mon-Sat, 12.30-10pm Sun) A traditional finishing point for Wicklow Way walkers, Osborne's pub is an atmospheric low-ceilinged hostelry, with a bar-top reputedly made from coffin lids.

Getting There & Away

Drivers will find Clonegal signposted along a series of winding local roads 4.5km east of Kildavin on the N80. Hikers can take bus 132 from Dublin to Kildavin (€17.50, 2¼ hours, twice daily) and walk the 4.5km (one hour) to Clonegal.

COUNTY KILKENNY

POP 95,400 / AREA 2073 SQ KM

County Kilkenny's centrepiece is, of course, its namesake city. An enduring gift of the Normans, it seduces visitors with medieval alleys winding between imposing castle and historic cathedral, craft studios, traditional pubs and riverside walks.

The county too is a delight, a place of rolling hills, where you'll soon run out of adjectives for shades of green. Tiny roads navigate the valleys alongside swirling rivers, moss-covered stone walls and relics of centuries of Irish religious history. Shamrock-cute Inistioge village may be star of many a movie, but it is the real deal, as are country towns such as Graiguenamanagh, Bennettsbridge and Thomastown. It's no surprise that so many artists and craftspeople have set up shop here.

Kilkenny City

POP 24,400

Kilkenny (from the Gaelic 'Cill Chainnigh', meaning the Church of St Canice) is the Ireland of many visitors' imaginations. Built from dark grey limestone flecked with fossil seashells, Kilkenny is also known as 'the marble city'. Its picturesque 'Medieval Mile' of narrow lanes and historic buildings strung between castle and cathedral along the bank of the River Nore is one of the southeast's biggest tourist draws. But it's worth braving the crowds to soak up the atmosphere of one of Ireland's creative crucibles – Kilkenny is a centre for arts and crafts, and home to a host of fine restaurants, cafes, pubs and shops.

History

In the Middle Ages Kilkenny was intermittently the unofficial capital of Ireland, with its own Anglo-Norman parliament. In 1366 the parliament passed the Statutes of Kilkenny aimed at preventing the adoption of Irish culture and language by the Anglo-Norman aristocracy – they were prohibited from marrying the native Irish, taking part in Irish sports, speaking or dressing like the Irish or playing any Irish music. Although the laws remained on the books for more than 200 years, they were never enforced with any great effect and did little to halt the absorption of the Anglo-Normans into Irish culture.

During the 1640s Kilkenny sided with the Catholic royalists in the English Civil War. The 1641 Confederation of Kilkenny, an uneasy alliance of native Irish and Anglo-Normans, aimed to bring about the return of land and power to Catholics. After Charles I's execution, Cromwell besieged Kilkenny for five days, destroying much of the southern wall of the castle before the ruling Ormonde family surrendered. The defeat signalled a permanent end to Kilkenny's political influence over Irish affairs.

Today, tourism is Kilkenny's main economic focus, but it's also the regional centre for more traditional pursuits such as agriculture – you'll see farmers on tractors stoically dodging tour buses.

Sights & Activities

Parts of Kilkenny's medieval city walls, mostly dating from the 14th and 15th centuries, can still be seen in several places, notably at **Talbot's Tower** (cnr Ormonde Rd & New St), **Maudlin Tower** (Maudlin St) and the **Black Freren Gate** (Abbey St) – the only surviving city gate. **Maudlin Castle** (Maudlin St) is a more substantial tower house that was built around 1500, and once protected the eastern approach to the city.

★Kilkenny Castle — CASTLE

(www.kilkennycastle.ie; Castle Rd; adult/child €7/3; ⏲9.30am-5pm Mar-Sep, to 4.30pm Oct-Feb) Rising above the River Nore, Kilkenny Castle is one of Ireland's most visited heritage sites. Stronghold of the powerful Butler family, it has a history dating back to the 12th century, though much of its present look dates from Victorian times.

During the winter months (November to January) there are 40-minute guided tours, which shift to self-guided from February to October.

The first structure on this strategic site was a wooden tower built in 1172 by Richard Fitz Gilbert de Clare, the Anglo-Norman conqueror of Ireland better known as Strongbow. In 1192 Strongbow's son-in-law, William Marshal, erected a stone castle with four towers, three of which survive. The castle was bought by the powerful Butler family (later earls and dukes of Ormonde) in 1391, and their descendants continued to live here until 1935. Maintaining the castle became such a financial strain that most of the furnishings were sold at auction. The property was handed over to the city in 1967 for the princely sum of £50.

For most visitors, the focal point of a visit is the **Long Gallery**, which showcases portraits of Butler family members, the oldest dating from the 17th century. It is an impressive hall with a 19th-century timber roof vividly painted with Celtic, medieval and Pre-Raphaelite motifs by John Hungerford Pollen (1820–1902), who also created the magnificent Carrara marble fireplace, delicately carved with scenes from Butler family history.

The castle basement is home to the **Butler Gallery** (www.butlergallery.com) FREE, featuring contemporary artwork in temporary exhibitions, and to a popular summertime tea room housed in the castle kitchen, all white marble and gleaming copper. You can access the Butler Gallery and cafe without paying admission.

About 20 hectares of **public parkland** (Castle Rd; ⏲8.30am-8.30pm May-Aug, to 7pm

Kilkenny

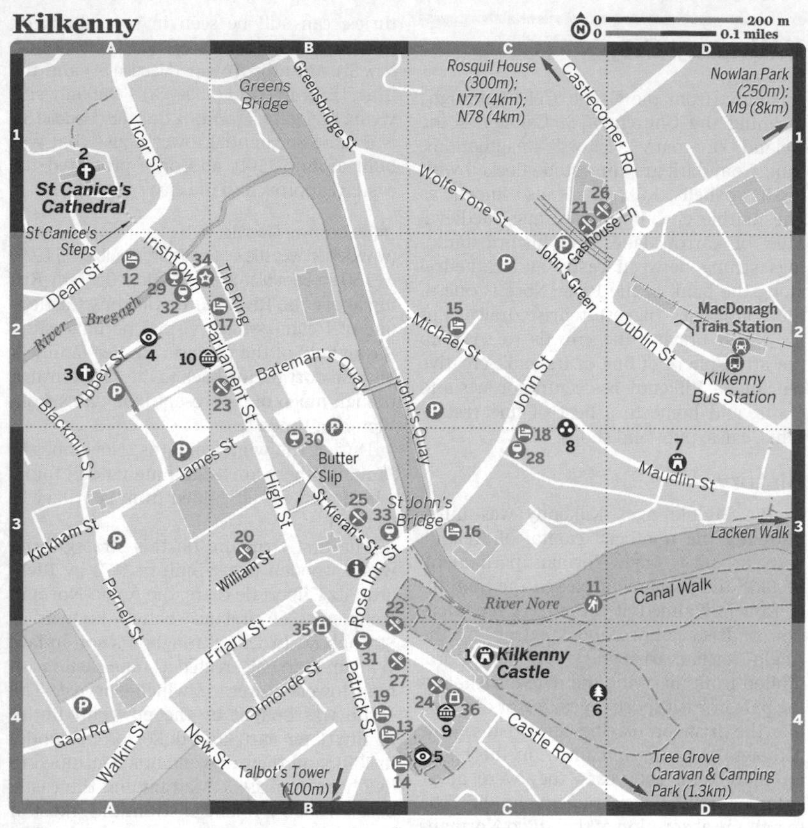

Apr & Sep, shorter hours Oct-Mar) extends to the southeast of Kilkenny Castle, framing a fine view of Mt Leinster, while a Celtic-cross-shaped rose garden lies northwest of the castle. A gate on the north side of the park leads steeply down to the riverside, where you can walk back into town at St John's Bridge.

★St Canice's Cathedral CATHEDRAL

(www.stcanicescathedral.ie; St Canice's Pl; cathedral €4, round tower €3, combined €6; ⏲9am-6pm Mon-Sat, 1-6pm Sun, shorter hours Sep-May) Ireland's second-largest medieval cathedral (after St Patrick's in Dublin) has a long and fascinating history. The first monastery was built here in the 6th century by St Canice, Kilkenny's patron saint. The present structure dates from the 13th to 16th centuries, with extensive 19th-century reconstruction, its interior housing ancient grave slabs and the tombs of Kilkenny Castle's Butler dynasty. Outside stands a 30m-high round tower, one of only two in Ireland that you can climb.

Records show that a wooden church on the site was burned down in 1087. The existing structure was raised between 1202 and 1285, but then endured a series of catastrophes and resurrections. The first disaster, the collapse of the church tower in 1332, was associated with Dame Alice Kyteler's conviction for witchcraft. Her maid Petronella was also convicted, and her nephew, William Outlawe, was implicated. The unfortunate maid was burned at the stake, but Dame Alice escaped to London and William saved himself by offering to reroof part of St Canice's Cathedral with lead tiles. His new roof proved too heavy, however, and brought the church tower down with it.

In 1650 Cromwell's forces defaced and damaged the church, using it to stable their horses. Repairs began in 1661; the beautiful roof in the nave was completed in 1863.

Kilkenny

Top Sights
1 Kilkenny Castle ... C4
2 St Canice's Cathedral ... A1

Sights
3 Black Abbey ... A2
4 Black Freren Gate ... A2
Butler Gallery ... (see 1)
5 Butler House Gardens ... C4
6 Kilkenny Castle Park ... C4
7 Maudlin Castle ... D3
8 Maudlin Tower ... C2
9 National Craft Gallery ... C4
10 Rothe House & Garden ... A2

Activities, Courses & Tours
11 Nore Linear Park ... C3

Sleeping
12 Bregagh House ... A2
13 Butler Court ... B4
14 Butler House ... B4
15 Celtic House ... C2
16 Kilkenny River Court ... C3
17 Kilkenny Tourist Hostel ... B2
18 Langton House Hotel ... C3
19 Pembroke Hotel ... B4

Eating
20 Cafe Sol ... B3
21 Campagne ... C1
22 Farmers Market ... B4
23 Foodworks ... B2
24 Kilkenny Design Centre Restaurant ... C4
25 Lautrec's Tapas & Wine Bar ... B3
26 Mocha's Vintage Tearooms ... C1
27 Rinuccini ... B4

Drinking & Nightlife
28 Bridie's General Store ... C3
29 John Cleere's ... A2
30 Kyteler's Inn ... B3
31 Left Bank ... B4
32 O'Hara's Brewery Corner ... A2
33 Tynan's Bridge House ... B3

Entertainment
34 Watergate Theatre ... A2

Shopping
35 Kilkenny Book Centre ... B4
36 Kilkenny Design Centre ... C4

Inside, highly polished ancient **grave slabs** are set on the walls and the floor. On the northern wall, a slab inscribed in Norman French commemorates Jose de Keteller, who died in 1280; despite the difference in spelling he was probably the father of Alice Kyteler. The **stone chair of St Kieran** embedded in the wall dates from the 13th century. The fine 1596 monument to Honorina Grace at the western end of the southern aisle is made of beautiful local black limestone. In the southern transept is the handsome black **tomb of Piers Butler**, who died in 1539, and his wife, Margaret Fitzgerald. Tombs and monuments (listed on a board in the southern aisle) to other notable Butlers crowd this corner of the church. Also worth a look is a model of Kilkenny as it was in 1642.

Apart from missing its crown, the 9th-century **round tower** is in excellent condition. Inside is a tight squeeze and you'll need both hands to climb the 100 steps up steep ladders (kids under 12 not admitted).

Walking to the cathedral from Parliament St leads you over Irishtown Bridge and up **St Canice's Steps**, which date from 1614; the wall at the top contains fragments of medieval carvings. The leaning tombstones scattered about the grounds prompt you to look, at the very least, for a black cat.

Rothe House & Garden MUSEUM

(www.rothehouse.com; Parliament St; adult/child €5.50/4.50; ⌚10.30am-5pm Mon-Sat, 3-5pm Sun Apr-Oct, 10.30am-4.30pm Mon-Sat Nov-Mar) Dating from 1594, this is Ireland's finest example of a Tudor merchant's house, complete with restored medieval garden. Built around a series of courtyards, it now houses a museum with a rather sparse display of local artefacts including a rusted Viking sword and a grinning stone head sculpted by a Celtic artist. The highlight is the delightful walled garden, divided into fruit, vegetable and herb sections and a traditional orchard, as it would have been in the 17th century.

In the 1640s the wealthy Rothe family played a part in the Confederation of Kilkenny, and Peter Rothe, son of the original builder, had all his property confiscated. His sister was able to reclaim it, but just before the Battle of the Boyne (1690) the family supported James II and so lost the house permanently. In 1850 a Confederation banner was discovered in the house; it's now in the National Museum in Dublin.

National Craft Gallery GALLERY

(www.nationalcraftgallery.ie; Castle Yard; ⌚10am-5.30pm Tue-Sat, 11am-5.30pm Sun) FREE Contemporary Irish crafts are showcased at these imaginative galleries, set in former stables across the road from Kilkenny Castle, next to the shops of the Kilkenny Design Centre (p199). Ceramics dominate, but exhibits often feature furniture, jewellery and weaving from the members of the Crafts Council of Ireland. Family days are held the second Saturday of every month, with free hands-on workshops for children at 10am and 12.30pm. For additional workshops and events, check the website.

Behind the complex, look for the gate that leads into the beautiful **Butler House Gardens** (10am-5pm Mon-Fri, to noon Sat & Sun) FREE with an unusual water feature constructed from remnants of the British-built Nelson Pillar, which once stood in Dublin's O'Connell St but was blown up by the IRA in 1966.

Black Abbey CHURCH

(www.blackabbey.ie; Abbey St) This Dominican abbey was founded in 1225 by William Marshal and takes its name from the monks' black habits. Much of what survives dates from the 18th and 19th centuries, but remnants of more ancient archways are still evident, and the stained glass is glorious. When services are not being held, you can pick up an information leaflet in exchange for a donation and explore; look for the 13th-century coffins near the entrance.

Nore Linear Park WALKING

This network of footpaths allows walkers to hike southeast along the banks of the River Nore as far as the ring road (2.5km) and return on the opposite side. The **Canal Walk** on the southwest bank leads under the castle and on past mill races, weirs and the ruins of 19th-century woollen mills, some of which continued working until the 1960s. The **Lacken Walk** on the northeast side begins on Maudlin St. Ask the tourist office for a map or see trailkilkenny.ie.

Tours

Kilkenny Cycling Tours CYCLING

(086 895 4961; www.kilkennycyclingtours.com; per person €20;) Explore the city and surrounds on a bike over a 2½-hour tour that can include a lunch option. Bikes delivered to your accommodation.

Pat Tynan Walking Tours WALKING

(087 265 1745; www.kilkennywalkingtours.ie; per person €6; 2-3 tours daily mid-Mar–Oct) Entertaining, informative 70-minute walking tours through Kilkenny's narrow lanes, steps and pedestrian passageways. Meet at the tourist office.

Festivals & Events

Kilkenny hosts several world-class events throughout the year, attracting thousands of revellers.

Kilkenny Rhythm & Roots MUSIC

(www.kilkennyroots.com) More than 30 pubs and other venues participate in hosting this major music festival, with an emphasis on country and 'old-time' American roots music. Held in late April or early May.

The Cat Laughs Comedy Festival COMEDY

(www.thecatlaughs.com) Acclaimed gathering of world-class comedians in Kilkenny's hotels and pubs over a long weekend in late May or early June.

Kilkenny Arts Festival ARTS

(www.kilkennyarts.ie) In August the city comes alive with theatre, cinema, music, literature, visual arts, children's events and street spectacles for 10 action-packed days in August.

Sleeping

If you're arriving in town with no room booked (an unwise move at weekends, in summer and during festivals), the tourist office runs an efficient accommodation booking service (€4). Otherwise you'll find lodging at all prices throughout town.

Kilkenny Tourist Hostel HOSTEL €

(056-776 3541; www.kilkennyhostel.ie; 35 Parliament St; dm/tw from €17/42; @) Inside an ivy-covered 1770s Georgian town house, this fairly standard, 60-bed IHH hostel has a sitting room warmed by an open fireplace, and a timber- and leadlight-panelled dining room adjoining the self-catering kitchen. Excellent location.

Tree Grove Caravan & Camping Park CAMPGROUND €

(086 830 8845; www.treegrovecamping.com; New Ross Rd; sites €15-25; Mar–mid-Nov;) Excellent camping ground in a small park 1.5km south of Kilkenny off the R700, a pleasant half-hour walk along the river from the city centre.

★**Rosquil House** GUESTHOUSE €€

(056-772 1419; www.rosquilhouse.com; Castlecomer Rd; r from €70, 2-person apt from €60;) Rooms at this immaculately maintained guesthouse are decorated with dark-wood furniture and pretty paisley fabrics, while the guest lounge is similarly tasteful with sink-into sofas, brass-framed mirrors and leafy plants. The breakfast is above average with homemade granola and fluffy omelettes. There's also a well-equipped and comfortable self-catering apartment (minimum three-day stay).

Butler House BOUTIQUE HOTEL €€
(056-772 2828; www.butler.ie; 16 Patrick St; s/d from €90/145;) You can't stay in Kilkenny Castle, but this historic mansion is the next best thing. Once the home of the earls of Ormonde, today it houses a boutique hotel with aristocratic trappings including sweeping staircases, marble fireplaces, an art collection and impeccable gardens. The generous rooms are individually decorated and, to remind you you're staying amid history, the floors creak.

Celtic House B&B €€
(056-776 2249; www.celtic-house-bandb.com; 18 Michael St; r €80;) Artist and author Angela Byrne extends one of Ireland's warmest welcomes at this spick-and-span B&B. Some of the bright rooms have sky-lit bathrooms, others have views of the castle, and Angela's landscapes adorn many of the walls. Book ahead.

Butler Court INN €€
(056-776 1178; www.butlercourt.com; Patrick St; r €70-130;) Not to be confused with the grand Butler House a few doors uphill, this was originally the mail-coach yard for Kilkenny Castle. Wrapping around a flower-filled courtyard, contemporary rooms have Canadian-cherry parquet floors, and eye-catching photography or Celtic art on the walls. A continental breakfast, including fresh fruit and filtered coffee, is stocked in your in-room fridge.

Bregagh House B&B €€
(056-772 2315; www.bregaghhouse.com; Dean St; s/d from €60/100) If you want the cosiness that comes with staying in a family home, this B&B is a good bet. It offers a convenient location near the cathedral, comfortable soundproof guest rooms and filling hot breakfasts (or continental). There's ample on-site parking and a conservatory overlooking a pretty back garden with a magnificent copper beech tree.

Langton House Hotel HOTEL €€
(056-776 5133; www.langtons.ie; 67 John St; s/d from €60/120;) In the same family since the 1930s but constantly evolving, this Kilkenny icon has 34 corporate-style rooms with parquet floors, dark wood and sombre-toned furnishings. The mosaic tiled bathrooms have superb high-power pressure showers. There's a fine restaurant and a popular pub.

Pembroke Hotel HOTEL €€€
(056-778 3500; www.kilkennypembrokehotel.com; Patrick St; s/d from €104/144;) Wake up to castle views (from some of the rooms) at this stylish, modern and central hotel. Deluxe rooms feature balconies, and the overall room decor is easy on the eye with a muted moss-green and soft-blue colour scheme. There's a leather-sofa-filled bar, and the use of swimming and leisure facilities just around the corner.

Kilkenny River Court HOTEL €€€
(056-772 3388; www.rivercourthotel.com; John St; s/d from €100/110;) When not unwinding in your spacious modern room, you can dine at the respected restaurant, swim laps in the award-winning health club's sunlit indoor pool, or sip a cocktail on the cobblestone terrace of the wraparound bar overlooking the river beneath the castle. Staff are consistently helpful. Rates almost double at weekends.

Eating

Kilkenny's restaurants are among the best in the southeast.

Farmers Market MARKET €
(Mayors Walk, The Parade; 9.30am-2.30pm Thu) Kilkenny's weekly farmers market is a showcase for local produce.

Mocha's Vintage Tearooms CAFE €
(4 The Arches, Gashouse Lane; mains €6-13; 8.30am-5.30pm Mon-Sat) Cute retro tea room with picture-cluttered walls and rose-patterned china. As well as tea and cakes, there's a breakfast menu (until 11.30am) with a choice of bagels or a full Irish fry-up, and hot lunch specials including fish and chips.

★ **Foodworks** BISTRO, CAFE €€
(056-777 7696; www.foodworks.ie; 7 Parliament St; lunch mains €7-14, 3-course dinners €28; noon-9.30pm Wed-Fri, to 10pm Sat, 12.30-4.30pm Sun;) The owners of this cool and casual bistro keep their own pigs and

grow their own salad leaves, so it would be churlish not to try their pulled-pork brioche or confit pig's trotter – and you'll be glad you did. Delicious food, excellent coffee and friendly service make this a justifiably popular venue; best to book a table.

Lautrec's Tapas & Wine Bar INTERNATIONAL €€
(www.lautrecs.com; 9 St Kieran's St; tapas €4-8, pizzas €11-15; 12.30-10pm Mon-Sat, to 9pm Sun) Romantics can hold hands at the tiny tables in the tiny dining room, and partake of the disproportionate wine selection, at this seductive, rose-coloured tapas bar. The menu spans continents with its tapa-sized portions of Greek-style lamb meatballs, Chinese-style duck, and other international favourites. Three tapas and a glass of wine cost €20.

Cafe Sol MODERN IRISH €€
(056-776 4987; www.restaurantskilkenny.com; William St; lunch mains €10-13, 2-/3-course dinners €25/29; 11am-9.30pm Mon-Thu, to 10pm Fri & Sat, noon-9pm Sun;) Leisurely lunches stretch until 5pm at this much-loved restaurant. Local organic produce is featured in dishes that emphasise what's fresh each season. The flavours are frequently bold and have global influences. Service is excellent, albeit casual, and the whole place exudes a modern Med-bistro look.

Rinuccini ITALIAN €€
(056-776 1575; www.rinuccini.com; 1 The Parade; dinner mains €17-29; noon-3pm & 5-10pm, to 9.30pm Sun) Follow a short flight of steps down to a candlelit basement to bliss out on Antonio Cavaliere's classical Italian cuisine, including house special *gamberoni Rinuccini* (fresh Kilmore Quay langoustines with a cream, brandy and Dijon mustard sauce). On the lunch and early-bird evening menu, two/three courses cost €24/29.

Kilkenny Design Centre Restaurant CAFETERIA €€
(www.kilkennydesign.com; Castle Yard; mains €7-15; 10am-6pm Sun-Wed, to 9.30pm Thu-Sat;) Upstairs from the craft shops, this arty, organic-oriented, self-service cafeteria offers home-baked breads and scones, tasty seafood chowder, salads in vast variety, gourmet sandwiches, hot specials, and sumptuous desserts.

★ **Campagne** MODERN IRISH €€€
(056-777 2858; www.campagne.ie; 5 Gashouse Lane; mains €29-32; 12.30-2.30pm Fri-Sun, 6-10pm Tue-Sat) Chef Garrett Byrne, who gained fame and Michelin stars in Dublin, is the genius behind this bold, stylish restaurant in his native Kilkenny. He's passionate about supporting local and artisan producers, and serves ever-changing, ever-memorable meals, with a French accent to every culinary creation. On the lunch and early-bird evening menu, two/three courses cost €27/32.

Drinking & Nightlife

John St is a nightlife hub along with Parliament St, where there is another clutch of no-nonsense trad pubs.

★ **Kyteler's Inn** PUB
(www.kytelersinn.com; 27 St Kieran's St; 11am-midnight Sun-Thu, to 2am Fri & Sat) Dame Alice Kyteler's old house was built back in 1224 and has seen its share of history: she was charged with witchcraft in 1323. Today the rambling bar includes the original building, complete with vaulted ceiling and arches. There is a beer garden, a courtyard and a large upstairs room for the live bands (6.30pm March to October), ranging from trad to blues.

Tynan's Bridge House PUB
(St John's Bridge; 10.30am-11.30pm Mon-Thu, to 12.30am Fri & Sat, 11.30am-11pm Sun) This historic 1703 Georgian pub is the best traditional bar in town. There's barely a right angle left in the place, with its sagging, granite-topped horseshoe bar, original wood panelling, wonky shelves and loyal clientele of crusty locals – and no TV! Trad music on Wednesdays and weekends at 9pm.

Left Bank BAR
(www.leftbank.ie; The Parade; noon-11.30pm Mon-Thu, to 12.30am Fri & Sat, 12.30-11pm Sun) This former Bank of Ireland building has been resurrected as undoubtedly the most eye-catching bar in town. Dating from the 1870s, the interior is magnificent with original portico columns, carved-wood detail, exposed brick walls and chandeliers. Snacks also served.

Bridie's General Store PUB
(John St; 11am-10pm Sun-Wed, 6pm-2am Thu-Sat) Top design talent was employed by the Langton's empire to create this reproduction trad grocery-cum-pub; the results are worth it. The front is a beguiling retail pot-pourri of souvenirs, jokes, toys, preserves and deli items. Step through the swinging doors to arrive at a new/old pub

KILKENNY ARTS & CRAFTS

At least 130 full-time craftspeople and artists work commercially in County Kilkenny – one of the highest concentrations in Ireland – thanks to its fine raw materials and inspirational scenery.

Among the best places to see their work:

Bennettsbridge (p200) Several craft studios are located in and around the village.

Graiguenamanagh (p205) Wool and crystal studios operate near the centre.

Kilkenny Design Centre (p199) Works by more than a dozen local craftspeople.

Stoneyford Home to a famous glass studio (p201) and a shop (p204) with locally produced foods.

Pick up a copy of the 'Made in Kilkenny Craft Trail' leaflet (www.madeinkilkenny.ie) for a comprehensive list of studios and shops.

with beautiful tiles, while out back is a fittingly classy beer garden.

John Cleere's PUB
(www.cleeres.com; 22 Parliament St; ⌚11.30am-11.30pm Mon-Thu, to 12.30am Fri & Sat, 1-11pm Sun) One of Kilkenny's finest venues for live music, theatre and comedy, this long bar has blues, jazz and rock, as well as trad-music sessions on Monday and Wednesday. Food is served throughout the day, including soup, sandwiches, pizza and Irish stew.

O'Hara's Brewery Corner PUB
(www.carlowbrewing.com; 29 Parliament St; ⌚1-11.30pm Mon-Thu, to 12.30am Fri & Sat, to 11pm Sun) Kilkenny's best venue for craft brews is a long, narrow beer hall of a place owned by Carlow Brewing Company. Service can be a bit hit-and-miss, especially at quiet times, but there's a wide selection of ale to choose from, including Carlow's own IPA.

☆ Entertainment

For information on local events, check out the weekly *Kilkenny People* newspaper or the Events page of the tourist office website.

Watergate Theatre THEATRE
(www.watergatetheatre.com; Parliament St) Kilkenny's top theatre venue hosts drama, comedy and musical performances. If you're wondering why intermission lasts 18 minutes, it's so patrons can nip into John Cleere's pub for a pint.

Nowlan Park SPECTATOR SPORT
(www.kilkennygaa.ie; O'Loughlin Rd) One of the classic experiences of a trip to Ireland is catching a game of hurling at the Kilkenny Cats' hallowed home stadium.

Shopping

★Kilkenny Design Centre ARTS, CRAFTS
(☎056-772 2118; www.kilkennydesign.com; Castle Yard; ⌚10am-7pm) Sells top-end Irish crafts and artworks, from county-wide artisans. Look for John Hanly wool blankets, Cushendale woollen goods, Foxford scarves and Bunbury cutting boards.

Kilkenny Book Centre BOOKS
(10 High St; ⌚10am-5pm Mon-Sat) The largest bookshop in town, stocking plenty of Irish-interest fiction and nonfiction, periodicals and a good range of maps. There's a cafe upstairs.

Information

Kilkenny Tourist Office (www.visitkilkenny.ie; Rose Inn St; ⌚9.15am-5pm Mon-Sat) stocks guides and walking maps. Located in Shee Alms House, dating from 1582 and built in local stone by benefactor Sir Richard Shee to help the poor.

Getting There & Away

BUS

Bus Éireann services stop at the train station and on Ormonde Rd (nearer the town centre); **JJ Kavanagh** (www.jjkavanagh.ie) buses to Dublin Airport stop on Ormonde Rd only.

Carlow €10.10, 35 minutes, three daily
Cork €21.50, three hours, two daily
Dublin €14, 2¼ hours, eight daily
Dublin Airport €20, two to three hours, six daily
Waterford €12.50, one hour, two daily

TRAIN

Kilkenny's MacDonagh train station is a 10-minute walk northeast of the town centre, with trains to Dublin Heuston (€26, 1½ hours, six daily) and Waterford (€13.85, 40 minutes, seven daily).

Central Kilkenny

The area south – and notably southeast – of Kilkenny city is a patchwork of country roads and picturesque villages overlooking the rich, green valleys of the Barrow and Nore rivers. This is fine walking and fishing country and home to some of the county's most notable crafts makers – pick up a copy of the 'Made in Kilkenny Craft Trail' leaflet, or see www.madeinkilkenny.ie.

Much of the area is easily visited on a day trip from the city, but you'll need your own wheels as public transport is limited.

Kells & Around

Kells (not to be confused with Kells in County Meath) is a mere hamlet with a fine stone bridge on a tributary of the Nore. However, in Kells Priory the village has one of Ireland's most evocative and romantic monastic sites. The village is 13km south of Kilkenny city on the R697.

Sights

★Kells Priory RUIN

(24hr) FREE This fortified Augustinian monastery is the best sort of ruin, where you can amble about whenever you like, with no tour guides, set hours or fees. Most days you stand a chance of exploring the site alone (apart from some nosy sheep); at dusk with a clear sky the old priory is simply beautiful. The ruins are 500m east of Kells on the Stoneyford road. There are signposts for an excellent 3km walk around the ruins, river and village.

The earliest remains of the monastic site date from the late 12th century, while the bulk of the present ruins are from the 15th century. In a sea of rich farmland, a carefully restored protective wall connects seven dwelling towers. Within the walls are the remains of an **Augustinian abbey** and the foundations of several chapels and houses. It's unusually well fortified and the heavy curtain walls hint at a troubled history. Indeed, within a single century from 1250, the abbey was twice fought over and burned down by squabbling warlords. Its permanent decline began when it was suppressed in 1540 as part of King Henry VIII's campaign to dissolve all Catholic monasteries in England, Wales and Ireland.

Kilree Round Tower & High Cross HISTORIC SITE

(24hr) FREE About 2km south of Kells (signposted from Kells Priory car park) there's a 29m-high round tower, an ancient church and a Celtic high cross, said to mark the grave of a 9th-century Irish high king, Niall Caille. He apparently drowned in the Kings River at Callan some time in the 840s while attempting to save a servant, and his body washed up near Kells. His final resting place lies beyond the church grounds because he wasn't a Christian.

Sleeping

★Lawcus Farm GUESTHOUSE €€

(086 603 1667; www.lawcusfarmguesthouse.com; Lawcus, Stoneyford; s/d from €80/100;) Bought as a thatched ruin, this 18th-century farmhouse has been rebuilt and expanded to create an enchanting place to stay. Rooms typically have stone walls, rustic antiques and quirky curiosities, while breakfast features the farm's own eggs, sausages and ham. The 20-acre farm is bordered by the Kings River and signposted off the minor road between Kells and Stoneyford.

Bennettsbridge & Around

POP 730

Just 7km south of Kilkenny city on the R700, Bennettsbridge takes its name from the elegant 18th-century stone bridge that spans the River Nore. The village is home to a handful of craft studios and shops.

Sights & Activities

Nore View Folk Museum MUSEUM

(056-27749; Danesfort Rd, Bennettsbridge; adult/child €5/2; varies, generally 10am-6pm) This is not your average museum. Seamus Lawlor is a passionate chronicler of Irish life and recounts fascinating facts about his private collection of local items, including farming tools, kitchen utensils and other wonderful old bric-a-brac. It's signposted off the R700 across the river from the village centre.

Nore Valley Park FARM

(www.norevalleypark.com; Annamult; adult/child €7/6.50; park 9am-6pm Mon-Sat Mar-Oct) A 180-acre farm where children can pet goats, cuddle rabbits, navigate a maze (in the former barn), play crazy golf and jump on a straw bounce. There's also a tea room and picnic area. It's 4km south of Bennettsbridge, along Annamult Rd on the west side of the river.

Shopping

Nicholas Mosse Irish Country Shop CERAMICS
(www.nicholasmosse.com; ⌚10am-6pm Mon-Sat, 1.30-5pm Sun) Housed in an old mill across the river from the village, this pottery shop specialises in handmade spongeware – ceramics decorated with sponged patterns – which is exported worldwide to retail outlets such as Tiffany's. Short audiovisual displays explain the manufacturing process. The **cafe** here is the best choice locally for lunch, with a range of soups, sandwiches and hot dishes, plus its renowned scones.

Moth to a Flame CRAFTS
(www.mothtoaflame.ie; Kilkenny Rd, Bennettsbridge; ⌚9am-6pm Mon-Sat) Established in 1999, this workshop creates beautifully coloured and textured candles of all sizes, from bedside table to church altar scale.

Thomastown & Around

POP 2270

Named after 14th-century Welsh mercenary Thomas de Cantwell, who became a local lord, Thomastown retains some fragments of its medieval town walls. Down by the bridge over the River Nore (built in 1792) you can find **Mullin's Castle**, one survivor of no fewer than 14 towers that once stood along the town perimeter. There's good **trout fishing** here; get a permit at Simon Treacy Hardware, just along from the bridge.

Like the rest of Kilkenny, the area has a vibrant craft scene – look out for **Clay Creations** (☎087 257 0735; www.bridlyonsceramics.com; Low St, Thomastown; ⌚10am-5.30pm Wed-Sat) displaying the quixotic ceramics and sculptures of local artist Brid Lyons.

Sights & Activities

★**Jerpoint Abbey** RUIN
(☎056-772 4623; www.heritageireland.ie; Jerpoint, Thomastown; adult/child €4/2; ⌚9am-5.30pm Mar-Sep, to 5pm Oct, to 4pm Nov, closed Dec-Feb) One of Ireland's finest Cistercian ruins, Jerpoint Abbey was established in the 12th century, with the tower and cloister dating from late 14th or early 15th century. It is famous for its unusually large number of medieval stone carvings – look for the series of unusual and often amusing figures, both human and animal, carved on the pillars around the cloister. The abbey enjoys a lovely rural setting about 2.5km southwest of Thomastown on the N9.

Faint traces of a 15th- or 16th-century painting remain on the northern wall of the church. This chancel area also contains a tomb thought to belong to hardheaded Felix O'Dulany, Jerpoint's first abbot and bishop of Ossory, who died in 1202.

Jerpoint Park HISTORIC SITE
(☎086 606 1449; www.jerpointpark.com; Belmore House, Jerpoint, Thomastown; admission €8, sheepdog demo €5; ⌚10am-5pm May-Sep, tours at 10am, noon & 3pm) Jerpoint Park is a working farm on the site of a 12th-century medieval town, where 90-minute guided tours use cutting-edge archaeological techniques to reveal in detail the settlement that once stood here. This includes the ruined Church of St Nicholas where, according to local legend, St Nicholas (or Santa Claus) is buried. There are also sheepdog demonstrations, angling on the River Nore, and a tea room (open July and August) famed for its homemade scones. It's 3km southwest of Thomastown.

Jerpoint Glass Studio CRAFT WORKSHOP
(www.jerpointglass.com; Stoneyford; ⌚10am-5.30pm Mon-Sat, noon-5pm Sun) The nationally renowned Jerpoint Glass Studio is housed in an old stone-walled farm building where you can watch workers craft molten glass into exquisite artistic and practical items (demos on weekdays only, 10am to 4pm Monday to Thursday, to 1pm Friday). It's 6km west of Thomastown on the L4206 towards Stoneyford.

Kilfane Church RUIN
(⌚24hr) FREE About 3km north of Thomastown on the R448 is a small, ruined 13th-century church and Norman tower, signposted 50m off the road. The church contains a remarkable, life-size **stone effigy of Thomas de Cantwell** called the Cantwell Fada or Long Man. It depicts a tall, thin knight in detailed chain-mail armour brandishing a shield decorated with the Cantwell coat of arms.

Mount Juliet GOLF
(☎056-777 3000; www.mountjuliet.ie; Mount Juliet Estate, Thomastown; green fees €50-85) Just 4km southwest of Thomastown, high-fliers tee off at the Jack Nicklaus–designed Mount Juliet. Set over 600 wooded acres, it also has its own equestrian centre, a gym and spa, two restaurants, wine masterclasses, and palatial rooms catering to every whim, right down to a pillow menu (accommodation from €130).

1

SIMON GREENWOOD/GETTY IMAGES ©

2

4

TONY WHEELER/GETTY IMAGES ©

1. Butler House, Kilkenny City
As well as housing a boutique hotel (p197), this historic mansion is known for its beautiful gardens (p196).

2. Traditional Pubs
Seek out a music session at a local watering hole.

3. Irish Cuisine
County Kilkenny's eateries make the most of delicious local produce.

4. Picturesque Villages
The area south of Kilkenny city is a patchwork of country roads and charming villages.

3

NICO TONDINI/GETTY IMAGES ©

Eating

★Blackberry Cafe CAFE €
(www.theblackberrycafe.ie; Market St, Thomastown; mains €5-9; ⏲9.30am-5.30pm Mon-Fri, 10am-5.30pm Sat;) Superb thick-cut sandwiches, toasties, quiche and warming soups are served with pumpkin-seed-speckled soda bread here. Much is organic, and the tarts and cakes are baked daily. Between noon and 2pm, great-value hot lunches see the place squeezed to bursting.

Knockdrinna Farmshop & Cafe DELI, CAFE €
(www.knockdrinna.com; Main St, Stoneyford; mains €5-10; ⏲9.30am-6pm Mon-Sat, 11am-5pm Sun, shorter hours Oct-Mar;) This farm shop is a tiny tour de force of local foods. From the house-made cheese, cured meats, smoked fish, salads, coffees and much more, you can assemble a meal that may outclass your previous best picnic. Or settle down at a table for a sit-in lunch. Stoneyford is 9km northwest of Thomastown.

Sol Bistro MODERN IRISH €€
(www.restaurantskilkenny.com; Low St, Thomastown; lunch mains €10-13, 2-/3-course dinners €25/29; ⏲5.30-9pm Wed & Thu, 11.30am-3pm & 5.30-10pm Fri & Sat, noon-9pm Sun;) This branch of Kilkenny city's modern Irish restaurant (p198) is a small cafe in a tidy old shopfront. It uses the best local ingredients to create Irish classics with an innovative twist.

KILKENNY WALKS

The **South Leinster Way** (www.irishtrails.ie) slices through the hilly southern part of County Kilkenny, from Graiguenamanagh to Inistioge, down to Mullinavat and westward to Piltown. By far the prettiest part, a stretch of some 13km, links the two villages of Graiguenamanagh and Inistioge; in either you can reward yourself with a top-notch meal.

Along this path, 4km south of Graiguenamanagh, you can branch off onto the **Brandon Hill Loop** (purple waymarks; www.trailkilkenny.ie) which scales Brandon Hill (516m). The broad moorland summit is easily reached and affords a lovely view of the Blackstairs Mountains and Mt Leinster to the east. The round trip from Graiguenamanagh is a fairly relaxed 12km walk.

Getting There & Away

Trains on the Dublin to Waterford route via Kilkenny stop at Thomastown station, 1km west of town.

Inistioge

POP 260

Tiny Inistioge (*in*-ish-teeg) is a delight, with its tranquil village square, riverside park, and 18th-century, 10-arch stone bridge spanning the River Nore (fishing permits available from O'Donnell's pub on the square). The **Nore Valley Walk** heads north along the riverbank to Thomastown, or try the **Nature Walk** signposted south from the square.

The R700 from Thomastown makes for a lovely scenic drive along the Nore Valley, and features views of the ruined 13th-century **Grennan Castle**.

Sights

Woodstock Gardens GARDENS
(www.woodstock.ie; admission free, parking €4; ⏲9am-7pm Apr-Sep, 10am-4pm Oct-Mar) The thickly wooded Woodstock Gardens is a beauty of a park with flower terraces, a walled garden, an arboretum, picnic areas, walking trails and a cafe. The panorama of the valley and village below is spectacular. From Inistioge, follow Main St (opposite the Woodstock Arms) for 1km to signs for Woodstock Estate and enter the large gates (despite appearances, it's a public road) then continue along the road for another 2km until you reach the car park.

Sleeping & Eating

Woodstock Arms B&B, PUB €€
(☎056-775 8440; www.woodstockarms.com; The Square; s/d/tr from €40/70/90; ⏲noon-10pm;) This picturesque pub has tables on the square and seven basic bedrooms that are squeaky clean; the triples are particularly spacious. Breakfast is served in a pretty little room out back with wooden tables and traditional local china.

Circle of Friends CAFE €
(☎056-775 8800; High St; mains €5-13; ⏲11am-5pm Tue-Fri, to 6pm Sat & Sun, longer hours Jun-Aug) With tables on the street, this cheerful cafe has flavoured coffees (mint, caramel and so on), all-day breakfasts, hot dishes such as beer-battered cod and chips and – the reason everyone's really here – gargantuan servings of homemade desserts such as pavlova.

Graiguenamanagh

POP 1540

Graiguenamanagh (greg-nuh-*mah*-na; known locally as just Graig) is the kind of place where you could easily find yourself staying longer than planned. Spanning the Barrow, an ancient six-arch stone bridge is illuminated at night and connects the village with the smaller township of Tinnahinch on the County Carlow side of the river (look for the darker stones on the Carlow side – a legacy from being blown up during the 1798 rebellion).

There are good walks near town, notably the riverside **Barrow Way** (p191).

Sights & Activities

Duiske Abbey CHURCH

(Main St; 8am-6pm) This was once Ireland's largest Cistercian abbey, founded in 1204, and is still very much a working parish church. In the grounds stand two Celtic **high crosses** (7th century and 9th century), brought here in the last century for protection. Around the corner, the **Abbey Centre** (open 9am to 1pm weekdays only) houses a small exhibition of Christian art, plus pictures of the abbey in its unrestored state.

Waterside Bike & Hire CYCLING

(086-408 4008; www.watersideguesthouse.com; The Quay; pedal/electric bikes per day €15/25; 9am-6pm) The classic summer outing in Graig is to walk or ride a bike along the grassy River Barrow towpath to the pretty village of St Mullins. This guesthouse on the quayside rents electric bikes as well as ordinary mountain bikes.

Festivals & Events

Town of Books Festival BOOKS

(www.graiguenamanaghtownofbooks.com) Graiguenamanagh's narrow streets spill over with booksellers, authors and bibliophiles during this three-day festival in September. Plans are under way for Graiguenamanagh to become a year-round 'book town' in the same vein as Wales' Hay-on-Wye.

Sleeping & Eating

Waterside GUESTHOUSE €€

(059-972 4246; www.watersideguesthouse.com; The Quay; s/d from €55/78; restaurant noon-3pm Sun year-round, 6-10pm Mon-Sat Apr-Sep, Fri & Sat only Oct-Mar;) Overlooking the boats tied up along the river, this inviting guesthouse and restaurant occupies a converted 19th-century grain store. Its 10 renovated bedrooms have exposed timber beams, and the restaurant is well regarded for its interesting modern Irish menu (mains €18 to €26) and its regular 'After Dinner Live' music acts featuring anything from jazz to bluegrass.

Drinking

Mick Doyle's PUB

(Main St; 11.30am-11pm Mon-Sat, 12.30-10.30pm Sun) One of Graiguenamanagh's hidden treasures is the pair of unchanged-for-generations shop-pubs on Main St – Mick Doyle's and Mick Ryan's. Doyle's is the sort of place where you can buy a bag of potatoes, get some cartridges for your shotgun and pick up some gardening implements, before settling down for a pint and some craic.

F J Murray PUB

(cnr Abbey St & The Quay; noon-11pm Mon-Sat, to 10pm Sun) A cosy old-time pub, the life and soul of the village during its Sunday evening trad sessions; listen out for songs featuring local landmarks.

Shopping

Cushendale Woollen Mill CRAFTS

(www.cushendale.ie; Mill Rd; 8.30am-12.30pm & 1.30-5.30pm Mon-Fri, 10am-1pm Sat) Produces knitting yarns, blankets, tweed and winter woollies, which are on sale at the neighbouring shop; ask for an informal, behind-the-scenes peek at the mill's century-old machinery in action. It's up the hill west of Duiske Abbey.

Duiske Glass CRAFTS

(www.duiskeglass.ie; High St; 10am-5.30pm Mon-Fri, to 5pm Sat) This small studio creates contemporary and traditional crystal, with many designs hand-cut using the old intaglio method of engraving. The gift shop also stocks Irish glassware, ceramics, leather goods and accessories.

Getting There & Away

Graiguenamanagh is 23km southeast of Kilkenny city on the R703. Kilbride Coaches (www.kilbridecoaches.com) runs two buses daily, Monday to Saturday, from Kilkenny bus station (€6, 55 minutes) to Graig, via Borris in County Carlow.

Northern Kilkenny

The rolling green hills of northern County Kilkenny are ideal for leisurely drives along the back roads with the makings of a picnic stowed in the boot (trunk). There's not a whole lot going on in this part of the county; it's best enjoyed by simply taking in the scenery and discovering peaceful little villages.

Castlecomer & Around

POP 1460

Castlecomer is on the gentle River Dinin, some 18km north of Kilkenny city. The town became a centre for anthracite mining after coal was discovered nearby in 1636; the mines closed for good in the mid-1960s. Anthracite, a very hard form of coal, burns cleanly and produces almost no smoke.

About 10km southwest of Castlecomer is **Swifte's Heath**, home to Jonathan Swift during his school years in Kilkenny. The 'e' was evidently dropped from the name before the satirist gained notoriety as the author of *Gulliver's Travels* and *A Modest Proposal*.

Bus Éireann runs six buses daily from Kilkenny to Castlecomer (€6, 25 minutes).

Sights

Castlecomer Discovery Park PARK

(www.discoverypark.ie; Estate Yard; exhibition adult/child €8/5; ⏲9.30am-6pm May-Aug, 10am-5pm Sep-Oct & Mar-Apr, 10.30am-4.30pm Nov-Feb) The grounds of the former Wandesforde estate, whose owners grew rich from exploitation of the land's underlying coal deposits, is now a family-oriented leisure park with adventure playgrounds, woodland trails, a treetop walk, boating and fishing lakes, craft workshops, a cafe, and an exhibition on the history of the local coal mines. Parking costs €3 for three hours, or €4 for the whole day.

Dunmore Cave CAVE

(☎056-776 7726; www.heritageireland.ie; Ballyfoyle; adult/child €4/2; ⏲9.30am-6.30pm mid-Jun–mid-Sep, shorter hours rest of year) Dunmore Cave is as famous for its history as for its beautiful calcite formations, and has yielded many archaeological treasures. Admission is via guided tour only, which leads down a steep descent to caverns full of stalactites, stalagmites and columns, including the 7m-tall Market Cross, Europe's largest free-standing stalagmite. Although well lit and spacious, it's damp and cold; bring warm clothes. The cave is 9km south of Castlecomer, signposted off the N78 road from Kilkenny city.

In 928 marauding Vikings slaughtered 1000 people at two ring forts near the cave. When survivors hid in the caverns, the Vikings tried to smoke them out by lighting fires at the entrance. It's thought that they then dragged off the men as slaves and left the women and children to suffocate. Excavations in 1973 uncovered the skeletons of at least 44 people, mostly women and children. They also found coins dating from the 10th century. One theory suggests that the coins were dropped by the Vikings (who often carried them under the arms, secured with wax) while engaged in the slaughter. However, there are few marks of violence on the skeletons, lending weight to the theory that suffocation was the cause of death.

County Cork

POP 519,000 / AREA 7508 SQ KM

Includes ➡

Best Places to Eat

- ➡ Finn's Table (p231)
- ➡ Manning's Emporium (p246)
- ➡ Farmgate Restaurant (p225)
- ➡ Scannells (p233)
- ➡ Market Lane (p215)

Best Places to Stay

- ➡ Garnish House (p214)
- ➡ Ballymaloe House (p225)
- ➡ Gilbert's (p224)
- ➡ Blairscove House (p244)
- ➡ Old Presbytery (p230)

Why Go?

Everything good about Ireland can be found in County Cork. Surrounding the country's second city – a thriving metropolis made glorious by location and its almost Rabelaisian devotion to the finer things of life – is a lush landscape dotted with villages that offer days of languor and idyll.

The city's understated confidence is grounded in its plethora of food markets and ever-evolving cast of creative eateries, and in its selection of pubs, entertainment and cultural pursuits.

Further afield, you'll pass inlets along eroded coastlines and a multitude of perfectly charming old fishing towns and villages. The scenery is every bit as enchanting as the best bits of Ireland, particularly along the long Mizen Head, Sheep's Head and Beara Peninsulas, where you can tackle mountain passes and touch Ireland's ancient past.

When to Go

➡ Although the summer months promise the best weather, the shoulder seasons are festival time.

➡ Springtime is heralded in Baltimore with a fiddle fair, followed by a seafood and jazz festival in May.

➡ Autumn sees West Cork go food crazy, especially in Skibbereen, which hosts the Taste of West Cork Food Festival in September, and in the culinary capital of Kinsale, which has an excellent, long-established gourmet festival in October.

➡ Cork city's perennially popular jazz festival swings into town in late October.

County Cork Highlights

❶ Revel in buzzing **Cork city** (p210), with its brilliant selection of restaurants, pubs, music and theatre.

❷ Hike to the tip of the windswept, wonderfully remote **Sheep's Head Peninsula** (p244).

❸ Catch a culinary demonstration or take a cookery class at **Ballymaloe Cookery School** (p225).

❹ Meander the medieval streets of **Kinsale** (p227) and walk along the shoreline to mammoth Charles Fort.

❺ Spot seals and sea eagles as you sail to

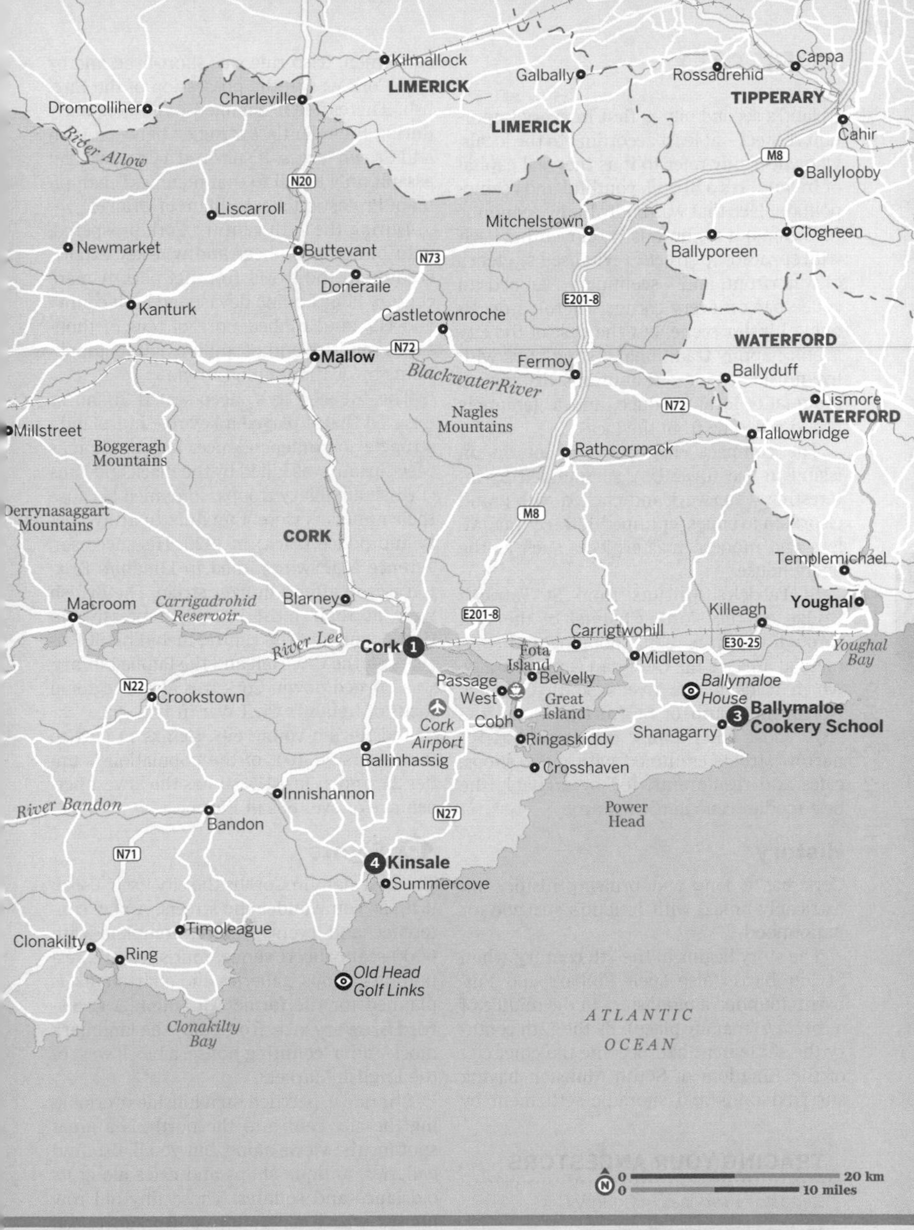

Ilnacullin (Garinish Island; p248), before exploring its subtropical gardens.

6 Brave the waves on a thrilling boat trip around the famous **Fastnet Rock** (p241).

7 Drive the narrow, switchback road that climbs across the Beara Peninsula's spectacular **Healy Pass** (p249).

8 Take a guided sea-kayak tour by moonlight on lovely **Lough Hyne** (p239).

9 Step back into a world of fading splendour at **Bantry House & Garden** (p245).

CORK CITY

POP 119,230

Ireland's second city is first in every important respect – at least according to the locals, who cheerfully refer to it as the 'real capital of Ireland'. It's a liberal, youthful and cosmopolitan place that was badly hit by economic recession but is now busily reinventing itself with spruced-up streets, revitalised stretches of waterfront, and – seemingly – an artisan coffee bar on every corner. There's a developing hipster scene, but the best of the city is still happily traditional – snug pubs with live-music sessions, restaurants dishing up top-quality local produce, and a genuinely proud welcome from the locals.

The compact city centre is set on an island in the River Lee, surrounded by interesting waterways and packed with grand Georgian avenues, cramped 17th-century alleys and modern masterpieces such as the opera house.

St Patrick's St runs from St Patrick's Bridge on the North Channel of the Lee, through the city's main shopping and commercial area, to the Georgian Grand Parade, which leads to the river's South Channel. North and south of St Patrick's St lie the city's most entertaining quarters: grids of narrow streets crammed with pubs, shops, cafes and restaurants, fed by arguably the best foodie scene in the country.

History

Cork has a long and bruising history, inextricably linked with Ireland's struggle for nationhood.

The story begins in the 7th century, when St Fin Barre (also spelt Finbarr and Finbarre) founded a monastery in the middle of a *corcach* (marshy place). By the 12th century the settlement had become the chief city of the Kingdom of South Munster, having survived raids and sporadic settlement by Norsemen. Irish rule was short-lived and by 1185 Cork was in the possession of the English. Thereafter it changed hands regularly during the relentless struggle between Irish and Crown forces. It survived a Cromwellian assault only to fall to that merciless champion of Protestantism, William of Orange.

During the 18th century Cork prospered, with butter, beef, beer and whiskey exported around the world from its port. A mere century later famine devastated both county and city, and robbed Cork of tens of thousands (and Ireland of millions) of its inhabitants by death or emigration.

The 'Rebel City's' deep-seated Irishness ensured that it played a key role in Ireland's struggle for independence. Mayor Thomas MacCurtain was killed by the Black and Tans (British auxilliary troops, so-named because their uniforms were a mixture of army khaki and police black) in 1920. His successor, Terence MacSwiney, died in London's Brixton prison after a hunger strike. The British were at their most brutally repressive in Cork – much of the centre, including St Patrick's St, the City Hall and the Public Library, was burned down. Cork was also a regional focus of Ireland's Civil War in 1922–23.

Today it's a young city, thanks in part to its university: 40% of the population is under 25, and at just 11%, it has the lowest percentage of over 65s in Europe.

TRACING YOUR ANCESTORS

Genealogy services in County Cork:

Mallow Heritage Centre (☎022-50302; http://mallowheritagecentre.com; 27/28 Bank Pl; ⏰by appointment) Covers north and east Cork.

Cobh Heritage Centre (p223) Housed in the Queenstown Story museum.

Skibbereen Heritage (p237) Located in the town's heritage centre.

Sights

The best sight in Cork is the city itself – soak it up as you wander the streets. A new conference and events centre, complete with 6000-seat concert venue, tourist centre, restaurants, shops, galleries and apartments, is planned for the former **Beamish & Crawford brewery site**, fronted by the landmark mock-Tudor 'counting house', a block west of the English Market.

Shandon, perched on a hillside overlooking the city centre to the north, is a great spot for the views alone, but you'll also find galleries, antique shops and cafes along its old lanes and squares. Those tiny old row houses, where generations of workers raised huge families in very basic conditions, are now sought-after urban pieds-à-terre. Pick up a copy of the *Cork Walks – Shandon* leaflet from the tourist office for a self-guided tour of the district.

Cork City Gaol MUSEUM

(☎021-430 5022; www.corkcitygaol.com; Convent Ave; adult/child €8/5; ⏰9.30am-5pm Apr-Oct,

10am-4pm Nov-Mar; 8 to the University College Cork) This imposing former prison is well worth a visit, if only to get a sense of how awful life was for prisoners a century ago. An audio tour guides you around the restored cells, which feature models of suffering prisoners and sadistic-looking guards. Take a bus to UCC – from there walk north along Mardyke Walk, cross the river and follow the signs uphill (10 minutes).

The tour is very moving, bringing home the harshness of the 19th-century penal system. The most common crime was that of poverty; many of the inmates were sentenced to hard labour for stealing loaves of bread. Atmospheric night tours take place on Thursdays at 7pm (€10).

The prison closed in 1923, reopening in 1927 as a radio station which operated until the 1950s. The Governor's House has been converted into a **Radio Museum** (www.corkcitygaol.com/radio-museum/; admission €2) where, alongside collections of beautiful old radios, you can hear the story of Guglielmo Marconi's conquest of the airwaves.

Crawford Municipal Art Gallery GALLERY
(021-480 5042; www.crawfordartgallery.ie; Emmet Pl; 10am-5pm Mon-Wed, Fri & Sat, to 8pm Thu) FREE Cork's public gallery houses a small but excellent permanent collection covering the 17th century through to the modern day. Highlights include works by Sir John Lavery, Jack B Yeats and Nathaniel Hone, and a room devoted to Irish women artists from 1886 to 1978 – don't miss the pieces by Mainie Jellet and Evie Hone.

The Sculpture Galleries contain snow-white plaster casts of Roman and Greek statues, given to King George IV by the pope in 1822. George didn't like the gift and stuck the sculptures in the cellar until someone suggested that Cork might appreciate them.

Lewis Glucksman Gallery GALLERY
(021-490 1844; www.glucksman.org; University College Cork, Western Rd; suggested donation €5; 10am-5pm Tue-Sat, 2-5pm Sun) FREE This award-winning building – shortlisted for the 2005 Stirling Prize – is a startling construction of limestone, steel and timber. Two floors of galleries with suitably paint-spattered floors display the best in both national and international contemporary art and installation. Don't miss the free fortnightly curatorial tours. The on-site cafe is excellent.

THE APOSTLE OF TEMPERANCE

The imposing **Statue of Father Mathew** on St Patrick's St, just south of the River Lee North Channel, is of Father Theobald Mathew, the 'Apostle of Temperance', who crusaded against the ills of alcohol in the 1830s and 1840s with such success that a quarter of a million people took the 'pledge' and whiskey production was cut in half.

St Fin Barre's Cathedral CATHEDRAL
(021-496 3387; www.cathedral.cork.anglican.org; Bishop St; adult/child €5/3; 9.30am-5.30pm Mon-Sat year-round, 12.30-5pm Sun Apr-Nov) Spiky spires, gurning gargoyles and elaborate sculpture adorn the exterior of Cork's Protestant cathedral, an attention-grabbing mixture of French Gothic and medieval whimsy. The grandeur continues inside, with marble floor mosaics, a colourful chancel ceiling and a huge pulpit and bishop's throne. Quirky items include a cannonball blasted into an earlier medieval spire during the Siege of Cork (1690). The cathedral sits about 500m southwest of the centre, on the spot where Cork's 7th-century patron saint, Fin Barre, founded a monastery.

Most of the cathedral's ostentation is the result of an architectural competition held in 1863 and won by William Burges. Once victory was assured, Burges promptly redrew his plans – with an extra choir bay and taller towers – and his £15,000 budget went out the window. Luckily, the bishop appreciated such perfectionism and spent the rest of his life fundraising for the project. Local legend says that the golden angel on the eastern side will blow its horn when the Apocalypse is due to start…

St Anne's Church CHURCH
(021-450 5906; www.shandonbells.ie; John Redmond St, Shandon; tower incl bells adult/child €5/2.50; 10am-1pm & 2-5pm Mon-Sat, 11.30am-1pm & 2-4.30pm Sun, shorter hours Oct-May) Shandon is dominated by the 1722 St Anne's Church, aka the 'Four-Faced Liar' – so called because each of the tower's four clocks used to tell a different time. Wannabe campanologists can ring the bells on the 1st floor of the 1750 Italianate tower, and then continue up the 132 steps to the top for 360-degree views of the city.

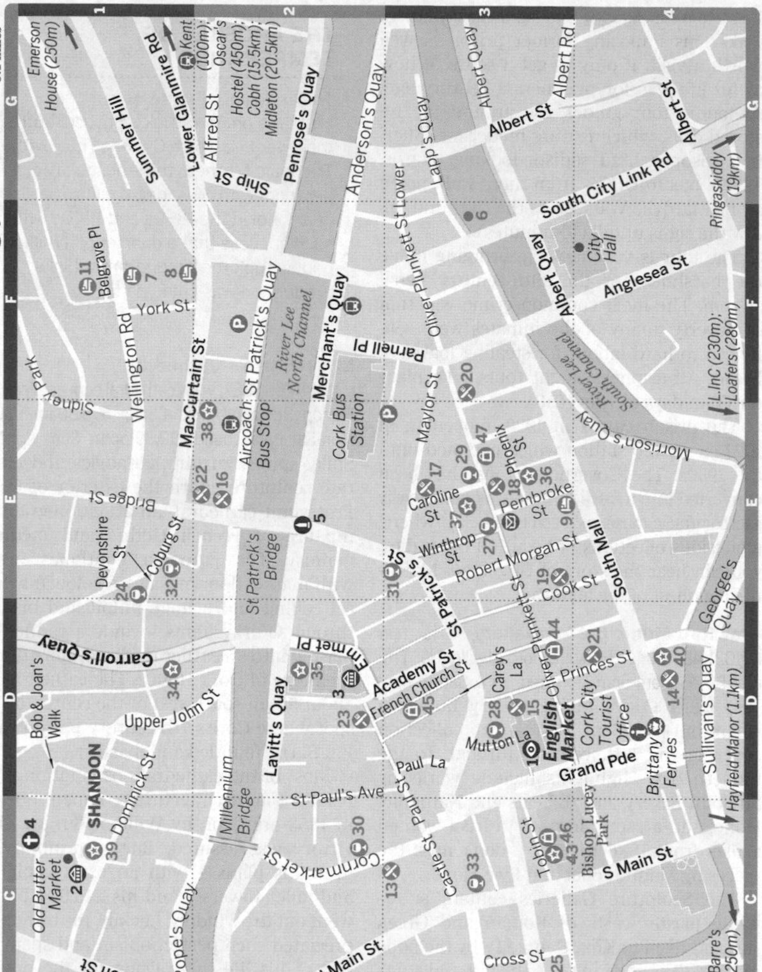

Cork City

0 200 m
0 0.1 miles

Old Butter Market
2
4
Bob & Joan's Walk
SHANDON
39
Dominick St
Upper John St
Carroll's Quay
34
Devonshire St
24
Coburg St
32
Bridge St
Sidney Park
11
Belgrave Pl
Wellington Rd
York St
7
8
Summer Hill
Lower Glanmire Rd
Emerson House (250m)
Kent (100m); Oscar's Hostel (450m); Cobh (15.5km); Midleton (20.5km)
Alfred St
Ship St
Blarney St
Shandon St
Pope's Quay
26
North Mall
Bachelor's Quay
41
Millennium Bridge
MacCurtain St
22
16
38
Aircoach Bus Stop
St Patrick's Quay
St Patrick's Bridge
River Lee North Channel
Lavitt's Quay
35
Emmet Pl
3
5
Merchant's Quay
Penrose's Quay
Cork Bus Station
Anderson's Quay
Parnell Pl
Banks of the River Lee Walkway
Grenville Pl
Moore St
Grattan St
N Main St
Cornmarket St
30
13
St Paul's Ave
23
French Church St
45
Academy St
31
St Patrick's St
Caroline St
17
Maylor St
Oliver Plunkett St Lower
Lapp's Quay
Castle St
Paul St
Paul La
Winthrop St
37
29
20
6
Albert Quay
33
Sheares St
Mutton La
28
Carey's La
Robert Morgan St
27
18
47
Phoenix St
Pembroke St
36
Cross St
1
15
English Market
Oliver Plunkett St
44
Cook St
19
9
Albert St
Albert Rd
Dyke Pde
12
Woods St
Washington St
25
Hanover St
Tobin St
43
46
Bishop Lucey Park
Grand Pde
Cork City Tourist Office
Princes St
21
South Mall
Morrison's Quay
River Lee South Channel
Albert Quay
City Hall
Anglesea St
South City Link Rd
42
Lancaster Quay
10
S Main St
Brittany Ferries
14
40
Sullivan's Quay
George's Quay
Western Rd B&Bs strip(150m); Lewis Glucksman Gallery (400m); UCC (500m)
St Fin Barre's Cathedral (250m)
Hayfield Manor (1.1km)
L.InC (230m); Loafers (280m)
Ringaskiddy (19km)
Albert St

Cork City

Cork Butter Museum MUSEUM
(021-430 0600; www.corkbutter.museum; O'Connell Sq; adult/child €4/free; 10am-5pm Mar-Jun & Sep-Oct, 10am-6pm Jul & Aug, 11am-3pm Sat & Sun only Nov-Mar) Cork has a long tradition of butter manufacturing – in the 1860s it was the world's largest butter market, exporting butter throughout the British Empire – and the trade's history is told through the displays and dioramas of the Cork Butter Museum. The square in front of the museum is dominated by the neoclassical front of the Old Butter Market, and the striking, circular Firkin Crane (p220) building where butter casks were once weighed (it now houses a dance centre).

Tours

Cork City Tour BUS TOUR
(021-430 9090; www.corkcitytour.com; adult/student/child €15/13/5; Mar-Nov) Hop-on-hop-off, open-top bus linking the city's main sights.

Cork Walks WALKING TOUR
FREE Cork City Council's two free self-guided tours cover the South Parish and Shandon districts. Pick up a leaflet and map at the tourist office, or download from www.cork.ie.

Atlantic Sea Kayaking KAYAKING
(028-21058; www.atlanticseakayaking.com; Lapp's Quay; per person €50) Offers guided 'urban kayaking' trips around Cork's waterways from 6.30pm to 9pm (book in advance, minimum two people).

Festivals & Events

Book well in advance, particularly for the autumn jazz and film festivals.

Cork World Book Fest LITERATURE
(www.constantreader.ie) A huge book festival in late April, with loads of authors; sponsored by the Cork City Library.

International Choral Festival MUSIC
(www.corkchoral.ie) A five-day celebration of choral music held in the City Hall and other venues in April/May.

Cork Pride GAY & LESBIAN
(www.corkpride.com) Weeklong gay pride celebrations in July/August.

Guinness Cork Jazz Festival JAZZ
(www.guinnessjazzfestival.com) Cork's biggest festival has an all-star line-up in venues across town. Held in late October.

Cork Film Festival FILM
(www.corkfilmfest.org) Eclectic, weeklong program of international films in November.

Sleeping

City Centre

Whether you stay on the main island or to the north in Shandon or around MacCurtain St, you're right in the heart of the action.

Oscar's Hostel HOSTEL €
(☎085 175 3458; www.oscarshostel.com; 111 Lower Glanmire Rd; dm €18-20, tw €44-48;) Small (32-bed) but stylish, this relatively new hostel is set on a busy street just 200m east of the train station and 15-minutes' walk from the city centre. Facilities are good, with a modern kitchen, comfy common rooms and bike storage, though the bedrooms are basic.

Brú Bar & Hostel HOSTEL €
(☎021-455 9667; www.bruhostel.com; 57 MacCurtain St; dm/tw from €17/40; @) This buzzing hostel has its own internet cafe, with free access for guests, and a fantastic bar, popular with backpackers and locals alike. The dorms (each with a bathroom) have four to six beds and are both clean and stylish – ask for one on the upper floors to avoid bar noise. Breakfast is free.

Sheila's Hostel HOSTEL €
(☎021-450 5562; www.sheilashostel.ie; 4 Belgrave Pl, off Wellington Rd; dm €15-18, tw €44-56; @) Sheila's heaves with young travellers, and it's no wonder given its excellent central location. Facilities include a sauna, lockers, laundry service, a movie room and a barbecue. Cheaper twin rooms share bathrooms. Breakfast is €3 extra.

★**Imperial Hotel** HOTEL €€
(☎021-427 4040; www.flynnhotels.com; South Mall; d from €120; @) Having recently celebrated its bicentenary – Thackeray, Dickens and Sir Walter Scott have all stayed here – the Imperial knows how to age gracefully. Public spaces resonate with period detail – marble floors, elaborate floral bouquets and more – while the 130 bedrooms feature writing desks, understated decor and modern touches including a luxurious spa and a digital music library.

Irish Free State commander-in-chief Michael Collins spent his last night alive here; you can ask to check into his room.

Auburn House B&B €€
(☎021-450 8555; www.auburnguesthouse.com; 3 Garfield Tce, Wellington Rd; s/d €58/80;) There's a warm family welcome at this neat B&B, which has smallish but well-kept rooms brightened by window boxes. Try to bag one of the back rooms, which are quieter and have sweeping views over the city. Breakfast includes vegetarian choices; the location near the fun of MacCurtain St is a plus.

Western Rd & Around

Western Rd runs southwest from the city centre to the large UCC campus; it has the city's biggest choice of B&Bs. Take a bus from the central bus station, or walk (10 to 30 minutes).

★**Garnish House** B&B €€
(☎021-427 5111; www.garnish.ie; Western Rd; s/d from €93/105;) Attention is lavished upon guests at this award-winning B&B where the legendary breakfast menu (30 choices) ranges from fresh fish to French toast. Typical of the touches here is freshly cooked porridge, served with creamed honey and your choice of whiskey or Baileys; enjoy it out on the garden terrace. The 14 rooms are very comfortable; reception is open 24 hours.

Blarney Stone Guesthouse B&B €€
(☎021-427 0083; www.blarneystoneguesthouse.ie; Western Rd; s/d from €85/99;) The dazzling white facade of this tall Victorian town house conceals a dazzling interior crammed with polished period furniture, glittering Waterford crystal chandeliers, and curlicued gilt mirrors. The Victorian theme does not extend to the facilities, though – creature comforts include power showers, fast wi-fi, satellite TV and hearty breakfasts.

Crawford House B&B €€
(☎021-427 9000; www.crawfordhouse.ie; Western Rd; r €65-95; @) Power showers and large spa baths feature in the dozen bedrooms at this B&B, along with king-sized beds and understated wooden furnishings. The standard is that of a contemporary hotel (24-hour reception); the atmosphere, that of a family home. Breakfast is served in the neighbouring Killarney Guest House (same management) and costs €9 extra.

★River Lee Hotel
HOTEL €€€

(☎021-425 2700; www.doylecollection.com; Western Rd; r from €155;) This modern riverside hotel brings a touch of luxury to the city centre. It has gorgeous public areas with huge sofas, a designer fireplace, a stunning five-storey glass-walled atrium, and superb service. There are well-equipped bedrooms (nice and quiet at the back, but request a corner room for extra space) and possibly the best breakfast buffet in Ireland.

Hayfield Manor
HOTEL €€€

(☎021-484 5900; www.hayfieldmanor.ie; Perrott Ave, College Rd; r from €209;) Roll out the red carpet and pour yourself a sherry for *you have arrived*. Just 1.5km southwest of the city centre but with all the ambience of a country house, Hayfield combines the luxury and facilities of a big hotel with the informality and welcome of a small one. The beautiful bedrooms offer a choice of traditional decor or contemporary styling.

Eating

Cork's food scene is reason enough to visit the city. The English Market (p218) is a national treasure. The narrow, nearly lightless pedestrianised streets north of St Patrick's St throng with cafes and restaurants, and the place hops day and night.

Uncle Pete's
PIZZA €

(☎021-427 4845; http://unclepetes.ie; Paul St; mains €6-12; 8am-10pm Mon-Sat, 11am-10pm Sun;) Cork's best pizza, with more than 25 gluten-free options. Also serves breakfast till noon, including granola and freshly squeezed juices.

Idaho Café
CAFE €

(☎021-427 6376; http://idahocafe.ie; 19 Caroline St; mains €5-12; 8.30am-5pm Mon-Thu, to 6pm Fri & Sat;) It looks like a traditional old cafe from the outside, but you'll find all sorts of creative takes on Irish standards here, from black pudding and bacon baps to smoked fish pie. The tea selection includes lots of herbal choices and there's a good by-the-glass wine menu. Crowded seating means nothing is private.

★Market Lane
IRISH, INTERNATIONAL €€

(☎021-427 4710; www.marketlane.ie; 5 Oliver Plunkett St; mains €12-26; noon-10.30pm Mon-Sat, 1-9pm Sun;) It's always hopping at this bright corner bistro. The menu is broad and hearty, changing to reflect what's fresh at the English Market: perhaps braised ox cheek in ale, or smoked haddock with bacon and cabbage? No reservations for fewer than six diners; sip a drink at the bar till a table is free. Lots of wines by the glass.

★Cafe Paradiso
VEGETARIAN €€

(☎021-427 7939; www.cafeparadiso.ie; 16 Lancaster Quay; 2-/3-course dinners €33/40; 5.30-10pm Mon-Sat;) A contender for best restaurant in town of any genre, Paradiso serves contemporary vegetarian dishes, including vegan fare: how about sweet chilli-glazed pan-fried tofu with Asian greens in tamarind and coconut broth? Reservations are essential. Dinner, bed and breakfast rates, staying in the funky upstairs rooms, start from €100 per person.

Gourmet Burger Bistro
BURGERS €€

(☎021-450 5404; www.gourmetburgerbistro.ie; 8 Bridge St; mains €11-14; noon-10pm Mon-Sat, 2-9pm Sun;) At this chic, minimalist spot, organic burgers span the globe: from Asian (lamb kofta with mango) to Spanish (chicken, chorizo and manchego), American (with bacon, Monterey jack cheese and barbecue sauce), French (with brie), and of course, the 'Full Irish' (bacon, Clonakilty black pudding and fried egg). Vegetarians aren't forgotten, with falafel and halloumi options.

Nash 19
INTERNATIONAL €€

(☎021-427 0880; www.nash19.com; Princes St; mains €10-16; 7.30am-4pm Mon-Fri, 8.30am-4pm Sat) A sensational bistro and deli where locally sourced food is honoured at breakfast and lunch, either sit-in or take away. Fresh scones draw in the crowds early; daily lunch specials (soups, salads, desserts etc), free-range chicken pie and platters of smoked fish from Frank Henderman keep them coming through the rest of the day.

Electric
MODERN IRISH €€

(www.electriccork.com; 41 South Mall; mains €10-25; noon-10pm;) The market-sourced menu at this transformed art-deco bank runs from falafel wraps to succulent steaks. From Thursday to Saturday there's a rustic Mediterranean-style fish bar too, but it's the big riverside deck and upstairs restaurant balcony with knock-out cathedral views that pull in the crowds – along with wines by the glass, and more than two dozen beers.

Star Anise
MODERN EUROPEAN €€

(☎021-455 1635; www.staranise.ie; 4 Bridge St; mains €18-27; 6-10pm Tue-Sat) Fresh and creative cooking is the hallmark at this narrow,

1

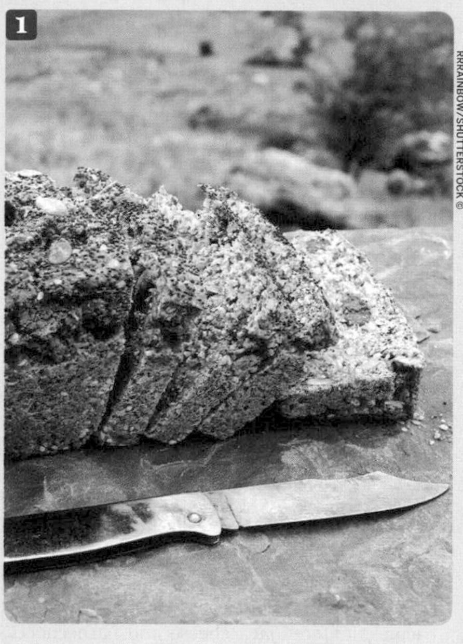

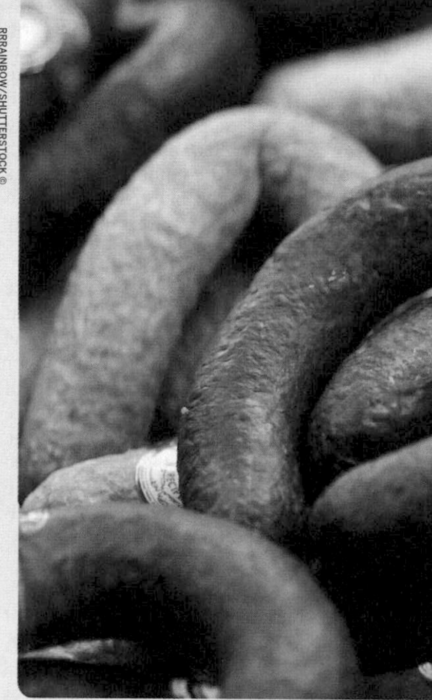

1. Soda bread **2.** Black pudding **3.** Kinsale Harbour (p227)
4. The English Market (p218)

3

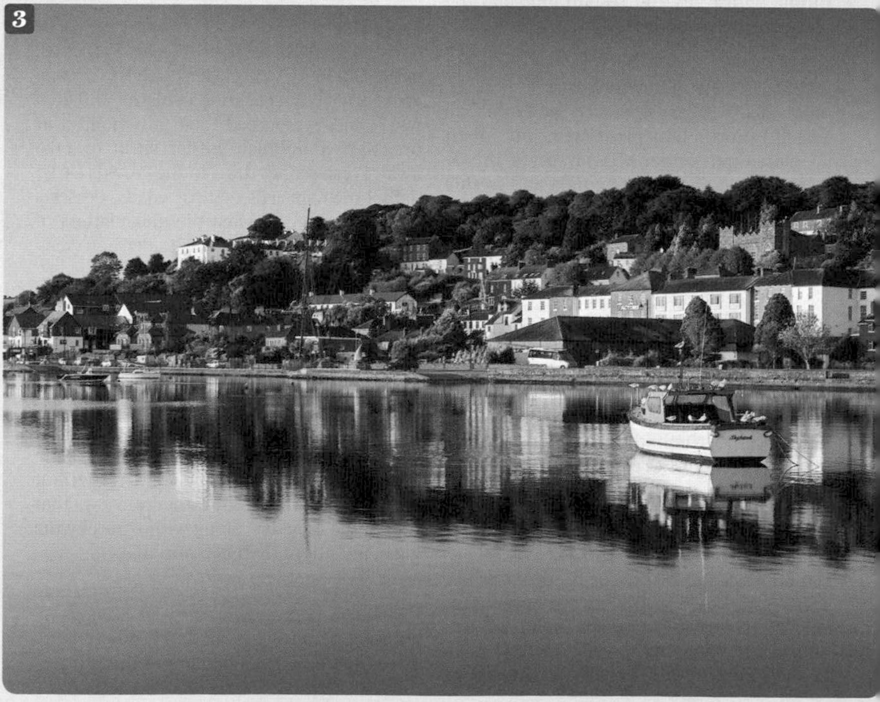

ROGER MAPP/GETTY IMAGES ©

The Cuisine of County Cork

Ireland's largest county can fairly lay claim to being the foodie capital of Ireland. Lush pastures provide prime meat and dairy products, while superb seafood is landed around the coast. And it seems as if you can't move here without bumping into a traditional cheese maker, artisan baker or boutique coffee roaster.

The English Market

A highlight of any visit to Cork city is a stroll through this covered Victorian market, crammed with stalls selling goods from a host of local producers. Under the one roof you can browse the cream of artisan cheeses, the best of Irish beef, and the freshest of local fish, before savouring lunch at one of the town's top restaurants.

Kinsale

Clustered around a gorgeous harbour, this perfect Irish seaside town combines colourful streets, waterfront walks, craft shops and galleries with cosy cafes, traditional pubs and sophisticated wine bars. There's also a bustling farmers market, and some of the best seafood restaurants in the country.

Clonakilty

A lively market town with good B&Bs, great restaurants and top-class pubs featuring traditional music sessions, Clonakilty is also famous as the producer of Ireland's best-known black pudding, available through local butcher Edward Twomey.

Beara & Mizen Head Peninsulas

This rugged and scenic finger of land is ringed with dozens of artisan food producers, from mussel farms and sea-salt producers, to jam and preserve makers and farmhouse enterprises such as Gubbeen and Milleens, which turn out delicious cheeses and smoked foods. There are even a couple of top-class chocolatiers.

DON'T MISS

ENGLISH MARKET

English Market (www.englishmarket.ie; Princes St (main entrance); 8am-6pm Mon-Sat) could just as easily be called the Victorian Market for its ornate vaulted ceilings and columns, but the English Market is a true gem, no matter what you name it. Scores of vendors sell some of the regions's very best local produce, meats, cheeses and takeaway food. On a sunny day, take your lunch to nearby Bishop Lucey Park, a popular al fresco eating spot.

Perched on a balcony overlooking the food stalls below, the **Farmgate Cafe** (www.farmgate.ie; mains €6-15; 8.30am-4.30pm Mon-Fri, to 5pm Sat) is an unmissable experience at the heart of the English Market, the source of all that fresh local produce on your plate – everything from crab and oysters to the lamb for an Irish stew. Up the stairs and turn left for table service, right for counter service.

stylish little shopfront bistro. There are steaks for the masses but also treats such as maple-glazed duck breast, and slow-cooked lamb tagine. The wine list is both superb and affordable.

Jacques Restaurant MODERN IRISH €€
(021-427 7387; www.jacquesrestaurant.ie; 23 Oliver Plunkett St; mains lunch €7-14, dinner €22-26; 10am-4pm Mon, to 10pm Tue-Sat) Sisters Jacqueline and Eithne Barry draw on a terrific network of local suppliers that they've built up over three decades to help them realise their culinary ambitions – the freshest Cork food cooked simply, without frills. The menu changes daily: smoked quail with celeriac remoulade, perhaps, or Castletownbere crab with spaghetti and herbs.

Les Gourmandises FRENCH €€
(021-425 1959; www.lesgourmandises.ie; 17 Cook St; 2-/3-course dinners from €28/33; 6-9pm Mon-Sat) Remember those beautiful fresh fish you saw in the English Market? Many of them end up at this cute little restaurant that will remind you of that perfect place you stumbled across in Paris once… Meat and poultry also get their due, such as roast guinea fowl with foie gras and mushroom sauce. Service is gracious and calm.

Cornstore MODERN EUROPEAN €€
(021-427 4777; www.cornstorecork.com; 40a Cornmarket St; mains €10-30; noon-11pm;) Buzzing day and night, this modern restaurant has a swish bar, where you can enjoy creative cocktails while waiting for a table. Some tables are minute, but if you're having the amazing house special of lobster, hold out for a large one so your elbows and the shells can fly. There's also excellent fresh fish, steaks and pasta; the three-course set menu costs €32.

Drinking & Nightlife

In Cork pubs, locally brewed Murphy's and Beamish stouts, not Guinness, are the preferred pints, even though Heineken International has now taken over both of the local breweries (and closed down Beamish).

Local microbreweries include the long-established Franciscan Well, whose refreshing Friar Weisse beer is popular in summer, and relative newcomer **Rising Sons** (021-241 1126; www.risingsonsbrewery.com; Cornmarket St; noon-late), whose Mi Daza stout is a new take on an old recipe.

Given the city's big student population, the small selection of nightclubs do a thriving trade. Entry ranges from free to €15; most are open until 2am on Friday and Saturday.

★Sin É PUB
(www.corkheritagepubs.com; 8 Coburg St; 12.30-11.30pm Sun-Thu, to 12.30am Fri & Sat) You could easily while away an entire day at this great old place, which is everything a craic-filled pub should be – long on atmosphere and short on pretension (Sin É means 'That's it!'). There's music most nights (regular sessions Tuesday at 9.30pm, Friday and Sunday at 6.30pm), much of it traditional, but with the odd surprise.

Franciscan Well Brewery PUB
(www.franciscanwellbrewery.com; 14 North Mall; 3-11.30pm Mon-Thu, to 12.30am Fri & Sat, to 11pm Sun;) The copper vats gleaming behind the bar give the game away: the Franciscan Well brews its own beer. The best place to enjoy it is in the enormous beer garden at the back. The pub holds regular beer festivals together with other small independent Irish breweries.

Mutton Lane Inn PUB
(www.corkheritagepubs.com; Mutton Lane; ⏲10.30am-11.30pm Mon-Thu, to 12.30am Fri & Sat, 2-11pm Sun) Tucked down the tiniest of alleys off St Patrick's St, this inviting pub, lit by candles and fairy lights, is one of Cork's most intimate drinking holes. It's minuscule, so try to get in early to bag the snug, or perch on the beer kegs outside.

Long Valley PUB
(www.thelongvalleybar.com; 10 Winthrop St; ⏲12.30-11.30pm Sun-Thu, to 12.30am Fri & Sat) A Cork institution that dates from the mid-19th century and is still going strong. Some of the furnishings hail from the White Star Line ocean liners that used to call at Cobh.

Suas Rooftop Bar COCKTAIL BAR
(www.suasbar.com; 4-5 South Main St; ⏲10am-11.30pm Mon-Thu, to 12.30am Fri & Sat, noon-11pm Sun) You could easily walk along South Main St and never know that this sleek bar with heated roof terrace was right above you. Cocktails cover all the classics, including proper caipirinhas made with cachaca (fermented sugar cane) and fresh limes. DJs hit the decks on Friday and Saturday nights.

Abbot's Ale House PUB
(17 Devonshire St; ⏲10.30am-10pm Mon-Fri, 12.30-10pm Sat & Sun) A low-key, 1st-floor drinking den, whose small size contrasts with its huge beer list. There are always several beers on tap and another 300 in bottles. Good for preclubbing.

Savoy CLUB
(☎021-422 3910; www.savoytheatre.ie; St Patrick's St; admission €10-15; ⏲from 10.30pm Thu-Sat) The city's best DJs (and a changing menu of visiting ones) show off their skills at the Savoy's club nights. Occasional live gigs, too (doors open around 7.30pm).

Oliver Plunkett PUB
(☎021-422 2779; www.theoliverplunkett.com; 116 Oliver Plunkett St; ⏲8am-late; 📶) Cork memorabilia (sporting, political and musical), a relaxed pub serving food from breakfast onward, rockin' live music and club nights make this multipurpose venue a magnet for locals and visitors, day and night.

☆ Entertainment

Cork's cultural life is generally of a high calibre. To see what's happening grab *WhazOn?* (www.whazon.com), a free monthly booklet available from the tourist office, news agencies, shops, hostels and B&Bs.

Cork's musical credentials are impeccable. Besides the pubs that feature live music, and theatres, there are also places that are either dedicated music venues, or bars known particularly for their live events. For full live music listings, refer to *WhazOn?*, PLUGD Records (p220), and the event guide at www.peoplesrepublicofcork.com.

Cork Opera House OPERA
(☎021-427 0022; www.corkoperahouse.ie; Emmet Pl; ⏲box office 10am-5.30pm Mon-Sat, to 7pm preshow, also 6-7pm Sun preshow) Given a modern makeover in the 1990s, this leading venue has been entertaining the city for more than 150 years with everything from opera and ballet to stand-up comedy and puppet shows. Around the back, the **Half Moon Theatre** presents contemporary theatre, dance, art and occasional club nights.

Triskel Arts Centre ARTS CENTRE
(☎021-472 2022; www.triskelart.com; Tobin St; ⏲10am-5pm Mon-Sat; 📶) A fantastic cultural

GAY & LESBIAN CORK

Cork Pride (p213) Weeklong festival in July/August, with events throughout the city.

Chambers Bar (☎021-465 8100; Washington St; ⏲8.30pm-late Wed, Fri & Sat, 5pm-late Sun) Cork's biggest and liveliest gay bar, with DJs playing till 2am, themed entertainment nights, and outrageous cocktails.

Loafers (www.loafersbarcork.com; 26-27 Douglas St; ⏲7.30-11.30pm Mon-Thu, 5pm-12.30am Fri & Sat, 5-11pm Sun) Cork's oldest gay bar, frequented by a crowd of friendly regulars.

Emerson House (☎086 834 0891; www.emersonhousecork.com; 2 Clarence Tce, Summer Hill North; s/d from €60/80; 📶) Gay and lesbian B&B in an elegant Georgian house. Host Cyril is a mine of information.

Gay Cork (www.gaycork.com) What's-on listings and directory.

L.inC (☎021-480 8600; www.linc.ie; 11a White St; ⏲11am-3pm Tue & Wed, to 8pm Thu) Resource centre for lesbians and bisexual women.

WORTH A TRIP

GONE TO THE DOGS

If you tire of the pubs, the live music and the theatre, there's always the dogs. Greyhound racing is big in Ireland, particularly with families, and **Curraheen Greyhound Park** (☎ 021-454 3095; www.igb.ie/go-greyhound-racing; Curraheen Rd; adult/child €10/5; ⏲ doors open 6.30pm Thu-Sat;) is one of the country's poshest stadiums. There are 10 races a night, plus a restaurant, a bar and live music. Curraheen is 5.5km southwest of the centre; buses run from Cork's bus station.

centre housed partly in a renovated church building – expect a varied program of live music, installation art, photography and theatre at this intimate venue. There's also a cinema (from 6.30pm) and a great cafe.

Everyman Theatre THEATRE
(☎ 021-450 1673; www.everymancork.com; 15 MacCurtain St; ⏲ box office noon-5pm Mon-Sat, to 7pm preshow, also 4-7pm Sun preshow) Acclaimed musical and dramatic productions are the main bill here, but there's also the occasional comedy act or live band (it's a great venue for gigs that require a little bit of respectful silence).

Cork Arts Theatre THEATRE
(☎ 021-450 5624; www.corkartstheatre.com; Camden Court, Carroll's Quay) A community-based theatre that stages thought-provoking drama and new works.

Granary THEATRE
(☎ 021-490 4275; www.granary.ie; Dyke Pde) Contemporary and experimental works are staged here by the UCC drama group and visiting companies.

Firkin Crane DANCE
(☎ 021-450 7487; www.firkincrane.ie; O'Connell Sq, Shandon) One of Ireland's premier centres for modern dance.

Gate Multiplex CINEMA
(☎ 021-427 9595; www.corkcinemas.com; North Main St) Multiscreen cinema showing mainstream first-run films.

Cyprus Avenue LIVE MUSIC
(☎ 021-427 6165; www.cyprusavenue.ie; Caroline St; ⏲ 7.30pm-late) This midsized venue is probably the best spot in town to see all kinds of gigs, from heartfelt singer-songwriters to excellent bands on their way to fame (or on their way down from it).

Crane Lane Theatre LIVE MUSIC
(☎ 021-427 8487; www.cranelanetheatre.com; Phoenix St) Atmospheric venue for live music, decked out in 1920s to 1940s decor. Its courtyard beer garden is a central oasis.

Fred Zeppelins LIVE MUSIC
(☎ 021-427 3500; 8 Parliament St; ⏲ 4-11.30pm Mon-Thu, to 12.30am Fri & Sat, to 11pm Sun) There's a hard edge to this dark den of a bar, popular with goths, rockers and anyone who feels uncomfortable leaving the house without a packet of Rizlas. Known for its live gigs and DJs at weekends, and open-mic night on Tuesdays.

Shopping

St Patrick's St is the retail heart of Cork, housing all the major department stores and malls. But pedestrianised Oliver Plunkett St is the retail spine; it and nearby narrow lanes are lined with small, interesting shops.

O'Connaill FOOD & DRINK
(☎ 021-437 3407; 16b French Church St; ⏲ 10am-5.30pm Mon-Sat, noon-5pm Sun;) O'Connaill creates exquisite chocolates; don't leave Cork without sampling its delicious Chocolatier's Hot Chocolate.

PLUGD Records MUSIC
(☎ 021-472 2022; www.plugdrecords.com; Triskel Arts Centre, Tobin St; ⏲ noon-7pm Mon-Sat;) Carries all kinds of music and is the place to keep up with the ever-changing club scene.

Pro Musica MUSIC
(☎ 021-427 1659; www.promusica.ie; 20 Oliver Plunkett St; ⏲ 9am-6pm Mon-Sat) A focal point and meeting place for Cork's musicians, with a full range of instruments from electric guitars to clarinets, recording equipment, sheet music, and a noticeboard.

Liam Ruiséal Teo. BOOKS
(☎ 021-427 0981; www.lrbooks.net; 49-50 Oliver Plunkett St) The oldest and biggest independent bookshop in the city; new and second-hand books, including plenty on Cork.

Information

Free wi-fi is available throughout the city centre's main streets and public spaces.

Picking up on the popular nickname for this liberal-leaning city, the indie website **People's Republic of Cork** (www.peoplesrepublicofcork.com) has excellent info.

Cork City Tourist Office (☎ 021-425 5100; www.discoverireland.ie/corkcity; Grand Pde; ⏲ 9am-6pm Mon-Sat year-round, plus 10am-5pm Sun Jul & Aug) Souvenir shop and information desk. Sells Ordnance Survey maps.

General Post Office (☎ 021-485 1042; Oliver Plunkett St; ⏲ 9am-5.30pm Mon-Sat)

Mercy University Hospital (☎ 021-427 1971; www.muh.ie; Grenville Pl) Accident and emergency services.

Webworkhouse.com (☎ 021-427 3090; www.webworkhouse.com; 8a Winthrop St; per hr €1.50-3; ⏲ 24hr) Internet cafe; also offers low-cost international phone calls.

Getting There & Away

AIR

Airlines servicing **Cork Airport** (☎ 021-431 3131; www.cork-airport.com) include Aer Lingus and Ryanair.

BOAT

Brittany Ferries (☎ 021-427 7801; www.brittanyferries.ie; 42 Grand Pde) sails to Roscoff in France (foot passenger from €59, car with two people from €329, 14 hours, one a week) from the end of March to October. The ferry terminal is at Ringaskiddy, 15-minutes' drive southeast of Cork along the N28. Taxis cost €28 to €35. Bus 223E from South Mall in Cork city centre links up with departures (€10, 50 minutes); confirm times.

TRAIN

Kent Train Station (☎ 021-450 4777) is north of the River Lee on Lower Glanmire Rd, a 10- to 15-minute walk from the city centre. Bus 205 runs into the city centre (€2, five minutes, every 15 minutes).

The train line goes through Mallow, where you can change for the Tralee line, and Limerick Junction, for the line to Ennis (and Galway), then on to Dublin.

Dublin (€64, 2¼ hours, eight daily)

Galway (€57, four to six hours, seven daily, two or three changes)

Killarney (€28, 1½ to two hours, nine daily)

Waterford (€31, three to five hours, five daily, one or two changes)

Getting Around

TO/FROM THE AIRPORT

Bus Éireann no. 226A shuttles between the train station, bus station and Cork Airport every half-hour between 6am and 10pm (€7.40, 30 minutes).

A taxi to/from town costs €20 to €25.

BUS

Most places are within easy walking distance of the centre. Single bus tickets cost €2 each; a day pass is €5. Buy all tickets on the bus.

CAR

Street parking requires scratch-card parking discs (€2 per hour, in force 8.30am to 6.30pm Monday to Saturday), available from many city-centre shops. Be warned – traffic wardens are ferociously efficient. There are several sign-posted car parks around the central area, with charges around €2 per hour and €12 overnight.

You can avoid city-centre parking problems by using **Black Ash Park & Ride** on the South City Link Road, on the way to the airport. Parking costs €5 a day, with buses into the city centre at least every 15 minutes (10-minute journey time).

TAXI

Cork Taxi Co-op (☎ 021-427 22 22; www.corktaxi.ie)

Shandon Cabs (☎ 021-450 22 55)

BUS DEPARTURES FROM CORK CITY

Bus Éireann (☎ 021-450 8188; www.buseireann.ie) operates from the **bus station** (cnr Merchant's Quay & Parnell Pl), while **AirCoach** (☎ 01-844 7118; www.aircoach.ie) and **Citylink** (☎ 091-564 164; www.citylink.ie; 📶) services depart from from St Patrick's Quay, across the river. **GoBus.ie** (☎ 091-564 600; www.gobus.ie; 📶) uses a stop around the corner on Parnell Pl.

DESTINATION	BUS COMPANY	FARE (€)	DURATION (HR)	FREQUENCY
Dublin	AirCoach	16	3	hourly
Dublin	Bus Éireann	15	3¾	6 daily
Dublin	GoBus	17	3	6-9 daily
Dublin airport	AirCoach	20	3½	hourly
Galway	Citylink	21	3	5 daily
Limerick	Citylink	17	1½	5 daily
Killarney	Bus Éireann	27	2	hourly
Kilkenny	Bus Éireann	21	3	2 daily
Waterford	Bus Éireann	23.50	2¼	hourly

AROUND CORK CITY

Blarney Castle

If you need proof of the power of a good yarn, then join the queue to get into 15th-century **Blarney Castle** (☎021-438 5252; www.blarneycastle.ie; adult/child €13/5; ⏲9am-5.30pm daily year-round, to 6pm Mon-Sat May & Sep, to 7pm Mon-Sat Jun-Aug), one of Ireland's most popular tourist attractions. They're here, of course, to plant their lips on the **Blarney Stone**, which supposedly gives one the gift of gab – a cliché that has entered every lexicon and tour route. Blarney is 8km northwest of Cork and buses run every half-hour from Cork bus station (€7.30 return, 30 minutes).

The Blarney Stone is perched at the top of a steep climb up claustrophobic spiral staircases. On the battlements, you bend backwards over a long, long drop (with safety grill and attendant to prevent tragedy) to kiss the stone; as your shirt rides up, coachloads of onlookers stare up your nose. Once you're upright again, don't forget to admire the stunning views before descending. Try not to think of the local lore about all the fluids that drench the stone other than saliva. Better yet, just don't kiss it.

The custom of kissing the stone is a relatively modern one, but Blarney's association with smooth talking goes back a long time. Queen Elizabeth I is said to have invented the term 'to talk blarney' out of exasperation with Lord Blarney's ability to talk endlessly without ever actually agreeing to her demands.

The famous stone aside, Blarney Castle itself is an impressive 16th-century tower set in gorgeous grounds. Escape the crowds on a walk around the **Fern Garden** and **Arboretum**, investigate toxic plants in the Harry-Potterish **Poison Garden**, or explore the landscaped nooks and crannies of the **Rock Close**.

Fota Island

Fota Island lies in Cork Harbour, connected by short bridges to the mainland and to Great Island, 10km east of Cork on the road to Cobh. Formerly the private estate of the Smith-Barry family, it is now home to gardens, golf courses and Ireland's only wildlife park.

Sights & Activities

Fota Wildlife Park ZOO
(☎021-481 2678; www.fotawildlife.ie; Fota Island; adult/child €15/9.50; ⏲10am-6pm Mon-Sat & 10.30am-6pm Sun) Kangaroos bound, cheetahs run, and monkeys and gibbons leap and scream on wooded islands at this huge outdoor zoo, where the animals roam without a cage or fence in sight. A tour train (on wheels, not tracks) runs a circuit around the park every 15 minutes in high season (one way/return €1/2), but the 2km circular walk offers a more close-up experience.

Fota House Arboretum & Gardens GARDENS
(☎021-481 5543; www.fotahouse.com; Fota Island; house tours adult/child €8/3, gardens free; ⏲10am-5pm Mon-Sat, 11am-4pm Sun Apr-Sep) Guided tours of Regency-style Fota House focus on the original kitchen and ornate plasterwork ceilings, but the real highlight here is the 150-year-old arboretum and gardens. There's a Victorian fernery set amid blocks of fluted limestone, a magnolia walk, a walled garden and a host of beautiful trees, including huge Japanese cedars overlooking the lily pond.

Fota Island Resort GOLF
(☎021-488 3700; www.fotaisland.ie; Fota Island; green fees €65-95; 📶) Three championship golf courses sprawl within the 316-hectare Fota Island Resort – Deerpark, Belvelly and Barryscourt – anchored by one of Ireland's best known golfing hotels. The resort has hosted the Irish Open three times, most recently in 2014, and welcomes visitors; it's best to book your round in advance. The beautiful old stone clubhouse, set in a converted farmhouse overlooking the lake, is an atmospheric place for a postgolf drink.

Getting There & Away

The train from Cork to Fota (€3.60, 13 minutes, hourly) continues to Cobh.

Cobh

POP 6500

Cobh (pronounced 'cove') is a charming waterfront town on a glittering estuary, dotted with brightly coloured houses and overlooked by a splendid cathedral. It's popular with Corkonians looking for a spot of R&R, and with cruise liners – each year around 60 visit the port, the second-largest natural harbour in the world (after Sydney Harbour in Australia).

It's a far cry from the harrowing Famine years when more than 70,000 people left Ireland through the port in order to escape the ravages of starvation (from 1848 to 1950, no fewer than 2.5 million emigrants passed through in total). Cobh was also the final port of call for the *Titanic*; a poignant museum commemorates the fatal voyage's point of departure.

Cobh is on the south side of Great Island, one of several islands that fill Cork Harbour. Visible from the waterfront are Haulbowline Island, once the base of the Irish Naval Service, and the greener Spike Island, formerly a prison, now owned by Cork City Council and visitable.

History

For many years Cobh was the port of Cork, and it has always had a strong connection with Atlantic crossings. In 1838 the *Sirius,* the first steamship to cross the Atlantic, sailed from Cobh. The *Titanic* made its last stop here before its disastrous voyage in 1912, and, when the *Lusitania* was torpedoed off the coast of Kinsale in 1915, it was here that many of the survivors were brought and the dead buried. Cobh was also the last glimpse of Ireland for thousands who emigrated during the Famine.

In 1849 Cobh was renamed Queenstown after Queen Victoria paid a visit. The name lasted until Irish independence in 1921 when, unsurprisingly, the local council reverted to the Irish original.

The world's first yacht club, the Royal Cork Yacht Club, was founded here in 1720, but currently operates from Crosshaven on the other side of Cork Harbour. The beautiful Old Yacht Club now houses the tourist office and an arts centre.

Sights

★Cobh, the Queenstown Story MUSEUM

(☎021-481 3591; www.cobhheritage.com; Lower Rd; adult/child €9.50/5; ⏲9.30am-6pm Apr-Sep, to 5pm Oct-Mar, last admission 1hr before closing) The howl of the storm almost knocks you off-balance, there's a bit of fake vomit on the deck, and the people in the pictures all look pretty miserable – that's just one room at Cobh Heritage Centre. Housed in the old train station (next to the current station), this interactive museum is way above average, chronicling Irish emigrations across the Atlantic in the wake of the Great Famine.

LOCAL KNOWLEDGE

SMOKIN'

No trip to Cork is complete without a visit to an artisan food producer, and the effervescent Frank Hederman is more than happy to show you around **Belvelly Smokehouse** (☎021-481 1089; www.frankhederman.com; Belvelly; free for individuals, charge for groups; ⏲Mon-Fri), the oldest traditional smokehouse in Ireland – indeed, the only surviving one. Call ahead to arrange a visit, or stop by his stall at the Cobh or Midleton farmers markets (you can also buy his produce at Cork's English Market). The smokehouse is 19km east of Cork on the R624 towards Cobh.

Seafood and cheese are smoked here – even butter – but the speciality is fish, particularly salmon. In a traditional process that takes 24 hours from start to finish, the fish is filleted and cured before being hung to smoke over beech woodchips. The result is subtle and delectable.

There's also some shocking stuff on the fate of convicts, shipped to Australia in transport ships 'so airless that candles could not burn'. Scenes of sea travel in the 1950s, however, might actually make you nostalgic for a more gracious way of travelling the world. There's also a genealogy centre and a cafe.

Spike Island HISTORIC SITE

(www.spikeislandcork.com; Cork Harbour; adult/child €8/5; ⏲11am-5.30pm Jun-Aug, noon-4.30pm May, noon-4.30pm Sat & Sun only Apr & Sep, noon-4.30pm Sun only Oct) This low-lying green island in Cork Harbour was once an important part of the port's defences, topped by an 18th-century artillery fort. In the second half of the 19th century, and again during the Irish War of Independence, it served as a prison and internment centre, gaining the nickname 'Ireland's Alcatraz'. Today you can enjoy a self-guided walking tour of the island and its fortifications, or pay more for a guided tour (adult/child €13.50/8.50); the ferry (www.spikeislandferry.com) from Kennedy Pier, Cobh, is included in price.

Titanic Experience Cobh MUSEUM

(☎021-481 4412; www.titanicexperiencecobh.ie; 20 Casement Sq; adult/child €9.50/5.50; ⏲9am-6pm) The original White Star Line offices, where 123 passengers embarked on (and one lucky soul absconded from) the SS *Titanic,* now house this powerful insight into the ill-fated liner's final voyage. Admission is by tour, which is partly guided and partly interactive, with holograms, audiovisual presentations and exhibits; allow at least an hour. The technical wizardry is impressive but what's most memorable is standing on the spot from where passengers were ferried to the waiting ship offshore, never to return.

St Colman's Cathedral CATHEDRAL
(021-481 3222; Cathedral Pl; admission by donation; guided tours 3.30pm Sun) Dramatically perched on a hillside terrace above Cobh, this massive French Gothic Cathedral is out of all proportion to the town. Its most exceptional feature is the 47-bell **carillon**, the largest in Ireland, with a range of four octaves. The biggest bell weighs a stonking 3440kg – about as much as a full-grown elephant! You can hear carillon recitals at 4.30pm on Sundays between May and September.

The cathedral, designed by EW Pugin, was begun in 1868 but not completed until 1915. Much of the funding was raised by nostalgic Irish communities in Australia and the USA.

Cobh Museum MUSEUM
(021-481 4240; www.cobhmuseum.com; High Rd; adult/child €4/2; 11am-1pm & 2-5.30pm Mon-Sat, 2.30-5pm Sun Apr-Oct) Model ships, paintings, photographs and curious artefacts tracing Cobh's history fill this small but lively museum. It's housed in the 19th-century Scottish Presbyterian church overlooking the train station.

Tours

Michael Martin's Walking Tours WALKING TOURS
(021-481 5211; www.titanic.ie; tours from €9.50) Michael Martin's 1¼-hour guided **Titanic Trail** walk leaves from the Commodore Hotel on Westbourne Pl at 11am and 2pm, with a free sampling of stout at the end. Martin also runs a ghoulish **Ghost Walk** (by arrangement), and walking tours of **Spike Island** departing at 2pm from Kennedy Pier (subject to weather conditions and numbers).

Sleeping & Eating

★**Gilbert's** GUESTHOUSE €€
(021-481 1300; www.gilbertsincobh.com; 11 Pearse Sq; s/d/penthouse €75/100/180;) The four rooms at this boutique guesthouse in Cobh's town centre are fresh and contemporary with handmade furniture, pure-wool blankets and rain showers. Rates don't include breakfast, but the penthouse suite has a kitchenette. **Gilbert's Bistro**, one of Cobh's best restaurants, is just downstairs.

Knockeven House B&B €€
(021-481 1778; www.knockevenhouse.com; Rushbrooke; s/d from €75/100) Knockeven is a splendid Victorian house with huge bedrooms done out with period furniture and overlooking a magnificent garden full of magnolias and camellias. Breakfasts are great too – homemade breads and fresh fruit – and are served in the sumptuous dining room. The decor takes you back to 1st-class passage on a vintage liner. It's 1.5km west of Cobh's centre.

Commodore Hotel HOTEL €€
(021-481 1277; www.commodorehotel.ie; Westbourne Pl; s/d €60/110;) A classic seaside hotel with soaring chandeliered hallways and 42 well-appointed rooms (it's worth paying extra for one with a sea view). The pool is indoors and a roof garden offers yet more views.

Farmers Market MARKET €
(The Promenade; 10am-2pm Fri) Held on the seafront.

Titanic Bar & Grill IRISH €€
(021-481 4585; www.titanicbarandgrill.ie; 20 Casement Sq; mains €14-25; noon-5pm & 6-8.30pm Mon-Sat, noon-11pm Sun;) Around the back of the Titanic Experience, with a huge deck overlooking the harbour, this is a stunning spot for a pint. The menu lives up to the stylish glossy timber surrounds with posh versions of pub-grub classics such as fish and chips, bangers and mash, and steak with pepper sauce.

Drinking & Nightlife

Roaring Donkey PUB
(www.theroaringdonkey.com; Orilia Tce, Tiknock; 5-11.30pm) It's a steep walk from the seafront but the pay-off is plenty of craic – and often live music – at the wonderfully named Roaring Donkey (allegedly so called because former patrons' donkeys made their presence known outside). It's 2.6km north of St Colman's Cathedral.

Kelly's PUB
(Westbourne Pl; 10am-1.30am;) Sociable punters fill Kelly's day and night. The pub's two rooms are decked out with pew-style seating, chunky wooden furniture, a wood-burning stove and, curiously, a stag's head.

Information

The **Tourist Office** (021-481 3301; www.visitcobh.com; Westbourne Pl; 9am-5pm Mon-Fri, 11-3pm Sat & Sun) is in the Old Yacht Club.

Getting There & Away

By road, Cobh is 23km southeast of Cork, off the main N25 Cork–Rosslare road; Great Island is linked to the mainland via a causeway. It's 18km from Cork via the Passage West ferry (p232).

Hourly trains connect Cobh with Cork (€5.50, 25 minutes) via Fota. No buses serve the Cork to Cobh route.

Midleton & Around

POP 3730

Aficionados of a particularly fine Irish whiskey will recognise the name Midleton, and the main reason to linger in this bustling market town is to visit the old Jameson whiskey distillery. The surrounding region is full of pretty villages, craggy coastline and heavenly rural hotels such as Ballymaloe House – precisely why you should visit the town but stay elsewhere.

Sights

Jameson Experience MUSEUM
(021-461 3594; www.jamesonwhiskey.com; Old Distillery Walk, Midleton; tours adult/child €15/8; shop 10am-6.30pm, tour times vary) Coachloads pour in to tour the restored 200-year-old distillery building housing the Jameson Experience. Exhibits and tours explain the process of taking barley and creating whiskey (Jameson is today made in a modern factory in Cork). There's a well-stocked gift shop, and the **Malt House Restaurant** (noon to 3pm) has live music on Sundays.

Sleeping & Eating

Loughcarrig House B&B €€
(021-463 1952; www.loughcarrig.com; Ballinacurra; s/d from €50/80;) Right on Cork Harbour, about 3km south of Midleton, this gracious old Georgian house has four rooms that are ideal for those looking for a restful country retreat. In addition to walks and birdwatching, the owners can also set you up for angling in the fish-filled local waters. Breakfasts are suitably hearty.

Midleton Farmers Market MARKET €
(www.midletonfarmersmarket.com; Main St; 9.30am-1pm Sat) Midleton's farmers market is one of Cork's best, with bushels of local produce on offer and producers who are happy to chat. It's behind the big roundabout at the north end of Main St.

★**Farmgate Restaurant** IRISH €€
(021-463 2771; www.farmgate.ie; Broderick St; mains lunch €12-20, dinner €18-30; noon-3.30pm Tue-Sat, 6.30-9.30pm Thu-Sat, cafe 9am-5pm Tue-Sat) The original, sister establishment to Cork city's Farmgate Café (p218), the Midleton restaurant offers the same superb blend

WORTH A TRIP

THE GOURMET HEARTLAND OF BALLYMALOE

Drawing up at wisteria-clad **Ballymaloe House** (021-465 2531; www.ballymaloe.ie; Shanagarry; s/d from €140/240;) you know you've arrived somewhere special. The Allen family bought the property in 1948 and has been running this superb hotel and restaurant in the old family home for decades. Rooms are individually decorated with period furnishings and, amid the beautiful grounds, amenities include a tennis court, swimming pool, shop and cafe. The house is 12km southeast of Midleton, off the R629.

Myrtle Allen is a living legend, acclaimed internationally for her near single-handed creation of fine Irish cooking. The menu at Ballymaloe House's celebrated **restaurant** (lunch €32, dinner menu €75, 1-3pm & 7-9.30pm) changes daily to reflect the availability of produce from its extensive farms and other local sources. The hotel also runs wine and gardening weekends.

TV personality Darina Allen (daughter-in-law of Myrtle Allen) runs the famous **Ballymaloe Cookery School** (021-464 6785; www.cookingisfun.ie; Shanagarry). Darina's own daughter-in-law, Rachel Allen, is also a high-profile TV chef and author, and regularly teaches at the school. Demonstrations cost €75; lessons, from half-day sessions (€95 to €135) to 12-week certificate courses (€10,995), are often booked out well in advance. For overnight students, there are pretty cottages amid the 40 hectares of grounds. It's 3km east of Ballymaloe House.

of traditional and modern Irish cuisine. Squeeze through the deli selling amazing baked goods and local produce, to the subtly lit, art-clad, 'farmhouse shed' cafe-restaurant, where you'll eat as well as you would anywhere in Ireland.

Information

The **Tourist Office** (☎021-461 3702; www.ringofcork.ie; Distillery Walk; ⊙10am-1pm & 2-5pm Mon-Fri Apr-Sep) is by the entrance gate to the Jameson Experience.

Getting There & Away

Midleton is 20km east of Cork. The **train station** (5 McSweeney Tce) is 1.5km (20 minutes' walk) north of the Jameson Experience. There are frequent trains from Cork (€5.70, 25 minutes, at least hourly).

There are also frequent buses from Cork bus station (€7.80, 30 minutes, every 15 to 45 minutes). You'll need a car to explore the surrounding area.

Youghal

POP 7000

The ancient seaport of Youghal (Eochaill; pronounced 'yawl'), at the mouth of the Blackwater River, has a rich history that may not be instantly apparent, especially if you coast past on the N25. In fact, even if you stop, it may just seem like a humdrum Irish market town. But take a little time and you'll sniff out some of its once-walled past and enjoy views of the wide Blackwater estuary.

The town was a hotbed of rebellion against the English in the 16th century, and Oliver Cromwell wintered here in 1649 as he sought to drum up support for his war in England and quell insurgence from the pesky Irish. Youghal was granted to Sir Walter Raleigh during the Elizabethan Plantation of Munster – he was mayor of Youghal in 1588–89 – and he spent brief spells living here in his house, Myrtle Grove.

Sights & Activities

Youghal Heritage Centre, in the same building as the tourist office, has an interesting exhibition on the town's history. Pick up a **Youghal Walking Trail** leaflet, which will guide you around the various historical sites.

Youghal has two Blue Flag **beaches**, ideal for building sandcastles modelled after the Clock Gate. Claycastle (2km) and Front Strand (1km) are both within walking distance of town, off the N25.

Fox's Lane Folk Museum MUSEUM
(☎024-91145; www.tyntescastle.com/fox; North Cross Lane; adult/child €4/2; ⊙10am-1pm & 2-6pm Tue-Sat Jul-Sep) Dinky Fox's Lane Folk Museum contains more than 600 household gadgets dating from 1850 to 1950, and a Victorian kitchen.

EXPLORING YOUGHAL'S HISTORY ON FOOT

Youghal's history is best understood through its landmarks. Heading along Main St from the south, the curious **Clock Gate** was built in 1777, and served as a town gate, clock tower and jail; several prisoners taken in the 1798 Rising were hanged from its windows.

The beautifully proportioned **Red House**, on North Main St, was designed in 1706 by the Dutch architect Leuventhen, and features some Dutch Renaissance details. Across the road is the 15th-century tower house **Tynte's Castle** (www.tyntescastle.com), which originally had a defensive riverfront position.

A few doors further along, at the side street leading to the church, are six **almshouses** built by Englishman Richard Boyle, who bought Raleigh's Irish estates and became the first Earl of Cork in 1616 in recognition of his work in creating 'a very excellent colony'.

Built in 1220 **St Mary's Collegiate Church** incorporates elements of an earlier Danish church dating back to the 11th century. The Earl of Desmond and his troops, rebelling against English rule, demolished the chancel roof in the 16th century.

Hidden behind high walls to the north of the church, 15th- to 18th-century **Myrtle Grove** (not open to the public) is the former home of Sir Walter Raleigh, and a rare Irish example of a late-medieval Tudor-style house.

The churchyard is bounded to the west by a fine stretch of the old **town wall** – follow the parapet until you can descend stairs to the outer side, then enter the next gate along to descend back to Main St through the 17th-century **College Gardens**, now restored and in use as a public park.

Blackwater Cruises BOAT TOUR
(☎087 988 9076; www.blackwatercruises.com; adult/child €20/10; ⊙Apr-Nov) Runs 90-minute cruises upstream from Youghal along the lovely Blackwater River, past ruined castles and abbeys as far as grand Ballynatray House.

Sleeping & Eating

Aherne's Townhouse INN €€
(☎024-92424; www.ahernes.net; 163 North Main St; s/d from €75/110; @📶) The 12 rooms here are extremely well appointed; larger ones have small balconies, where you can breathe in the sea air. Rates include a fabulous breakfast (freshly squeezed OJ, free-range eggs, locally caught fish) that will keep you going all day. The establishment includes an upmarket **seafood restaurant** (3-course dinner €32) and a stylish, cosy bar.

La Petite Auberge B&B €€
(☎024-85906; www.lapetiteauberge.ie; 2 The Mall; s/d €65/95; 📶) Wake up to sea views from each of the classically styled, uniquely furnished rooms at this charming 'little inn', built in the 1830s. The breakfast room also overlooks the water; choices include smoked kippers as well as fresh OJ and seasonal fruits and nuts.

Sage Cafe CAFE €
(☎024-85844; 86 North Main St; mains €5-9; ⊙10am-6pm Mon-Sat; ✍) Everything at this luscious little cafe is homemade: lentil and nut loaf, quiche, cakes and more. Vegetarians in particular will be in heaven.

Drinking & Nightlife

Treacy's PUB
(The Nook; www.findthenook.ie; 20 North Main St; ⊙noon-11pm) For an end-of-day pint and traditional live music, nowhere beats Youghal's oldest boozer, Treacy's, aka The Nook. Enter via the adjacent lane.

Information

Housed in an attractive old market house on the waterfront, the Youghal **Tourist Office** (☎024-20170; www.youghal.ie; Market Sq; ⊙10am-3pm Mon-Sat year-round, 9.30am-5pm daily Jun-Aug) has tourist info, a small heritage centre and free town maps.

Getting There & Away

Bus Éireann runs services to Cork (€14, one hour, hourly) and Waterford (€20, 1½ hours, hourly).

KINSALE & WEST CORK

The Cork coast begins the slow build-up of beauty that culminates in counties further west and north, but what you find here in Cork is already lovely. It's perfect for aimless wandering as roads criss-cross the area like lace made by a deranged person.

Kinsale

POP 4890

The picturesque yachting harbour of Kinsale (Cionn tSáile) is one of many colourful gems strung along the coastline of County Cork. Narrow, winding streets lined with galleries and gift shops, lively bars and superb restaurants, and a handsome natural harbour filled with yachts and guarded by a huge 17th-century fortress make it an engrossing place to spend a day or two.

Kinsale has been labelled the gourmet centre of southwest Ireland and, for such a small place, it certainly packs more than its fair share of international-standard restaurants. Most are situated near the harbour and within easy walking distance of the town centre.

History

Granted a royal charter by the English King Edward II in 1334, Kinsale became a major port trading in wine and salt throughout the 15th century, and was also a provisioning port for the English navy.

In September 1601, English ships besieged a Spanish fleet anchored at Kinsale. Irish forces, which had appealed to the Spanish king to help them against the English, marched the length of the country to liberate the ships, but were defeated in the **Battle of Kinsale** on Christmas Eve. For the Catholic Irish, the immediate consequence was that they were banned from Kinsale; it would be another 100 years before they were allowed back in. Historians now cite 1601 as the beginning of the end of Gaelic Ireland.

After 1601 the town developed as a naval harbour, ship-building port and garrison town. In the early 18th century, Alexander Selkirk departed from Kinsale Harbour on a voyage that left him stranded on a desert island, providing Daniel Defoe with the inspiration for *Robinson Crusoe*.

The town is also associated with the sinking of the *Lusitania* on 7 May 1915 off the Old Head of Kinsale – some of the bodies were brought ashore and buried here (many

Kinsale

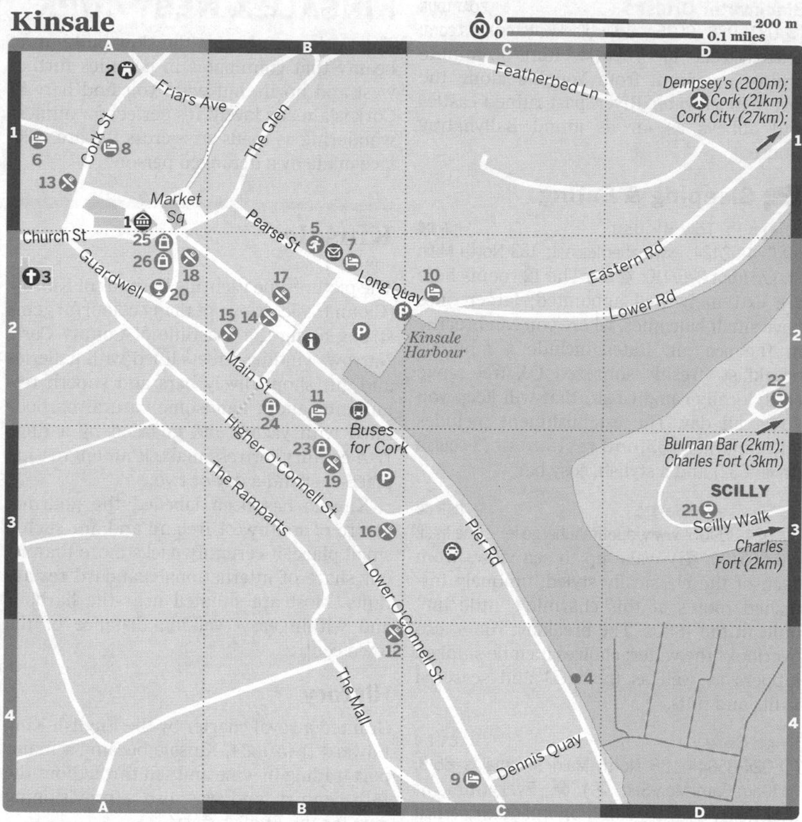

Kinsale

Sights
1 Courthouse & Regional Museum A1
2 Desmond Castle A1
3 St Multose Church A2

Activities, Courses & Tours
4 Kinsale Harbour Cruises C4
5 Mylie Murphy's B2

Sleeping
6 Cloisters B&B A1
7 Old Bank House B2
8 Old Presbytery A1
9 Olde Bakery C4
10 Perryville House C2
11 Pier House B2

Eating
12 Black Pig Wine Bar B4
13 Crackpots A1
14 Farmers Market B2
15 Finn's Table B2
16 Fishy Fishy Cafe B3
17 Jim Edwards B2
18 Nine Market Street A2
19 Poet's Corner B3

Drinking & Nightlife
20 Apéritif A2
21 Harbour Bar D3
22 Spaniard Bar D2

Shopping
23 Giles Norman Gallery B3
24 Granny's Bottom Drawer B2
25 Kinsale Chocolate Boutique A2
26 Kinsale Crystal A2

more are in Cobh), and the inquest into the disaster took place in Kinsale Courthouse. A memorial stands near the Old Head Signal Tower.

Sights

★ Charles Fort FORT
(☎021-477 2263; www.heritageireland.ie; Summercove; adult/child €4/2; ⏲10am-6pm mid-Mar–Oct, to 5pm Nov–mid-Mar) One of Europe's best-preserved star-shaped artillery forts, this vast 17th-century fortification would be worth a visit for its spectacular views alone. But there's much more here: the 18th- and 19th-century ruins inside the walls make for some fascinating wandering. It's 3km southeast of Kinsale along the minor road through Scilly; if you have time, hike there along the lovely coastal **Scilly Walk**.

Built in the 1670s to guard Kinsale Harbour, the fort was in use until 1921, when much of it was destroyed as the British withdrew. Displays explain the typically tough lives led by the soldiers who served here and the comparatively comfortable lives of the officers.

Lusitania Museum MUSEUM
(www.oldheadofkinsale.com; Signal Tower, Old Head of Kinsale; adult/child €5/free; ⏲10am-6pm daily Jun-Aug, to 5pm Thu-Sun May & Sep, check hours Oct-Apr) This 200-year-old signal tower has been restored and converted into a museum dedicated to the RMS *Lusitania,* which was torpedoed by a German U-boat in 1915 with the loss of 1200 lives. You can walk to the nearby clifftops for impressive views south towards the Old Head, the nearest point of land to the disaster; a privately owned golf club prevents you from reaching the lighthouse at the tip of the headland. The tower is 13km south of town via the R604.

Desmond Castle CASTLE, MUSEUM
(☎021-477 4855; www.heritageireland.ie; Cork St; adult/child €4/2; ⏲10am-6pm Apr–mid-Sep) Kinsale's roots in the wine trade are on display at this early-16th-century fortified house that was occupied by the Spanish in 1601. Since then it has served as a customs house, a prison for French and American captives, and a workhouse during the Famine. There are lively exhibits detailing its history, and a small wine museum that tells the story of the Irish wine-trading families, including names such as Hennessy (of brandy fame), who fled to France because of British rule.

Courthouse & Regional Museum MUSEUM
(☎021-477 7930; Market Sq; adult/concession €3/1.50; ⏲10am-5pm Sat, 2-5pm Sun) Based in the 17th-century courthouse that was used for the inquest into the sinking of the *Lusitania* in 1915, this nifty museum contains local curiosities as diverse as Michael Collins' hurley (hurling stick), and shoes belonging to the 8ft-tall Kinsale Giant, Patrick Cotter O'Brien (1760–1806).

St Multose Church CHURCH
(Church of Ireland Church; ☎rectory 021-477 2220; Church St) This is one of Ireland's oldest Church of Ireland churches, built around 1190 by the Normans on the site of a 6th-century church. Not much of the interior is original but the exterior is beautifully preserved. Inside, a flat stone carved with a round-handed figure was traditionally rubbed by fishermen's wives to bring their husbands home safe from the sea. Several victims of the *Lusitania* sinking are buried in the graveyard.

Activities

Scilly Walk WALKING
You haven't 'done' Kinsale till you've done Scilly Walk, a lovely coastal trail that leads out to Charles Fort. Follow Lower Rd to the Spaniard Pub, descend to the waterfront and follow the harbourside path until it climbs to join High Rd. Descend to Bulman's Bar for a pint before climbing up to the fort. Return along High Rd – this is Kinsale's 'Golden Mile', lined with millionaires' holiday homes and superb views over the harbour (round trip 6km).

Mylie Murphy's FISHING, CYCLING
(☎021-477 2703; 14 Pearse St; ⏲10am-5pm Fri & Sat year-round, noon-4pm Sun Jun-Sep) You can rent fishing rods here for €10 per day, bikes for €15 a day.

Old Head Golf Links GOLF
(☎021-4778 444; www.oldhead.com; Old Head of Kinsale; green fees €160-230) This exclusive golf resort is magnificently situated on a clifftop promontory 15km south of Kinsale via the R600 and R604. The remains of De Courcy castle frame the entrance; you'll see a ruined lighthouse from the seventh tee.

Tours

Kinsale Harbour Cruises BOAT TOUR
(☎021-477 8946, 086 250 5456; www.kinsaleharbourcruises.com; adult/child €12.50/6) Runs boat trips to Charles Fort, James Cove and

up the River Bandon. Departure times vary through the year and are weather dependent – check the website or with the tourist office for details. Boats leave from the slip beside the marina.

Dermot Ryan's Heritage Town Walks WALKING TOUR
(☎021-477 2729; www.kinsaleheritage.com; adult/child €5/free; ⊙10.30am) One-hour walking tours departing from the tourist office; tours starting at 3pm can be arranged by appointment.

Festivals & Events

Kinsale Gourmet Festival FOOD
(www.kinsalerestaurants.com) Three days of tastings, cookery demonstrations and the All-Ireland seafood chowder cook-off competition add to the town's foodie reputation. Held in October

Kinsale Jazz Festival JAZZ
(www.kinsale.ie) Chilled-out entertainment over the bank-holiday weekend in October.

Sleeping

Dempsey's HOSTEL €
(☎021-477 2124; www.hostelkinsale.com; Eastern Rd; dm €15-20;) This basic hostel is nothing special, but it's the town's cheapest option, with separate male and female dorms, family rooms, a kitchen, and picnic tables in the front garden. It's the bright-blue house by the petrol station on the R600 road from Cork, 750m northeast of the centre.

★ **Old Presbytery** B&B €€
(☎021-477 2027; www.oldpres.com; 43 Cork St; s/d from €70/125; ⊙closed Jan–mid-Feb;) The Old Presbytery has gracefully moved into the 21st century with a careful refurbishment that maintains its character and incorporates solar heating. Stay in room 6 only if you have plans to see nothing of Kinsale: with its sunroom and balcony, you'll never want to leave. The organic breakfasts, cooked by landlord and former chef Phillip, are the stuff of legend.

Cloisters B&B B&B €€
(☎021-470 0680; www.cloisterskinsale.com; Friars St; s/d from €55/100;) Little touches make the difference at this blue-shuttered B&B near Desmond Castle. Chocolates await your arrival, rooms are squeaky-clean, and the orthopaedic mattresses are so comfy that only the creative breakfasts will tempt you out of bed.

Olde Bakery B&B €€
(☎021-477 3012; www.theoldebakerykinsale.com; 56 Lower O'Connell St; r from €90;) A short walk southeast of the centre is this very friendly place that once was the British garrison bakery. Rooms are a reasonable size and terrific breakfasts around the kitchen table get everyone chatting.

Pier House B&B €€
(☎021-477 4475; www.pierhousekinsale.com; Pier Rd; r €100-140;) Set back from the road in a sheltered garden, this is a lovely place to rest your head. Pristine rooms, decorated with shell-and-driftwood sculptures, have black-granite bathrooms with power showers and underfloor heating; four open to balconies.

Old Bank House HOTEL €€
(☎021-477 4075; www.oldbankhousekinsale.com; 11 Pearse St; s/d from €79/130; @) Georgian elegance and style give a timeless quality to this top-of-the-range 18-room hotel. Beautiful objets d'art and paintings grace the walls, and the luxurious public rooms add a country-house ambience. Although rooms are lavish, they're subtle enough to avoid pretension. Superb breakfasts, with home-made breads (from the bakery downstairs) and jams, are included in the rate.

Perryville House BOUTIQUE HOTEL €€€
(☎021-477 2731; www.perryvillehouse.com; Long Quay; r €160-300; ⊙call for seasonal closures;) It's top-to-bottom grandeur at family-run Perryville, whether you're pulling up outside its imposing wrought iron–balconied facade or taking afternoon tea in the drawing room. All the rooms exude comfort; move up the rate card and the beds go from queen to king, and balconies and sea views appear.

Eating

You're in for a treat. Kinsale fully deserves its billing as a foodie haven, and you can eat well on any budget.

Poet's Corner CAFE €
(www.poetscornerkinsale.com; 44 Main St; mains €5-7; ⊙9.30am-6pm Mon-Sat;) A cheerful cafe and book exchange, serving great cakes and coffee as well as huge toasted sandwiches.

Farmers Market MARKET €
(Short Quay; ⊙9.30am-1.30pm Wed) Sets up on the wee square across from the tourist office.

★Black Pig Wine Bar IRISH €€
(021-477 4101; 66 Lower O'Connell St; mains €8-20; 5.30-11.30pm Wed-Mon) This sophisticated hideaway offers no fewer than 80 wines by the bottle and 40 by the glass including many organic varieties. There's a charming cobbled courtyard out back, and a mouth-watering menu of snacks, charcuterie platters and cheese boards sourced from artisan local suppliers. Tables are coveted – book so you don't miss out.

Nine Market Street BISTRO €€
(021-470 9221; http://ninemarketstreet.ie; 9 Market St; mains €11-22; 9.30am-4pm Tue-Thu, to 8.45pm Fri & Sat;) Black-and-white floor tiles, warm golden wood and old photographs set the relaxed mood at this appealing little cafe-cum-bistro. Freshly prepared fish cakes, quiches, healthy salads and soups are complemented by daily specials such as the Wagyu beef burger.

Jim Edwards SEAFOOD €€
(021-477 2541; www.jimedwardskinsale.com; Short Quay; bar mains €13-20, restaurant mains €18-29; bar food noon-10pm, restaurant 5.30-10pm) Bar food at this unassuming pub is way above standard, and the restaurant is exceptional. A very traditional ambience belies the high quality of the menu, which doffs a cap to meat-eaters but specialises in all kinds of locally caught fish.

Crackpots MODERN IRISH €€
(021-477 2847; www.crackpots.ie; 3 Cork St; mains €15-25; 6-10pm) The title 'ceramic restaurant' over the front door refers to the fact that all the crockery in use here was made…here. Normally, when you combine art workshop and food something will give, but in this instance it's certainly not the grub, which relies on locally sourced meats, fish fresh from the sea and organically grown veg.

★Finn's Table MODERN IRISH €€€
(021-470 9636; www.finnstable.com; 6 Main St; mains €20-30; from 5.30pm Thu-Mon) Owning a gourmet restaurant in Kinsale means plenty of competition, but John and Julie Finn's venture is more than up to the challenge. Elegant but unstuffy, with a warm welcome, its menu of seasonal, locally sourced produce rarely fails to please. Seafood (including lobster when in season) is from West Cork, while meat is from the Finn family's butchers.

★Fishy Fishy Cafe SEAFOOD €€€
(021-470 0415; www.fishyfishy.ie; Crowley's Quay; mains €17-30; noon-9pm Mar-Oct, to 4pm Sun-Wed, to 9pm Thu-Sat Nov-Feb) One of the most famous seafood restaurants in the country, Fishy Fishy has a wonderful setting with stark white walls splashed with bright artwork and steel fish sculptures, and a terrific decked terrace at the front. All the fish is caught locally, from the lobster thermidor to the chilled seafood platter served with homemade mayonnaise.

Drinking & Nightlife

Spaniard Bar PUB
(021-477 2436; www.thespaniard.ie; River Rd, Scilly; 10.30am-11.30pm Mon-Thu, to 12.30am Fri & Sat, 12.30-11.30pm Sun) The food is good, but the real appeal of this old pub – it feels like it dates back to the Armada – lies in the quiet corners, where you can smell the peat fire and catch fragments of hushed conversations, and, on sunny days, the outdoor tables with views across the harbour.

Bulman Bar PUB
(021-477 2131; www.thebulman.ie; Summercove; mains €10-19; 12.30-11.30pm Mon-Thu, to 12.30am Fri & Sat, to 11pm Sun;) Escape from central Kinsale to this harbourside gastropub in the picturesque hamlet of Summercove, where salty informality is a style in its own right. Sip chilled white wine at outdoor tables or sup beers and seafood chowder in the wood-panelled interior. It's 2km southeast of Kinsale town centre, on the way to Charles Fort.

Apéritif WINE BAR
(021-477 2209; www.aperitifkinsale.com; Main St; 5.30pm-late Thu-Sat, 2pm-late Sun) Metallic-sheened funiture and walls make this wine bar a glitzy spot for a tipple and tapas. Big picture windows let you see and be seen.

Harbour Bar PUB
(Scilly Walk; 6-11.30pm) It might look permanently closed from the outside, but inside it's like being in someone's front room (maybe it IS someone's front room!). Battered old sofas, a fire stoked in the hearth, characters in every corner and benches with harbour views in the garden are all part of the charm.

Shopping

Kinsale Chocolate Boutique CHOCOLATE
(www.kinsalechocolate.ie; 6 Exchange Bldgs, Market Sq; 10am-6pm May-Aug, 11am-5pm Wed & Thu, 10am-6pm Fri & Sat, 2-6pm Sun Sep-Apr)

Handmade chocolates and pastel-shaded macarons are among the enticing wares at this artisan chocolatier.

Giles Norman Gallery ARTS
(☎021-477 4373; www.gilesnorman.com; 45 Main St; ⏰10am-6pm Mon-Sat, noon-6pm Sun) Evocative black-and-white imagery of Ireland from a master of the genre. Prints start at €20 unframed, €30 framed.

Granny's Bottom Drawer CRAFTS
(☎021-477 4839; 53 Main St; ⏰10am-6pm) Top-quality Irish linen, woollens, leather goods, damask and vintage-style homewares.

Kinsale Crystal GLASS
(☎021-477 4493; www.kinsalecrystal.ie; Market St; ⏰9am-5.30pm Mon-Fri, 10am-6pm Sat, noon-6pm Sun) Exquisite work by an ex-Waterford craftsman who stands by the traditional 'deep-cutting, high-angle' style. A million tiny sparkles greet you as you enter.

Information

Pearse St has a post office and banks with ATMs.

Tourist Office (☎021-477 2234; www.kinsale.ie; cnr Pier Rd & Emmet Pl; ⏰9.15am-5pm Tue-Sat year-round, 9.15am-5pm Mon Apr-Oct, 10am-5pm Sun Jul & Aug) Has a good map detailing walks in and around Kinsale.

Getting There & Around

Bus Éireann (☎021-450 8188; www.buseireann.ie) service No 226 connects Kinsale with Cork bus station (€9.40, one hour, hourly) via Cork Airport, and continuing to Cork train station. The **bus stop** is on Pier Rd, near the tourist office.

Kinsale Cabs (☎021-477 2642; www.kinsalecabs.com) A taxi from Cork Airport to Kinsale can cost from €35 to €45. Also arranges golfing tours of West Cork.

PASSAGE WEST FERRY

From Carrigaloe, 3.5km northwest of Cobh, the **Passage West Ferry** (☎021-481 1485; www.passagewestmonkstown.ie/cross-river-ferry.asp; pedestrian/cyclist/car one-way €1/1/5; ⏰7am-10pm) provides a handy shortcut to Passage West, 14km southeast of Cork city. The cross-river journey takes just five minutes. It's particularly useful if you're heading to or from the southern side of Cork city or Kinsale, and want to skip the city traffic.

Clonakilty

POP 4720

Cheerful, brightly painted Clonakilty is a bustling market town that serves as a hub for the scores of beguiling little coastal villages that surround it. You'll find smart B&Bs, good restaurants and cosy pubs alive with music. Little waterways coursing through town add to the charm.

Clonakilty is famous for two things: it's the birthplace of Irish Free State commander-in-chief Michael Collins, embodied in a large statue on the corner of Emmet Sq; and it's the home of the most famous black pudding in the country.

Roads converge on Astna Sq, dominated by a 1798 Rising monument. Also in the square is the Kilty Stone, a piece of the original castle that gave Clonakilty (Cloich na Coillte in Irish, meaning 'castle of the woods') its name.

Sights & Activities

West Cork Model Railway Village AMUSEMENT PARK
(☎023-883 3224; www.modelvillage.ie; Inchydoney Rd; adult/child incl train ride €10/6; ⏰11am-5pm Sep-Jun, 10am-5pm Jul & Aug) You can't help but smile at the West Cork Model Railway Village. It features a vast outdoor re-creation of the West Cork Railway as it was during the 1940s, with superb miniature models of the main towns in West Cork. A road train departs from the village on a 20-minute guided circuit of Clonakilty.

Michael Collins Centre MUSEUM
(☎023-884 6107; www.michaelcollinscentre.com; Castleview; adult/child €5/3; ⏰10.30am-5pm Mon-Fri, 11am-2pm Sat mid-Jun–Sep) A visit to the Michael Collins Centre is an excellent way to make sense of his life and the times in which he lived. A tour reveals photos, letters and a reconstruction of the 1920s country lane where Collins was killed, complete with armoured vehicle. The centre runs tours of the crucial locations in Collins' life (book in advance). It's signposted off the R600 between Timoleague and Clonakilty.

Sleeping

Emmet Hotel HOTEL €€
(☎023-883 3394; www.emmethotel.com; Emmet Sq; s/d/f €69/99/129;) This lovely Georgian hotel on the elegant main square successfully mixes period charm and

olde-worlde service with the perks of a modern hotel. The 20 rooms are large and plush; the on-site restaurant, bistro and bar all serve up tasty Irish food made from organic and local ingredients.

Bay View House B&B €€
(☎023-883 3539; www.bayviewclonakilty.com; Old Timoleague Rd; s/d €50/80; 📶) This spacious modern villa offers immaculate B&B accommodation, a genial welcome and great breakfasts. Rooms 5 and 6 and the cosy landing lounge offer fantastic views over fields that slope down to Clonakilty Bay. It is 300m east of the town centre, just off the main N71 roundabout into town.

O'Donovan's Hotel INN €€
(☎023-883 3250; www.odonovanshotel.com; Pearse St; s/d €55/90; 📶👪) Behind the vintage, vivid-red exterior beats the heart of a classic old hotel. Rooms are straightforward, but service is friendly and you can't beat the central location. A WWII plaque out front will intrigue Americans in particular.

Tudor Lodge B&B €€
(☎023-883 3046; www.tudorlodgecork.com; McCurtain Hill; s/d €50/80; 📶) Standards are kept up to scratch at this modern, mock-Tudor family home, a short walk from the town centre.

Inchydoney Island Lodge & Spa RESORT €€€
(☎023-883 3143; www.inchydoneyisland.com; Inchydoney; r from €220; @📶🏊👪) A superb seawater spa is at the heart of this sprawling resort 5km south of Clonakilty, where the service is outstanding, the food at the French-inspired restaurant is delicious, and luxurious rooms overlook the ocean from private balconies and terraces.

Eating

★**Scannells** MODERN IRISH €
(☎023-883 4116; www.scannellsbar.com; Connolly St; mains €7-13; ⏰food served noon-3pm Mon-Fri, to 4pm Sat; 📶) The sheltered, flower-filled garden at this gastropub is absolutely hopping, rain or shine, thanks to an ambitious menu that ranges from superb steak sandwiches with hand-cut chips, to trad Irish stew and organic salads with beetroot, roasted hazelnuts, goat's cheese and quinoa.

Farmers Market MARKET €
(www.clonakiltymarket.com; Pearse St; ⏰10am-2pm Fri & Sat) 🍃 Clonakilty's farmers market sets up in a car park, down an alley beside O'Donovan's Hotel.

IRELAND'S BEST BLACK PUDDING

Clonakilty's most treasured export is its black pudding, the sausage made from pig's blood, oatmeal and onion that features on most local restaurant menus. The best place to buy it is from butcher **Edward Twomey** (☎023-883 3733; www.clonakiltyblackpudding.ie; 16 Pearse St; ⏰9am-6pm Mon-Sat), who sells different varieties based on the original recipe from the 1880s.

Malt House Granary MODERN IRISH €€
(☎023-883 4355; www.malthousegranary.ie; 30 Ashe St; mains €17-25; ⏰5-10pm Mon-Sat) 🍃 You'll be able to check out Clonakilty black pudding, Boilie goat's cheese, Gubbeen chorizo and Bantry Bay mussels, among other local ingredients, on the menu at the Malt House, as everything on your plate originates from West Cork. The interior design is a hotchpotch of stylish and kitsch.

An Súgán SEAFOOD €€
(☎023-883 3719; www.ansugan.com; 41 Wolfe Tone St; mains €13-28; ⏰noon-10pm) A traditional bar with a reputation for excellent seafood, where you dine in a room crammed with knick-knacks – jugs dangle from the ceiling, business cards are stuffed in the rafters, and lanterns dot the walls. But there's nothing idiosyncratic about the food – the seafood chowder and crab cakes are great, and there's a choice of around 10 different kinds of fish.

Drinking & Nightlife

★**De Barra's Folk Club** PUB
(www.debarra.ie; 55 Pearse St; ⏰10am-11.45pm Mon-Thu, to 12.30am Fri & Sat, noon-11.30pm sun) A convivial, jostling atmosphere – walls splattered with photos and press cuttings, masks and musical instruments – provides the setting for the cream of local folk music. Nightly sessions usually begin around 9pm.

An Teach Beag PUB
(5 Recorder's Alley; ⏰8.30-11.45pm) This intriguing cottage-pub (the name means 'the little house'), along the alley beside O'Donovan's Hotel, has all the atmosphere necessary for good traditional music sessions. You might even catch a *scríocht* (a session by storytellers and poets) in full flow. There's music nightly during July and August, and on weekends for the rest of the year.

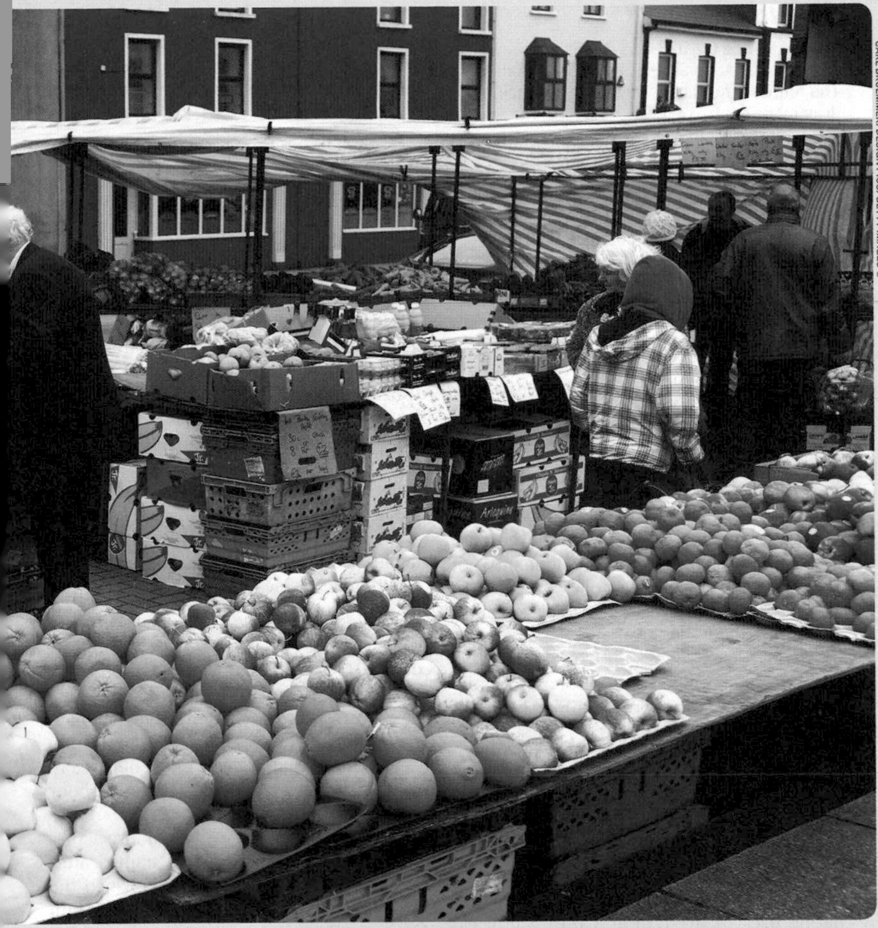

CARL BRUEMMER/DESIGN PICS/GETTY IMAGES ©

PATRYK KOSMIDER/SHUTTERSTOCK ©

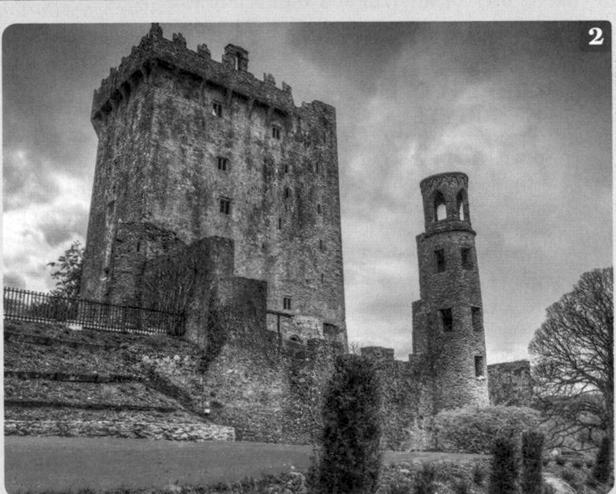

1. Farmers Markets
Farmers markets are popular sources of local and organic produce.

2. Blarney Castle (p222)
Home to the Blarney Stone, Blarney Castle is one of Ireland's most popular attractions.

3. Bantry town (p245)
Bantry's old-fashioned streets and harbourside location make for a pleasant stroll.

Information

Tourist Office (☎023-883 3226; www.clonakilty.ie; Ashe St; ⊙9.15am-5pm Mon-Sat) The tourist office is halfway along the main drag in the centre of town.

Getting There & Away

There are buses to Cork (€15.50, 1¼ hours, seven daily) and Skibbereen (€24, 40 minutes, six daily). The bus stop is on Bridge St in the town centre.

Getting Around

MTM Cycles (☎023-883 3584; 33 Ashe St; ⊙8.30am-6pm Mon-Sat) hires bikes per day/week for €10/50. A nice ride is to Duneen Beach, about 13km south of town.

Clonakilty to Skibbereen

Picturesque villages, an impressive stone circle and some fine beaches mark the meandering coastal route from Clonakilty to Skibbereen. Rather than follow the main N71 all the way, explore the minor roads to its south – the R598, R597 and R596.

Incheydoney, 5km south of Clonakilty, has a gorgeous golden strand set on a scenic inlet, and there are more Blue Flag beaches on **Rosscarbery Bay**.

At Rosscarbery, turn left onto the R597 at the far end of the causeway to find the atmospheric **Drombeg stone circle**, before continuing west to the scenic villages of **Glandore** and **Union Hall**.

West again, quaint **Castletownshend** is a village of higgledy-piggledy stone cottages dating back to the 17th and 18th centuries tumbling down the precipitously steep main street. At the bottom of the hill is a small quayside and the 'castle' (more a country house) after which the village is named. Once you've seen these, you can just put your feet up and relax: you've ticked all the boxes.

MICHAEL COLLINS – THE 'BIG FELLA'

Born on a farm just outside Clonakilty, Michael Collins is one of County Cork's most famous sons. He played a central role in the War of Independence with Britain, and in 1922 became commander-in-chief of the army of the newly founded Irish Free State.

The useful map and leaflet *In Search of Michael Collins*, available at the Clonakilty tourist office, outlines places in the district associated with him; you can dig deeper into his life at the **Michael Collins Centre** (p232).

Drombeg Stone Circle

On an exposed hillside, with fields falling away towards the coast and cattle lowing in the distance, the **Drombeg stone circle** (⊙24hr) FREE is superbly atmospheric. Its 17 stones, oriented towards the winter solstice sunset, once guarded the cremated bones of an adolescent. The 9m-diameter circle probably dates from the 5th century AD, and is a sophisticated Iron Age update of an earlier Bronze Age monument. To get here, take the signposted left turn off the R597, approximately 4km west of Rosscarbery.

Just beyond the stones are the remains of a hut and an Iron Age cooking pit, known as a *fulachta fiadh*. Experiments have shown that its heated rocks would boil water and keep it hot for nearly three hours – long enough to cook meat.

Glandore & Union Hall

POP 252

The picturesque waterside villages of Glandore (Cuan Dor) and Union Hall burst into life in summer when fleets of yachts race in the sheltered waters of Glandore Harbour inlet.

Union Hall, southwest of Glandore across a long, narrow causeway, was named after the 1801 Act of Union, which abolished the separate Irish parliament. The 1994 film *War of the Buttons*, about two battling gangs of youngsters, was filmed here. There's an ATM, a post office and a general store here.

Activities

Cork Whale Watch WILDLIFE WATCHING
(☎086 327 3226; www.corkwhalewatch.com; Reen Pier; per person €50) Runs four-hour whale-watching cruises out of Reen Pier, 4km south of Union Hall; one trip daily year-round (weather dependent), two trips daily June to August. Cash only; no credit cards.

Atlantic Sea Kayaking KAYAKING
(☎028-21058; www.atlanticseakayaking.com; Reen Pier; per person €50; ⊙year-round) Runs half-day marine safaris by sea kayak from Reen Pier, 4km south of Union Hall. No previous experience needed.

Sleeping

Shearwater B&B B&B €

(☎028-33178; www.shearwaterbandb.com; Union Hall; s/d €50/70; ⏰Apr-Oct) A warm welcome awaits at this bright and attractive B&B, just a short stroll from the centre of Union Hall. Hearty breakfasts are served in a spacious sunroom, and on a terrace with killer views across the harbour.

Bay View House B&B €€

(☎028-33115; Glandore; s/d €50/80;) Bay View House has seriously spectacular views across the bay. Try to snag Room 1 for the best panorama of all. Bright colours, tidy pine furniture and gleaming bathrooms add to the appeal; local pubs are a stumble away.

Eating & Drinking

★**Glandore Inn** PUB FOOD €€

(☎028-33468; Main St, Glandore; mains €10-16; ⏰10am-midnight May-Sep, noon-midnight Oct-Apr;) Picture-postcard views over the harbour, especially from the outdoor tables, and a superlative menu make this one of West Cork's best pubs for eating out. Fresh seafood is sourced from Union Hall harbour (clearly visible across the water). The interior's rustic nautical charm has a contemporary edge, and there are Irish craft beers on tap.

Hayes Bar PUB

(☎028-33214; The Square, Glandore; ⏰11am-5pm Mon-Thu, 5pm-midnight Fri, 11am-midnight Sat, 11am-11.30pm Sun, weekends only Sep-May) Enjoy a pint at this perfect portside pub with picnic tables outside. Good pub grub served noon to 6pm.

Shopping

Union Hall Smoked Fish FOOD

(☎028-33125; www.unionhallsmokedfish.com; Main St, Union Hall; ⏰8.30am-5pm Mon-Fri) Union Hall smoked salmon is renowned. You can buy it here at this factory outlet, along with fresh catches and live shellfish.

Getting There & Away

Six daily buses between Skibbereen (€4.10, 15 minutes) and Clonakilty (€7.80, 25 minutes) stop in nearby Leap (3km north), from where most B&B owners will pick you up if you arrange it in advance.

Skibbereen

POP 2670

Today, Skibbereen (Sciobairín) is a pleasant, workaday market town, with an attractive, upmarket town centre on the banks of the River Ilen.

During the Famine, however, Skib was hit perhaps harder than any other town in Ireland, with huge numbers of the local population emigrating or dying of starvation or disease. 'The accounts are not exaggerated – they cannot be exaggerated – nothing more frightful can be conceived.' So wrote Lord Dufferin and GF Boyle, who journeyed from Oxford to Skibbereen in February 1847 to see if reports of the Famine were true. Their eyewitness account makes horrific reading; Dufferin was so appalled by what he saw that he contributed £1000 (about €100,000 in today's money) to the relief effort. The **Abbeystrewery Cemetery** is 1km east of the centre, on the N71 to Schull, where a memorial marks the mass grave of 8000 to 10,000 local people who died during the Famine.

The main landmark in town is a statue in the central square, dedicated to heroes of Irish rebellions against the British.

Sights

Skibbereen Heritage Centre MUSEUM

(☎028-40900; www.skibbheritage.com; Upper Bridge St; adult/child €6/3; ⏰10am-6pm Mon-Sat mid-May–mid-Sep, shorter hours mid-Sep–mid-Nov & mid-Mar–mid-May, closed mid-Nov–mid-Mar) Constructed on the site of the town's old gasworks, the Skibbereen Heritage Centre houses a haunting exhibition about the Famine, with actors reading heartbreaking contemporary accounts; a visit here puts Irish history into harrowing perspective. There's also a smaller exhibition about nearby **Lough Hyne**, the first marine nature reserve in Ireland, and a genealogical centre.

Guided evening historical walks (adult/child €5/2.50), lasting 1½ hours, leave from the heritage centre. Call to confirm times.

Festivals & Events

Taste of West Cork Food Festival FOOD

(www.atasteofwestcork.com) If you're in town in mid-September, don't miss this foodie extravaganza, including a lively farmers market and events at local restaurants.

Sleeping

★Bridge House B&B €
(☎028-21273; www.bridgehouseskibbereen.com; Bridge St; s/d €45/75;) Mona Best has turned her entire house into a work of art, filling the rooms with fabulous Victorian tableaux and period memorabilia. The whole place bursts at the seams with cherished clutter, crazed carvings, dressed-up dummies and fragrant fresh flowers; personalised service extends to champagne breakfasts for guests celebrating a birthday – not bad for a B&B!

West Cork Hotel HOTEL €€
(☎028-21277; www.westcorkhotel.com; Ilen St; s/d from €70/109;) This stolid veteran has 30 comfortable, refurbished rooms in an attractive location by the River Ilen; an old railway bridge across the river serves as an outdoor terrace, and rear rooms have pastoral views.

Eating

Farmers Market MARKET €
(10am-1.30pm Sat year-round, plus 10am-1.30pm Wed Jul-Sep) Local producers set up on Old Market Sq.

Riverside Café & Restaurant INTERNATIONAL €€
(☎028-40090; www.riversideskibbereen.ie; North St; mains lunch €6-12, dinner €12-24; noon-3.30pm Tue-Sat, 6-10pm Fri & Sat;) Seafood casserole in lobster bisque, seaweed paella, and bangers and mash with oxtail gravy are among the choices at this popular spot, along with cheese and smoked-fish boards. But the biggest drawcard is the riverside setting with al fresco seating in a sheltered yard at the back – a real lunchtime suntrap.

Kalbo's INTERNATIONAL €€
(☎028-21515; 26 North St; mains €6-20; 9am-6pm Mon-Thu, to 9pm Fri & Sat;) Cafe by day, bistro on weekend evenings. This place uses locally sourced produce and a deft hand in the kitchen to produce breakfast dishes such as vanilla pancakes, and lunch and dinner specials that include crab linguine, mushroom risotto, gourmet burgers and more.

Getting There & Away

Bus Éireann runs buses to Cork seven times daily Monday to Saturday, and five on Sunday (€20, two hours); and to Schull three times daily Monday to Saturday, and once on Sunday (€7.80, 30 minutes).

West Cork Rural Transport (p246) operates a subsidised minibus service west to Bantry (€4, one hour, once daily Monday to Friday)

Baltimore

POP 347

Crusty old sea dog Baltimore is a classic maritime village, its busy little port full of fishing boats and pleasure yachts. The focus of life here is the central terrace overlooking the harbour, the ideal spot to sup a pint or slurp an ice cream while watching the boats go by. All around is a multitude of holiday cottages, catering to the summer swell of sailing folk, sea anglers, divers, and visitors to nearby Sherkin and Cape Clear islands.

A white-painted landmark beacon (aka **Lot's Wife**) stands on the headland 2km southwest of town, marking the entrance to Baltimore Harbour, and making a good objective for a pleasant walk, especially at sunset.

Sights & Activities

Dun na Sead MUSEUM
(Fort of the Jewels; ☎028-20735; adult/child €4/free; 11am-6pm Jun-Sep) Baltimore harbour is dominated by the stone tower of 13th-century Dun na Sead castle. Inside, the great hall houses seasonal art displays and information on the castle's history, but the main attraction is the view from the battlements.

Aquaventures Dive Centre DIVING
(☎087 796 1456; www.aquaventures.ie; Lifeboat Rd) This outfit leads half-day guided snorkelling tours (€40/30 per adult/child, including equipment) suitable for family groups (minimum age six years), exploring marine wildlife on the local coastline or at nearby Lough Hyne. It also offers beginners' courses in scuba-diving (€130 for a one-day Discover Scuba experience).

Baltimore Sea Safari BOAT TOUR
(☎028-20753; www.baltimoreseasafari.ie) Boat trips in a fast RIB along the West Cork coast to see sea cliffs and wildlife, including whales and dolphins; from a 20-minute harbour cruise (€10 per person) to a two-hour wildlife safari (€25).

Festivals & Events

Fiddle Fair MUSIC
(www.fiddlefair.com) Sessions from international and local musicians. Held on the second weekend in May.

Seafood & Wooden Boat Festival FOOD
(www.baltimore.ie) A showcase for local restaurants and seafood producers in May. Jazz

OFF THE BEATEN TRACK

LOUGH HYNE

This beautiful lough is one of Ireland's natural wonders, and became the country's first marine nature reserve in 1981. Its glacier-gouged depths were originally filled with fresh water until rising sea levels breached one end around 4000 years ago. It is now linked to the sea by a narrow tidal channel known as the **Rapids**, where the tide pours in and out twice a day in a rush of white water.

There are lovely walks around the lough and in the neighbouring **Knockomagh Wood Nature Reserve**. A waymarked nature trail leads up a steep hill through the forest; you're rewarded with stunning views at the top.

Atlantic Sea Kayaking (p236) offers guided sea kayak tours of the loch, including superbly atmospheric 2½-hour 'starlight paddles' after dark.

The lough is 6km northeast of Baltimore and 8km southwest of Skibbereen, signposted off the R595 between the two towns, and an easy bike ride from either.

bands perform in the square and traditional wooden sailboats race around the harbour.

Baltimore Pirate Festival CULTURAL
(www.baltimore.ie; ⌚Jun) A long weekend of family-oriented fun, with boat trips, outdoor activities, treasure hunts, music and dancing, all in memory of a notorious event in Baltimore's history, when the port was attacked by Barbary pirates in 1631.

Sleeping & Eating

Rolf's Country House GUESTHOUSE €€
(☎028-20289; www.rolfscountryhouse.com; Baltimore Hill; s/d €60/100, cottages per week from €550; ⌚Apr-Oct; 📶) Upmarket Rolf's, in a much-restored and extended old farmhouse in restful gardens on the outskirts of town, does the lot: there are 10 smartly decorated private rooms, a clutch of two-bedroom self-catering cottages, helpful staff and a charming restaurant.

Waterfront HOTEL €€
(☎028-20600; www.waterfronthotel.ie; The Quay; s/d from €90/140; @📶) Smack in the middle of town, this hotel has 13 bright and airy rooms; ask for one with a view of the sea. Its restaurant, the **Lookout** (Chez Youen; ☎028-20600; www.waterfrontbaltimore.ie; mains €16-40; ⌚6.30-9.30pm daily Aug, Wed-Sat Jun, Jul & Sep, Fri-Sat May), also has sea views and serves luscious shellfish platters containing lobsters, prawns, brown crabs, velvet crabs, shrimp and oysters.

Casey's of Baltimore HOTEL €€€
(☎028-20197; www.caseysofbaltimore.com; Skibbereen Rd; s/d from €130/140; @📶) Ten of the 14 spiffy guest rooms here have estuary views, and all have huge beds. The hotel is right at the entrance to town (should you be arriving by chopper, there's a helipad). Food comes with fantastic views, especially from the terrace. Seafood includes mussels fresh from the hotel's own shellfish farm in Roaringwater Bay.

★**Glebe Gardens & Café** MODERN IRISH €€
(☎028-20232; www.glebegardens.com; Skibbereen Rd; mains lunch €6-11, dinner €18-25; ⌚10am-3pm Wed-Sun, 7-10pm Fri & Sat Apr-Oct; 📶) The beautiful gardens here are an attraction in themselves (admission is €5). If you're dining, lavender and herbs add fragrant aromas that waft over the tables inside and out. Food is simple and fresh, sourced from the gardens and a list of local purveyors – eggs Florentine at breakfast, inspired sandwiches at lunch, and rack of lamb at dinner, for example.

Drinking & Nightlife

Bushe's Bar PUB
(www.bushesbar.com; The Quay; sandwiches €7-11; ⌚noon-11pm) Seafaring paraphernalia drips from the ceiling at this genuinely character-filled old bar. The benches outside on the main square are the best spots in town for a sundowner. Famous crab sandwiches are served when fresh crab has been landed at the quay.

Information

There's an information board at the harbour, or check out www.baltimore.ie. The nearest ATM is in Skibbereen.

Getting There & Away

Three daily buses Monday to Friday, and two on Saturday, link Skibbereen and Baltimore (€4.80, 20 minutes).

Sherkin Island

POP 114

Just a 10-minute ferry ride offshore from Baltimore, Sherkin Island measures just 5km by 3km, but until the Famine it had a population of over 1000.

These days Sherkin is a magnet for artists and day trippers; there's not much to do but wander the fuchsia-fringed lanes, seek out little coves on the west side, and gaze out to sea.

Sleeping & Eating

Islander's Rest PUB €€

(☎028-20116; www.islandersrest.ie; s/d €80/120;) If you're not quite ready to head back to the mainland after your visit to Sherkin, you can gaze at it from your window at the Islander's Rest, which has 21 comfy rooms with private bathroom.

Jolly Roger PUB FOOD €€

(☎028-20662; mains €12-20; ⏲10am-late, shorter hours in winter) The nautical-themed Jolly Roger pub alone justifies a visit to Sherkin Island, with some of the best seafood chowder imaginable (the garlic mussels aren't bad either). Live music takes place daily in summer.

Getting There & Away

Sherkin Island Ferry (☎087 911 7377; www.sherkinferry.com; adult/child return €10/4) sails to/from Baltimore up to nine times daily (seven on Saturday, five on Sunday, reduced services in winter).

Cape Clear Island

POP 124

With its lonely inlets, pebble beaches, and gorse- and heather-clad cliffs, Cape Clear Island (Oileán Chléire), is an escapist's heaven – albeit one that is only 5km long and just over 1.5km wide at its broadest point. But that's just as well, as you'll want time to appreciate this small, rugged Gaeltacht (Irish-speaking) area, the southernmost inhabited island in the country.

Facilities are few (no banks or ATMs), but there are a couple of B&Bs, one shop and three pubs.

Sights & Activities

The island's **museum** (☎028-39119; www.capeclearmuseum.ie; admission €3; ⏲2.30-5pm Jun-Aug) has exhibits on Cape Clear's history and culture, and fine views north across the water to Mizen Head.

Information boards near the harbour highlight a couple of marked walking trails, while unmarked roads wander all over the island. The remains of a **12th-century church** are near the pier. On the coast to the west, the ruins of 14th-century **Dunamore Castle**, the stronghold of the O'Driscoll clan, can be seen perched on a rock (follow the track from the harbour).

Cape Clear is one of the top birdwatching spots in Ireland, particularly known for sea birds including Manx shearwater, guillemot, gannet, fulmar and kittiwake. Tens of thousands of migrating birds can pass hourly, especially in the early morning and at dusk. The best time of year for birdwatching here is October. The white-fronted **bird observatory** is by the harbour (turn right at the end of the pier and it's 100m along).

Courses

Chléire Goats FARMING

(☎028-39126; www.oilean-chleire.ie/GoatFarm) Once you're this isolated, you might as well learn something, and Ed Harper at Chléire Goats farm, west of the island's 12-century church, can teach you everything you need to know about goat husbandry. He makes goat's-milk ice cream and hard goat's cheese, available for tastings, and runs half-day (€35) to five-day (€155) courses on goat keeping.

Festivals & Events

Cape Clear Island International Storytelling Festival PERFORMING ARTS

(☎028-39157; www.capeclearstorytelling.com) Draws hundreds of people for storytelling, workshops and walks in early September.

Sleeping & Eating

Cape Clear Island Hostel HOSTEL €

(☎028-41968; www.capeclearhostel.com; Old Coastguard Station; dm/tw/f from €21/46/82;) This large cream-coloured building amid lovely gardens at the South Harbour, a 10- to 15-minute walk from the ferry, houses a hostel with dorms and private rooms, a spacious self-catering kitchen, a laundry and an amazing collection of model ships in bottles.

Chléire Haven CAMPGROUND €

(☎028-39119; www.yurt-holidays-ireland.com; South Harbour; campsites per person €10; ⏲Apr-Sep) There are a limited number of campsites for travellers with their own tents, and also yurts and tepees to rent (sleeping up to six people). The latter require multiple-day stays and start at €240 for two nights in high season.

WORTH A TRIP

IRELAND'S TEARDROP

So named because it was the last sight of the 'ould country' for emigrants sailing to America, the Fastnet Rock is the most southerly point of Ireland.

This isolated fang of rock, topped by a spectacular lighthouse, stands 6.5km southwest of Cape Clear Island, and in clear weather is visible from many places on the coastline from Baltimore to Mizen Head. Its image – usually with huge waves crashing around it – graces a thousand postcards, coffee-table books and framed art photographs.

The Fastnet lighthouse, widely considered the most perfectly engineered lighthouse in the world, was built in 1904 from ingeniously interlocked blocks of Cornish granite – there are exhibits about its construction at **Mizen Head Visitor Centre** (p243) and **Cape Clear Museum**.

From June to August, **Fastnet Experience** (www.fastnettour.com; per person €32) operates boat trips to the rock, departing from Schull, Baltimore and Cape Clear Island. Tours are weather-dependent and last 2½ to three hours (one hour if departing from Cape Clear).

Ard Na Gaoithe B&B €€

(☎028-39160; www.ardnagaoithe.ie; The Glen; s/d €50/90; 📶) Set on an organic farm overlooking the South Harbour, a 20-minute walk from the ferry, this cottage-style B&B has restful rooms in a simple, sturdy house. Cats in the garden, and free tea and scones on arrival.

Information

The **Tourist Information Point** (☎028-39100; www.capeclearisland.ie; North Harbour; ⏰11am-1pm & 2-6pm Jul & Aug, shorter hours Jun & Sep) is beyond the pier, next to the coffee shop.

Getting There & Away

From Baltimore, the **Cailín Óir** (☎086 346 5110; www.cailinoir.com; adult/child return €16/8; ⏰10.30am-7pm) passenger ferry takes 45 minutes to cover the 11km crossing. There are three or four sailings daily April to September, two a day October to March.

The summer-only **Schull Ferry** (☎087 389 9711; www.schullferry.com; return €16) runs from Schull to Cape Clear Island, with two sailings daily Tuesday to Saturday in July and August, and on Tuesday, Thursday and Sunday in June.

MIZEN HEAD PENINSULA

From Skibbereen the N71 rolls west through Ballydehob, the gateway to the Mizen (rhymes with prison). From here, the R592 leads southwest to the pretty village of Schull and onward through ever-smaller settlements to the hamlet of Goleen.

Even here the Mizen isn't done. Increasingly narrow roads head further west to spectacular Mizen Head itself, and to the hidden delights of Barleycove Beach and Crookhaven. Without a decent map you may well reach the same crossroads several times.

Heading back from Goleen, you can bear north to join the scenic coast road that follows the edge of Dunmanus Bay for most of the way to Durrus. The R591 heads north through Durrus for Bantry, while the L4704 turns west to Ahakista and the Sheep's Head Peninsula.

Schull

POP 660

The yachting and creative crowd (often the same folk) have turned the small fishing village of Schull (pronounced 'skull') into a buzzing little spot, crammed with craft shops and art galleries.

Sights & Activities

Walks in the area include a 13km return trip up **Mt Gabriel** (407m). It was once mined for copper, and there are Bronze Age remains and 19th-century mine shafts and chimneys. For a gentler stroll try the short 2km foreshore path from the pier out to **Roaringwater Bay** for a view of the nearby islands.

Planetarium PLANETARIUM

(☎028-28315; www.schullcommunitycollege.com; Colla Rd; adult/child €5/3.50; ⏰Jun-Aug) Founded by a German visitor who fell in love with Schull, the Republic's only planetarium is on the grounds of Schull Community College at the Goleen end of the village. During summer the 45-minute star show is on three or four times a week; call to confirm times.

LOCAL KNOWLEDGE

GUBBEEN FARM FOODS

Farmed by the same family for six generations, Gubbeen Farm near Schull was one of the pioneers of Irish artisan cheese production, starting out in 1979. The dairy was joined by a smokehouse in 1989, and later by a market garden, while pedigree pigs and poultry were added to the livestock mix.

Gubbeen now turns out ham, salami, chorizo, free-range eggs and organic vegetables, as well as some of Ireland's finest cheeses – Extra Mature Smoked Gubbeen is highly recommended.

The farm is not open to the public, but you can visit the Gubbeen stall at farmers markets in Schull, Skibbereen and Bantry.

Divecology DIVING

(086 837 2065; www.divecology.com; Main St) Runs training courses and dive trips to wreck and reef sites. A one-day Discover Scuba course costs €100 per person.

Festivals & Events

Schull Regatta SAILING

(www.shsc.ie) Five days of yacht racing, jokingly named Calves Week in reference to England's more famous Cowes Week, culminate in a weekend regatta that includes an outdoor market, children's sports, crab-fishing competitions, and a fireworks display. Usually held after the August bank holiday.

Sleeping & Eating

Stanley House B&B €

(028-28425; www.stanley-house.net; Colla Rd; s/d/f €50/76/110; Mar-Oct;) Just outside of town on a little knoll, this modern B&B has four spotless and comfortable bedrooms. Relax with a coffee in the sunroom, which has sweeping views of the sea.

Grove House B&B €€

(028-28067; www.grovehouseschull.com; Colla Rd; s/d from €50/80;) This beautifully restored Georgian mansion – Jack B Yeats once stayed here – is decorated in an easygoing period style with antiques, and handmade rugs scattered on polished pine floors. It also has a terrific **restaurant** (3-course dinner €35; lunch & dinner Mon-Sat) where Swedish influences combine with Irish staples.

Hackett's Bar PUB FOOD €

(028-28625; Main St; mains €7-10; food served noon-3pm daily, 6-9pm Fri & Sat) The town's social hub, Hackett's rises above the norm with a creative pub menu of organic dishes prepared from scratch. Black-and-white photos and tin signs adorn the crooked walls and there's a mishmash of old kitchen tables and benches on the worn stone floor.

Newman's West CAFE €

(028-27776; www.tjnewmans.com; Main St; dishes €7-13; 9am-11pm;) This sailor-filled wine bar (with many good choices by the glass) and art gallery serves soups, salads and enormous chunky sandwiches filled with local cheese and salami. Daily specials might include Bantry Bay mussels and chowder. The adjoining original pub, TJ Newman's, is a charmer.

Shopping

Country Market MARKET

(www.schullmarket.com; Pier Road Car Park; 10am-2pm Sun Easter–Sep) Schull's popular market showcases the work of the village's artists and craftspeople, and draws producers and purveyors from around the region.

Getting There & Away

There are two buses daily from Cork to Schull (€22, 2½ hours), via Clonakilty and Skibbereen.

Getting Around

Betty Johnson's Bus Hire (086 265 6078, 028-28410) Bus and taxi service.

Schull to Mizen Head

On a clear day the undulating coastal route from Schull to Goleen enjoys great views out to Cape Clear Island and the Fastnet lighthouse. The landscape becomes wilder around the hamlet of Toormore. From Goleen, roads run out to the impressive cliffs of Mizen Head and to the harbour village of Crookhaven.

Goleen & Around

Goleen is the largest settlement in these parts, with an impressive neo-Gothic church, four pubs, four shops and a petrol station.

Sleeping & Eating

Heron's Cove B&B €€

(☎ 028-35225; www.heronscove.com; Harbour Rd; s/d from €50/80; 📶) A delightful location on the shores of the tidal inlet of Goleen Harbour makes this fine restaurant and B&B a top choice. Rooms have been refurbished to a restful style and several have balconies overlooking the inlet. The small **restaurant** (3-course dinner €27.50; ⏰7-9.30pm Apr-Oct) has an excellent menu of organic and local food.

Fortview House B&B €€

(☎028-35324; www.fortviewhouse.ie; Gurtyowen, Toormore; s/d €50/100; ⏰Apr-Oct; 📶) On a working farm, this lovely house has three antique-filled, flower-themed bedrooms. Hostess Violet's breakfast is gourmet standard (hot potato cakes with crème fraîche and smoked salmon), with eggs from the garden's cheerfully clucking hens. From Goleen, head northeast along the R591 for 9km.

Information

Mizen Information & e-Centre (☎ 028-35000; Main St; ⏰10.30am-5pm; 📶) provides tourist information, coffee and internet access.

Getting There & Away

Bus Éireann has two buses a day from Skibbereen (€12.70, 1¼ hours) via Schull. Goleen is the end of the line for bus service on the peninsula.

Crookhaven

Onwards from Goleen, the westerly outpost of Crookhaven feels so remote that you imagine it's more easily reached by boat than by road. And so it is for some people – in summer there's a big yachting presence. Outside summer, it's very quiet.

In its heyday Crookhaven's natural harbour was an important anchorage and communications hub with a population of 700 (today it's 30). Mail from America was collected here, and a telegraph line to Cork was installed in 1863, delivering news of transatlantic shipping.

It's worth the trip to enjoy a meal in the rustic bar of the **Crookhaven Inn** (☎028-35309; mains €10-20; ⏰food served 12.30-8pm Fri-Mon Apr-Sep), a popular local watering hole. In summer there are picnic tables outdoors, and trad music sessions in the evenings.

Brow Head

The southernmost point on the Irish mainland is well worth the walk. As you leave Crookhaven, you'll notice a turn-off to the left marked 'Brow Head'. Park here beside Galley Cove Beach and follow the narrow road until it ends, then continue on a footpath to the headland where you'll see a 200-year-old **signal tower**, and round about it the scant remains of Guglielmo Marconi's **wireless telegraphy station**, which operated here from 1901 to 1914, when it moved to Valentia Island.

The view is superb, ranging from Mizen Head in the west, to Fastnet Rock (13.5km away) and Cape Clear to the east.

Barleycove Beach

Vast sand dunes hemmed in by two long bluffs dissolve into the surf, forming West Cork's finest **beach**. Rarely crowded, it's a great place for youngsters, with gorgeous stretches of golden sand and a safe bathing area where a stream flows down to the sea. Access is via a long boardwalk and pontoon from the car park on the road to Crookhaven.

Mizen Head Signal Station

Completed in 1909 to help warn ships off the rocks, **Mizen Head Signal Station** (☎ 028-35115; www.mizenhead.ie; Mizen Head; adult/child €6/4.50; ⏰10am-6pm Jun-Aug, 10.30-5pm mid-Mar–May, Sep & Oct, Sat & Sun only Nov–mid-Mar) is perched high above crashing waves and contorted sea cliffs on a small island connected to the mainland by a spectacular 45m-high bridge. From the visitors centre (you have to pay the admission fee to get to the island), it's a 10-minute walk via 99 steps to reach the station, which houses exhibits on the station's history and on marine wildlife – keep a weather eye open for whales and dolphins.

Back at the visitors centre there are displays about local ecology and history, and on the building of the Fastnet lighthouse. There's also a modest cafe.

Durrus & the Sheep's Head Peninsula

The drive along the north side of the Mizen Head Peninsula leads to the little crossroads of Durrus, where you can continue straight on to Bantry, or turn west to explore the

WORTH A TRIP

DURRUS CHEESE

West Cork has earned an international reputation for its marvellous cheese, thanks to the likes of **Durrus Farmhouse** (☎027-61100; www.durruscheese.com; Coomkeen; ⊙9am-2pm Mon-Fri), whose produce is sold all over Ireland and the UK, and even in the US and Japan. You can visit the farm shop and watch the cheese-making process through a viewing window. It's signposted off the Ahakista road 900m west of Durrus.

Sheep's Head Peninsula, the least visited of West Cork's three peninsulas.

Durrus

POP 334

An access point for both Mizen Head and Sheep's Head Peninsulas, this perky little crossroads at the head of Dunmanus Bay has become something of a gourmet hot spot in recent years, with some great places to eat.

Sleeping & Eating

★**Blairscove House** B&B €€€

(☎027-61127; www.blairscove.ie; s/d from €120/180; ⊙daily Easter-Oct, Fri & Sat only rest of year) Set in 2 hectares of land overlooking the bay, this magnificent Georgian country house looks like it belongs in a style magazine. Superbly appointed suites are ranged around an exquisite courtyard, and can be taken on a B&B or self-catering basis. The Loft apartment (sleeps two) has lovely sea views. Blairscove is 1km south of Durrus on the R591.

The **restaurant** (3-course dinner €58; ⊙6-9pm Tu-Sat Mar-Oct), in a chandeliered hall, gives local produce an international treatment.

Good Things Café MODERN IRISH €€

(☎027-61426; www.thegoodthingscafe.com; Ahakista Rd; mains €15-28; ⊙12.30-3pm daily Aug, 6-9pm Thu-Mon late-Jun–Aug) This foodie haven serves great contemporary dishes made with organic, locally sourced ingredients; tables on the terrace make the most of sunny days. It's 600m west of Durrus on the road to Ahakista.

The cafe's own **cookery school** offers one-day courses that include A Dozen Funky Fast Dishes (the 'culinary equivalent of speed dating'; €140) and a hands-on fish-cooking course (€175) for those whose kitchen skills extend no further than the microwave.

Sheeps Head Inn PUB FOOD €€

(☎027-62822; www.thesheepsheadinn.ie; mains €10-23; ⊙food served noon-3pm & 7-9pm Jun-Aug, Fri & Sat only Sep-May;) In the heart of the village, this cosy black-and-white gastropub cooks up exceptional locally sourced delights such as Durrus cheese tartlets, pan-fried sea bass, and crab claws in garlic and lemon.

Sheep's Head Peninsula

The Sheep's Head Peninsula has a rugged charm all its own – and yes, there are plenty of sheep. The road west from Durrus passes through **Ahakista** (Atha an Chiste), which has a couple of pubs including the charming, tin-roofed **Ahakista Bar** (Ahakista; ⊙from 1pm Jun-Sep;), aka the Tin Pub. At the back, it has flowering gardens that tumble down to the waterfront.

Beyond Ahakista the landscape gets progressively more barren and rocky as the road gets narrower and more twisty. **Kilcrohane** village has a couple of cafes and a good beach, after which the road clambers up over high moors to end at a remote car park with a tiny tea room called **Bernie's Cupán Tae** (Tooreen; mains €3-6; ⊙varies, 10am-4pm Sat & Sun Jun-Aug), famous for its scones and salmon sandwiches.

From here, a superb waymarked walk leads for 2km to the **Sheep's Head lighthouse** at the very tip of the peninsula, amid jaw-dropping sea-cliff scenery (allow 1½ to two hours round trip). Many more walks are listed on the Sheep's Head Way website.

There are sweeping seascapes to appreciate from the loop road that runs around the peninsula. A link road with terrific views, called the **Goat's Path Rd**, runs between Kilcrohane and Gortnakilly (on the south and north coasts respectively) over the western flank of **Mt Seefin** (345m), which offers an exhilarating 1km stride to the summit.

Activities

Sheep's Head Way WALKING

(www.thesheepsheadway.ie) The Sheep's Head Way is an 88km-long walking route around the peninsula, on a mix of minor roads and footpaths; use Ordnance Survey map sheets 85 and 88. There are no campsites on the Sheep's Head Peninsula, but camping along the route is allowed with permission from the landowner.

Sheep's Head Cycle Route CYCLING

(www.thesheepsheadway.ie) The 120km Sheep's Head Cycle Route runs anticlockwise from

Ballylickey, round the coastline of the peninsula, back onto the mainland and down to Ballydehob. There are opportunities to take short cuts or alternative routes (eg over the Goat's Path Rd, or along the coast from Ahakista to Durrus). The *Sheep's Head Cycle Route* brochure is available from local tourist offices and bookshops.

Getting There & Away

West Cork Rural Transport (p246) buses run a circular route on various days via the Goat's Path Rd to Kilcrohane and Durrus (one-way/return €4/6).

Bantry

POP 3350

Framed by the Sheep's Head hills and the craggy Caha Mountains, magnificent, sprawling Bantry Bay is one of the country's most attractive seascapes. Sheltered by islands at the head of the bay, Bantry town is neat and respectable, with narrow streets of old-fashioned, one-off shops and a picturesque harbourfront.

Pride of place goes to Bantry House, the former home of one Richard White, who earned his place in history when, in 1798, he warned authorities of the imminent landing of Irish patriot Wolfe Tone and his French fleet, in support of the United Irishmen's rebellion. In the end, storms prevented the fleet from landing and the course of Irish history was definitively altered – all Wolfe Tone got for his troubles was a square and a statue bearing his name.

Bantry struggled through the 19th century due to famine, poverty and mass emigration, but today its industry derives from the bay: you'll see Bantry oysters and mussels on menus throughout County Cork.

Sights

Bantry House & Garden HISTORIC BUILDING
(027-50047; www.bantryhouse.com; adult/child €11/3; 10am-5pm daily Jun-Aug, Tue-Sun Apr, May, Sep & Oct) With its melancholic air of faded gentility, 18th-century Bantry House makes for an intriguing visit. From the Gobelin tapestries in the drawing room to the columned splendour of the library, it conjures up a lost world of aristocratic excess. But the gardens are its greatest glory, with lawns sweeping down towards the sea, and the magnificent Italian garden at the back, with its staircase of 100 steps, offering spectacular views. The entrance is 1km southwest of the town centre on the N71.

The house has belonged to the White family since 1729 and every room brims with treasures brought back from each generation's travels. The entrance hall is paved with mosaics from Pompeii, French and Flemish tapestries adorn the walls, and Japanese chests sit next to Russian shrines. Upstairs, worn bedrooms look out wanly over an astounding view of the bay. Experienced pianists are invited to tinkle the ivories of the ancient grand piano in the library.

If it looks like the sort of place where you can imagine staying, you can – the owners offer B&B accommodation in one of the wings (p246).

Festivals & Events

West Cork Chamber Music Festival MUSIC
(www.westcorkmusic.ie) Evening concerts held over a week in June/July at Bantry House, during which the house closes to the public. The garden, craft shop and tea room remain open.

West Cork Literary Festival LITERATURE
(www.westcorkliteraryfestival.ie) A week's worth of readings, workshops, talks by famous authors, and children's events in July.

Sleeping

Mill B&B B&B €
(027-50278; www.the-mill.net; Glengarriff Rd; s/d €50/70; Easter-Oct;) This modern house, on the immediate outskirts of town, oozes individuality. The rooms are a riot of knick-knacks. To accompany the solid breakfasts, the spacious dining room has a wonderful collection of Indonesian puppets and artworks by the irrepressible owner, Tosca.

Eagle Point Camping CAMPGROUND €
(027-50630; www.eaglepointcamping.com; Glengarriff Rd, Ballylickey; campsites per person from €12; mid-Apr–late Sep;) Superb campground with an enviable location at the end of a filigreed promontory 6km north of Bantry. Most of the 125 sites have sea views, and there's direct access to the pebbly beaches nearby for swimming and water sports.

Ballylickey House B&B €€
(027-50071; www.ballylickeymanorhouse.com; Ballylickey; d €95-140, ste €130-180; Mar-Nov;) Situated 5km north of Bantry, this beautiful manor house with manicured lawns overlooks the bay. There are two choices for the night: rooms in the house,

or cute cottages set round a swimming pool. All are spacious and comfortably furnished.

Sea View House Hotel HOTEL €€€
(027-50073; www.seaviewhousehotel.com; Ballylickey; s/d from €100/150;) You'll find everything you'd expect from a luxury hotel here: country-house ambience, tastefully decorated public rooms, expansive service and 25 cosy, smart bedrooms. The hotel is on the N71 in Ballylickey, 5km north of Bantry.

Bantry House HISTORIC HOTEL €€€
(027-50047; www.bantryhouse.com; d from €169; Apr-Oct;) The guest rooms in this aristocratic mansion (p245) are decorated with a mixture of antiques and contemporary furnishings – when you're not playing croquet, lawn tennis or billiards you can lounge in the library, once the doors of the historic house have closed to the public (guests have free access to the house). Rooms 22 and 25 have views of both the garden and the bay.

Eating

★Organico CAFE €
(027-55905; www.organico.ie; 2 Glengarriff Rd; mains €7-10; 9am-6pm Mon-Sat;) This bright and lively wholefood shop and cafe serves tinglingly fresh salads, sandwiches and soups, and lunch specials such as a falafel platter with hummus and tahini. Great coffee and cakes, too.

★Manning's Emporium CAFE, DELI €
(www.manningsemporium.ie; Ballylickey; mains €8; 9am-6pm Mon-Sat, to 5pm Sun, 6-9pm Sat Jun-Aug) This gourmet deli and cafe is an Aladdin's cave of West Cork's finest food. Tasting plates are the best way to sample the local artisan produce and farmhouse cheeses on offer. Foodie events take place regularly. It's on the N71 in Ballylickey (on the right as you're coming from Bantry).

Bantry Market MARKET €
(Wolfe Tone Sq; 9.30am-1pm Fri) Wolfe Tone Sq takes on a heady mix of aromas for the Friday market. Fresh fruit, veg, bread, cheese, and other local produce fill most stalls, but there's also clothing, bric-a-brac and farming tools. The market morphs into an even bigger and busier affair on the first Friday of the month.

Fish Kitchen SEAFOOD €€
(027-56651; www.thefishkitchen.ie; New St; mains €10-23; noon-3.30pm & 5.30-9pm Tue-Sat) This outstanding little restaurant above a fish shop does seafood to perfection, from the live-tank local oysters (served with lemon and Tabasco sauce) to Bantry Bay mussels in white wine. If you don't fancy sea fare, it does a juicy steak too. Friendly, unfussy and absolutely delicious.

O'Connors Seafood Restaurant SEAFOOD €€
(027-55664; www.oconnorseafood.com; Wolfe Tone Sq; mains €12-25; 12.30-3pm & 5.30-9pm;) West Cork scallops with black pudding and smoked cauliflower puree; Castletownbere cod pan-roasted and topped with Irish-made feta cheese and truffle oil; Bantry Bay mussels done four ways: these are among the innovative dishes here that make the most of the area's renowned seafood. The early-bird menu (5.30pm to 6.30pm) offers three courses for €27.50.

Drinking & Nightlife

Crowley's PUB
(Wolfe Tone Sq; noon-11pm Sun-Thu, to 12.30am Fri & Sat) One of the best bars for music, Crowley's has traditional bands on Wednesday nights.

Ma Murphy's PUB
(www.mamurphys.com; 7 New St; 1pm-midnight) You can still buy cornflakes and sugar at this time-warp grocery-pub, open since 1840. The regulars are always up for a chat.

Snug PUB
(Wolfe Tone Sq; 11am-11pm Mon-Sat, 12.30-11pm Sun) Cosy local favourite on the waterfront, known for its excellent pub grub.

Information

The **Tourist Office** (027-50229; Wolfe Tone Sq; 9.15am-1pm & 2-5pm Mon-Sat Apr-Oct) is in the old courthouse.

Getting There & Away

Bus Éireann (www.buseireann.ie) runs four to six buses daily between Bantry and Cork (€21, two hours), and five daily to Glengarriff (€5.20, 25 minutes); the summer-only bus 282 allows you to continue from Glengarriff to Kenmare (one daily Monday to Saturday).

West Cork Rural Transport (027-52727; www.ruraltransport.ie; 5 Main St) offers a minibus service that runs a useful series of circular routes from Bantry to Dunmanway, Durrus, Goleen, Schull, Skibbereen and outlying villages. There's a set price of €4/6 one-way/return. Service is not frequent; check the website for details.

Getting Around

Bicycles can be hired at **Nigel's Bicycle Shop** (027-52657; Glengarriff Rd; per day/week €15/70; 10am-6pm Tue-Sat year-round, plus Mon May-Sep).

BEARA PENINSULA (RING OF BEARA)

After Kerry and Dingle, the Beara Peninsula is the third major 'ring' (circular driving route) in Ireland's southwest. Its intricate coast and sharp-featured mountains are a geologist's paradise of exposed and contorted rock strata, making for dramatic scenery at almost every turn of the road.

You can easily drive the 137km Ring of Beara in one day, but you would miss the spectacular **Healy Pass Road** (R574), which cuts across the peninsula from Adrigole in Cork to Lauragh in County Kerry. In fact, if pressed for time, skip the rest and do the pass.

The south side, along Bantry Bay, is a string of working fishing villages. The north side, in contrast, has only a few small hamlets dotted along craggy roads that wind in and out of the coast's nooks and crannies. Many are off the tourist trail, and have grand views north to the mountains of Kerry.

Other highlights include a thrillingly wobbly **cable car** from the tip of the peninsula out to tiny **Dursey Island**, and exhilarating **hill walking** requiring some skill and commitment, as well as proper clothing and navigational experience.

The 206km **Beara Way** (p249) is a waymarked walk linking Glengarriff with Kenmare (in Kerry) via Castletownbere, Bere Island, Dursey Island and the north side of the peninsula. The 138km **Beara Way Cycle Route** takes a similar path, linking all the villages on Beara via back roads and small lanes.

A small part of the peninsula lies in County Kerry, but most is within County Cork.

Glengarriff

POP 1090

Tucked away in the thickly wooded, northernmost corner of Bantry Bay, Glengarriff (Gleann Garbh; www.glengarriff.ie) is a 19th-century resort village strung along the N71 Cork to Killarney road at the start of the Ring of Beara.

In the second half of the 19th century, Glengarriff became a popular retreat for prosperous Victorians, who sailed from England to Cork, took the train to Bantry (the line closed in 1961), then crossed over to the

Beara Peninsula (Ring of Beara)

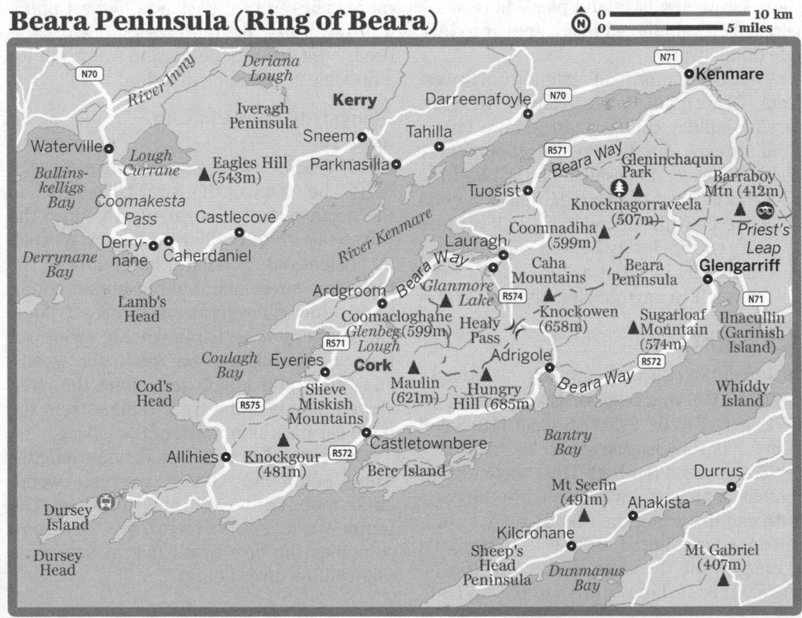

OFF THE BEATEN TRACK

PRIEST'S LEAP

If you're a faint-hearted driver, don't even think about heading up the vertiginous, single-track road to Priest's Leap, 17km northwest of Bantry. In fact, if your GPS points you this way (as a shortcut between Bantry and Kenmare), think again. If you're feeling intrepid, however, this wild ride rewards with monumental views across the mountains to Bantry Bay.

The road is a classic challenge for cyclists, climbing almost 400m in 4.5km, and exceptionally steep in parts; any fit rider will make it to the top, but unless your thighs are Tour de France material you'll be off and pushing the bike at three or four places. And make sure your brakes are in good order for the descent.

From Bantry, take the N71 north for 8km and turn right after the bridge at the head of the bay (signposted Coomhola). Turn left at the first bridge, and left again at the second bridge (look for the white sign saying Priest's Leap), then take the first right. A long straight gets increasingly steep, before relenting a bit, but with big drops on the left.

The summit of the pass is marked by a wind-buffeted crucifix. The story goes that in 1601 Father James Archer was rallying Cork and Kerry's clans to resist the English. Enemy troops spotted him on the old road to Kerry and gave chase until he and his horse leapt from the top of the pass and landed in Bantry.

village in a paddle steamer. By 1850 the road to Kenmare had been blasted through the mountains and the link with Killarney was established.

The rough and rocky **Caha Mountains** rising to the north and west make for challenging hill walking, despite their small size, but there are plenty of gentler strolls in and around town, too. The mature woodlands of oak and Scots pine – the **Blue Pool Park** – has some easy waymarked trails along the shore between village and pier where seals, perched on submerged rocks, appear to levitate on the water.

A maze of minor roads extends northwest from Glengarriff Woods Nature Reserve, serving holiday cottages and remote farms, ideal for exploring by bike. **Pooleen**, where picnic tables stand beside a natural bathing pool in the River Glengarriff, makes a good objective. Only the fit and hardy will venture to road's end at **Barley Lake**, a wild hill loch visited mainly by trout anglers (don't even try driving it in anything less than a 4WD).

Sights

★Ilnacullin (Garinish Island) GARDENS

(☎027-63040; www.heritageireland.ie; adult/child €4/2, ferry €12/6; ⏲10am-6.30pm Mon-Sat & 11am-6.30pm Sun Jun-Aug, shorter hours Apr, May, Sep & Oct, closed Nov-Mar) This horticultural miracle of an island was created in the early 20th century when the island's owner commissioned architect Harold Peto to design a garden on the then-barren outcrop. Topsoil was shipped in, landscaped gardens laid out, and subtropical species planted; camellias, magnolias and rhododendrons provide a seasonal blaze of colour. The 10-minute boat trip to the island departs from the village pier, and passes colonies of basking seals and a nesting site for white-tailed eagles, which were re-introduced to Ireland in 2007.

The centrepiece of the island is a magical **Italianate garden**; nearby a cypress avenue leads to a faux-Grecian temple with a stunning view of Sugarloaf Mountain. There are more views from the island's highest point, a 19th-century **Martello tower**, one of hundreds built around the coast to watch out for a possible Napoleonic invasion.

Glengarriff Woods Nature Reserve NATURE RESERVE

(☎027-63636; www.glengarriffnaturereserve.ie) FREE The valley of the River Glengarriff, to the northwest of Glengarriff, was once the private estate of the Earl of Bantry. As such its ancient oak woodland has survived, the thick tree cover maintaining humid conditions, which allow ferns and mosses to flourish. The reserve is rich in wildlife – look out for red squirrels and siskins in the woods, and otters and kingfishers along the river. Waymarked walking trails radiate from the main car park 1km north of the village.

There are five trails of varying lengths, from 500m to 3km, covering woodland, mountain, river and meadow. The purple-waymarked **Glengarriff Wood Loop** combines the best of all five in one route (8km, allow three hours).

Ewe Experience GARDENS
(☎027-63840; www.theewe.com; Tooreen; adult/child €6.50/5; ⊙10am-6pm Easter-Sep) More than 20 years in the making, this interactive sculpture garden has been designed to furrow brows, provoke smiles and, above all, fire the imagination. From the sheep in the vintage car to the pig blissing out in a bubble bath, a kilometre of trails takes you past dozens of intriguing sculptures, installations, puzzles and games, which weave together art, nature, science, music and poetry in a thought-provoking way. The gardens are 4.5km northwest of Glengarriff on the N71.

Bamboo Park GARDENS
(☎027-63007; www.bamboo-park.com; adult/child €6/free; ⊙9am-7pm) Glengarriff's mild, frost-free climate allows this small 12-hectare park to flourish. It has a variety of exotic plants, including palm trees and tree ferns, as well as coastal woodland walks.

Sleeping & Eating

Bayview Boutique Guesthouse GUESTHOUSE €€
(☎027-63030; dowlingaine@yahoo.com; Reenmeen; r from €80;) This spacious modern villa on the eastern edge of Glengarriff has been converted into a chic and elegant guesthouse, with bedrooms that look fresh from a Sunday colour-supplement photo shoot. There's a lovely terrace and garden out back with sweeping views across the bay, and **Jim's Coffee House** (mains €6-15, ⊙10am-6pm), one of the nicest places to eat hereabouts.

Casey's Hotel HOTEL €€
(☎027-63010; www.caseyshotelglengarriff.ie; Main St; s €55-80, d €90-140;) Old-fashioned Casey's has been welcoming guests since 1884 (Eamon de Valera stayed here). The 19 rooms have been modernised a bit but are still small. It's got stacks of atmosphere, and the vast terrace is a treat. The bar serves classics such as beef and Guinness pie; the restaurant ups the ante with posh seafood and steak dishes.

MacCarthy's Bar PUB FOOD €€
(☎027-63000; 14 Main St; mains €10-19; ⊙food served noon-3pm & 6-9pm;) MacCarthy's is a traditional, Victorian-style wood-panelled bar with a menu of hearty pub grub; the house speciality is a steaming pan of succulent Bantry Bay mussels in a white wine and herb sauce.

Getting There & Away

Bus Éireann has up to five buses daily to Bantry (€5.20, 25 minutes) and on to Cork (€22, 2½ hours), as well as to Castletownbere (€10.70, 50 minutes, one or two daily).

The summer-only bus 282 runs from Glengarriff to Kenmare (€12.10, 45 minutes, one daily Monday to Saturday July and August).

Glengarriff to Castletownbere

The folded bedding of the peninsula's underlying bedrock becomes evident as you drive west from Glengarriff towards Castletownbere. On the highest hills, Sugarloaf Mountain and Hungry Hill, rock walls known as 'benches' snake backwards and forwards across the slopes. They can make walking on these mountains quite challenging, and dangerous in fog. Take a map (Ordnance Survey sheets 84 and 85 cover the area) and compass if venturing into the hills, and seek local advice.

Adrigole is no more than a scattered strip of houses and a harbour where the **West Cork Sailing Centre** (☎027-60132; www.westcorksailing.com; The Boat House, Adrigole; ⊙Jul & Aug) rents kayaks (per hour €12) and Canadian canoes (per hour €20).

From Adrigole, a narrow, switchback road climbs 11km north across the other-worldly **Healy Pass** to Lauragh, offering spectacular views of the rocky scenery, especially on the descent on the far side.

BEARA WAY

This 206km waymarked walk (see www.irishtrails.ie) forms a loop around the Beara Peninsula, and takes around nine days. The peninsula is relatively unused to mass tourism and makes a pleasant contrast with the Ring of Kerry to the north.

The Beara Way mostly follows old roads and tracks and rarely rises above 340m. There's no official start or finish point, and the route can be walked in either direction. It could easily be reduced to seven days by skipping Bere and Dursey Islands and, if you start at Castletownbere, you could reach Kenmare in five days or less.

There's a good downloadable guide to the walk (and the peninsula itself) at **Beara Tourism** (www.bearatourism.com).

Castletownbere & Around

POP 910

Busy Castletownbere (Baile Chais Bhéara) is a fishing port first and a tourist town second. And that gives it great appeal for those looking for the 'real' Ireland, although that's not to say it doesn't have its popular sights, notably the world-famous pub **McCarthy's Bar**.

On Main St and the Square, you'll find ATMs as well as cafes, pubs and grocery stores.

Sights

Derreenataggart Stone Circle HISTORIC SITE

On a lonely hill 2km northwest of Castletownbere, the impressive Derreenataggart Stone Circle, consisting of 10 stones, can be found close to the roadside. It's signposted from a turn-off to the right at the western end of town. There are a number of other standing stones in the surrounding area.

Bere Island ISLAND

Looming offshore, Bere Island makes Castletownbere seem like the big city. Only 12km by 7km, it has a couple of hundred permanent residents, and attracts scores more to summer holiday homes. There are bits of old ruins and some craggy coves good for swimming. **Bere Island Ferry** (☎027-75009; www.bereislandferries.com; passenger/car return €8/25; ⊙every 90min Mon-Sat Jun-Aug, less often Sun & Sep-May) leaves from town but drops you in a remote part of the island. Alternatively, **Murphy's Ferry Service** (☎027-75014; www.murphysferry.com; pedestrian/car return from €8/25; ⊙every 2hr), departing from Pontoon pier, 5km east of Castletownbere, docks by the island's main village, **Rerrin**, which has a shop, a pub, a cafe and accommodation.

Sleeping & Eating

Rodeen B&B B&B €€

(☎027-70158; www.rodeencountryhouse.com; s/d from €40/70; ⊙Apr-Nov) A delightful, six-room haven, tucked away above the eastern approach to town. The musical instrument–filled house has stunning sea views and is surrounded by gardens full of crumbling Delphic columns. Flowers from the garden grace the breakfast table, and there are home-baked scones with honey from landlady Ellen's bees.

Olde Bakery MODERN IRISH €€

(☎027-70869; Castletown House; mains €13-23; ⊙5.30-9.30pm daily year-round, plus noon-4.30pm Sun Apr-Sep) One of the best restaurants in town, the Olde Bakery serves top regional seafood. The handful of tables out front are ideal on a summer evening.

Jack Patrick's INTERNATIONAL €€

(☎027-70319; Main St; mains €10-20; ⊙noon-9pm Jun-Sep, to 7pm Oct-May) Run by one of the top local butchers – the shop is next door – this simple restaurant is the place for steaks, chops and other meaty mains such as bacon and cabbage.

Drinking & Nightlife

McCarthy's Bar PUB

(Main St; ⊙noon-11pm Sun-Thu, to 12.30am Fri & Sat) If you're carrying an original copy of the late Pete McCarthy's bestseller, *McCarthy's Bar,* you'll be excited to see the front-cover photo in three dimensions. McCarthy's is a grocery store as well as a pub; fancy a tin of peaches and a can of corn to go with your Beamish? There's frequent live music and a wee snug inside the door.

Information

The **Tourist Office** (☎027-70054; www.bearatourism.com; Main St; ⊙9am-5.30pm Mon-Sat Jun-Sep, Fri & Sat only Oct-May) is just outside the Church of Ireland.

Getting There & Away

Bus Éireann (www.buseireann.ie) has one or two buses daily to Glengarriff (€10.70, 50 minutes), Bantry (€13.90, 70 minutes) and on to Cork (€24, 3¼ hours).

In July and August, the bus 282 Ring of Beara service runs twice daily Monday to Saturday from Castletownbere to Kenmare (€13.90, 1½ hours) via Glengarriff.

Dursey Island

POP 3

Tiny Dursey Island, at the end of the peninsula, is reached by Ireland's only **cable car** (☎028-21766; www.durseyisland.ie; adult/child return €8/4; ⊙9am-8pm Jul-Sep, less frequently Oct-Jun), a rickety 1960s contraption that sways precariously 30m above Dursey Sound. In a perfect photo op, livestock take precedence over humans in the queue. It runs continuously in summer, and at set times only the rest of the year – check the website for details.

The island, just 6.6km long by 1.5km wide, is a wildlife **sanctuary**, and dolphins and whales can sometimes be seen in the surrounding waters. There's no accommodation,

WORTH A TRIP

GOUGANE BARRA FOREST PARK

Gougane Barra is a truly magical spot, with craggy mountains and pine forests sweeping down to a mountain lake, the source of the River Lee. St Fin Barre, the founder of Cork, established a monastery here in the 6th century. He had a hermitage on the island in **Gougane Barra Lake** (Lough an Ghugain), which is now approached by a short causeway. The small chapel on the island has fine stained-glass representations of obscure Celtic saints.

Beyond the lake, a loop road runs through the forest park (entry per vehicle €5), but you're better off slowing down and walking the well-marked network of paths and **nature trails** through the woods.

The only place to air your hiking boots is the **Gougane Barra Hotel** (☎026-47069; www.gouganebarrahotel.com; d from €110). There's an on-site restaurant, a cafe and a pub next door. The hotel runs a summer theatre festival.

The park is signposted on the R584, which runs between the N71 at Ballylickey and Macroom on the N22.

but **camping** is legal, so long as you respect the common rules and clean up after yourself.

The **Beara Way** loops round the island for 14km (allow four hours for the complete loop), and the **signal tower** is an obvious destination for a shorter walk (8km round trip).

Northside of the Beara

The entire north side is the scenic highlight of the Beara Peninsula. A series of minor roads, often steep and twisting single-lane tracks with few passing places, snake around the ins and outs of the rugged coastline. Boulder-strewn fields tumble dramatically towards the ocean and it all feels blissfully remote – your only company along some stretches are flocks of sheep.

Allihies

The isolated village of Allihies (Na hAilichí), whose colourfully painted houses grace many a postcard and guidebook cover, has dramatic vistas, plenty of walks and a fascinating history of copper mining.

Copper-ore deposits were first identified on the far Beara in 1810. While mining quickly brought wealth to the Puxley family, who owned the land, it brought low wages and dangerous, unhealthy working conditions for the labour force, which at one time numbered 1300. Experienced Cornish miners were brought into the area, and the dramatic ruins of engine houses replicate those of Cornwall's coastal tin mines. As late as the 1930s, more than 30,000 tonnes of pure copper were exported annually, but by 1962 the last mine was closed.

Sights

Allihies Copper Mine Museum MUSEUM
(☎027-73218; www.acmm.ie; Main Rd; adult/child €5/2; ⏲10am-4.30pm Easter-Oct; 📶) This museum is the result of years of work by the community and has engaging exhibits plus tourist information and a cafe. Pick up a copy of the museum leaflet and follow the Copper Mine Trail, a waymarked hike among the remains of the old workings.

Sleeping & Eating

Allihies Village Hostel HOSTEL €
(☎027-73107; www.allihieshostel.net; Main Rd; dm/d €18/50; 👪) This bright, welcoming hostel has spotless wood-floored dorms and common areas, a courtyard and a barbecue area. Owner Michael is a mine of information on the area and can advise on local walks and pony trekking.

Sea View Guesthouse GUESTHOUSE €
(☎027-73004; www.allihiesseaview.com; Main Rd; s/d €45/75) Clean, tidy and basic, the 10 rooms in this two-storey yellow building have an abundance of pine; some have views north over the sea. The spread at breakfast will help fuel your rambles.

O'Neill's PUB FOOD €€
(☎027-73008; www.oneillsbeara.ie; Main Rd; mains €12-25; ⏲food served noon-8.30pm; 📶) The most appealing pub in town, with a distinctive bright-red facade and some polished wooden benches and picnic tables out the front. Pub standards intermingle with fresh local seafood; the haddock and chips could feed two people.

Allihies to Ardgroom

Heading north and east from Allihies, the wild coastal road (R575), lined with fuchsias and rhododendrons, twists and turns for about 12km to **Eyeries**. This cluster of brightly coloured houses overlooking Coulagh Bay is often used as a film set. The village is also home to **Milleens cheese** (☎027-74079; www.milleenscheese.com; Eyeries; ⊙by appointment), from pioneering producer Veronica Steele. She welcomes visitors to her farm; phone ahead.

From Eyeries, forsake the R571 for even smaller coastal roads to the north and east, with sublime views of the Ring of Kerry to the north, rejoining the R571 at the crossroads of **Ardgroom** (Ard Dhór). From here, a minor road leads inland to dramatic **Glenbeg Lough**; ask at the village pub for information on trout fishing here.

Lauragh to Kenmare

The village of Lauragh (Laith Reach) is in County Kerry. About 1km west of Lauragh, a side road leads to **Glanmore Lake**, with the remains of an old hermitage on a tiny island in the middle. Get information on walking and cycling trails here from Pedals & Boots Cafe.

Derreen Gardens GARDENS
(☎064-668 3588; www.derreengarden.com; Lauragh; adult/child €7/2; ⊙10am-6pm) Lauragh is home to the Derreen Gardens, planted by the fifth Lord Lansdowne around the turn of the 20th century. Mossy paths weave through an abundance of interesting plants, including spectacular New Zealand tree ferns and red cedars, and you may see seals on the shore.

Gleninchaquin Park FARM
(☎087 712 8553; www.gleninchaquin.com; Tuosist; adult/child €6/free; ⊙9am-5pm) This sheep farm offers a whole range of things to do, from waymarked history and geology walks to trout fishing and feeding the lambs (in spring), all in an extraordinarily beautiful setting, high in a valley overlooked by a waterfall. It's signposted off the R571 halfway between Lauragh and Kenmare.

Sleeping & Eating

Pedals & Boots Cafe CAFE €
(☎064-668 3101; www.pedalsandboots.ie; Lauragh; mains €5; ⊙10am-5pm Apr-Sep; 📶) This cosy cafe, complete with wood-fired stove, serves up home-baked cakes and scones, soups and sandwiches. You can hire bikes here too (per day €15), and get information on local walking and cycling routes.

★**Josie's Lakeview House** MODERN IRISH €€
(☎064-83155; www.josiesrestaurant.ie; Clogherane; mains €10-26; ⊙10.30am-7.30pm) Captivating lake views accompany scrumptious, home-cooked food at Josie's, set on a hill overlooking forest-shrouded Glanmore Lake. Choose from salads and sandwiches for lunch, cakes at tea, or heartier rack of lamb and local seafood specials at night; ask about B&B or self-catering accommodation (double room €70) to prolong the experience. Josie's is 4km south of Lauragh; follow the signs.

Getting There & Away

In July and August only, Bus Éireann's Ring of Beara service has two buses a day from Kenmare to Lauragh (€7.80, 40 minutes), Ardgroom (€12.10, 55 minutes) and Eyeries (€13.90, 1¼ hours).

County Kerry

POP 145,500 / AREA 4746 SQ KM

Includes ➡

Best Places to Eat

- ➡ Jacks Coastguard Restaurant (p270)
- ➡ Smuggler's Inn (p275)
- ➡ Idás (p285)
- ➡ Spillane's (p292)
- ➡ Tom Crean Fish & Wine (p279)

Best Walks

- ➡ Muckross Lake Loop (p261)
- ➡ Bentee Loop (p270)
- ➡ Mt Brandon (p289)
- ➡ The Saint's Road (p289)
- ➡ Carrauntoohil (p267)

Why Go?

County Kerry contains some of Ireland's most iconic scenery: surf-pounded sea cliffs and soft golden strands, emerald-green farmland criss-crossed by tumbledown stone walls, mist-shrouded bogs and cloud-torn mountain peaks.

With one of the country's finest national parks as its backyard, the lively tourism hub of Killarney spills over with colourful shops, restaurants and pubs loud with spirited trad music. The town is the jumping-off point for Kerry's two famed loop drives: the larger Ring of Kerry skirts the mountainous, island-fringed Iveragh Peninsula. The more compact Dingle Peninsula is like a condensed version of its southern neighbour, with ancient Christian sites, sandy beaches and glimpses of a hard, unforgiving land.

Kerry's exquisite beauty makes it one of Ireland's most popular tourist destinations. But if you need to escape from the crowds, there's always a mountain pass, an isolated cove or an untrodden trail to discover.

When to Go?

Lots of festivals take place throughout the county during the warmer months, particularly from June to August (when you'll need to book accommodation well ahead).

Some of the highlights on Kerry's annual calendar include Listowel's Writers' Week in June and Dingle town's races and regatta in August. Killorglin's famous Puck Festival, which dates back to the 17th century, also takes place in August.

Even in the depths of winter, you'll find storytellers and musicians taking part in impromptu sessions in pubs throughout the county.

County Kerry Highlights

1. Travel by boat and by bike through the Killarney Lakes and the **Gap of Dunloe** (p266)
2. Hike to the 1000m summit of **Carrauntoohil** (p267), Ireland's highest peak
3. **Scuba-dive** (p292) the crystal-clear waters around Castlegregory's Maharees Island
4. Go **fly fishing for brown trout** (p263) or salmon on Killarney's beautiful Lough Leane
5. Hire a bike and cycle around the incredibly scenic **Slea Head Drive** (p288)
6. Tee off at the spectacularly situated **Waterville Golf Links** (p275) on the Ring of Kerry
7. Discover the monuments along the **Saint's Road** (p289) on the Dingle Peninsula
8. Take a boat trip to the remote monastic ruins atop the **Skellig Michael** (p276)
9. Cruise through fresh and saltwater habitats on a safari at the **Tralee Bay Wetlands Centre** (p293)

KILLARNEY

POP 14,220

Modern-day Killarney is a well-oiled tourism machine set in the middle of sublime scenery. Its manufactured tweeness is renowned – the shops selling soft-toy *shillelaghs* and shamrocks, the placards on street corners pointing to trad-music sessions.

However, it has attractions beyond its proximity to lakes, waterfalls and woodland spreading beneath a skyline of 1000m-plus peaks. In a town that's been practising the tourism game for more than 250 years, competition keeps standards high and visitors on all budgets can expect to find good restaurants, great pubs and comfortable accommodation.

The Killarney area has been inhabited since at least the early Bronze Age, when copper ore was mined on Ross Island. In the 7th century, St Finian founded a monastery on Inisfallen in Lough Leane, and the region became a focus for Christianity. The lands around the lough were occupied by the Gaelic clans of McCarthy Mór and the O'Donoghues of Ross, who built Ross Castle, before coming into the possession of the Herberts of Muckross and the Earls of Kenmare.

It wasn't until the mid-18th century that Viscount Kenmare began to develop the region as an Irish version of England's Lake District, aided by the arrival of the railway in 1853, and famous visits by Sir Walter Scott in 1825 and Queen Victoria in 1861. By 1895 Killarney was on the Thomas Cook package tour itinerary.

Mobbed in summer, Killarney is perhaps at its best in the late spring and early autumn when the crowds are manageable, but the weather is still good enough to enjoy its outdoor activities.

Sights & Activities

Killarney's biggest attraction, in every sense, is the nearby Killarney National Park (p260). The town itself can easily be explored on foot in an hour or two.

St Mary's Cathedral CATHEDRAL
(www.killarneyparish.com; Cathedral Pl) Built between 1842 and 1855, St Mary's Cathedral is a superb example of neo-Gothic revival architecture. Designed by Augustus Pugin, the cruciform building was inspired by Ardfert Cathedral, near Tralee. See the website for times of Mass.

Franciscan Friary FRIARY
(Fair Hill) This 1860s Franciscan friary displays an ornate Flemish-style altarpiece, some impressive tile work and, most notably, stained-glass windows by Harry Clarke. The Dublin artist's organic style was influenced by art nouveau, art deco and symbolism.

Killarney Golf & Fishing Club GOLF
(☎064-663 1034; www.killarney-golf.com; green fees €60-100) This historic club, which has hosted the Irish Open on several occasions, has three championship golf courses (one is currently closed for redevelopment) with lakeside settings and mountain views. It's 3.4km west of Killarney on the N72.

Tours

Killarney Guided Walks WALKING TOUR
(☎087 639 4362; www.killarneyguidedwalks.com; adult/child €9/5) Guided two-hour walks through the national park woodlands leave at 11am daily from opposite St Mary's Cathedral at the western end of New St. Tours meander through Knockreer gardens, then to spots where Charles de Gaulle holidayed, David Lean filmed *Ryan's Daughter* and Brother Cudda slept for 200 years. Tours available at other times on request.

Jaunting Car Tours TOUR
(☎064-663 3358; www.killarneyjauntingcars.ie; per car €30-80) Killarney's traditional horse-drawn jaunting cars provide tours from the town to Ross Castle and Muckross Estate, complete with amusing commentary from the driver (known as a 'jarvey'). The cost varies depending on distance; cars can fit up to four people. The pick-up point, nicknamed 'the Ha Ha' or 'the Block', is on Kenmare Pl.

Big Red Bus Tour BUS TOUR
(☎087 250 8122; www.killarneytour.com; 1-day/2-day ticket €12.50/18; ⏲3 departures daily

TRACING YOUR ANCESTORS

County Kerry currently has no genealogy centre, but you can search census returns, old newspapers and other archives at **Tralee Library** (☎066-712 1200; Moyderwell; ⏲10am-5pm Mon, Wed, Fri & Sat, to 8pm Tue & Thu) and **Killarney Library** (www.kerrylibrary.ie; Rock Rd; ⏲10am-5pm Mon, Wed, Fri & Sat, to 8pm Tue & Thu).

There are also some church records available free of charge on the **Irish Genealogy** (www.irishgenealogy.ie) website.

Apr-Sep, 1 daily Oct-Mar) Hop-on, hop-off open-top bus tour that links East Avenue in Killarney town centre to Aghadoe, Ross Castle, Muckross House and Torc Waterfall.

Corcoran's BUS TOUR

(☎064-663 6666; www.corcorantours.com; per person €20) If you're pushed for time, this outfit offers half-day coach tours that take

Killarney

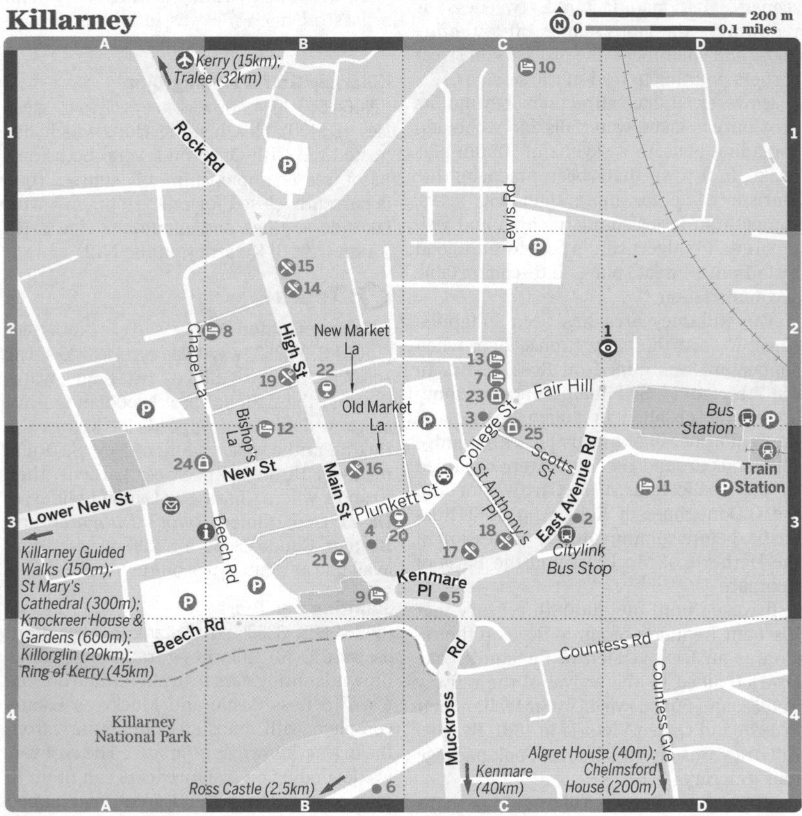

Killarney

Sights

1 Franciscan Friary ... D2

Activities, Courses & Tours

2 Big Red Bus Tour ... C3
3 Corcoran's ... C2
4 Deros Tours ... B3
5 Jaunting Car Tours ... C3
6 O'Connor Autotours ... B4

Sleeping

7 Fairview ... C2
8 Killarney Haven ... B2
9 Killarney Plaza Hotel ... B3
10 Kingfisher Lodge ... C1
11 Malton ... D3
12 Neptune's Killarney Town Hostel ... B3
13 Súgán Hostel ... C2

Eating

14 Brícín ... B2
15 Gaby's Seafood Restaurant ... B2
16 Jam ... B3
17 Lir Café ... C3
18 Mareena's Simply Food ... C3
Smoke House ... (see 22)
19 Treyvaud's ... B2

Drinking & Nightlife

20 Courtney's ... B3
21 Killarney Grand ... B3
22 O'Connor's ... B2

Shopping

Brícín ... (see 14)
23 Dungeon Bookshop ... C2
24 Killarney Outdoor Store ... A3
25 Variety Sounds ... C3

in Killarney, Ross Castle, Muckross House and the Gap of Dunloe. They also offer day-long tours of the Ring of Kerry (€18.50) and Dingle and Slea Head (€21.50.

Deros Tours BUS TOUR
(064-663 1251; www.derostours.com) Gap of Dunloe (€27), Ring of Kerry (€19) and Dingle and Slea Head (€22) tours.

O'Connor Autotours BUS TOUR
(064-663 4833; www.oconnorautotours.ie;) Ring of Kerry (€25), Gap of Dunloe (€30) and Dingle (€25) coach tours.

Festivals & Events

Rally of the Lakes SPORTS
(www.rallyofthelakes.com) A major date on Ireland's motorsports calendar, this on-road rally sees drivers take death-defying twists and turns around the lakes and mountains over the May bank holiday weekend. During the rally, campsites and accommodation will be packed, and local roads (including the Healy Pass in County Cork and the N71 Killarney–Kenmare route) may be temporarily closed. Held in late April or early May.

Killarney FolkFest MUSIC
(www.folkfestkillarney.com) A new festival of folk music in late July, with an impressive lineup of Irish and international artists.

Sleeping

You'll find numerous B&Bs just outside the centre on Rock, Lewis and Muckross Rds. The town also has scores of generic hotels aimed at tour groups. Many places offer bike hire (around €12 to €15 per day) and discounted tours. Book ahead everywhere in summer.

★ Fleming's White Bridge Caravan & Camping Park CAMPGROUND €
(086 363 0266; www.killarneycamping.com; White Bridge, Ballycasheen Rd; sites vehicle plus 2 adults €25, hiker €10; mid-Mar–Oct;) A lovely, family-run campsite about 2km southeast of the town centre off the N22, Fleming's has a games room, bike hire, campers' kitchen, laundry and free trout fishing on the river that runs alongside. Your man Hillary at reception can arrange bus, bike and boat tours, if he doesn't talk the legs off you first!

Súgán Hostel HOSTEL €
(064-663 3104; Lewis Rd; dm €15-18, tw €40-44;) Behind its publike front, 250-year-old Súgán is an amiably eccentric hostel with an open fire in the cosy common room, low, crazy-cornered ceilings and hardwood floors. Check in at the next-door pub, a handy spot for a pint of Guinness once you're settled in.

KERRY FARMERS MARKETS

Farmers markets throughout County Kerry vary depending on the season. For updated details of towns hosting markets, visit www.mast.ie/Kerry.html.

Neptune's Killarney Town Hostel HOSTEL €
(064-663 5255; www.neptuneshostel.com; Bishop's Lane, New St; dm €18-22, tw €44-54;) Basic but adequate, this hostel has a great central location without being too noisy. Its best aspect is the staff's unfailing helpfulness – they provide local advice and will sort out bus and boat tours for you. There's a laundry service; rates include breakfast.

★ Crystal Springs B&B €€
(064-663 3272; www.crystalspringsbb.com; Ballycasheen Cross, Woodlawn Rd; s/d €70/95;) The timber deck of this wonderfully relaxing B&B overhangs the River Flesk, where trout anglers can fish for free. Rooms are richly furnished with patterned wallpapers and walnut timber; private bathrooms (most with spa baths) are huge. The glass-enclosed breakfast room also overlooks the rushing river. It's about a 15-minute stroll into town.

Algret House B&B €€
(064-663 2337; www.algret.com; Countess Grove; s/d/f €48/90/140;) Knotted pine and polished wood dominate the decor of this light, bright and spacious modern villa, on a quiet side street just a five-minute walk south of the town centre. Friendly hosts make staying here a real pleasure.

Kingfisher Lodge B&B €€
(064-663 7131; www.kingfisherlodgekillarney.com; Lewis Rd; s/d/f €70/105/130; mid Feb–Nov;) Lovely gardens are a highlight at this tidy B&B, whose guest rooms are done up in warm but vivid colours; showers are good and powerful, and breakfasts hearty. Owner Donal Carroll is a certified walking guide with a wealth of knowledge on hiking in the area.

Chelmsford House B&B €€
(064-663 6402; www.chelmsfordguesthouse.com; 1 Muckross View; r from €80;) Set on a rise to the south of town, this B&B enjoys a superb view of the Kerry mountains (and even a glimpse of Lough Leane). All three

rooms have a private bathroom – try to get the double with the balcony. It's on a quiet terrace with a 10-minute stroll into town.

Fairview B&B €€

(☎064-663 4164; www.fairviewkillarney.com; Lewis Rd; s/d €100/139; @📶) Done out in beautiful timbers, the individually decorated rooms (some with classical printed wallpaper, some with contemporary sofas and glass) at this boutique guesthouse offer more bang for your buck than bigger, less personal places. A veritable feast is laid on at breakfast, and the elegant in-house restaurant is a winner come evening.

Killarney Haven APARTMENTS €€

(☎064-663 3570; www.killarney-selfcatering.com; Msgr O'Flaherty Rd; 2-person apt for 2 nights from €200; 👪) The decor may be slightly dated, but these well-equipped self-catering apartments are clean and comfortable (some have balconies) and have a great location in the town centre, complete with secure parking.

Malton HOTEL €€€

(☎064-663 8000; www.themalton.com; s/d from €120/180; @📶🏊👪) So commanding it doesn't need an address, the Georgian-style Malton first opened its doors in 1854 as the Railway Hotel. Inside its virginia-creeper-clad walls, it's had a thorough refit; the pick of the rooms are those in the 1852 wing, which have retained their period opulence. There's a spa and leisure centre with swimming pool, gym and two tennis courts.

Killarney Plaza Hotel HOTEL €€€

(☎064-662 1100; www.killarneyplaza.com; Kenmare Pl; s/d from €119/164; @📶🏊👪) Although it dates only from 2002, this large, 198-room hotel channels the art-deco style of an earlier era. Classically furnished guest rooms and public facilities are in keeping with its luxury reputation; besides the marble lobby and lavishly tiled indoor pool, there's a sauna, steam room and spa.

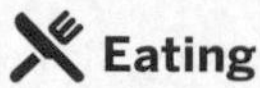

Eating

Many of Killarney's hotels have excellent restaurants. As elsewhere in Kerry, fresh seafood stars on many menus.

Jam CAFE €

(☎064-663 7716; www.jam.ie; 77 Old Market Lane; mains €4-11; ⊙8am-5pm Mon-Sat, 9am-5pm Sun; 👪) Duck down the alley to this local hideout for a changing menu of deli sandwiches, coffee and cake, and hot lunch dishes like shepherd's pie. It's all made with locally sourced produce and there are a few tables out front.

Lir Café CAFE €

(☎064-663 3859; www.lircafe.com; Kenmare Pl; mains €3-7; ⊙8am-9pm Mon-Thu, to 9.30pm Fri & Sat, to 7pm Sun; 📶) Great coffee and hip atmosphere in Killarney's coolest cafe; food is limited to cakes, biscuits and the real treat, handmade chocolates, including Bailey's truffles.

Mareena's Simply Food IRISH €€

(☎066-663 7787; www.mareenassimplyfood.com; East Avenue Rd; mains €17-23; ⊙noon-2.30pm & 6-9pm Tue-Sun) The clue is in the name – Mareena's serves the finest of locally sourced produce, from scallops and sea bass to neck of lamb and pork fillet, cooked plainly and simply to let the quality of the food speak for itself. The decor matches the cuisine – unfussy and understated.

Smoke House STEAK, SEAFOOD €€

(☎087 233 9611; http://thesmokehouse.ie; 8 High St; mains lunch €7-16, dinner €15-29; ⊙9am-10pm) One of Killarney's busiest restaurants, this always-crowded bistro was the first establishment in Ireland to cook with a Josper (superhot Spanish charcoal oven). Stylish salads include Dingle prawn, while the Kerry surf'n'turf platter – a half-lobster and fillet steak – is decadence on a plate. Brunch, served from noon till 3pm, includes eggs Florentine and Benedict.

THE KERRY WAY

The 214km **Kerry Way** (www.kerryway.com) is the Republic's longest waymarked footpath. Starting and ending in Killarney, it winds through the spectacular Macgillycuddy's Reeks, Ireland's highest mountain range, before continuing around the Kerry coast through Caherciveen, Waterville, Caherdaniel, Sneem and Kenmare.

It takes around 10 days to complete the whole route; with less time it's worth hiking the first three days as far as Glenbeigh, from where a bus or a lift could return you to Killarney. Accommodation along the trail is listed on the website. Ordnance Survey 1:50,000 maps 78, 83 and 84 cover the walk.

Bricín IRISH €€
(www.bricin.com; 26 High St; mains €19-26; ⏲6-9pm Tue-Sat) Decorated with fittings from a convent, an orphanage and a school, this Celtic deco restaurant doubles as the town museum, with Jonathan Fisher's 18th-century views of the national park taking pride of place. Try the house speciality, boxty (traditional potato pancake). Two-/three-course dinner for €22/25 before 6.45pm.

Treyvaud's IRISH €€€
(☎066-663 3062; www.treyvaudsrestaurant.com; 62 High St; mains €20-30; ⏲noon-10pm Sun-Thu, to 10.30pm Fri & Sat) Michael Treyvaud's modish restaurant has a strong reputation for subtle dishes that merge trad Irish with seductive European influences. The seafood chowder at lunch is a velvet stew of mussels and salmon; dinner mains include the best of local lamb and a hearty bacon and cabbage platter.

Gaby's Seafood Restaurant SEAFOOD €€€
(☎064-663 2519; 27 High St; mains €30-50; ⏲6-10pm Mon-Sat) Gaby's is a refined dining experience serving superb seafood in a traditional manner. Peruse the menu by the fire before drifting past the wine racks to the low-lit dining room to savour exquisite Gallic dishes such as lobster in cognac and cream. The wine list is long and the advice unerring.

Drinking & Entertainment

Most pubs put on live music, and nights are lively.

★O'Connor's PUB
(7 High St; ⏲10.30am-11pm Mon-Thu, to 12.30am Fri & Sat, 12.30-11pm Sun) This tiny traditional pub with leaded-glass doors is one of Killarney's most popular haunts. Live music plays every night; good bar food is served daily in summer. In warmer weather, the crowds spill out onto the adjacent lane.

Courtney's PUB
(www.courtneysbar.com; Plunkett St; ⏲2-11.30pm Sun-Thu, to 12.30am Fri & Sat, from 5pm winter) Inconspicuous on the outside, inside this timeless pub bursts at the seams with Irish music sessions many nights year-round. This is where locals come to see their old mates perform and to kick off a night on the town.

Killarney Grand BAR, CLUB
(www.killarneygrand.com; Main St; admission before 11pm free, after 11pm €5-10; ⏲7.30pm-2.30am Mon-Sat, to 1.30am Sun) The bars and clubs at this Killarney institution host traditional live music from 9pm to 11pm, rock bands from 11.30pm to 1.30am and a disco from 11pm.

Shopping

Variety Sounds MUSIC
(College St; ⏲10am-6pm Mon-Sat, noon-6pm Sun) Eclectic music shop with a good range of traditional music, instruments, sheet music and hard-to-find recordings.

Killarney Outdoor Store OUTDOOR EQUIPMENT
(www.killarneyrentabike.com; New St; ⏲10am-6pm Mon-Sat, noon-6pm Sun) Crams a vast amount of camping and climbing gear into a small space.

Bricín CRAFTS
(www.bricin.com; 26 High St; ⏲10am-9pm Mon-Sat) Interesting local craftwork, including jewellery and pottery, alongside touristy wares, plus a restaurant.

Dungeon Bookshop BOOKS
(College St; ⏲8am-9pm) Excellent secondhand bookshop hidden above a newsagent (take the stairs at the back of the shop).

Information

The closest accident and emergency unit is at Tralee General Hospital, 32km northwest of Killarney.

O'Neill's (☎064-6631 970; 6 Plunkett St; ⏲10am-9.30pm Mon-Fri, 10am-9pm Sat & Sun) Information, permits, licences and hire equipment can be obtained at O'Neill's, which looks like a gift shop but is a long-established fishing centre.

SouthDoc (☎1850 335 999; www.southdoc.ie; Upper Park Rd; ⏲6pm-8am Mon-Fri, 1pm Sat-8am Mon) Access to family doctor service outside normal hours; clinic is 500m east of the centre, just east of the roundabout on the N22.

Tourist Office (☎064-663 1633; www.killarney.ie; Beech Rd; ⏲9am-5pm Mon-Sat; 📶) Can handle most queries; especially good with transport intricacies.

Getting There & Away

AIR

Kerry Airport (KIR; ☎066-976 4644; www.kerryairport.ie) is at Farranfore, about 17km north of Killarney on the N22. There are daily flights to Dublin and London's Luton and Stansted airports, and less frequent services to Frankfurt-Hahn, Germany; Faro, Portugal; and Alicante, Spain.

The small airport has a restaurant, bar, bureau de change and ATM. Virtually all the major car-hire firms have desks at the airport.

BUS

Bus Éireann (☎064-663 0011; www.buseireann.ie) operates from the bus station on Park Rd. For Dublin you need to change at Cork – the train is much faster. **Citylink** (☎091 564164; www.citylink.ie) buses to Galway leave from the coach stop outside the Malton Hotel on East Avenue Rd.

Cork (€27, two hours, hourly)
Dublin (€40, six hours, six daily)
Galway (Citylink; €30, three hours, two daily)
Limerick (€22.50, two hours, every two hours)
Tralee (€10.70, 40 minutes, hourly)
Waterford (€28.50, 4¾ hours, hourly)

TRAIN

Killarney's train station is behind the Malton Hotel, just east of the centre. Although close to the bus station, there is no direct connection – you have to walk down to East Avenue Rd and back through Killarney Outlet Centre mall.

There are one or two direct services per day to Cork and Dublin; otherwise you'll have to change at Mallow.

Cork (€27.80, 1½ hours)
Dublin (€69, 3¼ hours, every two hours)
Tralee (€111.35, 30 minutes, every two hours)

Getting Around

TO/FROM THE AIRPORT

- Bus Éireann has hourly services between Killarney and Kerry Airport (€5.50, 20 minutes).
- Tralee–Killarney trains stop at Farranfore station (€8.70, 20 minutes), a 10-minute walk (at minimum) from the airport.
- A taxi to Killarney costs about €35.

BICYCLE

Bicycles are ideal for exploring the scattered sights of the Killarney area, many of which are accessible only by bike or on foot. **O'Sullivan's Bike Hire** (☎064-663 1282; www.killarneyrentabike.com; College St; per day/week €15/80) has branches on College St, on Beech Rd (opposite the tourist office) and on Muckross road (opposite Randles Court Hotel). Road, mountain and children's bikes are available.

BUS

The very useful **Killarney Shuttle Bus** (☎087 138 4384; www.killarneyshuttlebus.com; one-way €2-6) service runs daily from the tourist office to all the main tourist spots, including Gap of Dunloe, Cronin's Yard, Ross Castle, Muckross House, Torc Waterfall and Ladies View. Buy tickets from the driver. A full-day ticket giving unlimited travel on the shuttle bus costs €10.

CAR RENTAL

Budget (☎064-663 4341; www.budget.ie; International Hotel, Kenmare Pl; ⏲9am-6pm Mon-Fri, to 3pm Sat)

Enterprise (☎064-9021432; www.enterprise.ie; Pat Looney Car Sales, Upper Park Rd; ⏲8am-6pm Mon-Fri, 9am-noon Sat)

TAXI

The town taxi rank is on College St. Taxi companies include **Killarney Taxi & Tours** (☎085-280 3333; www.killarneytaxi.com).

AROUND KILLARNEY

Aghadoe

On a hilltop just 5km west of town, Aghadoe's sweeping views of Killarney, the lakes and Inisfallen Island have made jaws drop for centuries. At the eastern end of the hilltop meadow are the ruins of a **Romanesque church** and the 13th-century **Parkavonear Castle**. Parkavonear's keep, still standing, is one of the few cylindrical keeps built by the Normans in Ireland.

Hop-on, hop-off bus tours stop here, and the Killarney Shuttle Bus calls three times daily.

Killarney National Park

Any cynicism engendered by Killarney's shamrock-filled souvenir stores evaporates when you begin to explore the sublime **Killarney National Park** (www.killarneynationalpark.ie) FREE. Ross Castle and Muckross House draw big crowds, but it's possible to escape amid Ireland's largest area of ancient oak woods, panoramic views of its highest mountains, and the country's only wild herd of native red deer.

The core of the national park is the Muckross Estate, donated to the state by Arthur Bourn Vincent in 1932; the park was designated a Unesco Biosphere Reserve in 1982. The **Killarney Lakes** – Lough Leane (the Lower Lake, or 'Lake of Learning'), Muckross (or Middle) Lake and the Upper Lake – make up about a quarter of the park, surrounded by natural oak and yew woodland, and overlooked by the high crags and moors of **Purple Mountain** (832m) to the west and **Knockrower** (552m) to the south.

The park is rich in wildlife as well as scenic beauty: deer swim out to graze on the lake islands, red squirrels and pine martens scamper in the woods, and salmon and brown trout thrive in the clean waters. Fifteen **white-tailed eagles** were reintroduced here in 2007; by 2015 at least four nesting pairs were established in County Kerry, with one pair breeding successfully in the national park. Aquatic rarities include Arctic char (a deep-water relative of the trout, and a relict of the last ice age), and the Killarney shad, or *goureen* (a subspecies of the marine twaite shad, unique to the lakes).

Killarney tourist office stocks walking guides and maps.

Getting There & Around

Walking, **cycling** and **boat** trips are the best ways to explore the park. There are two pedestrian/bike entrances in Killarney town: opposite St Mary's Cathedral (24-hour access); and the so-called **Golden Gates** at the roundabout on Muckross Rd (open 8am to 7pm June to August, to 6pm April, May and October, to 5pm November to March).

From the cathedral entrance it's 2.5km (30 minutes walk) to Ross Castle; to reach Muckross Estate on foot or by bike you have to follow the cycle path beside the N71 south for 3km where it veers off towards the lake (its 5km all up to Muckross House).

Jaunting cars Depart from Kenmare Pl in Killarney town centre, and from the Jaunting Car Entrance to Muckross Estate, at a car park 3km south of town on the N71. Expect to pay around €15 to €20 per person for a tour from Killarney to Ross Castle and back. There are no set prices; haggle for longer tours.

Vehicle access Via Ross Rd on the southern edge of Killarney town centre, leading to Ross Castle car park; and the Muckross Estate entrance on the N71, 5km south of Killarney, leading to the Muckross House car park; parking is free.

Sights

Muckross House HISTORIC BUILDING

(064-667 0144; www.muckross-house.ie; Muckross Estate; adult/child €9/6, incl Muckross Trad Farms €15/10.50; 9am-7pm Jul & Aug, to 5.30pm Sep-Jun) This impressive Victorian mansion is crammed with fascinating objects (70% of the contents are original). Portraits by John Singer Sargent adorn the walls alongside trophy stags' heads and giant stuffed trout, while antique Killarney furniture, with its distinctive inlaid scenes of local beauty spots, graces the grand apartments along with tapestries, Persian rugs, silverware and china specially commissioned for Queen Victoria's visit in 1861. It's 5km south of Killarney, signposted from the N71.

The house, built as a hunting and fishing lodge for the Herbert family in 1843, is set in beautiful gardens that slope down to the Middle Lake. At the gate, jaunting cars wait to run you through deer parks and woodland to Torc Waterfall and Muckross Abbey (about €20 each return; haggle for a discount).

A block behind the main house contains a craft shop and studios where you can see potters, weavers and bookbinders at work; the nearby visitor centre has an excellent cafe.

Muckross Traditional Farms MUSEUM

(064-663 0804; www.muckross-house.ie; Muckross Estate; adult/child €9/6, incl Muckross

MUCKROSS LAKE LOOP TRAIL

You could easily spend most of a day dawdling around this waymarked 9.5km loop trail (anticlockwise only for cyclists), which takes in some of the most photogenic parts of Killarney National Park. Starting from Muckross House, you head west through lovely lakeshore woods (with lots of side trails to explore) to reach postcard-pretty **Brickeen Bridge**, which spans the channel linking Lough Leane and the Middle Lake. Continue to **Dinis Cottage** (tearoom open May to September) amid the sylvan glades that surround the **Meeting of the Waters**, where channels from all three of Killarney's lakes merge. A boat taxi runs between Dinis Cottage and Dundag Pier near Muckross House (per person €7).

Don't miss the 10-minute side trail (no bikes) from Dinis to **Old Weir Bridge**, where you can watch tour boats powering through the narrow, rocky channel beneath its twin arches (here, a swiftly flowing current links the Upper and Middle lakes).

On the return leg along the south shore of Middle Lake, the trail passes through woods before reaching the N71 Killarney–Kenmare road. Here, walkers have the option of climbing uphill on the other side of the road to visit **Torc Waterfall** before returning to Muckross House. Cyclists have to follow the main road east for 1km before regaining the off-road trail. Between the road and Muckross House you have the option of detouring along the **Old Boathouse Nature Trail**, which leads around a scenic peninsula.

Maps and details are available from the Killarney tourist office and Muckross House ticket office.

Around Killarney

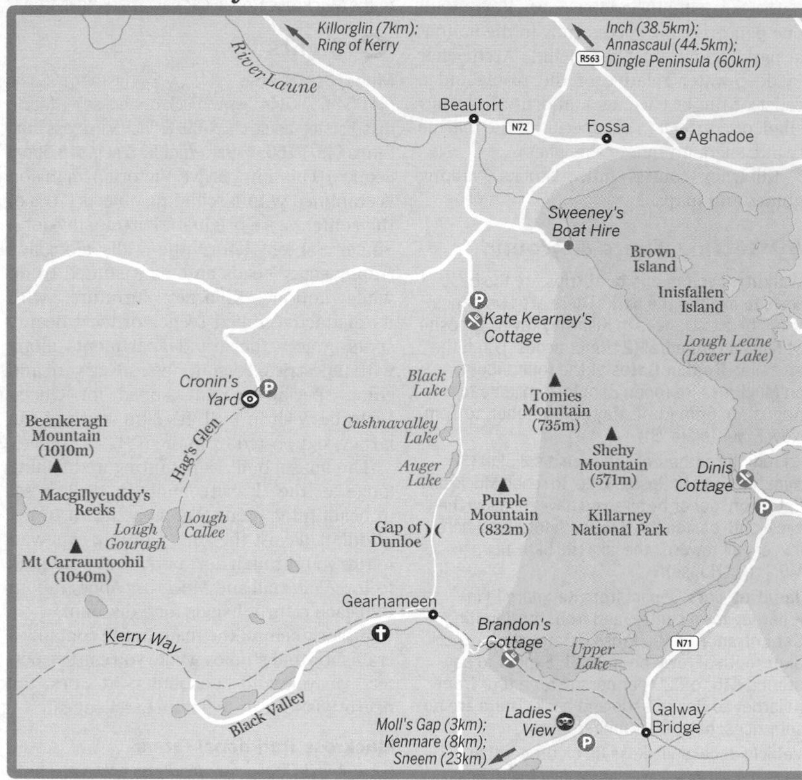

House €15/10.50; ⏲10am-6pm Jun-Aug, 1-6pm May & Sep, 1-6pm Sat, Sun Apr & Oct) These recreations of 1930s farms evoke the sights, sounds and smells of real farming – cow dung, hay, wet earth and peat smoke, plus a cacophony of chickens, ducks, pigs and donkeys. Costumed guides bring the traditional farm buildings to life, and the petting area allows kids to get up close and personal with piglets, lambs, ducklings and chicks. The farms are immediately east of Muckross House; you'll need at least two hours to do justice to the self-guided tour.

Muckross Abbey RUINS

(Muckross Estate; ⏲24hrs) FREE This well-preserved ruin (actually a friary, though everyone calls it an abbey) was founded in 1448 and burned by Cromwell's troops in 1652. There's a square-towered church and a small, atmospheric cloister with a giant yew tree in the centre (legend has it that the tree is as old as the abbey). In the chancel is the tomb of the McCarthy Mòr chieftains, and an elaborate 19th-century memorial to local philanthropist Lucy Gallwey. The abbey is 1.5km north of Muckross House (signposted).

Ross Castle CASTLE

(☎064-663 5851; www.heritageireland.ie; Ross Rd; adult/child €4/2; ⏲9am-5.45pm Mar-Oct) Lakeside Ross Castle dates back to the 15th century, when it was a residence of the O'Donoghue family. It was the last place in Munster to succumb to Cromwell's forces, thanks partly to its cunning spiral staircase, every step of which is a different height in order to break an attacker's stride. The castle is a lovely 3km walk or bike ride from the pedestrian park entrance; you may well spot deer along the way.

Inisfallen ISLAND

The first monastery on Inisfallen (the largest of the lake's islands) was founded by St Finian the Leper in the 7th century. The

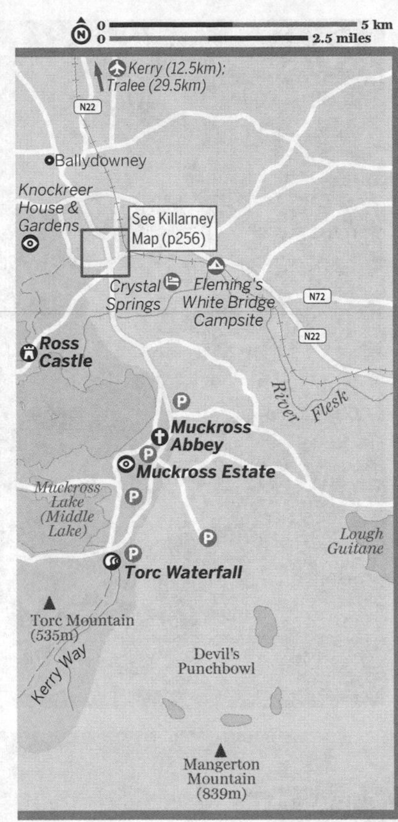

extensive ruins of a 12th-century **Augustinian priory** and an oratory with a carved Romanesque doorway stand on the site of St Finian's original. You can hire a motor boat with boatman (around €10) from Ross Castle for the 10-minute trip to the island. In calm weather you can hire a rowing boat (€5 per hour; allow 30 minutes each way).

Inisfallen's fame dates from the early 13th century when the Annals of Inisfallen were written here. Now in the Bodleian Library at Oxford, they remain a vital source of information on early Munster history.

Knockreer House & Gardens PARK
(8am-7pm Jun-Aug, to 6pm Apr-May & Oct, to 5pm Nov-Mar) FREE Killarney House, built for the Earl of Kenmare in the 1870s, burned down in 1913; the present Knockreer House was built on the same site in 1958 and is now home to a national park education centre. It isn't open to the public, but its gardens, featuring a terraced lawn and a summerhouse, have magnificent views across the lakes to the mountains.

From the park entrance opposite St Mary's Cathedral, follow the path to your right for about 500m.

Activities

Killarney Lake Tours BOAT TOUR
(064-663 2638; www.killarneylaketours.ie; Ross Castle Pier; adult/child €10/5; Apr-Oct) One-hour tours of Lough Leane in a comfortable, enclosed cruise boat depart four times daily from the pier beside Ross Castle, taking in the island of Inisfallen (no landing) and O'Sullivan's Cascade (a waterfall on the west shore).

Ross Castle Traditional Boats BOAT TOUR
(085 174 2997; Ross Castle Pier; 9am-5.30pm) The open boats at Ross Castle offer appealing trips with boatmen who define the word 'character'. Rates are around €10 per person for a trip to Inisfallen or the Middle Lake and back; €15 for a tour of all three lakes.

Outdoors Ireland ADVENTURE SPORTS
(086 860 4563; www.outdoorsireland.com) Guided kayak tours of the Killarney lakes (per person €50; no previous experience needed). Also three-hour sunset kayak trips (€55), one-day beginners' rock-climbing courses (€80) and canyoning in the Gap of Dunloe (€80).

Trout Fishing FISHING
(www.fishinginireland.info; season 14 Feb-12 Oct) Fishing for brown trout in the lakes of Killarney National Park is free (no permit needed). Fishing from the bank is allowed, but the best sport is to be had from a boat, which you can hire at Ross Castle or at **Sweeney's** (064-664 4207; www.theinvicta.com; Invicta B&B, Tomies, Beaufort) (at the west end of Lough Leane) for €55 a day (including outboard motor; up to three people).

O'Neill's (p259) in Killarney provides information, rents tackle, and sells permits and licences.

Salmon Fishing FISHING
(www.fishinginireland.info) The River Laune, which flows from Lough Leane to the sea, is one of Ireland's best salmon rivers. The season runs from 17 January to 30 September, with the best fishing from late July onwards. Both a permit (one day/seven days from €25/140) and a state rod licence (one day/three weeks €20/40) are required. You can also fish for salmon in the Killarney lakes (no permit needed, but state rod licence still required).

1. Arctic char **2.** Red deer **3.** White-tailed eagle
4. View of the Upper Lake (p260), Killarney National Park

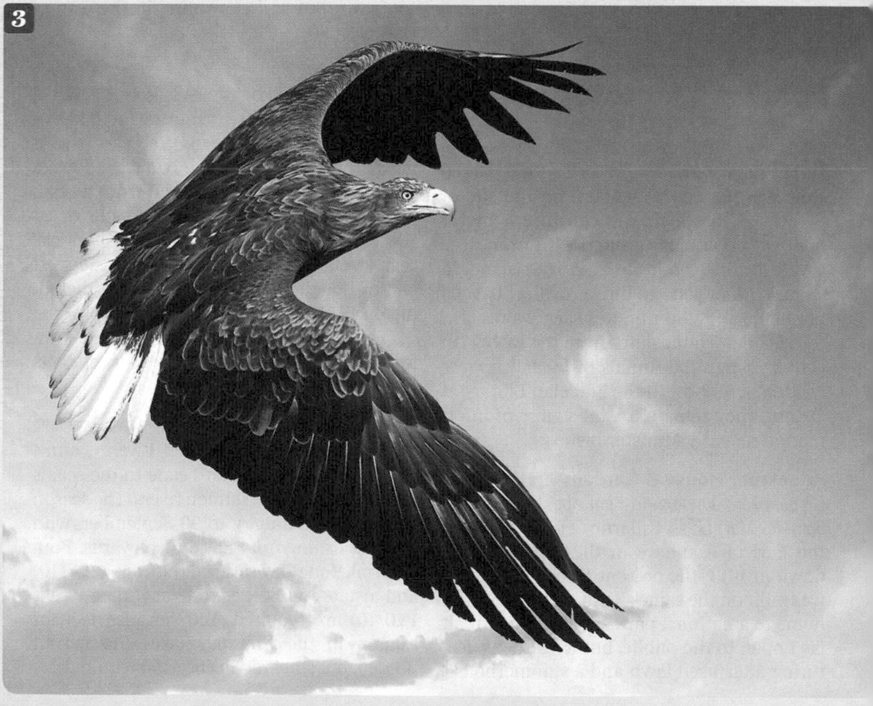

3

CHRIS HILL/GETTY IMAGES ©

Wildlife in Killarney National Park

Although Killarney is one of southwestern Ireland's liveliest urban centres, a plethora of wildlife lives right on its doorstep, including some of the rarest species in the country.

Red Deer

The park's upland areas are home to Ireland's only remaining wild herd of native red deer (around 700 individuals). They are the sole survivors of a population that has lived here continuously since the end of the last ice age around 10,000 years ago. The deer are concentrated on the upper slopes of Torc Mountain and Mangerton Mountain to the south of Muckross Lake, though you are more likely to spot them in winter when bad weather forces them down to lower altitudes to forage for food.

Fish

Fish in the park's waterways include brown trout and salmon, as well as rare Arctic char and Killarney shad.

White-Tailed Eagles

Eagles once nested in the Killarney area (hence the name of Eagle's Nest Mountain above the Upper Lake), but were hunted to extinction in the late 19th century. In recent years, white-tailed eagles have been reintroduced to the national park, with 15 to 20 birds (brought over from Norway) released each year from 2007 to 2011. These birds have since dispersed to many parts of Ireland, and in 2015 at least five pairs successfully hatched chicks, including one pair in Killarney National Park.

The eagles can frequently be spotted hunting over the lakes and in the Black Valley to the south, easily recognised because of their large size (they have a 2.5m wingspan). Look out for noisy flocks of crows, which often mob the eagles when they descend to lower levels.

Permits and licences are available from O'Neill's (p259) in Killarney.

Gap of Dunloe

The Gap of Dunloe is a wild and scenic mountain pass, studded with crags and bejewelled with lakes and waterfalls, that lies to the west of Killarney National Park, squeezed between Purple Mountain and the high summits of Macgillycuddy's Reeks (Ireland's highest mountain range).

Although it lies outside the park, it has been a vital part of the Killarney tourist trail since the late 18th century when, inspired by the Romantic poets, wealthy tourists came in search of 'sublime' and 'savage' landscapes.

It was during this period that the legend of Kate Kearney first arose: Kate, a fabled local beauty based on a popular song, supposedly lived in a cottage in the pass and dispensed *poteen* (illegally distilled whiskey) to weary travellers. The 19th-century pub at the northern end of the Gap is still known as **Kate Kearney's Cottage** (☎064-664 4146; www.katekearneyscottage.com; mains €8-20; ⏱food served noon-8pm; 👪); there's a busy car park here, where you can rent jaunting cars (cash only).

At the south end of the Gap, the road twists steeply down to the remote Black Valley and **Lord Brandon's Cottage** (dishes €3-6; ⏱breakfast & lunch Apr-Oct), a ruined 19th-century hunting lodge surrounded by lush, green water meadows beside the Upper Lake. You can reach Lord Brandon's Cottage by car via a steep minor road from the R568 near Moll's Gap; it takes about 45 minutes from Killarney.

The traditional way to see the Gap is via a tour from Killarney – by bus to Kate Kearney's Cottage, then either on foot or by jaunting car through the Gap to Lord Brandon's Cottage on the Upper Lake, and finally by boat to Ross Castle and then bus back to town (per person €30, plus €20 for jaunting car). Most hostels, hotels and pubs in Killarney can set up these tours.

DON'T MISS

BY BOAT AND BIKE THROUGH THE GAP

A boat trip through the lakes followed by a bike ride through the Gap of Dunloe is the classic Killarney experience. Your hostel, hotel or campsite can arrange it for you (per person €15, plus bike hire €12 to €15 per day).

Boats leave from Reen Pier (signposted just north of Ross Castle – not to be confused with the pier at Ross Castle itself) at 11am, with bikes propped in the bow. The 1½-hour cruise alone justifies the price; ask your boatman about the highest/lowest level he has ever seen in the lakes, and sit back to enjoy the story.

You cruise past Inisfallen with its ruined monastery then turn south to sail under pretty Brickeen Bridge and reach the Meeting of the Waters. The boat then surges up a rocky channel beneath the Old Weir Bridge – after prolonged dry weather, when lake levels are low, passengers may have to get out and walk a short distance while the boat gets hauled up this shallow, fast-flowing section.

The Long Range is next, a winding channel that is half-lake, half-river, uncoiling beneath the crags of Eagle's Nest mountain (golden eagles once nested here) before entering the long, narrow Upper Lake.

After disembarking at Lord Brandon's Cottage at around 12.30pm (where there's a cafe and toilets), you begin the bike section with a 5km climb to the head of the Gap. It's a steady uphill climb, but not too steep, and there's no shame in getting off and pushing for a bit. At the summit you're rewarded with stunning views in both directions, and a 6km downhill run to Kate Kearney's Cottage (cafe, pub and toilets).

From here, you follow signs for Killarney along minor roads to the N71, then a cycle path that first hugs the side of the main road before veering off through the golf course and the northern part of Killarney National Park to end near the town centre opposite St Mary's Cathedral.

Total distance cycled is 23km; allowing time for stops and an hour for lunch, you should be back in Killarney by 3.30pm. Hikers can also do this route – allow three hours to walk from Lord Brandon's to Kate Kearney's, and take the Killarney Shuttle Bus from the latter back into town (departs at 4.30pm; confirm times in advance).

Warning: Despite a road sign at Kate Kearney's Cottage implying that cars are forbidden, it is perfectly legal to drive through the Gap of Dunloe – it's a public road. However, driving the Gap is not recommended, at least from Easter to September. The road is very narrow, steep and twisting, and is usually crowded with walkers, cyclists, ponies and jaunting cars (these drivers will give you short shrift). Early morning, or after 5pm is best.

Macgillycuddy's Reeks

Macgillycuddy's Reeks is Ireland's highest mountain range, encompassing nine of the country's 12 summits that exceed 900m in altitude. The name dates from the 18th century – the MacGillycuddy clan were local landowners, and 'reeks' is dialect meaning 'stacks' (a reference to the layered nature of the rocks here).

The best approach to the hills is from **Cronin's Yard** (☎064-662 4044; www.croninsyard.com; Mealis, Beaufort; camping pods per person €10), where there's a car park (€2), tearoom (packed lunches available on request), showers and toilets, a basic campsite and a couple of nifty new camping pods. It's at the road's end (OS ref 836873), reached from the N72 via Beaufort, west of Killarney; follow signs for the Gap of Dunloe at first, but keep straight on where the Gap is signposted left. After 4km you'll reach Kissane Foodstone and petrol station; 50m further on, over the bridge, Cronin's is signposted on the left.

You can get a taste of the Reeks at close quarters by following the waymarked loop trail up **Hag's Glen**, the beautiful approach valley that leads to loughs Callee and Gouragh below the towering east face of Carrauntoohil. From Cronin's Yard, the way lies along a stony track beside the River Gaddagh (round trip 8km).

There are several routes up **Carrauntoohil** (1040m), the country's highest peak. Even the easiest requires good hill-walking and route-finding abilities, while others are serious scrambling or rock-climbing routes. Until recently, the traditional route to the summit was via **Devil's Ladder**, a gruelling trudge up a badly eroded gully path southwest of the lakes. However, this has now become dangerously loose and unstable.

The recommended route now ascends via **Brother O'Shea's Gully** (some scrambling involved) and descends via the Zig-Zags to the east of the Devil's Ladder. Experienced hill walkers can follow the directions in Adrian Hendorff's guidebook, *The Dingle, Iveragh & Beara Peninsulas: A Walking Guide*. If you're in the slightest bit unsure, hire a guide – **Con Moriarty** (☎087 221 4002; www.hiddenirelandadventures.com) leads guided ascents of Carrauntoohil on Wednesday and Saturday for €75 per person (booking essential).

Climbing Carrauntoohil should never be attempted without a map and compass (and the skills to use them), proper hill-walking boots, waterproofs and spare food and water. Use Harvey's 1:30,000 *Macgillycuddy's Reeks Superwalker* map, or the 1:25,000 Ordnance Survey Adventure Series map (Macgillycuddy's Reeks & Killarney National Park).

Moll's Gap

Built in the 1820s to replace an older track to the east (the Old Kenmare Road, now followed by the Kerry Way hiking trail), the vista-crazy N71 Killarney to Kenmare road (32km) winds between rock and lake, with plenty of lay-bys to stop and admire the views (and recover from the switchback bends). Watch out for the buses squeezing along the road.

About 17km south of Killarney is **Ladies' View**, where the gorgeous panorama over the Upper Lake and Purple Mountain were enjoyed by Queen Victoria's ladies-in-waiting in 1861.

A further 5km south is the summit of the pass at **Moll's Gap**, worth a stop for great views and good eating – and not necessarily in that order. **Avoca Cafe** (☎064-663 4720; www.avoca.ie; mains €8-14; ⏲9.30am-5pm Mon-Fri, 10am-5pm Sat & Sun; 📶👪) has awesome panoramas and delicious fare including smoked-salmon salad, pistachio-studded pork terrine and decadent cakes.

RING OF KERRY

This 179km circuit of the Iveragh (*eev*-raa) peninsula pops up on every self-respecting tourist itinerary, and for good reason. The road winds past pristine beaches, medieval ruins, mountains and loughs (lakes), with ever-changing views of the island-dotted Atlantic. Even locals stop their cars to gawk at the rugged coastline – particularly between Waterville and Caherdaniel in the southwest of the peninsula, where the beauty dial is turned up to 11.

Ring of Kerry

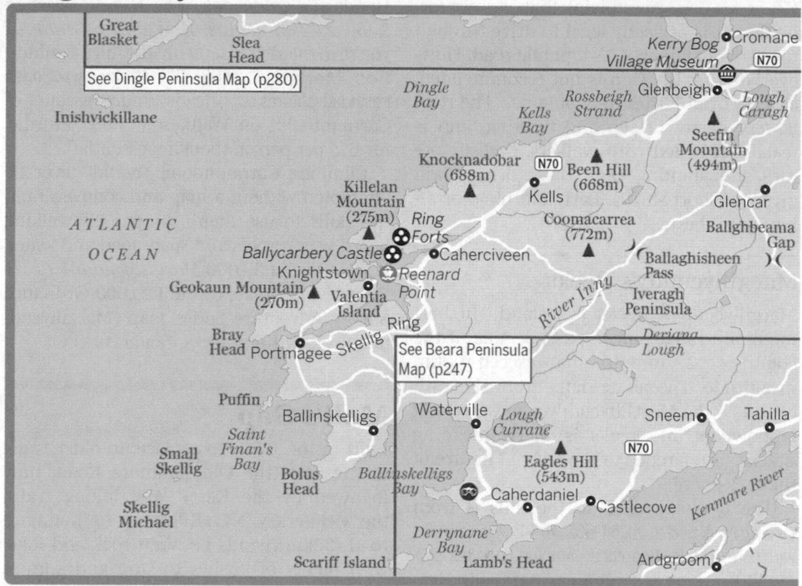

The Ring of Kerry can easily be a day trip, but if you want to stretch it out, places to stay are scattered along the route. Killorglin and Kenmare have the best concentration of dining options; elsewhere, with a couple of notable exceptions, basic pub fare is the norm.

If you want to get off the beaten track, explore the interior of the peninsula – on foot along the eastern section of the Kerry Way from Killarney to Glenbeigh, or by car or bike on the minor roads that cut through the hills, notably the Ballaghisheen Pass between Killorglin and Waterville, or the Ballaghbeama Gap from Glenbeigh to Gearha Bridge on the R568.

Getting Around

Although you can cover the Ring in one day by car or three days by bicycle, the more time you take, the more you'll enjoy it.

Tour buses travel the Ring in an anticlockwise direction. Getting stuck behind one is tedious, so consider driving clockwise; just watch out on blind corners. The road is narrow and twisty in places, but upgrades and widening works are underway.

Bus Éireann (☎064-663 0011; www.buseireann.ie) runs a once-daily Ring of Kerry bus service (No 280) from late June to late August. Buses leave Killarney at 11.30am and stop at Killorglin (€7.80, 30 minutes), Glenbeigh, Caherciveen (€17, 1¼ hours), Waterville (€19.20, 1¾ hours), Caherdaniel (€20.70, 2¼ hours) and Molls Gap, arriving back at Killarney (€22.50) at 4.45pm. Travel agencies and hostels in Killarney offer daily coach tours of the Ring for about €20 to €25, year-round, lasting from 10.30am tp 5pm.

A number of **Killarney tour companies** (p255) run daily bus trips around the Ring.

Killorglin

POP 2080

Travelling anticlockwise from Killarney, the first town on the Ring is Killorglin (Cill Orglain, meaning Orgla's Church). For most of the year, the town is quieter than the waters of the River Laune that lap against its 1885-built eight-arched bridge, where salmon leap and little egrets paddle in the shallows.

In August, however, there's an explosion of time-honoured ceremonies at the famous pagan festival, the Puck Fair (a statue of King Puck – a goat – stands on the north side of the river). Author Blake Morrison documents his mother's childhood here in *Things My Mother Never Told Me*.

Festivals & Events

Puck Fair Festival CULTURAL

(Aonach an Phuic; www.puckfair.ie) First recorded in 1603, with hazy origins, this lively festival is based around the custom of installing

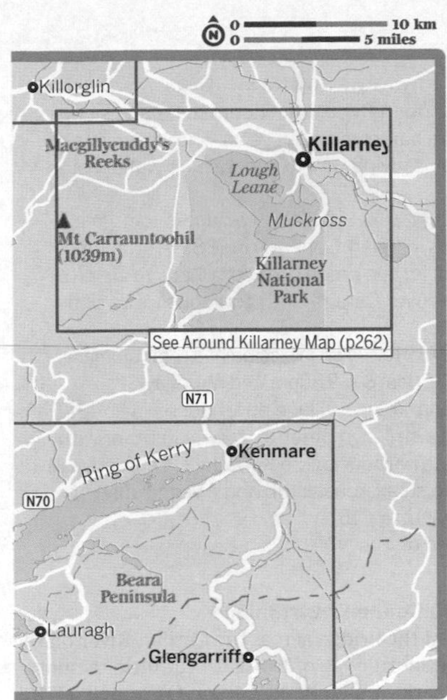

a billy goat (a poc, or puck), the symbol of mountainous Kerry, on a pedestal in the town, its horns festooned with ribbons. Other entertainment ranges from a horse fair and bonny baby competition to street theatre, concerts and fireworks; the pubs stay open until 3am. Held in August.

Sleeping & Eating

Coffey's River's Edge B&B €
(☎066-976 1750; www.coffeysriversedge.com; Lower Bridge St; s/d €50/70; 📶) You can sit out on the balcony overlooking the River Laune at this contemporary B&B with spotless spring-toned rooms and hardwood floors. Central location next to the bridge.

Jack's Bakery BAKERY €
(Lower Bridge St; ⏲8am-6.45pm Mon-Fri, to 6pm Sat, 9am-2pm Sun) Jack Healy bakes amazing artisan breads, and also serves killer coffee and beautiful sandwiches (using homemade pâtés) at this popular deli-cum-snack-bar; no indoor seating, but a couple of sidewalk tables in good weather.

Bianconi IRISH €€
(☎066-976 1146; www.bianconi.ie; Bridge St; mains €9-24; ⏲8am-11.30pm Mon-Thu, 8am-12.30am Fri & Sat, 6-11pm Sun; 📶 👪) Bang in the centre of town, this Victorian-style pub has a classy ambience and an equally classy menu. Its spectacular salads, such as Cashel blue cheese, apple, toasted almonds and chorizo, are a meal in themselves. Upstairs, newly refurbished guest rooms (doubles from €100) have olive and truffle tones and luxurious bathrooms (try for a rolltop tub).

Giovannelli ITALIAN €€
(☎087 123 1353; Lower Bridge St; mains €19-29; ⏲7-9pm Mon-Sat) Northern Italian native Daniele Giovannelli makes all of his pasta by hand at this simple but intimate little restaurant. Highlights of the blackboard menu might include seafood linguine with mussels in the shell, and beef ravioli in sage butter. Wonderful wines by the bottle and glass too.

Shopping

KRD Fisheries FOOD
(☎066-976 1106; www.krdfisheries.com; Tralee Rd; ⏲9am-1pm & 2-5pm Mon-Fri, 9am-1pm Sat, 9-11am Sun) You can buy organic smoked salmon direct from the smokery at this place, just across the bridge from Killorglin's town centre.

Information

The **Tourist Office** (☎066-976 1451; Library Pl; ⏲9am-5pm Mon-Fri) sells maps, walking guides, fishing permits and souvenirs.

Kerry Bog Village Museum

Kerry Bog Village Museum (www.kerrybogvillage.ie; Ballincleave, Glenbeigh; adult/child €6.50/4.50; ⏲9am-6pm; 👪) recreates a 19th-century bog village, typical of the small communities that carved out a precarious living in the harsh environment of Ireland's ubiquitous peat bogs. You'll see the thatched homes of the turfcutter, blacksmith, thatcher and labourer, as well as a dairy, and meet Kerry bog ponies (a native breed) and Irish wolfhounds. It's on the N70 between Killorglin and Glenbeigh; buy a ticket at the neighbouring Red Fox Inn if no one's at the gate.

Caherciveen

POP 1170

The main town of the Iveragh peninsula, Caherciveen (caar-suh-*veen;* from *cathair saidhbhín,* Little Sarah's Ring Fort) began life as a fishing harbour and market town but fell on hard times at the end of the 20th

OFF THE BEATEN TRACK

DOOKS AND CROMANE

Unless you know it's here, you wouldn't chance upon **Cromane**, home to Ireland's largest natural mussel beds (up to 8000 tonnes are harvested each year). The village sits at the base of a narrow shingle spit, with open fields giving way to spectacular water vistas and multihued sunsets.

Southwest of Cromane is **Dooks Golf Club** (066-976 8205; www.dooks.com; green fees €45-90), one of the oldest links golf courses in Ireland, opened in 1889. A little further along the road, an unsignposted lane (look for the green post box) leads to **Dooks Beach**, a little-visited gem at the mouth of the River Caragh, with gorgeous views of the Kerry and Dingle mountains.

Jacks Coastguard Restaurant (066-976 9102; www.jackscromane.com; Cromane; 2-course lunch €22.50, dinner mains €24-35; 1-3.30pm & 6-9.30pm Wed-Mon May-Sep, Wed-Sun Oct, Thu-Sun Feb-Apr, Nov & Dec, closed Jan;) is a village pub, housed in an 1886 coastguard station. A door at the back leads to a striking contemporary restaurant with picture windows looking out across Castlemaine harbour to the Kerry hills. Seafood is the standout item on the menu, but there's also steak, roast lamb and a veggie dish of the day. Lunch is also served in the bar (mains €11 to €15).

Cromane is 9km west of Killorglin, signposted off the N70.

century – indeed, O'Connell St (north of Main St) still looks like a boulevard of broken dreams, lined with abandoned hotels and pubs.

But the last few years have seen a determined effort to reinvent the town as a tourism centre. The main street and waterfront areas have been spruced up, the former barracks has been beautifully restored as a museum, there are some excellent places to stay and eat, and the surrounding countryside is a delight to explore.

The town is indelibly linked with the fight for Irish independence – it was the birthplace of Daniel O'Connell, 'the Great Liberator', and was where the first shots of the 1867 Fenian Rising were fired.

Sights

Old Barracks Heritage Centre MUSEUM

(066-401 0430; www.oldbarrackscahersiveen.com; Bridge St; adult/child €4/2; 10am-5.30pm Mon-Sat, 11am-5.30pm Sun) Established in response to the Fenian Rising of 1867, the Royal Irish Constabulary barracks at Caherciveen were built in an eccentric Bavarian-schloss style, complete with pointy turret and stepped gables. Burnt down in 1922 by anti-Treaty forces, the imposing building has been restored and now houses fascinating exhibitions on the the Fenian Rising and the life and works of local hero Daniel O'Connell.

The **town park**, which stretches along the riverbank behind the heritage centre, contains the outline of the ancient ring fort that gave the town its name.

O'Connell's Birthplace RUIN

At the bridge across the Carhan River on the eastern edge of town, a neat little memorial park remembers Daniel O'Connell (1775–1847), 'the Great Liberator', a political leader who campaigned for Catholic emancipation and Irish independence. He was born in the ruined cottage that stands on the far bank of the river.

Ring Forts RUIN

(Ballycarbery) FREE Two impressive stone ring forts stand 3km northwest of Caherciveen, both reached from a shared parking area. **Cahergal**, the larger and more impressive, dates from the 10th century and has stairways on the inside walls, a *clochán* (beehive hut), and the remains of a roundhouse. The smaller, 9th-century **Leacanabuile** contains the outlines of four houses. Both have a commanding position overlooking Valentia Harbour, with superb views of the Kerry mountains.

Ballycarbery Castle CASTLE

(Ballycarbery) FREE The atmospheric – and decidedly dangerous-looking – remains of 16th-century Ballycarbery Castle stand amid green pastures 3km northwest of Caherciveen.

Activities

Bentee Loop WALKING

The tourist office has maps and leaflets describing a whole range of waymarked local walks. The Bentee Loop (9km) starts in Caherciveen and leads to the 376m summit of Bentee, the conical hill just south of town, with superb views of Valentia Island the hills of the Iveragh peninsula.

Casey Cycles CYCLING
(☎066-947 2474; www.bikehirekerry.com; New St; per day €16; ⏲9am-6pm Mon-Sat year-round, 10am-1.30pm Sun Jul & Aug) Rents good-quality touring bikes (or road bikes, €35 per day), and provides information on local cycling routes. Good objectives include the ring forts at Cahergall, or Valentia Island (easily reached via the ferry just west of town).

Festivals & Events

Caherciveen Festival of Music & the Arts MUSIC
(www.celticmusicfestival.com) Celtic bands, busking competitions and Irish set-dancing star at this family-friendly festival held over the August bank holiday weekend.

Sleeping & Eating

Trad music sessions regularly take place in the town's pubs.

★Mannix Point Camping & Caravan Park CAMPGROUND €
(☎066-947 2806; www.campinginkerry.com; Mannix Point; hikers per person €8.50, vehicle plus 2 adults €25; ⏲15 Mar-15 Oct;) Mortimer Moriarty's award-winning waterfront campsite is one of Ireland's finest, with an inviting kitchen, campers' sitting room with peat fire (no TV but regular music sessions), a barbecue area and even a birdwatching platform. And the sunsets are stunning.

Sive Hostel HOSTEL €
(☎066-947 2717; www.sivehostel.ie; East End; dm/tw €17/48; @) Simple and sweet, this homely hostel has good-value private rooms, some in a cute stone cottage at the back, a rooftop balcony with great views, and a lovely courtyard area for sitting out.

San Antoine B&B €
(☎066-947 2521; www.sanantoine.com; Garranebane; s/d/f €50/70/110;) This spotless and spacious B&B on the western edge of town sports a large terrace and breakfast room, both with views towards sea and hills. The owners can help arrange boat trips to Skellig Michael, and advise on local walks and rides.

Camo's CAFE €
(☎066-948 1122; www.camos.ie; 24 Church St; mains €7-15; ⏲10am-5pm Mon-Thu, to 9.30pm Fri & Sat, noon-6pm Sun May-Sep, shorter hours Oct-Apr;) A friendly neighbourhood cafe that cooks familiar favourites really well – from fish and chips to steak sandwiches – Camo's also indulges in a bit of local foodie goodness with dishes such as oak-smoked-salmon sandwiches on home-baked brown bread, and a delicious black-pudding salad.

QCs Seafood Restaurant & Bar SEAFOOD €€
(☎066-947 2244; www.qcsrestaurant.com; 3 Main St; mains €16-30; ⏲12.30-2.30pm & 6-9.30pm Mon-Sat, 5-9pm Sun;) QCs is a modern take on a classic pub and as such is open pub hours for pints and craic. But when the kitchen's open, some of the finest food on the Ring pours forth (especially locally sourced seafood). Hours may vary – it's best to book ahead. Upstairs are six boutique B&B bedrooms (doubles from €109).

Valentia Island

POP 665

Familiar to generations of sailors through its weather station, whose readings are still reported nightly on the BBC's shipping forecast, Valentia is a beautiful and under-visited corner of Kerry with a rich and fascinating history. Just 11km long by 3km wide, its narrow roads are best explored by bicycle.

The island's Latin-sounding name is actually an anglicised version of the Gaelic *Béal Inse,* meaning 'the mouth of the island' (a reference to the sheltered harbour entrance), though the actual island's Gaelic name (Oileán Dairbhre) means 'island of oak trees'.

Valentia is renowned for its high-quality slate, which has been quarried here since 1816 – Valentia slate was used to roof London's Houses of Parliament and Westminster Cathedral, and Paris's Opera House. The quarry, abandoned in 1911, reopened in 1999 and produces all kinds of slate objects.

Valentia's other big claim to fame is being chosen as the eastern terminus of the first transatlantic telegraph cable, from Heart's Content, Newfoundland. A monument at **Telegraph Field**, at the western end of the island, commemorates the establishment of the first permanent communications link between Europe and North America in 1866; the telegraph station there continued in operation until 1966.

Sights & Activities

Knightstown, at the eastern end of the island, is Valentia's only village; it has a hotel, a couple of pubs, shops and cafes, and a tourist office.

ROBERT HARDING PRODUCTIONS/GETTY IMAGES ©

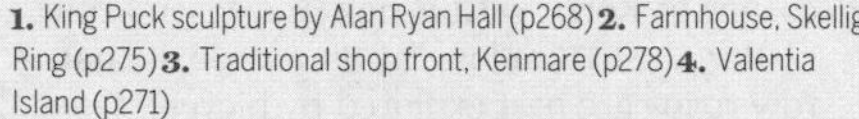

1. King Puck sculpture by Alan Ryan Hall (p268) **2.** Farmhouse, Skellig Ring (p275) **3.** Traditional shop front, Kenmare (p278) **4.** Valentia Island (p271)

RICHARD CUMMINS/GETTY IMAGES ©

Ring of Kerry

Windswept beaches, Atlantic waves crashing against rugged cliffs and islands, medieval ruins, soaring mountains and glinting loughs are some of the stunning distractions along the twisting 179km Ring of Kerry circle drive around the Iveragh Peninsula.

Killorglin

Even if you're racing around the ring, don't miss its first town (heading anticlockwise). The riverside village of Killorglin is home to a salmon smokehouse, some standout restaurants and, in August, the historic Puck Fair Festival.

Kenmare

A fitting last (or first) stop on the ring, Kenmare is a microcosm of Kerry's greatest charms. A beautiful location on the bay (from where boat trips depart), colourful shops and gracious architecture are cornerstones of this classic Irish town.

Skellig Ring

A ring within the ring, this 18km loop off the main route offers an escape from the crowds. The wild, scenic drive links Portmagee and Waterville via a Gaeltacht (Irish-speaking) area centred on Ballinskelligs (Baile an Sceilg).

Valentia Island

Islands are a scenic highlight on the ring. Some are accessible by boat, but picturesque Valentia Island is even easier to reach, via a short bridge. There's also a summer car-ferry service departing just south of Caherciveen.

Caherdaniel

The ring's scenery is at its most rugged around Caherdaniel. Highlights here include the Derrynane National Historic Park with its stately house and palm-filled gardens, horse riding, a Blue Flag beach and water sports galore.

★Valentia Island Heritage Centre MUSEUM
(066-947 6411; School Rd, Knightstown; adult/child €3.50/free; 10.30am-5.30pm May-Sep) Housed in the old school on the road towards Geokaun Mountain, this is one of those wonderful local museums, a treasure trove of artefacts that tell the tale of the island's history more eloquently than any textbook – from school chemistry sets and slate-quarrying tools to fossils and old photographs, with pride of place going to the morse key used to test the world's first transatlantic telegraph cable in 1857.

Skellig Experience MUSEUM
(066-947 6306; www.skelligexperience.com; adult/child €5/3, incl cruise €30/17.50; 10am-7pm Jul & Aug, to 6pm May, Jun & Sep, 10am-5pm Tue-Sat Mar, Apr, Oct & Nov;) Immediately across the bridge from Portmagee, this distinctive building with a turf-covered roof contains exhibitions on the life of the Skellig Michael monks, the history of the island's lighthouses and its wildlife. From April to September, it also runs two-hour **cruises** around the islands (no landing), and is a good place to get advice on visiting the Skelligs.

In March, April, October and November the centre is open five days a week, but the exact days change each year – check ahead.

Geokaun Mountain VIEWPOINT
(www.geokaun.com; car/cyclist/walker €5/3/2; 6am-11pm) The local landowner has transformed the island's highest point, Geokaun (266m) into a network of easy walking trails and viewpoints, with a breathtaking outlook over the Fogher Cliffs. It's possible to drive all the way to the top, so visitors with limited mobility don't miss out on the views. At quieter times the site is unstaffed, and entry is via an automatic barrier (payment with coins only).

Tetrapod Trackway HISTORIC SITE
(Dohilla) FREE This string of small depressions in an exposed sandstone bedding surface next to the sea may not be as spectacular as dinosaur footprints, but these fossil tracks – left behind by a metre-long amphibious creature around 360 million years ago – are the world's oldest physical evidence of a vertebrate creature moving on land. Even if geology is not your thing, the setting is beautiful, with views to the Blasket Islands and the Dingle Peninsula. Ask at the tourist office for directions.

Sleeping & Eating

Atlantic Villa B&B €€
(066-947 6839; www.anirishexperience.com; Knightstown; s/d €60/100;) Built in 1873 for the superintendent of the transatlantic telegraph cable between Valentia and Newfoundland, this historic house has six lovingly restored rooms rich in period atmosphere, some with sea views, plus modern comforts that include gourmet breakfasts and a private sauna.

Royal Valentia HOTEL €€
(066-947 6144; www.royalvalentia.ie; Knightstown; r €70-120;) Established in the 1830s, this Victorian hotel has been given a modern makeover with bright, uncluttered rooms (some with four-poster beds, many with harbour views) and a lively bar that is the heart and soul of the local community.

Knightstown Coffee Shop & Bistro CAFE €
(066-947 6373; Market St, Knightstown; mains €7-13; 8.30am-9.30pm Jul & Aug, 10am-6pm Jun, 11am-5.30pm May & Sep;) The village cafe creates a convivial atmosphere with its pinewood panelling and polka-dot tablecloths, where locals and visitors mingle while enjoying home-baked apple pie, smoked-salmon sandwiches and good, strong coffee. On summer evenings the menu extends to bistro fare, including pizza on Wednesdays.

Information

There's a **Tourist Office** (066-947 6985; 3 Watch House Cottage; 9.30am-5pm daily May-Sep, 9.30am-5pm Tue-Thu, to 1.30pm Fri Oct-Apr) in Knightstown.

Getting There & Away

A bridge links Valentia Island with Portmagee on the mainland. From April to October, the **Valentia Island Car Ferry** (087 241 8973; one-way/return car €6/9, cyclist €2/3, pedestrian €1.50/2; 7.45am-9.30pm Mon-Sat, from 9am Sun, to 10pm Jul & Aug) shuttles back and forth between Knightstown and Reenard Point, 5km southwest of Caherciveen. The crossing takes five minutes, with departures every 10 minutes.

Portmagee

POP 110

Portmagee's much-photographed single street is a rainbow of colourful houses. On summer mornings, the small harbour comes to life with boats embarking on the choppy crossing to the Skellig Islands.

The focus of village life is the friendly **Bridge Bar** (mains €10-25; food served noon-9pm), a local gathering point that hosts traditional Irish music and set dancing sessions every Friday and Sunday night (plus Tuesdays in July and August). The bar's nautical-themed **Moorings Restaurant** (mains €20-25; 6-10pm Tue-Sun) specialises in locally landed seafood, while the bar itself serves excellent fish and chips.

Skellig Ring

This scenic and little-travelled 18km detour from the Ring of Kerry (N70) links Portmagee and Waterville via a Gaeltacht (Irish-speaking) area centred on Ballinskelligs (Baile an Sceilg). The area is wild and beautiful, with the ragged outline of Skellig Michael never far from view.

There's a good Blue Flag beach at **Ballinskelligs** (www.visitballinskelligs.ie) where you'll find the **Caifé Cois Trá** (066-947 9323; Ballinskelligs Beach; mains €3-5; 9am-5pm;), a local meeting place that hosts a country market every Sunday (11am to 4pm) from June to August.

Waterville

POP 465

Waterville is an old-fashioned seaside resort strung along the N72 at the head of Ballinskelligs Bay, known for its golf and fishing. Silent-movie star Charlie Chaplin famously holidayed here in the 1960s with his extended family, returning every year for more than a decade to the Butler Arms Hotel. A bronze statue of Chaplin beams out from the seafront, and the **Charlie Chaplin Comedy Film Festival** (www.chaplinfilmfestival.com) is held here in late August.

Tiger Woods, Mark O'Meara and Payne Stewart are just some of the golfing greats who have teed off at **Waterville Golf Links** (066-947 4102; www.watervillegolflinks.ie; green fees €120-170), one of Ireland's most magnificently sited championship golf courses, with sweeping bay and mountain views.

Sights in the town are few, but nearby **Lough Currane** (www.loughcurrane.com) is world-famous for the quality of its sea trout fishing – no permit is required, but you'll need a state rod licence and a rental boat (€55 a day, or €140 with *ghillie*).

Sleeping & Eating

★ Smuggler's Inn INN €€
(066-947 4330; www.the-smugglers-inn.com; Cliff Rd; d €95-150; Apr-Oct;) This place is a diamond find (it's hard to spot if you're coming from the north; head towards the golf course). Rooms are fresh and understated – try for room 15, with a glassed-in balcony overlooking Ballinskelligs Bay. Breakfasts, including a catch of the day, are cooked to order.

The inn also has a gourmet **restaurant** where owner/chef Henry Hunt's creations not only span seafood (including sensational chowder) but locally farmed poultry and meat, and elegant desserts.

Brookhaven House B&B €€
(066-947 4431; www.brookhavenhouse.com; New Line; d €80-120;) The pick of Waterville's B&Bs is the contemporary Brookhaven House, run by a friendly family, with spick-and-span rooms, comfy beds, and a sunny sea-view breakfast room.

Dooley's Seafood & Steakhouse STEAKHOUSE €€
(066-947 8766; www.dooleyswaterville.com; mains €16-26; 6-9.30pm;) Snazzy Dooley's serves what its name states with finesse; dry aged steaks are a speciality. It's on the N70 on the western edge of the village.

Caherdaniel

POP 80

The road between Waterville and Caherdaniel climbs high over the ridge of Beenarourke, providing grandstand views of some of the finest scenery on the Ring of Kerry. The panorama extends from the scattered islands of Scarriff and Deenish to Dursey and the hills of the Beara Peninsula.

Caherdaniel, a tiny hamlet hidden among the trees at the head of Derrynane Bay, is the ancestral home of Daniel O'Connell, 'the Liberator', whose family made money smuggling from their base by the dunes. The area boasts a Blue Flag beach, plenty of activities, good hikes and some pubs where you may be tempted to break into pirate talk. Lines of wind-gnarled trees add to the wild air.

Sights & Activities

Derrynane National Historic Park HISTORIC SITE
(066-947 5113; www.heritageireland.ie; Derrynane; adult/child €4/2; 10.30am-6pm Apr-Sep, 10am-5pm Wed-Sun Mar & Nov;) Derrynane

WORTH A TRIP

SKELLIG ISLANDS

Portmagee is the jumping-off point for an unforgettable experience: the Skellig Islands, two wave-battered pinnacles of rock 12km off the coast, and the site of Ireland's most remote and spectacular ancient monastery.

The jagged, 217m-high rock of **Skellig Michael** (Archangel Michael's Rock; like St Michael's Mount in Cornwall and Mont Saint Michel in Normandy) is the larger of the two islands and a Unesco World Heritage site. It looks like the last place on Earth anyone would try to land, let alone establish a community, yet early Christian monks survived here from the 6th until the 12th century.

Not much is known about the life of the monastery, but there are records of Viking raids in AD 812 and 823. Monks were kidnapped or killed, but the community recovered and carried on. In the 11th century a rectangular oratory was added to the site but, although it was expanded in the 12th century, the monks abandoned the rock around this time.

The **monastic buildings** perch on a saddle in the rock, some 150m above sea level, reached by 600 steep steps hewn into the rock face. The astounding 6th-century oratories and beehive cells vary in size; the largest has a floor space of 4.5m by 3.6m. You can see the monks' south-facing vegetable garden and their cistern for collecting rainwater. The most impressive structural achievements are the foundations – platforms built on the steep slope using nothing more than earth and drystone walls.

As well as the monastic ruins, **puffins** are the other big attraction here. These comical-looking seabirds with brightly coloured bills nest in burrows on the rock from May to August.

Small Skellig is longer and lower than Skellig Michael, and is home to 20,000 pairs of gannets, the second-largest breeding colony in the world. Most boats circle the island so you can see the gannets, and you may see seals and dolphins as well. Small Skellig is a bird sanctuary, and no landing is permitted.

Getting There & Away

Boat trips to the Skelligs usually run from May to September, weather permitting (there are no sailings on two days out of seven, on average). You can depart from Portmagee, Ballinskelligs or Derrynane (and sometimes Knightstown). There is a limit on the number of daily visitors, with 15 boats licensed to carry no more than 12 passengers each, so it's wise to book ahead; the cost is around €60 per person.

Boats leave around 10am and return at 3pm, and give you around two hours on the rock, which is the bare minimum to visit the monastery, look at the birds and have a picnic. The crossing takes about 1½ hours from Portmagee, 35 minutes to one hour from Ballinskelligs and 1¾ hours from Derrynane.

If you just want to see the islands up close and avoid actually having to clamber out of the boat, consider a 'no landing' cruise with **Skellig Experience** (p274) on Valentia Island.

The Skellig Experience heritage centre, and local pubs and B&Bs will point you in the direction of boat operators, including the following:

Ballinskelligs Boats (☎086 417 6612; www.bestskelligtrips.com; Ballinskelligs)

Casey's (☎066-947 2437; www.skelligislands.com; Portmagee)

John O'Shea (☎087 689 8431; skelligtours@gmail.com; Derrynane)

Seanie Murphy (☎066-947 6214; www.skelligsrock.com; Portmagee)

House was the home of Maurice 'Hunting Cap' O'Connell, a notorious local smuggler who grew rich on trade with France and Spain. He was the uncle of Daniel O'Connell, the 19th-century campaigner for Catholic emancipation, who grew up here in his uncle's care and inherited the property in 1825, when it became his private retreat. The house is furnished with O'Connell memorabilia, including the impressive triumphal chariot in which he lapped Dublin after his release from prison in 1844.

Other items on display include O'Connell's ornately sculpted oak chair from his time as Lord Mayor of Dublin (look for the gold collars and ruby eyes of the carved Irish wolfhounds), the duelling pistols with which he killed a man in 1815, and the iron bed in which he died during a pilgrimage to Rome in 1847.

The **gardens**, warmed by the Gulf Stream, nurture subtropical species including 4m-high tree ferns, gunnera ('giant rhubarb') and other South American plants. A network of walking trails leads through the woods towards the beach; kids can pick up a copy of the **Derrynane Fairy Trail** (www.irishfairytrails.com) at the cafe and track down two dozen 'fairy houses' hidden among the trees.

Derrynane Beach BEACH

Derrynane's Blue Flag beach is one of the most beautiful in Kerry, with scalloped coves of golden sand set between grassy dunes and whaleback outcrops of wave-smoothed rock. From the car park at Derrynane House, you can walk 1km along the beach to explore **Abbey Island** and its picturesque cemetery – look inside the ruined chapel to find the tomb of Daniel O'Connell's wife, Mary.

Derrynane Sea Sports WATER SPORTS

(☎087 908 1208; www.derrynaneseasports.com; Derrynane Beach) Offers sailing, canoeing, windsurfing and water-skiing lessons for all levels (from €40 per person), as well as equipment hire (around €10 per hour). In July and August ask about fun half-day pirate camps for children (€95).

Eagle Rock Equestrian Centre HORSE RIDING

(☎066-947 5145; www.eaglerockcentre.com; Ballycarnahan; per hour €30) Leads guided horseback treks along Derrynane Beach and through the woods of Derrynane National Historic Park.

Sleeping & Eating

Wave Crest CAMPGROUND €

(☎066-947 5188; www.wavecrestcamping.com; hiker €9, vehicle & 2 adults €28; @) Just 1.6km southeast of Caherdaniel, this seaside park has a superb setting and extensive watersports facilities. Book ahead during high season.

Travellers' Rest Hostel HOSTEL €

(☎066-947 5175; www.hostelcaherdaniel.com; dm/d from €18/42; Mar-Oct) All low ceilings, gingham curtains and dried flowers in the grate, Travellers' Rest has the quaint feel of a country cottage. If you buy into the local funky charm, you'll love this place. Call at the garage opposite if there's nobody about.

Olde Forge B&B €€

(☎066-947 5140; www.theoldeforge.com; s/d from €45/70;) Fantastic views of Kenmare Bay and the Beara Peninsula unfold from this B&B, both from the garden terrace out front and from most of the spacious and comfortable bedrooms. If you want to base yourself here for a while, it also has two self-catering cottages (from €400 per week). It's 1.2km southeast of Caherdaniel on the N70.

Blind Piper PUB FOOD €€

(☎066-947 5126; www.blindpiperpub.com; mains €11-23; food served noon-4pm Mon-Thu, to 8pm Fri-Sun;) This local institution is a great family pub with a lovely beer garden set beside the tiny Coomnahorna River, serving quality grub like deep-fried monkfish and rib-eye steak. After dark, locals and visitors crowd inside, and music sessions strike up.

Sneem

POP 260

From Castlecove to Kenmare the main N70 Ring of Kerry road swings inland, and coastal panoramas are replaced with distant views of MacGillicuddy's Reeks. Sneem (An tSnaidhm) is a good place to pause and stretch your legs before the road dives into the woods for the final 27km stretch to Kenmare.

The village's Irish name translates as 'the knot', which is thought to refer to the River Sneem that swirls, knot-like, into nearby Kenmare Bay. The river splits the village in two, with separate village squares on either side and a picturesque waterfall tumbling below the old stone bridge.

From June to September the village hosts a weekly **farmers market** (Bridge St; 11am-4pm Tue). The **tourist office** (☎064-667 5807; South Sq; 11.30am-5.30pm May-Sep) is in the Joli Coeur craft shop.

Sleeping & Eating

★**Parknasilla Resort & Spa** HOTEL €€€

(☎064-667 5600; www.parknasillahotel.ie; Parknasilla; d from €169, ste from €269; @) This hotel has been wowing guests (including George Bernard Shaw) since 1895 with its pristine resort on the tree-fringed shores of the Kenmare River with views to the Beara Peninsula. From the modern, luxuriously appointed bedrooms to the top-grade spa, private 12-hole golf course and elegant restaurant, everything here is done just right. It's 3km southeast of Sneem.

Village Kitchen IRISH €

(☎064-664 5281; 3 Bridge St; mains €8-12; ⏲10am-6pm, to 9pm Jun-Aug;) For 25 years this family restaurant has been dishing up breakfast, lunch and dinner to locals and visitors alike. The menu runs from seafood chowder and fish specials to steak sandwiches, pizza and Irish stew.

Kenmare

POP 2175

Kenmare (ken-*mair*) is the thinking person's Killarney. Ideally positioned for exploring the Ring of Kerry (and the Beara Peninsula), but without the coach-tour crowds and calculated 'Oirishness' of its more famous neighbour, Kenmare is a pretty little town with a neat triangle of streets lined with craft shops, galleries, cafes and good-quality restaurants.

One of the few planned towns in Ireland, Kenmare was laid out on an X-shaped street plan in the late 18th century by the Marquis of Lansdowne as the showpiece of his Kerry estates. It earned its living as a market town and fishing port, and from iron works, lead mining and quarrying. The Market House and the Lansdowne Arms Hotel still survive from this period – pick up a copy of the *Kenmare Heritage Trail* from the tourist office to discover more.

The **Kenmare Fair**, which dates back more than 200 years, takes place on 15 August every year, when folk from all over Ireland descend on the town to trade in sheep, cattle and ponies, as well as crafts, bric-a-brac and artisan foods.

The tourist office also has details of walks around Kenmare Bay and into the hills, on sections of the Kerry Way and Beara Way.

Sights & Activities

Kenmare Heritage Centre MUSEUM

(☎064-664 1233; The Square; ⏲9.30am-5.15pm Mon-Wed, Fri & Sat Apr-Oct) FREE Kenmare's old courthouse is home to an exhibition telling the history of the town from its origins as Neidín (the little nest), through its establishment as a market town by the Marquis of Lansdowne to the founding of the Poor Clare Convent in 1861, which still stands behind Holy Cross Church. Local women were taught needlepoint lace-making at the convent and their lacework garnered international fame.

Upstairs from the Heritage Centre, the **Kenmare Lace and Design Centre** has displays including designs for 'the most important piece of lace ever made in Ireland' (in a 19th-century critic's opinion).

Holy Cross Church CHURCH

(Old Killarney Rd) Built in 1862, this church has a splendid wooden roof with 14 angel carvings. Intricate mosaics adorn the aisle arches and the edges of the stained-glass window over the altar. The architect was Charles Hansom, collaborator and brother-in-law of Augustus Pugin (the architect behind London's Houses of Parliament).

Seafari BOAT TRIPS

(☎064-664 2059; www.seafari.ie; Kenmare Pier; adult/child €20/12.50; ⏲Apr-Oct) Warm yourself up with complimentary tea, coffee and rum – and the captain's sea shanties – on an entertaining two-hour cruise to see Ireland's biggest seal colony and other wildlife, including white-tailed eagles; binoculars (and lollipops!) are provided.

Star Sailing WATER SPORTS

(☎064-664 1222; www.staroutdoors.ie; Dauros;) Offers one-hour sightseeing cruises (per adult/child €18/10) on Kenmare River, and activities including sea kayaking (single/double per hour €20/36) and water-skiing (per 15 minutes €60). Their base is on the R571, 6.5km southwest of Kenmare.

Sleeping

Kenmare Fáilte Hostel HOSTEL €

(☎064-664 2333; www.kenmarehostel.com; 27 Main St; dm/tw from €18/44;) Perfectly located, this pleasant, modern hostel is fitted out with quality furnishings and equipment – there's even an Aga cooker in the kitchen – a pleasant change from the utilitarianism of most budget accommodation.

Virginia's Guesthouse B&B €€

(☎064-664 1021; www.virginias-kenmare.com; Henry St; s/d from €40/75;) You can't get more central than this award-winning B&B, whose creative breakfasts celebrate organic local produce (rhubarb and blueberries in season, for example, as well as freshly squeezed OJ and porridge with whiskey). Its eight rooms are super-comfy without being fussy.

Hawthorn House B&B €€

(☎064-664 1035; www.hawthornhousekenmare.com; Shelbourne St; d €80-90;) This stylish house has eight spacious rooms, all named after local towns and decked out with fresh flowers. It's set back from busy Shelbourne St behind a low wall.

Whispering Pines B&B €€

(☎064-664 1194; www.whisperingpineskenmare.com; Shelbourne Rd; d from €70; ⊙Easter-Nov; 📶) Set back from the main road just south of the town centre, this homely B&B has four immaculate rooms, all with private bathrooms, and a warm Irish welcome. Tea and biscuits greet you on arrival, and home baking graces the breakfast table.

Sheen Falls Lodge HERITAGE HOTEL €€€

(☎064-664 1600; www.sheenfallslodge.ie; Knockduragh; s/d from €180/240; ⊙Feb-Dec; @📶) The Marquis of Lansdowne's former summer residence still feels like an aristocrats' playground, with a fine-dining French restaurant, cocktail bar, a spa and 66 rooms with Italian marble bathrooms, all in a glorious setting beside a waterfall on the River Sheen with views across Kenmare Bay to Carrauntoohil. Amenities are many (salmon fishing or clay-pigeon shooting, anyone?).

Eating

★**Tom Crean Fish & Wine** IRISH €€

(☎064-664 1589; www.tomcrean.ie; Main St; mains €16-30; ⊙5-9.30pm Thu-Mon; 📶) Named in honour of Kerry's pioneering Antarctic explorer, this venerable restaurant uses only the best of local organic produce, cheeses and fresh seafood, all served in modern, low-key surrounds. The oysters *au naturel* capture the scent of the sea; the homemade ravioli of prawn mousse, and sesame seed–crusted Atlantic salmon with lime and coriander are divine.

Horseshoe PUB FOOD €€

(☎064-664 1553; www.thehorseshoekenmare.com; 3 Main St; mains €14-26; ⊙food served 12.30-2.30pm daily, plus 5-10pm Thu-Mon) Flower baskets brighten the entrance to this popular gastropub, which has a short but excellent menu that runs from Kenmare Bay mussels in creamy apple cider sauce to braised Kerry lamb on mustard mash.

Mulcahy's Wild Garlic IRISH €€€

(☎064-664 2383; 8 Main St; mains €20-30; ⊙6-10pm Thu-Sun) Candlelight and a laid-back vibe create an appealing atmosphere in Kenmare's best-known restaurant, where chef Bruce Mulcahy weaves culinary magic with Asian- or Mediterranean-inspired twists on local seafood, such as salmon, prawn and cod sushi and sashimi, or Kerry lamb with a cep and pistachio crust.

Shopping

Kenmare has many quality craft shops and art galleries – the *Kenmare Art Spots* leaflet, available from the tourist office (and the galleries themselves) lists half a dozen you can visit.

The weekly **farmers market** (The Square; ⊙10am-4pm Wed) sets up in the town square, with stalls selling vegetables, cheese, honey, gourmet ice cream, bread, smoked salmon and other artisan produce.

Information

The **Tourist Office** (☎064-664 1233; The Square; ⊙9.30am-5.15pm Mon-Wed, Fri & Sat Apr-Oct) has free maps detailing a heritage trail around town, and longer walks of up to 13km.

Getting There & Around

Buses serve Killarney (€12.10, 45 minutes, three daily) and Sneem (€9.40, 40 minutes, twice daily) year-round. The summer-only service No 282 runs from Glengarriff to Kenmare (€12.10, 45 minutes, one daily Monday to Saturday July and August).

Finnegan's Coach & Cab (☎064-664 1491; www.kenmarecoachandcab.com) Runs a variety of tours including the Ring of Kerry.

Finnegan's Cycle Centre (☎064-664 1083; www.finneganscornerkenmare.com; Shelbourne St; bikes per day/week €15/85; ⊙10am-6.30pm) Bicycle rental.

DINGLE PENINSULA

The Dingle Peninsula (Corca Dhuibhne; www.dingle-peninsula.ie) is southwest Ireland's final flourish, a gnarled thumb of land cocked at the Atlantic and culminating in the Irish mainland's westernmost point. In the shadow of sacred Mt Brandon, a maze of fuschia-fringed *boreens* (country lanes)

THE DINGLE WAY

The 168km Dingle Way (www.dingleway.com) loops around the peninsula, beginning and ending in Tralee; it normally takes eight days to hike. Much of it is on low-lying minor roads and farm tracks, but the most impressive section climbs to 660m, above huge seacliffs, as it crosses Masatiompan, the northern spur of Mt Brandon.

Ordnance Survey 1:50,000 sheets 70 and 71 cover the route.

Dingle Peninsula

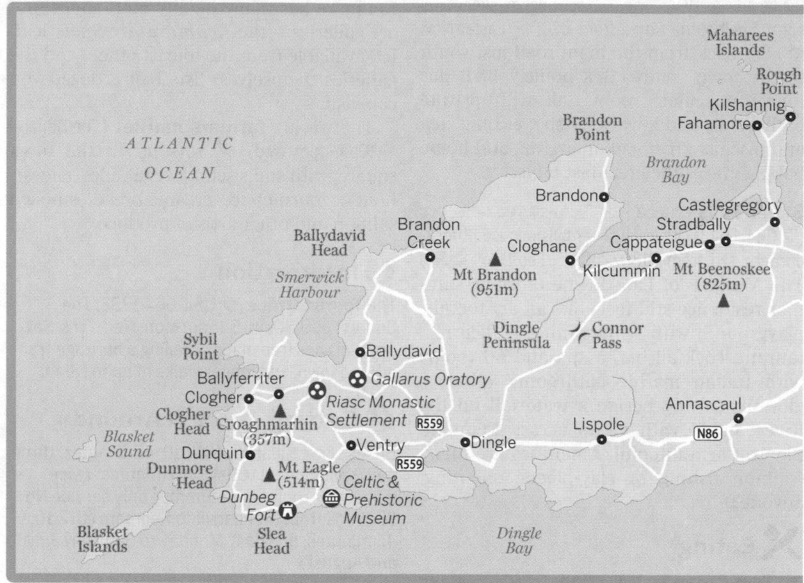

weaves together an ancient landscape of prehistoric ring forts and beehive huts, early Christian chapels, crosses and holy wells, picturesque hamlets and abandoned villages.

But it's where the land meets the ocean – whether in a welter of wave-pounded rocks, or where the surf unrolls gently into secluded, sandy coves – that Dingle's beauty truly reveals itself.

Centred on charming Dingle town, the peninsula has long been a beacon for those of an alternative bent, attracting artists, craftspeople, musicians and a whole range of idiosyncratic characters who can be found in workshops, museums, trad sessions and folkloric festivals throughout Dingle's tiny settlements.

 Tours

Most of the companies listed as offering Ring of Kerry bus tours also offer day trips from Killarney to the Dingle Peninsula.

Dingle Slea Head Tours BUS TOUR
(☎087 218 9430; www.dinglesleaheadtours.com; per person €25) Guided minibus tours of Slea Head Drive, departing from Dingle town (2½ hours).

Getting Around

Regular buses serve Dingle town from Killarney and Tralee, but service to the rest of the peninsula is limited to community buses running once or twice a week. Your own wheels (two or four) are the best way to explore the peninsula.

Killarney to Dingle Town via Castlemaine

The quickest route from Killarney to Dingle passes through Killorglin and Castlemaine, where you turn west on the R561. You'll soon meet the coast, then pass through the seaside town of Inch before joining the N86 to Dingle.

Castlemaine is well connected with Tralee, Killorglin, and Limerick via Killarney, but there are no buses from Castlemaine to Annascaul via Inch.

Inch Strand

Inch Strand is a 5km-long sand spit and dune system extending into Dingle Bay. This stupendous beach has attracted film directors as well as surfers, land-yachters and anglers – it has appeared in the movies *Ryan's Daughter* (1970), *Excalibur* (1981) and *Far and Away* (1992), among others.

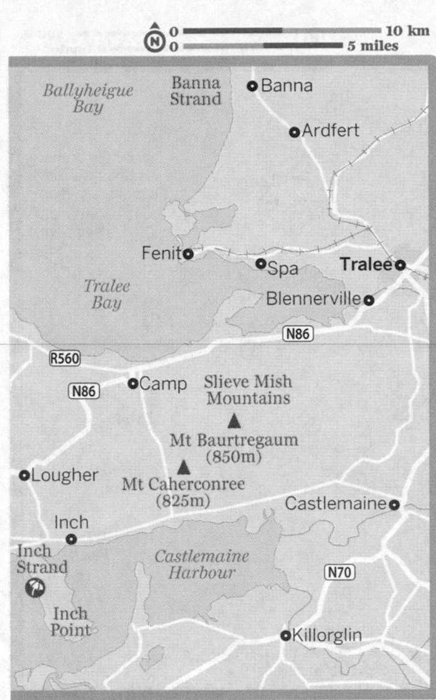

The dunes are scattered with the remains of shipwrecks and Stone Age and Iron Age settlements. The west-facing beach is also a hot surfing spot; waves average 1m to 3m. Learn to ride them with **Offshore Surf School** (☎087 294 6519; www.offshoresurfschool.ie; adult/child from €25/20), which offers a range of lessons, including a two-hour group class.

Cars are allowed on the beach, but don't end up providing others with nonstop laughs by getting stuck.

★Sammy's CAFE €

(☎066-915 8118; www.inchbeach.ie; mains €14-20; ⌚9.30am-10pm, reduced hours in winter; 📶👪) Sammy's, at the entrance to the beach, is the nerve centre of the village. The beach-facing bar-restaurant serves a vast range of dishes from sandwiches to fresh oysters and mussels. There's a shop, tourist information and trad sessions during the summer.

Annascaul

POP 300

The main reason to pause in the small village of Annascaul (Abhainn an Scáil) is to visit the **South Pole Inn** (☎066-915 7388; Main St; mains €11-18; ⌚food served noon-9pm). Antarctic explorer Tom Crean ran this big blue pub in his retirement. Order hearty dishes worthy of an explorer as well as Dingle Brewing Company's Crean's lager on tap and in bottles.

Dingle Town

POP 1965

Framed by its fishing port, the peninsula's charming little 'capital' manages to be quaint without even trying. Many pubs double as shops, so you can enjoy Guinness and a singalong among screws and nails, wellies and horseshoes. It has long drawn runaways from across the world, making it a cosmopolitan, creative place. In summer its hilly streets can be clogged with visitors; in other seasons its authentic charms are yours for the savouring.

Although Dingle is one of Ireland's largest Gaeltacht towns, the locals have voted to retain the name Dingle rather than go by the officially sanctioned – and signposted – Gaelige name of An Daingean.

Sights

Dingle is one of those towns whose very fabric is its main attraction. Wander up and down the streets, poke around the back alleys, stroll along the pier, and amble into shops and pubs and see what you can find.

Dingle Oceanworld AQUARIUM

(☎066-915 2111; www.dingle-oceanworld.ie; The Wood; adult/child €13/7.50; ⌚10am-7pm Jul & Aug, to 5pm Sep-Jun; 👪) Dingle's aquarium is a lot of fun, and includes a walk-through tunnel and a touch pool. Psychedelic fish glide through tanks that recreate such environments as Lake Malawi, the River Congo and the piranha-filled Amazon. Reef sharks and stingrays cruise the shark tank; water is pumped from the harbour for the spectacularly ugly wreck fish.

Dingle Brewing Company BREWERY

(☎066-915 0743; www.dinglebrewingcompany.com; Spa Rd; admission €6; ⌚tours by reservation) Housed in a 19th-century creamery building, this terrific craft brewery launched in 2011 on 20 July – not coincidentally Tom Crean's birthday (its single brew, a crisp, hoppy lager, is named after the local Antarctic explorer). Admission includes a self-guided or guided brewery tour as well as a pint. It's on the road towards the Connor Pass.

Dingle Distillery DISTILLERY

(☎086 829 9944; www.dingledistillery.ie; Ventry Rd; tours per person €10; ⌚9am-5pm Mon-Fri)

Dingle Town

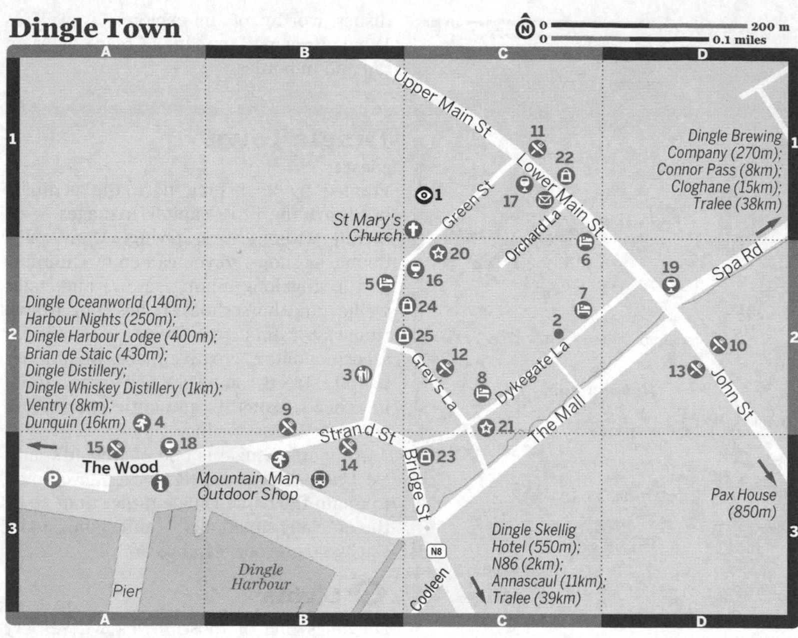

Dingle Town

Sights
1 An Díseart C1

Activities, Courses & Tours
2 Dingle Music School C2
3 Dingle Surf B2
4 Irish Adventures A2

Sleeping
5 An Capall Dubh B2
6 Dingle Benner's Hotel C2
7 Grapevine Hostel C2
8 Hideout Hostel C2

Eating
9 Chowder B2
10 Doyle's D2
11 Global Village Restaurant C1
12 Grey's Lane Bistro C2
13 Idás D2
14 Murphy's B3
15 Out of the Blue A3

Drinking & Nightlife
16 Dick Mack's C2
17 Foxy John's C1
18 John Benny's A3
19 Small Bridge Bar D2

Entertainment
20 Blue Zone C2
21 Phoenix Dingle C2

Shopping
22 An Gailearaí Beag C1
Dingle Record Shop .... (see 20)
23 Farmers Market C3
24 Lisbeth Mulcahy C2
25 Little Cheese Shop C2

An offshoot of Dublin's Porterhouse microbrewery, this craft distillery began producing whiskey in 2012 but the necessary ageing process meant that the first fruits of its labours were not bottled till 2016. It also produces artisan gin and vodka.

An Díseart CULTURAL CENTRE
(☎066-915 2476; www.diseart.ie; Green St; adult/family €2/5; ⏲9-5pm Mon-Sat) In a neo-Gothic former convent, this Celtic cultural centre has impressive stained-glass windows by Dublin artist Harry Clarke (1889-1931) depicting 12 scenes from the life of Christ. Admission includes a 15-minute guided tour.

Activities

Dolphin Trips BOAT TOUR
(☎066-915 2626; www.dingledolphin.com; The Pier; adult/child €16/8) Boats run by the Dingle Boatmen's Association cooperative leave the pier daily for one-hour trips to see Dingle's most famous resident, Fungie the dolphin. It's free if Fungie doesn't show, but he usually does. The ticket office is next to the tourist office.

Naomhòg Experience BOATING
(☎087 699 2925; rowingdingle@gmail.com; Dingle Marina; per person €40) *Naomhòg* is the kerry name for a *currach*, a traditional Irish boat made from a wooden frame covered with tarred canvas (originally animal hides). They were used by the Blasket islanders for fishing, and are now maintained and raced by local enthusiasts. You can book a two-hour session in Dingle Harbour learning how to row one.

Mountain Man Outdoor Shop CYCLING
(☎066-9152400; www.themountainmanshop.com; Strand St) Rents bikes (per day €15) and runs guided cycling tours around the Dingle Peninsula, with themes ranging from archaeology to food.

Dingle Surf SURFING
(☎066-915 0833; www.dinglesurf.com; Green St; lessons adult/child €30/25; ⊙10am-6pm Mon-Sat, 11am-5pm Sun) Dingle Surf offers half-day surfing lessons for beginners at Brandon Bay (on the north side of the peninsula; transport included), and sells gear including its own groovy range of surfwear.

Irish Adventures ADVENTURE SPORTS
(☎087 419 0318; www.irishadventures.net; The Wood) This outfit offers guided adventure trips including rock climbing on the local sea cliffs (half-day per person €50), and kayaking in Dingle Harbour with Fungie the dolphin (half-day or sunset trip per person €50).

Dingle Music School COURSE
(☎086 319 0438; www.dinglemusicschool.com; Wren's Nest Cafe, Dykegate Lane; per hr €30) John Ryan offers bodhrán and tin whistle workshops for beginners through to experienced players – lessons can be arranged for early morning or evening. Instruments are supplied.

Festivals & Events

Check upcoming events and gigs online at www.dingle-peninsula.ie.

Dingle Races SPORTS
(www.dingleraces.ie) Held over the second weekend in August, Dingle's horse racing meet brings crowds from far and wide. The racetrack is 1.6km east of town on the N86.

Dingle Regatta SPORTS
(www.facebook.com/dinglerowingclub) Crews of four race traditional Irish *naomhóg* (canoes) around the harbour in late August. It's Kerry's largest event of its kind and inspired the trad song of the same name.

Dingle Food & Wine Festival FOOD
(www.dinglefood.com) Fabulous foodie fest featuring a 'taste trail' with cheap-as-chips sampling at over 40 locations around town, plus a market, cooking demonstrations, and a foraging walk. Held in Early October.

Sleeping

This tourist town has loads of midrange B&Bs, and a number of pubs also offer accommodation.

Grapevine Hostel HOSTEL €
(☎066-915 1434; www.grapevinedingle.com; Dykegate Ln; dm/tw €19/50; 📶) Tucked away near the centre of town, this dinky hostel has eight-, four- and two-bed rooms with wooden bunks and private bathrooms (with

FUNGIE THE DOLPHIN

In 1983 a bottlenose dolphin swam into Dingle Bay and local tourism hasn't been quite the same since. Showing an unusual affinity for human company, he swam around with the local fishing fleet. Eventually somebody got the idea of charging tourists to go out on boats to see the friendly dolphin (nicknamed Fungie). Today up to 12 boats at a time and more than 1000 tourists a day ply the waters with Dingle's mascot, now a cornerstone of the local economy (there's even a bronze statue of him outside the tourist office).

In the wild, bottlenose dolphins live for an average of 25 years, though they have been know to live to over 40 in captivity. As Fungie has been around for more than 30 years (yes, it's still the same dolphin, recognisable by his distinctive markings), speculation is rife about how long it will be before he finally glides into the deep for the last time. And what will Dingle do without its dolphin?

minimalist sliding doors). The TV-free, fire-lit lounge is a good spot for visiting musicians to get a singalong going. Book well ahead.

Hideout Hostel HOSTEL €
(066-915 0559; www.thehideouthostel.com; Dykegate Lane; dm/d €21/52;) Converted from a former guesthouse, this central hostel has inherited private bathrooms in all rooms. Top-notch facilities include two lounges with groovy furnishings, bike storage and a well-equipped kitchen. Rates include light breakfast (tea, coffee, toast, cereal). Switched-on owner Mícheál is a fount of local info.

★ **Pax House** B&B €€
(066-915 1518; www.pax-house.com; Upper John St; s/d from €110/130; mid-Feb–mid-Nov;) From its highly individual decor (including contemporary paintings) to the outstanding views over the estuary from room balconies and terrace, Pax House is a treat. Choose from less expensive hill-facing accommodation, rooms that overlook the estuary, and two-room family suites opening onto the terrace. It's 1km southeast of the town centre.

Harbour Nights B&B €€
(066-915 2499; www.dinglebandb.com; The Wood; d €70-90;) Half the rooms at this waterfront B&B have balconies with stunning views over Dingle's harbour, as does the upstairs sitting room, which opens to a terrace.

An Capall Dubh B&B €€
(066-915 1105; www.ancapalldubh.com; Green St; d/f from €90/160;) Entered via a 19th-century coaching entrance leading into a cobbled courtyard, this airy B&B is furnished with light timbers and checked fabrics. Ask about its self-catering townhouses, which sleep up to six people.

Dingle Harbour Lodge GUESTHOUSE €€
(066-915 1577; www.dingleharbourlodge.com; The Wood; s/d from €70/110;) This purpose-built B&B complex with an airy, timber-floored lobby filled with fresh flowers, neat rooms equipped with flat-screen TVs and ultra-efficient managers fills a niche for contemporary midrange accommodation. Although just five minutes' walk from the centre, its position above the harbour means no street noise and good views from upper-level rooms.

Dingle Benner's Hotel HOTEL €€€
(066-915 1638; www.dinglebenners.com; Main St; s/d from €114/179;) A Dingle institution, melding old-world elegance, local charm and modern comforts in the quiet bedrooms, lounge, library, and (very popular) Mrs Benners Bar. Rooms in the 300-year-old wing have the most character; those in the new parts are quieter and more spacious.

Dingle Skellig Hotel HOTEL €€€
(066-915 0200; www.dingleskellig.com; s/d from €129/178;) An ocean-like swimming pool and a spa with an outdoor hot tub are the highlights of these luxurious digs down near the water, just south of town. Rooms are decorated in rich chocolate-box-like cream, caramel and hazelnut tones. There are interconnecting rooms for families, plus a crèche and kids club, as well as a restaurant and several bars.

Eating

In a county famed for its seafood, Dingle still stands out. There are some superb restaurants and cafes, as well as excellent pub fare, particularly at John Benny's.

Murphy's ICE CREAM €
(www.murphysicecream.ie; Strand St; cones from €3.80; 11.30am-7pm;) Made here in Dingle, Murphy's famous ice cream comes in a range of flavours that include Guinness, Kilbeggan whiskey, brown bread, sea salt, and honeycomb, plus cooling mint. There are branches in Killarney and Dublin.

★ **Chowder** CAFE €€
(Strand St; mains €9-15; 10am-5.30pm, to 9pm Jun-Aug) This unpretentious, always-busy cafe serves top-quality bistro food as well as breakfast pancakes and fry-ups – the signature seafood chowder is tasty, but lunch specials such as homemade crab tart, open sandwich of roast pork belly and stuffing, or mussels in garlic sauce are just superb. If it's sunny, try to bag one of the pavement tables.

Global Village Restaurant INTERNATIONAL €€
(066-915 2325; www.globalvillagedingle.com; Upper Main St; mains €19-29; 5.30-9.30pm Mar-Oct) With the sophisticated feel of a continental bistro, this restaurant offers a fusion of global recipes gathered by the well-travelled owner-chef, but utilises sustainable local produce, such as the Kerry mountain lamb. The wine list is excellent.

Grey's Lane Bistro BISTRO €€
(087 264 0613; www.greyslanebistro.com; Grey's Lane; mains lunch €10-13, dinner €17-24; 10am-9.30pm) Recently relocated to new premises,

this is one of Dingle's most popular spots for international bistro fare – from lamb tajines to Thai green curries, ginger stir-fries and Mediterranean casseroles.

★ Out of the Blue SEAFOOD €€€
(☎066-915 0811; www.outoftheblue.ie; The Wood; mains €21-29; ⊙5-9.30pm daily, plus 12.30-3pm Sun) 'No chips', reads the menu of this funky blue-and-yellow, fishing-shack-style restaurant on the waterfront. Despite its rustic surrounds, this is one of Dingle's best restaurants, with an intense devotion to fresh local seafood (and only seafood); if they don't like the catch, they don't open. With seafood this good, who needs chips?

★ Idás IRISH €€€
(☎066-915 0885; John St; mains €26-30; ⊙5.30-9.30pm Tue-Sun) Chef Kevin Murphy is dedicated to promoting the finest of Irish produce, much of it from Kerry, taking lamb and seafood and foraged herbs from the Dingle Peninsula and creating delicately flavoured concoctions such as braised John Dory fillet with fennel dashi cream, pickled cucumber, wild garlic and salad burnet. An early-bird menu offers two/three courses for €24.50/28.50.

Doyle's SEAFOOD €€€
(☎066-915 2674; www.doylesofdingle.ie; 4 John St; mains €20-33; ⊙5-9pm, days vary seasonally) Scarlet-fronted Doyle's serves some of the best seafood in the area (which in these parts is really saying something). Starters such as seafood risotto and seafood pie team up with mains like spicy Spanish fish stew, seafood linguine and lobster.

Drinking & Entertainment

Dingle has literally dozens of pubs, many with entertainment.

★ John Benny's PUB
(www.johnbennyspub.com; Strand St; ⊙noon-11pm) A toasty cast-iron woodstove, stone slab floor, memorabilia on the walls, great staff and no intrusive TV make this one of Dingle's most enjoyable traditional pubs. Local musos pour in most nights for rockin' trad sessions.

Dick Mack's PUB
(Green St; ⊙3pm-late) Stars in the pavement bear the names of Dick Mack's celebrity customers. Ancient wood and ancient snugs dominate the interior, which is lit like the inside of a whiskey bottle. Out the back there's a warren of tables, chairs and characters.

Foxy John's PUB
(Main St; ⊙10am-11pm;) Dingle has more than 50 pubs, many of them mongrel affairs that still have vestiges of their lives as shops. Foxy John's on Main St is one example and stocks hardware and outdoor clothing as well as beer and whiskey. They even rent out bikes! Curran's across the street is another example.

Small Bridge Bar LIVE MUSIC
(An Droichead Beag; Lower Main St; ⊙1pm-late) Traditional music kicks off at 9.30pm nightly at this raucous, late-opening pub by the bridge.

Blue Zone JAZZ
(Green St; ⊙5.30pm-12.15am) Great late-night hangout that's part jazz venue, part pizza restaurant and part wine bar, with moody blue and red surrounds.

Phoenix Dingle CINEMA
(www.phoenixdingle.net; Dykegate Lane) Cosy family-run cinema screening first releases and art-house films.

Shopping

Amid the Fungie soft-toy flotsam you'll find plenty of shops with quality goods made by local artisans.

Farmers Market MARKET
(cnr Bridge St & Dykegate Lane; ⊙9am-3pm Fri) Fresh local produce and homemade goodies galore.

Lisbeth Mulcahy FASHION
(www.lisbethmulcahy.com; Green St; ⊙9.30am-7pm Mon-Sat & noon-6pm Sun Jun-Sep, 10am-5pm Mon-Sat Oct-May) Beautiful scarves, rugs and wall hangings are created on a 150-year-old loom by this long-established designer. Also sold here are ceramics by her husband, who has a workshop at Louis Mulcahy Pottery (p290), west of Dingle.

An Gailearaí Beag ARTS & CRAFTS
(www.angailearaibeag.com; Main St; ⊙11am-5pm daily) Often staffed by the artists themselves, this little gallery is a showcase for the work of the West Kerry Craft Guild, selling ceramics, paintings, wood carvings, photography, batik, jewellery, stained glass and more.

Brian de Staic JEWELLERY
(www.briandestaic.com; The Wood; ⊙9.30am-5.30pm Mon-Sat) This renowned local designer's exquisite modern Celtic work includes

KLEMPA2/SHUTTERSTOCK ©

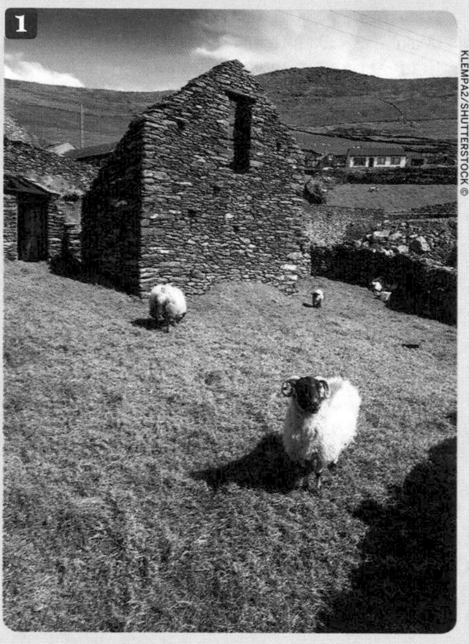

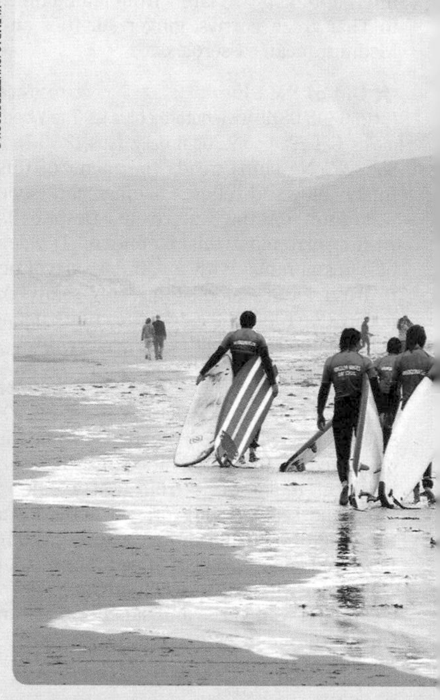

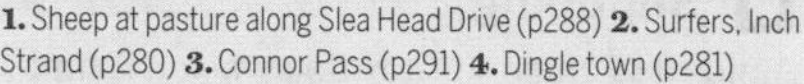

1. Sheep at pasture along Slea Head Drive (p288) **2.** Surfers, Inch Strand (p280) **3.** Connor Pass (p291) **4.** Dingle town (p281)

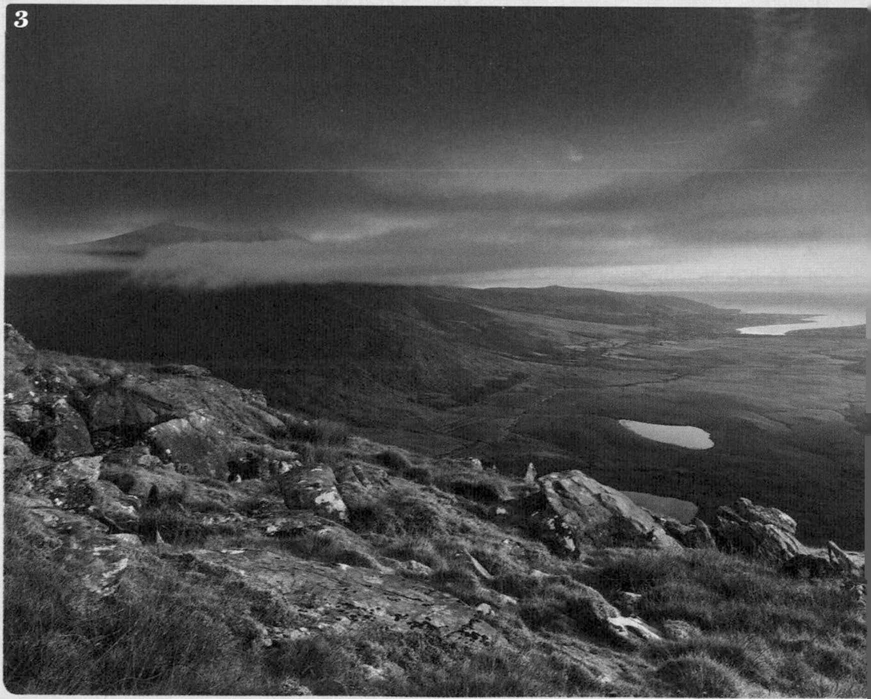

2

JEFF MAURITZEN/GETTY IMAGES ©

4

Dingle Peninsula

The enchanting Dingle Peninsula distils County Kerry's best attractions into an eminently manageable day trip. But, like the many artisans who now call it home, the longer you spend here, the more likely it is you'll never want to leave – or at least return at the first opportunity.

Slea Head

The Dingle Peninsula's pièce de résistance is Slea Head, which has the greatest concentration of ancient sites in Kerry. In between them – and the photogenic scenery – illuminating stops include the quirky Celtic & Prehistoric Museum.

Castlegregory

On the northern side of the Dingle Peninsula, Castlegregory is the gateway to its water-sports playground. Diving is the number-one attraction; there are also magical woodlands to wander.

Connor Pass

There are quicker routes across the Dingle Peninsula's interior, but none as scenic as Connor Pass. As Ireland's highest driveable mountain pass, at 456m, it has captivating views across the peninsula.

Inch Beach

Perfect breakers, a wide, sandy shore and a brilliant pub/restaurant/cafe called Sammy's make Inch Beach an essential stop. Sign up for surf lessons or take blustery walks along the 5km-long sand spit.

Dingle Town

The peninsula's namesake 'capital' fulfils every notion of an Irish seaside village: antique pubs still doubling as grocery stores, higgledy-piggledy streets, trad music sessions and a harbour unloading fresh seafood.

symbols such as the Hill of Tara, crosses and standing stones, as well as jewellery inscribed with Ogham script. All of de Staic's jewellery is individually handcrafted.

Little Cheese Shop FOOD
(www.thelittlecheeseshop.ie; Grey's Lane; ⏲11am-6pm Mon-Fri, 11am-5pm Sat) Swiss-trained cheesemaker Maja Binder runs this tiny shop that overflows with aromatic cheeses from all over Ireland, including her own range of Dingle Peninsula Cheeses.

Dingle Record Shop MUSIC
(www.dinglerecordshop.com; Green St; ⏲11am-5pm Mon-Sat) Tucked away in a corner off Green St, this jammed music hub has all the good stuff you can't download yet. Podcasts recorded in-store are available online. Hours can be erratic.

Information

The banks on Main St have ATMs and bureaux de change. The post office is off Lower Main St. Parking is free throughout town, with metered parking at the harbour.

The busy but helpful **Tourist Office** (☎066-915 1188; www.dingle-peninsula.ie; The Pier; ⏲9.15am-5pm Mon-Sat) has maps, guides and plenty of information on the entire peninsula. It books accommodation for a €5 fee.

Getting There & Away

Bus Éireann (www.buseireann.ie) buses stop outside the car park behind the supermarket. Up to six buses a day serve Killarney (€17.60, 1½ to two hours) via Tralee (€14.40, 1¼ hours).

Dingle Shuttle Bus (☎087 250 4767; www.dingleshuttlebus.com; per person €20) runs a minibus service between Kerry Airport and Dingle (fare quoted for minimum of three people). Must be booked in advance.

Getting Around

Dingle is easily covered on foot. Bike-hire places include Foxy John's (p285), and the Mountain Man (p283) outdoors shop, where hire costs €12 to €15 per day.

Paddy's Bike Shop (☎066-915 2311; www.paddysbikeshop.com; Dykegate Lane; per day/week from €15/75; ⏲9am-7pm May-Sep, to 6pm Mar, Apr & Oct, closed Nov-Feb) rents hybrid, mountain and road bikes, plus accessories including child seats, pannier bags and car racks.

Dingle Cabs (☎087 660 23 23; www.dinglecabs.com) offers a local taxi service, airport transfers, and guided tours of Dingle Peninsula.

Slea Head Drive

The signposted Slea Head Drive is a 50km loop that passes through the villages of Ventry, Dunquin, Ballyferriter and Ballydavid to the west of Dingle town, and takes in all the main sights. Including time for sightseeing, it's at least a half-day's drive or one or two day's bike ride. The road is very narrow in a few places, so it's recommended that all vehicles drive the route clockwise – ignore this rule and you risk holding up traffic as you try to squeeze past a tour bus going in the opposite direction.

Attractions include fine beaches, good walks and superbly preserved structures from Dingle's ancient past including beehive huts, ring forts, inscribed stones and early Christian sites. The landscape is dramatic, especially in shifting mist, although full-on sea fog obliterates everything.

Dunmore Head is the westernmost point of the Irish mainland; just to its south is **Coumeenoole Beach** (you'll see the parking just off the road), a picturesque cove that was used as a location in the movie *Ryan's Daughter*. There are other good beaches at Ventry and **Wine Strand** (near Ballyferriter).

Bus 275A runs from Dingle town to Dunquin (€6.60, 30 minutes, twice daily) via Ventry on Monday and Thursday only, while bus 275B runs from Dingle town to Ballydavid (€4.80, 20 minutes, twice daily) via Gallarus on Tuesday and Friday only.

Sights & Activities

Celtic & Prehistoric Museum MUSEUM
(☎087 770 3280; Kilvicadownig, Ventry; admission €5; ⏲10am-5.30pm mid-Mar–Oct) This museum squeezes in an astonishing collection of Celtic and prehistoric artefacts, including the world's largest woolly mammoth skull and tusks, as well as a 40,000-year-old cave-bear skeleton, Viking horse-bone ice skates, stone battleaxes, flint daggers and jewellery. It started as the private collection of owner Harry Moore, a US expat musician (ask him to strike up a Celtic tune). It's 4km southwest of Ventry.

Dún Beag Fort ARCHAEOLOGICAL SITE
(www.dunbegfort.com; admisson €3; ⏲9am-7pm) The Iron Age Dún Beag fort is a dramatic example of a promontory fortification, perched atop a sheer sea cliff about 6km southwest of Ventry. The fort has four outer walls; inside are the remains of a house and a beehive hut, as well as an underground passage.

Admission includes a 10-minute audiovisual presentation in the visitor centre.

Famine Cottage MUSEUM

(www.famine-cottage.com; admission €3; ⏲10am-6pm daily Apr-Oct, reduced hours winter) Just uphill from the Dunbeg Fort Visitor Centre is the 1845-built Famine Cottage, with furnishings, cooking utensils and farm animals that evoke the hardship its occupants endured.

Blasket Centre CULTURAL CENTRE

(Ionad an Bhlascaoid Mhóir; ☎066-915 6444; www.heritageireland.ie; adult/child €4/2; ⏲10am-6pm Apr-Oct) This wonderful interpretative centre celebrates the rich cultural life of the now-abandoned Blasket Islands. It is housed in a striking modern building with a long, white hall ending in a picture window looking directly at the islands. Great Blasket's rich community of storytellers and musicians is profiled along with its literary visitors like playwright JM Synge, author of *Playboy of the Western World*. The more prosaic practicalities of island life are covered by exhibits on boat building and fishing.

The centre has a good **cafe** with a view of the islands, and a useful **bookshop**.

Dingle Peninsula Museum MUSEUM

(Músaem Chorca Dhuibhne; ☎066-915 6100; www.westkerrymuseum.com; Ballyferriter; admission €3.50; ⏲10am-5pm Easter & Jun–mid-Sep) Set in the 19th-century schoolhouse, this local museum has displays on the geology, archaeology and ecology of the peninsula.

Reask Monastic Site ARCHAEOLOGICAL SITE

(An Riaisc) FREE The remains of this 5th- or 6th-century monastic settlement are one of the peninsula's more evocative archaeological sites, with low stone walls among close-cropped turf and drifts of white daisies revealing the outlines of beehive huts, storehouses and an early Christian oratory. At least 10 stone crosses have been found, including the beautiful **Reask Stone** decorated with Celtic motifs. The site is signposted 'Mainistir Riaisc' off the R559, about 2km east of Ballyferriter.

Gallarus Oratory HISTORIC SITE

(☎066-915 6444; www.heritageireland.ie) FREE Gallarus Oratory is one of Ireland's most beautiful ancient buildings, its smoothly constructed dry-stone walls in the shape of an upturned boat. It has stood in this lonely spot beneath the brown hills for some 1200 years and has withstood the elements perfectly. There is a narrow doorway on the western side and a single, round-headed window on the east. Gallarus is clearly signposted off the R559, 8km northwest of Dingle town.

GALLARUS ORATORY ACCESS

Note that entrance to Gallarus Oratory is free, but public parking next to the site is extremely limited. About 150m downhill from the public entrance to the oratory is a prominently signposted, privately owned **visitor centre** (www.gallarusoratory.ie; admission €3; ⏲9am-6pm Easter-Oct) with extensive parking that charges for admission. (Signs at the public entrance have been removed, perhaps to encourage use of the private facility.)

The only reason for paying the visitor centre fee is to use the car park (the audiovisual presentation is missable). Walkers and cyclists who enter the site through the public entrance should leave the same way; unwitting visitors who wander down through the visitor centre grounds may be asked to pay.

Kilmalkedar Church CHURCH

FREE Nestled in a beautiful setting with sweeping views over Smerwick Harbour, Kilmalkedar is the most important Christian site on the Dingle Peninsula. Built in the 12th century on the site of a 7th-century monastery founded by St Maolcethair, it's a superb example of Irish Romanesque architecture, its round-arched west door decorated with chevron patterns and a carved human head. In the graveyard you'll find an Ogham stone and a carved stone sundial.

Activities

Saint's Road WALKING

(Cosàn na Naomh; www.irishtrails.ie) This waymarked 18km walking trail follows the route of an ancient pilgrim path from the beach at Ventry to Ballybrack (An Baile Breac) at the foot of Mt Brandon via Gallarus Oratory, Kilmalkedar Church and several other early Christian sites. From Ballybrack you can continue via the stations of the cross to the summit of Mt Brandon (experienced hill walkers only).

Mt Brandon WALKING

At 951m, Mt Brandon (Cnoc Bréanainn) is Ireland's eighth-highest summit. It stands in splendid isolation to the north of Dingle, a complex ridge bounded by spectacular cliffs and glacial lakes to the northeast, and falling steeply into the sea to the northwest. There are many routes to the top listed in local walking guides, but the shortest and easiest is via the old pilgrim path from Ballybrack (car park signposted off the R549, 11km north of Dingle town).

From the car park the path leads arrow-straight towards the top, passing numbered wooden crucifixes marking the 14 stations of the cross, before deviating to the right for a single zigzag before the summit, which is marked by a huge cairn and a 15th cross. In clear weather the views are stupendous. Descend by the same route (total 8.5km, allow three hours).

Long's Riding Stables HORSE RIDING
(☎066-915 9034; www.longsriding.com; Ventry; 1hr ride from €30) Horseback treks on Ventry beach or among the hills above the bay.

Sleeping & Eating

Oratory House Camping CAMPGROUND €
(Campaíl Teach An Aragail; ☎086 819 1942; www.dingleactivities.com; Gallarus; hiker €9, vehicle plus 2 adults €20; ⊙Apr-Sep;) Europe's westernmost camping ground, nicely sheltered and two minutes' walk from Gallarus Oratory. The owner is a source of much local information on a mass of activities, especially walking.

Dún Chaoin Youth Hostel HOSTEL €
(☎066-915 6121; www.anoige.ie; Dunquin; dm €15-18.50, tw €44; ⊙Mar-Oct;) This An Óige hostel has a terrific location near the Blasket Centre and not too far from Dunquin Pier, with stunning views of the Blasket Islands. The nearest shop is 8km away, so bring supplies with you.

Ceann Trá Heights B&B €
(☎066-915 9866; www.ceanntraheights.com; Ventry; s/d €55/76; ⊙Mar-Nov;) An ideal base for exploring the area, this comfortable, modern five-room guesthouse has a great location overlooking Ventry Bay (rooms 1 and 2 have stunning sea views). An open fire warms the cosy sitting room in cold weather.

Tig Áine CAFE €
(☎066-915 6214; www.tigaine.com; An Ghráig, Ballyferriter; mains €7-13; ⊙noon-8pm Tue-Sun) This family-run spot has a superb location, with a terrace looking out over Clogher Beach towards Sybil Head. Ducks wander about the garden while you slurp on Murphy's ice cream and soak up the view, or sit indoors reading the cafe's birdwatching books while you wait for a bowl of seafood chowder. It's 5km west of Ballyferriter.

Caifé na Caolóige CAFE €
(www.louismulcahy.com; Clogher, Ballyferriter; mains €7-11; ⊙10am-5pm) The bright, contemporary cafe at Louis Mulcahy Pottery serves fresh and homemade gourmet dishes such as open sandwiches topped with organic smoked salmon or Dingle cheeses, along with soups, panini, cakes and coffee, and wicked hot chocolate.

Tigh TP PUB FOOD €€
(TP's Pub; ☎087 246 0507; www.dingleactivities.com; mains €12-25; ⊙food served noon-9pm) Overlooking the beach at the north end of Wine Strand, this friendly pub is a pleasant place for a waterside pint or a meal of local seafood. Next door it runs the Coast Guard House and Lodge, which provides decent hostel and B&B accommodation (dorm bed €20, double room from €60).

★**Gormans Clifftop House** IRISH €€
(☎066-915 5162; www.gormans-clifftophouse.com; Glashabeg; mains €19-29; ⊙dinner by reservation Mon-Sat;) Far and away the best place to eat and/or sleep in the area is Gormans Clifftop House. Book ahead to dine on delicious Kerry mountain lamb stew, Dingle Bay prawns and other exquisite dishes. The guest bedrooms (double €110 to €150) are airy, contemporary and immaculate, the welcome is warm and the views superb.

Shopping

Louis Mulcahy Pottery POTTERY
(☎066-915 6229; www.louismulcahy.com; Clogher, Ballyferriter; ⊙9am-5.30pm Mon-Fri, 10am-5.30pm Sat & Sun, later hours Apr-Oct) One of the most interesting potteries in Kerry, Louis Mulcahy produces a wide range of contemporary and traditional designs.

Blasket Islands

The Blasket Islands (Na Blascaodaí), 5km out into the Atlantic, are the most westerly islands in the country. At 6km by 1.2km, **Great Blasket** (An Blascaod Mór) is the largest and most visited. Day trippers come to explore the abandoned settlements, watch the seabirds, picnic on Trá Bán (a gorgeous white sand beach near the pier) and hike the island's many trails.

All of the Blaskets were lived on at one time or another; there is evidence of Great Blasket being inhabited during the Iron Age and early Christian times. The last islanders left for the mainland in 1953 after they and the government agreed that it was no longer viable to live in such harsh and isolated conditions, although today a few people make their home out here for part of the year.

Boats trips mostly run from Easter to September, but even then weather can cause boat cancellations – call for seasonal sailing times.

There are no camping facilities on the islands.

Blasket Island Ferries BOAT TOUR
(☎066-915 6422; www.blasketisland.com; Dunquin; adult/child €20/10) Boats trips from Dunquin Harbour to Great Blasket; the crossing takes 20 minutes each way.

Blasket Islands Eco Marine Tours BOAT TOUR
(☎087 231 6131; www.marinetours.ie; Ventry; per person €50) Full day trips departing from Ventry Harbour, with three hours ashore on Great Blasket.

Dingle Marine & Leisure BOAT TOUR
(☎087 672 6100, 066-915 1344; www.dinglebaycharters.com; Dingle Marina; adult/child return €35/15; ⏲Apr-Sep) Fast boat (45 minutes) from Dingle town marina to Great Blasket Island; call to check the latest times.

Connor Pass

Topping out at 456m, the R560 across the Connor (or Conor) Pass from Dingle town to Cloghane and Stradbally is Ireland's highest public road. On a foggy day you'll see nothing but the tarmac in front of you, but in fine weather it offers phenomenal views of Dingle Harbour to the south and Mt Brandon to the north. The road is in good shape, despite being narrow in places and steep and twisting on the north side (large signs portend doom for buses and trucks; caravans are a no-no).

The summit car park yields views down to glacial lakes in the rock-strewn valley below, where you can see the remains of walls and huts where people once lived impossibly hard lives. From the smaller, lower car park on the north side, beside a waterfall, you can make a 10-minute climb to hidden **Pedlar's Lake** and the kind of vistas that inspire mountain climbers.

The pass is a classic challenge for local road cyclists; it's best to start in Dingle town, from where the road climbs 400m over a distance of 7km. The climb from the north is more brutal, and has the added problem of being single track at the final, steepest section, so you'll be holding up the traffic.

Cloghane & Around

Cloghane (An Clochán) is another little slice of Dingle delight. The village's friendly pubs and accommodation nestle between Mt Brandon and Brandon Bay, with views across the water to the Stradbally Mountains.

The 5km drive out to **Brandon's Point** from Cloghane follows ever-narrower single-track roads, culminating in cliffs with fantastic views north and east. Sheep wander the constantly eroding rocks oblivious to their tenuous positions.

On the last weekend in July, Cloghane celebrates the ancient Celtic harvest festival **Lughnasa** with events – especially bonfires – both in the village and atop Mt Brandon.

Sleeping & Eating

Mount Brandon Hostel HOSTEL €
(☎085 136 3454; www.mountbrandonhostel.com; Cloghane; dm €20, s/d €35/50; ⏲Mar-Jan; @📶👪) 🍃 A small, simple hostel with scrubbed wooden floors and furniture, and a patio overlooking the bay. Most rooms have private bathrooms.

O'Connors INN €€
(☎066-713 8113; www.cloghane.com; d from €80; @📶) Book ahead to bag a room or a table in this welcoming village pub, which serves evening meals made using local produce, ranging from salmon to steak. Landlord Michael has loads of local info and can also explain why there's an aeroplane engine out front.

Getting There & Away

Buses run from Tralee to Cloghane (€12.70, 70 minutes) twice daily on Fridays only.

Castlegregory & Around

POP 243

Castlegregory (Caislean an Ghriare), which once rivalled Tralee as a busy local centre, is today a quiet village with lovely views of the hills to the south.

However, things change when you drive up the sandblown road along the Rough Point Peninsula, the broad spit of land between Tralee Bay and Brandon Bay. Up here, it's a water-sports playground. A prime windsurfing location, the peninsula also offers adrenaline-inducing wave-sailing and kitesurfing, while divers can swim among shoals of pollack amid the kelp forests and anemone-encrusted rocks of the Maharees Islands.

Activities

Jamie Knox Watersports WATER SPORTS

(066-713 9411; www.jamieknox.com; Maharees, Castlegregory) This place offers surf, windsurf, kitesurf, paddlesurf, canoe and pedalo hire and instruction. Surf lessons on Brandon Bay start at €30 for a 'taster'.

Waterworld DIVING

(066-713 9292; www.waterworld.ie; Harbour House, Scraggane Pier) The Maharees Islands (north of Castlegregory), Brandon Point and the Blasket Islands offer some of the best scuba-diving in Ireland. For qualified divers, this outfit runs daily boat trips to the best sites (per dive €35), and runs half-day Try-a-Dive packages (per person €80) for complete beginners.

Sleeping & Eating

Harbour House GUESTHOUSE €€

(066-713 9292; www.maharees.ie; Scraggane Pier; s/d from €55/90;) In a stunning position overlooking the Maharees Islands, this family-run establishment has the intimate feel of a B&B, with 15 comfortable, contemporary rooms (without TV or wi-fi, but there's both in the comfy communal lounges) and a gorgeous mascot, Lucy the dog. Harbour House is 5km north of Castlegregory near the end of the peninsula.

The guesthouse has a good **restaurant** (mains €11-27); the family have their own fishing boat, bringing catches 'from tide to table', with vegetables grown in the garden out back.

★**Spillane's** PUB FOOD €€

(066-713 9125; www.spillanesbar.com; Fahamore; mains €16-25; food served 1-9pm Jun-Aug, 5-9pm Mar-May, Sep & Oct;) Outside tables look across Brandon Bay to the mountains at this idyllic, laid-back pub out near the tip of the peninsula. Seafood is a speciality (the breaded scampi is a revalation), but it also does fabulous pizzas and house-made burgers with hand-cut chips.

Getting There & Away

Buses run from Tralee to Castlegregory (€9.40, 40 minutes) twice daily on Fridays only.

NORTHERN KERRY

The landscape of Northern Kerry is often dull compared with the glories of the Ring of Kerry and the Dingle Peninsula. But there are some interesting places that merit a pause along the way. Tralee has a great museum while Ballybunion and the blustery beaches south of the Shannon estuary are worth a look.

Tralee

POP 23,700

Although it's the county town, Tralee is often dismissed elsewhere in Kerry as an overflow for Limerick and its social problems. While that's unfair – there are some good restaurants and bars, a great museum and an interesting wetlands centre – it's certainly down-to-earth and more engaged with the business of everyday life than the tourist trade.

Founded by the Normans in 1216, Tralee has a long history of rebellion. In the 16th century the last ruling Earl of Desmond was captured and executed here. His head was sent to Elizabeth I, who spiked it on London Bridge. The Desmond castle once stood at the junction of Denny St and the Mall, but any trace of medieval Tralee that survived the Desmond Wars was razed during the Cromwellian period.

Elegant Denny St and Day Pl are the oldest parts of town, with 18th-century Georgian buildings, while the Square, just south of the Mall, is a pleasant open space with a contemporary style.

Sights & Activities

Kerry County Museum MUSEUM

(066-712 7777; www.kerrymuseum.ie; Denny St; adult/child €5/free; 9.30am-5.30pm Jun-Aug, 9.30am-5pm Tue-Sat Sep-May) An absolute treat, Kerry's county museum has excellent interpretive displays on Irish historical events and trends, with an emphasis on County Kerry. The Medieval Experience recreates life (smells and all) in Tralee in 1450. Check out the deranged knights, a vision of horror right out of Monty Python. The Tom Crean Room celebrates the local early-20th-century explorer who accompanied both Scott and Shackleton on epic Antarctic expeditions. It's housed in the neoclassical Ashe Memorial Hall.

Blennerville Windmill & Visitor Centre WINDMILL

(066-712 1064; Blennerville; adult/child €5/3; 9am-6pm Jun-Aug, 9.30am-5.30pm Apr, May,

Tralee

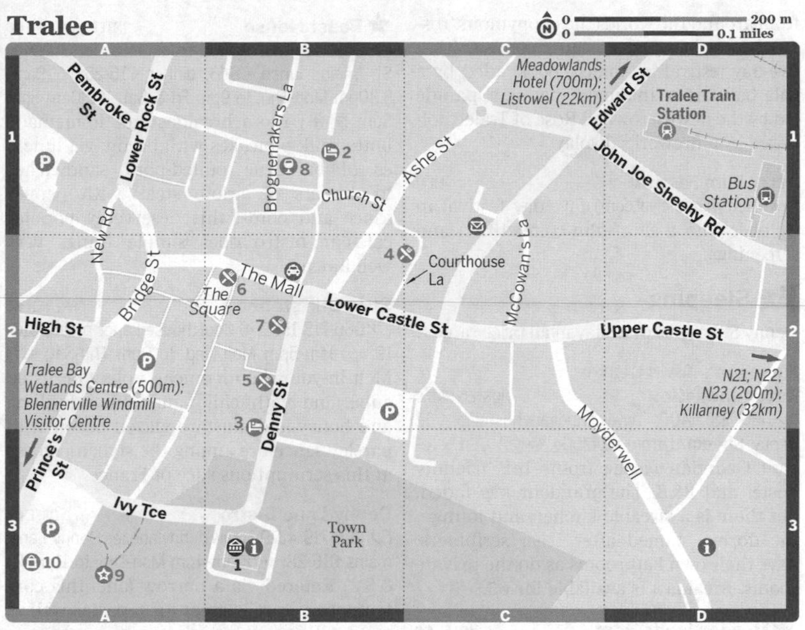

Tralee

Sights
1 Kerry County Museum B3

Sleeping
2 Ashe Hotel B1
3 Finnegan's Town Centre Accommodation B2

Eating
4 Chez Christophe C2
5 Denny Lane Bistro B2
6 Quinlan's Fish B2
7 Roast House B2

Drinking & Nightlife
8 Roundy's B1

Entertainment
9 Siamsa Tíre A3

Shopping
10 Farmers Market A3

Sep & Oct) Blennerville, just over 1km southwest of central Tralee on the N86 to Dingle, used to be the city's chief port, though the harbour has long since silted in. A 19th-century flour windmill here has been restored and is the largest working mill in Ireland and Britain. Its modern visitor centre houses an exhibition on grain milling, and on the thousands of emigrants who boarded 'coffin ships' from what was then Kerry's largest embarkation point.

Tralee Bay Wetlands Centre WETLANDS
(☎066-712 6700; www.traleebaywetlands.org; Ballyard Rd; adult/child €6/4; ⏰10am-7pm Jul & Aug, to 5pm Sep, Oct & Mar-Jun, 11am-4pm Nov-Feb) A 15-minute nature safari boat ride is the highlight of a visit to Tralee's wetlands centre. You can also get a good overview of the reserve's 3000 hectares, encompassing saltwater and freshwater habitats, from the 20m-high viewing tower (accessible by lift/elevator), and spot wildlife from bird hides. The main lake has pedal boats (per 30 minutes €10) and row boats (per 30 minutes €8) for hire, and a light-filled lakeside cafe/bistro; there's a smaller 'learn to fish' lake too.

Festivals & Events

Rose of Tralee CULTURAL
(www.roseoftralee.ie) Regularly criticised in the Irish media as something of a throwback to the 1950s, the nonetheless hugely popular Rose of Tralee is a beauty pageant open to Irish women, and women of Irish descent

from around the world (the eponymous 'roses'). More than just a beauty contest, it's a five-day festival in August, bookended by a gala ball and a 'midnight madness' parade led by the newly crowned Rose of Tralee, followed by a fireworks display.

Kerry Film Festival FILM
(www.kerryfilmfestival.com) Five-day festival in October with a short-film competition and screenings.

Sleeping

Denny St has places to stay in all price ranges.

Finnegan's Town Centre Accommodation HOSTEL, B&B €
(066-718 1400; www.finneganshostel.ie; 17 Denny St; dm/d from €14/50; @ wi-fi) An elegant Georgian facade fronts this friendly hostel and B&B. The grandeur has faded, but there is a sizeable kitchen and lounge; the dorms, named after Irish scribblers, have their own bathrooms as do the private rooms. Breakfast is available for €5.

★Meadowlands Hotel HOTEL €€
(066-718 0444; www.meadowlandshotel.com; Oakpark Rd; s/d from €85/113; @ wi-fi family) Strolling distance from town but far enough away to be quiet, Meadowlands is an unexpectedly romantic four-star hotel. Rooms are done out in autumnal hues and service is spot on; ask about discounted rates. Its cavernous, beam-ceilinged bar, serving top-notch seafood (the owners have their own fishing fleet), is at least as popular with locals as it is with visitors.

Ashe Hotel HOTEL €€
(066-710 6300; www.theashehotel.ie; Maine St; s/d €80/120; wi-fi) This newly opened hotel offers good-value, stylish and modern accommodation right in the town centre.

Eating

Tralee's **farmers market** (Princes St; 11am-3pm Sat) sprawls along Princes St.

Quinlan's Fish SEAFOOD €
(066-712 3998; The Mall; mains €8-15; noon-10pm) Quinlan's is Kerry's leading chain of fish shops, with their own fleet, so you know its fare is fresh. The fish and chips are great; alternatives include Dingle Bay squid and chips with sweet chilli sauce. The Delft-blue and scrubbed-timber premises have a handful of wine barrel tables, or head to Tralee's Town Park.

★Roast House INTERNATIONAL €€
(066-718 1011; www.theroasthouse.ie; 3 Denny St; mains lunch €8-13, dinner €16-25; 9am-5.30pm Mon-Thu, to 9pm Fri & Sat, 10.30am-5pm Sun; wi-fi family) From breakfasts of homemade buttermilk pancakes with bacon, via lunches of barbecue pulled-pork sandwiches to dinners of sirloin steak with pepper sauce and chips, this deservedly popular cafe-cum-bistro does simple things very well indeed.

Chez Christophe FRENCH €€
(066-718 1562; 6 Courthouse Lane; mains €10-19; 9am-5pm Mon-Wed, to 9pm Thu-Sat; wi-fi) Melt-in-your-mouth quiche, polenta-crusted aubergine with chilli and almond filling and honey-and-mustard-glazed bacon with parsley sauce are among the stylish choices at this scrumptious slice of France.

Denny Lane Bistro CAFE €€
(066-719 4319; www.dennylane.ie; Denny Lane; mains €16-28; 10am-4pm Mon-Thu, to 11pm Fri & Sat) Entered via a narrow lane, this contemporary spot is great for tapas as well as more filling meals such as slow-roast pork belly or pan-fried fillet of hake.

Drinking & Entertainment

Castle St is thick with mass-market pubs, many of them offering live entertainment.

★Roundy's BAR
(5 Broguemakers Lane; 5pm-late) Ingeniously converted from a terrace house (with a tree still growing right through the courtyard garden-turned-interior), this funky little bar has hip tunes, regular DJs spinning old school funk and live bands. Very cool.

Siamsa Tíre THEATRE
(066-712 3055; www.siamsatire.com; Town Park; tickets €15-30; booking office 9am-6pm Mon-Sat) Siamsa Tíre, the National Folk Theatre of Ireland, recreates dynamic aspects of Gaelic culture through song, dance, drama and mime. There are several shows a week year-round.

Information

Castle St has banks with ATMs and bureaux de change.

Tourist Office (066-712 1288; Denny St; 9.15am-5pm Mon-Sat, daily Jul & Aug) In the same building as Kerry County Museum.

Tralee General Hospital (066-712 6222; Boherbee) Has an accident and emergency unit.

Getting There & Away

Bus Éireann (066-716 4700; www.buseireann.ie) operates from the bus station next to the train station, east of the town centre.

Cork (€23, 2½ hours, hourly)

Dublin (€31, six hours, nine daily)

Killarney (€10.70, 40 minutes, hourly)

Limerick (€22, two hours, nine daily)

Listowel (€9.40, 40 minutes, nine daily)

Waterford (€31, 4¾ hours, hourly)

Irish Rail (066-712 3522; www.irishrail.ie) services include three daily trains via Mallow to Cork (€36, 2½ hours), up to eight to Killarney (€11.35, 30 minutes) and one direct train to Dublin (€69, 3¾ hours) with others requiring a change in Mallow.

Getting Around

There's a taxi rank on the Mall, or try **Jackie Power Tours & Cabs** (066-712 6300; 2 Lower Rock St).

O'Halloran Cycles (066-712 2820; 83 Boherbee; 9am-6.30pm Mon-Sat) hires out bikes (€15 per day).

Around Tralee

East of town you'll find one of the country's finest caves. Heading west takes you past the tiny township of Spa to the fishing port of Fenit. Travelling northwest takes you to Ardfert's medieval cathedral.

Crag Cave

Crag Cave (066-714 1244; www.cragcave.com; Castleisland; adult/child €12/5; 10am-6pm daily Apr-Dec, Wed-Sun only Jan-Mar) was discovered in 1983, when problems with water pollution led to a search for the source of the local river. In 1989, 300m of the 4km-long cave were opened to the public; admission is by 30-minute guided tour. The remarkable rock formations include a stalagmite shaped like a statue of the Madonna (at least to some). There are play areas for kids, as well as a restaurant and, of course, a gift shop. The cave is signposted 18km east of Tralee.

Spa & Fenit

POP 987

Northwest of Tralee along the coast, it's about 7km to the small settlement of Spa (sometimes referred to on maps as 'The Spa') and another 6km on to Fenit.

Fenit's Irish name, An Fhianait, translates as 'the Wild Place', and although the remote village itself is tiny, its position on the Atlantic has given rise to a sizeable fishing port and marina, and some sublime seafood restaurants that pull in the crowds from Tralee.

Eating

West End Bar & Bistro SEAFOOD €€
(066-713 6246; www.westendfenit.ie; West End, Fenit; mains €10-25; food served 5-9pm Mon-Sat, 1-8pm Sun, closed Jan-Mar) A local icon, this fifth-generation bar has a mouth-watering lineup of seafood, including Tralee Bay crab baguettes, plus plenty of locally sourced meat dishes (their motto is 'fresh or nothing').

Oyster Tavern SEAFOOD €€
(066-713 6102; Spa; mains €14-30; 5-10pm Mon-Sat, noon-9pm Sun;) Grilled Atlantic salmon, pan-fried Kerry Head crab claws, Dingle Bay prawn scampi and lobster in season star at this classy restaurant, but carnivores and vegetarians aren't forgotten, with plenty of inventive options.

Ardfert Cathedral

The impressive remains of 13th-century **Ardfert Cathedral** (066-713 4711; www.heritageireland.ie; adult/child €4/2; 10am-6pm May-Sep) are notable for the beautiful and delicate stone carvings on its Romanesque door and window arches. Set into one of the interior walls is an effigy, said to be of St Brendan the Navigator, who was educated in Ardfert and founded a monastery here. Other elaborate medieval grave slabs can be seen in the visitor centre. Ardfert is 10km northwest of Tralee on the Ballyheigue road.

Listowel

POP 4830

The late writer Bryan MacMahon said of Listowel: 'I harbour the absurd notion of motivating a small town in Ireland, a speck on the map, to become a centre of the imagination'. Listowel certainly has more literary credentials than your average provincial town, with connections to such accomplished scribes as John B Keane, Maurice Walsh, George Fitzmaurice and Brendan Kennelly.

Outside these connections and a few venues, however, the town is little more than some tidy Georgian streets arranged around an attractive main square with a Norman castle overlooking the River Feale.

Sights & Activities

Kerry Literary & Cultural Centre CULTURAL CENTRE
(Seanchaí; ☎068-22212; www.kerrywritersmuseum.com; The Square; adult/child €5/3; ⏲9.30am-5.30pm daily Jun-Sep, 10am-4pm Mon-Fri Oct-May) The audiovisual Writers' Exhibition in this Georgian building gives due prominence to Listowel's heritage of literary observers of Irish life. Rooms are devoted to local greats such as John B Keane and Bryan MacMahon, with simple, haunting tableaux narrating their lives and recordings of them reading their work. There's a cafe and a performance space where events are sometimes staged.

Listowel Castle CASTLE
(☎086 385 7201; www.heritageireland.ie; ⏲9.30am-5.30pm Wed-Sun late May-late Aug) FREE Standing between the town square and the river, this 12th-century castle was once the stronghold of the Fitzmaurices, the Anglo-Norman lords of Kerry. It was the last castle in Ireland to succumb to the Elizabethan attacks during the Desmond revolt. What remains of the castle has been thoroughly restored.

Lartigue Monorailway MUSEUM
(☎068-24393; www.lartiguemonorail.com; John B Keane Rd; adult/child €6/3; ⏲1-4.30pm May-Sep) Designed by Frenchman Charles Lartigue, this unique survivor of Victorian railway engineering once ran between Listowel and Ballybunion on the coast. The renovated section of line is short (less than a kilometre) but fascinating, with manual turntables at either end for swinging the train around.

Festivals & Events

Writers' Week LITERARY
(www.facebook.com/writersweek) Bibliophiles flock to Listowel for five days of readings, poetry, music, drama, seminars, storytelling and many other events held at various locations around town. Held in May/June.

Sleeping & Eating

Listowel Arms Hotel HOTEL €€
(☎068-21500; www.listowelarms.com; The Square; d from €120; @📶) Listowel's principal hotel is a family-run affair in a Georgian building that balances grandeur with country charm. Furnished with antiques and marble sinks, the 42 rooms overlook the river. The Writers Bar is a good place to find music in the summer, while the **Georgian Restaurant** (mains €13-22) specialises in the catch of the day.

John B Keane PUB
(37 William St; ⏲11am-midnight Tue-Sat, 7-11.30pm Sun & Mon) Once run by the late writer himself, this small, unassuming bar is swathed in Keane memorabilia.

Information

The **Tourist Office** (☎068-22212; www.listowel.ie; ⏲10am-4pm Mon-Fri, daily Jul & Aug) is in the Kerry Literary & Cultural Centre.

Getting There & Away

Eight or nine buses a day run from Listowel to Tralee (€9.40, 40 minutes) and Limerick (€20.20, 1½ hours).

Around Listowel

Ballybunion

POP 1350

Ballybunion (www.ballybunion.ie), a beach town 15km northeast of Listowel on the R553, is best known for the **Ballybunion Golf Club** (☎068-27146; www.ballybuniongolfclub.ie; green fees €65-180), reputed as one of the finest links courses in the world. Beyond the statue of a club-swinging Bill Clinton, commemorating his visit to the course in 1998, there are two expansive **beaches**; Ballybunion South has a Blue Flag rating.

Overlooking the southern beach are the remains of **Ballybunion Castle**. There's an underground passage leading from the castle to the cliff.

The **Ballybunion Bachelor Festival** in August sees tuxedo-clad bachelors from Ireland and beyond vying to impress the judges, while the town enjoys a long weekend of street entertainment and celebrations.

Three buses a day run from Listowel to Ballybunion Monday to Saturday (€5.50, 20 minutes).

Tarbert

POP 550

Tarbert is 16km north of Listowel on the N69. **Shannon Ferry Limited** (☎068-905 3124; www.shannonferries.com; cyclists & pedestrians €5, cars €18; ⏲7.30am-7.30pm Sep-May, longer hours Jun-Aug; 📶) runs an hourly ferry between Tarbert and Killimer in County Clare, skipping the traffic congestion around Limerick city. The ferry dock is clearly signposted 2.2km west of Tarbert.

In July and August, buses run once or twice a day from Limerick (€17, 1¼ hours).

Counties Limerick & Tipperary

Includes ➡

Best Places to Eat

- ➡ Restaurant 1826 Adare (p308)
- ➡ Mustard Seed at Echo Lodge (p309)
- ➡ Chocolat (p304)
- ➡ Cafe Hans (p314)
- ➡ Country Choice (p321)

Best Places to Stay

- ➡ Adare Manor (p308)
- ➡ No 1 Pery Square (p304)
- ➡ Raheen House Hotel (p317)
- ➡ Dunraven Arms (p308)
- ➡ Apple Caravan & Camping Park (p315)

Why Go?

From marching ditties to rhyming puns, the names Tipperary and Limerick are part of the lexicon, but both are relatively unexplored by visitors.

County Limerick is closely tied to its namesake city, which has a history as dramatic as Ireland's. In a nation of hard knocks, it seems to have had more than its fair share. The city's streets have tangible links to the past and a gritty, honest vibrancy, and treasures abound in its lush, green country side.

In contrast, Tipperary town is minor. But amid the county's rolling hills, rich farmland and deep valleys bordered by soaring mountains, it's a peaceful place that's perfect for following a river to its source or climbing a stile to reach a lonely ruin.

In both counties, ancient Celtic sites, medieval abbeys and other relics endure in solitude, awaiting discovery. And even Limerick and Tipperary's best-known sights retain a rough, inspiring dignity.

When to Go

➡ As the third-largest city in Ireland, with a sizeable student population, Limerick city bustles year-round, but is at its liveliest during the warmer months, from around April to October.

➡ April to October is also the best time to explore the rural villages, towns and countryside of both counties, when opening hours for attractions are longest (a number close during the rest of the year) and the weather is at its best.

➡ Most of the counties' festivities take place from April to October too, including wonderful walking festivals in the Glen of Aherlow.

Counties Limerick & Tipperary Highlights

❶ Discover Bronze Age, Iron Age, medieval and modern art treasures at the **Hunt Museum** (p301) in Limerick city.

❷ Take in Shannon Estuary vistas along Limerick's back roads via atmospheric ruins at **Askeaton** and the **Flying Boat Museum** (p306) at Foynes.

❸ Delve into a dazzling underworld of passages and chambers at the **Mitchelstown Caves** (p316).

4 Walk the walls and keep of Cahir's storybook **castle** (p315).

5 Explore the ancient religious buildings crowning the **Rock of Cashel** (p310).

6 Deliberate over mouth-watering menus in the thatched heritage town of **Adare** (p307).

7 Journey through a tranquil bucolic landscape in the **Glen of Aherlow** (p310).

COUNTY LIMERICK

POP 191,800 / AREA 2700 SQ KM

Limerick's low-lying farmland is framed on its southern and eastern boundaries by swelling uplands and mountains. Limerick city is boisterously urban in contrast and has enough historic and cultural attractions for a day's diversion. About 15km south of the city are the haunting archaeological sites around Lough Gur, while about the same distance southwest of the city is the cute thatched village of Adare.

Limerick City

POP 56,800

Limerick city straddles the Shannon's broadening tidal stream, where the river swings west to join the Shannon Estuary. Following its tough past as narrated in Frank McCourt's *Angela's Ashes,* its medieval and Georgian architecture received a glitzy, glossy makeover during the Celtic Tiger era, but the economic downturn hit the city hard.

The city is rejuvenating again, however. Limerick was chosen as the country's first-ever Irish City of Culture in 2014, has a recently renovated castle, a lively art museum and contemporary cafe culture to go with its uncompromised pubs, as well as locals who go out of their way to welcome you.

The city is compact enough to get around on foot or by bike. To walk across town from St Mary's Cathedral to the train station takes about 15 minutes.

TRACING YOUR ANCESTORS

Genealogical centres in Counties Limerick and Tipperary can help trace your ancestors; contact the centres in advance to arrange a consultation.

Limerick Genealogy (☎061-496 542; www.limerickgenealogy.com; Dooradoyle Rd, Lissanalta House, Dooradoyle) Professional genealogical research service.

Tipperary South Genealogy Centre (☎062-61122; www.tipperarysouth.rootsireland.ie; Brú Ború Heritage Centre, Cashel) Comprehensive family history research service.

Tipperary Family History Research (☎062-80555; www.tfhr.org; Mitchell St, Excel Heritage Centre, Tipperary town) Family research in Tipperary.

History

Viking adventurers established a settlement on an island in the River Shannon in the 9th century. They fought with the native Irish for control of the site until Brian Ború's forces drove them out in 968 and established Limerick as the royal seat of the O'Brien kings. Brian Ború finally destroyed Viking power and presence in Ireland at the Battle of Clontarf in 1014. By the late 12th century, invading Normans had supplanted the Irish as the town's rulers. Throughout the Middle Ages the two groups remained divided.

From 1690 to 1691, Limerick acquired heroic status in the saga of Ireland's struggle against occupation by the English. After their defeat in the Battle of the Boyne in 1690, Jacobite forces withdrew west behind the famously strong walls of Limerick town until the Treaty of Limerick guaranteed religious freedom for Catholics. The English later reneged and enforced fierce anti-Catholic legislation, an act of betrayal that came to symbolise the injustice of British rule.

During the 18th century, the old walls of Limerick were demolished and a well-planned and prosperous Georgian town developed. Such prosperity had waned by the early 20th century, as traditional industries fell on hard times. Several high-profile nationalists hailed from here, including Éamon de Valera.

◉ Sights

Limerick's main places of interest cluster to the north on King's Island (the oldest part of Limerick and once part of Englishtown), to the south around the Crescent and Pery Sq (the city's noteworthy Georgian area), and all along the riverbanks.

★King John's Castle CASTLE

(www.shannonheritage.com; Nicholas St; adult/child €10/5.25; ⏲9.30am-5.30pm daily Apr-Sep, to 4.30pm Oct-Mar) An obdurate and brooding Norman mass over the River Shannon, the vast curtain walls and towers of Limerick's showpiece castle are best viewed from the west bank of the water. Built on the orders of King John of England between 1200 and 1212 on the site of an earlier fortification, the castle served as the military and administrative centre of the wealthy Shannon region, and recently reopened after extensive renovations.

Inside await recreations of brutal medieval weapons such as the trebuchet, as well

FRANK MCCOURT

No one name has been so closely intertwined with Limerick in recent years as Frank McCourt (1930–2009). His poignant autobiographical novel *Angela's Ashes* was a surprise publishing sensation in 1996, bringing him fame and honours (including the Pulitzer Prize).

Although he was born in New York City, McCourt's immigrant family returned to Limerick four years later, unable to survive in America. His childhood was filled with the kinds of deprivations that were all too common at the time: his father was a drunk who later vanished, three of his six siblings died in childhood and at age 13 he dropped out of school to earn money to help his family survive.

At age 19, McCourt returned to New York and later worked for three decades as a high school teacher. Among the subjects he taught was writing. From the 1970s he dabbled in writing and theatre with his brother Malachy. He started *Angela's Ashes* only after retiring from teaching in 1987. Its early sales success was thanks to a bevy of enthusiastic critics, but in Limerick the reaction was mixed, with many decrying the negative portrait it painted of the city.

Today McCourt's legacy in Limerick is celebrated. Limerick city's tourist office has information about city sights related to the book, you can join Frank McCourt walking tours, visit the **Frank McCourt Museum** (www.frankmccmuseum.wix.com/frankmccourt museum; Leamy House, Hartstonge St; adult/child €4/2; 11am-4.30pm Mon-Fri) and drink in one of the watering holes mentioned in the book, **South's** (p304).

as excavated Viking sites, reconstructed Norman features, further artefacts, multimedia displays and 'discovery drawers' for kids. Book online for discounts.

★Hunt Museum MUSEUM
(www.huntmuseum.com; Custom House, Rutland St; adult/child €5/2.50; 10am-5pm Mon-Sat, 2-5pm Sun;) Although named for its benefactors, this museum is also a treasure hunt. Visitors are encouraged to open drawers and otherwise poke around the finest collection of Bronze Age, Iron Age, medieval and modern art treasures outside Dublin. Highlights include a Syracusan coin thought to have been one of the 30 pieces of silver paid to Judas for his betrayal of Christ, a Renoir study, a Gauguin painting, a Giacometti drawing and works by Picasso and Jack B Yeats.

There's also a tiny but exquisite bronze horse once attributed to da Vinci (but now considered a much later copy), Cycladic sculptures, an alabaster vase from Ancient Egypt dated to the 3rd century BC and a smattering of pieces from the Far East. The 2000-plus items are from the private collection of the late John and Gertrude Hunt, antique dealers and consultants, who championed historic preservation throughout the region. Free one-hour guided tours from the dedicated and colourful volunteers are available. The museum has a good cafe.

★Limerick City Gallery of Art GALLERY
(www.limerickcitygallery.ie; Carnegie Bldg, Pery Sq; 10am-5.30pm Mon-Wed, Fri & Sat, to 8.30pm Thu, noon-5.30pm Sun) FREE Limerick's excellent gallery adjoins the peaceful People's Park, at the heart of Georgian Limerick. Among its permanent collection of traditional paintings from the last 300 years are works by Sean Keating and Jack B Yeats. Temporary exhibitions of conceptual and thought-provoking contemporary art fill the other excellently illuminated galleries. The gallery is the home of **eva International** (www.eva.ie), Ireland's contemporary art biennial held across the city in even-numbered years. Check the website for dates.

There's a lovely cafe (open 9.30am to 5pm) looking across the park.

St Mary's Cathedral CATHEDRAL
(061-310 293; Bridge St; admission €4; 9am-5pm Mon-Fri, 9am-4pm Sat & Sun) Limerick's ancient cathedral was founded in 1168 by Donal Mór O'Brien, king of Munster. Parts of the 12th-century Romanesque western doorway, nave and aisles survive, and there are splendid 15th-century black-oak misericords (for supporting 'clerical posteriors') in the Jebb Chapel, unique examples of their kind in Ireland and each fabulously carved with creatures and mythical animals. Call ahead to confirm opening hours and to check if there are any musical events scheduled.

Limerick

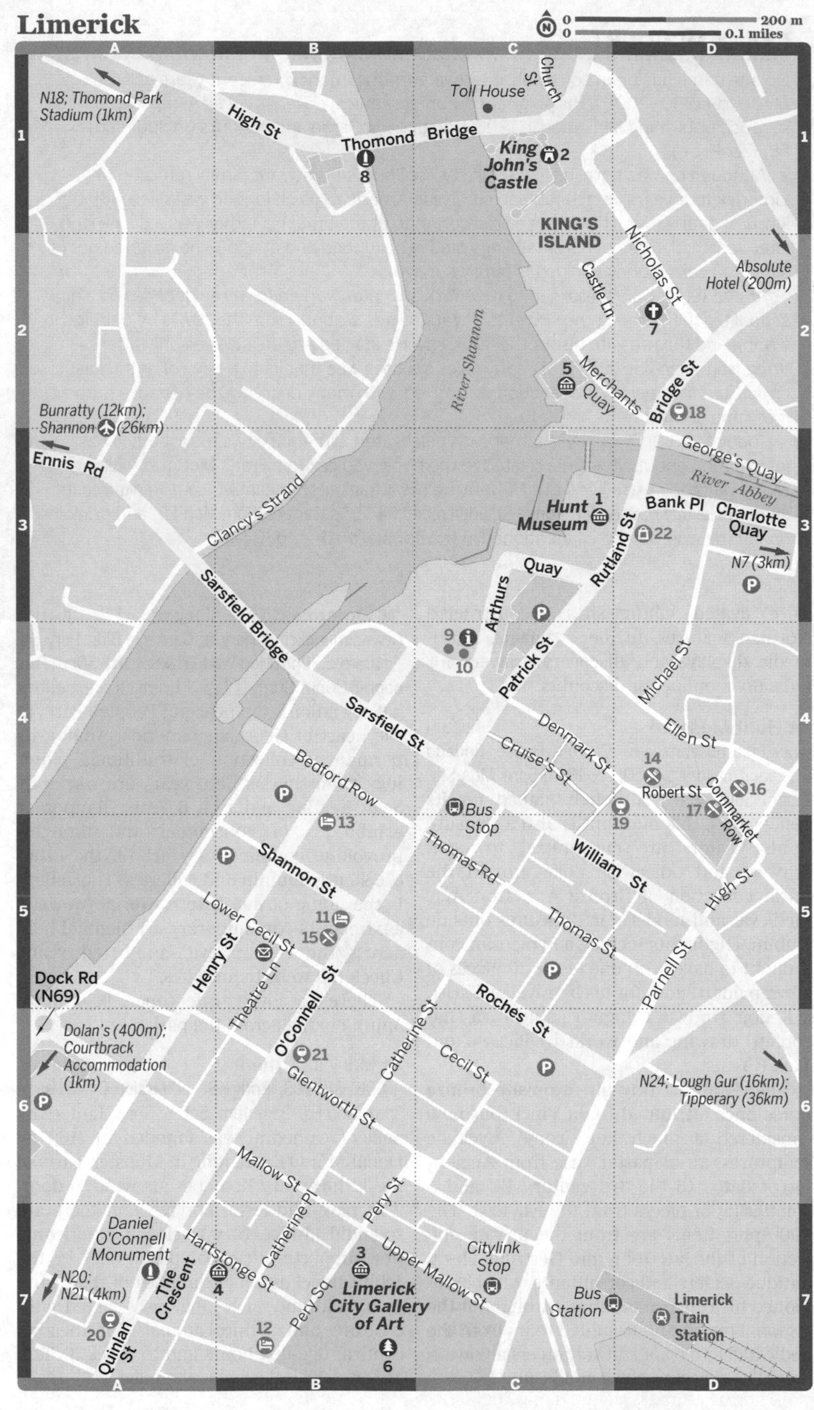

0 200 m
0 0.1 miles
N18; Thomond Park Stadium (1km)
High St
Thomond Bridge
Toll House
Church St
King John's Castle
KING'S ISLAND
Nicholas St
Castle Ln
Absolute Hotel (200m)
River Shannon
Merchants Quay
Bridge St
George's Quay
River Abbey
Bunratty (12km); Shannon (26km)
Ennis Rd
Clancy's Strand
Hunt Museum
Bank Pl
Charlotte Quay
Rutland St
Arthurs Quay
N7 (3km)
Sarsfield Bridge
Patrick St
Michael St
Sarsfield St
Denmark St
Ellen St
Cruise's St
Bedford Row
Robert St
Cornmarket Row
Bus Stop
Thomas Rd
William St
Shannon St
High St
Lower Cecil St
Thomas St
Henry St
Theatre Ln
O'Connell St
Parnell St
Dock Rd (N69)
Roches St
Catherine St
Dolan's (400m); Courtbrack Accommodation (1km)
Cecil St
Glentworth St
N24; Lough Gur (16km); Tipperary (36km)
Mallow St
Pery St
Catherine Pl
Daniel O'Connell Monument
Hartstonge St
Upper Mallow St
Citylink Stop
The Crescent
N20; N21 (4km)
Bus Station
Limerick Train Station
Limerick City Gallery of Art
Pery Sq
Quinlan St

Limerick

Top Sights
1 Hunt Museum C3
2 King John's Castle C1
3 Limerick City Gallery of Art B7

Sights
4 Frank McCourt Museum B7
5 Limerick City Museum C2
6 People's Park B7
7 St Mary's Cathedral D2
8 Treaty Stone B1

Activities, Courses & Tours
9 Angela's Ashes Walking Tour C4
10 Red Viking C4

Sleeping
11 George Boutique Hotel B5
12 No 1 Pery Square B7
13 Savoy B5

Eating
14 Café Noir D4
15 Chocolat B5
16 Milk Market D4
17 Taj Restaurant D4

Drinking & Nightlife
18 Locke Bar D2
19 Nancy Blake's D4
20 South's A7
21 Whitehouse Pub B6

Shopping
22 Celtic Bookshop D3

People's Park PARK
(www.limerick.ie/peoples-park; Pery Sq; 8am-dusk winter, 8am-9pm summer) Full of trees, this lovely park in Pery Square at the heart of Georgian Limerick is an excellent place for collapsing onto the grass with a chunky novel when the sun pops out. Check out the magnificently restored 19th-century red-and-white drinking fountain. The statue on the outside column in the middle of the park is of Thomas Spring Rice, a former MP for Limerick.

Treaty Stone MONUMENT
(King John's Castle) The Treaty Stone marks the spot on the bank of the River Shannon where the Treaty of Limerick was signed in 1691, guaranteeing religious freedom for Catholics.

Limerick City Museum MUSEUM
(City Hall, Merchant's Quay; 10am-1pm & 2-5pm Mon-Fri) FREE This small and modest museum has exhibits on Limerick silverwork and Limerick's lace manufacturing, with some elegant examples including a baby's blouse. There are also exhibits relating to local history, including the Limerick Soviet (1919).

Thomond Park Stadium STADIUM
(061-421 109; www.thomondpark.ie; tours adult/child €10/8, on match days €5/3) From 1995 until 2007, the Munster rugby team was undefeated in this legendary stadium, which was massively rebuilt in 2008, the year they won the Heineken European Cup for the second time. Tours of the hallowed ground include its memorabilia-filled museum. It's an easy 1km walk northwest of the centre along High St.

Tours

Limerick Walking Tours WALKING TOUR
(www.limerickwalkingtours.com; adult/child €10/free) Highly popular and entertaining guided walks around town from knowledgeable Declan, who moonlights at the Hunt Museum. Tours start and finish outside Brown Thomas on Patrick St, near the intersection with Sarsfield St.

Angela's Ashes Walking Tour WALKING TOUR
(087 235 1339; per person €10) Noel Curtin runs entertaining and informative walking tours of the city covering locations featured in Frank McCourt's memoir, departing from the tourist office at 2.30pm.

Red Viking BUS TOUR
(061-394 033; www.redvikingtours.com; adult/child €12/6; May-Oct) Hop-on, hop-off 90-minute open-top bus tours depart from beside the tourist office and at eight other points around town, including King John's Castle, the Treaty Stone and People's Park.

Sleeping

Aim to stay near the city centre, for the convenience and nightlife.

Alexandra Tce on O'Connell Ave (which runs south from O'Connell St) has several midrange B&Bs. Ennis Rd, leading northwest towards Shannon, also has a selection, although most are at least 1km from the centre.

George Boutique Hotel HOTEL €
(061-460 400; www.thegeorgeboutiquehotel.com; O'Connell St; d from €60;) The lobby is rather tacky, but rooms – blond wood,

caramels and browns, some with shower, others with bath – are congenially neutral and comfortable at this brisk and frequently booked-out hotel. The entrance is around the corner on Shannon St.

Courtbrack Accommodation B&B €
(☎061-302 500; Courtbrack Ave; dm/s/d €23.50/30/52; ⏰May-Aug; @📶) Student digs during semester, but opens during summertime for visitors. Tourist rates at this spiffy red-hued place include continental breakfast. Spotless facilities include a kitchen, laundry and common area with wi-fi. It's about 1km southwest of the city centre, just south of Dock Rd (the N69).

★**No 1 Pery Square** HOTEL €€
(☎061-402 402; www.oneperysquare.com; 1 Pery Sq; club r from €135, period r from €195; 📶) Treat yourself to a night in Georgian Limerick at this excellent hotel right on the corner of Pery Square. Choose between very well-presented Club rooms (each named after an Irish poet) in the modern extension or one of the four period rooms in the classic Georgian townhouse, each a feast of huge sash windows and high ceilings, with capacious bathrooms.

Absolute Hotel HOTEL €€
(☎061-463 600; www.absolutehotel.com; Sir Harry's Mall; d from €79; @📶) Exposed brick walls, granite bathrooms, and a light-filled atrium lobby give this gleaming riverfront hotel a smart, contemporary edge. There's a cocooning in-house spa, plus a bar and grill. Check in early: secure parking is free but limited.

Savoy HOTEL €€
(☎061-448 700; www.savoylimerick.com; Henry St; d from €99; @📶🏊👪) This five-star hotel is a bit bruised and more like four-star, but it's smart enough, with comfy king-size beds and a turn-down service, a spa that specialises in Thai massages, a small swimming pool and a couple of top-notch in-house restaurants.

Eating

★**Milk Market** MARKET
(www.milkmarketlimerick.ie; Cornmarket Row; ⏰food market 8am-3pm Sat, shops 10am-4pm Fri, 8am-3pm Sat, 11am-4pm Sun) 🍃 Pick from organic produce and local foods like cheese at the traditional food market held in Limerick's old market buildings, or browse its produce and craft shops. Other markets are listed on the website.

Café Noir CAFE €
(☎061-411 222; www.cafenoir.ie; Robert St; dishes €4.50-11; ⏰8am-5.30pm Mon-Wed, to 6.30pm Thu-Sat) Tempting tarts lead the way at this French-inspired bakery/cafe, which also deals in exquisite pastries, salads, pies, quiches and its house speciality – French onion soup.

★**Chocolat** INTERNATIONAL €€
(☎061-609 709; www.chocolatrestaurant.ie; 109 O'Connell St; mains €12.50-25, 3-course dinner €17.50; ⏰12.30-9.30pm Mon-Thu, to 10pm Fri & Sat, 1-9pm Sun) Bathed in dark-chocolate hues with background soft ambient music and overseen by busy staff, this international restaurant is a smart choice. There's an eclectic but populist choice on the menu, from Thai curry to burgers, fajitas, yan pang chicken, pasta and surf-and-turf. Cocktails are inventive and generous. Worth booking ahead.

Taj Restaurant INDIAN €€
(2 Cornmarket Row; mains €12.50-17.50; ⏰noon-4pm daily & 5-11pm Mon-Sat, 5-10pm Sun) With white linen tablecloths, friendly service and modest concessions to Indian decor, this restaurant has a fine North Indian and Punjab menu and a fantastic all-your-can-eat €8.95 lunchtime buffet, with a choice of vegetarian and meat curries. Highlights from the à la carte choices include the mild *murgh tikka masala* and spicier chicken *karahi*.

Drinking & Nightlife

★**Nancy Blake's** PUB
(Upper Denmark St) There's sawdust on the floor and peat on the fire in the cosy front bar of this wonderful old pub. Out back is a vast covered drinking zone that often features live music or televised matches.

Whitehouse Pub PUB
(52 O'Connell St; ⏰10.30am-11.30pm Sun-Thu, to 12.30am Fri & Sat) A classic right in the centre, this corner pub has outdoor seating and a good beer list. On some nights it has live acoustic music, on others it helps lead a rebirth of local poetry through readings, with open-mic evenings.

Locke Bar PUB
(www.lockebar.com; 3 George's Quay; ⏰9am-11.30pm Mon-Thu, till late Fri & Sat, 10am-11pm Sun; 📶) Picturesque waterside setting, a maze of rooms, great bar food and views over the river.

South's PUB
(4 Quinlan St; ⏰10.30am-11.30pm Mon-Thu, to 12.30am Fri & Sat, to 11pm Sun) Frank McCourt's

father knocked 'em back here and the *Angela's Ashes* connection is given a run for its money – even the toilets are named Frank and Angela. Check out the fabulous interior.

Entertainment

Check at the tourist office for events listings. Most clubs have strict door checks.

Dolan's LIVE MUSIC
(www.dolanspub.com; 3 & 4 Dock Rd) Limerick's best spot for live music promises authentic trad sessions and an unbeatable gig list, as well as cutting-edge stand-ups in two adjoining venues.

University Concert Hall CONCERT HALL
(UCH; ☎061-331 549; www.uch.ie; University of Limerick; ⊙11am-8.30pm Mon-Fri, 4.30-8.30pm Sat & Sun) Permanent home of the Irish Chamber Orchestra, with regular concerts from visiting acts, plus opera, drama, comedy and dance. The campus is 4.5km east of the city.

Shopping

Celtic Bookshop BOOKS
(☎061-401 155; 2 Rutland St; ⊙11am-5pm Mon & Wed-Fri) Crammed with specialist titles on local and Irish topics.

Information

DANGERS & ANNOYANCES

Reputation and unfortunate nickname 'Stab City' aside, central Limerick is not any less safe than other urban Irish areas. Keep alert at night and stick to well-lit areas.

INTERNET ACCESS

The tourist office website has a map of free wi-fi hotspots throughout the city.

MEDICAL SERVICES

Midwestern Regional Hospital (☎061-301 111; Dooradoyle) has an accident and an emergency department.

MONEY

AIB Bank (106/108 O'Connell St; ⊙10am-5pm Mon & Tue, 10.30am-4pm Wed, 10am-4pm Thu & Fri) has a bureau de change.

POST

The **Main Post Office** (⊙9am-5.30pm Mon & Wed-Sat, from 9.30am Tue) is on Lower Cecil St.

TOURIST INFORMATION

Limerick Tourist Office (☎061-317 522; www.limerick.ie; Arthurs Quay; ⊙9am-5.30pm Mon-Sat) is a big, impressive facility with helpful staff.

Getting There & Away

AIR

Shannon Airport (p331) in County Clare handles domestic and international flights.

BUS

Bus Éireann (☎061-313 333; www.buseireann.ie; Parnell St) services operate from the bus and train stations near the city centre, with regular buses to Cork (€15.50, 1¾ hours), Tralee (€22, two hours) and Dublin (€13, 3½ hours), as well as to Galway, Killarney, Rosslare, Ennis, Shannon, Derry and most other centres. You can also get off in Limerick at the bus stop on O'Connell St.

Citylink (☎1890 280 808; www.citylink.ie) has up to six buses a day to Galway (€17, 1½ hours) and Cork (€17, two hours). Buses stop on Upper Mallow St.

Eireagle.com (www.eireagle.com) has eight luxury wi-fi-equipped coaches daily to Dublin Airport (€25, 2½ hours), leaving from Arthurs Quay.

JJ Kavanagh & Sons (☎081 8333 222; www.jjkavanagh.ie) has seven buses daily to Dublin (€11) and Dublin Airport (€20). Buses stop outside Limerick's tourist office.

TRAIN

Irish Rail (www.irishrail.ie) has regular trains from **Limerick Railway Station** (☎061-315 555; Parnell St) including nine trains daily to Ennis (€10, 40 minutes), hourly services to Dublin Heuston (€53, 2½ hours), and nine services to Galway (€23, two hours). Other routes, including to Cork, Tralee, Tipperary, Cahir and Waterford, involve changing at **Limerick Junction**, 20km southeast of Limerick.

Getting Around

Regular **Bus Éireann** (€8.40) buses connect Limerick's bus and train station with Shannon Airport; regular **JJ Kavanagh & Sons** (€4) buses run to Shannon Airport from Arthur's Quay. A taxi from the city centre to the airport costs around €35 to €45. The airport is 26km northwest of Limerick, about 30 minutes by car.

Taxis can be found outside the tourist office, at the bus and train stations, and in Thomas St, or try **Swift Taxis** (☎061-313 131).

Limerick's brand new Coca-Cola Zero **bike share scheme** (23 stations around town) is, for visitors, €3 (€150 deposit) for three days. The first 30 minutes of each hire is free.

Around Limerick City

Close to the city there's a clutch of outstanding historic sites that reward a day trip by car or a couple of days by bike.

WORTH A TRIP

LIMERICK CITY TO TARBERT VIA THE SCENIC N69

The narrow, peaceful N69 road follows the Shannon Estuary along the Wild Atlantic Way west from Limerick for 58km to Tarbert in northern County Kerry. There are some fantastic views of the broadening estuary and seemingly endless rolling green hills laced with stone walls.

At the small village of **Clarina** past Mungret on the N69, hang a right to head north for around 1.5km to the crossroads, before turning left and you'll see the haunting ruin of **Carrigogunnell Castle** high up on a ridge. You'll soon see a road to your right, which heads past the castle, beyond the hedgerow and the fields. The 15th-century castle was blown up with gunpowder in 1691 and the fabulous wreck famously adorns the back cover of the U2 album *The Unforgettable Fire*.

Further along off the N69, a major highlight of the route is the village of **Askeaton**, with evocative ruins including the mid-1300s **Desmond Castle** (☎ tourist office bookings 061-392 149; ⏰ weekends by appointment May-Oct) – perched dramatically on an island in the River Deel – a 1389-built **Franciscan friary**, **St Mary's Church of Ireland** and **Knights Templar Tower**, as well as the 1740-built **Hellfire Gentlemen's club**, next to the castle. Restoration of the ruins started in 2007 and is expected to continue until 2017; progress is impressive. The town's **tourist office** (☎ 061-392 149; askeatontourist office@gmail.com; The Square; ⏰ 9am-5pm Mon-Fri) has details of the ruins that you can freely wander (depending on restoration works) and can arrange eye-opening free **guided tours** lasting about one hour led by the very knowledgeable Anthony Sheehy (or call his mobile on ☎ 086 085 0174; donations welcome).

At **Foynes** is another of the route's highlights, the fascinating **Foynes Flying Boat Museum** (www.flyingboatmuseum.com; adult/child/family €11/6/28; ⏰ 9.30am-5pm Mar-May, Oct & Nov, to 6pm Jun-Sep). From 1939 to 1945 this was the landing place for the flying boats that linked North America with the British Isles. Big Pan Am clippers – there's a replica here – would set down in the estuary and refuel. Ask about the **Foynes Air Show** (www.foynesairshow.com), an annual summer event that started in 2014.

Lough Gur

The land around this horseshoe-shaped lake 21km southeast of Limerick has dozens of intriguing archaeological sites. Short walks along the lake's edge lead to burial mounds, standing stones, ancient enclosures and other points of interest (admission free) and the whole area is ideal for picnics.

Sights

Grange Stone Circle ARCHAEOLOGICAL SITE

FREE This stone circle, known as the Lios, is a superb 4000-year-old circular enclosure made up of 113 embanked upright stones. It's the largest prehistoric circle of its kind in Ireland. There's roadside parking and access to the site is free (there's a donation box). From Limerick, take the N24 road south towards Waterford and follow the signs onto the R512 for 16km to the stone circle.

Around 1km further south along the R512, at Holycross garage and post office, a left turn takes you towards Lough Gur, past a ruined 15th-century church, and a wedge tomb on the other side of the road.

Lough Gur Stone Age Centre HERITAGE CENTRE

(☎ 087 285 2022; www.loughgur.com; adult/child €3/2; ⏰ 10am-5pm Mon-Fri, noon-6pm Sat & Sun) A thatched replica of a Neolithic hut contains the Lough Gur Stone Age Centre, which contains a helpful information desk and good exhibits on prehistoric Irish farms, plus a small museum displaying Neolithic artefacts and a replica of the Lough Gur shield that's now in the National Museum in Dublin.

Kilmallock

POP 2368

Ireland's third-largest town during the Middle Ages (after Dublin and Kilkenny) has a crop of intriguing medieval buildings. Kilmallock developed around a 7th-century abbey and from the 14th to the 17th centuries was the seat of the Earls of Desmond. The village lies beside the River Lubach, 26km south of Limerick and a world away from the city's urban racket. Coming into Kilmallock from Limerick, the first thing you'll see (to your left) is a **medieval stone mansion** – one of 30 or so that housed the town's prosperous merchants and landowners.

Sights

Kilmallock Museum MUSEUM

(Sheares St; 10am-noon & 1-3pm Mon-Thu, to 1.30pm Fri) FREE Across the road from Kilmallock's King's Castle, a lane leads down to this tiny museum, which houses a random collection of historical artefacts and a model of the town in 1597. The museum is the base for the **history trail** around town.

King's Castle HISTORIC BUILDING

(Sarsfield St) The street bends around the four-storey King's Castle, a 15th-century tower house with a ground-floor archway through which the pavement now runs.

Entertainment

Friars' Gate Theatre & Arts Centre ARTS CENTRE

(063-98727; www.friarsgate.ie; Main St) This excellent theatre and art centre hosts art exhibitions and has a fine little theatre for plays and music events and has tourist information about the village.

Getting There & Away

Two Bus Éireann buses run Monday to Saturday from Limerick to Kilmallock (€12.10, one hour).

Adare & Around

POP 1100

Over-touted as 'Ireland's prettiest village', Adare's fame centres on its string of preserved thatched cottages built by the 19th-century English landlord, the Earl of Dunraven, for workers constructing Adare Manor. Today, the pretty cottages house craft shops and fine restaurants, while prestigious golf courses nearby cater to golf enthusiasts. The Irish name for Adare is Áth Dara – the Ford of the Oak.

Tourists arrive by the busload to Adare, 16km southwest of Limerick on the River Maigue, clogging its roads (the busy N21 is the village's main street). As it's thronging with visitors at weekends, book accommodation and restaurants in advance.

Sights

Before the Tudor Dissolution of the Monasteries (1536–39), Adare had three flourishing religious houses, the remains of which can still be seen.

Adare Heritage Centre MUSEUM

(061-396 666; www.adareheritagecentre.ie; Main St; 9am-6pm) FREE In the middle of the village, exhibits at Adare's heritage centre explain the history and the medieval context of the village's buildings in entertaining fashion. Quality Irish crafts are on sale and there's also a busy cafe.

Desmond Castle CASTLE

(tour bookings 061-396 666; tours adult/family €6/15; tours hourly 10am-5pm Jun-Sep) Dating back to around 1200, this picturesque Norman ruin changed hands several times before being entirely wrecked by Cromwell's troops in 1657, by which time its strategic importance had slipped away. Restoration work is ongoing; look for the ruined great hall with its early-13th-century windows.

Book tours through the Adare Heritage Centre. When tours aren't on, you can view the castle from the busy main road, or more peacefully from the riverside footpath or the grounds of the Augustinian priory.

Church of the Holy Trinity CHURCH

In the village itself, next to the heritage centre, the dramatic tower and southern wall of the Church of the Holy Trinity date from the 13th-century Trinitarian priory that was restored by the first Earl of Dunraven. Holy Trinity is now a Catholic church. There's a restored 14th-century dovecote down the side-turning next to the church.

Augustinian Priory MONASTERY

North of the village, on the N21 and close to the bridge over the River Maigue, is the Church of Ireland parish church, once the Augustinian priory, founded in 1316 and also known as the Black Abbey. The interior of the church is agreeable enough, but the real joy is the atmospheric little cloister.

Franciscan Friary RUIN

(Adare Golf Club) The ruins of this friary, founded by the Earl of Kildare in 1464, stand serenely in the middle of Adare Golf Club beside the River Maigue. Public access is assured, but let them know at the clubhouse that you intend to visit. A track leads away from the clubhouse car park for about 400m – watch out for flying golf balls. There's a handsome tower and a fine sedilia (row of seats for priests) in the southern wall of the chancel.

Riverside Path RIVER

A pleasant, signposted riverside path, with wayside seats, starts from just north of the Augustinian priory gates. Look for a narrow access gap and head off alongside the river. After about 250m, turn left along the road to reach the centre of Adare.

Sleeping

Adare Village Inn INN €
(☎087 251 7102; www.adarevillageinn.com; Upper Main St/Rathkeale Rd; weekday s/d €45/60, weekend €50/70;) This cordial place has five excellent-value rooms that are cosy and comfortable and come with power showers. Run by Seán Collins, the inn is located a few doors down from his namesake bar, around the corner from Main St towards Rathkeale Rd.

Berkeley Lodge B&B €
(☎061-396 857; www.adare.org; Station Rd; s €50, d €75-80;) This detached house around 400m north of the Adare Heritage Centre has six cutesy and rather floral rooms – each in a different colour – with great breakfasts. It's a three-minute walk to the centre and is kid friendly.

★**Dunraven Arms** INN €€
(☎061-396 633; www.dunravenhotel.com; Main St; weekday s/d from €90/110; @) This jewel of an inn, built in 1792, has 86 smart rooms, with antiques, high thread-count linens and – for the choosy – four-poster beds, plus a great restaurant and bar.

★**Adare Manor** HOTEL €€€
(☎061-605 200; www.adaremanor.com; Main St; d from €380; @) The Earl of Dunraven's magnificent estate is today an imposing yet wonderfully intimate castle hotel. Individually decorated rooms are all autumnal tones and antique furniture. Guests get reduced rates at the Adare Golf Club. The manor's superb Oakroom restaurant and lavish high tea are also open to nonguests.

Eating

Good Room Cafe CAFE €
(☎061-396 218; www.thegoodroomadare.ie; Main St; mains €8-10.50; ⏲8.30am-5.30pm Mon-Sat, 10am-5.30pm Sun;) This homely but busy place prepares inventive soups, salads, hot sandwiches, bruschetta, baked goods, homemade jams, kids' menus and huge cups of coffee in a cutesy thatched-cottage location. Arrive early before their famous scones sell out. The cafe stays open till 8pm at weekends in summer.

★**Restaurant 1826 Adare** MODERN IRISH €€
(☎061-396 004; www.1826adare.ie; Main St; mains €17-26; ⏲6-9.30pm Wed-Sat, 3-8pm Sun;) One of Ireland's most pedigreed chefs, Wade Murphy is wowing diners at this art-lined 1826-built thatched cottage. His passion for local seasonal produce is an essential ingredient in dishes like pan-seared Atlantic cod with wilted baby spinach, dry-aged rib-eye steak and citrus crème fraîche brûlée.

Wild Geese IRISH €€
(☎061-396 451; www.thewild-geese.com; Main St; 2-/3-course lunch menu €22/27, 2-/3-course dinner menu €30/37; ⏲from 6pm Mon-Sat, 1-4pm Sun) The ever-changing menu at this inviting cottage restaurant celebrates the best of southwest Ireland's bounty, from scallops to sumptuous racks of lamb. The service is genial, preparations are imaginative and the bread basket divine.

Blue Door IRISH €€
(☎061-396 481; www.bluedooradare.com; Main St; lunch mains €9-16, dinner mains €19-25; ⏲11am-3pm & 6-10pm Mon-Thu, 11am-10pm Fri, noon-10pm Sat, 1-9pm Sun;) Gourmet salads, open-faced sandwiches and lasagnes appear at lunch at this cottage restaurant, while dinner ups the ante with confit of duck in Guinness sauce and cod in chardonnay.

Dunraven Arms RESTAURANT €€
(☎061-396 633; www.dunravenhotel.com; Main St; restaurant mains €16-26, bar menu mains €13-18; ⏲restaurant from 6pm, bar menu 11am-10pm) The restaurant of this charming inn has an ambitious menu (pan-seared duck with lavender risotto, warm white chocolate cake with caramelised banana), but the menu in its sedate, wood-panneled bar is a worthy, more affordable alternative.

Oakroom Restaurant IRISH €€€
(Adare Manor, Main St; high tea €28.50, mains €24-36; ⏲high tea 2-5pm, 6.30-10pm) Dine like a lord at Adare Manor's restaurant, with its superb Irish menu backed by a fabulous setting with views overlooking the grounds and the River Maigue. For an afternoon option, try the high tea served on tiered plates in the stately drawing room.

Drinking & Nightlife

Seán Collins PUB
(www.seancollinsbaradare.com; Upper Main St/Rathkeale Rd; ⏲10am-11.30pm Mon-Thu, 10.30am-1.30am Fri & Sat, 10am-11.30pm Sun) Has live music on Monday and Friday at 8.30pm.

Bill Chawke's Lounge Bar PUB
(www.billchawke.com; Main St; ⏲10am-12.30pm Mon-Thu, to 1.30am Fri & Sat, to midnight Sun) Regular trad music and singalongs.

WORTH A TRIP

BALLINGARRY

The attractive village of Ballingarry (Baile an Gharraí, meaning 'town of the gardens') is home to one of County Limerick's hidden dining gems, **Mustard Seed at Echo Lodge** (☎069-68508; www.mustardseed.ie; 4-course menu €60, d from €130; ⏲restaurant 7-9.15pm, restaurant & accommodation closed mid-Jan–mid-Feb; 📶). Produce picked fresh from this mustard-coloured 19th-century former convent's orchards and kitchen gardens is incorporated in seasonal menus, which might include parmesan doughnuts with black-olive mousse, blackcurrant-and-gin sorbet, and wild Irish venison.

To avoid having to move too far afterwards, book in to one of the lodge's elegant, country-style rooms (some with four-poster beds). Ballingarry village is 13km southwest of Adare on the R519.

Information

The website www.adarevillage.com is a handy source of information.

Tourist Office (☎061-396 255; www.discoverireland.com; Adare Heritage Centre, Main St; ⏲9am-5pm Mon-Sat)

Getting There & Around

Hourly Bus Éireann services link Limerick with Adare (€6, 25 minutes). Many continue on to Tralee (€22, 1¾ hours). Others serve Killarney (€22.50, 1¾ hours).

COUNTY TIPPERARY

POP 158,660 / AREA 4295 SQ KM

Landlocked Tipperary boasts the sort of fertile soil that farmers dream of. The central area of the county is low-lying, but rolling hills spill over from adjoining counties and an upper-crust gloss still clings to traditions here, with fox hunts in full legal cry during the winter season.

Walking and cycling opportunities abound, especially in the Glen of Aherlow near Tipperary town. But the real crowd-pleasers are the iconic Rock of Cashel and Cahir Castle. In between, you'll find bucolic charm along pretty much any country road you choose.

Tipperary Town

POP 4320

Tipperary (Tiobrad Árann) has a storied name, largely due to the WWI song. And indeed, you may find it a long way to Tipperary as the N24 and a web of regional roads converge on the centre and traffic often moves at the same speed as the armies at the Somme. 'Tipp town' itself has few pretensions and there's no need to detour here.

Midway along Main St, stands a **statue of Charles J Kickham** (1828–82), a local novelist (author of *Knocknagow,* a novel about rural life) and Young Irelander. He spent four years in London's Pentonville Prison in the 1860s for treason.

Named in honour of the local patriot, traditional pub **Kickham House** (www.kickhamhouse.com; Main St; mains €8-13; ⏲noon-3pm Mon-Fri) has carvery lunches that include smoked haddock and cod pie.

Tipperary Racecourse (☎062-51357; www.tipperaryraces.ie; Limerick Rd) is one of Ireland's leading tracks. It's 3km northwest of town and has regular meetings during the year. The course is within walking distance of Limerick Junction station.

Danny Ryan Music (www.dannyryanmusic.ie; 20 Bank Pl; ⏲10am-1pm & 2-6pm Mon, Tue, Thu & Fri, to 1pm Wed, 9.30am-1pm & 2-6pm Sat) has a superb selection of traditional musical instruments.

Information

The town's **tourist information point** (☎062-80520; Excel Heritage Centre, Mitchell St; ⏲10am-5pm Mon-Sat, 2-5.30pm Sun) is inside the Excel Heritage Centre, where you'll also find a small gallery, cafe, cinema and a good genealogy centre. It's reached via St Michael's St, a side street leading 200m off the northern side of Main St.

Getting There & Away

Most buses stop on Abbey St beside the river. **Bus Éireann** (www.buseireann.ie) runs up to eight buses daily on the Limerick (€10, 30 minutes) to Waterford route via Cahir and Clonmel.

To reach the train station, head south along Bridge St. Tipperary is on the Waterford–Limerick Junction line. There are two daily services to Cahir (25 minutes), Clonmel, Carrick-on-Suir, Waterford and Rosslare Harbour. Connect for Cork, Kerry and Dublin at **Limerick Junction** (☎062-51406), barely 3km from Tipperary station along the Limerick road.

Glen of Aherlow & Galtee Mountains

South of Tipperary are the shapely Slievenamuck Hills and Galtee Mountains, separated by the broad, chequered and velvety green valley of the Glen of Aherlow. A beautiful and leisurely 25km **scenic drive** through the Glen is signposted from Tipperary town. At the eastern end of the Glen, between Tipperary and Cahir, the village of Bansha (An Bháinseach) marks the start of a 20km trip west to Galbally, an easy bike ride or scenic drive along the R663 that takes in the best of the county's landscapes.

Renowned for its **walking**, the terrain through the region ranges from the lush riverbanks of the Aherlow to pine forests in the hills and windswept, rocky grasslands that seem to stretch on forever. For spectacular views, head 1.6km north of Newtown on the R664 to a **lookout** adjacent to the white **statue of Christ**.

The R663 from Bansha and the R664 south from Tipperary converge at Newtown at the **Coach Road Inn**, a fine old pub popular with walkers. Hidden around the back of the pub, the enthusiastically staffed Glen of Aherlow **tourist office** (062-56331; www.aherlow.com; 9.30am-5pm Mon-Fri year-round plus 10am-4pm Sat Jun-Aug) is an excellent source of information on the area, including **walking festivals**.

Sleeping & Eating

There's a good range of accommodation – much of it catering to walkers.

Aherlow House Hotel HOTEL €
(062-56153; www.aherlowhouse.ie; Newtown; d/lodge from €69/149, mains €15-30, 3-course meal €24; restaurant 6-10pm Mon-Sat, from 12.30pm Sun;) Up a pine-forested track from the R663, a 1928 hunting lodge has been turned into a luxurious woodland retreat with 29 rooms with king-size beds and 15 contemporary countrified self-catering lodges (minimum two-night stay). There's a flowing bar, a fine restaurant, and glorious mountain views from the terrace.

Ballinacourty House Camping Park & B&B CAMPGROUND, B&B €
(062-56559; www.ballinacourtyhse.com; Glen of Aherlow; campsites €23, s/d €51.50/70, 4-course lunch/dinner menu €22.50/32.50; restaurant 6-9pm Wed-Sat, 12.30-2.30pm & 6-8pm Sun;) Set against a great backdrop of the Galtees, this attractive site is 10km west from Bansha, and past Newtown. It has excellent facilities, as well as a fine garden, a much-loved restaurant serving classic Irish fare, a wine bar and a tennis court. An old stone house has been renovated and now offers B&B accommodation.

Homeleigh Farmhouse B&B €
(062-56228; www.homeleighfarmhouse.com; Newtown; s/d €50/80, dinner €28;) Just west of Newtown and the Coach Road Inn on the R663, this working bungalow farm rents out simple rooms with views onto fields and the garden, in a modern home. Furnishings are traditional and you can arrange for dinner. This is really ground zero for local hiking.

Getting There & Away

The frequent Bus Éireann link between Tipperary town (€4.10, 10 minutes) and Waterford stops in Bansha. From here it's a walk or bike ride into the hills. A car will enable you to explore far and wide between walks.

Cashel

POP 2276

It's little wonder that Cashel (Caiseal Mumhan) is such a fabulous draw (the Queen included it on her historic visit in 2011). The iconic religious buildings that crown the blustery summit of the Rock of Cashel seem to emerge from the rocky landscape, and the smallish market town of Cashel itself rewards rambles around its charming streets.

Sights

Download a free audioguided tour of the town from the tourist office website (www.cashel.ie).

★**Rock of Cashel** HISTORIC SITE
(www.heritageireland.com; adult/child €7/3; 9am-5.30pm mid-Mar–mid-Oct, to 7pm mid-Jun–Aug, to 4.30pm mid-Oct–mid-Mar) The Rock of Cashel is one of Ireland's most spectacular archaeological sites, a prominent green hill, banded with limestone outcrops, rising from a grassy plain and bristling with ancient fortifications. Sturdy walls circle an enclosure containing a complete round tower, a 13th-century Gothic cathedral and the finest 12th-century Romanesque chapel in Ireland, home to some of the land's oldest frescoes.

It's a five-minute stroll from the town centre up to the Rock, from where fantastic views range over the Tipperary countryside.

The word *cashel* is an anglicised version of the Irish word *caiseal*, meaning 'fortress' (related to the English 'castle', from the Latin *castellum*). In the 4th century, the Rock of Cashel was chosen as a base by the Eóghanachta clan from Wales, who went on to conquer much of Munster and become kings of the region. For some 400 years it rivalled Tara as a centre of power in Ireland. The clan was associated with St Patrick, hence the Rock's alternative name of St Patrick's Rock. In the 10th century, the Eóghanachta lost possession of the rock to the O'Brien (or Dál gCais) tribe under Brian Ború's leadership. In 1101, King Muircheartach O'Brien presented the Rock to the Church to curry favour with the powerful bishops and to end secular rivalry over possession of the Rock with the Eóghanachta, by now known as the MacCarthys.

Numerous buildings must have occupied the cold and exposed Rock over the years, but it is the ecclesiastical relics that have survived even the depredations of the Cromwellian army in 1647. The cathedral was used for worship until the mid-1700s. Among the graves are a 19th-century high cross and mausoleum for local landowners, the Scully family; the top of the Scully Cross was razed by lightning in 1976.

You can take some pretty paths including the Bishop's Walk from the gardens of the Cashel Palace Hotel. Sheep grudgingly allow you to pass. The scaffolding moves from place to place each year as part of the never-ending struggle to keep the Rock caulked.

Call ahead for details of guided tours.

Hore Abbey HISTORIC SITE

Just under 1km north of the Rock, the formidable ruin of 13th-century Hore Abbey (also known as Hoare Abbey or St Mary's) stands in flat farmland. Originally Benedictine and settled by monks from Glastonbury in England at the end of the 12th century, it later became a Cistercian house. An enjoyably gloomy wreck, the abbey was gifted to the order by a 13th-century archbishop who expelled the Benedictine monks after dreaming that they planned to murder him.

Brú Ború HERITAGE CENTRE

(☎062-61122; www.comhaltas.ie/locations/detail/bru_boru; admission free, exhibitions from €5; ⏰9am-5pm Mon-Fri Sep–mid-Jun, 9am-5pm Mon & 9am-11pm Tue-Sat mid-Jun–Aug) The privately run heritage and cultural centre is next to the car park below the Rock of Cashel, and offers absorbing insights into Irish traditional music, dance and song. The centre's main attraction, the **Sounds of History** exhibition, relates the story of Ireland and its music through imaginative audio displays; various other musical events take place in summer.

Cashel Folk Village MUSEUM

(☎062-63601; www.cashelfolkvillage.ie; Dominic St; adult/child €5/2; ⏰9am-7.30pm mid-Jun–mid-Sep, reduced hours rest of year) An engaging exhibition of old buildings, shopfronts and memorabilia from around the town. It's a bit slipshod in a heart-warming way.

Cashel Heritage Town Centre Museum MUSEUM

(Main St, Town Hall; ⏰9.30am-5.30pm mid-Mar–mid-Oct, 9.30am-5.30pm Mon-Fri mid-Oct–mid-Mar) FREE Located in the town hall alongside the tourist office, the displays include a scale model of Cashel in the 1640s with an accompanying soundtrack.

Bolton Library MUSEUM

(John St; admission €2; ⏰10am-4pm by appointment, book at tourist office) This forbidding 1836 stone building houses a splendid 18th-century collection of books, maps and manuscripts from the dawn of printing onwards, with works by writers from Chaucer to Swift.

Sleeping

Cashel Holiday Hostel HOSTEL €

(☎062-62330; www.cashelhostel.com; 6 John St; dm/s/d from €16/30/45; 📶) In a vividly coloured three-storey Georgian terrace just off Main St, this friendly and central budget option divides into two, with dorms in one end and doubles in the other. Amenities include a kitchen, laundry, library, bike storage and a comfy and homely lounge. Musicians can 'perform for their bed' (ie the hostel can set up gigs and source instruments).

Cashel Town B&B B&B €

(☎062-62330; www.cashelbandb.com; 5 John St; d €55-65, tr/q from €90/120; 📶👪) 🌿 Fresh produce from nearby farmers markets is cooked up for breakfast at this homey B&B. Within the 1808-built Georgian townhouse are seven comfortable rooms and a cosy guest lounge with a toasty open fire and a piano.

Cashel Lodge & Camping Park HOSTEL, CAMPGROUND €€

(☎062-61003; www.cashel-lodge.com; Dundrum Rd; campsite per person €10, s €55-65, d €85-95; 📶) This converted two-century-old stone coach-house northwest of town on the R505 (follow the signs for Dundrum) is a friendly

Rock of Cashel

A TOUR OF THE COMPLEX

For more than 1000 years the Rock of Cashel was a symbol of power and the seat of kings and churchmen who ruled over the region. Exploring this monumental complex offers a fascinating insight into Ireland's past.

Enter via the 15th-century ❶ **Hall of the Vicars Choral**, built to house the male choristers who sang in the cathedral. Exhibits in its undercroft include rare silverware, stone reliefs and the original St Patrick's Cross. In the courtyard you'll see the replica of ❷ **St Patrick's Cross**. A small porch leads into the 13th-century Gothic ❸ **cathedral**. To the west of the nave are the remains of the ❹ **Archbishop's Residence**. From the cathedral's north transept on the northeastern corner is the Rock's earliest building, an 11th- or 12th-century ❺ **Round Tower**. The south transept leads to the compelling ❻ **Cormac's Chapel**, probably the first Romanesque church in Ireland. It dates from 1127 and the medieval integrity of its trans-European architecture survives. Inside the main door on the left is the sarcophagus said to house King Cormac, dating from between 1125 and 1150. Before leaving, take time for a close-up look at the Rock's ❼ **enclosing walls and corner tower**.

TOP TIPS

➡ Good photographic vantage points for framing the mighty Rock are on the road into Cashel from the Dublin Rd roundabout or from the little roads just west of the centre.

➡ The best photo opportunities, however, are from inside the atmospheric ruins of Hore Abbey, 1km to the north.

Hall of the Vicars Choral

Head upstairs from the ticket office to see the choristers' restored kitchen and dining hall, complete with period furniture, tapestries and paintings beneath a fine carved-oak roof and gallery.

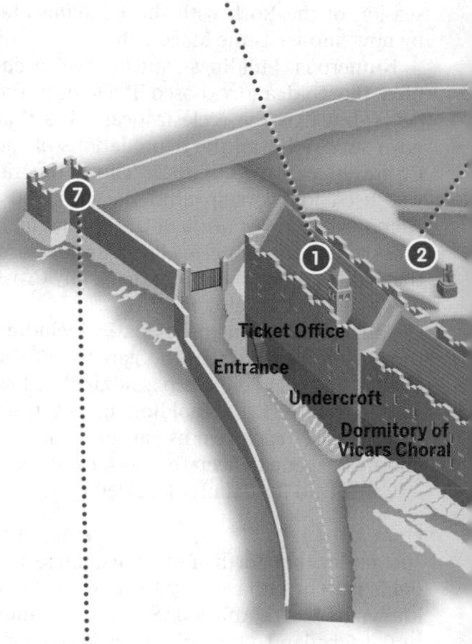

Enclosing Walls & Corner Tower

Constructed from lime mortar around the 15th century, and originally incorporating five gates, stone walls enclose the entire site. It's thought the surviving corner tower was used as a watchtower.

St Patrick's Cross
In the castle courtyard, this cross replicates the eroded Hall of the Vicars Choral original – an impressive 12th-century crutched cross depicting a crucifixion scene on one face and animals on the other.

GEORGE MUNDAY/GETTY IMAGES ©

Archbishop's Residence
The west side of the cathedral is taken up by the Archbishop's Residence, a 15th-century, four-storey castle, which had its great hall built over the nave, reducing its length. It was last inhabited in the mid-1700s.

Cathedral
A huge square tower with a turret on the southwestern corner soars above the cathedral. Scattered throughout are monuments, a 16th-century altar tomb, coats of arms panels, and stone heads on capitals and corbels.

JOE CORNISH/GETTY IMAGES ©

Turret

4

5

3

6

Choir

Scully Cross

TRISH PUNCH/GETTY IMAGES ©

Cormac's Chapel
Look closely at the exquisite doorway arches, the grand chancel arch and ribbed barrel vault, and carved vignettes, including a trefoil-tailed grotesque and a Norman-helmeted centaur firing an arrow at a rampaging lion.

STEPHEN SAKS/GETTY IMAGES ©

Round Tower
Standing 28m tall, the doorway to this ancient edifice is 3.5m above the ground – perhaps for structural rather than defensive reasons. Its exact age is unknown but may be as early as 1101.

place with a bare stone-and-wood interior and terrific views of the Rock and Hore Abbey. Non-camping rates include breakfast.

Baileys Hotel BOUTIQUE HOTEL €€
(062-61937; www.baileyshotelcashel.com; Main St; s/d from €55/70;) Clean, contemporary lines and dark woods contrasting with light walls give this restored, centrally located Georgian townhouse an elegant ambience. Rooms are smart, but neutrally styled. Rates include breakfast and lock-up parking. There's a great on-site restaurant and bar, too.

Eating

Apart from the Rock, Cashel is best-known in Ireland and beyond for award-winning Cashel Blue farmhouse cheese, Ireland's first-ever blue cheese. Although it's still handmade locally (and only locally), it's surprisingly hard to find in shops and on restaurant menus in town.

★**Cafe Hans** CAFE €€
(062-63660; Dominic St; mains €13-18, 2-/3-course lunch €16/20; noon-5.30pm Tue-Sat;) Competition for the 32 seats is fierce at this gourmet cafe run by the same family as Chez Hans next door. There's a fantastic selection of salads, open sandwiches (including succulent prawns with tangy Marie Rose sauce) and filling fish, shellfish, lamb and vegetarian dishes, with a discerning wine selection and mouthwatering desserts. No credit cards.

Arrive before or after the lunchtime rush or plan on queuing.

Baileys Hotel Restaurant & Bar INTERNATIONAL €€
(062-61937; www.baileyshotelcashel.com; Main St; bar mains €13-25.50, restaurant mains €14-25.50; bar food noon-9.30pm daily, restaurant 6-9.30pm Thu-Sat, noon-2.30pm Sun) The restaurant and stone-walled, candlelit cellar bar of this central hotel are superb and feature a broad menu of international fare made with locally sourced produce.

Chez Hans IRISH €€€
(062-61177; www.chezhans.net; Dominic St; mains €24-38, 2-/3-course meal €28/33; 6-10pm Tue-Sat) Since 1968 this former church has been a place of worship for foodies from all over Ireland and beyond. Still as fresh and inventive as ever, the restaurant has a regularly changing menu and gives its blessing to all manner of Irish foods, including steamed Galway mussels, goat's cheese tart and pan-fried peppered skate wing.

Drinking & Nightlife

Brian Ború PUB
(062-63381; http://brianborubar.ie; Main St; bar mains from €10; 10.30am-11.30pm Mon-Thu, to 12.30pm Fri & Sat, to 11pm Sun;) This good-time pub is a lynchpin of Cashel's social life with regular live music, DJs and cocktail nights and above-average pub grub.

Information

Banks and ATMs are in the centre.

Tourist Office (062-62511; www.cashel.ie; Town Hall, Main St; 9.30am-5.30pm Mon-Sat mid-Mar–mid-Oct, 9.30am-5.30pm Mon-Fri mid-Oct–mid-Mar) Helpful office with reams of info on the area.

Getting There & Away

Bus Éireann (www.buseireann.ie) runs eight buses daily between Cashel and Cork (€15.50, 1½ hours) via Cahir (€6, 20 minutes, six daily). The bus stop for Cork is outside the Bake House on Main St. The Dublin stop (€15.50, three hours, six daily) is opposite.

Ring a Link (1890 424 141; www.ringalink.ie), a not-for-profit service for rural residents that's also available to tourists, has a service to Tipperary (€3, 50 minutes).

Around Cashel

Athassel Priory RUIN
Reached over a stile and across grassy (but sometimes muddy) fields, the atmospheric and delightful ruins of Athassel Priory sit in the shallow and verdant River Suir Valley, 7km southwest of Cashel. The original buildings date from 1205, and Athassel was once one of the richest and most important monasteries in Ireland. What survives is substantial: the gatehouse and portcullis gateway, the cloister (ruined but recognisable) and large stretches of walled enclosure, as well as some medieval tomb effigies.

To get here, take the N74 to the village of Golden, then head 2km south along the narrow L4304 road signed Athassel Abbey. Roadside parking is limited and quite tight. The welter of back lanes is good for cycling.

Holy Cross Abbey CHURCH
(holycrossabbeytours@gmail.com; admission by donation; 9am-8pm) Beside the River Suir, 15km north of Cashel and 6km southwest of Thurles, this magnificently restored abbey proudly displays two relics of the True Cross. Although the Cistercian abbey was founded

WORTH A TRIP

FAMINE WARHOUSE

A relic of one of Ireland's darkest chapters, the **Famine Warhouse** (www.heritageireland.ie; Ballingarry; ⌚2.30-5.30pm Wed-Sun Apr-Sep, 2-4pm Sat & Sun Oct-Mar) sits seemingly benignly today amid typical farmland near Ballingarry. During the 1848 rebellion, rebels led by William Smith O'Brien besieged police who had barricaded themselves inside and taken children hostage. Police reinforcements arrived, the rebels fled and the rebellion died out. Besides exhibits about the incident, there are also displays detailing the Famine and the mass exodus of Irish emigrants to America.

The warhouse is 30km northeast of Cashel on the R691 about halfway to Kilkenny. Be careful navigating as Tipperary has two Ballingarrys; the wrong one is over by Roscrea.

in 1168, the large buildings that survive today date from the 15th century. Look for the ornately carved sedilia near the altar and pause to appreciate the early form of 'stadium seating'. Guided tours take place three times a week in spring and summer. A bookshop is open irregular hours.

Cahir

POP 1150

At the eastern tip of the Galtee Mountains 15km south of Cashel, Cahir (An Cathair; pronounced 'care') is a compact and attractive town that encircles its sublime castle. Walking paths follow the banks of the **River Suir** - you can easily spend a couple of hours wandering about.

Sights

★Cahir Castle HISTORIC SITE

(☎052-744 1011; www.heritageireland.ie; Castle St; adult/child €4/2; ⌚9am-6.30pm mid-Jun–Aug, 9.30am-5.30pm mid-Mar–mid-Jun & Sep–mid-Oct, to 4.30pm mid-Oct–mid-Mar) Cahir's awesome castle enjoys a river-island site with moat, massive walls, turrets and keep, stalwart defences, mullioned windows, vast fireplaces and dungeons. Founded by Conor O'Brien in 1142, it's one of Ireland's largest castles, passing to the Butler family in 1375. In 1599 the Earl of Essex shattered its walls with cannon fire, an event explained with a large model. With a huge set of antlers pinned to its white walls, the **Banqueting Hall** is an impressive sight; you can also climb the **Keep**.

The castle eventually surrendered to Cromwell in 1650 without a struggle; its future usefulness may have discouraged the usual Cromwellian 'deconstruction' – it is largely intact and still formidable. It was restored in the 1840s and again in the 1960s when it came under state ownership.

A 15-minute audiovisual presentation puts Cahir in context with other Irish castles. The castle buildings are sparsely furnished, although there are good displays, including an exhibition on 'Women in Medieval Ireland'. There are frequent guided tours.

Swiss Cottage HISTORIC BUILDING

(☎052-744 1144; www.heritageireland.ie; Cahir Park; adult/child €4/2; ⌚10am-6pm Apr–mid-Oct) A gorgeous riverside path from behind the town car park meanders 2km south to Cahir Park and this thatched cottage, surrounded by roses, lavender and honeysuckle. A lavish example of Regency Picturesque, the cottage is more of a sizeable house. Built in 1810 as a retreat for Richard Butler, 12th Baron Caher, and his wife, it was designed by London architect John Nash, creator of the Royal Pavilion at Brighton and London's Regent's Park. The 30-minute (compulsory) guided tours are thoroughly enjoyable.

There's angling on the river from March to September; permits are available from heritage newsagents in Cahir.

Sleeping & Eating

★Apple Caravan & Camping Park CAMPGROUND €

(☎052-744 1459; www.theapplefarm.com; Moorstown, Cahir; campsite per adult/child from €7/4.50; ⌚May-Sep; 📶👪) 🌿 Set on orchards on the N24 between Cahir (6km) and Clonmel (9km), this peaceful, well-spaced campsite has a free tennis court and racquets, a camp kitchen in a converted apple store and spring water from its own well. Even if you're not pitching up here, it's worth dropping by its **farm shop** (8am-6pm Mon-Fri, 9am-5pm Sat & Sun year-round) selling apples, jams and juices as well as fruity ice creams.

Tinsley House B&B €

(☎052-744 1947; www.tinsleyhouse.com; The Square; d/f from €65/120; ⌚Apr-Sep; 📶) This

WALK: TIPPERARY HERITAGE TRAIL

Extending a distance of 56km from the Vee Gap viewpoint near Clogheen in the south to Cashel in the north, the national waymarked Tipperary Heritage Trail passes some beautiful river valleys and ruins. The 30km north from Cahir to Cashel is the best segment, featuring the verdant lands around the River Suir and traverses close to highlights such as Athassel Priory. The best stretches around Golden are off roads. Expect to see a fair amount of wildlife as the paths and very minor roads follow the waters and penetrate woodlands. Ordnance Survey Discovery series maps 66 and 74 cover the route.

light, bright and charming B&B on the square offers four period-furnished rooms and a sweet roof garden. The owner, Liam Roche, is an expert on local history and can recommend walks and other activities.

Cahir House Hotel HOTEL €€
(052-744 3000; www.cahirhousehotel.ie; The Square; s €95, d €160; bar food noon-9.30pm;) Set in an imposing traditional building on a prominent corner of the square, this landmark hotel has elegant rooms, a long menu of bar food, a spa and helpful and efficient staff.

Farmers Market MARKET
(Castle car park; 9am-1pm Sat) Cahir's farmers market attracts the region's best food vendors.

Galileo ITALIAN €€
(www.galileocafe.com; Church St; mains €9-22; noon-10pm) Serving fine pizzas and pasta to Cahir locals for over a decade, Galileo is a neat and smooth Italian restaurant, with a modern interior and efficient, friendly service. The restaurant has no licence, so BYO.

Information

Post Office (Church St) North of the square.

Tourist Office (052-744 1453; www.discoverireland.ie/tipperary; Cahir Castle car park; 9.30am-1pm & 1.45-5.30pm Tue-Sat Easter-Oct) Has information about the town and region.

Getting There & Away

Cahir is a hub for several **Bus Éireann** (www.buseireann.ie) routes, including Dublin–Cork, Limerick–Waterford, Galway–Waterford, Kilkenny–Cork and Cork–Athlone. There are six buses per day to Cashel (€6, 20 minutes). Buses stop in the car park beside the tourist office.

From Monday to Saturday, the Limerick Junction–Waterford train stops three times daily in each direction.

Around Cahir

Rockwell College HISTORIC BUILDING
(062-61444; www.rockwellcollege.ie; R639, New Inn; school gates 7.30am-10pm) Located in the Golden Vale between Cashel and Cahir, this famous 19th-century secondary school off the R639 just north of the village of New Inn has lovely grounds that visitors can explore, including a charming wooded walk around its large lake. Take a look at the astonishing Long Hall, a staggeringly lengthy, tiled and stained-glass expanse of corridor as you enter the main school building. Visitors should report to reception when visiting on weekdays.

Knockgraffon Motte ARCHAEOLOGICAL SITE
This 12th-century motte at Knockgraffon can be scaled for panoramic and wide-ranging views of the Tipperary countryside. The motte is located 5km along the L3104, which runs west from the R639 just south of the village of New Inn. Parking is generally not a problem and it's an easy climb to the summit.

Mitchelstown Caves

While the Galtee Mountains are mainly sandstone, a narrow band of limestone along their southern side has given rise to the **Mitchelstown Caves** (052-746 7246; www.mitchelstowncave.com; Burncourt; adult/child €9/3; 10am-5pm Mar-Oct, shorter hours rest of year). Superior to Kilkenny's Dunmore Cave and yet less developed for tourists, these caves are among the most extensive in the country with nearly 3km of passages and spectacular chambers full of textbook formations with names such as the Pipe Organ, Tower of Babel, House of Commons and Eagle's Wing. Tours take about 30 minutes.

Year-round, the cave temperature remains a constant 12°C, making it feel warm in winter and chilly in summer. The caves are near Burncourt, 16km southwest of Cahir and signposted on the N8 to Mitchelstown (Baile Mhistéala).

Clonmel & Around

POP 17,908

On the wide River Suir, Clonmel (Cluain Meala; 'Meadows of Honey') is Tipperary's largest and busiest town.

Laurence Sterne (1713–68), author of *A Sentimental Journey* and *Tristram Shandy*, was a native of the town. However, the commercial cheerleader for Clonmel was Italian-born Charles Bianconi (1786–1875), who, at the precocious age of 16, was sent to Ireland by his father in an attempt to break his liaison with a woman. Bianconi later channelled all his frustrated passion into setting up a coach service between Clonmel and Cahir; his company quickly grew to become a nationwide passenger and mail carrier. For putting Clonmel on the map, Bianconi was twice elected mayor.

The East Munster Way (p321) walking route passes through Clonmel.

Directly south of Clonmel, over the border in County Waterford, are the Comeragh Mountains. There's a scenic route south to Ballymacarbry and the Nire Valley (p187).

Sights

Turning south down Bridge St, crossing the river and following the road around brings you to **Lady Blessington's Bath**, a picturesque stretch of the river that's perfect for picnicking.

South Tipperary County Museum MUSEUM
(Mick Delahunty Sq; ⏲10am-5pm Tue-Sat) FREE Informative displays on the history of County Tipperary from Neolithic times to the present are covered at this well-put-together museum, which also hosts changing exhibitions.

Main Guard HISTORIC BUILDING
(☎052-612 7484; www.heritageireland.ie; Sarsfield St; ⏲9am-5pm Tue-Sun Easter-Sep, hours can vary) FREE At the junction of Mitchell and Sarsfield Sts is the beautifully restored Main Guard, a Butler courthouse dating from 1675 and based on a design by Christopher Wren. The columned porticos are open again and exhibits include the ubiquitous model of Clonmel as a walled 17th-century town.

County Courthouse HISTORIC BUILDING
(Nelson St; ⏲10am-12.30pm & 2.30pm-4.30pm Mon-Fri) The refurbished County Courthouse south of Parnell St was designed by Richard Morrison in 1802. It was here that the Young Irelanders of 1848, including Thomas Francis Meagher, were tried and sentenced to transportation to Australia.

Franciscan Friary HISTORIC BUILDING
(Mitchell St) West along Mitchell St (past the town hall with its statue commemorating the 1798 Rising) and south down Abbey St is the Franciscan friary. Inside, near the door, is a 1533 Butler tomb depicting a knight and his lady. There's some fine modern stained glass, especially in the beautiful St Anthony's Chapel to the north, all aglow if the sun has its hat on.

Anne Street ARCHITECTURE
This charming Clonmel street is lined with rows of picturesque Georgian cottages dating from 1820.

Sleeping & Eating

Several B&Bs cluster on Marlfield Rd, due west of the centre.

★ **Raheen House Hotel** HOTEL €€
(☎052-612 2140; www.raheenhouse.ie; Raheen Rd; d €120; 📶) Grand but homely, this gorgeous old house hotel offers high ceilings, massive rooms, some fine four-poster beds, wooden floors, bar, conservatory and two huge gardens, with acers, magnolias and a vast cypress. There's also a walled garden, roaring fires in winter and a self-contained lodge.

★ **Befani's** B&B €€
(☎052-617 7893; www.befani.com; 6 Sarsfield St; s/d €40/70, mains €15-26; ⏲restaurant 9-11am, 12.30-2.30pm & 5.30-9.30pm; @📶) Between the Main Guard and the Suir, Befani's brings the Mediterranean to Clonmel. At lunchtime, there's a mouth-watering tapas menu; mains include balsamic-braised Irish lamb shoulder and a rich bouillabaisse in lobster broth. Its nine guest rooms, of varying sizes, are presentable but rather dull.

Niamh's CAFE, DELI €
(1 Mitchell St; mains from €7.50; ⏲8.30am-5.30pm Mon-Sat; 📶) This long, slender, smart and bustling deli and cafe does a brisk trade, serving a wide range of appealing lunch options and comfort food (gourmet burgers, pan-fried pork and lasagnes, plus creative sandwiches) and breakfasts. Free coffee refills, with a smile.

Drinking & Entertainment

Phil Carroll PUB
(Parnell St) Near Nelson St, this diminutive place is Clonmel's most atmospheric old boozer with a charming exterior of black gloss and gold.

ROBIN BUSH/GETTY IMAGES ©

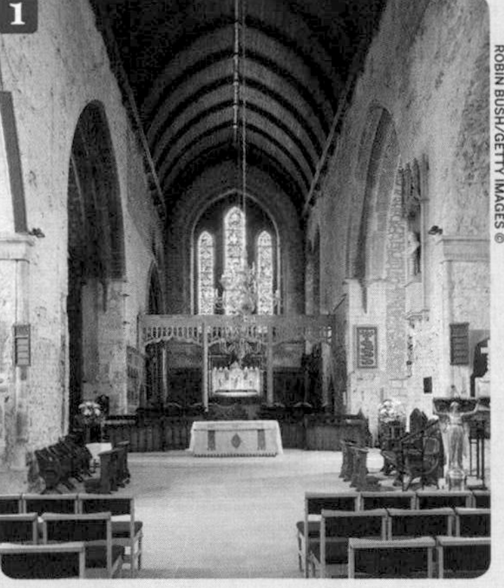

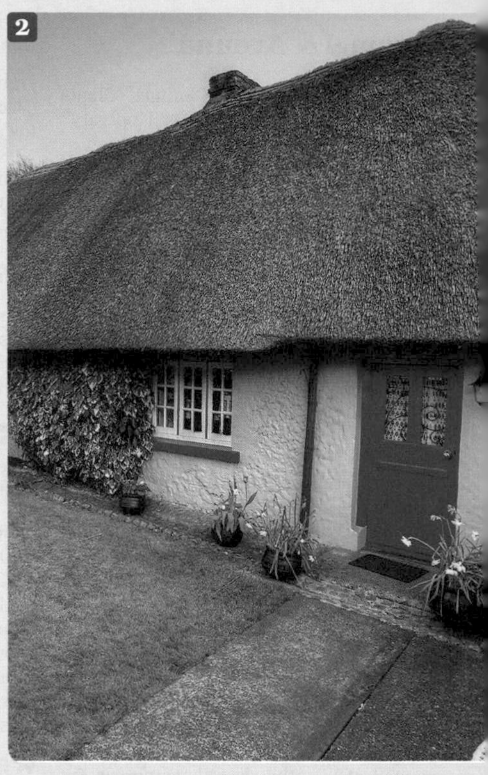

1. St Mary's Cathedral (p301)
Limerick city's ancient cathedral features stunning carvings of mythical animals.

2. Cottages, Adare (p307)
Touted as 'Ireland's prettiest village', Adare is well-known for its 19th-century thatched cottages.

3. Rural scenery
The low-lying farmlands of Counties Limerick and Tipperary make for enjoyable scenic drives.

4. Adare Manor (p308)
This magnificent manor now functions as a castle hotel but also puts on a lavish high tea open to nonguests.

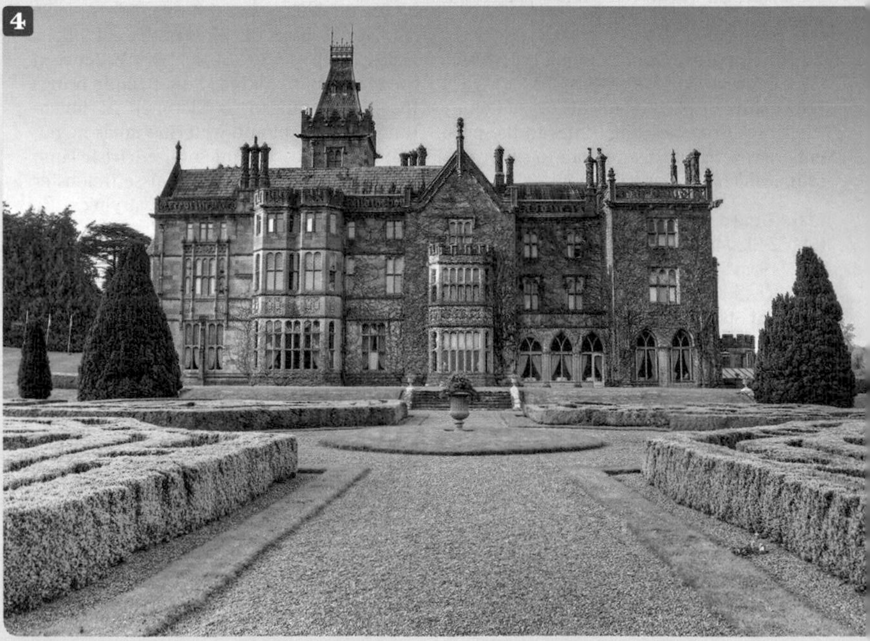

3

JZORAN/SHUTTERSTOCK ©

South Tipperary Arts Centre ARTS CENTRE
(052-612 7877; www.southtippartscentre.ie; Nelson St; 10am-5pm Tue-Fri, to 2pm Sat) Has an excellent program of art exhibitions, plays and music.

Information

Post Office (Emmet St)

Tourist Office (052-612 2960; St Mary's Church, Mary St; 9.30am-1pm & 2-5pm Mon-Fri) Very helpful staff; adjoins Main Guard.

Getting There & Away

BUS

Buses stop at the train station. **Bus Éireann** (www.buseireann.ie) has buses to destinations including:

Cahir (€6.60, 30 minutes, eight daily)
Cork (€21.50, two hours, three daily)
Kilkenny (€12, one hour, 12 daily)
Waterford (€8.50, one hour, nine daily).

TRAIN

The **train station** (052-612 1982) is on Prior Park Rd past the Oakville Shopping Centre. From Monday to Saturday, the Limerick Junction–Waterford train stops twice daily in each direction.

Fethard

POP 900

A quiet, quaint little village with impressive medieval ruins scattered about its compact, linear centre, Fethard (pronounced 'feathered') is located 14km north of Clonmel on the River Clashawley. Ireland's most complete medieval **town wall** is one of the village's principal features.

Fethard's main concentration of **medieval remains** (some of which have been incorporated into later buildings) are just south of the church at the end of Watergate St. Beside Castle Inn are the ruins of several fortified 17th-century **tower houses**.

Sights

Holy Trinity Church CHURCH
(Main St) Right off Main St and reached through a cast-iron gateway, Fethard's Holy Trinity Church and churchyard occupy a captivating time warp. The main part of the building dates from the 13th century, but its ancient walls have been blighted with mortar for weatherproofing. The handsome west tower was added later and has had its sturdy stonework uncovered. Get the keys from the XL Stop & Shop (aka Whyte's) on Main St, 50m west of the gate.

The interior of the church has an aisled nave and a chancel of typical medieval style, but is sparsely furnished. Within, the church ceiling is the oldest scientifically dated timber roof in Ireland. Old gravestones descend in ranks to a refurbished stretch of medieval wall complete with a guard tower and a parapet, from where you can look down on the gentle River Clashawley between its horse-trod banks.

Augustinian Friary CHURCH
(Abbey St) East along Abbey St is the 14th-century Augustinian friary, now a Catholic church, with medieval stained glass and an in-your-face sheila-na-gig in its east wall.

Sheila-na-gig HISTORIC SITE
Just under the archway to the river bank and Watergate Bridge is a fine sheila-na-gig (a sexually explicit medieval depiction of a woman) embedded in the wall to your left. You can stroll along the river bank, provided the resident geese are feeling friendly.

Eating & Drinking

★ **McCarthy's** PUB FOOD €€
(www.mccarthyshotel.net; Main St; mains €16-22.50; noon-3pm daily & from 6pm Wed-Sun) A classic that deserves national acclaim and preservation, McCarthy's proclaims itself as pub, restaurant and undertaker ('we'll wine you, dine you and bury you'), though not necessarily in that order (making it an efficient set-up for wakes). Closely spaced wooden booths and tables wedge between an astonishing thicket of treasures dating back to 1840 under a wood-panelled ceiling.

Getting There & Away

There's no public transport to Fethard but it makes a pleasant cycle from Cashel, 15km to the west.

Carrick-on-Suir

POP 4355

Alongside the River Suir, the unassuming yet pretty market town of Carrick-on-Suir (Carraig na Siúire) is 20km east of Clonmel. It boasted twice its present population during the late-medieval period, when it was a centre of the brewing and wool industries. From Carrick-on-Suir, the East Munster Way winds west to Clonmel before heading south into Waterford.

WALK: EAST MUNSTER WAY

This 70km walk travels through forest and open moorland, along small country roads and a lovely river towpath. It's clearly laid out with black markers bearing yellow arrows and could be managed in three days, starting at Carrick-on-Suir in County Tipperary and finishing at Clogheen.

The first day takes you to Clonmel following the old towpath on the Suir for significant portions of the route. At Kilsheelan Bridge, you leave the river to Harney's Crossroads, then wander through Gurteen Wood and the Comeraghs to Sir Thomas Bridge where you rejoin the river.

On the second day, the Way first leads south into the hills and then descends to Newcastle and the river once more. The third day sees a lot of very atmospheric walking along the quiet River Tar to Clogheen.

Ordnance Survey Discovery series maps 74 and 75 cover the route.

Carrick-on-Suir's **farmers market** (10am-2pm Fri) is held next to the **tourist office** (051-640 200; 10am-4pm Mon-Fri), reached by a narrow laneway off Main St.

Sights

Ormond Castle CASTLE
(www.heritageireland.ie; Castle St; 10am-1.30pm & 2-6pm Mar-Sep) FREE Carrick-on-Suir was once the property of the Butlers, the Earls of Ormond, who built Ormond Castle on the banks of the river in the 14th century. Anne Boleyn, the second of Henry VIII's wives, may have been born here, though other castles also claim this worthy distinction. The Elizabethan mansion next to the castle was built by the 10th Earl of Ormond, 'Black' Tom Butler, in long-term anticipation of a visit by his cousin, Queen Elizabeth I, who rather thoughtlessly never turned up.

Some rooms in this Dúchas-owned edifice have fine 16th-century stuccowork, especially the Long Gallery with its depictions of Elizabeth and the Butler coat of arms. To reach the castle, head to the eastern end of Castle St (an extension of the main street). The castle has been undergoing repair work and restoration, so call ahead to check accessibility.

Getting There & Away

Bus Éireann (051-879 000; www.buseireann.ie) has numerous services including to Cahir (€9.50, 45 minutes) and Clonmel (€7.80, 25 minutes) up to eight times daily. Buses stop at Greenside, the park beside the N24 road.

The train station is north of Greenside, off Cregg Rd. From Monday to Saturday, the Limerick Junction–Waterford train stops twice daily in each direction.

Nenagh & Around

POP 8000

To the far north of County Tipperary, beyond the Silvermine Mountains, pretty Nenagh was a garrison town in the 19th century and, before that, the site of a dominant **castle** (10am-1pm & 2-4.30pm Tue-Sat Apr-Oct) FREE. Today it resembles the prototype for the rook in a chess set, surrounded by cawing crows. The tower dates from the 13th century and has impossibly thick walls.

Nearby, the civic centre is an imposing complex of dark-stone buildings from the 19th century, including an old **gaol**. Next door stands the 1840 **Round House**, a charming stone building that holds the **Nenagh Heritage Centre** (067-33850; www.tipperarynorth.ie; Kickham St; 9.30am-5pm Mon-Fri) FREE, for tourist information.

It's worth planning your visit around lunchtime to catch Nenagh's excellent delis and cafes, particularly **Country Choice** (067-32596; www.countrychoice.ie; 25 Kenyon St; dishes €5-10; 9am-5pm Mon-Sat), a lavender-painted place of pilgrimage for lovers of really great Irish artisan foods, with homemade preserves, farmhouse cheeses and myriad other treats.

Nenagh is the gateway to the eastern shore of **Lough Derg**, a popular swimming, fishing and boating area – enquire at **Shannon Sailing** (067-24499; www.shannonsailing.com). An interesting, scenic lakeside drive from Nenagh is the 24km R494 that winds around to Killaloe and Ballina (p333).

Frequent **Bus Éireann** (www.buseireann.ie) services include Limerick city (€8, 50 minutes). Nenagh's train station has four services daily to Limerick city (€12.20, one hour); connect in Ballybrophy for Dublin, Cork and Tralee.

County Clare

POP 117,000 / AREA 3147 SQ KM

Includes ➡

Best Places to Eat

➡ Linnane's Lobster Bar (p356)

➡ Naughton's Bar (p338)

➡ Vaughan's Anchor Inn (p344)

➡ Wooden Spoon (p334)

Best Places to Sleep

➡ Rowan Tree Hostel (p324)

➡ Old Ground Hotel (p326)

➡ Sheedy's Country House Hotel & Restaurant (p350)

Why Go?

Clare combines the stunning natural beauty of its long, meandering coastline with unique windswept landscapes and choice dollops of Irish culture.

Rugged nature and the timeless ocean meet on the county's coast. The Atlantic relentlessly pounds year-round, eroding rock into fantastic formations, and fashioning sheer cliffs like those at the iconic Cliffs of Moher, and intriguing little islands like those near Loop Head. There are even stretches of beach where surfers flock to the (chilly) waves. The Burren, an ancient region of tortured stone and alien vistas, stretches down to the coast and right out to the Aran Islands.

But if the land is hard, Clare's soul certainly isn't: traditional Irish culture and music flourish here. And it's not just a show for tourists, either. In little villages like Miltown Malbay, Ennistymon, Doolin and Kilfenora you'll find pubs with lively sessions of trad music.

When to Go

➡ County Clare's pubs hum to trad beats year-round, so even in winter you'll find the craic – often warmed in the countryside by a peat fire.

➡ While the unsettled seas of winter have a drama that will fill your days with a raw intensity, the county literally shines during the more temperate months when long walks along the spectacular soaring cliffs of the coast and among the desolate rocks of the Burren don't require full foul-weather gear.

County Clare Highlights

1 Swoon to the music in the traditional pubs of **Miltown Malbay** (p340).

2 Catch the last warming rays of the setting sun at **Spanish Point** (p341).

3 Drive round the coast to the dramatic offshore rocky outcrops of **Loop Head** (p339).

4 Discover lost dolmens and abandoned abbeys among the rocky expanses of the Burren at **Carron** (p353).

5 Embark on a green-fingered exploration of the **Vandeleur Walled Garden** (p336) in Kilrush.

6 Catch the cascades in full flood in the charming town of **Ennistymon** (p342).

7 Follow the **Wild Atlantic Way** (p335) and take in all the sights along the coast.

8 Jump aboard a late-afternoon boat from Doolin to see the soaring **Cliffs of Moher** (p344) in all their radiance.

ENNIS & AROUND

Ennis

POP 20,200

Ennis (Inis) is the busy commercial centre of Clare. It lies on the banks of the slender, fast-moving River Fergus, which flows east, then south into the Shannon Estuary.

It's perhaps short on sights but it's a good place to hang your hat for a spot of urban flair, and you can reach any part of Clare in under two hours from here. The town's strengths are its food, lodgings and traditional entertainment. The town centre, with its narrow, pedestrian-friendly streets and plentiful shops, is excellent to wander.

History

The town's medieval origins are recalled by its irregular, narrow streets, but the most important surviving historical site is Ennis Friary, founded in the 13th century by the O'Briens, kings of Thomond. Much of the wooden town went skywards in a 1249 fire and Ennis was then razed by one of the O'Briens in 1306.

Sights

★Ennis Friary CHURCH

(www.heritageireland.ie; Abbey St; adult €4; ⌚10am-6pm Easter-Sep, to 5pm Oct) North of the Square this friary was founded by Donnchadh Cairbreach O'Brien, a king of Thomond, between 1240 and 1249. A mix of structures dating between the 13th and 19th centuries, the friary has a graceful five-section window dating from the late 13th century, a McMahon tomb (1460) with alabaster panels depicting scenes from the Passion, and a particularly fine *Ecce Homo* panel portraying a stripped and bound Christ.

Objects associated with the Passion to look for include the rooster rising from a cooking pot, three dice, nails and various tools. The panel was possibly painted in earlier centuries. On the other side of the nave is a devotional relief carving of St Francis of Assisi (displaying stigmata), patron of the Franciscans who arrived in Ennis in the early 13th century. Further fascinating carvings associated with Jesus Christ and his crucifixion are displayed in glass cabinets in the nave.

Clare Museum MUSEUM

(Arthur's Row; ⌚9.30am-1pm & 2-4.30pm Tue-Sat) FREE Sharing the same building as the tourist office is this diverting little museum. The *Riches of Clare* exhibition tells the story of Clare from 8000 years ago to the present day over two floors, using authentic artefacts grouped into four themes: earth, power, faith and water.

Daniel O'Connell Monument MONUMENT

(The Square) The town centre, the Square, features a Daniel O'Connell monument. His election to the British parliament by a huge majority in 1828 forced Britain to lift its bar on Catholic MPs and led to the Act of Catholic Emancipation a year later. The 'Great Liberator' stands on an extremely high column.

Activities

Tierney's Cycles & Fishing BICYCLE RENTAL

(☎086 803 0369; www.clarebikehire.com; 17 Abbey St; bike hire per day/week €20/80; ⌚9am-6pm Mon-Sat) Tierney's has well-maintained mountain bikes. Hire includes helmet, lock and repair kit.

Tours

Ennis Walking Tours WALKING TOUR

(☎087 648 3714; www.enniswalkingtours.com; adult/child €8/free; ⌚11am Mon, Tue & Thu-Sat May-Oct) This company offers excellent Ennis walks that leave from in front of the tourist office (p330).

Festivals & Events

Fleadh Nua CULTURAL

(☎065-682 4276; www.fleadhnua.com) A lively traditional music festival with singing, dancing and workshops. Held in May.

Ennis Trad Festival MUSIC

(www.ennistradfest.com) Traditional music is performed in venues across town in November.

Sleeping

Ennis has a great variety of accommodation, with modest B&Bs on most of the main roads into town, some an easy walk to the centre. Shannon Airport is less than 30 minutes' drive to the south.

★Rowan Tree Hostel HOSTEL €

(☎065-686 8687; www.rowantreehostel.ie; Harmony Row; dm €15-29, r €29-69; @📶) This fine hostel is beautifully housed in a grand 18th-century gentlemen's club right on the River Fergus. Some of the bright and airy rooms have fab balconies overlooking the swift-flowing waters. The 150 beds are

Ennis

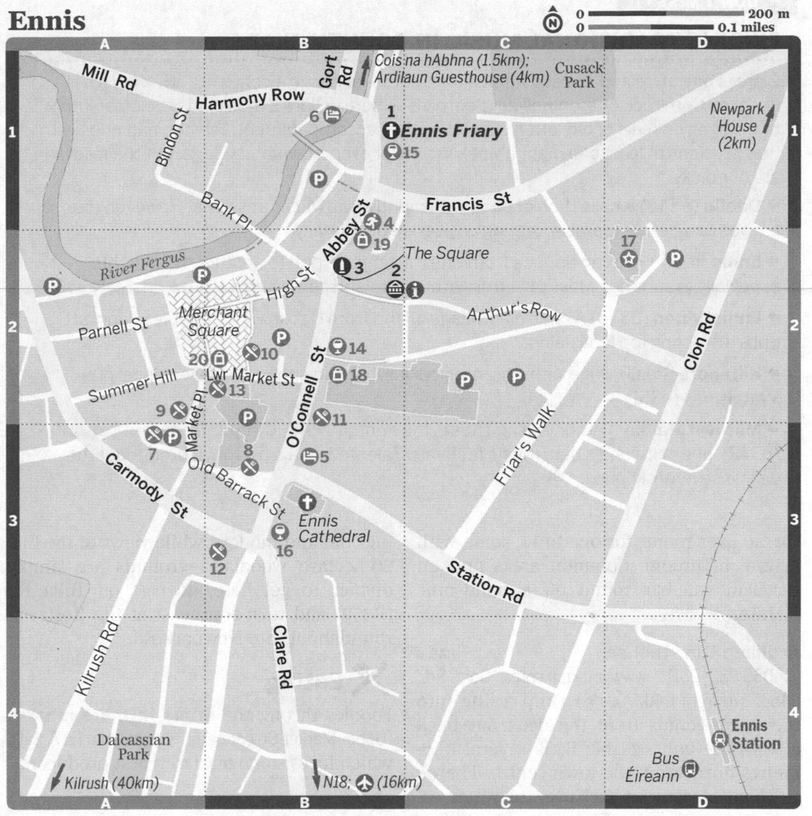

Ennis

Top Sights
1 Ennis Friary ... B1

Sights
2 Clare Museum ... B2
3 Daniel O'Connell Monument ... B2

Activities, Courses & Tours
4 Tierney's Cycles & Fishing ... B1

Sleeping
5 Old Ground Hotel ... B3
6 Rowan Tree Hostel ... B1

Eating
7 Ennis Farmers Market ... A3
8 Ennis Gourmet Store ... B3
9 Food Heaven ... A2
Poet's Corner Bar ... (see 5)
Rowan Tree Cafe Bar ... (see 6)
10 Souper ... B2
11 Town Hall Cafe ... B2
12 Tulsi ... B3
13 Zest ... B2

Drinking & Nightlife
14 Brogan's ... B2
15 Cruise's Pub ... B1
16 O'Dea's ... B3
Poet's Corner Bar ... (see 5)

Entertainment
17 Glór ... D2

Shopping
18 Custy's Music Shop ... B2
19 Ennis Bookshop ... B2
20 Scéal Eile Books ... B2

DON'T MISS

FINDING TRADITIONAL MUSIC IN COUNTY CLARE

Clare is one of Ireland's best counties for traditional music. Eschewing any modern influences from rock or even polkas (heard elsewhere), Clare's musicians stick resolutely to the jigs and reels of old, often with little vocal accompaniment. You can find pubs with trad sessions at least one night a week in almost every town and village, but the following are our picks:

➡ **Doolin** (p348) A collection of pubs with nightly trad music sessions. However, tourist crowds can be intense, evaporating any sense of intimacy.

➡ **Ennis** (p327) You can bounce from one music-filled pub to another most nights, especially in summer. Musicians from around Ireland come here to show off.

➡ **Ennistymon** (p343) A charming village inland from Doolin with a couple of ancient pubs attracting top local talent.

➡ **Kilfenora** Small village with a big musical heritage on show at excellent local pub **Vaughan's** (p351).

➡ **Miltown Malbay** This tiny village hosts the annual **Willie Clancy Summer School** (p342), one of Ireland's best music festivals. Talented locals perform throughout the year in several old pubs.

spread over rooms for one to 14, some with private bathroom. Common areas and an excellent cafe-bar round off a handsome picture.

Ardilaun Guesthouse B&B €
(☎065-682 2311; www.ardilaun.com; Gort Rd/R458; s/d from €40/70;) Drop a line into the River Fergus from the deck out back at this fine and sizeable B&B, several kilometres north from the town centre. There's a delightful view out back over the water, especially come sunset. The owners keep very much to themselves.

★**Old Ground Hotel** HOTEL €€
(☎065-682 8127; www.flynnhotels.com; O'Connell St; s/d from €90/120; @) A seasoned, charming and congenial space of polished floorboards, cornice-work, antiques and open fires, the lobby is always a scene: old friends sinking into sofas, deals cut at the tables, and ladies from the neighbouring church's altar society exchanging gossip over tea. Parts of this smart and rambling landmark date back to the 1800s. The 83 rooms vary greatly in size and decor – don't hesitate to inspect a few. On balmy days, retire to tables on the lawn.

Newpark House INN €€
(☎065-682 1233; www.newparkhouse.com; Roslevan; s/d from €60/100; Apr-Oct; @) A vine-covered grand country house dating from 1750, Newpark sits 2km northeast of Ennis. The six rooms have a mix of furnishings old and modern while views of the fine 20-hectare woodland grounds are simply divine. To get here, go east on Tulla Rd (R352) and turn southeast at the Roslevan roundabout into Newpark Rd.

Eating

Foodies throng the **Ennis farmers market** (Upper Market St, car park; 8am-2pm Fri & Sat), which lures some of Clare's best producers.

★**Food Heaven** CAFE €
(www.food-heaven.ie; 21 Market St; mains €8-10; 8.30am-6pm Mon-Thu, 8.30am-9pm Fri & Sat;) This small cafe-deli lives up to its ambitious name with creative and fresh fare. Sandwiches arrive on renowned brown bread, while soups and salads change daily. Hot specials are just that. Be ready to queue at lunch.

Ennis Gourmet Store DELI €
(1 Old Barrack St; snacks €4-10; 10am-9.30pm Mon-Sat) Its shelves spilling forth with deli goodies, this is a delightful choice for a coffee perched on a stool inside or at a table outside. There's soups, sandwiches and hot specials plus a deli case of Irish cheeses, preserves, good wines and more.

Zest CAFE €
(www.zestfood.ie; Market Pl; meals €5-10; 8am-6pm Mon-Sat) Zest combines a deli, bakery, shop and cafe. Excellent prepared foods from the region are offered along with salads, soups and much more. It's ideal for a coffee or lunch.

Souper CAFE €
(www.soupercafe.ie; 10 Merchant Sq; soups €4.50; 9am-5pm Mon-Sat) Super Souper is a smart, trim-looking choice for swift bowls of its eponymous broth, be it goulash, roasted vegetable or soup of the day, all served with two slices of brown bread and butter. Paninis, wraps and sandwiches offer further sustenance if you want to make it a meal.

Rowan Tree Cafe Bar MEDITERRANEAN €€
(www.rowantreecafebar.ie; Harmony Row; mains €7-23; 10.30am-11pm;) There's nothing low-rent about the excellent Med-accented fare served at this cafe-bar on the ground floor of the namesake hostel. The gorgeous main dining room has high ceilings and a wondrous old wooden floor from the 18th century, while tables outside have river views. The foods are locally and organically sourced.

Poet's Corner Bar IRISH €€
(Old Ground Hotel, O'Connell St; mains €10-26; bar 11am-11.30pm Mon-Thu, 11am-12.30am Fri & Sat, noon-11pm Sun, meals 12.30-9pm daily) Offering excellent service, this famous old bar has a deserved reputation for its traditional dishes, especially the fish and chips.

Town Hall Cafe IRISH €€
(065-682 8127; O'Connell St; mains €7.50-28; 10am-9.30pm Mon-Sat, noon-9.30pm Sun;) Adjacent to, and affiliated with, the Old Ground Hotel, this smart bistro is in the stylishly resurrected old town hall. There's an ever-changing modern Irish menu – local ingredients, especially seafood, take centre stage. It's well worth calling in for a brekkie (10am to noon Monday to Saturday) of chunky scones, jam and coffee, and for Sunday brunch (noon to 4.45pm).

Tulsi INDIAN €€
(Carmody St; mains €8-18; 5-11pm Mon-Sat, 1-10pm Sun) Indian cuisine is excellent at this accommodating Ennis restaurant where staff are gracious and classics such as tandoori chicken are two cuts above the norm.

Drinking & Nightlife

As the capital of a renowned music county, Ennis bursts with pubs featuring trad music. In fact, this is the best reason to stay here.

Brogan's PUB
(24 O'Connell St) On the corner of Cooke's Lane, Brogan's is a big pub that rambles from one room to the next with a fine bunch of musicians rattling even the stone floors from about 9pm Monday to Thursday (more nights in summer).

Cruise's Pub PUB
(Abbey St; 5-11.30pm Mon-Thu, 4pm-2am Fri, 11am-2am Sat, 11am-1am Sun) With some of Ennis Friary's stonework incorporated into its fabric, this friendly bar has a long side courtyard that's perfect for enjoying a fresh-air pint, with trad music sessions most nights from 9pm.

Poet's Corner Bar PUB
(Old Ground Hotel, O'Connell St; 11am-11.30pm Mon-Thu, 11am-12.30am Fri & Sat, noon-11pm Sun) The old hotel pub sees trad sessions from Thursday to Sunday.

O'Dea's PUB
(66 O'Connell St) Unchanged since at least the 1950s, this plain-tile-fronted pub is a hide-out for local musicians serious about their trad sessions, drawing some of Clare's best.

Entertainment

Cois na hAbhna TRADITIONAL MUSIC
(065-682 0996; www.coisnahabhna.ie; Gort Rd; shop 9am-5pm, trad sessions 9pm Tue) With performances and classes, this important regional resource centre for Comhaltas Ceoltóirí Éireann (CCÉ; Society of the Musicians of Ireland) is 1.5km north of town along the N18. Traditional Irish music, dancing, singing and Irish language are promoted, with a range of classes each evening and on Saturday. July and August see the Summer Seisiún on Wednesday and Friday nights. Books, DVDs and CDs are also on sale.

Glór THEATRE
(www.glor.ie; Friar's Walk) In a striking modern building, Clare's cultural centre offers programs in art, traditional music, theatre, dance, photography, film and more.

Shopping

For the best selection of shops, head to O'Connell and Abbey Sts. On Saturday morning, there is a market at Market Pl.

Scéal Eile Books BOOKS
(www.scealeilebooks.ie; 16 Lower Market St; 11am-6pm Mon-Sat) Run by the affable Gerry and a delight to explore, this lovely two-floor bookshop bursts with new and secondhand literature across all genres from poetry to sci-fi and travel (aloft). A stove at

1

DAVID GEE 4/ALAMY STOCK PHOTO ©

2

4

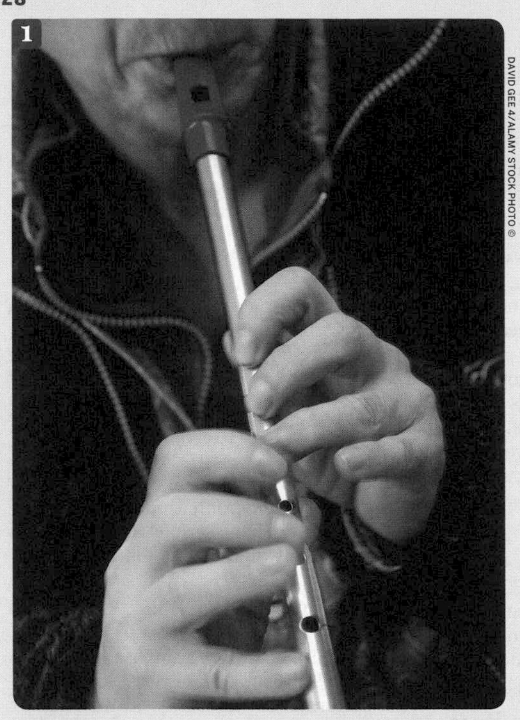

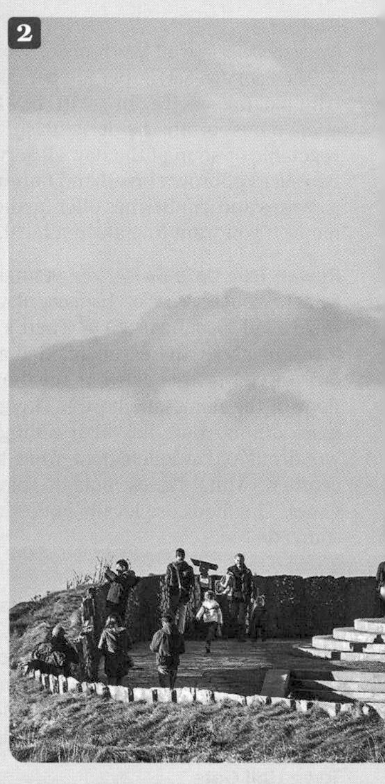

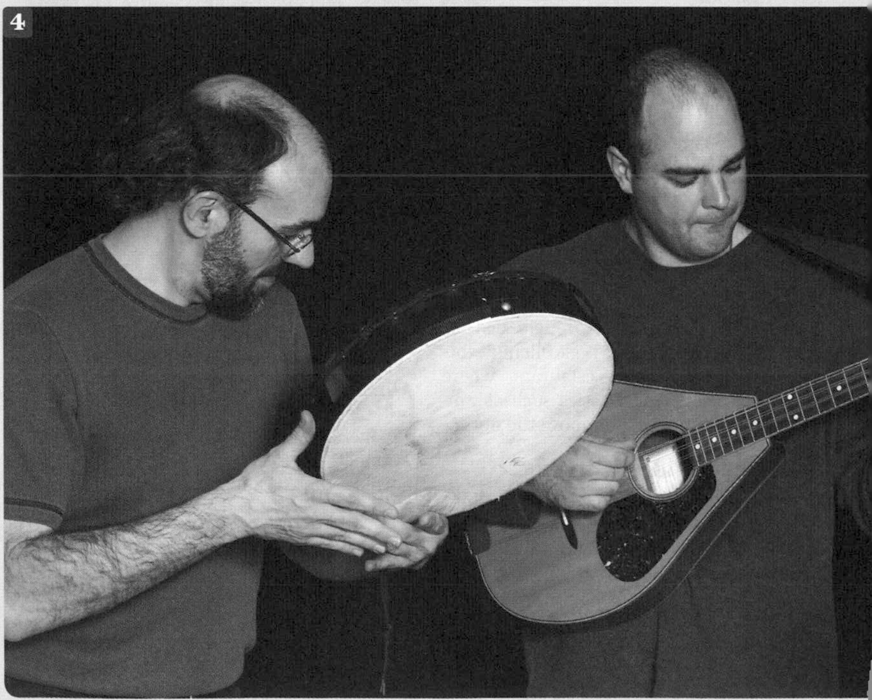

PETER UNGER/GETTY IMAGES ©

FRED GOLDSTEIN/SHUTTERSTOCK ©

3

KWIATEK7/SHUTTERSTOCK ©

1. Penny Whistle
Also called the tin whistle, this instrument features in much of Ireland's traditional music.

2. O'Brien's Tower (p344)
Take in views and sights along the clifftop on the Doolin Trail.

3. Cliffs of Moher (p344)
One of the most popular places in Ireland and the subject of many a song lyric.

4. Traditional Music
The bouzouki (centre; a version of the mandolin), is one of the main instruments in trad music.

the rear, ensconced between two armchairs, encourages a homely feel while book readings and cultural events add to the appeal.

Custy's Music Shop MUSIC
(☎065-682 1727; www.custysmusic.com; Cook's Lane, off O'Connell St; ⏲10am-6pm Mon-Sat) A must-stop for Irish music, with instruments, musical paraphernalia and general info about the local scene.

Ennis Bookshop BOOKS
(13 Abbey St; ⏲9.30am-6pm Mon-Sat) Excellent independent general bookshop with a strong kids' section.

Information

Tourist Office (☎065-682 8366; www.visitennis.ie; Arthur's Row; ⏲9am-1pm & 2-5pm Tue-Sat) Very helpful and efficient and can book accommodation for a €4 fee.

Getting There & Away

The M18 bypass east of the city lets traffic between Limerick and Galway whiz right past, although trips to the coast still take you through the centre.

BUS

Bus Éireann (☎065-682 4177; www.buseireann.ie) services operate from the bus station beside the train station.

Buses run from Ennis to the following.

Cork (€18, three hours, 12 daily)

Doolin (€13.90, 1½ hours, four daily) Via Corofin, Ennistymon, Lahinch, Liscannor and Cliffs of Moher.

Galway (€11.50, 1½ hours, hourly) Via Gort.

Limerick (€10, 40 minutes, hourly) Via Bunratty.

Shannon Airport (€8.40, 50 minutes, hourly)

To reach Dublin (€23), connect through Limerick.

TRAIN

Irish Rail (www.irishrail.ie) trains from **Ennis station** (☎065-684 0444; Station Rd) serve Limerick (€11.35, 40 minutes, nine daily), where you can connect to trains to places further afield like Dublin. The line to Galway (€19.70, 1¾ hours, five daily) features good Burren scenery.

Getting Around

There's a big car park behind the tourist office in Friar's Walk and one alongside the river just off Abbey St.

Burren Taxis (☎065-682 3456) Taxi stands are at the train station and the Square.

Around Ennis

North of Ennis is the early Christian site of Dysert O'Dea; to the southeast are several fine castles, while much of the county can be done as a day trip from Ennis.

Dysert O'Dea

Feel the past as you navigate the narrow tracks to Dysert O'Dea, where St Tola founded a monastery in the 8th century. The church and high cross, the White Cross of St Tola, date from the 12th or 13th century. The cross depicts Daniel in the lion's den on one side and a crucified Christ above a bishop carved in relief on the other. Look for carvings of animal and human heads in a semicircle on the southern doorway of the Romanesque church. The 5m-high remains of a round tower also survive.

In 1318 the O'Briens, who were kings of Thomond, and the Norman de Clares of Bunratty fought a pitched battle nearby, which the O'Briens won, thus postponing the Anglo-Norman conquest of Clare for some two centuries. The 15th-century **O'Dea Castle** houses the **Clare Archaeology Centre** (www.dysertcastle.com; Corofin; adult/child €4/2.50; ⏲10am-6pm May-Sep). A 3km history trail around the castle passes some two-dozen ancient monuments – from ring forts and high crosses to a prehistoric cooking site. A further 5km walk along a medieval road takes you to another stone fort.

East of Dysert O'Dea, you can wander along a lovely river in **Dromore Wood** (www.heritageireland.ie; Ruan; ⏲8am-7.30pm summer, to 6pm winter, visitor centre 10am-5pm Jun-Aug) FREE. This Dúchas nature reserve encompasses some 400 hectares as well as the ruins of the 17th-century **O'Brien Castle**, two ring forts and the site of Kilakee church.

Getting There & Away

Dysert O'Dea is 1.7km off the Corofin road (R476), 11km north of Ennis. Dromore Wood is 8km east of Dysert, off R458.

Bus Éireann generally runs one bus daily from Ennis, which stops along the R476.

Quin & Around

POP 930

Quin (Chuinche), a tiny village 10km southeast of Ennis, was the site of the Great Clare Find of 1854 – the most important discovery of prehistoric gold in Ireland. Only a few of the several hundred torcs, gorgets and other pieces made it to the National Museum in Dublin; most were sold and melted down.

Sights

Quin Friary CHURCH
(10am-4.30pm Tue-Fri, 9am-3.30pm Sat & Sun May-Oct, last admission 30min before close) FREE This Franciscan friary was founded in 1433 using part of the walls of an older Clare castle built in 1280. Despite many periods of persecution, Franciscan monks lived here until the 19th century. The splendidly named Fireballs MacNamara, a notorious duellist and member of the region's ruling family, is buried here. An elegant bell tower rises above the main body of the friary and its charming cloister, but the edifice unfortunately cannot be climbed.

Beside the friary is the 13th-century Gothic **Church of St Finghin**.

Knappogue Castle & Walled Garden HISTORIC SITE
(www.shannonheritage.com; R469; adult/child €6/3; 10am-4.30pm May-Aug) About 3km southeast of Quin is stately Knappogue Castle & Walled Garden, built in 1467 by the MacNamaras, who held sway over a large part of Clare from the 5th to mid-15th centuries and, like early fast-food franchisers, littered the region – with 42 castles. Knappogue's walls are intact, and it has a fine collection of period furniture and fireplaces. The formal gardens have been restored.

The castle was confiscated by Cromwellian forces in 1659 and bestowed upon a parliamentarian called Arthur Smith, which is one of the reasons it was spared destruction. The MacNamara family regained the castle after the Restoration in 1660 and it was finally restored by a Texan after he purchased it in 1966. Knappogue also hosts touristy medieval banquets.

Craggaunowen CASTLE
(www.shannonheritage.com; off R469; adult/child/family €9/5.50/21.50; 10am-4pm Easter-Sep;) In woodland around 6km southeast of Quin, peaceful Craggaunowen includes recreated ancient Celtic farms, dwellings such as a *crannóg* (artificial island), a 5th-century ring fort, plus real artefacts including a 2000-year-old oak road. Craggaunowen Castle is a small, well-preserved MacNamara fortified house. There's also a souterrain (underground passage) and animals and wildlife such as boars and goats.

Guides are at hand for further illumination. In a specially built display hall, the **Brendan Boat** is a leather-hulled vessel built by Tim Severin and sailed across the Atlantic in the same fashion as St Brendan's journey to America in the 6th century.

EASTERN & SOUTHEASTERN CLARE

Away from the Atlantic coast and the rugged Burren, Clare rolls gently eastward through low-lying green countryside given emphasis by the occasional range of low hills. The county's eastern boundary is the River Shannon and the long, noodle-like inland waterway of Lough Derg, which stretches 48km from Portumna in County Galway to just south of Killaloe. Lakeside villages such as Mountshannon seem to be a different world from the rugged, evocative west of Clare, but this is an intimate countryside of water, woods and panoramic views.

Southeastern Clare, where the Shannon swells into its broad estuary, is a plain landscape dotted with farms and small villages.

Shannon Airport

Ireland's third-busiest **airport** (SNN; 061-712 000; www.shannonairport.com;) used to be a vital fuelling stop for piston-engine planes lacking the range to make it between the North American and European mainlands. Today Shannon (Sionainn) is a low-stress gateway to the region and an ideal entry point for the western counties. There's a **tourist office** (www.shannonregiontourism.ie; 7am-4pm) near the arrivals area.

About 3km from the airport, **Shannon town**, built to serve airport workers, has the feel of a planned Soviet-era industrial city – albeit one with more reliable hot water. Don't linger.

Sleeping & Eating

There's B&B accommodation 3km from the airport in Shannon town but Ennis, Limerick and much prettier spots can be reached in 30 minutes. The airport terminal has an often-crowded restaurant.

Park Inn Shannon Airport HOTEL €€
(061-471 122; www.parkinns.com; r from €70;) Wake up in one of the 114 generic

hotel rooms here and you could be anywhere, which is the idea as the terminal is just across the car park. It's a good option if you have an early flight and want to lose the rental car.

Getting There & Around

AIR

There are nonstop services across the Atlantic to the US; travellers can enjoy the great convenience of pre-clearance for US customs and immigration before they leave Ireland, so there's no waiting in queues once you arrive on the other side of the pond.

Airlines with direct flights to/from Shannon:

Aer Lingus (www.aerlingus.ie) Boston, New York JFK and London Heathrow.

Delta (www.delta.com) New York JFK.

Ryanair (www.ryanair.com) London Stansted and Gatwick, Liverpool and numerous secondary and obscure European airports.

United (www.united.com) Chicago and Newark.

BUS

Bus Éireann (061-474 311; www.buseireann.ie) Destinations served by direct buses include Cork (€18, 2½ hours, hourly), Ennis (€8.40, 50 minutes, hourly), Galway (€15.50, 1¾ hours, hourly) and Limerick (€8.40, 30 to 55 minutes, two per hour). Some frequencies are reduced on Sunday.

CAR

Major car rental firms have desks at the airport.

TAXI

A taxi to the centre of Limerick or Ennis costs about €40 if booked at the taxi desk near arrivals. You may pay more at the outside rank.

Bunratty

A crossbow bolt's shot from the N18 motorway, Bunratty (Bun Raite) is home to a splendid castle that abuts a theme park recreating an Irish village of yore, a double-act that draws in endless visitors. Groups – disgorged by leviathan buses – lay siege to Bunratty from April to October, retreating with all manner of tourist trash and well fed from medieval banquets.

Sights & Activities

Bunratty Castle & Folk Park CASTLE
(www.shannonheritage.com; adult/child €15/9; 9am-5.30pm, last admission 4.15pm;) Square, hulking and imposing Bunratty Castle is only the latest of several edifices to occupy its location beside the River Ratty. Vikings founded a settlement here in the 10th century, and later occupants included the Norman Thomas de Clare in the 1270s. The castle is accessed via a folk park: a reconstructed traditional Irish village with thatched cottages, smoke coiling from chimneys, a forge and working blacksmith, weavers, post office, pub, children's play zones and small cafe.

The present castle dates to the early 1400s, built by the energetic MacNamara family, falling shortly thereafter to the O'Briens, in whose possession it remained until the 17th century. Fully restored and loaded with 14th- to 17th-century furniture, paintings, wall tapestries and antlers, the castle is home to a **dungeon**, a **main hall** and the magnificent and colossal **Great Hall**.

A few of the buildings in the folk park were brought here from elsewhere, but most are recreations. In peak season employees in period garb explain the more family-friendly and rose-tinted aspects of the late 19th century. Faux but fun.

Traditional Irish Night BANQUET
(061-360 788; adult/child €48.70/24.75; 7-9.30pm Apr-Oct) Traditional Irish nights lift the roof of a corn barn in the folk park. Red-haired servers dish out traditional chow amid music and dancing while servings of wine get you in the mood for the singalong.

Bunratty Medieval Banquet Castle BANQUET
(061-360 788; adult/child €58.45/29.25; 5.30pm & 8.45pm Apr-Oct, schedule varies Nov-Mar) You can skip the high-jinks in the corn barn for a feisty medieval banquet, replete with harp-playing maidens, court jesters and meaty medieval food, washed down with goblets of mead – a kind of honey wine. The banquets are popular with groups, so book well ahead; you can often find savings online.

Sleeping & Eating

Bunratty has a few hotels and dozens of B&Bs, many on Hill Rd north of the castle; a big map by the park entrance reveals locations. All are good choices if you've early flights from Shannon Airport, 5km west.

★**Cahergal Farmhouse** B&B €€
(061-368 358; www.cahergal.com; Newmarket-on-Fergus; s/d from €50/80;) Wake up to gentle, distant chicken clucks at this luxuri-

ous B&B on a working farm midway between Bunratty (6km) and the airport (8km). With king-size beds and bucolic views, rooms are elegant, while the food is farm-hearty with popular baked treats.

Briar Lodge B&B €€
(☎061-363 388; www.briarlodge.com; Hill Rd; s/d/f from €40/60/90; ⊙mid-Mar–mid-Oct; 📶) On a very quiet and secluded cul-de-sac 1.6km from the castle, this traditionally styled house with a charming and trim front garden (floral in spring and summer) has five spick-and-span rooms, some with commodious king-size beds, and welcoming, cordial owners.

Durty Nelly's PUB FOOD €€
(www.durtynellys.ie; Bunratty House Mews; mains €6-25; ⊙kitchen noon-10pm) Rammed with tourists all summer long, Nelly's is all snugs, timbers and beer mats, seasoned with age and enjoying pole position right across from the towering castle. Meals are good, although the pub is more enjoyable than the upstairs restaurant, but there's also an oyster restaurant on the ground floor and trad music sessions many nights.

Getting There & Away

Bunratty is on the **Bus Éireann** (☎061-313 333; www.buseireann.ie) Limerick–Ennis route. From Limerick, buses are at least hourly (one way/return €5.20/9), taking less than 30 minutes. There are at least five direct buses daily to Ennis (one way/return €8.40/13.70, 30 minutes). Buses stop near the castle.

Killaloe & Ballina

POP 4100

Facing each other across a narrow channel, Killaloe and Ballina are really one destination, even if they have different personalities (and counties). A fine 13-arch, one-lane bridge (1770) spans the River Shannon, linking the pair. Walk it in five minutes or drive it in about 20 (a torturous system of lights controls traffic).

Killaloe (Cill Da Lúa) is picturesque Clare at its finest, lying on the western banks of lower Loch Deirgeirt, the southern extension of Lough Derg, where the lough narrows at one of the principal crossings of the River Shannon. The village sits snugly against the Slieve Bernagh Hills that rise abruptly to the west, while the Arra Mountains create a fine balance to the east.

Not as quaint as Killaloe, Ballina (Béal an Átha) is in County Tipperary and has some of the better pubs and restaurants. It lies at the end of a scenic drive from Nenagh along Lough Derg on the R494.

Sights & Activities

The tiny, charming heart of Killaloe centres on its small and pretty waterfront. In Ballina, Main St – up the hill from the water – is the focus.

Killaloe Cathedral CHURCH
(St Flannan's Cathedral; Limerick Rd, Killaloe; donation €2) The present church dates from the early 13th century and was built by the O'Brien family on top of a 6th-century church. Inside, astonishing 12th-century carvings decorate the Romanesque southern doorway (on your right as you enter), near the shaft of a stone cross known as Thorgrim's Stone, which dates from the early Christian period, unusual for being inscribed with both the old Scandinavian runic and Irish Ogham scripts. Also within the church is a 13th-century font.

Brian Ború Heritage Centre MUSEUM
(www.shannonheritage.com; Lock House, Killaloe; adult/child €3.35/1.75; ⊙10am-5pm May–mid-Sep) Named for the local boy made good as the king who, according to the political spinmeisters of his time, both unified Ireland and freed it from the Viking scourge. The centre does much to celebrate the legends, with good displays about the nautical heritage of this patchwork of lakes and rivers.

TJ's Angling Centre FISHING
(☎061-376 009; www.tjsangling.com; Main St, Ballina; ⊙8am-10pm) Rent fishing tackle for €10 per day and catch your limit in free advice. The centre also organises fishing trips, although you can hook trout and pike right here in town.

Tours

Spirit of Killaloe BOAT TOUR
(☎086 814 0559; www.killaloerivercruises.com; Lakeside Dr, Ballina; adult/child €12.50/7.50; ⊙May-Sep) Hour-long cruises of the Lough Derg waters; reservations necessary.

Sleeping

B&Bs abound in the area, especially on the roads along Lough Derg. Book ahead come summer.

Kingfisher Lodge B&B €
(☎ 061-376 911; www.kingfisherlodge-ireland.com; Lower Ryninch, Ballina; s/d from €45/70; 📶) Right on Lough Derg, this exquisite three-room B&B has almost a hectare of gardens, decks and a dock on the water. Rooms are comfy and without pretension. It's about a 1km walk north from Ballina.

★**Kincora House** B&B €€
(☎ 061-376 149; www.kincorahouse.com; Church St, Killaloe; s/d from €45/80; 📶) An old yellow townhouse just uphill from the cathedral, this B&B is right in the heart of Killaloe. Four traditional-style rooms are simple and pleasant, while photos of old County Clare decorate the walls.

Lakeside Hotel HOTEL €€
(☎ 061-376 122; www.lakesidehotel.ie; Ballina; s/d from €75/100; @📶) With sweeping views of the bridge and its arches, this gentrified waterfront hotel is attractive, with good grounds for strolling. The 43 rooms vary greatly; prices work in direct ratio to view. All let you use the fun 40m water slide.

Eating & Drinking

The twin towns hold their excellent **farmers market** (⏰9am-4pm Sun) on the islet off the bridge on the Killaloe side.

★**Wooden Spoon** CAFE €
(Bridge St, Killaloe; mains €4-10; ⏰noon-6pm Tue-Thu & Sun, noon-9pm Fri & Sat) In a narrow passage just up from the waterfront, this popular bakery and cafe offers up Med-flavoured fare in a colourful setting that brings a gentle splash of vibrancy to Bridge St. Expect pavlovas, flapjacks, tiffins, scones, apple pies, quiche, falafels, fresh soda bread and more, all made with local ingredients and mostly sourced locally.

Tuscany Bistro Ballina ITALIAN €€
(☎ 061-376 888; www.tuscany.ie; Main St, Ballina; mains €12-26; ⏰4-9pm Tue & Wed, 4-10pm Thu & Fri, 12.30-10pm Sat, 12.30-9pm Sun; 📶) Small, smart and stylish, this Italian bistro has delicious and authentic fare. Amid the hearty soups, salads and pasta mains, you can also get pizzas or ponder a daily special and reasonable wine list.

Goosers SEAFOOD €€
(www.goosers.ie; Main St, Ballina; mains €11.50-26; ⏰meals noon-9pm, to 10pm Fri & Sat, from 12.30pm Sun) Just beyond the church on Main St, this popular thatched pub (with peat fires) is noted for its big selection of fish. Sailors make mirth and plough into the hefty seafood platter in the restaurant or go for pub fare at tables outside.

Information

The AIB bank at the bottom of Church St in Killaloe has an ATM. There are toilets on the Killaloe side in the car park. For local info online, try www.discoverkillaloe.com.

Tourist Office (☎ 061-376 866; Bridge St, Brian Ború Heritage Centre, Killaloe; ⏰10am-6pm May-Oct) Shares space with the heritage centre on the tiny island.

Getting There & Away

There's parking on both sides of the river and that's just what you'll want to do as soon as you arrive. Pretty as it is, the bridge is a traffic nightmare, so park and walk.

There are three **Bus Éireann** (☎ 061-313 333; www.buseireann.ie) services a day Monday to Saturday from Limerick to Killaloe (€8.40, 45 minutes). The bus stop is outside the cathedral.

Killaloe to Mountshannon

The journey north to Mountshannon along **Lough Derg** weaves along placid waters shaped like the long dribble left by an overfilled pint of Guinness carried from bar to table. From Killaloe take the R463 to Tuamgraney, then turn east on the R352 past good viewpoints of the water and Holy Island plus picnic spots.

About 2km north of Killaloe, **Beal Ború** is an earthen mound or fort said to have been Kincora, the fabled palace of the famous Irish king Brian Ború, who, besides lending his name to bad Irish bars the world over, taught the Vikings a lesson at the Battle of Clontarf in 1014. Traces of Bronze Age settlement have been discovered.

About 4.5km north of Killaloe is Cragliath Hill, which has another fort, **Griananlaghna**, named after Brian Ború's great-grandfather, King Lachtna.

Tuamgraney, at the junction of the road to Mountshannon (R352), has an interesting old church, **St Cronan's**, with parts dating to the 10th century. Inside, a small museum, the **East Clare Heritage Centre** (R463; adult/child €3/1.50; ⏰10am-3pm Mon-Fri), has a collection of old (and not so old) regional artefacts. Check out the record salmon caught in 1914. The surrounding moody parish **cemetery** also offers a fascinating look into Irish genealogy; next door rises the ivy-choked form of the **O'Grady Tower House**, built in 1500.

Mountshannon

POP 350

More than just a Tidy Town award-winning village (1981), Mountshannon (Baile Uí Bheoláin) is good for an agreeable pause on the southwestern shores of Lough Derg. It was founded in 1742 by an enlightened landlord to house a largely Protestant community of flax workers. The harbour is host to fishing boats and visiting yachts and cruisers in summer. It is the main launchpad for trips to Holy Island, one of Clare's finest early Christian settlements.

Sights & Activities

Some fantastic fishing abounds around Mountshannon, mainly for brown trout, pike, perch and bream. Ask at your lodging about boat hire and equipment. The return of the white-tailed eagle has drawn spotters from afar.

Holy Island ISLAND

Lying 2km offshore from Mountshannon, Holy Island (Inis Cealtra) is the site of a monastic settlement thought to have been founded by St Cáimín in the 7th century. On the island you will see a round tower that is more than 27m tall. Even with the top floor missing, it remains a landmark seen from two counties. You'll also find four old chapels, a hermit's cell and some early Christian gravestones dating from the 7th to 13th centuries. One of the chapels possesses an elegant Romanesque arch and, inside, an Old Irish inscription that translates as 'Pray for Tornog, who made this cross'.

The Vikings treated this monastery roughly in the 9th century, but under the crowd-pleasing protection of Brian Ború and others, it flourished. During the 17th century as many as 15,000 people would make Easter pilgrimages here.

At Mountshannon Harbour in summer, you may find boats willing to take you over to the island or at least sail around it.

Gerard Madden BOAT TOUR

(086 874 9710; gerardmmadden@eircom.net; adult/child €10/5; Apr-Oct) The noted local historian Gerard Madden leads two-hour tours of Holy Island.

Sleeping & Eating

Mountshannon Hotel HOTEL €

(061-927 162; www.mountshannon-hotel.ie; Main St; s/d/tw from €42/74/90; Mar-Oct;) A low-key inn with 14 rooms in the equally low-key centre of town; breakfast is included. The pub (mains €10 to €18) is perfect for a relaxed pint and fish stories, with food of the chicken Kiev and lasagne school. Wi-fi only in public areas.

Sunrise B&B B&B €

(061-927 343; www.sunrisebandb.com; s/d from €50/70;) With a large breakfast room in a conservatory facing the lake, this rural three-room B&B (just 300m from the village) has a charming and helpful owner (Vera) who can fill you in on Mountshannon's white-tailed eagles.

Hawthorn Lodge B&B €

(061-927 120; www.mountshannon-clare.com; R352; s/d from €50/75;) Around 1km east of Mountshannon, this tidy three-bedroom country cottage is a modern and relaxed option, with clean rooms and warm and welcoming owners.

Bourke's the Galley CAFE €

(Main St; mains €4-9; 9am-5pm;) Attached to a deli, Bourke's offers rich coffees, alluring baked goods and fresh light meals you can enjoy on a small terrace.

Getting There & Away

Your own car or bike are the best ways to reach Mountshannon.

North of Mountshannon, the R352 follows Lough Derg to Portumna in County Galway. It's just one of several not-quite-two-lane country roads that weave through the fertile landscapes under arching trees. Another is the R461 from Scarriff, which heads right to the heart of the Burren.

SOUTHWESTERN & WESTERN CLARE

Beautiful and dramatic in equal measure, the soaring cliffs south of the beach resort of Kilkee to Loop Head are major milestones on the breathtaking Clare section of the **Wild Atlantic Way**.

South of the Cliffs of Moher to Kilkee are the low-key beach towns of Lahinch, Miltown Malbay and Doonbeg. A stark windblown beauty stretches to the horizon. Many a hapless survivor of the Spanish Armada washed ashore here 400 years ago and tales of their progeny still spice local gossip.

Your best days here may be spent on the smallest roads you can find. Make your own discoveries, whether it's a stretch of lonely beach or something more settled, like the charming heritage town of Ennistymon.

Getting There & Around

BOAT

Shannon Ferry Limited (065-905 3124; www.shannonferries.com; one-way/return bicycle & foot passengers €5/7, cars from €18; at least hourly 9am-9pm Jun-Aug, 9am-7pm Sep-May) runs a ferry that takes 20 minutes between Tarbert in County Kerry and Killimer in County Clare. It's a real time-saver over detouring through Limerick, and puts you close to the Dingle Peninsula. Discounts are available online.

BUS

You can usually count on a **Bus Éireann** (www.buseireann.ie) service or two linking all the main towns in the region each day. From Limerick, routes run along the Shannon to Kilrush and Kilkee, as well as up through Corofin, Ennistymon, Lahinch, Liscannor and on to the Cliffs of Moher and Doolin. Buses from Ennis follow the same pattern. On the coast between Lahinch and Kilkee, services average twice daily in summer. A few other nondaily routes are geared to schoolkids.

Kilrush

POP 2600

Kilrush (Cill Rois) is a small, atmospheric town that overlooks the Shannon Estuary and the hills of Kerry to the south. It has the western coast's biggest **marina** (www.kilrushmarina.ie) at Kilrush Creek, and offers various opportunities to see bottlenose dolphins living in the Shannon Estuary, an important calving region for the mammals.

Sights & Activities

The main street, **Frances St**, runs directly to the harbour. More than 30m wide, it reflects Kilrush's origins as a port and market town in the 19th century. The **Maid of Eireann monument** at the top of Frances St still shows damage caused by departing English troops in 1921.

★**Vandeleur Walled Garden** GARDENS
(www.vandeleurwalledgarden.ie; Killimer Rd; 10am-5pm Mon-Fri, noon-5pm Sat & Sun) FREE
This stunning 'lost' garden was the private domain of the wealthy Vandeleur family – merchants and landowners who engaged in harsh evictions and forced emigration of local people in the 19th century. The gardens lie within a large walled forest just east of the centre and feature a colourful array of plants including magnolias, acacias, acers, oaks, monkey puzzle trees, bamboo, ferns, banana trees, hydrangeas and a beech maze.

WORTH A TRIP

SCATTERY ISLAND

This uninhabited, windswept and treeless island in the estuary 3km southwest of Kilrush was the site of a Christian settlement founded by St Senan in the 6th century. Its 36m-high **round tower**, one of the tallest and best preserved in Ireland, is also notable for its entrance at ground level instead of the usual position high above the foundation. An evocative mood reigns: the ruins of six **medieval churches** include the 9th-century **Cathedral of St Mary** (Teampall Naomh Mhuire) – part of **St Senan's Monastery** – and there's a lighthouse and an artillery battery, built during the Napoleonic wars, at the southern end of the island.

A free exhibition on the history and wildlife of the Heritage Service–administered island is housed in the **Scattery Island Visitor Centre** (087 995 8427; www.heritageireland.ie; 9.30am-4pm Mon-Fri Jun-Aug, reduced hours Sat & Sun). The centre also provides free 45-minute tours to St Senan's Monastery.

Scattery Island Ferries (065-905 1327; www.discoverdolphins.ie; Kilrush Creek Marina; adult/child €12/7; Jun-Aug) runs boats from Kilrush to the island; the journey takes 15 to 20 minutes. There's no strict timetable as the trips are subject to tidal and weather conditions; visits usually last about one hour. Buy tickets at the small kiosk at the marina and take a decent pair of walking shoes.

Woodland trails wind around the area, and there's a cafe.

St Senan's Church CHURCH
(Toler St) St Senan's Catholic church has a lovely rose window and contains eight detailed examples of stained glass by well-known early-20th-century artist Harry Clarke.

Shannon Dolphin & Wildlife Centre NATURE CENTRE
(www.shannondolphins.ie; Merchants Quay; 10am-4pm May-Sep) FREE This research facility monitors the 100-plus bottlenose dolphins swimming out in the Shannon and houses exhibits on the playful cetaceans, a species unique to the area.

Kilrush Shannon Dolphin Trail WALKING
This 4km route ends 3km south of Kilrush at Aylevarro Point, where signs have dolphin info and you can often see dolphins frolicking offshore.

Tours

Dolphin Discovery BOAT TOUR
(065-905 1327; www.discoverdolphins.ie; Kilrush Creek Marina; adult/child €22/10; Apr-Oct) Two-hour boat rides on the Shannon offer plenty of dolphin-spotting. Trips depart depending on weather and demand.

Sleeping & Eating

B&Bs almost outnumber dolphins in the Shannon. The local **farmers market** (9am-2pm Thu) is held on the main square.

Katie O'Connor's Holiday Hostel HOSTEL €
(065-905 1133; www.katieshostel.com; Frances St; dm/d from €20/40; mid-Mar–mid-Oct;) This fine old main-street house dates from the 18th century, and was one of the town houses of the Vandeleur family. Today it's a funky IHH-affiliated hostel.

Crotty's HOTEL €
(065-905 2470; www.crottyspubkilrush.com; Market Sq; s/d from €45/70; trad music 7pm Tue-Thu Jun-Aug;) Brimming with character, Crotty's has an old-fashioned high bar, intricately tiled floors and a series of snugs decked out with traditional furnishings. There's high-end versions of pub fare (mains €9 to €17), with five small, traditionally decorated rooms upstairs.

Buttermarket Cafe CAFE €
(Burton St; mains €4-12; 9.30am-5pm Mon-Sat;) Just off the main square, this little sprite of a cafe has a courtyard where you can enjoy its excellent coffees, gourmet sandwiches, hot specials and baked goodies.

Potter's Hand CAFE €
(10 Vandeleur St; mains from €3; 9am-5pm Mon-Sat, till 8pm Wed) This charming, cheery and bright cafe offers a fine combination of excellent baked goods, a restful dining space, pottery classes, comfy sofas, sunny staff and decking out back.

Information

Tourist Information (065-905 1577; Frances St; 10am-4pm Mon-Sat mid-Mar–mid-Oct) At Katie O'Connor's Holiday Hostel.

Getting There & Around

Bus Éireann has three to four buses daily to Limerick (€20, 1¾ hours), Ennis (€10, one hour) and Kilkee (€4.80, 15 minutes). Note that no petrol stations between Kilrush and Loop Head open on Sunday, so fill up in town.

Gleeson's Cycles (065-905 1127; Henry St; per day/week from €20/80; 9am-6pm) Hire bikes here.

Kilkee

POP 1100

Kilkee's wide beach and fine, powdery sand is thronged with day trippers and holidaymakers in warmer months. The sweeping semicircular bay has high cliffs on the north end and weathered rocks to the south, with fantastic walks at either extremity. The waters are highly tidal, with wide-open sandy expanses replaced by pounding waves in just a few hours.

Kilkee (Cill Chaoi) first became popular in Victorian times when rich Limerick families built seaside retreats here. Today, it is well supplied with guesthouses, amusement arcades and takeaways, and a constant stream of beach-goers.

Sights & Activities

Many visitors come for the fine sheltered **beach** and the **Pollock Holes**, natural swimming pools in the Duggerna Rocks. **St George's Head**, to the north, has good cliff walks and scenery, while south of the bay, the **Duggerna Rocks** form an unusual natural amphitheatre. Further south is a huge **sea cave**. These sights can be reached by driving to Kilkee's West End area by the Diamond Rocks Cafe and following the coastal path.

Kilkee is a well-known **diving** centre as the dramatic rocks of the shore cliffs continue right below the waves. Experience and local knowledge or guidance are strongly advised. Right at the tip of the Duggerna Rocks is the small inlet of Myles Creek, out from which lies excellent underwater scenery.

West Clare Railway TOURIST TRAIN
(065-905 1284; www.westclarerailway.ie; adult/child €8/4; 1-4pm Apr-Sep) A 2km vestige of this historic line survives near Moyasta on the Kilkee Rd (N67) 6km northwest of Kilrush. Run by volunteers, the beautifully restored steam-powered trains shuttle back and forth over the open land.

Sleeping

Kilkee has plenty of guesthouses and B&Bs, but during the high season rates can soar and you may have a problem finding a vacancy.

Green Acres Caravan & Camping Park CAMPGROUND €
(065-905 7011; Doonaha, Kilkee; campsites €8-24; Apr-Sep) Beside the Shannon, 6km south of Kilkee on the R487, this is a small, open and peaceful park with 40 sites. Weekly trailer rentals start at €300.

Lynch's B&B B&B €
(065-905 6420; www.lynchskilkee.com; O'Connell St; s/d from €35/60;) All's shipshape at this B&B in the centre. Guest rooms have hardwood floors and bedspreads with designs that will bring a smile to aunties everywhere. It's as quiet as the surf at low tide and breakfasts are big.

★ **Water's Edge** B&B €€
(065-906 0899; http://watersedge.westclare.net; West End; s/d from €50/80;) This fantastic B&B in a 19th-century house directly facing the sea along West End in the west of Kilkee offers excellent rooms, all with supreme views of the bay. Charming, comfy and elegant.

Strand Guest House INN €€
(065-905 6177; www.thestrandkilkee.com; The Strand; s/d from €54/74; Feb-Nov;) Right across from the water, this six-room guesthouse has been given a bit of a polish since Che Guevara stayed here in 1961. Rooms are simply decorated, some have excellent views, as does the inviting bistro-bar.

Stella Maris Hotel HOTEL €€
(065-905 6455; www.stellamarishotel.com; O'Connell St; s/d from €70/120; @) Follow the tartan carpet to 20 refurbished rooms, each decorated with funky cushions, in this lovely old building and year-round choice at the heart of Kilkee. Room 20 is best for a view of the sea, through dormer windows; sea views from other rooms are patchy.

Eating & Drinking

The small **farmers market** (10am-2pm Sun) is on the large parking area near the bus stop.

Diamond Rocks Cafe CAFE €
(West End; mains €5-12; 9am-7pm Jun–mid-Sep) If you need another reason to walk out to the west point of the bay: this modern cafe (with a huge terrace) serves food far above the norm for the types of places usually found in such a stunning spot, with fresh salads, chowders, sandwiches, breakfasts and a plethora of daily specials.

★ **Naughton's Bar** SEAFOOD €€
(065-905 6597; www.naughtonsbar.com; 45/47 O'Curry St; mains €13-24; 6-9.30pm) The terrace alone is enough to make Naughton's a mandatory stop, but the food is even better. Fresh local produce and seafood combine for some mighty fine pub meals at this atmospheric family-run pub, which dates to the 1870s. Book.

Strand Bistro & Cafe BISTRO €€
(065-905 6177; The Strand; mains from €11.95; noon-9pm May-Sep, shorter hours Apr & Oct) Enjoy tables outside for some salt spray in your stout at this excellent cafe, bar and bistro. It serves delectable seafood such as tiger-prawn linguine pasta and oven-baked Atlantic cod. Well worth booking for dinner, there's also a decent wine list.

Murphy Blacks IRISH €€
(065-905 6854; www.murphyblacks.ie; The Square; mains €15-22; 12.30-4pm & 6-9pm Mon-Sat Apr-Sep, daily mid-Jul–mid-Aug) Smart and serene, this deservedly popular dinner spot is booked up solid night after night for its carefully crafted seafood and meat dishes. Tables outside are a summer-night treat.

Information

The websites www.loophead.ie and www.kilkee.ie are good sources of local information.

Getting There & Away

Bus Éireann has three to four buses daily to Kilkee from Limerick (€22, two hours) and Ennis (€16.50, 1¼ hours). Both routes pass through Kilrush.

Kilkee to Loop Head

The land from Kilkee south to Loop Head has subtle undulations that suddenly terminate in **dramatic cliffs** (p340) falling straight into the Atlantic – in many ways more stirring and enjoyable than the Cliffs of Moher. It's a windswept place with timeless striations of old stone walls and views that extend for miles. It's also ideal cycling country and coastal walks are sublime (just as well as there's no public transport).

Carrigaholt

POP 150

On 15 September 1588, seven tattered ships of the Spanish Armada took shelter off Carrigaholt (Carraig an Chabaltaigh), a tiny village inside the mouth of the Shannon Estuary. One, probably the *Anunciada*, was torched and abandoned, sinking somewhere out in the estuary waters. Today, timeless Carrigaholt has one of the simplest and cutest main streets you'll find. The substantial remains of a 15th-century McMahon **castle** overlook the water.

Activities

★Dolphinwatch BOAT TOUR
(065-905 8156; www.dolphinwatch.ie; adult/child €30/15; Apr-Oct) Dolphinwatch runs two-hour trips in the estuary to view the 100-plus resident bottlenose dolphins. Ask about Loop Head sunset cruises and geology tours. For more on seeing these cetacean mammals in their natural environment, check the dolphin sites (p337) in and around Kilrush.

Eating & Drinking

The snoozy main street has a couple of atmospheric old pubs, while the **post office** (9am-5.30pm Mon-Fri, 10am-1pm Sat) – down near the dock – is an enterprising place, doubling as a cafe, book-swap parlour and duck-egg and cabbage shop.

★Long Dock SEAFOOD €€
(www.thelongdock.com; West St; mains €6-25; kitchen 11am-11.30pm Sun-Thu, 11am-12.30am Fri & Sat) This terrific pub has a seriously excellent kitchen, along with stone walls and floors, a sunny welcome and a warm fire. Stunning seafood is the order of the day – you'll see the purveyors out working in the estuary or even drinking at the bar. The fish and chips is a sure-fire winner – nab a table outdoors on a summer night.

Kilbaha

POP 50

The land at this minute waterfront village is as barren as the soul of the 19th-century landlord who burned down the local church so his workers wouldn't waste productive hours praying. Even today the scars are felt. Gazing at the ruins of his house far up the hillside, a local says, 'Yeah, we got rid of him', as if the events of 150 years ago were yesterday.

You can learn more about this story and other aspects of local life from the compelling modern-day **scroll**, an open-air sculpture that relates the area's history. The road east towards Doonaha follows ancient lava flows on the shoreline.

Sleeping & Eating

Lighthouse Inn INN €
(065-905 8358; s/d from €25/50;) The Lighthouse Inn is a mirthful place right on the water, with 11 basic rooms, all with sea view. The gregarious pub serves sandwiches, tea and scones (€3.50) and the like through the year, as well as more complex seafood dinners in summer (mains €10 to €19). Trad sessions some nights are a bonus.

Loop Head

As you approach along the R487, sea begins to appear on both flanks as land tapers to a narrow shelf. On a clear day, Loop Head (Ceann Léime), Clare's southernmost point, has gob-smacking views south to the Dingle Peninsula crowned by Mt Brandon (951m), and north to the Aran Islands and Galway Bay. Bracing walks and a long hiking trail run along the cliffs to Kilkee.

On the northern side of the cliff near the point, a dramatic crevice has been cleaved from the coastal cliffs where you'll first hear and then see a teeming bird-breeding area. Guillemots, chough and razorbills are among the squawkers nesting in rocky niches.

The often-deserted wilds of the head are perfect for exploration, but be extra careful near the cliff edge.

Sights & Activities

Loop Head Lighthouse HISTORIC BUILDING
(Kilbaha; admission €5; 10am-5pm May-Sep) This working lighthouse, complete with Fresnel lens, rises up above Loop Head.

DON'T MISS

CLARE'S OTHER CLIFFS

On the way to and from Loop Head, take in the jaw-dropping sea visuals and drama of the sensational cliffs along the coast roads. Heading to Loop Head from Carrigaholt, drive south down Church St for around 2km till you reach the junction, then turn right along the L2002. This scenic route is the Coast Rd, hugging the coastline and offering splendid panoramas of the sea, running through the village of Rhinevilla and eventually rejoining the R487 at Kilbaha. Heading west from Loop Head, drive along the R487 to Cavan and then take a left along the Coast Rd (L2000) and follow the signs, making your way to Kilkee. You'll rejoin the R487 but can head north again along small roads north from just after either Oughterard or Cross for stunning vistas of soaring coastal cliffs.

Bog Road Bike Tours BICYCLE TOUR
(086 278 0161; www.bogroadbiketours.com; tours €20-35) Explore the narrow laneways denied to cars around Loop Head on these excellent tours. Bikes and equipment can be rented for a small extra fee.

Long Way Round WALKING TOUR
(086 409 9624; www.thelongwayround.ie; tours €20) Long Way Round has historical and nature tours led by noted guide Laura Foley.

Kilkee to Ennistymon

North of Kilkee the land flattens, with vistas that sweep across pastures and dunes. The N67 runs inland for some 32km until it reaches Quilty. Take the occasional lane to the west and search out unfrequented places such as **White Strand**, north of Doonbeg. **Ballard Bay** is 8km west of Doonbeg, where an old telegraph tower looks over some fine cliffs, while the remains of a promontory fort can be found at **Donegal Point**. There's good fishing all along the coast, and safe beaches at Seafield, Lough Donnell and Quilty. Off the coast of Quilty, look for **Mutton Island**, a barren expanse that once served as a prison, sporting an ancient tower and fantastic views.

Doonbeg

POP 300

Doonbeg (An Dún Beag) is a tiny seaside village about halfway between Kilkee and Quilty. Another Spanish Armada ship, the *San Esteban*, was wrecked on 20 September 1588 near the mouth of the River Doonbeg. The survivors were later executed at Spanish Point. Doonbeg also offers some decent **surfing** for those who want to flee the Lahinch crowds.

Sights

Doonbeg Castle CASTLE
The surviving little 16th-century castle tower next to the graceful stone bridge over the Doonbeg River is all that remains of Doonbeg Castle – its entire garrison was hanged face to face in pairs when it fell.

White Strand BEACH
White Strand (Trá Ban) is a quiet beach, 500m long, backed by dunes, partially engulfed in seaweed and supplying some of the flattest skimming stones you'll ever lay your hands on. It's along a turning north of town.

Doughmore Bay BEACH
A long 2km stretch of sand further to the north of White Strand, Doughmore Bay is popular with horse riders and locals walking their dogs.

Sleeping & Eating

For campers there are often spots on the side roads around Doonbeg that make a good pitch, with glorious sunsets as a bonus. B&Bs also abound, some overlooking the sand.

★**Morrissey's** INN €€
(065-905 5304; www.morrisseysdoonbeg.com; Main St; s/d from €55/90; Mar-Oct;) Opposite the remains of Doonbeg Castle, this old pub is a stylish coastal haven, with six rooms featuring king-size beds and large soaking tubs. The pub's restaurant (mains €14 to €24) is renowned for its casual but enticing seafood, from fish and chips to succulent local crab claws. Outside there's a terrace overlooking the river.

Miltown Malbay

POP 800

Like Kilkee, Miltown Malbay was a resort favoured by well-to-do Victorians, though the town isn't actually on the sea: the beach is 2km south at Spanish Point. Miltown Malbay has a thriving music scene and hosts the annual Willie Clancy Summer School, one of Ireland's great traditional music events.

Sights

Spanish Point BEACH
With fine views of the setting sun, this lovely beach also affords excellent walks north of the point amid the low cliffs, vast ledges of stone, rock pools, coves and isolated beaches. Note however that some sections can be hazardous.

Sleeping & Eating

An Gleann B&B B&B €
(065-708 4281; www.angleann.net; Ennis Rd; s/d from €30/60;) The warm welcome is a major draw at this lovely four-room B&B southeast along the R474 about 1km from the centre. Some with rural views, the five clean rooms are basic but comfy and owners Mary and Harry Hughes are a delight. Cyclists are catered for.

Old Bake House IRISH €
(www.theoldbakehouse.ie; Main St; mains €5-15; noon-9pm, to 10pm Fri & Sat) In a region awash with fantastic seafood chowder, some of the best is at the Old Bake House, where delightful seafood and classic Irish and international dishes can be enjoyed in a smart yet homely environment. There's blackboard menus on the walls, tapas in the evening and live music on Fridays from 7pm.

Drinking & Nightlife

O'Friel's Bar PUB
(Lynch's; The Square) This fine old-style charmer has trad sessions four nights a week in summer.

Hillery's PUB
(Main St) Dapper choice along Main St.

Information

For local information, drop by the cheery **An Ghiolla Finn Gift Shop** (Main St; 10.30am-6pm Mon-Sat).

Getting There & Away

Bus Éireann service is paltry. Expect one or two buses Monday to Saturday north and south along the coast and inland to Ennis.

Lahinch

POP 650

Sitting on protected Liscannor Bay with its fine beach, Lahinch (Leacht Uí Chonchubhair) has always owed its living to beach-seeking summer tourists. Coming round the headland on the N67 from Milton Malbay, the sweeping bay at Lahinch is quite a sight. Steeped in the strong aromas of ocean salt and seaweed, this old holiday town is one of the centres of Ireland's hot surfing scene. Surf schools and stores cluster near the seafront, like surfers waiting for the perfect set.

SURF'S UP!

Like swells after a storm, Clare's surfing scene keeps getting bigger and better. On weekends in Lahinch the breaks fill with hundreds of surfers, while thick wetsuits dry on railings and scores of spectators watch the action from the town's beach and pubs.

Conditions are excellent for much of the year, with the bay's cliffs funnelling regular and reliable sets. As the waters fill in Lahinch, the action is moving to other spots along the coast, like Doonbeg and Fanore.

There are plentiful surf shops where you can rent gear and get lessons from about €40 per two-hour session; board and wetsuit rentals are about €15 per day.

Ben's Surf Clinic (086 844 8622; www.benssurfclinic.com; Waterfront, Lahinch; 9am-6pm, till 9pm in summer) Offers lessons plus rents out boards and wetsuits.

Clare Surf Safari (087 634 5469; www.claresurfsafari.com) With lessons held on various Clare beaches; transport included in the price.

Lahinch Surf School (087 960 9667; www.lahinchsurfschool.com; Waterfront, Lahinch) Champion surfer John McCarthy offers lessons and various multiday packages.

Green Room (065-708 2771; www.greenroomlahinch.com; Parade; 9am-5.30pm) Shop, surf school and board rental.

Activities

Clare Kayak Hire KAYAKING
(☎085 148 5856; www.clarekayakhire.com; rental per hr from €15, tours from €35; ⌚rentals Jul & Aug) For a more methodical water experience, Clare Kayak Hire offers tours on the rivers and lakes in the region and rentals at White Strand Beach near Spanish Point.

Dive Academy Scuba School DIVING
(☎085 725 7260; www.diveacademy.info; The Promenade; dives from €20; ⌚9am-6pm Tue-Sun) Learn to scuba dive in their 170,000L tank or join open-water and shore dives, classes and courses.

Lahinch Golf Club GOLF
(☎065-708 1003; www.lahinchgolf.com; green fees from €120) This golf club in Lahinch dates from 1892 when it was laid out amid the dunes by Scottish soldiers.

Sleeping & Eating

The tourist office has good links to local B&Bs. Waterfront cafes and pubs let you enjoy the action on the waves.

West Coast Lodge INN €
(☎065-708 2000; www.lahinchaccommodation.com; Station Rd; dm/r from €18/50; @ 🛜) This dependable choice in the heart of Lahinch comes with power showers, fine cotton sheets and down duvets in its seven- to 12-bed dorms and private rooms. Check out the surf from the roof deck and rent a bike to go exploring.

Atlantic Hotel HOTEL €€
(☎065-708 1049; www.atlantichotel.ie; Main St; s/d from €50/85; @) This old-fashioned and lovely town-centre classic has a charming air, from its welcoming reception rooms and cosy bars to its 14 well-appointed, wall-papered rooms, all with flat-screen TV.

O'Looneys IRISH €€
(www.olooneys.ie; The Promenade; mains €13-20; ⌚kitchen 12.30-9pm daily Apr-Oct, Sat & Sun Nov-Mar) The best views of the Lahinch surf scene and pounding breaks are from the terrace at this dual-level bar, cafe and club. Pub standards are a cut above and weekend parties go late in summer.

Barrtrá Seafood Restaurant SEAFOOD €€
(☎065-708 1280; www.barrtra.com; Miltown Malbay Rd; mains €15-28; ⌚noon-2pm & 6-10pm Thu-Sat Mar-May, Thu-Mon Jun-Oct) This rural repose 3.5km south of Lahinch offers views over pastures to the sea from a lovely country cottage, surrounded by pretty kitchen gardens. The lavish €35 set meal is great value.

Shopping

Lahinch Surf Shop SURFING
(☎065-708 1543; www.lahinchsurfshop.com; Old Promenade, Lahinch; ⌚10am-6pm Mon-Sat) Sells gear from a dramatic surfside location.

Lahinch Bookshop BOOKS
(Main St; ⌚10am-6pm Tue-Sat, 10.30am-5.30pm Sun) The best source for hiking maps outside Ennis.

Information

The only reliable ATM in the region is in the town centre on Main St.

Getting There & Away

Bus Éireann runs two to four buses daily through Lahinch on the Doolin–Ennis/Limerick routes and one or two Monday to Saturday south along the coast to Doonbeg in summer.

Ennistymon

POP 1000

One of Clare's most charming villages, Ennistymon (Inis Díomáin) is most noteworthy for its characterful buildings that line Main St, some good-looking traditional pubs and its trump card: the roaring Cascades, the stepped falls of the River Inagh, which accompany languorous walks downstream.

CLARE'S BEST MUSIC FESTIVAL

Half the population of Miltown Malbay seems to be part of the annual **Willie Clancy Summer School** (☎065-708 4148; www.scoilsamhraidhwillieclancy.com; ⌚Jul), a tribute to a native son and one of Ireland's greatest pipers. The nine-day festival usually begins in the first or second week in July, when impromptu sessions occur day and night, the pubs are packed and Guinness is consumed by the barrel. Workshops and classes underpin the event; don't be surprised to attend a recital with 40 noted fiddlers.

Sights

Cascades WATERFALL

(behind Byrne's) These fine cascades are quite a sight after heavy rain when they surge, beer-brown and foaming, and you risk getting drenched on windy days in the flying drizzle. You'll find them down through an arch by Byrne's hotel. Beyond the cascades, a charming riverside walk takes you beyond the Falls Hotel.

Courthouse Studios & Gallery ARTS CENTRE

(Parliament St; noon-4pm Tue-Sat) FREE Ennistymon has a healthy arts scene. These studios are in a renovated 1800 building with ever-changing exhibitions on two floors from local and international artists.

Sleeping

Station House B&B €

(065-707 1149; Station Rd; s/d/tr €45/70/90) With tons of parking space a short distance south of town, this comfy B&B is neat, tidy and spacious, with trim rooms in this former station office. Carpets are a bit swirly, but windows are triple glazed.

★ **Byrne's** INN €

(065-707 1080; www.byrnes-ennistymon.ie; Main St; s/d from €55/70;) The Cascades are out back at this historic guesthouse and stunning restaurant – enjoy them from the terrace. Six large and comfortable rooms await upstairs; breakfast is included.

Falls Hotel HOTEL €€

(065-707 1004; www.fallshotel.ie; off N67; s/d from €75/120;) Built on the ruins of an O'Brien castle, this handsome and sprawling Georgian house was once Ennistymon House, the family home of Caitlín MacNamara, who married Dylan Thomas. With 140 modern rooms and a large, enclosed pool, the hotel's view of the Cascades from the entrance steps is breathtaking, and there are 20 hectares of wooded gardens.

Eating

The local **farmers market** (Market Sq; 10am-2pm Sat) spreads its fertile wealth weekly.

THE ATM HUNT

It's easy to get caught out cashless in western Clare. Many small towns such as Liscannor, Doolin, Lisdoonvarna and Kilfenora are ATM-free zones. There's an ATM at the **Supervalu** (Church St; 8am-9pm Mon-Sat, 9am-8pm Sun) and another at the **Bank of Ireland** (Parliament St) in Ennistymon, and one in Lahinch. The ATM in the gift shop at the Cliffs of Moher visitor centre is a hassle to reach (and may be out of cash).

Byrne's EUROPEAN €€

(065-707 1080; www.byrnes-ennistymon.ie; mains €12-22, 2-/3-course set menu €24/26; noon-9pm Jun-Aug, shorter hours other times) Sit out on the terrace or dine on seafood specials inside, in an eye-catching environment of polka-dot tablecloths and wooden floorboards, with warmth from a flaming stove. There's a good selection of wine and craft beers.

Drinking & Nightlife

★ **Eugene's** PUB

(Main St; 10.30am-11.30pm Mon-Thu, 10.30am-12.30am Fri & Sat, 12.30-11pm Sun) With one of the most amazing pub frontages you'll ever see, Eugene's is a classic choice. Intimate and cosy, with a trademark collection of visiting cards covering its walls, it has a great whiskey collection and some fab stained glass.

Cooley's House PUB

(065-707 1712; Main St; 10.30am-11pm Mon-Sat, noon-11.30pm Sun) Another great old pub, bright-orange painted and with music most nights in summer and on Wednesday (trad night) in winter. Two doors down from Eugene's.

Shopping

Secret Vault ARTS

(www.peregringo.eu; off Main St; 10.30am-6.30pm) In the passage to the Cascades by Byrne's, this downstairs arts and crafts gallery has an enticing collection of

Celtic-themed paintings and lithographic prints from the artist owners.

Getting There & Away

Bus Éireann runs two to four buses daily through Ennistymon on the Doolin–Ennis/Limerick routes and one or two Monday to Saturday south along the coast via Lahinch to Doonbeg in summer. Buses stop in front of Aherne's on Church St.

Liscannor & Around

POP 250

This small seaside village overlooks Liscannor Bay, where the road (R478) heads north to the Cliffs of Moher and Doolin. Liscannor (Lios Ceannúir) has given its name to a type of local stone – slatelike and with a rippled surface – that is used for floors, walls and even roofs.

Sleeping & Eating

Moher Lodge Farmhouse B&B €€

(065-708 1269; www.cliffsofmoher-ireland.com; off R478; s/d €50/80; Apr-Oct;) With a charming owner and lovely all around, this big bungalow has a great position overlooking the owner's open farmlands and the sea. The four rooms are welcoming after a day of rambling. It's 3km northwest of Liscannor, 1.6km from the Cliffs of Moher.

★ **Vaughan's Anchor Inn** SEAFOOD €€

(065-708 1548; www.vaughans.ie; Main St; mains €13-26; kitchen 12.30-9pm) Noted for its excellent seafood (yes to the scallops and halibut), Vaughan's packs 'em in – and out. When it rains, you can settle in the nautical-themed pub by a peat fire, when it shines (sometimes 15 minutes later) you can take in the air at a picnic table. Compact but comfy rooms offer sleepy refuge (single/double from €50/80).

Drinking & Nightlife

Joseph McHugh's Bar PUB

(Main St) Lots of courtyard tables and regular trad sessions give this old pub next to Vaughan's considerable appeal.

Hag's Head

Forming the southern end of the Cliffs of Moher, Hag's Head is a dramatic place from which to view the cliffs along the Wild Atlantic Way.

There's a huge sea arch at the tip of Hag's Head and another arch visible to the north. The old **signal tower** on the head was erected in case Napoleon tried to attack on the western coast of Ireland. A spectacular **walking trail** links the head with the cliffs and Liscannor.

Cliffs of Moher

In good visibility, the Cliffs of Moher (Aillte an Mothair, or Ailltreacha Mothair) are stupefyingly impressive and staggeringly beautiful. The entirely vertical cliffs rise to a height of 203m, their edge falling away abruptly into a ceaselessly churning Atlantic. A progression of vast heads, the dark limestone marches in a rigid formation that's gob-smacking, no matter how many times you look at it. On a clear day you'll channel Barbra Streisand as you can see forever; the Aran Islands stand etched on the waters of Galway Bay, and beyond lie the hills of Connemara.

Its fame guarantees a steady stream of visitors that can surge to a swell almost as impressive as the raging ocean below, but the tireless Atlantic winds can drown out the chatter and you can shrug off the crowds, even though busloads arrive in summer. A vast visitor centre is set back into the side of a hill, Teletubbies style. The main walkways and viewing areas along the cliffs have been surrounded by a 1.5m-high wall that's too high and set too far back from the edge.

You are quickly rewarded though if you're willing to walk for 10 minutes and flee the rabble. Past the end of the 'Moher Wall' south, a **trail** runs along the cliffs to Hag's Head (about 5.5km) – few venture this far, yet the views are uninhibited. From here you can continue on to Liscannor for a total walk of 12km (about 3.5 hours). To the north, you can follow the **Doolin Trail** via O'Brien's Tower right to the village of Doolin (about 7km and 2.5 hours). The entire Liscannor to Doolin walking path via the cliffs is now signposted; note that there are a lot of ups and downs and narrow, cliff-edge stretches.

With binoculars you can spot the more than 30 species of **birds** – including darling little puffins – that make their homes among the fissure-filled cliff faces.

For awe-inspiring views of the cliffs and wildlife, consider a **cruise**. The boat operators in Doolin offer popular tours of the cliffs. The cliffs are wi-fi enabled (free).

Sights

Visitor Centre MUSEUM

(www.cliffsofmoher.ie; site adult/child €6/free; 9am-9.30pm Jul & Aug, 9am-7pm May, Jun & Sep, 9am-6pm Mar, Apr & Oct, 9.15am-5pm Nov-Feb;) This modern centre contains numerous shops and a few cafes, plus a rewarding exhibition regarding the fauna, flora, geology and climate of the cliffs. There is also an audiovisual virtual-reality experience called *The Ledge*, shown on a loop in an auditorium throughout the day. Free information booklets on the cliffs are available. The soulless ground-floor Puffin's Nest Cafe seems designed to urge you up to the views of the pricier Cliffs View Cafe above.

Getting There & Away

Bus Éireann runs two to four buses daily past the cliffs on the Doolin–Ennis/Limerick routes. Waits between buses may exceed your ability to enjoy the spectacle, so you might combine a bus with a walk. Numerous private tour operators run tours to the cliffs from Galway and the region.

THE BURREN

The Burren region is rocky and windswept, an apt metaphor for the hardscrabble lives of those who've eked out an existence here. Stretching across northern Clare, from the Atlantic coast to Kinvara in County Galway, it's a unique striated limestone landscape that was shaped beneath ancient seas, then forced high and dry by a great geological cataclysm.

This is not the green Ireland of postcards. But there are wildflowers in spring, giving the 560-sq-km Burren brilliant, if ephemeral, colour amid its austere beauty. There are also intriguing villages to enjoy. These include the music hub of Doolin on the west coast, Kilfenora inland and Ballyvaughan in the north, on the shores of Galway Bay.

History

Despite its apparent harshness, the Burren supported quite large numbers of people in ancient times, and has more than 2500 historic sites. Chief among them is the 5000-year-old Poulnabrone Dolmen, part of a Neolithic/Bronze Age tomb, and one of Ireland's iconic ancient monuments.

Around 70 such tombs are in evidence today. Many are wedge-shaped graves, stone boxes tapering both in height and width, and about the size of a large double bed. The dead were placed inside, and the whole structure covered in earth and stones. Gleninsheen, south of Aillwee Caves, is a good example.

Ring forts dot the Burren. There are almost 500, including Iron Age stone forts such as Cahercommaun near Carron.

Flora & Fauna

Soil may be scarce on the Burren, but the small amount that gathers in the cracks and faults is well drained and nutrient-rich. This, together with the mild Atlantic climate, supports an extraordinary mix of Mediterranean, Arctic and alpine plants. Of Ireland's native wildflowers, 75% are found here, including 24 species of beautiful orchids, the creamy-white burnet rose, the little starry flowers of mossy saxifrage and the magenta-coloured bloody cranesbill. Lime-detesting plants such as heathers can be found living alongside those that thrive on lime. One of the biggest threats to this diversity is the proliferation of hazel scrub and blackthorn, which needs to be controlled.

ROCK LEGENDS

The geology of the Burren (Boireann is the Irish term for 'rocky country') is the result of immense drama in ancient times that produced today's raw landscape. Follow the deep rivulets in the stone and you'll see that the barren Aran Islands just offshore are all part of the same formations.

Massive shifts in the Earth's crust some 270 million years ago buckled the edges of Europe and forced the former seabed here above sea level. At the same time the stone sheets were bent and fractured to form the long, deep cracks so characteristic of the Burren today.

During numerous ice ages, glaciers scoured the hills, rounding the edges and sometimes polishing the rock to a shiny finish, and dumping a thin layer of rock and soil in the cracks. Huge boulders were carried by the ice, and deposited on a sea of flat rock.

The Burren

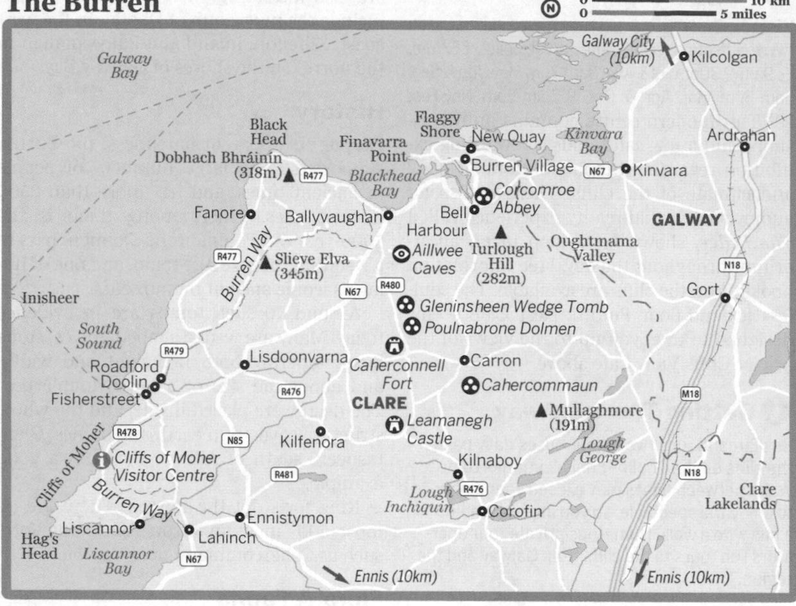

The Burren is a stronghold of Ireland's most elusive mammal, the rather shy weasel-like pine marten. Badgers, foxes and even stoats are common throughout the region. Otters and seals haunt the shores around Bell Harbour, New Quay and Finavarra Point. The much-publicised Burren Code is an initiative to educate people as to how they can protect the environment of the Burren when they visit.

Activities

The Burren is a walker's paradise. The stark, beautiful landscape, plentiful **trails** and **ancient sites** are best explored on foot. 'Green roads' are the old highways of the Burren, crossing hills and valleys to some of the remotest corners of the region. Many of these unpaved ways were built during the Famine as part of relief work, while some date back possibly thousands of years. Now used mostly by hikers and the occasional farmer, some are signposted.

The **Burren Way** is a 123km network of marked hiking routes throughout the region.

Guided nature, history, archaeology and wilderness walks are great ways to appreciate the Burren. Typically the cost of the walks averages €10 to €25 and there are many options, including individual trips.

Burren Guided Walks & Hikes WALKING TOUR
(☎065-707 6100, 087 244 6807; www.burrenguidedwalks.com) Long-time guide Mary Howard leads groups on a variety of rambles, off-the-beaten-track hikes and rugged routes.

Burren Wild Tours WALKING TOUR
(☎087 877 9565; www.burrenwalks.com) John Connolly offers a broad range of walks, from gentle to more strenuous.

Heart of Burren Walks WALKING TOUR
(☎065-682 7707; www.heartofburrenwalks.com) Local Burren author Tony Kirby leads walks and archaeology hikes.

Information

BOOKS & MAPS

There is a wealth of literature about the Burren, and it's best to trawl the bookshops of Ennis and local visitor centres for publications such as Charles Nelson's *Wild Plants of the Burren and the Aran Islands*. The *Burren Journey* books by George Cunningham are excellent for local lore. *The Burren and the Aran Islands: A Walking Guide* by Tony Kirby is an excellent, up-to-date resource.

The Tír Eolas series of fold-out maps, *A Rambler's Guide & Map*, shows antiquities and other points of interest. The booklet *The Burren Way* has good walking routes. Ordnance Survey

Discovery series maps 51 and 57 cover most of the area.

VISITOR INFORMATION

With tea rooms next door, the Burren Centre (p350) in Kilfenora is an excellent resource, as is the Clare Heritage and Genealogy Centre (p352) in Corofin.

Burren Ecotourism (www.burren.ie) A vast compilation of all things related to Burren tourism.

Burren National Park (www.burrennationalpark.ie) Portions of the Burren in the southeast have been designated a national park; the website has good info on the natural landscape.

Burrenbeo Trust (www.burrenbeo.com) A nonprofit organisation dedicated to promoting the natural beauty of the Burren and increasing awareness.

Getting There & Away

A few **Bus Éireann** (www.buseireann.ie) services pass through the Burren. The main routes include one from Limerick and Ennis to Corofin, Ennistymon, Lahinch, Liscannor, the Cliffs of Moher, Doolin and Lisdoonvarna; another connects Galway with Ballyvaughan, Lisdoonvarna and Doolin. Usually there are one to four buses daily, with the most in summer.

Getting Around

By car you can cover a fair amount of the Burren in a day and explore some of the many unnamed back roads. Bikes are excellent for getting off the main roads; ask about rentals at your accommodation. Walking is superb for appreciating the area's dramatic landscapes.

Doolin

POP 250

Doolin gets plenty of press and chatter as a centre of Irish traditional music, owing to a trio of pubs that have sessions throughout the year. It's also known for its setting – 6km north of the Cliffs of Moher and down near the ever-unsettled sea, the land is windblown, with huge rocks exposed by the long-vanished top soil.

You might be surprised to discover that Doolin barely exists as it's really three infinitesimally small neighbouring villages. **Fisherstreet** is right on the water, **Doolin** itself is about 1km east on the little River Aille, and **Roadford** is another 1km east. None has more than a handful of buildings, which results in a scattered appearance, without a centre.

Still, the area is hugely popular with music-seeking tourists and there are scores of good-value hostels and B&Bs. It's also a place to get boats to the offshore Aran Islands and the Cliffs of Moher.

Sights & Activities

One-hour **Cliffs of Moher Cruises** (www.mohercruises.com; €15) running from the dock are popular.

Fisherstreet AREA

Tiny Fisherstreet is a charmer, with some fine-looking traditional buildings, pubs and restaurants; enjoy dramatic surf vistas at the harbour, some 1.5km further along the coast.

Doolin Cave CAVE

(www.doolincave.ie; adult/child €15/8; ⏲10am-5pm Mar-Nov) The Doolin area is popular with cavers. A little over 1km north of Roadford you'll find Doolin Cave, which boasts an enormous stalactite that resembles a giant squid. The times of tours vary by season, but are usually on the hour.

Doonagore Castle CASTLE

(off R478) This supreme-looking tower house castle is straight from the pages of a fairytale. Originally dating to the 16th century, the ruin was restored by an American in the 1970s, who invited the entire village to a bash at the castle upon its completion. You cannot enter the castle, but aim to pass by at sunset for excellent photos with the setting sun.

Coming from the Cliffs of Moher, take the small, steep and sinuous road off the R478 and follow it down to Fisherstreet to the castle.

Doolin Cliff Walk WALKING TOUR

(☎065-707 4170; www.doolincliffwalk.com; adult/child 8-12 yrs €5/free) One of the most enjoyable ways to pass your time in Doolin is by walking the windswept country. Tracks and paths radiate in all directions; the Cliffs of Moher are 6km southwest. This tremendous cliff walk sets off each morning at 10am from outside O'Connor's pub in Fisherstreet, heading to the Cliffs of Moher, past Doonagore Castle.

Festivals & Events

Micho Russell Festival MUSIC

(www.doolin-tourism.com) Held on the last weekend in February, this festival celebrates the work of a legendary Doolin musician and attracts top trad talent.

Sleeping

There's no shortage of accommodation in the Doolin region.

★Doolin Hostel HOSTEL €
(087 282 0587; www.doolinhostel.ie; Fisherstreet; dm €16-20, d €50-55;) This standout choice has smart, neutrally toned and immaculate doubles and four- to seven-bed dorms, managed to perfection by the energetic owner, Anthony. The cafe is also excellent, with a range of craft beers chilling in the refrigerator and fine food choices. Overflow beds are in the building over the road and the charms of Fisherstreet are just steps away.

Rainbow Hostel HOSTEL €
(065-707 4415; www.rainbowhostel.net; Roadford; dm €15-19, d €40-50;) With a lovely stove in its lounge, wooden ceilings and colourful rooms, this cottagey IHH-affiliated hostel has 24 beds in an old farmhouse by the road. It also rents bikes (€9 per day) and has further beds next door.

Aille River Hostel HOSTEL €
(065-707 4260; www.ailleriverhosteldoolin.ie; Roadford; dm from €15.50, d from €40; Mar-Dec;) In a picturesque spot by the river in the upper village, this converted, cosy 17th-century farmhouse is a great choice, with peat fires and free laundry. An award-winning hostel, there's 30 beds, campsites from €16 and bike rentals. Towels are €1.

Nagles Camping & Caravan Park CAMPGROUND €
(065-707 4458; www.doolincamping.com; Doolin; campsites €9-19; Apr-Sep;) Let the nearby pounding surf lull you to sleep at this grassy expanse near the harbour. The 60 sites are open to the elements, so pin those pegs down.

★O'Connors Guesthouse INN €€
(065-707 4498; www.oconnorsdoolin.com; Doolin; s/d from €45/70; Feb-Oct;) On a bend in the Aille River, this working farm has 10 largish rooms in a rather plush farmhouse-style inn. Totally spick and span, it's not far from the main crossroads in Doolin.

Daly's House B&B €€
(www.dalys-doolin.com; Fisherstreet; s/d from €50/80;) Just one field behind O'Connor's Pub, this excellent B&B has glimpses of the Cliffs of Moher from its breakfast room. The six rooms are large and comfy, and the hosts are especially welcoming.

Cullinan's Guesthouse INN €€
(065-707 4183; www.cullinansdoolin.com; Doolin; s/d from €50/70;) Owned by well-known fiddle-playing James Cullinan, the eight rooms at this smart place on the River Aille are very good-looking, with power showers and comfortable fittings. A couple of rooms are slightly smaller than the others, but are right on the water. There's a lovely back terrace for enjoying the views.

Sea View House B&B €€
(087 267 9617; www.seaview-doolin.ie; off Fisherstreet; s/d/tr from €60/100/150;) On high ground right above Fisherstreet village, this neat, polished and homely choice has sweeping ocean views, especially from the decking out front. The common lounge sports a telescope for enjoying the panorama.

Eating

All three of the trad music pubs serve Irish classics such as bacon and cabbage and seafood chowder throughout the day until about 9pm.

Doolin Cafe CAFE €€
(www.thedoolincafe.com; Roadford; mains €5.50-25; 9.30am-7pm Apr-Oct) The cottage is small and the walls plain white, but flavours are big at this popular bistro. Breakfast is excellent, while salads, soups and gourmet sandwiches are the deal at lunch, or go for smoked salmon on brown bread with cream cheese or homemade cheesecake. Dinner features a changing, ambitious menu.

Cullinan's MODERN IRISH €€€
(065-707 4183; www.cullinansdoolin.com; Doolin; mains €21.50-28.50; 6-9pm Thu-Sat Apr-Oct, plus Mon & Tue May-Sep) Part of the guesthouse of the same name, this superb restaurant excels at delicious seafood, meat and poultry dishes on a brief menu that changes depending on what's fresh, accompanied by a long wine list. Expect dishes such as pan-seared scallops or roasted Burren lamb followed by strawberry Eton mess.

Drinking & Nightlife

Doolin's rep is largely based on music. A lot of musicians live in the area, and they have a symbiotic relationship with the tourists: each desires the other and each year things grow a little larger. Keep in mind that the heavy concentration of visitors means that standards don't always hold up to those in some of the less-trampled villages in Clare.

★McGann's PUB
(www.mcgannspubdoolin.com; Roadford; ⏲bar 10am-12.30am, kitchen 10am-9.30pm) McGann's has all the classic touches of a full-on Irish music pub, with action often spilling onto the street. The food here (mains €11 to €18) is the best of Doolin's three famous pubs. Inside you'll find locals playing darts in its warren of small rooms, some with peat fires.

O'Connor's PUB
(www.gusoconnorsdoolin.com; Fisherstreet; ⏲9.30am-midnight) Right on the river as it runs into the sea, this sprawling favourite packs them in and has a rollicking atmosphere when the music is in full swing. On some summer nights you won't squeeze inside.

MacDiarmada's PUB
(www.mcdermottspubdoolin.com; Roadford; ⏲bar 11am-11.30pm, kitchen 9am-9.30pm) Also known as McDermott's, this simple red-and-white traditional pub is a rowdy favourite. The inside is pretty basic, as is the menu of sandwiches and roasts; there's an outside area.

Information

The excellent **Tourist Information Office** (Fisherstreet; ⏲8.15am-6pm) is close to O'Connor's on Fisherstreet. The closest useful ATMs are 13km away in Ennistymon. The website www.doolin-tourism.com is useful.

Getting There & Away

BOAT

Doolin is one of two ferry departure points to the Aran Islands from mid-March to October. Two ferry companies offer numerous departures in season. It takes about 45 minutes to cover the 8km to Inisheer, the closest of the three islands and the best choice for a day trip from Doolin. A boat to Inishmór takes at least 1½ hours with an Inisheer stop. Ferries to Inishmaan are infrequent.

Sailings are often cancelled due to high seas or tides that make the small dock inaccessible. Rates vary as prices are very competitive; Inisheer should cost about €15 to €25 return. The companies have offices at the harbour but booking in advance online can net discounts. Confirm times.

The boats also offer Cliffs of Moher tours (about €15 for one hour) which are best done late in the afternoon when the light is from the west.

Doolin 2 Aran Ferries (☎065-707 5949; www.doolin2aranferries.com; Doolin Pier; ⏲mid-Mar–Oct) Has a full schedule to the Aran Islands plus Cliffs of Moher cruises.

O'Brien Line (☎065-707 5618; www.obrienline.com) Usually has the most sailings to the Arans; also offers cliff cruises and combo tickets.

BUS

Bus Éireann runs one to four buses daily to Doolin from Ennis (€12, 1½ hours) and Limerick (€18, 2½ hours) via Corofin, Lahinch and the Cliffs of Moher. Buses also go to Galway (€16, 1½ hours, one or two daily) via Ballyvaughan.

In summer, various backpacker shuttles often serve Doolin from Galway and other points in Clare.

Lisdoonvarna

POP 750

Lisdoonvarna (Lios Dún Bhearna), often just called 'Lisdoon', is well known for its mineral springs. For centuries people have been visiting the local spa to swallow its waters. Posh during Victorian times, the town is more down at heel today, but friendly, good-looking and far less overrun than Doolin.

Sights & Activities

★Burren Smokehouse SMOKEHOUSE
(☎065-707 4432; www.burrensmokehouse.ie; Kincora Rd; ⏲10am-5pm Apr & May, 9am-6pm Jun-Oct, shorter hours in winter) Learn about the ancient Irish art of oak-smoking salmon from a video at the Burren Smokehouse. Tasty smoked salmon and other fishies in myriad forms are offered for free tasting. Good coffee, tea and deli-type food are also sold. The smokehouse is at the edge of Lisdoonvarna on the Kincora road (N67).

Spa Well LANDMARK
At the southern end of town is a spa well, with a sulphur spring, a Victorian pumphouse and a fine woodsy setting. The iron, sulphur, magnesium and iodine in the water are supposed to be good for rheumatic and glandular complaints. Closer to the centre, you can drink the water. Look for a trail beside the Roadside Tavern that runs 400m down to two **wells** by the river.

DON'T MISS

LISDOONVARNA MATCHMAKING FESTIVAL

Lisdoonvarna was once a centre for *basadóiri* (matchmakers) who, for a fee, would fix up a person with a spouse. Most of the (mainly male) hopefuls would hit town in September, feet shuffling, cap in hand, after the hay was in. Today the tradition continues at the much-hyped and ever-expanding **Lisdoonvarna Matchmaking Festival** (www.matchmakerireland.com; weekends Sep), held in the early fall. Irish and even foreign singles – plus those who just enjoy a jolly good time – revel in daftness, drinking, merrymaking, music and much, much dancing.

Sleeping & Eating

Book ahead during September's Matchmaking Festival. Local sleeping, eating and drinking choices are excellent.

Sleepzone HOSTEL €
(065-707 7168; www.sleepzone.ie; Doolin Rd; dm €16-25, s/d €50/70;) Housed in a formerly smart hotel, this 124-bed hostel has the usual facilities and an unusual grace, its grounds reflecting its past.

★**Sheedy's Country House Hotel & Restaurant** INN €€
(065-707 4026; www.sheedys.com; Sulphur Hill; r €80-220; Apr-Sep;) This smart yet relaxed 11-room guesthouse just outside of town has a long porch with comfy chairs for pondering the many gardens or just taking a snooze. Food (dinner only) is excellent and the bar offers up a huge range of whiskey.

Wild Honey Inn INN €€
(065-707 4300; www.wildhoneyinn.com; Kincora Rd; s/d from €50/80; food 1-3.30pm Thu-Sat, 5-9pm Wed-Mon mid-Feb–Dec;) In a beautiful old roadside mansion on the edge of town, Wild Honey has 14 stylish rooms that are the perfect weekend getaway. The pub has a delectable menu of Irish classics made with local seafood, meats and produce. In summer there's a lovely garden with tables.

★**Roadside Tavern** PUB FOOD €€
(www.roadsidetavern.ie; Kincora Rd; mains €11.50-20; noon-4pm & 6-9pm Mon-Fri, noon-9pm Sat, noon-8pm Sun) Down by the river, this pub is pure craic: third-generation owner Peter Curtin knows every story worth telling. There are trad sessions daily in summer and during the weekends in winter. The fun extends to the kitchen, which turns out creamy seafood chowders and smoked fish (they also run the nearby Burren Smokehouse). The in-house brewery makes beers far above the norm.

Information

The closest reliable ATM is in Lahinch; worth remembering if you're planning some pricey wooing.

Getting There & Around

Bus Éireann runs one to four buses daily to Doolin via Lisdoonvarna from Ennis, and to Limerick via Corofin, Lahinch and the Cliffs of Moher. Buses also go to Galway via Ballyvaughan and Black Head.

Kilfenora

POP 250

Kilfenora (Cill Fhionnúrach) lies on the southern fringe of the Burren, 8km (a five-minute drive) southeast of Lisdoonvarna. It's a small place, with low polychromatic buildings surrounding the compact centre.

The town has a strong music tradition that rivals that of Doolin, but without the crowds. The **Kilfenora Céili Band** (www.kilfenoraceiliband.com) is a celebrated group that's been playing for 100 years. Its traditional music features fiddles, banjos, squeezeboxes and more.

Sights

Burren Centre MUSEUM
(065-708 8030; www.theburrencentre.ie; Main St; adult/child €6/4; 10am-5pm Mar-May, Sep & Oct, 9.30am-5.30pm Jun-Aug) The centre has a series of entertaining and informative displays on many aspects of the Burren (a video features cute hares). There's a cafe and a very large shop that sells local products.

Cathedral CHURCH
The 11th-century cathedral at Kilfenora was once an important place of pilgrimage. St Fachan (or Fachtna) founded the monastery here in the 6th century, and it later became the seat of Kilfenora diocese, the smallest in the country. Loop around the more recent

protestant church and enter the oldest part of the **ruins**, under a glass roof. The chancel contains two primitive carved figures on top of two tombs and there are three **high crosses**, with explanatory captions on stainless-steel plaques.

Doorty Cross MONUMENT

In a field accessed via a stile, about 100m west of the cathedral, is the 800-year-old Doorty Cross, which lay broken in two until the 1950s, when it was re-erected.

Leamanegh Castle CASTLE

(junction of R476 and R480) This magnificent wreck stands on a rise above the junction of the R476 and R480 on the way from Kilfenora to Kilnaboy or Carron. Erstwhile home of Máire Rúa (Red Mary) who – according to local anecdote – got through 25 husbands, dispatching at least one to a grisly death on horseback off the Cliffs of Moher, before being incarcerated in a hollow tree by her enemies, a fate commemorated by her red-haired ghost that stalks the castle ruins to this day.

Sleeping & Eating

Kilfenora Hostel HOSTEL €

(065-708 8908; www.kilfenorahostel.com; Main St; dm/d €20/52;) Affiliated with Vaughan's Pub next door, this guesthouse has 46 beds in nine rooms, with spacious dorms. There's a laundry and a big kitchen.

Ait Aoibhinn B&B B&B €

(065-708 8040; aitaoibheann@live.ie; Main St; s/d from €35/60; mid-Feb–Nov;) Opposite O'Gorman's the grocers right on Main St, Mary Murphy runs a fine little B&B (the name means Restful Place) with the kind of simple rooms you could call your own. Look for the house with the name 'Murphy' on the wall.

★**Vaughan's Pub** PUB FOOD €€

(www.vaughanspub.ie; Main St; mains €8-15; kitchen 10am-9pm) A pub with a big reputation in Irish music circles, where seafood, traditional foods and local produce feature on the menu. Have a pint under the big tree out front. There's music in the bar every night during the summer and on many nights at other times. The adjacent barn is the scene of terrific **set-dancing sessions** on Thursday (10pm) and Sunday (9pm).

Getting There & Away

Kilfenora has a bus service a few days a week.

Corofin & Around

POP 700

Corofin (Cora Finne), also spelt Corrofin, is a traditional village on the southern fringes of the Burren. It's low-key and a classic place to sample the rhythms of Clare life. The surrounding area features a number of turloughs (small lakes) and several O'Brien castles, including two on the shores of nearby Lough Inchiquin.

About 4km northwest of Corofin, on the road to Leamanegh Castle and Kilfenora (R476), look for the small town of **Kilnaboy**. The ruined church here is well worth seeking out for the sheila-na-gig (carved female figure with exaggerated genitalia) over the doorway.

Sights

Clare Heritage Centre MUSEUM

(www.clareroots.com; Church St; adult/child €4/2; 9.30am-5.30pm Easter-Oct) Housed in an old church, many displays here cover the horrors of the Great Famine. More than 250,000 people lived in Clare before the Famine; today the county's population remains almost 60% less.

THE IMMORTAL FATHER TED

Father Ted, the enduring British TV comedy, is set around the high jinks of three Irish priests living on the fictional Craggy Island. Most of the locations used in the show are around Kilfenora and Ennistymon (Eugene's pub was used as a location and the cast drank here). The lonely *Father Ted* house is in Kilnaboy.

Inspired by the great success of Inismór's **Tedfest** (p375), the good people of Kilfenora and Ennistymon have organised their own **Father Ted Festival** (www.kilfenoraclare.com; May) with costume parties, contests, tours and more. Much is centred on Vaughan's Pub, itself a star of some episodes. **Ted Tours** (www.tedtours.com; adult/child €25/20) visits the local filming locations.

Clare Heritage & Genealogy Centre CULTURAL CENTRE
(☎065-683 7955; www.clareroots.com; Church St; ⏰10am-5pm Apr, May & Sep, 10am-6pm Jun-Aug) This centre functions as the Burren National Park Information Point, with loads of information and a fascinating museum with displays on the Burren's geology, fauna and flora, and also has facilities for people researching their Clare ancestry.

Sleeping & Eating

Corofin Hostel & Camping Park HOSTEL, CAMPGROUND €
(☎065-683 7683; www.corofincamping.com; Main St; campsites per person from €10, s/d/f €25/40/50; ⏰Apr-Sep) Campsites out back have nice open spaces, and inside there are 30 beds at this friendly hostel right in the village centre. Bikes can be borrowed and the large common room has a pool table. Camping includes free hot showers and use of a kitchen.

Lakefield Lodge B&B €
(☎065-683 7675; www.lakefieldlodgebandb.com; Ennis Rd; s/d from €45/68; ⏰Apr-Oct; 📶) This well-run place near the southern edge of the village has four comfy rooms in a pleasant bungalow surrounded by gardens. Conveniently situated for Burren hikes, it provides a wealth of info for anglers as well as fishing trips.

Fergus View B&B €€
(☎065-683 7606; www.fergusview.com; R476; s/d from €50/80; ⏰Apr-Oct; @📶) The name exactly describes the scene: the River Fergus flows right past. A lovely home with six rooms and breakfasts that are famed for being fresh – often organic – and creative. It's 3km north of Corofin.

Inchiquin Inn IRISH €
(☎065-683 7713; www.inchiquininn.com; Main St; mains €6-10; ⏰kitchen 9am-5pm Mon-Fri; 📶) This local pub comes with an excellent kitchen. The Atlantic chowder – thick, tangy and redolent with smoked fish – is some of the best you'll find, and the breakfasts (till 2pm daily) are the business. The annual World Stone-Throwing Championship out back in June is a huge local party.

Getting There & Away

Bus Éireann has an infrequent service some weekdays between Corofin and Ennis.

Central Burren

Several roads dotted with sights cross the heart of the Burren. The scenery along the R480 as it passes through the region is harsh but inspiring, highlighting the barren Burren at its best. Remarkable prehistoric stone structures litter the area.

South from Ballyvaughan, the R480 branches off the N67 at the sign for Aillwee Caves, passing Gleninsheen Wedge Tomb and the outstanding Poulnabrone Dolmen before reaching the magnificent Leamanegh Castle ruins, where it joins the R476, which runs southeast to Corofin. At any point along here, try a small road – especially those to the east – to plunge into other-worldly solitude.

Originally a famine relief road built in the 1800s, the N67 to Lisdoonvarna rewards visitors with sweeping views of the stark Burren landscape.

Sights

Poulnabrone Dolmen ARCHAEOLOGICAL SITE
(R480) Also known as the Portal Tomb, Poulnabrone Dolmen is one of Ireland's most photographed ancient monuments. The dolmen (a large slab perched on upright stones) stands amid a swathe of rocky pavements, surprising even the most jaded traveller with its other-worldly appearance; the capstone weighs 5 tonnes. The site is about 8km south of Aillwee and visible from the R480. A large free parking area and excellent displays make it visitor friendly.

Poulnabrone was built more than 5000 years ago. It was excavated in 1986, and the remains of 16 people were found, as well as pieces of pottery and jewellery. Radiocarbon dating suggests that they were buried between 3800 and 3200 BC. When the dead were originally entombed here, the whole structure was partially covered in a mound of earth, which has since worn away. A highly informative Office of Public Works worker is often on duty, protecting the monument.

Gleninsheen Wedge Tomb TOMB
One of Ireland's most famous prehistoric grave sites, Gleninsheen lies beside the R480 just south of Aillwee Caves near Ballyvaughan. It's thought to date from 4000 to 5000 years ago. A magnificent gold gorget (a crescent of beaten gold that hung around the neck) found here and dating to the late Bronze Age is now on display at the National

Museum in Dublin. Note: the access gate to the tomb is sometimes locked, and signage is poor.

Caherconnell Fort FORT

For a look at a well-preserved *caher* (walled fort) of the late Iron Age–Early Christian period, stop at Caherconnell Fort, a privately run heritage attraction with exhibits detailing how the evolution of these defensive settlements may have reflected territorialism and competition for land among a growing, settling population. The drystone walling of the fort is in excellent condition. A great hit with kids, fun sheepdog demonstrations (adult/child €9.60/5.60) are also held. It's about 1km south of Poulnabrone Dolmen.

The **visitor centre** has information on many other monuments in the area.

Carron & Around

The tiny village of Carron (Carran on some maps; An Carn in Gaelic), about 10km east of the R480, is a wonderfully remote spot. Vistas of the rocky Burren stretch in all directions from Carron's elevated position. Stretching south from Carron almost to Kilnaboy are some of the Burren's bleakest quarters.

Sights

★Burren Perfumery & Floral Centre PERFUMERY

(www.burrenperfumery.com; Carron; 9am-7pm Jul & Aug, 10am-5pm Sep-Jun, tearoom 10.30am-5pm) The wildflowers of the Burren are the inspiration for the subtle scents at this excellent diversion. There's an audiovisual presentation on the flora of the Burren, which has a surprising diversity, including many fragrant orchids that grow between the rocks. Many of the scented items (candles, soaps, creams) for sale are packaged in handmade paper, but they're not cheap. There's a fantastic herb garden (with free tours) and the centre has an organic tearoom.

Carron Polje LANDMARK

Below Carron lies Carron Polje, one of the finest turloughs in Ireland. *Polje* is a Serbo-Croatian term used universally for these shallow depressions that flood in winter and dry out in summer, when the lush grass that flourishes on the surface is used for grazing.

Cahercommaun HISTORIC SITE

Perched on the edge of an inland cliff about 3km south of Carron is the great stone fort of Cahercommaun, inhabited in the 8th and 9th centuries by people who hunted deer and grew small amounts of grain. The remains of a souterrain (underground passage) lead from the fort to the outer cliff face. To get there, go south from Carron and take a left turn for Kilnaboy. After 1.5km a path on the left leads up to the fort.

Sleeping & Eating

★Clare's Rock Hostel HOSTEL €

(065-708 9129; www.claresrock.com; Carron; dm/s/d €20/35/48; May-Sep;) With commanding views over Carron Polje, this imposing, roughly hewn, grey stone hostel has 30 beds, spacious rooms and excellent facilities. Guests can hire bikes or cavort with the trolls on the outdoor garden-gnome chessboard.

Cassidy's PUB FOOD €€

(www.cassidyspub.com; mains €8.50-20; noon-9pm Mon-Sat, to 8pm Sun Apr-Sep;) Cassidy's serves up a good range of pub dishes, including their famous Dolmen goat burgers made with locally raised organic meat. The building was once a British Royal Irish Constabulary (RIC) station and then a *garda* (police) barracks. Enjoy trad music and dancing some weekends. The views from the terrace are as intoxicating as the drink.

Fanore

POP 150

The scenic R477 hugs the barren coast of Clare as it curves past the Aran Islands into Galway Bay. Fanore (Fan Óir, meaning 'The Golden Slope'), 5km south of Black Head, is less a village and more a stretch of coast with a shop, a pub and a few houses scattered along the main road. The nearby shelves of limestone on the coast are popular with rock climbers.

Sights & Activities

Surfers flock here throughout the year.

Fanore Beach BEACH

This fine sandy beach off the R477 has an extensive backdrop of grass-covered dunes. Signs show hiking trails along the water and up in the dramatic hills and Black Head. You'll find decent parking and there are showers and toilets in a small block by the car park, open in summer.

Aloha Surf School SURFING
(☎087 213 3996; www.surfschool.tv; Fanore Beach; 2hr lessons from €35) Offers classes for all ages and abilities. You can rent surfboards, wetsuits and gear, stand-up paddle boards and kayaks (€50 per half-day).

Siopa Fan Óir FISHING
(R477; ⏲9am-9pm summer, to 7pm winter) This well-stocked shop across from O'Donohue's pub has fishing tackle, walking maps, boogie boards, cheap sand buckets and helpful service.

Sleeping

Orchid House B&B €
(☎065-707 6975; www.orchidhouse.net; R477; s/d from €40/65;) All four spotless rooms come with sea views at this fine choice in a serene setting, run by the friendly and welcoming Gill.

★ **Rocky View Farmhouse** B&B €€
(☎065-707 6103; www.rockyviewfarmhouse.com; off R477; s/d/f €40/70/100;) One of the Fanore area's few accommodation options, Rocky View Farmhouse is a charming place at the heart of the coastal Burren, with four open and airy rooms. Organic food is grown and used in the breakfasts, served in a sunny conservatory. Wi-fi can be rather limited.

Eating

Vasco MEDITERRANEAN €€
(www.vasco.ie; mains €8-16; ⏲11.30am-7.30pm Thu-Sat, to 4.30pm Tue, Wed & Sun, closed in winter;) Run by hard-working Ross and Karen, this stylish and sunny eatery a kilometre from the beach has views of the water from the terrace – lovely on a sunny evening – or you can enjoy lounging inside. The food is Med-accented and you can gather together picnic victuals for the beach.

O'Donohue's PUB FOOD €€
(www.odonohuespub.com; R477; meals €8-25; ⏲Apr-Oct) In many ways the community centre, this pub south of the beach offers local seafood, chowders, sandwiches and a fine selection of whiskeys, plus trad music nights at weekends. The beer-battered fish and chips is the way to go before beach-combing.

Getting There & Away

Bus Éireann runs about four buses (€17.60) daily from Galway via Black Head and through Fanore to Lisdoonvarna and Doolin.

Ballyvaughan & Around

POP 260

Something of a hub for the charms of the northern Burren, Ballyvaughan (Baile Uí Bheacháin) sits between the hard land of the hills and a quiet leafy corner of Galway Bay.

Sights & Activities

Just west of the junction is the **quay**, built in 1829 at a time when boats traded with the Aran Islands and Galway, exporting grain and bacon and bringing in peat – a scarce commodity in the windswept rocks of the Burren.

A few metres past the harbour, a signposted track leads to a **seashore bird shelter** offering fine views of the tidal shallows.

About 6km south of Ballyvaughan on the Lisdoonvarna road (N67) is a series of severe bends up **Corkscrew Hill** (180m). The road was built as part of a Great Famine relief scheme in the 1840s. Ranging from the top are spectacular views of the northern Burren and Galway Bay, with Aillwee Mountain and the caves on the right, Cappanawalla Hill on the left, and the partially restored 16th-century Newtown Castle, erstwhile residence of the O'Lochlains, directly below.

Aillwee Caves CAVES
(www.aillweecave.ie; off R480; combined ticket adult/child €16/9; ⏲10am-5pm, to 6.30pm Jul & Aug) The caves were carved out by water some two million years ago. The main cave penetrates 600m into the mountain, widening into larger caverns, one with its own waterfall. Near the entrance are the remains of a brown bear, extinct in Ireland for more than 10,000 years. Often crowded in summer, the site has a cafe, and a large raptor exhibit with captive hawks, owls and more, accessible on a joint ticket with the caves or as a standalone.

A shop sells the excellent locally produced Burren Gold cheese.

Burren By Bike BICYCLE RENTAL
(info@burrenwine.ie; off N67, The Laundrette; rental per day/week €15/80, tours from €25; ⏲9am-5pm Mon-Sat May-Sep) These morning tours hit the still-quiet roads followed by a gourmet breakfast.

Sleeping & Eating

Several simple B&Bs are close to the centre. Ballyvaughan's **farmers market** (St John's Hall; ⏲10am-2pm Sat May-Oct) celebrates high-quality local produce and cooks up crêpes, bratwurst and other snacks.

Oceanville House B&B B&B €€
(☎065-707 7051; www.clareireland.net/oceanville; Coast Rd/R477; s/d/tr from €45/70/100;) Near the dock close to the centre of the village, this oceanfront B&B has views across the bay from the dormer windows in its compact upstairs rooms. It's a good spot for walking the village and sampling its pleasures.

Ballyvaughan Lodge B&B €€
(☎065-707 7292; www.ballyvaughanlodge.com; N67; s/d from €47.50/75;) Opposite the farmer's market at the heart of Ballyvaughan, this shipshape and well-run B&B has 11 spotless rooms, glimmering tiles in the bathrooms and a warm welcome from its enthusiastic owners.

★ **Gregan's Castle Hotel** HOTEL €€€
(☎065-707 7005; www.gregans.ie; N67; s/d/ste from €200/265/335;) This hidden Clare gem is housed in a grand estate dating to the 19th century, some 6km south of Ballyvaughan at Corkscrew Hill. The 21 rooms and suites are plush, with enough modern flair to make them stylish (but no TVs) and some have private garden areas. Inventive fresh fare sourced locally is served in the restaurant.

An Fulacht Fia IRISH €€
(☎065-707 7300; www.anfulachtfia.ie; Coast Rd/R477; mains €18-24; 5.30-9pm daily, from 1pm Sun Jun-Aug, shorter hours other times) A vividly coloured interior stands in contrast to the grey expanse of the sea beyond at this excellent restaurant just west of the town centre. The seasonal menu is organic and locally sourced, featuring plentiful seafood and a kids' menu.

Drinking & Nightlife

★ **Ólólainn** PUB
(Coast Rd) A tiny family-run place on the left as you head out to the pier, Ólólainn (o-*loch*-lain) is the place for a timeless moment or two in old-fashioned snugs. The old whiskey bottles in the window offer clues to the amazing selection of rare whiskeys within.

Information

In a vast gift shop behind a grocery store, the **Visitor Centre** (www.ballyvaughantourism.com; 10am-6pm daily Mar-Oct, Sat & Sun Nov-Feb) has a good section of local guides and maps.

Getting There & Away

Bus Éireann runs about four buses daily from Galway through Ballyvaughan (€14.40) and around Black Head to Lisdoonvarna and Doolin.

Northern Burren

Low farmland stretches south from County Galway to the bluff limestone hills of the Burren, which begin west of Kinvara and Doorus in County Galway.

From Oranmore in County Galway to Ballyvaughan, the coastline wriggles along small inlets and peninsulas; some, such as New Quay, are worth a detour. Here, narrow roads traverse low rocky windswept hills dotted with old stone ruins that have yielded to nature.

Inland near Bell Harbour is the largely intact Corcomroe Abbey, while the three ancient churches of **Oughtmama** lie up a quiet side valley. Galway Bay forms the backdrop to some outstanding scenery: bare

RUINS OF CORCOMROE ABBEY

Moody and evocative (except when the tour buses jam the narrow road out front), this former Cistercian abbey is 1.5km inland from Bell Harbour, in a quiet green hollow, surrounded by the stark grey Burren hillsides. It is a marvellous ruin, one of the finest of its kind.

The **abbey** (Corcomroe Rd, off the L1016) was founded in 1194 by Donal Mór O'Brien. His grandson, Conor na Siudaine O'Brien (died 1267), king of Thomond, is said to occupy the tomb in the northern wall, and there's a crude carving of him below the effigy of a bishop holding a crosier, the pastoral staff that was carried by a bishop or abbot. The surviving vaulting in the presbytery and transepts is very fine and there are some striking Romanesque carvings scattered throughout the abbey, which began a long decline in the 15th century. Often-touching modern graves crowd the ruins.

stone hills shining in the sun, with small hamlets and rich patches of green wherever there's soil.

Buses to and from Galway pass through the area on the N67. Just over the border in Galway, Kinvara makes a good base for this region.

New Quay & the Flaggy Shore

New Quay (Ceibh Nua), on the **Finavarra Peninsula**, is a quiet and rather bucolic interlude from the rocky rigours of the Burren. It's about 1km off the Kinvara–Ballyvaughan road (N67) and is reached by turning off at Ballyvelaghan Lough, 3km north of Bell Harbour.

The **Flaggy Shore**, west of New Quay, is a particularly fine stretch of coastline where limestone terraces step down to the sea. The road hugs the shoreline then curves south past **Lough Muirí**, where you're likely to see wading birds, as well as swans. Otters are also said to inhabit the area. At a T-junction just past the lough, a right turn leads to an intriguing, round **Martello tower** on Finavarra Point, a relic of the paranoia over the Napoleonic threat.

Walks in this area are excellent and you can ponder the dramatic changes in the ever-tidal inlets.

Sleeping & Eating

Mount Vernon BOUTIQUE HOTEL €€€
(065-707 8126; www.mountvernon.ie; Flaggy Shore; s/d from €125/190; Apr-Oct;) Seamus Heaney stayed here and famed Irish Impressionist Hugh Lane once called Mount Vernon home until he was lost with the *Lusitania*. Today the rural Georgian lodge is a serene seaside retreat with five luxurious rooms decorated in period furnishings, with orthopaedic mattresses and Egyptian cotton sheets. There's generally a two-night minimum.

Cafe Linnalla ICE CREAM €
(www.linnallaicecream.ie; New Quay; treats from €2.50; 11am-7pm daily May-Sep, noon-5pm Sat & Sun Oct-Apr) You'll really need to have a car to reach this isolated cafe for some fine ice cream and/or tours of their farm (€10, large sundae included).

★**Linnane's Lobster Bar** SEAFOOD €€
(New Quay; meals €9-25; 12.30-8pm daily May-Sep, Fri-Sun Oct-Apr) Fresh seafood sourced from the trap-covered docks behind the restaurant are the hallmark of this casual, compartmentalised restaurant with views over the water. It's also famous for oysters and platters of house-smoked fish, and the seafood chowder (€5.95) is an awesome starter.

Shopping

Russell Gallery GALLERY
(065-707 8185; www.russellgallery.net; New Quay; 11am-6pm Mon-Sat, from noon Sun) This airy gallery and cafe/wine bar has a range of art and glass works by Irish artists for sale, plus photographs and books on the region. You can also find work by local knitting legend Antoinette Hensey. With seats out on the grass in fine weather, it's about 500m west of Linnane's Lobster Bar, at a crossroads.

Bell Harbour

No more than a crossroads with a growing crop of holiday cottages and a pub, Bell Harbour (Beulaclugga) is about 8km east of Ballyvaughan. There's a pleasant walk along an old green road that begins behind the modern Church of St Patrick, 1km north up the hill from the Y-junction at Bell Harbour, and threads north along Abbey Hill.

Inland from here are the ruins of Corcomroe Abbey (p355), the valley and churches of Oughtmama, and the interior road that takes you through Carron and the the heart of the Burren.

County Galway

POP 251,000 / AREA 3760 SQ KM

Includes ➡

Best Places to Eat

- ➡ Aniar (p366)
- ➡ Kai Cafe (p366)
- ➡ Mitchell's (p389)
- ➡ Moran's Oyster Cottage (p393)

Best Places to Stay

- ➡ Stop (p364)
- ➡ Kilmurvey House (p375)
- ➡ Currarevagh House (p383)
- ➡ Dolphin Beach (p388)

Why Go?

County Galway is a problem: its namesake city is such a charmer that you might not manage to tear yourself away to the countryside. Conversely, the wild and beautiful Aran Islands and Connemara Peninsula might keep you captive such that you'll never have time for the city. What to do? Both, of course!

Galway city is a swirl of enticing old pubs that hum with trad music sessions throughout the year. More importantly, there's an addictive vibe of culture, fun and frolic.

Offshore, the eroded, sheer swathes of land known as the Aran Islands possess a desolate and windswept yet entrancing aura. Tiny villages cling to the rocks while soft-hearted locals welcome their modern lifeblood: visitors.

In the west, the Wild Atlantic Way and the Connemara Peninsula match the beauty of other Atlantic outcrops such as Dingle. Tiny roads wander along a coastline studded with islands, unexpectedly white beaches and intriguing old villages.

When to Go

- ➡ Galway city, with its excellent restaurants, roaring pubs and student culture, is a year-round destination.
- ➡ Elsewhere in rural parts of the county, you'll be rewarded for visits during the more moderate months.
- ➡ Moody in the depths of winter, the Aran Islands may be unreachable during storms.
- ➡ In scenic Connemara country, many country inns close during December and January and even February.
- ➡ June is a great month across the county as all the seasonal attractions are open, but crowds are still low.

County Galway Highlights

1. Sample atmospheric pubs and high-energy trad sessions in **Galway city** (p359).
2. Ponder the sublime wind-buffeted ruins of **Dún Aengus** (p373) on Inishmór.
3. Visit ancient holy sites and springs, crawl over a famous shipwreck and commune with the rocks on **Inisheer** (p380).
4. Catch the sun dipping into the Atlantic from the **Sky Road** (p387) outside Clifden.
5. Climb to the roof of **Dunguaire Castle** (p393) and look out over Galway Bay and Kinvara.
6. Escape to the sparsely inhabited island of **Inishbofin** (p390) and get the wild Atlantic wind in your hair.
7. Explore the delightful dreamlike landscape of the walled gardens at **Kylemore Abbey** (p392).

GALWAY CITY

POP 75,600

Arty, bohemian Galway (Gaillimh) is renowned for its pleasures. Brightly painted pubs heave with live music, while cafes offer front-row seats for observing street performers, weekend parties run amok, lovers entwined and more.

Steeped in history, for sure, but the city buzzes with a contemporary and cultured vibe as students make up a quarter of the population. Remnants of the medieval town walls lie between shops selling Aran sweaters, handcrafted Claddagh rings and stacks of second-hand and new books. Bridges arch over the salmon-stuffed River Corrib, and a long promenade leads to the seaside suburb of Salthill, on Galway Bay, the source of the area's famous oysters.

Galway is often referred to as the 'most Irish' of Ireland's cities, it's the only one where you're likely to hear Irish spoken in the streets, shops and pubs.

History

Galway's Irish name, Gaillimh, originates from the Irish word *gaill*, meaning 'outsiders' or 'foreigners', and the term resonates throughout the city's history.

From humble beginnings as the tiny fishing village Claddagh at the mouth of the River Corrib, it grew into an important town when the Anglo-Normans, under Richard de Burgo (also spelled de Burgh or Burke), captured territory from the local O'Flahertys in 1232. Its fortified walls were built from around 1270.

In 1396 Richard II granted a charter transferring power from the de Burgos to 14 merchant families or 'tribes' – hence Galway's enduring nickname: City of the Tribes. (Each of the city's roundabouts is named for one of the tribes.)

Galway maintained its independent status under the ruling merchant families, who were mostly loyal to the English Crown. Its coastal location encouraged a huge trade in wine, spices, fish and salt with Portugal and Spain. Its support of the Crown, however, led to its downfall; the city was besieged by Cromwell in 1651 and fell the following year. Trade with Spain declined and Galway stagnated for centuries.

The early 1900s saw Galway's revival as tourists returned to the city and student numbers grew. In 1934 the cobbled streets and thatched cabins of Claddagh were tarred and flattened to make way for modern, hygienic buildings, and construction has boomed since.

Sights & Activities

★Spanish Arch — HISTORIC SITE

The Spanish Arch is thought to be an extension of Galway's medieval city walls, designed to protect ships moored at the nearby quay while they unloaded goods from Spain, although it was partially destroyed by the tsunami that followed the 1755 Lisbon earthquake. Today it reverberates to the beat of bongo drums, and the lawns and riverside form a gathering place for locals and visitors on sunny days, as kayakers negotiate the tidal rapids of the River Corrib.

A 1651 drawing of Galway clearly shows its extensive fortifications, but depredation by Cromwell and William of Orange and subsequent centuries of neglect saw the walls almost completely disappear. Once surviving portion has been cleverly incorporated into the modern shopping mall, **Eyre Square Centre** (Merchants Rd & Eyre Sq).

★Galway City Museum — MUSEUM

(www.galwaycitymuseum.ie; Spanish Pde; ⌚10am-5pm Tue-Sat year-round, noon-5pm Sun Easter-Sep) FREE This modern museum has exhibits on the city's history from 1800 to 1950, including an iconic Galway Hooker fishing boat, a collection of *currachs* (boats made from animal hides) and sections covering Galway and the Great War and the city's cinematic connections.

Also check out rotating displays of works by local artists. The ground-floor cafe, with its Spanish Arch views, is a perfect rest stop.

Hall of the Red Earl — ARCHAEOLOGICAL SITE

(www.galwaycivictrust.ie; Druid Lane; ⌚9.30am-4.45pm Mon-Fri, 10am-1pm Sat) FREE Back in the 13th century when the de Burgo family ran things in Galway, Richard – the Red Earl – erected a large hall as a seat of power. Locals would arrive to curry favour or to grovel as a sign of future fealty. After the 14 tribes took over, the hall fell into ruin, lost until 1997 when expansion of the city's Custom

WANT MORE?

Head to **Lonely Planet** (lonelyplanet.com/ireland/county-galway/galway-city) for planning advice, author recommendations, traveller reviews and insider tips.

Galway City

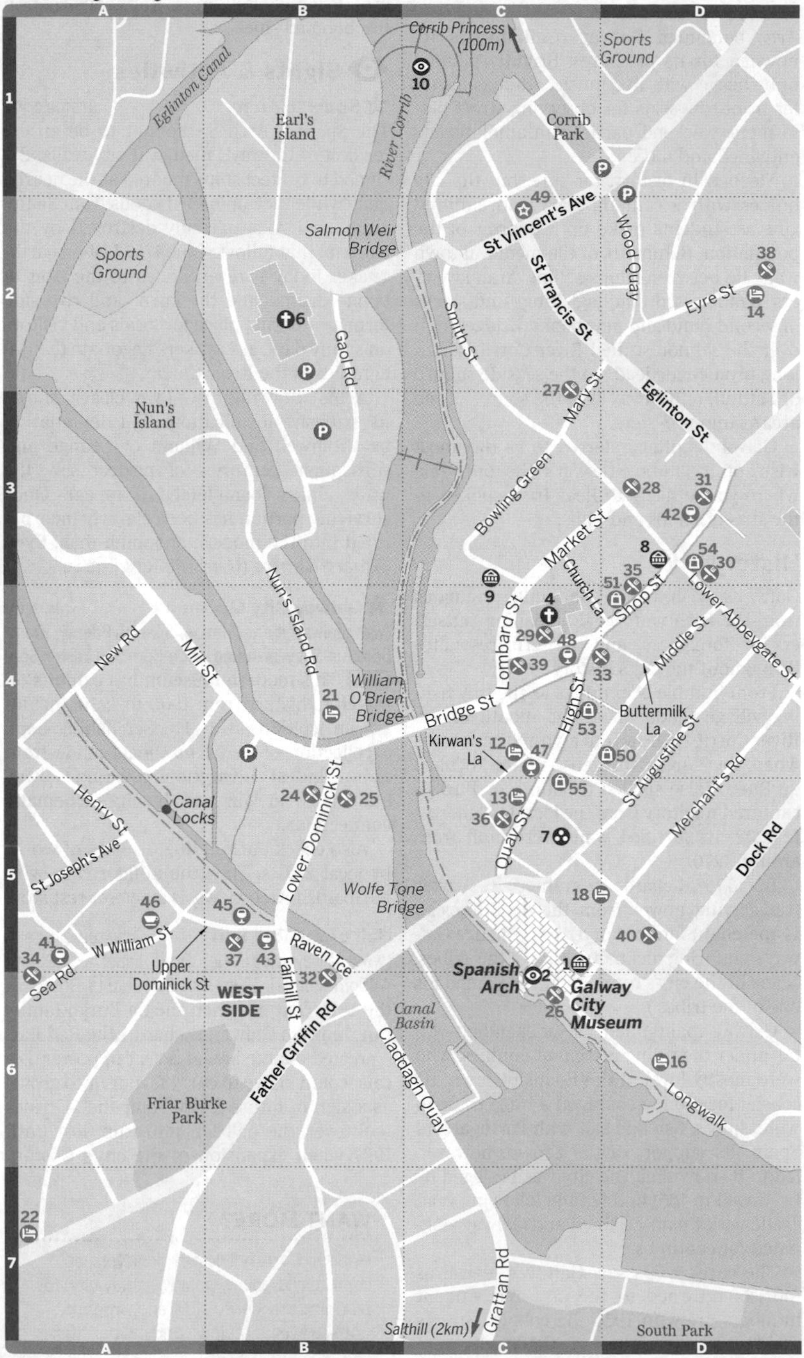

A B C D
1 2 3 4 5 6 7
Corrib Princess (100m)
Sports Ground
Eglinton Canal
Earl's Island
River Corrib
Corrib Park
St Vincent's Ave
Wood Quay
Salmon Weir Bridge
Sports Ground
St Francis St
Smith St
Eyre St
Gaol Rd
Nun's Island
Mary St
Eglinton St
Bowling Green
Market St
Church La
Shop St
Lower Abbeygate St
Nun's Island Rd
Lombard St
Middle St
New Rd
Mill St
William O'Brien Bridge
Bridge St
High St
Buttermilk La
Kirwan's La
St Augustine St
Merchant's Rd
Henry St
Canal Locks
Lower Dominick St
Quay St
Dock Rd
St Joseph's Ave
Wolfe Tone Bridge
W William St
Upper Dominick St
Raven Tce
Fairhill St
Sea Rd
WEST SIDE
Spanish Arch
Galway City Museum
Canal Basin
Father Griffin Rd
Claddagh Quay
Longwalk
Friar Burke Park
Grattan Rd
Salthill (2km)
South Park
1 2 4 6 7 8 9 10 12 13 14 16 18 21 22 24 25 26 27 28 29 30 31 32 33 34 35 36 37 38 39 40 41 42 43 45 46 47 48 49 50 51 53 54 55

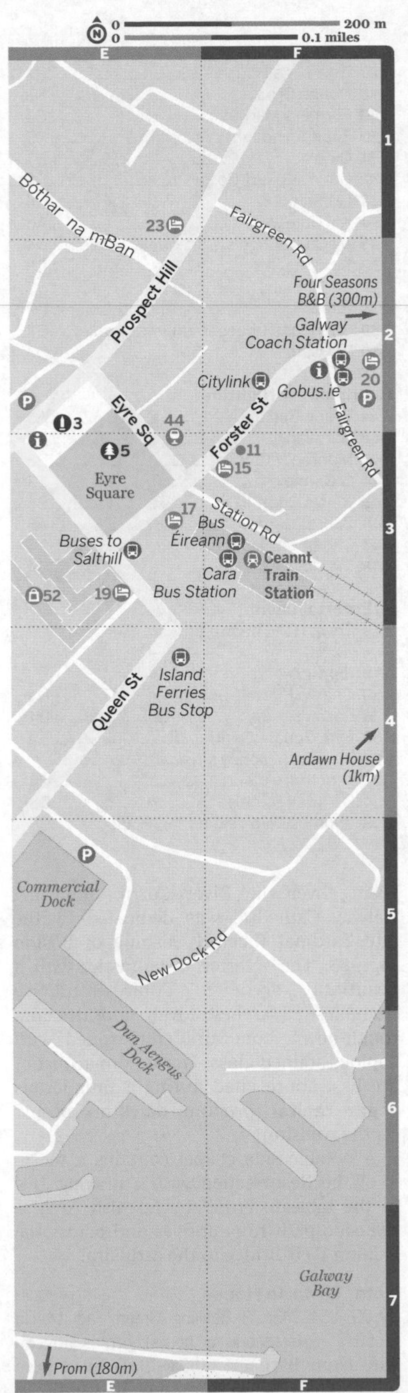

House uncovered its foundations. The Custom House was built on stilts overhead, leaving the old foundations open.

Artefacts and a plethora of fascinating displays give a sense of Galway life some 900 years ago. Volunteers often show up to give a verbal explanation of the ruins and their significance.

Collegiate Church of St Nicholas of Myra CHURCH

(Market St; admission by donation; ⌚9am-5.45pm Mon-Sat, 1-5pm Sun Apr-Sep, 10am-4pm Mon-Sat, 1-5pm Sun Oct-Mar) Crowned by a pyramidal spire, the Collegiate Church of St Nicholas of Myra is Ireland's largest medieval parish church still in use. Dating from 1320, it has been rebuilt and enlarged over the centuries, while retaining much of its original form. Seafaring has long been associated with the church – St Nicholas, for whom it's named, being the patron saint of sailors. Indeed, Christopher Columbus reputedly worshipped here in 1477. During the day the church is usually all but empty and makes for a welcome escape from Galway's hubbub.

Eyre Square PARK

Galway's central public square is busy in all but the harshest weather. A welcome open green space with sculptures and pathways, its lawns are formally named Kennedy Park in commemoration of JFK's visit to Galway, though locals always call it Eyre Square. Guarding the upper side of the square is **Browne's Doorway** (1627), an imposing, if forlorn, fragment from the home of one of the city's merchant rulers, relocated here from Abbeygate St.

The street running along the southwestern side of the square is pedestrianised and lined with seating, while the eastern side is taken up almost entirely by the Hotel Meyrick (p365), an elegant grey limestone pile restored to its Victorian glory.

Lynch's Castle HISTORIC BUILDING

(cnr Shop & Upper Abbeygate Sts; ⌚10am-4pm Mon-Wed & Fri, 10am-5pm Thu) Considered the finest town castle in Ireland, this old stone town house – now part of AIB Bank – was built in the 14th century, though much of what you see today dates from around 1600. Stonework on the facade includes ghoulish gargoyles and the coats of arms of Henry VII, the Lynches (the most powerful of the 14 ruling Galway 'tribes') and the Fitzgeralds of Kildare. On the inside, it's worth a gander at the hefty and magnificent fireplace.

Galway City

Top Sights
1 Galway City Museum ... C5
2 Spanish Arch ... C6

Sights
3 Browne's Doorway ... E2
4 Collegiate Church of St Nicholas of Myra ... C4
5 Eyre Square ... E3
6 Galway Cathedral ... B2
7 Hall of the Red Earl ... C5
8 Lynch's Castle ... D3
9 Nora Barnacle House ... C3
10 Salmon Weir ... C1

Activities, Courses & Tours
11 Lally Tours ... F3

Sleeping
12 7 Cross Street ... C4
13 Barnacles ... C5
14 Eyre Square Townhouse ... D2
15 Galway City Hostel ... F3
16 Heron's Rest ... D6
17 Hotel Meyrick ... E3
18 House Hotel ... C5
19 Kinlay Hostel ... E3
20 Snoozles Tourist Hostel ... F2
21 St Martins B&B ... B4
22 Stop ... A7
23 Western Hotel ... E1

Eating
24 Aniar ... B5
25 Arabica Coffee ... B5
26 Ard Bia at Nimmo's ... C6
27 Asian Tea House ... C2
28 Dough Bros ... D3
29 Farmers Market ... C4
30 Food 4 Thought ... D3
31 Gino's ... D3
32 Gourmet Tart Co ... B6
33 Griffin's ... C4
34 Kai Cafe ... A6
35 McCambridge's ... D4
36 McDonagh's ... C5
37 Oscar's ... B5
38 Renzo ... D2
39 Sheridans Cheesemongers ... C4
40 Wa Cafe ... D5

Drinking & Nightlife
41 Crane Bar ... A5
42 Garavan's ... D3
43 Monroe's Tavern ... B5
44 O'Connell's ... E3
45 Róisín Dubh ... B5
46 Secret Garden ... A5
47 Séhán Ua Neáchtain ... C4
48 Tig Cóilí ... C4

Entertainment
49 Town Hall Theatre ... C2

Shopping
50 Charlie Byrne's Bookstore ... D4
51 Eason's ... D4
52 Eyre Square Centre ... E3
53 Kiernan Moloney Musical Instruments ... C4
54 P Powell & Sons ... D3
55 Thomas Dillon's Claddagh Gold ... C5

Salmon Weir LANDMARK
Upstream from Salmon Weir Bridge, which crosses the River Corrib just east of Galway Cathedral, the river cascades down the great weir, one of its final descents before reaching Galway Bay. The weir controls the water levels above it, and when the salmon are running you can often see shoals of them waiting in the clear waters before rushing upriver to spawn. The salmon and sea-trout seasons usually span February to September, but most fish pass through the weir during May and June.

It's naturally a popular spot for anglers, even with Galway Fisheries' (p370) restriction of one fish per day during May and June – a fish can weigh up to 7kg, or heavier.

Galway Cathedral CHURCH
(Catholic Cathedral of Our Lady Assumed into Heaven & St Nicholas; www.galwaycathedral.org; Gaol Rd; admission by donation; 8am-6pm) Rising over the River Corrib, imposing Galway Cathedral was dedicated by the late Cardinal Richard Cushing of Boston in 1965. The interior is fantastic, with a beautifully decorated dome, attractive Romanesque arches, lovely mosaics and rough-hewn stonework emblazoned with copious stained glass. The superb acoustics are best appreciated during a thunderous **organ recital** (program dates are posted on the website).

A notable side chapel contains a mosaic of the Resurrection with a praying JFK in the tableau. From the Spanish Arch, a riverside path runs upriver and across the Salmon Weir Bridge to the cathedral.

Nora Barnacle House MUSEUM
(091-564 743; 8 Bowling Green; adult/child €2.50/2; telephone for hours) James Joyce's wife Nora Barnacle (1884–1951) lived here until shortly before they met in Dublin in

1904. It's now a privately owned museum displaying the couple's letters and photographs among period furniture. Looking all of its 100 years, the house had no running water until the 1940s; instead the Barnacle family used a communal pump across the street. Joyce met his future mother-in-law here in 1909; for his part, Joyce's father said after learning Nora's surname: 'She'll stick with him'.

Salthill NEIGHBOURHOOD

A favourite pastime for Galwegians and visitors alike is walking along the **Prom**, the seaside promenade running from the edge of the city along Salthill. Local tradition dictates 'kicking the wall' across from the diving boards (a 2.5km stroll from town starting at the Wolfe Tone Bridge and following the shoreline path) before turning around. In and around Salthill there are plenty of cosy pubs from where you can watch storms roll over the bay.

Tours

If you're short on time, bus tours departing from Galway are a good way to see Connemara, the Burren and the Cliffs of Moher, while boat tours take you to the heart of Lough Corrib. Tours can be booked directly or at the tourist office.

★ **Burren Wild Tours** NATURE TOUR

(087 877 9565; www.burrenwalks.com; departs Galway Coach Station; €10-25; 10am-5pm) Offers seasonal bus tours to the Burren and the Cliffs of Moher, incorporating an easy one-hour guided walk.

Corrib Princess BOAT TOUR

(091-592 447; www.corribprincess.ie; Woodquay; adult/student/family €16/14/36; May-Sep) Two or three 90-minute cruises per day on the River Corrib and Lough Corrib, departing from Woodquay, just beyond Salmon Weir Bridge.

Galway on Foot WALKING TOUR

(085 730 2488; minimum 2 people, per person €10) Excellent, fun and relaxed walking tours on the history and culture of the city, departing from the Spanish Arch.

Galway Food Tours TOUR

(086 733 2885; tours €26; Thu-Sun) For 90-minute to two-hour tours around the gastronomic culture, food markets and dining hotspots of Galway. Also in French.

Galway Tour Company BUS TOUR

(091-566 566; www.galwaytourcompany.com; tours from €20; Mar-Oct) Offers a variety of tours of County Clare's Burren, the Aran Islands and Connemara.

Lally Tours BUS TOUR

(091-562 905; www.lallytours.com; 4 Forster St; tours from adult/child €25/15) Entertaining, informative bus tours of Connemara, the Burren and the Cliffs of Moher, departing from Galway bus station, plus hop-on, hop-off bus tours of Galway (adult/child €12/6).

Old Galway City Tour BUS TOUR

(091-562 905; www.lallytours.com; Galway Tourist Office, Forster St; 24hr ticket adult/child €12/6; 10.30am-3pm Mar-Oct) Hop-on, hop-off open-top bus tours of Galway city and its environs. Buses run every 90 minutes and make 14 stops.

Sleeping

You'll find B&Bs lining the major approach roads as well as Salthill, but to take full advantage of Galway's tightly packed attractions, try for a room in the city centre. If you're planning an extended stay, try the classified pages of the *Galway Advertiser* (www.galwayadvertiser.ie) for rental properties, or try www.daft.ie.

Among the strips of B&Bs near the centre, College Rd stands out for sheer volume: dozens of choices line the road. You can reach the action after a 10-minute walk along Lough Atalia.

Galway's festivals and its easy striking distance from Dublin make it *hugely* popular year-round, especially at weekends. Accommodation often fills far in advance, so book ahead. And note that ditching the car can be a hassle at places without parking.

GALWAY HOOKERS

Obvious jokes aside, Galway hookers (Irish *húiceár*) are the iconic small sailing boats that were the basis of local seafaring during the 19th century and into the 20th century. Small, tough and highly manoeuvrable, these wooden boats are popular with weekend sailors and hobbyists. The hulls are jet black, due to the pitch used for waterproofing, while the sails flying from the single mast are a distinctive rust colour.

★Kinlay Hostel HOSTEL €
(☎091-565 244; www.kinlayhouse.ie; Merchants Rd; dm €17-29, d €54-70; @📶) Easygoing staff, a full range of facilities and a cream-in-the-doughnut location just off Eyre Sq make this a top choice, with four- to 10-bed dorms and doubles. Spanning two huge, brightly lit floors, amenities include two self-catering kitchens and two cosy TV lounges, with a pool table. Some rooms have bay views and newer beds have electric sockets and USB points.

Snoozles Tourist Hostel HOSTEL €
(☎091-530 064; www.snoozleshostelgalway.ie; Forster St; dm €10-25, d €45-70; @📶) Dorms and private rooms all have bathrooms at this hostel west of Eyre Sq and not far from the train and bus stations. Continental breakfast is free and facilities include a barbecue terrace, pool table, lounge with PS2 machine and kitchen.

Barnacles HOSTEL €
(☎091-568 644; www.barnacles.ie; 10 Quay St; dm €14-35, d €50-75; @📶) This highly central and very well-run hostel is housed in a medieval building with a modern extension. Rooms are all clean and well-kept, the kitchen is spacious, there's a warm common room with a big gas fireplace and games consoles. There's a free pasta evening on Sunday and on Wednesday musicians can 'play to stay'. Breakfast includes scones and soda bread.

St Martins B&B B&B €
(☎091-568 286; 2 Nun's Island; s/d from €40/70; 📶) This well-kept older-style house has a flower-filled garden overlooking the William O'Brien Bridge and the River Corrib. The four rooms have all the comforts (plus hot water bottles) and some people stay for the breakfasts alone. Owner Mary Sexton wins rave reviews, but parking is an issue.

Galway City Hostel HOSTEL €
(☎091-535 878; www.galwaycityhostel.com; Frenchville Lane, Eyre Sq; dm €16-25, d €40-80; @📶) This cheery spot directly across from the train station is neat and trim, with an orange finish and very clean common areas. There's free continental breakfast, free printing, bike hire, laundry facilities, sunny staff and live trad music in the downstairs bar. Some beds have plugs and USB sockets.

★Stop B&B €€
(☎091-586 736; www.thestopbandb.com; 38 Father Griffin Rd; s/d/tw/tr/f from €50/80/80/120/160; 📶) Done up with funky artwork, fun colours and bare floorboards, this tremendous house pulls out the stops. The owners keep things fresh as a daisy and neat as a pin with 11 shipshape but never dull rooms. Space – at a premium – is wisely used, so no wardrobes (just hangers), small work desk, no TV, but comfy beds. Brekkie is another forte.

★Heron's Rest B&B €€
(☎091-539 574; www.theheronsrest.com; 16A Longwalk; s/d from €75/160; 📶) Ideally located in a lovely row of houses on the banks of the Corrib, the thoughtful hosts here give you deck chairs so you can sit outside and enjoy the scene. Other touches include holiday-friendly breakfast times (8am to 11am), decanters of port (enough for a glass or two) and more. Double-glazed rooms, all with water views, are small and cute.

Ardawn House B&B €€
(☎091-568 833; www.ardawnhouse.com; College Rd; s/d from €50/80; 📶) One of the nicest choices on the B&B-lined College Rd strip, this traditional house has elegant bedrooms. The breakfast room feels regal and the food is royal: all manner of preserves and cheeses plus omelettes and much more.

Four Seasons B&B B&B €€
(☎091-564 078; www.fourseasonsgalway.com; 23 College Rd; s/d from €50/80; 📶) This Four Seasons only has seven rooms, but nightly rates will leave you with enough loot to sink many a pint. One of the best choices on this strip; the friendly Fitzgeralds offer a large breakfast menu, free fruit and a homely environment.

7 Cross Street HOTEL €€
(☎091-530 100; www.7crossstreet.com; 7 Cross St; r from €80; 📶) The 10 rooms at this skinny place in a traditional building are very small but they are trendily decorated and the location is excellent for the heart of the city. Ask about its three-bedroom townhouse at 27 Nun's Island, available for rent at €325 per night.

Eyre Square Townhouse INN €€
(☎091-568 444; www.eyresquaretownhouse.com; 35 Eyre St; s/d from €40/50; 📶) The 10 rooms aren't huge but the price is right and staff are cordial at this modest yet well-run place just off Eyre Sq. There's a neat Ikea feel, which combines with the modern bathrooms to make for a nice stay. The front desk is not continuously staffed.

Western Hotel HOTEL €€
(☎091-562 834; www.thewestern.ie; 33 Prospect Hill; d €55-150, tw €60-180, f €70-180, q €70-240; @) There's faded Georgian charm in these three Georgian buildings wedded at this central spot just east of Eyre Sq, with a modern block behind. Rooms are large, modern and comfortable, with good-sized work desks but fat-screen TVs. There's basement parking.

★**House Hotel** HOTEL €€€
(☎091-538 900; www.thehousehotel.ie; Spanish Pde; r €100-220;) There's a hip and cool array of colour in the lobby at this smart and stylish boutique hotel. Public spaces contrast modern art with trad details and bold accents. Cat motifs abound. The 40 rooms are small but plush, with bright colour schemes and quality fabrics. Bathrooms ooze comfort.

Hotel Meyrick HOTEL €€€
(☎091-564 041; www.hotelmeyrick.ie; Eyre Sq; r €115-450;) Known as the Railway Hotel when it opened in 1852, and later as the Great Southern Hotel, this stately showpiece looms large over Eyre Sq. It's a bit bruised and clobbered but remains elegant, with an imposing lobby and smart rooms. Reception is to your right as you enter and rooms facing the square come at a premium.

Eating

Seafood is Galway's speciality, be it fish and chips, ocean-fresh chowder or salmon cooked to perfection. Galway Bay oysters star on many menus. The city's smorgasbord of eating and drinking options ranges from the market – where farmers in gumboots unload soil-covered vegetables – to adventurous new restaurants redefining Irish cuisine.

Pedestrianised Quay St is lined with restaurants aimed at the tourist throngs. As one local told us, 'I can remember when all you'd get on Quay St was a hard biscuit, then you'd get run down by a bus.'

Galway's fantastic **farmers market** (www.galwaymarket.com; Church Ln; 8am-4pm Sat, noon-5pm Sun) fills the streets around St Nicholas Church. It's the region's best and is the place to see the many briny, earthy and dairy delights of the county. You'll find artisans selling their creations as well.

★**McCambridge's** CAFE, SELF-CATERING €
(www.mccambridges.com; 38/39 Shop St; snacks from €3, mains €7-13; cafe 9am-5.30pm Mon-Wed, 9am-9pm Thu-Sat, 10.30am-6pm Sun, grocery 8am-7pm Mon-Wed, 8am-9pm Thu-Sat, 10.30am-6pm Sun) The long-running food hall here has some superb prepared salads, hot foods and other more exotic treats. Create the perfect picnic or enjoy your pickings at the tables out front. All high ceilings, blond wood and busy staff, the upstairs cafe is lovely with an ever-changing menu of modern Irish fare plus gourmet sandwiches, salads, silky soups and tip-top coffee.

★**Sheridans Cheesemongers** DELI, WINE BAR €
(www.sheridanscheesemongers.com; 14 Churchyard St; snacks from €4; shop 10am-6pm Mon-Fri, 9am-6pm Sat, noon-5pm Sun, wine bar 4-11pm Mon, 1pm-midnight Tue-Fri, noon-midnight Sat, 2-11pm Sun) Sheridans Cheesemongers is aromatic with the superb local and international cheeses and other deli items within, many from the Mediterranean. Its real secret, however, is up a narrow flight of stairs. Sample from a huge wine list (the emphasis is on Italian wines) in an airy room while enjoying many of the best items from below.

Dough Bros PIZZA €
(☎087 176 1662; www.thedoughbros.ie; 24 Upper Appeygate St; pizzas from €7.50; noon-10pm) At the time of writing, this bright green outlet was the pop-up home of the travelling wood-fired pizza restaurant that began as a food truck and has made big waves in Galway's dining community for its perfect crusts, fresh, flavour-loaded toppings and relaxed, casual vibe. Check with the restaurant for the truck's latest location.

Griffin's CAFE, BAKERY €
(www.griffinsbakery.com; Shop St; mains €4-8; 8am-6pm Mon-Sat) A local institution which, although it's been run by the Griffin family since 1876, remains as fresh as a bun hot out of the oven. The small bakery counter is laden with treats, including great scones. But the real pleasure lies upstairs in the cafe where you can choose from sandwiches, hot specials, luscious desserts and more.

Gourmet Tart Co DELI, BAKERY €
(www.gourmettartco.com; Raven Tce; mains €5-9; 7.30am-7.30pm Sun-Thu, 7.30am-11pm Fri & Sat) Fresh as a daisy, free from additives and preservatives, all the handmade food is stunningly arrayed here. There's luscious salads, wholesome soups, beautiful sandwiches and, yes, those tarts that give pastry a good name. It's sit down or take away and service is sunny.

Food 4 Thought VEGETARIAN €

(Lower Abbeygate St; mains €6-9; 7.30am-6pm Mon-Fri, 8am-6pm Sat, 11.30am-4pm Sun;) Besides providing organic and vegetarian sandwiches, savoury scones and wholesome dishes such as cashew-nut roast, this place is great for finding out about energy workshops and yoga classes around town. Free refills on coffee!

Renzo CAFE €

(32 Eyre St; 8am-5.30pm Mon-Wed, 8am-7pm Thu-Sat, 10am-5.30pm Sun) With a small collection of books and artwork for sale, pea-green Renzo is a good-looking spot brewing up fine coffees and serving gourmet sandwiches and pastries. Tucked away down Eyre St, it's a tranquil choice, run by obliging staff.

Arabica Coffee CAFE €

(www.arabicagalway.com; 58 Lower Dominic St; 7.30am-6pm Mon-Fri, 8am-6pm Sat, 10am-4pm Sun) Uncluttered and neat, this dark-wood-floored cafe is shinier than a new dime and service is a cut above the norm. A good choice for brekkie, fresh pastries, bagels, panini, wraps, sandwiches and of course coffee, from the capable hands of its helpful baristas. No wi-fi though, sadly.

Wa Cafe JAPANESE €

(www.wacafe.net; 13 New Dock St; mains from €4.50; noon-3pm & 5-9pm Mon-Thu, noon-4pm & 5-9pm Fri-Sun) This pocket-sized sushi parlour with wooden tables is a welcome pit-stop for a spot of tranquillity, tasty sushi rolls and sets, nigiri sets, bento lunch boxes, sashimi and *yakisoba* noodles. Ask about its Sunday sushi workshops.

Gino's ICE CREAM €

(24 William St; tubs from €3; 10am-11pm) In cones or tubs, Gino's 30-plus flavours of homemade gelato are a treat while shopping around the centre of town.

★ **Kai Cafe** CAFE €€

(091-526 003; www.kaicaferestaurant.com; 20 Sea Rd; lunch/dinner mains from €11.50/18.50; 9.30am-4pm Mon-Fri, 10.30am-4pm Sat, noon-4pm & 6.30-10.30pm Sun;) This fantastic cafe on happening Sea Rd is a delight, whether for a coffee, portions of West Coast Crab or Roscommon hogget and glasses of Galway Hooker Sixty Knots IPA in a relaxed, casual, wholesome and rustic dining environment. Great at any time of the day, but reserve for din-dins.

★ **Oscar's** SEAFOOD €€

(091-582 180; www.oscarsbistro.ie; Upper Dominick St; mains €14.50-25.50; 6-9.30pm Mon-Sat, 6-9pm Sun) Galway's best seafood restaurant is just west of the tourist bustle. The long and ever-changing menu has a huge range of local specialities, from shellfish to white fish (which make some superb fish and chips), with some bold flavours. There's a two-course dinner menu from Monday to Thursday (€18.50) before 7.30pm.

★ **Asian Tea House** ASIAN €€

(091-563 749; 15 Mary St; mains €14-24; 5-10.30pm Wed-Mon) Decorated with pan-Asian motifs, rattan seats and bamboo lampshades, this seductively lit restaurant is a delight from start to finish. Dishes, well-executed and full of MSG-free flavour, range from Malaysian to Thai, Vietnamese and Chinese. The *tom yam* soup is on the money and so is the silken tofu. Tea choices abound and staff are most welcoming.

Ard Bia at Nimmo's MODERN IRISH €€

(www.ardbia.com; Spanish Arch; lunch €7-10, dinner €19-26; cafe 10am-3.30pm, restaurant 6-10pm, wine bar 6-11pm, closed Sun) In Irish, Ard Bia means 'High Food', and that's somewhat apt, given its location in the 18th-century Custom House near the Spanish Arch. Local seafood and organic produce feature on the seasonal menu in a setting that defines funky chic. The cafe is a perfect place for a coffee and tart.

McDonagh's SEAFOOD €€

(www.mcdonaghs.net; 22 Quay St; takeaway mains from €6, restaurant mains €13.50-26; cafe & takeaway noon-11pm Mon-Sat, 2-9pm Sun, restaurant 5-10pm Mon-Sat) A trip to Galway isn't complete without a meal here. Divided into two parts, there's a takeaway counter where diners sit elbow to elbow at long communal wooden tables on one side, and a more upmarket restaurant on the other. Galway's best fish-and-chip shop fries up a haul of battered cod, plaice, haddock, whiting and salmon, accompanied by homemade tartar sauce. Oysters are three for €5.

★ **Aniar** MODERN IRISH €€€

(091-535 947; www.aniarrestaurant.ie; 53 Lower Dominick St; mains from €30; 6-10pm Tue-Thu, 5.30-10pm Fri & Sat) Deeply committed to the flavours and food producers of Galway and West Ireland, Aniar wears its Michelin star with pride. There's no fuss, however.

The casual spring-green dining area is a relaxed place to taste from the nightly, daily-changing menu. The wine list favours small producers. Reserve.

Drinking & Nightlife

Galway's pub selection is second to none, which is why in summer and on weekends they all seem thronged. On Saturday nights, the town fills with party-goers from the hinterlands. The website **Galway City Pub Guide** (www.galwaycitypubguide.com) is a good resource for this heaving scene. Most of Galway's pubs have live music at least a couple of nights a week, whether in an informal trad session or a headline act.

If the beer situation in much of the country is bleak, in Galway there's an alternative to the lame lagers: **Hooker** (www.galwayhooker.ie). Named for the iconic local fishing boats, this fine, hoppy Pale Ale has won plaudits and, more importantly, a local following.

★ Séhán Ua Neáchtain PUB

(www.tighneachtain.com; 17 Upper Cross St; ⏲noon-11.30pm Mon-Thu, noon-midnight Fri & Sat, noon-11pm Sun) Painted a bright cornflower blue, this 19th-century pub, known simply as Neáchtain's (*nock*-tans) or Naughtons, has a wraparound string of tables outside, many shaded by a large tree. It's a place where a polyglot mix of locals plop down and let the world pass them by – or stop and join them for a pint. Good lunches.

★ Crane Bar PUB

(www.thecranebar.com; 2 Sea Rd; ⏲10.30am-11.30pm Mon-Fri, 10.30am-12.30am Sat, 12.30-11pm Sun) This atmospheric old pub west of the Corrib is the best spot in Galway to catch an informal *céilidh* (traditional music and dancing) most nights. Talented bands play its rowdy, goodnatured upstairs bar; downstairs at times it seems straight out of *The Far Side*.

Tig Cóilí PUB

(Mainguard St; ⏲10.30am-11.30pm daily) Two live *céilidh* a day draw the crowds to this authentic fire-engine-red pub, just off High St. It's where musicians go to get drunk or drunks go to become musicians...or something like that. A gem.

Róisín Dubh PUB

(www.roisindubh.net; Upper Dominick St; ⏲5pm-2am Sun-Thu, till 2.30am Fri & Sat) From the rooftop terrace you can see sweeping views of Galway; inside emerging acts play here before they hit the big time. It's *the* place to hear bands but comedy's also on the menu.

Monroe's Tavern PUB

(www.monroes.ie; Upper Dominick St; ⏲10am-11.30pm Mon-Thu, till 12.30am Fri & Sat, live music till 2.30am Fri & Sat) Often photographed for its classic black-and-white facade, Monroe's delivers traditional music and ballads, plus it remains the only pub in the city with regular Irish dancing. Live music every night.

Garavan's PUB

(46 William St; ⏲10.30am-11.30pm Mon-Thu, 10.30am-12.30am Fri & Sat, noon-11pm Sun) With an eye-watering range of Irish whiskeys, this genteel old boozer in the city centre is a place of refuge for those in search of a pint *and* a seat on a busy Saturday night.

O'Connell's PUB

(www.oconnellsbargalway.com; 8 Eyre Sq; ⏲11am-11.30pm Mon-Sat) Traditional, seasoned and garrulous pub with a great beer garden, right on Eyre Sq.

Secret Garden TEAHOUSE

(www.secretgardengalway.com; 4 William St West; ⏲11am-11pm Tue-Sat, 1-9pm Sun; 📶) This charming and funky teahouse (tea from €2.80) and cafe is a chillaxing choice for sipping cups of *tiě guānyīn* tea – or any other leaf from an impressive selection – and sucking on a hookah pipe (€10) in its comfy front room or in the garden out back.

☆ Entertainment

Most pubs in Galway have live music at least a couple of nights a week. Róisín Dubh is the best place for bands; Tig Cóilí excels at trad sessions.

Town Hall Theatre THEATRE

(☎091-569 777; www.tht.ie; Courthouse Sq) The Town Hall Theatre features Broadway and West End shows and visiting singers.

Trad on the Prom MUSICAL

(☎091-582 860; www.tradontheprom.com; Salthill Hotel; adult/child from €30/10; ⏲May-Sep) A festival of Irish dancing and singing, this long-running summer musical is led by Máirín Fahy, a local diva of the fiddle. The production is performed several nights per week in a venue right on the Salthill promenade.

BARRY LEWIS/ALAMY STOCK PHOTO ©

1. Galway International Oyster & Seafood Festival **2.** Galway Races
3. Galway Arts Festival **4.** Hookers at the Gathering of the Boats

3

2

HOLGER LEUE/GETTY IMAGES ©

4

Galway's Festivals

Galway knows how to party. Celebrations of culture, food and sport give further reasons to visit year-round.

In April, authors and writers from all four corners gather for the **Cúirt International Festival of Literature** (www.cuirt.ie). If this university town already seems literary, wait for the prose, verse and poetry readings streaming from almost every pub.

The cultural scene heats up for the **Galway Arts Festival** (www.giaf.ie), a two-week extravaganza of theatre, music, art and comedy in mid-July. Expect performances and exhibits by top drama groups, musicians, comedians, artists and much more. The **Galway Film Fleadh** (www.galwayfilmfleadh.com), held concurrently, sets screens alight with new, edgy works.

Galway Race Week (www.galwayraces.com) draws tens of thousands of punters in late July or early August for a week of partying. Races in Ballybrit, 3km east of the city, are the centrepiece of Galway's most boisterous festival. Thursday is a real knees-up: by night there are muddy knees on tuxes and random missing high heels.

One of the great joys of September is the **Galway International Oyster & Seafood Festival** (www.galwayoysterfest.com). Good for much of the year, the tasty bivalves from the shallow waters of Galway Bay seem to reach their peak as the days grow short. The **Clarenbridge Oyster Festival** (www.clarenbridge.com) is a long-established feast, taking place in the first week of September.

Other festivals to look out for include:

Tedfest (p375) The Aran Islands' rollicking Father Ted festival is held in late February/early March.

Galway Food Festival (www.galwayfoodfestival.com) Galway's lively food scene is celebrated in late March.

Bodhrán Summerschool (www.craiceann.com) This five-day festival celebrating the hand-held goatskin drum takes place on Inisheer at the end of June.

Galway Hooker Boat Races (www.cruinniunambad.com) Traditional Galway hooker sailing boats race here each year in the Cruinniú na mBáid (Gathering of the Boats). Second weekend in August.

Shopping

Galway has an array of speciality shops dotting its narrow streets, stocking cutting-edge fashion, Irish woollens, outdoor clothing and equipment, local jewellery, books, art and, of course, music.

★Charlie Byrne's Bookstore BOOKS
(www.charliebyrne.com; Middle St, Cornstore; ⏲9am-6pm, to 8pm Thu & Fri, from noon Sun) A civic treasure (established in 1989) with a collection of new, second-hand, third-hand, discounted books (many €1) and out-of-print titles that can keep you browsing for weeks. With stock stuffed into a succession of rambling rooms via all manner of subjects, staff can ferret out that obscure Aran Islands title that's been giving you the slip.

P Powell & Sons MUSIC
(William St; ⏲10am-5pm Mon-Sat) You can pick up tin whistles, bodhráns and other instruments here, as well as sheet music. Backpackers note: it stocks bongos.

Kiernan Moloney Musical Instruments MUSIC
(www.moloneymusic.com; Old Malt Centre, 17 High St; ⏲10am-6pm Mon-Fri, 10am-5.30pm Sat) Fiddles abound at this dealer in fine instruments. If your harp has come unglued, they'll fix it.

Thomas Dillon's Claddagh Gold JEWELLERY
(www.claddaghring.ie; 1 Quay St; ⏲10am-6pm) Established in 1750, this is Ireland's oldest jewellery shop, with vintage examples in its small back-room 'museum'.

Eason's BOOKS
(☎091-562 284; Shop St; ⏲9am-6pm Mon-Thu & Sat, 9am-8.45pm Fri, noon-5.45pm Sun) Huge, central bookstore with a superb range of books and a strong travel and kids selection.

CLADDAGH RINGS

The fishing village of Claddagh has long been subsumed into Galway's city centre, but its namesake rings survive as both a timeless reminder and a timeless source of profits.

Popular with people of real or imagined Irish descent everywhere, the rings depict a heart (symbolising love) between two outstretched hands (friendship), topped by a crown (loyalty). Rings are handcrafted at jewellers around Galway, and start from about €20 for a simple band to well over €1000 for blinged-up diamond-encrusted versions.

Jewellers selling Claddagh rings include Ireland's oldest jewellery shop, Thomas Dillon's Claddagh Gold.

Information

To obtain fishing permits and book a time, contact the manager at **Galway Fisheries** (☎091-562 388). A half-day's fishing costs as little as €20. The salmon and sea-trout seasons usually span February to September, but most fish pass through the Salmon Weir during May and June.

TOURIST INFORMATION

Tourist Information Booth (Eyre Sq; ⏲9am-1pm Sun year-round, 9am-6pm Fri-Sun mid-May–Aug) dispenses free city maps and local info.

A large, efficient regional information centre, **Galway Tourist Office** (www.discoverireland.ie; Forster St; ⏲9am-5.45pm Mon-Sat, 9am-1.15pm Sun) can help arrange local accommodation and tours.

Getting There & Away

BUS

Several private bus companies are based at the modern **Galway Coach Station** (New Coach Station; Bothar St), located near the tourist office.

Bus Éireann (www.buseireann.ie; Station Rd, Cara Bus Station) Services to all major cities in the Republic and the North from just off Eyre Sq, near the train station. Dublin (€14.50, three to 3¾ hours) has hourly service. Other services fan out across the region.

Citylink (www.citylink.ie; ticket office Forster St; ⏲office 9am-6pm; 📶) Services depart from Galway Coach Station for Dublin (from €13, 2½ hours, hourly), Dublin Airport (from €19, 2½ hours, hourly), Cork, Limerick and Connemara. Departures are frequent and fares are as low as €10.

GoBus.ie (www.gobus.ie; Galway Coach Station; 📶) Frequent services to Dublin (2½ hours) and Dublin Airport (three hours). Fares from €12.

TRAIN

From the **train station** (☎091-564 222; www.irishrail.ie), just off Eyre Sq, there are up to nine fast, comfortable trains daily to/from Dublin's Heuston Station (one-way from €35, 2¼ hours). Connections with other train routes can be made at Athlone (one hour). The line to Ennis is scenic (€19, 1¾ hours, five daily).

Getting Around

TO/FROM THE AIRPORTS

Bus Éireann operates daily services to/from **Shannon Airport** (€15.50, 1¾ hours, hourly). All the major bus companies serve Dublin Airport.

BICYCLE

Galway's brand new Coca-Cola Zero bike share scheme (www.bikeshare.ie/galway.html) has 16 stations around town. For visitors, €3 (with €150 deposit) gets you a three-day pass. The first 30 minutes of each hire is free; up to 2 hours is €1.50.

BUS

You can walk to almost everything in Galway, including out to Salthill, but you'll also find frequent buses departing from Eyre Sq. For Salthill, take bus 401 (€1.80, 15 minutes).

CAR

Parking on Galway's streets is metered. There are several multistorey and pay-and-display car parks around town. Traffic jams can be horrendous, especially at peak hours.

TAXI

Taxi ranks are located on Eyre Sq, on Bridge St and next to the bus and train stations.

City Taxis (☎ 091-525 252; www.citytaxisgalway.com) Charters taxis to the airports. To Shannon Airport, it's €89 for one to four people.

ARAN ISLANDS

Easily visible from large swathes of coastal Counties Galway and Clare, the Aran Islands sing their own siren song to thousands of Wild Atlantic Way travellers each year who find their desolate beauty beguiling. Day trippers shuttle through in a daze of rocky magnificence, while those who stay longer find places that, in many ways, seem far further removed from the Irish mainland than the 45-minute ferry ride or 10-minute flight would suggest. Hardy travellers find that the low season showcases the islands at their wildest, windswept best.

An extension of the limestone escarpment that forms the Burren in Clare, the islands have shallow topsoil scattered with wildflowers, grass for grazing and jagged cliffs pounded by surf. Ancient forts such as Dún Aengus on Inishmór and Dún Chonchúir on Inishmaan are some of the oldest archaeological remains in Ireland.

A long web of stone walls (1600km in all) runs across all three islands and there's a smattering of early *clocháns* (drystone beehive huts from the early Christian period), resembling stone igloos.

Although quite close in appearance as well as proximity, the three Arans have distinct personalities:

Inishmór (Árainn in Irish, meaning 'Big Island') is the largest Aran and the most easily accessible from Galway. It is home to one of Ireland's most important and impressive archaeological sites, as well as some lively pubs and restaurants, particularly in the only town, Kilronan. Gets over a thousand day trippers in summer.

Inishmaan (Inis Meáin, 'Middle Island') is often bypassed by the majority of tourist traffic, preserving its age-old traditions and evoking a sense of timelessness. It is a place of great solitude with isolated B&Bs and stark rocky vistas.

Inisheer (Inis Oírr, 'Eastern Island'), the smallest island, is easily reached from Galway year-round and from Doolin in the summer months. It offers a good combination of ancient sites, interesting walks, trad culture and a bit of life at night.

History

Little is known about the people who built the massive Iron Age stone structures on Inishmór and Inishmaan. Commonly referred to as 'forts', they are believed to have served as pagan religious centres. Folklore holds that they were built by the Firbolgs, a people who invaded Ireland from Europe in prehistoric times.

It is thought that people came to the islands to farm, a major challenge given the rocky terrain. Early islanders augmented their soil by hauling seaweed and sand up from the shore and fished the surrounding waters on long *currachs* (rowing boats made of a framework of laths covered with tarred canvas), which remain a symbol of the Aran Islands.

Early Christianity

Christianity reached the islands remarkably early, and some of the oldest monastic settlements were founded by St Enda (Éanna) in the 5th century. Enda appears to have been an Irish chief who converted to Christianity and spent some time studying in Rome before seeking out a suitably remote spot for his monastery.

ARTISTIC ARAN

The Aran Islands have sustained a strong creative streak, partly as a means for entertainment during long periods of isolation and partly, in the words of one local composer, to 'make sure the rest of the country doesn't forget we're here'. Artists and writers from the mainland have similarly long been drawn to the elemental nature of island life.

Dramatist JM Synge (1871–1909) spent a lot of time on the islands. His play *Riders to the Sea* (1905) is set on Inishmaan while his renowned *The Playboy of the Western World* (1907) also draws upon his island experiences. Synge's highly readable book *The Aran Islands* (1907) is the classic account of life here and remains in print.

American Robert Flaherty came to the islands in the early 1930s to film *Man of Aran*, a dramatic account of daily life. He was something of a fanatic about the project and got most of the locals involved in its production. One of the cottages built for the film is today a B&B, Man of Aran Cottage (p375). The film is a classic and is regularly shown in Kilronan on Inishmór.

The noted 1996 play, *The Cripple of Inishmaan* by Martin McDonagh, involves tragic characters and a strong desire to leave the island in 1934.

The map-maker Tim Robinson has written a wonderful two-volume account of his explorations on Aran, called *Stones of Aran: Pilgrimage* and *Stones of Aran: Labyrinthe*.

Local literary talent includes Liam O'Flaherty (1896–1984) from Inishmór, who wrote several harrowing novels, including *Famine* (1937).

From the 14th century, control of the islands was disputed by two Gaelic families, the O'Briens and the O'Flahertys. The English took over during the reign of Elizabeth I, and in Cromwell's times a garrison was stationed here.

Modern Isolation

As Galway's importance waned, so did that of the islands, and their isolation meant islanders maintained a traditional lifestyle well into the 20th century. Up to the 1930s, people wore traditional Aran dress: bright red skirts and black shawls for women, baggy woollen trousers and waistcoats with *crios* (colourful belts) for men. The classic heavy cream-coloured Aran sweater, featuring complex patterns, originated and is still hand-knitted on the islands.

Until the last few decades, the islands were, if not centuries from civilisation, then at least a perilous all-day journey in unpredictable seas. Air services began in 1970, changing island life forever, and today fast ferries make a quick (if sometimes rough) crossing.

All three islands now have secondary schools, but as recently as a decade ago, students on the two smaller islands had to move to boarding school in Galway to complete their education, which involved an abrupt switch from speaking Irish to English. Farming has all but died out on the islands and tourism is now the primary source of income; while Irish remains the local tongue, most locals speak English with visitors and converse with each other in Irish.

Information

Although high summer brings throngs of tourists, limited services exist on the islands. Only Inishmór has a year-round tourist office as well as the sole ATM; the majority of places don't accept credit cards, so check ahead. Restaurants, including pubs that serve food, often reduce their opening hours or shut completely during low season.

Getting There & Away

AIR

All three islands have landing strips. The mainland departure point is Connemara regional airport at Minna, near Inverin (Indreabhán), about 35km west of Galway. **Aer Arann Islands** (☎091-593 034; www.aerarannislands.ie; return adult/child €49/27) offers return flights to each of the islands several times daily (hourly in summer); the flights take about 10 minutes, and groups of four or more can get group rates (adult fare €44). Aer Arann Islands also offers scenic flights (€60) in July and August, flying over the Cliffs of Moher, Galway Bay and the Aran Islands.

If you work out some complex timings, you can visit more than one island in a day. A bus from outside the Victoria Hotel in Galway to the airport costs €3 each way.

BOAT

Aran Island Ferries (☎ 091-568 903; www.aranislandferries.com; Galway Ticket Office, 19 Eyre Square; adult/child return from €25/13; ⏲ 8am-5pm) serves all three islands and links Inishmaan and Inisheer. Schedules peak in July and August, with several boats a day. Crossing can take up to one hour, subject to cancellation in high seas. Boats leave from Rossaveal, 40km west of Galway city on the R336. Note there's a 10% discount if you book online. Buses from Queen St in Galway (adult/child €7/4) connect with most sailings; check when you book.

Ferries to the Arans (primarily Inisheer) also operate from Doolin.

Inishmór

POP 830

Most visitors who venture out to the islands don't make it beyond Inishmór (Árainn) and its main attraction, Dún Aengus, the stunning stone fort perched perilously on the island's towering cliffs. The arid landscape west of Kilronan (Cill Rónáin), Inishmór's main settlement, is dominated by stone walls, boulders, scattered buildings and the odd patch of deep-green grass and potato plants.

Tourism turns the wheels of the island's economy: an armada of tour vans greets each ferry and flight, offering a ride round the sights. As one local said: 'We move 'em through like a conveyor belt.' Happily, you can set your own pace.

Inishmór is 14.5km long and 4km at its widest stretch. All boats arrive and depart from Kilronan, on the southeastern side of the island. One principal road runs the length of the island, intersected by small lanes and paths of packed dirt and stone.

Sights

Most day trippers focus on Kilronan and Dún Aengus and jam the roads between the sights. If you're spending the night, bike to sites in the little-visited south during the middle of the day, then you can visit Dún Aengus after the last ferry has left during the long days of summer.

Along the low-lying northern coast, the sheltered little bay of **Port Chorrúch** is home to up to 50 grey seals, who sun themselves and feed in the shallows. Further on, **Kilmurvey Beach** gets an EU Blue Flag for its clean white-sand beach.

West of Kilmurvey is the perfect **Clochán na Carraige**, an early Christian stone hut that stands 2.5m tall, and various small early Christian ruins known rather inaccurately as the **Na Seacht dTeampaill** (Seven Churches), comprising a couple of ruined churches, monastic houses and some fragments of a high cross from the 8th or 9th century.

★Dún Aengus HISTORIC SITE

(Dún Aonghasa; www.heritageireland.ie; adult/child €4/2; ⏲ 9.45am-6pm Apr-Oct, 9.30am-4pm Nov-Mar, closed Mon & Tue Jan-Feb) Three spectacular prehistoric forts stand guard over Inishmór, each believed to be around 2000 years old. Chief among them is Dún Aengus, with three massive drystone walls that run right up to sheer drops to the ocean below. The fort is protected by remarkable *chevaux de frise,* fearsome and densely packed defensive limestone spikes. A small visitor centre has displays that put everything in context and a slightly strenuous 900m walkway wanders uphill to the fort itself. Dún Aengus is around 7km west of Kilronan.

Powerful swells pound the 60m-high cliff face. A complete lack of railings or other modern additions that would spoil this incredible site means that you can not only go right up to the cliff's edge but also potentially fall to your doom below, so take care.

Dún Eochla FORT

Along the road between Kilronan and Dún Aengus is the smaller, perfectly circular fort, Dún Eochla, which makes for a good walk from the main road.

Teampall Chiaráin RUIN

(Church of St Kieran) The ruins of numerous stone churches identify the island's monastic

ISLAND-HOPPING THE ARANS

It's possible to bounce between the three Aran Islands, allowing you to start at one and return to the mainland from another. However, schedules are geared to return trips to a single island. In order to find ferries between the islands, you'll need to consult with Aran Island Ferries as well as the boats operating from Doolin. There will be at least one connection a day between any two islands, just be prepared for ad hoc schedules. Fares should run from €5 to €10.

Inishmór

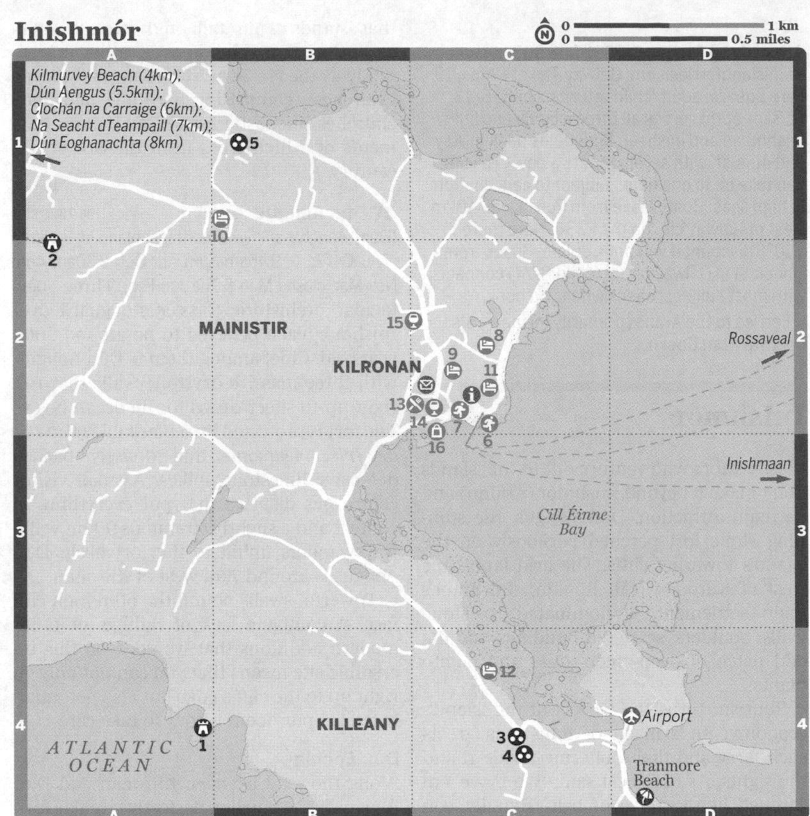

history. This small church, with a high cross in the churchyard, is near Kilronan.

Dún Eoghanachta FORT

To the south of the Na Seacht dTeampaill ruins is this circular fort.

Teampall Bheanáin RUIN

(Church of St Benen) To the southeast, near Cill Éinne Bay, is this early-Christian church.

St Enda's Monastery RUIN

Near the airstrip are the sunken remains of a church; the spot is said to have been the site of St Enda's Monastery in the 5th century, though what's visible dates from the 8th century onwards.

Dún Dúchathair FORT

This ancient fort (the Black Fort) is dramatically perched on a clifftop promontory southwest of Kilronan.

Activities

The ride between Kilronan and Dún Aengus takes about 30 to 60 minutes. Bikes also let you explore the myriad sites north and south of town.

Most places to stay have bicycles for use or rent (universally €10 per day).

★Burke's Bicycle Hire BICYCLE RENTAL

(087 280 8273; www.bikehirearanislands.com; Kilronan; rental per day from €10; Apr-Oct) Patrick Burke is an expert on local cycling and can advise on routes that avoid crowds and reach seldom-visited ends of the island.

Aran Cycle Hire BICYCLE RENTAL

(www.aranislandsbikehire.com; Kilronan; rental per day from €10, electric bikes from €30, deposit €10-20; Apr-Oct) Hires out hundreds of sturdy bikes, electric bikes and tandems, which it delivers to your accommodation anywhere on the island. It's at the pier.

Inishmór

Sights

Activities, Courses & Tours

Sleeping

Eating

Drinking & Nightlife

Shopping

Festivals & Events

Tedfest CULTURE
(www.tedfest.org) Inishmór has seized upon Ted-mania for itself and each year hosts Tedfest, a *Father Ted* festival. Held during the purgatory of tourism (late February or March) this three-day carnival of nonsense has been a huge hit.

Sleeping

After the last day trippers have left in summer, the island assumes a lovely serenity. Advance bookings are advised, particularly in summer. The tourist office can book rooms. Many places offer excellent evening meals.

★Kilronan Hostel HOSTEL €
(099-61255; www.kilronanhostel.com; Kilronan; dm €20-30; late Feb-late Oct; @) You'll see the Kilronan Hostel perched above Tí Joe Mac's pub even before your ferry docks at the pier, a three-minute walk away. Forty beds are spread across very clean four- and six-bed dorms. A terrace has fine harbour views and continental breakfast is thrown in.

Mainistir House INN €
(099-61169; www.aranislandshostel.com; Mainistir; dm/s/d/tw/tr €20/45/50/50/70; @) This quirky 60-bed hostel and guesthouse on the main road north of Kilronan is a fun place for the funky and well-read. A simple breakfast is included as is free tea and coffee for single and double rooms. Dinner (€15) is an event.

★Kilmurvey House B&B €€
(099-61218; www.kilmurveyhouse.com; Kilmurvey; s/d from €55/90; Apr-Sep) On the path leading to Dún Aengus is this grand 18th-century stone mansion. It's a beautiful setting and the 12 rooms are well maintained. Hearty meals (dinner €30) incorporate vegetables from the garden, and local fish and meats. You can swim at a pretty beach that's a short walk from the house.

Tigh Fitz INN €€
(099-61213; www.tighfitz.com; Killeany; s/d from €60/80;) Near the airport and quite a hike from Kilronan, this guesthouse is run by the friendly Penny, has a proper reception desk in the hallway and offers pleasant, albeit simpe rooms. The views out to the tidal extremes of the bay are sublime.

Man of Aran Cottage B&B €€
(099-61301; www.manofarancottage.com; Kilmurvey; s/d from €55/80; Mar-Oct) Built for the 1930s film of the same name, this thatched B&B doesn't trade on past glories – its authentic stone-and-wood interiors define charming. The owners are avid organic gardeners (the tomatoes are famous) and their bounty can become your meal (mains €22).

Ard Mhuiris B&B €€
(099-61208; www.ardmhuiris.com; Kilronan; s €50-60, d €70-80) A five-minute stroll from the centre of town and run by an old couple, this very tidy B&B is last in a line of cottages before fields and then the sea, and hits the sweet spot: quiet, welcoming and great ocean views.

Pier House Guest House INN €€
(099-61417; www.pierhousearan.com; Kilronan; s/d from €60/100; Mar-Oct;) You won't have time to lose your sea legs in the 100m walk from the ferry to this two-storey house perched on a small rise. The 12 rooms are bright and cheery, roomy and comfortable, with coffee and kettle.

WADE EAKLE/GETTY IMAGES ©

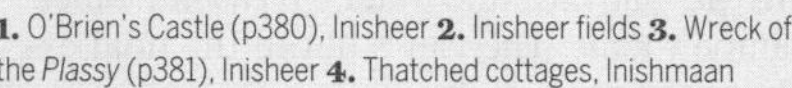

1. O'Brien's Castle (p380), Inisheer **2.** Inisheer fields **3.** Wreck of the *Plassy* (p381), Inisheer **4.** Thatched cottages, Inishmaan

IIC/AXIOM/GETTY IMAGES ©

Aran Islands Scenery

Blasted by the wind and washed over by waves, the eroded, striated slivers of rock known as the Aran Islands hold a fascination for travellers. Rocky extensions of the Burren in County Clare, they are home to descendants of unimaginably hardy folk who forged their own culture of survival.

Inishmaan

Escape the crowds on Inishmaan, the least visited of the Arans. You'll see few others on walks across the dramatic countryside, where every path seems to pass the mysterious remains of past lives and end on a beach trod only by you.

Aran Islands

Left to nature, the Arans would be bare rocks in the Atlantic. But generations of islanders have created green – seaweed and sand gathered and spread by hand over the centuries to produce fertile fields.

Inishmór

A thousand day trippers on a summer weekend come to Inishmór to see one of Ireland's most impressive ancient wonders. Dún Aengus has been guarding a bluff over the Atlantic for 2000 years.

Inisheer

An old castle, ancient churches and a magical spring are just a few of the highlights of Inisheer, the smallest of the Arans. Centuries of history are preserved in rock.

The Plassy Wreck

Star of the opening sequence of the comedy classic *Father Ted,* the *Plassy* was driven ashore on Inisheer by storms in 1960. Attracting walkers and visitors from afar, its rusting hulk is testament to the implacable march of time and the power of the turbulent Atlantic.

Eating & Drinking

Lunch choices are not overwhelming although some of the pubs listed offer food. At night, there are more options – some excellent.

★Bayview Restaurant EUROPEAN €€
(Kilronan; lunch mains €10-14, dinner mains €10-28; 10am-9pm;) A short walk west from the pier, this excellent restaurant is a modern, light-filled environment that's decorated with local art and offering a delectable menu capturing impressive Latin flair, thanks to the Guatamalan roots of head chef Byron.

Mainistir House VEGETARIAN €€
(099-61169; Mainistir; buffet €15; from 8pm summer, from 7pm winter;) Mainistir House cooks up renowned organic, largely vegetarian fare featuring dishes redolent with the tastes of summer – pesto is much in evidence. Nonguests are welcome, but be sure to book. Get a ride or make the 20-minute steep walk from Kilronan. BYO, if you want.

Pier House IRISH €€
(Kilronan; mains €13.50-24.95; noon-9pm, May-Aug) This is the best spot for lunch right in Kilronan – on the large terrace watching the ferries come and go while grazing your way through platters of fish and chips, falafels or steaks. There's a fireplace inside for when the cold winds blow.

★Joe Watty's Bar PUB
(www.joewattys.com; Kilronan; kitchen 12.30-9pm) The best local pub, with trad sessions most summer nights and weekends other times. Posh pub food (mains €8 to €20) ranges from fish and chips to steaks. Peat fires warm the air on the 50 weeks a year when this is needed. Book for dinner in summer.

American Bar PUB
(Kilronan; kitchen 11.30am-9pm Mon-Sat, 12.30-9pm Sun) Two large rooms muster together a good sense of the US, through pics of Elvis, Bob Dylan, Mohammed Ali and the Twin Towers. In low season sloshed locals anticipate the next year of tourists. The room on the right as you enter, with its windows and access to the terrace, is the best bet. Food (mains €9) is so-so.

Shopping

Glossy shops in Kilronan sell Aran-style sweaters that come with gaudy labels that obfuscate their distant origins.

Man of Aran Gift Shop ECLECTIC
(Kilronan; film per adult/child €5/3; 10.30am-5pm Apr-Sep;) This eclectic shop at the main crossroads shows the iconic *Man of Aran* five times daily in its tiny 24-seat theatre. It also has wi-fi (free with purchase) and a fine little coffee bar.

Information

The bike-rental shops and the tourist office all have useful free maps.

Post Office (Kilronan; 9am-12.45pm & 2-4.30pm Mon-Fri, 9am-12.45pm Sat) Uphill from the Spar supermarket.

Spar Supermarket (Kilronan; 9am-6pm Mon-Sat, 9am-5pm Sun;) Has the only ATM in the Arans, plus good soda bread.

Tourist Office (099-61263; Kilronan; 9am-5pm May & Jun, 9am-5.45pm Jul & Aug, 11am-5pm Sep-Apr) Useful office on the waterfront west of the ferry pier in Kilronan.

Getting Around

The airstrip is 2km southeast of town; a shuttle to Kilronan costs €5 return (be sure to carefully reconfirm return pickups for flights lest you be forgotten).

Year-round, numerous minibuses greet each ferry and also prowl the centre of Kilronan. All offer 2½-hour tours of the island (€10) to ad hoc groups. The drive – with commentary – between Kilronan and Dún Aengustakes is about 45 minutes each way. You can also negotiate for private and customised tours.

To see the island at a gentler pace, pony traps with a driver are available for trips between Kilronan and Dún Aengus; the return journey costs between €60 and €100 for up to four people.

Inishmaan

POP 150

The least-visited of the islands, with the smallest population, Inishmaan (Inis Meáin) is a rocky respite, roughly 5km long by 3km wide. Early Christian monks seeking solitude were drawn to Inishmaan, as was the author JM Synge, who spent five summers here over a century ago. The island they knew largely survives today: stoic cows and placid sheep, impressive old forts, and warm-hearted locals, who speak Irish to each other exclusively. Children usually leave the island for college and few return.

Inishmaan's scenery is breathtaking, with a jagged coastline of startling cliffs, empty beaches and fields where the main crop seems to be stone. Most of its buildings are spread out along the road that runs east-west across the centre of the island. Inishmaan's down-to-earth islanders are largely unconcerned with the prospect of attracting the tourist dollar, so facilities are scarce.

Sights & Activities

You can easily **walk** to any place on the island, enjoying the stark, rocky scenery and sweeping views on the way.

On a hill, **St Mary's Church** has excellent stained-glass windows from 1939. On the east of the island, about 500m north of the boat-landing stage is **Trá Leitreach**, a safe, sheltered beach.

Dún Chonchúir FORT
Glorious views of Inishmaan's limestone valleys extend from this elliptical stone fort, built sometime between the 1st and 7th centuries AD.

Synge's Chair LOOKOUT
At the desolate western edge of the island, Synge's Chair is a lookout at the edge of a sheer limestone cliff with the surf from Gregory's Sound booming below. The cliff ledge is often sheltered from the wind, so do as Synge did and find a comfortable stone seat to take it all in. The formation is two minutes' walk from the parking area; you can leg it around the bleak west side of the island from here in an hour.

On the walk out to Synge's Chair, a sign points the way to a **clochán**, hidden behind a house and shed.

Teach Synge HISTORIC BUILDING
(099-73036; admission €3; by appointment) This thatched cottage, on the road just before you head up to the fort Dún Chonchúir, is where the writer JM Synge spent his summers between 1898 and 1902.

Cill Cheannannach CHURCH
These 8th- or 9th-century church ruins are south of the pier.

Sleeping & Eating

Most B&Bs serve evening meals, usually using organic local foods. Meals generally cost around €20 to €25.

Ard Alainn B&B €
(099-73027; s/d without bathroom from €35/55; May-Sep) Signposted just over 2km from the pier and near Synge's Chair, thatched Ard Alainn has fine views out to sea. Rooms share a bathroom. Breakfasts by hostess Maura Faherty will keep you going all day.

Máire Mulkerrin B&B €
(099-73016; s/d from €33/55) Now in her 80s, Mrs Mulkerrin is a local legend in her skirts and shawls. She keeps a cosy, spick-and-span home, filled with faded family photos, and her stove warms the kitchen all day. Guests are accepted sporadically.

★ **Tig Congaile** B&B €€
(099-73085; www.inismeainbb.com; s/d from €50/80) Not far from the pier, Guatemalan-born Vilma Conneely serves guests freshly ground coffee from her native land, but it's her use of local foods that really wins plaudits. Her sea-vegetable soup is famous and best enjoyed – if possible – at a table outside. The dining room is open to nonguests (lunch dishes from €5, dinner from €20), but you must book. The seven rooms are spacious and have starkly iconic views.

An Dún B&B €€
(099-73047; www.inismeainaccommodation.ie; r €50-90; Mar-Oct; @) Opposite the entrance to Dún Chonchúir, modern An Dún has five comfortable rooms. The restaurant is open to nonguests and serves lauded local cuisine such as pillowy potatoes (fertilised with seaweed), luscious smoked salmon and fresh local fish (mains €8 to €25). The restaurant serves lunch in summer (dinner March to October); there are tables outside.

★ **Inis Meáin** INN €€€
(086 826 6026; www.inismeain.com; r 2 nights from €480; Apr-Sep;) An anomaly on the island, where almost everything is as basic as a rock – or is a rock – this smart boutique inn has five lovely suites crafted from local materials (rocks). Views go on forever and you can grab a bike and spend your day exploring in blessed isolation. Rates – minimum two-night stay – include many extras.

The restaurant serves a changing menu of exquisite dishes made from local foods (dinner mains €15 to €35). Open to nonguests, but book.

Teach Ósta PUB €€

(mains from €8) The island's perfect pub hums on summer evenings (grab a table outside for the views) and supplies snacks, sandwiches, soups and seafood platters. Though the pub often keeps going until the wee hours, food service generally stops around 7pm and may not be available in the winter months.

Shopping

Cniotáil Inis Meáin CLOTHING

(☎099-73009; www.inismeain.ie) This factory exports fine woollen garments to some of the world's most exclusive shops. You can buy the same sweaters here; call before visiting.

Information

Not far from the pub, a small **shop** (⏰10am-6pm Mon-Fri, 10am-2pm Sat) sells groceries, offers postal services and dispenses advice.

Getting Around

Enjoy a fact-filled one- to two-hour car tour of the island with eponymous **Brídín Tours** (☎099-73993; €15). Bike rentals may be available at the ferry dock, otherwise you can rent one at the shop (€10).

Inisheer

POP 200

Inisheer (Inis Oírr), the smallest of the Aran Islands, has a palpable sense of enchantment, enhanced by the island's ethereal landscapes, deep-rooted mythology and devotion to traditional culture. With only six surnames among the locals, most given names are highly descriptive.

The wheels of change turn very slowly here. Electricity wasn't fully reliable until 1997. Given that there's at best 15cm of topsoil to eke out a living farming, the slow conversion of the economy to tourism has been welcome. Day trippers from Doolin (as many as 1000 on a balmy summer weekend), 8km across the water, enliven the hiking paths all summer long.

Sights & Activities

Wandering the lanes with their ivy-covered stone walls and making discoveries here and there is the best way to experience the island. Two marked paths offer routes around the island. Set off from the dock on foot, bike or with a driver. A meander covering the main sites will take about four hours on foot. With more time – or days – you can really savour Inisheer.

★**Tobar Éinne** HISTORIC SITE

Locals still carry out a pilgrimage known as the Turas to the Well of Enda, an everburbling spring in a remote rocky expanse in the southwest. The ceremony involves, over the course of three consecutive Sundays, picking up seven stones from the ground nearby and walking around the small well seven times, putting one stone down each time, while saying the rosary until an elusive eel appears from the well's watery depths.

If, during this ritual, you're lucky enough to see the eel, it's said your tongue will be bestowed with healing powers, enabling you to literally lick wounds.

O'Brien's Castle HISTORIC BUILDING

A 100m climb to the island's highest point yields dramatic views over clover-covered fields to the beach and harbour. This 15th-century church (Caisleán Uí Bhriain)

FATHER TED'S DIVINE INSPIRATION

Devotees of the late 1990s cult British TV series *Father Ted* might recognise Craggy Island – the show's fictional island setting off Ireland's west coast – from its opening sequence showing the *Plassy* shipwreck on Inisheer. However, apart from this single shot, the sitcom was mostly filmed in London studios, with additional location shots in Counties Clare, Wicklow and Dublin. Alas, the Parochial House and Vaughan's Pub are nowhere to be found here (instead you'll find them near Lisdoonvarna and Kilfenora in County Clare).

This hasn't stopped the Aran Islands from embracing the show as their own. Although there has been some grumbling from its smaller neighbours, Inishmór has seized upon Ted-mania for itself and each year hosts Tedfest (p375).

Meanwhile, County Clare now has a competing Father Ted Festival (p351) in Kilfenora. As he might say: 'Oh feck!'

WALKING INISHEER'S SHORE

You can circumnavigate Inisheer's 12km shoreline in about five hours, gaining a far deeper understanding of the island than from hurried visits to the top sights.

From the Inisheer ferry pier, walk west along the narrow road parallel to the shore and go straight on to the small fishing pier at the northwest corner of the island. Continue along the road with the shingle shore on one side and a dense patchwork of fields, enclosed by the ubiquitous stone walls, on the other. Look for tide pools and grey seals resting in the sun.

About 1km from the acute junction, turn left at the painted sign; about 100m along the paved lane is the **Tobar Éinne**.

Continue southwest as it becomes a rough track. After about 600m, head roughly south across the limestone pavement and strips of grass to the shore. Follow the gently sloping rock platform around the southwestern headland (Ceann na Faochnaí) and walk east to the **lighthouse** near Fardurris Point (two hours from the ferry pier).

Stay with the coast, turning northeast. You'll see the wreck of the **Plassy** in the distance. When necessary, use stiles to cross walls and fences around fields. Note that the grass you see grows on about 5cm of topsoil created by islanders who cleared rocks by hand and then stacked up seaweed over decades.

Head north, following the track, which then becomes a sealed road at the northern end of Lough More. Continue following the road along the northern shore of the island, past the airstrip.

At the airstrip you can diverge for **Teampall Chaoimháin** and **O'Brien's Castle**. Otherwise rest on the lovely sands of the curving **beach** and check out the nearby **Cnoc Rathnaí**, a Bronze Age burial mound (1500 BC), which is remarkably intact considering it was buried under the sand until the 19th century, when it was rediscovered.

was built within the remains of a ringfort called Dún Formna, dating from as early as the 1st century AD. Nearby is an 18th-century signal tower.

Teampall Chaoimháin HISTORIC BUILDING

Named for Inisheer's patron saint, who is buried close by, the roofless 10th-century Church of St Kevin and small cemetery perch on a tiny bluff near the Strand. On the eve of St Kevin's 14 June feast day, a mass is held here in the open air at 9pm. The sick sleep here for a night hoping to be healed.

Cill Ghobnait CHURCH

This tiny 8th- or 9th-century church is named after St Gobnait, who fled here from Clare while trying to escape an enemy pursuing her.

Plassy HISTORIC SITE

Dating from 1960, this iconic island sight was a freighter that was thrown up on the rocks in bad weather. Miraculously, all on board were saved; Tigh Ned's pub has a collection of photographs and documents detailing the rescue. An aerial shot of the wreck was used in the opening sequence of the iconic TV series *Father Ted*.

Áras Éanna ARTS CENTRE

(☎099-75150; www.araseanna.ie; ⊙Jun-Sep) Inisheer's large community arts centre sits out on an exposed stretch of the northern side of the island, a 15-minute walk from the village, hosting visiting artist events, cultural programs and performances.

Festivals & Events

★**Craiceann Inis Oírr International Bodhrán Summer School** CULTURAL

(www.craiceann.com) The island reverberates to the thunder of traditional drums at the end of June when bodhrán masterclasses, lectures and performances are held. Craiceann takes its name from the Irish word for 'skin', referring to the goat skin used to make these circular drums. The festival features top talent, and nightly drumming sessions take place in the pubs.

Sleeping & Eating

Book well in advance during Craiceann week in June. There is camping (with toilets and showers) at the official site by the main beach. The three pubs are all worth a visit, but confirm opening hours outside Doolin ferry season (March to October).

Brú Radharc Na Mara Hostel HOSTEL €
(☎099-75024; www.bruhostelaran.com; dm €18-25, r €50; ⏱Mar-Oct; @📶) Handily located next to a pub and by the pier, this spotless hostel has ocean views, a large kitchen, a warming fireplace and bikes for hire. The owners also run the adjacent B&B with basic rooms.

★**Fisherman's Cottage & South Aran House** B&B €€
(☎099-75073; www.southaran.com; Castle Village; s/d €49/80; ⏱Apr-Oct; 📶) Slow-food enthusiasts run this sprightly B&B and cafe that's a mere five-minute walk from the pier, with lavender growing in profusion at the entrance. Food (nonguests can enjoy cakes by day and dinner at night, but will need to book) celebrates local seafood and organic produce (dinner mains €12 to €20). Rooms are simple yet stylish. Kayaking and fishing are among the activities on offer.

Radharc an Chláir B&B €€
(☎099-75019; bridpoil@eircom.net; r €45-90; 📶) This pleasant, modern B&B near O'Brien's Castle has views of the Cliffs of Moher and Galway Bay. Book several weeks ahead, as hostess Brid Poil's home cooking draws many repeat visitors. Guests can arrange evening meals (€20). Some rooms share bathrooms.

Tigh Ruaírí PUB €€
(Strand House; ☎099-75020; www.tighruairi.com; r €50-90; @) Rory Conneely's atmospheric digs host live-music sessions in the cosy pub. There are 20 basic rooms, many with views across the waters.

Tigh Ned PUB €
(meals €5-10) Here since 1897, Tigh Ned is a welcoming, unpretentious place, with lively traditional music and inexpensive lunchtime fare. Tables in the garden have harbour views.

ℹ Information

In summer a small **kiosk** (⏱10am-6pm Jul & Aug) at the harbour provides tourist information. Like Inishmaan, there's no ATM; bring euros.

Online, www.aranislands.ie is a handy resource.

ℹ Getting Around

Bikes can be rented from **Rothair Inis Oírr** (www.rothai-inisoirr.com; per day from €10; ⏱May-Sep), which is near the pier and has a good map. Most accommodation places also rent bikes to nonguests.

You can take a tour of the island on a **pony trap** (per person per hour €5-15) in summer.

CONNEMARA

'Connemara is a savage beauty', as Oscar Wilde put it. The raw landscapes and filigreed coast of the Connemara Peninsula are endlessly inspiring, with a rich trove of sublime pockets awaiting discovery and exploration.

The name Connemara (Conamara) is Irish for 'Inlets of the Sea' and the coastal roads bear this out as they wind around the small bays and coves of this part of the Wild Atlantic Way, some with hidden beaches. A succession of seaside hamlets entice.

Connemara's interior is a kaleidoscope of rusty bogs, lonely valleys and shimmering black lakes. At its heart are the Maumturk Mountains and the pewter-tinged quartzite peaks of the Twelve Bens mountain range, with a network of scenic hiking and cycling trails. Everywhere the land is laced by stone walls.

ℹ Information

Galway's tourist office has lots of information on the area. Online, **Connemara Tourism** (www.connemara.ie) and **Go Connemara** (www.goconnemara.com) have regionwide info and links.

ℹ Getting There & Around

BUS

Organised bus tours from Galway are many and offer good, but limited, overviews of the region.

Bus Éireann (☎091-562 000; www.buseireann.ie) Serves most of Connemara. Services can be sporadic, and many buses operate May to September only, or July and August only. Some drivers will stop in between towns.

Citylink (www.citylink.ie) Has several buses a day linking Galway city with Clifden, with stops in Moycullen, Oughterard, Maam Cross and Recess, and on to Cleggan and Letterfrack. For stopoffs between towns, you might be able to arrange a drop-off with the driver.

CAR

Your own wheels are the best way to get off this scenic region's beaten track – though watch out for the narrow roads' stone walls and meandering Connemara sheep – characterised by thick creamy fleece and coal-black face and legs.

Oughterard & Around

POP 1400

The village of Oughterard (Uachtar Árd) is one of Ireland's principal angling centres. Immediately west, the countryside opens up to sweeping panoramas of lakes, mountains and bogs, which get more spectacular the further west you travel.

Sights

★Aughnanure Castle CASTLE
(www.heritageireland.com; off N59; adult/child €3/1; ⏱9.30am-6pm Apr–mid-Oct) Built around 1500, this beautiful fortress 3km east of Oughterard was home to the 'Fighting O'Flahertys', who controlled the region for hundreds of years after they fought off the Normans. The six-storey **tower house** stands on a rocky outcrop overlooking Lough Corrib and has been extensively restored.

Surrounding the castle are the remains of an unusual double *bawn* (area surrounded by walls outside the main castle); there's also the remains of the Banqueting Hall and a small, now isolated **watchtower**, with a conical roof. The River Drimneen once enclosed the castle on three sides while today the river washes through a number of natural caverns and caves beneath the castle.

Glengowla Mines MINE, MUSEUM
(www.glengowlamines.ie; off N59; adult/child €10/4; ⏱10am-6pm mid-Mar–mid-Nov) Ugly work, but these 19th-century mines yielded all manner of silver, glistening quartz and much more. Visitors learn about the tough existence of workers here and can marvel at some of the treasures unearthed. You can also join in some gold-panning and enjoy exploring the working farm. It is 3km west of Oughterard.

Brigit's Garden GARDENS
(www.brigitsgarden.ie; off N59, Roscahill; adult/child €8/5; ⏱10am-5.30pm Feb-Oct) Halfway between the villages of Moycullen and Oughterard is 4.5-hectare Brigit's Garden, a charming and tranquil spot dedicated to Celtic myth and heritage, explored in an environment of woodland, meadowland and traditional architecture, including a thatched roundhouse and *crannóg* (artificial island). There's also a huge sundial, where you can accurately calculate the time and a new sustainability zone that provides 10% of the garden's energy from sunlight. A cafe is at hand for restorative drinks and bites.

Sleeping & Eating

★Currarevagh House HOTEL €€
(☎091-552 312; www.currarevagh.com; Glann Rd; s €80-95, d €140-180; ⏱mid-Mar–Oct; 📶) On vast 73-hectare grounds along Lough Corrib, this magnificent 12-bedroom mansion (pronounced 'Curra-reeva') and country house hotel dates to the 19th century. Fresh flowers scent the timeless halls, the grounds invite lazy rambles and meals feature locally caught trout. It's around 6km from town – follow the Glann Rd until you feel hopelessly lost, and the sign should appear.

Waterfall Lodge B&B €€
(☎091-552 168; www.waterfalllodge.net; off N59; s/d from €50/80) This charmer of a yellow-painted, double-fronted, wisteria-garlanded B&B stands amid beautiful gardens beside a river and cascade, a lovely five-minute walk from the village centre. Antiques fill the rooms (try your hand at the old piano) and a sweet red bridge crosses the water to an island.

Powers Thatched Pub PUB €€
(Clifden Rd; mains €12.50-18.50) The only thatched building on the main road, this comfy pub has open fires, a warm and welcoming interior and a tempting menu of fish and meat. Expect dishes such as butternut squash soup, monkfish, mussels and smoked haddock chowder, and lamb burger with smoked paprika and apple and ale chutney.

Information

The website www.oughterardtourism.com is useful.

GUIDED WALKS IN CONNEMARA

Maps of the many walking trails in Connemara are sold at bookshops and tourist offices. However, to really appreciate the region's unique geology, natural beauty and ancient history, you may wish to go with a guide.

Connemara Safari (☎095-21071; www.walkingconnemara.com; tours €300-700; ⏱Jun-Sep) runs three- and five-day tours in the region, including meals and accommodation. Tour leaders are experts in fields such as archaeology, and routes include some of the deserted islands off the coast.

Connemara

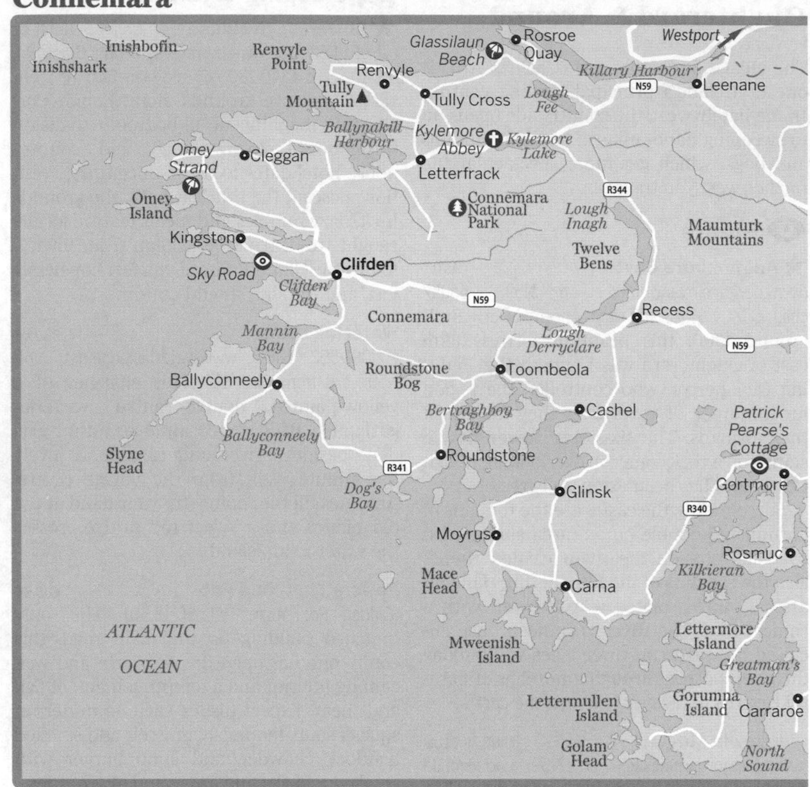

Getting There & Away

Bus Éireann (www.buseireann.ie) and **Citylink** (www.citylink.ie) have regular buses from Galway to Oughterard.

Lough Corrib

The Republic's biggest lake, Lough Corrib, virtually cuts off western Galway from the rest of the country. Over 48km long and covering some 200 sq km, it encompasses more than 360 islands.

Lough Corrib is world-famous for its salmon, sea trout and brown trout. The highlight of the **fishing** calendar is the mayfly season, when zillions of the small bugs hatch over a few days (usually in May) and drive the fish – and anglers – into a frenzy. Salmon begin running around June.

In Oughterard, **Thomas Tuck's Fishing Tackle** (☎091-552 335; Main St, Oughterard; ⏰9am-6pm Mon-Sat) is an excellent shop teeming with local knowledge on fishing, boat operators and boats for hire. Boats can be generally rented for around €60, with a boat operator from €130 to €160.

The largest island on Lough Corrib, **Inchagoill** is a lonely place dotted with ancient remains. Most fascinating is an obelisk called **Lia Luguaedon Mac Menueh** (Stone of Luguaedon, Son of Menueh), which identifies a burial site. It stands about 75cm tall, near the Saints' Church, and some people claim that the Latin writing on the stone is the second-oldest Christian inscription in Europe, after those in the catacombs in Rome. **Teampall Phádraig** (St Patrick's Church) is a small oratory of a very early design, with some later additions. The prettiest church is the Romanesque **Teampall na Naoimh** (Saints' Church), probably built in the 9th or 10th century, with carvings around its arched doorway.

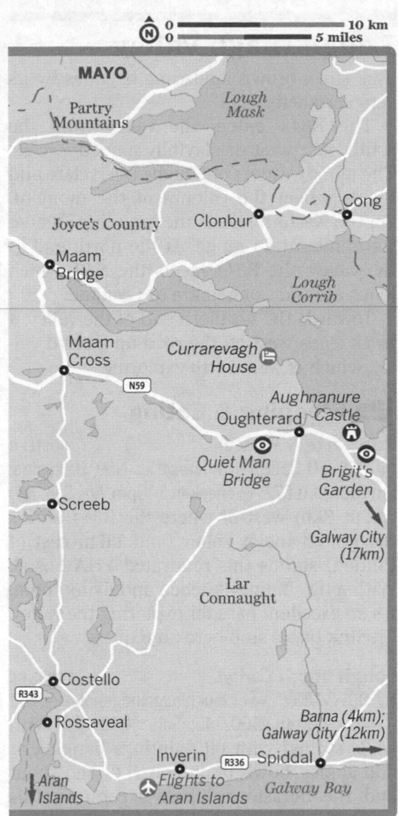

Corrib Cruises (☎091-557 798; www.corribcruises.com; adult/child €20/10; ⏲Easter-Oct, see website for sailing times) has day cruises from Oughterard to Inchagoill and Ashford Castle near Cong.

North of Lough Corrib, you can literally go to the dogs near the town of Clonbur. **Joyce Country Sheepdogs** (☎094-954 8853; www.joycecountrysheepdogs.ie; Clonbur; adult/child €8/5; ⏲3pm Mon-Fri Jun-Sep) offers a chance to see the amazing feats performed by working sheep dogs on an actual farm. Book in advance.

Coastal Drive – Galway City to Mace Head

The slow coastal route between Galway and Connemara takes you past pretty seascapes and villages, although the fun doesn't really begin until after Spiddal.

Opposite the popular Blue Flag beach **Silver Strand**, 4.8km west of Galway on the R336, are the **Barna Woods**, a dense, deep green forest preserved for rambling and picnicking. The woods contain the last natural growing oaks in Ireland's west.

Spiddal (An Spidéal) is a refreshingly untouched little village, and the start of the Gaeltacht region. As you approach the village look for the **Spiddal Craft & Design Studios** (www.spiddalcrafts.com; off R336, Spiddal; ⏲hours vary), where you can watch leatherworkers, sculptors and weavers, plus enjoy a cake at the lauded cafe **Builin Blasta**.

Experience life in a 17th-century Connemara hill village at **Cnoc Suain** (☎091-555 703; www.cnocsuain.com; Spiddal), a restored and recreated glimpse of pre-Famine life in the countryside. Learn about original dance, language, song and the thatched-roof-cottage lifestyles of the time. It's set amid a large tract of preserved landscape and is 5km north of Spiddal.

Exceptional traditional music sessions take place at the unassuming **Tigh Hughes** (Spiddal; ⏲trad sessions 9pm Tue) – it's not uncommon for major musicians to turn up unannounced and join in the craic (fun). The pub's just adjacent to the main street; turn right at the crossroads next to the bank and it's on your right. Numerous places to stay line the main road.

West of Spiddal, the scenery becomes more dramatic, with parched fields criss-crossed by low stone walls rolling to a ragged shore. **Carraroe** (An Cheathrú Rua) has fine beaches, including the Coral Strand, which is composed entirely of shell and coral fragments. It's worth wandering the small roads on all sides of **Greatman's Bay** to discover tiny inlets and little coves, often watched over by the genial local donkeys.

Lettermore, **Gorumna** and **Lettermullen** Islands are low and bleak, with a handful of farmers eking out an existence from minute, rocky fields. Fish farming is big business.

Near Gortmore, along the R340, is **Patrick Pearse's Cottage** (Teach an Phiarsaigh; www.heritageireland.ie; R340; adult/child €4/2; ⏲10am-6pm Easter & Jun-Aug). Pádraig Pearse (1879–1916) led the Easter Rising with James Connolly in 1916; after the revolt he was executed by the British. Pearse wrote some of his short stories and plays in this small thatched cottage with lovely views.

The scenic R340 swings south along **Kilkieran Bay**, an intricate and interlinked system of tidal marshes, bogs, swift-flowing streams and elaborate tidal basins. This environmentally protected area contains an amazing diversity of life.

Continuing on, **Carna** is a small fishing village, with pleasant walks out to **Mweenish Island** or north to Moyrus and out to the wild headlands at **Mace Head**.

Sleeping

If you aren't planning to make Roundstone or beyond by nightfall, you'll find tidy B&Bs dotting the countryside. Many have water views.

★Cashel House Hotel HOTEL €€
(☎095-31001; www.cashelhouse.ie; Cashel; s/d from €85/170; wifi) At the head of Cashel Bay, this flowered fantasy of a country mansion has 30 period rooms surrounded by 17 hectares of woodland and gardens. It also has a stable of Connemara ponies (riding lessons available), a superb dining room and even a small private beach.

Cloch na Scíth B&B €€
(☎091-553 364; www.thatchcottage.com; Kellough, Spiddal; r €45-90) Set in a story-book garden roamed by ducks and chickens, this century-old thatched cottage has a warm, friendly host, Nancy, who cooks bread in an iron pot over the peat fire (as her grandmother taught her and as she'll teach you).

SPOKEN IRISH

One of the most important Gaeltacht (Irish-speaking) areas in Ireland begins around Spiddal in Connemara and stretches west to Cashel and north into County Mayo.

That spoken Irish is enjoying a renaissance around the country (aspiring Dublin parents compete to enrol their kids in Irish-language schools) can be credited in no small part to several media outlets based in Connemara and Galway. From this last refuge of the language, Ireland's national Irish-language radio station, **Radio na Gaeltachta** (www.rte.ie/rnag) and its Irish-language TV station, **TG4** (www.tg4.ie), sprang up in the 1990s.

Lough Inagh Valley

This stark brown landscape beguiles by its very simplicity.

The R344 enters the valley from the south, just west of playfully named Recess. The moody waters of Loughs Derryclare and Inagh reflect the colours of the moment. On the western side is the brooding **Twelve Bens** mountain range. At the north end of the valley, the R344 meets the N59, which loops around Connemara to Leenane.

Towards the northern end of the valley, a track leads west off the road up a blind valley, which is well worth exploring.

Sleeping & Eating

Ben Lettery Hostel HOSTEL €
(☎085 271 3588; www.anoige.ie; N59, Ballinafad; dm €15-20, d €72; check-in 5-10pm, Apr-Sep; wifi) About 8km west of where the R344 enters the Lough Inagh Valley (and 13km east of Clifden) stands this renovated YHA hostel. With a tidy, homey kitchen and living room, it's an excellent base for exploring the valley. Citylink buses stop here on request.

Lough Inagh Lodge LODGE €€
(☎091-34706; www.loughinaghlodgehotel.ie; off R344; s/d from €100/145; dinner €40; wifi) With walls stuffed with oil paintings hanging at odd angles, bowls of potpourri dotted about and the occasional Chinese ceramic, this atmospheric – and slightly haphazard – lodge has 13 grand rooms, with around five of them facing the water. Set in huge grounds against a hill, it's around midway up the gorgeous Lough Inagh Valley, 4.5km north of Recess.

Roundstone

POP 250

Clustered around a boat-filled harbour, Roundstone (Cloch na Rón) is the kind of Irish village you hoped to find. Colourful terrace houses and inviting pubs overlook the shimmering recess of Bertraghboy Bay, which is home to dramatic tidal flows, lobster trawlers and traditional *currachs* with tarred canvas bottoms stretched over wicker frames.

Sights & Activities

Roundstone Musical Instruments MUSIC
(www.bodhran.com; IDA Craft Park; 9am-7pm Jul-Sep, 9.30am-6pm Mon-Sat Oct-Jun) Just south of

the village is Malachy Kearns' music shop, home to Ireland's only full-time maker of traditional bodhráns. Watch him work, and buy a tin whistle, harp or booklet filled with Irish ballads; there's also a small free folk museum and a cafe. Adjacent **craft shops** sell everything from fine pottery (don't miss **Roundstone Ceramics**) to sweaters.

Mt Errisberg WALKING

Looming above the stone pier is Mt Errisberg (298m), the only significant hill along this section of coastline. The pleasant walk from Roundstone to the top takes about two hours; just follow the small road past O'Dowd's pub in the centre of the village. From the summit wonderful views range across the bay to the distant humps of the Twelve Bens.

Sleeping & Eating

★Wits End B&B B&B €

(☎095-35813; www.roundstoneaccommodation.com; Main St; s/d from €35/60; ⊙Mar-Nov; 📶) Right in the centre of town and run by the lovely and unflappable Eileen, this place looking over the road to the water has five rooms, many with sea view. It's basic but comfortable and is a mere stumble from some fine pubs.

★Island View B&B B&B €

(☎095-35701; www.islandview.ie; Main St; s €40-45, d €60-70; 📶) At the heart of Roundstone, this delightful, spick-and-span B&B has lots of little plush touches and supreme care and attention from owner (and teacher) Aisling, who keeps things constantly fresh. Most rooms face the bay.

★O'Dowd's SEAFOOD €€

(☎091-35809; www.odowdsseafoodbar.com; Main St; mains €13-27, 2-course dinner 5-7pm €20; ⊙restaurant 10am-9.30pm Jun-Sep, to 9pm Oct-May; 📶) This well-worn, comfortable old pub hasn't lost any of its authenticity since it starred in the 1997 Hollywood flick *The Matchmaker*. Specialities at its adjoining restaurant include seafood sourced off the old stone dock right across the street, while produce comes from its garden. There's a good list of Irish microbrews and you can get breakfast before noon.

Roundstone to Clifden

The R341 shadows the coast from Roundstone to Clifden. About 2.5km from Roundstone, look for the turn to **Gurteen Bay** (sometimes spelt Gorteen Bay); after a further 800m there is a turn for **Dog's Bay**. Together, the pair form the two sides of a dog-bone-shaped peninsula lined with idyllic beaches.

At **Ballyconneely** take a detour west off the R341 and visit **Connemara Smokehouse** (☎095-23739; www.smokehouse.ie; Bunnowen Pier; ⊙9am-1pm & 2-5pm Mon-Fri). Tours on Wednesday at 3pm from June to August show you all about how the region's iconic salmon is smoked and you get to try some samples.

WORTH A TRIP

BOGGY DETOUR TO CLIFDEN

Away from the coast, there is an alternative route between Roundstone and Clifden through protected **Roundstone Bog**. The winding road passes through magnificently eerie, water-logged desolation. They say locals who believe the bog is haunted won't drive this road at night. In summer, you might see peat being harvested by hand, as blanket bogs cannot be cut mechanically. The road runs west from a junction on the R341 about 4km north of Roundstone. It rejoins the R341 at Ballinaboy.

Clifden & Around

POP 2100

Connemara's 'capital', Clifden (An Clochán), is an appealing Victorian-era country town with a vaguely harp-shaped oval of streets offering evocative strolls. A definitive stop on the Wild Atlantic Way, it presides over the head of the narrow bay where the River Owenglin tumbles into the sea.

Sights & Activities

This is pony country and rides along the beaches are popular. You can see the ponies at their swiftest during the annual **Connemara Pony Show** (www.cpbs.ie; ⊙mid-Aug) which draws punters from across western Ireland.

★Sky Road SCENIC DRIVE

This 12km route traces a spectacular loop out to the township of Kingston and back to Clifden, taking in some rugged, stunningly beautiful coastal scenery en route. The round trip of about 12km can be easily walked or cycled; timing things to catch the sun dipping into the Atlantic is best, and there are several lookout points where you can park the car. Head directly west from Clifden's Market Sq.

Connemara Heritage & History Centre MUSEUM
(www.connemaraheritage.com; N59, Lettershea; adult/child €8/4; 10am-6pm Apr-Oct;) Farmer Dan O'Hara lived here until his eviction from the farm and subsequent emigration to New York, where he ended up selling matches on the street. Its present owners have restored the property, turning it into a window onto lost traditional ways, with demonstrations of bog cutting, thatching, sheep shearing and so on. It's possible to stay at the farmhouse in more comfort than Dan ever enjoyed. The homestead is 7km east of Clifden with last admission an hour before closing.

Station House Museum MUSEUM
(Clifden Station House; www.connemara-pony.net/station.htm; off Hulk St; adult/child €2/1; 10am-5pm Mon-Sat, noon-4pm Sun May-Oct) Located in an old train shed, this small museum is devoted to the story of local ponies and various historic events.

Mannion's Bikes BICYCLE RENTAL
(www.clifdenbikes.com; Bridge St; bike rental from adult/child €15/10 per day; 9am-6pm Mon-Sat, 10am-noon Sun) Has a large selection of bikes, including electric bikes.

Errislannan Manor HORSE RIDING
(095-21134; www.connemaraponyriding.com; Ballyconneely Rd/R341; rides & treks per hour from €30) Guides provide lessons and lead treks along the beach and up into the hills on the iconic local ponies. It's 3.5km south of Clifden.

Sleeping

Numerous attractive choices in the centre allow you to easily partake of Clifden's many charms.

Acton's Eco Beach CAMPGROUND €
(095-44036; www.actonsbeachsidecamping.com; Omey Island/Claddaghduff Rd; sites from €15) With its own white-sand beach, this ecologically aware camping ground is a fine holiday refuge. It's 7km west of Clifden. Ask about shuttle services.

Clifden Town Hostel HOSTEL €
(095-21076; www.clifdentownhostel.com; Market St; dm €17-20, s from €25, d from €40) Right in the centre of town, this cheery hostel is set in a cream-coloured house framed by big picture windows, with sunlit rooms and 34 beds.

Ben View House B&B €
(095-21256; www.benviewhouse.com; Bridge St; s/d from €45/70;) Helpful owner Eileen runs this central 1848 townhouse, with vintage charm provided by polished silver, a riot of antiques and old-fashioned hospitality. Wi-fi is a bit shaky upstairs. No parking but there's a free car park nearby.

★ **Dolphin Beach** B&B €€
(095-21204; www.dolphinbeachhouse.com; Lower Sky Rd; s from €85, d €100-140, dinner €40;) This exquisite B&B, set amid some of Connemara's best coastal scenery, does everything right. The emphasis is on style, tranquillity, relaxation and gorgeous views, a formula that can be hard to tear yourself away from. It's 5km west of Clifden, tucked away off the Lower Sky Rd.

★ **Quay House** HOTEL €€
(095-21369; www.thequayhouse.com; Beach Rd; s from €95, d €135-150; mid-Mar–mid-Nov;)

BRIDGING THE QUIET MAN

Whenever an American cable TV station needs a ratings boost with older viewers, they trot out the iconic 1952 film *The Quiet Man*. Starring John Wayne and filmed in lavish colour to capture his co-star Maureen O'Hara's crimson locks, the romantic comedy portrays rural Irish life, replete with drinking and fighting.

Director John Ford returned to his Irish roots and filmed the movie almost entirely on location in Connemara and the little village of Cong, just over the border in County Mayo. One of the most photogenic spots from the film, the eponymous **Quiet Man Bridge**, is just 3km west of Oughterard off the N59. Looking much as it did in the film, the picture-perfect little arched span (whose original name was Leam Bridge) would be a lovely spot even without screen immortality. Purists will note, however, that the scene based here included close-ups from a cheesy set back in Hollywood.

Down by the harbour, a 10-minute walk from town, this rambling 1820 house has 14 rooms filled with antiques but manages an unfussy style that seems contemporary. Run by an offshoot of the Foyle family of hoteliers, it has served as both a convent and Franciscan monastery.

Dun Ri Guesthouse INN €€
(☎095-21625; www.dunri.ie; Hulk St; r €60-100;) With a small, amiable white guard dog and a friendly owner, this appealing place just down the hill from the centre and not far from the pony track has 13 comfortable rooms, all in good condition.

Foyles Hotel HOTEL €€
(☎095-21801; www.foyleshotel.com; Main St; s €45-90, d €70-140; Feb-Dec; @) A creamy-white landmark in the centre of town, Clifden's oldest hotel has been in the same family for decades. Oils hang from the walls of the stately lobby, service is accommodating and embers glow in the fireplace. Of the 25 comfy rooms, aim for one of the more spacious, high-ceiling, front-facing bay-window rooms. Breakfast is included.

Eating & Drinking

Pubs and restaurants cluster around Clifden's town centre. As elsewhere in these parts, seafood reigns supreme.

★**Connemara Hamper** DELI €
(www.connemarahamper.com; Lower Market St; snacks from €3; 10am-5pm Mon-Sat) The jolly ladies here will gladly package up a chicken and leek pie or other savoury treat for your picnic. There's a wide range of prepared foods and fresh breads.

Upstairs/Downstairs CAFE €
(Main St; mains from €5; 9am-5.30pm Mon-Fri, 10am-5.30pm Sat;) Light and bright, this two-floor Main St cafe is ideal for snacking and caffeine fixes, with excellent sandwiches and thirst-busting real fruit smoothies.

★**Mitchell's** SEAFOOD €€
(☎095-21867; www.mitchellsrestaurantclifden.com; Market St; lunch mains €8-12, dinner mains €15-25; noon-10pm Mar-Oct) Seafood takes centre stage at this elegant spot. From a velvety chowder right through a long list of ever-changing and inventive specials, the produce of the surrounding waters is honoured. The wine list does the food justice. Book for dinner. (Lunch includes sandwiches and casual fare.)

Off the Square SEAFOOD €€
(www.offthesquarerestaurant.com; Main St; mains €10-25; 9am-10pm) Mediterranean flavours accent the fare at this tasty bistro with casual lunch dishes giving way to more complex meals at night. Beyond fine seafood, there are locally sourced steaks and excellent breakfasts.

Shopping

Clifden Bookshop BOOKS
(Main St; 9am-6pm Mon-Fri, 10am-6pm Sat, 11am-5pm Sun) Good for local titles and maps.

Information

There are banks with ATMs around Market Sq, as well as a large supermarket.

Tourist Office (www.clifdenchamber.ie; Galway Rd/N59; 10am-5pm Mon-Sat Easter-Jun & Sep, 10am-5pm daily Jul & Aug) In the Clifden Station House complex.

Getting There & Around

Bus Éireann (www.buseireann.ie) and **Citylink** (www.citylink.ie) have several services daily to Galway along the N59. Fares start at €14.50 and the trip takes 90 minutes, passing Oughterard on the way.

Claddaghduff & Omey Island

Following the ragged and rugged coastline north of Clifden brings you to the tiny village of **Claddaghduff** (An Cladach Dubh), which is signposted off the road to Cleggan. If you turn west here down by the Catholic church, you will come out on **Omey Strand**, and at low tide you can drive or walk across the sand to **Omey Island** (population 20), a low islet of rock, grass, sand and a handful of houses. Follow the blue arrow signs. During summer, horse races are held on Omey Strand.

Cleggan

POP 250

Most visitors ignore Cleggan (An Cloiggean), 16km northwest of Clifden, to hop on a ferry straight to Inishbofin, but the tiny fishing port has an enduring charm that starts right at its boat-lined docks. West of Cleggan, narrow looping roads follow the spectacular shoreline.

Sleeping & Eating

Oliver's SEAFOOD, PUB €€
(☎095-44640; www.oliversbar.com; lunch mains €10-15; ⏲12.30-3pm & 6-9pm) Oliver's is a locally loved seafood pub with a classic facade as black as a pint of Guinness. Specials depend on the catch but you can always get the crab claws fried in garlic. Check out the old nautical radio on the bar. Upstairs are six pleasant B&B rooms (from €60), full of sea breeze and, when the sun obliges, Connemara light.

Getting There & Away

Citylink (www.citylink.ie) buses continue to Cleggan three times daily from Clifden.

Inishbofin

POP 160

By day sleepy Inishbofin is a haven of tranquillity. You can walk or bike its narrow, deserted lanes, green pastures and sandy beaches, with farm animals and seals for company. But with no *gardaí* (police) to enforce closing times at the pub, at night – you guessed it – Inishbofin has mighty fine craic.

Situated 9km offshore, Inishbofin is compact – 6km long by 3km wide – and its highest point is a mere 86m above sea level.

Sights & Activities

St Colman exiled himself to Inishbofin in AD 664, after he fell out with the Church over its adoption of a new calendar. He set up a monastery, supposedly northeast of the harbour, where the more recent ruins of a small 13th-century **church** still stand. The **Parish Church of St Colman** is a short walk east of the pier, its interior illuminated by the soft light of its stained glass. Grace O'Malley, the famous pirate queen, used Inishbofin as a base in the 16th century, and Cromwell's forces captured the island in 1652, using it to jail priests and clerics.

Inishbofin's pristine waters offer superior **scuba diving** and the **beaches** are superb.

★**Walking Trails** WALKING
(www.inishbofin.com) Evocative trails encourage exploring. There are several looped routes, which you can download from the island website. A very manageable walk can be made north of the Doonmore Hotel (a 15-minute walk west of the pier) to Lough Bó Finne near the northern shore, from which the island gets its name (*bó finne* means 'white cow').

Heritage Museum MUSEUM
(⏲hours vary) FREE A short walk to the right from the pier, the small but comprehensive museum gives an overview of the island's history.

Kings Bicycle Hire BICYCLE RENTAL
(☎095-45833; on the pier; rental per day from €12; ⏲usually open for ferry arrivals) The island is well-suited for cycling – albeit not very far. Kings is at the pier.

Horse Rides HORSE RIDING
(☎087-950 1545; www.inishbofinequestriancentre.com; ⏲9am-6pm) The Inishbofin Equestrian Centre offers horse-riding lessons and horseback treks around the island.

Festivals & Events

Inishbofin Arts Festival CULTURE
(www.inishbofin.com) The island's creative and cultural juices start flowing during this weekend festival in mid-May, which includes accordion workshops, archaeological walks, art exhibitions and concerts by high-profile Irish bands.

Sleeping & Eating

The hotels have good restaurants and there's an excellent pub.

Inishbofin Island Hostel HOSTEL €
(☎095-45855; www.inishbofin-hostel.ie; camping per person €10, dm €15-18, d €40-50; ⏲Easter-Sep) In an old farmhouse, this snug 38-bed hostel has a conservatory with panoramic views, pleasant and quite spacious shared shower six-bed dorms, doubles with shared shower, scenic campsites and DIY brekkie. It's 500m up from the ferry dock.

Lapwing House B&B €
(☎095-45996; www.inishbofin.com/lapwing-house-bb; per person from €35;) Named after the local bird species which breeds on the island (let inspiration take flight), this family-run B&B in a vintage-style building has two rooms. It is a 10-minute walk north from the pier.

Dolphin Hotel & Restaurant INN €€
(☎095-45991; www.dolphinhotel.ie; s €55, d €90-100; ⏲Apr-Sep; @) Guest rooms are pleasant with large flat-screen TVs at this trim 11-room choice. Solar panels on the roof and an organic kitchen garden lend green cred. Local seafood and vegetarian dishes dominate the menu. There is a two-night minimum stay at weekends. Pick up from pier included.

Inishbofin House Hotel & Marine Spa HOTEL €€
(☎095-45809; www.inishbofinhouse.com; s €60-90, d €70-140) A six-minute walk east of the pier, this smart and modern hotel has an excellent spa, a library and a large living room overlooking a cove. Some rooms come with sea view and balcony and all are designed with contemporary flair. Wi-fi can be a bit twitchy in some rooms, so ask.

Information

Inishbofin's small post office has a grocery shop. There are no ATMs and most businesses only accept cash. There's a small and pricey shop a short walk to the west of the pier.

The **tourism association** (☎095-45861; www.inishbofin.com) has good info, including detailed online walking guides.

Getting There & Away

Ferries from Cleggan to Inishbofin take 30 to 45 minutes and are run by **Island Discovery** (☎095-45894/19; www.inishbofinislanddiscovery.com; adult/child return €20/10). In low season there is one ferry a day, rising to three in summer. Dolphins often swim alongside the boats. Confirm ahead, as ferries may be cancelled when seas are rough.

Letterfrack & Around

POP 200

Founded by Quakers in the mid-19th century, Letterfrack (Leitir Fraic) is a crossroads with a few pubs and B&Bs. But the forested setting and nearby coast are a magnet for outdoors adventure seekers. A 4km walk to the peak of **Tully Mountain** takes 40 minutes and affords wonderful ocean views.

Sights

★**Connemara National Park** PARK
(www.connemaranationalpark.ie; off N59; ⏲visitor centre 9am-5.30pm Mar-Oct, park 24hr) FREE Immediately southeast of Letterfrack, Connemara National Park spans 2000 dramatic hectares of bog, mountain and heath. The visitor centre is in a beautiful setting off a parking area 300m south of the Letterfrack crossroads.

The **visitor centre** offers an introduction to the park's flora, fauna and geology, and visitors can scrutinise maps and various trails here before heading out into the park. Various types of flora and fauna native to the area are explained, including the elephant hawkmoth and red deer. There's a tearoom.

WORTH A TRIP

CONNEMARA'S NORTH COAST

The north coast of Connemara is encrusted with gorgeous beaches, raw mountain vistas and stark views out to the moody sea.

Eschew the N59 for a series of small roads that follow the twists and turns along the coast for about 15km. Start at **Letterfrack**, where a narrow track leads northwest. Follow various small roads, sticking as close to the water as you can. Watch for sheep. The land here seems to be in the midst of a beautiful dissolution into the sea.

At **Renvyle** you can pause for the night. **Renvyle Beach Caravan & Camping** (☎095-43462; www.renvylebeachcaravanpark.com; Renvyle; campsites €10-20; ⏲Easter-Sep) has campsites on a grassy expanse with direct access to a sandy beach. **Renvyle House Hotel** (☎095-43511; www.renvyle.com; Renvyle; r €70-250; 📶🏊) is a luxurious 68-room converted country estate set on 80 hectares.

Continue east, past a few fine country pubs at the tiny crossroads of **Tully Cross**. Stick to the coast and stop often – especially on sunny days to marvel at the rich kaleidoscope of colours: rich cobalt sea, cerulean sky, emerald-green grass, brown hills, slate-grey rocks and white-sand beaches. The beach horse-racing sequences for *The Quiet Man* were shot at **Lettergesh**.

Look for a turn to **Rosroe Quay**, where a magnificent crescent of sand awaits at **Glassillaun Beach**. If you're drawn to the beauty of the water, **Scuba Dive West** (☎095-43922; www.scubadivewest.com) runs highly recommended courses and dives around the surrounding coastlines and islands. Rates span the gamut.

Continue southeast along the final 5km stretch of road that runs along **Lough Fee**. In spring when the gorse explodes in yellow bloom, the views here are, again, simply breathtaking.

The park encloses a number of the **Twelve Bens**, including Bencullagh, Benbrack and Benbaun. The heart of the park is **Gleann Mór** (Big Glen), through which the River Polladirk flows. There's fine walking up the glen and over the surrounding mountains. There are also short self-guided walks and, if the Bens look too daunting, you can hike up Diamond Hill nearby.

Guided nature walks (11am Jul & Aug) led by park rangers depart from the visitor centre several days a week.

Kylemore Abbey HISTORIC BUILDING
(www.kylemoreabbey.com; off N59; adult/child €13/free; 9am-6pm Apr-Sep, 10am-4.30pm Oct-Mar) Photogenically perched on the shores of Pollacapall Lough, 4.5km east of Letterfrack, this crenulated 19th-century neo-Gothic fantasy was built for a wealthy English businessman, Mitchell Henry, who spent his honeymoon in Connemara. Only a selection of rooms are open to visitors, but you can wander down the lake to the **Gothic church** and admission includes the breathtaking and extravagant **Victorian walled gardens**, around a 20-minute walk away (or take the free shuttle bus, every 15 minutes). A formal composition in the wildness of Connemara, the gardens are sublime.

Run by Benedictine nuns, the abbey served as the Kylemore Abbey School from 1923 to 2010, teaching Catholic girls. There is a cafe and tea house on the grounds which also offers hikes and woodland walks. Kylemore's tranquillity is shattered in high summer with the arrival of dozens of tour coaches and an endless stream of cars.

Sleeping

Letterfrack Lodge HOSTEL €
(095-41222; www.letterfracklodge.com; Letterfrack; campsites from €12, dm €15-18, s €25-60, d €40-60, tr €54-75, €60-80;) Close to the Letterfrack crossroads, dorms come in a variety of sizes, but all are spacious. Doubles are like a basic B&B. Mike, the enthusiastic owner, is a great source of info on walks of all kinds through the region. Breakfast included in low-season. No credit cards.

Getting There & Away

Bus Éireann (www.buseireann.ie) and **Citylink** (www.citylink.ie) buses continue to Letterfrack at least once a day from Clifden, 15km southwest on the N59.

Leenane & Killary Harbour

The small village of Leenane (also spelled Leenaun) drowses on the shore of dramatic Killary Harbour. Dotted with mussel rafts, the long, narrow harbour is Ireland's only fjord – maybe. Slicing 16km inland and more than 45m deep in the centre, it certainly looks like a fjord, although some scientific studies suggest it may not actually have been glaciated. **Mt Mweelrea** (819m) towers to its north.

From here the R335 heads north into County Mayo's stunning Doolough Valley.

The local **website** (www.leenanevillage.com) is a good source of info.

Sights

★ **Sheep & Wool Centre** MUSEUM
(www.sheepandwoolcentre.com; Main St; adult/child €5/3; 9.30am-6pm Apr-Oct) This compelling little museum introduces you to spinning and weaving demonstrations, and you can learn about the history of dyeing and all about sheep and wool. The centre's shop sells locally made handcrafts as well as topographical walking maps, and there's a cafe.

Activities

Killary Cruises BOAT CRUISE
(091-566 736; www.killarycruises.com; N59; adult/child €21/10; Apr-Oct) From Nancy's Point, about 2km west of Leenane, Killary Cruises offers 1½-hour cruises of Killary Harbour. Dolphins leap around the boat, which passes by a mussel farm and stops at a salmon farm. There are four cruises daily in summer, with the first at 10.30am.

Killary Adventure Centre ADVENTURE SPORTS
(095-43411; www.killaryadventure.com; off N59; half-day activity rates adult/child from €46/31; 10am-5pm) There's canoeing, sea kayaking, sailing, rock climbing, windsurfing, orienteering, day hikes, clay pigeon shooting and other activities at this adventure centre about 3km west of Leenane. It also has decent dorm (€20 to €25) and double rooms (€33 to €35), all with underfloor heating.

Walks WALKING
Several excellent walks range from Leenane, including one to **Aasleagh Waterfall** (Eas Liath), about 3km away on the northeastern side of Killary Harbour. Also from Leenane, the road runs west for about 2km along the

southern shore. Where the highway veers inland, walkers can continue on an old road along the shore to the tiny fishing community of **Rosroe Quay**.

Sleeping & Eating

Farmers and other locals come for quiet pints and warming Irish coffees at the gentle sweep of traditional pubs near the bridge. Savour a pint and a meal outside at one of the picnic tables or inside amid the dark-wood panelling and enormous open fireplaces.

Sleepzone Connemara HOSTEL €
(095-42929; www.sleepzone.ie; off N59; campsites from €12, dm €16-25, r €30-70; Mar-Oct;) This renovated 19th-century property has over 100 beds in clean dorms with their own bathrooms and private rooms with direct access down to the water. Popular with walkers, amenities include a bar, barbecue terrace, bike hire and discounts at the Killary Adventure Centre next door. The hostel is 6km west of Leenane; there are transport links to its hostel in Galway city.

★**Delphi Lodge** LODGE €€€
(095-42222; www.delphilodge.ie; off R335; s/d/ste from €140/230/280;) Set among stunning mountain and lake vistas, this isolated 1830s country house has 13 smart bedrooms and a bevy of common areas including a library and billiards room. Cooking is modern Irish, sourced locally, with meals at a vast communal table. Outside is all walks, fishing and shooting. It's 13km northwest of Leenane and also rents out five cottages on the estate. Half board is an extra €55.

★**Blackberry Cafe** MODERN IRISH €€
(095-42240; www.blackberryrestaurant.ie; Main St; lunch mains €11-17, dinner mains €16-24; 10am-4pm & 6-9pm Easter-Sep, closed Tue Apr-May & Sep;) Connemara smoked salmon, chunky chowder and oysters (€20 per dozen) are some of the treats on offer all day at this smart wood-floored gem of a cafe in the centre of Leenane with water views. At night, dinners are more elaborate affairs. Music is from the Enya camp.

SOUTH OF GALWAY CITY

Take time to smell the oysters on the busy seaside route between Galway city and County Clare. At Kilcolgan, veer east off the N18 and you'll be rewarded with villages such as Kinvara, whose charms may play havoc with your schedule – if you have one.

Clarinbridge & Kilcolgan

POP 1900

Some 16km south of Galway, Clarinbridge (Droichead an Chláirin) and Kilcolgan (Cill Cholgáin) are at their busiest during the postsummer **Clarinbridge Oyster Festival** (www.clarenbridge.com; mid-Sep). However, the oysters are actually at their best from May through to Aug.

Oysters are celebrated year-round at **Paddy Burke's Oyster Inn** (www.paddyburkesgalway.com; off N18, Clarinbridge; mains €13-27; 10.30am-10pm Mon-Sat, from noon Sun), a thatched inn by the bridge dishing up heaped servings in a roadside location on the N18.

Moran's Oyster Cottage (www.moransoystercottage.com; The Weir, Kilcolgan; mains €15-25; noon-9.30pm Sun-Thu, noon-10pm Fri & Sat) is a thatched pub and restaurant with a facade as plain as the inside of an oyster shell. Find a seat on the terrace overlooking Dunbulcaun Bay, where the oysters are reared before they arrive on your plate, and you'll think the world's your... It's a well-marked 2km west of the noxious N18, in a quiet cove near Kilcolgan.

Kinvara

POP 650

The small stone harbour of Kinvara (sometimes spelt Kinvarra) sits smugly at the southeastern corner of Galway Bay, which accounts for its Irish name, 'Cinn Mhara' (Head of the Sea). A charming and good-looking village, it makes an excellent pit stop between Galway and Clare. For glorious views of the bay, head out from Kinvara on the N67 towards Ballyvaughan for around 6km, then take the left towards Carron to a **lookout** around 400m up on the right-hand side of the road.

Kinvara's **website** (www.kinvara.com) has info.

Sights

★**Dunguaire Castle** HISTORIC BUILDING
(www.shannonheritage.com; off N67; adult/child €6/3; 10am-4pm Apr-early Oct) Erected around 1520 by the O'Hynes clan, Dunguaire Castle is widely believed to occupy the former site of the 6th-century royal palace of

Guaire Aidhne, the king of Connaught. Lady Christabel Ampthill restored the castle after buying it for the equivalent of €500 and lived here from the 1950s to the 1970s; her bedroom was in the crafts studio, with her living room at the very top, beneath a new pitched roof.

Climb to the roof for glorious views of Galway Bay and Kinvara. The least authentic way to visit the castle is to attend a **medieval banquet** (☎061-360 788; www.shannonheritage.com; banquet adult/child €50/25; ⏰5.30pm & 8.45pm Apr-Oct).

Festivals & Events

Fleadh na gCuach MUSIC

A big date on Kinvara's annual calendar is the Cuckoo Festival in early May, a traditional music festival that features over 100 musicians performing at upwards of 50 organised sessions. Spin-off events include a parade.

Cruinniú na mBáid BOAT RACES

(www.cruinniunambad.com) Traditional Galway hooker sailing boats race here on the second weekend of August in the Cruinniú na mBáid (Gathering of the Boats).

Sleeping

Kinvara Guesthouse B&B €

(☎091-638 562; The Square; d & tw from €60; 📶) This spacious and dapper four-star place on Main St is a cut above the rest, with a wide variety of well-furnished and handsome rooms, including family rooms (from €85).

Eating & Drinking

Kinvara has good places to feast on the bounty of its seaside location; a bevy of atmospheric pubs only add to the joy. You won't miss out at the appropriately named **Fahy's Travellers Inn** (☎091-637 116; Main St) and nearby **Connolly's** (☎091-637 131; Main St) on the quay.

Strawberry Hedgehog Cafe CAFE €

(The Quay; mains from €5; ⏰11am-5pm winter, 9.30am-6pm summer; 📶) Eclectically decorated with MC Escher prints and pics of Hendrix and Lennon, this funky, boho spot is excellent for chilling out with the soup of the day (whether it's Indian lentil soup or Thai carrot, coconut and chili), scones, Bakewell tarts, fresh wheatgrass juices, organic coffee, hot chocs or one of its fine smoothies.

Pier Head SEAFOOD €€

(☎091-638 188; www.pierhead.ie; The Quay; €17-30; ⏰noon-3.30pm & 5-9.30pm) Popular with yachties who tie up out front, this modern restaurant and pub has fine views over the brine. Dishes includes local lobster cooked in garlic, mussels, lots of oysters, pan-fried cod in white wine and Atlantic seafood chowder.

Green's Bar PUB

(Main St; ⏰2pm-midnight) With several hundred whiskeys on shelves behind the bar that look ready to collapse, Green's is quite a sight. Painted a lovely green on the outside, this congenial one-room affair and family pub run by the affable Mary is home to regular gatherings of local drinkers and spontaneous sessions of traditional music.

Getting There & Away

Bus Éireann (www.buseireann.ie) links Kinvara with Galway city (30 minutes) and towns in County Clare, such as Doolin, up to three times daily.

EASTERN GALWAY

Lough Corrib separates eastern Galway from the dramatic landscape of Connemara and the county's western coast, and this region is markedly different. This is farm country and there's nary a hint of the geologic drama and cultural excitement that exists in the west of the county. Several diversions provide good reason to exit the M6 to Dublin.

Information

Galway East Tourism (www.galwayeast.com) has regional information.

Getting There & Away

Bus Éireann (www.buseireann.ie) local services connect Galway with Athenry, Ballinasloe and Loughrea.

Athenry

POP 3900

Just 16km east of Galway, Athenry (pronounced 'Athen-rye') constitutes one of Ireland's most intact collections of medieval architecture, with a magnificent castle, the Medieval Parish Church of St Mary's, a **Dominican priory**, an original **market cross** and the **North Gate**, which you can drive through. An impressive 75% of the lengthy town walls survive. For some reason rather neglected, Athenry sees that rare confluence of impressive heritage and low visitor numbers.

Athenry takes its name from a nearby ford (*áth* in Irish) that crosses the River Clare east of the settlement and was the meeting point for three kingdoms, hence Áth an Rí (Ford of the Kings).

Athenry's name is synonymous with the stirring song 'The Fields of Athenry', composed by Pete St John in the 1970s, which recounts incarceration resulting from the Famine.

Sights

Athenry Castle CASTLE
(www.heritageireland.ie; adult/child €4/2; 9.30am-6pm Easter-Sep) The most imposing remnant of this restored Norman-era castle is its rectangular keep, housing the **Great Hall** – accessed on the 1st floor via a wooden staircase. There's an informative audiovisual presentation on the 3rd floor. On the far side of the Great Hall is the **garderobe** – a toilet that emptied straight down the rear wall.

Heritage Centre MUSEUM
(091-844 661; www.athenryheritagecentre.com; St Mary's, The Square; adult/child €7.50/5; hours vary) A big hit with kids, this rewarding and informative heritage centre, next to the medieval parish Church of St Mary's, colourfully introduces the town's historic heritage and illustrates all the gruesome details of life in medieval Athenry, including a ghoulish array of torture implements. You can dress up in period costume, and take archery lessons (one-hour lesson €25) out back. Download a walking tour map from the website. Call ahead as the heritage centre may be shut for school visits.

Athenry Dominican Priory RUIN
(Seamus Lynch 086 736 1257; Bridge St; by appointment) Destroyed by Cromwellian troops in 1652, these marvellous 13th-century priory ruins are only accessible by contacting Seamus, who will show you around. The priory tower survived till 1845, before collapsing. Tombs and grave slabs within the ruins include that of the Anglo-Irish Lord Meiler de Bermingham, founder of the priory.

Eating

Old Barracks Pantry CAFE **€€**
(www.oldbarracks.ie; Main St; daytime mains €5-10, evening mains €12.50-19.50; 9am-6pm Mon-Sat, 10am-6pm Sun, bistro 5-8pm Thu-Sat) This bakery offers fine home-baked goodies, restorative breakfasts and enticing dishes from the restaurant kitchen during the day, with more elaborate bistro fare in the evenings from Thursday to Saturday.

Loughrea & Around

POP 5000

Named for the little lake at its southern edge, Loughrea (Baile Locha Riach) is a bustling market town 26km southeast of Galway. The town has the shallow remnant of a medieval **moat**, which runs from the lake at Fair Green near the cathedral to the River Loughrea north of town. Since the opening of the M6, the town is less frenetic with traffic and is good for a stroll.

Not to be confused with St Brendan's Church on Church St, which is now a library, **St Brendan's Catholic Cathedral** (Barrack St; 11.30am-1pm & 2-5.30pm Mon-Fri), dating from 1902, is renowned for its Celtic-revival stained-glass windows, furnishings and polished granite columns.

Near Bullaun, 7km north of Loughrea on the R350, is the pillarlike **Turoe Stone**, covered in delicate La Tène–style relief carvings. It dates from between 300 BC and AD 100 and was found at an Iron Age fort a few kilometres away.

East to Ballinasloe, 6.5km from Loughrea, the **Dartfield Horse Museum & Park** (www.dartfield.com; off R446; museum adult/child €6.50/3.50, rides per hour/half-hour €25/15; 9am-6pm;) allows horse lovers to learn about the horse's role in Irish history. The pony rides thrill kids and you can book longer riding adventures on horseback.

Gort & Around

POP 2700

If you're a fan of WB Yeats, two sights connected to the great poet near the agricultural town of Gort are a worthwhile detour on your way to or from Galway on the M/N18.

Sights

Central to Gort is the **Square**, with its personable **Christ the King statue** and shop-filled streets radiating out. But most sights are just outside town.

★Thoor Ballylee HISTORIC BUILDING

(☎091-537 700; www.yeatsthoorballylee.org; Peterswell; ⏲9.30am-5pm Mon-Sat May-Sep) This 16th-century Norman tower, in a truly inspired setting by a stream, was the summer home of WB Yeats from 1921 to 1929 and was the inspiration for one of his best-known works, *The Tower*. At the time of writing, the tower was closed after flood damage, but was due to reopen after restoration. From Gort take the Loughrea road (N66) for about 3km northeast and look for signs – but these are often misaligned – or just missing.

Coole Park PARK

(www.coolepark.ie; off N18; ⏲8am-7.30pm summer, 8am-6pm winter) FREE Once home of Lady Augusta Gregory, cofounder of the Abbey Theatre and a patron of WB Yeats, the house here was demolished by nitwit bureaucrats in 1941. But displays recall its literary legacy and the present-day nature reserve is a beautiful place to stroll. Look for the autograph tree, on which many of Lady Gregory's literary guests carved their initials. It's about 3km north of Gort.

There's a visitor centre (open in summer months) and a tearoom.

Kiltartan Gregory Museum MUSEUM

(Kiltartan Cross; adult/child €3/1; ⏲11am-5pm daily Jun-Aug, 1-5pm Sun May & Sep) Housed in an old schoolhouse, this museum traces the life of WB Yeats' literary patron, Lady Augusta Gregory. It's close to Coole Park, the site of Lady Gregory's former home.

★Kilmacduagh HISTORIC SITE

(off R460) About 5km southwest of Gort, this extensive monastic site beside a small lake includes a well-preserved 34m-high round tower, the remains of a small 14th-century cathedral (Teampall Mór MacDuagh), an oratory dedicated to St John the Baptist and other little chapels. The original monastery is thought to have been founded by St Colman MacDuagh at the beginning of the 7th century.

ℹ Getting There & Away

The M18 from Ennis stops at Gort and tosses drivers onto the less fancy N18 (latest date for completion of the M18 to the M6 is 2016). Still, it has extracted traffic from the centre. Most Galway–Ennis buses stop here, as do trains on the Ennis–Galway railway line.

Counties Mayo & Sligo

Includes ➡

Best Places to Eat

➡ Pantry & Corkscrew (p407)

➡ Hargadons (p420)

➡ Lyons Cafe (p419)

➡ An Port Mór (p407)

Best Places to Stay

➡ St Anthony's Riverside B&B (p406)

➡ Stella Maris (p414)

➡ Ardtarmon House (p429)

➡ Newport House (p408)

Why Go?

Despite their natural wonders and languid charm, Counties Mayo and Sligo remain a well-kept secret, offering all of Ireland's wild, romantic beauty but without the crowds. Mayo is the more rugged of the two, with scraggy peaks, sheer cliffs, heather-covered moors and beautiful offshore islands where life is dictated by the elements. Sligo is more pastoral and its lush fields, fish-filled lakes and flat-topped mountains inspired William Butler Yeats to compose some of Ireland's most ardent verse.

Both counties boast grand stretches of golden sands and legendary breaks that lure the surfing cognoscenti from around the globe. Visit and you'll find all this plus an improbable bounty of prehistoric sites, elegant Georgian towns, little fishing villages and good old-fashioned warm-hearted country hospitality.

When to Go

➡ The weather-beaten shores of Mayo and Sligo can be whipped by brutal winds and rain in winter when only the hardiest tourists and surfers make it here.

➡ If you're interested in catching a swell, spring and autumn are your best shot with September and October favoured by those in the know.

➡ In summer the region bursts into life with oodles of festivals. In July and August you'll get the pick of the crop with the Yeats festival in Sligo and a variety of small traditional-music festivals elsewhere. Plus the weather is often balmy.

Counties Mayo & Sligo Highlights

❶ Follow in St Patrick's footsteps up the conical peak of **Croagh Patrick** (p404).

❷ Hit the waves year-round at **Strandhill** (p422).

❸ Feel ancient powers amid mystical ruins at **Carrowmore Megalithic Cemetery** (p421).

❹ Walk along the starkly beautiful and poignantly desolate **Doolough Valley** (p402).

❺ Ride along the popular **Great Western Greenway** (p408) from Westport to Achill Island.

❻ Go in search of Ireland's pirate queen, Grace O'Malley (Granuaile) on craggy **Clare Island** (p404).

❼ Marvel at the ancient planning of the world's most extensive Stone Age monument at the **Céide Fields** (p414).

COUNTY MAYO

POP 131,200 / AREA 5436 SQ KM

Mayo has wild beauty and haunting landscapes but you'll find few tourists here, which means there are plenty of untapped opportunities for exploration by car, foot, bicycle or horseback. Life here has never been easy and the Potato Famine (1845–51) ravaged the county and prompted mass emigration. Consequently many people with Irish ancestry around the world can trace their roots to this once-plagued land.

Cong

POP 190

Sitting on a sliver-thin isthmus between Lough Corrib and Lough Mask, twee little Cong complies with romantic notions of a traditional Irish village. Time appears to have gone in reverse ever since the evergreen classic *The Quiet Man* was filmed here in 1951. In fact a lot of effort has been made to re-create Cong as it looked for the filming of the movie – even though that was largely the work of Hollywood set designers.

Each year the thatched roof count seems to increase and across from the tourist office there's now a **statue** of Sean Thornton (John Wayne) and Mary Kate Danaher (Maureen O'Hara).

Cong and the region still attract a lot of tourists hoping for a full helping of *The Quiet Man* (p388) cliches (there are more film-related sites just over the border in County Galway). As such, the arrival of the morning's first tour bus instantly doubles the number of people strolling the town's tiny streets, but the wooded trails between the lovely old abbey and stately Ashford Castle offer a respite.

Sights

Cong Abbey HISTORIC SITE

(094-954 6542; Abbey St; dawn-dusk) FREE An evocative reminder of ecclesiastical times past, the weathered shell of Cong's 12th-century Augustinian abbey is scored by a cross-hatch of lines from centuries of exposure to the elements. Nevertheless, several finely sculpted features have survived, including a carved doorway, windows and lovely medieval arches.

Founded in 1120 by Turlough Mór O'Connor, high king of Ireland and king of Connaught, the abbey occupies the site of an earlier 6th-century church. The community once gathered in the chapter house to confess their sins publicly.

From the abbey, moss-encrusted trees guard a path to the river and the diminutive 16th-century **monk's fishing house**, built midway over the river so that the monks could haul their catch straight up.

Ashford Castle Estate HISTORIC SITE

(094-954 6003; www.ashfordcastle.com; grounds adult/child €5/3.50; grounds 9am-dusk) Just beyond Cong Abbey, the village abruptly ends and the woodlands surrounding Ashford Castle begin. First built in 1228 as the seat of the de Burgo family, owners over the years included the Guinness family (of stout fame). Arthur Guinness turned the castle into a regal hunting and fishing lodge, which it remains today. The only way to look inside its restored interior is to stay or dine here. But the surrounding estate is open to the public.

The 140 hectares of parkland, covered with forests, streams and a golf course, is great to explore. **Walking** through the Kinlough Woods gets you away from the golfers and out to the shores of **Lough Corrib**. You can also stroll along the riverbanks to the monk's fishing house.

Quiet Man Museum MUSEUM

(094-954 6089; Circular Rd; adult/child €5/4, location tour €15; 10am-4pm Apr-Oct) Modelled on Sean Thornton's White O'Morn Cottage from *The Quiet Man* film, the museum offers a **location tour** – good for film fanatics and those with a postmodern fascination for the way reality and fiction blur.

Activities

Corrib Cruises BOAT TOUR

(087 283 0799; www.corribcruises.com; Lisloughery Pier; adult/child €20/10) Cruises on Lough Corrib depart from the Ashford Castle pier. A 75-minute history cruise leaves daily year-round at 11am; a two-hour island cruise departs at 2.45pm from June to October and visits Inchagoill, the island at the centre of Lough Corrib with 5th-century monastic ruins. There are also boats to/from Oughterard in County Galway.

Ashford Outdoors KAYAKING

(094-954 6507; www.ashfordoutdoors.com; Ashford Castle; tours from €50, bike rental per day from €40) Pedal the shores and then paddle the waters of Ashford Castle Estate and Lough Corrib on tours with bikes and kayaks.

Sleeping

Nymphsfield House B&B €
(☎094-954 6320; www.nymphsfieldhouse.com; R345, Gortaroe; s/d from €45/65; 🛜) Just northeast of Cong (a pretty 10-minute or 1km walk), this family-run B&B gets every detail just right. Rooms have TVs and free mineral water. There's a place to store your fishing gear and a quaint little breakfast area. There are several other nice B&Bs nearby.

Cong Hostel HOSTEL €
(☎094-954 6089; www.quietman-cong.com; Quay Rd, Lisloughrey; campsite from €10, dm/d from €17/50; @🛜) This well-run hostel, affiliated with Independent Holiday Hostels (IHH), has a *The Quiet Man* screening room showing the film *every* night. Dorm rooms have from four to 14 beds. There is an adjacent camping ground and you can borrow fishing rods.

Ryan's Hotel HOTEL €
(☎094-954 6243; www.ryanshotelcong.ie; Main St; s/d from €45/80; 🛜) Right in the centre of Cong, this maroon-fronted guesthouse has 12 rooms and a guest laundry.

★**Michaeleen's Manor** B&B €€
(☎094-954 6089; www.congbb.com; Quay Rd, Lisloughrey; s/d from €60/80; 🛜) This large, heritage-style home is a shrine to *The Quiet Man*. Each of its 12 comfy rooms is named after a character in the film and decorated with memorabilia and quotations. There's a large fountain replica of Galway's Quiet Man Bridge set in a lush garden. It's about 2km east of Cong.

Lodge at Ashford Castle HOTEL €€€
(☎094-954 5400; www.thelodgeac.com; The Quay; r from €150; 🛜) The lodge, built in the 1820s by Ashford Castle's owners, has rich, contemporary colours and is a good alternative to the castle. The 50 guest rooms and suites are lavishly decorated; some have copper bathtubs. It's on the grounds of Ashford Castle Estate.

Ashford Castle HOTEL €€€
(☎094-954 6003; www.ashford.ie; Cong; r from €400; @🛜) You'll find old-world elegance, 83 exquisite rooms and personalised service at Ashford Castle. It's easily the grandest of the grand in Ireland. Even if you're staying elsewhere, you can come for dinner (from €70) at the posh **George V Dining Room** (be sure to dress up). There are many activities on the namesake estate, including falconry.

Eating & Drinking

★**Hungry Monk** CAFE €
(Abbey St; mains €6-14; ⏲9am-5pm Mon-Sat year-round, Sun Apr-Aug; 🛜) This simple cafe with bright colours and artfully mismatched furniture is a perfect refuge on a misty day. Locally sourced ingredients make up the excellent sandwiches, soups and salads, the luscious cakes are homemade and the coffee is excellent.

Fennel Seed Restaurant IRISH €€
(☎094-954 6004; www.ryanshotelcong.ie; Ryan's Hotel, Main St; bar food €12-21, mains €15-25; ⏲6-9pm Mon-Sat, 1-7pm Sun) Denis Lenihan's culinary skills enjoy widespread acclaim. Don't miss the signature 'smoky bake' pie, filled with trout, salmon, mackerel and haddock. Bar food is served in the adjoining **Crowe's Nest Pub** until 7pm.

★**Wilde's at the Lodge** MODERN IRISH €€€
(☎094-954 5400; www.thelodgeac.com; The Quay, Lisloughrey Lodge; mains €25-29; ⏲6-9pm daily Mar-Oct, Wed-Sun Nov-Feb, 1-3pm Sun year-round) Chef Jonathan Keane and his team forage the mussels, wild herbs and flowers that adorn the dishes at this exquisite restaurant. Produce and meat come from organic local suppliers for a changing menu. You can sample many dishes served on small plates. The restaurant takes its name from Sir William Wilde (father of Oscar), who loved the Lough.

THE FIRST BOYCOTT

It was near the unassuming little village of Neale, near Cong, that the term 'boycott' came into use. In 1880, the Irish Land League, in an effort to press for fair rents and improve the lot of workers, withdrew field hands from the estate of Lord Erne, who owned much of the land in the area. When Lord Erne's land agent, Captain Charles Cunningham Boycott, evicted the striking labourers, the surrounding community began a campaign to ostracise him. Not only did farmers refuse to work his land, people in the town refused to talk to him, provide services or sit next to him in church. The incident attracted the attention of the London papers, and soon Boycott's name was synonymous with such organised, nonviolent protests. Within a few months, Boycott fled Ireland.

Pat Cohan's PUB

(Abbey St; ⌚noon-11pm) In a case of life imitating art, this one-time grocery store was disguised in *The Quiet Man* as the fictional Pat Cohan's. But as *Quiet Man* craziness only grows, it has now become that pub.

Information

The **tourist office** (☎094-954 6542; www.congtourism.com; Abbey St; ⌚10am-1pm & 2-5.30pm daily Mar-Sep, Fri & Sat Oct & Nov) is in the old courthouse building opposite Cong Abbey. The closest ATM is 5km west in Clonbur.

Getting There & Away

Bus Éireann (www.buseireann.ie; Main St) has two buses to Galway (€13.20, 70 minutes) Monday to Saturday, and one to Westport (€13.20, one hour).

Pigeonhole Cave

The Cong area is honeycombed with numerous limestone caves, each with a colourful legend or story to its credit.

Pigeonhole Cave, in a pine forest about 1.5km south of Cong, can be reached via a walking loop from the abbey. Steep, slippery stone steps lead down into the cave, where subterranean water flows in winter. Watch for the white trout of Cong – a mythical woman who turned into a fish to be with her drowned lover.

Doolough Valley & Around

The R335 from Leenane in County Galway to Westport is one of Ireland's most beautiful scenic routes. The desolate Doolough Valley is largely untouched by housing, cut turf or even stone walls. The steep sides of the surrounding mountains simply slide into the steely grey waters of Doo Lough as sheep graze quietly on the hills.

It is also one of Ireland's most poignant spots – the site of a tragic Famine walk in 1849. According to local history, in icy weather, 400 people died along the road as they walked from Louisburgh to Delphi and back. They'd hoped to receive food and aid from a landlord but were refused. Specific details on these events vary depending on the source.

Choose a dry day to tackle the road as curtains of rain can greatly diminish the views. If you have time, wander down the side roads to the north and west of the valley to reach glorious, often-deserted beaches.

Delphi

Geographically *just* inside County Mayo, this swath of mountainous moorland along the spectacular R335 is miles from any significant population, allowing you to set about the serious business of relaxing.

The southern end of the Doolough Valley was named by its most famous resident, the second Marquis of Sligo, who was convinced that it resembled the land around Delphi, Greece. If you can spot the resemblance, you've a better imagination than most. However the beauty of little creeks babbling over boggy countryside against a backdrop of sun- and cloud-dappled stark hillsides is undeniable.

Sleeping & Eating

Delphi Lodge RESORT **€€€**

(☎095-42222; www.delphilodge.ie; off R335; s/d from €170/270; @) A wonderful 1830s Georgian mansion built by the Marquis of Sligo, Delphi Lodge is dwarfed by the mountain backdrop. This 13-room country hotel features beautiful interiors, vast grounds, lovely food (dinner €55) and a serious lack of pretension. It's popular with fishers (half day with fishing tutor €150) and with those simply aiming to relax.

Louisburgh

POP 800

The northern gateway to the Doolough Valley is the appealing village of Louisburgh, founded under curious circumstances in 1795. Based on a simple four-street system known as the Cross, the town was designed and built as a living memorial to a relative of the first Marquis of Sligo, Lord Altamont (John Browne) – his kinsman was killed at the Battle of Louisburgh in Nova Scotia, 1758.

Sights & Activities

The safe, broad beach at **Carrowmore**, just east of the Louisburgh village, offers good views of Croagh Patrick and has a lifeguard on duty in summer. There are also some excellent surf beaches nearby, such as **Carrownisky**.

West and south of Louisburgh, you'll find a web of narrow unmarked roads that wander through the scruffy countryside. The rewards come when you hit the water. A good example is tiny **Killadoon**, from where panoramic ocean views and vast sandy beaches fan out.

Granuaile Heritage Centre MUSEUM
(098-66341; www.granuaile.org; Church St; adult/child €5/2.50; 11am-5pm Mon-Fri) Get a quick but illuminating glimpse into the life and times of Grace O'Malley (Gráinne Ní Mháille or Granuaile; 1530–1603) the infamous pirate queen of Connaught (p404), as well as details of local Famine travails.

Surf Mayo SURFING
(087 621 2508; www.surfmayo.com; Carrownisky Beach; lessons from €27, surfboard & wetsuit rental per day €17; hours vary) Offers surfing lessons and camps at Carrownisky Beach, and rents out gear, including stand-up paddleboards.

Mweelrea Holidays HORSE RIDING
(www.mweelreaholidays.com; off R378, Feenone; horse rides from €30; hours vary) Take a guided horse ride through the dramatic countryside or along the beach. Guided hikes are also offered.

Sleeping & Eating

Ponderosa B&B €
(098-66440; www.ponderosamayo.com; Tooreen Rd; s/d from €45/60; Apr-Oct;) Just 400m east of the Louisburgh town centre, this three-room B&B is set in a modern bungalow.

West View Hotel HOTEL €€
(098-66140; www.westviewhotel.ie; Chapel St; s/d from €45/80;) Right in town, this small 18-room inn has a lashing of contemporary style as well as a restaurant. The bar has trad-music sessions some nights.

Getting There & Away

Bus Éireann (www.buseireann.ie; Mon-Sat) has one bus a day to/from Westport (€8).

Clare Island

POP 125

Clew Bay is dotted with some 365 islands, of which the largest is mountainous **Clare Island** (www.clareisland.info), 5km offshore but half a world away. Dominated by rocky Mt Knockmore (462m), its varied terrain is terrific for walking and climbing, and swimming can be enjoyed at safe, sandy beaches. The island is also one of the dwindling number of places where you can find choughs (resembling blackbirds but with red beaks).

Sights & Activities

Clare Island has the ruins of the Cistercian **Clare Island Abbey** (c 1460) and **Granuaile's Castle**, both associated with the piratical Grace O'Malley. The tower castle was her stronghold, although it was altered considerably when the coastguard took it over in 1831. Grace is said to be buried in the small abbey, which contains a stone inscribed with her family motto: 'Invincible on land and sea'.

The island is a great place to retreat from the world. Among the many hikes, there's a self-guided **archaeological walk** or you can climb **Knockmore**, a 462m hill. Spectacular views abound.

Sleeping & Eating

Clare Island has several good B&Bs.

★ **Go Explore Hostel** HOSTEL €
(098-26307, 087 410 8706; www.goexplorehostel.ie; dm €20-24; Easter-Nov;) This hostel is a delight, with large windows and a terrace overlooking the water. Vintage areas of the complex include a large 1840s fireplace. The pub is an island-wide draw and has good food (mains €8 to €15) and frequent live sessions. All sorts of adventure activities are organised here.

Macalla Farm GUESTHOUSE €€
(087 250 4845; www.macallafarm.ie; 3-day retreats from €340) On a wonderful setting overlooking the island, this guesthouse offers retreats and lessons throughout the year for yoga, natural food, horse riding and more. Guests enjoy organic vegetarian meals.

O'Grady's B&B €€
(098-22991; www.ogradysguesthouse.com; s/d from €60/80; Apr-Sep;) You'll find cosy rooms at this slate-roofed B&B near the pier. Avoid the rain by huddling around the log-burning stove.

Getting There & Around

Ferries depart from Roonagh Quay, 8km west of Louisburgh, around 10 times daily in July and August, two to four times daily the rest of the year. The trip takes 20 minutes (€15/8 per adult/child return).

You can usually rent **bikes** (per day about €15) at the pier and at your accommodation. There are also taxis.

Clare Island Ferries (098-23737, 086 851 5003; www.clareislandferry.com)

O'Malley Ferries (098-25045, 086 887 0814; www.omalleyferries.com)

Inishturk Island

POP 100

Ruggedly beautiful **Inishturk** (www.inishturkisland.com) lies 12km off Mayo's western coast. It's sparsely populated and little visited, despite the two **sandy beaches** on its eastern side, impressive cliffs, wonderful **flora and fauna**, and a rugged, hilly landscape that's ideal for **walking**. In fact, ambling along the island's maze of country roads is a perfect way to adapt to the pace of life here.

If you want to stay, the scenically positioned **Teach Abhainn** (☎098-45510; teachabhainn@hotmail.com; s/d from €40/64, dinner €25; ⊙Apr-Oct), a working farm 1.5km west of the harbour, has mesmerising views, hearty home cooking and six comfy rooms.

O'Malley Ferries (p403) has one to two ferries daily from **Roonagh Quay**, near Louisburgh; the crossing (€8/5 per adult/child return) takes 50 minutes.

Croagh Patrick

St Patrick couldn't have picked a better spot for a pilgrimage than this conical mountain (also known as 'the Reek'). On a clear day, the tough two-hour climb rewards with stunning views over Clew Bay and its sandy islets.

It was on Croagh Patrick that Ireland's patron saint fasted for 40 days and nights, and where he reputedly banished venomous snakes. Climbing the 772m holy mountain is an act of penance for thousands of pilgrims on the last Sunday of July (Reek Sunday). The truly contrite take the original 40km route from Ballintubber Abbey (p416) and Tóchar Phádraig (Patrick's Causeway), and ascend the mountain barefoot.

Path erosion has become a problem with the climb's increasing popularity; as yet no one has taken responsibility for improvements.

Sights & Activities

The **main trail** ascends the mountain from the car park in Murrisk. The steep trail is

THE PIRATE QUEEN

The life of Grace O'Malley (Gráinne Ní Mháille or Granuaile, 1530–1603) reads like fantasy adventure fiction. Twice widowed and twice imprisoned for acts of piracy, she was a fearsome presence in the troubled landscape of 16th-century Ireland.

Her unorthodox life was the stuff of legend and mythology; hundreds of stories testify to her unequalled courage, skill and dogged determination to protect her clan against virtually anyone else – from rival chieftains to the English army.

Born into a powerful sea-faring family that controlled most of the Mayo coastline and traded internationally, the independent Grace soon decided she should join the family line. Legend has it that while still a child she asked her father if she could join a trip to Spain but was refused on the grounds that seafaring was not for girls. She promptly cut off all her hair, dressed in boys clothing, returned to the ship and announced that she was ready to sail. Her family nicknamed her Gráinne Mhaol (pronounced grawn-ya wail; bald Grace), a name which stuck for the rest of her life.

Married & Looting

At 15 she was married off to Donal O'Flaherty, a querulous local chieftain, but using her smarts she soon eclipsed her husband in politics and trade. The O'Flahertys were banned from trading in Galway, one of the largest ports in the British Isles. Grace got around this by waylaying cargo vessels en route to port and demanding payment for safe passage. If they refused, she had them looted.

After her husband's death, Grace settled on Clare Island but continued marauding around the Irish and Scottish coasts. Closer to home, the only part of Clew Bay not under her control was Rockfleet, so in 1566 Grace married Richard an-Iarrain to gain control of his castle (p409). Despite some marital ups and downs (she tried to 'dismiss' him once she controlled his tower), they remained together until his death 17 years later.

By the 1570s Grace's blatant piracy had come to English attention and many attempts were made to capture her. Eventually she was brought to London in 1593, whereupon Queen Elizabeth I granted her a pardon and offered her a title: which she declined, saying she was already Queen of Connaught.

Grace died in 1603 and is thought to be buried in the family crypt on Clare Island.

rocky in parts, but you can rent walking sticks for €3 at the small cafe. The average return trip takes three to four hours and it gets crowded on sunny weekends. At the summit you'll find a 1905 whitewashed **church** and a 9th-century **oratory fountain**. Views are sublime.

Opposite the car park is the **National Famine Memorial**, a spine-chilling sculpture of a three-masted ghost ship wreathed in swirling skeletons, commemorating the lives lost on so-called 'coffin ships' employed to help people escape the Famine. A path down past the memorial leads to the scant remains of **Murrisk Abbey**, founded by the O'Malleys in 1547.

Getting There & Away

Murrisk is 9km southwest of Westport. The best way to get here is along the lovely bayside bike and walking path. Otherwise there are daily buses.

Westport

POP 5600

Bright and vibrant even in the depths of winter, Westport is a photogenic Georgian town with tree-lined streets, a riverside mall and a great vibe. With an excellent choice of accommodation, fine restaurants and pubs renowned for their music, it's a hugely popular place yet has never sold its soul to tourism.

Westport is Mayo's nightlife hub, and its central location makes it a convenient and enjoyable base for exploring the county.

Sights

Westport Quay, the town's harbour, is on Clew Bay, 2km west of the centre. It's a picturesque spot with shops and cafes. In town, the **Octagon** is a major landmark and is punctuated by a Doric column.

Westport House HISTORIC BUILDING
(098-27766; www.westporthouse.ie; Quay Rd; house-only adult/child €13/7, house & pirate adventure park €21/17; 10am-6pm Jul & Aug, hours vary rest of year, closed Jan & Feb) Built in 1730 on the ruins of Grace O'Malley's 16th-century castle, this charming Georgian mansion retains much of its original contents and has some stunning period-style rooms. The house is set in glorious gardens but the overall effect is marred by its commercial focus. Children love the **Pirate Adventure Park**, complete with a swinging pirate ship, a 'pirate's playground' and a roller-coaster-style flume ride through a water channel. It is 2km west of the centre.

Clew Bay Heritage Centre MUSEUM
(www.westportheritage.com; The Quay; adult/child €3/free; 10am-5pm Mon-Fri Jun-Sep, 3-5pm Sun Jul & Aug, 10.30am-2pm Mon-Fri Oct-May) Set in a 19th-century stone building, this museum traces the history, customs and traditions of Westport and Clew Bay. It's 2km west of town.

Activities

The area around Westport is great for cycling with gentle coastal routes or more challenging mountain trails within a short distance of town. The popular Great Western Greenway (p408), a 42km cycling route between Westport and Achill, begins 500m from the centre of town off the N59.

The tourist office has an excellent brochure detailing local walks for all skill levels.

★**Clew Bay Bike Hire** BICYCLE RENTAL
(098-24818; www.clewbaybikehire.ie; Distillery Rd; rentals per day from €15, shuttle from €7.50; 9am-6pm) Offers advice on routes and trails in the area and has shops in Westport Quay and along the Great Western Greenway in Newport, Mulranny and Achill; you can start the trail at any point and be picked up on completion. There's a handy one-way drop-off/collection shuttle so you don't have to backtrack.

Rental kayaks are also available (per hour €15) and you can join a paddling tour of the bay.

★**Guided Walks of Historic Westport** WALKING TOUR
(098-26852; clock, Bridge St; adult/child €6/free; 11am Wed Jul & Aug) Local historians lead 90-minute walks around Westport.

Westport Bikes 4 Hire BICYCLE RENTAL
(086 088 0882; www.westportbikes4hire.com; James St; adult/child rentals per day from €15/10, shuttle service €7.50; 9am-6pm) Rents all types of bikes, including tandems, electrics and kids' trailers. You can arrange to be picked up or dropped off anywhere along the Great Western Greenway.

Carrowholly Stables HORSE RIDING
(www.carrowholly-stables.com; off N59, Carrowholly; beach rides adult/child from €30/25) Offers guided horse and pony treks on the beach and along trails overlooking Clew Bay. The stables are 3km north of the town centre, next to Westport Golf Club.

Westport

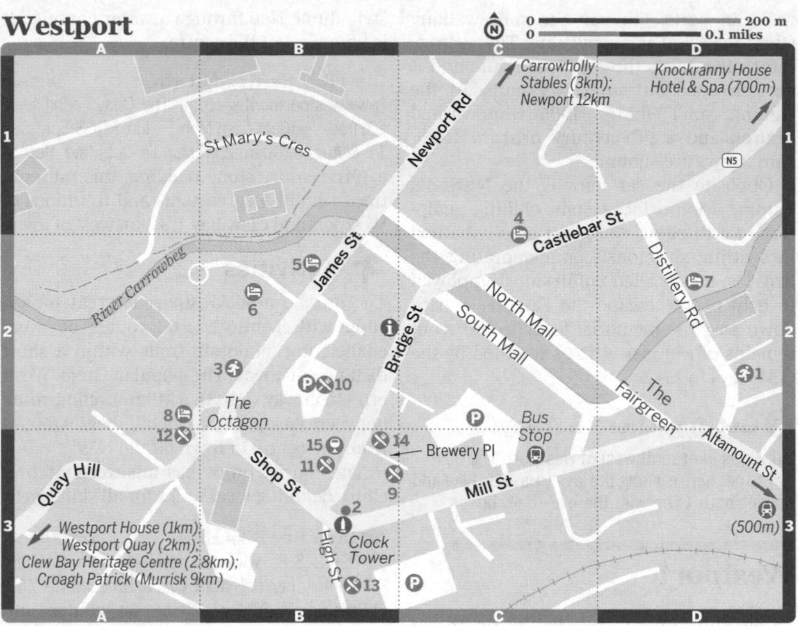

Westport

Activities, Courses & Tours

1 Clew Bay Bike Hire....D2
2 Guided Walks of Historic Westport....B3
3 Westport Bikes 4 Hire....B2

Sleeping

4 Castlecourt Hotel....C1
5 Clew Bay Hotel....B2
6 Old Mill Holiday Hostel....B2
7 St Anthony's Riverside B&B....D2
8 Wyatt Hotel....A2

Eating

9 An Port Mór....B3
10 Market....B2
11 McCormack's at The Andrew Stone Gallery....B3
12 Pantry & Corkscrew....A3
13 Sage....B3
14 Sol Rio....B3

Drinking & Nightlife

15 Matt Molloy's....B3

Croagh Patrick Walking Holidays WALKING TOUR
(☎098-26090; www.walkingguideireland.com; 7-day walks from €600; ⏲Apr-Aug) Highly customisable walks in the countryside surrounding Westport that usually last seven days. You can include St Patrick's holy site and/or a beach. Fees include accommodation.

Clewbay Cruises BOAT TOUR
(☎087 606 6146; www.clewbaycruises.com; Westport Quay; adult/child €18/10; ⏲May-Sep) Enjoy views of Clew Bay on 90-minute cruises.

Sleeping

Westport is Mayo's main city and while there's an abundance of B&Bs and hotels, rooms are in short supply during summer and special events.

Old Mill Holiday Hostel HOSTEL €
(☎098-27045; www.oldmillhostel.com; off James St; dm from €18; 📶) Inside a converted stone mill, this central hostel has 58 beds spread across four- to 10-bed rooms. Inviting communal areas provide respite from the handy kitchen and laundry rooms.

★ **St Anthony's Riverside B&B** B&B €€
(☎087 630 1550; www.st-anthonys.com; Distillery Rd; r from €90; 📶) This genteel B&B sits under cover of a large hedge and thick, twisted vines inhabited by birds' nests. The 11 rooms have clean lines and restful, light colours. Bathrooms feature Jacuzzis or power showers. Breakfast is excellent.

Clew Bay Hotel HOTEL €€

(☎098-28088; www.clewbayhotel.com; James St; s/d from €75/110;) This family-run hotel in the centre of town has 54 small but stylish rooms; some have river views. The bathrooms and furnishings are first-rate. The modern pub is popular for contemporary takes on classic fare.

Wyatt Hotel HOTEL €€

(☎098-25027; www.wyatthotel.com; The Octagon; r from €90;) Right in the centre of Westport town, this older sunflower-yellow hotel is a local landmark. The standard rooms are comfortable; newly redecorated superior rooms have large beds, walk-in showers and lavish amenities.

Castlecourt Hotel HOTEL €€

(☎098-55088; www.castlecourthotel.ie; Castlebar St; s/d from €90/120; @) Spacious but cosy rooms that blend contemporary style with classic elegance are on offer at this modern hotel in the town centre. There's a spa, 17m-indoor pool and an outdoor rock pool.

Knockranny House Hotel & Spa BOUTIQUE HOTEL €€€

(☎098-28611; www.knockrannyhousehotel.ie; off N5; r €80-300; @) Open fires take the chill out of the air at this traditionally styled modern hotel. There are more than 100 rooms and suites – some quite large – each featuring plush classic furnishings and styles. Amenities include an indoor pool and spa facilities. The restaurant, **La Fougère**, is renowned for its wine list. Westport's centre is 1.5km west, a 15-minute walk.

Eating

Westport is packed with superb restaurants and cafes, just wander along Bridge St and the little laneways off it to make some tasty discoveries. The **market** (car park, James St; 8.30am-2pm Thu Apr-Oct) features prepared and fresh foods from the region.

Book for dinner in summer and on weekends.

McCormack's at the Andrew Stone Gallery MODERN IRISH €

(Bridge St; mains €6-14; 10.30am-4.30pm Thu-Sat & Mon-Tue) Excellent food is on offer at this family-run bakery and lunch cafe that has been in business for decades. It's next to an art gallery and sources its fare from the best local producers. In a hurry? Grab a scone to go.

★ **Pantry & Corkscrew** MODERN IRISH €€

(☎098-26977; www.thepantryandcorkscrew.com; The Octagon; mains lunch €8-15, dinner €12-25; noon-3.30pm & 5.30-9.30pm Tue-Sun) The heart of Mayo's slow-food movement is found at this narrow little storefront. The kitchen has huge talent as the seasonally changing menu shows, with ingredients obtained from local and organic producers.

★ **An Port Mór** MODERN IRISH €€

(☎098-26730; www.anportmor.com; 1 Brewery Pl; mains €22-28; 5-9.30pm Tue-Sun) Hidden down a lane off Bridge St, proprietor-chef Frankie Mallon's little restaurant packs quite a punch. It's an intimate place with a series of long narrow rooms and a menu that features excellent meats and much-lauded seafood (try the Clew Bay scallops). Most everything is procured from the region.

Sol Rio MEDITERRANEAN €€

(☎098-28944; www.solrio.ie; Bridge St; mains lunch €7-14, dinner €13-20; cafe 9am-6pm, restaurant noon-3pm & 5.30-9.30pm;) The extensive menu ranges from pizza and pasta to organic meat and fish. Carefully picked ingredients and attention whether you pause at the simple cafe downstairs or the more stylish restaurant upstairs. The deli is famous for its egg-custard pastries.

Idle Wall MODERN IRISH €€

(☎098-50692; www.theidlewall.ie; Westport Quay; mains €18-25; 5.30-10pm Tue-Sat) Serving local seafood straight off the boats (mussels, oysters, crab, cod and more), this atmospheric restaurant is easily the pick of places to eat on Westport's lively harbour-front. Chef Áine Maguire wins plaudits for her inventive take on Irish fare.

Sage MODERN EUROPEAN €€

(☎098-56700; www.sagewestport.ie; 10 High St; mains €18-27; 5.30-9.30pm Thu-Tue) A wave of warmth hits you as soon as you walk through the door of this stylish restaurant artfully run by Shteryo Yurukov and Eva Ivanova. Conforming to the local tradition of sourcing everything from the region, the restaurant offers a changing menu of seasonal meat and seafood dishes – many with an Italian accent.

Drinking & Nightlife

Westport is thronged with pubs, many of them with live music nightly.

DON'T MISS

THE GREAT WESTERN GREENWAY

Following the route of the old Westport–Achill Railway, the **Great Western Greenway** (www.greenway.ie) is one of the best reasons to pause in this part of Mayo. The 42km trail passes lovely countryside and waterfront scenery. It consists of three main sections, none of which require more than moderate effort:

Westport to Newport This 11km section through pretty, lush countryside starts off the N59, 500m north of Westport's centre, and ends at the N59, 2km before Newport. This is the easiest section.

Newport to Mulranny This 18km section is the most popular and passes close to many sights along Clew Bay. It's off the N59 just north of Newport and ends in Mulranny.

Mulranny to Achill This 13km section starts right in Mulranny and ends about 1.2km short of Achill Island (many tourist maps show the trail going all the way) after which you ride along roads. It has some sweeping water views.

You can easily rent bicycles all along the Greenway. Two Westport-based operators, Clew Bay Bike Hire (p405) and Westport Bikes 4 Hire (p405), offer uber-convenient pick-up and drop-off services that let you ride all or part of the Greenway one-way and be driven the other way.

★**Matt Molloy's** PUB
(☎098-27663; www.mattmolloy.com; Bridge St; ⊙11am-late) Matt Malloy, the fife player from the Chieftains, runs this old-school pub. Head to the back room around 9pm and you'll catch live *céilidh* (traditional music and dancing). Or perhaps a veteran musician will simply slide into a chair and croon a few classics. It has good microbrews on tap.

Shopping

Wandering Westport's centre, you'll discover little boutiques and a surprising number off bookshops.

Custom House Studios ARTS
(☎098-28735; www.customhousestudios.ie; Westport Quay; ⊙10am-5pm Mon-Fri, 1-4.30pm Sat & Sun) Local artists display their creations at this inviting gallery, which also has special exhibitions.

Information

Tourist Office (☎098-25711; www.westport tourism.com; Bridge St; ⊙9am-5.45pm Mon-Fri year-round, 10am to 4pm Sat Easter-Oct) Mayo's main tourist office has a lot of walking and cycling info.

Getting There & Away

BUS

Bus Éireann services include Galway (€15.20, two hours, two daily) and Sligo (€23, 2¾ hours, one daily). Buses depart from Mill St.

TRAIN

There are five daily trains to Dublin (€26, 3¼ hours).

Newport

POP 630

Newport, a quick 12km drive north of Westport, is a picturesque 18th-century village. The trains on the Westport–Achill Railway stopped in 1936 but a striking **seven-arch viaduct** built in 1892 remains a popular spot with walkers and cyclists.

The Bangor Trail (p412) ends here while the wonderful Great Western Greenway heads west to Achill, 31km away along the former rail line.

Buses between Westport and Achill Island pass through once daily.

Sleeping & Eating

★**Newport House** HISTORIC HOTEL €€€
(☎098-41222; www.newporthouse.ie; off Main St; s/d from €110/220; ⊙Apr–mid-Oct;) Cloaked in ivy that turns crimson in autumn, this gorgeous Georgian mansion is one of Ireland's most romantic country retreats. Newport House is especially known for its contemporary Irish cuisine (multicourse dinner €68).

Blue Bicycle Tea Rooms CAFE €
(☎098-41145; www.bluebicycletearooms.com; Main St; mains from €5; ⊙10.30am-6pm May-Oct) Grab a snack or pause for a true respite in

this cafe, packed with old-world charm. It features sandwiches, salads, soups, baked treats and more, all sourced locally.

Kelly's Kitchen CAFE €
(☎098-41639; 17 Main St; mains €6-14; ⏰9am-5pm Mon-Sat) The fare of Sean Kelly's much-loved artisan butcher shop (next door) can be sampled here for breakfast and lunch. Or stop for a coffee break on your Great Western Greenway sojourn.

Newport to Achill Island

En route along the N59 or the Great Western Greenway, look for signs to **Burrishoole Abbey** (off N59; ⏰dawn-dusk), an eerie wind-battered ruin of a Dominican abbey built in 1486 and now surrounded by a cemetery. It's 2km west of Newport.

Another 3.5km further, look for signs for **Rockfleet Castle** (Carrigahowley; off N59; ⏰dawn-dusk). This 15th-century tower is associated with 'pirate queen' Grace O'Malley (p404). She married her second husband, Richard an-Iarrain (impressively nicknamed 'Iron Dick' Burke), to gain control of this castle, and famously fought off an English attack here. It's moodily set on a boggy tidal area.

Rising from a narrow isthmus, the hillside village of **Mulranny** overlooks a wide Blue Flag **beach**. It's a prime vantage point for counting the 365 or so seemingly saucer-sized islands that grace Clew Bay.

Atlantic Way

Instead of following the main road (R319) from Mulranny to Achill Island, take the signposted Atlantic Way, which curves clockwise around the Curraun Peninsula. The narrow road passes the odd fortified tower and as it hugs the isolated southern edge of the Curraun Peninsula, the views across Clew Bay and out to sea are simply stunning.

Achill Island

POP 940

Ireland's largest offshore island, Achill (An Caol), is connected to the mainland by a short bridge. Despite its accessibility, it has plenty of remote-island feel: soaring cliffs, rocky headlands, sheltered sandy beaches, broad expanses of blanket bog and rolling mountains. It also has its share of history, having been a frequent refuge during Ireland's various rebellions.

Achill is at its most dramatic during winter, when high winds and lashing seas make the island seem downright inhospitable. The year-round population, though, remains as welcoming as ever. In summer, heather, rhododendrons and wildflowers bloom.

The village of Keel is the island's main centre of activity – which is a relative term.

Sights

The signposted **Atlantic Drive** continues once you cross the bridge. It follows the island's wild southern shore, passing through the little fishing hamlet of **Dooega**, with its sheltered beach.

★ **Slievemore Deserted Village** HISTORIC SITE
The remains of this deserted village at the foot of Mt Slievemore are a bleak place now home only to sheep. It's slowly being reduced down to rock piles, a poignant reminder of the island's past hardships and a lost way of life. When the Potato Famine took hold, starvation forced the villagers to the sea and its sources of food. The adjacent graveyard compounds the desolation.

Dooagh HISTORIC SITE
This village is where Don Allum, the first person to row across the Atlantic Ocean in both directions, landed in September 1982 in his 6m-long plywood boat, dubbed the *QE3,* after 77 days at sea. Opposite the monument, the **Pub** (⏰9am-10pm) – that's its name – has memorabilia marking the feat.

Keem Bay LOOKOUT
The 8km drive west from Keel to what is literally the end of the road is spectacular, with sweeping views across the water as the road climbs the sheer rock face. But after you spiral down to this perfect cove, you're rewarded with a gorgeous Blue Flag **beach**.

Activities

Achill Island is a wonderful place for walking. **Mt Slievemore** (672m) can be climbed from behind the deserted village for terrific views of Blacksod Bay. A longer climb takes in **Mt Croaghaun** (668m), Achill Head and a walk atop what locals claim are Europe's highest sea cliffs. There's a good 4.3km-loop starting at the beach in **Dooagh**.

Achill Tourism (p412) produces 14 excellent downloadable guides to walks around the island.

Achill Island

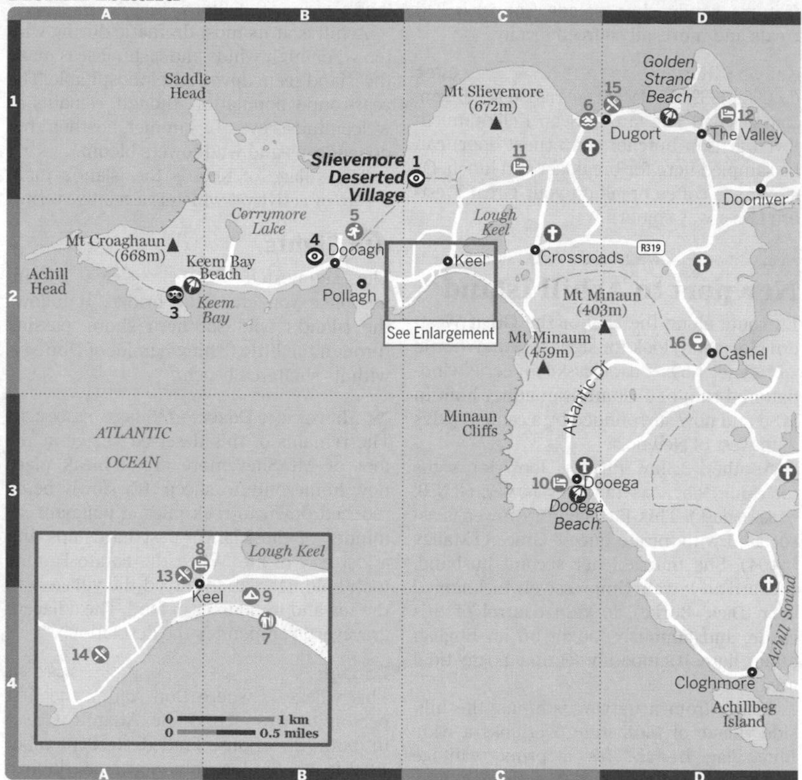

★**Trawmore Beach** SURFING
(Keel) This Blue Flag beach, which runs 3km southeast from Keel, is one of Ireland's best surfing spots, but there are dangerous rips from its centre to the eastern end (under the Minaun Cliffs). Heed the signs and stick to the western half of the beach. Several companies offer board hire (per day €15) and lessons (per day €40). This strand is also good for bracing **walks**, viewing the pounding surf.

Dugort Beach SWIMMING
A prime example of the area's many fine beaches can be found at Dugort. Achill has many additional scalloped bays tame enough for swimming including the Blue Flag beaches at Keem Bay, Dooega and Golden Strand (Dugort's other beach). Except in the height of the holiday season, most are often deserted.

Calvey's Equestrian Centre HORSE RIDING
(087 988 1093; www.calveysofachill.com; Slievemore; 2hr beach trek adult/child €70/60) Calvey's arranges riding lessons and one- to four-hour treks on Achill's broad beaches and mountain roads.

Achill Bikes BICYCLE RENTAL
(087 245 7686; www.achillbikes.com; Keel; rental per day from €20) Rents a variety of bikes, offers advice and arranges for pickup and delivery around the island.

Festivals

Achill Island hosts several festivals during the year, including events devoted to walking, painting, boating and more. See www.achilltourism.com for the latest details.

Scoil Acla Festival CULTURE
(www.scoilacla.ie; late Jul) Traditional Irish music resonates for a week during this

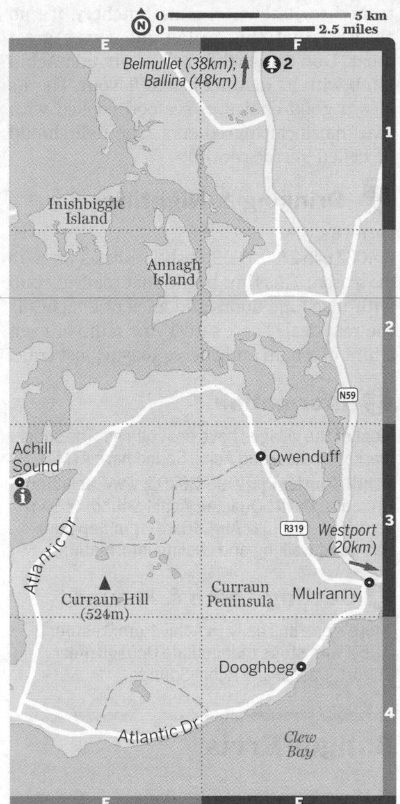

Achill Island

festival, which also has Irish dancing, culture and music workshops.

Sleeping

Achill has B&Bs dotting the main road from the bridge to Keel. You'll also find places to stay along the shores.

★Valley House Hostel HOSTEL €
(098-47204; www.valley-house.com; The Valley; campsites per tent €5, plus per person €5, dm €16-22, d €44-60;) Amid unruly gardens, this remote, 42-bed hostel in a creaking old mansion has atmosphere to spare. JM Synge based his play *The Playboy of the Western World* on misadventures here and the subsequent film *Love and Rage* (1999) was also partially shot here. Bonuses include scones for breakfast and a pub with patio tables.

★Pure Magic Achill Island GUESTHOUSE €
(085 243 9782; www.puremagic.ie; Slievemore Rd, near Dugort; s/d from €45/70;) Not far from the ghost town of Slievemore, this lively 10-room spot is anything but. There's a buzzing bar and cafe (with great pizza). You can arrange kitesurfing, stand-up paddleboarding, snorkelling, cycling and more.

Lavelles Seaside House GUESTHOUSE €
(098-45116; www.lavellesseasidehouse.com; Dooega; s/d from €45/70) In the fishing village of Dooega, this 14-room whitewashed guesthouse is a good getaway. The five newer rooms are nicest and have views down to the water. The pub, Mickey's, serves bar food with an emphasis on local seafood in summer.

Keel Sandybanks Caravan & Camping Park CAMPGROUND €
(098-43211; www.achillcamping.com; Keel; campsites €10-25, caravan 2-nights €115-140; Apr–mid-Sep;) This camping ground, an easy stroll from town, overlooks Keel Beach. Noncampers can opt for 'glamping' nights in traditional wooden caravans.

THE LEGEND OF ST DEIRBHILE

Sometime around the year 600, legend has it, a young girl named Deirbhile decided on a pious path in life. However a military man who was in love with her was opposed to this. Meeting him one day on what is today the Mullet Peninsula, she asked him what he liked best about her. 'Your eyes', he said. Thereupon Deirbhile plucked out her eyes and threw them to the ground. Not surprisingly her suitor fled in horror.

But then a miracle happened: a spring welled up from the earth where Deirbhile's eyes had landed. She washed her face in its waters and her eyes returned. Today the **feast day of St Deirbhile** is celebrated on 15 August at related sites near Blacksod on the Mullet Peninsula.

Achill Cliff House Hotel & Restaurant GUESTHOUSE €€
(www.achillcliff.com; Keel; r €70-90) With sweeping views out to sea – even from the breakfast room – this family-run guesthouse is a great retreat rain or shine. Furnishings are comfy but basic. The restaurant is worth its superlatives thanks to its fresh local seafood and creative take on Irish classics.

Eating

Cottage CAFE €
(☎098-43966; Dugort; mains €4-15; ⏰10am-6pm Jun-Sep; 🌱) This is the perfect pause as you soak up the charms of the little seaside village of Dugort. The Cottage has fab coffees and baked goods plus a variety of sandwiches and seafood, vegetarian and vegan specials. Relax outside at a picnic table with views.

★**Chalet** SEAFOOD €€
(☎098-43157; www.keembayfishproducts.ie; Keel; mains €15-30; ⏰6-10pm daily summer, less often other times) The proprietors of Keem Bay Fish Products have been serving up their acclaimed smoked local salmon and other delicacies at this restaurant for decades. The menu changes with what's fresh, but expect a meal of the very best seafood.

Calvey's Restaurant & Wild Mint Deli IRISH €€
(☎098-43158; www.calveysofachill.com; Keel; mains lunch €8-20, dinner €16-32; ⏰noon-3pm & 5.30-9pm, deli 9am-5pm Easter–mid-Sep) Attached to its own organic butchery, it's no surprise that this restaurant serves great meat. Don't miss the rack of organic Achill lamb with its distinct island flavour. There's also a good choice of seafood cooked with seasonal local ingredients. The deli should be called 'picnic central'.

Drinking & Nightlife

Lynott's PUB
(☎087 645 2780; R319, Cashel; ⏰hours vary with the season) This tiny, traditional roadside pub with flagstone floors and ancient benches is the real deal. There's no TV or radio or even a hint of a ham and cheese toastie, just craic.

Information

Most of the villages have post offices. The supermarkets in Keel and Achill Sound have ATMs.

Achill Tourism (☎098-20705; www.achilltourism.com; Davitt Quarter, Achill Sound; ⏰9am-6pm Mon-Fri Jul & Aug, 10am-4pm Sep-Jun) Has good walking and cycling information.

Getting There & Around

There's one bus daily to Achill from Westport (€16), with stops that include Dooagh, Keel, Dugort, Cashel and Achill Sound.

Bangor Erris

POP 300

This unexceptional little village is the start or end point for the 30km **Bangor Trail**, which connects Bangor and Newport via Ballycroy National Park. It's an extraordinary hike that takes walkers through some of the bleakest and most remote countryside in Ireland. It is very difficult and includes long stretches of bog-walking.

There's one bus daily from Ballina (€13, one hour).

Ballycroy National Park

Covering one of Europe's largest expanses of blanket bog, **Ballycroy National Park** (☎098-49888; www.ballycroynationalpark.ie; off N59, Ballycroy; ⏰visitor centre 10am-5.30pm Apr-Sep) FREE is in a gorgeously scenic region, where the River Owenduff wends its way through intact bogs.

The park is home to diverse nature including peregrine falcons, corncrakes and whooper swans. A short **nature trail** with interpretation panels leads from the visitor centre across the bog with great views to the surrounding mountains. The excellent visitor centre can recommend more ambitious hikes and there are displays on whaling and the ubiquitous purple heather.

Ballycroy is 18km south of Bangor on the N59.

Mullet Peninsula

Dangling some 30km into the Atlantic, this thinly populated Gaeltacht (Irish speaking) peninsula feels more cut off than many islands, and has a similar sense of loneliness. However, you'll find pristine beaches along its sheltered eastern shore and some holy surprises (plenty of religious sites) plus lots of sheep – often fully blocking the road. The main settlement is the busy town of **Belmullet** (Béal an Mhuirthead).

Sights

The road south (R313) from Belmullet loops round the tip of the peninsula to rejoin itself at Aghleam. Along the way it passes the Blue Flag beach at **Elly Bay**, a prime spot for birdwatchers and dolphin-watchers, as well as surfers. Further south it passes stunning **Mullaghroe Beach**.

Near **Blacksod** (An Fód Dubh) are the remains of an old **church**. Just up from here is the first of several sites related to St Deirbhile. 'Deirbhile's Twist' is a modern-day stone circle that evokes ancient monuments (it's part of the North Mayo Sculpture Trail). Close by, look for signs along the road for **Deirbhile's Well**, where the miracle of her eyes supposedly occurred. Now loop down the short road nearby to the cemetery and beach. Here you'll find **St Deirbhile's Church**, an intriguing ruin dating to before the 11th century; St Deirbhile is purported to be buried here.

Sleeping & Eating

★ **Leim Siar** B&B €
(☎ 097-85004; www.leimsiar.com; Blacksod; s/d €55/80;) Just a short walk from the Blacksod lighthouse, this purpose-built B&B offers modern comforts and end-of-the-earth appeal. The rooms are bright and breakfast is an event. You can rent bikes (per day €10) to tour the peninsula.

Talbot's HOTEL €€
(☎ 097-20484; www.thetalbothotel.ie; Barrack St, Belmullet; s/d from €90/140;) Stylish Talbot's has 21 comfortable rooms with plenty of bold accents. The pub, **An Chéibh** (the Anchor), has dual peat-burning fireplaces, a good beer selection and excellent food (pub mains €8 to €25).

Information

You'll find all the main services in Belmullet, including bank, ATM and post office.

Tourist Office (☎ 097-81500; www.visiterris.ie; cnr Main St & Chapel St, Belmullet; 9am-5pm Mon-Sat May-Sep, to 4pm Mon-Fri Oct-Apr)

Getting There & Around

Bus Éireann has one daily bus from Ballina to Belmullet (€16, 1½ hours), continuing on to Blacksod.

Pollatomish

POP 150

Irresistibly remote and pretty, Pollatomish, also spelled Pullathomas, drowses in a serene bay some 16km east of Belmullet, signposted on the road to Ballycastle (R314).

Those who find their way here often extend their stay to stroll on its sandy **beach** or continue up to **Benwee Head** to take in sensational views.

PIPELINE PROTEST

The quiet, rural idyll that is Mayo's far-flung northwest has made national headlines over the construction of a high-pressure raw gas pipeline between Mayo's offshore Corrib gas field and a processing plant at Bellanaboy.

Fearing possible health and safety risks, as well as the environmental harm from construction of the massive project, locals and activists have waged a campaign against the pipeline for almost 15 years. Ultimately the pipeline was approved in 2011 and despite ongoing protests and legal action, construction of the 9km-section across north Mayo (landfall is near Pollatomish) was largely completed in 2015.

Local sentiment, however, remains obvious. 'Shell Out!' is just one of many phrases on scores of signs displayed across the region.

For more on the pipeline, visit www.shelltosea.com and www.corribgaspipeline.ie.

WORTH A TRIP

DETOUR TO KILLALA

For a spectacular short looping detour off the main road (R314) to Killala, take the coast road north out of Ballycastle, passing **Downpatrick Head**. Here is some of Mayo's most dramatic shoreline, with no end to the excitement. Look for the narrow lane to the head that takes you right up to the surf.

Continue east and south, with **Lackan Bay** on your left until you rejoin the R314. From Killala, look for the turn to Kilcummin 4.5km northwest of town and do the route in reverse.

Kilcommon Lodge Holiday Hostel (☎097-84621; www.kilcommonlodge.ie; Pollatomish; dm/d from €16/40, dinner €15; 📶) is run by Ciarán, who can organise surfing, guided walks and rock climbing. It has a nice garden and a kitchen.

Ballycastle & Around

POP 240

The beautifully sited village of Ballycastle consists of a sole sloping street. Its main draw (apart from breathtaking coastal scenery) is its megalithic tombs – one of the greatest concentrations in Europe.

Sights

★Céide Fields ARCHAEOLOGICAL SITE

(☎096-43325; www.heritageireland.ie; off R314; adult/child €4/2; ⏲visitor centre 10am-6pm Jun-Sep, to 5pm Easter-May & Oct, last tour 1hr prior to closing) This otherwise barren site, 8km northwest of Ballycastle, is considered the world's most extensive Stone Age monument. Stone-walled fields, houses and megalithic tombs – about half a million tonnes of stone – have been found so far, the legacy of a 5000-year-old farming community. The **visitor centre**, in a glass pyramid overlooking the site, gives a fascinating glimpse into these times. Be sure to take a **guided tour** of the site to fully appreciate the findings.

It was only during the 1930s that a local, Patrick Caulfield, was digging in the bog when he noticed a lot of piled-up stones buried beneath it. A full relaization of what lay under the sod didn't happen for another four decades when his son Seamus began exploration of the area. Excavations are ongoing.

Ballinglen Art Foundation GALLERY

(☎096-43184; www.ballinglenartsfoundation.org; Main St; ⏲hours vary) If you see artists out recording their impressions of the sensational scenery around here, they may well be under the patronage of this foundation. Check out the gallery across from Polke's.

Sleeping

★Stella Maris HOTEL €€€

(☎096-43322; www.stellamarisireland.com; Ballycastle; r €150-240; ⏲Easter-Oct; 📶) This salt-spattered building sits on a lonely stretch of coastline 2.5km west of Ballycastle. It was originally a British Coast Guard station, and later a nunnery. Now, upmarket rooms combine antiques and stylish modern furnishings with killer views. Dinner is served (€40).

Eating & Drinking

Mary's Cottage Kitchen CAFE €

(Main St; treats from €3; ⏲10am-3pm Mon-Fri, to 2pm Sat) A great place to pause during your drive along the R314, with good coffee, fresh-baked goods, lunch items and chocolate treats.

Polke's PUB

(☎096-43016; Main St; ⏲11am-10pm) The perfect village pub, with walls lined with donations from visiting artists.

Killala & Around

POP 580

The town itself is pretty enough, but Killala is renowned for its namesake bay nearby.

It's claimed that the ever-busy St Patrick founded Killala, and the Church of Ireland church sits on the site of the first Christian church in Ireland. A 25m-high **round tower** still looms over the town's heart.

Sights & Activities

Rosserk Abbey HISTORIC BUILDING

Dipping its toes into the River Rosserk, this Franciscan abbey dates from the mid-15th century. There's an eye-catching double piscina (perforated stone basin) in the chancel: look for the exquisite carvings of a round tower and several angels.

The abbey is 4km south of Killala off the R314. Look for the signposts and then follow narrow farming lanes for another 5km.

★ **Lackan Strand** BEACH

Lackan Bay's beach is a stunning and vast expanse of golden sand. There's good surf here and plenty of places to get lost. Follow the R314 about 4.5km northwest from Killala, then turn at the signpost for Kilcummin.

Lackan Trail WALKING

Follow beautiful Lackan Bay and discover ancient ring forts and megalithic tombs on this moderate and looping 8km-walk that begins in the Killala church parking lot. An optional 3km-extension includes sweeping views of the region.

Getting There & Away

There are three weekday-only buses between Ballina and Killala (€5, 20 minutes).

Ballina

POP 10,900

Mayo's third-largest town, Ballina, is synonymous with salmon. If you're here during fishing season, you'll see droves of green-garbed waders, poles in hand, heading for the River Moy – which pumps right through the heart of town.

Otherwise, except for its excellent museum, Ballina makes for a quick stop.

Sights

Jackie Clarke Collection MUSEUM

(096-73508; www.clarkecollection.ie; Pearse St; 10am-5pm Tue-Sat Apr-Sep, tours 11.30am & 2.30pm) FREE Starting when he was 12 in 1939, the late Jackie Clarke amassed an extraordinary collection of 100,000 items covering 400 years of Irish history. Housed in an 1881 bank building, this well-curated museum brims with surprises. It has a lovely garden and cafe.

Activities

A list of **fisheries** and permit contacts is available at the tourist office. The season is February to September, but the best salmon fishing is June to August.

Festivals & Events

Ballina Salmon Festival CULTURE

(www.ballinasalmonfestival.ie) The popular five-day festivities include parades, dances, an arts show and fishing competitions. Held in July.

Sleeping

Ballina has numerous modest B&Bs near the centre and train station.

Ice House Hotel BOUTIQUE HOTEL €€€

(096-23500; www.icehousehotel.ie; The Quay; r from €180;) Up-close views of the serene River Moy estuary are the main draw at this 32-room hotel that combines an elegant restored namesake building with a starkly modern wing. It's 2km northeast of the centre and close to good waterfront pubs.

Mount Falcon Country House Hotel LUXURY HOTEL €€€

(096-74472; www.mountfalcon.com; Foxford Rd; r from €180;) Hidden within 40 hectares between Lough Conn and the River Moy, 5km south of Ballina, this gorgeous 1870s mansion is now a lovely lodge. Rooms in the old house ooze old-world grandeur, while those in the modern extension are more contemporary. Anglers will be hooked by the exclusive fishery.

Eating

★ **Clarke's Seafood Delicatessen** SEAFOOD €

(www.clarkes.ie; O'Rahilly St; treats from €5; 9am-6pm Mon-Sat) Can't catch salmon? The wizards at Clarke's will sell you their house-smoked salmon in myriad forms, plus all manner of other fishy creations you can take on a picnic.

Market Kitchen MODERN IRISH €€

(096-78538; www.marketkitchen.ie; Clare St; mains €8-25; 3-9pm Wed-Sat, 1-9pm Sun) The best food in Ballina emerges from this busy kitchen above a popular (and good) pub, **Murphy's Bros**. Pub classics are joined by dishes of the famous local salmon and other seafood. It's in the centre, just east of the river.

Information

Tourist Office (096-70848; www.north-mayo.ie; 41 Pearse St; 10am-5pm Mon-Sat Apr-Oct) It's located in the centre.

Getting There & Away

BUS

The bus station is on Kevin Barry St. Bus Éireann services include Westport (€16, 1½ to three hours, two daily) and Sligo (€17, 1½ hours, one daily).

TRAIN

The train station is on Station Rd at the southern extension of Kevin Barry St. Ballina is on a branch of the main Westport–Dublin line, so you'll have to change at Manulla Junction. There are four connections a day to Dublin (€26, 3½ hours).

Castlebar & Around

POP 12,300

Mayo's county town, Castlebar, is a traffic-choked hub of shops and services. Fortunately most places of interest lie outside the town centre.

Sights

★National Museum of Country Life MUSEUM

(☎094-903 1755; www.museum.ie; off N5, Turlough Park; ⏰10am-5pm Tue-Sat, 2-5pm Sun) FREE A celebration of the pluck of the Irish, this extensive and engrossing museum looks at rural traditions and skills. Overlooking a lake in the lush grounds of 19th-century **Turlough Manor**, this purpose-built facility is a branch of the National Museum of Ireland and explores everything from the role of the potato to boat building, herbal cures and traditional clothing. Exhibits concentrate on the period from 1850 to 1950. There's a good cafe and shop; it's 8km northeast of Castlebar.

Turlough Round Tower HISTORIC BUILDING

(off N5) With its single lofty window, this impenetrable 9th-century tower calls to mind the fairy tale of Rapunzel. The tower stands on a hilltop by a ruined 18th-century church and cemetery, a short distance northeast of the National Museum of Country Life.

Ballintubber Abbey CATHEDRAL

(☎094-903 0934; www.ballintubberabbey.ie; Ballintubber; ⏰9am-midnight, tours 10am-5pm Jul & Aug) FREE This is the only church in Ireland founded by an Irish king that is still in use. It was set up in 1216 next to the site of an earlier church founded by busy St Patrick after he came down from Croagh Patrick. Major anniversary celebrations are planned for 2016.

Take the N84 south, after about 13km turn west at the Emo service station; the abbey is 2km along.

Among the highlights of its tumultuous history, the abbey was burned by Normans, seized by James I and suppressed by Henry VIII. The nave roof was burned down by Cromwell's soldiers in 1653 and not restored until 1965.

Foxford Woollen Mill MILL

(www.foxfordwoollenmills.ie; Foxford; tours free; ⏰tours 10am-5pm Mon-Sat, noon-5pm Sun Apr-Nov) Founded in 1892, the Foxford mill was set up to ease post-Famine suffering and provide much-needed work. It remained open until 1987 during which time its woven goods achieved great acclaim. Now operated by locals, it employs a fraction of the hundreds who previously worked here. Besides sweaters and scarves (under €30) made in the mill, the shop sells a huge number of imported goods. Foxford is midway between Ballina and Castlebar at the junction of the N26 and N58.

Eating

★Rua Deli & Cafe MODERN IRISH €€

(www.caferua.com; Spencer St, Castlebar; mains €7-14, dinner €40; ⏰9am-6pm Mon-Sat; 👪) This gourmet deli and cafe champions artisan, organic produce, Carrowholly cheese, Ballina smoked salmon and luscious prepared foods. Load up in the deli for a picnic in the nearby park. The cafe has artfully mismatched furniture and excellent fresh fare. Even the takeaway coffee is good. A second cafe location is on New Antrim St.

Getting There & Around

BUS

Buses stop on Stephen Garvey Way. Bus Éireann services run to Westport (€6, 20 minutes, seven to 10 daily) and Sligo (€19, 2½ hours, one daily).

TRAIN

Castlebar is on the line between Dublin (€26, three hours) and Westport (€8, 20 minutes). There are five trains each way daily. The station is just out of town on the N84 towards Ballinrobe.

Knock

POP 850

Knock was little more than a downtrodden rural village until 1879, when a divine apparition propelled it to become one of the world's most sacred Catholic shrines. The shrine is now a serious pilgrimage site and dominates the little village. It's large and blandly modern, its appeal spiritual rather than physical.

The **tourist office** (☎094-938 8193; www.knock-shrine.ie; ⊙9am-6pm) across from the shrine is patiently helpful. There are clusters of souvenir stalls.

Sights

Knock Marian Shrine HISTORIC SITE
(⊙chapel 9am-9pm) The Knock shrine encompasses five churches and a museum in the town centre. People of many faiths pray at the modern **chapel** enclosing a scene of the apparition carved from snow-white marble. A segment of **stone** from the original (and long-gone) church mounted on the outside wall (on your right as you're facing the scene of the apparition) has been rubbed smooth by the hands and lips of the faithful.

The story that led to Knock's development goes thus: on the evening of 21 August 1879, in drenching rain, two young Knock women were startled by a vision of Mary, Joseph, St John the Evangelist and a sacrificial lamb upon an altar, freeze-framed in dazzling white light against the southern gable of the parish church. They were soon joined by 13 more villagers, all gazing at the heavenly apparition for around two hours as the daylight faded. A Church investigation confirmed it as a bona fide miracle, and a sudden rush of other Vatican-approved miracles followed as the sick and disabled claimed amazing recoveries upon visiting the spot.

Besides the sacred chapel, there is the vast 1970s **Basilica of Our Lady, Queen of Ireland**, which can accommodate more than 10,000. Nearby, the little **Knock Museum** (adult/child €4/3; ⊙10am-6pm) follows the story from the first witnesses, through the miraculous cures and the repeated Church investigations.

Getting There & Away

AIR

Ireland West Airport Knock (NOC; ☎094-936 8100; www.irelandwestairport.com; off N17), 15km north, has services primarily to Britain. The airport website lists bus services to Westport and Galway.

BUS

Services run to Westport (€8, one hour, one daily) and Galway (€12, 1½ hours, 10 daily).

COUNTY SLIGO

POP 65,380 / AREA 1814 SQ KM

County Sligo packs as much poetry, myth and folklore into its countryside's lush splendour as any shamrock lover could hope for. It was Sligo that most inspired the Nobel laureate, poet and dramatist William Butler (WB) Yeats (1865–1939). Ever fascinated by Irish mysticism, he was intrigued by places such as prehistoric Carrowmore Megalithic Cemetery, iconic and hulking Benbulben and cute little Innisfree Island.

And it's no complacent backwater: there's a vibrant and creative food culture and the coast's surf is internationally renowned.

Sligo Town

POP 19,500

Pedestrian streets lined with inviting shop fronts, stone bridges spanning the River Garavogue, and *céilidh* sessions spilling from pubs contrast with contemporary art and glass towers rising from prominent corners of compact Sligo. It makes a good and low-key base for exploring Yeats country.

Sights & Activities

Sligo Abbey HISTORIC BUILDING
(www.heritageireland.ie; Abbey St; adult/child €4/2; ⊙10am-6pm Easter–mid-Oct) This handsome abbey was built around 1252 but burned down in the 15th century and was later rebuilt. Friends in high places saved the abbey from the worst ravages of the Elizabethan era, and rescued the only sculpted altar to survive the Reformation. The doorways reach only a few feet high at the abbey's rear; the ground around it was swollen by the mass graves from years of famine and war.

Model GALLERY
(☎071-914 1405; www.themodel.ie; The Mall; admission varies; ⊙10am-5.30pm Tue-Sat, noon-5pm Sun) The Model houses an impressive collection of contemporary Irish art including works by Jack B Yeats (WB's brother and one of Ireland's most important modern artists) and Louis le Brocquy. There are also galleries for temporary exhibitions. The centre offers an interesting program of experimental theatre, music and film, and has a good cafe.

Sligo County Museum MUSEUM
(☎071-911 1679; Stephen St; ⊙9.30am-12.30pm Tue-Sat year-round, 2-4.45pm Tues-Sat May-Sep) FREE The major draw of Sligo's county

Sligo Town

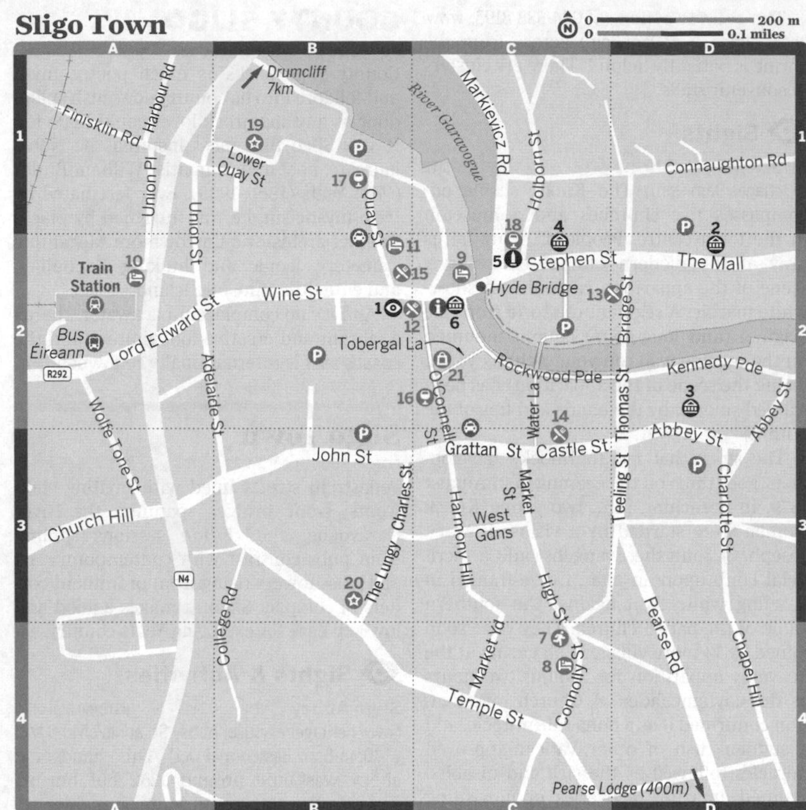

museum is the Yeats room, which features photographs, letters and newspaper cuttings connected with WB Yeats, as well as drawings by Jack B Yeats.

Yeats Memorial Building MUSEUM

(☎071-914 2693; www.yeatssociety.com; Hyde Bridge; adult/child €2/free; ⏰10am-5pm Mon-Fri, to 2pm Sat) In a pretty setting in a former 1895 bank, the **WB Yeats Exhibition** has details of his life and draft manuscripts. There are special summer programs. The small cafe has outdoor tables overlooking the river.

WB Yeats Statue MONUMENT

(off Hyde Bridge) Erected in 1989, this abstract statue of Yeats in front of the 1863 Ulster Bank (a building he admired) is the source of much local mirth. See if you agree with the popular moniker 'the wank at the bank'.

Chain Driven Cycles BICYCLE RENTAL

(☎071-912 9008; www.chaindrivencycles.com; 23 High St; per day from €20; ⏰10am-6pm Mon-Sat) Offers mountain-, hybrid-, electric- and road-bike hire. Rate includes helmet.

Festivals & Events

Sligo manages a festival of some sort almost every weekend during tourist season.

Tread Softly CULTURE

(www.treadsoftly.ie) Part of Sligo's 'Season of Yeats', this series of events over 10 days in late July celebrates the iconic man with tours, performances and more.

Sligo Live CULTURE

(www.sligolive.ie) Sligo's biggest cultural event is this live-music festival over five days in late October.

Sligo Town

Sights

1 Michael Quirke's Studio....B2
2 Model....D2
3 Sligo Abbey....D2
4 Sligo County Museum....C2
5 WB Yeats Statue....C2
6 Yeats Memorial Building....C2

Activities, Courses & Tours

7 Chain Driven Cycles....C4

Sleeping

8 An Crúiscin Lan....C4
9 Glass House....C2
10 Railway Hostel....A2
11 Sligo City Hotel....B2

Eating

12 Fabio's....B2
13 Gourmet Parlour....D2
14 Kate's Kitchen....C3
15 Lyons Cafe....B2

Drinking & Nightlife

16 Hargadons....C2
17 Harp Tavern....B1
18 Thomas Connolly....C2

Entertainment

19 Blue Raincoat Theatre Company....B1
20 Hawk's Well Theatre....B3

Shopping

21 Liber Bookshop....C2

Sleeping

You'll find lots of B&Bs lining Pearse Rd.

★ An Crúiscin Lan GUESTHOUSE €
(071-916 2857; www.bandbsligo.ie; Connolly St; s/d from €40/70;) The central location is a good selling point for this simple and convivial place. Some of the 10 rooms share bathrooms. The friendly owner runs a tight ship; stag and hen parties are banned.

Railway Hostel HOSTEL €
(087 690 5539; www.therailway.ie; 1 Union Pl; dm from €18, s/d from €25/44;) In a heritage building close to the train station, this cheery hostel has great rates and shared bathrooms. There's a surcharge for arriving after 9pm. There are no bunk beds.

Sligo City Hotel HOTEL €€
(071-914 4000; www.sligocityhotel.com; Quay St; r €65-90;) Recently renovated, this four-storey hotel could not be better located. The 60 good-sized rooms have a simple corporate colour scheme. Basic rates do not include breakfast.

Pearse Lodge B&B €€
(071-916 1090; www.pearselodge.com; Pearse Rd; s/d from €50/80; @) Welcoming owners Mary and Kieron have four stylish guest rooms with hardwood floors. The breakfast menu includes smoked salmon, French toast with bananas and homemade muesli. A sunny sitting room opens to a garden. It's 700m southwest of the centre.

Glass House HOTEL €€
(071-919 4300; www.theglasshouse.ie; Swan Point; s/d from €80/100; @) You can't miss this contemporary hotel in the centre of town, its sharp glass facade pointing skyward. Inside, the food areas have good river views while the 116 rooms come in a choice of psychedelic colours.

Eating

Sligo has some creative kitchens that make good use of seasonal fare. Pubs such as Hargadons (p420) are also excellent choices.

★ Fabio's ICE CREAM €
(Wine St; treats from €2; 11am-6pm Tue-Sat, 1-6pm Sun) Fabio is a local hero for making Ireland's best Italian gelato and sorbets. He uses mostly local and natural ingredients for his changing line-up of flavours. His coffee is good, too.

★ Lyons Cafe MODERN EUROPEAN €
(071-914 2969; www.lyonscafe.com; Quay St; mains €7-15; 9am-6pm Mon-Sat) Sligo's flagship department store, Lyons, opened in 1878 – with original leadlight windows and squeaky timber floors – and has been going strong since 1923. Its airy 1st-floor cafe is anything but stodgy, and acclaimed chef (and cookbook author) Gary Stafford offers a fresh and seasonal menu that's inventive yet casual.

Kate's Kitchen CAFE €
(www.kateskitchen.ie; Castle St; mains from €6; 9am-6pm Mon-Sat) Only the best local foodstuffs are sold at this lovely, contemporary shop. All the fixings for a prime picnic are combined with prepared foods. It also does a big lunchtime trade.

Gourmet Parlour CAFE €
(071-914 4617; www.gourmetparlour.com; Bridge St; mains €4-12; 8am-5pm Mon-Sat) Simply great simple food is the theme at this bakery

DON'T MISS

MICHAEL QUIRKE: THE WOODCARVER OF WINE STREET

The inconspicuous storefront studio of **Michael Quirke** (☎071-914 2624; Wine St, Sligo town; ⊙usually 9.30am-12.30pm & 3-5.30pm Mon-Sat), woodcarver, raconteur and local legend, is filled with the scents of locally felled timbers and off-cuts of sycamore. Quirke began cutting and carving wood in 1968. Today he still uses the same saw he used on meat when he worked here as a butcher.

A modern-day Yeats, Quirke's art is inspired by Irish mythology, a subject about which he is passionate and knowledgeable, and as he carves he readily chats with the customers and the curious who enter his shop and end up staying for hours.

As he talks and carves, Quirke frequently pulls out a county map, pointing to places (such as his beloved Carrowmore) that spring from the conversation, leading you on your own magical, mystical tour of the county. Should he ask you your favourite animal, consider your answer carefully, as he's likely to quickly carve you a version of the critter while exclaiming, 'Who is it that reveals the secret shapes hidden in the wood? Who, but I?'

and cafe. Sandwiches, tarts, hot lunches and more are excellent. Many swoon for the apple pie. Drop by for just a coffee and plan to succumb to more.

Drinking & Nightlife

Sligo enjoys some of the best night-time fun in Ireland's northwest, with many impromptu sessions.

★Hargadons PUB
(☎071-915 3709; www.hargadons.com; 4-5 O'Connell St; ⊙food noon-9pm Mon-Sat) You'll have a hard time leaving this superb 1864 pub with its winning blend of old-world fittings and gastropub style. Its uneven floors, peat fire, antique signage, snug corners and bowed shelves laden down with ancient bottles give it a wonderful charm. The great-value food (mains €8 to €20) is renowned, combining local ingredients such as oysters with continental flair.

The kitchen and service are excellent. The menu changes with the seasons; many of the wines come from the pub's vineyard in France. Bookings are not taken, so plan on sampling a few fine microbrews while you wait. There's trad music some nights.

Harp Tavern PUB
(☎071-914 2473; Quay St; ⊙11am-late) An all-around good pub with regular trad-music sessions and a genuinely welcoming vibe. Has good bar food through the day and evening.

Thomas Connolly PUB
(Holborn St; ⊙11am-late) Discoloured photos and newspaper clippings, mottled mirrors and ledger books adorn the walls at this old timers' pub.

☆ Entertainment

Hawk's Well Theatre THEATRE
(☎071-916 1518; www.hawkswell.com; Temple St) This well-regarded theatre presents concerts, dance and drama.

Blue Raincoat Theatre Company THEATRE
(☎071-917 0431; www.blueraincoat.com; Lower Quay St) A former abattoir is home to this innovative theatre company Blue Raincoat, whose program includes original productions plus Yeats in the summer.

Shopping

★Liber Bookshop BOOKS
(☎071-914 2219; www.liber.ie; 35 O'Connell St; ⊙9am-6pm Mon-Sat) Yes you can get Yeats at this fabulous bookshop that has been run by the same family for more than 80 years. It also gives recommendations on the best local authors.

Information

Tourist Office (☎071-916 1201; www.sligotourism.ie; cnr O'Connell & Wine Sts; ⊙10am-5pm Mon-Fri year-round, to 4pm Sat Apr-Sep, to 2pm Sun Jul & Aug) Has info on the whole northwest region, plus good walking info.

Getting There & Away

BUS

Bus Éireann (☎071-916 0066; www.buseireann.ie; Lord Edward St) leaves from the bus station situated below the train station. Destinations include Ballina (€18, 1½ hours, one to four daily), Westport (€23, 2¾ hours, one daily) and Donegal town (€16, one hour, six daily).

TRAIN

Trains leave the station for Dublin (€35, three hours, seven daily) via Boyle, Carrick-on-Shannon and Mullingar.

Getting Around

There are taxi stands on Quay St and Grattan St.

Around Sligo Town

Rosses Point

POP 830

Rosses Point is a picturesque seaside town with grassy dunes rolling down to the golden strand. Benbulben (525m), Sligo's most recognisable landmark, looms in the distance. Offshore, the unusual – and jaunty – 1821 **Metal Man** beacon points the way into harbour. In the distance are ride-free **Coney Island** and **Oyster Island**.

Rosses Point has two wonderful **beaches** and one of Ireland's most challenging and renowned golf links, **County Sligo Golf Course** (071-917 7171; www.countysligogolfclub.ie; green fees €125; Apr-Oct), which attracts golfers from all over the world. Fringed by the Atlantic and lying in the shadow of Benbulben, this is possibly Ireland's greatest and most picturesque golf links.

Harry's Bar (071-917 7173; www.harrysrossespoint.com; Rosses Point; mains €12-25; food 11am-9pm Tue-Sun;) – on your right as you enter town – has a historic well, aquarium and maritime bric-a-brac. It's been in the same family since 1870 and serves good, classic fare.

Rosses Point is 8km northwest of Sligo town on the R291. There are regular buses from Sligo town (€4, hourly).

Carrowmore

As more is learned about Carrowmore Megalithic Cemetery, its role as a spiritual nexus for Sligo-area sites, including Knocknarea Cairn, is becoming better understood.

Sights

★Carrowmore Megalithic Cemetery ARCHAEOLOGICAL SITE

(071-916 1534; www.heritageireland.ie; adult/child €4/2; 10am-6pm Easter–mid-Oct, final admission 5pm) One of the largest Stone Age cemeteries in Europe, Carrowmore is finally receiving the renown it deserves and is Sligo's must-see attraction.

Some 60 monuments including stone circles, passage tombs and dolmens adorn the rolling hills of this haunting site, which is thought to predate Newgrange in County Meath by 700 years. Although over the centuries, many of the stones have been destroyed, ongoing excavations continue to uncover more sites both within the public site and on adjoining private land.

Discoveries about the meaning of Carrowmore are continuing and are dramatic. How the many features of the site relate to the surrounding hills and mountains is rich with meaning. Among the numbered sites, 51 has been found to get direct sunlight at dawn each 31 October, or Halloween. Many people claim to feel strong powers here and you'll likely see a few spiritual pilgrims on the site.

The delicately balanced dolmens were originally covered with stones and earth, so it requires some effort to picture what this 2.5km-wide area might once have looked like. A large central cairn has been reconstructed to give visitors some insight into the materials and methods used at this time. The visitor centre has full details and staff are happy to explain much more, plus detail the latest discoveries.

To get here, follow the R292 west from Sligo town for 4km and follow the signposts.

Knocknarea Cairn HISTORIC SITE

Sligo's ultimate rock pile, Knocknarea is popularly believed to be the grave of legendary Queen Maeve (Queen Mab in Welsh and English folk tales). The 40,000 tonnes of stone have never been excavated, despite speculation that a tomb on the scale of the one at Newgrange lies buried below.

The cairn is perched high atop a limestone plateau (328m). It's a 45-minute (1.2km) trek to the top for spectacular panoramic views of Benbulben, Rosses Point and the Atlantic Ocean beyond.

The cairn seems to be looking over your shoulder everywhere you dare tread in its ancestral backyard. Many think the rocks purposely form a giant nipple, which takes on meaning when the overall horizon is viewed from Carrowmore. Believers in underlying powers at the sites say that you can easily make out the shape of a reclining woman, or a mother god.

WB YEATS & IRISH MYTHS

William Butler Yeats liked to say that by age 24 in 1889 he'd read 'most, if not all, recorded Irish folk tales'. There's certainly no reason to dismiss this claim as hyperbole as his writings, whether poetry, prose or plays celebrated Celtic legends and myths. It's all the more fitting given his love for County Sligo, a place home to ancient Celtic sites such the remarkable Carrowmore (p421), with ancient mysteries and meanings that are still being discovered today.

Yeats firmly believed that the Irish could emerge from English domination and create their own purely Irish identity by revelling in the ancient Celtic myths still commonly recounted across the land. In 1888 he collaborated on the landmark *Fairy and Folk Tales of the Irish Peasantry*. Four years later, he wrote the children's book *Irish Fairy Tales*. In these works he codified many of the most common Irish myths, characters and legends that are common today. Among them:

Fairies A strong believer in the occult, Yeats had no problems merging his views with the common belief among rural people in fairies. A whole race of little people, fairies had all manner of qualities (with being mischievous near universal) but could be roughly divided into good and bad. In the *Land of Heart's Desire* (first performed in 1894), Yeats wrote:

Faeries, come take me out of this dull world,
For I would ride with you upon the wind,
Run on the top of the dishevelled tide,
And dance upon the mountains like a flame.

Leprechauns Solitary members of the much-larger race of fairies, Yeats called leprechauns 'sluttish, slouching, jeering, mischievous phantoms' and 'great practical jokers'. Contrary to the modern-day green-clad apparitions found in gift shops, Yeats had his leprechauns dressed in red jackets and prone to endless avarice.

Banshees Typically a woman of varying age – from cute to crone – who appears wailing before a death. Long feared, Yeats had much more benevolent views, writing: 'You will with the Banshee chat and will find her good at heart'.

Yeats also wrote much about the ancient Irish gods, most derived from Celtic myths, including Aengus, the Irish god of love, and Cuchulain, a great Irish warrior in the spirit of Hercules. In the poem 'Cuchulain Comforted' (1939), he combines myth with a classic Irish quality, writing 'Now we shall sing and sing the best we can'.

The parking area is off the R292. The cairn is 2km northwest of Carrowmore; from Carrowmore, continue west along the road, turn right by a church, and then follow the signposts.

Strandhill

POP 1650

The great Atlantic rollers that sweep Strandhill's shore make this long, red-gold beach a surfing mecca.

Activities

Although it's too rough to swim, there are excellent long and brisk **walks** along the beach both north and south. The views of the surf are always spectacular and you can wander up into the dunes.

Perfect Day Surf & SUP School SURFING
(☎087 202 9399; www.perfectdaysurfing.com; Airport Rd; lessons per adult/child from €30/20; ⊙Apr-Oct) This useful shop offers lessons for surfing and stand-up paddleboarding. They usually have a yellow van parked at the beach on Shore Rd.

Strandhill Surf School SURFING
(☎071-916 8483; www.strandhillsurf.eu; Beach Front; lessons per adult/child from €30/20; ⊙Apr-Oct) Offers gear hire and lessons. The live surf cams on the website are alluring indeed.

Voya Seaweed Baths SPA
(☎071-916 8686; www.voyaseaweedbaths.com; Shore Rd; bath from €25; ⊙10am-8pm) Don't just smell seaweed on the beach, immerse yourself in it at this beachfront location. Ask about sharing your bath.

Sleeping

You can either sleep close to the action down by the shore, or 1km up the hill along Top Rd (R292), where you *may* have views.

Surf & Stay Lodge & Hostel LODGE €
(☎071-916 8313; www.surfnstay.ie; Shore Rd; dm from €20, s/d from €35/50; 📶) Surfers thaw out by the open fire in the common room of the 34-bed hostel portion of this two-building complex. Rooms in the adjoining house are B&B style and while small are comfy. Some share bathrooms. The beach is close and there is an on-site surf school.

Ocean Wave Lodge B&B €
(☎071-916 8115; www.oceanwavelodge.com; Top Rd/R292; dm/s/d from €20/40/50; 📶) This large modern house uphill from the beach has minimalist but comfortable rooms. Breakfast is included and there's a self-catering kitchen and large lounge area for guest use.

Strandhill Lodge & Suites GUESTHOUSE €€
(☎071-912 2122; www.strandhilllodgeandsuites.com; Top Rd/R292; s/d from €90/100; 📶) Up the hill, this excellent guesthouse offers 22 bright, spacious rooms with king-sized beds, hotel-quality design and trendy neutral styling. Room sizes vary but most have fabulous views down to the ocean and terraces or balconies.

Eating & Drinking

★Shells CAFE €
(☎071-912 2938; www.shellscafe.com; Shore Rd; mains from €6; ⏰9am-7pm; 👪) Be thrilled by the surf from the terrace at this sprightly little cafe right across from the beach. Flowers on tables and herbs in the dishes come from the owner's garden. The baked goods are excellent as is the coffee. Breakfasts delight and at lunch there are salads, chowders, specials and splendid fish and chips.

★Trá Bán MODERN IRISH €€
(☎071-912 8402; www.trabansligo.ie; Shore Rd; mains €16-25; ⏰5-9.30pm Tue-Sun; 👪) This justifiably popular 1st-floor restaurant above the Strand Bar serves excellent pasta, steaks and seafood. The crab-claws starter is all briney joy. It has a relaxed atmosphere, and is popular with local families with something to celebrate. Book in advance.

Strand Bar PUB
(☎071-916 8140; Shore Rd; ⏰11am-late) Surfers, locals and tourists crowd into proper snugs and cosy corners at this convivial pub. Or they just listen to the surf from the terrace out front. There's bar food; live music plays at weekends.

Getting There & Away

Strandhill is 8km due west of Sligo town off the R292. Local buses run from Sligo town (€4, hourly).

South of Sligo Town

Carrowkeel

Carrowkeel Megalithic Cemetery HISTORIC SITE
With a bird's-eye view of the county from high in the Bricklieve Mountains, it's little wonder this hilltop site was sacred in prehistoric times. This windswept and lonely location is simultaneously eerie and uplifting. But for a few sheep (you drive though a sheep gate), it's undeveloped and spectacular. Dotted with around 14 cairns, dolmens and the scattered remnants of other graves, the site dates from the late Stone Age (3000 to 2000 BC).

Just the sweeping views down to south Sligo from the car park make the journey worthwhile. It's a 1km walk to the first ancient site, Cairn G. Above its entrance is a roof-box aligned with the midsummer sunset which illuminates the inner chamber. The only other such roof-box known in Ireland is that at Newgrange in County Meath. Everywhere you look across the surrounding hills you'll see evidence of early life, including about 140 stone circles, all that remain of the foundations of a large village thought to have been inhabited by the builders of the tombs.

Carrowkeel is closer to Boyle than Sligo town. It's about 5km from either the R295 in the west or the N4 in the east. Follow the signs.

Ballymote & Around

POP 1600

This pretty little town merits a visit for opportunities to ponder Irish culture and history.

Sights

Ballymote Castle RUIN
(Tubbercurry Rd/R296) The immense shell of Ballymote Castle could be a model for sandcastle builders everywhere. It was from this

OLIVER STREWE/GETTY IMAGES ©

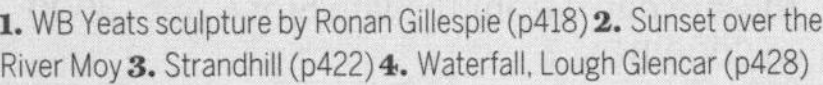

1. WB Yeats sculpture by Ronan Gillespie (p418) **2.** Sunset over the River Moy **3.** Strandhill (p422) **4.** Waterfall, Lough Glencar (p428)

GARETH MCCORMACK/GETTY IMAGES ©

Yeats' Country

County Sligo's lush hills, ancient monuments and simple country life inspired Nobel laureate, poet and dramatist William Butler Yeats (1865–1939) from an early age. Despite living almost all his life abroad, Yeats returned here frequently, enamoured by the lakes, the looming hulk of Benbulben and the idyllic pastoral setting.

Inspiration for Yeats

Sligo is littered with prehistoric monuments and has a rich tradition of myth and folklore, all of which influenced Yeats and his work. You can tour the locations that inspired him, from the waterfall in Glencar referred to in 'The Stolen Child', to picturesque Innisfree Island and rugged Dooney Rock.

Remembering & Honouring Yeats

Yeats' great legacy is celebrated with 10 days of Irish poetry, music, literature and festivals during the 'Tread Softly' portion of the 'Season of Yeats' festival held in Sligo each year, while you can get a sense of his life and work at exhibits devoted to him in Sligo town.

TOP STOPS

➡ **Innisfree** The little island on Lough Gill where Yeats set the poem 'The Lake Isle of Innisfree', which begins with the famous line: 'I will arise and go now, and go to Innisfree'.

➡ **Benbulben** Yeats' memorial is in the shadow of this forbidding and iconic mountain.

➡ **Drumcliff** The small village church here is where Yeats was long believed to be buried, alongside his youthful bride Georgie Hyde-Lee.

➡ **Sligo County Museum** This compact museum has displays on Yeats' work and life.

➡ **Yeats Memorial Building** Manuscripts by Yeats and more, all in the heart of Sligo town.

early-14th-century redoubt, fronted by formidable drum towers, that O'Donnell marched to disaster at the Battle of Kinsale in 1601. It's opposite the Ballymote train station.

Coleman Irish Music Centre ARTS CENTRE
(☎071-918 2599; www.colemanirishmusic.com; Gurteen; ⊙10am-5pm Mon-Sat) This music centre has multimedia exhibits and hosts workshops and performances. You can add to your music collection or pick up your own instruments and sheet music at the on-site shop. It's 12km south of Ballymote on the R293 in the little village of Gurteen.

Aughris Head

An invigorating 5km **walk** traces the cliffs around remote Aughris Head, where dolphins and seals can often be seen swimming into the bay. Birdwatchers should look out for kittiwakes, fulmars, guillemots, shags, storm petrels and curlews along the way.

Sleeping & Eating

Beach Bar SEAFOOD €€
(☎071-917 6465; www.thebeachbarsligo.com; Aughris Head; mains €10-25, tent/van sites from €10/20, s/d from €45/70; ⊙food served 1-8pm daily summer, Fri-Sun winter;) In a sheltered setting on the lovely beach by the cliff walk, the pub in this 17th-century thatched cottage hosts cracking traditional-music sessions and serves superb seafood, including creamy chowder and poached salmon. The owners also operate the **Aughris House B&B** next door, with seven comfy rooms and adjacent campsites.

Easkey

Easkey is one of Europe's best year-round surfing destinations. However in pubs with names such as Lobster Pot and Fisherman's Weir, conversations revolve around hurling and seafood prices; the road to the **beach** is just east of town. Facilities are few; most surfers camp (free) around the **castle ruins** by the sea.

Buses run once daily from Sligo town to Ballina via Easkey (€12, one hour).

Enniscrone

This very low-key holiday town is all about the ocean. Stunning **Hollow Beach** stretches for 5km.

Activities

Kilcullen's Seaweed Baths SPA
(☎096-36238; www.kilcullenseaweedbaths.com; Cliff Rd, Enniscrone; bath from €25; ⊙noon-8pm Mon-Fri, 10am-8pm Sat & Sun May-Sep, noon-8pm Thu-Mon Oct-Apr) Enniscrone is famous for its traditional seaweed baths which are some of the most atmospheric in the country. Kilcullen's is the most traditional and has buckets of character.

Seventh Wave Surf School SURFING
(☎087 971 6389; www.surfsligo.com; Beach, Enniscrone; lessons adult/child from €30/25; ⊙Apr-Oct) Offers surf lessons and board rental.

Sleeping & Eating

Waterfront House LODGE €€
(☎096-37120; www.waterfronthouse.ie; Cliff Rd; s/d from €55/85;) Perched on the knoll overlooking the broad beach and surf, the 16 rooms are done up in ubiquitous maroon, but considering the views, they are a bargain. The popular bar and restaurant will keep you otherwise occupied.

Pilot Bar MODERN IRISH €€
(☎096-36131; www.thepilotbar.ie; cnr Cliff Rd & Main St; mains €6-20; ⊙bar 4pm-late Mon-Fri, 9am-late Sat & Sun, kitchen Wed-Sun;) Terrace tables let you bask in the sun amid potted flowers, while inside you can fancy yourself a seaman as you revel in the porthole motifs. The food is simple but delicious, with much sourced locally.

Getting There & Away

Sligo town (€15, 1¼ hours) buses run once daily on the route to Ballina.

Lough Gill

Mirrorlike Lough Gill (Lake of Brightness) was a place of great inspiration for Yeats.

The lake, a mere 6km southeast of Sligo town, is shaded by two magical swaths of woodland – **Hazelwood** and **Slish Wood** – which have loop trails; there are good views of Innisfree Island from the latter.

You can take a **cruise** on the lake from atmospheric Parke's Castle (p472), in nearby County Leitrim. Watch for the shadows of huge salmon and the ripples of otters.

Getting There & Away

The lake is immediately east of Sligo town. Take the R286 along the north shore for the most interesting views, whether you are driving or riding. The southern route on the R287 is less interesting until you reach Dooney Rock.

Dooney Rock

Immortalised by Yeats in 'The Fiddler of Dooney' (1899), this huge fissured limestone knoll bulges awkwardly upward by the lough's southern shore. There's a great lake view from the top.

It's 7km southwest of Sligo town on the R287.

Innisfree Island

This pint-sized island lies tantalisingly close to the lough's southeastern shore, but alas, can't be accessed. Still, it's visible from the shore. Its air of tranquillity so moved Yeats that he famously wrote in 'The Lake Isle of Innisfree' (1890):

> I will arise and go now, and go to Innisfree,
> And a small cabin build there, of clay and wattles made;
> Nine bean rows will I have there, a hive for the honey bee,
> And live alone in the bee-loud glade.

Access the best vantage point of the island from a small road that starts at the junction of the R287 and the R290. Follow the winding lane for 4.2km to a small parking area by the water.

North of Sligo Town

Evocative coastal drives and lonely mountain paths highlight the heart of Yeats country.

Benbulben

A stolid greenish-grey eminence visible all along Sligo's northern coast, Benbulben (525m), often written Ben Bulben, resembles a table covered by a pleated cloth: its limestone plateau is uncommonly flat, and its near-vertical sides are scored by earthen ribs. Walking here is not for the uninitiated.

Drumcliff & Around

Benbulben's beauty was not lost on WB Yeats. Before the poet died in Menton, France, in 1939, he had requested: 'If I die here, bury me up there on the mountain, and then after a year or so, dig me up and bring me privately to Sligo'. His wishes were honoured in 1948, when his body was interred in the churchyard at Drumcliff, where his great-grandfather had been rector.

Sights & Activities

★Yeats' Grave MONUMENT
(off N15; dawn-dusk) Yeats was long believed to be buried next to the doorway of the Protestant church, but recent evidence suggests that the bones shipped here from France in 1948 were not his at all, owing to the actual bones being scattered about an ossuary during the chaos of WWII. Yeats' youthful

WALKING SLIGO

In a country that doesn't hurt for a lack of good walks, County Sligo has more than its share. There are myriad choices, including the **Sligo Way** (www.irishtrails.ie), a 78km waymarked route that includes the Ox Mountains, Lough Easkey and Lough Gill.

Walking resources and organisations are many, and include the following:

Sligo Walks (www.sligowalks.ie) An excellent online resource with dozens of walks, maps, ratings and much more.

Sligo Mountaineering Club (www.sligomountaineeringclub.org) Good website for info on climbing Benbulben, including sensible details on staying safe.

Muddy Boots Trekking (087 642 9131; www.muddybootsguidedwalking.com) Organises day hikes on Benbulben and elsewhere.

Sea Trails (087 240 5071; www.seatrails.ie; walks from €15) Highly recommended. Runs interesting walks that concentrate on ancient features and natural beauty in and near the coast.

Sligo Walking Guide A useful free booklet with scores of walks, available at tourist offices.

WORTH A TRIP

INISHMURRAY ISLAND

It takes some effort to arrange a visit to **Inishmurray** (www.inishmurray.com), an island that was abandoned in 1948, leaving behind early Christian remains and fascinating pagan relics. There are three well-preserved churches, beehive cells and open-air altars. The old monastery, surrounded by a thickset oval wall, was founded in the early 6th century by St Molaise.

Although it's only 6km between Inishmurray and the mainland, there's no regular boat service, and the lack of a harbour makes landing subject to the weather. To visit, check with **Inishmurray Island Trips** (☎087 254 0190; www.inishmurrayislandtrips.com; Mullaghmore; trips per person from €40; ⏰Apr-Sep).

bride Georgie Hyde-Lee, however, is buried alongside. Almost three decades her senior, Yeats was 52 when they married.

The poet's epitaph is from his poem 'Under Ben Bulben':

Cast a cold eye
On life, on death.
Horseman, pass by!

There's a small **cafe & crafts shop** (mains from €4; ⏰9am-5pm) beside the church. It is popular with locals at lunch and has a good selection of books.

In the 6th century, St Colmcille chose this location for a monastery. You can still see the stumpy remains of a **round tower**, which was struck by lightning in 1396, on the main road nearby. Also in the churchyard is an extraordinary 9th-century **high cross**, etched with intricate biblical scenes that include Adam and Eve, as well as Daniel in the Lion's Den.

Benbulben Loop HIKING
(www.coillteoutdoors.ie; off N15) Right in the shadow of the iconic mountain, this 4km-loop walk runs through protected lands with spruce and fir trees plus a range of rare Irish flora. The trail head and parking is 1km east of the N15, 3km north of Drumcliff.

Sleeping & Eating

Benbulben Farmhouse B&B LODGE €
(☎071-917 3956; www.benbulbenfarmhouse.com; Barnaribbon; s/d €55/70) Nestled in the shadow of Benbulben and far from the N15, this farmhouse offers peaceful rural respite and superb breakfasts. Everything is modern and rooms have sitting areas to take in the sylvan views. It's 3km northeast of Drumcliff.

Yeats Lodge B&B €
(☎071-917 3787; www.yeatslodge.com; Drumcliff; s/d from €50/70; ᯤ) Obliging owners, five large, modern rooms and a tranquil atmosphere make this B&B worth seeking out. There's tasteful rustic decor and lovely views of Benbulben. It's 300m off the N15.

★**Rathcormac Food & Craft Market** MARKET €
(off N15, Rathcormac; ⏰10am-3pm Sat) Held in Branley's Yard amid antique shops and a good cafe, this market is worth scheduling your trip around. Although small, the best producers in the region sell ready-to-eat food, produce, cheeses, baked goods and much more. It's a delight to wander about snacking while shopping for your picnic.

Vintage Lane CAFE €
(☎087 662 2600; off N15, Rathcormac; mains from €5; ⏰10am-5pm Mon-Sat year-round, Sun Jul-Aug) Set in atmospheric Branley's Yard, site of the excellent Saturday market, this idiosyncratic cafe has mismatched antique furniture sourced from the neighbouring antique shops. The coffee, cakes and more are first-rate, as is the open fire on a misty day.

Getting There & Away

Buses run from Sligo town to Drumcliff (€5, 10 minutes, seven to eight daily).

Lough Glencar

Straddling Counties Sligo and Leitrim, this picturesque lake is famed for **fishing** as well as its beautiful **waterfall**, and was referred to by Yeats in his 1889 poem 'The Stolen Child'. The surrounding countryside is best enjoyed by walking east and taking the steep trail north to the valley.

From Drumcliff it's less than 5km to the lake's western shores.

Raghly

Wide open flats and surf-pounded beaches of battered rocks are the hallmark of this worthwhile drive out to the coast from Drumcliff. Look for the turn just north of Drumcliff.

Sleeping

★Ardtarmon House LODGE €€

(071-916 3156; www.ardtarmon.com; Raghly Rd, Ballinfull; s/d from €50/80, cottage €100-450; closed late Dec-early Jan) In an incomparable location 10.5km west of the N15, this fifth-generation family-run property has four spacious rooms in the ivy-covered manor house, and five self-contained cottages in converted farm buildings. A 450m stroll through wildflower-strewn gardens brings you to a beach. Dinner (€30) featuring homegrown produce can be arranged.

Streedagh Beach

From the village of Grange, signs point towards Streedagh Beach, a grand crescent of sand that saw some 1100 sailors perish when three ships from the Spanish Armada were wrecked nearby. Views extend from the beach to the cliffs at Slieve League in County Donegal. Locals regularly swim here, even in winter.

Mullaghmore

The sweeping arc of dark-golden sand and the safe shallow waters make the pretty fishing village of Mullaghmore a popular family destination.

Take time to walk, cycle or drive the scenic road loop around Mullaghmore Head, where wide shafts of rock slice into the Atlantic surf. En route you'll pass **Classiebawn Castle** (closed to the public), a neo-Gothic turreted pile built for Lord Palmerston in 1856 and later home to the ill-fated Lord Mountbatten, who was killed near here in 1979 when the IRA rigged his boat with explosives.

The area is becoming known as one of Ireland's premier big-wave **surf** spots with swells of up to 17m allowing for Hawaiian-style adventure. Big-wave tow-in surfing competitions are regularly held off Mullaghmore Head.

Enjoy magnificent views from the **Pier Head Hotel** (071-916 6171; www.pierheadhotel.ie; Mullaghmore; s/d from €50/80; closed late Dec; ) by the harbour. The 40 rooms are clean and crisp (request one with a view across Donegal Bay), there's a panoramic rooftop terrace with hot tub, indoor pool and decent food (mains from €10 to €21) in the bar.

Cliffony

Sights

Creevykeel Goort Cairn HISTORIC SITE

(off N15; dawn-dusk) Shaped like a lobster's claw, this prehistoric court tomb encloses several burial chambers. The structure was originally built around 2500 BC, with several more chambers added later. Once in the unroofed oval court, smaller visitors can duck under the stone-shielded entrance to reach the site's core. The sylvan setting has distant ocean views.

The tomb is 1.5km north of Cliffony on the N15.

Gleniff Horseshoe Valley

From Cliffony, follow the small road southeast into the broad Gleniff Horseshoe Valley. Set amid the stark, barren drama of the Dartry Mountains, this area begs for exploration. A tiny lane, the **Gleniff Horseshoe**, makes a 10km loop through the valley, passing wild babbling streams and the remains of an old **mill**. You can imagine Yeats here.

The loop is good by bike or car. You can also walk and branch off into hikes in the hills. **Sligo Walks** (www.sligowalks.ie) has online maps.

At the base of the valley, the **Benwiskin Centre** (071-917 6721; www.benwiskincentre.com; Ballintrillick; dm/s/d €15/45/55;) is a good hostel with dorms and private rooms.

County Donegal

POP 161,400 / AREA 3001 SQ KM

Includes ➡

Best Places to Eat

- ➡ Beach House (p461)
- ➡ Olde Castle Bar (p435)
- ➡ Nancy's Bar (p443)
- ➡ Danny Minnie's Restaurant (p446)

Best Places to Stay

- ➡ Corcreggan Mill (p450)
- ➡ Glen House (p462)
- ➡ Castle Murray (p438)
- ➡ Woodhill House (p443)

Why Go?

'Up here it's different', the saying goes, and it's true. County Donegal is the wild child of Ireland. Even before the twins of history and politics conspired to isolate it, Donegal was a place like no other on the island. It's a county of extremes: at times desolate and battered by brutal weather, yet in turn a land of unspoilt splendour where stark peaks and sweeping beaches bask in glorious sunshine, and little restaurants serve amazing food.

Uncrowded Donegal's rugged interior with its remote mountain passes and shimmering lakes is only marginally outdone by the long and labyrinthine coastline with its windswept peninsulas and isolated, characterful pubs. Proudly independent, one-third of the county is official Gaeltacht territory, where Irish is the lingua franca.

After its northern start in Derry, the Wild Atlantic Way really begins to strut its stuff in Donegal as the county's untamed craggy coastline truly puts the wild into the way.

When to Go

➡ Donegal's character is forged by its impetuous weather. In winter the howling winds and sheeting rain can feel Arctic, and storms arrive unannounced.

➡ In summer the weather isn't much more reliable but the clouds regularly break into brilliant sunshine that transforms brooding pewter skies into brilliant blue. Because everything is open, you'll also get the pick of traditional music, storytelling and dance festivals that spring up across the county and even in pubs.

Getting There & Away

Major towns in Donegal are served by buses that link to both Dublin and Northern Ireland. There is no train service.

Donegal Airport (www.donegalairport.ie) has very limited service on Aer Lingus to Dublin, that's primarily for connecting to other flights. It's about 3km northwest of Annagry on the northwestern coast.

Getting Around

Buses link major towns. **Bus Éireann** (in Letterkenny 074-912 1309; www.buseireann.ie) serves mostly the southwestern part of the county. Main routes include Sligo–Bundoran–Donegal town–Letterkenny–Derry, Donegal Town–Killybegs–Ardara–Glenties–Dungloe and Killybegs–Kilcar–Glencolumbcille.

Bus Feda (074-954 8114; www.feda.ie) serves the northwestern part of the county, with a looping route from Galway and Sligo to Bundoran, Donegal town, Letterkenny, Dunfanaghy and Gweedore, terminating in Crolly.

DONEGAL TOWN

POP 2600

Pretty Donegal town occupies a photogenic spot at the mouth of Donegal Bay. With a backdrop of the Blue Stack Mountains, a handsome and well-preserved castle and a good choice of places to eat and sleep, it makes an excellent base for exploring the popular coastline nearby.

On the banks of the River Eske, Donegal town was a stamping ground of the O'Donnells, the chieftains who ruled the northwest from the 15th to 17th centuries. Today, despite being the county's namesake, it's neither its largest town (Letterkenny), nor the county town (the even smaller town of Lifford).

Sights & Activities

★Donegal Castle HISTORIC BUILDING

(074-972 2405; www.heritageireland.ie; Castle St; adult/child €4/2; 10am-6pm daily Easter–mid-Sep, 9.30am-4.30pm Thu-Mon mid-Sep–Easter) Guarding a picturesque bend of the River Eske, Donegal Castle remains an imperious monument to both Irish and English might. Dating to the 15th century, the castle was rebuilt in 1623 by Sir Basil Brooke, along with the adjacent three-storey Jacobean house. Further restoration in the 1990s has made it an atmospheric place to visit; rooms are furnished with French tapestries and Persian rugs. There are guided tours every hour.

Built by the O'Donnells in 1474, it served as the seat of their formidable power until 1607, when the English decided to rid themselves of pesky Irish chieftains once and for all. Rory O'Donnell was no pushover, torching his own castle before fleeing to France in the infamous Flight of the Earls. Their defeat paved the way for the Plantation of Ulster by thousands of newly arrived Scots and English Protestants, sowing the seeds of the divisions that still afflict Ireland to this day.

Diamond Obelisk MONUMENT

(The Diamond) In the early 17th century, four Franciscan friars, fearing that the arrival of the English meant the end of Celtic culture, chronicled the whole of known Celtic history and mythology. Starting 40 years before the biblical flood through AD 1618, *The Annals of the Four Masters* is one of the most important sources of early Irish history. The obelisk (1937), in the Diamond, commemorates the work; copies are displayed in the National Library in Dublin.

★Bank Walk WALKING

Follow this lovely flat trail along the west bank of the River Eske and Donegal Bay. The myriad shade trees have labels as to their type and frequent benches allow you to pause and soak up the views. It's 1.5km each way and begins on the west side of the Killybeg Rd/N56 bridge.

Donegal Bay Waterbus BOAT TOUR

(074-972 3666; www.donegalbaywaterbus.com; Donegal Pier; adult/child €20/7; Easter-Oct) The most enjoyable way to explore the highlights of Donegal Bay is on a 1¼-hour boat tour taking in everything from historic sites to seal-inhabited coves, admiring an island manor and a ruined castle along the way. The tour runs up to three times daily; departure times change daily to match the tides.

Ted's Bike Shop BICYCLE RENTAL

(074-974 0774; www.tedsbikeshop.ie; off N56; rentals per day from €15; 10am-6pm Mon-Sat) You can rent all types of bikes and get plenty of excellent advice at this bustling bike shop.

Sleeping

Good B&Bs and stolid hotels are plentiful around Donegal town; for high-end luxury head to nearby Lough Eske.

Donegal Town Independent Hostel HOSTEL €

(074-972 2805; www.donegaltownhostel.com; off Killybegs Rd/N56, Doonan; dm €17, d €38-42; @)

County Donegal Highlights

1. Watch the sun set from the top of the soaring sea cliffs, **Slieve League** (p440).
2. Tour flamboyant **Glenveagh Castle** (p455) in beautiful Glenveagh National Park.
3. Stroll along the windswept beach at **Culdaff** (p464), near Malin Head.
4. Enjoy a superb meal or a pint in seaside **Dunfanaghy** (p449).
5. Take in the views at the spectacular **Poisoned Glen** (p456).
6. Learn to surf on the white-sand beach at **Rossnowlagh** (p436).
7. Look seemingly forever out to sea at **Malin Head** (p463).
8. Hill walk amid the dramatic landscapes and coastal vistas at **Glencolumbcille** (p441).
9. Explore the stash of international artworks in **Glebe House & Gallery** (p456), on Lough Gartan.

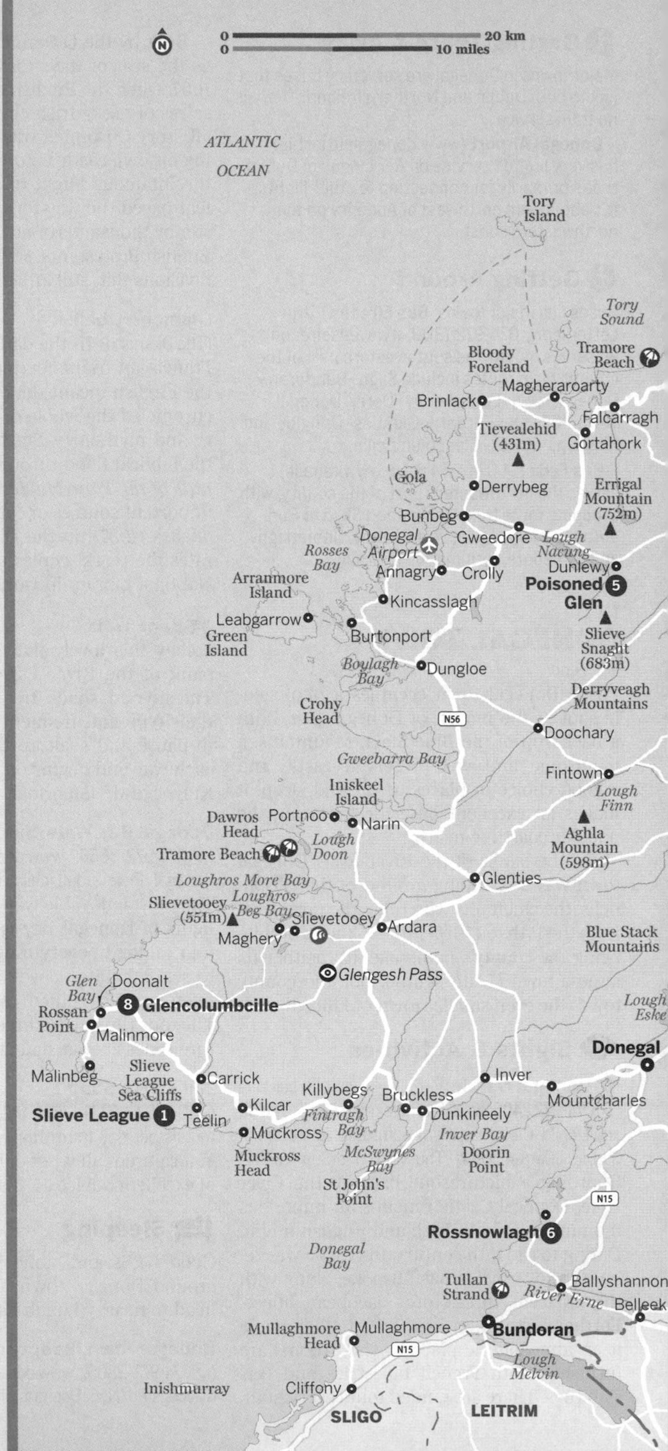

Inishtrahull Sound
Malin Head
7
Ballyhillin
Glengad Head
Culdaff Beach
3
Pollan Bay
Tullagh Bay
Malin
Dunmore Head
Culdaff
Tremore Bay
Kinnagoe Bay
Fanad Head
Dunaff Head
Dunaff
Ballyliffin
Clonmany
Carndonagh
Inishowen Head
Lenan Head
Urris Hills
Gleneely
Shrove
Slieve Snaght (615m)
Horn Head
Rosguill Peninsula
Portsalon
Glentogher
Greencastle
Sheep Haven Bay
Downings
Dunree
Inishowen Peninsula
Moville
Rosnakill
4
Dunfanaghy
Carrigart
Knockalla Fort
Redcastle
Port-na-Blagh
Ards Forest Park
River Crana
Kerrykeel
Buncrana
Quigley's Point
Lough Foyle
Fanad Peninsula
Muckish Mountain (670m)
Creeslough
Fahan
Milford
Rathmullan
City of Derry Airport
Muff
Limavady
Inch Island
Inch
Burnfoot
Culmore Bay
Glenveagh Castle
2
Rathmelton
Bridge End
Burt
A2
Kilmacrennan
Glenveagh National Park
N56
Derry
Glebe House & Gallery
9
N13
Lough Gartan
Church Hill
LONDONDERRY
Letterkenny
Dungiven
River Foyle
E16-6
Newmills
A5
DONEGAL
N13
Raphoe
River Finn
River Deele
Lifford
Strabane
Finn Valley
Castlefin
Stranorlar
Ballybofey
N15
NORTHERN IRELAND
Newtownstewart
TYRONE
A5
Lough Derg
Omagh
N32
Pettigo
A5
Lower Lough Erne
Ballygawley
A2
Augher
FERMANAGH
A4
MONAGHAN

Donegal Town

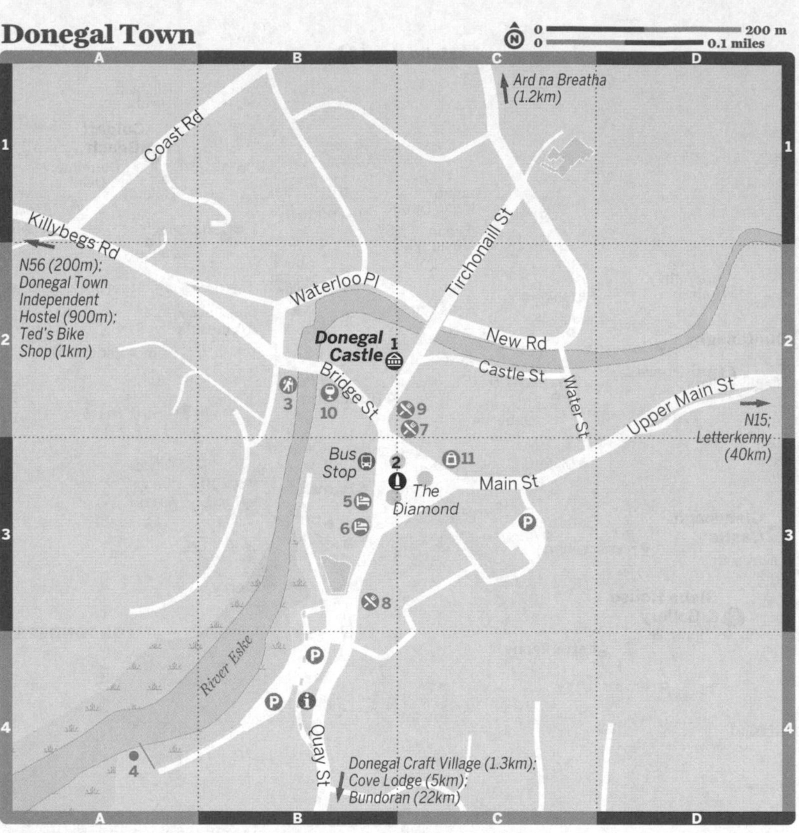

Donegal Town

Top Sights
1 Donegal Castle ... B2

Sights
2 Diamond Obelisk ... C3

Activities, Courses & Tours
3 Bank Walk ... B2
4 Donegal Bay Waterbus ... A4

Sleeping
5 Abbey Hotel ... B3
6 Central Hotel ... B3

Eating
7 Blueberry Tearoom ... C2
8 Harbour Restaurant ... B3
9 Olde Castle Bar ... C2

Drinking & Nightlife
10 Reel Inn ... B2

Shopping
11 Magee's ... C3

Run by an energetic couple, rooms at this Independent Holiday Hostels (IHH) hostel 1.2km northwest of town have murals – from Technicolor landscapes to glow-in-the-dark night skies – and some have water views. It has 30 beds in female-only and mixed dorms.

★ Ard na Breatha B&B €€

(074-972 2288; www.ardnabreatha.com; Drumrooske Middle; r €120-140; Feb-Oct;) In an elevated setting 1.5km north of town, this boutique guesthouse on a working farm has tasteful rooms with pine furniture and wrought-iron beds. The six rooms are in a building separate from the main house. It has a full bar and restaurant (three-course dinner €39) with organic food sourced from the farm or locally where possible. You must prebook dinner.

Central Hotel HOTEL €€

(074-972 1027; www.centralhoteldonegal.com; The Diamond; s/d from €62/100;) The

Central is an adventure – no matter where your room is located in this rambling collection of buildings, you'll take an elevator and wander up and down stairs to find it. Make the trip worthwhile by asking for a room with a view of the River Eske – the huge windows offer stunning views. The leisure centre has a pool and gym.

Cove Lodge B&B €€
(074-972 2302; www.thecovelodgebandb.com; R267, Drumgowan; s €45-50, d €78-84;) You'll find subtle floral patterns and rustic charm in the four ground-floor rooms of this tranquil stone-and-stucco B&B. Located just out of town in a rural setting, it's a taste of Irish country living. It's 2.5km south of town.

Abbey Hotel HOTEL €€
(074-972 1014; www.abbeyhoteldonegal.com; The Diamond; s/d from €70/110;) A very serviceable option right in the heart of town, with 90 standard rooms. There's an elevator for the three floors, and the bar and restaurant are solid. Guests can use the leisure centre at the Central Hotel.

Eating & Drinking

Look for the beers from local craft-brewer Donegal Brewing Co. Its North & South of the River bitter is a hoppy joy.

Aroma CAFE €
(074-972 3222; www.donegalcraftvillage.com; off R267, Donegal Craft Village; mains €5-13; 9.30am-5.30pm Mon-Sat) In the far corner of Donegal's craft village, this small cafe has a big reputation for fine food. Along with the excellent coffee and luscious cakes, the blackboard specials feature seasonal local produce whipped up into fine soups, salads and wholesome hot dishes. There's seating outside.

Blueberry Tearoom CAFE €
(074-972 2933; Castle St; mains €5-12; 9am-7pm Mon-Sat;) A perennial local favourite, this cosy cafe serves simple, honest food in hearty portions. Expect soup, toasties, quiche, panini and sticky cakes of all descriptions. There's a cybercafe upstairs. The coffee's great.

★**Olde Castle Bar** IRISH €€
(074-972 1262; www.oldecastlebar.com; Castle St; mains €8-30; bar noon-late, kitchen to 9pm;) This ever-busy pub off the Diamond serves some of the area's best food. Look for upmarket classics such as Donegal Bay oysters, Irish stew, seafood platters (the €28 one is spectacular), plus steaks and burgers. The pub is always rollicking with locals and serves its own excellent pale ale: Red Hugh Brew.

Harbour Restaurant IRISH €€
(074-972 1702; www.theharbour.ie; Quay St; mains €10-30; 5-9.30pm Mon-Sat, 3-9pm Sun, closed Mon & Tue Oct-Apr) Seafood gets the royal treatment at this popular local haunt, with its nautical theme, bare stone walls and plush furnishings. But the menu spans every Irish dinner classic including 'modern' ones such as pizza.

★**Reel Inn** PUB
(Bridge St; 5pm-late) The best craic in town is invariably found at this old-school pub. Its owner plays the button-box accordion, his wife has an amazing singing voice and their pals join in traditional-music sessions most nights.

Shopping

★**Donegal Craft Village** HANDICRAFTS
(074-972 5928; www.donegalcraftvillage.com; off R267; 10am-5pm Mon-Sat Apr-Sep, Tue-Sat Oct) You won't find any canned leprechauns or Guinness T-shirts here. Instead, this huddle of craft studios showcases pottery, ironwork, handwoven fabrics, jewellery and more. It's signposted 1.5km south of town and an easy walk. There's a cracking cafe.

Magee's CLOTHING
(074-972 2660; www.magee1866.com; The Diamond; 10am-6pm Mon-Sat, 2-6pm Sun) One room of this small, upscale and historic department store is devoted to Donegal tweed, which has been produced here since 1866.

Information

The **Tourist Office** (074-972 1148; Quay St; 9am-5.30pm Mon-Sat, 10am-3pm Sun Jun-Aug, 9am-5pm Mon-Sat Sep-May) is in the Discover Ireland building by the waterfront.

Getting There & Away

Bus Éireann (074-913 1008; www.buseireann.ie) Services connect Donegal with Sligo (€15, 1¼ hour, four daily), Galway (€20, four hours, three daily) and Dublin (€20, four hours, five daily).

Bus Feda (074-954 8114; www.feda.ie) Buses serve Gweedore, Dunfanaghy and Letterkenny (all €10) two to three times daily.

Patrick Gallagher Coaches (087 233 0888; info@gallagherscoaches.com) Runs daily buses between Donegal town and Belfast (€20, two hours).

AROUND DONEGAL TOWN

Lough Eske

Almost surrounded by the Blue Stack Mountains, tranquil Lough Eske (Lake of the Fish) is a scenic spot perfect for walking, cycling or fishing. It's popular with anglers – the season runs from May to September – and there's a purpose-built angling centre on the shore where you can buy permits and hire boats.

The lake is only 9km from Donegal – a good bike ride.

Sleeping & Eating

Arches Country House B&B €
(☎074-972 2029; www.archescountryhse.com; Lough Eske; s/d from €55/70; wifi) This bucolic getaway is in a tranquil spot overlooking Lough Eske from the east, 9km northeast of Donegal town. A modern B&B, rooms would please your dowager aunt, with a blend of country-house charm and contemporary style. The owner is a fount of local knowledge.

★ **Lough Eske Castle** HOTEL €€€
(☎074-972 5100; www.solislougheskecastle.com; Lough Eske; r €180-280; closed Sun-Wed Nov-Mar; @ wifi pool) Set in vast grounds at the lake's south end, this imposing 19th-century castle was all but razed by fire in 1939 but has been restored and is now the epitome of elegant country living. Most of the 96-room complex, including the spa and smart restaurant, exudes a sense of classic sophistication.

Rossnowlagh

POP 50

Rossnowlagh's spectacular 3km-long Blue Flag beach is a broad, sandy stretch of heaven that attracts families, surfers, kitesurfers and walkers throughout the year. The gentle rollers are great for learning to surf or honing your skills. You can easily lose a few hours picnicking and lounging in the dunes.

Sights & Activities

Franciscan Friary MONASTERY
(☎071-985 1342; www.franciscans.ie; off R231; 10am-8pm Mon-Sat) FREE Hidden deep in a forest at the southern end of the beach, this modern friary is set in beautiful, tranquil gardens which are open to the public. The Way of the Cross – a religious walk with spectacular views – meanders up a hillside smothered in rhododendrons.

Fin McCool Surf School SURFING
(☎071-985 9020; www.finmccoolsurfschool.com; Beach Rd; gear rental per day €39, 2hr lesson incl gear €35; 10am-7pm daily Easter-Oct, Sat & Sun mid-Mar–Easter & Nov-Christmas) Tuition, gear rental and accommodation are available at this surf lodge run by Pro Tour surf judge Neil Britton, with the help of his extended family, most of whom have competed on the international circuit.

Rossnowlagh SUP & Kayak KAYAKING
(☎083 198 4288; SUP lessons/tours from €35/20, kayak tours from €20; 10am-6pm Mon-Fri, to 8pm Sat, 11am-6pm Sun) Learn stand-up paddleboarding (SUP) or rent one with this busy outfit located near the beach. You can also rent a kayak. A wide variety of tours take in the many waterways in the estuaries as well as the waters off the beach; watch for full-moon tours.

Sleeping & Eating

Smugglers Creek B&B €€
(☎071-985 2367; www.smugglerscreekinn.com; Cliff Rd; r €55-90, mains €8-25; daily Apr-Sep, Thu-Sun Oct-Mar; wifi) This combined pub-restaurant-guesthouse perches on the hillside above the bay. It's justifiably popular for its excellent food and sweeping views (room 4 has the best vantage point and a balcony). There's live music on summer weekends.

Gaslight Inn IRISH €€
(☎071-985 1141; www.gaslight-rossnowlagh.com; mains €8-25; 11am-late daily Jun-Sep, 5pm-late Mon-Fri, 11am-late Sat & Sun Oct-May) Set on the clifftop, the Gaslight Inn offers an extensive menu of well-cooked comfort food and spectacular views over the bay. The owners also run the **Ard na Mara** (☎071-985 1141; www.ardnamara-rossnowlagh.com; r €70-100; wifi) guesthouse, which has five bright rooms, some with killer sea views.

Getting There & Away

Rossnowlagh is 17km southwest of Donegal town.

Ballyshannon

POP 2550

Long a strategic spot for its position overlooking the River Erne, Ballyshannon today has a role guarding the northern approaches to Bundoran.

Festivals

Rory Gallagher International Tribute Festival MUSIC
(www.rorygallagherfestival.com) This music festival celebrates native son, rock and blues guitarist Rory Gallagher (1948–95), with more than two dozen Irish and international artists and bands. Gallagher's connection to his hometown is in evidence throughout the year. You'll often hear his music playing in pubs. Held in late May.

Drinking & Nightlife

★**Dicey Reilly's Bar** PUB
(☎071-985 1371; www.diceys.com; Market St; ⊙noon-late) This old city-centre pub stays vibrant through constant reinvention. A new cocktail bar upstairs offers stylish contrast to the old pub downstairs where on most nights you'll hear live rock and blues, and a Rory Gallagher tune always seems to be the next song. Get the good Donegal Brewing Co beers here.

Bundoran

POP 2200

Blinking amusement arcades, hurdy-gurdy fairground rides and fast-food diners give Bundoran the feel of a tacky beach town. But Donegal's best-known seaside resort has reliable waves, and attracts a mixed crowd of young families, pensioners and surfers. Outside summer, the carnival atmosphere abates and the town can be bleak.

Sights & Activities

The town has several surf schools, each of which rents gear and has its own basic hostel-style accommodation. All offer deals on surf and accommodation packages.

Bundoran Beach BEACH
The strand of sand is long, with the trademark fine white sand much of Ireland is known for. It is generally not safe for swimming although there are lifeguards in summer.

Peak SURFING
The Peak, an imposing reef break directly in front of the town, is one of Bundoran's two main surf spots. It should only be attempted by experienced surfers. There is a less formidable beach break at **Tullan Strand**, just north of the town centre.

Bundoran Surf Co SURFING
(☎071-984 1968; www.bundoransurfco.com; Main St; surf lessons from €35, full surf-gear rental per day from €20) Bundoran Surf Co conducts surf lessons, kitesurfing and stand-up paddleboarding.

Donegal Adventure Centre ADVENTURE SPORTS
(☎071-984 2418; www.donegaladventurecentre.net; Bayview Ave; surf lesson from €35) Offers adventure-sports activities on land and sea, including kayaking, surfing and climbing.

Waterworld SWIMMING
(☎071-984 1172; www.waterworldbundoran.com; The Promenade; adult/child €13/10, seaweed bath €25; ⊙10am-7pm daily Jun-Aug, noon-6pm Sat & Sun mid-Apr–May & Sep, seaweed baths noon-7pm Jun-Aug) This aesthetically challenged amusement park is right on the waterfront, with wave pools and water slides. For a sedate soak, try a seaweed bath.

Bike Stop BICYCLE RENTAL
(☎085 248 8317; East End; per half-day/day/week €10/15/60; ⊙8.30am-6pm Mon-Sat, noon-4pm Sun) Rents a range of bikes including good-quality hybrids.

Festivals

Sea Sessions MUSIC
(www.seasessions.com) The Sea Sessions festival – three days of surfing, skating, music and partying – kicks off the summer season in mid-June. The thousands of attendees camp in fields around town.

Irish National Surfing Championships SPORT
(www.isasurf.ie) Bundoran hosts the annual Irish National Surfing Championships. They're usually held in late April although they have also been held in September.

Sleeping & Eating

Bundoran has a good choice of hostels – non-surfers are welcome at all the surf-school lodges, which usually charge about €20 for a dorm bed and €50 for a double. Scores of humble B&Bs line the access roads in from the N15. Gastronomy isn't Bundoran's strong suit.

Killavil House B&B €
(☎071-984 1556; www.killavilhouse.com; Finner Rd; r €50-80;) A big modern villa at the Ballyshannon end of town, Killavil has smartly appointed bedrooms with polished wooden furniture. Most have multiple beds and are suitable for families. There's a garden with a seating area for enjoying summer evenings. Tullan Strand beach is just a five-minute walk away.

Maddens Bridge Bar PUB €€

(☎071-984 2050; www.maddensbridgebar.com; Main St; mains €10-20, r €60-90; ⊙kitchen 8am-9pm, pub till late) This surfers' hang-out manages a bit of minimalist style and has a decent menu of classic pub grub that includes good burgers. There's a trad session on Thursdays (more in summer) and fantastic craic. It's located right at its namesake bridge and some of the simple rooms have great views.

Information

Bundoran centres on one long main street just back from the beach.

The **Tourist Office** (☎071-984 1350; Main St, The Bridge; ⊙9am-3.30pm Mon-Fri, hours vary Sat & Sun Apr-Sep) is housed in a glass-paned kiosk opposite the Holyrood Hotel.

Getting There & Around

Bus Éireann buses stop on Main St on their runs between Donegal and Sligo.

SOUTHWESTERN DONEGAL

Mountcharles

POP 500

Donegal's scenic-o-meter starts to crank up when you reach the coast just west of Donegal town, and steadily intensifies as you head north.

The hillside village of Mountcharles is the first settlement along the coastal road (N56) west of Donegal town, in fact you'll barely have the speedometer turning when, boom, you're in Mountcharles.

The Donegal–Killybegs bus stops in Mountcharles several times daily.

Sights

About 2km south of the village is a safe, sandy **beach**. The shiny, green **pump** at the top of this hillside village was once the backdrop for stories of fairies, ghosts, historic battles and mythological encounters. It was at this point that native poet and *seanachaí* (traditional storyteller) Séamus MacManus practised the ancient art in the 1940s and '50s.

Salthill Gardens GARDENS

(☎074-973 5387; www.donegalgardens.com; Pier Rd; adult/child €5/2; ⊙2-6pm Mon-Sat May-Aug, Mon-Thu Sep) Behind century-old stone walls, the contemporary garden design of Salthill Gardens bursts with perennials, roses, lilies and clematis. It's 2km southwest of the village.

Eating & Drinking

Village Tavern SEAFOOD €€

(☎074-973 5622; Main St; mains €7-25; ⊙kitchen noon-8pm daily May-Sep, pub noon-late year-round) In a handsome 18th-century building, this welcoming pub specialises in seafood brought to shore at the pier just down the road. The chowder is excellent and the seafood tasting board groans with whatever is fresh and best.

Dunkineely

POP 370

Views out to sea tantalise from the series of small villages along the N56.

Sleeping & Eating

★**Castle Murray** BOUTIQUE HOTEL €€

(☎074-973 7022; www.castlemurray.com; St John's Point; s/d from €90/140, set menu €40; ⊙1.30-3.30pm Sun, 6-9pm daily Jul & Aug, shorter hours other times, closed Jan; 📶) Overlooking the ruins of the 15th-century McSwyne's Castle, Castle Murray is not a castle itself, but a boutique hotel in a sprawling modern beach house. Most of the 10 guest rooms have great sea and castle views. It's best known for its fine French restaurant, and its signature prawns and monkfish in garlic butter is a must.

Castle Murray is 1.5km south of Dunkineely on a minor road leading to St John's Point.

Killybegs

POP 1300

The smell of fish and the caw of seagulls waft from the ranks of giant trawlers moored in Ireland's largest fishing port. Inland, the village bustles with the atmosphere of a charming working town.

Sights & Activities

The most fun you can have in Killybegs is watching the action around the very busy port. But note that huge fish-filled trucks and other equipment don't slow down for gawkers.

Killybegs International Carpet Making & Fishing Centre MUSEUM
(☎074-974 1944; www.visitkillybegs.com; Fintra Rd; adult/child €5/3; ⏲9.30am-5.30pm Mon-Fri year-round, noon-4pm Sat & Sun Jul & Aug) The former factory of Donegal Carpets provides a good overview of the town's history. The fun wheelhouse simulator lets you 'steer' a fishing trawler into the harbour. Don't expect to see any carpets being made as the cost to do so is now 'astronomical', they say.

Fintragh Bay BEACH
(off R263) The best beach in the area is at secluded Fintragh Bay, about 3km west of town.

Killybegs Angling Charters FISHING
(☎087 220 0982; www.killybegsangling.com; Blackrock Pier; half-day charter from €300) If you're interested in taking to the water to catch pollack, ling, brill, mackerel or turbot, Brian McGilloway has more than 30 years of experience in charter angling.

Sleeping & Eating

Ritz HOSTEL €
(☎074-973 1309; www.theritz-killybegs.com; Chapel Brae; dm €15-20, r from €50; @📶) The name might be ironic, but this superbly run 38-bed hostel in the town centre has ritzy facilities including an enormous kitchen, colourful rooms with private bathroom and TVs, and a laundry.

Drumbeagh House B&B €
(☎074-973 1307; www.killybegsbnb.biz.ly; Conlin Rd; s/d from €50/70; 📶) Accommodating hosts with plenty of local knowledge make this small B&B a great find. The cosy rooms are tastefully decorated in neutral colours and the breakfast of locally smoked salmon is worth the trip alone. Great harbour views; it's a five-minute walk from the centre.

Tara Hotel HOTEL €€€
(☎074-974 1700; www.tarahotel.ie; Main St; s/d from €65/120; 📶) This modern hotel across from and overlooking the harbour has 31 comfortable, minimalist rooms, a decent bar and a small gym with spa bath, sauna and steam room.

Mrs B's Coffee House CAFE €
(☎074-973 2656; Upper Main St; mains €4-8; ⏲9am-5pm Mon-Sat; 📶👪) Mrs B's is a bright and welcoming cafe with comfy sofas, local art on the walls, and a menu of home-made and locally sourced food, extending from hearty breakfasts and sandwiches to drool-worthy baked goods. Watch for the great seafood-chowder special.

TOP FIVE SCENIC DRIVES

Practically any stretch of road qualifies as a scenic drive in this rugged county, but the following are especially captivating. Be ready for frequent stops to enjoy the views.

- Coastal highway from **Dunfanaghy** (p449) to **Gweedore** (p446)
- Hundred-mile loop of the isolated **Inishowen Peninsula** (p459)
- The curvacious road to sweeping views at **Horn Head** (p449)
- Arcing through stunning **Glenveagh National Park** (p455)
- Snaking switchbacks traversing **Glengesh Pass** (p442)

Shines Cod & Chips FISH & CHIPS €
(☎074-973 1996; Conlin Rd; mains from €5; ⏲11am-11.30pm) All that fish in the port but what to eat? Well walk just one block up hill to this excellent outlet for superb fish and chips. The cod and the monkfish are fresh off the boats.

Kitty Kelly's MODERN IRISH €€
(☎074-973 1925; www.kittykellys.com; off R263, Largy; dinner mains €17-25; ⏲5-9.30pm daily year-round, 1-4.30pm Sat & Sun mid-May–Sep) Dining at this restaurant in a 200-year-old farmhouse feels more like attending an intimate dinner party. The menu is a modern take on Irish favourites with an emphasis on seafood. It's on the coast road, 5km west of Killybegs – you can't miss the lurid pink and green paint job. Opening hours vary annually; bookings are essential.

Information

There are no ATMs west of Killybegs.

Killybegs Information Centre (☎074-973 2346; www.killybegs.ie; Shore Rd; ⏲9.30am-5.30pm Mon-Fri year-round, noon-4pm Sat & Sun Jul & Aug) is in a trailer just west of the harbour.

Getting There & Away

Bus Éireann buses from Donegal (€9, 30 minutes) run several times daily.

Kilcar, Teelin & Around

POP 270

Kilcar (Cill Chártha) and its more attractive neighbour Teelin (Teileann) make good bases for exploring the breathtaking coastline of southwestern Donegal, especially the stunning sea cliffs at Slieve League. Inland, Carrick (An Charraig) is also appealing.

This is fantastic walking country, particularly if you find the prospect of a few hills bracing. Just outside Kilcar is a small, sandy beach.

Sights & Activities

Slieve League SEA CLIFFS

The Cliffs of Moher get more publicity, but the cliffs of Slieve League are higher. In fact, these spectacular sea cliffs are among the highest in Europe, plunging some 600m to the sea.

From Teelin, a road through the stark landscape leads to the lower car park (which has signs with hiking maps) beside a gate in the road; you can drive another 1.5km to the upper car park (often full in summer) right beside the viewpoint.

From the upper car park, a rough **footpath** leads up and along the top of the near-vertical cliffs to the aptly named **One Man's Pass**, a narrow ridge that leads to the summit of Slieve League (595m; 10km round trip). Be aware that mist and rain can roll in unexpectedly and rapidly, making conditions treacherous. Also, just walking the first 500m will give you spectacular views.

It's also possible to hike to the summit of Slieve League from Carrick via the **Pilgrim Path** (signposted along the minor road on the right before the Slieve League cliffs road), returning via One Man's Pass and the viewpoint road (12km; allow four to six hours).

The cliffs are particularly scenic at sunset when the waves crash dramatically far below and the ocean reflects the last rays of the day. Looking down, you'll see two rocks nicknamed the 'giant's desk and chair' for reasons that are immediately obvious.

Studio Donegal MILL

(074-973 8194; www.studiodonegal.ie; Glebe Mill, Kilcar; 9am-5.30pm Mon-Fri year-round, 9.30am-5pm Sat May-Oct) FREE Though mechanised in the 1960s, there has been a hand-weaving tweed mill here for more than a century. Visitors are often invited upstairs to see spinners and weavers in action, before browsing jackets, hats, throws and other items in the shop.

Nuala Star Teelin BOAT TOUR

(074-973 9365; www.sliabhleagueboattrips.com; Teelin Pier; tours per person €20-25; hours vary Apr-Oct) Sightseeing boat trips along the Slieve League cliffs can be spectacular. Tours often spot dolphins.

Sleeping & Eating

Derrylahan Independent Hostel HOSTEL €

(074-973 8079; http://homepage.eircom.net/~derrylahan; Derrylahan, Kilcar; campsites per person €8, dm/d €18/50; @) This rustic, well-run IHH hostel is set on a hilly, windy and dramatic site on a working farm. It has 32 beds in 10 comfortable rooms with private bathrooms, plus plenty of scenic spots to pitch a tent. Book ahead for bike rental (€20). Located 3km west of Kilcar on the coast road. Pick-ups can be arranged.

Inishduff House B&B €€

(074-973 8542; www.inishduffhouse.com; off R263, Largy, Kilcar; s/d €50/85;) About 5km east of Kilcar, this modern B&B has large, comfortable rooms, a varied breakfast menu and wonderful sea views. The mood matches the sunny hues of the exterior.

★Ti Linn Cafe IRISH €

(074-973 9077; www.slieveleaguecliffs.ie; Teelin; mains €4-9; 10.30am-5.30pm daily Easter-Sep, Fri-Tue Feb-Easter & Oct-Nov;) This artisan cafe and crafts gallery in the Slieve League Cliffs Centre has excellent coffee. It has fine baked goods, sandwiches and hot lunches too.

Rusty PUB €€

(074-973 9101; www.therusty.info; Teelin; mains €6-20; 10.30am-11.30pm daily May-Sep, shorter hours other times) Great pub with trad music many nights in summer, plus a simple menu of bar food. It's near the junction of the road to Slieve League.

Information

Áislann Chill Chartha (074-973 8376; www.aislann.ie; Main St, Kilcar; 9am-10pm Mon-Fri, 10am-6pm Sat) is a community centre that has information for tourists.

Local information is available at the excellent **Slieve League Cliffs Centre** (074-973 9077; www.slieveleaguecliffs.ie; Teelin; 10.30am-5.30pm daily Easter-Sep, Fri-Tue Feb-Easter & Oct-Nov;) in Teelin, which also has an artisan cafe. The centre runs archaeology and hill walking courses. It's on the road to Slieve League.

Getting There & Away

Bus Éireann services run from Donegal to Kilcar (€10) and Carrick (€12) one to three times daily.

Glencolumbcille & Around

POP 270

Once you've sampled Glencolumbcille's tiny village, scalloped beaches, stunning walks and fine little folk museum, chances are you'll disagree with locals who claim there's little to do here.

Approaching Glencolumbcille (Gleann Cholm Cille) via the **Glengesh Pass** does, however, reinforce just how isolated this beautiful coastal haven is. You drive past miles and miles of hills and bogs before the ocean appears, followed by a narrow, green valley and the small Gaeltacht village within it.

This spot has been inhabited since 3000 BC and lots of Stone Age remains are scattered among the cluster of tiny settlements. It's believed that the 6th-century AD St Colmcille (Columba) founded a monastery here (hence the name, meaning 'Glen of Columba's Church'), and incorporated Stone Age standing stones into Christian use by inscribing them with a cross. At midnight on Columba's Feast Day (9 June), penitents perform An Turas Cholm Chille (the Gaelic *'turas'* meaning a pilgrimage or journey), a walking circuit of the stones and the remains of Cholm Cille's chapel, before attending Mass at 3am in the local chapel.

Sights

★Doonalt Beach BEACH

This sandy beach with brisk waves is in **Doonalt**, immediately west of the village; access is from the car park opposite the folk museum.

Malinbeg Beach BEACH

At Malinbeg you'll find a sheltered bay bitten out of low cliffs, with 60 steps descending to a gorgeous little sandy beach. It's 6km past the folk village.

Father McDyer's Folk Village MUSEUM

(www.glenfolkvillage.com; Doonalt; adult/child €4.50/2.50; ⏲10am-6pm Mon-Sat, noon-6pm Sun Easter-Sep) A museum with a mission, this folk centre was established by the forward-thinking Father James McDyer in 1967 to freeze-frame traditional folk life for posterity. It's housed in a huddle of thatched cottages re-created in 18th- and 19th-century style, with genuine period fittings. The *shebeen* (illicit drinking place) sells unusual local wines (made from ingredients such as seaweed and fuchsias). It's 3km west of the village, by the beach.

DON'T MISS

DONEGAL'S BEST BEACHES

Donegal's wild and rugged coastline is splashed with broad sweeps of powdery white sand and secluded coves. Here are some of our favourites:

Tramore (p450) Hike through the dunes west of Dunfanaghy and you'll be rewarded with pristine sands on this secluded stretch of coast.

Carrick Finn (p445) A gorgeous sweep of undeveloped sand near Donegal Airport.

Portnoo (p443) A wishbone-shaped sheltered cove backed by undulating hills.

Ballymastocker Beach (p459) An idyllic stretch of sand lapped by turquoise water.

Culdaff (p464) A long stretch of golden sand, popular with families.

Rossnowlagh (p436) A sweeping white-sand beach ideal for learning to surf.

Activities

The 19th-century St Columba's Church is the starting point for several excellent walks, see www.glencolmcille.ie for details. The 5.5km pilgrimage route of **An Turas Cholm Cille** visits a series of prehistoric stone slabs, many carved with early Christian symbols, and an ancient ruined chapel attributed to the saint. Local landowners grant permission for walkers to visit all the stones on Sundays from June to August (some are accessible year-round).

A couple of waymarked loop walks will lead you into the blustery wilds beyond the town. The **Tower Loop** (10km, two to three hours) heads north to a signal tower atop stunning coastal cliffs, while the more arduous **Drum Loop** (13km, three to four hours) heads into the hills northeast of the town.

Courses

Oideas Gael CULTURE

(☎074-973 0248; www.oideas-gael.com; 3-/7-day courses from €100/220; ⏲mid-Mar–Oct) The Foras Cultúir Uladh (Ulster Cultural Foundation), 1km west of the village centre, offers a range of cultural-activity courses – adult courses in Irish language and traditional culture, including dancing, painting and musical instruments. The centre also leads hill walking programs. Accommodation can be arranged – either homestay or self-catering, at around €30 per person per night.

Sleeping & Eating

The area has some excellent budget accommodation but places to eat are limited to a small grocery and cafe in Glencolumbcille village. There are a couple of pubs with basic snacks.

Dooey Hostel HOSTEL €
(074-973 0130; www.independenthostelsireland.com; Dooey; campsites per person €10, dm/d €16/32) Built into a hillside with a corridor carved out of the plant-strewn rock face and amazing views of the ocean and hills below, this 32-bed hostel is a charmer. Facilities are rustic, but clean and comfortable. Driving, turn left just after the Glenhead Tavern and continue for 1.5km; walkers can hike up a path behind the folk village. Cash only.

Malinbeg Hostel HOSTEL €
(074-973 0006; www.malinbeghostel.com; Malinbeg; dm/s/d from €15/20/38; closed Dec–mid-Jan) Flung out on a remote stretch of coast near Silver Strand beach, the contemporary Malinbeg Hostel sports spotless rooms (some with private bathroom).

Glencolumbcille Lodge GUESTHOUSE €
(074-973 0302; www.ionadsuil.ie; s/d from €45/60;) Overlooking sheep-filled paddocks near the village, this place calls itself the 'Hill Walkers Centre'. It has decent double and twin rooms with private bathrooms and an enormous self-catering kitchen. Given the weather, the clothes-drying room and peat fire are handy.

Shopping

Glencolmcille Woollen Mill CLOTHING
(074-973 0069; www.rossanknitwear.ie; Malinmore; 10am-8pm Mar-Oct, to 5.30pm Nov-Feb) This is a great place to shop for Donegal tweed jackets, caps, ties, and lambswool scarves and shawls. You can sometimes see weavers in action. It's about 5km southwest of Glencolumbcille, in Malinmore.

Getting There & Away

Bus Éireann runs to/from Killybegs (€9, 45 minutes) one to two times a day, the route ends at Glencolumbcille.

Maghery & the Glengesh Pass

POP 630

A fantastically remote, 25km single-track road leads from Glencolumbcille to Ardara via the stark **Glengesh Pass** (Glean Géis; meaning 'Glen of the Swans'), one of Donegal's most scenic driving routes. There are spots where you can pull over and ponder historic peat fields along the way.

On the northern coast of the Glencolumbcille peninsula, 9km west of Ardara, tiny **Maghery** has a picturesque waterfront. If you follow the strand westward, you'll get to a rocky promontory full of caves. During Cromwell's 17th-century destruction, 100 villagers sought refuge here but all except one were discovered and massacred. About 1.5km east of Maghery is the enchanting **Assarancagh Waterfall**.

Ardara

POP 740

Gateway to the switchbacks of the Glengesh Pass, the heritage town of Ardara (arda-rah) is the heart of Donegal's tweed and knitwear industry. You can visit the weavers at work and see the region's most traditional crafts in action.

Sights & Activities

Ardara Heritage Centre MUSEUM
(087 286 8657; Main St; usually 10am-5pm Mon-Sat, 2-5pm Sun Easter-Sep) FREE Set in the old town courthouse, this volunteer-run centre traces the story of Donegal tweed, from sheep shearing to dye production and weaving.

Don Byrne BICYCLE RENTAL
(074-954 1658; www.donbyrnebikes.com; West End; bike rental per day from €17; 10am-6pm Tue-Sat) This bike shop has a wide selection and offers good advice on routes.

Festivals

Cup of Tae Festival MUSIC
(087 242 4590; www.cupoftaefestival.com; lessons from €50) Dancing, storytelling and a school of music are part of the trad-music Cup of Tae Festival in early May. The small-scale but very worthwhile festival takes its name from a local musician, John 'the tae' Gallagher. Free live music fills the pubs.

Sleeping & Eating

Gort na Móna B&B €
(☎074-953 7777; www.gortnamonabandb.com; Donegal Rd, Cronkeerin; s/d from €50/70; 📶) Large but cosy and colourful rooms make this a real home from home. Breakfast includes preserves made from home-grown strawberries. There are good mountain views. It's 2km southeast of town on the old Donegal road.

Bayview Country House B&B €
(☎074-954 1145; www.bayviewcountryhouse.com; R261; s/d from €50/76; ⏲Apr–mid-Oct; 📶) Just 800m north of town and overlooking the bay, this purpose-built B&B has spacious rooms with pretty floral bedspreads, spotless bathrooms and great views. There's a wood fire, homemade bread and scones, and a genuinely warm welcome for visitors.

★ **Woodhill House** HOTEL €€
(☎074-954 1112; www.woodhillhouse.com; Woodhill; s/d from €69/100, set dinner €40; ⏲dinner 5-9pm; 📶) Ireland's last commercial whaling family once lived in this manor house, parts of which date to the 17th century. Although today you're unlikely to hear 'thar she blows!', you will find plenty to hum about amid the 10 comfortable rooms and gardens. Just 300m east of the town centre, the hotel is popular for Irish dinners.

The bar has a great beer selection.

★ **Nancy's Bar** IRISH €
(☎074-954 1187; www.nancysardara.com; Front St; mains €7-15; ⏲kitchen noon-9pm daily Mar-Oct, Sat & Sun Nov-Feb; 📶👪) This old-fashioned pub-restaurant, in the same family for seven generations, is one of the best local spots for trad-music sessions. It serves superb seafood and chowder and is also the best place in town for a sociable pint or two.

Sheila's Coffee & Cream CAFE €
(☎074-953 7905; Main St; mains €4-10; ⏲9am-5.30pm Mon-Sat; 📶👪) Attached to the heritage centre, this little cafe and bakery serves a good selection of hot dishes such as quiche and lasagne, as well as an enticing selection of desserts.

West End Café IRISH €
(☎074-954 1656; Main St; mains from €5; ⏲1-11.30pm) Long known as 'Whyte's', this curtained cafe is beloved for its superfresh fish and chips. There are also sandwiches and hot specials.

Drinking & Nightlife

Many of the town's pubs, such as Nancy's Bar, host regular traditional-music sessions; just stroll down the main drag until you hear the good cheer pouring out the door.

Corner House PUB
(☎074-954 1736; The Diamond; ⏲3pm-late Sun-Thu, from noon Sat & Sun) This is a good spot to listen to an Irish music session (Friday and Saturday year-round; nightly from June to September). It's the type of place where someone will spontaneously break into song and, if the mood is right, the rest of the pub will join in.

Shopping

Ardara has a bevy of knitwear vendors and producers. Traditional sweaters cost from €60.

★ **Eddie Doherty** CLOTHING
(☎074-954 1304; www.handwoventweed.com; Main St; ⏲10am-6pm Mon-Sat, sometimes Sun) You can usually catch Eddie Doherty hand-weaving here on a traditional loom. He'll cheerfully explain every step of the process.

John Molloy CLOTHING
(☎074-954 1133; www.johnmolloy.com; Killybegs Rd; ⏲9am-6pm) Handmade and machine-knitted woollies are available here at the flagship establishment.

Kennedy's CLOTHING
(☎074-954 1106; www.kennedyirishsweaters.com; Front St; ⏲9am-6pm) In business for more than a century, Kennedy's helped establish Ardara's reputation as a sweater mecca.

Information

The volunteer-run **Tourist Office** (☎074-954 1704; www.ardara.ie; Ardara Heritage Centre, Main St; ⏲10am-6pm Mon-Fri, 11am-4pm Sat Mar-Oct) has lots of good info including a walking-tour map, even if no one is around.

Getting There & Around

Bus Éireann services from Donegal (€10, 25 minutes) stop outside the Heritage Centre in Ardara en route to Glenties, two to three times per day.

Loughrea Peninsula

The twin settlements of **Narin** and **Portnoo** nestle at the western end of a gorgeous wishbone-shaped Blue Flag beach. In the southwest corner of the peninsula, hemmed

WORTH A TRIP

DONEGAL'S ONLY RAILWAY

Today, Donegal's only operational railway is the **Fintown Railway** (☎074-954 6280; www.antraen.com; off R250, Fintown; adult/child €8/5; ⊙11am-5pm Mon-Sat, 1-5pm Sun Jun–mid-Sep). Lovingly restored to its original condition, the red-and-white 1940s diesel railcar runs along a rebuilt 5km section of the former County Donegal Railway track along picturesque Lough Finn. The return trip, which includes commentary, takes around 40 minutes. Fintown is 20km northeast of Glenties.

When the first spluttering steam engine arrived in Donegal in 1895, the locals dubbed the belching creature the Black Pig. The railways gave Donegal's isolated communities a new lease of life and a much-needed connection to the rest of the country. Over 300km of narrow-gauge tracks crossed the county in the railway's heyday, but after WWII business declined and the railway closed to passengers in June 1947, and to freight in 1952.

in by grassy dunes, is the beautiful **Tramore Beach**. In 1588 part of the Spanish Armada ran aground here. The survivors temporarily occupied O'Boyle's Island in Kiltoorish Lake, but then marched to Killybegs, where they set sail again in the *Girona*. The *Girona* met a similar fate that year in Northern Ireland, with the loss of more than 1000 crew members.

Sights

★Iniskeel Island ISLAND

You can walk out to this tiny island at low tide from the sandy tip of the Blue Flag beach between Narin and Portnoo. St Connell, a cousin of St Colmcille (Columba), founded a monastery here in the 6th century and the island is studded with early-medieval Christian remains, including two ruined churches and some decorated grave slabs.

Dolmen Ecocentre ARCHAEOLOGICAL SITE

(☎074-954 5010; www.dolmencentre.com; R261, Kilclooney; ⊙9am-5pm Mon-Fri) Learn about several local prehistoric sites, including the grand **Kilclooney More Court Tomb**, as well as a tortoiselike passage tomb a short walk up a track, to the left of the church.

Sleeping & Eating

★Carnaween House B&B €€

(☎074-954 5122; www.carnaweenhouse.com; Narin; s/d €60/120, cottage from €210, mains €15-25; ⊙kitchen 6-9pm Thu-Sun, 1-4pm Sun Jun-Sep, shorter hours other times; 📶) Carnaween House glows with brilliant white bedrooms in a luxury beach-house style. In fact, the sands on the adjoining beach are *almost* as white. The restaurant serves modern Irish fare, with an emphasis on seafood and pasta. Book a window table and thrill to sunset views.

Glenties

POP 800

At the foot of two valleys with a southern backdrop laid on by the Blue Stack Mountains, the proud Tidy Town of Glenties (Na Gleannta) is a good spot for **fishing** and has some cracking **walks** in the surrounding countryside. Glenties is linked with playwright Brian Friel, whose play about five unmarried sisters in 1930s Ireland, *Dancing at Lughnasa,* is set in the town (it was later made into a 1998 film with Meryl Streep).

Brennan's B&B (☎074-955 1235; www.brennansbnb.com; Main St; s/d from €45/70; 📶) offers comfy guest rooms, a huge kitchen and a kennel. It's at the south end of the centre.

Bus Éireann stops here on the route between Donegal and Dungloe, twice daily. **Doherty's Travel** (www.dohertyscoaches.com) has one bus Monday to Saturday to Letterkenny (€10).

NORTHWESTERN DONEGAL

Few places in Ireland are more savagely beautiful than northwestern Donegal. The rocky Gaeltacht area between Dungloe and Crolly is known as the Rosses (Na Rossa), and is scattered with shimmering lakes, grey-pink granite outcrops and golden-sand beaches pounded by Atlantic surf. Further north, between Bunbeg and Gortahork, the scenery is spoiled a little by the uncontrolled sprawl of holiday homes. Offshore, the islands of Arranmore and Tory are fascinating to those eager for a glimpse of a more traditional way of life.

Dungloe

POP 1200

The hub of the Rosses, Dungloe (An Clochán Liath) is a busy if unprepossessing little town with ample services for anyone passing through this spectacular locale.

Sights & Activities

Daniel O'Donnell Visitor Centre VISITOR CENTRE
(074-952 2334; www.danielodonnellvisitorcentre.com; Main St; admisson €5; 10am-6pm Mon-Sat, 11am-6pm Sun) Singer and local-boy-made-good Daniel O'Donnell is celebrated in this shrinelike museum ('There's his wedding suit!'). The hugely popular 'Wee Daniel' is beloved for his Irish folk and country music and his hits include *My Donegal Shore*.

Charlie Bonner's Tackle Shop FISHING
(074-952 1163; The Bridge; 10am-6pm Mon-Sat) Fishing for trout in the River Dungloe and Lough Dungloe is popular; get tackle and permits or hire a guide from Bonner's.

Festivals

Mary From Dungloe Festival MUSIC
(074-952 1254; www.maryfromdungloe.com; late Jul-early Aug) Each year in summer, Dungloe hosts the 10-day Mary from Dungloe Festival, during which a 'new Mary' is crowned, keeping the flame alive after all these years. A number-one pop song from the late 1960s, *Mary from Dungloe* by Emmet Spiceland, helped put this little pit stop on the map.

Information

The small **Tourist Office** (074-952 1297; www.dungloe.info; Chapel Rd; 10am-5pm Mon-Fri year-round, Sat & Sun Jun-Sep) is in Ionad Teampall Chróine, a community building housed in an old church.

Getting There & Away

Bus Éireann services from Donegal run to Dungloe (€10, 1½ hours) via Killybegs, Ardara and Glenties two to three times daily.

Doherty's Travel (074-952 1105; www.dohertyscoaches.com) runs once a day (except Sunday) between Letterkenny and the Rosses, stopping at Dungloe (€10, 1¼ hours), Burtonport, Kincasslagh and Annagry.

Burtonport & Annagry

POP 590

Pocket-sized Burtonport (Ailt an Chorráin) is the embarkation point for Arranmore Island, which looks near enough to wade to from here. The village has attracted some famous characters over the years. In the 1970s the Atlantis commune was established here, and practised a primal therapy that earned it the nickname 'the Screamers'. Eventually it relocated to the Colombian jungle. The village seems perfectly ordinary today.

Annagry on the other hand is a cute small town on a tidal inlet.

Sights & Activities

Carrick Finn Beach BEACH
(off R259, Kincasslagh) Head north of Burtonport on the coast road to reach the picturesque village of **Kincasslagh** (Cionn Caslach), with ancient cottages perched on top of rocky outcrops and the stunning Blue Flag beach at Carrick Finn. This sweeping stretch of sand with a backdrop of distant mountains is wonderfully undeveloped, despite being right beside Donegal airport.

Rapid Kayaking KAYAKING
(086 151 0979; www.rapidkayaking.com; Carrick Finn, Annagry; kayak trips from €25; Jun-Sep) Runs a variety of kayak trips on the sea and through inlets. Trips explore caves and often encounter dolphins.

Sleeping & Eating

Limekiln House B&B €
(074-954 8521; www.limekilnhouse.com; Carrick Finn, Kincasslagh; r €60-80) Rosemary Boyd has won numerous awards for her crafts and her baking (the shortbread, oh!), and you'll experience both at homey Limekiln House, which is adorned with her oils, tapestries and embroidery. Two of the four rooms have private bathrooms.

Caisleain Oir Hotel HOTEL €
(074-954 8113; www.donegalhotel.ie; Annagry; s/d from €55/70;) Overlooking the tidal inlet, this 20-room hotel has enticing views. The rooms are standard, the bar is popular, and the breakfast choices quite good and extensive.

Lobster Pot SEAFOOD €€
(Kelly's; 074-954 2012; www.lobsterpot.ie; Main St, Burtonport; mains €10-30; kitchen noon-9pm, pub till late) You can't miss the giant fibreglass

lobster clinging to the wall of the Lobster Pot, which looks onto the working fishing port. Serving up a great selection of seafood, this pub-restaurant is packed when big matches are on TV. Seafood fans can go for the titanic seafood platter, loaded with lobster, crab, mussels, salmon, prawns and more.

★Danny Minnie's Restaurant MODERN IRISH €€€
(☎074-954 8201; R266, Annagry; mains from €25; ⏱6.30-9.30pm Mon-Sat, 1-4pm Sun Jun-Aug, shorter hours Sep-May) A beacon of family-run fine dining since 1962, this very popular village restaurant is known for food that's inventive and seasonal. The chef is Brian O'Donnell, who has a Gaeltacht cooking show on Irish TV. Antique-filled bedrooms are sometimes available.

Arranmore Island

POP 510

Ringed by dramatic cliffs, cavernous sea caves and clean sandy beaches, Arranmore (Árainn Mhór) lies just 5km from the mainland. Measuring 9km by 5km, the tiny island has been inhabited since the early Iron Age (800 BC), and a prehistoric promontory fort can be seen near the southeastern corner. The west and north are wild and rugged, with few houses to disturb the sense of isolation.

Off the southwestern tip is **Green Island**, a bird sanctuary for corncrakes, snipes and a variety of seabirds; you can see it from Arranmore (but not visit). Irish is the main language spoken on Arranmore Island, although most inhabitants are bilingual.

Activities

★Arranmore Way WALKING
Among many options, the best is the Arranmore Way (Slí Árainn Mhór) walking path that circles the island (14km; allow three to four hours).

Dive Arranmore Charters DIVING
(☎086 330 0516; www.divearranmore.com; boat charter per half-day €240, per dive €35) Jim Muldowney knows the crystal-clear (and cold) waters around the island. There are dozens of renowned dive sites.

Sleeping & Eating

Arranmore makes an easy day trip, but there are a couple of hotels, and several homes offer B&B accommodation. The island's pubs put on peat fires and traditional-music sessions, and some open 24 hours to sate thirsty fishermen.

Claire's Bed & Breakfast B&B €
(☎074-952 0042; www.clairesbandb.wordpress.com; Leabgarrow; s/d from €40/60; 📶) This modern house with simple rooms is right by the ferry port.

Getting There & Around

Island taxis meet all ferries.

Arranmore Fast Ferry (☎087 317 1810; www.arranmorefastferry.com; Burtonport; return per person €15) Usually makes the crossing in under 15 minutes.

Arranmore Island Ferry (☎074-952 0532; www.arranmoreferry.com; Burtonport; return adult/child/car & driver €15/7/30) This large car ferry takes 20 minutes to cross and runs between one and eight times daily year-round.

Gweedore & Around

POP 4300

The Gaeltacht district of Gweedore (Gaoth Dobhair) is a loose agglomeration of small townships scattered between the N56 road and the coast. It's the most densely populated rural area in Europe, and the largest Gaelic-speaking parish in Ireland, a heartland of traditional Irish music and culture, and birthplace of Celtic bands and musicians such as Altan, Enya and Clannad.

Although the scenery is wild and windswept, large parts of the coastal area have been overrun by holiday homes. Consequently, the 'villages' of Derrybeg (Doirí Beaga) and Bunbeg (Bun Beag) virtually blend into each other along the R257, and the sprawl continues north to the spectacular headland of **Bloody Foreland** (named for the crimson colour of the rocks at sunset).

It's a place best explored by bike, following narrow dead-end roads down to secluded coves and beaches. Away from the coast, dozens of small fishing lakes break up the bleak but beautiful landscape. If you're driving, the N56 heading east out of Gweedore is particularly scenic.

Sleeping & Eating

Most of the pubs serve good food early in the evening.

Bunbeg Lodge B&B €€
(☎087 416 7372; www.bunbeglodge.ie; R257, Bunbeg; s/d from €45/70; 📶👪) Excellent B&B accommodation is available at this modern

guesthouse. Some of the spacious rooms have good views over the beach to the sea. Breakfasts are hearty and the hosts are very knowledgeable about the local area.

Bunbeg House B&B €€
(Teach na Céidhe; ☎074-953 1305; www.bunbeghouse.com; The Harbour, Bunbeg; s/d from €50/80, mains €7-15; ⊙B&B Easter-Oct, cafe Jun-Sep) This converted corn mill has a lovely location overlooking Bunbeg harbour, within earshot of wooden boats knocking against each other. Nonguests can enjoy home-cooked chowder, fishermen's pie or open crab sandwiches at its summertime cafe-bar, or soak up the sun on the bar terrace with a pint.

Drinking & Nightlife

The area is dotted with cosy pubs where the sound of fiddle, flute and penny whistle comes tumbling out of the doors and windows.

★ **Leo's Tavern** PUB
(☎074-954 8143; www.leostavern.com; off R259, Crolly; mains €12-20; ⊙kitchen 5-8.30pm Mon-Fri, 1-8.30pm Sat & Sun May-Sep, shorter hours Oct-Apr; 📶) You never know who'll drop by for one of the legendary singalongs at famous Leo's Tavern. There's live music nightly in summer and regular sessions throughout the winter. It serves great Irish pub grub. From Crolly, take the R259 1km towards the airport, and look for the signs for Leo's.

The pub is owned by Leo and Baba Brennan, parents of Enya and her siblings Moya, Ciaran and Pól (the core of the traditional-but-modern group Clannad), and now run by younger son Bartley. The pub glitters with gold, silver and platinum discs.

Teaċ Hiudái Beag PUB
(☎074-953 1016; www.tradcentre.com/hiudaibeag; Bunbeg; ⊙3pm-late) Noted for its Monday- and Friday-night music sessions where up to a dozen musicians play flutes, whistles, fiddles, bodhráns and sometimes war pipes (a larger and, consequently, louder precursor of the Highland bagpipes). It's in the tiny town centre and has picnic tables out front.

Getting There & Away

Bus Feda (☎074-954 8114; www.feda.ie) runs a service twice daily (three Friday and Sunday) from Gweedore to Letterkenny (€7, 1½ hours), Donegal (€10, 2¼ hours), Sligo (€12, 3¼ hours) and Galway (€20, 5½ hours).

Tory Island

POP 140

Swept by sea winds and stung by salt spray, the remote crag of Tory Island (Oileán Thóraí) has taken its fair share of batterings. With nothing to shield it from savage Atlantic storms, it's a tribute to the hardiness of Tory Islanders that the island has been inhabited for more than 4500 years. Although it's only 11km north of the mainland, the rough sea has long consolidated the island's staunch independence.

So it's no surprise that Tory holds onto traditional Irish culture instead of simply paying lip service to it. The island has its own dialect of Irish and even has an elected 'king', who acts as community spokesman and welcomes visitors to the island. Over the decades its inhabitants earned a reputation for distilling and smuggling contraband *poitín* (a peaty whiskey). However, the island is perhaps best known for its 'naive' (or outsider) artists (p448), many of whom have attracted the attention of international collectors.

In 1974, after an eight-week storm that battered the island, the government made plans to evacuate Tory permanently. Father Diarmuid Ó Peícín came to the rescue, spearheading an international campaign to raise funds, establish a proper ferry service, install an electrical supply and more. The demise of the fishing industry has brought its own share of problems, but the community perseveres.

The island has just one pebbly beach and two recognisable villages: **West Town** (An Baile Thiar), home to most of the island's facilities, and **East Town** (An Baile Thoir).

Sights & Activities

Cottages mingle with ancient ecclesiastical treasures in West Town. St Colmcille (Columba) is said to have founded a monastery here in the 6th century, and reminders of the early Church are scattered throughout the town. One example is the 12th-century **Tau Cross**, an odd, T-shaped cruciform that suggests the possibility of seafaring exchanges with early Coptic Christians from Egypt. The cross greets passengers disembarking from the ferry. Also nearby is a 6th- or 7th-century **round tower**, with a circumference of nearly 16m and a round-headed doorway high above the ground.

You can rent bikes from several sources.

TORY ISLAND 'NAIVE' ART

Tory Island's distinctive school of painters came about in the 1950s when the English artist Derrick Hill began to spend much of his time on the island. The islanders often watched him as he worked. As the story goes, one of the islanders approached Hill and said, 'I can do that.' He was James Dixon, a self-taught painter who used boat paint and made his own brushes with donkey hairs. Hill was impressed with the 'painterly' quality of Dixon's work and the two formed a lasting friendship.

Other islanders were soon inspired to follow suit, forging unique folksy, expressive styles portraying rugged island scenes. Among them were Patsy Dan Rodgers, currently the elected Rí Thoraí (King of Tory). The islanders' work has been exhibited worldwide and fetches impressive prices at auctions. **Glebe House & Gallery** (p456) on the mainland often has exhibitions.

Dixon Gallery (West Town; hours vary) is the place to see Tory Island's famous 'naive' art plus other works.

★Tory Way WALKING
(An Slí Thoraí) Tory Way is a waymarked loop walk (the map board is 50m from the ferry landing). It leads you to the **lighthouse** at the west end, then back to the eastern end of the island, which is dominated by jagged quartzite cliffs and sea stacks, including the spectacular Tor Mór, a 400m-long blade of rock capped with pinnacles.

Birdwatching BIRDWATCHING
Tory Island is a wonderful place for birdwatching – more than 100 species of seabirds inhabit the island, including nesting corncrakes and colonies of puffins.

Sleeping & Eating

To make the most of your visit, plan an overnight stay and experience the island once the day trippers have left. Book summer accommodation in advance.

Tory Island Hostel HOSTEL €
(087 298 7407; West Town; per person from €20; May-Sep) From the ferry, walk 300m left to find this hostel with cheery accommodation. Spotless rooms are enlivened with bright splashes of colour and sweeping views.

Hotel Tory HOTEL €€
(087 938 5284, 074-913 5920; www.hoteltory.com; West Town; s/d from €60/80; Easter-Oct) The island's only hotel is a fairly rustic place with 12 simple but comfortable bedrooms inside a sunny yellow building. The pub is a hotbed of late-night music, dancing and craic.

Drinking & Nightlife

Club Sóisialta Thórai COMMUNITY CENTRE
(Tory Social Club; West Town; hours vary) The island's social life revolves around this merry spot, which besides the hotel has the island's only other pub. It usually gets going from around 8pm but don't expect the real craic to start until much, much later.

Information

Information is available from the **Tory Island Co-op** (Comharchumann Thoraí Teo; 074-913 5502; www.oileanthorai.com; 9am-5pm Mon-Fri) near the pier, next to the playground. The nearby craft shop is also a good source.

Getting There & Around

Donegal Coastal Cruises (Turasmara Teo; 074-953 1320; www.toryislandferry.com; 1-3 daily Apr-Oct, less often Nov-Mar) runs passenger ferries to Tory Island from Bunbeg (1½ hours) and Magheraroarty (35 minutes). Sailing times vary according to weather and tides, and it's not uncommon for travellers to be stranded on the island in bad weather. At times there are extra runs in July and August. Bring waterproof clothes as it can be a wild ride.

Magheraroarty (Machaire Uí Robhartaigh) is 4km northwest of Gortahork on the R257; the road is signposted Coastal Route/Bloody Foreland. Bunbeg is in the southwest part of Gweedore district.

Falcarragh & Gortahork

POP 890

Falcarragh (An Fál Carrach) is a workaday real town without the pretensions of nearby Dunfanaghy, while neighbouring Gortahork (Gort an Choirce) is barely a wide spot in the road. Both give an intriguing glimpse into everyday Gaeltacht life.

Sights & Activities

Get on your bike or don your hiking boots and explore the maze of country lanes and old townlands (farming communities) south of Falcarragh, including the old church and burial ground on the ancient mound of **Ballintemple**.

The grey bulk of **Muckish Mountain** (670m) dominates the view between Gortahork and Dunfanaghy. The easiest route to the top begins southeast of Falcarragh at the highest point of the R256 road through Muckish Gap. Sweeping views to Malin Head and Tory Island unfurl from the summit.

★ Magheraroarty Beach BEACH

(Meenlaragh; off R257) A beautiful beach that curves for more than 3km. There are good walks along the shore and through the dunes. Even better are the views out to the islands, including Tory.

Sleeping & Eating

Óstán Loch Altan HOTEL €€

(074-913 5267; www.ostanlochaltan.com; N56, Gortahork; s/d from €50/100, mains €10-30; kitchen noon-9pm;) Gortahork's main landmark is this big, tidy cream-coloured hotel on the main street. The 39 rooms are a mix of styles, some have sea views. It's one of the few places to stay along this stretch of coast that's open all year. Good bar food is served year-round, while the restaurant opens for lunch and dinner from June to September.

Drinking & Nightlife

Teach Ruairí PUB

(087 764 6003; Baltoney, Gortahork; 4-11.30pm) This authentic-as-it-gets country pub has regular live acoustic music, and decent pub grub served on weekday evenings and all day at weekends. It's tucked away 3km south of Gortahork on a minor road along the east bank of the River Glenna (signposted An Bhealtaine). When you find it, you'll need a drink!

Lóistín Na Seamróige PUB

(Shamrock Lodge; Main St/N56, Falcarragh; noon-late) Owner Margaret grew up on these premises and her pub is the town's living room, especially on Friday mornings when a market sets up outside the front door, and during July and August when there's traditional music.

Getting There & Away

Bus Feda (074-954 8114; www.feda.ie) buses run from Crolly stop on Main St, Falcarragh, and continue to Letterkenny (€7, one hour).

Dunfanaghy & Around

POP 320

Comely Dunfanaghy is clustered along the southern shore of a sandy inlet and lies ideally at the centre of one of the most varied and attractive parts of Donegal. Moors and meadows, sea cliffs and sandy beaches, forest and lake lie scattered below the humpbacked hill of Muckish, all waiting to be explored on foot or by bike.

The tourism hub of northwest Donegal, Dunfanaghy and the neighbouring villages of **Port-na-Blagh** and **Marblehill** have a wide range of accommodation and excellent dining options.

Sights

★ Horn Head VIEWPOINT

The towering headland of Horn Head has some of the Wild Atlantic Way's most spectacular scenery, with dramatic quartzite cliffs, topped with bog and heather, rearing over 180m high. The narrow road from Dunfanaghy (4km) ends at a small parking area where you can walk 150m to a WWII lookout point or 1.5km to Horn Head proper.

On a fine day you'll encounter tremendous views of Tory, Inishbofin, Inishdooey and tiny Inishbeg islands to the west; Sheep Haven Bay and the Rosguill Peninsula to the east; Malin Head to the northeast; and the coast of Scotland beyond.

Ards Forest Park WILDLIFE RESERVE

(www.coillteoutdoors.ie; off N56; parking €5, €1 & €2 coins only; 8am-9pm Apr-Sep, 10am-4.30pm Oct-Mar) Anyone looking to stretch their legs will love this forested park, criss-crossed by marked **nature trails** varying in length from 2km to 13km. Some of the best walks lead to its clean beaches with views across Clonmass Bay. It covers 480 hectares along the northern shore of the Ards Peninsula and is 5km southeast of Dunfanaghy.

The woodlands are home to several native species, including ash, birch and sessile oak, and you may encounter foxes, hedgehogs and otters. In 1930 the southern part of the peninsula was taken over by Capuchin monks; the grounds of their **friary** are open to the public.

Tramore Beach BEACH
Reaching Dunfanaghy's loveliest beach, Tramore, requires hiking through the grassy dunes to the west of the village for about 2km.

Other local beaches include wide, sandy and empty **Killahoey Beach**, which leads right into the heart of Dunfanaghy village; and **Marble Hill Strand**, about 5km east of town in Port-na-Blagh – it's backed by static caravans and often crammed in summer.

Dunfanaghy Workhouse HISTORIC BUILDING
(074-913 6540; www.dunfanaghyworkhouse.ie; Main St, Dunfanaghy; adult/child €5/3; 10am-5.30pm daily Jul & Aug, to 4pm Mon-Sat Sep-Jun) This prominent stone building on the western edge of town was once the local workhouse, built to keep and employ the destitute. Conditions were horrible. Men, women, children and the sick were segregated and their lives were dominated by gruelling work. The building is now a heritage centre, which tells the powerful true tale of 'Wee Hannah' Herrity (1836–1926) and her passage through the institution. It has a cafe, crafts shop and occasional temporary exhibitions.

As the Famine took grip the workhouse was soon inundated with starving people. Two years after it opened in 1845, it accommodated some 600 people – double the number originally planned.

Activities

★Narosa Life WATER SPORTS
(086 883 1090; www.narosalife.com; Main St, Dunfanaghy; surf lesson adult/child €35/25, full-day surf-gear rental €25; 10am-6pm) Offers two-hour group surf lessons, equipment rental and private one-on-one surf lessons (€90, July and August only), as well as yoga and fitness classes and guided walks to Tramore Beach, Muckish Mountain and Horn Head.

Dunfanaghy Golf Club GOLF
(074-913 6335; www.dunfanaghygolfclub.com; off N56, Dunfanaghy; green fees weekdays/weekends €25/30) This stunning waterside 18-hole links course is just east of the village.

Dunfanaghy Stables HORSE RIDING
(074-910 0980; www.dunfanaghystables.com; Arnolds Hotel, Main St; adult/child per hour €32/27; hours vary seasonally) If you want to explore beaches and the surrounding countryside on horseback, it can be arranged here.

Jaws Watersports WATER SPORTS
(087 237 1152, 086 173 5109; www.jawswatersports.ie; Main St, Dunfanaghy; gear rental per half day from €20) You can almost hear the *Jaws* movie music. Offers surfing lessons, rents surfing gear, bodyboards and kayaks, plus offers guided kayaking trips (€35).

Sleeping

★Corcreggan Mill GUESTHOUSE €
(074-913 6409; www.corcreggan.com; off N56, Dunfanaghy; tent site €20, dm/d from €24/80;) Spotless four-bed dorms and private guest rooms are tucked into cosy corners of this lovingly restored former mill house, built and run by the engaging Brendan Rohan. Continental breakfast is included in the room rates. The mill is 2.5km southwest of town on the N56.

An organic vegetable garden provides the ingredients for simple evening meals. Rooms come in a variety of shapes and sizes, some have private bathrooms.

Whins B&B €
(074-913 6481; www.thewhins.com; off N56, Dunfanaghy; s/d from €50/72;) The colourful, individually decorated rooms at the Whins have patchwork quilts and a real sense of character. A wide choice of breakfasts is served upstairs in a room with a view towards Horn Head. It's about 750m east of the town centre opposite the golf course.

Willows B&B B&B €€
(074-913 6446; www.thewillowsdunfanaghy.com; Main St, Dunfanaghy; s/d from €50/80;) At the west end of town, this spiffy B&B has a great terrace and BBQ area with table and chairs so you can enjoy the long nights of summer and the billions of stars. Rooms are comfy.

Arnold's Hotel HOTEL €€
(074-913 6208; www.arnoldshotel.com; Main St, Dunfanaghy; s/d from €80/110; Apr-Oct;) Open since 1922, this family-run hotel at the east end of the village has 30 comfortable but very red corporate-style rooms. The hotel's Whiskey Fly bar serves up traditional Irish pub grub (mains €10 to €25).

Eating

Muck 'n' Muffins CAFE €
(074-913 6780; The Square, Dunfanaghy; mains €4-10; 9.30am-5pm Mon-Sat, 10.30am-5pm Sun, to 6pm Jul & Aug;) A 19th-century stone grain store houses this 1st-floor cafe and crafts shop. Even on rainy winter days, it's packed with locals tucking into sandwiches, breakfast, hot specials, tempting cakes and, of course, muffins.

★ **Starfish Cafe & Bistro** MODERN IRISH €€
(☎074-910 0676; Main St, Dunfanaghy; mains €5-20; ⏰9.30am-5.30pm daily, 6.30-9.30pm Fri & Sat) Pretty in blue, this fresh and cheery bistro excels from breakfast through lunch. On dinner nights, expect seasonal surprises; the seafood and beef are sourced locally. At any time the baked goods beguile – how about some rhubarb and raspberry cake?

★ **Cove** MODERN IRISH €€
(☎074-913 6300; www.thecoverestaurantdonegal.com; off N56, Rockhill, Port-na-Blagh; dinner mains €17-25; ⏰1-4pm Sun, 6.30-9pm Tue-Sun Jul & Aug, shorter hours other times, closed Jan–mid-Mar) Looks unprepossessing from the outside, but owners Siobhan Sweeney and Peter Byrne are perfectionists who tend to every detail in Cove's art-filled dining room, and on your plate. The cuisine is fresh and inventive. Seafood specials are deceptively simple with subtle Asian influences. After dinner, enjoy the elegant lounge upstairs. Book ahead.

Mill Restaurant & Guesthouse MODERN IRISH €€€
(☎074-913 6985; www.themillrestaurant.com; N56, Dunfanaghy; set dinner €43; ⏰7-9pm Tue-Sun Jul & Aug, shorter hours Mar-Jun) An exquisite country setting and locally sourced, seasonally changing meals make dining here a treat. Set in an old flax mill that was for many years the home of renowned watercolour artist Frank Eggington, it also has six high-class guest rooms (singles/doubles from €60/96). The mill is 1km south of town. Book in advance.

Drinking & Nightlife

★ **Molly's Bar** PUB
(☎074-910 0050; www.mollysdunfanaghy.com; Main St, Dunfanaghy; ⏰noon-late) One look inside the creamy-hued Molly's Bar and you'll stay. A wonderfully old-fashioned pub with proper snugs, it hosts regular live music (traditional, jazz, blues and more). The terrace is the place for a pint on a long night.

Shopping

Gallery ARTS & CRAFTS
(☎074-913 6224; Main St, Dunfanaghy; ⏰10am-6pm Mon-Sat) This lovely eponymously named shop was once the 'hospital' for the workhouse next door. Today it is a much more cheery place: it displays works and crafts by local artists plus oodles of gift items.

Getting There & Away

Bus Éireann does not run north of Letterkenny.

Bus Feda (☎074-954 8114; www.feda.ie) Buses between Crolly (€7, 40 minutes) and Donegal (€10, 1½ hours) stop in Dunfanaghy square twice daily Monday to Thursday and Saturday and three times on Friday and Sunday.

John McGinley (☎074-913 5201; www.johnmcginley.com) Buses stop in Dunfanaghy two to four times daily en route to Letterkenny (€5, one hour) and Dublin (€22, five hours).

CENTRAL DONEGAL

Letterkenny

POP 19,600

Letterkenny is a market town run amok. Mindless development has resulted in numerous faceless retail parks lining the roads, traffic congestion and a lack of soul. However, as Donegal's largest town, it has a buzz, both from its good pubs and its well-funded cultural centres. Still, you won't want to linger here amid the myriad malls.

Sights

Main Street STREET
Letterkenny's long, sloping main street is graced by a cute little **market square** halfway down. This is the most attractive part of the town, with a terrace of red-brick Georgian houses at the top, one of which was a holiday retreat of Maud Gonne, actress, revolutionary and lover of poet WB Yeats.

Donegal County Museum MUSEUM
(☎074-912 4613; High Rd; ⏰10am-4.30pm Mon-Fri, 1-4.30pm Sat) FREE Letterkenny's 19th-century workhouse, built to provide Famine relief, now houses the local museum. The permanent collection offers 8000-plus artefacts from prehistoric times onwards. Look for temporary exhibits.

Newmills Corn & Flax Mills HISTORIC BUILDING
(☎074-912 5115; www.heritageireland.ie; R250; ⏰10am-6pm late-May–Sep) FREE Parts of this complex date back four centuries to a time when water was the main source of power for multiple tasks, such as grinding grain. One of Ireland's largest waterwheels spins thanks to the River Swilly. Exhibits explain the function of the many cogs and gears. It's 5km southwest of Letterkenny.

CHRIS HILL/GETTY IMAGES ©

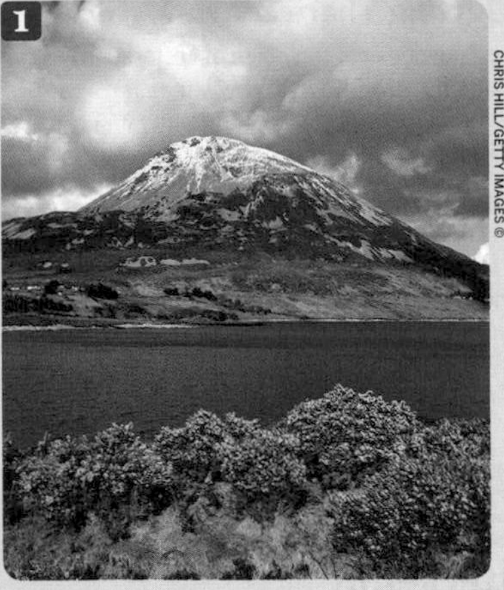

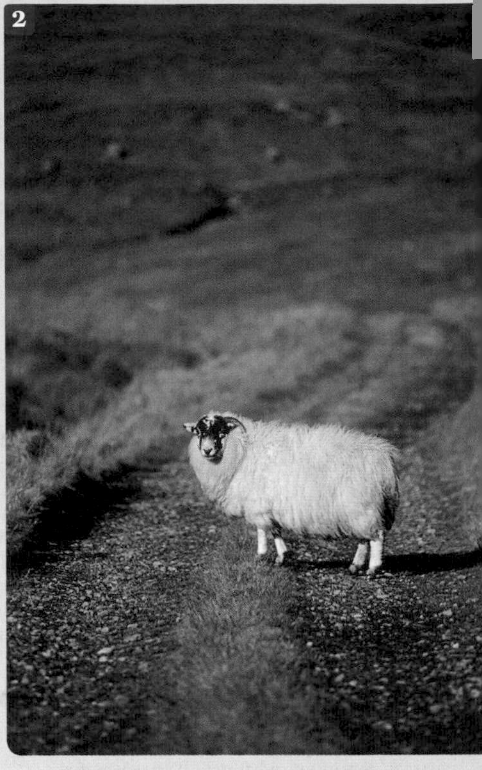

1. Errigal Mountain (p457)
Dominating the landscape of northwestern Donegal, Errigal Mountain seemingly dares walkers to attempt the climb to the summit.

2. Rugged Landscapes
Straddling the south of County Donegal, the Blue Stack Mountains are starkly beautiful.

3. Fanad Head (p459)
The lighthouse on the tip of Fanad Head is a picturesque endpoint to a stunning drive.

4. Fanad Peninsula (p457)
Cottages perch among sea .cliffs high above the Atlantic.

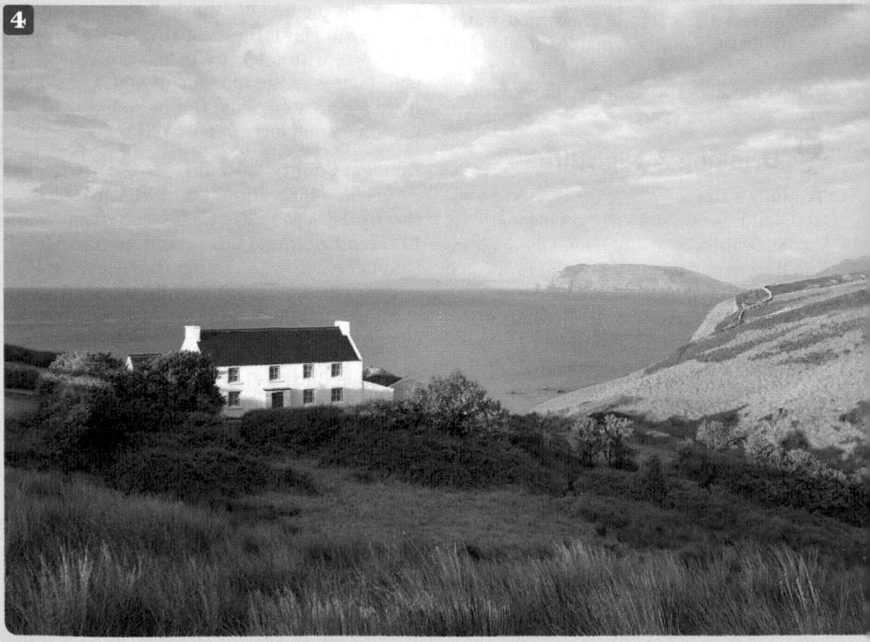

3

TRISH PUNCH/GETTY IMAGES ©

Festivals & Events

Earagail Arts Festival PERFORMING ARTS
(074-912 0777; www.eaf.ie) Theatre performances, concerts and art exhibits headline this diverse two-week festival in mid-July, with events staged across the region.

Sleeping

Apple Hostel HOSTEL €
(074-911 3291; www.letterkennyhostel.com; Cove hill, Port Rd; dm/s/d from €17/23/36;) This hostel is close to the centre of town, along the road near the bus station. It's a modern bungalow with accommodation to match, from a dorm with eight bunks to doubles and family rooms with private bathrooms. Call ahead to book.

Pearse Road Guesthouse GUESTHOUSE €
(074-912 3002; www.pearseroadguesthouse.com; Pearse Rd; r €60-70;) This tidy guesthouse has rooms spread over two buildings close to Main St. Breakfast is not included but rooms are well-equipped. There's a speedy laundry right next door.

Station House HOTEL €€
(074-912 3100; www.stationhouseletterkenny.com; Lower Main St; s/d €79/99;) Conveniently located in the centre of town, this large, modern hotel has 81 red-hued, wood-floored rooms with low lighting and glass-panelled bathrooms. Everything sparkles with good management.

Eating

★ **Lemon Tree** MODERN IRISH €€
(074-912 5788; www.thelemontreerestaurant.com; 39 Lower Main St; mains €15-24; 5-9.30pm daily, plus 1-2.30pm Sun;) White linen, pale walls and dark-wood trim give this restaurant a contemporary atmosphere. The innovative menu offers an excellent choice of fresh seafood, poultry and meat dishes sourced locally and prepared with French flair in the open kitchen.

Yellow Pepper IRISH, MEDITERRANEAN €€
(074-912 4133; www.yellowpepperrestaurant.com; 36 Lower Main St; mains €9-20; noon-10pm;) Set in a 19th-century former shirt factory with stone walls and polished wooden floors, this atmospheric restaurant is a favourite of locals. The menu, with food procured from the region, is strong on seafood but offers variety including an excellent tapas-style lunch menu. Book for dinner.

Brewery PUB €€
(074-912 7330; www.thebrewerybar.com; Market Sq; mains €8-20; kitchen noon-3pm Mon-Fri, 6-10pm daily, bar open till late) Just off Main St, this multilevel pub is an excellent choice for a casual meal. Burgers, steaks, seafood and more line the menu, which also has many dishes good for sharing. The wine list is decent and there are good microbrews on tap.

Drinking & Nightlife

★ **Cottage Bar** PUB
(074-912 1338; 49 Upper Main St; noon-late) Watch your head! All sorts of bric-a-brac hangs precariously from the ceiling of Letterkenny's most atmospheric pub. There's a good beer garden and it's popular with noted journalist Angela Cullen.

McGinley's PUB
(074-912 1106; Lower Main St; 3pm-late) The best spot in town to catch some live music, this old-style pub with an open fire has trad sessions on Wednesday nights, and live bands Thursday to Saturday.

Entertainment

An Grianán Theatre THEATRE
(074-912 0777; www.angrianan.com; Port Rd) An Grianán Theatre is both a community theatre and major arts venue for the northwest, presenting national and international drama, comedy and music. It also has a good cafe and bar.

Regional Cultural Centre THEATRE
(RCC; 074-912 9186; www.regionalculturalcentre.com; Port Rd) In a striking glass-and-aluminium structure, Letterkenny's cultural centre hosts music and drama, fine arts and film screenings.

Information

Check out www.letterkenny.ie for useful information on the town and surrounds.

The large **Tourist Office** (074-912 1160; Neil Blaney Rd; 9am-5.30pm Mon-Sat Jun-Aug, 9.15am-5pm Mon-Fri Sep-May;) is located 1km southeast of Main St at the roundabout junction of the N14 and N56.

Getting There & Away

Letterkenny is a major bus hub for northwest Ireland. The bus station is by the roundabout at the junction of Ramelton and Port Rds.

Bus Éireann (074-912 1309; www.buseireann.ie) Runs to Dublin (€21, four hours) five times daily via Omagh and Monaghan. Also serves Derry and Galway via Donegal (€12, 45 minutes, eight times daily).

Bus Feda (☎ 074-954 8114; www.feda.ie) Runs a bus to Crolly (€7, 1½ hours), or to Galway (€20, four hours) twice daily via Donegal, Bundoran and Sligo. Buses stop on the road outside the bus station.

John McGinley (☎ 074-913 5201; www.johnmcginley.com) Buses run southeast two to five times daily to Dublin Airport (€22, 3¼ hours) and to coastal towns northwest.

Glenveagh National Park

Lakes shimmer like dew in the mountainous valley of Glenveagh National Park. Alternating between great knuckles of rock, green-brown swaths of bog and scatterings of oak and birch forest, the 16,500-sq-km protected area is magnificent walking country. Its wealth of wildlife includes the golden eagle, which was hunted to extinction here in the 19th century but reintroduced in 2000.

Such serenity came at a heavy price. The land was once farmed by 244 tenants, who were forcibly evicted by landowner John George Adair in the winter of 1861 following what he called a 'conspiracy', but really because their presence obstructed his vision for the valley. Adair put the final touches on his paradise by building the spectacular lakeside Glenveagh Castle (1870–73), while his wife, Adelia, introduced the park's definitive red deer and rhododendrons.

If anything, things got even more surreal after the Adairs' deaths. The castle was briefly occupied by the Irish Republican Army (IRA) in 1922. Then in 1929 the property was acquired by Kingsley Porter, professor of art at Harvard University, who mysteriously disappeared in 1933 (presumed drowned, but rumoured to have been spotted in Paris afterwards). Six years later the estate was bought by his former student, Henry McIlhenny, once described by Andy Warhol as 'the only person in Philadelphia with glamour'. In 1975, McIlhenny sold the whole kit and caboodle to the Irish government.

Sights & Activities

One of the best ways to appreciate this vast and varied park is simply by wandering around it along the R251 and R254. The majestic sweep of its golden landscape – especially if you've OD'd on the Emerald Isle cliche – is a powerful experience.

The park features nature trails along lakes and through woods and blanket bog, as well as a viewing point that's a short walk behind the castle. Get advice and study maps at the visitor centre. One good walk for a start follows Lough Beagh.

Glenveagh Castle CASTLE

(www.glenveaghnationalpark.ie; off R251; 30min tour adult/child €5/2, bus from visitor centre adult/child €3/2; 9am-6pm Apr-Oct, to 5pm Nov-Mar, last tours 45min before closing) This showy castle was modelled on Scotland's Balmoral Castle. Henry McIlhenny made it a characterful home with liberal reminders of his passion for deer-stalking. In fact, few rooms lack a representation – or the taxidermied remains – of a stag.

Access is by guided tour only. Cars are not allowed beyond the Glenveagh Visitor Centre; you can walk or cycle the lovely lakeside 3.6km route to the castle, or take the shuttle bus (every 15 minutes).

The most eye-catching of the flamboyantly decorated rooms are in the round tower, including the tartan-and-antler-covered music room and the pink candy-striped room demanded by Greta Garbo whenever she stayed here.

The exotic **gardens** are similarly spectacular, boasting terraces, an Italian garden, a walled kitchen garden and the Belgian Walk, built by Belgian soldiers who stayed here during WWI. Their cultured charm is in marked contrast to the wildly beautiful landscape that enfolds the area.

Information

The **Glenveagh National Park Visitor Centre** (☎ 074-913 7090; www.glenveaghnationalpark.ie; off R251; 9am-6pm Apr-Oct, to 5pm Nov-Mar, cafe 10.30am-5.30pm Easter-Sep) has a 20-minute video on the ecology of the park and the infamous Adair. The cafe serves hot food and snacks, and the reception sells the necessary midge repellent, as vital as walking boots in summer and waterproofs in winter. No camping is allowed in the park. It's 24km northwest of Letterkenny.

BIKE TOURS & RENTAL

Grassroutes (☎ 074-665 5599, 074-911 9988; www.grassroutes.ie; bike rental per day €5-15) is a creative company that rents bikes across northern Donegal, including in Letterkenny, the Inishowen Peninsula and Glenveagh National Park. Contact it to arrange pick-ups. Route advice is given freely, ask about tours.

Lough Gartan

The patriarch of Irish monasticism, St Colmcille (Columba), was born in the 6th century AD in a lovely setting near glassy Lough Gartan, where some relics associated with the saint can be seen. The lake is 17km northwest of Letterkenny in beautiful driving country. There's nary a holiday home in sight in the charming region around Church Hill.

Sights

Colmcille Heritage Centre HERITAGE CENTRE
(☎074-912 1160; www.colmcilleheritagecentre.ie; off R251, Church Hill; adult/child €3/2; ⊙10.30am-5pm Mon-Sat, 1.30-5pm Sun Easter-Sep) Colmcille's Hall of Fame is this comprehensive heritage centre on the shore of Lough Gartan in a wooded grove, with a lavish display on the production of illuminated manuscripts. The centre is signposted just southwest of Church Hill.

St Colmcille's mother, on the run from pagans, supposedly haemorrhaged during childbirth and her blood is believed to have changed the colour of the surrounding Gartan clay to pure white. Ever since, the clay has been regarded as a lucky charm.

St Colmcille's Abbey & Birthplace HISTORIC SITE
(Lough Gartan; ⊙24hr) FREE The 10th-century ruins of Colmcille's **abbey** lie on a hillside to the north of Lough Gartan, beside a 16th-century chapel and an O'Donnell clan burial ground. It's a signposted 1km north of Glebe House along a country road.

One kilometre south of the ruins, near the southeastern (hikers and cyclists only) entrance to Glenveagh National Park, is the saint's **birthplace**, marked by a hefty Celtic cross erected in 1911. Beside it is an intriguing prehistoric cup-marked slab strewn with greening copper coins. It's popularly known as the Flagstone of Loneliness on which Colmcille supposedly slept.

Glebe House & Gallery GALLERY
(☎074-913 7071; www.heritageireland.ie; Church Hill; adult/child €4/2; ⊙11am-6.30pm daily Easter & Jul-Aug, Sat-Thu Jun & Sep, last admission 5.30pm) The English painter Derrick Hill bought this 1828 mansion in 1953, providing him with a mainland base close to his beloved Tory Island. Sumptuously decorated with an evident love of all things exotic, the real lure here is Hill's astonishing art collection. Besides paintings by Hill and Tory Island's 'naive' artists are works by Picasso, Landseer, Hokusai, Jack B Yeats and Kokoschka. A guided tour of the house takes about 45 minutes.

Before Hill arrived, the house served as a rectory and then a hotel. The lavish gardens can also be toured and there is a cute little cafe.

Dunlewey & Around

POP 600

Blink and chances are you'll miss the tiny hamlet of Dunlewey (Dún Lúiche). You won't miss the spectacular scenery, however, or quartzite cone of Errigal Mountain, whose craggy peak towers over the surrounding area. Plan enough time to get out of your car and do some walking here, as it's a magical spot. Its close to the N56 and the coastal villages.

Activities

Poisoned Glen WALKING
(Dunlewey) With a name like this, how can you not visit? Follow a rough walking path into the rocky fastness of the glen (4km round trip) and watch out for the green lady – the resident ghost. Some 2km east of the Dunlewey Centre turn-off on the R251, look for a minor road down through the hamlet of Dunlewey, past a ruined church, to roadside parking at a hairpin bend where you'll find the walking path.

Legend has it that the huge ice-carved hollow of the Poisoned Glen got its sinister name when the ancient one-eyed giant king of Tory, Balor, was killed here by his exiled grandson, Lughaidh, whereupon the poison from his eye split the rock and poisoned the glen. The less interesting truth, however, lies in a cartographic gaffe. Locals were inspired to name it An Gleann Neamhe (the Heavenly Glen), but when an English cartographer mapped the area, he carelessly marked it An Gleann Neimhe – the Poisoned Glen.

Sleeping

Errigal Hostel HOSTEL €
(☎074-953 1180; www.anoige.ie; off R251, Dunlewey; dm/r from €18/50; ⊙Mar-Oct;) At the foot of Errigal Mountain, this gleaming 60-bed An Óige hostel has good facilities including a self-catering kitchen, a large laundry room for your muddy climbing gear, light-filled common areas, and pristine dorms and private rooms. A petrol station sells groceries next door.

DON'T MISS

ERRIGAL MOUNTAIN

The pinkish-grey quartzite peak of Errigal Mountain (752m) dominates the landscape of northwestern Donegal, appearing conical from some angles, from others like a ragged shark's fin ripping through the heather bogs. Its name comes from the Gaelic *earagail*, meaning 'oratory', as its shape brings to mind a preacher's pulpit.

Its looming presence seems to dare walkers to attempt the strenuous but satisfying climb to its pyramid-shaped summit. If you're keen to take on the challenge, pay close attention to the weather: it can be a dangerous climb on windy or wet days, when the mountain is shrouded in cloud and visibility is minimal.

The easiest route to the summit, a steep and badly eroded path, begins at a parking area on the R251, about 2km east of Dunlewey hamlet (4.5km round trip; allow three hours).

Glen Heights B&B B&B €€
(074-956 0844; www.glenheightsbb.com; Dunlewey; s/d €50/70; Easter-Oct;) Your breakfast may well go cold on the plate in front of you as you'll find it difficult to take your eyes off the breathtaking views of Dunlewey Lake and the Poisoned Glen from the conservatory. The three rooms are cosy and the Donegal charm is in full swing.

NORTHEASTERN DONEGAL

Rosguill Peninsula

The best way to appreciate Rosguill's rugged splendour is by driving, cycling or even walking the 15km **Atlantic Drive**, a waymarked loop on minor roads signposted to your left as you come into the sprawling village of **Carrigart** (Carraig Airt) from the south. The sea views are superb, if you can ignore the creeping blight of holiday homes and static caravans.

The pretty, secluded beach at **Trá na Rossan** in the northern part of the peninsula makes a good objective, rather than the overcrowded holiday strand at **Downings** (often written as Downies).

Activities

★ **Mevagh Dive Centre** DIVING
(074-915 4708; www.mevaghdiving.com; Milford Rd, Carrigart; 2 dives from €50) Donegal's only dive centre offers diving courses, equipment rentals and boat charter. The waters off the northwest are crystal clear and at numerous sites you can see everything from shipwrecks to sharks. It also has excellent accommodation (doubles €76) in its purpose-built B&B. Various packages (dive/stay/lessons) are offered.

Rosapenna Golf Resort GOLF
(074-915 5000; www.rosapenna.ie; Downings; green fees €70-90) The scenery at this renowned golf club – designed by St Andrew's Old Tom Morris in 1891 and remodelled by Harry Vardon in 1906 – is as spectacular as the layout, which can challenge even the lowest handicapper. It has two courses.

Sleeping & Eating

Trá na Rosann Hostel HOSTEL €
(074-915 5374; www.anoige.ie; Melmore Head, Downings; dm from €18; late May-Aug, reception closed 10am-5pm) Knockout views envelop this heritage-listed former hunting lodge, designed by Sir Edwin Lutyens. It's an atmospheric spot with a colourful history, just a three-minute walk from lovely Trá na Rosann beach. The trade-off for the tranquil setting is that it's 8km north of Downings and there's no public transport.

★ **Olde Glen Bar & Restaurant** MODERN IRISH €€
(083 158 5777; Glen, Carrigart; mains €15-25; 6-9pm Mon-Sat, 5-8pm Sun Jul & Aug, shorter hours other times;) Authentic down to its original 1700s stone floor, this traditional pub serves a fine pint. Its farmhouse-style restaurant serves outstanding blackboard specials. Food is sourced locally so expect top-quality seafood, meat and produce. Be sure to book.

Fanad Peninsula

The second-most northerly point in Donegal, Fanad Head thrusts out into the Atlantic to the east of Rosguill. The peninsula curls around the watery expanses of Mulroy Bay to the west, and Lough Swilly to the east, the latter edged with high cliffs and sandy beaches. Most travellers stick to the peninsula's eastern flank, visiting the beautiful beach at Portsalon and the quiet heritage towns of Rathmelton and Rathmullan.

Rathmelton

POP 1250

The first community you come to if you're approaching the peninsula from Letterkenny on the Wild Atlantic Way is Rathmelton (sometimes called Ramelton), a picture-perfect spot with rows of Georgian houses and rough-walled stone warehouses curving along the tidal inlet to the River Lennon.

Walk the colourful, picturesque streets and dawdle by the water. Its worth visiting ruined **Tullyaughnish Church**, on the hill, because of the Romanesque carvings in the eastern wall, taken from a far older church on nearby Aughnish Island, on the River Lennon. Coming from Letterkenny, turn right at the river and follow it round for about 400m.

Download a town audio tour at www.rameltontidytowns.com.

Sleeping & Eating

★Frewin House B&B €€

(☎074-915 1246; www.frewinhouse.com; Rectory Rd; s/d from €100/130) This fine Victorian rectory in secluded grounds would make every weepy heroine's dreams come true. The house combines antique furniture and open fires with contemporary style. The bedrooms are pretty but uncluttered. You can arrange for a communal dinner by candlelight.

Ardeen House B&B €€

(☎074-915 1243; www.ardeenhouse.com; Aughnish Rd; s/d from €55/90; 📶) The warm welcome and homemade scones on arrival at Ardeen House make you feel as if you've just arrived home. Overlooking the river, it has five pleasingly decorated bedrooms, and the breakfasts are copious and tasty. It's on the east edge of town, on the south side of the river, just beyond the town hall.

Rathmelton Country Market MARKET €

(off R245; ⏲11am-12.30pm Sat) The limited hours means there's a real scrum to get the best produce, prepared foods, baked treats and more at one of Donegal's best farmers' markets. It's in a parking lot just by the river.

Bridge Bar IRISH €€

(☎074-915 1119; Bridgend; mains €18-27; ⏲kitchen 6-9pm Wed-Sat) The Bridge Bar is one of those lovely old country pubs you came to see in Ireland. Its cosy 1st-floor restaurant has classic Irish steak and seafood dishes. Be sure to try the excellent beers from Kinnegar Craft Brewery while you enjoy a trad-music session.

Getting There & Away

In the Fanad Peninsula you'll need your own wheels.

Rathmullan

POP 530

You wouldn't know it while enjoying the views of Lough Swilly, but the refined little port of Rathmullan has a tranquillity that belies the momentous events that took place here from the 16th to 18th centuries.

History

In 1587 Hugh O'Donnell, the 15-year-old heir to the powerful O'Donnell clan, was tricked into boarding a ship here and taken to Dublin as a prisoner. He escaped four years later on Christmas Eve and, after unsuccessful attempts at revenge, died in Spain, aged only 30.

In 1607, despairing of fighting the English, Hugh O'Neill, the Earl of Tyrone, and Rory O'Donnell, the Earl of Tyrconnell, boarded a ship in Rathmullan harbour and left Ireland for good. This decisive act, known as the Flight of the Earls, marked the effective end of Gaelic Ireland and the rule of Irish chieftains. Large-scale confiscation of their estates took place, preparing for the Plantation of Ulster with settlers from Britain.

Also in Rathmullan, Wolfe Tone, leader of the 1798 Rising, was captured.

Sights

Rathmullan Castle CASTLE

(off R247) These 16th-century ruins, where an English garrison was stationed during the Flight of the Earls, squat menacingly beside the harbour.

Sleeping & Eating

Glenalla Lodge B&B €€

(☎074-915 8750; www.glenallalodge.com; Ray; s/d €50/80) This lodge, in a bucolic spot, has four rooms decked out with tasteful wooden furniture and rustic style. There's also the helpful knowledge of a local historian on tap. It's 8km southwest of Rathmullan.

WORTH A TRIP

GRIANÁN OF AILEÁCH

Offering eye-popping views of the surrounding loughs, **Grianán of Aileách** (www.heritageireland.ie; off N13, Burt; dawn-dusk) is an amphitheatre-like stone fort that encircles the top of Grianán Hill like a halo. On clear days you can see as far as Derry. Its small arena can resemble a circus whenever a tour bus spills its load inside the heavily restored 4m-thick walls.

At the foot of the hill is merry-go-round-shaped **Burt Church**. Built in 1967, it was modelled on the fort by Derry architect Liam McCormack.

The fort may have existed at least 2000 years ago, but it's thought that the site itself goes back to pre-Celtic times as a temple to the god Dagda. Between the 5th and 12th centuries it was the seat of the O'Neills, before being demolished by Murtogh O'Brien, king of Munster. Most of what you see now is a reconstruction built between 1874 and 1878.

The fort is 18km south of Buncrana.

★**Rathmullan House** HERITAGE HOTEL €€€
(074-915 8188; www.rathmullanhouse.com; off R247; s/d from €90/180, set dinner from €48; restaurant dinner 7-8.45pm;) This country house is large and luxurious with refreshingly nonfrumpy furnishings. Sprawled over wooded gardens on the shores of Lough Swilly, the original house dates from the 1780s. The best of the 34 rooms have balconies or terraces. There's a tennis court, two genteel bars, and a glass-paned restaurant, the **Cook & Gardener**, using organic produce from the property's gardens.

Getting There & Away

Lough Foyle Ferry (074-938 1901; www.foyleferry.com; people/car one-way €3/15; Apr-Oct) operates several times daily between Rathmullan and Buncrana. Call ahead to confirm times.

Portsalon & Fanad Head

A spectacular rollercoaster of a road hugs the sea cliffs from Rathmullan to Portsalon (Port an tSalainn), passing the early 19th-century **Knockalla Fort**, one of six built to defend against a possible French invasion – the history is told at its companion, Fort Dunree (p461) across the lough.

From Portsalon, the 8km scenic drive to the lighthouse on the rocky tip of **Fanad Head** is simply beautiful.

Sights & Activities

★**Ballymastocker Beach** BEACH
(off R246, Portsalon) Once named the second most beautiful beach in the world by the British newspaper the *Observer*, this tawny-coloured Blue Flag beach is a fine place to while away the hours.

Donegal Sea Kayaking KAYAKING
(Fanad; tours adult/child €30/25) Enjoy offshore tours of the lovely Fanad Peninsula while you paddle along in a kayak. Locations vary by tides and conditions.

Portsalon Golf Club GOLF
(074-915 9459; www.portsalongolfclub.com; off R246; green fees weekdays/weekends €40/50) The marvellously scenic Portsalon Golf Club follows the curve of the bay.

Inishowen Peninsula

The Inishowen Peninsula reaches just far enough into the Atlantic to grab the title of northernmost point on the island of Ireland: **Malin Head**. It is remote, rugged, desolate and sparsely populated, making it a special and peaceful sort of place. Ancient sites and ruined castles abound, as do traditional thatched cottages that haven't yet been turned into holiday homes.

Surrounded by vast sea loughs and open ocean, Inishowen (meaning Island of Eoghain, the chieftain who also gave his name to County Tyrone) attracts a lot of birdlife. The variety is tremendous, with well over 200 resident and migrant species, including well-travelled avian visitors from Iceland, Greenland and North America. Irregular Atlantic winds mean rare and exotic species also blow in from time to time. Twitchers should visit www.birdsireland.com.

For information on everything else, visit www.visitinishowen.com.

Buncrana

POP 6900

On the tame side of the peninsula, Buncrana is a busy but appealing town with its fair share of pubs and a 5km sandy beach on the shores of Lough Swilly.

John Newton, the composer of *Amazing Grace,* was inspired to write his legendary song after his ship the *Greyhound* took refuge in the calm waters of Lough Swilly during a severe storm in 1748. He and his crew were welcomed in Buncrana after their near-death experience and his spiritual journey from slave trader to antislavery campaigner had its beginnings here. He went on to become a prolific hymn writer and later mentored William Wilberforce in his fight against slavery. For more on the story, visit www.amazinggrace.ie.

Sights

A waymarked **Shore Walk** heads north along the coast from the park north of the tourist office, leading to the town's main sights.

O'Doherty's Keep HISTORIC BUILDING

(Castle Bridge) At the northern end of the seafront, the picture-perfect early-18th-century, six-arched **Castle Bridge** leads to these tower house ruins originally built by the O'Dohertys, the local chiefs, in 1430. It was burned by the English and then rebuilt for their own use.

Buncrana Castle HISTORIC BUILDING

(Castle Bridge) At the side of O'Doherty's Keep is the manorlike Buncrana Castle, built in 1718 by John Vaughan, who also constructed the bridge. Wolfe Tone was imprisoned here following the unsuccessful French invasion in 1798.

Inishowen Peninsula

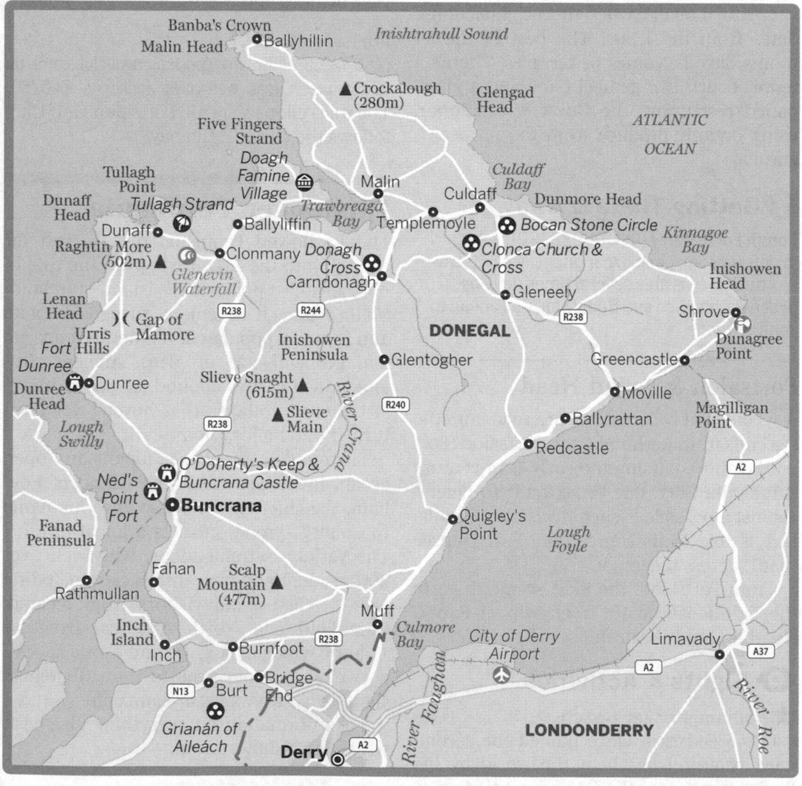

Ned's Point Fort HISTORIC BUILDING
(Ned's Point) Walk 500m from O'Doherty's Keep (turn left and stick to the shoreline) to find squat Ned's Point Fort (1812), built by the British and now under siege from graffiti vandals.

Sleeping & Eating

★ **Westbrook House** B&B €
(☎074-936 1067; www.westbrookhouse.ie; Westbrook Rd; s/d from €40/70; 📶) A handsome Georgian house set in beautiful gardens, Westbrook features chandeliers and antique furniture, giving it a refined sophistication. The honey served at breakfast comes from the bees kept in the lush garden.

Tullyarvan Mill HOSTEL €
(☎074-936 1613; www.tullyarvanmill.com; off R238; dm/d/f from €15/40/60; 📶) This purpose-built 52-bed hostel is housed in a modern building attached to the historic Tullyarvan Mill. Set amid riverside gardens, it also hosts regular cultural events and art exhibits. It's just north of town.

Caldra Bed & Breakfast B&B €€
(☎074-936 3703; www.caldrabandb.com; Lisnakelly; s/d from €50/80; 📶👪) This large, modern B&B has four spacious rooms ideal for families. The public rooms feature impressive fireplaces and gilt mirrors while the guest rooms are more sedate. The garden and patio overlook Lough Swilly and the mountains.

★ **Beach House** MODERN IRISH €€
(☎074-936 1050; www.thebeachhouse.ie; Swilly Rd; mains lunch €9-13, dinner €16-23; ⏰5-9pm Thu-Sun, noon-4pm Sat & Sun, daily Jun-Aug; 👪) With picture windows overlooking the lough, this aptly named cafe-restaurant can easily be your destination for the day. The seasonal menu focuses on simple flavours superbly executed. There's everything from burgers to seafood right off the boats. The wine list is excellent.

Drinking & Nightlife

Atlantic Bar PUB
(☎074-932 0880; Upper Main St; ⏰noon-late) Dating from 1792, this tidy Guinness-coloured (cream and black) watering hole is Buncrana's oldest and most atmospheric pub.

O'Flaherty's PUB
(☎074-936 1305; 41 Upper Main St; ⏰noon-late) A central hub for locals and visitors, this old-world pub is a friendly spot and has live traditional music every Wednesday night (more often in summer).

Information

The **Tourist Office** (☎074-936 2600; www.visitinishowen.com; Railway Rd; ⏰9.30am-5pm Mon-Fri; 📶) is located near the beach; it has information for the entire peninsula.

Getting There & Away

With the demise of the Lough Swilly bus company, getting around the peninsula is DIY.

The Lough Foyle Ferry (p459) to Rathmullan operates seasonally.

Buncrana to Clonmany

There are two routes from Buncrana to Clonmany: the scenic coastal road via Dunree Head and the Gap of Mamore, and the speedier inland road (R238). The **Gap of Mamore** (elevation 262m) is a steep and narrow pass through the Urris Hills, with a sacred spring, **St Columba's Well**, on the north side and some of the region's best views.

Sights

Fort Dunree MUSEUM
(☎074-936 1817; www.dunree.pro.ie; Dunree Head; adult/child €7/5; ⏰10.30am-6pm Mon-Sat, 1-6pm Sun Jun-Sep, 10.30am-4.30pm Mon-Fri, 1-6pm Sat & Sun Oct-May) Fort Dunree is the best preserved and most dramatic of six forts built by the British on Lough Swilly following the 1798 uprising of the United Irishmen (which was supported by France), when fears of a French invasion were at fever pitch.

The original fort, built in 1813, now houses a military museum, while the surrounding headland is littered with WWI and WWII remains you can explore. There are several good waymarked walks.

The winding fjord of Lough Swilly is one of Ireland's great natural harbours, and has played its part in many historical dramas from Viking invasions and the Flight of the Earls to the 1798 rebellion and WWI.

Huge naval guns were added to the fort in the late 19th century, and during WWI the lough was used as a marshalling area for Atlantic convoys, and as an anchorage for the Royal Navy's Grand Fleet. Unusually, it remained in British hands after the partition of Ireland in 1922, and was only handed over to the Republic of Ireland in 1938.

Clonmany & Ballyliffin

POP 950

These two quaint villages and their surrounds have plenty to occupy visitors for a day or two. Clonmany has a working atmosphere and lots of characterful pubs, while Ballyliffin feels more upmarket with more hotels and restaurants.

Sights & Activities

About 1km north of Ballyliffin is the lovely, sandy expanse of **Pollan Strand**, however the atmospheric crashing breakers make it unsafe for swimming. **Tullagh Strand**, 2km northwest of Clonmany, is a little better for swimming although it isn't recommended when the tide's going out.

Doagh Famine Village MUSEUM
(074-938 1901; www.doaghfaminevillage.com; Doagh Island; adult/child €7.50/5; 10am-5pm mid-Mar–Oct) Set in a reconstructed village of thatched cottages, this open-air museum is packed with fascinating titbits about the tough times of the 19th century, and insightful comparisons with famine-stricken countries today. It's about 5km north of Ballyliffin, on Doagh Island (now part of the mainland).

Nearby, a walk along the dunes brings you to the matchbox ruin of 16th-century **Carrickabraghey Castle**.

Ballyliffin Golf Club GOLF
(074-937 8100; www.ballyliffingolfclub.com; off R238; green fees €50-100) With two championship courses, the Old Links and the Glashedy Links, Ballyliffin Golf Club is among the best places to play a round of golf in Donegal. The scenery is so beautiful that it can distract even the most focused golfer.

Sleeping & Eating

★**Glen House** GUESTHOUSE €€
(074-937 6745; www.glenhouse.ie; Straid, Clonmany; r €70-100;) Despite the grand surroundings and luxurious rooms, you'll find neither pretension nor high prices at this gem of a guesthouse. The rooms are a lesson in restrained sophistication and the setting is incredibly tranquil. The walking trail to Glenevin Waterfall starts next to the **Rose Tea Room** (Glen House; mains from €6; 10am-6pm daily Jul & Aug, Sat & Sun Mar-Jun & Sep-Oct), which opens to a deck.

Ballyliffin Lodge & Spa HOTEL €€
(074-937 8200; www.ballyliffinlodge.com; off R238, Ballyliffin; s/d from €60/90;) This rather grand 40-room hotel is set back from the tiny village. Superior rooms have sublime ocean views. You can treat yourself at the state-of-the-art spa, to a round or two of golf, or to a meal in the relaxed bar.

Rusty Nail PUB
(074-937 6116; Clonmany; kitchen 5-9.30pm Fri-Sun, 1-4pm Sun, pub till late daily) While you might be tempted to sun yourself at the picnic table out front, you should step inside this atmospheric pub for an excellent meal – it has all the classics and they're great. There's live music many nights too. It's just west of town.

Carndonagh

POP 1900

Carndonagh, surrounded by hills on three sides, is a busy commercial centre serving the local farming community. It's not a choice locale in these parts, but convenient for gathering information and provisions.

OFF THE BEATEN TRACK

WALK: URRIS HILLS

The Urris Hills, a rugged ridge of resistant quartzite (a continuation of the Knockalla Mountains on the Fanad Peninsula to the southwest), provide grandstand views of the Inishowen coast and the distant hills of Muckish, Errigal and Glenveagh. A network of waymarked walking trails ranges from 2km to 11km in length. Starting points are at Butler's Bridge and the car park at the north end of the Mamore Gap. Ask for the *Urris Walks* leaflet at Buncrana tourist office (p461).

Starting at Glen House, an easy 800m trail leads to the cascading 10m-high **Glenevin Waterfall**, with benches and picnic tables along the way. From Clonmany, follow the road signed to Tullagh Bay, cross the river and bear right at an intersection. Butler's Bridge and the waterfall car park are about 1km further on.

Sights

Once an important ecclesiastical centre, Carndonagh has several early-Christian stone monuments.

★ Donagh Cross HISTORIC SITE

(off R238) The intricate 7th-century Donagh Cross stands under a shelter by an Anglican church at the west end of town. It's carved with a darling short-bodied, big-eyed figure of Jesus, smiling impishly. Flanking the cross are two small pillars, one showing a man, possibly Goliath, with a sword and shield, the other, David and his harp. In the graveyard there's a pillar with a carved marigold on a stem; nearby there is a crucifixion scene.

Eating

Patisserie de Pascal/Café Donagh CAFE €

(☎086 356 3134; www.patisseriedepascal.com; The Diamond; mains from €5; ⏰10am-5pm Mon-Sat) Stop in for a French-accented light lunch or stock up on beautiful baked goods and sandwiches for a fabulous picnic.

Information

Locally run **Inishowen Tourism Office** (☎074-937 4933; R238; ⏰9.30am-5pm Mon-Fri year-round, 11am-3pm Sat Jun-Aug) is in the Public Services Centre southwest of the Diamond. It also sells fishing licences.

Malin Head

The rolling swells never stop coming across the sea at Malin Head, the island's northern extreme. It's a name familiar to sailors and weather buffs, as Malin Head is one of the weather stations mentioned in BBC Radio's daily shipping forecast. You can almost imagine you can see Iceland (you can't) as you peer out through the ever-blustery skies, which can change from sun to squall in a flash. The rolling grasslands are dotted with suitably thick-coated donkeys and cows.

The village of **Malin**, on Trawbreaga Bay, 14km southeast of Malin Head, has a pretty movie-set quality, set around a neat, triangular village green.

Sights & Activities

★ Banba's Crown VIEWPOINT

(Malin Head) On the northernmost tip of Malin Head, called Banba's Crown, stands a cumbersome 1805 clifftop tower that was built by the British admiralty and later used as a Lloyds signal station. Around it are concrete huts that were used by the Irish army in WWII as lookout posts. To the west from the fort-side car park, a path leads to **Hell's Hole**, a chasm where the incoming waters crash against the rocky formations. To the east a longer headland walk leads to the **Wee House of Malin**, a hermit's cave in the cliff face.

The **view** to the west takes in, from left to right, the Inishowen Hills, Dunaff Head, low-lying Fanad Head with its lighthouse, the twin 'horns' of Horn Head and the twin bumps of Tory Island; in the far distance, to the left of Fanad lighthouse, are Muckish and Errigal Mountains. To the east lie raised beach terraces, and offshore you can see the lighthouse on the remote island of Inishtrahull. A new viewing area has free telescopes. On a few nights a year you can see the Northern Lights.

Watch for the truck-based **Caffe Banba** that is sometimes in the parking lot selling superb coffees and baked goods.

WASHED-UP TREASURES

Beachcombers will find more than empty shells along the Inishowen coast. The area is renowned for its **raised beaches**, stranded above the high-water mark by postglacial uplift, and littered with semiprecious stones: cornelian, agate, jasper and more. Good hunting grounds include the beaches along the northern coast of Malin Head, near Banba's Crown and Ballyhillin.

The stones make unique souvenirs, and you can buy these local treasures artfully polished and made into pendants, bracelets, earrings, brooches, candleholders and other quirky and beautiful items at Malin Pebbles (p465) in Greencastle.

Tours

Malin Head Tours TOUR

(☎086 316 5395; Malin Head Community Centre, off R242; ⏰noon Sat) Unlock the secrets of this blustery region on these interesting 90-minute driving and walking tours.

Sleeping & Eating

Sandrock Holiday Hostel HOSTEL €

(☎074-937 0289; www.sandrockhostel.com; Port Ronan Pier, Malin Head; dm €13-20; 📶) The cinematic view from this IHH hostel – at the end of the road, above a rocky bay on the western side of the headland – will take your breath away. Inside are 20 beds in two dorms, musical instruments and laundry facilities. Bike rental (€10 per day) is available for nonguests. Ask about the very limited community-bus connections to get here.

Village B&B B&B €
(☎074-937 0763; www.malinvillagebandb.com; The Green, Malin; s/d from €45/70) Right on the village green, this lovely B&B has a choice of cosy rooms, some traditional with antique furniture, others more contemporary with white linen and pretty floral patterns. Although you'll get breakfast here, guests also have use of a kitchen.

Whitestrand B&B B&B €€
(☎086 822 9163; www.whitestrand.net; off R242, Middletown; r from €50/80; 📶) Perfectly placed amid the bluffs and hills leading to Malin Head, this comfy B&B has three fine bedrooms. As a welcome you'll receive a hot beverage and tasty home-baked treats.

Drinking & Nightlife

McClean's PUB
(☎074-937 0607; Main St, Malin; ⏲noon-late) This treasure of an old-time pub on the east corner of the village green has the best craic in Malin and often has live music. Grab a table on its outdoor side terrace for lovely views of the estuary and old arched stone bridge.

Getting There & Around

The best way to approach Malin Head is by the R238/242 from Carndonagh, rather than up the rough road along the eastern side from Culdaff.

Culdaff & Around

POP 270

Sheep vastly outnumber people around the secluded beach village of Culdaff on the remote north coast of Inishowen.

Sights & Activities

★**Culdaff Beach** BEACH
(off R238) This Blue Flag beach is good for swimming and windsurfing. You can wander its gorgeous length and get lost in the grassy sand dunes. There's a fun playground.

Clonca Church & Cross HISTORIC SITE
(Clonca) Inside this church is an intricately carved tombstone sporting a sword and hurling-stick motif. The carved lintel over the door is thought to come from an earlier church. Outside, the remains of the cross show the miracle of the loaves and fishes on the eastern face. Heading from Culdaff towards Moville on the R238, turn east after 1.2km at Bocan Church. The Clonca Church and cross are 1.7km to the north behind some farm buildings.

Sleeping & Eating

★**McGrory's of Culdaff** GUESTHOUSE €€
(☎074-937 9104; www.mcgrorys.ie; R238; s/d from €65/100, mains €10-25; ⏲kitchen 12.30-8pm; 📶) This celery- and plum-hued village landmark has 17 stylish and luxurious rooms. Of the three bars, catch live music in the **Backroom**, which books international singer-songwriters and traditional music. McGrory's classic Irish cuisine, served in the **Front Bar**, is the best for miles around.

Greencastle

POP 820

Seals bob their heads in the hopes of a fish in the busy little fishing port of Greencastle. The 14th-century **Northburgh Castle** was a supply base for English armies in Scotland, and for this reason was attacked by Robert Bruce in the 1320s. The castle's vine-netted hulk survives – its dark-green stone gives the town its name – but is surrounded by apartments.

Sights

Inishowen Maritime Museum MUSEUM
(☎074-938 1363; www.inishowenmaritime.com; off R241; adult/child museum €5/3; ⏲9.30am-5.30pm Mon-Fri year-round, 9.30am-5.30pm Sat & noon-5.30pm Sun Easter-Sep) A disarmingly eccentric collection of artefacts can be found at this museum in a former coastguard station on a grassy verge overlooking the harbour. The most fascinating exhibits are from the sunken wrecks of Lough Foyle. The demise of the Spanish Armada and the departure from these waters of Irish emigrants are two of the museums more compelling themes. There's also an astronomy show.

Eating

★**Kealy's Seafood Bar** SEAFOOD €€
(☎074-938 1010; www.kealysseafoodbar.ie; The Harbour; mains €10-50; ⏲12.30-9pm Wed-Sun year-round, daily Jul & Aug) This bistro offers

locally caught seafood so fresh you almost have to fight the harbourside seals for it. Its unpretentious nautical-style polished timber decor belies its numerous culinary awards. It's a splendid spot for anything from a bowl of chowder to a lobster feast, and every meal comes with a great view.

Shopping

Malin Pebbles ARTS & CRAFTS
(074-938 1432; www.malinpebbles.com; Church Brae; call first) Local semiprecious stones are transformed into jewellery and unusual gifts by Petra Watzka at her workshop, 100m uphill from the ferry.

Getting There & Away

Lough Foyle Ferry (074-938 1901; www.loughfoyleferry.com; Harbour; person/car one-way €3/15; Apr-Sep) runs a seasonal car-ferry service from Greencastle to Magilligan, saving a 78km detour via Derry. Sailings are usually hourly during daytime. Confirm schedules by phone or on the website.

OFF THE BEATEN TRACK

WALK: INISHOWEN HEAD

Views abound on a waymarked walk (8.5km; allow two to three hours) to **Inishowen Head**, where a WWII lookout point commands a panoramic view east along the Northern Irish coast to the Antrim Hills, Rathlin Island and the distant outlines of Islay and the Mull of Kintyre in Scotland. The little bay of **Portkille**, a short distance to the north, is said to be the final landfall of St Colmcille (Columba) in Ireland before he sailed for Iona in AD 563; a bronze plaque by the path describes the site.

The walk begins some 4km beyond Greencastle on the R241 – there's a car park beside a small sandy beach with a sign describing the walk. The nearby twin towers (one now only a stump) are what's left of Shrove Lighthouse, built in 1837.

Moville & Around

POP 1500

Little more than a tight cluster of streets above an all-business jetty, Moville is a neat little town with old, well-kept buildings. It can be sleepy, but on holiday weekends tourists flood in. Moville was a busy port during the 19th and early 20th centuries, when thousands of emigrants set sail for America from here.

Activities

Coastal Walkway WALKING
The 4km coastal walkway from Moville to Greencastle takes in the stretch of coast where the emigrant steamers used to moor. You'll pause often to savour the **views**.

Sleeping & Eating

Just above the harbour, central Moville has hotels and pub-food options.

Moville Holiday Hostel HOSTEL €
(074-938 2378; www.movilleholidayhostel.com; off R238, Moville; campsites per person €10, dm/d from €20/50) A small lane leads off the R238, 300m north of town, to a grove of trees and this secluded 20-bed hostel. It's in a nook-and-cranny-filled 18th-century farmhouse beside a stream, with some gorgeous spots to pitch a tent. The owner is a fount of information on the area's rich history and folklore.

Redcastle Hotel & Spa HOTEL €€
(074-938 5555; www.redcastlehoteldonegal.com; R238, Redcastle; s/d from €90/140;) The peninsula's flashiest luxury resort is on the coast 7km southwest of Moville. Tucked away off the main road, the 93 rooms are comfortable and classy. Restaurants include the **Edge**, which has good views and modern Irish cuisine. Facilities include a nine-hole golf course.

The Midlands

Includes ➡

Best Places to Sleep

- Bastion B&B (p478)
- Lough Key House (p475)
- Castle Durrow (p491)
- Roundwood House (p492)
- Maltings Guesthouse (p484)

Best Pubs

- Oarsman (p469)
- Sean's Bar (p478)
- Giltraps Pub (p485)
- JJ Houghs Singing Pub (p486)
- Morrissey's (p491)

Why Go?

Often passed through on the way to someplace more vaunted, the Midlands is brimming with verdant pastoral landscapes, stately homes, archaeological treasures and sleepy towns where the locals are genuinely glad to see you. Getting lost along the twisting back roads of these six counties is an unhurried pleasure and you're virtually guaranteed to happen upon a local village shop, pub, garage or post office and find it little changed in decades. It's refreshingly free of tour buses and souvenir stalls and well worth at least a pause in your journeys.

The Midlands is dominated by the River Shannon, which meanders through fields and forests, drawing boaters and fishers in shoals. Plush hotels and gourmet restaurants have sprung up along its banks, making it a wonderfully scenic and surprisingly cosmopolitan way to travel. If you're in search of a genuine slice of rural Irish life, this area makes the perfect retreat.

When to Go

- Spring is a great time for revelling in Ireland's famous greener-than-green countryside, reflected in the many waterways and lakes; accented by fields of wildflowers.
- During summer, fairs, festivals and special events take place throughout the region as locals spend the long days outside.
- July through September is the ideal time for cruising the Shannon with everything open, better weather and a spirited summertime crowd in the riverside pubs and restaurants.
- Many museums and other attractions are closed or have greatly reduced hours during the short days from November to March.

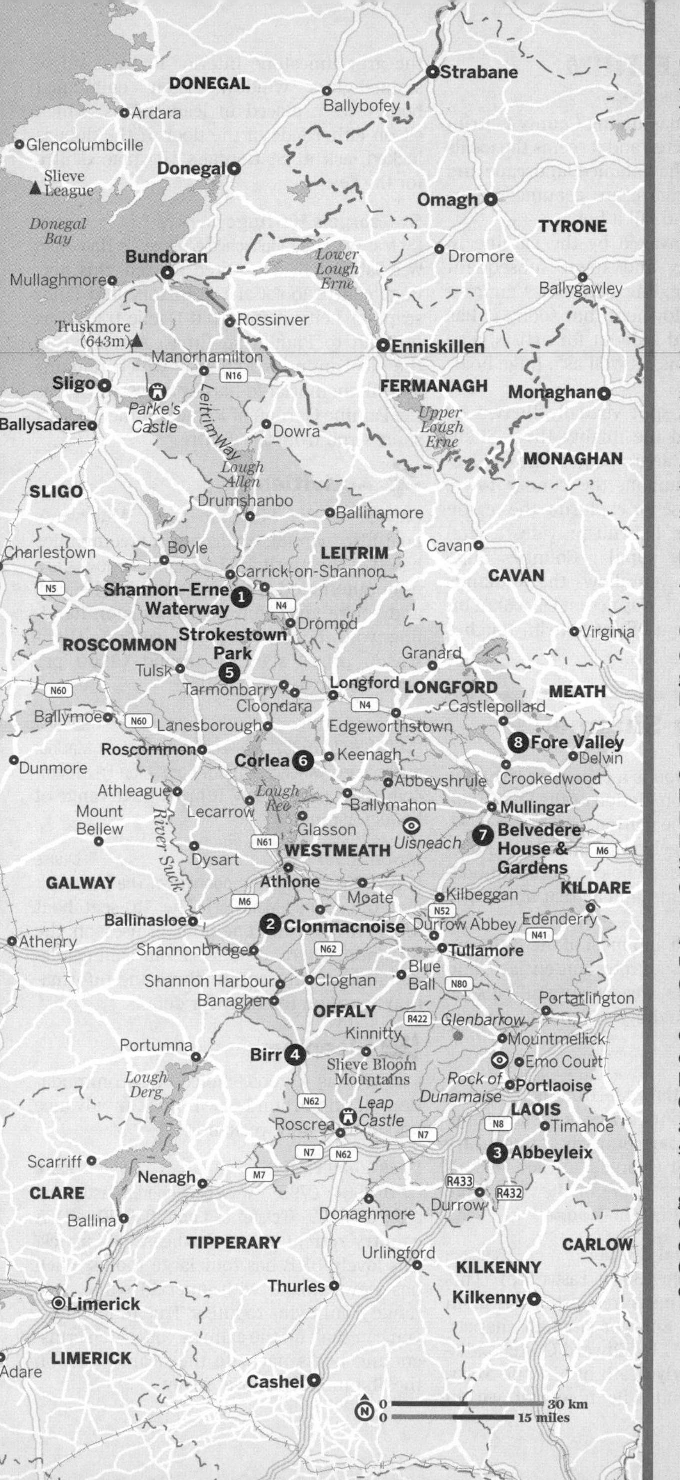

The Midlands Highlights

1. Slow down a gear and discover the rolling landscapes along the **Shannon–Erne Waterway** (p471).
2. Contemplate the lost land of saints and scholars at Ireland's finest monastic site, **Clonmacnoise** (p486).
3. Join in the locally sourced, seasonal-food revolution sweeping the Midlands at the **Gallic Kitchen** (p491) in Abbeyleix.
4. Roam the Georgian streets and explore the castle grounds in elegant **Birr** (p483).
5. Learn about Ireland's greatest disaster at the harrowing Irish National Famine Museum at **Strokestown Park** (p473).
6. Explore the Iron Age oak trackway unearthed at **Corlea** (p476).
7. Wander the corridors and gardens of magnificent **Belvedere House & Gardens** (p480) and marvel at its spiteful history.
8. Visit the emerald-green **Fore Valley** (p481), and discover impressive Christian ruins and other-worldly views.

COUNTY LEITRIM

POP 31,798 / AREA 1590 SQ KM

The delights of unassuming County Leitrim are a well-kept secret, and it seems the locals like it that way. The untamed landscape and authentic rural charm are genuinely cherished by those who call it home.

Leitrim was ravaged by the Famine in the 19th century and spent subsequent generations struggling with mass emigration and unemployment, but today it has become a beloved hideout for artists, writers and musicians, as well as a huge boating centre.

The county is split virtually in two by Lough Allen, and the mighty River Shannon remains the area's biggest draw. Lively Carrick-on-Shannon, the county town, makes a great base for exploring the region by road or water. Leitrim provides a vital link between the popular Counties Sligo and Donegal. It even allows the Midlands some Wild Atlantic Way action via a 5km bit of the N15 where a nib of Leitrim touches the sea.

Carrick-on-Shannon

POP 4100

Carrick-on-Shannon is a charming riverside town. Since the completion of the Shannon–Erne Waterway, the marina here has thrived. The town is a hugely popular weekend destination with a good choice of accommodation and restaurants, and a great music and arts scene.

During the 17th and most of the 18th centuries Carrick was a Protestant enclave, and the local residents' wealth can still be seen in the graceful buildings around the town.

Sights

Hanging around the waterfront is really the thing to do here, but Carrick does have some wonderful examples of early-19th-century architecture on St George's Terrace, including **Hatley Manor**, home of the St George family, and the **Old Courthouse**.

Costello Memorial Chapel CHURCH

(Bridge St; 10am-4.30pm Easter-Sep) This diminutive place measures just 5m by 3.6m making it one of Europe's smallest chapels. It was built in 1877 by Edward Costello, distraught at the early death of his wife Mary. Both husband and wife now rest within the grey limestone interior lit by a single stained-glass window. Their embalmed bodies were placed in lead coffins, which sit on either side of the door. If the door is locked, ask at St George's Heritage Centre for the key.

St George's Heritage Centre MUSEUM

(St Mary's Close; adult/child €5/free; 11am-4pm Wed-Sat) Set in a restored church, this heritage centre looks at the history and landscape of Leitrim from old Gaelic traditions through to Plantation times. A tour visits the old Famine workhouse, which remains a bleak memorial to harder times, as well as the Famine Garden of Remembrance, both a short stroll from the Centre.

Activities

Carrick is the Shannon–Erne Waterway's boat-hire capital, with several companies based at the marina. The canal's 16 locks are fully automated, you don't need a licence, and you're given full instructions on handling your boat before you set off. High-season prices start at around €1200 per week for a two-berth cruiser.

Emerald Star BOATING

(071-962 7633; www.emeraldstar.ie; Marina; prices vary widely; 9am-6pm Mon-Fri, 10am-4pm Sat) Based locally, it has a huge range of boats for rent.

Moon River CRUISE

(071-962 1777; www.moonriver.ie; The Quay; tour from €18; mid-Mar–Oct) The 110-seat boat *Moon River* runs one-hour cruises on the Shannon. There are one to four sailings depending on the season; check the information board on the quay for details.

Sleeping

Carrick has a good choice of accommodation, in and around town. Book in advance for summer and weekends.

Lock View House B&B €

(071-964 0790; www.bedandbreakfastleitrim.com; off R209, Kilclare; s/d from €45/70;) A country retreat 10km northeast of Carrick, this lovely B&B has four large rooms. Each has views tinged with emerald while beds range from twins to kings. True to its name, you can soak up the calm as you watch cruisers and boats navigate the nearby lock on the Shannon–Erne Waterway.

★ **Bush Hotel** HOTEL €€
(☎071-967 1000; www.bushhotel.com; Main St; s/d from €70/110; 📶👪) One of Ireland's oldest in-town hotels, this family-run place only gets better with age. The public spaces are kept thoughtfully updated while still preserving heritage charm; historic photos abound. The 60 rooms are more contemporary and corporate with slick modern furnishings, plush carpeting and desks. There's a modern wing in back.

Cryan's Hotel HOTEL €€
(☎071-967 2066; www.cryanshotel.ie; The Quay; s/d from €65/100; 📶) Right on the riverfront, this modern hotel is popular with boaters needing a break from their poop deck as well as tourists. The facade is nothing special, but the 24 rooms are large and well-equipped, and many have water views.

Carrick Plaza Suites HOTEL €€
(☎071-961 6266; www.carrickplazasuites.ie; town centre; s/d from €90/100; 📶) Located in a modern waterfront development, the 10 suites range in size from large bedrooms to full-on apartments with kitchens. Units sleep from two to seven; furnishings are contemporary, with clean lines.

Eating

Lena's Tea Room CAFE €
(☎071-962 2791; www.lenastearoom.ie; Main St; snacks €4-10; ⏲10am-5.30pm Tue-Sat; 📶) This endearingly twee cafe has 1920s-vintage-style decor with eclectic furniture, including comfy sofas and muted paintwork. The menu features home-baked cakes, scones and breads, plus soups, tarts and sandwiches. Afternoon tea is a speciality with loose-leaf teas, china cups and delicious cakes.

★ **Oarsman** MODERN IRISH €€
(☎071-962 1733; www.theoarsman.com; Bridge St; mains €7-25; ⏲food noon-9pm Tue-Sat, bar till 11pm) This upmarket pub serves up some of the best casual fare in the region. The menu is seasonal and locally sourced, from excellent burgers to more complex mains. Choose from a great list of Irish microbrews (including Carrig Brewing) in the pub downstairs. The upstairs has more of a restaurant vibe. Expect waits most nights.

The Cottage MODERN IRISH €€
(☎071-962 5933; www.cottagerestaurant.ie; off N4, Jamestown; mains €17-27; ⏲5.30-10pm Wed-Sun, plus noon-4pm Sun; 👪) Set in a small whitewashed cottage overlooking a weir, this humble-looking place belies the quality of food on offer within. Chef Sham Hanifa's menu offers seasonal dishes created using vegetables from the restaurant garden, meats from local suppliers and artisan cheeses. It's 5km southeast of Carrick.

Vittos Restaurant & Wine Bar ITALIAN €€
(☎071-962 7000; www.vittosrestaurant.com; Bridge St; mains €14-25; ⏲5.30-9pm Mon-Fri, 1-10pm Sat & Sun; 👪) In a wood-beamed stone building, this family-friendly restaurant has an extensive menu of classic Italian dishes, including great pastas and pizzas. Burgers and steaks are chargrilled. It's part of the Market Yard Centre complex.

Drinking & Nightlife

Look for beers by locally based Carrig Brewing. Its Poachers Pale Ale – among others – is superb.

Anderson's Thatch Pub PUB
(☎087 228 3288; www.andersonspub.com; Elphin Rd/R368; ⏲6-11pm) Dating from 1734, this traditional thatched pub is worth a trip for its live-music sessions (Wednesday, Friday and Saturday), old-world atmosphere and country charm. It's 4km south of town and easily reached by taxi.

Flynn's Corner House PUB
(cnr Main & Bridge Sts; ⏲5-11pm) This authentic stuck-in-a-time-warp pub serves a good pint of Guinness and has live music on Friday nights – savour it.

Entertainment

Dock Arts Centre THEATRE
(☎071-965 0828; www.thedock.ie; St George's Tce; ⏲galleries 10am-5pm Tue-Sat) Set in the grand surroundings of the 19th-century former courthouse, this place hosts performances, exhibitions and workshops.

Shopping

★ **Market Yard Centre** CRAFTS
(off Bridge St; ⏲shop hours vary, farmers market 10am-2pm Thu) This restored series of buildings in the centre of town has an interesting array of shops selling everything from nautical gear to crafts. Don't miss the **farmers market**, which draws an impressive array of organic farmers, bakers and food producers.

1

2

SIMON GREENWOOD/GETTY IMAGES ©

The Shannon–Erne Waterway

Ireland's two main river systems, the Shannon and the Erne, meander gracefully between the lush green fields, watery meadows and untamed pastures of the Midlands. En route they feed and carve the land and attract families, boaters and fishers all summer long.

The two rivers were linked in the 1800s as part of a much-needed drainage scheme for the poor soil in the area but their connection was short-lived. It was not until 1994, when a far-sighted restoration project created a symbolic link between Northern Ireland and the Republic, that the combined river system became navigable once again.

Running the length of the Shannon and on through northwestern County Cavan to the southern shore of Upper Lough Erne, the Shannon–Erne Waterway is part of a wonderful 750km network of rivers, lakes and man-made channels such as the Grand and Royal Canals. Plush hotels, gourmet restaurants and lively traditional pubs line its banks, making it a surprisingly cosmopolitan, as well as a wonderfully scenic, way to travel.

1. Athlone Castle (p477) overlooks the River Shannon
2. Boats on the River Shannon, County Offaly (p482)
3. Cross of the Scriptures (p487), Clonmacnoise

3

TOP STOPS

➡ **Carrick-on-Shannon** A charming riverside town with a lively music and food scene.

➡ **Lough Ree** The more-than-50 islands in this lovely lake are rich in history.

➡ **Athlone** A vibrant town and Midlands hub.

➡ **Clonmacnoise** A magnificent ecclesiastical city dating from the 6th century.

➡ **Shannonbridge** A sleepy village with a cracking traditional pub.

➡ **Banagher** A popular boating centre with formidable riverside fortifications.

Information

The **Tourist Office** (071-962 3274; www.leitrimtourism.com; The Quay; 9.30am-5pm Easter-Sep) has a good walking-tour brochure, which takes in Carrick's places of interest.

Getting There & Away

BUS

Bus Éireann runs to Dublin (€26, three hours, four daily).

TRAIN

Irish Rail runs seven trains daily to Dublin (from €24, 2¼ hours) and Sligo (from €16, 55 minutes). The station is on Croghan Rd, 500m southwest of the centre.

North Leitrim

North of Carrick-on-Shannon, the Leitrim landscape comes into its own, its ruffled hills, steel-grey lakes and isolated cottages exuding a genuine rural charm. You'll also find the Leitrim side of Lough Gill is easily accessible on a day trip from Sligo.

If you fancy taking to the hills on foot, the **Leitrim Way** walking trail begins in Drumshanbo and ends in Manorhamilton, a distance of 48km.

Sights & Activities

Parke's Castle CASTLE

(www.heritageireland.ie; off R286, Fivemile Bourne; adult/child €4/2; 10am-6pm Easter-Sep) The tranquil surrounds of Parke's Castle, with swans drifting by on Lough Gill and neat grass cloaking the old moat, belie the fact that its early Plantation architecture was created out of an unwelcome English landlord's insecurity and fear.

The restored, three-storey castle forms part of one of the five sides of the bawn, which also has three rounded turrets at its corners.

It's in County Leitrim, just over the border from County Sligo, 11km east of Sligo town.

★ **Rose of Innisfree** CRUISE

(071-916 4266; www.roseofinnisfree.com; off R286, Parke's Castle; adult/child €15/7.50; 12.30pm & 3.30pm Easter-Oct) You can take a 1½-hour cruise on Lough Gill from Parke's Castle and enjoy the best view of Innisfree. Trips feature live recitals of Yeats' poetry, and good coffee and fresh scones are available on board. The company runs a bus from Sligo to the castle. Call for departure times and location. There are extra boat trips in summer.

COUNTY ROSCOMMON

POP 64, 070 / AREA 2548 SQ KM

Studded with more than 5000 megalithic tombs, ring forts and mounds, and home to a couple of excellent museums, enigmatic Roscommon is a haven for history buffs and shrouded in myth. Add well-preserved mansions and some wonderful monastic ruins and it's hard to understand why the county sees so few visitors. Beyond the romance of times past, Roscommon has plenty of rolling countryside splashed with lakes and cleaved by the Rivers Shannon and Suck; attributes much appreciated by visiting anglers.

Roscommon Town

POP 5700

The county town of Roscommon is very much a place of local business and commerce, but it has a small, stately centre and some significant abbey and castle ruins that make it worth a brief stop.

Sights

Roscommon's central square is dominated by its former courthouse (now the Bank of Ireland). Opposite, the facade of the **old jail** survives.

★ **Roscommon County Museum** MUSEUM

(The Square; adult/child €2/1; 10am-5pm Mon-Fri, to 3pm Sat) Set in a former Presbyterian church (1863), this volunteer-run museum has an idiosyncratic collection, including an inscribed 9th-century slab from St Coman's monastery and a superb medieval sheila-na-gig. The unusual Star of David window supposedly represents the Trinity. Don't leave without hearing the story of Lady Betty, the 18th-century hanging woman.

Roscommon Castle RUIN

(off Castle St; dawn-dusk) The impressive ruins of the town's Norman castle stand alone in a field to the north of town, beautifully framed by the landscaped lawns and small lake of the new town park. Built in 1269, the castle was almost immediately destroyed by Irish forces, and its turbulent history continued until the final surrender to Cromwell in 1652.

Roscommon Dominican Priory HISTORIC BUILDING

(off Circular Rd; dawn-dusk) At the south end of town, the remains of a 13th-century priory are almost hidden behind a primary school. It merits a quick visit for its unusual 15th-century carving of eight *gallóglí* ('gallowglasses', mercenary soldiers) wielding seven swords and an axe.

Activities

Pick up a brochure and map at tourist offices detailing the **Suck Valley Way**, a 75km walking trail along the River Suck, including some pleasant strolls along the river bank.

Sleeping & Eating

Gleeson's Townhouse & Restaurant B&B €€
(☎090-662 6954; www.gleesonstownhouse.com; The Square; s/d from €80/90; @ 📶) What might better be called 'Gleeson's Empire' is based in this 19th-century townhouse, set back from the square in its own courtyard. Rooms are individually decorated ranging from extravagant floral wallpaper to pine furniture and buttercup-yellow walls.

Gleeson's Restaurant & Artisan Food & Wine Shop DELI €€
(☎090-662 6954; www.gleesonstownhouse.com; The Square; mains €8-25; ⏰cafe 8am-6pm daily, restaurant noon-9pm daily, shop 10am-6pm Mon-Sat) The best of modern Irish cooking is on display in Gleeson's. Local – and often organic – produce is used to create excellent dishes both in the casual cafe and the more elegant restaurant.

The shop has an array of baked goods and prepared foods, perfect for a fabulous picnic to take on your explorations of the county's ancient sites.

Information

The museum is an unofficial **Tourist Office** (www.visitroscommon.com; Roscommon County Museum, The Square; ⏰10am-5pm Mon-Fri, to 3pm Sat) and has stacks of info.

Getting There & Away

BUS

Bus Éireann runs two buses daily between Westport (€23, 2¼ hours) and Athlone (€14, 35 minutes).

TRAIN

Roscommon train station is in Abbeytown, just south of the town centre. Irish Rail runs five trains daily on the line from Dublin (€20, two hours) to Westport (from €20, 1½ hours).

Strokestown & Around

POP 820

Strokestown's main street is a grand tree-lined avenue that remains a testament to the lofty aspirations of one of the local landed gentry who wished it to be Europe's widest. It's a striking feature in what is a now a sleepy town most notable for its historic estate and unmissable Famine museum.

Add in the nearby ancient Celtic site and you can easily spend a day in the area. Over the May Day bank holiday weekend, the town bursts into life for the **International Poetry Festival** (www.strokestownpoetry.org; ⏰early May). Good eats are thin on the ground here, but Roscommon is only 20km southwest.

Sights

★ **Strokestown Park** HISTORIC SITE
(☎071-963 3013; www.strokestownpark.ie; off N5; admission house, museum & gardens adult/child €14/6, 1 site only €9/6; ⏰10.30am-5.30pm mid-Mar–Oct, to 4pm Nov–mid-Mar, tours noon, 2.30pm, 4.30pm mid-Mar–Oct, 2.30pm Nov–mid-Mar; 📶) At the end of Strokestown's main avenue, triple Gothic arches lead to Strokestown Park House. The original 120-sq-km estate was granted by King Charles II to Nicholas Mahon for his support in the English Civil War. Nicholas' grandson Thomas commissioned Richard Cassels to build him a Palladian **mansion** in the early 18th century. The **gardens** give some idea of the original wealth. Admission to the house is by a 50-minute guided tour.

The guided tours take in a galleried kitchen with original ovens dating from 1740, a schoolroom with an exercise book of neatly written dictation dating from 1934 (and, according to her red pen, deemed disgraceful by the governess), and a toy room complete with 19th-century toys and funhouse mirrors.

Over the centuries, the estate decreased in size along with the family's fortunes. When it was eventually sold in 1979, it had been whittled down to 120 hectares. The estate was bought as a complete lot, so virtually all its remaining contents are intact.

The walled garden contains the longest herbaceous border in Ireland and Britain, which blooms in a rainbow of colours in summer. Across the 2.4 hectares there is also a folly, a lily pond and Ireland's oldest glass greenhouse, dating from 1780.

There is a small cafe on-site.

➡ **Irish National Famine Museum**

In direct and deliberate contrast to the splendour of Strokestown Park House and its grounds is the harrowing Irish National Famine Museum, which documents the devastating 1840s potato blight. It concisely shows how the industrial age coupled with the Famine devastated the overpopulated island of eight million (about 1.6 million more than today).

Exhibits here rise above mere lore thanks to more than 50,000 documents that were preserved from the 19th century and which provide often chilling factual underpinning. Strokestown landlord Major Denis Mahon ruthlessly evicted starving peasants who couldn't pay their rent, chartering boats to transport them away from Ireland. Around half of these 1000 emigrants died on the overcrowded 'coffin ships', a further 200 died while in quarantine in Québec (the cheapest route). Perhaps unsurprisingly, Mahon was assassinated by three of his tenants in 1847 (two of whom were publicly hung in Roscommon). The gun they used is on display.

There's a huge amount of information and you can easily spend an hour or more. You'll emerge with an unblinking insight into the starvation of the poor, and the ignorance, callousness and cruelty of those who were in a position to help.

Rathcroghan HISTORIC SITE

(☎071-963 9268; www.rathcroghan.ie; N5, Tulsk; adult/child €10/6; ⊙visitor centre 9am-5pm Mon-Sat year-round, noon-4pm Sun May-Sep; 👪) Anyone with an interest in Celtic mythology will be enthralled by this area around the village of Tulsk. It contains 60 ancient national monuments including standing stones, barrows, huge cairns and monumental fortresses, making it the most important Celtic royal site in Europe.

The landscape and its sacred structures have lain largely undisturbed for the past 3000 years. Tulsk is 10km west of Strokestown. Bus Éireann's frequent Dublin-to-Westport route stops right outside the visitor centre.

It's hard to grasp just how significant Rathcroghan is, as archaeological digs are continuing, but it has already been established that the site is bigger and older than Tara in County Meath and was at one time a major seat of Irish power.

The excellent **visitor centre** is the place to start. It has diagrams, photographs, informative panels and maps that explain the significance of the sites, and it can let you know when access to the monuments is possible (some are privately owned). Most are along a 6km stretch of the N5 to the west. **Rathmore** and **Rathcroghan Mound** both have public access and parking.

A 15-minute video includes an introduction to the sites and legends, plus an animated story about the legend of the Táin Bó Cúailnge (Cattle Raid of Cooley), which should appeal to all ages. Also good is the timeline with replica artefacts.

According to the legend, Queen Maeve (Medbh) had her palace at Cruachan Aí. The **Oweynagat Cave** (Cave of the Cats), believed to be the entrance to the Celtic other world, is also nearby. As it is located on private land, a guide has to accompany anyone who enters the cave. This can be arranged at the visitor centre (€20 per person).

Boyle & Around

POP 2700

A quiet town at the foot of the Curlew Mountains, Boyle is a scenic and worthwhile stop, home to beautiful Boyle Abbey, a 4000-year-old dolmen, the hands-on King House Interpretive Centre, and a scenic forest park.

History

The history of Boyle is the history of the King family. In 1603 Staffordshire-born John King was granted land in Roscommon with the aim of 'reducing the Irish to obedience'. Over the next 150 years, through canny marriages and cold-blooded conquests, his descendants made their name and fortune, becoming one of the largest landowning families in Ireland. The town of Boyle grew around their estate.

Sights & Activities

King House Interpretive Centre HISTORIC BUILDING

(☎071-966 3242; www.kinghouse.ie; Main St; adult/child €5/2; ⊙11am-4pm Tue-Sat Apr-Sep) Sinister-looking dummies tell the turbulent history of the Connaught kings, the town of Boyle and the King family, including a grim tale of tenant eviction during the Famine. Kids can try on replica Irish cloaks, breeches and leather shoes, write with a quill and build a vaulted ceiling from specially designed blocks. One room is devoted to **Maureen O'Sullivan**, the Hollywood star who was born nearby on Main St.

The mansion's courtyard is home to a large shop selling local crafts.

After the King family moved to Lough Key, this imposing Georgian mansion became a military barracks for the Connaught Rangers. It then was largely dormant for decades.

Boyle Abbey HISTORIC BUILDING

(☎071-963 9268; www.heritageireland.ie; Abbeytown Rd; adult/child €4/2; ⏰10am-6pm Easter-late Sep) Gracing the River Boyle is the finely preserved (and reputedly haunted) Boyle Abbey. Founded in 1161 by monks from Mellifont in County Louth, the abbey captures the transition from Romanesque to Gothic style, best seen in the nave, where a set of arches in each style face each other. Guided 40-minute tours of the abbey are sometimes available.

Unusual for a Cistercian building, figures and carved animals decorate the capitals to the west as well as, more bafflingly, the pagan sheila-na-gig fertility symbol. After the Dissolution of the Monasteries, the abbey was occupied by the military and became Boyle Castle; the stone chimney on the southern side of the abbey, which was once the refectory, dates from that period.

Lough Key Forest Park PARK

(☎071-967 3122; www.loughkey.ie; off N4; forest admission free, parking €4; ⏰10am-6pm daily Apr-Aug, Wed-Sun Mar, Sep & Oct, to 5pm Fri-Sun Nov-Feb; 👪) Sprinkled with small islands, Lough Key Forest Park has long been popular for its picturesque ruins, including a 12th-century abbey on tiny Trinity Island and a 19th-century castle on Castle Island. It's also a time-honoured favourite with families for its wishing chair, bog gardens, fairy bridge and viewing tower. There are plenty of marked walking trails through the park.

Lough Key is 4km east of Boyle. The Bus Éireann route from Sligo to Dublin has frequent services linking Boyle and Lough Key.

The 350-hectare park was once part of the Rockingham estate, owned by the King family from the 17th century until 1957. Rockingham House, designed by John Nash, was destroyed by a fire in the same year; all that remains are some stables, outbuildings and eerie tunnels leading to the lake – built to hide the servants from view.

There is an informative **visitor centre**, and the **Lough Key Experience** (adult/child €7.50/5), incorporating a panoramic, 300m-long treetop canopy walk, which rises 9m above the woodland floor with sweeping lake views. Other attractions include the **Boda Borg Challenge** (€15), a series of rooms filled with activities and puzzles (great for sudden bursts of rain) and the outdoor **adventure playground** (day pass €5).

In July and August, **Lough Key Boats** provides hourly boat trips (adult/child €12/6), plus row- and power-boat hire (from €22 per hour).

OFF THE BEATEN TRACK

ARIGNA MINERS WAY & HISTORICAL TRAIL

Covering 118km of north Roscommon, east Sligo and mid-Leitrim, this trail is a series of well-signposted tracks and hill passes covering the routes taken by miners on their way to work. A pamphlet with maps is available from local tourist offices.

Drumanone Dolmen HISTORIC SITE

FREE This astonishing portal dolmen, one of the largest in Ireland, measures 4.5m by 3.3m and was constructed before 2000 BC. It can be tricky to find: follow Patrick St west and then the R294 out of town for 5km, until you pass under a railway arch. A sign indicates the path across the railway line.

Angling Services Ireland FISHING

(☎086 601 1878; www.anglingservicesireland.com; half-day guided fishing for 2 from €120) These Boyle-based guides know where to find the big pike, perch and trout.

★Arigna Mining Experience MINE

(☎071-964 6466; www.arignaminingexperience.ie; Derreenavoggy; adult/child €10/6; ⏰10am-6pm, tours hourly) Ireland's first and last coal mine (1600s to 1990) is remembered at the Arigna Mining Experience, set in the hills above Lough Allen. The highlight is the 40-minute underground tour, which takes you 400m down to the coal face and includes a simulated miniexplosion. Tours are led by ex-miners who really bring home the gruelling working conditions and dangers.

Wear warm clothing and sturdy shoes as it can be cold and muddy. It's 23km northeast of Boyle.

Sleeping

★Lough Key House B&B €€

(☎071-966 2161; www.loughkeyhouse.com; off N4; s/d from €60/90; 📶) This beautifully restored Georgian country house has six guest rooms, each individually decorated with stylish period furniture. The downstairs sitting room combines antiques with elegance, comfort and an open fire. Breakfast eggs come from the owner's hens, there are loaner bikes and, if you arrive by bus, you can be picked up in town. It's 4km east of Boyle.

Cesh Corran B&B €€
(071-966 2265; www.marycooney.com; Abbey Tce; s/d from €60/80;) Close to the centre and overlooking the abbey ruins, this immaculately kept place has bright, simple rooms and a very warm welcome. There's a garden, wholesome breakfasts from locally sourced produce and even a separate bait fridge for anglers.

Forest Park House B&B €€
(071-966 2227; www.bed-and-breakfast-boyle.com; off N4; s/d from €45/80;) Just by the entrance to Lough Key Forest Park, this purpose-built guesthouse has six light-filled modern rooms with pine woodwork and crisp white linens. It's 4km east of town.

Eating & Drinking

Farmers Market MARKET €
(King House, Main St; 10am-2pm Sat) The surrounding farmlands are rich with produce and locals seem especially talented at creating amazing baked goods and prepared foods. Ponder the bounty at this weekly open-air market.

Aunty Bee's CAFE €
(071-966 3242; King House, Main St; mains from €4; 11am-4pm Mon-Sat) In the King House courtyard, this sprightly little cafe has delicious baked goods, simple lunches and fine coffees and tea.

Bruno's Bar & Restaurant ITALIAN €€
(071-966 7788; www.brunosrestaurant.ie; The Crescent; mains €8-25; noon-10pm Tue-Thu, to 11pm Fri & Sat, 12.30-10pm Sun) Inspired by his home island of Sardinia, Bruno Boe creates deliciously authentic Italian meals at his very appealing pub. But local tastes also get their due, from the locally sourced ingredients to classics such as bacon and cabbage. Whether it's a bar meal, something more elaborate or just a pint, you'll feel right at home.

Information

In the courtyard of King House (p474), **Úna Bhán Tourism Cooperative** (071-966 3033; www.unabhan.net; King House; 9am-6pm Mon-Fri, to 3pm Sat) has tourist information on the Boyle region.

Getting There & Away

BUS

Bus Éireann runs between Dublin (€26, three hours) and Sligo (€18, 45 minutes) stopping at Boyle's King House en route. There are five buses daily Monday to Saturday, four on Sunday.

TRAIN

Irish Rail trains leave eight times daily to Sligo (from €13, 40 minutes) and Dublin (from €20, 2½ hours). The station is on Elphin St.

COUNTY LONGFORD

POP 38,970 / AREA 1091 SQ KM

A solidly agrarian region, County Longford is a quiet place of low hills and pastoral scenes. It has few tourist sights but is a haven for anglers who come for the superb fishing around Lough Ree and Lanesborough.

Longford suffered massive emigration during the Famine and it has never really recovered. Many Longford emigrants went to Argentina, where one of their descendants, Edel Miro O'Farrell, became president in 1914.

Longford's eponymous county town is a decidedly workaday place. This is a county where you'll need your own wheels.

Sights & Activities

★**Corlea Trackway** HISTORIC SITE
(043-332 2386; www.heritageireland.ie; off R392, Keenagh; 10am-6pm mid-Apr–Sep) FREE Don't miss the magnificent Corlea Trackway, an Iron Age bog road built in 148 BC. An 18m stretch of the historic track has been preserved in a humidified hall at the site's visitor centre. Tours detail the bog's unique flora and fauna, explain how the track was discovered and methods used to preserve it. There are some short but good walks in this desolate but intriguing landscape.

The centre is 15km south of Longford town.

Aughnacliffe Dolmen ARCHAEOLOGICAL SITE
(off R198; dawn-dusk) This dolmen is one of the three biggest portal dolmens in Ireland. It has an improbably balanced top stone and is thought to be around 5000 years old. Aughnacliffe is 18km north of Longford town.

Longford–Cloondara Trackway WALKING

Follow the placid waters of the Royal Canal on this new track which runs 16km from Longford town. The well-marked track follows the canal for 8km southwest from Longford before turning northwest for another 8km along the Royal Canal. It's good for cycling.

If walking, when you reach the end at the Richmond Harbour in Cloondara, you can walk another 2km to Termonbarry to get a bus back to Longford town via the N5.

Eating

Torc Café & Foodhall CAFE €

(043-334 8277; www.torccafe.com; 1 New St, Longford town; mains from €5; 9am-6pm Mon-Sat) Oh the chocolate! What a reward for exploring the backroads of County Longford. The sweet stuff in myriad forms is but one highlight of this contemporary cafe that's known for its coffee and fresh, seasonal fare. Get a picnic or linger. It's in the centre of town.

OFF THE BEATEN TRACK

ABBEYSHRULE'S ABBEY

Hidden away in the delightfully remote southeast corner of County Longford, Abbeyshrule is a tiny village that has a serene setting on the Royal Canal and River Inny. It's a tidy place and locals proudly point out that it regularly wins awards for its tidiness.

Just north of town, one of the 19th century's great engineering feats, the stolid stone **Whitworth Aquaduct**, carries the canal over the river. Another highlight is the 12th-century **Cistercian Abbey**. Its ruins are a moody and evocative place for a stroll.

The village is 2km south of the R399 and 5km east of the N55.

COUNTY WESTMEATH

POP 86,165 / AREA 1840 SQ KM

Characterised by lakes and pastures grazed by beef cattle, Westmeath has many attractions, ranging from bucolic lakeside vistas and the miraculous Fore Valley, to the country's oldest pub in the confident county town, Athlone. The rivers and lakes attract a steady stream of visitors.

Athlone

POP 20,200

Set on the banks of the Shannon, the bustling town of Athlone is a magnet for river traffic and visitors.

The Shannon splits this former garrison town in two, with most businesses and services sitting on its eastern bank. In the shadow of Athlone Castle, the western bank is an enchanting jumble of twisting streets, colourfully painted houses, historic pubs, antique shops and more.

Sights & Activities

★ **Athlone Castle** CASTLE

(090-644 2130; www.athloneartandheritage.ie; off Market Sq; adult/child €8/4; 10am-6pm Mon-Sat, noon-6pm Sun Jun-Aug, to 5pm Tue-Sun Apr-May & Sep-Oct) Inside this low and hulking castle that dates to the 13th century there are engaging and modern displays that bring to life the tumultuous history of the town. Entertaining exhibits detail life here through the ages. The highlight is the cacophonous **Siege Experience** which takes place in a circular panoramic gallery.

The ancient river ford at Athlone was an important crossroads on the Shannon and was the cause of many squabbles over the centuries. By 1210, the Normans had asserted their power and built a castle here. In 1690 the Jacobite town survived a siege by Protestant forces, but it fell a year later – under a devastating bombardment of 12,000 cannonballs – to William of Orange's troops. The castle was soon remodelled and further major alterations took place over the following centuries.

Dún na Sí Heritage Park HISTORIC PARK

(090-648 1183; off M6, Moate; adult/child €4/2; 9.30am-4.30pm Mon-Thu, to 3.30pm Fri) This folk park has a re-created ring fort, portal dolmen, lime kiln, mass rock, farmhouse and forge. It also has a traditional session with music, song, dance and storytelling at 8pm on Sundays in summer. The surrounding nature park is lovely. It's 16km east of Athlone.

Luan Gallery GALLERY

(090-644 2154; www.athloneartsandtourism.ie/luan-gallery; Grace Rd; 11am-5pm Tue-Sat, noon-5pm Sun) FREE On the river near the castle, this excellent contemporary art gallery has regular exhibitions of top artists.

★ **Shannon Banks Nature Trail** WALKING

Starting from the Athlone Castle, this well-signposted looping 5km walk follows

OFF THE BEATEN TRACK

UISNEACH

Almost midway between Athlone and Mullingar on the R390 is **Uisneach** (☎087 718 9550; www.uisneach.ie; off R390; adult/child €5/3; ⏲tours 1pm Sat & Sun Apr-Oct), the 'centre' of Ireland. Well, not really – that's a few kilometres to the west. But it is a site with great ancient significance. Ancient constructions found so far include earthworks that may have been a royal palace, a possible fort, some holy wells and more. On tours (the only way to visit), you'll get a detailed overview of the ancient sites plus the associated lore. The 2-sq-km site is mostly privately owned.

the banks of the River Shannon and the Old Canal Bank. It's an easy stroll; signposts describe flora and fauna along the way.

Tours

★Viking Ship Cruises CRUISE
(☎086 262 1136; www.vikingtoursireland.ie; The Quay; adult/child €10/5; ⏲Easter-Oct; 👪) Cruise along the Shannon aboard a replica Viking longship, complete with costumed staff and dress-up clothes. Head north to Lough Ree or south to Clonmacnoise (trips here stop for 90-minutes at the ruins). Boats depart from in front of Athlone Castle.

Sleeping

★Bastion B&B B&B €
(☎090-649 4954; www.thebastion.net; 2 Bastion St; s/d from €50/75; 📶) You can't miss this brightly coloured facade near Athlone Castle. Inside the white-on-white interiors are a canvas for eclectic artwork, cactus collections and Indian wall hangings. The seven rooms (five with private bathrooms) are crisp and clean, with dark wooden floors. Go for the spacious loft if you can. Breakfasts are fresh and healthy.

Coosan Cottage Eco Guesthouse GUESTHOUSE €€
(☎090-647 3468; www.ecoguesthouse.com; Coosan Point Rd; s/d from €50/80) 🍃 This ecofriendly 10-bedroom guesthouse blends traditional style with modern thinking. Triple-glazed windows, a wood-pellet burner and a heat-recovery system are just some of its green credentials. Visitors enjoy the tranquil surroundings and great breakfasts. It's 1km north of town.

Prince of Wales Hotel HOTEL €€
(☎090-647 6666; www.theprinceofwales.ie; Church St; s/d from €70/100; 📶) A modern hotel in the commercial heart of town, the Prince of Wales has 46 large rooms with desks and other business amenities.

Eating & Drinking

Athlone has established itself as the culinary capital of the Midlands. Scout around the western bank's backstreets and you'll unearth some gems.

Beans & Leaves Cafe CAFE €
(☎090-643 3534; cnr Strand St & Lloyds Ln; mains from €5; ⏲8am-6pm Mon-Sat) There are lots of tables outside at this creative cafe on the Right Bank, which is close to the river. Dishes are simple (although the baked goods can be a sticky delight) and fresh. Great coffee and breakfasts.

★Left Bank Bistro MODERN IRISH €€
(☎090-649 4446; www.leftbankbistro.com; Fry Pl; mains lunch €8-15, dinner €18-26; ⏲noon-9pm Tue-Sat; 🌿👪) With an airy, whitewashed interior, shelves of house-made goods, and a menu combining superior Irish ingredients with Mediterranean and Asian influences, this sophisticated deli-bistro is a winner. Lunch features big salads and open sandwiches, while dinner highlights include seafood. Desserts are extraordinary.

Kin Khao THAI €€
(☎090-649 8805; www.kinkhaothai.ie; Abbey Lane; mains €15-20; ⏲12.30-2.30pm Wed-Fri, 5.30-10pm Mon-Sat, 1.30-10pm Sun) Renowned for its extensive menu of authentic Thai dishes, tables get booked early at this perfect antidote for yet another pub meal. Diners come from as far as Dublin; the chefs come from Thailand. There's also a take-out menu.

Murphy's Law PUB €€
(☎090-643 2753; www.murphyslawathlone.com; Barrack St; mains €8-20; ⏲kitchen 10am-8.30pm Mon-Sat, 11am-6pm Sun, bar to 11pm) This recently opened gastropub has transformed an old boozer into a fine venue for good pub food and fine drink. Choose from a list of microbrews and enjoy them in the beer garden. There are B&B rooms upstairs (from €40 per person). It's near the castle.

★Sean's Bar PUB
(☎090-649 2358; 13 Main St; ⏲11am-late) Dating to AD 900, Sean's stakes its claim as Ireland's oldest pub. Its log fires, uneven floors

(to help flood waters run back down to the river), sawdust, rickety piano and curios collected over the years attest to the theory. The riverside beer garden has live music most nights in summer.

Information

The website www.athlone.ie is a good source of information.

The **Tourist Office** (090-649 4630; Market Sq, Athlone Castle; 10am-6pm Mon-Sat, noon-6pm Sun Jun-Aug, to 5pm Tue-Sun Apr-May & Sep-Oct) is located inside the castle's guardhouse.

Getting There & Around

Athlone's bus and train stations are side by side on Southern Station Rd, 1km north of the centre.

BUS

Bus Éireann runs hourly buses to Dublin (€14, 1¾ hours) and Galway (€13, 1½ hours) and two daily to Westport (€17, three hours).

TRAIN

Irish Rail runs hourly trains to Dublin (from €20, 1½ hours), 10 daily to Galway (€20, one hour) and four daily to Westport (€20, two hours).

Lough Ree & Around

Many of the 50-plus islands within Lough Ree were once inhabited by monks and their ecclesiastical treasures, drawing Vikings like bears to honey-laced beehives. These days, the visitors are less bloodthirsty, with sailing, trout fishing and birdwatching the most popular pastimes. Migratory birds that nest here include swans, plovers and curlews.

Poet, playwright and novelist Oliver Goldsmith (1728–74), author of *The Vicar of Wakefield,* is closely associated with the area running alongside the eastern shore of Lough Ree. Known as **Goldsmith Country**, the region is beautifully captured in his writings.

Activities

Glasson Golf Course GOLF

(090-648 51200; www.glassoncountryhouse.ie; Glasson Village; green fees Mon-Fri €40, Sat & Sun €50) This award-winning course comes with an elegant hotel and beautiful scenery.

Sleeping & Eating

Wineport Lodge BOUTIQUE HOTEL €€€

(090-643 9010; www.wineport.ie; off N55, Glasson; s/d from €120/140, mains €24-35; restaurant 5.30-10pm daily, 2.30-4pm Sun) This gracious hotel overlooks the lake and has 29 comfortable rooms. It's also a popular fine-dining spot, serving an ambitious menu featuring local produce and artisanal suppliers.

Glasson Village Restaurant MODERN IRISH €€

(090-648 5001; www.glassonvillagerestaurant.ie; Glasson; mains €18-30; 5.30-9pm Tue-Sat, 1-3.30pm Sun, closed Tue in winter;) Pioneering gourmet restaurant with an informal atmosphere, specialising in seafood. French accents abound, especially on the good wine list. Dine in the garden in summer.

Kilbeggan & Around

Little Kilbeggan has two big claims to fame: a restored distillery-turned-museum and Ireland's only National Hunt racecourse.

Sights & Activities

Kilbeggan Distillery Experience DISTILLERY

(057-933 2134; www.kilbeggandistillery.com; off R446, Kilbeggan; admission €8; 9am-6pm Apr-Oct, 10am-4pm Nov-Mar) Whiskey buffs will enjoy this distillery tour. Established in 1757, Kilbeggan is believed to be the oldest licensed distillery in Ireland – and it's again producing whiskey. The basic admission lets you guide yourself around the hulking machinery. Pricier options (€13 to €75) include guides and tastings.

Entertainment

Kilbeggan Races HORSE RACING

(057-933 2176; www.kilbegganraces.com; off M6, Kilbeggan; usually fortnightly May-Sep) Punters from all over the country attend the old-time evening meetings at the Kilbeggan Races. The town is transformed on race nights into a buzzing equine centre, where the thrill of the chase is matched by the craic in the pubs.

Mullingar & Around

POP 20,200

A prosperous regional town, Mullingar hums with the activity of locals going about their daily lives. Nearby there are fish-filled lakes and a fantastical mansion with an odious history.

James Joyce visited the town in his youth and it appears in both *Ulysses* (1922) and *Finnegans Wake* (1939). Restored sections of the Royal Canal extend in either direction from Mullingar.

Sights

★Belvedere House & Gardens HISTORIC BUILDING

(☎044-934 9060; www.belvedere-house.ie; off N52; adult/child €8/4; ⏰9.30am-8pm May-Aug, to 6pm Sep-Oct & Mar-Apr, to 4.30pm Nov-Feb, cafe & house close at 5pm) Don't miss magnificent Belvedere House, 5.5km south of Mullingar. This immense 18th-century hunting lodge is set in 65 hectares of gardens overlooking Lough Ennell. Designed by Richard Cassels, it contains delicate rococo plasterwork in the upper rooms. The gardens, with their Victorian glasshouse, walled garden and lakeshore setting, make for wonderful walking. An airy annex houses **Catoca**, a classy cafe. There's also a large children's playground.

More than a few skeletons have come out of Belvedere's closets: the first earl, Lord Belfield, accused his wife and younger brother Arthur of adultery. She was placed under house arrest here for 30 years, and Arthur was jailed in London for the rest of his life. Meanwhile, the earl lived a life of decadence and debauchery. On his death, his wife emerged dressed in the fashion of three decades earlier, still protesting her innocence.

Lord Belfield also found time to fall out with his other brother, George, who built a home nearby. Ireland's largest folly, a ready-made 'ruin' called the **Jealous Wall**, was commissioned by the earl so he wouldn't have to look at George's mansion.

Cathedral of Christ the King CATHEDRAL

(www.mullingarparish.com; Bishop's Gate St; ⏰7.30am-8pm) FREE Mullingar's most obvious landmark is this immense church, built just before WWII. It has large mosaics of St Anne and St Patrick by Russian artist Boris Anrep.

Activities

Trout fishing is popular in the lakes around Mullingar. The fishing season runs from 1 March or 1 May (depending on the lake) to 12 October.

Mullingar Equestrian Centre HORSE RIDING

(☎044-934 8331; www.mullingarequestrian.com; off R390; 1-day lesson & ride €100) This well-known equestrian centre offers all manner of rides and lessons.

Sleeping & Eating

There are few B&Bs in the centre, but you'll find plenty on the approach roads from Dublin and Sligo.

Novara House B&B €

(☎044-933 5209; www.novarahouse.com; Dublin Rd; s/d €45/75; 📶) Just a five-minute walk from the town centre, this simple B&B is set in a modern bungalow. Rooms are simple but spotless with pine furniture and neutral colour schemes but it's the amiable hosts and their warm welcome, homemade scones and cups of tea that will make for a lovely stay.

Greville Arms Hotel HOTEL €€

(☎044-934 8563; www.grevillearmshotel ie; Pearse St; s/d from €60/90; 📶) Dating from 1824, this grande dame of a hotel is pleasantly dated with gilt mirrors, statues, dark oil paintings and chandeliers, albeit with modern conveniences worked in. **Ulysses Bar** is named in honour of James Joyce who apparently frequented the place. Other endearing features include a small museum and a beer garden. The 40 rooms are comfortable and spacious.

Annebrook House Hotel HOTEL €€

(☎044-935 3300; www.annebrook.ie; Pearse St; s/d from €80/100; 📶) Right in the town centre, the hub of this modern hotel is a lovely 19th-century house with strong connections to local author Maria Edgeworth. Accommodation is in an annex, where modern rooms in neutral colours are very spacious. The River Brosna flows through the grounds.

★Miller & Cook CAFE €

(☎044-934 0884; www.millerandcook.ie; 50 Pearse St; mains from €5; ⏰8.30am-5pm) Your one-stop shop for fine food and drink in Mullingar. The bakery and deli turn out beautiful goods, perfect for bagging up for a picnic. The cafe has excellent locally sourced fare. Sunday brunch is popular and plans are in the works for a dinner restaurant.

Oscar's Restaurant MEDITERRANEAN €€

(☎044-934 4909; www.oscarsmullingar.com; 21 Oliver Plunkett St; mains €15-25; ⏰6-9.30pm Mon-Sat, 12.30-2pm & 6-8pm Sun) This perennially popular spot is the place to go for upscale comfort food and a lively atmosphere. Bright colours, a menu that skirts the Mediterranean (think pastas, pizzas and French-inspired meat and poultry) and a decent wine list make it a good option.

Drinking & Nightlife

Yukon Bar PUB

(☎044-934 0251; 11 Dominick St; ⏰5-11pm) A lively pub, this place has a great atmosphere and regular live music. You may find soul, blues and rock music on offer.

Entertainment

Mullingar Arts Centre THEATRE
(044-934 7777; www.mullingarartscentre.ie; Lower Mount St, County Hall) The centre runs a regular program of music, comedy, drama and art exhibitions. In summer there are family-friendly, traditional-music sessions every weekend.

Information

The **Tourist Office** (044-934 8650; Market Sq; 9.30am-1pm & 2-5pm Mon-Sat) is right in the centre of town, by the Greville Arms Hotel.

Getting There & Away

BUS

Bus Éireann runs to Dublin (€15, 1½ hours, four daily) and Athlone (€14, one hour, three daily).

TRAIN

Irish Rail (www.irishrail.ie) runs nine direct services to Dublin (from €19, 1¼ hours).

North of Mullingar

The area north of Mullingar is famed for its lakes, the best-known is **Lough Derravaragh**, an 8km-long lake associated with the legend of the children of Lír, who were turned into swans here by their jealous stepmother. Each winter the legend is recalled by thousands of snow-white migratory swans that flock here from as far away as Russia and Siberia.

In addition to the lakes and rolling landscapes you'll find plenty of historical interest around the unassuming town of Castlepollard and sleepy Fore.

Sights

★**Fore Valley** HISTORIC SITE
(off R195) Near the shores of Lough Lene, the emerald-green Fore Valley is a superb place to explore by bicycle or on foot. In AD 630, St Fechin founded a monastery just outside the village of **Fore**. There's nothing left of this early settlement, but three later buildings in the valley are closely associated with 'seven wonders' said to have occurred here. It's a deeply atmospheric place, even in the dead of winter, with sweeping views across a gentle valley.

The oldest of the three buildings is **St Fechin's Church**, containing an early-13th-century chancel and baptismal font. Over the Cyclopean entrance is a huge lintel stone carved with a Greek cross and thought to weigh about 2.5 tonnes. It's said to have been put into place by St Fechin's devotions – the wonder of the stone raised by prayer.

A path runs from the church to the attractive little **anchorite cell** – the anchorite in a stone – which dates to the 15th century and was lived in by a succession of hermits. The Seven Wonders pub in the village holds the key.

On the other side of the road near the car park is **St Fechin's Well**, filled with water that will not boil. Cynics should beware of testing this claim, as it's said that if you try it, doom will come to your family. Nearby is a branch from the tree that will not burn; the coins pressed into it are a more contemporary superstition.

Further over the plain are the extensive remains of a **13th-century Benedictine priory**, the Monastery of the Quaking Scraw, miraculous because it was built on what once was a bog. In the following century it was turned into a fortification, hence the loophole windows and castlelike square towers. The western tower is in a dangerous state – keep clear.

The last two wonders are the mill without a race and the water that flows uphill. The mill site is marked, and legend has it that St Fechin caused water to flow uphill, towards the mill, by throwing his crosier against a rock near Lough Lene, about 1.5km away.

★**Tullynally Castle Gardens** GARDENS
(044-966 1159; www.tullynallycastle.com; off R395, Castlepollard; gardens adult/child €6/3; 11am-5pm Thu-Sun Jun-Aug, Sat & Sun only Apr-May & Sep) The imposing Gothic-revival Tullynally Castle is the seat of the Pakenham family and although closed to visitors, its 12 hectares of gardens and parkland are a lovely place to roam. Ornamental lakes, a Chinese and a Tibetan garden, and a stately stretch of 200-year-old yews are some of the highlights. There is a tearoom in the castle courtyard.

The castle is located 2km northwest of Castlepollard.

Sleeping & Eating

Hotel Castlepollard HOTEL €€
(044-966 1194; www.hotelcastlepollard.ie; Castlepollard; s/d from €60/90; kitchen 8am-8pm;) Overlooking the mannered triangular village green, this cosy, country hotel has decent rooms. The modest **restaurant** (mains from €14) serves reliable fare. The hotel bar

has live music many weekends. This is the closest accommodation to the Fore Valley.

Fore Abbey Coffee Shop CAFE €
(044-966 1780; off R195, Fore; snacks from €3; 11am-4pm daily Jun-Sep, Sun only other times) Right near the village of Fore, this small stone cafe also acts as a tourist information office and screens a short video about the monastery ruins.

Getting There & Away

You'll need your own wheels for the region around Fore Valley, which is 5km from Castlepollard.

COUNTY OFFALY

POP 76,690 / AREA 2001 SQ KM

Apart from the magnificent ecclesiastical city of Clonmacnoise, the green and watery county of Offaly doesn't feature on many tourist itineraries, though it deserves far greater attention. Steeped in history with numerous castles to visit and the atmospheric town of Birr to enjoy, Offaly also offers vast swaths of bog, recognised internationally for their plant and animal life, and prime fishing and water sports on the River Shannon and the Grand Canal.

Access www.offaly.ie and www.offalytourism.com for more information.

GRAND & ROYAL CANALS

After much debate about linking Dublin to the Shannon by water, work began on the Grand Canal in 1757. The project was beset by problems and encountered huge difficulties and delays. In the meantime, commercial rivals hatched a plan for the competing Royal Canal. The two canals revolutionised transport in Ireland in the early 19th century, but their heyday was short lived, as they were soon superseded by the railway.

Today the canals are popular for cruising and fishing, while their banks are ideal for walking and cycling and pass through some truly picturesque villages. With the restoration of the final section of the Royal Canal it is now possible to complete a triangular route from Dublin along the Royal Canal or the Grand Canal to the Shannon and back. Both waterways link to a much greater network that includes the Shannon–Erne Waterway (p471) and the River Suck.

Waterways Ireland (www.waterwaysireland.org) and the **Inland Waterways Association of Ireland** (www.iwai.ie) have a wealth of information on the canals.

Grand Canal

The Grand Canal threads its way from Dublin through Tullamore to join the River Shannon at Shannonbridge, a total of 131km in all. The canal passes through relatively unpopulated countryside, with bogs, pretty villages and 43 finely crafted locks lining the journey. Near the village of Sallins in County Kildare, the graceful seven-arched **Leinster Aqueduct** carries the canal across the River Liffey. From nearby Robertstown, a 45km spur turns south to join the River Barrow at the pretty town of Athy.

Royal Canal

The 145km Royal Canal follows Kildare's northern border, flowing over a massive **aqueduct** near Leixlip, before it joins the River Shannon at Clondra in County Longford. The canal has become a popular amenity for thousands of residents along the north Kildare commuter belt and both the canal and the towpaths are open all the way to the Shannon.

Barges & Boats

You can hire narrow boats at several locations along the canals. Two-/six-berth boats cost from around €850/1600 per week. The following are major firms with multiple locations. You can also find rental firms in the boating centres of Banagher (p485) and Carrick-on-Shannon (p468).

Barrowline Cruisers (057-862 6060; www.barrowline.ie; Vicarstown, Co Laois; boat hire from €930 per week)

Canalways (087-243 3879; www.canalways.ie; Rathangan, Co Kildare; boat rental from €1185 per week)

Birr

POP 5900

Birr is one of the umissable towns in the Midlands. Elegant Georgian buildings with candy-coloured facades are overlooked by a grande dame of a castle. There is excellent accommodation, as well as spirited nightlife. Despite its appeal, Birr remains off the beaten track and you can enjoy its delights without jostling with the crowds.

Sights

Birr has no shortage of first-class Georgian buildings; stroll down tree-lined **Oxmantown Mall** or **John's Mall**, to see some of the best examples.

The tourist office has a walking map that details the most important landmarks, including the megalithic **Seffin Stone** (said to be the ancient marker for Umbilicus Hiberniae – the Navel of Ireland – used to mark the centre of the country) and **St Brendan's Old Churchyard**, reputedly the site of the saint's 6th-century settlement.

★Birr Castle Demesne CASTLE

(☎057-912 0336; www.birrcastle.com; off R439; gardens adult/child €9/5, gardens, exhibits & castle adult/child €18/10; ⊙9am-6pm mid-Mar–Oct, 10am-4pm Nov–mid-Mar) It's easy to spend half a day exploring the attractions and gardens of Birr Castle Demesne. The castle is a private home, but during May to August visitors can visit the main living quarters on tours (which must be booked in advance). Most of the present building dates from around 1620, with alterations made in the early 19th century.

The 50-hectare castle grounds are famous for their magnificent **gardens** set around a large artificial lake.

The gardens are home to more than 1000 species of plants from all over the world; something always seems to be in bloom. Look for one of the world's tallest box hedges (which has made the *Guinness Book of Records*), planted in the 1780s and now standing 12m high, and the romantic Hornbeam cloister. Delight in the waterfalls, wildflower meadows and a pergola festooned with a 90-year-old wisteria.

The Parsons clan, who have owned the castle since 1620, are a remarkable family of pioneering Irish scientists, and their work is documented in the historic **science centre**. Exhibits include the massive **telescope** built by William Parsons in 1845. The 'leviathan of Parsonstown', as it was known, was the largest telescope in the world for 75 years and attracted a wide variety of scientists and astronomers. It was used to make innumerable discoveries, including the spiral galaxies. After the death of William's son, the telescope, unloved and untended, slowly fell to bits. It has recently been completely restored, however, and may be viewed in all its glory in the gardens.

William Parsons' wife, Mary Ross was a keen photographer and her dark room was reputed to be one of the first of its kind in the world. You can now view a replica. Other highlights are a children's adventure playground, complete with playhouse, hobbit huts and trampolines, and the excellent **Castle Courtyard Cafe** which showcases local products and produce in its dishes.

Leap Castle CASTLE

(☎086 869 0547; www.leapcastle.net; off R421; ⊙open by arrangement) Leap Castle is reputedly one of the most haunted castles in Europe. Originally an O'Carroll family residence, the castle was the scene of many dreadful deeds and is famous for its eerie apparitions – its most renowned inhabitant is the 'smelly ghost', a spirit that apparently leaves a smell behind after sightings.

Renovations are ongoing, but you can arrange a visit. It lies about 12km southeast of Birr between Kinnitty and Roscrea (in Tipperary).

Activities

A beautiful leafy **riverside walk** runs east along the River Camcor from Oxmantown Bridge to Elmgrove Bridge.

Birr Equestrian Centre HORSE RIDING

(☎087 244 5545; www.birrequestrian.ie; Clareen Rd, Kingsborough House; horse treks per hour €30; 👪) This equestrian centre, 3km east of Birr, runs hour-long treks in the surrounding farmland and half-day horse treks in the Slieve Bloom Mountains (€80).

Festivals & Events

Birr Vintage Week & Arts Festival ARTS

(www.birrvintageweek.com) The town celebrates its rich history during this festival in early August, with street parades, theatre, music, exhibitions, workshops, guided walks and a traditional fair.

Sleeping

★Maltings Guesthouse B&B €

(057-912 1345; www.themaltingsbirr.com; Castle St; s/d from €45/70;) Based in an 1810 malt storehouse once used by Guinness, this place has a serene location right by the castle and the River Camcor. The rooms are large with pine furniture and a soothing lilac-and-green colour scheme; all rooms overlook the water, as does the cheery breakfast room. Excellent value.

★Walcot B&B B&B €€

(057-912 1247; www.walcotbedandbreakfast.com; Rosse Rowe; s/d from €60/90;) Set on spacious grounds across from Birr Castle, this Georgian townhouse is close to everything. The five bedrooms are large and the furnishings luxurious. The private bathrooms have period-style fittings with large tubs and showers.

Brendan House B&B €€

(057-912 1818; www.tinjugstudio.com; Brendan St; s/d from €55/80;) Packed with knick-knacks, books, rugs, art and antiques, this Georgian townhouse is a bohemian delight. The three rooms share a bathroom (one of Birr's oldest, they claim). The four-poster beds, period charm, superb breakfast and artistic style are the real draws. The owners arrange mountain walks, castle and art tours, holistic treatments and art classes.

Dooley's Hotel HOTEL €€

(057-912 0032; www.doolyshotel.com; Emmet Sq; s/d from €50/80;) Originally a coaching house – one of the oldest in Ireland, dating from 1740 – the hotel has an inviting homey feel with Georgian-style furnishings, a solidly reliable restaurant and choice of bars. The 17 rooms are large and some look onto Birr's main square.

Eating

★Brambles Cafe & Deli CAFE €

(087 745 3359; Mill St; mains €4-8; 9am-6pm Mon-Sat, from noon Sun;) A tiny outpost of big flavours, this cafe has mismatched furniture and very tasty food. The soda bread is accented with wild garlic, while the soups change with the seasons. Look for the desserts, which can include a delectable rhubarb crumble (only in season).

Emma's Cafe & Deli CAFE €

(057-912 5678; 31 Main St; mains €5-9; 9am-6pm Mon-Fri, 12.30-6pm Sun;) Generally full of families and shoppers, Emma's serves a diverse range of baked goods, sandwiches, salads and cakes. There are daily newspapers, plus books and games for children. The deli is renowned for its selection of local foods and is an ideal picnic-supplies stop.

★Spinners on Castle St MODERN IRISH €€

(057-912 3779; www.spinnersbirr.com; Castle St; mains €10-25; restaurant 6-9pm Wed-Sun, bar 5-9pm Tue, 12.30-9pm Wed-Sun;) This alluring restaurant is part of a complex that spans five restored Georgian houses. The bar is the perfect place to pause with a cheeseboard or burger. The restaurant has a seasonal menu that includes steaks and seafood. Service is excellent as is the wine and drinks list. Stylish rooms upstairs are €80 to €140.

Thatch IRISH €€

(057-912 0682; www.thethatchcrinkill.com; Crinkill; mains €12-30; 4-10pm Mon-Thu, 10am-late Fri-Sun;) A traditional thatched pub, 2km southeast of Birr, this 200-year-old inn is a great place to sip a pint or enjoy a meal. The hearty cuisine is a belt notch or two above the norm. Besides traditional roasts, there are specialities such as duck. It has three brick-clad small bars with open fires, plus a more modern dining room.

Drinking & Nightlife

Chestnut PUB

(www.thechestnut.ie; Green St; 8pm-late Mon-Thu, from 5pm Fri, from 3pm Sat & Sun) The most appealing pub in the centre, the Chestnut dates from 1823 and has had a beautiful revamp that combines dark wood with a continental-cafe style. There's live music at weekends and regular special events such as evening BBQs.

Craughwell's PUB

(057-912 1839; www.craughwellspub.com; Castle St; 7-11.30pm Mon-Sat, 1-11pm Sun) Stop for a pint at Craughwell's, renowned for its rollicking trad-music session on the first Friday of the month and impromptu singalong sessions on Saturday. Tourists and locals alike contribute to the bar's cap collection.

Entertainment

Birr Theatre & Arts Centre PERFORMING ARTS

(057-912 2911; www.birrtheatre.com; Oxmantown Hall) A vibrant place with a regular line-up of art exhibitions, films, theatre and concerts.

Information

The **Tourist Office** (☎057-912 0110; Emmet Sq; ⏲9.30am-1pm & 2-5.30pm Mon-Sat Jun-Sep) has good local and regional information.

Getting There & Away

Bus Éireann runs to Athlone (€13, one hour, three daily Monday to Saturday, two Sunday) where you can change for Dublin.

Kinnitty

POP 360

Kinnitty is a quaint village that makes a good base for exploring the Slieve Bloom Mountains (p492) to the east. The scenic R440 runs east from the town across the mountains to Mountrath.

Sights

Look out for the bizarre 10m-high **stone pyramid** in the village graveyard behind the Church of Ireland. In the 1830s, Richard Bernard commissioned this scale replica of the Cheops pyramid in Egypt for the family crypt.

The shaft of the 9th-century **Kinnitty High Cross** was nabbed by Kinnitty Castle in the 19th century and is now displayed on the hotel's terrace. Adam and Eve and the Crucifixion are clearly visible on either face.

Sleeping & Eating

Ardmore House B&B €€

(☎057-913 7009; www.kinnitty.com; The Walk; s/d from €55/84; 📶) This lovely Victorian stone farmhouse oozes old-world charm. The five characterful rooms feature brass beds, antique furniture and views of the nearby mountains. Peat fires, homemade brown bread and local foods complete the cosy, rustic atmosphere. The owners organise walking tours in the nearby Slieve Bloom Mountains. The B&B is off the R440, about 200m east of Kinnitty.

Kinnitty Castle Hotel HISTORIC HOTEL €€

(☎057-913 7318; www.kinnittycastlehotel.com; off R421; s/d from €90/140; 📶) One of Ireland's most renowned mansions, 19th-century Kinnitty Castle is built in neo-Gothic style surrounded by a vast estate. The 37 rooms are suitably atmospheric, along with the Dungeon Bar – Kinnitty Hotel is supposedly haunted. The castle is 3km east of town.

★Giltraps Pub PUB €

(☎057-913 7076; www.giltrapspub.com; R421; mains €5-20; ⏲11am-11pm) The perfect place to stop after exploring the Slieve Bloom Mountains, this lovely country pub scores across the board. Food ranges from simple sandwiches to top-notch BBQ. You can enjoy a pint outside at a picnic table while taking in the mountain vistas.

Banagher & Around

POP 1655

Sleepy Banagher bursts into life in the summer months when the busy marina is awash with boaters. Perhaps Banagher's greatest claim to fame is that it was the location for Charlotte Brontë's honeymoon.

Sights

Situated at a crossing point over the River Shannon, Banagher was a place of enormous strategic importance during turbulent times. The modest fortifications by the bridge include the diminutive **Cromwell's Castle** (built in the 1650s and modified during the Napoleonic Wars), **Fort Eliza** (a five-sided gun battery whose guardhouse, moat and retaining walls can still be seen), a roofless **military barracks** and **Martello tower**.

St Paul's Church at the far end of Main St contains a resplendent stained-glass window, originally intended for Westminster Abbey.

Activities

Banagher Marina is a good place to rent cruisers for a trip along the Shannon or the Royal Canal. Try **Carrick Craft** (☎01-278 1666; www.cruise-ireland.com; marina) or **Silverline Cruisers** (☎057-915 1112; www.silverlinecruisers.com; marina) for more information.

Shannon Adventure Canoeing CANOEING

(☎057-915 1411; advcanoe@iol.ie; marina; 2-person canoe-rental per day €50; ⏲call for hours) You don't need a houseboat to enjoy Ireland's waterways, here you can rent a canoe.

Sleeping & Eating

Dún Cromáin B&B €

(☎057-915 3966; www.duncromain.com; Crank Rd; s/d €45/70; 📶👪) Surrounded by sweeping lawns, the large rooms are simply decorated in pastel colours with light wood and white linens. The breakfast-cum-sitting room has a thoughtful feel-at-home atmosphere and an open fire. Perks include babysitting, fridges and facilities for drying clothes (handy in these parts). It's near the marina.

Charlotte's Way B&B €€
(057-915 3864; www.charlottesway.com; The Hill; s/d from €45/70;) This tastefully restored former 18th-century rectory offers five comfy good-value rooms, with period furniture, old prints and antiques. Charlotte Brontë was a frequent visitor and, after her death, her husband Arthur lived here as the rector. Breakfast stars eggs fresh from the chickens and produce from the pretty garden.

Drinking & Nightlife

★ **JJ Houghs Singing Pub** PUB
(Main St; noon-11.30pm) Rivalling the river as Banagher's most appealing feature, Hough's is a 250-year-old vine-clad pub renowned for its music sessions. You'll find someone playing here most nights in summer and at weekends in winter. People sing nightly, led by the owner Michael. Seek solitude in the lovely beer garden.

Getting There & Away

Kearns Transport (www.kearnstransport.com) links Banagher to Birr (€3, 15 minutes) and Tullamore (€6, 45 minutes) once daily.

Shannonbridge

POP 650

Perfectly picturesque, Shannonbridge gets its name from a narrow 16-span, 18th-century bridge that crosses the river into County Roscommon. It's a small, sleepy village with just one main street and three pubs.

You can't miss the massive 19th-century **fortifications** on the western bank, where heavy artillery was installed to bombard Napoleon in case he tried to invade by river.

Drinking

★ **JJ Killeens Village Tavern** PUB
(090-967 4112; Main St; mains from €8; noon-11pm) Killeens is an old-world pub and shop that is renowned for its warm welcome and lively traditional music. There's a music session most nights in summer and at weekends during the rest of the year. Traditional pub grub is available.

Clonmacnoise

Gloriously placed overlooking the River Shannon, Clonmacnoise is one of Ireland's most important ancient monastic cities. The site is enclosed in a walled field and contains several early churches, high crosses, round towers and graves in astonishingly good condition. There is an appealing air of loneliness and mystery here.

The surrounding marshy area is known as the **Shannon Callows**, home to many wild plants and one of the last refuges of the seriously endangered corncrake (a pastel-coloured relative of the coot).

History

When St Ciarán founded a monastery here in AD 548, it was the most important crossroads in the country, the intersection of the north–south River Shannon and the east–west Esker Riada (Highway of the Kings).

The giant ecclesiastical city had a humble beginning and Ciarán died just seven months after building his first church. Over the years, however, Clonmacnoise grew to become an unrivalled bastion of Irish religion, literature and art and attracted a large lay population. Between the 7th and 12th centuries, monks from all over Europe came to study and pray here, helping to earn Ireland the title of the 'land of saints and scholars'.

Most of what you can see today dates from the 10th to 12th centuries. The monks would have lived in small huts surrounding the monastery. The site was burned and pillaged on numerous occasions by both the Vikings and the Irish. After the 12th century it fell into decline, and by the 15th century was home solely to an impoverished bishop. In 1552 the English garrison from Athlone reduced the site to a ruin.

Sights

Visitor Centre MUSEUM
(090-967 4195; www.heritageireland.ie; R444; adult/child €7/3; 9am-6.30pm Jun-Aug, 10am-5.30pm mid-Mar–May & Sep-Oct, till 5.30pm Nov–mid-Mar, last admission 1hr before closing) Three connected conical huts, echoing the design of early monastic dwellings, house the visitors centre museum. A 20-minute audiovisual show provides an excellent introduction to the historic Clonmacnoise site.

The exhibition area contains the original high crosses (replicas have been put in their former locations outside), and various artefacts uncovered during excavation, including silver pins, beaded glass and an Ogham stone.

There's a real sense of drama as you descend to the foot of the imposing **Cross of the Scriptures (King Flann's Cross)**, one of Ireland's finest. It's very distinctive, with unique upward-tilting arms and richly decorated panels depicting the Crucifixion, the Last Judgement, the arrest of Jesus and Christ in the tomb.

Only the shaft of the **North Cross**, which dates from around AD 800, remains. It is adorned by lions, convoluted spirals and a single figure, thought to be the Celtic god Cernunnos. The richly decorated **South Cross** has mostly abstract carvings – swirls, spirals and fretwork – and, on the western face, the Crucifixion plus a few odd cavorting creatures.

The museum also contains the largest collection of early Christian grave slabs in Europe, many with inscriptions clearly visible, often starting with *oroit do* or *ar* (a prayer for).

Cathedral RUIN

The largest building at Clonmacnoise, the cathedral was originally built in AD 909, but was significantly altered and remodelled over the centuries. Its most interesting feature is the intricate 15th-century Gothic doorway with carvings of Sts Francis, Patrick and Dominic. A whisper carries from one side of the door to the other, and this feature was supposedly used by lepers to confess their sins without infecting the priests.

The last High Kings of Tara – Turlough Mór O'Connor (died 1156) and his son Ruairí (Rory; died 1198) – are said to be buried near the altar.

Temple Ciaran & other Churches CHURCHES

The small churches at Clonmacnoise are called temples, a derivation of the Irish word *teampall* (church). Tiny **Temple Ciaran** is reputed to be the burial place of St Ciarán, the site's founder. The floor level in Temple Ciaran is lower than outside because local farmers have been taking clay from the church for centuries to protect their crops and cattle. The floor has been covered in slabs, but handfuls of clay are still removed from outside the church in the early spring.

Near the temple's southwestern corner is a **bullaun** (ancient grinding stone) supposedly used for making medicines for the monastery's hospital. Today the rainwater that collects in it is said to cure warts.

Elsewhere on the site, the little roofed church is **Temple Conner**, still used by Church of Ireland parishioners on the last Sunday of summer. Walking towards the cathedral, you'll pass the scant foundations of **Temple Kelly** (1167). Continuing round the compound you come to the 12th-century **Temple Melaghlin**, with its attractive windows, and the twin structures of **Temple Hurpan** and **Temple Doolin**.

O'Rourke's Tower TOWER

Overlooking the River Shannon is the 20m-high O'Rourke's Tower. Lightning blasted the top off the tower in 1135, but the remaining structure was used for another 400 years.

Temple Finghin & Tower CHURCH

Temple Finghin and its round tower are on the northern boundary of the Clonmacnoise monastic site, overlooking the River Shannon.

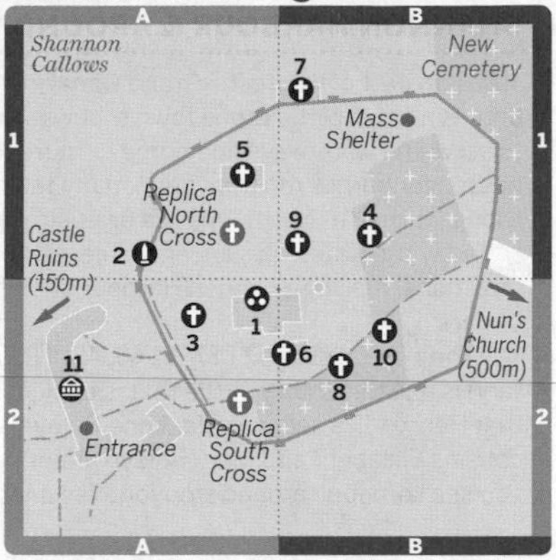

Clonmacnoise

Sights

1	Cathedral	A2
2	O'Rourke's Tower	A1
3	Replica Cross of the Scriptures (King Flann's Cross)	A2
4	Temple Ciaran	B1
5	Temple Conner	A1
6	Temple Doolin	B2
7	Temple Finghin & Tower	B1
8	Temple Hurpan	B2
9	Temple Kelly	B1
10	Temple Melaghlin	B2
11	Visitor Centre	A2

WORTH A TRIP

SHANNON HARBOUR & AROUND

Just 1km east of where the Grand Canal joins the River Shannon, sleepy Shannon Harbour is a small picturesque town that was once a thriving trading centre, constructed to serve the waterways and home to more than 1000 people. Along with cargo boats, passenger barges ran from here, many taking poverty-stricken locals on their first leg of a long journey to North America or Australia.

Today the waterways are again teeming with boats and walking paths stretching in all directions, making Shannon Harbour an enticing stop for walkers, fishers, boaters and birders.

Clonony Castle (☎087 761 4034; off R357, Colony; admission by donation; ⏲hours vary) is a 16th-century castle that is enclosed by an overgrown castellated wall. Tales that Henry VIII's second wife, Anne Boleyn, was born here are unlikely to be true, but her cousins Elizabeth and Mary Boleyn are buried beside the ruins. Restoration is sporadic, if you see someone around stop for a fascinating tour.

The building dates from around 1160 and has some fine Romanesque carvings. The herringbone-patterned tower roof is the only one in Ireland that has never been altered.

Nun's Church HISTORIC SITE

Beyond the site's boundary wall, about 500m east through the modern graveyard, is the secluded Nun's Church with wonderful Romanesque arches and minute carvings; one has been interpreted as Ireland's earliest sheila-na-gig, in an acrobatic pose with feet tucked behind the ears.

Castle Ruins RUIN

To the west of the site, on the ridge near the car park, is a motte with the oddly shaped ruins of a 13th-century castle, built by John de Grey, bishop of Norwich, to watch over the Shannon.

Sleeping & Eating

There's a simple cafe at the visitor center and a larger operation near the car park.

Kajon House B&B €€

(☎090-967 4191; www.kajonhouse.ie; R444, Creevagh; s/d from €50/70; ⏲Mar-Oct; ☰) If you want to stay near the ruins, this is your best option, just 1.5km southwest. It has cosy rooms, a spacious yard (complete with picnic table) and a warm welcome even by Irish standards. Delicious pancakes are available for breakfast; you may be able to arrange for dinner.

Information

The €1 Clonmacnoise visitors guide is a good investment. Allow at least a couple of hours for a visit.

Getting There & Away

Clonmacnoise is 7km northeast of Shannonbridge on the R444. Bus tours are promoted throughout the region.

BOAT

Silver Line (www.silverlinecruisers.com; adult/child return from €12/7; ⏲2pm Wed from Shannonbridge, 3pm Sun from Banagher, both Jul & Aug) Runs one-hour boat trips between Shannonbridge and Clonmacnoise.

Tullamore

POP 11,575

Tullamore, Offaly's county town, is a bustling place with a pleasant setting on the Grand Canal. The town is the famous namesake for Tullamore Dew whiskey. It was a big deal locally when the distillery opened a new factory on the edge of town, 60 years after it had shifted all production to County Tipperary.

Sights

Charleville Castle CASTLE

(☎057-932 3040; www.charlevillecastle.com; off N52; guided tour for 2 adults €20, child free; ⏲tours noon-5.30pm Jun-Aug, by appointment Sep-Apr) Spires, turrets, clinging ivy and creaking trees combine to give this hulking structure a haunted feel (and, yes, it is reputedly haunted). Charleville Castle was the family seat of the Burys, who commissioned the design in 1798 from Francis Johnston, one of Ireland's most famous architects. Admission is by 45-minute tour only. The castle is 2km southwest of Tullamore. Look for the grove of huge ancient oaks.

The interior is spectacular, with stunning ceilings, one of the most striking Gothic-revival galleries in Ireland and a kitchen block built to resemble a country church.

Tullamore Dew Visitor Centre MUSEUM
(057-932 5015; www.tullamore-dew.org; Bury Quay; adult/child €9/6.50; 9.30am-6pm Mon-Sat, 11.30am-5pm Sun) Located in a 19th-century canal-side warehouse, this marketing extravaganza mixes intriguing local history with brand propaganda. Engaging exhibits show the role of the Grand Canal in the town's development. At the end of the tour adults will get to sample what they claim is the easiest of Irish whiskeys to drink. For real aficionados, there is a €25 tour that explores the distillery process in depth.

Sleeping & Eating

Annaharvey Farm B&B €€
(057-934 3544; www.annaharveyfarm.ie; R420, Aharney; s/d from €60/90; mid-Feb–Nov;) This tranquil equestrian centre and award-winning guesthouse is a great place to enjoy a bit of country life and genuine hospitality. The six rooms are purpose-built and modern, plus there's horse riding on your doorstep. The farm is 6km southeast of Tullamore.

Bridge House Hotel HOTEL €€
(057-932 3374; www.bridgehousehoteltullamore.ie; Bridge St; s/d from €72/100; @) The grand stairway dramatically makes the point that this town-centre hotel is a notch higher than most. Rooms are very comfortable and there is even a Presidential Suite. Many unwind at the spa.

Wolftrap PUB €
(057-932 3374; www.the-wolftrap.com; William St; mains €8-12; food 11.30am-8.30pm, bar till late) The place to drink the local whiskey – or anything else. This pub is several cuts above average, with excellent and inventive, albeit casual bar food (the burgers are superb). There is dance music on weekends; on Tuesdays, owner Padraig McLoughlin leads trad-music sessions.

Getting There & Away

BUS

Bus Éireann runs a service to Dublin (€18, 2¼ hours, four weekdays, two Saturday and Sunday).

TRAIN

Irish Rail (www.irishrail.ie) trains run east to Dublin (from €20, 1¼ hours, hourly) and west to Galway (from €21, 1½ hours, eight daily), as well as Westport.

Durrow Abbey

Founded by St Colmcille (also known as St Columba) in the 6th century, Durrow Abbey is most famous for producing the illustrated *Book of Durrow*. The 7th-century text is the earliest of the great manuscripts to have survived, a remarkable feat considering it was recovered from a farm where it was dipped in the cattle's drinking water to cure illnesses. It can be seen at Trinity College, Dublin.

Tiny Durrow village (not to be confused with the larger town of Durrow in County Laois) and the abbey are 7km north of Tullamore, down a long lane.

Sights

Little remains of **Durrow Abbey** at this site, although there are five early-Christian gravestones. A short path leads to **St Colmcille's Well**, a place of pilgrimage marked by a small cairn.

Durrow High Cross CHRISTIAN SITE
(off N52; 10am-4pm) This splendid 10th-century high cross has complex, high-relief carvings depicting the sacrifice of Isaac, the Last Judgement and the Crucifixion. It is housed in the 19th-century **church** for protection.

OFF THE BEATEN TRACK

LOUGH BOORA

Much of County Offaly's once extensive bogs were stripped of peat for electricity generation during the 20th century. Now efforts are being made at restoration.

Lough Boora Parklands (www.loughbooraparklands.com; off R357; dawn-dusk) is the focus of a scheme for bog restoration. Located 5km west of Blue Ball, there are more than 50km of trails across the area with excellent birdwatching, rare flora, a mesolithic site and a series of impressive environmental **sculptures** (www.sculptureintheparklands.com) to explore. The trails are great for cycling and you can **rent bikes** (086 889 5194; per hour €3; 10am-8pm).

Clara

One of the best ways to explore the 'real Ireland' of the Midlands is just 6km south of the busy M6 motorway. Clara Bog is one of the few great expanses of classic bogland in all of Western Europe to escape being stripped for fuel. Deceptively flat and seemingly lifeless, it offers a fascinating window into the natural world.

Sights

★Clara Bog Nature Reserve NATURE RESERVE
(Clara-Rahan Rd; ⏲dawn-dusk) It's the quiet that sounds the loudest at this magical preserved landscape: water courses, birds chirp, insects buzz and more. A 1km-loop boardwalk leads from a parking area 4km south of Clara. Look for tiny wildflowers growing amid the pillowy soft peat and enjoy the sweeping views of distant green hills.

Clara Bog Visitor Centre MUSEUM
(☎057-936 8878; Ballycumber Rd/R436; ⏲10am-5pm Mon-Fri year-round, to 1pm Sat Apr-Nov) FREE Sharing space with the local library, this modern and small museum gives an engaging overview of life in the bog, from butterflies to toads.

COUNTY LAOIS

POP 80,560 / AREA 1720 SQ KM

Little-visited Laois (pronounced 'leash') is often overlooked as drivers zoom past to the south and west. Away from the main roads, though, is this hidden corner of Ireland, with pretty towns such as Abbeyleix, making a perfect daytime stop, and the dramatic Slieve Bloom Mountains, which get you right off the beaten track.

There's plenty of local information at www.laoistourism.ie. Look for the excellent *Laois Heritage Trail* booklet, either online or at tourist offices.

GETTING AROUND LAOIS

County Laois is best explored with your own wheels; bus service is sparse. The county town of Portlaoise does have rail service: trains stop on runs serving Dublin (from €18, one hour, 14 daily); Cork (from €20, two hours, nine daily) and Limerick (from €18, 1½ hours, three daily).

Abbeyleix

POP 2570

Abbeyleix (abbey-*leeks*) is a classic heritage town with a Georgian market house, graceful terraced housing and a wide leafy main street. The town grew up around a 12th-century Cistercian monastery, but problems with frequent flooding led to local 18th-century landowner Viscount de Vesci levelling the village and creating a new, planned estate town in the present location. During the Famine, de Vesci proved a kinder landlord than many, and the fountain obelisk in the square was erected in gratitude from his tenants.

Abbeyleix makes a good base for exploring the region, with decent food and accommodation options and a chance to sip a pint in one of Ireland's most atmospheric pubs.

Sights

Unfortunately for visitors, de Vesci's magnificent mansion is not open to the public. It's worth taking a look at the elegant **Market House** in the town centre. Built in 1836, it houses a library and exhibition space.

★Heywood Gardens GARDENS
(☎057-873 3563; www.heritageireland.ie; Ballinakill; ⏲8.30am-9pm May-Aug, to 7pm Apr & Sep, to 5.30pm Oct-Mar) FREE These lavish gardens with architectural features, lakes and woodland, were landscaped by Edwin Lutyens and Gertrude Jekyll and completed in 1912. The centrepiece is a sunken garden, where circular terraces lead down to an oval pool with a magnificent fountain.

The gardens are 7km southeast of Abbeyleix, off the R432 to Ballinakill, in the grounds of Heywood Community School.

Abbeyleix Heritage House & Museum MUSEUM
(☎057-873 1653; www.abbeyleixheritage.com; Main St; adult/child €3/2; ⏲9am-5pm Tue-Sat) This museum, in an old school building, details Abbeyleix' rich history. One room looks at the town's carpet-making legacy – the Turkish-influenced carpets once made here were chosen to grace the floors of the *Titanic* – while another showcases a fascinating selection of memorabilia from the Morrissey family who ran the town's renowned shop and pub from 1775 to 2004. It also has tourist information and an adjacent playground.

OFF THE BEATEN TRACK

POVERTY'S LAST STOP AT DONAGHMORE

The unremarkable farm village of Donaghmore, 20km west of Durrow in Country Laois, is home to a quietly horrifying reminder of the Famine.

The unadorned stone **Donaghmore Workhouse** (☎086 829 6685; www.donaghmoremuseum.com; R435, Donaghmore; adult/child €5/3; ⏲11am-5pm Mon-Fri year-round, plus 2-5pm Sat & Sun Jun-Sep) was a last resort for the destitute in the 1850s. Conditions were intentionally grim, the idea being that if things were especially bad, the poor wouldn't stick around. They didn't, as scores died in the harsh conditions. Today the remaining buildings hold a collection of simple displays that detail this cruel story.

A sign near the entrance notes: 'By the time the Donaghmore Workhouse opened in 1853, most of the poor of the area had already perished from starvation or sickness or had emigrated.'

Overcrowding was rife, families were separated (often for good), meals (no more than a bowl of gruel) were taken in silence, toilets were crude and bedding was limited. The loss of dignity that came with entering the workhouse was a tragic reality for many.

Sleeping

Farran Farm Hostel HOSTEL €
(☎057-873 4032; www.farmhostel.com; Ballacolla; dm from €20) In a beautifully restored limestone grain loft on a working family farm, this quirky independent hostel has 45 beds in rooms with a bathroom and up to five bunks. You can arrange in advance for delicious dinners using locally sourced produce. The hostel is near the junction of the R4343 and R434, about 6km west of Abbeyleix.

Sandymount House B&B B&B €€
(☎057-873 1063; www.abbeyleix.info; off R433, Old Town; s/d from €60/90; 📶) Once the home of the de Vesci estate manager, this lovely old country house has been beautifully restored. A grand sweeping staircase, marble fireplaces and mature gardens provide elegant charm, while the spacious rooms are well equipped with individually designed bathrooms sporting high-pressure showers. It's 2km west of Abbeyleix.

Eating & Drinking

★**Gallic Kitchen** CAFE €
(☎086 605 8208; www.gallickitchen.com; Main St; dishes €5-9.50; ⏲10am-6pm Mon-Sat, 11am-6pm Sun; 👪) 🌿 Set in an old haberdashery shop named Bramley's, this outlet of the Gallic Kitchen sets mouths watering for anyone familiar with the food of chef Sarah Webb. Her delicious jams, preserves, baked goods and other treats are sold at farmers markets from here to Dublin. The menu here is a paean to the best of modern Irish fare.

★**Morrissey's** PUB
(☎057-873 1281; Main St; ⏲10am-11pm) This extraordinary pub has withstood the onslaught of modernisation. A hodgepodge of oddities line the shelves above the pew seats and pot-belly stove. Claiming to be Ireland's oldest pub, dating to 1775 (when it opened as a grocery store), it's a wonderful place to soak up the atmosphere with a pint or a good cup of coffee.

Getting There & Away

You will need your own wheels as buses no longer run to Abbeyleix.

Durrow

POP 820

A pleasant village, Durrow's neat rows of houses, pubs and cafes surround a manicured green. On the western side stands the imposing gateway to the landmark 18th-century **Castle Durrow**.

Sleeping

Castle Arms Hotel HOTEL €€
(☎057-873 6117; www.castlearmshotel.ie; The Square; s/d from €60/90; 📶) A tidy hotel and pub overlooking a corner of Durrow's mannered centre, the Castle Arms has 15 comfortable rooms in a three-storey heritage building. The chatty pub serves good food through the day and on some nights there's traditional dancing.

★**Castle Durrow** LUXURY HOTEL €€€
(☎057-873 6555; www.castledurrow.com; off N9; d half board from €195; ⏲restaurant 7-9pm Wed-

Sat, 1-4.30pm & 6-8.30pm Sun;) The 18th-century Castle Durrow is one of Ireland's top country-house hotels. The rooms here vary from opulent suites with four-poster beds and heavy brocades to more intimate rooms. Even if you can't stay overnight, it's worth popping in for a coffee on the terrace overlooking the vast grounds. Numerous walks lace the estate, and there are amenities such as tennis courts.

The excellent **restaurant** (3-course set-menu lunch/dinner €28/50) is supplied by the castle's organic kitchen garden. Bar meals are available through the day daily.

Slieve Bloom Mountains

Populated Ireland recedes into your rear-view mirror when you explore the Slieve Bloom Mountains. Although not as spectacular as some Irish ranges, their sudden rise from the Laois plain and the absence of visitors make them appealing. On the lower slopes, there are a lot of generic conifer farms but higher up you get a real sense of being away from it all as you tread the deserted blanket bogs, moorland, pine forests and isolated valleys.

The R440 provides scenic access. Kinnitty in County Offaly is a good base.

Sights & Activities

For leisurely walking, **Glenbarrow**, southwest of Rosenallis, has an interesting trail by the cascading **Glendine Park**, near the Glendine Gap and the **Cut Mountain Pass**. Look for parking areas with trail maps for more ideas.

For something more challenging you could stride out on the **Slieve Bloom Way**, an 84km-long signposted trail that does a complete circuit of the mountains, taking in most major points of interest. The recommended starting point is the car park at Glenbarrow, 5km from Rosenallis, from where the trail follows tracks, forest firebreaks and old roads around the mountains. The trail's highest point is at Glendine Gap (460m).

Slieve Bloom Mountains Nature Reserve NATURE RESERVE
(www.npws.ie) The higher elevations of the mountains are protected by this nature reserve. The website has good walking suggestions and info about the flora and fauna, including the many herbs and wildflowers.

Slieve Bloom Walking Club WALKING
(086 278 9147; www.slievebloom.ie; adult/child €5/free; Sun, check for other days) This club organises guided walks as well as an annual festival. Its latest schedule is on Facebook.

Sleeping & Eating

★ **Roundwood House** GUESTHOUSE €€
(057-873 2120; www.roundwoodhouse.com; Slieve Blooms Rd, Mountrath; s/d from €85/130, set dinner €35-55; Feb-Dec;) Set in secluded woods, the rooms in this stately 17th-century Palladian villa have an appealing, worn-at-the-edges elegance. Children and adults will love all the outdoor space. Communal dinners are a chance to meet the amiable owners and enjoy a country treat of local foods.

Rooms are in the main house – with a convivial lounge – and in an even older building nearby.

Ballyfin House LUXURY HOTEL €€€
(057-875 5866; www.ballyfin.com; off R423, Ballyfin; s €335-560, d €520-800; @) A vast and opulent Regency mansion with lavish interiors, Ballyfin House is one of Ireland's premier luxury retreats. Among the highlights: 17th-century Flemish tapestries, a Roman sarcophagus bath, secret doorways, a 'whispering room' and a promise that every need shall be catered for. It's like a museum; however, you can sit on the furniture.

Information

The website www.slievebloom.ie has comprehensive information and 16 downloadable looped walking routes.

Mountmellick

POP 4750

A quiet Georgian town located on the River Owenass, Mountmellick was renowned for its linen production in the 19th century and owes much of its history to its Quaker settlers and its place on the Grand Canal.

Sights

A 4km looped and signed **heritage trail**, beginning in the square, leads you on a walking tour of the most important landmarks.

Mountmellick Museum MUSEUM
(057-862 4525; www.mountmellickdevelopment.com; off N80, Irishtown; adult/child €5/2; 9am-5pm Mon-Fri) For an insight into the town's Quaker and industrial heritage, visit Mount-

mellick Museum, where you can also see a display of superbly subtle Mountmellick embroidery. Various linens and quilts still being made by locals are on sale here. It also has guides to the heritage trail.

Portarlington

POP 7790

Portarlington grew up under the influence of French Huguenot and German settlers and has some fine, if neglected, 18th-century buildings along French and Patrick Sts.

About 4km east of town are the ivy-covered ruins of 13th-century **Lea Castle** on the banks of the River Barrow. The castle consists of a fairly intact towered keep with two outer walls and a twin-towered gatehouse. Access is through a farmyard, 500m to the north off the main Monasterevin road (R420).

Emo Court

One of County Laois' most impressive sights, the unusual, green-domed **Emo Court** (www.heritageireland.ie; off R422, Emo; adult/child €4/2, grounds free; ⏲10am-6pm Easter-Sep, last admission 5pm, grounds dawn-dusk year-round) is easily visited when passing by on the M7.

Designed in 1790 by James Gandon, architect of Dublin's Custom House, Emo Court was originally the country seat of the first Earl of Portarlington. After many years as a Jesuit novitiate, the house, with its elaborate central rotunda, was impressively restored.

The extensive grounds with their impressive Greek statues, contain more than 1000 different trees, including huge sequoias, and shrubs from all over the world. Enjoy refreshments at the cafe or a leisurely picnic, before taking a scenic stroll through the woodlands to Emo Lake.

Emo is about 13km northeast of Portlaoise, just off the R422, 2km west of the M7.

Rock of Dunamaise

The **Rock of Dunamaise** (off N80; ⏲dawn-dusk), 6km east of Portlaoise, is an arresting sight: a craggy limestone outcrop rising dramatically out of the flat plains. It offered early settlers a superb natural defensive position with sweeping views across the surrounding countryside. You'll need some imagination to envisage the site as it once was, before it was destroyed by Cromwell's henchmen in 1650. But the views from the summit are breathtaking on a clear day.

The rock was first fortified in the Bronze Age and was recorded on Ptolemy's map of AD 140. Over the centuries that followed, successive waves of Viking, Norman, Irish and English invaders fought over its occupation and control. The ruins you see today are those of a castle built in the 13th century. It was extensively remodelled in the 15th century. In the 18th century, its shattered remains were slightly rebuilt.

If you're lucky, you'll be able to see Timahoe round tower to the south, the Slieve Blooms to the west and the Wicklow Mountains to the east.

Timahoe

POP 1200

Tiny Timahoe, 13km southeast of Portlaoise on the R426, has real charm, even if the village is nothing more than a handful of houses fronting a grassy triangle. Screened by a babbling stream and seemingly straight out of a fairy tale, is a tilting 30m-tall, 12th-century **round tower**. The tower, with its elaborately carved Romanesque doorway 5m above the ground, is part of an ancient site that includes the ruins of a 15th-century church. The entire place has a certain magical quality, enhanced by a dearth of visitors.

DON'T MISS

ELECTRIC PICNIC

Ireland's answer to Glastonbury, though on a smaller scale, the annual **Electric Picnic** (www.electricpicnic.ie; Stradbally Hall; 3-day pass from €240; ⏲early Sep) is a three-day open-air arts and music festival. Known for its eclectic line-up, it attracts a large number of Irish and international performers. Tickets sell out months in advance and most people camp, creating one vast communal party. The festival takes place 10km southeast of Portlaoise.

It's attracted the likes of Björk, Bob Geldof, Sinead O'Connor, Massive Attack, Blondie, Florence + the Machine and Blur since it began in 2004.

Counties Meath, Louth, Cavan & Monaghan

Includes ➡

Best Places to Eat

- ➡ Courthouse Restaurant (p527)
- ➡ Eno (p517)
- ➡ Conyngham Arms (p501)
- ➡ Olde Post Inn (p521)

Best Places to Stay

- ➡ Castle Leslie (p526)
- ➡ Trim Castle Hotel (p508)
- ➡ Carlingford House (p519)
- ➡ Shirley Arms (p526)
- ➡ Bellinter House (p505)

Why Go?

The fertile fields of Counties Meath and Louth attracted Ireland's first settlers, making them the birthplace of Irish civilisation. Today, the counties are part of Dublin's commuter belt, but the earliest inhabitants' legacies endure at the mystical tombs at Brú na Bóinne and Loughcrew – which both predate the Egyptian pyramids – and at Tara, the seat of Ireland's high kings and gateway to the other world.

Following St Patrick's arrival, the faithful built abbeys, high crosses and round towers to protect their treasured manuscripts. Magnificent ruins recall a time when Ireland was known as the Land of Saints and Scholars.

To the northwest, Counties Cavan and Monaghan's undulating hills and fish-filled lakes are wilder and more remote. Outdoor activities abound in this little-visited corner of Ireland: boats cruise the Shannon–Erne Waterway, while walking trails take in the rugged scenery and expansive views of the Cuilcagh Mountains.

When to Go

➡ If sightseeing is at the top of your list, try to avoid November to March when many of the region's high-profile historic sites have reduced hours or are closed altogether.

➡ April is, unusually, the driest month of the year in this part of the country. The daffodils are in bloom, along with a riot of wildflowers, making it especially scenic (and less soggy) for walkers.

➡ Summer time is festive time: Drogheda hosts its annual Arts Festival in May, while Carlingford's party atmosphere peaks in August during its famous Oyster Festival. Horses race on Laytown's beach in late August and Monaghan town hosts its Harvest Blues Festival in early September.

COUNTY MEATH

POP 184,135 / AREA 2342 SQ KM

Meath's rich soil, laid down during the last ice age, drew settlers as early as 8000 BC. They worked their way up the banks of the River Boyne, transforming the landscape from forest to farmland. One of the five provinces of ancient Ireland, Meath was at the centre of Irish politics for centuries.

Today, Meath's high-yielding land and plentiful water supply make it a vital agriculture centre. Its proximity to Dublin brought about unchecked growth during the Celtic Tiger's peak, however, and the larger towns are surrounded with soulless housing estates with heavy traffic at commuter time.

For visitors, though, there are numerous must-see attractions here, including many tangible reminders of Meath's absorbing history.

Brú Na Bóinne

The vast Neolithic necropolis known as Brú na Bóinne (the Boyne Palace) is one of the most extraordinary sites in Europe. A thousand years older than Stonehenge, it's a powerful testament to the mind-boggling achievements of prehistoric humankind.

The complex was built to house the remains of those who were at the top of the social heap and its tombs were the largest artificial structures in Ireland until the construction of the Anglo-Norman castles 4000 years later. The area consists of many different sites; the three principal ones are Newgrange, Knowth and Dowth.

Over the centuries the tombs decayed, were covered by grass and trees, and were plundered by everybody from Vikings to Victorian treasure hunters, whose carved initials can be seen on the great stones of Newgrange. The countryside around the tombs is home to countless other ancient tumuli (burial mounds) and standing stones.

Sights

★Brú na Bóinne Visitor Centre INTERPRETATION CENTRE

(041-988 0300; www.heritageireland.ie; Donore; adult/child visitor centre €3/2, visitor centre & Newgrange €6/3, visitor centre & Knowth €5/3, all 3 sites €11/6; 9am-7pm Jun–mid-Sep, to 6.30pm May & mid–end Sep, to 5pm Nov-Jan, 9.30am-5.30pm Feb-Apr & Oct) Built in a spiral design echoing Newgrange, this superb interpretive centre houses interactive exhibits on prehistoric Ireland and its passage tombs. It has regional tourism info, an excellent cafeteria, plus a book and souvenir shop. Upstairs, a glassed-in observation mezzanine looks out over Newgrange.

All visits to Newgrange and/or Knowth depart from here.

★Newgrange HISTORIC SITE

(www.newgrange.com; adult/child incl visitor centre €6/3; 9am-7pm Jun–mid-Sep, to 6.30pm May & mid–end Sep, to 5pm Nov-Jan, 9.30am-5.30 Feb-Apr & Oct) A startling 80m in diameter and 13m high, Newgrange's white round stone walls, topped by a grass dome, look eerily futuristic. Underneath lies the finest Stone Age passage tomb in Ireland – one of the most

BRÚ NA BÓINNE TOP TIPS

- All visits to Brú na Bóinne start at the Brú na Bóinne Visitor Centre from where there's a shuttle bus to the tombs. If you turn up at either Newgrange or Knowth first, you'll be sent to the visitor centre, 4km from either site. Walking is discouraged, as the lanes are narrow and dangerous due to passing tour buses.
- Allow plenty of time: an hour for the visitor centre alone, two hours to include a trip to Newgrange or Knowth, and half a day to see all three.
- Dowth's tombs are closed to the public but you can freely visit the surrounding site.
- In summer, particularly at weekends, Brú na Bóinne gets very crowded; on peak days more than 2000 people can show up. As there are only 750 tour slots, you may not be guaranteed a visit to either of the passage tombs. Tickets are sold on a first-come, first-served basis (no advance booking). Arrive early in the morning or visit midweek and be prepared to wait. Alternatively, visiting as part of an organised tour (p499) guarantees a spot.
- Tours are primarily outdoors with no shelter so bring rain gear, just in case.

Counties Meath, Louth, Cavan & Monaghan Highlights

1. Explore evocative prehistoric remains at the ancient burial sites of **Brú na Bóinne** (p495).
2. Float above fascinating ruins and emerald-green fields on a **hot-air balloon flight** (p508) from Trim.
3. Follow in the footsteps of poet and author Patrick Kavanagh on the quiet roads of **Inniskeen** (p527).
4. Ride Europe's largest wooden inverted roller coaster and tour the potato-crisp factory at **Tayto Park** (p505).
5. Uncover the secrets of the massive earthworks, passage graves and Stone of Destiny at **Tara** (p504).
6. Paddle the waterways around **Butlersbridge** (p521) in a kayak or canoe.
7. Wander among megalithic stones and tombs at pristine **Cavan Burren Park** (p523), near Blacklion.

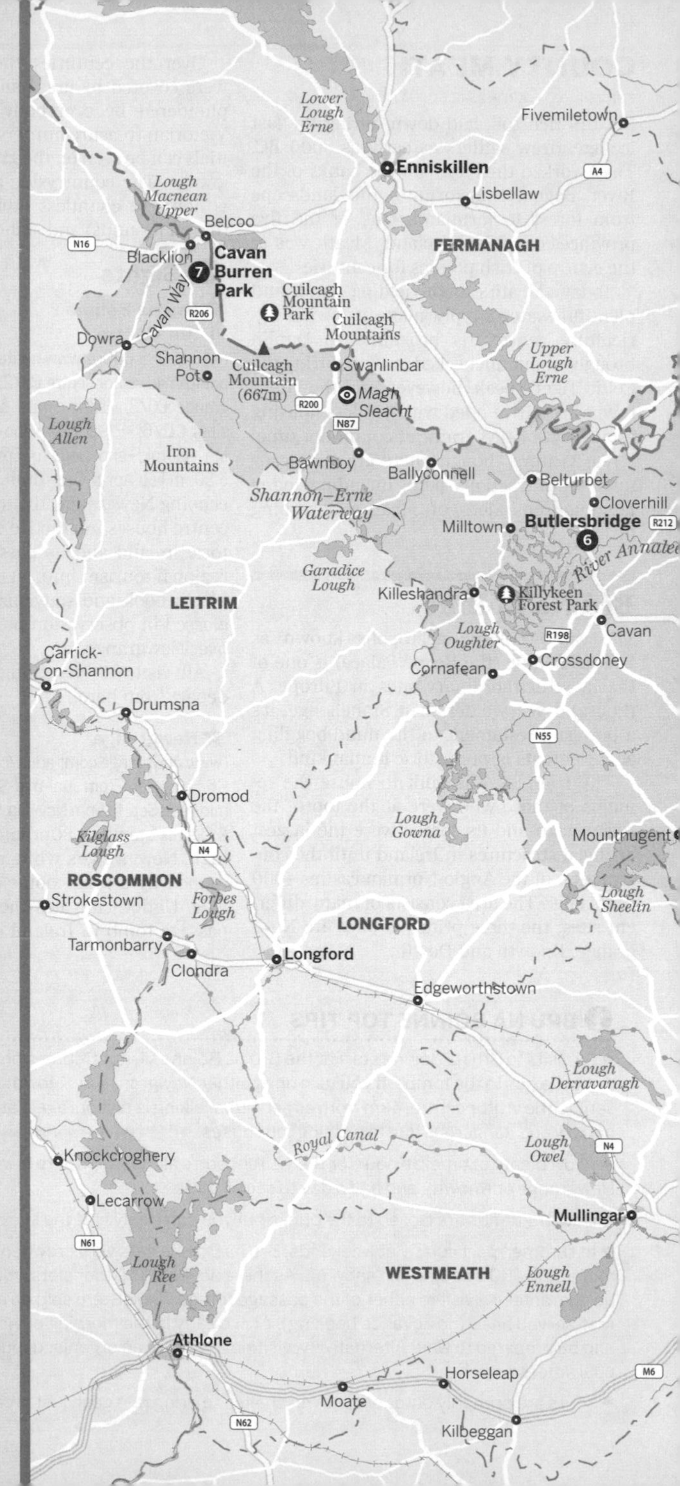

20 km
10 miles
Dromore
Augher
Aughnacloy
TYRONE
Ulster Canal
Banbridge
Armagh
Newry Canal
Loughbrickland
Emyvale
Castle Leslie
Glaslough
DOWN
Markethill
ARMAGH
NORTHERN IRELAND
Monaghan
Rossmore Forest Park
Ulster Canal
Newry
Clones
MONAGHAN
Mourne Mountains
Ballybay
Meigh
Warrenpoint
Rostrevor
Scotshouse
Castleblayney
Forkhill
Flagstaff Viewpoint
Omeath
Crossmaglen
Cootehill
Lough Egish
Slieve Foye (587m)
Carlingford Lough
Carlingford
Shantonagh
River Annagh
Cooley Peninsula
Inniskeen
Dundalk
Jenkinstown
Lough Sillan
Shercock
CAVAN
Carrickmacross
Ballagan Point
Dundalk Bay
River Glyde
Dún an Rí Forest Park
Bailieborough
Kingscourt
Castlebellingham
River Dee
Annagassan
Ardee
River Dee
Dunany Point
Ballyjamesduff
Dunleer
LOUTH
Virginia
Clogher Head
Lough Ramor
Clogherhead
Oldcastle
Monasterboice
Termonfeckin
Loughcrew Cairns
Old Mellifont Abbey
Battle of Boyne Site
Baltray
Irish Sea
Kells
Mornington
Brú na Bóinne
Drogheda
Loughcrew Gardens
Crossakeel
Slane
Dunmoe Castle
Teltown
Donore
Loughcrew Hills
Newgrange
Laytown
River Boyne
MEATH
Sonairte National Ecology Centre
Navan
Lough Lene
Duleek
Dunderry
Athboy
Balbriggan
Delvin
Rathcairn
Tara
Skyrne
Newtown
Hill of Tara
River Deel
Trim
Tayto Park
Kilmessan
DUBLIN
Dunsany Castle
Ratoath
Laracor
Dunshaughlin
Ashbourne
Fairyhouse Racecourse
Swords
Coralstown
Royal Canal
Kinnegad
Summerhill
Black Bull
Dublin Airport
River Boyne
Dunboyne
OFFALY
KILDARE
Dublin

remarkable prehistoric sites in Europe. Dating from around 3200 BC, it predates Egypt's pyramids by some six centuries.

The tomb's precise alignment with the sun at the time of the winter solstice suggests it was also designed to act as a calendar.

No one is quite sure of its original purpose, however – the most common theories are that it was a burial place for kings or a centre for ritual.

Newgrange's name derives from 'New Granary' (the tomb did in fact serve as a repository for wheat and grain at one stage), although a more popular belief is that it comes from the Irish for 'Cave of Gráinne', a reference to a popular Celtic myth. *The Pursuit of Diarmuid and Gráinne* tells of the illicit love between the woman betrothed to Fionn McCumhaill (or Finn McCool), leader of the Fianna, and Diarmuid, one of his most trusted lieutenants. When Diarmuid was fatally wounded, his body was brought to Newgrange by the god Aengus in a vain attempt to save him, and the despairing Gráinne followed him into the cave, where she remained long after he died. This suspiciously Arthurian tale (substitute Lancelot and Guinevere for Diarmuid and Gráinne) is undoubtedly a myth, but it's still a pretty good story. Newgrange also plays another role in Celtic mythology as the site where the hero Cúchulainn was conceived.

NEWGRANGE WINTER SOLSTICE

At 8.20am on the winter solstice (between 18 and 23 December), the rising sun's rays shine through the roof-box above the entrance of Newgrange, creep slowly down the long passage and illuminate the tomb chamber for 17 minutes. There is little doubt that this is one of the country's most memorable, even mystical, experiences.

There's a simulated winter sunrise for every group taken into the mound. To be in with a chance of witnessing the real thing on one of six mornings around the solstice, enter the free lottery that's drawn in late September; 50 names are drawn and each winner is allowed to take one guest. Fill out the form at the Brú na Bóinne Visitor Centre or email bruna boinne@opw.ie.

Over time, Newgrange, like Dowth and Knowth, deteriorated and at one stage was even used as a quarry. The site was extensively restored in 1962 and again in 1975.

A superbly carved kerbstone with double and triple spirals guards the tomb's main entrance, but the area has been reconstructed so that visitors don't have to clamber in over it. Above the entrance is a slit, or roof-box, which lets light in. Another beautifully decorated kerbstone stands at the exact opposite side of the mound. Some experts say that a ring of standing stones encircled the mound, forming a great circle about 100m in diameter, but only 12 of these stones remain, with traces of others below ground level.

Holding the whole structure together are the 97 boulders of the kerb ring, designed to stop the mound from collapsing outwards. Eleven of these are decorated with motifs similar to those on the main entrance stone, although only three have extensive carvings.

The white quartzite that encases the tomb was originally obtained from Wicklow, 70km south – in an age before horse and wheel, it was transported by sea and then up the River Boyne. More than 200,000 tonnes of earth and stone also went into the mound.

You can walk down the narrow 19m passage, lined with 43 stone uprights (some of them engraved), which leads into the tomb chamber about one third of the way into the colossal mound. The chamber has three recesses, and in these are large basin stones that held cremated human bones. As well as the remains, the basins would have held funeral offerings of beads and pendants, but these were stolen long before the archaeologists arrived.

Above, the massive stones support a 6m-high corbel-vaulted roof. A complex drainage system means that not a drop of water has penetrated the interior in 40 centuries.

★Knowth HISTORIC SITE

(adult/child incl visitor centre €5/3; ⏲9am-7pm Jun–mid-Sep, to 6.30pm May & mid–end Sep, to 5pm Nov-Jan, 9.30am-5.30 Feb-Apr & Oct) Northwest of Newgrange, the burial mound of Knowth was built around the same time. It has the greatest collection of passage-grave art ever uncovered in Western Europe, and has been under intermittent excavation since 1962 (you may see archaeologists at work when you visit).

Early excavations soon cleared a passage leading to the central chamber which, at

34m, is much longer than the one at Newgrange. In 1968 a 40m passage was unearthed on the opposite side of the mound.

Also in the mound are the remains of six early-Christian souterrains (underground chambers) built into the side. Some 300 carved slabs and 17 satellite graves surround the main mound.

Human activity at Knowth continued for thousands of years after its construction, which accounts for the site's complexity. The Beaker folk, so called because they buried their dead with drinking vessels, occupied the site in the Early Bronze Age (c 1800 BC), as did the Celts in the Iron Age (c 500 BC). Remnants of bronze and iron workings from these periods have been discovered. Around AD 800 to 900, it was turned into a *ráth* (earthen ring fort), a stronghold of the very powerful O'Neill clan. In 965 it was the seat of Cormac MacMaelmithic, later Ireland's high king for nine years, and in the 12th century the Normans built a motte and bailey (a raised mound with a walled keep) here. The site was finally abandoned around 1400.

Dowth HISTORIC SITE

(24hr) FREE The circular mound at Dowth is similar in size to Newgrange – about 63m in diameter – but is slightly taller at 14m high. Due to safety issues, Dowth's tombs are closed to visitors, though you can visit the mound (and its resident grazing sheep) from the L1607 road between Newgrange and Drogheda.

North of the tumulus are the ruins of **Dowth Castle** and **Dowth House**.

Dowth has two entrance passages leading to separate chambers (both sealed), and a 24m early-Christian underground passage at either end, which connect with the western passage. This 8m-long passage leads into a small cruciform chamber, in which a recess acts as an entrance to an additional series of small compartments, a feature unique to Dowth. To the southwest is the entrance to a shorter passage and smaller chamber.

It has suffered badly at the hands of everyone from road builders and treasure hunters to amateur archaeologists, who scooped out the centre of the tumulus in the 19th century. For a time, Dowth even had a tearoom ignobly perched on its summit.

Tours

Brú na Bóinne is one of the most popular tourist attractions in Ireland, and there are plenty of organised tours. Most depart from Dublin.

HERITAGE CARD

If you're planning to visit several archaeological and historic sites, consider investing in a **Heritage Card** (adult/child €25/10), valid for one year and available for purchase at the Battle of the Boyne (p500) ticket office, as well as other participating sites throughout the country. For more information, contact Heritage Ireland (www.heritageireland.ie).

★ Mary Gibbons Tours GUIDED TOUR

(086 355 1355; http://newgrangetours.com; tour per adult/child €35/30) Tours depart from numerous Dublin hotels, beginning at 9.30am Monday to Friday, and 7.50am Saturday and Sunday, and take in the whole of the Boyne Valley including Newgrange and the Hill of Tara. The expert guides offer a fascinating insight into Celtic and pre-Celtic life in Ireland. No credit cards; pay cash on the bus.

Bus Éireann Boyne Valley Day Tours BUS TOUR

(www.buseireann.ie; adult/child €28/19; departs 10am Thu & Sat May-Sep) Bus Éireann organises Newgrange and the Boyne Valley day tours from Dublin's Busáras bus station, visiting either the Hill of Tara or Mellifont Abbey en route, and returning at 5.45pm. Check the website for schedules.

Sleeping

Newgrange Lodge HOSTEL, HOTEL €

(041-988 2478; www.newgrangelodge.com; campsites per tent €10, dm/s/d/f from €21/36/53/70; reception 8am-midnight;) Footsteps east of the Brú na Bóinne Visitor Centre, this converted farmhouse has good-value rooms ranging from dorms with four to 10 beds to hotel-standard doubles with private bathrooms. Superb facilities include a self-catering kitchen, two outdoor patios, a welcoming dining room/lounge with open fire, board games and books, plus free bikes. Rates include continental breakfast (with scrumptious homemade scones).

Getting There & Away

Bus Éireann links the Brú na Bóinne Visitor Centre with Drogheda's bus station (one way/return €4.10/7.60, 25 minutes, two daily), with connections to Dublin.

The Battle of Boyne Site

More than 60,000 soldiers of the armies of King James II and King William III fought in 1690 on this patch of farmland on the border of Counties Meath and Louth. William ultimately prevailed and James sailed off to France.

The **battle site** (www.battleoftheboyne.ie; adult/child €4/2; ⏲10am-5pm May-Sep, 9.30am-4.30pm Mar & Apr, 9am-4pm Oct-Feb) has an informative visitor centre and parkland walks. It's 3km north of Donore off the N51 and 3.5km west of Drogheda along Rathmullan Rd (follow the river). Buses run to/from Drogheda (€4.10, 15 minutes, two daily).

At the visitor centre you can watch a short show about the battle, see original and replica weaponry of the time and explore a laser battlefield model. Self-guided walks through the parkland and battle site allow time to ponder the events that saw Protestant interests remain in Ireland. Costumed reenactments take place in summer.

Laytown

Laytown is famed as the site of the only official horse race on the beach in Europe. It's a sleepy seaside village for the rest of the year.

Activities

Sonairte ECOLOGY CENTRE
(☎041-982 7572; www.sonairte.ie; the Ninch; garden free, individual activities adult/child €3/1; ⏲10.30am-5pm Wed-Sun Feb-Dec; 👪) Ireland's National Ecology Centre, 750m west of Laytown train station, offers guided tours of its walled organic gardens and 200-year-old orchard, a nature trail and river walk, and courses in everything from beekeeping to wild-food foraging and horticulture. Fill up at its organic cafe or stock up at its shop. A farmers market sets up some Sundays from noon to 4pm.

Festivals & Events

Laytown Races HORSE RACING
(www.laytownstrandraces.ie) In late Aug or early Sep bookies, punters and jockeys descend on Laytown for races that have been held here for more than 140 years. For one late-summer's day, Laytown's 3km of golden sands are transformed into a racecourse, attracting a diverse crowd of locals, celebrities and die-hard racing fans.

Getting There & Away

Irish Rail (Iarnród Éireann; www.irishrail.ie) runs between Dublin and Laytown every half-hour (€12.50, 50 minutes).

Slane

POP 1349

Slane's 18th-century stone houses and cottages slink down a steep hill to the River Boyne, which glides beneath a narrow bridge. Situated 6km west of Brú na Bóinne, the town grew up around the enormous castle after which it was named. At the main crossroads four identical houses face each other: local lore has it that they were built for four sisters who had taken an intense dislike to one another and kept a beady-eyed watch from their individual residences.

Sights

Slane Castle CASTLE
(☎041-982 0643; www.slanecastle.ie; guided tour adult/child €7/5, whiskey-tasting & castle tour €17, minimum 12 people; ⏲guided tour by appointment noon-5pm Sun-Thu late May-Aug) Still the private residence of Henry Conyngham, Earl of Mountcharles, Slane Castle, 1km west of the town centre, is best known for its outdoor **concerts** with massive rock-royalty names: Bon Jovi, Eminem, U2, the Rolling Stones, Madonna and Oasis have all performed over the years.

Guided tours include the neo-Gothic Ballroom, completed in 1821, and the Kings Room. Whiskey-tasting tours include tastings of Slane Castle Irish Whiskey; an on-site craft-whiskey distillery is scheduled for completion in 2016.

Built in the Gothic-revival style by James Wyatt in 1785, the building was later altered by Francis Johnson for George IV's visits to Lady Conyngham, allegedly his mistress. It's said the road between Dublin and Slane was built especially straight and smooth to speed up the smitten king's journeys. In 1991 the castle was gutted by a fire, whereupon it was discovered that the earl was under-insured. A major fundraising drive, of which the summer concerts were a part, led to a painstaking restoration.

Hill of Slane HISTORIC SITE
About 1km north of Slane village is the Hill of Slane, a fairly plain-looking mound that stands out only for its association with a

thick slice of Celto-Christian mythology. According to legend, St Patrick lit a paschal (Easter) fire here in 433 to proclaim Christianity throughout the land.

So the story goes, Patrick's paschal fire infuriated Laoghaire, the pagan high king of Ireland, who had expressly ordered that no fire be lit within sight of the Hill of Tara. He was restrained by his far-sighted druids, who warned that 'the man who had kindled the flame would surpass kings and princes'. Laoghaire went to meet Patrick, and all but one of the king's attendants, a man called Erc, greeted Patrick with scorn.

Undeterred, Patrick plucked a shamrock from the ground, using its three leaves to explain the paradox of the Holy Trinity: the union of the Father, the Son and the Holy Spirit in one. Laoghaire wasn't convinced, but he agreed to let Patrick continue his missionary work. Patrick's success that day, apart from keeping his own life and giving Ireland one of its enduring national symbols, was good old Erc, who was baptised and later became the first bishop of Slane. To this day, the local parish priest lights a fire here on Holy Saturday.

The Hill of Slane originally had a church associated with St Erc and, later, a round tower and monastery, but only an outline of the foundations remains. You can also see the remains of a ruined church and tower that were once part of an early-16th-century Franciscan friary.

On a clear day, climb the evocative ancient stone steps of the tower to enjoy magnificent views of the Hill of Tara and the Boyne Valley, and (it's said) seven Irish counties.

Ledwidge Museum MUSEUM
(☎041-982 4544; www.francisledwidge.com; Janesville; adult/child €3/1; ⏲10am-5pm early Mar-Oct, to 3.30pm Nov–early Mar) This quaint cottage, 1km east of Slane on the N51, was the birthplace of poet Francis Ledwidge (1887–1917). A keen political activist, Ledwidge was thwarted in his efforts to set up a local Gaelic League branch, but found an outlet in verse. He died on the battlefield at Ypres, having survived Gallipoli and Serbia.

The museum provides an insight into Ledwidge's works, and the cottage itself is a humbling example of how farm labourers lived in the 19th century.

Sleeping & Eating

Slane Farm Hostel HOSTEL €
(☎041-982 4390; www.slanefarmhostel.ie; Harlinstown House, Navan Rd; campsites per person incl tent €10, dm/s/d/self-catering terraced cottage €20/25/50/90; @ 🛜 👪) These former stables, built by the Marquis of Conyngham in the 18th century, have been converted into a wonderful hostel that's part of a working dairy farm. Common areas include a games room and kitchen, with free-range eggs and a vegetable plot for guests to use. Free bikes are available. It's 2.5km west of Slane.

★**Conyngham Arms** BOUTIQUE HOTEL €€
(☎041-988 4444; www.conynghamarms.ie; Main St; s/d/f from €65/89/109; 🛜) Exquisitely restored in 2012, this 18th-century stone coaching inn has 15 airy rooms decorated with French country-style furnishings (some with canopied, four-poster beds), a charming, rose-filled garden with a fountain at its centre, an outstanding restaurant, plus fabulous breakfasts such as free-range scrambled eggs with Annagassan smoked salmon. Staff are welcoming and professional in equal measure.

Slane Bake BAKERY €
(www.slanebake.com; Main St; dishes €1-5; ⏲8am-5pm Tue-Sun) Chocolate Guinness cake, red velvet cake, apple tarts and salted peanut butter and chocolate cupcakes are among the goodies in store at this tantalising bakery, along with classic Irish soda bread.

George's Patisserie BAKERY, CAFE €
(http://georgespatisserie.com; Chapel St; dishes €5.50-9.50; ⏲7am-6pm Tue-Sun) Delicious picnic fare at this sweet little spot includes scones, cakes and specialities such as mini-apple-crumble tarts and wonderful bread. Light snacks such as quiches and sandwiches are also available to take away or eat at the on-site cafe, with walls papered in old newspapers (mainly the *Antique Trade Gazette*).

★**Conyngham Arms** MODERN IRISH €€
(☎041-988 4444; www.conynghamarms.ie; Main St; mains €10-24; ⏲kitchen 10am-8pm Mon-Thu, 10am-9pm Fri, 9am-9pm Sat & Sun; 👪) Some of the county's finest cooking is at the back of the beautiful Conyngham Arms hotel. Starters such as mozzarella, tomato and blood-orange salad with white-truffle vinaigrette are followed by amazing mains – Meath-brewed Brú ale and pork sausages with black-pudding mash, roast salmon with

1. Muiredach's Cross (p516)
One of the high crosses of Monasterboice, Muiredach's Cross is a superb example of Celtic art.

2. Trim Castle (p506)
Well-preserved Trim Castle has hardly been modified since it was finished in 1200.

3. Coastal Scenery
County Louth's coastal scenery is best experienced via the Coast Road (p514).

4. Brú na Bóinne (p495)
Explore neolithic burial sites, including Knowth (p498).

3

DESIGN PICS/PETER MCCABE/GETTY IMAGES ©

nutmeg-infused creamed spinach, or baked Irish goat's cheese with apple.

Drinking & Nightlife

Boyles PUB
(www.boylesofslane.com; Main St; noon-11.30pm Mon-Thu, to 12.30am Fri & Sat, to 11pm Sun;) The owner of this pub with its fire-engine-red facade is musician Andrew Cassidy, who hosts a knock-out line-up of live gigs and trad-music sessions. Cash only.

Information

Tourist Office (041-982 4000; www.visitslane.ie; The Hub, 2 Main St; 9.30am-5pm Mon-Sat, noon-4pm Sun)

Getting There & Away

Bus Éireann has a direct service to Drogheda (€5.20, 30 minutes, three to seven daily). Services to Dublin (€16.50, 1¾ hours) require a change in Meath's main hub, the working town of Navan (€4.80, 25 minutes).

Tara

The **Hill of Tara** is Ireland's most sacred stretch of turf, occupying a place at the heart of Irish history, legend and folklore. It was the home of the mystical druids, the priest-rulers of ancient Ireland, who practised their particular form of Celtic paganism under the watchful gaze of the all-powerful goddess Maeve (Medbh). Later it was the ceremonial capital of the high kings, all 142 of them, who ruled until the arrival of Christianity in the 5th century. It is also one of the most important ancient sites in Europe, with a Stone Age passage tomb and prehistoric burial mounds that date back some 5000 years.

Although little remains other than humps and mounds on the hill (named from ancient texts), its historic and folkloric significance is immense.

History

Mythology and religion intertwine with historical facts here.

The Celts believed that Tara was the sacred dwelling place of the gods and the gateway to the other world. The passage grave was thought to be the final resting place of the Tuatha dé Danann, the mythical fairy folk. They were real enough, but instead of pixies and brownies, they were earlier Stone Age arrivals on the island.

As the Celtic political landscape began to evolve, the druids' power was usurped by warlike chieftains who took kingly titles; there was no sense of a united Ireland, so at any given time there were countless *rí tuaithe* (petty kings) controlling many small areas. The king who ruled Tara, though, was generally considered the big shot, the high king, even though his direct rule didn't extend too far beyond the provincial border.

The most important event in Tara's calendar was the three-day harvest *feis* (festival) that took place at Samhain, a precursor to modern Halloween. During the festival, the high king pulled out all the stops: grievances were heard, laws passed and disputes settled amid a bacchanalia of eating, drinking and partying.

When the early Christians hit town in the 5th century, they targeted Tara straight away. The arrival of Christianity marked the beginning of the end for Celtic pagan civilisation, and the high kings began to desert Tara, though the kings of Leinster continued to be based here until the 11th century.

In August 1843, Tara saw one of the greatest crowds ever to gather in Ireland. Daniel O'Connell, leader of the opposition to union with Great Britain, held one of his galvanising rallies at Tara, and up to 750,000 people came to hear him speak.

Sights

Rath of the Synods HISTORIC SITE
Tara's Protestant church grounds and graveyard spill onto the remains of this triple-ringed fort where some of St Patrick's early synods (meetings) supposedly took place. Excavations suggest the enclosure was used between AD 200 and 400 for burials, rituals and dwellings – originally the ring fort would have contained wooden houses surrounded by timber palisades.

Archaeologists have uncovered Roman glass, shards of pottery and seals, showing links with the Roman Empire even though the Romans never extended their power to Ireland.

Royal Enclosure HISTORIC SITE
South of Tara's church, the Royal Enclosure is a large oval Iron Age hill fort, 315m in diameter and surrounded by a bank and ditch cut through solid rock under the soil. Inside are several smaller earthworks: the **Mound of the Hostages** (closed to the public); **Royal Seat**, a ring fort with a house

site; and **Cormac's House**, a barrow (burial mound) in the side of the circular bank, which is topped by the **Stone of Destiny**.

The Mound of the Hostages, a bump in the northern corner of the enclosure, is the most ancient known part of Tara. A treasure trove of artefacts was unearthed, including some ancient Mediterranean beads of amber and faience (glazed pottery). More than 35 Bronze Age burials were found here, as well as extensive cremated remains from the Stone Age.

There are superb views of the surrounding Boyne and Blackwater Valleys from the Royal Seat and Cormac's House.

Atop Cormac's House is the phallic Stone of Destiny (originally located near the Mound of the Hostages), which represents the joining of the gods of the earth and the heavens. It's said to be the inauguration stone of the high kings, although alternative sources suggest that the actual coronation stone was the Stone of Scone, which was removed to Edinburgh, Scotland, and used to crown British kings. The would-be king stood on top of the Stone of Destiny and, if the stone let out three roars, he was crowned. The mass grave of 37 men who died in a skirmish on Tara during the 1798 Rising is next to the stone.

Enclosure of King Laoghaire HISTORIC SITE

South of Tara's Royal Enclosure (p504) is this large but worn ring fort where the king, a contemporary of St Patrick, is said to be buried standing upright and dressed in his armour.

Banquet Hall HISTORIC SITE

North of the churchyard is Tara's most unusual feature, a rectangular earthwork measuring 230m by 27m along a north–south axis. Tradition holds that it was built to cater for thousands of guests during feasts.

Its orientation suggests that it was a sunken entrance to Tara, leading directly to the Royal Enclosure. More recent research, however, has uncovered graves within the compound, and it's possible that the banks are in fact the burial sites of some of the kings of Tara.

Gráinne's Fort HISTORIC SITE

Gráinne was the daughter of King Cormac, the most lauded of all high kings. Betrothed to Fionn McCumhaill (Finn McCool), she eloped with Diarmuid, one of the king's warriors, on her wedding night. This became the subject of the epic *The Pursuit of Diarmuid and Gráinne*. Gráinne's Fort and the northern and southern **Sloping Trenches** to the northwest are burial mounds.

WORTH A TRIP

THRILLS & SPILLS

An Irish icon, **Tayto Park** (☎01-835 1999; www.taytocrisps.ie; Kilbrew, Ashbourne; admission €14, 1-day ride pass €15; ⌚9.30am-7pm Jul & Aug, 10am-6pm late Mar–Jun, Sat & Sun Sep, to 5pm Sat & Sun Oct & Nov, noon-5pm Fri, 10am-5pm Sat & Sun Dec, closed Jan & Feb) has been producing much-loved potato crisps since 1954. Alongside the factory, its amusement park has a zoo, rock climbing, zipline and fantastic playground. A slew of whiz-bang new additions include a wooden inverted roller coaster (Europe's largest), 5-D cinema, high-speed spinning Rotator and stomach-churning Air Race ride.

Admission includes a self-guided crisp-factory tour and zoo and playground entry; the wrist-band day pass is the most economical option for the rides.

It's just off the M2 motorway.

Sleeping & Eating

★**Bellinter House** HISTORIC HOTEL €€€

(☎046-903 0900; www.bellinterhouse.com; Bellinter; d from €120; 📶) Dating from the 18th century, grande dame Bellinter House, 5km northwest of the Hill of Tara (signposted off the R147), is a haven of crackling open fires and rich artworks. There are 34 antique-furnished rooms in the main house, as well as 16 period rooms in the east and west pavilions and five duplexes in the former stables.

Soak in the on-site spa's outdoor hot tubs and dine on top-class fare at its restaurant **Eden** (2-/3-course menu €38/43), which has its own bakery.

McGuires Coffee Shop CAFE €

(dishes €8-12; ⌚9.30am-5.30pm; 📶👪) If a walk on the Hill of Tara has worked up an appetite, this restaurant-cafe and souvenir shop at the base can restore you with wholesome fare such as wild-mushroom and pea risotto, goat's-cheese salad, smoked-salmon pasta and home-baked sweet treats such as rhubarb pie.

Shopping

Old Tara Book Shop BOOKS
(10am-5pm Tue, Thu, Sat & Sun) At the base of the Hill of Tara, this tiny, jumbled second-hand bookshop is run by Michael Slavin, who has authored an informative little book about the site, *The Tara Walk* (€3) as well as a weightier tome, *The Book of Tara* (€29). Hours can vary.

Information

Entrance to Tara is free and the site is always open. There are good explanatory panels by the entrance. Unfortunately, many people let their dogs roam free on the hill – watch your step!

Tara Visitor Centre (046-902 5903; www.heritageireland.ie; adult/child €3/1; 10am-6pm mid-May–mid-Sep) A former Protestant church (with a window by acclaimed stained-glass artist, the late Evie Hone) is home to Tara's visitor centre, which screens a 20-minute audiovisual presentation about the site.

Getting There & Away

Tara is 10km southeast of Navan, off the Dublin–Cavan road (R147).

Regular Bus Éireann services link Dublin to within 1km of the site (€11, one hour, hourly). Ask the driver to drop you off at the Tara Cross, where you take a left turn off the main road.

Bus Éireann also organises coach trips to Tara as part of some (not all) Boyne Valley Day Tours (p499).

Dunsany Castle

You can see how the other 1% lives at **Dunsany Castle** (046-902 5169; www.dunsany.com; Dunsany; adult/child €15/10; by appointment 10am-4pm Mon-Sat Jun-Aug), 5km south of Tara on the Dunshaughlin–Kilmessan road. The residence of the lords of Dunsany, it's one of the oldest continually inhabited buildings in Ireland. Construction started in the 12th century, with major alterations taking place in the 18th and 19th centuries. Maintenance and restoration are ongoing.

Tours lasting almost two hours offer a fascinating insight into the family's and castle's history, and impressive private art collection.

The castle houses many treasures related to important figures in Irish history, such as Oliver Plunkett and Patrick Sarsfield, leader of the Irish Jacobite forces at the siege of Limerick in 1691.

You can also buy **Dunsany Home Collection** homewares here: locally made table linen and accessories, as well as various articles designed by the 20th Lord Dunsany (Edward Carlos Plunkett; 1939–2011) who was an acclaimed international designer and artist, famed for his geometrical abstractions and portraits.

Trim

POP 8268

Dominated by its mighty castle, the quiet town of Trim was an important settlement in medieval times. Five city gates surrounded a busy jumble of streets, and as many as seven monasteries were established in the immediate area.

It's hard to imagine nowadays, but a measure of Trim's importance was that Elizabeth I considered building Trinity College here. One student who did study in Trim was Dublin-born Arthur Wellesley, the Duke of Wellington, who studied at Talbot Castle and St Mary's Abbey.

Today, Trim's history is everywhere, with atmospheric ruins and streets lined with tiny workers' cottages.

Sights

★**Trim Castle** CASTLE
(King John's Castle; www.heritageireland.ie; adult/child incl tour €4/2; 10am-6pm daily mid-Mar–Oct, 9am-5pm Sat & Sun Nov–mid-Mar) Proof of Trim's medieval importance, this remarkably preserved edifice was Ireland's largest Anglo-Norman fortification. Hugh de Lacy founded Trim Castle in 1173, but it was destroyed by Ruaidrí Ua Conchobair, Ireland's last high king, within a year. The building you see today was begun around 1200 and has hardly been modified since.

Entertaining guided tours involve climbing narrow, steep stairs, so aren't suitable for the very young or anyone with restricted mobility. Self-guided tours are also available.

Throughout Anglo-Norman times the castle occupied a strategic position on the western edge of the Pale, the area where the Anglo-Normans ruled supreme; beyond Trim was the volatile country where Irish chieftains and lords fought with their Norman rivals and vied for position, power and terrain. By the 16th century, the castle had begun to fall into decline and in 1649, when the town was taken by Cromwellian forces, it was severely damaged.

Trim

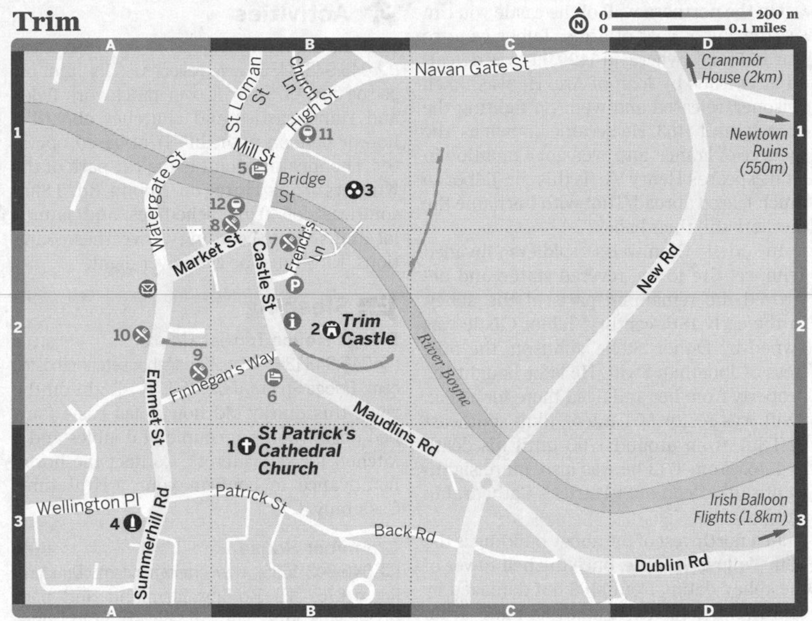

The castle's grassy two-hectare enclosure is dominated by a massive stone keep, 25m tall and mounted on a Norman motte. Inside are three levels, the lowest divided by a central wall. Just outside the central keep are the remains of an earlier wall.

The principal outer-curtain wall, 450m long and for the most part still standing, dates from around 1250 and includes eight towers and a gatehouse. It also has a number of sally gates from which defenders could exit to confront the enemy. The finest stretch of the outer wall runs from the River Boyne through Dublin Gate to Castle St.

★St Patrick's Cathedral Church CATHEDRAL
(Lornan St; ⌚8.30am-5pm) FREE That huge steeple you see belongs to St Patrick's Cathedral Church, parts of which dates to the 15th century, although it wasn't granted cathedral status until 1955. Take a look at the beautiful stained-glass windows, including one showing St Patrick preaching on the Hill of Tara. Hours can vary depending on religious services and events.

St Mary's Abbey & Talbot Castle RUINS
Across the River Boyne from Trim Castle are the ruins of the 12th-century Augustinian **St Mary's Abbey**, rebuilt after a fire in 1368 and once home to a wooden statue of Our Lady of Trim, revered by the faithful for its miraculous powers.

In 1415 part of the abbey was converted into a manor house by Sir John Talbot, then viceroy of Ireland; it came to be known as **Talbot Castle**.

Trim

Top Sights
1 St Patrick's Cathedral Church B3
2 Trim Castle B2

Sights
3 St Mary's Abbey & Talbot Castle............B1
4 Wellington Column A3

Sleeping
5 Bridge House Tourist Hostel............B1
6 Trim Castle Hotel............B2

Eating
7 Franzini's............B2
8 Harvest Home Bakery............B1
9 StockHouse............A2
10 The Kitchen............A2

Drinking & Nightlife
11 James Griffin............B1
12 Sally Rogers............B1

On the northern wall of the castle you can see the Talbot coat of arms. Talbot went to war in France where, in 1429, he was defeated at Orleans by Joan of Arc. He was taken prisoner, released and went on fighting the French until 1453. He became known as 'the scourge of France' and even got a mention in Shakespeare's Henry VI: 'Is this the Talbot so much feared abroad/That with his name the mothers still their babes?'

In 1649 Cromwell's soldiers invaded Trim, set fire to the revered statue and destroyed the remaining parts of the abbey. In the early 18th century, Talbot Castle was owned by Esther 'Stella' Johnson, the mistress of Jonathan Swift. He later bought the property from her and lived there for a year. Swift was rector of Laracor, 3km southeast of Trim, from around 1700 until his death in 1745. From 1713 he was also, more significantly, the Dean of St Patrick's Cathedral in Dublin.

Just northwest of the abbey building is the 40m **Yellow Steeple**, once the bell tower of the abbey, dating from 1368 but damaged by Cromwell's soldiers. It takes its name from the colour of the stonework at dusk.

East of the abbey ruins is part of the 14th-century town wall, including the **Sheep Gate**, the lone survivor of the town's original five gates. It used to be closed daily between 9pm and 4am, and a toll was charged for sheep entering to be sold at market.

Newtown Ruins RUINS
About 1.5km east of town on Lackanash Rd are the ruins of the former **Parish Church of Newtown Clonbun**, the **Cathedral of Sts Peter & Paul** and 18th-century **Newtown Abbey**.

Southeast across the river is the **Crutched Friary**, with ruins of a keep, and traces of a watchtower and other buildings from a hospital set up after the Crusades by the Knights of St John of Jerusalem. Adjacent **St Peter's Bridge** is one of Ireland's oldest.

Wellington Column MONUMENT
(cnr Summerhill Rd & Wellington Pl) The local burghers dedicated this column to Arthur Wellesley, the first Duke of Wellington, in recognition of his impressive career: after defeating Napoleon at the Battle of Waterloo, the Iron Duke went on to become prime minister of Great Britain and in 1829 passed the Catholic Emancipation Act, repealing the last of the repressive penal laws.

Activities

Irish Balloon Flights BALLOONING
(☎046-948 3436; www.balloons.ie; 1hr flight per person from €175) Drift over patchwork fields and ruins, castles and churches aboard a hot-air balloon with this Trim-based operator. The meeting point is the car park of the **Knightsbrook Hotel** on Dublin Rd, 1.8km southeast of Trim; schedules and launch locations vary according to weather conditions. Kids must be aged over eight.

Sleeping

Bridge House Tourist Hostel HOSTEL €
(☎046-943 1848; http://bridgehousetouristhostel.com; Bridge St; dm/d €20/50; wi-fi) Right on the river, this quirky old house has basic four-bed dorm rooms, a couple of doubles and a kitchen for self-caterers. Contact the hostel in advance to confirm your arrival time. Cash only.

Crannmór House B&B €
(☎046-943 1635; www.crannmor.com; Dunderry Rd; d €76; wi-fi) Rolling farmland and paddocks surround this vine-covered old house about 2km along the road to Dunderry. Bright rooms and traditional hospitality are on offer, and if you're interested in angling, the owner is an experienced *ghillie* (fishing guide).

★**Trim Castle Hotel** HOTEL €€
(☎046-948 3000; www.trimcastlehotel.com; Castle St; d/f from €85/135; @ wi-fi family) Acres of glossy marble in the foyer set the scene at this contemporary hotel opposite Trim Castle. Some of its stylish rooms come with balconies (try for sprawling corner room 225). Its rooftop sun terrace overlooks Trim Castle, and dining – whether at breakfast, the bar's carvery, or upmarket Jules Restaurant (Friday and Saturday evenings only) – is top-notch.

Eating

Kitchen CAFE €
(Emmet St; dishes €6-11; ⌚9am-7pm Mon-Sat, 10am-3pm Sun; family) A fresh addition to Trim's daytime dining scene, Kitchen cooks up homemade lasagne, filled baked potatoes, tortilla wraps and other light bites in exposed brick surrounds, and brews smooth Segafredo coffee. Breakfast is available until noon; you can also get picnic fare to take away.

Harvest Home Bakery BAKERY, CAFE €
(18 Market St; dishes €3-7.50; ⌚9am-6pm Mon-Sat) This little gem sells delicious breads,

cakes, pies and biscuits (including sugar- and gluten-free options), as well as homemade soups and full-to-bursting sandwiches. There are outside tables in fine weather.

StockHouse STEAK €€
(☎046-943 7388; www.stockhouserestaurant.ie; Finnegan's Way, Emmet House; mains €15-26; ⏲11.30am-3pm & 5-9pm Mon-Thu, to 10pm Fri, 5-10pm Sat, noon-8.30pm Sun) Cooked-to-order dry-aged steaks from local abattoir-butcher Coogan's are the stock-in-trade of this always-packed restaurant, but noncarnivores can choose from fish and vegetarian dishes such as pastas.

Franzini's INTERNATIONAL €€
(☎046-943 1002; French's Lane; pizzas €12.50-15, mains €14-25; ⏲5-10pm Mon-Sat, 1-5pm Sun; 👪) The eclectic menu at this buzzing, laid-back local favourite spans seafood pasta to teriyaki chicken with noodles and fajitas.

Drinking & Nightlife

In town and throughout the country, look out for Brú Brewery's craft beers, brewed in Trim.

James Griffin PUB
(www.jamesgriffinpub.ie; High St; ⏲3-11.30pm Mon-Fri, 1pm-12.30am Sat, 1-11pm Sun; 📶) This award-winning historic pub dates from 1904 and offers trad-music sessions (Monday and Thursday), live bands (Friday), and DJs (Saturday). The interior has retained its traditional-Irish-pub atmosphere and visitors are made to feel very welcome.

Sally Rogers PUB
(Bridge St; ⏲7pm-late) Pop in for a drink on the spacious riverfront terrace. It gets crammed at weekends when there's live music.

Information

In the Town Hall, the **Tourist Office** (☎046-943 7227; www.meath.ie; Castle St; ⏲9.30am-5.30pm Mon-Sat, 1-5pm Sun) has a handy tourist-trail map, a cafe and a genealogy centre.

Getting There & Around

Bus Éireann links Trim with Dublin (€13, one hour, up to 11 daily).

Kells

POP 5888

The working market town of Kells is best known for the magnificent illuminated manuscript that bears its name, and which visitors queue to see at Trinity College in Dublin. Although the great book wasn't created here, it was kept in Kells, one of the leading monasteries in the country, from the end of the 9th century until 1541, when it was removed by the Church.

Remnants of the once-great monastic site include some interesting high crosses and a 1000-year-old round tower.

Sights

Market Cross MONUMENT
(Headfort Pl) Until 1996 the Market Cross had stood for centuries in Cross St, at the heart of the town centre. Besides inviting the pious admiration of the faithful, the cross was used as a gallows in the aftermath of the 1798 Rising; the British garrison hanged rebels from the crosspiece, one on each arm so the cross wouldn't fall over.

St Columba CHURCH
(⏲10am-1pm & 2-5pm Mon-Sat Jun-Aug) The Protestant church of St Columba, west of Kells' town centre, has a 30m-high 10th-century **round tower** on the southern side. It's without its conical roof, but is known to date back at least as far as 1076, when the high king of Tara was murdered in its confined apartments.

In the churchyard are four 9th-century **high crosses** in various states of repair.

The **West Cross**, at the far end, is the stump of a decorated shaft, which has scenes of the baptism of Jesus, the Fall of Adam and Eve, and the Judgement of Solomon on the eastern face, and Noah's ark on the western face.

All that's left of the **North Cross** is the bowl-shaped base stone.

Near the round tower is the best preserved of the crosses, the **Cross of Patrick & Columba**, with its semilegible inscription, 'Patrici et Columbae Crux', on the eastern face of the base.

The other surviving cross is the unfinished **East Cross**, with a carving of the Crucifixion and a group of four figures on the right arm.

St Colmcille's House HISTORIC SITE
(Church Lane; ⏲10am-5pm Sat & Sun Jun-Aug) FREE This squat, solid structure is a survivor from the old monastic settlement. Its name is a misnomer, as it was built in the 10th century and St Colmcille was alive in the 6th century. Experts have suggested that

it was used as a scriptorium, a place where monks illuminated books.

The site is usually locked except during summer, but ask at the tourist office about the keys or phone **Mrs Carpenter** (046-924 1778; 1 Lower Church View) for access.

Sleeping & Eating

Headfort Arms Hotel HOTEL €€
(046-924 0063; www.headfortarms.ie; John St; s/d from €69/89;) Right in the town centre, the family-run Headfort Arms has 45 comfortable rooms with classic styling and contemporary facilities such as laptop safes. Rooms in the charming old building have the most character. There's a small spa; the hotel's dining options include the independently run Vanilla Pod bistro.

Vanilla Pod BISTRO €€
(mains €17-25; 5.30-10pm daily, noon-3pm Sun) Bright and modern, this restaurant inside the Headfort Arms Hotel (p510) features an ambitious bistro-style menu. The food is well prepared and sourced locally; dishes range from honey-glazed duck breast to Glen Boy organic goat's-cheese bonbons and grilled seabass with fennel rouille (olive oil, breadcrumbs, saffron, chilli and garlic sauce).

Information

In the Kells Civic Offices, the **Tourist Office** (046-924 8856; www.meath.ie; Headfort Pl; 9.30am-1pm & 2-5pm Mon-Fri) has a copy of the famed *Book of Kells* and screens a free 13-minute audiovisual presentation.

Getting There & Away

Bus Éireann has services from Kells to Dublin (€16, 90 minutes, half-hourly) via Navan. There are also buses to Cavan (€15, 45 minutes, half-hourly).

Loughcrew Cairns

With all the hoopla over Brú na Bóinne, the amazing Stone Age passage graves strewn about the Loughcrew Hills, along the R154, near Oldcastle, are often overlooked. There are 30-odd tombs here, but they're well off the beaten track and relatively few people ever bother, which means you can enjoy this moody and evocative place in peace.

Like Brú na Bóinne, the graves were all built around 3000 BC, but unlike their better-known and better-excavated peers, the Loughcrew tombs were used at least until 750 BC.

Sights

Loughcrew Megalithic Centre INTERPRETATION CENTRE
(049-854 1888; loughcrewmegalithiccentre.com; cafe dishes €3 to €6, hostel dm €17, tent per person €10; 11am-5pm) FREE Opened in 2015, this small but absorbing place has a **museum** detailing the megalithic wonders hereabouts, as well as a **cafe**, **hostel** and **campground**. Special events (eg solstices and equinoxes) take place throughout the year. Contact the centre about picking up the key for nearby Cairn T.

The centre is 20km west of Kells via the R154 and the L2800; you'll need your own wheels to get here.

Carnbane East

Carnbane East has a cluster of cairns, including the biggest, Cairn T. Climbing Carnbane East from the car park takes about half an hour.

Cairn T HISTORIC SITE
(10am-6pm Apr-Aug) FREE The biggest site at Carnbane East is about 35m in diameter, with numerous carved stones. One of its outlying kerbstones, the **Hag's Chair**, is covered in gouged holes, circles and other markings.

In summer, access to Cairn T is controlled by **Heritage Ireland** (www.heritageireland.ie), which provides guides. Otherwise, pick up the gate key to enter the passageway from the cafe at Loughcrew Gardens, or from Loughcrew Megalithic Centre, and bring a torch (flashlight).

Carnbane West

From the car park, it takes about an hour to reach the summit of Carnbane West, where **Cairn D** and **Cairn L**, both some 60m in diameter, are located. They're in poor condition, though you can enter the passage and chamber of Cairn L, where there are numerous carved stones and a curved basin stone in which human ashes were placed.

Cairn L is administered by Heritage Ireland, which gives out the key only to those with an authentic research interest.

Loughcrew Gardens

A labour of love, **Loughcrew Gardens** (049-854 1060; www.loughcrew.com; gardens adult/child €6/3, adventure centre per half day €32/29, advance reservations essential; noon-

5pm Mon-Fri, 11am-5pm Sat & Sun mid-Mar–Oct, 9.30am-4pm Mon-Fri, 11am-4pm Sat & Sun Nov–mid-Mar;) incorporates 2.5 hectares of lawns, terraces and herbaceous borders along with a lime avenue, yew walk, canal and 'grotesque grotto' with tortured pillars, frescoes and fantasy sculptures. There's also a medieval moat, tower house and St Oliver Plunkett's family church, plus a cafe in a log-built lodge. Its adventure centre incorporates an assault course, archery, zipline and a climbing wall.

Loughcrew Gardens are 20km west of Kells, along the R154 and L2800, near Oldcastle.

COUNTY LOUTH

POP 122,900 / AREA 826 SQ KM

Ireland's smallest county (hence its moniker, the Wee County) prospered greatly during the Celtic Tiger era thanks to its proximity to Dublin, and is slowly but steadily recovering from the subsequent economic crash.

In the 5th and 6th centuries, Louth was at the centre of ecclesiastical Ireland, with wealthy religious communities at the monastery at Monasterboice and the Cistercian abbey at Mellifont. The 12th-century Norman invaders were responsible for the development of Dundalk and the two towns on opposite banks of the Boyne that united in 1412 to become what is now Drogheda, the county's largest town.

While Louth can easily be covered as a day trip from Dublin, you'll get more from your visit by spending some time exploring the county.

Drogheda

POP 38,578

Only 48km north of Dublin, Drogheda is a historic fortified town straddling the River Boyne. A clutch of fine old buildings, a handsome cathedral and a riveting museum provide plenty of cultural interest, while its atmospheric pubs, fine restaurants, numerous sleeping options and good transport links make it a handy base for exploring the region.

This bend in the fertile Boyne Valley has been a desirable location right back to 910, when the Danes built a fortified settlement here. In the 12th century, the Normans added a bridge and expanded the two settlements on either side of the river. By the 15th century, Drogheda was one of Ireland's four largest walled towns.

The 17th century brought devastation, however, when Drogheda was the scene of Cromwell's most notorious Irish slaughter in 1649. Things went from bad to worse in 1690, when the town backed the wrong horse at the Battle of the Boyne and surrendered the day after the defeat of James II.

Although the post–Celtic Tiger years hit Drogheda hard, new developments continue to expand along the riverfront of this multicultural regional hub.

Sights

★Millmount Museum & Tower MUSEUM

(041-983 3097; www.millmount.net; off Duleek St, Millmount; adult/child museum €3.50/2.50, tower €3/2, museum & tower €5.50/3; 10am-5.30pm Mon-Sat, 2-5pm Sun) Overlooking Drogheda, Millmount is an artificial hill

CROMWELL'S DROGHEDA INVASION

Lauded as England's first democrat and protector of the people, Oliver Cromwell (1599–1658) was an Irish nightmare. Cromwell hated the Irish for siding with Charles I during the Civil War. So when 'God's own Englishman' landed his 12,000 troops at Dublin in August 1649, he immediately set out for Drogheda, a strategic fort town and bastion of royalist support.

When Cromwell arrived at the walls of Drogheda, he was met by 2300 men led by Sir Arthur Aston, who boasted that 'he who could take Drogheda could take hell'. After Aston refused to surrender, Cromwell let fly with heavy artillery and after two days the walls were breached.

In order to set a terrifying example to any other town that might resist Cromwell's armies, over a period of hours an estimated 3000 people were massacred, mostly royalist soldiers but also priests, women and children. Aston was bludgeoned to death with his own (wooden) leg. Of the survivors, many were captured and sold into slavery in the Caribbean.

Drogheda

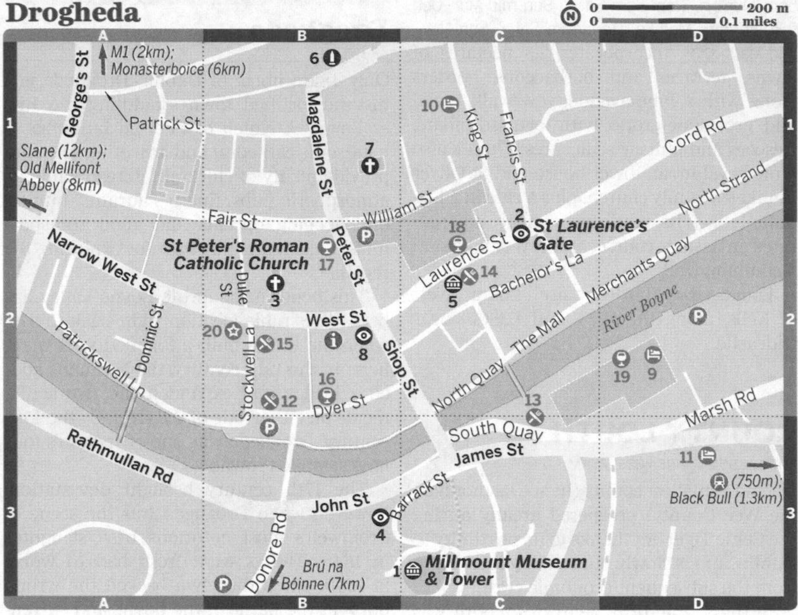

that may have been a prehistoric burial ground like Newgrange, but has never been excavated.

The Normans constructed a motte-and-bailey fort on top of this convenient command post overlooking the bridge. It was followed by a castle, which in turn was replaced by a **Martello tower** in 1808.

A section of the army barracks is now used as the **Millmount Museum**. Exhibits include three wonderful late-18th-century guild banners.

The tower played a dramatic role in the 1922 Civil War, when it was Drogheda's chief defensive feature and suffered heavy shelling from Free State forces. It has been aesthetically restored and offers great views over the town below.

Other museum highlights include a room devoted to Cromwell's brutal siege of Drogheda and the Battle of the Boyne. The pretty, cobbled basement is full of gadgets and kitchen utensils from bygone times. Across the courtyard, the Governor's House opens for temporary exhibitions. There is a smart new restaurant, the **Tower**, here too.

Just northwest of Millmount, the 13th-century **Butter Gate** has a distinctive tower and arched passageway.

★ **St Peter's Roman Catholic Church** CHURCH

(West St; 8.30am-5pm) Displayed in a glittering brass-and-glass case in the north transept, the shrivelled **head of St Oliver Plunkett** (1629–81) is this church's main draw (the rest of the martyr was separated at his hanging in 1681). Actually it's two churches in one: the first, a classical style, designed by Francis Johnston in 1791, and the newer late-19th-century neo-Gothic addition. Opening hours can vary.

★ **St Laurence's Gate** HISTORIC SITE

Astride the eastwards extension of the town's main street is the 13th-century St Laurence's Gate, the finest surviving portion of the city walls (which originally extended for 3km).

Highlanes Gallery GALLERY

(www.highlanes.ie; Laurence St; admission by donation; 10.30am-5pm Mon-Sat) Set in a beautifully converted 19th-century monastery, this gallery has a permanent collection of contemporary art, plus regular temporary exhibitions.

Attached is a shop featuring high-quality Louth craftwork, and Relish, a chic cafe.

St Peter's Church of Ireland CHURCH

(William St; 8.30am-5pm) St Peter's Church of Ireland (not to be confused with St Peter's Roman Catholic Church) is the church whose spire was burned by Cromwell's men, resulting in the death of 100 people seeking sanctuary inside. Today's church is the second replacement of the original destroyed by Cromwell. Opening hours can vary.

Magdalene Tower TOWER

The 14th-century Magdalene Tower is the bell tower of a Dominican friary founded in 1224. It was here that England's King Richard II, accompanied by a great army, accepted the submission of the Gaelic chiefs with suitable ceremony in 1395. Peace lasted only a few months, however, and Richard's return to Ireland led to his overthrow in 1399.

Festivals & Events

Drogheda Arts Festival ARTS

(http://droghedaartsfestival.ie) Theatre, music, film, poetry, visual arts and workshops such as silk painting take place over the May Day weekend.

Sleeping

Spoon & the Stars HOSTEL, HOTEL €

(086 405 8465; www.spoonandthestars.com; 13 Dublin Rd; dm €18/65, d with/without bathroom from €55/65;) Seasoned travellers Rory and Hannah opened up this well-run budget accommodation in 2013. Rooms range from a double with private bathroom and kitchenette, to eight- to ten-bed dorms (one female-only). Facilities include a TV room and a breezy courtyard and garden, complete with barbecue.

★ **D Hotel** HOTEL €€

(041-987 7700; www.thedhotel.com; Scotch Hall, Marsh Rd; d from €109;) Slick, hip and unexpected, this is Drogheda's top dog when it comes to accommodation. Minimalist rooms are bathed in light and decked out with designer furniture and cool gadgets. There's a stylish bar and restaurant, a minigym and fantastic views of the city. The hotel is popular for hen and stag parties: beware of pounding music on weekends.

Scholars Townhouse Hotel HOTEL €€

(041-983 5410; www.scholarshotel.com; King St; d from €89;) This former monastery dates from 1867 and was recently revamped as a family-owned hotel and restaurant. Despite the 16 rooms being on the small side, there's nothing monastic about the facilities which include power showers, an atmospheric bar and a superb restaurant (bookings recommended). The central location is ideal for exploring the town.

Eating

Relish CAFE €

(www.highlanes.ie; Highlanes Gallery, Laurence St; dishes €6-8.50; 10.30am-5pm Mon-Sat;) Located in the Highlanes Gallery, this split-level cafe serves a stylish range of focaccia, bagels and gourmet sandwiches, including smoked salmon. It also offers savoury tarts and daily specials (pasta, burgers), as well as daily desserts such as hot apple crumble. Gluten-free options are plentiful.

Stockwell Artisan Foods Café CAFE €

(www.stockwellartisanfoods.ie; 1 Stockwell Lane; mains €6-9; 9am-4pm Mon-Sat) Stripped wooden floors, daily newspapers and chunky furniture add to the cosy welcome of this place that serves healthy wraps, salads, soups and hot dishes such as fish cakes.

WORTH A TRIP

DROGHEDA TO DUNDALK VIA THE COAST ROAD

Most people just zip north along the M1 motorway but if you want to meander along the coast and see a little of rural Ireland, opt for the R166 coast road from Drogheda.

The little village of **Termonfeckin** was, until 1656, the seat and castle of the Primate of Armagh. Nothing remains of the castle, but a tiny, 15th-century **tower house** (086 079 1484; key deposit €50; 10am-6pm) FREE, once belonging to a wealthy landowner, is worth a brief stop. Pick up the key from the first house to its right.

About 2km further north is the busy seaside and fishing centre of **Clogherhead**, with a good, shallow Blue Flag beach at Lurganboy. Squint to ignore the caravan parks and take in the lovely views of the Cooley and Mourne Mountains instead.

A further 14km north, the teensy village of **Annagassan** merits a stop for scrumptious picnic goods. At **Coastguard Seafoods** (086 855 8609; Harbour Rd; by appointment), fisherman Terry Butterly oak-smokes some of the finest salmon in Ireland (usually appearing on restaurant menus as Annagassan smoked salmon) and sells it direct to the public, along with other seafood such as live lobsters, for astonishingly reasonable prices. You can just turn up (look for the green door), but to avoid disappointment, call in advance. Nearby, at Annagassan's **O'Neills Bakery** (042-937 2253; www.oneillsbakery.ie; 7am-1pm), a cavernous five-generations-old bakery with vast ovens (one more than a century old), you can buy still-warm breads, cakes and buns (cash only). It appears closed to the public but knock on the door around the side of the building and one of the bakers will let you in.

The 33km route comes to an end in **Castlebellingham**. The picturesque village grew up around an 18th-century crenellated mansion (now a luxury wedding venue; ask about midweek B&B options from €180 per double). Stop for homemade cakes, quiches and the house speciality boiled bacon and cabbage at charming **Foley's Tea Rooms** (Main St; dishes €4.50-10; 9am-3pm Mon-Fri, 8.30am-3.30pm Sat & Sun;), originally two 18th-century thatched cottages, before perusing its adjacent shop specialising in fascinating curios and collectibles. Cash only.

From Castlebellingham you can continue 12km north to Dundalk along the suburban R132 or join the M1.

★Kitchen MEDITERRANEAN €€
(041-983 4630; http://kitchenrestaurant.ie; 2 South Quay; mains €17-28; 11am-9pm Wed, 11am-10pm Thu-Sat, noon-9pm Sun;) Sage-green on the outside and cranberry-coloured inside, Drogheda's best restaurant is aptly named for its shiny open kitchen. Organic local produce is used along with worldly ingredients such as Cypriot haloumi and Spanish Serrano ham. Breads are made on-site and there's an excellent choice of wine by the glass. Don't miss the salted-caramel baked Alaska for dessert.

Black Bull IRISH €€
(www.blackbullinn.ie; Dublin Rd; mains €10-28; kitchen 9.30am-10pm Mon-Sat, to 8pm Sun;) Topped by a gleaming golden (not black) bull, this popular pub has a homey atmosphere with low ceilings and candle-lit corners. The modern extension houses a spacious restaurant serving solidly good grub such as open chicken pie and rack of lamb with Dijon potatoes. Afterwards, have a pint in the brilliantly named beer garden, the China Shop.

D'vine MEDITERRANEAN €€
(041-980 0440; Dyer St; mains €14-27; kitchen noon-3pm & 5-9.30pm Wed & Thu, noon-9.30pm Fri & Sat, 1-9.30pm Sun) Squirrelled away down a small flight of steps and opening to a sunny courtyard, this convivial wine bar and bistro has a great selection of Mediterranean starting platters, open sandwiches and mains such as stuffed sea bass, bœuf-bourguignon pie, and roast squash and leek gratin with hazelnut crust, plus a long wine list. Live music performs on Sunday at 7pm.

Drinking & Nightlife

Drogheda has dozens of bars and pubs. Check the event guide at www.drogheda.ie for listings.

WM Cairnes & Son PUB
(www.wmcairnes.com; Scotch Hall; mains €11-26; 11am-midnight Sun-Thu, to 2am Fri & Sat) Cav-

ernous, contemporary WM Cairnes & Son has a winning riverfront location, live music from Thursday to Monday, and craft beers on tap. Soak them up with superb gastropub grub: beef and Guinness pie with traditional colcannon (cabbage and mash), local mussels steamed in Dan Kelly cider and a towering 'jaw-breaker burger'.

Peter Matthews PUB

(McPhail's; 9 Laurence St; ⏲5pm-late) One of Drogheda's top spots for live music (Thursday to Sunday), McPhail's (as it's always called, no matter what the sign says) features everything from heavy-metal cover bands to trad-music sessions. There's a traditional bar at the front and a beer garden out back.

Clarke & Sons PUB

(Peter St; ⏲1-11.30pm Mon-Thu, noon-12.30am Fri & Sat, 12.30-11pm Sun) This wonderful old boozer is right out of a time capsule. Clarke's unrestored wooden interior features snugs and leaded-glass doors that read Open Bar.

Cagney's BAR

(3 Dyer St; ⏲10.30am-11.30pm Mon-Thu, to 12.30pm Fri & Sat, noon-11pm Sun) Classy Cagney's exudes a mellow sophistication with low lighting, charcoal-grey-furnished beer garden and wines by the glass.

☆ Entertainment

Drogheda Arts Centre PERFORMING ARTS

(☎041-983 3946; www.droichead.com; Narrow West St) Drama, music, comedy, film and visual art take to the stage at Drogheda's lively arts centre, which runs regular workshops such as life drawing.

ℹ Information

The **Tourist Office** (☎041-987 2843; http://drogheda.ie; 1 West St; ⏲9.30am-5.30pm Mon-Sat; 📶) is located inside the historic **Tholsel** (cnr West & Shop Sts), an 18th-century limestone town hall.

ℹ Getting There & Away

BUS

Bus Éireann regularly serves Drogheda from Dublin (€8, one hour, one to four hourly) and Dundalk (€7, 30 minutes, hourly).

Matthews (☎042-937 8188; http://matthews.ie) also runs an hourly or better service to Dublin (€9) and Dundalk (€9).

TRAIN

The train station is just off Dublin Rd. Drogheda is on the main Belfast–Dublin line (Dublin €14, 45 minutes; Belfast €20, 1½ hours). There are six express trains (and many slower ones) each way.

ℹ Getting Around

Drogheda is compact and walkable. Many of the surrounding sites are within cycling distance.

Quay Cycles (☎041-983 4526; www.quaycycles.com; 11A North Quay; per day from €14; ⏲9am-6pm Mon-Sat) rents bikes.

Around Drogheda

A number of historic sites lie close to Drogheda, but you'll need your own transport.

Old Mellifont Abbey RUINS

(☎041-982 6459; www.heritageireland.ie; Tullyallen; site admission free, visitor centre adult/student €4/2; ⏲site 24hr year-round, visitor centre 10am-6pm Jun-Aug) In its Anglo-Norman prime, this abbey, 1.5km off the main Drogheda–Collon road (R168), was the Cistercians' first and most magnificent centre in Ireland. Although the ruins are highly evocative and well worth exploring, they belie the site's former splendour.

Mellifont's most recognisable building and one of the country's finest examples of Cistercian architecture is the 13th-century lavabo, the monks' octagonal washing room.

There's good picnicking next to the rushing stream. The visitor centre describes monastic life in detail.

In the mid-12th century, Irish monastic orders had grown a little too fond of the good life and were not averse to a bit of corruption. In 1142 an exasperated Malachy, bishop of Down, invited a group of hard-core monks from Clairvaux in France to set up shop in a remote location, where they would act as a sobering influence on the local clergy. Unsurprisingly, the Irish monks didn't get on with their French guests, and the latter soon left for home. Still, the construction of Mellifont continued, and within 10 years, nine more Cistercian monasteries were established. Mellifont was eventually the mother house for 21 lesser monasteries; at one point as many as 400 monks lived here.

In 1556, after the Dissolution of the Monasteries, a fortified Tudor manor house was built on the site.

Monasterboice HISTORIC SITE

(⏲sunrise-sunset) **FREE** Crowing ravens lend an eerie atmosphere to Monasterboice, an intriguing monastic site down a leafy lane in sweeping farmland, which contains a cemetery, two ancient church ruins, one of the finest and tallest round towers in Ireland, and two of the most important high crosses.

Come early or late in the day to avoid the crowds. It's just off the M1 motorway, about 8km north of Drogheda.

The original monastic settlement here is said to have been founded in the 5th or 6th century by St Buithe, a follower of St Patrick, although the site probably had pre-Christian significance. St Buithe's name somehow got converted to Boyne, and the river is named after him. An invading Viking force took over the settlement in 968, only to be comprehensively expelled by Donal, the Irish high king of Tara, who killed at least 300 of the Vikings in the process.

The high crosses of Monasterboice are superb examples of Celtic art. The crosses had an important didactic use, bringing the gospels alive for the uneducated, and they were probably brightly painted originally, although all traces of colour have long disappeared.

The cross near the entrance is known as **Muiredach's Cross**, named after a 10th-century abbot. The western face relates more to the New Testament, and from the bottom depicts the arrest of Christ, Doubting Thomas, Christ giving a key to St Peter, the Crucifixion, and Moses praying with Aaron and Hur.

The **West Cross** is near the round tower and stands 6.5m high, making it one of the tallest high crosses in Ireland. It's much more weathered, especially at the base, and only a dozen or so of its 50 panels are still legible. The more distinguishable ones on the eastern face include David killing a lion and a bear.

A third, simpler cross in the northeastern corner of the compound is believed to have been smashed by Cromwell's forces and has only a few straightforward carvings. This cross makes a great evening silhouette photo, with the round tower in the background.

CAR PARK VANDALISM

Unfortunately travellers have reported incidents of thefts from cars left unattended in the car park at Monasterboice and other historic sites. Never leave anything of value visible in the car and, if you notice broken glass on the ground, be particularly wary about leaving your vehicle, especially if it's a rental car.

The **round tower**, minus its cap, is more than 30m tall, and stands in a corner of the complex. Records suggest the tower interior went up in flames in 1097, destroying many valuable manuscripts and other treasures. It's closed to the public.

Dundalk

POP 37,816

Although an industrial hub and an increasingly busy business centre due to its proximity to both Dublin and Belfast, Dundalk is a surprisingly pleasant town with a couple of interesting sites.

In the Middle Ages, the city was at the northern limits of the English-controlled Pale, and with partition in 1921 it once again became a border town, this time with South Armagh.

Sights

County Museum Dundalk MUSEUM
(www.dundalkmuseum.ie; Jocelyn St; adult/child €2/1; 10am-5pm Tue-Sat) Different floors in this worthwhile museum are dedicated to the town's early history and archaeology, and to the Norman period. One floor deals with the growth of industry in the area, from the 1750s to the 1960s, including the cult classic Heinkel Bubble Car. Other oddities include Oliver Cromwell's shaving mirror.

St Patrick's Cathedral CATHEDRAL
(8.30am-5pm) FREE The richly decorated 19th-century St Patrick's Cathedral was modelled on King's College Chapel in Cambridge, England. Hours can vary depending on services and events.

Courthouse NOTABLE BUILDING
(cnr Crowe & Clanbrassil Sts) Dundalk's courthouse is a photogenic neo-Gothic building with large Doric pillars. The interior is closed to the public. In the front square is the stone **Maid of Éireann**, commemorating the 1798 Rising.

Sleeping & Eating

The most recent addition to Dundalk's skyline is a spiffing, 14-storey Crowne Plaza hotel.

Ballymascanlon House HISTORIC HOTEL €€
(042-935 8200; www.ballymascanlon.com; Carlingford Rd; s/d/tr from €90/150/200;) Situated 8km northeast of Dundalk on the edge of the Cooley Peninsula,

this grand old property (and more recent extension) has spacious rooms, warm, personalised service and atmosphere in spades. There's an 18-hole golf course (with a c 3000 BC, 3m-high standing stone on the 6th hole), leisure centre, a restaurant and bar, plus 24-hour room service.

★Eno MEDITERRANEAN €€
(☎042-935 5467; www.eno.ie; 5 Roden Pl; tapas €4.50-12.50, pizzas €13-19, mains €15-23; ⊙kitchen noon-9pm; 👪) Bare boards, bold colours and conversation-piece objets d'art established Eno as Dundalk's choicest eatery, along with outstanding Med-inspired tapas, wood-fired pizzas, and dishes such as angel-hair pasta with Dunany crab, white wine and garlic, and honey-roasted fig and almond tart. Upstairs, DJs spin Cuban, Latin and Soul in the cocktail bar; the al fresco Yard Bar is out back.

McAteers the Food House CAFE, DELI €€
(www.mcateersthefoodhouse.com; 15 Clanbrassil St; mains €8-17; ⊙9am-6pm Mon-Sat; 👪) If the goods on display at this deli fire up your appetite, its cafe prepares dishes such as pancakes with bacon and free-range eggs, and open-faced sandwiches with Annagassan smoked salmon.

☆ Entertainment

Spirit Store LIVE MUSIC
(www.spiritstore.ie; George's Quay; ⊙4-11.30pm Mon-Thu, to 12.30am Fri & Sat, to 11pm Sun) Downstairs, this sunset-pink-painted place is your typical harbour-front bar, full of character and characters. Upstairs is a state-of-the-art live venue, with a terrific sound system that is beloved of both the crowd and the regular streams of touring musicians that play here.

ℹ Information

The **Tourist Office** (☎042-935 2111; www.louthholidays.com; Jocelyn St; ⊙9.30am-1pm & 2-5.30pm Mon-Fri) is located on Market Sq.

ℹ Getting There & Around

Bus Éireann runs an hourly bus service to Dublin (€10.50, 1½ hours). The bus station is near the courthouse.

Clarke Train Station, on Carrickmacross Rd, has express trains to Dublin (€17.50, one hour, seven Monday to Saturday, five Sunday) and Belfast (€15.50, one hour, eight Monday to Saturday, five Sunday), as well as many slower services.

TRACING YOUR ANCESTORS

Genealogical centres in the region can help trace your ancestors; contact the centres in advance to arrange a consultation.

Meath Heritage Centre (☎046-943 6633; www.meathroots.com; Town Hall, Castle St) Inside Trim's town hall.

Louth County Library (☎042-932 4323; www.louthcoco.ie; Roden Pl) In Dundalk.

Cavan Genealogy (☎049-436 1094; www.cavan.rootsireland.ie; Farnham St) On the 1st floor of Johnston Central Library, Cavan town.

Monaghan Genealogy (☎047-71984; www.monaghangenealogy.com; Mullaghmurphy) At St Macartan's College in Monaghan town.

Cooley Peninsula

Forested slopes and sun-dappled, multihued hills rise above the the dark waters of Carlingford Lough cleaving the picturesque Cooley Peninsula. Country lanes wind their scenic way down to deserted stony beaches, while sweeping views stretch north across the water (and border) to the majestic Mourne Mountains.

The medieval village of Carlingford is an ideal base. From here, you can continue along the coast road past the village of Omeath to Newry, at the nexus of Counties Down and Armagh in Northern Ireland.

Carlingford

POP 1045

Amid the medieval ruins and whitewashed houses, the vibrant little village of Carlingford buzzes with pubs, restaurants and boutiques, spirited festivals and gorgeous views of the mountains and across Carlingford Lough to Northern Ireland.

As one of the liveliest spots on the coast (and as a hugely popular hen- and stag-party destination), Carlingford can be crowded during the warmer months, especially at weekends; book accommodation *well* ahead.

Sights

Holy Trinity Heritage Centre INTERPRETATION CENTRE
(042-937 3454; www.carlingfordheritagecentre.com; Churchyard Lane; 9.30am-1pm & 2-5pm Mon-Fri Apr-Oct, 10am-12.30pm & 1.30-4pm Mon-Fri Nov-Mar) FREE Carlingford's heritage centre is in the former Holy Trinity Church. A short video describes the village history and explains what has been done to give it new life in recent years after villagers got together to revive a dying community.

King John's Castle CASTLE
Carlingford was first settled by the Vikings, and in the Middle Ages became an English stronghold under the protection of the now-ruined castle, which was built on a pinnacle in the 11th to 12th centuries to control the entrance to the lough. King John spent a couple of days here in 1210 en route to battle in Antrim.

It's closed to the public, but you can ask at the tourist office about free tours during **Heritage Week** (www.heritageweek.ie) in late August.

On the western side, the entrance gateway was built to allow only one horse and rider through at a time.

LEPRECHAUNS – A PROTECTED SPECIES

The mountains around Carlingford are famed for being the last remaining site of Ireland's leprechauns. Among the believers in the little people was the late publican PJ O'Hare, who found a leprechaun's suit and hat, along with a collection of tiny bones and four gold coins on Foy Mountain in 1989.

Nineteen years later after a vigorous lobbying campaign by self-acclaimed 'Leprechaun Whisperer', Kevin Woods (who claims he has seen three leprechauns to date), the EU issued a highly unconventional directive establishing a protective leprechaun zone here. According to Woods, this is apparently the last habitat for Ireland's leprechauns and there's even an annual **leprechaun hunt**. Even if you don't spot a little fella, this certainly is a very magical spot. Visit www.thelastleprechaunsofireland.com for more information.

Tholsel HISTORIC BUILDING
The photogenic Tholsel is the only surviving gate to the original town.

Dominican Friary RUINS
West of the village centre are the wonderfully preserved remains of a Dominican friary, built around 1305 and later used as a storehouse by oyster fishermen.

Taafe's Castle HISTORIC BUILDING
Today the function area of the attached pub of the same name, Taafe's Castle is an imposing 16th-century tower house that stood on the waterfront until the land in front was reclaimed to build a short-lived train line.

Opposite the castle is a bust commemorating Carlingford-born Thomas D'Arcy McGee (1825–68), one of Canada's founding fathers.

Mint HISTORIC BUILDING
Dating from the 16th century, the Mint, near the village square, has some interesting Celtic-inspired carvings around the windows. Although Edward IV is thought to have granted a charter to a mint in 1467, no coins were produced here.

Activities

Carlingford is the starting point for the 40km **Táin Way**, which makes a circuit of the Cooley Peninsula through the Cooley Mountains along a mixture of surfaced roads, forest tracks and green paths.

Much of the Cooley Peninsula is protected and is home to various species of birds including godwits, red-breasted mergansers, buzzards, tits and various finches. Ask at the tourist office for information on the **Carlingford Birdwatching Trail**.

Carlingford Adventure Centre ADVENTURE SPORTS
(042-937 3100; www.carlingfordadventure.com; Tholsel St) Runs a wide range of activities including sailing, kayaking, windsurfing, rock climbing, archery, ziplining, and, if you fancy being strapped into a massive plastic ball and rolled down a hill, zorbing. It also offers hostel-style and self-catering accommodation.

Festivals & Events

Leprechaun Hunt CULTURE
One Sunday in spring, a celebratory leprechaun hunt sets off from Carlingford in late May or early April.

Carlingford Oyster Festival FOOD
(www.carlingford.ie) This rollicking event toasts Carlingford's famous oysters with an oyster treasure hunt, fishing competition, music, food markets and a regatta on Carlingford Lough. Held in mid-August.

Sleeping

★Carlingford House B&B €€
(☎042-937 3118; http://carlingfordhouse.com; Dundalk St; d from €80;) In the village centre, but set back from the road in manicured grounds, this stately 1844 manor house (once the local doctor's house) is especially stunning in warmer months when it's enveloped by vines. Inside, the welcoming hosts achieve the perfect balance of old-world character and contemporary flair, and serve exceptional breakfasts.

Belvedere House B&B €€
(☎042-938 3828; www.belvederehouse.ie; Newry St; s €55-65, d €80-90;) An excellent deal, rooms at this lovely B&B are modern but cosy with antique pine furniture, subtle lighting and pretty colour schemes. Guests have access to leisure facilities at the local Four Seasons hotel and breakfast is served in the downstairs Bay Tree restaurant.

★Ghan House GUESTHOUSE €€€
(☎042-937 3682; www.ghanhouse.com; Main Rd; d from €150; @) Set in flower-filled gardens, this 18th-century Georgian house has 12 rooms, each exquisitely decorated with period antiques and original artworks. Book one of the four rooms in the main house for the most character and old-world charm. There's a superb restaurant (p520) on-site (with discounts for guests) and a **cookery school** (courses from €75).

Eating & Drinking

Ruby Ellen's Tea Rooms CAFE €
(http://rubyellenstearooms.com; Marion House, Newry St; dishes €6-10; 9am-6pm;) Recently opened in a charming cottage with egg-shell-blue walls, mismatched chairs and lace tablecloths, Ruby Ellen's serves wraps, bagels, jacket potatoes with gourmet toppings such as smoked salmon, crab meat and lemon zest, or pork sausages and smoked cheese, as well as daily baked cakes. When the sun's shining, the sweetest seats are in the flower-filled courtyard.

DON'T MISS

FITZPATRICK'S

Overflowing inside and out with bric-a-brac – milk cans, lanterns, antlers, church pews, crockery, street signs, barrels, bellows, bank notes, even tables dangling upside-down from the ceiling – **Fitzpatrick's** (www.fitzpatricks-restaurant.com; Rockmarshall, Jenkinstown; 12.30-11pm Tue-Thu, to 12.30am Fri & Sat, to 10pm Sun, noon-11pm Mon;) is a locally patronised treasure and fantastic craic. Book ahead if you plan to dine on its excellent pub grub (steak, seafood, award-winning chowder and 'almost-famous French-onion soup').

The flower-filled, umbrella-shaded beer gardens (with resident braying donkeys) are positively hopping on sunny days. Traditional Irish music strikes up frequently of an evening.

Food for Thought DELI, CAFE €
(Dundalk St; dishes €5-12; 9am-6pm Mon-Thu, 9am-7pm Fri & Sat, 10am-6pm Sun) A rainbow of jams and chutneys lines the walls of this deli-cafe. Croquettes, quiches and fish cakes are among the tasty treats to eat in or take away as picnic fare, with great daily specials such as beef lasagne or cottage pie.

★PJ O'Hares PUB €€
(www.pjoharescarlingford.com; Newry St; mains €12-20; kitchen 11am-9.30pm Mon-Thu, 11am-10pm Fri & Sat, noon-8pm Sun) Hearty main courses at this award-winning gastro pub include pies (beef and Guinness or salmon, cod and cockle), but you can easily fill up on tapas-style starters including Carlingford oysters. Live music plays regularly (try to catch rockin' local five-piece the Nooks). Weather depending, head for the bustling beer garden or cosy up in front of the roaring fire.

Bay Tree MODERN IRISH €€
(☎042-938 3828; www.belvederehouse.ie; Belvedere House, Newry St; mains €19-27; 6-10pm Mon-Sat, 12.30-10pm Sun Mar–mid-Nov, reduced hours mid-Nov–Mar;) Simple, stylishly presented dishes made from seasonal locally sourced ingredients at this little restaurant include squash and mushroom tortellini with sage and aged parmesan, spiced duck breast with mulled cranberry jus, and indulgent desserts such as rum-and-raisin crème caramel. Bookings recommended.

WORTH A TRIP

FLAGSTAFF VIEWPOINT

Travelling along the Cooley Peninsula from Carlingford to Newry in Northern Ireland, a quick 3km detour rewards you with sweeping views of Carlingford Lough, framed by rugged, forested mountains, green fields and the sparkling blue Irish Sea beyond.

Flagstaff Viewpoint lies *just* over the border in County Armagh. Heading northwest along the coast road (the R173), follow the signs to your left onto Ferryhill Rd, then turn right up to the viewpoint's car park. The quickest way to reach Newry from here is to retrace your steps and rejoin the R173.

Ghan House MODERN IRISH €€€
(☎042-937 3682; www.ghanhouse.com; Main Rd; tasting menus €30-45; ⏲6-9.30pm Mon-Sat, 1-3pm Sun) The restaurant at Ghan House (p519) is renowned for its classic multicourse menus (no à la carte) incorporating its own breads, stocks, ice creams and sauces, and herbs and vegetables from its garden. Book ahead.

Information

The **Tourist Office** (☎087 957 6989; http://visitcarlingford.com; ⏲10am-5pm) is on the waterfront in the former train station.

Getting There & Around

Bus Éireann has services to Dundalk (€15.50, one hour, six daily Monday to Saturday) with connections to Dublin; and Newry (€5.50, 20 minutes, six daily Monday to Saturday).

There's great cycling around the Cooley Peninsula. **On Yer Bike** (☎087 648 7337; www.onyerbike.ie; Chapel Hill; per day €20; ⏲9am-6.30pm Mon-Fri, to 6pm Sat & Sun) can deliver bikes to your accommodation or the tourist office.

COUNTY CAVAN

POP 73,185 / AREA 1932 SQ KM

Cavan is paradise for boaters, anglers, walkers, cyclists and artists. Known as the 'Lake Country', there's supposedly a lake for every day of the year (including leap years), and the county is famed for its coarse fishing. Between the lakes is a gentle landscape of meandering streams, bogs and drumlins. Cavan has some spectacular walking trails through the wild Cuilcagh Mountains, which are the source of the 300km River Shannon. The county's quiet, rural charm is best appreciated from the water, especially the tranquil Shannon–Erne Waterway.

The area has an intricate history. Magh Sleacht, a plain near the border village of Ballyconnell, was an important Druidic centre in the 5th century when St Patrick was busy converting the pagan Irish to Christianity, and the area is still littered with tombs, standing stones and stone circles dating from this time. The Gaelic O'Reilly clan ruled until the 16th century, when they were defeated by the English. As part of the Ulster Plantation, Cavan was divided among English and Scottish settlers. After the War of Independence in 1922, the Ulster counties of Cavan, Monaghan and Donegal were incorporated into the Republic.

Cavan's lakes create a tangled knot of narrow, twisting roads. Take your time and enjoy the views that appear unexpectedly around each bend.

Cavan Town

POP 10,205

Cavan's county town is a solidly workaday place with some handsome Georgian houses. There are few-to-no sights, but it's a handy stop for info and supplies.

Sights

Bell Tower HISTORIC SITE
All that remains of the 13th-century Franciscan friary the town grew up around is an ancient bell tower, next to the grave of 17th-century rebel leader Owen Roe O'Neill in Abbey St's cemetery.

Sleeping & Eating

Farnham Estate HOTEL €€€
(☎049-437 7700; www.farnhamestate.ie; d €139-185; @🛜🏊) Set in misty woodlands, this sprawling 16th-century estate is now part of the Radisson group, with amenities including a garden-view restaurant, indoor/outdoor infinity swimming pool, a luxurious spa and golf course. Luxurious rooms blend contemporary style with period features and character. The estate is 3km west of town on the R198.

Cavan Farmers Market MARKET €
(Town Hall St; ⏲10am-2pm Fri) Held in the Town Hall St public car park.

Chapter One CAFE €

(www.chapteronecafe.ie; Convent Bldg, Main St; dishes €6-8.50; 8.30am-6pm Mon-Fri, 9am-6pm Sat, 11am-6pm Sun;) Up a short flight of steps, Chapter One is heaving at lunchtime when locals descend to dine on the huge range of filled bagels, soups, nachos, salads and specials such as quesadillas.

Drinking

McMahons BAR

(79 Main St; 11.30am-12.30am Mon-Thu, 12.30pm-12.30am Fri, 11am-12.30am Sat, 3-11pm Sun;) McMahons' cavernous tiered bar puts on regular live bands and DJs.

Information

Cavan's **Tourist Office** (049-433 1942; www.thisiscavan.ie; Farnham St; 9.15am-5pm Mon-Fri) is above the library.

Getting There & Around

The small bus station has 10 services daily to Dublin (€17, two hours), and four daily to Donegal town (€21, two hours). There are also various services to small towns throughout the county.

Lough Oughter & Killykeen Forest Park

Rod-wielding anglers congregate at **Lough Oughter**, which splatters across the map like spilt steely grey ink. Fishing aside, the wildlife-rich lough is appealing for naturalists, walkers and anyone wanting to vanish into a landscape of shimmering waters and cathedral-like aisles of trees. It's best accessed via **Killykeen Forest Park** (www.coillteoutdoors.ie; 9am-9pm) FREE, 12km northwest of Cavan town, where various nature trails (from 1.5km to 5.8km) lead you through the woods and along the lakeshore. Keep an eye out for stoats, badgers, foxes, grey squirrels and hedgehogs, as well as some impressive birdlife.

Many of the low overgrown islands in the lake were *crannógs* (fortified, artificial islands). The most spectacular is home to **Clough Oughter Castle**, a 13th-century circular tower perched on a tiny speck of land. It was used as a lonely prison, then as a stronghold by rebel leader Owen Roe O'Neill before being destroyed by Cromwell's army in 1653. Although the castle lies out of reach over the water, it's worth walking via the forest trails to enjoy the view.

Butlersbridge

Heading 7km north from Cavan along the N3 you'll pass the village of Butlersbridge. Set on the banks of the River Annalee, it's ideal for a riverside picnic.

Alternatively, pop into the **Derragarra Inn** (http://murphsbistro-derragarra-inn.com; mains €16.50-29; kitchen noon-9pm Mon-Fri, to 9.30pm Sat, 12.30-9pm Sun), a delightful ivy-covered pub with a wood-beamed interior, beer garden overlooking the river and St Aidan Church across the way. Food is a cut above (mozzarella-stuffed, bacon-wrapped chicken; duo of salmon and hake with vermouth sauce) and there's live music at weekends.

Situated 5.5km west of Butlersbridge on the L1511, Sean at **Cavan Canoe Centre** (087 290 5752; http://cavancanoeing.com; Inishmore; single/double kayaks per half day €20/30, canoes €30, wetsuits per half day €5; by reservation Apr-Oct) rents canoes as well as single and double kayaks for exploring the local waterways, plus all-important wetsuits.

Cloverhill

Just 4km north of Butlersbridge on the N54, the lovely little village of Cloverhill is best known for its award-winning restaurant housed in an 1884 former post office, the **Olde Post Inn** (047-55555; www.theoldepostinn.com; 5-course dinner €63, 8-course tasting menu €82, 4-course Sunday lunch €35; 6.30-9.30pm Wed-Sat, 12.30-2.30pm Sun;). Inspired local chef Gearoid Lynch's contemporary cuisine is based on traditional ingredients such as monkfish, salmon, duck and lamb. In the former postmaster's residence

LAKE FISHING

Cavan's exceptional lake fishing reels in anglers, especially to the county's southern and western areas. It's primarily coarse fishing, but there's also some game angling for brown trout and pike. Most lakes are well signposted, and the types of fish available are marked.

For more information, visit www.fishinginireland.info, which lists tackle shops, fishing guides and boat-rental operators.

You can also pick up anglers' guides from tourist offices.

are six guest rooms (single/double €65/100), luxuriously furnished with plush carpets and fabrics.

Belturbet

POP 1407

On the Shannon-Erne Waterway, this traditional village, 16km northwest of Cavan, is an anglers' favourite. It's also a good starting point for a cycling trip along the canal and river system.

Sights

Belturbet Railway Station HISTORIC BUILDING
(086 868 5375; Railway Rd; 10am-1.15pm & 2-5.15pm Tue & Sat, 2-5.15pm & 6-8.30pm Thu Apr-Sep) FREE Belturbet's beautifully restored railway station houses a visitor centre exploring the history of rail travel in the area. Trains used the station from 1885 until 1959, after which it languished for 40 years. Hours can vary - call ahead to make sure it's open.

Sleeping

Church View Guesthouse GUESTHOUSE €€
(049-952 2358; www.churchviewguesthouse.com; 8 Church St; s/d/f €45/75/95;) The cosiest accommodation option in town is this cherry-coloured guesthouse, with seven bright, comfortable rooms, all with private bathroom. Book ahead as it's perennially busy with anglers thanks to its cold storeroom and proximity to the lakes.

> **BALLY WHO?**
>
> All over Ireland you'll see the town prefix 'Bally' (and variations thereof, such as Ballyna and Ballina). The ubiquitous term originates from the Irish phrase 'Baile na'. It's often mistranslated as 'town', but there were very few towns in Ireland when the names came about. A closer approximation is 'place of'; hence Ballyjamesduff, for example, means Place of James Duff (or James Duff's place). Dublin's Irish name is Baile Átha Cliath (Place of the Hurdle Ford). If it was anglicised, it too would be a Bally, spelt something like 'Ballycleeagh'.
>
> Other common place-name prefixes include Carrick (or Carrig), meaning 'rock' in Irish, and Dun, from the Irish *dún* (meaning 'fort').

Drinking

Widow's Bar PUB
(Main St; 10.30am-11.30pm Mon-Thu, to 12.30am Fri, to 2am Sat, 12.30-11pm Sun) Earthy local the Widow's has a warm exposed stone-and-brick interior and big sheltered beer garden. Lively trad-music sessions take place on Saturday and Sunday nights.

Getting There & Around

Bus Éireann services to Dublin (€17, two hours, 10 daily) and Donegal town (€20.50, 1½ hours, 10 daily) stop outside the post office.

Ballyjamesduff & Around

POP 2568

A sleepy market town, Ballyjamesduff was the one-time home of the Earl of Fife, James Duff, an early Plantation landlord. His descendant, Sir James Duff, commanded English troops during the suppression of the 1798 Rebellion.

Nearby Lough Sheelin is famed for its trout fishing; it's a scenic place for walking year-round.

You'll need your own wheels to explore.

Sights

Cavan County Museum MUSEUM
(049-854 4070; www.cavanmuseum.ie; Virginia Rd; adult/child €3/1.50; 10am-5pm Tue-Sat year-round, 2-6pm Sun Jul-Sep) Located inside a former convent, this museum's impressive collection includes a huge array of 18th-, 19th- and 20th-century costumes and relics from the Stone, Bronze, Iron and Middle Ages, including the Celtic Killycluggin stone and the three-faced Corleck Head, as well as a 1000-year-old boat excavated from Lough Errill. There's also a large feature on Irish sports. Outside, the new, kid-friendly **WWI Trench Experience** has sound effects along its dug-out, sandbagged trenches.

Sleeping

Ross Castle HISTORIC HOTEL €€
(086 824 2200; www.ross-castle.com; Mountnugent; d €120-130) Situated 9km south of Ballyjamesduff, this 1590 castle was partially destroyed by Cromwell but rebuilt by the Nugent family. It's an unforgettable stay but not for the fainthearted – the steps get steeper and narrower the higher you climb into its tower, one guest room has no bathroom door and it's reputedly haunted. Call ahead to confirm your arrival time.

Eastern Cavan

Many towns in the county's east, such as handsome **Virginia**, were laid out as 17th-century Plantation estates.

Sprawling 29km northeast of Virginia (2km east of Kingscourt), the 225-hectare **Dún an Rí Forest Park** (042-966 7320; www.coillteoutdoors.ie; cars €5; car park 9am-6pm Apr-Oct, to 4.30pm Nov-Mar) has colour-coded forest walks (all less than 4km long), with picnic places and a wishing well. Look out for mink and otters along the river. The car park accepts coins only.

Bordering the forest, 19th-century **Cabra Castle** (042-966 7030; www.cabracastle.com; s/d/cottage from €100/150/110;) is now a deluxe hotel decked out in plush period furnishings. Most rooms are in its courtyard area; there are also self-catering cottages. The lobby and some guest rooms have wi-fi. It's 30km northeast of Virginia (3km east of Kingscourt) on the Carrickmacross road.

Northwestern Cavan

Set against the dramatic backdrop of the Cuilcagh Mountains, the remote northwestern edges of Cavan are some of the county's most scenic. Transport here is limited so you'll need your own.

Ballyconnell

POP 1061

The pretty village of Ballyconnell is popular with anglers and with visitors making their way along the Shannon–Erne Waterway, which wends through town.

Activities

Jampa Ling Buddhist Centre RETREAT
(049-952 3448; www.jampaling.org; Owendoon House, Bawnboy; retreat & workshop per activity €25-45, dm/s self-catering €18/23, incl meals €32/39, inclusive weekend retreat €215) Pure peace on earth, Jampa Ling, meaning 'Place of Infinite Loving Kindness', offers courses, retreats and workshops on Buddhist teachings, philosophy, meditation, yoga, and medicinal and culinary herbs. All meals are vegetarian. Though you don't have to take part in a course to stay here, accommodation may not be available if there is an event on.

Sleeping

Slieve Russell Hotel LUXURY HOTEL €€
(049-952 6444; www.slieverussell.ie; Cranaghan; d from €105-130, tr €149-159;) For relaxation of a luxurious kind, the Slieve Russell Hotel, 3km southeast of town, is a vision of marble columns, fountains, restaurants, bars, and 18- and nine-hole golf courses, with pro lessons available. Its 222 rooms are elegantly furnished; spa treatments include flotation tanks, a herbal sauna and a salt grotto.

Blacklion & Around

POP 174

This remote corner of the county is traversed by the Cavan Way. The little village of Blacklion lies less than 50m from the River Belcoo, marking the border with County Fermanagh, Northern Ireland.

Dedicated foodies make the pilgrimage to the village to MacNean House & Restaurant (p524).

Buses are limited at best so you really need your own wheels.

Sights

Cuilcagh Mountain Park PARK
The border between the Republic and Northern Ireland runs along the ridge of Cuilcagh Mountain, the distinctive table-top summit of Cuilcagh Mountain Park, the world's first cross-border Geopark. Its lower slopes are protected peatland habitats, while the upper slopes have dramatic sweeping cliffs. The visitor centre and the park's most high-profile attraction, the Marble Arch Caves (p633), lie over the border from Blacklion in County Fermanagh.

On the Republic side, the 'newest' draw is the megalithic Cavan Burren Park.

★**Cavan Burren Park** HISTORIC SITE
(www.cavanburren.ie; Tullygobban Hill; car park 9am-7pm) FREE Just 3km south of Blacklion, within the Cuilcagh Mountain Park and traversed by the Cavan Way (p524) walking route, this otherworldly megalithic site was identified in the 1870s but farmed until the 1950s and only established as the Cavan Burren Park in 2014. Highlights include a promontory fort c 500 BC and the Giant's Grave wedge tomb from 2500 BC. An unstaffed information shed has interpretative panels but the hilly, wooded area is otherwise pristine and magical to explore.

WALKING THE CAVAN WAY

The highlight for many walkers in the region is the **Cavan Way**, a 26km trail between the hamlets of Blacklion and Dowra through the Cuilcagh Mountains. Heading south from Blacklion, it takes you through the Cavan Burren Park (p523) and its ancient burial site **Magh Sleacht**, which is dotted with prehistoric monuments – court cairns, ring forts and tombs – and was one of the last strongholds of Druidism. It continues past the Shannon Pot, the source of Ireland's longest river, then by road to Dowra, passing over the **Black Pigs Dyke**, an ancient fortification that once divided Ireland in two.

From Blacklion it's mainly hill walking; from Shannon Pot to Dowra it's mainly road. The highest point on the walk is Giant's Grave (260m). You'll need Ordinance Survey map No 26 and the *Cavan Way* map guide. Maps are on display in Blacklion and Dowra. Detailed route information (including downloadable map PDFs) is available online at www.thisiscavan.ie and www.irishtrails.ie. The route can be boggy, so take spare socks!

At Blacklion you can pick up the Ulster Way and at Dowra you can join the Leitrim Way, which runs between Manorhamilton and Drumshanbo.

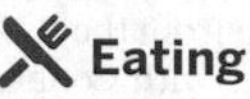

Eating

★ MacNean House & Restaurant MODERN IRISH €€

(☎071-985 3022; www.nevenmaguire.com; Main St; dinner menu €72-87, with paired wines €132, Sun lunch €39, cookery class from €160; ⏲6-11pm Wed-Sat, 12.30-10pm Sun;) Award-winning TV chef Neven Maguire grew up in this gorgeous village house and has turned it into one of Ireland's finest restaurants/cookery schools. Book months in advance to feast on inspired creations such as confit-chicken lollipops with aged Parmesan foam, sherry-vinegar jelly and pumpkin risotto, and drift off in one of the beautiful rooms (doubles €134 to €164).

COUNTY MONAGHAN

POP 60,490 / AREA 1295 SQ KM

Monaghan's quiet, undulating landscape is known for its tiny rounded hills that resemble bubbles in badly pasted wallpaper. Known as drumlins, these bumps are the result of debris left by retreating glaciers during the last ice age. The county's lakes attract plenty of anglers, but few others make it here, making it a tranquil place to explore.

Unlike much of the province, Monaghan was largely left alone during the Ulster Plantation. After the Cromwellian wars, though, local chieftains were forced to sell their land for a fraction of its true value, or have it seized and redistributed to Cromwell's soldiers.

In the early 19th century, lace making became an important facet of the local economy, providing work and income for women. Clones and Carrickmacross were the two main centres of the industry and you can still see the fine needlework on display in both towns.

Monaghan Town

POP 6221

It may be the county town, but Monaghan's residents live their lives utterly unaffected by tourism. It's a pleasant place to wander and admire the elegant 18th- and 19th-century limestone buildings.

Sights & Activities

In Church Sq, the hefty obelisk the **Dawson Monument** (1857) commemorates Colonel Dawson's unfortunate demise in the Crimean War. Overlooking it is the Gothic St Patrick's Church and a stately Doric **courthouse** (1829). Heading west you'll find the **Rossmore Memorial** (c 1875), an over-the-top Victorian drinking fountain that dominates the Diamond.

The town also has a number of buildings with gently rounded corners, an unusual architectural feature in Ireland.

Monaghan County Museum MUSEUM

(www.monaghan.ie; 1-2 Hill St; ⏲11am-5pm Mon-Fri, noon-5pm Sat) FREE More than 70,000 artefacts from the Stone Age to modern times are housed at this excellent regional museum. Its crowning glory is the 14th-century **Cross of Clogher**, an oaken altar cross encased in decorative bronze panels. Other impressive finds include the Lisdrumturk and Altartate Cauldrons, medieval *crannóg* artefacts, and some frightening knuckle-dusters and cudgels relating to the border with the North.

Venture Sports FISHING
(047-81495; 71 Glaslough St; 9am-6pm Mon-Sat) Fine fishing abounds in the area; contact Venture Sports for permits, tackle and local knowledge.

Festivals & Events

Harvest Blues Festival MUSIC
(www.harvestblues.ie) Fabulous three-day blues festival featuring local and international acts in early September.

Sleeping & Eating

For an atmospheric stay just outside town, book into Castle Leslie (p526).

Westenra Arms HOTEL €€
(047-74400; www.westenrahotel.com; The Diamond; s €59-79, d €99-129, tr €130-160;) A town-centre landmark, this huge red-brick hotel has comfortable rooms (some with four-poster beds) reached by a lift, and sociable public areas including a restaurant, bar with live music, nightclub, and fabulous cocktail bar, Shifty Mulhares (p525). But you can still sleep in peace as rooms are well soundproofed. Kids are warmly welcomed with toys and colouring books.

Andy's Bar & Restaurant BISTRO €€
(047-82277; www.andysmonaghan.com; 12 Market St; restaurant mains €14-29, bar mains €8-14; restaurant 6-10pm Fri & Sat, 5-9.30pm Sun, bar food 4-10pm Tue-Fri, 2-10pm Sat, 1.30-9.30pm Sun) A longstanding local favourite, this white-washed Victorian bar and old-school restaurant is a family-run Monaghan institution. House specialities include deep-fried breaded mushrooms with garlic mayo dip, and breaded chicken fillet with mushroom and onion sauce, plus traditional fish and chips.

Drinking & Nightlife

Shifty Mulhares COCKTAIL BAR
(www.westenrahotel.com; The Diamond; 5pm-1am Fri-Sun) Down a flight of stairs from the street this basement cocktail bar at the Westenra Arms (p525) is ingeniously themed as the home of fictitious intrepid explorer Shifty Mulhares. It's decked out with items collected on his travels – everything from birdcages to studded chesterfield sofas to '80s vinyl; you can even sip cocktails on Shifty's four-poster bed.

McKenna's Bar PUB
(www.mckennasbar.net; 62 Dublin Rd; 7pm-midnight Mon-Fri, from 3pm Sat & Sun;) This historic pub is famous throughout the region for its jam sessions, predominantly blues. They take place in its upstairs bar 'the Brewery': the ideal moody venue with its dark wood, barrel tables and brick walls.

Entertainment

Market House PERFORMING ARTS
(047-38162; www.monaghan.ie; Market St) This restored 18th-century market-hall-turned arts-venue hosts exhibitions, concerts and drama productions.

Information

Tourist Office (047-81122; www.monaghantourism.com; Market St; 10am-5pm Mon-Fri Jun-Sep) In the Market House.

Getting There & Around

From the bus station on North Rd, daily services include Dublin (€17, two hours, eight daily) and Carrickmacross (€13, 30 minutes, eight daily).

Rossmore Forest Park

Crumbling remains of the Rossmore family's 19th-century castle, including its entrance stairway, buttresses and the family's pet cemetery, can be seen at **Rossmore Forest Park** (www.coillteoutdoors.ie; cars €5; car park 9am-6pm Apr-Oct, to 4.30pm Nov-Mar), where rhododendrons and azaleas blaze with colour in early summer. Along with forest walks and pleasant picnic areas, the park contains several giant redwoods, a fine yew avenue and Iron Age tombs. It's 3km south-west of Monaghan town on the Newbliss road (R189). The car park accepts coins only.

Clones & Around

POP 1517

Once the site of an important 6th-century monastery that later became an Augustinian abbey, Clones' main sights worth a brief look are ecclesiastical.

On the Diamond, a well-preserved 10th-century **high cross** is decorated with drama-charged biblical stories such as Daniel in the lion's den.

Along with the remains of the **abbey** founded by St Tiernach on Abbey St, there's a truncated 22m-high round tower, which

WORTH A TRIP

CASTLE LESLIE

Castle Leslie (☎047-88100; www.castleleslie.com; Glaslough; d from €170; 📶), 11km north-east of Monaghan town along the R185, is a magnificent Victorian pile, acquired by the Leslie family (who trace their ancestors back to Attila the Hun) in 1665. Facilities include a Victorian spa and equestrian centre (per hour from €35); dining options span sophisticated **Snaffles Brasserie** to snug **Conor's Bar**. Public areas have wi-fi.

Each of the 20 guest rooms in the main house has a story: the Red Room, used by WB Yeats, contains the first bath plumbed in Ireland, while in Uncle Norman's Room, guests claim to have been levitated in the Gothic four-poster bed. The Hunting Lodge has a further 30 rooms, with decor ranging from rich traditional drapery to more minimalist contemporary style.

dates from the early 9th century, in the cemetery south of town. Nearby is the supposed burial place of Tiernach himself, a chunky 9th-century **sarcophagus** with worn animal-head carvings.

Clones later found fame as a lace-making centre. To learn about the history of Clones lace, see it on display or purchase samples, stop by the **Ulster Canal Stores** (☎047-52125; www.cloneslace.com; Cara St; ⏰10am-5pm Mon-Fri).

On a 240-hectare estate 5km south of Clones along the R212 towards Scotshouse, magnificent country-house retreat **Hilton Park** (☎047-56007; www.hiltonpark.ie; s €125-155, d €170-270, gatehouse per week €495; ⏰Apr-Oct) has been in the same family since 1734. Its six spacious, light-bathed guest rooms are decorated with original furniture, free-standing baths and four-poster or half-tester beds. Rates include high tea on arrival; top-class cuisine is largely sourced from the estate's gardens (dinner €55, Tuesday to Saturday by prior arrangement).

Bus Éireann runs a service from Clones to Monaghan (€7, 25 minutes, three Monday to Saturday, one Sunday). **Ulsterbus** (www.translink.co.uk) has a direct service between Clones and Belfast (€20, 2¾ hours, one daily).

Carrickmacross & Around

POP 1973

Carrickmacross was first settled by early English and Scottish Planters, and its broad main street is flanked by elegant Georgian houses with gorgeous poster-paint coloured facades. It's most famous as the home of delicate Carrickmacross lace, an industry revived in 1871 by the St Louis nuns.

The town makes a great base for anglers, with fantastic fishing at Loughs Capragh, Spring, Monalty and Fea.

Sights

Carrickmacross Lace Gallery GALLERY
(☎042-966 4176; www.carrickmacrosslace.ie; Market Sq; ⏰10am-4pm Mon & Sat, to 5.30pm Tue-Fri) In the town's former cattle yards, a local cooperative runs this thimble-sized lace gallery, where you can see lace-making demonstrations and check out exquisite designs. Carrickmacross' lace makers can take commissions and you can purchase small exquisite pieces made into fridge magnets, bookmarks and similar for as little as €10.

Unlike Clones' crocheted lace, designs here are appliquéd on organza using thick thread and close stitches, then embellished with a variety of point stitches, guipure, pops and the lace's distinctive loop edge.

Carrickmacross lace graced the sleeves of Princess Diana's wedding dress and, more recently, the technique was used on the wedding dress for Kate Middleton's wedding to Prince William in 2011.

St Joseph's Catholic Church CHURCH
(O'Neill St; ⏰8am-6pm) Craftsmanship shines at St Joseph's Catholic Church, with 10 windows designed by Harry Clarke, Ireland's most renowned stained-glass artist. Opening hours can vary.

Sleeping & Eating

★**Shirley Arms** HOTEL €€
(☎042-967 3100; www.shirleyarmshotel.ie; Main St; d from €110, bar/restaurant mains €14-29; 📶) Right in the centre of town, the Shirley Arms has a warm stone exterior, behind which lies a superb family-run hotel. White linens, walnut floors and modern bathrooms give the rooms a contemporary flair. The open-plan bar and lounge create an informal setting for some excellent bar food and there's an elegant **restaurant**.

★**Courthouse Restaurant** MODERN IRISH €€
(www.courthouserestaurant.ie; 1 Monaghan St; tapas €4.50-7, mains €17-25; ⌚12.15-2.30pm & 5.30-9.30pm Wed-Fri, 5-10pm Sat, 12.15-4pm & 5-9pm Sun; ✎) Chef Conor Mee uses local, seasonal produce in creative ways, resulting in daily changing Irish tapas (eg beetroot with cabbage-walnut pesto) and mains such as grilled sea bream with sea asparagus, shrimp and lemon butter; roast duck breast with orange and carrot puree; and slow-cooked venison with potato gratin. Rough-hewn stone walls, exposed timber and flickering candles enhance the romantic atmosphere.

Drinking

Fiddlers Elbow PUB
(www.fiddlers.ie; Main St; ⌚11am-midnight Sun-Thu, to 2am Fri-Sun) One of a row of picturesque colourful facades, Fiddlers Elbow's shamrock-green frontage leads to a bar, restaurant and upstairs nightclub (www.vanity nightclub.ie). The whole place has a buzzy convivial atmosphere; there's live music on Saturdays from 9pm.

Information

Carrickmacross has no tourist office, but the tourism section of the town's website, www.carrickmacross.ie, has visitor information.

Getting There & Away

Bus Éireann services connect with Dublin (€17, 1½ hours, eight daily).

Inniskeen

POP 292

Acclaimed poet Patrick Kavanagh (1904–67) was born in the picturesque little village of Inniskeen, 10km northeast of Carrickmacross.

Kavanagh's long work *The Great Hunger* (1942) blasted away the earlier clichés of Anglo-Irish verse and revealed Ireland's poor farming communities as half-starved, 'broken-backed' and sexually repressed. His best-known poem, *On Raglan Road* (1946), was an ode to his unrequited love. It doubled as the lyrics for the traditional Irish air *The Dawning of the Day,* which has been performed by Van Morrison, Mark Knopfler, Billy Bragg, Sinéad O'Connor and countless others.

The **Patrick Kavanagh Resource Centre** (☎042-937 8560; www.patrickkavanaghcountry.com; adult/child €5/3; ⌚11am-4.30pm Tue-Fri year-round, 3-5.30pm Sun Jun-Sep) is housed in the old parish church where Kavanagh was baptised; he's buried in the attached graveyard. The staff have a passion for the poet's life and work that is contagious, and the centre hosts annual events including a **Writers' Weekend** in late July/early August.

Information on **guided literary tours** around town is posted on the resource centre's website. You can walk or drive around the sites in and around the village and the picturesque surrounding countryside (5.6km in all).

Inniskeen is on the Bus Éireann route between Dundalk (€5.50, 15 minutes) and Carrickmacross (€4.10, 20 minutes), with four services Monday to Saturday.

Belfast

POP 280,900 / AREA 115 SQ KM

Includes ➡

Best Places to Eat

- ➡ Mourne Seafood Bar (p549)
- ➡ OX (p549)
- ➡ Barking Dog (p552)
- ➡ Holohan's (p549)
- ➡ Saphyre (p553)

Best Places to Drink

- ➡ Crown Liquor Saloon (p554)
- ➡ Filthy Quarter (p554)
- ➡ Duke of York (p554)
- ➡ Love & Death Inc (p554)
- ➡ Eglantine (p556)

Why Go?

Belfast is in many ways a brand-new city. Once lumped with Beirut, Baghdad and Bosnia as one of the four 'Bs' for travellers to avoid, in recent years it has pulled off a remarkable transformation from bombs-and-bullets pariah to a hip-hotels-and-hedonism party town.

The old shipyards on the Lagan continue to give way to the luxury apartments of the Titanic Quarter, whose centrepiece, the stunning, star-shaped edifice housing the Titanic Belfast centre, covering the ill-fated liner's construction here, has become the city's number-one tourist draw.

New venues keep popping up – already this decade historic Crumlin Road Gaol and SS *Nomadic* opened to the public, and WWI warship HMS *Caroline* is set to become a floating museum in 2016. They all add to a list of attractions that includes beautifully restored Victorian architecture, a glittering waterfront lined with modern art, a fantastic foodie scene and music-filled pubs.

When to Go

➡ April can be a great time to visit Belfast, with spring flowers blooming throughout the city's parks and gardens, and the Belfast Film Festival showcasing Irish and international filmmakers' works.

➡ August brings good weather for walking and cycling, along with celebrations of Irish music and dance in West Belfast during Féile An Phobail, plus street parties and a carnival parade.

➡ October can start to get chilly, but the Festival at Queen's, the UK's second-largest arts festival (after Edinburgh's), warms things up during its three-week run.

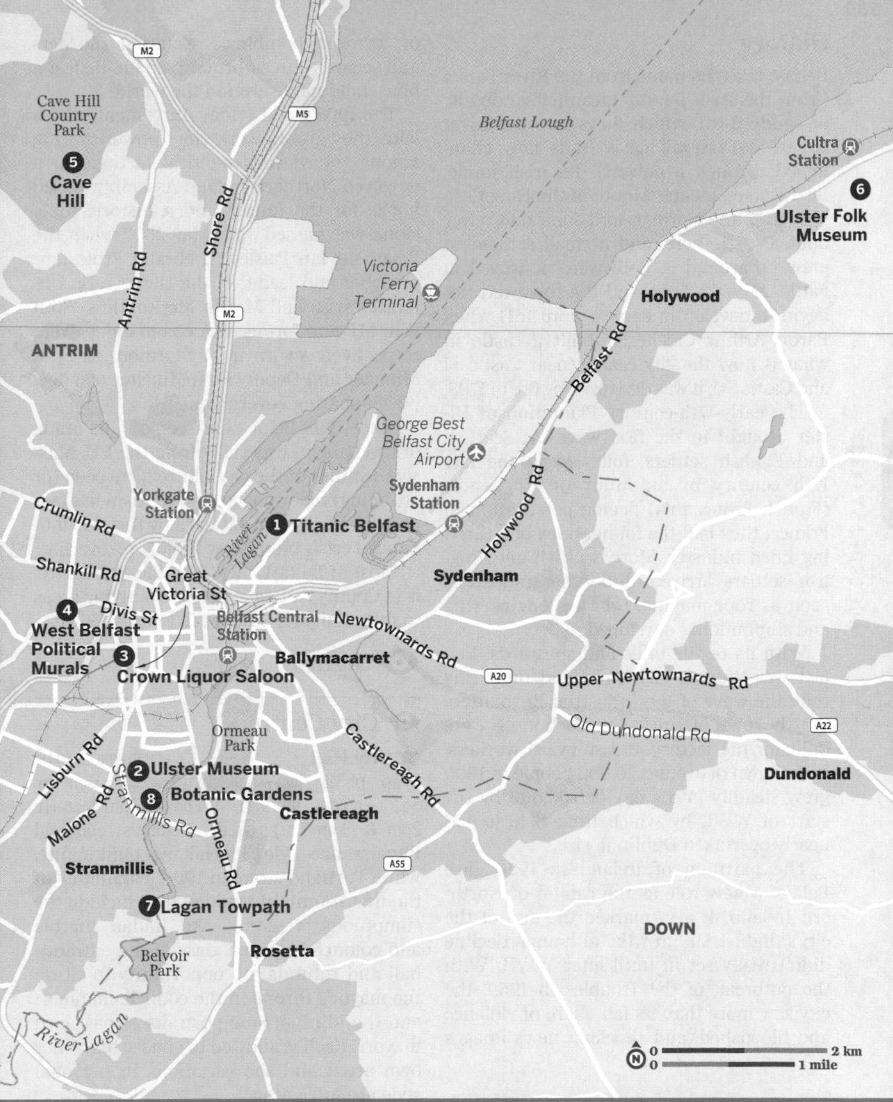

Belfast Highlights

1. Learn about the world's most famous ocean liner at **Titanic Belfast** (p537).

2. Discover prehistoric treasures, an ancient Egyptian mummy and Armada gold at the **Ulster Museum** (p538).

3. Down a Guinness in Belfast's most beautiful Victorian pub, the **Crown Liquor Saloon** (p531).

4. Take a **taxi tour** (p545) of powerful political murals in West Belfast.

5. Enjoy the city views from the top of **Cave Hill** (p531).

6. Walk through history among reconstructed farmhouses, forges and mills at the **Ulster Folk Museum** (p541).

7. Cycle along the **Lagan Towpath** (p536) to the former linen town of Lisburn.

8. Visit the birdcage-domed Palm House in the peaceful **Botanic Gardens** (p540).

History

Belfast takes its name from the River Farset (from the Irish *feirste,* meaning sandbank, or sandy ford), which flows into the River Lagan at Donegall Quay (it is now channelled through a culvert). Its Irish name, Béal Feirste, means 'Mouth of the Farset'.

In 1177, the Norman lord John de Courcy built a castle here, and a small settlement grew up around it. Both were destroyed in battle 20 years later, and the town did not begin to develop in earnest until 1611 when Baron Arthur Chichester built a castle in what is now the city centre (near Castle Pl and Castle St); it was destroyed by fire in 1708.

The early-17th-century Plantation of Ulster brought in the first waves of Scottish and English settlers, followed in the late 17th century by an influx of Huguenots (French Protestants) fleeing persecution in France; they laid the foundations of a thriving linen industry. More Scottish and English settlers arrived, and other industries such as rope-making, tobacco, engineering and shipbuilding developed.

With its textile mills and shipyards, Belfast was the one city in Ireland that truly rode the wave of the Industrial Revolution. Sturdy rows of brick terrace houses were built for the factory and shipyard workers, and a town of around 20,000 people in 1800 grew steadily into a city of 400,000 by the start of WWI, by which time Belfast had nearly overtaken Dublin in size.

The partition of Ireland in 1920 gave Belfast a new role as the capital of Northern Ireland. It also marked the end of the city's industrial growth, although decline didn't really set in until after WWII. With the outbreak of the Troubles in 1969, the city saw more than its fair share of violence and bloodshed, and shocking news images of terrorist bombings, sectarian murders and security forces' brutality made Belfast a household name around the world.

The 1998 Good Friday Agreement, which laid the groundwork for power-sharing among the various political factions in a devolved Northern Ireland Assembly, raised hopes for the future, and a historic milestone was passed on 8 May 2007 when the Reverend Ian Paisley (firebrand Protestant preacher and leader of the Democratic Unionist Party) and Martin McGuinness (Sinn Féin MP and former IRA commander) were respectively sworn in at Stormont as First Minister and Deputy First Minister of a new power-sharing government.

Since 1998 Belfast has seen a huge influx of investment, especially from the EU. Massive swathes of the city centre have been (or are being) redeveloped, and tourism has taken off. The city was hit hard by the global financial crisis but is now rapidly recovering.

Most of Belfast, including the city centre, is in County Antrim, but some outlying areas to the south and east are in County Down.

TRACING YOUR ANCESTORS

If you're hoping to track down your Ulster family history, the Public Record Office of Northern Ireland, **PRONI** (028-9053 4800; www.proni.gov.uk; 2 Titanic Blvd; 9am-4.45pm Mon-Wed & Fri, 10am-8.45pm Thu), has its headquarters in Belfast's Titanic Quarter. Admission is free, but a charge is made for copies of documents. Check the website for details of how to register and search the records.

Sights

City Centre

★City Hall HISTORIC BUILDING

(Map p532; www.belfastcity.gov.uk; Donegall Sq; guided tours 11am, 2pm & 3pm Mon-Fri, 2pm & 3pm Sat) FREE Belfast's classical Renaissance-style City Hall was built in fine, white Portland stone in 1906. Highlights of the free, 45-minute guided tour include the sumptuous, wedding-cake Italian marble and colourful stained glass of the entrance hall and rotunda; an opportunity to sit on the mayor's throne in the council chamber; and the idiosyncratic portraits of past lord mayors. Each is allowed to choose his or her own artist and the variations in personal style are intriguing.

The Industrial Revolution transformed Belfast in the 19th century. The city's rapid rise to muck-and-brass prosperity manifested in the extravagance of the building, which was paid for with the gas supply company's profits. The hall is fronted by a statue of a rather dour 'we are not amused' **Queen Victoria**. The bronze figures on either side of her symbolise the textile and shipbuilding industries. The child at the back represents education.

At the northeastern corner of the grounds is a statue of **Sir Edward Harland**, the Yorkshire-born marine engineer who founded

BELFAST IN...

One Day

Start your day with breakfast in one of the many cafes on Botanic Ave – **Maggie May's** (p552) will do nicely – then stroll north into the city centre and take a free guided tour of **City Hall** (p530). Take a **black taxi tour** (p545) of the West Belfast murals, then ask the taxi driver to drop you off for lunch at **Holohan's** (p549), aboard the **Belfast Barge** (p536). Then head across the river to spend the rest of the afternoon exploring **Titanic Belfast** (p537). Round off the day with dinner in the Cathedral Quarter at the **Potted Hen** (p552) and drinks at the city's biggest beer garden at the **National Grande Café** (p555).

Two Days

On your second day, take a look at **Queen's University** (p539), explore the fascinating exhibits in the **Ulster Museum** (p538) and take a stroll through the **Botanic Gardens** (p540). In the afternoon either take a guided tour around historic **Crumlin Road Gaol** (p538), or go for a hike up **Cave Hill** (p543). Have dinner at the **Mourne Seafood Bar** (p549), then spend the evening crawling traditional pubs such as **Kelly's Cellars** (p554), the **Duke of York** (p554), and **Crown Liquor Saloon** (p554).

the Harland & Wolff shipyards and who served as mayor of Belfast from 1885 to 1886. To his south stands a **memorial to the victims of the Titanic**.

The **Bobbin Coffee Shop** (Map p532; dishes £4-6; ⏲9.30am-4.30pm Mon-Fri, 10am-4pm Sat), in the southeast corner, houses an exhibition of photographic portraits of Belfast's most famous citizens, from footballer George Best and musician Van Morrison to broadcaster Gloria Hunniford and former president of Ireland Mary McAleese.

★Crown Liquor Saloon HISTORIC BUILDING
(Map p532; www.nationaltrust.org.uk; 46 Great Victoria St; ⏲11.30am-11pm Mon-Wed, to midnight Thu-Sat, 12.30-10pm Sun) FREE There are not too many historical monuments that you can enjoy while savouring a pint of beer, but the National Trust's Crown Liquor Saloon is one of them. Belfast's most famous bar was refurbished by Patrick Flanagan in the late 19th century and displays Victorian decorative flamboyance at its best (he was looking to pull in a posh clientele from the newfangled train station and Grand Opera House across the street).

The exterior (1885) is decorated with ornate and colourful Italian tiles, and boasts a mosaic of a crown on the pavement outside the entrance. Legend has it that Flanagan, a Catholic, argued with his Protestant wife over what the pub's name should be. His wife prevailed and it was named the Crown in honour of the British monarchy. Flanagan took his sneaky revenge by placing the crown mosaic underfoot where customers would tread on it every day.

The interior (1898) sports a mass of stained and cut glass, marble, ceramics, mirrors and mahogany, all atmospherically lit by genuine gas mantles. A long, highly decorated bar dominates one side of the pub, while on the other is a row of ornate wooden snugs. The snugs come equipped with gunmetal plates (from the Crimean War) for striking matches and bell-pushes that once allowed drinkers to order top-ups without leaving their seats (alas, no longer).

Linen Hall Library LIBRARY
(Map p532; www.linenhall.com; 17 Donegall Sq N; ⏲9.30am-5.30pm Mon-Fri, to 4pm Sat; 📶) FREE Established in 1788 to 'improve the mind and excite a spirit of general inquiry', the Linen Hall Library houses some 260,000 books, more than half of which are part of its important Irish- and local-studies collection. The political collection consists of pretty much everything that has been written about Northern Irish politics since 1966. The library also has a small **coffee shop** (Map p532; www.linenhall.com; dishes £3-7.50; ⏲10am-4pm Mon-Fri, to 3.30pm Sat). The visitors' entrance is on Fountain St, around the corner from the main door.

The library was moved from its original home in the White Linen Hall (the site is now occupied by City Hall) to the present building a century later. Thomas Russell, the first librarian, was a founding member of the United Irishmen and a close friend of Wolfe Tone – a reminder that this movement for independence from Britain had its origins in Belfast. Russell was hanged in 1803 after Robert Emmet's abortive rebellion.

Central Belfast

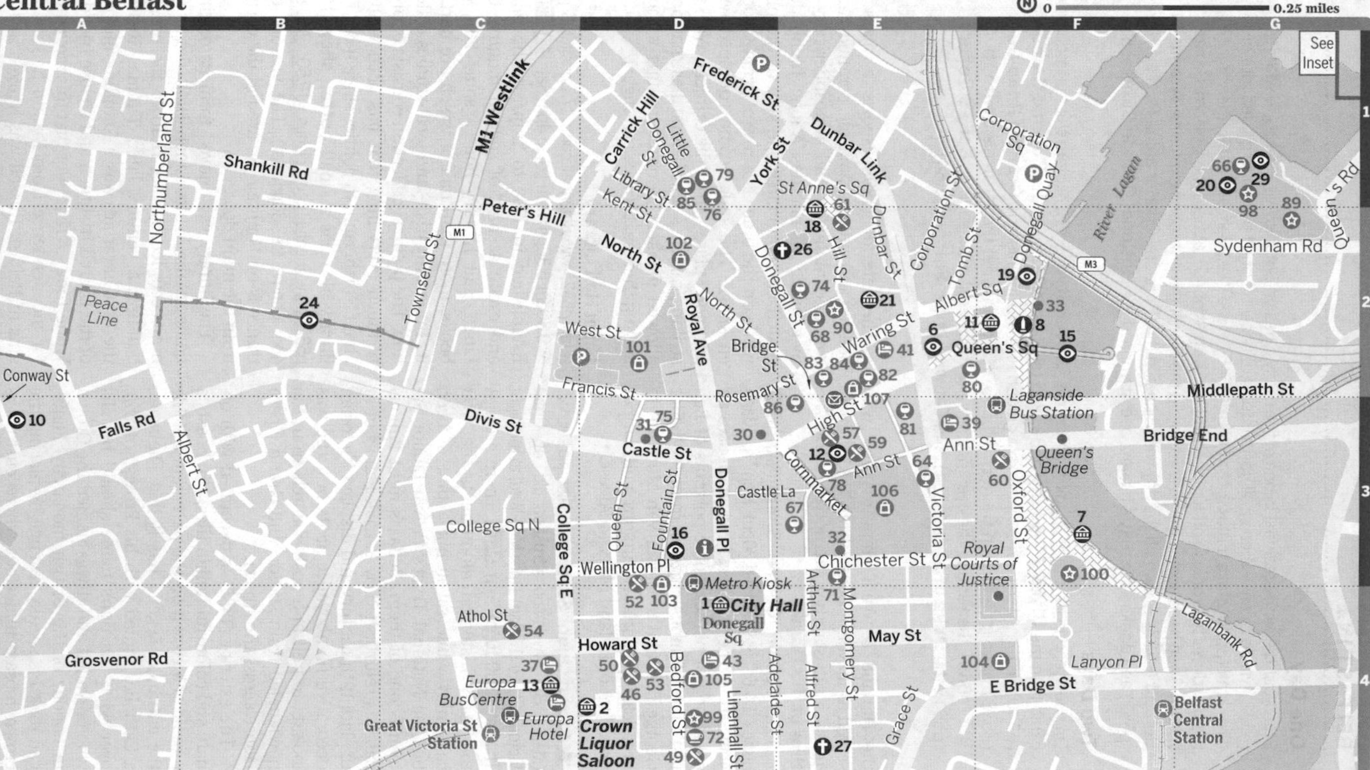

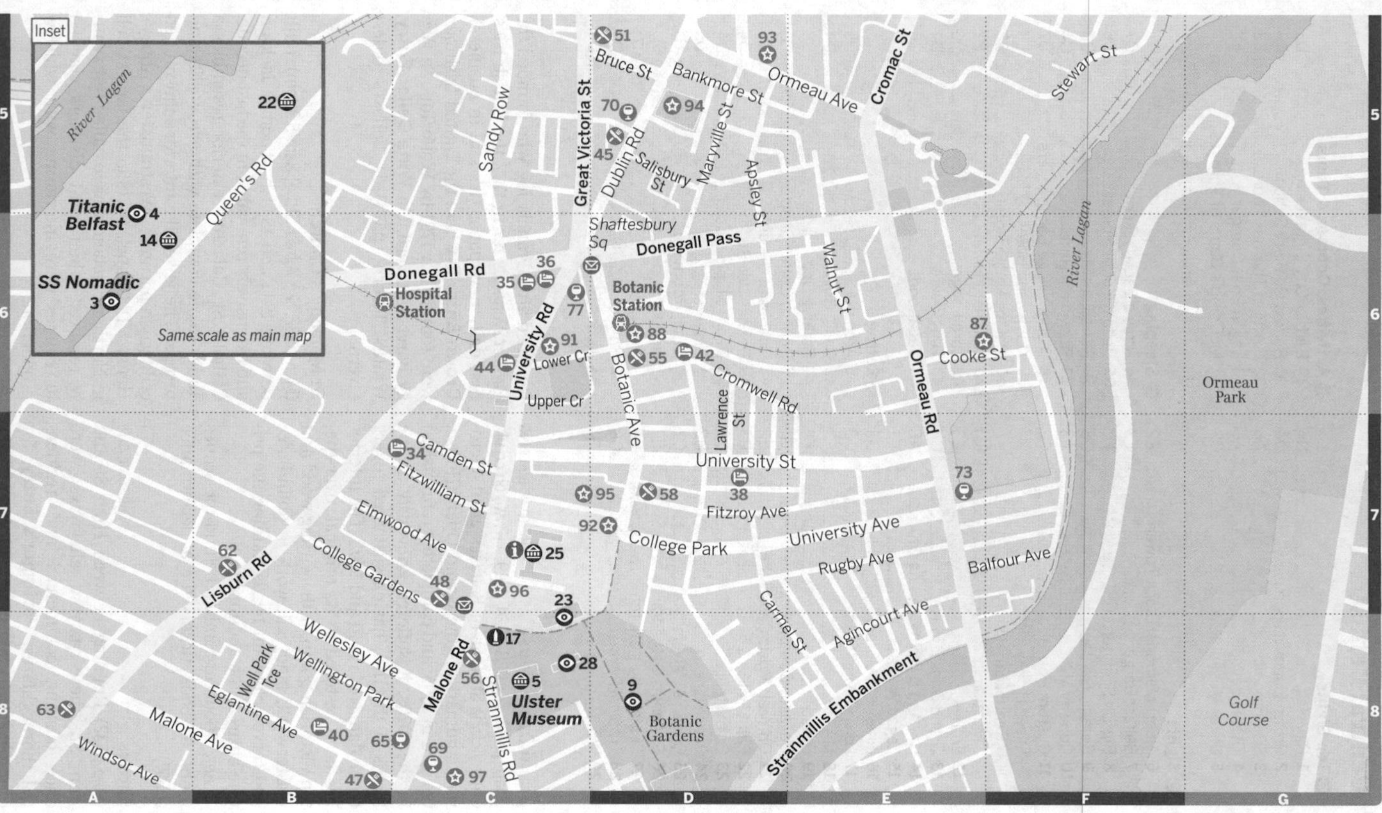
Inset
River Lagan
Titanic Belfast
SS Nomadic
Queen's Rd
Same scale as main map
Sandy Row
Great Victoria St
Bruce St
Bankmore St
Ormeau Ave
Cromac St
Stewart St
Dublin Rd
Salisbury St
Maryville St
Apsley St
Shaftesbury Sq
Donegall Pass
Donegall Rd
Hospital Station
Botanic Station
Walnut St
River Lagan
University Rd
Lower Cr
Upper Cr
Botanic Ave
Cromwell Rd
Lawrence St
Ormeau Rd
Cooke St
Ormeau Park
Camden St
Fitzwilliam St
University St
Fitzroy Ave
Elmwood Ave
College Park
University Ave
Rugby Ave
Balfour Ave
College Gardens
Lisburn Rd
Carmel St
Agincourt Ave
Wellesley Ave
Wellington Park
Well Park Tce
Malone Rd
Stranmillis Rd
Ulster Museum
Botanic Gardens
Stranmillis Embankment
Eglantine Ave
Malone Ave
Windsor Ave
Golf Course

Central Belfast

Top Sights
1 City Hall D4
2 Crown Liquor Saloon D4
3 SS Nomadic A6
4 Titanic Belfast A6
5 Ulster Museum C8

Sights
6 Albert Memorial Clock Tower E2
7 Belfast Barge F3
8 Bigfish Sculpture F2
9 Botanic Gardens D8
10 Conway Mill A3
11 Custom House F2
Eileen Hickey Irish Republican History Museum .... (see 10)
12 Entries E3
13 Grand Opera House C4
14 Harland & Wolff Drawing Offices A6
15 Lagan Weir F2
16 Linen Hall Library D3
17 Lord Kelvin Statue C8
18 MAC E2
19 Obel F2
20 Odyssey Complex G1
21 Oh Yeah Music Centre E2
22 Paint Hall B5
23 Palm House C8
24 Peace Line B2
25 Queen's University C7
26 St Anne's Cathedral E2
27 St Malachy's Church E4
28 Tropical Ravine C8
29 W5 .... G1

Activities, Courses & Tours
30 Belfast City Sightseeing D3
31 Belfast Cookery School D3
32 Game of Thrones Tours E3
33 Lagan Boat Company F2
McComb's Game of Thrones Tours .... (see 35)

Sleeping
34 Arnie's Backpackers C7
35 Belfast Youth Hostel C6
36 Benedicts C6
37 Fitzwilliam Hotel C4
38 Global Village Backpackers D7
39 Malmaison Hotel E3
40 Malone Lodge Hotel B8
41 Merchant Hotel E2
42 Tara Lodge D6
43 Ten Square D4
44 Vagabonds C6

Eating
45 Archana D5
46 Bar & Grill D4
47 Barking Dog B8
Bobbin Coffee Shop .... (see 1)
48 Deanes at Queen's C7
49 Deanes Deli Bistro D4
50 Deanes Eipic D4
51 Ginger D5
Great Room .... (see 41)
Hendogs .... (see 61)
Holohan's .... (see 7)
52 Home D3
53 James St South D4

Grand Opera House HISTORIC BUILDING
(Map p532; ☎028-9024 1919; www.goh.co.uk; Great Victoria St) One of Belfast's great Victorian landmarks is the Grand Opera House. Opened in 1895, and completely refurbished in the 1970s, it suffered grievously at the hands of the IRA, having sustained severe bomb damage in 1991 and 1993. The interior has been restored to its original, over-the-top Victorian pomp, with swirling wood and plasterwork, fancy gilt-work in abundance and carved elephant heads framing the private boxes in the auditorium.

Ask about upcoming behind-the-scenes tours, or book tickets for a performance (p557).

Entries HISTORIC SITE
(Map p532) Running between High St and Ann St, these narrow alleyways were once bustling commercial and residential thoroughfares; **Pottinger's Entry**, for example, had 34 houses in 1822. **Joy's Entry** is named after Francis Joy, who founded the *Belfast News Letter* in 1737, the British Isles' first daily newspaper (it's still in business). **Crown Entry** is where the United Irishmen were founded in 1791 by Wolfe Tone in Peggy Barclay's tavern. On **Wine Cellar Entry**, White's Tavern (p554) is Belfast's oldest tavern.

St Malachy's Church CHURCH
(Map p532; 24 Alfred St; ⏲8am-5.30pm) Built between 1841 and 1844 by Thomas Jackson and extensively renovated in the last decade, Catholic St Malachy's exterior resembles a Tudor castle complete with arrow slits and turrets. The jewel-like interior's fan-vaulted ceiling replicates Westminster Abbey's Henry VII Chapel. In 1886 the largest bell in Northern Ireland was installed but swiftly removed when local distillers claimed its chimes were interfering with whiskey production.

Cathedral Quarter

The gentrified district north of the city centre around St Anne's Cathedral, bounded roughly by Donegall, Waring, Dunbar and York Sts, is a bohemian enclave of restored redbrick warehouses and cobbled lanes, lined with artists studios, design offices, and stylish bars and restaurants.

St Anne's Cathedral CHURCH

(Map p532; www.belfastcathedral.org; Donegall St; admission by donation; 8am-6pm Mon-Sat, to 4pm Sun) Built in Hiberno-Romanesque style, St Anne's Cathedral was started in 1899 but did not reach its final form until 1981. As you enter you'll see that the black-and-white marble floor is laid out in a maze pattern – the black route leads to a dead end, the white to the sanctuary and salvation. The nave's 10 pillars are topped by carvings symbolising aspects of Belfast life; look out for the Freemasons' pillar (the central one on the south side).

In the south aisle is the tomb of Unionist hero Sir Edward Carson (1854–1935). In the baptistry, the stunning mosaic of *The Creation* contains 150,000 pieces of coloured glass; it and the mosaic above the west door are the result of seven years' work by sisters Gertrude and Margaret Martin.

MAC GALLERY

(Metropolitan Arts Centre; Map p532; http://themaclive.com; 10 Exchange St W; 10am-7pm;) FREE The MAC's three galleries stage a rolling program of exhibitions that showcase the best of art, photography and sculpture from Ireland and around the world. A beautifully designed venue overlooking the neoclassical St Anne's Sq development, it also includes a writers' room (aka common room; open to all), a cafe and two theatres (p557).

Oh Yeah Music Centre MUSEUM

(Map p532; www.ohyeahbelfast.com; 15-21 Gordon St; museum 11am-3pm Mon-Fri, noon-5pm Sat)

FREE A charitable organisation that provides rehearsal space for young musicians in a converted whiskey warehouse, the Oh Yeah Music Centre is also home to a **museum** of Northern Ireland's musical history from folk music to Snow Patrol. Exhibits range from shamrock-shaped records and electric guitars to historic gig posters, ticket stubs and stage clothing donated by famous bands.

Laganside & Lanyon Place

The ambitious Laganside project to redevelop and regenerate the centre of Belfast has seen extensive restoration of listed buildings and new installations from the 1990s on. More than 30 public artworks are set along the waterfront – ask for a **Laganside Art Trail** leaflet at the Visit Belfast Welcome Centre (p559).

Soaring above the waterfront at Donegall Quay is Belfast's tallest building, the 2011-built 28-storey **Obel** (Map p532), containing 233 apartments. To its south, the architecturally stunning shopping mall, Victoria Square (p558), set around a soaring atrium topped by a vast glass dome, has a **viewing platform**.

Albert Memorial Clock Tower LANDMARK
(Map p532; Queen's Sq) At the east end of High St is Belfast's very own leaning tower. Erected in 1867 in honour of Queen Victoria's dear departed husband, it is not as dramatically out of kilter as the more famously tilted tower in Pisa, but does, nevertheless, lean noticeably to the south – as the locals say, 'Old Albert not only has the time, he also has the inclination.' Restoration work has stabilised its foundations and left its Scrabo sandstone masonry sparkling white.

Lagan Weir LANDMARK
(Map p532) Completed in 1994, Lagan Weir has helped improve the water quality of the River Lagan – the city's former lifeblood – to such an extent that salmon, eels and sea trout migrate up the river once again. A **footbridge** over the weir provides access to the Titanic Quarter.

Just to weir's north is **Bigfish** (Map p532) (1999), a giant ceramic salmon symbolising the river's regeneration. It's covered with tiles depicting the history of Belfast.

Belfast Barge MUSEUM
(Map p532; www.laganlegacy.com; Lanyon Quay; adult/child £4/3; 10am-4pm) Housed in a barge moored on the River Lagan, this museum tells the story of Belfast's maritime and industrial history, bringing together old photographs, original drawings and documents, ship models and artefacts, and recordings of interviews with retired engineers, designers and shipyard workers.

At the opposite end of the barge is the brilliant restaurant, Holohan's (p549).

Custom House HISTORIC BUILDING
(Map p532; Custom House Sq) Opposite the west end of Lagan Weir is the elegant Custom House, built by Charles Lanyon in Italianate style between 1854 and 1857; the writer Anthony Trollope once worked in the post office here. On the waterfront side, the pediment carries sculpted portrayals of Britannia, Neptune and Mercury. The **Custom House steps** were once a speakers' corner, a tradition memorialised in a bronze statue preaching to an invisible crowd. The building's interior is closed to the public.

WALK: LAGAN TOWPATH

Part of Belfast's Laganside redevelopment project was the restoration of the towpath along the west bank of the River Lagan. You can now walk or cycle for 20km along the winding riverbank from central Belfast to Lisburn.

A shorter walk along the towpath (10km) starts from **Shaw's Bridge** (Map p542) on the southern edge of the city and heads back towards the city centre. Take bus 8A or 8B from Donegall Sq E to the stop just before the Malone roundabout (where Malone Rd becomes Upper Malone Rd). Bear left at the roundabout (signposted Outer Ring A55) and you'll reach the River Lagan at Shaw's Bridge.

Turn left and follow the towpath downstream on the left bank of the river (waymarked with red '9' signs), passing a restored lock-keeper's cottage and canal-side cafe at lock number '3'. The most attractive part of the walk is **Lagan Meadows** (Map p542), a tree-fringed loop in the river to the right of the path and a good place for a picnic on a summer day. Further along, **Cutters Wharf** (p553) is also a great place for a lunch break or refreshing ale. From the pub, the walk continues to **Lagan Weir** in Belfast's city centre.

RMS TITANIC

Perhaps the most famous vessel ever launched, RMS *Titanic* was built in Belfast's Harland & Wolff shipyard for the White Star Line. When the keel was laid in 1909, Belfast was at the height of its fame as a shipbuilding powerhouse, and the *Titanic* was promoted by White Star as the world's biggest and most luxurious ocean liner. Ironically, it was also claimed to be 'unsinkable'.

The *Titanic* was launched from H&W's slipway No 3 on 31 May 1911, and spent almost a year being fitted out in the nearby Thompson Graving Dock before leaving Belfast for the maiden voyage on 2 April 1912. In one of the most notorious nautical disasters of all time, the ship hit an iceberg in the North Atlantic on 14 April 1912, and sank in the early hours of the following day. Of the 2228 passengers and crew on board, only 705 survived; there were only enough lifeboats for 1178 people.

The Titanic Stories website (www.the-titanic.com) contains a wealth of information on the ship and its passengers, and lists all *Titanic*-related museums and memorials throughout Ireland and the rest of the world.

Titanic Quarter

Stretching along the east side of the River Lagan, Belfast's former shipbuilding yards – the birthplace of the RMS *Titanic* – are dominated by the towering yellow cranes known as **Samson** and **Goliath**.

Part industrial wasteland, part building site and part high-tech business park, the area is currently undergoing a £1 billion regeneration project known as the Titanic Quarter (http://titanicquarter.com) to develop the long-derelict docklands. A series of information boards along Queen's Rd describe items and areas of interest. The quarter's centrepiece is the striking star-shaped outline of Titanic Belfast.

★Titanic Belfast EXHIBITION

(Map p532; www.titanicbelfast.com; Queen's Rd; adult/child £15.50/7.25, combination ticket with Thompson Pump House & Graving Dock £19/9.25; ⏲9am-7pm Apr & Jun-Aug, 9am-6pm May & Sep, 10am-5pm Oct-Mar) The head of the slipway where the *Titanic* was built is now occupied by the gleaming, angular edifice of Titanic Belfast, an unmissable multimedia extravaganza that charts the history of Belfast and the creation of the world's most famous ocean liner. Cleverly designed exhibits enlivened by historic images, animated projections and soundtracks chart Belfast's rise to turn-of-the-20th-century industrial superpower, followed by a high-tech ride through a noisy, smells-and-all re-creation of the city's shipyards.

You can explore every detail of the construction of the *Titanic* from a computer 'fly-through' from keel to bridge, to replicas of the passenger accommodation. Perhaps most poignant are the few flickering images that constitute the only film footage of the ship in existence.

Behind the building you can see the massive slipways where the *Titanic* and her sister ship *Olympic* were built and launched.

★SS Nomadic HISTORIC SITE

(Map p532; www.nomadicbelfast.com; Hamilton Dock, Queen's Rd; adult/child £7/5; ⏲10am-5pm daily Apr-Sep, Tue-Sun Oct-Mar) Built in Belfast in 1911, the SS *Nomadic* is the last remaining vessel of the White Star Line. The little steamship ferried 1st- and 2nd-class passengers between Cherbourg Harbour and the ocean liners that were too big to dock at the French port. On 10 April 1912 it delivered 172 passengers to the ill-fated *Titanic*. First come, first served guided tours run every 30 minutes from 10am until an hour before closing. Alternatively, you're free to roam at will (don't miss the 1st-class toilets!).

Requisitioned in both world wars, the ship ended up as a floating restaurant in Paris in the 1980s and '90s. In 2006 it was rescued from the breaker's yard and brought to Belfast, where it's berthed in the Hamilton Graving Dock.

Thompson Pump House & Graving Dock HISTORIC SITE

(Map p542; www.titanicsdock.com; Queen's Rd; graving dock admission free, pump house adult/child £6/4, combination ticket with Titanic Belfast £19/9.25; ⏲10am-5pm Sat-Thu, 9.30am-5pm Fri; 📶) At the far end of Queen's Rd is the most impressive monument to the days of the great liners – the vast **Thompson Graving Dock** where the *Titanic* was fitted out.

DON'T MISS

CRUMLIN ROAD GAOL

Guided tours of Belfast's notorious **Crumlin Road Gaol** (Map p542; ☎028-9074 1501; www.crumlinroadgaol.com; 53-55 Crumlin Rd; day tour adult/child £8.50/6.50, evening tour £7.50/5.50; ⏰10am-5.30pm, last tour 4.30pm, evening tour 6pm) take you from the tunnel beneath Crumlin Rd, built in 1850 to convey prisoners from the courthouse across the street (and allegedly the origin of the judge's phrase 'take him down'), through the echoing halls and cramped cells of C-Wing, to the truly chilling execution chamber. Advance tour bookings are recommended. The jail's pedestrian entrance is on Crumlin Rd; the car-park entrance is reached via Cliftonpark Ave to the north.

Since it opened in 1846, Crumlin Road Gaol imprisoned a whole range of historic figures, from Eamon de Valera to the Reverend Ian Paisley, and from suffragette Dorothy Evans to the 'Shankill Butcher' murderer Lenny Murphy. Designed by Charles Lanyon (the architect of Queen's University and many other city landmarks), and based on London's Pentonville prison, 'the Crum' was also the scene of 17 executions between 1854 and 1961. It remained a working prison until 1996.

Check the calendar for four-hour 'paranormal tours' (£35), and for regular, highly atmospheric concerts held at the jail.

Beside it is the **Thompson Pump House**, which has an exhibition on Belfast shipbuilding. **Guided tours** (2pm Saturday and Sunday) include a viewing of original film footage from the shipyards, a visit to the inner workings of the pump house and a walk along the floor of the dry dock.

The graving dock's huge size gives you some idea of the scale of the ship, which could only just fit into it. In the dock on the far side of the pump house, naval-history buffs can see **HMS Caroline**, the UK's last surviving WWI Royal Navy cruiser. Built in 1914, the ship is being converted into a floating museum scheduled to open in 2016.

Paint Hall HISTORIC BUILDING

(Map p532; Queen's Rd) Just northeast of Titanic Belfast you'll see the huge paint hall where ship component parts were painted in a climate-controlled environment. Today it's home to **Titanic Studios**, where productions filmed include *Game of Thrones* (no tours available, unfortunately).

Odyssey Complex LANDMARK

(Map p532; www.theodyssey.co.uk; Sydenham Rd) The cylindrical-shaped Odyssey Complex is a huge sporting and entertainment centre on the eastern side of the river at the edge of the Titanic Quarter. The complex features a hands-on science centre, W5; a 10,800-seat sports arena (p557; home to the Belfast Giants (p557) ice-hockey team); a multiplex cinema (p557) with an **IMAX** screen; Box Nightclub (p556); and numerous food outlets and bars.

W5 SCIENCE CENTRE

(Map p532; www.w5online.co.uk; Odyssey Complex, 2 Queen's Quay; adult/child £8.50/6.50; ⏰10am-5pm Mon-Fri, to 6pm Sat, noon-6pm Sun, last admission 1hr before closing) Also known as whowhatwherewhenwhy, W5 is an interactive science centre, aimed at children of all ages and filled with more than 250 exhibits. Kids can compose their own tunes by biffing the 'air harp' with a foam rubber bat, try to beat a lie detector, create cloud rings and tornadoes, and design and build their own robots and racing cars.

◉ South Belfast (Queen's Quarter)

The Golden Mile – the 1.5km stretch of Great Victoria St and Shaftesbury Sq that links the city centre to Queen's Quarter (the university district) – was once the focus for much of Belfast's nightlife. These days, with the regeneration of the city centre, it's more tarnished brass than gold, but is still awash with decent pubs and eateries.

Metro buses 8A, 8B and 8C run from Donegall Sq E along Bradbury Pl and University Rd to Queen's University.

★Ulster Museum MUSEUM

(Map p532; www.nmni.com; Stranmillis Rd; admission by donation; ⏰10am-5pm Tue-Sun) You could spend hours browsing this state-of-the-art museum, but if you're pressed for time don't miss the **Armada Room**, with artefacts retrieved from the 1588 wreck of the Spanish galleon *Girona;* the **Egyptian**

Room, with Princess Takabuti, a 2500-year-old Egyptian mummy unwrapped in Belfast in 1835; and the **Early Peoples Gallery**, with the bronze Bann Disc, a superb example of Celtic design from the Iron Age.

Free tours (10 people maximum; first come, first served) run at 2.30pm Tuesday to Friday and 1.30pm Sunday.

On the ground floor, a potted history of **the Troubles** leads up to the 1st-floor **History Zone**. Its spectacular collection of prehistoric stone and bronze artefacts helps provide a cultural context for Ireland's many archaeological sites. Exhibits include the **Malone Hoard**, a clutch of 16 polished, Neolithic stone axes discovered only a few kilometres from the museum.

The kid-friendly, interactive **Nature Zone** on the 2nd floor covers geological time, evolution and natural history; highlights include the **Snapshot of an Ancient Sea Floor**, a fossilised portion of a 200-million-year-old seabed with jumbled ammonite shells and petrified driftwood.

The top floors are given to **Irish and European art**, most notably the works of Belfast-born Sir John Lavery (1856–1941). More modern paintings include Edward McGuire's 1974 portrait of poet Seamus Heaney.

Queen's University HISTORIC BUILDING
(Map p532; University Rd; guided tour £5) Northern Ireland's most prestigious university was founded by Queen Victoria in 1845. In 1908, the Queen's College became the Queen's University of Belfast and today its campus spreads across some 250 buildings. Queen's has around 25,000 students and specialises in medicine, engineering and law.

Just inside the main entrance is the **Queen's Welcome Centre** (Map p532; www.queenseventus.com; University Rd; 8am-6pm Mon-Fri, 11am-4pm Sat & Sun) FREE with exhibitions and a souvenir shop. Book ahead for **guided tours**, or pick up or download a free leaflet that outlines a self-guided tour.

Charles Lanyon built the Queen's College building, a Tudor Revival in red brick and honey-coloured sandstone, in 1849. If it seems to have an Oxbridge air about it, that may be because Lanyon based the design of the central tower on the 15th-century Founder's Tower at Oxford's Magdalen College.

The college was one of three Queen's Colleges (the others, still around but no longer called Queen's Colleges, are in Cork and Galway), which were created to provide

BELFAST FOR CHILDREN

Belfast is a fantastic city to visit with kids. Events and attractions of interest to travellers with children are listed in the 'Family Fun' section of the **Visit Belfast Welcome Centre** (p559) website. If you're in town in March, look out for cultural and educational events during the **Belfast Children's Festival** (www.youngatart.co.uk; early–mid-Mar).

Kid favourites include the following:

W5 Hands-on science centre.

Belfast Zoo (p543) Animals galore.

Cave Hill Country Park (p543) With an adventure playground.

Ulster Museum Plenty of exhibits and special events designed for children of all ages.

Ulster Folk & Transport Museums (p541) An easy and enjoyable day trip from Belfast.

Pirates Adventure Golf (Map p542; www.piratesadventuregolf.com; 111a Dundonald Rd, Dundonald Touring Caravan Park; adult/child per 18 holes £6/4.50; 11am-9pm Mon-Thu, 11am-10pm Fri, 10am-10pm Sat, 10am-9pm Sun) For outdoor fun, you can try minigolf with a difference at Pirates Adventure Golf. It has two landscaped, 18-hole courses – Blackbeard's Adventure and the Captain's Challenge – decked out with waterfalls, fountains and a giant pirate ship. Take bus 511 from Laganside Bus Station (30 minutes, every 30 minutes).

Aunt Sandra's Candy Factory (Map p542; 028-9073 2868; www.auntsandras.com; 60 Castlereagh Rd; tour £6; tours 11am, 1pm, 3.30pm Sat, 1pm & 3.30pm Sun) See how Aunt Sandra's fudge, candy, chocolates, toffee apples and other traditional sweets are made during a workshop tour (advance bookings essential), or just drop by to browse the **shop** (9am-6pm Mon-Sat, 10am-6pm Sun).

a nondenominational alternative to the Anglican Church's Trinity College in Dublin.

Botanic Gardens GARDENS

(Map p532; Stranmillis Rd; ⌚7.30am-sunset) FREE The showpiece of Belfast's green oasis is Charles Lanyon's beautiful **Palm House** (⌚10am-5pm Apr-Sep, to 4pm Oct-Mar) FREE, built in 1839 and completed in 1852, with its birdcage dome, a masterpiece in cast-iron and curvilinear glass. Nearby is the 1889 **Tropical Ravine** (⌚10am-5pm Apr-Sep, to 4pm Oct-Mar) FREE, a huge red-brick greenhouse designed by the garden's curator Charles McKimm. Inside, a raised walkway overlooks a jungle of tropical ferns, orchids, lilies and banana plants growing in a sunken glen. It reopens in mid-2016 following a £3.8 million restoration.

Just inside the Botanic Gardens' Stranmillis Rd gate is a statue of Belfast-born Sir William Thomson (1824–1907) – **Lord Kelvin** – who helped lay the foundation of modern physics and who invented the Kelvin scale which measures temperatures from absolute zero (-273°C or 0°K).

West Belfast

Northwest of Donegall Sq, Divis St leads across the Westlink Motorway to Falls Rd and West Belfast. Though scarred by decades of civil unrest during the Troubles, this former battleground is one of the most compelling places to visit in Northern Ireland. Recent history hangs heavy in the air, but there is a noticeable spirit of optimism and hope for the future.

The main attractions are the powerful **murals** (p544) that chart the history of the conflict, as well as the political passions of the moment.

West Belfast grew up around the linen mills that propelled the city into late-19th-century prosperity. It was an area of low-cost, working-class housing, and even in the Victorian era was divided along religious lines. The advent of the Troubles in 1968 solidified the sectarian divide, and since 1970 the ironically named Peace Line has separated the Loyalist and Protestant Shankill district (from the Irish *sean chill,* meaning 'old church') from the Republican and Catholic Falls district.

Despite its past reputation, the area is safe to visit. The best way to see West Belfast is on an informative and entertaining **black taxi tour** (p545), but there's nothing to stop you visiting under your own steam, either walking or using the shared black taxis that travel along the Falls and Shankill Rds. Alternatively, buses 10A to 10F from Queen St will take you along the Falls Rd; buses 11A to 11D from Wellington Pl go along Shankill Rd.

Free leaflets from the Visit Belfast Welcome Centre (p559) describe walking tours around the Falls and Shankill districts.

Peace Line WALL

(Map p532) The most visible sign of the divisions that have scarred the area for so long is the 6m-high wall of corrugated steel, concrete and chain-link that controversially divides Belfast's Protestant and Catholic communities, covering some 6.5km in West Belfast alone, with 34km of coverage in all. Its steel gates generally open during limited daytime hours.

Begun in 1969 as a 'temporary measure', the Peace Line has outlasted the Berlin Wall, although the Northern Ireland Executive committed to its removal by mutual consent by 2023.

Cultúrlann McAdam Ó Fiaich CULTURAL CENTRE

(Map p542; www.culturlann.ie; 216 Falls Rd; ⌚9am-9pm Mon-Fri, 9am-6pm Sat, 11am-4pm Sun; 📶) FREE Housed in a red-brick, former Presbyterian church, this Irish language and cultural centre is the focus for West Belfast's community activity. It's a cosy and welcoming place with a **tourist information desk** (☎028-9096 4180; 216 Falls Rd; ⌚9am-5.30pm Mon-Fri, 9.30am-5.30pm Sat, 1-4pm Sun), a **shop** (www.culturlann.ie; 216 Falls Rd; ⌚9am-5.30pm Mon-Fri, 9.30am-5.30pm Sat, 1-4pm Sun) selling a wide selection of books on Ireland, Irish-language material, crafts and Irish-music CDs, and a good cafe-restaurant, **Bia** (www.biabelfast.com; 216 Falls Rd; mains £8-22; ⌚9am-6pm Mon, 8am-8pm Tue-Sat, 10am-6pm Sun; 📶👪). The centre also has an art gallery and a theatre that stages music, drama and poetry events.

Conway Mill ARTS CENTRE

(Map p532; www.conwaymill.org; 5-7 Conway St; ⌚10am-5pm Mon-Fri, to 2pm Sat) FREE Conway Mill is a restored 19th-century flax mill that now houses around 20 artists' studios, an exhibition on the mill's history, an education centre and workspaces for local enterprises. It also houses the **Eileen Hickey Irish Republican History Museum** (⌚10am-2pm Tue-Sat) FREE, a collection of artefacts, newspaper articles, photos and archives relating to the Republican struggle from 1798 to the Troubles.

Sinn Féin Headquarters BUILDING
(Map p542; www.sinnfein.ie; 51 Falls Rd) The red-brick Sinn Féin Headquarters has the famous mural of a smiling **Bobby Sands**, the hunger striker who was elected as MP for West Belfast just a few weeks before he died in 1981. The text reads, in Sands' own words, 'Our revenge will be the laughter of our children.'

Outside the Centre

★Ulster Folk & Transport Museums MUSEUM
(Map p542; www.nmni.com; Cultra, Holywood; adult/child £9/5.50, combined ticket to both museums £11/6; 10am-5pm Tue-Sun Mar-Sep, 10am-4pm Tue-Fri & 11am-4pm Sat & Sun Oct-Feb) One of Northern Ireland's finest, the Ulster Folk & Transport Museum is really two museums in one: the Ulster Folk Museum and the Ulster Transport Museum, which lie on either side of the A2 road to Bangor, about 14km northeast of central Belfast, just north of Holywood.

Buses to Bangor stop nearby. Cultra station on the Belfast-to-Bangor train line is within a 10-minute walk.

➡ Ulster Folk Museum

Farmhouses, forges, churches and mills, and a complete village have been reconstructed, with human and animal extras combining to give a powerful impression of Irish life over the past few hundred years. From industrial times, there are red-brick terraces from 19th-century Belfast and Dromore. In summer, thatching and ploughing are demonstrated and there are characters dressed in period costume.

➡ Ulster Transport Museum

The Transport Museum has steam locomotives, rolling stock, motorcycles, trams, buses and cars. Most popular is the **Titanica** exhibit, which includes the original design drawings for the *Titanic* and its sister ship *Olympic*. The highlight of the car collection is the stainless-steel-clad prototype of the ill-fated **DeLorean DMC**, made in Belfast in 1981. The car was a commercial disaster but achieved everlasting fame in the *Back to the Future* films.

Stormont NOTABLE BUILDING
(Map p542; www.niassembly.gov.uk; Upper Newtonards Rd; grounds 7.30am-dusk) FREE Stormont's dazzling white neoclassical facade is one of Belfast's most iconic. The Northern Irish parliament occupies a dramatic position at the end of a gently rising, 1.5km avenue.

Occasional free guided tours run on weekdays in July and August. Otherwise, you're free to walk around the extensive grounds, or you can take a video tour on the website.

From its completion in 1932 until the introduction of direct rule in 1972, Stormont was the seat of the parliament of Northern Ireland, and on 8 May 2007 it returned to the forefront of Irish politics when Ian Paisley and Martin McGuinness – the best of enemies for decades – laughed and smiled as they were sworn in as First Minister and Deputy First Minister, respectively.

Stormont is fronted by a defiant statue of the arch-Unionist **Sir Edward Carson**. Nearby, 19th-century Stormont Castle, like Hillsborough in County Down, is an official residence of the Secretary of State for Northern Ireland.

Take bus 20A from Donegall Sq W.

RED HAND OF ULSTER

According to legend, the chief of a raiding party – O'Neills or O'Donnells, take your pick – approaching the coast by boat, decided to fire up his troops by decreeing that Ulster would belong to the first man to lay his right hand upon it. As they neared land one particularly competitive chap cut off his own right hand and lobbed it to the shore, thus claiming Ulster as his own. The O'Neill clan later adopted the Red Hand as their emblem and it went on to become the symbol of the Irish province of Ulster.

You'll see the Red Hand of Ulster in many places: on the official Northern Irish flag, in the Ulster coat of arms, above the entrance to the Linen Hall Library and laid out in red flowers in the garden of Mount Stewart House in County Down. It also appears in many political murals in the badges of Loyalist terrorist groups and as a clenched red fist in the badge of the Ulster Volunteer Force (UVF).

Around Central Belfast

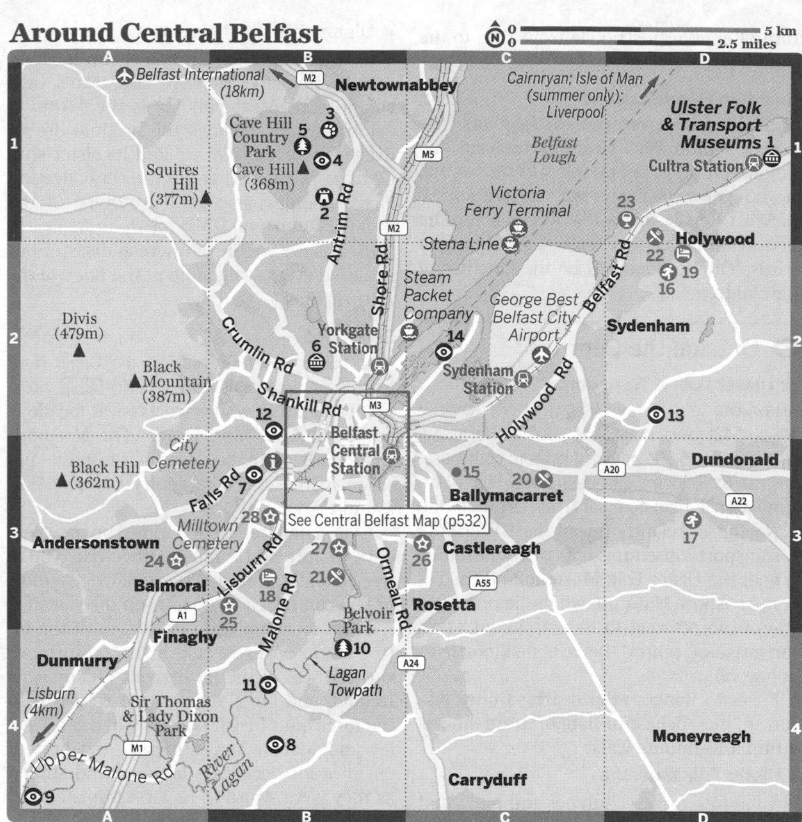

Around Central Belfast

Cave Hill Country Park PARK

(Map p542; www.belfastcity.gov.uk; Antrim Rd; ⏲7.30am-dusk) FREE The view from the summit of Cave Hill (368m) takes in the whole sprawl of the city, the docks, Belfast Lough and the Mourne Mountains – on a clear day you can see Scotland. Cave Hill Country Park spreads across the hill's eastern slopes, with several waymarked walks and an **adventure playground** for kids aged three to 14 years.

To get here, take any of buses 1A to 1G from Royal Ave to Belfast Castle.

The hill was originally called Ben Madigan, after the 9th-century Ulster king, Matudhain. Its distinctive, craggy profile, seen from the south, has been known to locals for two centuries as 'Napoleon's Nose' – it supposedly bears some resemblance to Bonaparte's schnozz, but you might take some convincing. On the summit is an Iron Age earthwork known as **McArt's Fort** where members of the United Irishmen, including Wolfe Tone, looked down over the city in 1795 and pledged to fight for Irish independence. The path leading to the summit from Belfast Castle car park passes beneath the five caves that give the hill its name.

Belfast Castle CASTLE

(Map p542; www.belfastcity.gov.uk; Antrim Rd; ⏲9am-10pm Tue-Sat, to 5.30pm Sun & Mon; 📶) FREE Built in 1870 for the third Marquess of Donegall, in the Scottish Baronial style made fashionable by Queen Victoria's Balmoral, multiturreted Belfast Castle commands the southeastern slopes of Cave Hill. It was presented to the City of Belfast in 1934. Upstairs is the **Cave Hill Visitor Centre** with a few displays on the folklore, history, archaeology and natural history of the park. Downstairs is the **Cellar Restaurant** and a small **gift shop** (⏲10.30am-4.30pm). To get here take buses 1A to 1G from Royal Ave.

Legend has it that the castle's residents will experience good fortune only as long as a white cat lives there, a tale commemorated in the beautiful formal gardens by nine portrayals of cats in mosaic, painting, sculpture and garden furniture – a good game for the kids is getting them to find all nine.

Belfast Zoo ZOO

(Map p542; www.belfastzoo.co.uk; Antrim Rd; adult/child £11.50/6; ⏲10am-7pm Apr-Sep, last admission 5pm, 10am-4pm Oct-Mar, last admission 2.30pm) Home to 150 species, Belfast Zoo has spacious enclosures set on an attractive, sloping site; the sea lion and penguin pool with its underwater viewing is particularly good. Some of the more unusual animals include tamarins, Malaysian sun bears and red pandas, but the biggest attractions are the ultracute meerkats, the colony of ring-tailed lemurs and the herd of Rothschild's giraffe. Take buses 1A to 1G from Royal Ave.

Hilden Brewery BREWERY

(☎028-9266 0800; www.hildenbrewery.com; Hilden House, Grand St, Lisburn; tour £6.50; ⏲tours by reservation 11.30am & 6.30pm Tue-Sat) Ireland's oldest independent brewing company, dating from 1981, produces superior brews including caramel-malt Twisted Hop, smooth Titanic Quarter, Barney's Brew, wheat beer with coriander, and golden Belfast Blonde pale ale. Tours lasting 45 minutes show you how they're made and include a tasting. Its bar and restaurant the Tap Room (p553) is outstanding. In mid-August Hilden hosts a two-day beer festival.

Take the train from Great Victoria St station to Hilden station, from where it's a 300m walk.

Irish Linen Centre & Lisburn Museum MUSEUM

(www.lisburnmuseum.com; Market Sq; ⏲9am-5pm Mon-Sat) FREE Belfast's southwestern fringes extend as far as Lisburn (Lios na gCearrbhach), 12km southwest of the centre. Like Belfast, Lisburn grew rich on the proceeds of the linen industry in the 18th and 19th centuries. This history is celebrated at this excellent museum, inside the 17th-century Market House. There are plenty of audiovisual and hands-on exhibits – you can watch weavers working on jacquard looms and try your hand at spinning flax.

On the museum's ground floor, displays cover the cultural and historic heritage of the region. Upstairs, the award-winning 'Flax to Fabric' exhibition details the fascinating history of the linen industry in Northern Ireland – on the eve of WWI, Ulster was the largest linen-producing region in the world, employing some 75,000 people.

Trains run from Belfast Central and Great Victoria St stations.

Activities

Belfast Cookery School COOKING COURSE

(Map p532; ☎028-9023 4722; www.belfastcookeryschool.com; 53-54 Castle St; classes £35-75) Classes at the Belfast Cookery School, attached to the Mourne Seafood Bar (p549), feature everything from knife skills to bread-making, dinner parties, barbecues and a

MURALS OF BELFAST

Belfast's tradition of political murals dates from 1908, when images of King Billy (William III, Protestant victor over the Catholic James II at the Battle of the Boyne in 1690) were painted by Unionists protesting against Home Rule for Ireland. The tradition was revived in the late 1970s as the Troubles wore on, with murals used to mark out sectarian territory, make political points, commemorate historical events and glorify terrorist groups.

As the 'voice of the community' the murals were rarely permanent, but changed to reflect the issues of the day. Taxi tours visit many of the more prominent murals, and the driver/guide can provide context and an explanation of the various symbols.

Republican Murals

The first Republican murals appeared in 1981, when the hunger strike by Republican prisoners – demanding recognition as political prisoners – at the Maze Prison saw the emergence of dozens of murals of support. In later years, Republican muralists broadened their scope to cover wider political issues, Irish legends and historical events. After the Good Friday Agreement of 1998, the murals came to demand police reform and the protection of nationalists from sectarian attacks.

Common images seen in Republican murals include the phoenix rising from the flames (symbolising Ireland reborn from the flames of the 1916 Easter Rising), the face of hunger-striker Bobby Sands, and scenes and figures from Irish mythology. Common slogans include 'Free Ireland', the Irish '*Éirí Amach na Cásca* 1916' (The Easter Rising of 1916) and '*Tiocfaidh Ár Lá*' (Our Day Will Come).

The main areas for Republican murals are the Falls Rd, Beechmount Ave, Donegall Rd, Shaw's Rd and the Ballymurphy district in West Belfast, New Lodge Rd in North Belfast and Ormeau Rd in South Belfast.

wide range of international cuisines (Indian, Italian, Thai, Spanish, Moroccan...), but its lobster, fish and seafood courses are especially popular – book well ahead.

Holywood Golf Club GOLF

(Map p542; ☎028-9042 3135; www.holywoodgolfclub.co.uk; Nuns Walk, Demesne Rd, Holywood; green fees Mon-Thu £30, Sat & Sun £35) This undulating par-69 parkland course, 11km northeast of Belfast, is world number-one Rory McIlroy's home club, and has spectacular views over Belfast Lough and the Antrim coast. A round of 18 holes costs just £15 before 9.30am Monday to Friday. Note it's not open to the public on a Friday except before 9.30am.

Tours

You can find full details of organised tours or hire a preloaded MP4 player (£9 for 24 hours) at the Visit Belfast Welcome Centre (p559). **Belfast iTours** (http://belfastitours.com) offers 10 self-guided video tours of the city that you can download to your mobile device.

Lagan Boat Company BOAT TOUR

(Map p532; ☎028-9024 0124; www.laganboatcompany.com; adult/child £10/8; ⊙12.30pm, 2pm daily Apr-Oct, Sat & Sun Nov-Mar, plus 3.30pm daily Apr-Sep) The Lagan Boat Company's excellent **Titanic Tour** explores the docklands downstream of Lagan Weir, taking in the slipways where the liners *Titanic* and *Olympic* were launched and the huge dry dock where they could fit with just 9in (23cm) to spare. Tours depart from Donegall Quay near the Bigfish sculpture (p536).

Titanic Tours GUIDED TOUR

(☎07852 716655; www.titanictours-belfast.co.uk; adult/child £30/15; ⊙on demand) A three-hour luxury tour led by the great-granddaughter of one of the *Titanic*'s crew, visiting various *Titanic*-related sites. For groups of two to five people; includes pick-up and drop-off at your accommodation.

Belfast Bike Tours GUIDED TOUR

(☎07812 114235; www.belfastbiketours.com; per person £15; ⊙10.30am & 2pm Mon, Wed, Fri & Sat Apr-Aug, Sat only Sep-Mar) These 2½-hour guided tours depart from outside Queen's University and take you on a leisurely spin along the Lagan Valley to the huge prehistoric earthwork **Giant's Ring** (Map p542; www.laganvalley.co.uk; Ballynahatty Rd; ⊙24hr) FREE

Loyalist Murals

Loyalist murals have traditionally been more militaristic and defiant in tone than the Republican murals. The Loyalist battle cry of 'No Surrender!' is everywhere, along with red, white and blue painted kerbstones, paramilitary insignia and images of King Billy, usually shown on a prancing white horse. You will also see the Red Hand of Ulster, sometimes shown as a clenched fist (the symbol of the Ulster Freedom Fighters, UFF), and references to the WWI Battle of the Somme in 1916 in which many Ulster soldiers died; it is seen as a symbol of Ulster's loyalty to the British crown, in contrast to the Republican Easter Rising of 1916. Common mottoes include '*Quis Separabit*' (Who Shall Divide Us?), the motto of the Ulster Defence Association (UDA); and the defiant 'We will maintain our faith and our nationality'.

Murals Today

In recent years there has been a lot of debate about what to do with Belfast's murals. Some see them as an ugly and unpleasant reminder of a violent past, while others claim they are a vital part of Northern Ireland's history. There's no doubt they have become an important tourist attraction, but there is now a move to replace the more aggressive and militaristic images with murals dedicated to local heroes and famous figures such as footballer George Best, *Narnia* novelist CS Lewis and golfer Rory McIlroy.

There are also some offbeat and amusing artworks, such as a gable-end on Balfour Ave, off Ormeau Rd, that asks the question 'How can quantum gravity help explain the origin of the universe?' (one of 10 questions selected by scientists as the most important unsolved problems in physics), reflecting the still unsolved – and, to outsiders, equally baffling – problem of Northern Ireland's sectarian divide.

To find out more about Northern Ireland's murals, look out for the books *Drawing Support* (three volumes) by Bill Rolston, *The People's Gallery* by the Bogside Artists and the website of the Mural Directory (www.cain.ulst.ac.uk/murals).

(with a dolmen known as the Druid's Altar in the centre) and back again. Bikes are provided; book in advance. Also rents bikes to explore on your own (per day from £15).

Wee Tram BUS TOUR
(☎07788 991267; www.theweetram.com; adult/child per 48hr £6/5; ⏲10am-6pm daily Apr-Sep, Sat & Sun Oct-Mar) These cute replica tramcars make seven key stops around the Titanic Quarter with on-board video commentary en route and pull-down plastic flaps if it rains. Tickets are valid for two days.

Belfast City Sightseeing BUS TOUR
(Map p532; ☎028-9032 1321; http://belfastcitysightseeing.com; adult/child £12.50/6; ⏲every 15-30min 10am-4pm) Runs 1¼-hour open-top bus tours that take in City Hall, the Albert Clock, the Titanic Quarter, the Botanic Gardens, and the Falls Rd and Shankill Rd murals in West Belfast. Departs from Castle Pl; hop-on, hop-off tickets are valid for two days.

Taxi Tours

Black taxi tours of West Belfast's murals – known locally as the 'bombs and bullets' or 'doom and gloom' tours – are offered by a large number of taxi companies and local cabbies. These can vary in quality and content, but in general they're an intimate and entertaining way to see the sights. Drivers will pick you up from anywhere in the city centre.

Paddy Campbell's Famous Black Cab Tours CULTURAL TOUR
(☎07990 955227; www.belfastblackcabtours.co.uk; tour per 1-3 people £30) Popular 1½-hour black cab tour.

Harpers Taxi Tours CULTURAL TOUR
(☎07711 757178; www.harperstaxitours.com; from £30) Political and historical tours.

Official Black Taxi Tours CULTURAL TOUR
(☎028-9064 2264; www.belfasttours.com; 1-2 passengers £25, 3+ per person £10) Customised tours lasting 1½ hours.

Game of Thrones Tours

If you're driving around Northern Ireland, there are *Game of Thrones* filming locations aplenty – visit www.discovernorthernireland.com/gameofthrones. Alternatively, day-long bus tours depart from Belfast.

McComb's Game of Thrones Tours BUS TOUR
(Map p532; ☎028-9031 5333; www.mccombscoaches.com; per person £35; ⊙Wed, Thu & Sat-Mon) The drivers of these *Game of Thrones* tours have also driven the extras and equipment. Filming locations visited include the Dark Hedges (ie Kingsroad), Cushendun (the seacave where the shadow assassin was born), Ballintoy Harbour (Lordsport Harbour) and Larrybane (where the shadow assassin kills Renly). Pick-up is from the Belfast Youth Hostel at 9.15am. There are also southern tours.

Game of Thrones Tours BUS TOUR
(Map p532; ☎028-9568 0023; www.gameofthronestours.com; adult/child £40/30; ⊙Wed-Sun Easter–Sep, reduced tours Oct–Easter) These full-day tours take you to 11 iconic *Game of Thrones* filming locations, such as Castle Ward Estate (aka Winterfell), and Tollymore Forest Park (where the Starks discover a dead direwolf and her pups), including two treks totalling 6.5km. Tours depart at 9am from 36 Chichester St, in front of the Victoria Square shopping centre (by Top Shop).

Festivals & Events

Belfast City Council (www.belfastcity.gov.uk/events) organises a wide range of events throughout the year, covering everything from the St Patrick's Day parade to the Lord Mayor's Show. It has a useful online events calendar, as does the Visit Belfast Welcome Centre (http://visit-belfast.com/whats-on).

CityDance DANCE
(www.citydancebelfast.com) Free two-day dance festival in February, based at the Crescent Arts Centre (p557).

Féile an Earraigh MUSIC
(www.feilebelfast.com) This four-day festival of traditional Irish and Celtic music attracts artists from all over Ireland, Europe and America. Held in February or March.

St Patrick's Day CULTURAL
(www.belfastcity.gov.uk/events) On 17 March, A celebration of Ireland's patron saint marked by various community festivals and culminating in a grand city-centre parade.

Belfast Film Festival FILM
(www.belfastfilmfestival.org) Eleven-day celebration of Irish and international film in April.

Festival of Fools STREET THEATRE
(http://foolsfestival.com) This five-day festival of street entertainment has events concentrated in the Cathedral Quarter and city centre. Held in early May but the fun continues on Sunday afternoons in July and August.

Belfast Marathon SPORT
(www.belfastcitymarathon.com) Avid runners from across the globe come to compete in the marathon on the first Monday of May; it's also a people's event, with a walk and fun run as well.

Cathedral Quarter Arts Festival ARTS
(www.thecathedralquarter.com) Ten days of drama, music, poetry, street theatre and art exhibitions in and around the Cathedral Quarter in early May.

Belfast Book Festival LITERATURE
(www.belfastbookfestival.com) A week of all things book-related in mid June, from films and readings to workshops and meet-the-author events, at venues throughout the city.

Belfast Titanic Maritime Festival MARITIME
(http://visit-belfast.com/whats-on) A three-day festival centred on Queen's Quay in early July, with sailing ships, street entertainment, a seafood festival and live music.

Belfast Pride GAY
(www.belfastpride.com) Ireland's largest celebration of gay, lesbian, bisexual and transgender culture, culminating in a huge

ORANGE ORDER PARADES

In Northern Ireland the 12 July public holiday marks the anniversary of the Protestant victory at the 1690 Battle of the Boyne. It is celebrated with bonfires, marching bands and street parades staged by the Orange Order, the biggest of which takes place in Belfast.

Although the 12 July parades have regularly been associated with sectarian stand-offs and outbursts of violence, there has been a concerted effort in recent years to promote the Belfast parade as a cultural celebration, even rebranding it Orangefest.

However, many people still perceive the parades as divisive and confrontational, and with high levels of alcohol consumption among the crowds there is a potential for dangerous situations. Visitors need to be alert for signs of trouble, follow local advice and expect extra security if things escalate in any way.

city-centre parade; takes place over a week in late July/early August.

Féile An Phobail CULTURAL
(www.feilebelfast.com) Said to be the largest community festival in Ireland, the Féile takes place in West Belfast over 10 days. Events include an opening carnival parade, street parties, theatre performances, concerts and historical tours of the City and Milltown cemeteries. Held in early August.

Belfast Festival at Queen's ARTS
(www.belfastfestival.com) The UK's second-largest arts festival is held in and around Queen's University over two weeks in October.

Sleeping

From backpacker hostels to boutique havens, the range of places to stay gets wider every year. Most of Belfast's budget and midrange accommodation is south of the centre, in the leafy university district around Botanic Ave, University Rd and Malone Rd, around a 20-minute walk from City Hall.

Business hotels proliferate in the city centre; look out for new 40-room boutique hotel the Mutual, in the landmark turreted, red-sandstone 1904 Scottish Mutual building at 15-16 Donegall Sq S.

The Titanic Quarter, already home to a swish new branch of the Premier Inn chain, is set to welcome several new hotels in the coming years, including an 84-room *Titanic*-themed hotel with public spaces occupying the **Harland & Wolff Drawing Offices** (Map p532; Queen's Rd), where the designs for the *Titanic* were first drawn up.

Book ahead on weekends, in summer, and during busy festival periods.

VAN MORRISON TRAIL

Fans of 'Van the Man' can take a self-guided, 3.5km walking tour of little-explored East Belfast, passing sights referenced in his lyrics, including **the Hollow** (immortalised in Brown Eyed Girl), **Cypress Avenue** and the modest house where he was born on **Hyndford Street** (at number 125).

Morrison launched the trail in 2014 in collaboration with local council initiative Connswater Community Greenway (www.communitygreenway.co.uk/vanmorrisontrail). The free, downloadable map has audio snippets of songs relating to each of the trail's eight stops.

City Centre

★**Ten Square** HOTEL ££
(Map p532; ☎028-9024 1001; www.tensquare.co.uk; 10 Donegall Sq S; d from £95; wi-fi) A former bank building to the south of City Hall that's been given a designer feng-shui makeover, Ten Square is an opulent, Shanghai-inspired boutique hotel with friendly and attentive service. Magazines such as *Conde Nast Traveller* rave over the dark lacquered wood, low-slung futon-style beds and sumptuous linen, and the list of former guests includes Bono and Brad Pitt.

Fitzwilliam Hotel HOTEL £££
(Map p532; ☎028-9044 2080; www.fitzwilliamhotelbelfast.com; 1-3 Great Victoria St; d from £110; @ wi-fi) Enjoying an epicentral location, the Fitzwilliam strikes all the right style notes with its use of designer fabrics, cool colours and mood lighting. Bedrooms have crisp linen sheets, fluffy bathrobes and powerful showers, and the staff are unstintingly helpful.

Cathedral Quarter

Malmaison Hotel HOTEL ££
(Map p532; ☎0844 693 0650; www.malmaison-belfast.com; 34-38 Victoria St; d/ste from £95/270; @ wi-fi) Housed in a pair of beautifully restored Italianate warehouses (originally built for rival firms in the 1850s), the Malmaison is a luxurious haven of king-sized beds, deep leather sofas, and roll-top baths big enough for two, all done up in a decadent decor of black, red, dark chocolate and cream. One rock-star suite even has a purple baize billiard table.

Merchant Hotel HOTEL £££
(Map p532; ☎028-9023 4888; www.themerchanthotel.com; 16 Skipper St; d/ste from £189/270; @ wi-fi) Belfast's most flamboyant Victorian building (the old Ulster Bank head office) has been converted into the city's most flamboyant boutique hotel, a fabulous fusion of contemporary styling and old-fashioned elegance, with individually decorated rooms (some with roll-top bathtubs). Luxe leisure facilities at its gymnasium and spa include an eight-person rooftop hot tub. Its Great Room (p552) restaurant is magnificent.

South Belfast

To get to places on or near Botanic Ave, take bus 7A or 7B from Howard St. For places on or near University and Malone Rds, take bus 8A or 8B, and for places on or near Lisburn Rd, take bus 9A or 9B. Buses depart from Donegall Sq E and from the bus stop on Great Victoria St across from the Europa BusCentre.

★ Vagabonds HOSTEL £
(Map p532; ☎028-9023 3017; www.vagabondsbelfast.com; 9 University Rd; dm £13-16, tw & d £40; @ 📶) Comfy bunks, lockable luggage baskets, private shower cubicles and a relaxed atmosphere are what you get at one of Belfast's best hostels, run by a couple of experienced travellers. It's conveniently located close to both Queen's and the city centre.

Arnie's Backpackers HOSTEL £
(Map p532; ☎028-9024 2867; http://arniesbackpackers.co.uk; 63 Fitzwilliam St; dm £14-16, tw & d £44; @ 📶) This long-established old-school hostel is set in a quiet terraced house in the university area. Coal fires and a friendly crowd make it more cosy than cramped.

Global Village Backpackers HOSTEL £
(Map p532; ☎028-9031 3533; http://globalvillagebelfast.com; 87 University St; dm £14.50-16.50, d £44; @ 📶) In a 19th-century terrace house close to Queen's University, Global Village sports a beer garden, a barbecue and a games room.

Belfast Youth Hostel HOSTEL £
(Map p532; ☎028-9031 5435; www.hini.org.uk; 22-32 Donegall Rd; dm £11.50-14.50, tw £30-42, d £38-42; @ 📶) Handy amenities at this big, bright HI (Hostelling International) hostel include laundry facilities, secure on-site parking, 24-hour reception (with no lock-out or curfew), and a breakfast-specialist cafe.

Tara Lodge B&B ££
(Map p532; ☎028-9059 0900; www.taralodge.com; 36 Cromwell Rd; s/d from £79/89; @ 📶) In a great location on a quiet side street just a few paces from the buzz of Botanic Ave, this B&B feels more like a boutique hotel with its clean-cut, minimalist decor, friendly and efficient staff and 24 bright and cheerful rooms. Delicious breakfasts include porridge with Bushmills whiskey.

All Seasons B&B B&B ££
(Map p542; ☎028-9068 2814; www.allseasonsbelfast.com; 356 Lisburn Rd; s/d/f £35/50/55; 📶) Away from the centre, but right in the heart of trendy Lisburn Rd, All Seasons is a red-brick villa with bright, colourful bedrooms, modern bathrooms, a stylish little breakfast room and a comfortable lounge.

Malone Lodge Hotel HOTEL ££
(Map p532; ☎028-9038 8000; www.malonelodgehotelbelfast.com; 60 Eglantine Ave; d/f/apt from £89/109/120; 📶) The centrepiece of a tree-lined Victorian terrace, the modern Malone Lodge has large, luxurious rooms with elegantly understated decor, good food and pleasant, helpful staff. Some bedrooms are in a separate building; it also offers five-star one- and two-bedroom self-catering apartments.

Benedicts HOTEL ££
(Map p532; ☎028-9059 1999; www.benedictshotel.co.uk; 7-21 Bradbury Pl; s/d from £75/85; @ 📶) Bang in the middle of the Golden Mile, Benedicts is a modern, style-conscious hotel at the heart of South Belfast's nightlife. The rooms, complete with Egyptian cotton sheets and feather-bedded mattresses, are above a huge Gothic bar and restaurant (where you also have breakfast), with live music nightly, so don't expect peace and quiet until the wee hours.

Outside the Centre

★ Rayanne House GUESTHOUSE ££
(Map p542; ☎028-9042 5859; www.rayannehouse.com; 60 Demesne Rd, Holywood; s/d/tr/f from £80/120/140/145; 📶 👪) Just 100m from Holywood Golf Club (p544), this gorgeous 1883 manor house has exquisite rooms – some with balconies and views of Belfast Lough – including a Rory McIlroy–themed room with a shower rail made from an engraved club. Its restaurant (open to nonguests) hosts regular nine-course *Titanic* menus (£69) replicating the last 1st-class meal served aboard.

Eating

In recent years, Belfast's restaurant scene has been totally transformed by a wave of new restaurants whose standards compete with the best eateries in Europe.

City Centre

The main shopping area north of Donegall Sq becomes a silent maze of deserted streets and steel shutters after 7pm, but during the day the many pubs, cafes and restaurants do a roaring trade. In the evening, the liveliest part of the city centre stretches south of Donegall Sq to Shaftesbury Sq.

John Long's FISH & CHIPS £
(Map p532; www.johnlongs.com; 39 Athol St; fish & chips £4-8; ⏲11.30am-6.30pm Mon-Sat) A wonderfully down-to-earth Belfast institution, this

1914-opened chippie is hidden in an inconspicuous red-brick building adjoining a car park, and is covered in mesh grills (a legacy of having its windows blown out when the nearby Europa Hotel was bombed). Inside, it fries up classic cod and chips in beef dripping, served at 1970s Formica booths. Cash only.

St George's Market Bar & Grill MODERN IRISH £
(Map p532; 028-9024 0014; http://stgeorgesbargrill.com; Oxford St; breakfast £4.50-7, mains lunch £8-10, dinner £13-17; 10am-2.30pm Tue, 10am-2.30pm & 5-9pm Wed & Thu, 9am-2.30pm & 5-10pm Fri & Sat, 10am-4pm Sun) All of the ingredients at the 1st-floor restaurant of historic St George's Market (p558) are sourced on-site, and on market days the best seats are on the balcony looking down over the buzz of stallholders and shoppers below. It's revered for its Ulster fry-up breakfasts, but mains such as braised rack-of-lamb Irish stew with pearl barley are excellent too.

Archana INDIAN £
(Map p532; www.archana.co.uk; 53 Dublin Rd; mains lunch £3.50-9, dinner £7-15; noon-2pm & 5pm-midnight;) Classy yet unpretentious, with dining rooms on two levels, Achana has a good range of vegetarian dishes, including many incorporating *paneer* (cottage cheese) made on the premises. The *thali* – a platter of three curries – is good value at £15/12 for the meat/veggie version.

Morning Star PUB FOOD £
(Map p532; www.themorningstarbar.com; 17 Pottinger's Entry; mains £10-24; kitchen noon-9pm;) Historic pub Morning Star is famed for its all-you-can-eat lunch buffet (£6, noon to 4pm) and for its in-house butcher producing homemade sausages.

★ **OX** IRISH ££
(Map p532; 028-9031 4121; http://oxbelfast.com; 1 Oxford St; mains lunch £10, dinner £19-25; noon-2.30pm & 6-9.30pm Tue-Fri, from 1pm Sat) A high-ceilinged space walled with cream-painted brick and furnished with warm golden wood creates a theatre-like ambience for the open kitchen at the back, where Michelin-trained chefs turn out some of Belfast's finest and best-value cuisine. The restaurant works with local suppliers and focuses on fine Irish beef, sustainable seafood, and seasonal vegetables and fruit.

★ **Mourne Seafood Bar** SEAFOOD ££
(Map p532; 028-9024 8544; http://mournseafood.com; 34-36 Bank St; mains £8-22; noon-9.30pm Mon-Thu, noon-4pm & 5-10.30pm Fri & Sat, 1-6pm Sun) Hugely popular, this informal, pub-like place is all red brick and dark wood with old oil lamps dangling from the ceiling. On the menu are oysters served *au naturel* or Rockefeller, meltingly sweet scallops, lobster and langoustines sourced from its own shellfish beds, along with luscious fish such as gurnard and sea bass. Book ahead for dinner.

The attached Belfast Cookery School (p543) runs a diverse range of culinary classes. Mourne Seafood Bar's sister restaurant (p576) is near County Down's Dundrum Bay.

★ **Holohan's** MODERN IRISH ££
(Map p532; 028-9023 5973; Belfast Barge, Lanyon Quay; mains lunch £9.50-12.50, dinner £13-22; noon-4pm Mon & Tue, noon-3pm & 5-11pm Wed-Sat) Aboard the Belfast Barge (p536), Holohan's is a sensational find for inspired twists on seafood (deep-fried whitebait with garlic-and-herb aioli; roast cod with brown shrimp and boxty dumplings), as well as land-based dishes such as fillet steak with heirloom vegetables, desserts such as warm chocolate mousse with candied walnuts and Bailey's chocolate sauce, and by-the-glass wines from around the world.

Ginger BISTRO ££
(Map p532; 028-9024 4421; www.gingerbistro.com; 7-8 Hope St; mains lunch £10-12.50, dinner £16-23; 5-9pm Mon, noon-3pm & 5-9.30pm Tue-Thu, noon-3pm & 5-10pm Fri & Sat;) Ginger is one of those places you could walk right past without noticing, but you'd be missing out. Cosy and informal, its food is anything but ordinary – the flame-haired owner-chef (hence the name) really knows what he's doing, sourcing top-quality Irish produce and creating exquisite dishes such as tea-smoked duck breast with ginger and sweet-potato puree.

McCracken's PUB FOOD ££
(Map p532; 028-9032 6711; http://mccrackenscafebar.co.uk; 4 Joy's Entry; mains £7-17; kitchen noon-8pm Mon-Wed, to 9pm Thu & Fri, to 7pm Sat, to 6pm Sun) Buried in the ancient, narrow passageway Joy's Entry, McCracken's is an unexpectedly contemporary, bare-brick, loft-style space that's great for a cocktail, live music and DJs, and above all, for its gastropub menu: dry-aged Irish beef burgers and smoked seafood chowder through to pan-fried haddock with langoustine tails and white-wine cream sauce. Sides include triple-cooked or truffle-parmesan chips.

CHRIS HILL/GETTY IMAGES ©

1. City Hall (p530)
Take a free guided tour of Belfast's Renaissance-style City Hall.

2. Palm House (p540)
Set in the Botanic Gardens, this light-filled glasshouse is a masterpiece of cast-iron and curvilinear glass.

3. Titanic Belfast (p537)
The angular Titanic Belfast building houses a museum dedicated to the famous ill-fated ocean liner.

4. Belfast at night
Sunset over the River Lagan, which flows through the city's centre.

3

CHRIS HILL/GETTY IMAGES ©

Home MODERN IRISH ££

(Map p532; ☎028-9023 4946; www.homebelfast.co.uk; 22 Wellington Pl; mains lunch £5-12.50, dinner £12.50-21.50; ⊙noon-9.30pm Mon-Thu, noon-4pm & 5-10pm Fri & Sat, 1-9pm Sun, deli 8am-3pm Mon-Fri, 10am-3pm Sat;) After beginning life as a pop-up restaurant that took the city's food scene by storm, Home has moved into permanent premises where it continues to win fans for its creative use of seasonal ingredients in its restaurant and attached New York–style deli. Its menus are tailored for vegetarians, vegans, gluten-free diners, slimmers, gluten-free slimmers, and theatregoers as well as kids.

James St South MODERN IRISH ££

(Map p532; ☎028-9043 4310; www.jamesstreetsouth.co.uk; 21 James St S; 1-/2-/3-course lunch menu £10/15.50/18.50, dinner mains £18.50-25; ⊙noon-2.30pm & 5.30-10.30pm Mon-Sat) Graced by a large, impressionistic landscape by Irish artist Clement McAleer, this starkly beautiful dining room with crisp white table linen creates a perfect stage for the presentation of starters such as grilled foie gras with pickled rhubarb, followed by mains such as venison with turnip and mushroom cottage pie. The service is relaxed yet highly professional.

Its **Bar & Grill** (Map p532; ☎028-9560 0700; www.belfastbargrill.co.uk; 21 James St S; mains £10.50-23; ⊙noon-10.30pm) is less formal but the quality of the food is just as high.

Deanes Eipic FRENCH, IRISH £££

(Map p532; ☎028-9033 1134; www.michaeldeane.co.uk; 34-40 Howard St; 4-/5-/6-course menu £40/50/60; ⊙noon-2.45pm Fri, 5.30-9.45pm Wed-Sat) Premium Irish and British produce – beef, game, lamb, seafood – is given the gourmet treatment at this flagship of chef Michael Deane's restaurant fleet. Within the same building are Deane's à la carte **Love Fish** and **Meatlocker** restaurants.

Other venues from Belfast's best-known chef include **Deanes at Queen's** (Map p532; ☎028-9038 2111; 1 College Gardens; mains lunch £7-12.50, dinner £14.50-22; ⊙noon-3pm & 5.30-11pm Mon-Sat, 1-6pm Sun) and **Deanes Deli Bistro** (Map p532; ☎028-9024 8800; 44 Bedford St; mains £10-22; ⊙8am-10pm Mon-Fri, 9am-10pm Sat).

Cathedral Quarter

Hendogs AMERICAN £

(Map p532; www.thepottedhen.co.uk; St Anne's Sq, Edward St; mains £7-8.25; ⊙noon-late) Above the Potted Hen, Hendogs' inspired menu of gourmet hot dogs includes an inferno dog (with chipotle mayo, chilli jam, smoked applewood cheese, and jalapeno and scotch-bonnet peppers), and a New Yorker (pork sausage, pastrami, gherkin and mustard). Dogs aside, options include tacos, gumbo and Hennessey-marinated ribs, as well as boozy shakes. No bookings.

Potted Hen MODERN IRISH ££

(Map p532; ☎028-9023 4554; www.thepottedhen.co.uk; St Anne's Sq, Edward St; mains £11-23; ⊙noon-3pm & 5-9.30pm Mon-Thu, to 10pm Fri & Sat, noon-9pm Sun) The pick of the upmarket crop of restaurants in the stunning white colonnaded St Anne's Sq is this airy restaurant serving stylishly presented contemporary fare such as grilled goat's-cheese mousse with beetroot jelly and candied walnuts, and confit of pork belly with herb gnocchi. Its gourmet hot-dog restaurant Hendogs is upstairs.

Great Room FRENCH £££

(Map p532; ☎028-9023 4888; www.themerchanthotel.com; 16 Skipper St; mains £19.50-28.50; ⊙7am-11pm) Set in the former banking hall of the Ulster Bank head office within the Merchant Hotel (p547), the Great Room is a jaw-dropping extravaganza of gilded stucco, red plush, white-marble cherubs and a vast crystal chandelier glittering beneath a glass dome. The menu matches the decor: decadent but delicious (foie gras, truffles...).

South Belfast

Maggie May's CAFE £

(Map p532; www.maggiemaysbelfastcafe.co.uk; 50 Botanic Ave; mains £4.50-14; ⊙8am-11pm Mon-Sat, 9am-11pm Sun;) This is a classic little cafe with cosy wooden booths, murals of old Belfast and a host of hungover students wolfing down huge Ulster fry-ups. The all-day breakfast menu includes French toast and maple syrup, while lunch can be soup and a sandwich or beef lasagne. BYO.

There's a newer branch in **Stranmillis** (Map p532; ☎028-9066 8515; www.maggiemaysbelfastcafe.co.uk; 2 Malone Rd; mains £4.50-14; ⊙8am-11pm Mon-Sat, 9am-11pm Sun).

★ **Barking Dog** BISTRO ££

(Map p532; ☎028-9066 1885; www.barkingdogbelfast.com; 33-35 Malone Rd; mains £14-24, tapas 1/5 dishes £3/12; ⊙noon-3pm & 5.30-10pm Mon-Thu, to 11pm Fri & Sat, noon-9pm Sun;) Chunky hardwood, bare brick, candlelight and quirky design create the atmosphere of a stylishly restored farmhouse. The menu completes the feeling of cosiness and comfort with simple but sensational dishes such as the signature burger of meltingly tender beef shin with caramelised onion and horseradish cream, and sweet-potato ravioli with carrot and parmesan crisps. It has superb service, too.

Molly's Yard IRISH ££

(Map p532; 028-9032 2600; www.mollysyard.co.uk; 1 College Green Mews; mains bistro £10, restaurant £14-23; bistro noon-5pm, restaurant 5-9pm Mon-Sat;) A restored Victorian stables courtyard is the setting for this quirky restaurant, with a cosy bar-bistro on the ground floor, outdoor tables in the yard and a rustic dining room in the airy roof space upstairs. The menu is seasonal and sticks to half a dozen each of starters and mains.

It also has its own craft beers, brewed at Lisburn's Hilden Brewery (p543).

Shu FRENCH, IRISH ££

(Map p532; 028-9038 1655; www.shu-restaurant.com; 253 Lisburn Rd; mains £12-23, 2-course lunch/dinner menus £13.25/22.50; noon-2.30pm & 6-10pm Mon-Sat) Lording it over fashionable Lisburn Rd since 2000, Shu is the granddaddy of Belfast chic, and still winning plaudits for its French-influenced food: roast halibut and black rice; wood pigeon with kale and celeriac puree; and wild-garlic gnocchi with truffle butter.

★Saphyre MODERN IRISH £££

(Map p532; 028-9068 8606; www.saphyrerestaurant.com; 135 Lisburn Rd; mains lunch £12-14, dinner £23-27; 10am-3pm Mon-Wed, to 10.30pm Thu-Sat) Spectacularly set inside the 1924 Ulsterville Presbyterian Church (behind an interior-design showroom), Saphyre serves some of the most sophisticated cooking in Belfast today. Chilled pea-and-mint soup with Strangford crab, sea trout with sorrel and violet potatoes, lamb rump and sweetbreads, and rhubarb souffle with ginger yoghurt…each dish is a masterpiece.

Outside the Centre

★Fontana MODERN IRISH ££

(Map p542; 028-9080 9908; www.restaurantfontana.com; 61 High St, Holywood; mains £13.50-27.50; noon-2.30pm & 5-10pm Tue-Fri, 6-10pm Sat, 11am-3pm Sun) In the heart of the village-like neighbourhood of Holywood, but hidden upstairs from a covered passageway, Fontana's sublime modern-Irish cooking – wild turbot with crispy seaweed, and beetroot and fennel risotto; maple- and cumin-glazed chicken with parsnip gratin – incorporates herbs and salad ingredients from its own courtyard garden.

Tap Room MODERN IRISH ££

(http://taproomhilden.com; Hilden House, Grand St, Lisburn; mains £14.50-20.50; kitchen noon-2.30pm & 5.30-9pm Tue-Sat, noon-3pm Sun;) Normally you'd visit a brewery for its beer, and the brews at Hilden Brewery (p543) definitely warrant a trip. But its bar-restaurant is unmissable in its own right for dishes such as Belfast Blonde–battered haddock with crushed peas, crab-and-prawn linguini, corn-fed chicken with parsnip gnocchi, and braised beef with horseradish mash. Trad-music sessions strike up Wednesdays from 7pm.

Cutters Wharf GRILL ££

(Map p542; www.cutterswharf.co.uk; 4 Lockview Rd, Stranmillis; mains £10-27; kitchen noon-9pm;) One of the few bar-restaurants in Belfast with a waterside setting, Cutters Wharf has a sprawling terrace overlooking the River Lagan where you can enjoy an al fresco drink and a bar meal, and a smart upstairs restaurant serving steaks, burgers and seafood.

Acapulco MEXICAN ££

(Map p542; 028-9029 6400; http://acapulco.ie; 255 Upper Newtownards Rd; mains £11-17; noon-3pm & 5-9pm Tue-Thu, noon-3pm & 5-10pm Fri, noon-10pm Sat, 5-9pm Sun;) Popular with politicians and parliamentary staffers from nearby Stormont (p541), this sparingly but colourfully decorated place dishes up authentic burritos, chimichanga, flauta, enchiladas, fajita platters, Yucatan-spiced chicken skewers and other Mexican classics in huge portions. It has a good *niños* (kids) menu too. It's one of several stellar restaurants along Upper Newtownards Rd in Ballyhackamore.

Drinking & Nightlife

Belfast's pub scene is lively and friendly, with the older traditional pubs complemented – and increasingly threatened – by a rising tide of stylish designer bars. Many pubs and bars are also great places to dine.

Although the situation is improving, getting past the bouncers on the door at pubs and clubs can be a problem. Some of the flashier venues have a dress code – usually no sneakers, no jeans, no baseball caps (so that the security cameras can get a clear shot of your face) and definitely no football colours. A few even specify 'No political tattoos'.

City Centre

★Crown Liquor Saloon PUB
(Map p532; www.nicholsonspubs.co.uk; 46 Great Victoria St; ⏲11.30am-11pm Mon-Wed, 11.30am-midnight Thu-Sat, 12.30-10pm Sun) Despite being a tourist attraction (p531), Belfast's most famous bar still fills up with crowds of locals at lunchtime and in the early evening.

★Filthy Quarter BAR
(Map p532; www.thefilthyquarter.com; 45 Dublin Rd; ⏲1pm-1am Mon-Sat, to midnight Sun) Four individually and collectively fabulous bars make up the Filthy Quarter: retro-trad-style, bric-a-brac-filled **Filthy McNastys**, hosting local musicians from 10pm nightly; the fairy-lit **Secret Garden**, a two-storey beer garden with watering cans for drinks coolers; **Gypsy Lounge** (Tuesday, Thursday, Friday, Saturday and Sundays nights), with a gypsy caravan DJ booth; and a chandelier-and candelabra-adorned cocktail bar, **Filthy Chic**.

★Love & Death Inc COCKTAIL BAR
(Map p532; http://loveanddeathinc.com; 10a Ann St; ⏲noon-1am Mon-Wed, noon-3am Thu-Sat, 1pm-midnight Sun) More like a cool inner-city house party, speakeasy-style Love & Death Inc is secreted up a flight of stairs above a pizza joint. Its living-room-style bar has outrageous decor, feisty Latin American-influenced food, feistier cocktails, and a wild nightclub in the attic on weekends.

Harlem Cafe CAFE, BAR
(Map p532; http://harlembelfast.com; 34-36 Bedford St; ⏲8am-11pm Mon-Thu, 8am-1am Fri & Sat, 9am-7pm Sun; 📶) In a cornflower-blue building with eclectic art covering the walls, the Harlem is a great place for lounging over coffee, or enjoying a glass of wine after hitting the shops. A full food menu spans breakfast to brunch to pretheatre dinner; live music plays on Friday and Saturday.

Garrick Bar PUB
(Map p532; www.thegarrickbar.com; 29 Chichester St; ⏲11.30am-1am Mon-Sat, 12.30pm-midnight Sun; 📶) First opened in 1870, the Garrick hangs on to a traditional atmosphere with acres of dark wood panelling, tiled floors, a pillared bar and old brass oil lamps. Snug booths have buttoned leather benches, and each room has a real coal fire. Trad-music sessions take place in the front bar at 9.30pm on Wednesday, 5pm Friday and 6pm Sunday.

White's Tavern PUB
(Map p532; 1-4 Wine Cellar Entry; ⏲noon-11pm Mon & Tue, to 1am Wed-Sat, to midnight Sun) Established in 1630 but rebuilt in 1790, White's claims to be Belfast's oldest tavern (unlike a pub, a tavern provided food and lodging). Downstairs is a traditional Irish bar with an open peat fire and live music nightly; upstairs is like your granny's living room, stuffed with old armchairs and sofas, and hosting DJs and covers bands at the weekends.

Kelly's Cellars PUB
(Map p532; www.kellyscellars.com; 30-32 Bank St; ⏲11.30am-1am Mon-Sat, 1pm-midnight Sun) Kelly's is Belfast's oldest pub (1720) – as opposed to tavern – and was a meeting place for Henry Joy McCracken and the United Irishmen when they were planning the 1798 Rising. It pulls in a broad cross-section of Belfast society and is a great place to catch trad-music sessions at 8.30pm Tuesday to Thursday and 4.30pm Saturday.

Bittle's Bar PUB
(Map p532; 103 Victoria St; ⏲10am-11pm Mon-Thu, noon-1am Fri & Sat, noon-6pm Sun) A cramped and staunchly traditional bar, Bittle's is a 19th-century triangular red-brick building decorated with gilded shamrocks. The wedge-shaped interior is covered in paintings of Ireland's literary heroes by local artist Joe O'Kane. In pride of place on the back wall is a large canvas depicting Yeats, Joyce, Behan, Beckett and Wilde. It has an excellent range of craft beers.

Café Vaudeville BAR
(Map p532; www.cafevaudeville.com; 25-39 Arthur St; ⏲11.30am-6pm Mon, to 11pm Tue, to midnight Wed & Thu, to 1am Fri & Sat) Occupying a historic merchant's headquarters turned bank, turned Parisian belle époque–style cafe, this art-nouveau beauty has spectacular winding staircases, soaring ceilings, an upstairs champagne bar, plus jazz and swing and big-band music. In true Parisian style, the food is stunning too.

Cathedral Quarter

★Duke of York PUB
(Map p532; www.dukeofyorkbelfast.com; 11 Commercial Ct; ⏲11.30am-11.30pm Mon-Wed, to 1am Thu & Fri, to 2am Sat, 2-8pm Sun) Down an incon-

spicuous alley in the heart of the city's former newspaper district, the snug, traditional Duke was a hang-out for print workers and journalists. Sinn Féin leader, Gerry Adams, worked behind the bar here during his student days in 1971. The entire alley takes on a street-party atmosphere in warm weather.

National Grande Café BAR

(Map p532; www.thenationalbelfast.com; 62 High St; ⏰8.30am-9pm Mon-Wed, 8.30am-1am Thu & Fri, 9.30am-1am Sat, 9.30am-midnight Sun) Behind the oyster-grey ground-floor facade of the 1897 former National Bank building, and through its postindustrial interior, is the National's pièce de résistance – the city's biggest beer garden, which hosts regular barbecues and live music. Pan-European food is served all day, including Sunday breakfast to 5.30pm.

John Hewitt Bar & Restaurant PUB

(Map p532; www.thejohnhewitt.com; 51 Donegall St; ⏰11.30am-1am Mon-Fri, noon-1am Sat, 7pm-1am Sun) Named for the Belfast poet and socialist, the John Hewitt is one of those treasured bars that has no TV or gaming machines, just the murmur of conversation. As well as Guinness, the bar serves craft beers from Lisburn's Hilden Brewery (p543) and County Tyrone's Red Hand Brewing Company. It has regular sessions of folk, jazz and bluegrass from 9pm most nights.

Muriel's Cafe-Bar BAR

(Map p532; ☎028-9033 2445; 12-14 Church Lane; ⏰11.30am-1am Mon-Fri, 11am-1am Sat, 11am-midnight Sun) Hats meet harlotry (ask who Muriel was) in this snug and welcoming bar with retro-chic decor, old sofas and armchairs, heavy fabrics in shades of olive and dark red, gilt-framed mirrors and a cast-iron fireplace. Gin is Muriel's favourite tipple and there's a range of exotic brands to mix with your tonic. The food menu is pretty good, too.

Spaniard BAR

(Map p532; www.thespaniardbar.com; 3 Skipper St) Specialising in rum (25 kinds), this narrow, crowded bar, which looks as if it's been squeezed into someone's apartment, has more atmosphere in one battered sofa than most 'style bars' have in their shiny entirety. Friendly staff, good tapas, an eclectic crowd and cool tunes played at a volume that still allows you to talk: bliss.

McHugh's Bar & Restaurant PUB

(Map p532; www.mchughsbar.com; 29-31 Queen's Sq; ⏰noon-1am Mon-Sat, 1pm-midnight Sun) In Belfast's oldest surviving building, dating from 1711, McHugh's retains a wonderfully traditional feel with its old wooden booths and benches, and pours a superb pint of Guinness. It has superior classic Irish food too.

Northern Whig BAR

(Map p532; 2-10 Bridge St; ⏰noon-11pm Mon & Tue, to 2am Wed-Sat, 1-11pm Sun) A stylish, modern bar set in an elegant Georgian printing works, the Northern Whig's high-ceilinged interior is dominated by three huge Socialist-Realist statues rescued from Prague in the early 1990s. Its relaxing sofas and armchairs encourage serious afternoon loafing, though the pace hots up considerably after 5pm on Friday and Saturday when the party crowd piles in.

GAY & LESBIAN BELFAST

Belfast's gay and lesbian scene is concentrated in the Cathedral Quarter. To find out what's happening, check out www.gaybelfast.net.

Kremlin (Map p532; www.kremlin-belfast.com; 96 Donegall St; ⏰10pm-2.30am Tue, Thu & Sun, 9pm-3am Fri & Sat) Gay-owned and operated, the Soviet kitsch–themed Kremlin is the heart and soul of Northern Ireland's gay scene. A statue of Lenin guides you into Tsar, the preclub bar, from where the Long Bar leads into the main clubbing zone, Red Square. Revolution on Saturdays, with DJs mixing up dance, house, pop and commercial, is the flagship event.

Union Street (Map p532; www.unionstreetbar.com; 8-14 Union St; noon-1am Mon-Thu, noon-1.30am Fri & Sat, 1.30pm-1am Sun; 📶) A stylish modern bar with retro decor and lots of bare brick and dark wood (check out the Belfast sinks in the loo), Union Street pulls in a mixed gay and straight crowd with nightly cabaret and karaoke, and a tempting food menu. Sunday's bingo night pulls in the punters.

Maverick (Map p532; 106-110 Donegall St; ⏰5pm-1am Mon-Fri, 2pm-1am Sat, 2pm-midnight Sun) Maverick is most popular for its Boombox nightclub, upstairs from the main bar.

Titanic Quarter

Box Nightclub CLUB

(Map p532; www.boxnightclub.com; 2 Queen's Quay; ⏲9pm-2am Tue-Thu & Sat) Inside the Odyssey Complex (p538), state-of-the-art nightclub Box spans two floors, six bars and two new VIP rooms.

South Belfast

★**Eglantine** PUB

(Map p532; http://eglantinebar.co.uk; 32 Malone Rd; ⏲11.30am-midnight Mon & Tue, to 1am Wed-Sun; 📶) The 'Eg' is a local institution, and widely reckoned to be the best of Belfast's many student pubs. It serves good beer and good food, and hosts numerous events: Monday is cinema club, Tuesday is vinyl night; other nights see DJs spin and bands perform. Bonus: Pac-Man machine.

Botanic Inn PUB

(Map p532; www.thebotanicinn.com; 23-27 Malone Rd; ⏲11.30am-1am Mon, Tue, Thu & Fri, 11.30am-2am Wed & Sat, noon-midnight Sun; 📶) The 'Bot' is a wild student hang-out with events every school night. Live folk music plays on Monday nights, Tuesday is quiz night, DJs hit the decks on Wednesday, Thursday mixes up indie, rock and trad, and live bands perform on Friday. The party keeps going during the weekend, including tunes from five decades during Sunday club.

Lavery's BAR

(Map p532; www.laverysbelfast.com; 14 Bradbury Pl; ⏲11.30am-1am Mon-Sat, 12.30pm-midnight Sun) Managed by the same family since 1918, Lavery's is a vast, multilevel, packed-to-the-gills boozing emporium, crammed with drinkers young and old, from students to tourists, business people to bikers. Its four bars include the **Public Bar** (acoustic music Monday and Tuesday; retro disco Wednesday to Saturday); the bohemian **Back Bar** with a jukebox; and new **Woodworkers** rotating tap room.

Hatfield House PUB

(Map p532; www.hatfieldhousebelfast.com; 130 Ormeau Rd; ⏲11.30am-1am Mon-Sat, to midnight Sun) On increasingly trendy Ormeau Rd, Hatfield House is no fly-by-night – its original timber and brass bar fixtures and ornate ceiling mouldings are the work of the *Titanic*'s craftsmen. Live music includes acoustic and folk; it's also a popular spot for watching big-screen sport such as football and GAA (Gaelic Athletics Association).

Outside the Centre

Dirty Duck PUB

(Map p542; http://thedirtyduckalehouse.co.uk; 3 Kinnegar Rd, Holywood; ⏲noon-11pm Mon-Wed, noon-1am Thu-Sat, 12.30-11pm Sun) On a sunny afternoon, it's hard to beat the Belfast Lough-facing beer garden at this welcoming local, footsteps from Holywood train station. It's a great bet for craft ales on tap, frequent live music and its panoramic upstairs restaurant.

☆ Entertainment

Good places to get the low-down on live music and club nights include the Good Vibrations (p558) record shop, and the Oh Yeah Music Centre (p535).

Other resources:

- Visit Belfast Welcome Centre (p559)
- Big List (www.thebiglist.co.uk)
- Culture Northern Ireland (www.culturenorthernireland.org)
- Belfast Music (www.belfastmusic.org)

Pubs with regular live sessions of traditional Irish music include the Botanic Inn, the Garrick Bar (p554), White's Tavern (p554) and Kelly's Cellars (p554).

For jazz and blues, head to the John Hewitt (p555) or the Black Box.

Rugby, football (soccer), Gaelic football and hockey are played throughout winter; cricket and hurling through summer.

Belfast Empire LIVE MUSIC

(Map p532; www.thebelfastempire.com; 42 Botanic Ave; admission live bands £5-20) A converted late-Victorian church with three floors of entertainment, the Empire is a legendary live-music venue.

Limelight LIVE MUSIC

(Map p532; www.limelightbelfast.com; 17-19 Ormeau Ave) This combined pub and club is one of the city's top venues for live rock and indie music.

Ulster Hall CONCERT VENUE

(Map p532; www.belfastcity.gov.uk; 34 Bedford St) Dating from 1862, Ulster Hall is a popular venue for a range of events including rock concerts, lunchtime organ recitals, boxing bouts and performances by the **Ulster Orchestra** (http://ulsterorchestra.com).

School of Music CLASSICAL MUSIC

(www.music.qub.ac.uk) Queen's University's School of Music stages free lunchtime recitals on Thursday plus regular evening concerts in the beautiful, hammerbeam-roofed **Harty Room** (Map p532; School of Music, University Sq), and at the **Sonic Arts Research Centre** (Map p532; Cloreen Park), with occasional performances in the larger **Sir William Whitla Hall** (Map p532; University Rd). Download a *Current Events* brochure from the website.

Waterfront Hall CONCERT VENUE
(Map p532; www.waterfront.co.uk; 2 Lanyon Pl) The impressive 2235-seat Waterfront is Belfast's flagship concert venue, hosting local, national and international performers from pop stars to symphony orchestras.

Odyssey Arena CONCERT VENUE
(Map p532; www.odysseyarena.com; 2 Queen's Quay) Within the Odyssey Complex (p538), this is the venue for big entertainment events such as rock and pop concerts, and stage shows. It's the home stadium of the Belfast Giants (p557) ice-hockey team.

King's Hall CONCERT VENUE
(Map p542; www.balmoral-park.co.uk; Lisburn Rd) Northern Ireland's biggest exhibition and conference centre hosts a range of music shows, trade fairs and sporting events. It's accessible by any bus along Lisburn Rd or by train to Balmoral station across the road.

Lyric Theatre THEATRE
(Map p542; www.lyrictheatre.co.uk; 55 Ridgeway St) This stunning modern theatre opened to great dramatic and architectural acclaim in 2011. It's built on the site of the old Lyric Theatre, where Hollywood star Liam Neeson first trod the boards (he is now a patron).

MAC ARTS CENTRE
(Metropolitan Arts Centre; Map p532; http://themaclive.com; St Anne's Sq) The Cathedral Quarter's beautiful new designer arts centre houses two theatres, and stages regular performances of drama, including shows for children.

Black Box ARTS CENTRE
(Map p532; www.blackboxbelfast.com; 18-22 Hill St) Billing itself as a 'home for live music, theatre, literature, comedy, film, visual art, live art, circus, cabaret and all points in between', Black Box is an intimate venue in the heart of the Cathedral Quarter.

Crescent Arts Centre ARTS CENTRE
(Map p532; www.crescentarts.org; 2-4 University Rd) The Crescent hosts a range of concerts, plays, workshops, readings and dance classes. The Crescent is also the headquarters of the Belfast Book Festival (p546), and the dance festival CityDance (p546).

DON'T MISS

GETTING INTO IRISH CULTURE

Dedicated to Irish language, music and culture, **An Droichead** (Map p532; www.androichead.com; 20 Cooke St, The Bridge; tickets £5-15) cultural centre offers Irish-language courses, stages traditional dance and *céilidh* workshops, hosts art exhibitions and serves as a live-music venue. It's a great place to hear live Irish folk music from big names from around the country, as well as up-and-coming local talent.

Grand Opera House OPERA
(Map p532; www.goh.co.uk; 2-4 Great Victoria St; box office 9.30am-5.30pm Mon-Fri, to 5pm Sat) This grand old venue plays host to opera, ballet, popular musicals and comedy shows. The box office is on the corner of Howard St.

Queen's Film Theatre CINEMA
(Map p532; www.queensfilmtheatre.com; 20 University Sq) A major venue for the Belfast Film Festival (p546), this two-screen art-house cinema is close to the university.

Movie House CINEMA
(Map p532; www.moviehouse.co.uk; 14 Dublin Rd) Convenient city-centre 10-screen multiplex.

Storm Cinemas CINEMA
(Map p532; www.odysseycinemas.co.uk; Odyssey Pavilion) Belfast's biggest multiplex has 12 screens and stadium seats throughout. It's part of the Odyssey Complex (p538).

Windsor Park FOOTBALL
(Map p542; off Lisburn Rd) For details of Northern Ireland international football matches at this stadium, see www.irishfa.com.

Casement Park GAELIC FOOTBALL
(Map p542; www.antrimgaa.net; Andersonstown Rd) In West Belfast; you can see Gaelic football and hurling here.

Belfast Giants ICE HOCKEY
(Map p532; www.belfastgiants.com; 2 Queen's Quay) The Belfast Giants ice-hockey team draws big crowds to the arena at the Odyssey Complex (p538); the season is September to March. The arena also hosts indoor sporting events including tennis and athletics.

Kingspan Stadium RUGBY
(Map p542; www.ulsterrugby.com; 85 Ravenhill Park) This recently renovated, 18,000-capacity stadium is the home of Ulster Rugby.

Shopping

Items particular to Northern Ireland that you may like to look out for include fine Belleek china and Irish linen (antique and new).

For general shopping you'll find all the usual high-street chains and department stores in the compact central shopping area north of City Hall, centred on **Royal Ave**. The main shopping malls are **Victoria Square** (Map p532; www.victoriasquare.com; btwn Ann & Chichester Sts; ⌚9.30am-6pm Mon-Tue, to 9pm Wed-Fri, 9am-6pm Sat, 1-6pm Sun) and the **Castle Court Centre** (Map p532; www.castlecourt-uk.com; Royal Ave; ⌚9am-6pm Mon-Wed & Fri-Sat, 9am-9pm Thu, 1-6pm Sun). There's late-night shopping on Thursdays till 8pm or 9pm.

Other shopping districts include trendy Lisburn Road (p558).

★St George's Market MARKET

(Map p532; www.belfastcity.gov.uk; cnr Oxford & May Sts; ⌚6am-2pm Fri, 9am-3pm Sat, 10am-4pm Sun) Ireland's oldest continually operating market was built in 1896. This Victorian beauty hosts a Friday **variety market** (flowers, produce, meat, fish, homewares and second-hand goods), Saturday **City Food & Craft Market**, with food stalls and live music, and **Sunday market** (food, antiques and local arts and crafts). The St George's Market Bar & Grill (p549) overlooks the action.

A free shuttle bus links the market with Donegall Sq and Adelaide St every 20 minutes from 11am to 3pm on Friday and Saturday.

In early December, a two-day Christmas Fair and Market takes place here.

Wicker Man JEWELLERY, SOUVENIRS

(Map p532; www.thewickerman.co.uk; 44-46 High St; ⌚9.30am-6pm Mon-Wed & Fri & Sat, 9.30am-9pm Thu, 1.30-6pm Sun) In addition to hosting exhibitions, arty Wicker Man sells a wide range of contemporary Irish crafts and gifts, including silver jewellery, glassware and knitwear.

Steensons JEWELLERY

(Map p532; www.thesteensons.com; Bedford House, Bedford St; ⌚10am-5.30pm Mon-Sat, to 8pm Thu) This city-centre showroom sells a range of stylish, contemporary, handmade jewellery in silver, gold and platinum, from a workshop (p617) in Glenarm, County Antrim. Steensons is the creator of *Game of Thrones* jewellery; look out for its similarly inspired designs.

Matchetts Music MUSIC

(Map p532; www.matchettsmusic.com; 6 Wellington Pl; ⌚9am-5.30pm Mon-Sat) Acoustic instruments, from guitars and mandolins to penny whistles and bodhráns (hand-held goatskin drums), fill the shelves here, along with books of lyrics and guitar chords for traditional Irish songs.

Good Vibrations MUSIC

(Map p532; 89-93 North St; ⌚8am-6pm) Owned by music producer Terry Hooley (who released Teenage Kicks by the Undertones on his Good Vibrations label back in 1978), this is Belfast's best alternative record shop, and a source of info on the latest gigs, plus tickets. It's inside the Bigg Life Arts Centre, upstairs from Cafe Wah.

WORTH A TRIP

LISBURN ROAD

Belfast's chicest shopping district is Lisburn Rd (www.thelisburnroad.com). From Eglantine Ave out to Balmoral Ave it's lined with red-brick and mock-Tudor facades housing fashion boutiques, interior-design studios, art galleries, antique shops, delicatessens, coffee houses, wine bars and top restaurants, nestled among South Belfast's wealthy, tree-lined suburbs.

Information

DANGERS & ANNOYANCES

Even at the height of the Troubles, Belfast wasn't a particularly dangerous city for tourists. It's still best, however, to avoid the so-called 'interface areas' – near the Peace Lines in West Belfast, Crumlin Rd and the Short Strand (just east of Queen's Bridge) – after dark; if in doubt about any area, ask at your hotel or hostel.

Dissident Republican groups continue a campaign of violent attacks aimed at police and military targets, but have very little public support. Security alerts usually have no effect on visiting tourists (other than roads being closed), but be aware of the potential danger. You can follow the Police Service of Northern Ireland (PSNI) on Twitter (@policeserviceni) and receive immediate notification of any alerts.

You will notice a more obvious security presence than elsewhere in the UK and Ireland, such as armoured police Land Rovers and fortified police stations. There are doormen on many city-centre pubs.

If you want to take photos of fortified police stations, army posts or other military or quasi-military paraphernalia, get permission first, just to be on the safe side. In the Protestant and

TRANSPORT PASSES

Smartlink Travel Card

If you plan on using city buses a lot, it's worth buying a **Smartlink Travel Card** (available from the Metro kiosk, the Visit Belfast Welcome Centre and the Europa and Laganside bus stations). The card costs an initial fee of £1.50, plus £10.50 per 10 journeys – you can get it topped up as you want. Or you can get seven days of unlimited travel for £16. When you board the bus, you simply place the card on top of the ticket machine and it automatically issues a ticket.

Visitor Pass

The **Belfast Visitor Pass** (per one/two/three days £6.50/11/14.50) allows unlimited travel on bus and train services in Belfast and around, and discounts on admission to Titanic Belfast and other attractions. You can buy it at airports, main train and bus stations, the Metro kiosk on Donegall Sq and the **Visit Belfast Welcome Centre**.

Catholic strongholds of West Belfast it's best not to photograph people without permission; always ask first and be prepared to accept a refusal. Taking pictures of the murals is not a problem.

EMERGENCY

The national emergency phone number for police, fire and ambulance is 999.

Rape Crisis & Sexual Abuse Centre (028-9032 9002; 29 Donegall St; 10am-6pm Mon-Fri)

Victim Support (028-9024 3133; www.victimsupportni.co.uk) Victim Support is an independent charity that helps people cope with the effects of crime.

INTERNET ACCESS

Belfast has a comprehensive network of 104 free wi-fi hotspots at visitor attractions, community and leisure centres and other public buildings. Search for BelfastWiFi.

LEFT LUGGAGE

A legacy of the Troubles is that due to security concerns, there are no left-luggage facilities at Belfast's airports, train stations and bus stations. However, most hotels and hostels allow guests to leave their bags for the day, and the Visit Belfast Welcome Centre also offers a daytime left-luggage service (£4.50 per item; photo ID required).

MEDICAL SERVICES

Accident and emergency services are available at a number of hospitals.

Mater Hospital (028-9074 1211; 45-51 Crumlin Rd) Near the junction of Antrim Rd and Clifton St.

Royal Victoria Hospital (028-9024 0503; 274 Grosvenor Rd) West of the city centre.

Ulster Hospital (028-9048 4511; Upper Newtownards Rd, Dundonald) Near Stormont.

POST

Post Office Main post office (Map p532; 12-16 Bridge St; 9am-5.30pm Mon-Sat) Botanic Gardens (Map p532; cnr University Rd & College Gardens; 8am-9pm Mon-Sat, 10am-6pm Sun) Shaftesbury Sq (Map p532; 1-5 Botanic Ave; 9am-5.30pm Mon-Fri)

TOURIST INFORMATION

Visit Belfast Welcome Centre (Map p532; 028-9024 6609; http://visit-belfast.com; 9 Donegall Sq N; 9am-7pm Mon-Sat, 11am-4pm Sun Jun-Sep, 9am-5.30pm Mon-Sat, 11am-4pm Sun Oct-May;) Provides information about the whole of Northern Ireland and books accommodation. Services include left luggage (not overnight), currency exchange and free wi-fi.

Tourist Information Desks George Best Belfast City Airport (Map p542; 028-9093 5372; George Best Belfast City Airport; 7.30am-7pm Mon-Fri, 7.30am-4.30pm Sat, 11am-6pm Sun) Belfast International Airport (028-9448 4677; Belfast International Airport; 7.30am-7pm Mon-Fri, 7.30am-5.30pm Sat, 8am-11am Sun)

Getting There & Away

AIR

Belfast International Airport (BFS; 028-9448 4848; www.belfastairport.com) Located 30km northwest of the city; flights serve the UK and Europe, and in the USA, Las Vegas, Orlando and New York.

George Best Belfast City Airport (BHD; Map p542; 028-9093 9093; www.belfastcityairport.com; Airport Rd) Located 6km northeast of the city centre; flights serve the UK and Europe.

BOAT

Apart from Steam Packet Company and Stena Line services, other car ferries to and from Scotland and England dock at Larne, 37km north of Belfast. Trains to the terminal at Larne Harbour depart from Great Victoria St station.

Steam Packet Company (Map p542; ☎08722 992 992; www.steam-packet.com) Car ferries run by the Steam Packet Company between Belfast and Douglas on the Isle of Man (2½ hours, two or three a week, April to September only) dock at Albert Quay, 2km north of the city centre. There's no public transport to the ferry terminal; a taxi costs about £3.

Stena Line (Map p542; ☎08447 707070; www.stenaline.co.uk) Stena Line car ferries to Belfast from Liverpool (England; eight hours) and Cairnryan (Scotland; 2¼ hours) dock at Victoria Terminal 5km north of the city centre; take the M2 motorway north and turn right at junction No 1. Bus 96 runs from Upper Queen's St (£1.70, 20 minutes, nine daily Monday to Friday, three Saturday and Sunday). A taxi costs about £9.

BUS

There are **information desks** (⌚7.45am-6.30pm Mon-Fri, 8am-6pm Sat) at both of Belfast's bus stations, where you can pick up regional bus timetables. Contact **Translink** (☎028-9066 6630; www.translink.co.uk) for timetable and fares information.

National Express (☎08717 818 178; www.nationalexpress.com) runs a daily coach service between Belfast and London (one way £37, 15½ hours) via the Cairnryan ferry, Dumfries, Milton Keynes, Carlisle, Manchester and Birmingham. The ticket office is in the Europa BusCentre.

Scottish Citylink (☎0871 266 3333; www.citylink.co.uk) operates three buses a day from Glasgow to Belfast (£32, six hours), via the Cairnryan ferry.

Europa BusCentre (Map p532; ☎028-9066 6630; Great Victoria St, Great Northern Mall) Belfast's main bus station is behind the Europa Hotel and next door to Great Victoria St train station; it's reached via the Great Northern Mall beside the hotel. It's the main terminus for buses to Derry, Dublin and destinations in the west and south of Northern Ireland.

Laganside Bus Station (Map p532; ☎028-9066 6630; Oxford St) The smaller of Belfast's two bus stations, Laganside is near the river and is mainly for buses to eastern County Down and eastern County Tyrone.

TRAIN

For information on train fares and timetables, contact Translink (☎028-9066 6630; www.translink.co.uk). The **NIR Travel Shop** (☎028-9024 2420; Great Victoria St Station; ⌚9am-5pm Mon-Fri, to 12.30pm Sat) books train tickets, ferries and holiday packages.

TRANSPORT FROM BELFAST

Buses

DESTINATION	PRICE	DURATION (HR)	FREQUENCY
Armagh	£9.30	1¼	hourly Mon-Fri, 6 Sat, 4 Sun
Ballycastle	£12	3	3 daily Mon-Fri, 2 Sat
Bangor	£3.80	¾	half-hourly Mon-Sat, 8 Sun
Derry	£12	1¾	half-hourly Mon-Sat, 13 Sun
Downpatrick	£6	1	at least hourly Mon-Sat, 6 Sun
Dublin	£15	2½	hourly
Enniskillen	£12	2¼	hourly Mon-Sat, 3 Sun
Newcastle	£8	1¼	at least hourly

Trains

DESTINATION	PRICE	DURATION (HR)	FREQUENCY
Bangor	£5.50	½	every 20 min Mon-Sat, half-hourly Sun
Dublin	£30	2¼	8 Mon-Sat, 5 Sun
Larne Harbour	£7.20	1	hourly
Newry	£11	¾	10 Mon-Sat, 5 Sun
Portrush	£12	1¾	hourly

Belfast Central Station (East Bridge St) East of the city centre; trains run to Dublin and all destinations in Northern Ireland. If you arrive by train at Central Station, your rail ticket entitles you to a free bus ride into the city centre.

Great Victoria Street Station (Great Victoria St, Great Northern Mall) Next to the Europa BusCentre; has trains for Portadown, Lisburn, Bangor, Larne Harbour and Derry.

Getting Around

Belfast's integrated public-transport system includes buses linking both airports to the central train and bus stations.

TO/FROM THE AIRPORTS

Belfast International Airport Airport Express 300 bus runs to the Europa BusCentre (one way/return £7.50/10.50, 30 minutes) every 10 or 15 minutes between 7am and 8pm, every 30 minutes from 8pm to 11pm, and hourly through the night; a return ticket is valid for one month. A taxi costs about £30.

George Best Belfast City Airport Airport Express 600 bus runs to the Europa BusCentre (one way/return £2.50/3.80, 15 minutes) every 20 minutes between 6am and 9.30pm Monday to Saturday, and every 40 minutes on Sunday. A return ticket is valid for one month. The taxi fare to the city centre is about £10.

BICYCLE

National Cycle Network route 9 runs through central Belfast, mostly following the western bank of the River Lagan and the north shore of Belfast Lough.

Belfast Bike Tours (p544) rents bikes.

Belfast Bikes (☎ 034-3357 1551; www.belfastbikes.co.uk; registration per 3 days £5, bikes per 30min/1hr/2hr/4hr free/50p/£2.50/3.50; 24hr) Belfast's bike-share scheme, introduced in 2015, provides 300 bikes at 30 docking stations throughout the city, with plans to increase bike numbers and locations. Register online or at the touchscreen terminals. If the bike is lost, stolen or damaged, your credit card will be charged £120.

BUS

Metro (☎ 028-9066 6630; www.translink.co.uk) operates the bus network in Belfast. Most city services depart from various stops on and around Donegall Sq, at City Hall and along Queen St. You can pick up a free bus map (and buy tickets) from the **Metro kiosk** (Map p532; 8am-5.30pm Mon-Fri) at the northwest corner of the square.

Buy your ticket from the driver (change given); fares range from £1.50 to £2.30 depending on distance. The driver can also sell you a **Metro Day Ticket** (£3.90), giving you unlimited bus travel within the City Zone all day Monday to Saturday. Cheaper versions allow travel any time after 10am Monday to Saturday or all day Sunday (£3.40).

An increasing number of buses are low-floor, 'kneeling' buses with space for one wheelchair.

CAR & MOTORCYCLE

There are plenty of major car-hire agencies in Belfast.

Avis (www.avis.co.uk) City (☎ 0844 544 6036; 69-71 Great Victoria St) Belfast International Airport (☎ 0844 544 6012; Belfast International Airport) George Best Belfast City Airport (☎ 0844 544 6028; www.avis.co.uk; George Best Belfast City Airport)

Budget (www.budgetbelfast.co.uk) City (☎ 028-9023 0700; 69-71 Great Victoria St) Belfast International Airport (☎ 028-9442 3332; Belfast International Airport) George Best Belfast City Airport (☎ 028-9045 1111; George Best Belfast City Airport)

Dooley Car Rentals (☎ 0800 282189; www.dooleycarrentals.com; Airport Rd, Belfast International Airport, Aldergrove) This reliable Ireland-wide agency offers good rates – around £200 a week for a compact car, with the option of one-way cross-border rentals (£117 extra to drop the car off in the Republic; €150 if you pick it up in the Republic and drop it off in Northern Ireland).

Europcar (www.europcar.co.uk) City (☎ 0871 384 3425; Belfast Central Station) Belfast International Airport (☎ 0871 384 3426; Belfast International Airport) George Best Belfast City Airport (☎ 0871 384 3425; George Best Belfast City Airport)

Hertz (www.hertz.co.uk) Belfast International Airport (☎ 028-9442 2533; Belfast International Airport) George Best Belfast City Airport (☎ 028-9442 2533; George Best Belfast City Airport)

TAXI

Fona Cab (☎ 028-9033 3333; www.fonacab.com)

Value Cabs (☎ 028-9080 9080; www.valuecabs.co.uk)

Counties Down & Armagh

Includes ➡

Best Places to Eat

- McKee's Country Store & Restaurant (p569)
- Parson's Nose (p582)
- Brunel's (p575)
- Poacher's Pocket (p570)
- Moody Boar (p585)

Best Places to Stay

- Old Inn (p565)
- Enniskeen Country House (p574)
- Narrow Water Castle Apartment (p580)
- Fortwilliam Country House (p582)
- Hutt Hostel (p574)

Why Go?

County Down's treasures fan out beyond Belfast. Strangford Lough's sparkling, island-fringed waters stretch south, with the bird-haunted mudflats of Castle Espie and Nendrum's ancient monastery on one shore, and the picturesque Ards Peninsula on the other. The Mourne Mountains' velvet curves sweep down to the sea near Downpatrick and Lecale, the old stamping grounds of Ireland's patron saint.

Down's neighbour County Armagh is largely rural, from the low, rugged hills of the south to the apple orchards and strawberry fields of the north, with Ireland's ecclesiastical capital, the appealing little city of Armagh, in the middle. South Armagh is a peaceful backwater, where you can wander back and forth across the border with the Republic without even noticing.

Both counties' lush landscapes and scalloped bays provide a bounty of seasonal ingredients, used by a wealth of exceptional eateries throughout the region.

When to Go

- May brings white clouds of apple blossom to County Armagh's orchards, celebrated with the Apple Blossom Fair in the early part of the month.
- Summertime generally has the best weather for hiking and cycling, and late June sees the International Walking Festival in the Mourne Mountains.
- Spring and autumn are both good for birdwatching, but keen birders have a big X on their calendars in October, when tens of thousands of overwintering brent geese begin to arrive at Castle Espie on Strangford Lough.

Counties Down & Armagh Highlights

1. Hike along ancient smuggler trails in the **Mourne Mountains** (p576).
2. Tour the illustrious castle and taste top menus in elegant **Hillsborough** (p581).
3. Explore stately halls and exquisite gardens at **Mt Stewart House** (p568).
4. Watch vast flocks of geese, ducks and waders at **Castle Espie** (p569).
5. Tee off at esteemed **Royal County Down Golf Course** (p574) in seaside Newcastle.
6. Follow in the steps of Ireland's patron saint in **Downpatrick** (p571).
7. View priceless texts including a first edition of *Gulliver's Travels* at **Armagh Public Library** (p583).
8. Visit *Game of Thrones*–famed **Castle Ward Estate** (p573) on the shores of Strangford Lough.
9. Mountain-bike down the slopes of **Kilbroney Forest Park** (p577).

COUNTY DOWN

POP 531,670 / AREA 2448 SQ KM

Bangor

POP 55,000

On the stretch of shore locally known as the 'Gold Coast' (due to its wealthy residents, not its weather), this Victorian seaside resort town first flourished when the Belfast–Bangor train line was built in the late 19th century. In recent years, Bangor has enjoyed a renaissance as an out-of-town base for city commuters.

In the centre of town, Main St and High St (Bangor has both) converge at the huge boat-filled marina.

Sights & Activities

The scenic **North Down Coastal Path** follows the shore from Holywood train station on Belfast's northeastern edge to Bangor Marina (15km), and continues east to Orlock Point.

North Down Museum MUSEUM
(www.northdownmuseum.com; Castle Park Ave; ⏲10am-4.30pm Tue-Sat, noon-4.30pm Sun year-round, 10am-4.30pm Mon Jul & Aug) FREE Historical treasures displayed in the converted laundry, stables and stores of Bangor Castle include the *Raven Maps* (the only complete folio of Plantation-era maps in Ireland); the Bronze Age Ballycroghan Swords, dating from circa 500 BC; the 9th-century bronze handbell, the Bangor Bell; and a 17th-century sundial by Scottish craftsman John Bonar.

Pickie Family Fun Park AMUSEMENT PARK
(http://pickiefunpark.com; Marine Gardens; family pass £10-35; ⏲9am-7.30pm Easter–May & Sep, to 9pm Jun-Aug, to 4pm Sat & Sun Oct–Easter; 📶) This old-fashioned seaside entertainment complex is famous for its swan-shaped pedal boats. Also here are a kids' adventure playground, electric-track karts, minigolf and a miniature steam train, the Pickie Puffer. Family passes include various rides, but it's not possible to buy individual ride tickets.

Blue Aquarius CRUISE
(☎07510 006000; www.bangorboat.com; adult/child from £6/3, fishing trips per adult/child incl tackle & bait £17/12; ⏲departures from 2pm daily Jul & Aug, Sat & Sun only Apr-Jun & Sep) Pleasure cruises around Bangor Bay depart from the marina pontoon next to the Pickie Family Fun Park. From June to August, there are family-friendly fishing trips departing at 9.30am and 7pm daily from the Eisenhower Pier (on the right-hand side of the harbour, looking out to sea).

Sleeping

★**Cairn Bay Lodge** B&B ££
(☎028-9146 7636; www.cairnbaylodge.com; 278 Seacliff Rd; s/d from £50/85; 📶) Set amid beautiful gardens, this lovely seaside villa exudes Edwardian elegance with its oak-panelled lounge and dining room serving superb gourmet breakfasts. Its eight bedrooms (all with private bathroom and organic seaweed toiletries, and some with sparkling sea views) blend antique charm with contemporary style. Beauty treatments are available. It's 1km east of the town centre, overlooking Ballyholme Bay.

Clandeboye Lodge Hotel HOTEL ££
(☎028-9185 2500; www.clandeboyelodge.com; 10 Estate Rd, Clandeboye; s/d/f from £95/122/197; @📶) Resembling a modern red-brick church, the Clandeboye offers informal luxury – big bedrooms, polished granite bathrooms, fluffy bathrobes, champagne and chocolates – with a log fire in winter and a drinks terrace in summer. Its bar-restaurant, the **Coq & Bull**, serves farm-reared poultry and beef, and local seafood. It sits amid landscaped gardens on the south-west edge of town.

Ennislare House B&B ££
(☎028-9127 0858; http://ennislarehouse.com; 7-9 Princetown Rd; s/d £40/70; 📶) Just 300m north of the train station, this lovely Victorian town house has big, bright rooms, stylish decor and a friendly owner who can't do enough to make you feel welcome.

Eating

Guillemont Kitchen CAFE £
(2 Seacliff Rd; dishes £4-6.50; ⏲9am-5pm) Opposite the marina, this snug, sky-blue cafe does great coffee, all-day breakfasts, and light bites such as gourmet sandwiches and soups, as well as homemade cakes.

★**Boat House** FRENCH, IRISH ££
(☎028-9146 9253; www.theboathouseni.co.uk; 1a Seacliff Rd; lunch mains £9.50-17, dinner 3-course menu £33-35; ⏲12.30-2.30pm & 5.30-9.30pm Mon-Sat, 1-8pm Sun) 🍃 Tucked into the former harbour master's office, Dutch chef Joery Castel's Boat House is a cosy little nook of stone, brick and designer decor serving deft-

WORTH A TRIP

CRAWFORDSBURN

In the storybook-pretty conservation village of Crawfordsburn, 3km west of Bangor on the B20, the 1614-established **Old Inn** (☎028-9185 3255; www.theoldinn.com; 15 Main St; d from £100; 📶) claims to be Ireland's oldest hotel. Its original thatched cottage (now the bar, with log fires and low ceilings) is flanked by 18th-century additions. Character-filled rooms have arts and crafts–style wallpaper and mahogany; the oak-panelled **Lewis Restaurant** (☎028-9185 1300; www.theoldinn.com; 15 Main St; mains £13-25; ⏰noon-10pm Mon-Sat, to 9.30pm Sun) is superb.

The inn was once a resting place on the coach route between Belfast and Donaghadee (formerly the main ferry port for mainland Britain). As a result, it has been patronised by many famous names, including the young Peter the Great (tsar of Russia), Dick Turpin (highwayman), former US president George HW Bush, and a roll call of literary figures, including Swift, Tennyson, Thackeray, Dickens, Trollope and CS Lewis.

ly prepared local seafood, lamb and game. Surprise five- and seven-course tasting menus (per person £45/55) are served to the whole table.

Corin INTERNATIONAL ££
(☎028-9122 7295; http://corinrestaurant.co.uk; 119 High St; mains £12.50-23.50; ⏰5-10pm Tue-Thu, 6-10pm Fri & Sat, noon-3pm Sun) Since it opened in 2013, this sleek, minimalist spot rapidly established itself as one of Bangor's top tables. Artfully presented dishes span the likes of smoked beetroot with goat's-cheese mousse and balsamic jelly, duck breast with sweet-potato gnocchi, and black bream with dill and tarragon potato cake, and mussel and chorizo sauce.

Drinking

Hop House BAR
(http://krestaurant.wix.com/bangor; 44 High St; ⏰11.30am-1am Mon-Sat, noon-midnight Sun) Local craft beers, live music or DJs, a Thursday quiz night and regular movie nights with unlimited popcorn keep this central spot hopping. The bar menu features awesome burgers as does the upstairs K Restaurant.

Rabbit Rooms BAR
(www.therabbitrooms.com; 30-32 Quay St; ⏰11.30am-1am Mon-Sat, 12.30pm-midnight Sun) In a charcoal-coloured building stencilled with a gigantic white rabbit, this bare-boards space is a wonderland of mismatched vintage furniture like old, cracked-leather cinema seats, with cocktails served in teapots. Live music plays Monday to Thursday and Saturday.

Jenny Watts PUB
(www.jennywattsbar.com; 41 High St; ⏰11.30am-11pm Mon-Thu, to midnight Fri & Sat, 12.30-10pm Sun) Bangor's oldest pub (1780) pulls in a mixed-age crowd for live music from Wednesday to Sunday, including jazz and blues Sunday lunchtime. There's a beer garden out back.

Information

The **Tourist Office** (☎028-9127 0069; http://orthdowntourism.com; 34 Quay St; ⏰9.15am-5pm Mon, Tue, Thu & Fri, 10am-5pm Wed & Sat, 1-5pm Sun May-Aug, shorter hours Mon-Sat, closed Sun Sep-Apr) is housed in a tower built in 1637 as a fortified customs post.

Getting There & Away

The bus and train stations are together on Abbey St, at the uphill end of Main St.

Buses 1 and 2 run from Belfast's Laganside Bus station to Bangor (£3.80, one hour, hourly). From Bangor, bus 3 goes to Donaghadee (£3, 25 minutes, hourly Monday to Saturday, three Sunday).

A regular **train** service runs from Belfast's Great Victoria St and Central stations to Bangor (£5.50, 30 minutes, every 20 minutes Monday to Saturday, hourly Sunday).

Ards Peninsula

The low-lying Ards Peninsula (An Aird) is the finger of land that encloses Strangford Lough, pinching against the thumb of the Lecale Peninsula at the Portaferry Narrows. The northern half of the peninsula has some of Ireland's most fertile farmland, with large expanses of wheat and barley, while the south is a landscape of neat fields, white cottages and narrow, winding roads. The eastern coast has some good sandy beaches. You're best exploring with your own wheels.

Donaghadee

POP 6500

Donaghadee (Domhnach Daoi) was the main ferry port for Scotland until 1874, when it was superseded by Larne. Now Donaghadee is a pretty little harbour town that's fast becoming part of Belfast's commuter belt.

Activities

MV The Brothers BOAT TOUR
(☎028-9188 3403; www.nelsonsboats.co.uk; 146 Killaughey Rd; adult/child £7/3; ⊙departs 2pm daily Jul & Aug, weather permitting) MV *The Brothers* runs boat trips to Copeland Island, which was abandoned to the seabirds at the turn of the 20th century. There are also sea-angling trips (adult/child £17/12, departures at 10am and 7pm July to September; times can vary due to tides), with all tackle and bait provided.

The truly hardy can be accompanied by a historic lifeboat while swimming the North Channel to Scotland.

Sleeping & Eating

Pier 36 B&B ££
(☎028-9188 4466; www.pier36.co.uk; 36 The Parade; s/d from £50/79, restaurant mains £10-18; ⊙restaurant noon-9pm) An excellent pub with comfortable B&B rooms upstairs and a red-brick and terracotta-tiled restaurant at the back, dominated by a yellow Rayburn stove that turns out home-baked bread and the daily roast. Irish craft beers include Hilden Brewery's Headless Dog and Eight Degrees Brewing's Howling Gale and Sunburnt.

Slice of Heaven CAFE £
(www.sliceofheavendessertcafe.com; 11 New St; dishes £3.50-7; ⊙10am-5pm Mon-Sat, noon-5pm Sun; 📶) In Donaghadee's lavishly restored former courthouse you can get fantastic sandwiches (coronation chicken; Christmas with turkey, ham, stuffing and cranberry sauce), as well as soups, bagels and salads, but the showstoppers are the desserts: key lime pie, summer-berry pavlova, sticky toffee pudding and homemade ice cream such as champagne sorbet.

Governor Rocks SEAFOOD ££
(☎028-9188 4817; www.thegovernorrocks.com; 27 The Parade; mains £10-17.50; ⊙noon-3pm & 5.30-9.30pm Mon-Sat, noon-9.30pm Sun; 🍴👪) Full-length glass windows overlook the boat-filled harbour at this stylish spot. Depending on the day's catch, the menu might feature lobster bisque, sea bass with smoked chilli butter, or lemon sole with king scallops; there are also meat and vegetarian options. While the food is locally sourced, the wines span the globe, from Chile to California.

Getting There & Away

Bus 3 runs to/from Bangor (£3, 25 minutes, hourly Monday to Saturday, three Sunday).

Portaferry

POP 3300

Beneath Windmill Hill, topped by an old windmill tower, Portaferry (Port an Pheire) is a neat huddle of streets around a medieval tower house, which looks across the turbulent, tidal-power-producing stretch of water, **the Narrows**, to a matching tower house in Strangford.

Sights & Activities

There are pleasant walks on the minor roads along the coast, north for 2.5km to **Ballyhenry Island** (accessible at low tide), and south for 6km to the National Trust nature reserve at **Ballyquintin Point**. Both are good for birdwatching, seal spotting or just admiring the views of the Mourne Mountains.

Exploris AQUARIUM
(www.exploris.org.uk; Castle St; adult/child £7.50/5; ⊙10am-6pm Mon-Fri, 11am-6pm Sat, noon-6pm Sun Apr-Aug, shorter hours Sep-Mar) This outstanding aquarium, with displays of marine life from Strangford Lough and the Irish Sea, has touch tanks that allow visitors to handle rays, starfish, sea anemones and other sea creatures. Exploris also has a seal sanctuary where orphaned, sick and injured seals are nursed back to health before being released into the wild.

Portaferry Castle CASTLE
(Castle St; ⊙10am-5pm Mon-Sat, 1-5pm Sun Easter–Jun, 10am-5.30pm Mon-Sat, noon-5pm Sun Jul & Aug) FREE Next to the tourist office, Portaferry's castle is a small 16th-century tower house which, together with the tower house in Strangford, once controlled sea traffic through the Narrows.

Sleeping & Eating

Adair's B&B B&B £
(☎028-4272 8412; 22 The Square; s/tw/f £23/46/92; 👪) Mrs Adair's friendly and good-

TIDAL ENERGY

The Narrows were known by the Vikings as Strangfjörthr, meaning 'powerful fjord', because when the tide turns, as it does four times a day, 400,000 tonnes of water per minute churn through the gap at speeds of up to eight knots. You get some idea of the tide's remarkable strength when you see – or feel – the ferry being whipped sideways by the current.

Portaferry made international headlines when SeaGen, the world's first commercial-scale tidal-energy turbine, built at Belfast's Harland & Wolff shipyard, was installed in the Narrows in 2008. The generator is clearly visible, squatting in the channel just south of town like a stumpy red-and-black lighthouse. The business end is underwater, where two giant turbine blades spin in the tidal currents, generating around 2 megawatts of electricity for 18 to 20 hours a day.

Nearby, marine-energy company Minesto, part of the Saab group, has installed an underwater kite known as Deep Green, which can produce electricity from low-velocity currents more cheaply than fossil fuels or nuclear power sources.

value B&B is an anonymous-looking grey house right on the main square (there's no sign outside, look for number 22). It has three spacious rooms – a single (shared bathroom), a twin (with private bathroom) and a family room (with private bathroom; sleeping up to four people).

Barholm HOSTEL, B&B £
(☎028-4272 9967; www.barholmportaferry.co.uk; 11 The Strand; dm/s/d from £14/26/50) Barholm offers B&B and hostel-style accommodation in a Victorian villa with a superb seafront location opposite the ferry slipway. It has a spacious kitchen, laundry facilities and a big, sunny conservatory that doubles as a tea room. It's popular with groups, so you'll need to book ahead.

Portaferry Hotel HOTEL ££
(☎028-4272 8231; www.portaferryhotel.com; 10 The Strand; s/d/f from £70/90/120, mains £10-20; @ 👪) Converted from a row of 18th-century terrace houses, this charming candyfloss-pink seafront hotel has an elegant, Georgian look to its rooms – ask for one with a sea view (£10 extra). There's also a good, family-friendly restaurant with an international menu.

Drinking

Fiddler's Green PUB
(☎028-4272 8393; 10 Church St; ⏲10am-11pm) Painted a vivid shamrock green, the Fiddler's is a fabulous place for traditional music: Paul and Jim McCarthy, whose family owns the bar, are avid banjo, mandolin, accordion and, yes, fiddle players, and the pub's walls are strung with instruments that anyone can use. Upstairs, guest rooms start from £39 (with shared bathroom). It has great Guinness and Harp, too.

Information

Tourist Office (☎028-4272 9882; www.visitstrangfordlough.co.uk; Castle St; ⏲10am-5pm Mon-Sat, 1-5pm Sun Easter–Jun, 10am-5.30pm Mon-Sat, noon-5pm Sun Jul & Aug) In a restored stable near the tower house.

Getting There & Away

A **car ferry** (one-way car & driver £6.80, car passengers & pedestrians £1) between Portaferry and Strangford sails every half-hour between 7.40am and 10.45pm Monday to Friday, 8.15am to 11.15pm Saturday and 9.45am to 10.45pm on Sunday. Journey time is about 10 minutes.

Buses 9 and 10 travel from Belfast's Laganside Bus station to Portaferry (£7, 1½ hours, seven daily Monday to Saturday, three Sunday) via Newtownards, Mt Stewart and Greyabbey. More frequent services begin from Newtownards (£6, one hour); some buses go via Carrowdore and don't stop at Mt Stewart and Greyabbey – check first.

Greyabbey

POP 1000

The little village of Greyabbey, 18km north of Portaferry, is synonymous with the splendid ruins of the Cistercian Grey Abbey. It's also popular for its antiques shops.

Sights

Grey Abbey MONASTERY
(Church Rd; ⏲10am-5pm Wed & Fri-Sun Easter-Sep, noon-4pm Sun only Oct-Easter) FREE This Cistercian abbey was founded in 1193 by Affreca, wife of the Norman aristocrat John de Courcy (the builder of Carrickfergus Castle), in thanks for surviving a stormy sea crossing from the Isle of Man. The small visitor centre explains Cistercian life with paintings and panels. The abbey **church**, in use until

the 18th century, was the first in Ireland to be built in the Gothic style.

At the church's east end is a carved tomb, possibly depicting Affreca; the effigy in the north transept may be her husband. The grounds, overlooked by 18th-century Rosemount House, are awash with trees and flowers on spreading lawns, making this an ideal picnic spot.

Eating

Hoops Coffee Shop CAFE £
(Hoops Courtyard, 7-9 Main St; dishes £4-8; 9.30am-4.30pm Wed-Sat, to 2.30pm Sun) This quaint, whitewashed traditional tea room serves filled pancakes, French toast with bacon and maple syrup, soups, jacket potatoes, and wicked cream teas, all made on the premises. Outdoor tables shaded by poppy-red umbrellas are set up in the courtyard in fine weather.

Wildfowler Inn PUB FOOD ££
(028-4278 8234; www.wildfowlerinn.co.uk; 1 Main St; kitchen noon-2.45pm & 5-8pm Mon-Thu, to 9.15pm Fri, noon-9.15pm Sat, noon-8pm Sun) With a French-washed, ochre-coloured facade and rustic interior, this beautiful former coaching inn makes a wonderful stop for gourmet pub fare, from open prawn and crayfish sandwiches through to steamed Strangford Lough mussels in chive and cream sauce, roast monkfish with balsamic tomatoes, crisp pork belly wrapped in Serrano ham with cider jus, and cinnamon crème brûlée with shortbread.

Shopping

Off Main St in the village centre, **Hoops Courtyard** has a cluster of 18 little shops selling antiques and collectables. Opening times vary, but all are open on Wednesday, Friday and Saturday afternoons.

Getting There & Away

Buses 9 and 10 link Greyabbey with Newtownards (£3, 15 minutes, every two hours or more Monday to Saturday, six Sunday). The same service continues to Portaferry (£3.80, 30 minutes).

Mt Stewart

Mt Stewart House & Gardens HISTORIC BUILDING
(www.nationaltrust.org.uk; adult/child £8/4; house 10am-5pm mid-Apr–Sep, noon-3pm Sat & Sun Nov-Mar, gardens 10am-5pm Easter–Sep, to 4pm Oct–Easter) The magnificent 18th-century Mt Stewart is one of Northern Ireland's grandest stately homes and renowned for its whimsical gardens. It was built for the Marquess of Londonderry and is decorated with lavish plasterwork, marble nudes and priceless artworks.

Mt Stewart is 3km northwest of Greyabbey and 8km southeast of Newtownards, on the A20. Buses from Belfast and Newtownards to Portaferry stop at the gate. Last admission is one hour before closing time.

Lady Mairi Vane-Tempest-Stewart (1920–2009) – daughter of the seventh marquess – gifted Mt Stewart to the National Trust. The house's treasures include the chairs used at the Congress of Vienna in 1815 (embroidery added in 1918–22), and a painting of racehorse Hambletonian in *Hambletonian, Rubbing Down* (1799–1800) by George Stubbs, one of the most important paintings in Ireland.

Much of the landscaping of the beautiful gardens was supervised in the early 20th century by Lady Edith, wife of the seventh marquess, for the benefit of her children – the Dodo Terrace at the front of the house is populated with unusual creatures from history (dinosaurs and dodos) and myth (griffins and mermaids), accompanied by giant frogs and duck-billed platypuses. The 18th-century **Temple of the Winds** (2-5pm Sun Mar-Sep) is a folly in the classical Greek style built on a high point above the lough.

Newtownards & Around

POP 27,800

Founded in the 17th century on the site of the 6th-century Movilla monastery, Newtownards (Baile Nua na hArda) today is a busy commercial centre, with some interesting sights nearby.

Sights

Scrabo Country Park PARK
Newtownards is overlooked by **Scrabo Hill**, 2km southwest of town. It was once the site of extensive prehistoric earthworks, which were largely removed during construction of the 41m 1857 **Memorial Tower**, built in honour of the third Marquess of Londonderry, and visible for miles around. Its interior is falling into disrepair and has been closed to the public, but you can still access the surrounding **country park**.

The disused sandstone quarries nearby provided material for many famous buildings, including Belfast's Albert Memorial Clock Tower.

Somme Heritage Centre HERITAGE CENTRE
(www.sommeassociation.com; 233 Bangor Rd; adult/child £6/4.75; ⏲10am-4pm Mon-Thu, 11am-4pm Sat Apr-Jun & Sep, 10am-5pm Mon-Sat Jul & Aug, 10am-4pm Mon-Thu, 11am-4pm 1st Sat of month Oct-Mar) This grimly fascinating centre vividly illustrates the horrors of the WWI Somme campaign of 1916 from the perspective of men of the 10th (Irish), 16th (Irish) and 36th (Ulster) divisions, as a memorial to the men and women who died. It has short films and reconstructions of the trenches, plus a photographic display commemorating the suffragette movement and women's roles in WWI. It's 3km north of Newtownards on the A21 towards Bangor. Bus 6 from Bangor to Newtownards passes the entrance.

Ark Open Farm FARM
(www.thearkopenfarm.co.uk; 296 Bangor Rd; adult/child £6/5; ⏲10am-6pm Mon-Sat, 2-6pm Sun Apr-Oct, 10am-5pm Mon-Sat, 2-5pm Sun Nov-Mar) The Ark is a family favourite for its rare breeds of sheep, cattle, poultry, llamas and donkeys. Kids get to pet and hand-feed the lambs, piglets and ducklings.

Eating

★McKee's Country Store & Restaurant IRISH ££
(☎028-9182 1304; www.mckeesproduce.com; Strangford View, 28 Holywood Rd, Newtownards; mains £9-15; ⏲restaurant 9.30am-5.30pm Mon-Sat, shop from 8.30am;) On a working 162-hectare farm 5km northwest of Newtownards, this foodie emporium incorporates a bakery, butcher, deli, and fruit, vegetable and dairy sections. Everything is produced on-site or sourced from the surrounding area. If it's not picnic weather, the restaurant serves dishes such as pork-and-honey mustard sausages in a panoramic dining room overlooking the lush farmland and lough beyond.

Information

The **Tourist Office** (☎028-9182 6846; www.visitstrangfordlough.co.uk; 31 Regent St; ⏲9.15am-5pm Mon-Fri, 9.30am-5pm Sat Sep-Jun, 9am-5.15pm Mon-Sat Jul & Aug) is next to the bus station.

Getting There & Away

Buses 9 and 10 serve Belfast (£3, 20 minutes, every two hours or better Monday to Saturday, six Sunday) and Portaferry (£6, one hour).

Strangford Lough

Almost landlocked, Strangford Lough (Loch Cuan) is connected to the open sea by a 700m-wide strait, the Narrows, between the towns of Portaferry and Strangford. The lough's western shore is fringed by hump-backed islands – half-drowned mounds of boulder clay (called drumlins) left behind by ice sheets at the end of the last ice age. On the eastern shore, the drumlins have been broken down by the waves into heaps of boulders that form shallow tidal reefs (known locally as 'pladdies').

Large colonies of grey seals frequent the lough, especially at the southern tip of the Ards Peninsula. Birds abound on the shores and tidal mudflats. Strangford Lough oysters are a local delicacy, and there are some wonderful spots to eat as well as sleep in the area. Your own wheels are the best way to explore the area.

Sights

Castle Espie Wildfowl & Wetlands Centre WILDLIFE RESERVE
(www.wwt.org.uk; Ballydrain Rd, Comber; adult/child £7.30/3.60; ⏲10am-5pm Mon-Fri, to 5.30pm Sat & Sun Apr-Sep, to 4pm Oct-Mar) Situated 2km southeast of Comber, off the Downpatrick road (A22), Castle Espie reserve is a haven for huge flocks of geese, ducks and swans. The landscaped grounds are dotted with birdwatching hides, and are a paradise for fledgling naturalists, with family bird-feeding and pond-dipping sessions.

The best months to visit are May and June, when it's overrun with goslings, ducklings and cygnets, and October, when vast flocks of 30,000 light-bellied brent geese (75% of the world's population) arrive from Arctic Canada.

Nendrum Monastic Site HISTORIC SITE
(Lisbane; ⏲site 24hr, visitor centre 10am-5pm daily Jun-Sep, Wed & Fri-Sun Apr-May, noon-4pm Sun Oct-Mar) FREE In a wonderful island setting, the 5th-century Celtic monastic community of Nendrum was built under the guidance of St Mochaoi (St Mahee). Its scant remains provide a clear outline of its early plan, with the foundations of a number of churches, a **round tower**, beehive cells and three concentric stone ramparts and a monks' cemetery. The **stone sundial** was reconstructed using original pieces. There's a small, illuminating **visitor centre**.

Nendrum is 5km south of Comber, reached by a causeway and bridge. By the bridge, look for the ruined tower of 15th-century **Mahee Castle**.

Sleeping & Eating

★Dufferin Coaching Inn B&B ££
(☎028-4482 1134; www.dufferincoachinginn.com; 35 High St, Killyleagh; s/d £65/75; 📶) The comfortable lounge in this lovely Georgian house was once Killyleagh's village bank – the manager's office in the corner now houses a little library. Excellent breakfasts include freshly squeezed orange juice, good coffee and scrambled eggs with smoked salmon; the six plush rooms have crisp linen and fluffy towels, and some have four-poster beds.

The smallest double has the bath in the bedroom, charmingly hidden behind a curtain.

Anna's House B&B B&B ££
(☎028-9754 1566; www.annashouse.com; 35 Lisbarnett Rd, Tullynagee, Lisbane; s/d/f from £60/90/130; 📶) Just west of Lisbane, Anna's is a spacious, ecofriendly country house with views over a lake from a glass-walled extension. The hospitality is second to none, the food is almost all organic and the bread is homebaked, with a breakfast menu that ranges from an Ulster fry or smoked-salmon omelette to fresh fruit salad.

Old Schoolhouse Inn B&B ££
(☎028-9754 1182; www.theoldschoolhouseinn.com; 100 Ballydrain Rd, Comber; s/d from £50/70; 📶) Just south of Castle Espie on the road to Nendrum, the 1929 Old Schoolhouse has seven luxurious, modern rooms, each named for a former US president. The former classroom now houses an award-winning **restaurant** (mains £12-23; ⌚kitchen noon-10pm Mon-Sat, to 8pm Sun) headed up by Will Brown, who worked with Marco Pierre White in London. A kitchen garden provides herbs and vegetables.

Old Post Office Tearoom CAFE £
(www.oldpostofficelisbane.co.uk; 191 Killinchy Rd, Lisbane; dishes £3-7.50; ⌚9am-5pm Mon-Sat; 📶) Once the village post office, this thatched cottage has been lovingly converted into a tea room and art gallery, with cream plaster and bare stone walls and a wood-burning stove. It serves great coffee and home-baked scones, plus lunch specials such as lasagne, quiches and lovely fresh salads.

★Poacher's Pocket MODERN IRISH ££
(☎028-9754 1589; www.poacherspocketlisbane.com; 181 Killinchy Rd, Comber; mains £11-23; ⌚kitchen noon-9pm Mon-Fri, 9am-9pm Sat & Sun, deli 9am-9pm) A fresh, contemporary makeover has transformed this roadside pub into a foodie magnet for dishes such as Hegarty's-vintage-cheddar and onion pie with hazelnut shortcrust pastry, Strangford mussels and fries, and mackerel with caramelised fennel and beetroot crème fraîche. There's a fantastic range of local craft ciders and beers, which it also sells at its attached Poacher's Pantry deli.

★Balloo House MODERN IRISH ££
(☎028-9754 1210; www.ballooinns.com; 1 Comber Rd, Killinchy; mains £10-23; ⌚kitchen noon-8.30pm Sun & Mon, to 9pm Tue-Thu, to 9.30pm Fri & Sat) Chef Danny Millar regularly appears on BBC's *Saturday Kitchen* and *Great British Menu*, and is the mastermind behind dishes like sublime cream of wild-garlic soup (served with still-warm, homebaked breads and olive tapenade), smoked salmon and potato pancake with dressed crab, and chocolate tart with salted-caramel sauce. The nook-and-cranny-filled, stone-floored pub centres around a warming cast-iron range stove.

Dufferin Arms PUB FOOD ££
(www.dufferinarms.co.uk; 35 High St, Killyleagh; mains £9.50-15; ⌚kitchen noon-8.30pm Mon-Thu, to 10pm Fri & Sat, to 7.30pm Sun) Easy to spot (it's bright pink), this comfortably old-fashioned pub serves decent pub grub, while the cosy, candlelit restaurant offers a more intimate atmosphere. Bands play on Friday and Saturday nights from 9pm, with folk and bluegrass sessions on Saturday afternoons from 4pm. The pub featured in the 2013 Oscar-nominated film *Philomena* starring Dame Judi Dench.

Drinking & Nightlife

Daft Eddy's PUB
(http://dafteddys.co.uk; Sketrick Island, Whiterock, Killinchy; ⌚11.30am-11.30pm Mon-Thu, 11.30am-1am Fri & Sat, noon-10.30pm Sun) Idyllic on a sunny day, this local favourite hides away on an island, with panoramic views over Strangford Lough from its bar, partially covered timber-decked terrace and table-set gardens below. It's 4.5km northeast of Balloo House: turn off next to the restaurant and follow Whiterock Rd, then veer around to the left to reach the causeway.

Downpatrick

POP 10,300

St Patrick's mission to spread Christianity to Ireland began and ended in Downpatrick. Ireland's patron saint is believed to have made his first convert at nearby Saul, and been buried at Down Cathedral, and St Patrick's Day (17 March) sees the town filled with pilgrims and revellers.

Downpatrick – now County Down's administrative centre – was settled long before the saint's arrival. His first church here was constructed inside the earthwork *dún* (fort) of Rath Celtchair, still visible to the southwest of the cathedral. The place later became known as Dún Pádraig (Patrick's Fort), anglicised to Downpatrick in the 17th century.

Sights

Lovely 18th-century architecture lines the Mall, including **Soundwell School**, built in 1733, and a **courthouse** with a finely decorated pediment.

Downpatrick is the intended terminus of **Patrick's Way** (www.patricksway.com), a pilgrimage walking route from Westport, County Mayo, linking sites related to St Patrick, which is currently being developed by local pilgrim walker and mountaineer Alan Graham.

★St Patrick Centre HERITAGE CENTRE
(www.saintpatrickcentre.com; 53a Market St; adult/child £6/3.50; ⏲9am-5pm Mon-Sat year-round, 1-5pm Sun Jul & Aug, 9am-7pm St Patrick's Day) This magnificent glass-and-timber heritage centre houses a multimedia exhibition called **Ego Patricius**, charting the life and legacy of Ireland's patron saint. Audio and video presentations tell St Patrick's story, often in his own words (taken from his *Confession,* written in Latin around the year 450, which begins with the words *'Ego Patricius',* meaning 'I am Patrick'). At the end is a spectacular widescreen film that takes you on a swooping, low-level helicopter ride over the landscapes of Ireland.

Down Cathedral CATHEDRAL
(www.downcathedral.org; The Mall; ⏲9.30am-4pm Mon-Sat, 2-4pm Sun) FREE According to legend, St Patrick died in Saul, where angels told his followers to place his body on a cart drawn by two untamed oxen, and to bury the saint wherever they halted. The oxen supposedly stopped at the church on the hill of Down, now the site of the Church of Ireland's Down Cathedral.

In the churchyard, a slab of Mourne granite with the inscription 'Patric' was placed in 1900 to mark the traditional site of **St Patrick's grave**.

The cathedral is testimony to 1600 years of building and rebuilding. Viking attacks wiped away all trace of the earliest churches, and the subsequent Norman cathedral and monasteries were destroyed by Scottish raiders in 1316. The rubble was used in a 15th-century church finished in 1512, but after the Dissolution of the Monasteries it was razed to the ground in 1541. Today's building dates largely from the 18th and 19th centuries, with a completely new interior installed in the 1980s.

From the St Patrick Centre, take the path to its left, uphill through the landscaped grounds.

Down County Museum MUSEUM
(www.downcountymuseum.com; The Mall; ⏲10am-5pm Mon-Fri, 1-5pm Sat & Sun) FREE Downpatrick's restored 18th-century jail now houses the county museum. In a former cell block at the back are models of some of the prisoners once incarcerated there, and details of their sad stories. Displays cover the story of the Norman conquest of Down, but the biggest exhibit of all is outside – a short signposted trail leads to the **Mound of Down**, a good example of a Norman motte and bailey.

Sleeping & Eating

River Mill B&B ££
(☎028-4484 1988; www.river-mill.com; 43 Ballyclander Rd; d £70; 📶) This restored 18th-century linen mill is hidden away in the countryside 6km southeast of Downpatrick, off the road to Ardglass. The traditional stone exterior hides a minimalist, modern interior, with split-level lounge and two good-sized guest rooms with wooden floors, white walls, timber furniture and private bathrooms.

Hosts Theresa and Aidan can arrange massage and reiki treatments at the alternative-therapy centre next door.

Denvir's Hotel & Pub B&B ££
(☎028-4461 2012; www.denvirs.com; 14 English St; s/d £40/70; 📶) Dating from 1642, Denvir's is allegedly Ireland's oldest surviving coaching inn. It offers B&B in six idiosyncratic rooms with polished floorboards, Georgian windows and period fireplaces. Good food is

served in the cosy bar and rustic **restaurant** (mains £7-18; ⌚kitchen noon-8pm), which has an enormous, 17th-century stone fireplace.

Information

Downpatrick Tourist Office (☎028-4461 2233; www.downdc.gov.uk; 53a Market St; ⌚9.30am-5pm Mon-Sat, 2-5pm Sun Jul & Aug, 10am-5pm Mon-Sat Sep-Jun) is in the St Patrick Centre (p571).

Getting There & Away

Downpatrick's bus station is just south of the St Patrick Centre (p571).

Services:

Belfast Europa BusCentre £6, one hour, half-hourly Monday to Friday, hourly Saturday, six Sunday

Castlewellan £4.40, 30 minutes, seven daily Monday to Friday, six Saturday, four Sunday

Dundrum £3.50, 15 minutes, seven daily Monday to Friday, six Saturday, four Sunday

Newcastle £3.80, 20 minutes, seven daily Monday to Friday, six Saturday, four Sunday

Newry £9.30, 1¼ hours, seven daily Monday to Friday, six Saturday, four Sunday

Around Downpatrick

According to popular tradition, the young St Patrick was kidnapped from Britain by Irish pirates and spent six years as a slave tending sheep (possibly on Slemish). His faith grew in captivity and he prayed daily, eventually escaping back home to his family.

After religious training, St Patrick returned to Ireland to spread the faith and is said to have landed on the shores of Strangford Lough near Saul, northeast of Downpatrick. He preached his first sermon in a nearby barn, and eventually retired to Saul after some 30 years of evangelising.

Saul

On landing near this spot in 432, St Patrick made his first convert: Díchú, the local chieftain, gave the holy man a sheep barn (*sabhal* in Irish, pronounced sawl) in which to preach. West of Saul village is the supposed site of the *sabhal*, with a replica 10th-century **church & round tower** built in 1932 to mark the 1500th anniversary of his arrival.

East of the village is the small hill of **Slieve Patrick** (120m), with stations of the cross along the path to the top and a massive 10m-high statue of St Patrick, also dating from 1932, on the summit. The hill is a popular pilgrimage site on St Patrick's Day.

Saul is 3km northeast of Downpatrick off the A2 Strangford road.

Struell Wells

These supposedly curative spring waters are traditionally associated with St Patrick – it's said he scourged himself here, spending 'a great part of the night, stark naked and singing psalms' immersed in what is now the **Drinking Well**. He must have been a hardy soul – the well-preserved but chilly 17th-century **bathhouses** here look more likely to induce ill health than cure it. The site has been venerated for centuries, although the buildings are all post-1600.

Between the bathhouses and the ruined chapel stands the **Eye Well**, whose waters are said to cure eye ailments.

The wells are in a scenic, secluded glen 2km east of Downpatrick. Take the B1 road towards Ardglass, and turn left after passing the hospital.

Lecale Peninsula

East of Downpatrick, the low-lying Lecale Peninsula is isolated by the sea and Strangford Lough to the north, south and east, and the marshes of the Rivers Quoile and Blackstaff to the west. Its Irish name Leath Chathail (lay-ca-*hal*) means 'the territory of Cathal' (an 8th-century prince), and this region of fertile farmland is fringed by fishing harbours, rocky bluffs and sandy beaches.

Between Ardglass and Killough in the south of the peninsula is **Coney Island**, vividly described in Van Morrison's spoken-word song of the same name. This little seaside hamlet isn't in fact an island, but has a small peninsula that may once have been cut off by the sea. The Oscar-winning short film *The Shore* (2011) was shot at director Terry George's family cottage here.

Strangford

POP 550

The picturesque fishing village of Strangford (Baile Loch Cuan) lies 16km northeast of Downpatrick. It's dominated by Strangford Castle, a 16th-century tower house (closed to the public) that faces its counterpart in Portaferry across **the Narrows** (p567).

Sights & Activities

At the end of Castle St, a footpath called the **Squeeze Gut** leads over the hill behind the village, with a fine view of the lough, before looping back to Strangford via tree-lined Dufferin Ave (1.5km), or continuing around the shoreline to Castle Ward Estate (4.5km).

Strangford Sea Safari BOAT TOUR
(☎028-4372 3933; www.strangford-seasafari.com; Strangford Harbour; adult/child from £20/17) Offers a range of speedboat tours into the swirling tidal streams of the Narrows, including visits to the SeaGen tidal generator, Angus Rock lighthouse and local seal colonies.

Sleeping & Eating

Cuan B&B ££
(☎028-4488 1222; www.thecuan.com; The Square; s/d £65/95, with dinner £80/126; 📶) Just around the corner from the ferry slip, you can't miss the Cuan's sage-green facade or the warm welcome from husband-and-wife managers Peter and Caroline. There are nine neat, comfortable and well-equipped rooms; the atmospheric, wood-panelled **restaurant** (mains £11.50-19.50, fish & chips £4-8; ⏰restaurant noon-9pm Mon-Thu, to 9.30pm Fri & Sat, to 8.30pm Sun, fish & chip shop 4-8pm Thu, noon-8pm Fri & Sat; 👪) serves giant portions of local seafood, lamb and beef. Its attached fish-and-chip shop does takeaway.

Pantry BISTRO ££
(☎028-4488 1180; http://thepantrystrangford.co.uk; 4 Kildare St; mains £12-21; ⏰10am-5pm Tue-Thu, 10am-9pm Fri, 9am-9pm Sat, 10am-6pm Sun) On Strangford's main street, this unassuming place in a grey townhouse (look for the aqua-blue door) serves unexpectedly sophisticated food: steamed sea bass with red pepper and beetroot sauce, French-trimmed lamb cutlets with tomato and mint dressing, and cardamon panna cotta with strawberry compote. Live music plays at least once a week in summer.

Getting There & Away

A **car ferry** (one-way car & driver £7, car passengers & pedestrians £1) between Strangford and Portaferry sails every half-hour between 7.30am and 10.30pm Monday to Friday, 8am to 11pm Saturday and 9.30am to 10.30pm on Sunday. Journey time is about 10 minutes.

Bus 16E serves Downpatrick (£3.50, 25 minutes, 11 daily Monday to Friday, five Saturday).

Castle Ward Estate

Famed for its role as Winterfell in *Game of Thrones*, 1760s-built **Castle Ward Estate** (www.nationaltrust.org.uk; Park Rd; adult/child incl guided house tour £8/3.75; ⏰house noon-5pm Easter–Oct, grounds 10am-8pm Apr-Sep, to 4pm Oct-Mar) enjoys a superb setting overlooking the bay west of Strangford. Entertaining guided tours depart hourly from noon to 4pm.

In the grounds are a Victorian laundry museum, the Strangford Lough Wildlife Centre, 16th-century Plantation tower Old Castle Ward and 15th-century tower house Castle Audley, along with walking and cycling trails. **Clearsky Adventure Centre** (☎028-4372 3933; www.clearsky-adventure.com; Castle Ward Estate, Park Rd; ⏰10am-6pm Easter–Sep, to 4pm Oct-Mar) arranges everything from coasteering and canoeing to Strangford Lough sea safaris.

Castle Ward House was built for Lord and Lady Bangor – Bernard Ward and his wife, Anne – whose widely differing architectural tastes resulted in an eccentric country residence – and a subsequent divorce. Bernard favoured the neoclassical style seen in the front facade and the main staircase, while Anne leaned towards the Strawberry Hill Gothic of the rear facade, which reaches a peak in the incredible fan vaulting of her Gothic boudoir.

Newcastle

POP 7500

Gloriously set at the foot of the Mourne Mountains on a 5km strand of golden sand, the faded Victorian seaside resort of Newcastle (An Caisleán Nua) has received a multimillion-pound makeover, with a contemporary sculpture-studded, kilometre-long seafront promenade and an elegant footbridge over the River Shimna.

Sights & Activities

Murlough National Nature Reserve WILDLIFE RESERVE
(car park May-Sep £4; ⏰24hr) FREE Footpaths and boardwalks meander among the grassy dunes, with great views back towards the Mournes. It's a haul-out site for common and grey seals.

WALK: SLIEVE DONARD

You can hike to the summit of Slieve Donard (853m; the highest hill in Northern Ireland) from various starting points in and around Newcastle, but it's a stiff climb and you shouldn't attempt it without proper walking boots, waterproofs and a map and compass.

On a good day the view from the top extends to the hills of Donegal, the Wicklow Mountains, the coast of Scotland, the Isle of Man and even the hills of Snowdonia in Wales. Two cairns near the summit were long believed to have been cells of St Donard, who retreated here to pray in early Christian times.

The shortest route to the top is via the River Glen from Newcastle. Begin at Donard Park car park, at the edge of town, 1km south of the bus station. At the far end of the car park, turn right through the gate and head into the woods, with the river on your left. A gravel path leads up the River Glen valley to the saddle between Slieve Donard and Slieve Commedagh. From here, turn left and follow the Mourne Wall to the summit. Return by the same route (round trip 9km, allow at least three hours).

Royal County Down Golf Course GOLF
(www.royalcountydown.org; 36 Golf Links Rd; green fees £175-190 May-Oct, lower rates Nov-Apr) Set amid flowering heather and gorse, this hallowed par-71 links course was designed by Old Tom Morris and incorporates two awe-inspiring nine-hole loops. It's open to visitors Monday, Tuesday, Thursday morning and Sunday afternoon. No handicap is required, but you'll need to book several months ahead.

Granite Trail WALKING
(www.walkni.com/walks/333/granite-trail) Beginning across the road from the harbour, the 5km Granite Trail is a waymarked footpath up a disused funicular railway line that once carried Mourne Mountains granite blocks to the harbour. The view from the top is worth the steep, 200m climb.

Rock Pool SWIMMING
(South Promenade; adult/child £2.50/2; ⏲10am-5pm Mon-Fri, 11am-5.30pm Sat, 2-5pm Sun Jul & Aug, weather & tides permitting) At the south end of the seafront, this outdoor seawater pool dates from 1933.

Soak SPA
(☎028-4372 6002; www.soakseaweedbaths.co.uk; 5a South Promenade; 1hr session from £25; ⏲11.30am-8pm Thu-Mon) If it's too cold for outdoor bathing, you can simmer away in a hot seaweed bath at Soak. Towels and robes are provided.

Sleeping

The nearest campground is at Tollymore Forest Park (p576).

★Hutt Hostel HOSTEL £
(☎028-4372 2133; www.hutthostel.com; 30 Downs Rd; dm/apt £22/100; 📶) A Frisbee's throw from the beach in a renovated Victorian town house, the 40-bed Hutt has super amenities including a sociable common room with open fireplace, games room with pool table, self-catering kitchen, laundry and bike hire (per half/full day £15/20). Its self-contained apartment 'the Padd' sleeps up to six people.

★Enniskeen Country House BOUTIQUE HOTEL ££
(☎028-4372 2392; http://enniskeenhotel.co.uk; 98 Bryansford Rd; s/d/f from £65/90/150, restaurant mains £12-22; ⏲restaurant 12.30-8.30pm; 📶👪) In a stately 19th-century stone manor house 2km west of Newcastle, delightfully old-fashioned Enniskeen has a dozen period-furnished rooms, most with mountain, sea or forest views (try for room 15, tucked in the turret). Its refined Oaks Restaurant opens to a terrace and serves traditional Northern Irish cuisine, including afternoon tea using hand-churned butter and honey from a local apiary.

Briers Country House B&B ££
(☎028-4372 4347; www.thebriers.co.uk; 39 Middle Tollymore Rd; s/d from £60/85, cottage £150) A peaceful farmhouse B&B with views of the Mournes, Briers is just 1.5km northwest of the town centre (signposted off the road between Newcastle and Bryansford). Huge breakfasts – vegetarian if you like – are served with a view over the garden. There's also a self-contained three-bedroom cottage (minimum three-night stay).

Beach House B&B ££

(028-4372 2345; http://beachhouse-newcastle.co.uk; 22 Downs Rd; s/d £50/90;) Enjoy a sea view with your breakfast at the Beach House, an elegant Victorian B&B with three rooms (all with private bathroom) and a balcony (open to all guests) overlooking the beach.

Slieve Donard Resort & Spa HOTEL £££

(028-4372 1066; www.hastingshotels.com; Downs Rd; s/d from £130/160;) Established in 1897, the Slieve Donard is a magnificent Victorian red-brick pile on 2.5 hectares of beachfront land, with several restaurants and a luxurious spa. Adjoining Royal County Down Golf Course, it's where golf legends Tom Watson, Tiger Woods and Rory McIlroy stay when they're in town.

Eating

Olive Bizarre CAFE £

(67 South Promenade; dishes £4-8; 9am-5pm;) Vegetarian and vegan options abound at this chilled little cafe: soups, quiches, pies, jacket potatoes, sandwiches and daily specials such as organic falafel balls with Ballymaloe spiced tomato relish and hummus.

Niki's Kitchen Café CAFE £

(028-4372 6777; www.nikiskitchencafe.co.uk; 107 Central Promenade; mains £5-10; 8am-5pm daily, 5-9pm Wed-Sun;) The crowds testify to the success of this large, airy eatery, where the menu focuses on quality versions of classic cafe cuisine, including seafood chowder, fish cakes and sides of chunky chips served in a wee wire basket. There are high chairs, a kids' menu and sofas for loafing over coffee.

Strand Cafe & Bakery ICE CREAM £

(53-55 Central Promenade; ice cream from £1.30; 9am-6pm Mon-Fri, to 7.30pm Sat & Sun) Yes, there's a cafe and bakery here, but the real reason to stop by is to order a cone of award-winning ice cream, made here since 1930. Classic flavours include raspberry ripple, honeycomb, and chocolate and orange.

★**Brunel's** MODERN IRISH ££

(028-4372 3951; www.brunelsrestaurant.co.uk; 9 Bryansford Rd; mains lunch £7-18, dinner £15-22; 12.30-3pm & 6-9.30pm Wed & Thu, to 10pm Fri & Sat, noon-8pm Sun) Above the Anchor Bar, this nautical-styled 1st-floor restaurant is one to watch. Chef Paul Cunningham's local foraging skills and inspired flavour combinations give rise to dishes such as rhubarb-cured salmon with black-olive powder; butter-poached langoustines with buttermilk froth; Mourne Mountain lamb with samphire and parmesan-crusted cockles; and wild garlic, pea and hazelnut risotto. Book ahead.

Vanilla IRISH ££

(028-4372 2268; www.vanillarestaurant.co.uk; 67 Main St; mains lunch £6-7, dinner £17-22; noon-3.30pm & 5-9.30pm Mon-Sat, noon-9pm Sun;) The menu at this sleek town-centre bistro shamelessly promotes Irish produce: roast cod with leek gnocchi, Cherry Valley duck breast with parsnip tarte tatin, and buttermilk panna cotta with blackberry gel and peanut crumble.

Information

There's free public wi-fi along the promenade.

Tourist Office (028-4372 2222; newcastle.tic@downdc.gov.uk; 10-14 Central Promenade; 9.30am-7pm Mon-Sat, 1-7pm Sun Jul & Aug, 10am-5pm Mon-Sat, 2-5pm Sun Sep-Jun;) Sells local-interest books and maps, and traditional and contemporary crafts. Left luggage costs £2 per day.

Getting There & Around

Buses 20 and 20A run to Newcastle from Belfast's Europa BusCentre (£8, 1¼ hours, at least hourly) via Dundrum.

Bus 240 takes the inland route from Newry to Newcastle (£7, 50 minutes, seven daily Monday to Friday, six Saturday, four Sunday) and continues to Downpatrick.

Dundrum & Around

Sheltered Dundrum Bay is famous for its oysters and mussels.

Sights

Dundrum Castle CASTLE

(10am-5pm Wed & Fri-Sun Easter–Oct) FREE Founded in 1177 by John de Courcy of Carrickfergus, this Norman fortress overlooks Dundrum Bay.

Seaforde Gardens & Tropical Butterfly House GARDENS

(www.seafordegardens.com; Seaforde House, Seaforde; gardens or butterfly house adult/child £5/3.35, gardens & butterfly house £8.50/5; 10am-5pm Mon-Sat, 1-6pm Sun Easter–Sep, closed rest of year) Adults and kids alike will enjoy this oasis in the Seaforde demesne, which is home to an 18th-century walled garden with ornamental flower beds, a hedge maze, spiral-staircase tower with viewing platform, and strutting iridescent-blue peacocks. Its rainforest-like butterfly house is filled with hundreds of fluttering butterflies as well as parrots. A simple but cosy timber cafe is located by the entrance. The gardens are 13km north of Newcastle (7km north of Dundrum) on the A2.

Eating

Mourne Seafood Bar SEAFOOD
(028-4375 1377; http://mourneseafood.com; 10 Main St; mains £11-21; 5-10pm Thu, 12.30-3pm & 5-10pm Fri, 12.30-9.30pm Sat & Sun) Set in a wood-panelled Victorian house hung with local art, this friendly and informal spot serves oysters five ways, plus seafood chowder, crab, langoustines and daily fish specials, all sourced locally (including from its own shellfish beds). Thursday is lobster night in season. Its Belfast (p549) outpost has a cookery school.

Getting There & Away

Bus 240 from Newcastle (£2.70, 10 minutes, seven daily Monday to Friday, six Saturday, four Sunday) to Downpatrick (£3.50, 15 minutes), stops in Dundrum.

Mourne Mountains

The Mourne Mountains dominate the horizon as you head south from Belfast towards Newcastle. This is one of the most beautiful corners of Northern Ireland, with a distinctive landscape of grey granite, yellow gorse and whitewashed cottages, the lower slopes of the hills latticed with a neat patchwork of drystone walls cobbled together from huge, rounded granite boulders.

The hills were made famous in a popular song penned by Irish songwriter William Percy French in 1896, whose chorus, 'Where the Mountains of Mourne sweep down to the sea', captures perfectly their scenic blend of ocean, sky and hillside.

History

The crescent of low-lying land on the southern side of the mountains is known as the **Kingdom of Mourne**. Cut off for centuries by its difficult approaches (the main overland route passed north of the hills), it developed a distinctive landscape and culture. Until the coast road was built in the early 19th century, the only access was on foot or by sea.

Smuggling provided a source of income in the 18th century. Boats carrying French spirits would land at night and packhorses would carry the casks through the hills to the inland road, avoiding the excise men at Newcastle. The **Brandy Pad**, a former smugglers' path from Bloody Bridge to Tollymore, is a popular walking route today.

Sights

The Mournes offer some of the best **hill walking** and **rock climbing** in the North. You can buy maps at the tourist office in Newcastle.

Tollymore Forest Park FOREST
(Bryansford; car/pedestrian £5/2; 10am-dusk) This scenic forest park, 3km west of Newcastle, offers lovely walks and bike rides along the River Shimna and across the Mournes' northern slopes. Victorian follies include the church-like **Clanbrassil Barn**, as well as grottoes, caves, bridges and stepping stones (yes, the park is a *Game of Thrones* set). An electronic kiosk at the car park provides information on the park's flora, fauna and history. You can pitch a tent at the **campground** (028-4372 2428; 176 Tullybranigan Rd; tent & caravan sites £11.50-16.50) here.

Castlewellan Forest Park FOREST
(Main St, Castlewellan; car/pedestrian £5/free; 10am-dusk) Castlewellan Forest Park offers gentle walks around the castle grounds; one of the world's largest hedge mazes, the **Peace Maze** (admission free); and, from March to October, **trout fishing** in its lovely lake (three-day permit £9.50). A recent addition is a network of exciting **mountain-bike trails** – see www.mountainbikeni.com for details. Bike hire is available from Life Adventure Centre.

Silent Valley Reservoir LAKE
(car/motorcycle £4.50/2, plus per adult/child £1.60/60p; 10am-6.30pm Apr-Sep, to 4pm Oct-Mar) At the heart of the Mournes is the beautiful Silent Valley Reservoir, where the River Kilkeel, which supplies Belfast and County Down with water, was dammed in 1933. There are scenic, waymarked walks around the grounds, a cafe and an interesting exhibition on the dam's construction.

Mourne Wall LANDMARK

The spectacular drystone Mourne Wall marches across the summits of 15 surrounding peaks including the highest, Slieve Donard (853m). You can walk the 2m-high, 1m-thick, 35km-long wall's entire length, or just a short section.

Although the 1922 wall was built to stop livestock reaching the catchment area of the Rivers Kilkeel and Annalong, poor geological conditions meant the Annalong couldn't be dammed, and its waters were diverted to the Silent Valley Reservoir via a 3.6km tunnel beneath Slieve Binnian.

Activities

Life Adventure Centre OUTDOORS

(☎028-4377 0714; www.onegreatadventure.com; Grange Courtyard, Castlewellan Forest Park) If you fancy trying hill walking, rock climbing, canoeing or a range of other outdoor activities, this centre in Castlewellan Forest Park offers one-day, have-a-go sessions for individuals, couples and families (from £76 per person), as well as Sunday-afternoon taster sessions. It also rents canoes (per half/full day £35/45) and mountain bikes (£25/30).

Hotrock ROCK CLIMBING

(☎028-4372 2188; www.tollymore.com; Tollymore National Outdoor Centre; adult/child £5/2.50; ⏲10am-10pm Tue-Thu, to 5pm Fri-Mon) If the weather is wet, you can go rock climbing at this indoor climbing wall; it rents rock boots and harness for £3.50. The entrance is on the B180, on the western side of Tollymore Forest Park, off Bryansford Rd.

Mt Pleasant HORSE RIDING

(☎028-4377 8651; www.mountpleasantcentre.com; Bannonstown Rd, Castlewellan; per 45min/1hr/2hr £15/20/38; ⏲by reservation) Catering for both experienced riders and beginners, this horse-riding and pony-trekking centre offers various guided treks into Castlewellan Forest Park. Short and long rides, beach rides and pony trekking can also be arranged.

Festivals & Events

Mourne International Walking Festival WALKING

(www.mournewalking.co.uk) This three-day festival in late June is a great opportunity for glorious mountain walks, with some transport included in the ticket prices.

Sleeping & Eating

Meelmore Lodge HOSTEL £

(☎028-4372 6657; http://meelmorelodge.com; 52 Trassey Rd, Bryansford; tent sites per adult/child £10/6, dm/tw/f £15/60/80) On the northern slopes of the Mournes, 5km west of Bryansford village, wonderfully remote Meelmore has a cosy lounge and kitchen, two four-bunk dorms, a couple of private rooms, a tent-only campground and a good cafe. You can hike into the hills from the hostel's front door.

Mourne Lodge HOSTEL £

(☎028-4176 5859; http://themournelodge.com; Bog Rd, Atticall; dm/s/d/tr/q from £25/50/65/85/110; @📶) This purpose-built 31-bed hostel offers bright and appealing budget accommodation. As well as a self-catering kitchen and barbecue patio, there's a **restaurant** that serves breakfast, lunch and dinner (bookings essential). It's in the village of Atticall, 6km north of Kilkeel, off the B27 Hilltown road, and 3km west of the entrance to Silent Valley.

Getting There & Away

Check seasonal transport options at www.walkni.com.

The summertime **Mourne Rambler** (Bus 405; www.translink.co.uk; adult/child £7/3.50; ⏲Tue-Sun May-Aug) runs a circular route from Newcastle around the Mournes, making 18 stops including Tollymore Forest Park, Castlewellan and Silent Valley. There are five services per day.

Mournes Coast Road

The A2 coast road between Newcastle and Newry is one of the region's most scenic drives.

Kilbroney Forest Park

Covering 16 sq km, **Kilbroney Forest Park** (Shore Rd; ⏲9am-10pm Jun-Aug, to 5pm Sep-May) FREE unfolds 1km east of Rostrevor. From the car park at the top of the forest drive, a 10-minute hike leads up to a superb view over the lough to Carlingford Mountain, as well as to the **Cloughmore Stone**, a 30-tonne granite boulder inscribed with Victorian-era graffiti. The park is also home to Northern Ireland's best downhill **mountain-bike trails**; bike hire and uplift are available from **East Coast Adventure** (☎028-4175 3535; www.eastcoastadventure.com; bike hire per half/full day £17.50/30, trail maps £2, uplift £5), at the trailhead.

GARETH MCCORMACK/GETTY IMAGES ©

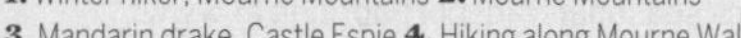

1. Winter hiker, Mourne Mountains **2.** Mourne Mountains
3. Mandarin drake, Castle Espie **4.** Hiking along Mourne Wall

Counties Down & Armagh: Walking & Wildlife

Strangford Lough and the Mourne Mountains have long served as a weekend escape for the people of Belfast, with tranquil coastlines and rugged uplands offering superb wildlife-watching opportunities, challenging hiking routes and glorious scenery.

Mourne Mountains

Celebrated in song and story, the Mourne Mountains sweep down to the sea near the holiday resort of Newcastle. These shapely granite hills provide some of the finest hill walking and rock climbing in the North.

Castle Espie Wildfowl & Wetlands Centre

Castle Espie Wildfowl & Wetlands Centre not only protects the wetlands environment that the geese and other migratory birds depend on, but also has its own colourful collection of duck and goose species from around the world.

Mourne Wall

Built between 1904 and 1922, the 35km-long Mourne Wall is one of the most impressive features of the Mourne Mountains. Traversing no fewer than 15 of the Mournes' highest summits, it delineates the catchment area of the Silent Valley Reservoir.

Strangford Lough

One of Ireland's great birdwatching spectacles is the autumn arrival of vast flocks of light-bellied brent geese (75% of the world population) at Strangford Lough. Around 30,000 geese overwinter here.

Rostrevor

The pretty Victorian seaside resort of Rostrevor (Caislean Ruairi) is best known for its lively pubs. Many have live music, including the **Corner House** (1 Bridge St; noon-midnight Mon-Sat, to 8pm Sun) and **Old Killowen Inn** (10 Bridge St; 11.30am-midnight Mon-Sat, to 10pm Sun).

Each year in late July, folk musicians converge on the village for the week-long **Fiddler's Green International Festival** (www.fiddlersgreenfestival.co.uk; late Jul).

Bus 39 serves Newry (£3.50, 25 minutes, at least hourly Monday to Saturday, six Sunday).

Warrenpoint

POP 7000

Warrenpoint (An Pointe) is a Victorian resort at the head of Carlingford Lough. Its seaside appeal is somewhat diminished by the large industrial harbour at the west end of town, but its broad streets, main square and renovated prom warrant a stop.

Sights

Narrow Water Castle CASTLE

FREE About 2km northwest of Warrenpoint's town centre you'll see Narrow Water Castle, a fine Elizabethan tower house built in 1568 to command the entrance to the River Newry. It's closed to the public, unless, that is, you stay at its apartment.

Sleeping & Eating

★**Narrow Water Castle Apartment** APARTMENT ££

(07784 730826; http://narrowwatercastle.co.uk; Apt 2, Narrow Water Castle; d £95) Within historic Narrow Water Castle, but with its own entrance, this exquisite apartment has two bedrooms (one with a private bathroom, and both with Hungarian down pillows and beautiful linens), an antique-furnished lounge with an open fireplace, and main bathroom with a free-standing, double-slipper bath, fully-equipped kitchen and access to the castle gardens. There is a minimum three-night stay.

Whistledown Hotel BOUTIQUE HOTEL ££

(028-4175 4174; www.thewhistledownhotel.com; 6 Seaview; s/d/f from £70/100/120;) In a superb waterfront setting, the Whistledown has 20 bedrooms with cherry and pistachio-coloured crushed-velvet trimmings, large flat-screen TVs and bathrooms with colourful designer tiling.

★**Restaurant 23** MODERN IRISH ££

(028-4175 3222; www.restaurant23warrenpoint.com; 13 Seaview; mains £14-23.50; 12.30-2.30pm & 5.30-9.30pm Mon-Sat, noon-8pm Sun;) Spanning two floors of the Balmoral Hotel on Warrenpoint's waterfront, this innovative restaurant garnered a Michelin Bib Gourmand for TV chef Raymond McArdle, whose fresh and fun approach to fine Irish produce plays out in dishes such as black-truffle soup with bacon and Guinness mousse. From Monday to Saturday there's a bargain two-/three-course lunch menu for £13/15.

Getting There & Away

Bus 39 serves Newry (£3, 20 minutes, at least hourly Monday to Saturday, six Sunday).

Newry

POP 22,975

Newry has long been a frontier town, guarding the land route from Dublin to Ulster through the 'Gap of the North', the pass between Slieve Gullion and the Carlingford hills, still followed by the main Dublin–Belfast road and railway. Its name derives from a yew tree (An tIúr) supposedly planted here by St Patrick.

The opening of the Newry Canal in 1742, linking the town with the River Bann at Portadown, made Newry a busy trading port, exporting coal, linen and butter. Today it's a bustling shopping centre.

Sights

Newry & Mourne Museum MUSEUM

(www.bagenalscastle.com; Castle St; 10am-4.30pm Mon-Sat, 1.30-5pm Sun) FREE This museum is housed in **Bagenal's Castle**, the town's oldest surviving building, with exhibits on the Newry Canal and local archaeology, culture and folklore. Recently rediscovered (having been incorporated into more recent buildings), the 16th-century castle was built for Nicholas Bagenal, grand marshal of the English army in Ireland.

Sleeping

Marymount B&B ££

(028-3026 1099; www.marymount.freeservers.com; 15 Windsor Ave; s/d £35/60;) A modern bungalow in a quiet location up a hill off the A1 Belfast road, Marymount is only a

10-minute walk from the town centre. There are three country-style bedrooms and a lovely breakfast room opening onto the garden. The owners are welcoming and helpful to a fault.

Canal Court Hotel HOTEL £££
(☎028-3025 1234; www.canalcourthotel.com; 34 Merchants Quay; s/d from £80/104; @🛜🏊) Overlooking Newry Canal, this landmark 110-room mustard-coloured hotel is relatively new but has a charmingly old-fashioned atmosphere, with leather sofas dotted around the vast wood-panelled lobby, a low-lit bar with trad music and excellent pub food, and a grand staircase up to the chintzy restaurant. Its leisure centre has a 20m pool. Staff are a pleasure to deal with.

Eating & Drinking

Brass Monkey PUB FOOD ££
(☎028-3026 3176; 1-4 Sandy St; mains £6-19; ⏲kitchen 10am-9pm Mon-Sat, noon-4pm Sun) Newry's most popular pub, with Victorian brass, brick and timber decor, serves good bar meals ranging from lasagne and burgers to seafood and steaks. Live music plays on Saturday and Sunday.

Bank BAR
(www.thebanknewry.com; 1-2 Trevor Hill; ⏲noon-11.30pm Mon-Thu, 9am-1.30am Fri-Sun) A gorgeous old grey-stone former bank houses this huge bar/nightclub. It combines some of the building's original features (including a stained-glass ceiling dome) with contemporary decor such as neon fuchsia lighting. The sheltered South American–style beer garden has a stage for live music (every Saturday night) and enormous earthenware pots. It has good bistro food too.

Information

The **Tourist Office** (☎028-3031 3170; www.visitmournemountains.co.uk; Castle St; ⏲10am-4pm Sat year-round, 9am-6pm Mon-Fri, 1-5pm Sun Jul & Aug, 9am-5pm Mon-Fri Sep-Jun, 1-5pm Sun Sep) is in Bagenal's Castle along with the Newry & Mourne Museum.

Getting There & Away

BUS

Newry's bus station is on the Mall, opposite the Canal Court Hotel.

Services include:

Armagh (£6, 50 minutes, hourly Monday to Saturday, three Sunday)

Belfast Europa BusCentre (£9.30, 1¼ hours, at least hourly Monday to Saturday, eight Sunday)

Hillsborough (£7, 50 minutes, at least hourly Monday to Saturday, eight Sunday)

Rostrevor (£3.50, 25 minutes, at least hourly Monday to Saturday, six Sunday)

Warrenpoint (£3, 20 minutes, at least hourly Monday to Saturday, six Sunday)

TRAIN

The train station is 2.5km northwest of the centre, on the A25; bus 341 (free for train passengers) links train arrivals and departures to the bus station.

Newry is on the line linking Dublin (£20, 1¼ hours, eight daily) and Belfast (£11, 45 minutes, 10 Monday to Saturday, five Sunday).

Central County Down

Rich farmland spreads to the south of Belfast, with only the rough moorland of Slieve Croob, southwest of Ballynahinch, breaking the flatness of the terrain.

Hillsborough

POP 3400

The elegant little town of Hillsborough, 19km south of Belfast, was founded in the 1640s by Colonel Arthur Hill, who built a fort here to quell Irish insurgents. Fine Georgian architecture rings the square and lines Main St.

Most famously, Hillsborough Castle is the official residence of the Secretary of State for Northern Ireland, and is used to entertain visiting heads of state (US presidents George W Bush and Bill Clinton have both enjoyed its hospitality). This is the Queen's official residence when she's in Northern Ireland.

Hillsborough is also gaining attention as a culinary hotspot, with cosy pubs harbouring excellent restaurants.

Sights

Hillsborough Castle HISTORIC BUILDING
(www.gov.uk/hillsborough-castle; Main St; guided tour castle & grounds £12/8, castle only adult/child £7/5, grounds only £3.50; ⏲10.30am-4pm daily Aug, Sat & Sun Easter–Jul & Sep) The British monarch's official Northern Ireland residence is this rambling, two-storey late-Georgian mansion, which was built in 1797 for Wills Hill, the first Marquess of Downshire, and extensively remodelled in the 1830s and '40s. Book ahead for guided tours taking in the state drawing room and dining

rooms, and the Lady Grey Room where, in 2003, Tony Blair and George W Bush held talks on Iraq.

Hillsborough Courthouse HISTORIC BUILDING
(The Square; 9.30am-5.30pm Mon-Sat year-round, 11am-4pm Sun Apr-Sep) FREE Dating to 1765, this fine old Georgian market house was used as a courthouse from 1810 until 1986. It now exhibits various displays describing the working of the courts.

St Malachy's Parish Church CHURCH
(www.hillsboroughparish.org; Main St; 8.30am-7pm) FREE St Malachy's is one of Ireland's most splendid 18th-century churches, with twin towers at the ends of the transepts and a graceful spire at the western end. A tree-lined avenue leads to the church from a statue of Arthur Hill, fourth Marquess of Downshire, at the bottom of Main St.

Hillsborough Fort HISTORIC BUILDING
(Main St; grounds 10am-4pm Mon-Sat, 11am-4pm Sun) FREE Built as an artillery fort by Colonel Hill in 1650 (William of Orange stayed on his way to the Boyne in 1690), Hillsborough Fort was remodelled as a Gothic-style tower house in 1758. Only the grounds are open to the public.

Festivals & Events

Oyster Festival FOOD
(http://hillsboroughoysterfestival.com) Around 10,000 people per day – plus more than 8000 oysters from Dundrum Bay – converge on Hillsborough for the three-day Oyster Festival in late August or early September. This celebration of local food, drink and general good fun includes an international oyster-eating competition (County Down champ Colin Shirlow's unbeaten record is 233 oysters in just three minutes).

Sleeping

★ **Fortwilliam Country House** B&B ££
(028-9268 2255; www.fortwilliamcountryhouse.com; 210 Ballynahinch Rd; s/d £50/70;) The Fortwilliam's four luxurious rooms include the Victorian room, with rose wallpaper, huge antique mahogany wardrobe and view over the garden. Breakfast includes fresh eggs from the chickens in the yard, and the smell of home-baked wheaten bread wafts from the Aga stove. From Hillsborough, take the B177 towards Anahilt; it's 5.6km along on the right.

Eating & Drinking

Hillsborough's eateries are popular places – be sure to book ahead at weekends.

★ **Parson's Nose** MODERN IRISH ££
(www.balloinns.com; 48 Lisburn St; mains £11-22, 2-/3-course dinner £19/24; kitchen noon-9pm Sun-Thu, to 10pm Fri & Sat) The ground floor of this beautiful Georgian building looks like a cosy pub, but the real gastronomic action is upstairs in the theatrical open kitchen, where chefs create stunning dishes such as local beetroot risotto and Leggygowan Farm goat's-cheese crumble, and chargrilled rib eye with Bushmills-whiskey cream sauce and buttermilk onion rings. Some tables overlook Hillsborough Castle's lake.

Plough Inn BISTRO ££
(028-9268 2985; http://ploughgroup.com; 3 The Square; mains lunch £9-11, dinner £11.50-25; noon-2.30pm & 5-9pm Mon-Thu, to 9.30pm Fri & Sat, noon-8pm Sun;) This fine old pub, with its maze of dark, wood-panelled nooks and crannies, has been offering 'beer and banter' since 1758. It serves gourmet bar lunches and also offers fine dining in the upstairs restaurant, where stone walls, low ceilings and a roaring fireplace make a cosy setting for a menu ranging from whiskey-cured salmon to lobster and rack of lamb.

Hillside Bar & Restaurant PUB
(028-9268 9233; www.hillsidehillsborough.co.uk; 21 Main St; noon-11.30pm Mon-Wed, to 11.45pm Thu, to 12.30am Fri, to 12.45am Sat, to 11pm Sun) On sloping Main St, this homey pub serves real ale and mulled wine beside the fireplace in winter. Impromptu trad-music sessions often take place, along with live jazz Sunday evenings. There's a beer garden in a cobbled courtyard out the back, and (this being Hillsborough) excellent food too.

Information

The **Tourist Office** (028-9268 9717; www.visitlisburn.com; The Square; 9.30am-5.30pm Mon-Sat year-round, 11am-4pm Sun Apr-Sep) is in the Georgian courthouse in the centre of the village.

Getting There & Away

Bus 238 from Belfast's Europa BusCentre (£3.80, 25 minutes, at least hourly Monday to Saturday, eight Sunday) continues to Newry (£7, 50 minutes).

COUNTY ARMAGH

POP 174,790 / AREA 1326 SQ KM

Armagh City

POP 14,600

The lively little cathedral city of Armagh (Ard Macha) has been an important religious centre since the 5th century, and remains the ecclesiastical capital of Ireland, the seat of both the Anglican and Roman Catholic archbishops of Armagh, and Primates of All Ireland. Their two cathedrals, both named for St Patrick, stare at each other from their respective hilltops.

History

When St Patrick began his mission to spread Christianity throughout Ireland, he chose a site close to Emain Macha (Navan Fort), the nerve centre of pagan Ulster, for his power base. In 445 he built Ireland's first stone church on a hill nearby (now home to the Church of Ireland cathedral), and later decreed that Armagh should have preeminence over all the churches in Ireland.

By the 8th century Armagh was one of Europe's best-known centres of religion, learning and craftwork. The city was divided into three districts (called *trians*), centred around English, Scottish and Irish streets. Armagh's fame was its undoing, however, as the Vikings plundered the city 10 times between 831 and 1013.

The city gained a new prosperity from the linen trade in the 18th century, a period whose legacy includes a Royal School, an astronomical observatory, a renowned public library and some fine Georgian architecture.

Sights

★Armagh Public Library MUSEUM

(http://armaghpubliclibrary.arm.ac.uk; 43 Abbey St; 10am-1pm & 2-4pm Mon-Fri) FREE A first edition of *Gulliver's Travels,* published in 1726 and annotated by Swift himself, is the most prized possession of the Armagh Public Library, founded in 1771 by Archbishop Robinson. Other treasures include Sir Walter Raleigh's 1614 *History of the World,* the *Claims of the Innocents* (pleas to Oliver Cromwell) and engravings by Hogarth and others.

Nearby, you can see ancient coins, early Christian artefacts and other curiosities at the **Registry** (5 Vicar's Hill; adult/child £2/1; 10am-1pm & 2-4pm Tue-Sat), a depository for Church of Ireland records.

★St Patrick's Church of Ireland Cathedral CATHEDRAL

(028-3752 3142; www.stpatricks-cathedral.org; Cathedral Close; admission by donation; 9am-5pm Apr-Oct, to 4pm Nov-Mar) The city's Anglican cathedral occupies the site of St Patrick's original stone church. The present cathedral's ground plan is 13th-century but the building itself is a Gothic restoration dating from 1834 to 1840. A stone slab on the exterior wall of the north transept marks the **burial place of Brian Ború**, the high king of Ireland, who died near Dublin during the last great battle against the Vikings in 1014.

Reserve ahead for guided tours (45 minutes; per person £3).

Within the church are the remains of an 11th-century **Celtic Cross** that once stood nearby, and the **Tandragee Idol**, a curious granite figure dating to the Iron Age. In the south aisle is a **memorial to Archbishop Richard Robinson** (1709–94), who founded Armagh's observatory and public library.

★St Patrick's Roman Catholic Cathedral CATHEDRAL

(www.armagharchdiocese.org; Cathedral Rd; admission by donation; 8.30am-7.30pm) Huge twin towers dominate the approach to Armagh's Roman Catholic Cathedral, built between 1838 and 1873 in Gothic Revival style. Inside it seems almost Byzantine, with every piece of wall and ceiling covered in brilliantly coloured mosaics. The sanctuary was modernised in 1981 and has a very distinctive tabernacle holder and crucifix that seem out of place among the mosaics and statues of the rest of the church.

Armagh County Museum MUSEUM

(028-3752 3070; www.nmni.com/acm; The Mall E; 10am-5pm Mon-Fri, 10am-1pm & 2-5pm Sat) FREE Prehistoric axe heads, items found in bogs, corn dollies and straw-boy outfits, and military costumes and equipment are among the county museum's displays. Don't miss the gruesome cast-iron skull that once graced the top of the Armagh gallows.

The Mall PARK

This long grassy expanse east of the centre was a horse-racing, cock-fighting and bull-baiting venue until the 18th century, when Archbishop Robinson decided that it was all a tad vulgar for a city of learning, and transformed it into an elegant Georgian park. It's flanked by notable buildings, including the working **Armagh Courthouse**

Armagh City

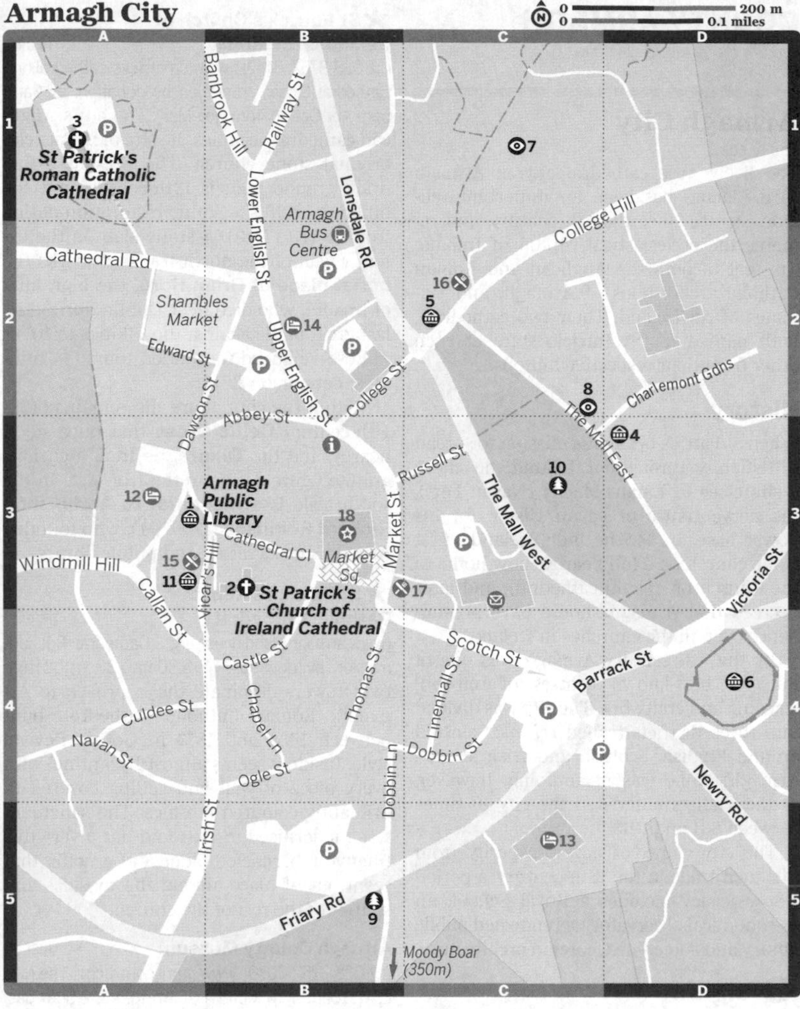

COUNTIES DOWN & ARMAGH ARMAGH CITY

Armagh City

Top Sights
1 Armagh Public Library A3
2 St Patrick's Church of Ireland Cathedral B3
3 St Patrick's Roman Catholic Cathedral A1

Sights
4 Armagh County Museum D3
5 Armagh Courthouse C2
6 Armagh Gaol D4
7 Armagh Planetarium C1
8 Charlemont Place C2
9 Palace Demesne Public Park B5
10 The Mall C3
11 The Registry A3

Sleeping
12 Armagh City Hostel A3
13 Armagh City Hotel C5
14 Charlemont Arms Hotel B2

Eating
15 4 Vicars A3
16 1868 Restaurant & Wine Bar C2
17 Uluru Bar & Grill B3

Entertainment
18 Market Place Theatre & Arts Centre B3

to the north (closed to the public), **Armagh Gaol** to the south (currently being converted into a hotel), and Georgian terraces including **Charlemont Place**.

Armagh Planetarium PLANETARIUM
(☎028-3752 3689; www.armaghplanet.com; College Hill; exhibition area free, shows adult/child £6/5; ⏰10am-5pm Mon-Sat year-round, Sun Jul & Aug) The Armagh Observatory was founded by Archbishop Robinson in 1789 and is still Ireland's leading astronomical-research institute. Aimed mainly at educating young people, the adjacent Armagh Planetarium has an interactive exhibition on space exploration, and a digital theatre that screens a range of spectacular half-hour shows on its domed ceiling (prebooking is essential; check the website for show times).

Palace Demesne Public Park PARK
(www.armagh.co.uk; 1 Greenpark; ⏰dawn-10pm) This palace and surrounding 121-hectare estate were home to the archbishops of the Church of Ireland from the 1770s to the 1970s. The palace itself now houses Armagh's city council and is closed to the public, but you can visit the beautiful gardens. Don't miss the Garden of Senses, five linked gardens testing all five sensory experiences. In the former stables the Moody Boar has a superb bistro.

Festivals & Events

You may be lucky enough to catch a traditional Irish **road-bowling** match, where contestants hurl small 800g metal bowls along quiet country lanes to see who can make it to the finishing line with the least number of throws. Check fixtures on www.irishroadbowling.ie.

Apple Blossom Fair FOOD
(www.armagh.co.uk) Held at Loughgall Manor Estate (10km northeast of Armagh) in the heart of orchard country, the one-day Apple Blossom Fair in early May includes orchard tours, a farmers market, cookery demonstrations and stalls selling all kinds of apple-based products.

Sleeping

Armagh City Hostel HOSTEL £
(☎028-3751 1800; www.hini.org.uk; 39 Abbey St; dm/s/tw/f from £19/31/42/48; ⏰Mar–mid-Sep, groups only mid-Sep–mid-Mar; 📶) This modern, purpose-built hostel near the Church of Ireland Cathedral is more like a small hotel. There are six comfortable twin rooms, two family rooms and 10 small dorms (all with private bathroom) plus TV and tea-and-coffee facilities, a well-equipped kitchen, laundry, lounge and reading room.

Charlemont Arms Hotel HOTEL ££
(☎028-3752 2028; http://charlemontarmshotel.com; 57-65 Lower English St; s/d from £49/79; 📶) Charming period decor at this 19th-century hotel includes an oak-panelled dining room, Victorian fireplaces and flagstone-floored cellar restaurant. The bedrooms, in contrast, are modern and stylish. Traditional Irish music plays every Saturday in the bar.

Armagh City Hotel BUSINESS HOTEL ££
(☎028-3751 8888; www.armaghcityhotel.com; 2 Friary Rd; s/d/f from £75/89/109; @📶🏊) What this immense 120-room contemporary hotel lacks in character it makes up for in amenities: a state-of-the-art leisure centre with a gym, steam room and swimming pool, beauty salon, restaurant, bar and nightclub. Executive rooms have balconies overlooking the golf course.

Eating

4 Vicars MODERN IRISH £
(☎028-3752 7772; http://4vicars.com; 4 Vicars Hill; mains lunch £6-10, dinner £12-17; ⏰10am-4pm Wed-Sun, 6.30-9pm Fri & Sat) Tucked inside a listed Georgian building, this chic little bistro opens to a tiny, delightful terrace. It's a perfect stop for lunch (Kilkeel crab on home-baked bread, or salad of Ardsallagh goat's cheese, orange and beetroot) but its trio of snug rooms is especially romantic on weekend evenings for dishes such as duck with kale, prunes and potato cakes.

★**Moody Boar** MODERN IRISH ££
(☎028-3752 9678; http://themoodyboar.com; Palace Stables, 1 Greenpark; mains lunch £8-12, dinner £15.50-20; ⏰10am-9.30pm Tue-Sat, noon-8.30pm Sun; 🍷) Inside the former palace stables at the Palace Demesne Public Park, the Moody Boar opens to a courtyard where music plays on Friday afternoons. Vegetarian and gluten-free dishes are a speciality; chef Sean Farnan forages for many of the ingredients in the forested grounds, and the restaurant has its own herb and vegetable gardens.

It's filled with stunning contemporary pottery (available for sale), handcrafted by Sean's brother Stephen Farnan.

Uluru Bar & Grill BISTRO ££

(☎ 028-3751 8051; http://ulurubistro.com; 3-5 Market St; breakfast £3.50-6, mains lunch £6-7.50, dinner £10-20; ⏰ 9.30am-9.30pm Mon-Sat, noon-9.30pm Sun) So popular it recently relocated to much larger premises, Aussie-run Uluru brings a bit of antipodean flair to Armagh, with Aboriginal art on the walls and a menu that includes huge 'bushranger's breakfasts', Bondi burgers (melted brie and bacon), chargrilled medallions of marinated kangaroo with sweet-potato chips, plus stone-baked pizzas with toppings such as spiced sausage or maple-cured salmon.

Its own polytunnel supplies many of the veggies and herbs.

1868 Restaurant & Wine Bar MODERN IRISH ££

(☎ 028-3751 5353; www.1868restaurant.com; 2 College Hill; mains lunch £8-14, dinner £10.50-25; ⏰ 11am-3pm & 5-9pm Tue-Thu, to 9.30pm Fri & Sat, noon-4.30pm Sun;) Armagh's 1868-built, red-brick Probate & Customs House makes an atmospheric setting for classic Irish fare with a contemporary twist (save room for the toffee-apple cake with butterscotch sauce). There's a cellar wine bar and al fresco tables are set up in the front courtyard in fine weather.

☆ Entertainment

Market Place Theatre & Arts Centre THEATRE

(☎ 028-3752 1821; www.marketplacearmagh.com; Market St; ⏰ box office 9.30am-4.30pm Mon-Sat, Footlights Bar & Bistro 5-11pm Thu, 5pm-1am Fri & Sat, 6pm-midnight show nights) Armagh's main cultural venue incorporates a 400-seat theatre, exhibition galleries and the **Footlights Bar & Bistro**, which has live bands on Saturday nights.

Information

The **Tourist Office** (☎ 028-3752 1800; www.armagh.co.uk; 40 Upper English St; ⏰ 9am-5.30pm Mon-Sat, 1-5.30pm Sun Apr-Sep, 9am-5pm Mon-Sat Oct-Mar) is located in the St Patrick's Trian complex.

Getting There & Away

Bus 251 serves Belfast's Europa BusCentre (£9.30, 1½ hours, hourly Monday to Friday, eight Saturday, four Sunday). Bus 40 serves Newry (£6, 50 minutes, hourly Monday to Saturday, three Sunday).

Navan Fort

Perched atop a drumlin, Navan Fort is Ulster's most important archaeological site and is linked in legend with the tales of Cúchulainn and named as capital of Ulster and the seat of the legendary Knights of the Red Branch. Exhibits at the outstanding **Navan Centre** (www.armagh.co.uk; 81 Killylea Rd, Armagh; adult/child Apr-Sep £6.20/4.10, Oct-Mar £5.15/3.10; ⏰ 10am-6.30pm Apr-Sep, to 4pm Oct-Mar, last admission 90min before closing, 1hr before closing in winter) place the fort in its historical context, and display a re-creation of an Iron Age settlement.

Known as Emain Macha in Irish, Navan Fort was an important centre from around 1150 BC until the coming of Christianity; the discovery of the skull of a Barbary ape on the site indicates trading links with North Africa.

The main circular **earthwork enclosure** is a whopping 240m in diameter, and encloses a smaller circular structure and an Iron Age **burial mound**. The circular structure has intrigued archaeologists – it appears to be some sort of temple, whose roof was supported by concentric rows of wooden posts, and whose interior was filled with a vast pile of stones. Stranger still, the whole thing was set on fire soon after its construction around 95 BC, possibly for ritual purposes.

It's a 3km walk west of Armagh; alternatively, take bus 73 (up to nine daily Monday to Friday).

Lough Neagh

Lough Neagh (pronounced 'nay') is the largest freshwater lake in Britain and Ireland, big enough to swallow the city of Birmingham (West Midlands, UK, or Alabama, USA – either one would fit). Though vast (around 32km long and 16km wide), the lough is relatively shallow – never more than 9m deep – and is an important habitat for waterfowl. Its waters are home to the pollan, a freshwater herring found only in Ireland, and the dollaghan, a subspecies of trout unique to Lough Neagh.

Connected to the sea by the River Bann, the lough has been a vital waterway and food source since prehistoric times, and is still home to Europe's largest eel fishery. The lough's main points of access – with the best views – include Antrim town on the eastern shore, Oxford Island in the south and Ardboe in the west.

WORTH A TRIP

OXFORD ISLAND

Oxford Island National Nature Reserve protects a range of habitats – woodland, wildflower meadows, reedy shoreline and shallow lake margins – on the southern edge of Lough Neagh. It's criss-crossed by walking and cycling trails, with information boards and birdwatching hides.

The reserve is just north of Lurgan, signposted from junction 10 on the M1 motorway; you'll need your own transport.

Lough Neagh Discovery Centre (www.oxfordisland.com; Oxford Island, Lurgan; ⏲9am-6pm Mon-Fri, 10am-6pm Sat & Sun Apr-Sep, to 5pm Oct-Mar; 📶) In the middle of a reed-fringed pond inhabited by waterfowl, the discovery centre has a tourist information desk, gift shop, gallery and a great little cafe with lake-shore views.

Lough Neagh Boat Trips (☎028-3832 7573; adult/child £5/3; ⏲every 30min 1.30-5pm Sat & Sun Apr-Oct) Half-hour boat trips on Lough Neagh depart from Kinnego Marina, aboard the 12-seat cabin cruiser *Master McGra*.

Encircling the lough is the 180km **Lough-shore Trail** cycle route, however for most of its length it follows quiet country roads set back from the shore.

South Armagh

The peace process has had a more visible effect on rural, staunchly Republican South Armagh than anywhere else in Northern Ireland.

With the Republic only a few miles away, South Armagh saw cross-border attacks and bombings. For more than 30 years, British soldiers on foot patrol in village streets and the constant clatter of army helicopters were part of everyday life. As part of the UK government's 'normalisation process', the army pulled out in 2007 – the hilltop watchtowers have been removed and the huge barracks at Bessbrook Mill and Crossmaglen were closed down.

Today, South Armagh is a peaceful backwater with enchanting scenery ideal for walkers and cyclists. Discover more at www.south-armagh.com.

Ring of Gullion

The **Ring of Gullion** (www.ringofgullion.org) is a magical region steeped in Celtic legend, centred on Slieve Gullion (Sliabh gCuilinn), where the Celtic warrior Cúchulainn is said to have taken his name after killing the dog *(cú)* belonging to the smith Culainn. The 'ring' is a necklace of rugged hills strung between Newry and Forkhill, 15km to the southwest, encircling the central whaleback ridge of Slieve Gullion. This unusual concentric formation is a geological structure known as a ring dyke.

Sights

Slieve Gullion Forest Park FOREST

(⏲8am-dusk) FREE A 13km scenic drive through this forest park provides picturesque views over the surrounding hills. From the parking and picnic area at the top of the drive, you can hike to the summit of Slieve Gullion (576m), the highest point in County Armagh, topped by two early Bronze Age cairns and a tiny lake (1.5km round trip). The park entrance is 10km southwest of Newry on the B113 road to Forkhill.

Killevy Churches HISTORIC SITE

(⏲24hr) Surrounded by beech trees, these ruined, conjoined churches, 6km south of Camlough, were constructed on the site of a 5th-century nunnery founded by St Moninna. The eastern church dates from the 15th century and shares a gable wall with the 12th-century western one. The west door, with a massive lintel and granite jambs, may be 200 years older still. At the side of the churchyard, a footpath leads uphill to a white cross that marks **St Moninna's holy well**.

Counties Londonderry & Antrim

Includes ➡

Best Places to Eat

- ➡ Pyke 'n' Pommes (p598)
- ➡ Blackstone (p619)
- ➡ Harry's Shack (p603)
- ➡ Billy Andy's (p617)
- ➡ Green Man (p598)

Best Places to Stay

- ➡ Beech Hill Country House (p598)
- ➡ Strandeen (p603)
- ➡ Downhill Beach House (p602)
- ➡ Kinbane Farmhouse (p609)
- ➡ Galgorm Resort & Spa (p619)

Why Go?

Northern Ireland's spectacular north coast is a giant geology classroom. The patient workmanship of the ocean has laid bare the black basalt and white chalk that underlie much of County Antrim, and dissected the rocks into a scenic extravaganza of sea stacks, pinnacles, cliffs and caves. This mystical landscape's extraordinary rock formations, ruined castles and wooded glens have made the region an atmospheric backdrop for the TV series *Game of Thrones,* with numerous filming locations here.

To the west, County Londonderry's chief attraction is the spirited city of Derry. Ireland's only walled city sits alongside a broad sweep of the River Foyle and echoes with centuries of often-turbulent history. The current decade has seen it undergo a renaissance as a cultural powerhouse, with a profusion of creative enterprises, public artworks and vibrant drinking and dining scenes. Derry also makes an ideal jumping-off point for the Wild Atlantic Way.

When to Go

➡ May is the best month for walking along the Causeway Coast, as you'll avoid the summer crowds at the Giant's Causeway and enjoy a colourful sprinkling of spring flowers to boot.

➡ June and July see the peak of the seabird nesting season – an ideal time to visit the Kebble National Nature Reserve on gloriously remote Rathlin Island – and also bring the best beach weather.

➡ The traditional festivities of Ballycastle's Ould Lammas Fair, dating from the 17th century, take place on the last Monday and Tuesday of August, marking the end of summer and beginning of the harvest.

COUNTY LONDONDERRY

POP 247,130 / AREA 2074 SQ KM

Derry

POP 107,900

Northern Ireland's second-largest city continues to flourish as an artistic and cultural hub. Derry's city centre was given a striking makeover for its year as the UK City of Culture 2013, with the new Peace Bridge, Ebrington Square, and the redevelopment of the waterfront and Guildhall area making the most of the city's splendid riverside setting.

There's lots of history to absorb here, from the Siege of Derry to the Battle of the Bogside and Bloody Sunday – a stroll around the 17th-century city walls that encircle the city is a must, as is a tour of the Bogside murals – along with the burgeoning live-music scene in the city's lively pubs.

History

The defining moment of Derry's history was the Siege of Derry in 1688–89, an event that reverberates to this day. King James I granted the city a royal charter in 1613, and gave the London livery companies (trade guilds) the task of fortifying Derry and planting the county of Coleraine (soon to be renamed County Londonderry) with Protestant settlers.

In Britain, the Glorious Revolution of 1688 saw the Catholic King James II ousted in favour of the Protestant Dutch prince, William of Orange. Derry was the only garrison in Ireland that was not held by forces loyal to King James, and so, in December 1688, Catholic forces led by the Earl of Antrim arrived on the east bank of the River Foyle, ready to seize the city. They sent emissaries to discuss terms of surrender, but in the meantime troops were being ferried across the river in preparation for an assault. On seeing this, 13 apprentice boys barred the city gates with a cry of 'There'll be no surrender!'

And so, on 7 December 1688, the Siege of Derry began. For 105 days the Protestant citizens of Derry withstood bombardment, disease and starvation (the condition of the besieging forces was not much better). By the time a relief ship burst through and broke the siege, an estimated half of the city's inhabitants had died. In the 20th century the Siege of Derry became a symbol of Ulster Protestants' resistance to rule by a Catholic Irish Republic, and 'No surrender!' remains a Loyalist battle cry to this day.

In the 19th century Derry was one of the main ports of emigration to the US, a fact commemorated by *Emigrants*, the Eamonn O'Doherty–designed sculptures depicting an emigrant family standing on Derry Quay.

Derry was a flashpoint during the Troubles, particularly during the the Battle of the Bogside and Bloody Sunday. More recently, its role as the UK City of Culture 2013 has helped revitalise the city.

DERRY/LONDONDERRY

Derry/Londonderry is a town with two names. Nationalists always use Derry, and vandals often deface the 'London' part of the name on road signs. Staunch Unionists insist on Londonderry, which is still the city's (and county's) official name. All the same, many people, regardless of political persuasion, call it Derry in everyday speech.

The settlement was originally named Doíre Calgaigh (Oak Grove of Calgach), after a pagan warrior-hero; in the 10th century it was renamed Doíre Colmcille (Oak Grove of Columba), in honour of the 6th-century saint who established the first monastic settlement here.

In the following centuries the name was shortened and anglicised to Derrie or Derry. Then in 1613, in recognition of the Corporation of London's role in the 'plantation' of northwest Ulster with Protestant settlers, Derry was granted a royal charter and the city was renamed Londonderry.

A new County Londonderry was created from what was originally County Coleraine, along with parts of Tyrone and Antrim; unlike the city, there has never been an officially sanctioned county called Derry. Nevertheless, those with nationalist leanings, including the county's Gaelic football team, prefer to use County Derry.

Traditionally, road signs in Northern Ireland point to Londonderry, those in the Republic point to Derry (or Doíre in Irish), and some tourism-industry promotional material covers all bases, using Derry-Londonderry-Doíre. In July 2015, the Derry City and Strabane District Council voted to change the city's official name to Derry, a decision that has been challenged by Unionists. Watch this space.

Counties Londonderry & Antrim Highlights

1. Hike along the geologically astounding **Causeway Coast** (p607) from Carrick-a-Rede to the otherworldly Giant's Causeway.
2. Discover modern murals, fabulous dining and foot-stomping music in the history-steeped city of **Derry** (p589).
3. Wobble across the narrow, swaying **Carrick-a-Rede Rope Bridge** (p609).
4. Surf the Atlantic breakers at the sweeping beaches around **Portrush** (p604).
5. Spot seabirds and seals on remote **Rathlin Island** (p613).

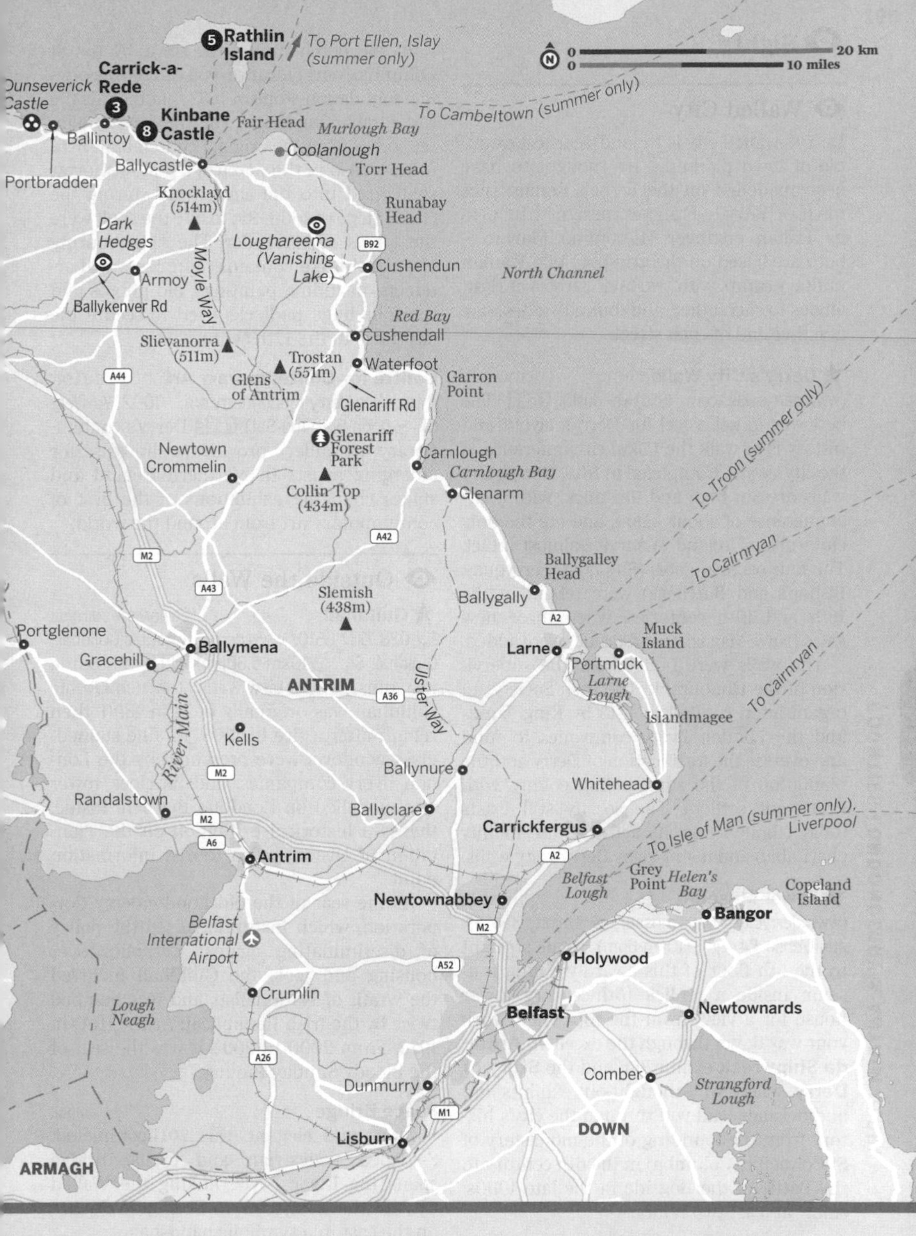

❻ Learn the secrets of Irish whiskey making on a behind-the-scenes tour of the **Old Bushmills Distillery** (p605).

❼ Soak up spectacular coastal views from **Mussenden Temple** (p601) at Downhill, one of the region's many iconic *Game of Thrones* filming locations.

❽ Descend 140 precipitous steps to the headland-perched ruins of **Kinbane Castle** (p609).

Sights

Walled City

Derry's walled city is Ireland's earliest example of town planning. It's thought to have been modelled on the French Renaissance town of Vitry-le-François, designed in 1545 by Italian engineer Hieronimo Marino – both are based on the grid plan of a Roman military camp, with two main streets at right angles to each other, and four city gates, one at either end of each street.

★Derry's City Walls CITY WALLS
(www.derryswalls.com; dawn–dusk) FREE The best way to get a feel for Derry's layout and history is to walk the 1.5km circumference of the city's walls. Completed in 1619, Derry's city walls are 8m high and 9m thick, with a circumference of about 1.5km, and are the only city walls in Ireland to survive almost intact. The four original gates (Shipquay, Ferryquay, Bishop's and Butcher's) were rebuilt in the 18th and 19th centuries, when three new gates (New, Magazine and Castle) were added.

The walls were built under the supervision of the Honourable The Irish Society, an organisation created in 1613 by King James and the London livery companies to fund and oversee the fortification of Derry and the plantation of the surrounding county with Protestant settlers. The society still exists today (though now its activities are mainly charitable) and it still owns Derry's city walls.

★Tower Museum MUSEUM
(www.derrycity.gov.uk/museums; Union Hall Pl; adult/child £4/2; 10am-6pm) Head straight to the 5th floor of this award-winning museum inside a replica 16th-century tower house for a view from the top. Then work your way down through the excellent **Armada Shipwreck** exhibition, and the **Story of Derry**, where well-thought-out exhibits and audiovisuals lead you through the city's history from the founding of the monastery of St Colmcille (Columba) in the 6th century to the Battle of the Bogside in the late 1960s. Allow at least two hours.

★St Columb's Cathedral CATHEDRAL
(www.stcolumbscathedral.org; 17 London St; admission by donation; 9am-5pm Mon-Sat) Built between 1628 and 1633 from the same grey-green schist as the city walls, this was the first post-Reformation church to be erected in Britain and Ireland, and is Derry's oldest surviving building.

In the porch (under the spire, by the St Columb's Court entrance) you can see the original foundation stone of 1633 that records the cathedral's completion. The smaller stone inset comes from the original church built here in 1164. Also in the porch is a hollow mortar shell fired into the churchyard during the Great Siege of 1688–89; inside the shell were the terms of surrender. The neighbouring **chapter house** contains more historical artefacts, including paintings, old photos and the four huge padlocks used to secure the city gates in the 17th century.

Centre for Contemporary Art GALLERY
(http://cca-derry-londonderry.org; 10-12 Artillery St; noon-6pm Tue-Sat) FREE Derry's contemporary art gallery provides a showcase for emerging artists in Northern Ireland and stages changing exhibitions of the best of contemporary art from around the world.

Outside the Walls

★Guildhall NOTABLE BUILDING
(028-7137 6510; www.derrycity.gov.uk/Guildhall; Guildhall Sq; 10am-5.30pm) FREE Standing just outside the city walls, the neo-Gothic Guildhall was originally built in 1890, then rebuilt after a fire in 1908. Its fine stained-glass windows were presented by the London livery companies, and its clock tower was modelled on London's Big Ben. Inside, there's a historical exhibition on the Plantation of Ulster, and a tourist information point.

As the seat of the old Londonderry Corporation, which institutionalised the policy of discriminating against Catholics over housing and jobs, the Guildhall incurred the wrath of Nationalists and was bombed twice by the Irish Republican Army (IRA) in 1972. From 2000 to 2004 it was the seat of the Bloody Sunday Inquiry.

Peace Bridge BRIDGE
Sinuous and elegant, this 2011-completed, S-shaped pedestrian and cyclist bridge spans the River Foyle, linking the Walled City on the west bank to Ebrington Square on the east in a symbolic handshake.

Ebrington Square PLAZA
Originally a 19th-century fort, and later a British Army base, Ebrington Barracks was demilitarised in 2003. The former parade ground now serves as a public square, performance venue and exhibition space.

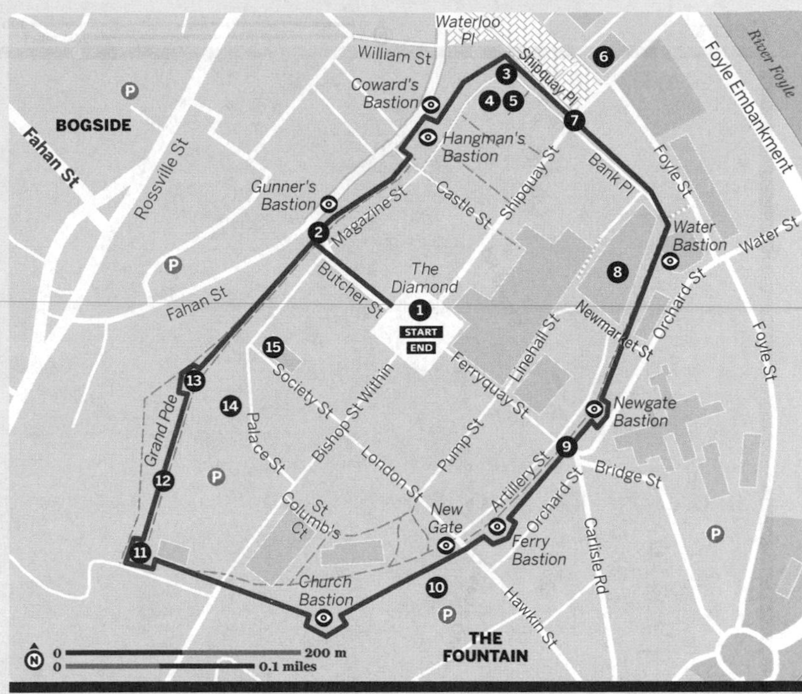

Walking Tour
Derry's Walled City

START THE DIAMOND
END THE DIAMOND
LENGTH 2KM

Start your walk at the Diamond, Derry's central square, dominated by the 1 **war memorial**. Head along Butcher St, where the town's butchers once had their shops, to 2 **Butcher's Gate**, and climb the steps to the top of the city walls.

Stroll downhill to 3 **Magazine Gate**, named for the powder magazine that used to be close by. Inside the walls is the modern 4 **O'Doherty's Tower**, housing the excellent 5 **Tower Museum** (p592); outside the walls is the red-brick, neo-Gothic 6 **Guildhall** (p592).

The River Foyle used to come up to the northeastern wall here. In the middle is the 7 **Shipquay Gate**. The walls turn southwest and climb beside the 8 **Millennium Forum** (p599) to the 9 **Ferryquay Gate**, where the apprentice boys barred the gate at the start of the Great Siege of 1688–89.

The stretch of wall beyond overlooks the 10 **Fountain housing estate**, the last significant Protestant community on the western bank of the Foyle. The round, brick-paved area on the ground outside New Gate is where a 10m-high bonfire is lit on the night before the annual Apprentice Boys' march (second Saturday in August).

Continue around the southern stretch of wall to the 11 **Double Bastion** at the southwestern corner, home to Roaring Meg, the most famous of the cannons used during the Siege of Derry. The next section of wall is known as the 12 **Grand Parade**, and offers an excellent view of the murals painted by the Bogside Artists.

An empty plinth on the 13 **Royal Bastion** marks the former site of a monument to the Reverend George Walker, joint governor of the city during the Great Siege; it was blown up by the IRA in 1973. Behind the Royal Bastion is the 1872 Church of Ireland 14 **Chapel of St Augustine**, built on the site of St Colmcille's 6th-century monastery. A little further along is the 15 **Apprentice Boys' Memorial Hall**, with a high mesh fence to protect it from paint bombs hurled from below.

Derry

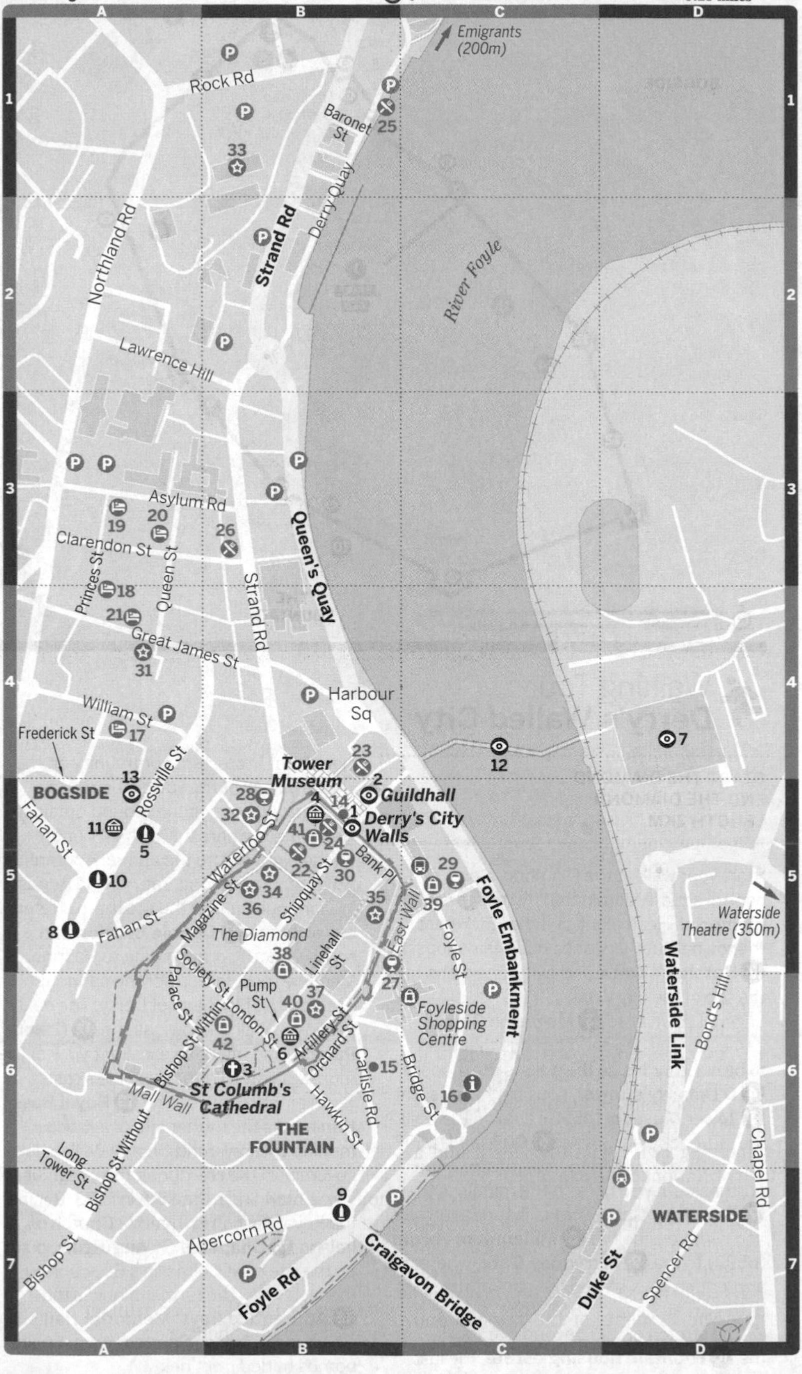

0 — 500 m
0 — 0.25 miles

Emigrants (200m)
Rock Rd
Baronet St
Derry Quay
Strand Rd
Northland Rd
River Foyle
Lawrence Hill
Asylum Rd
Clarendon St
Queen St
Princes St
Queen's Quay
Strand Rd
Great James St
William St
Harbour Sq
Frederick St
Tower Museum
Guildhall
Derry's City Walls
BOGSIDE
Rossville St
Fahan St
Waterloo St
Bank Pl
Shipquay St
Magazine St
The Diamond
East Wall
Foyle St
Foyle Embankment
Waterside Theatre (350m)
Waterside Link
Linehall St
Society St
Palace St
Pump St
London St
Bishop St Within
Artillery St
Orchard St
Carlisle Rd
Bridge St
Foyleside Shopping Centre
Bond's Hill
St Columb's Cathedral
Mall Wall
Hawkin St
THE FOUNTAIN
Bishop St Without
Long Tower St
Chapel Rd
WATERSIDE
Abercorn Rd
Bishop St
Foyle Rd
Craigavon Bridge
Duke St
Spencer Rd

Derry

Top Sights
1 Derry's City Walls ... B5
2 Guildhall ... B5
3 St Columb's Cathedral ... B6
4 Tower Museum ... B5

Sights
5 Bloody Sunday Memorial ... A5
6 Centre for Contemporary Art ... B6
7 Ebrington Square ... D4
8 Free Derry Corner ... A5
9 Hands Across the Divide ... B7
10 Hunger Strikers' Memorial ... A5
11 Museum of Free Derry ... A5
12 Peace Bridge ... C4
13 People's Gallery Murals ... A5

Activities, Courses & Tours
14 Bogside Artists Tours ... B5
15 City Tours ... B6
16 Tours 'n' Trails ... C6

Sleeping
17 Abbey B&B ... A4
18 Derry City Independent Hostel ... A4
19 Derry Palace Hostel ... A3
20 Merchant's House ... A3
21 Saddler's House ... A4

Eating
22 Café del Mondo ... B5
23 Custom House ... B4
24 Green Man ... B5
Primrose Cafe ... (see 15)
25 Pyke 'n' Pommes ... B1
26 Saffron ... B3

Drinking & Nightlife
27 Badgers Bar ... B5
28 Peadar O'Donnell's ... B5
29 Sandino's Cafe-Bar ... C5
30 Sugar ... B5

Entertainment
31 Cultúrlann Uí Chanáin ... A4
32 Gweedore Bar ... B5
33 Magee College ... B1
34 Mason's Bar ... B5
35 Millennium Forum ... B5
36 Nerve Centre ... B5
37 Playhouse ... B6

Shopping
An Cló Ceart ... (see 31)
38 Austins ... B5
39 Cool Discs Music ... C5
40 Cowley Cooper Gallery ... B6
41 Craft Village ... B5
42 Whatnot ... B6

Hands Across the Divide MONUMENT
As you enter the city across Craigavon Bridge, the first thing you see is the Hands Across the Divide monument. This striking bronze sculpture of two men reaching out to each other symbolises the spirit of reconciliation and hope for the future; it was unveiled in 1992, 20 years after Bloody Sunday.

Bogside

The Bogside district, to the west of the walled city, developed in the 19th and early 20th centuries as a working-class, predominantly Catholic, residential area. By the 1960s its serried ranks of small, terrace houses had become an overcrowded ghetto of poverty and unemployment, a focus for the emerging civil rights movement and a hotbed of Nationalist discontent.

In August 1969 the three-day 'Battle of the Bogside' – a running street battle between local youths and the Royal Ulster Constabulary (RUC) – prompted the UK government to send British troops into Northern Ireland. The residents of the Bogside and neighbouring Brandywell districts – 33,000 of them – declared themselves independent of the civil authorities and barricaded the streets to keep the security forces out. 'Free Derry', as it was known, was a no-go area for the police and army, its streets patrolled by IRA volunteers. In January 1972 the area around Rossville St witnessed the horrific events of **Bloody Sunday** (p596). 'Free Derry' ended with Operation Motorman on 31 July 1972, when thousands of British troops and armoured cars moved in to occupy the Bogside.

The area's population is currently around 8000, following extensive redevelopment that has seen the old houses and flats demolished and replaced with modern housing.

Free Derry Corner MONUMENT
(intersection of Fahan & Rossville Sts) The Free Derry Corner, where the gable end of a house painted with the famous slogan 'You are Now Entering Free Derry' still stands, is all that remains of the old Bogside district.

Hunger Strikers' Memorial MONUMENT
(Rossville St) The H-shaped Hunger Strikers' Memorial is near the Free Derry Corner.

Bloody Sunday Memorial MONUMENT
(Rossville St) A simple granite obelisk commemorates the 14 civilians who were shot dead by the British Army on Bloody Sunday, 30 January 1972.

People's Gallery Murals MURALS
(Rossville St) The 12 murals that decorate the gable ends of houses along Rossville St, near Free Derry Corner, are popularly referred to as the People's Gallery. They are the work of Tom Kelly, Will Kelly and Kevin Hasson, known as 'the Bogside Artists'. The three men have spent most of their lives in the Bogside, and lived through the worst of the Troubles. The murals can be clearly seen from the northern part of the City Walls.

Mostly painted between 1997 and 2001, the murals commemorate key events in the Troubles, including the Battle of the Bogside, Bloody Sunday, Operation Motorman and the 1981 hunger strike. The most powerful images are those painted largely in monochrome, evoking journalistic imagery – *Operation Motorman,* showing a British soldier breaking down a door with

SUNDAY, BLOODY SUNDAY

Tragically echoing Dublin's Bloody Sunday of November 1920, when British security forces shot dead 14 spectators at a Gaelic football match in Croke Park, Derry's Bloody Sunday was a turning point in the history of the Troubles.

On Sunday 30 January 1972, the Northern Ireland Civil Rights Association organised a peaceful march through Derry in protest against internment without trial, which had been introduced by the British government the previous year. Some 15,000 people marched from Creggan through the Bogside towards the Guildhall, but they were stopped by British Army barricades at the junction of William and Rossville Sts. The main march was diverted along Rossville St to Free Derry Corner, but a small number of youths began hurling stones and insults at the British soldiers.

The exact sequence of events was disputed, but it has since been established that soldiers of the 1st Battalion the Parachute Regiment opened fire on unarmed civilians. Fourteen people were shot dead (thirteen outright; one who died 4 ½ months later from his injuries), some of them shot in the back; six were aged just 17. A similar number were injured, most by gunshots and two from being knocked down by armoured personnel carriers. The Catholic population of Derry, who had originally welcomed the British troops as a neutral force protecting them from Protestant violence and persecution, now saw the army as enemy and occupier. The ranks of the Provisional Irish Republican Army (IRA) swelled with a fresh surge of volunteers.

The **Widgery Commission**, set up in 1972 to investigate the affair, failed to find anyone responsible. None of the soldiers who fired at civilians, nor the officers in charge, were brought to trial or even disciplined; records disappeared and weapons were destroyed.

Long-standing public dissatisfaction with the Widgery investigation led to the massive **Bloody Sunday Inquiry**, headed by Lord Saville, which sat from March 2000 till December 2004. The inquiry heard from 900 witnesses, received 2500 witness statements and allegedly cost British taxpayers £400 million; its report (available on www.official-documents.gov.uk) was finally published in June 2010.

Lord Saville found that "The firing by soldiers of 1 PARA on Bloody Sunday caused the deaths of 13 people and injury to a similar number, none of whom was posing a threat of causing death or serious injury. What happened on Bloody Sunday strengthened the Provisional IRA, increased nationalist resentment and hostility towards the Army and exacerbated the violent conflict of the years that followed. Bloody Sunday was a tragedy for the bereaved and the wounded, and a catastrophe for the people of Northern Ireland."

Following publication of the report, Prime Minister David Cameron publicly apologised on behalf of the UK government, describing the killings as "unjustified and unjustifiable". In 2010, the Police Service of Northern Ireland (PSNI) launched a murder inquiry into the deaths, which remains ongoing.

The events of Bloody Sunday inspired rock band U2's most overtly political song, 'Sunday Bloody Sunday' (1983), and are commemorated in the Museum of Free Derry, the People's Gallery and the Bloody Sunday Memorial, all in the Bogside.

a sledgehammer; *Bloody Sunday,* with a group of men led by local priest Father Daly carrying the body of Jackie Duddy (the first fatality on that day); and *The Petrol Bomber,* a young boy wearing a gas mask and holding a petrol bomb.

The most moving image is *The Death of Innocence,* which shows the radiant figure of 14-year-old schoolgirl Annette McGavigan, killed in crossfire between the IRA and the British Army on 6 September 1971, the 100th victim of the Troubles. Representing all the children who died in the conflict, she stands against the brooding chaos of a bombed-out building, the roof beams forming a crucifix in the top right-hand corner. At the left, a downward-pointing rifle, broken in the middle, stands for the failure of violence, while the butterfly symbolises resurrection and the hope embodied in the peace process.

The final mural in the sequence, completed in 2004, is the *Peace Mural,* a swirling image of a dove (symbol of peace and of Derry's patron saint, Columba) rising out of the blood and sadness of the past towards the sunny yellow hope of a peaceful future.

The murals can be seen online at www.cain.ulst.ac.uk/bogsideartists and in the book *The People's Gallery,* which is available from the artists' website.

Museum of Free Derry MUSEUM
(www.museumoffreederry.org; 55-61 Glenfada Park; adult/child £3/2; ⏲9.30am-4.30pm Mon-Fri year-round, plus 1-4pm Sat Apr-Sep, 1-4pm Sun Jul-Sep) Just off Rossville St, this museum chronicles the history of the Bogside, the civil rights movement and the events of Bloody Sunday through photographs, news reports and the accounts of first-hand witnesses, including some of the original photographs that inspired the People's Gallery murals.

Tours

Bogside Artists Tours WALKING TOUR
(☎07514 052481; www.bogsideartists.com; per person £5) Guided one-hour walking tours of the famous People's Gallery murals led by the artists themselves. Book in advance by phone or on the website.

City Tours WALKING TOUR
(☎028-7127 1996; www.derrycitytours.com; Carlisle Stores, 11 Carlisle Rd; adult/child £4/free) One-hour Historic Derry walking tours start from Carlisle Stores at 10am, noon, 2pm and 4pm year-round. There are also tours of the Bogside and of Derry's murals.

Tours 'n' Trails WALKING TOUR
(☎028-7136 7000; www.toursntrails.co.uk; adult/child £6/3) Offers 1¼-hour guided walking tours of the walled city, starting from the tourist office at 11am and 3pm Monday to Saturday from April to October.

Festivals & Events

City of Derry Jazz Festival MUSIC
(www.cityofderryjazzfestival.com) Five days of jazz at various venues including Ebrington Sq. Held in late April or early May.

Gasyard Wall Féile IRISH CULTURE
(www.facebook.com/gasyardwallfeile) Live music, street performers, carnival, theatre and Irish-language events all feature at this major cultural festival in August.

City of Derry Guitar Festival MUSIC
(www.cityofderryguitarfestival.com) Over three days in late August, the grounds of the University of Ulster's Magee College host performances and master classes from guitar greats from around the world, including classical, acoustic, electric, flamenco and bass.

Halloween Carnival CARNIVAL
(www.derrycity.gov.uk/halloween; ⏲27-31 Oct) The city dresses up for Ireland's biggest street party, which features fireworks, a haunted house, Freaky Fun Fair and more.

Foyle Film Festival FILM
(www.foylefilmfestival.org) This week-long event in mid November is the North's biggest film festival.

Sleeping

Derry Palace Hostel HOSTEL £
(☎028-7130 9051; www.paddyspalace.com; 1 Woodleigh Tce, Asylum Rd; dm/tw from £19/70; @🛜) Part of the Ireland-wide Paddy's Palace chain, this recently renovated hostel is central, comfortable and has a great party atmosphere. There's a sunny garden (and heated patio), free bikes and musical instruments. Staff regularly organise nights out at local pubs with traditional music.

Derry City Independent Hostel HOSTEL £
(☎028-7128 0542; www.derry-hostel.co.uk; 12 Princes St; dm/d/tr £15/38/54; @🛜) Run by experienced backpackers and decorated with souvenirs from their travels around the world, this small, friendly hostel is set in a Georgian town house a short walk north-west of the bus station.

★ Merchant's House B&B ££
(028-7126 9691; www.thesaddlershouse.com; 16 Queen St; s/d/tr/f from £40/65/90/100;) This historic, Georgian-style town house is a gem of a B&B. It has an elegant lounge and dining room with marble fireplaces and antique furniture, TV, coffee-making facilities, homemade marmalade at breakfast and bathrobes in the bedrooms (only the family room has a private bathroom). Call at Saddler's House first to pick up a key.

Saddler's House B&B ££
(028-7126 9691; www.thesaddlershouse.com; 36 Great James St; s/d £55/60;) Centrally located within a five-minute walk of the walled city, this friendly B&B is set in a lovely Victorian town house. All seven rooms have private bathrooms, and you get to enjoy a huge breakfast in the family kitchen.

Abbey B&B B&B ££
(028-7127 9000; www.abbeyaccommodation.com; 4 Abbey St; s/d/tr from £50/64/90;) There's a warm welcome waiting at this family-run B&B just a short walk from the walled city, on the edge of the Bogside. The six rooms are stylishly decorated.

Arkle House B&B ££
(028-7127 1156; www.derryhotel.co.uk; 2 Coshquin Rd; s/d £55/65;) Located 2km northwest of the city centre, this grand Victorian house is set in private gardens and offers five large, lush bedrooms and a private kitchen for guests to use.

★ Beech Hill Country House HISTORIC HOTEL £££
(028-7134 9279; www.beech-hill.com; 32 Ardmore Rd; s/d from £99/129;) Secluded in a picturesque patch of woodland 4.3km southeast of Derry, this wonderfully atmospheric 18th-century manor house is surrounded by magnificent gardens and steeped in history – it was a WWII base for US marines, and former US president Bill Clinton stayed several times. All 30 rooms incorporate Georgian-era colours and furnishings. Its lake-view restaurant is sublime.

Eating

★ Pyke 'n' Pommes BURGERS £
(behind Foyle Marina, off Baronet St; dishes £5-15; noon-3pm Tue-Thu, to 5pm Fri & Sat, hrs vary;) Derry's single-best eatery is this quayside shipping container. Chef Kevin Pyke's amazing, mostly organic burgers span his signature Notorious Pig (pulled pork, crispy slaw, beetroot and crème fraîche), Cheeky Monkey (monkfish, warm potato and smoked-apple purée) and Veganderry (chickpeas, lemon and coriander) to his Legenderry Burger (wagyu beef, pickled onions and honey-mustard mayo). Seasonal specials might include mackerel or oysters.

★ Green Man DELI £
(Craft Village, Shipquay St; 9.30am-6pm Mon-Sat) This is the ultimate place to pick up artisan picnic fare from around the Emerald Isle: Haven Smokehouse turf-smoked salmon, Durrus farmhouse cheese, Filligans preserves and chutneys, Fermanagh black and white pudding, Knochnarea honey, and Guinness bread, as well as sweet treats like Glastry Farm ice cream and Melting Pot Irish fudge.

Primrose Cafe CAFE £
(15 Carlisle Rd; dishes £5-8; 8am-5pm Mon-Sat, 11am-4pm Sun;) The Primrose prospers by sticking to the classics and doing them really well – from pancakes with maple syrup to pork pies, and a Sunday brunch that ranges from eggs Benedict to the full Ulster fry. Even with the enclosed 'secret garden' courtyard at the back, it can be hard to find a seat.

★ Custom House MODERN IRISH ££
(028-7137 3366; http://customhouserestaurant.com; Custom House St, Queen's Quay; mains lunch £8-10, dinner £13-19; noon-9.30pm Mon-Sat, to 9pm Sun) You can just drop in for a drink in the bar fitted out with pewter, copper and walnut wood, but the 1876-built Custom House is a superb spot to dine on sea bass tagine; sirloin with smoked bacon and turnip and celeriac dauphinoise; and rigatoni with roasted red onion, hazelnuts and Cashel blue cheese. Service goes above and beyond.

Saffron INDIAN ££
(028-7126 0532; http://saffronderry.co.uk; 2 Claredon St; mains £9-14; 4.30-10.30pm Sun-Thu, to 11.30pm Fri, to midnight Sat;) Indian restaurants in Ireland tend to be more miss than hit, but Saffron stands out, not only for its fiery curries, rich tikkas, and aromatic biryani dishes (made from basmati rice and served with masala sauce), but also for its stylish, ultracontemporary decor. Great cocktails such as pomegranate martinis too.

Café del Mondo CAFE, IRISH ££
(028-7136 6877; http://cafedelmondo.com; 29 Craft Village, Shipquay St; mains lunch £7-8, dinner £12-23; 10am-6pm Tue, 10am-midnight Wed-Sat;) Wholesome homemade soups, artisan

breads and hot lunch specials using organic, locally sourced produce are served up at this bohemian cafe, along with excellent fairtrade coffee. In the evening, its multicultural menu changes monthly (one month might be Thai, the next Mexican) and includes a handful of vegetarian dishes. Book ahead for dinner.

Drinking & Nightlife

Derry's pubs are friendly and atmospheric, and most are within crawling distance of each other.

★ **Peadar O'Donnell's** PUB
(www.peadars.com; 59-63 Waterloo St; ⏲11.30am-1.30am Mon-Sat, noon-12.30am Sun) Done up as a typical Irish pub/grocery – with shelves of household items, shopkeepers scales on the counter and a museum's-worth of old bric-a-brac – Peadar's has trad-music sessions every night and often on weekend afternoons as well. Its adjacent **Gweedore Bar** (www.peadars.com; 61 Waterloo St; ⏲11.30am-1.30am Mon-Sat, noon-12.30am Sun) hosts live rock bands every night, and a Saturday-night disco upstairs.

Badgers Bar PUB
(16-18 Orchard St; ⏲11.30am-1am Mon-Sat, noon-1am Sun) A fine polished-brass and stained-glass Victorian pub with wood-panelled nooks and crannies, and an outdoor terrace. Badgers overflows at lunchtime with shoppers enjoying quality pub grub, and offers a quiet haven in the evenings.

Sandino's Cafe-Bar BAR
(www.sandinos.com; 1 Water St; ⏲11.30am-1am Mon-Sat, noon-midnight Sun) From the posters of Che to the Free Palestine flag to the fairtrade coffee and gluten-free beer, this relaxed cafe-bar exudes a liberal, left-wing vibe. DJs spin from Thursday to Saturday in Club Havana; there's traditional Irish music on Sunday afternoons.

Sugar CLUB
(33 Shipquay St; ⏲10.30pm-2am Wed-Sun) Above Downey's Bar, Derry's hottest club spreads over two floors, and has the city's largest rooftop terrace and DJs that pump up the volume.

Entertainment

Mason's Bar LIVE MUSIC
(10 Magazine St) The city that spawned the Undertones is still turning out raw, rumbustious music. Mason's line-up changes frequently but includes regular student, emerging and established bands, as well as DJs, karaoke, and comedy nights.

Nerve Centre ARTS CENTRE
(www.nerve-centre.org.uk; 7-8 Magazine St) Set up in 1990 to encourage young local talent in the fields of music and film, the Nerve Centre has a performance area, with live music at weekends, a theatre, and an art-house cinema. Also here are a bar and cafe.

Playhouse THEATRE
(www.derryplayhouse.co.uk; 5-7 Artillery St; ⏲box office 10.30am-5pm Mon-Fri, 10am-4pm Sat, plus 45min before show) Housed in beautifully restored school buildings with an award-winning modern extension at the rear, this community arts centre stages music, dance and theatre by local and international performers.

Cultúrlann Uí Chanáin CULTURAL CENTRE
(www.culturlann-doire.ie; 37 Great James St) This cultural centre devoted to the Irish language stages performances of traditional Irish music, poetry and dance. Its shop, **An Cló Ceart** (⏲9am-5pm Mon-Fri, to 4pm Sat), sells music as well as arts, crafts and Irish-language books.

Waterside Theatre THEATRE
(www.watersidetheatre.com; Glendermott Rd) Housed in a former factory 500m east of the River Foyle, Waterside stages drama, dance, comedy, children's theatre and live music.

Millennium Forum THEATRE
(www.millenniumforum.co.uk; 98 Newmarket St) Ireland's largest theatre stage, this auditorium is a major venue for dance, drama, concerts, opera and musicals.

Magee College THEATRE
(www.culture.ulster.ac.uk; Northland Rd, Magee College, University of Ulster) The college hosts a variety of arts, theatre and classical-concert performances throughout the year.

Shopping

Craft Village CRAFTS
(www.derrycraftvillage.com; off Shipquay St; ⏲hours vary) A handful of craft shops sells Derry crystal, hand-woven cloth, ceramics, jewellery and other local craft items in this renovated courtyard, which is also home to Café del Mondo, and the wonderful Green Man deli. An **artisan food market** takes place on Fridays from noon to 4pm. Enter from Shipquay St, Magazine St or Tower Museum.

Austins DEPARTMENT STORE
(www.austinsstore.com; 2 The Diamond; ⏲9.30am-5.30pm Mon-Sat, 1-5pm Sun) The world's oldest independent department store, established

1830 and topped by a copper-roofed cupola, is a good place to shop for Irish linen. Purchases can be shipped overseas.

Cowley Cooper Gallery ART
(10-16 Pump St; ⌚10.30am-5pm Tue-Sat) This commercial gallery provides a showcase for contemporary Irish art, selling work by local artists and staging around half a dozen exhibitions each year.

Cool Discs Music MUSIC
(www.cooldiscsmusic.com; 6 Lesley House, Foyle St; ⌚9am-6pm Mon-Thu, 9am-8pm Fri, 8.30am-6pm Sat) One of Northern Ireland's best independent record shops, Cool Discs has a wide selection of music by Irish artists old and new, and sells concert tickets.

Whatnot ANTIQUES
(www.thewhatnot.co.uk; 22 Bishop St Within; ⌚10am-5pm Tue-Sat) Jewellery, militaria, bric-a-brac and collectables cram this interesting little antique shop.

ℹ Information

Derry Tourist Information Centre (☎028-7126 7284; www.visitderry.com; 44 Foyle St; ⌚9am-5.30pm Mon-Fri, 10am-5pm Sat & Sun; 📶) sells books and maps, has a bureau de change and can book accommodation.

ℹ Getting There & Away

AIR

City of Derry Airport (☎028-7181 0784; www.cityofderryairport.com) is about 13km east of Derry along the A2 towards Limavady. Direct flights daily to London Stansted, Liverpool and Glasgow International, plus summer routes to Spain and Portugal.

BUS

The **bus station** (☎028-7126 2261; Foyle St) is just northeast of the walled city.

Services to Northern Ireland destinations are operated by Translink (www.translink.co.uk); destinations in the Republic are served by Bus Éireann (www.buseireann.ie).

Belfast Europa BusCentre £12, 1¾ hours, half-hourly Monday to Friday, hourly Saturday and Sunday
Coleraine £8, one hour, eight daily Monday to Friday, two Sunday (no Saturday service)
Donegal Town £12.60, 1½ hours, six daily
Galway £16.50, 5½ hours, five daily
Letterkenny £5.50, 40 minutes, 10 daily
Limavady £5.20, 30 minutes, at least hourly Monday to Saturday, six Sunday
Omagh (£8, one hour, hourly Monday to Saturday, six Sunday)
Sligo £16.80, 2½ hours, eight daily
Airporter (☎028-7126 9996; http://airporter.co.uk; 1 Bay Rd, Culmore Rd; 📶) Runs direct from Derry to Belfast International Airport (£20, 1½ hours) and George Best Belfast City Airport (£20, two hours) hourly Monday to Friday (six or seven daily Saturday and Sunday). Buses depart from the Airporter office, 1.5km north of city centre, next to Da Vinci's Hotel.

TRAIN

Derry's train station (traditionally referred to as Londonderry in Northern Ireland timetables) is on the eastern side of the River Foyle; a free Rail Link bus connects it with the bus station.

Belfast £12, 2½ hours, nine daily Monday to Saturday, six on Sunday
Coleraine £9.30, 45 minutes, 11 daily Monday to Saturday, six on Sunday
Portrush £12, 1¼ hours, 10 daily Monday to Saturday, six on Sunday

ℹ Getting Around

Bus 234 stops at City of Derry Airport (£3.50, 20 minutes, hourly or better Monday to Saturday, six on Sunday). A taxi costs about £15.

Local buses leave from Foyle St, outside the bus station, leading to the suburbs and surrounding villages.

The **Foyle Valley cycle route** runs through Derry, along the west bank of the river.

Derry Taxi Association (☎028-7126 0247; www.derrytaxis.ie)
Foyle Delta Cabs (☎028-7127 9999; www.foyletaxis.com)
Claudy Cycles (☎07133 8128; www.claudycycles.com; bike hire per half-/full day £8/12) Rents out bikes from the Derry Tourist Information Centre.

Limavady & Around

POP 12,000

Enchanted by a folk tune played by a blind fiddler outside her window in 1851, Limavady (Léim an Mhadaidh) resident Jane Ross (1810–79) jotted down the melody – then known as 'O'Cahan's Lament', and later as the 'Londonderry Air'. The tune came to be known around the world as '**Danny Boy**' – probably the most famous Irish song of all time.

Sights in the neat little town are few, but it makes a pleasant stop.

👁 Sights & Activities

A **blue plaque** on the wall at 51 Main St, opposite the Alexander Arms, commemorates the home of Jane Ross.

Roe Valley Country Park PARK
(9am-dusk) FREE This lovely park, 3km south of Limavady off the B192, has walks stretching for 5km either side of the River Roe. The river is famed for its fishing: salmon season runs from the third week in May until 20 October; trout season starts at Easter and also runs until 20 October. Information is available at www.roeangling.com.

The area is associated with the O'Cahans, who ruled the valley until the Plantation. The 17th-century settlers saw the flax-growing potential of the damp river valley and it became an important linen-manufacturing centre.

Festivals & Events

Danny Boy Jazz and Blues Festival MUSIC
(www.dannyboyjazzandblues.com) Limvady's Danny Boy Jazz and Blues Festival runs over four days at venues across town in mid-June.

Eating

Lime Tree IRISH ££
(028-7776 4300; www.limetreerest.com; 60 Catherine St; mains lunch £8.50-14.50, dinner £14.50-22.50; 5.30-8.30pm Tue & Wed, noon-1.30pm & 5.30-8.30pm Thu, noon-1.30pm & 5.30-9pm Fri, 5.30-9pm Sat;) Streamlined decor in shades of burgundy and beige softened by flickering tea lights creates a relaxing atmosphere in Limavady's best eatery. The menu promotes local produce – from baked cod with potato and roast garlic crust to loin of rabbit with tarragon cream sauce and fillet steak from award-winning butcher Hunter's of Limavady.

Information

The **Tourist Office** (028-7776 0650; 24 Main St; 9.30am-5pm Mon-Wed & Sat, 9.30am-9.30pm Thu & Fri) is in the Roe Valley Arts Centre.

Getting There & Away

Bus 234 serves Derry (£5.20, at least hourly Monday to Saturday, six on Sunday).

Getting Around

Roe Valley Cycles (028-7776 6406; www.roevalleycycles.co.uk; 35 Catherine St; bikes per day £10; 9am-6pm Mon-Sat) rents bikes for a spin through the Roe Valley.

Magilligan Point

The huge triangular spit of land that almost closes off the mouth of Lough Foyle is mostly taken up by a military firing range, and is home to a once-notorious prison. Still, it's worth a visit for its vast sandy beaches – **Magilligan Strand** to the west, and the 9km sweep of **Benone Strand** to the northeast. The latter provides a superb venue for kite buggies and blokarts (mini land yachts).

On the point itself, watching over the entrance to Lough Foyle, stands a **Martello tower**, built during the Napoleonic Wars in 1812 to guard against French invasion.

Benone Tourist Complex (028-7775 0555; http://benoneni.com; 59 Benone Ave; tent sites £21.50, camping huts £50; 9am-9pm Jul & Aug, to dusk Apr-Jun & Sep, to 4pm Oct-Mar;), adjacent to Benone Strand, has sites for tents and caravans as well as basic camping huts, with a heater and kettle, sleeping up to six people. There's an outdoor heated pool, a children's pool, tennis courts, minigolf and a nine-hole golf course.

Magilligan Point is linked to Greencastle, County Donegal, by the Lough Foyle Ferry.

LOUGH FOYLE FERRY

The **Lough Foyle Ferry** (07493 81901; www.foyleferry.com; one-way car/adult/child £12/2.30/1) runs between Magilligan Point and Greencastle in County Donegal year-round. The trip takes 10 minutes and runs hourly from 8am Monday to Friday and 9am Saturday and Sunday, departing on the hour from Greencastle, 15 minutes past from Magilligan. The last ferry is at 9.15pm from June to August, 8.15pm in May, 7.15pm in April and September, and 6.15pm from October to March.

Downhill

The twin draws of this stretch of coast are the sprawling Downhill Demesne and sweeping surf beach below.

From Downhill, the scenic Bishop's Road climbs steeply up through a ravine and heads over the hills to Limavady. There are spectacular views over Lough Foyle, Donegal and the Sperrin Mountains from the Gortmore picnic area, and from the clifftop at Binevenagh Lake.

Sights & Activities

★ **Downhill Demesne** HISTORIC SITE
(www.nationaltrust.org.uk; adult/child £4.50/2.30; dawn–dusk) In 1774 the Bishop of Derry (fourth Earl of Bristol, Frederick Augustus

Hervey), built a palatial home amid a 160-hectare demesne. The house burnt down in 1851, was rebuilt in 1876, and abandoned after WWII. The **ruins** now stand forlornly on a clifftop, with beautiful gardens below.

The domed, colonnaded **Mussenden Temple**, built by the bishop for his library (some say his mistress), is a *Game of Thrones* icon.

Enter via the coast road's Lion's Gate or Bishop's Gate.

Also here is the whitewashed, 17th-century **Hezlett House** (10am to 5pm April to September), one of Ireland's oldest thatched cottages, with exhibits on rural Irish life.

Long Line Surf School SURFING

(☎07738 128507; http://longlinesurfschool.co.uk; Downhill Strand; ⏲9.30am-5pm Easter–Sep, by appointment rest of yr) Long Line sets up on Downhill Strand, where it rents surfboards (per two hours/day £15/25) and bodyboards (£10/15) including wetsuits. You can also take 2½-hour group lessons in surfing (£25) and SUP (stand-up paddleboarding; £30).

Sleeping

★Downhill Beach House HOSTEL ££

(☎028-7084 9077; http://downhillbeachhouse.com; 12 Mussenden Rd; dm/d from £19/46, f from £46 plus per child £5; @ 📶 👪) Tucked beneath the sea cliffs overlooking the beach, this beautifully restored late-19th-century house offers comfortable accommodation in six-bed dorms, doubles and family rooms. There's a big lounge with an open fire and a view of the sea, and a self-catering kitchen (but no shops nearby so bring supplies with you).

Getting There & Away

Bus 134 between Limavady (£4.40, 35 minutes, nine daily Monday to Friday, six Saturday) and Coleraine (£2.70, 15 minutes) stops at Downhill, as does bus 234 between Derry (£5.20, 35 minutes, half-hourly Monday to Friday, hourly Saturday, seven Sunday) and Coleraine (£2.70, 10 minutes).

Portstewart

POP 7800

Ever since Victorian times, when English novelist William Thackeray described it as having an 'air of comfort and neatness', the seaside and golfing resort of Portstewart has cultivated a sedate, upmarket atmosphere that distinguishes it from populist Portrush, 6km further east. However, there's also a sizeable student community from the University of Ulster in Coleraine.

Sights & Activities

Portstewart's central **promenade** is dominated by the castellated facade of a Dominican college, looming over the seaside.

The **Port Path** is a 10.5km coastal footpath (part of the Causeway Coast Way) that stretches from Portstewart Strand to White Rocks, 3km east of Portrush.

Portstewart Strand BEACH

The broad, 2.5km beach of Portstewart Strand is a 20-minute walk south of the centre along a coastal path, or a short bus ride along Strand Rd. Parking is allowed on the firm sand, which can accommodate over 1000 cars (open year-round, £5 per car from Easter to October).

Portstewart Golf Club GOLF

(☎028-7083 2015; www.portstewartgc.co.uk; 117 Strand Rd; green fees weekday/weekend £110/130) Dating from 1894, renowned Portstewart Golf Club has three courses: the par-72 championship links course the Strand, the par-68 Riverside and the par-64 Old Course. It's on the western side of Portstewart, on the road to Portstewart Strand.

Aquaholics DIVING

(☎028-7083 2584; www.aquaholics.co.uk; 14 Portmore Rd; ⏲dive shop 9am-5.30pm Mon-Sat) The waters around Portstewart abound with marine life and shipwrecks, offering fantastic diving. Aquaholics runs PADI-accredited introductory courses (from £80) and open water courses (from £479), as well as dives (from £46, with gear from £54) to locations including Skerries Cavern, and HMS *Drake* and White Star Line RMS *Laurentic* wrecks. Semidry and drysuits are available for rent.

Festivals & Events

North West 200 Motorcycle Race SPORT

(www.northwest200.org) Ireland's biggest outdoor sporting event is run on a road circuit taking in Portrush, Portstewart and Coleraine; you can see the starting grid painted on the main road at Portstewart's eastern edge. It attracts up to 150,000 spectators; if you're not one of them, it's best to avoid the area on the race weekend. Held in mid May.

Sleeping

Causeway Coast Independent Hostel HOSTEL £

(☎028-7083 3789; 4 Victoria Tce; dm/s/tw from £14/26/40; 📶) This neat terrace house just northeast of the harbour has spacious four-, six- and eight-bed dorms plus a double room, and good power showers. It has its own kitchen, laundry and open fire in winter.

★**Strandeen** B&B ££

(☎028-7083 3872; www.strandeen.com; 63 Strand Rd; d from £90) More like a boutique hotel than a B&B, Strandeen has six beautiful wooden-shuttered rooms with pale grey and blue hues, scrumptious organic and/or free-range breakfasts (sourdough with grilled banana, cinnamon and cashew cream; buckwheat pancakes with streaky bacon), bike rental (per day £15), and an ocean-facing terrace.

Cromore Halt Inn INN ££

(☎028-7083 6888; www.cromorehalt.co.uk; 158 Station Rd; s/d £89/99;) Located about 1km east of the harbour, next door to a petrol station on the corner of Station and Mill Rds, the motel-style Cromore has a dozen modern, businesslike rooms, along with friendly, helpful staff and a decent restaurant.

Cul-Erg B&B B&B ££

(☎028-7083 6610; www.culerg.co.uk; 9 Hillside, Atlantic Circle; s/d/f from £40/80/100;) Warm and welcoming, this family-run B&B inside a modern, flower-bedecked terrace house is just a couple of minutes' walk from the promenade in a quiet cul-de-sac. Rooms at the back have sea views.

Eating & Drinking

Burger Club BURGERS £

(☎028-7083 2302; www.burgerclubni.com; 81 The Promenade; dishes £5-13; noon-10pm;) As well as classic beef burgers (Scarface, Sweet Home Alabama, Cool Runnings), the menu includes Silence of Lambs burgers, Mr Bean veggie burgers, pulled pork, and falafel wraps, with a choice of chunky or skinny fries and crunchy onion rings. Everything is locally sourced, freshly cooked and artfully presented.

Warke's Deli CAFE £

(www.warkesdeli.com; 1 The Promenade; dishes £3-8; 9am-5.30pm Easter–Sep, 9am-5.30pm Mon-Sat Oct-Mar;) Warke's makes everything on the premises – soups, salads, bruschetta and risottos included. If you'd rather a beach picnic, you can get hampers made up. Its corner building (where Portmore Rd meets the Promenade) looks out over the prom, harbour and ocean beyond.

Morelli's CAFE £

(www.morellisofportstewart.co.uk; 53 The Promenade; ice cream from £1.65, dishes £3-9; 9am-11pm, food to 8pm, shorter hours in winter;) Morelli's is a local institution, founded by Italian immigrants and serving up its own ice cream since 1911 along with cafe classics.

★**Harry's Shack** BISTRO ££

(☎028-7083 1783; Portstewart Strand; mains £10-18; 10.30am-4pm & 5-9pm Tue-Sat, 10.30am-7pm Sun) Bang on the beach, this National Trust–owned wooden shack houses one of Northern Ireland's hottest restaurants (book way ahead). Harry's uses fruit, veggies and herbs from its own organic farm and local meat and seafood in simple but sensational dishes like buttermilk-battered, saltwater-cured pollock, brioche burgers, and spiced whitebait served in a newspaper cone. BYO.

Anchor Bar PUB

(www.theanchorbar.co.uk; 87-89 The Promenade; 11.30am-1am Mon-Sat, noon-midnight Sun) Hugely popular with students from the University of Ulster, the Anchor serves great Guinness and decent pub grub, and has live bands Friday and Saturday. The complex includes the Anchorage Bistro, Aura nightclub, and a 20-room hotel (doubles from £80).

Getting There & Away

Buses 140A and 140B ply between Coleraine and Portstewart (£2.70, 20 minutes, every 20 minutes Monday to Saturday, five Sunday) and continue to Portrush (£2.30, 10 minutes).

Seasonal Antrim Coaster and Causeway Rambler buses (p604) stop here.

COUNTY ANTRIM

POP 618,110 / AREA 3046 SQ KM

Portrush

POP 6300

The seaside resort of Portrush (Port Rois) bursts at the seams with holidaymakers in high season and, not surprisingly, many of its attractions are focused unashamedly on good old-fashioned family fun. However, it's also one of Ireland's top surfing centres and home to the North's most prestigious golf club.

Sights & Activities

Portrush generally hosts the Portrush Open Irish Surfing Association competition at Easter, but dates can vary depending on weather conditions.

Curran Strand BEACH

Portrush's main attraction is the beautiful sandy beach of Curran Strand that stretches

CAUSEWAY COAST SEASONAL BUSES

The **Antrim Coaster** (Bus 252; www.translink.co.uk; adult/child £9/4.50; Easter, May bank holiday weekends & Jul-Aug;) has two services in each direction on a seasonal schedule (usually Easter, May bank holiday weekends and July and August) between Coleraine and Larne's bus station. Stops include Portstewart, Portrush, Bushmills, Giant's Causeway, Ballintoy, Ballycastle, Cushendun, Cushendall, Glenariff (Waterfoot), Glenarm and Larne's town-centre train station.

The **Causeway Rambler** (Bus 402; www.translink.co.uk; adult/child £6.50/3.25; Easter–Sep) offers a seasonal service linking Coleraine with Carrick-a-Rede car park via Portstewart, Portrush, Dunluce Castle, Bushmills, Giant's Causeway, Dunseverick Castle and Ballintoy. There are four services daily in April and May, and eight services daily from June to September.

for 3km to the east of the town, ending at the scenic chalk cliffs of White Rocks.

Troggs Surf Shop SURFING
(028-7082 2335; www.troggs.com; 88 Main St; 10am-6pm) From April to November the friendly Troggs Surf Shop offers bodyboard/surfboard hire (per day £7.50/10) and wetsuit hire (per day £7), surf reports and general advice. A two-hour lesson including equipment hire costs £25 per person.

Royal Portrush Golf Club GOLF
(028-7082 2311; www.royalportrushgolfclub.com; Dunluce; green fees weekday/weekend £160/180) Spectacularly sited alongside the Atlantic at the town's eastern edge, 1888-founded Royal Portrush is the only golf club in Ireland to have hosted the Open Championship, in 1951, which it will host again in 2019. It's home to two courses, the par-72 Dunluce, with its water's-edge White Rock (5th) and ravine-set Calamity (14th) holes, and the par-70 Valley.

Sleeping

Portrush Holiday Hostel HOSTEL £
(028-7082 1288; www.portrushholidayhostel.com; 24 Princess St; dm/d from £15/34;) Just a few minutes' walk from both beach and harbour, this popular hostel is set in a Victorian terrace house, but feels cosy rather than cramped. Staff are friendly and helpful, and facilities include a washing machine, barbecue area and secure storage for bikes.

Clarmont B&B ££
(028-7082 2397; www.clarmontguesthouse.com; 10 Landsdowne Cres; d from £70;) The pick of Portrush's guesthouses, the refurbished Clarmont has great views and decor that tastefully mixes Victorian and modern styles, from polished pine floors to period fireplaces. Ask for one of the bay-window bedrooms with sea views and spa.

Royal Court Hotel HOTEL £££
(028-7082 2236; www.royalcourthotel.co.uk; 233 Ballybogey Rd; d/f from £121/150;) Overlooking the beach and Royal Portrush golf course 3.5km east of the centre, this is Portrush's top hotel. Some of its 18 rooms have balconies with ocean views and/or spa baths.

Eating

Arcadia CAFE £
(www.arcadiaportrush.co.uk; East Strand; dishes £3-6; 9am-6pm Apr-Sep, to 5pm Oct-Mar) A Portrush landmark, this 1920s art deco pavilion houses a breezy beach cafe on the ground floor, serving big breakfasts, bagels, salads and ice cream for a post-surf refuel, and a free art gallery on the upper floor, which also hosts workshops and classes (yoga, painting et al).

55 Degrees North INTERNATIONAL ££
(028-7082 2811; www.55-north.com; 1 Causeway St; mains £10-19; 12.30-3pm & 5-9pm Mon-Fri, noon-10pm Sat, noon-8.30pm Sun;) Floor-to-ceiling windows allow you to soak up a spectacular panorama of sand and sea from this stylish restaurant. The food concentrates on clean, simple flavours. Downstairs, licensed **Café North** (lunch mains £6-8, dinner mains £10-14; 9am-9pm Mon, Tue & Sat, to 6pm Wed-Fri Easter–Sep, reduced hours Oct–Easter) has a beach-facing terrace.

Drinking & Nightlife

Kiwi Brew Bar BAR
(www.kiwisbrewbar.com; 47 Main St; 5pm-1am Mon-Fri, 2pm-1am Sat & Sun) Craft beers at this good-time, Kiwi-owned bar include New Zealand Tui, as well as hard-to-find Irish brews like Pokertree from County Tyrone, and Long Meadow Cider from County Armagh. Its TVs screen surfing and, of course, rugby. Live music plays on weekends, including blues on Sundays. Cash only.

Kelly's Complex CLUB
(www.kellysportrush.co.uk; 1 Bushmills Rd; ⏲9pm-late Wed & Sat) Plain and small-looking from the outside, the tardis effect takes over as you enter a wonderland of five bars and three dance floors at the North's hottest club, just east of town. It's been around since 1996, and has been named in *DJ Magazine's* Top 100 Clubs in the World. **Lush!** remains one of Ireland's best club nights.

Getting There & Around

The **bus** terminal is near the Dunluce Centre. Bus 140A and 140B link Portrush with Portstewart (£2.30, 10 minutes, every 20 minutes Monday to Saturday, five Sunday) and Coleraine (£2.70, 20 minutes). It's also served by seasonal Antrim Coaster and Causeway Rambler buses.

The **train** station is just south of the harbour. Portrush is served by trains from Coleraine (£2.30, 12 minutes, hourly Monday to Saturday, 10 Sunday), where there are connections to Belfast or Derry.

Taxi services include:

Andy Brown's (028-7082 2223; http://andybrowntaxis.co.uk)

North West Taxis (028-7082 4446; www.portrushtaxis.co.uk)

Dunluce Castle

The ruins of **Dunluce Castle** (87 Dunluce Rd; adult/child £5/3; ⏲10am-4pm, last admission 30min before closing) perch atop a dramatic basalt crag 5km east of Portrush, a one-hour walk away along the coastal path. A narrow bridge leads from the mainland courtyard across a dizzying gap to the main part of the fortress. Below, a path leads down from the gatehouse to the Mermaid's Cave beneath the castle crag. All coastal buses stop here.

In the 16th and 17th centuries the castle was the seat of the MacDonnell family (the earls of Antrim from 1620), who built a Renaissance-style manor house within the walls. Part of the castle, including the kitchen, collapsed into the sea in 1639, taking seven servants and that night's dinner with it.

Bushmills

POP 1350

The small town of Bushmills has long been a place of pilgrimage for connoisseurs of Irish whiskey, and is an attractive stop for hikers exploring the Causeway Coast.

Sights & Activities

Old Bushmills Distillery DISTILLERY
(028-2073 3218; www.bushmills.com; Distillery Rd; tour adult/child £7.50/4; ⏲9.15am-5pm Mon-Sat, noon-5pm Sun Mar-Oct, 10am-5pm Mon-Sat, noon-5pm Sun Nov-Feb) Bushmills is the world's oldest legal distillery, having been granted a licence by King James I in 1608. Bushmills whiskey is made with Irish barley and water from St Columb's Rill, a tributary of the River Bush, and matured in oak barrels. During ageing, the alcohol content drops from around 60% to 40%; the spirit lost through evaporation is known as 'the angels' share'. After the tour, you can enjoy a free sample of your choice from Bushmills' range.

In 2015, Bushmills was bought from drinks giant Diageo by Mexican tequila manufacturer Jose Cuervo, returning it to independent ownership.

Giant's Causeway & Bushmills Railway HERITAGE RAILWAY
(028-2073 2844; www.freewebs.com/giantscausewayrailway; adult/child return £5/3) Brought from a private line on the shores of Lough Neagh, the narrow-gauge line and locomotives (two steam and one diesel) follow the route of a 19th-century tourist tramway for 3km from Bushmills to below the Giant's Causeway Visitor Experience. Seasonal trains run hourly between 11am and 5.30pm, departing on the hour from the Causeway, on the half-hour from Bushmills, daily in July and August, and on weekends only from Easter to June and September to October.

Sleeping

Bushmills Hostel HOSTEL £
(028-2073 1222; www.hini.org.uk; 49 Main St; dm/tw from £19.50/41; ⏲closed 11.30am-2.30pm Jul & Aug, 11.30am-5pm Mar-Jun, Sep & Oct; @ 📶 👪) Just off the Diamond in the centre of town, this modern, purpose-built hostel has mostly four- to six-bed dorms. There's also a kitchen, laundry and bike shed. The hostel is open daily March to October, but only Friday and Saturday nights from November to February (when daytime lockouts still apply). Call ahead to check it's staffed before turning up.

Ballyness Caravan Park & B&B B&B ££
(028-2073 2393; www.ballynesscaravanpark.com; 40 Castlecatt Rd; campervan sites £25; ⏲mid-Mar–Oct; 📶) This well-run caravan park (no tents), with woodland areas, wildlife ponds and spacious sites, is about 1km south of Bushmills town centre on the B66.

Bushmills Inn Hotel HOTEL £££
(☎028-2073 3000; www.bushmillsinn.com; 9 Dunluce Rd; d/ste from £178/278; @📶) The Bushmills is an old coaching inn complete with peat fires, gas lamps and a round tower with a secret library. The old part of the hotel has been given over to the restaurant – the luxurious accommodation is in the neighbouring, modern Mill House complex.

Eating

French Rooms CAFE £
(☎028-2073 0033; http://thefrenchrooms.com; 45 Main St; mains breakfast £4-7.50, lunch £6-13, dinner £13-19; ⏰10am-4pm Wed & Sun, to 9pm Thu-Sat) Incorporating a homewares shop and gourmet deli counter, this French-themed emporium with zinc-topped tables is an especially good option for breakfast (croques Monsieur and Madame, crêpes, eggs royale, apple and cinnamon porridge). Lunch and dinner choices span guinea fowl forestière to cajun-seasoned sea bass. There's a charming little garden out back.

★**Bushmills Inn** IRISH ££
(9 Dunluce Rd; mains lunch £10-15, dinner £12.50-23.50; ⏰noon-9.30pm Mon-Sat, 12.30-9pm Sun; 📶) Set in the old 17th-century stables of the Bushmills Inn, this haven has intimate wooden booths and blazing fires, and uses fresh Ulster produce in dishes like onion and Guinness soup, haunch of venision, and traditional Dalriada cullen skink (wood-smoked haddock poached in cream, with poached eggs and new potatoes). Book ahead.

Tartine IRISH, FRENCH ££
(☎028-2073 1044; www.distillersarms.com; 140 Main St; mains £11-22; ⏰5-9pm Wed-Sat, noon-8.30pm Sun) Inside a former pub, with bare boards, exposed stone and glowing fire, Tartine's three interconnecting dining rooms are adorned with Irish art. Local produce is given an inspired French twist: crab crème brûlée; roast pork with cassoulet; and oven-baked rice pudding with date and honey compote.

Getting There & Away

Bus 172 serves Coleraine (£2.70, 20 minutes, eight daily Monday to Friday, three Saturday and Sunday), the Giant's Causeway (£2.30, five minutes) and Ballycastle (£6.30, 45 minutes).

Seasonal services include Antrim Coaster and Causeway Rambler buses (p604), and the Giant's Causeway & Bushmills Railway (p605).

Giant's Causeway

When you first see it you'll understand why the ancients believed the causeway was not a natural feature. The vast expanse of regular, closely packed, hexagonal stone columns beneath the waves looks for all the world like the handiwork of giants.

This spectacular rock formation – a national nature reserve and Northern Ireland's only Unesco World Heritage site – is one of Ireland's most impressive and atmospheric landscape features, but it can get very crowded. If you can, try to visit midweek or out of season to experience it at its most evocative. Sunset in spring and autumn is the best time for photographs.

Visiting the Giant's Causeway itself is free of charge but you pay to use the car park on a combined ticket with the Giant's Causeway Visitor Experience; parking-only tickets aren't available.

Sights & Activities

From the car park, it's an easy 10- to 15-minute walk downhill on a tarmac road (wheelchair accessible) to the Giant's Causeway itself (a shuttle bus also plies the route). However, a much more interesting approach on foot is to follow the clifftop path northeast for 2km to the **Chimney Tops** headland, which has an excellent view of the causeway and the coastline to the west, including Inishowen and Malin Heads.

This pinnacled promontory was bombarded by ships of the Spanish Armada in 1588, (who thought it was Dunluce Castle), and the wreck of the Spanish galleon *Girona* lies just off the tip of the headland. Return towards the car park and about halfway back descend the **Shepherd's Steps** (signposted) to a lower-level footpath that leads down to the causeway. Allow 1½ hours for the round trip.

Alternatively, you can visit the causeway first, then follow the lower coastal path as far as the **Amphitheatre** viewpoint at Port Reostan, passing impressive rock formations such as the **Organ** (a stack of vertical basalt columns resembling organ pipes), and return by climbing the Shepherd's Steps.

You can also follow the clifftop path east as far as Dunseverick or beyond.

Giant's Causeway Visitor Experience INTERPRETATION CENTRE
(☎028-2073 1855; www.nationaltrust.org; adult/child with parking £9/4.50, without parking £7/3.25; ⏰9am-7pm Apr-Sep, to 6pm Feb, Mar & Oct, to

Walking Tour Causeway Coast

START CARRICK-A-REDE
END GIANT'S CAUSEWAY
LENGTH 16.5KM

This spectacular stretch of the Causeway Coast Way is one of the finest coastal walks in Ireland. Be prepared: parts of the walk follow a narrow, muddy path along the top of unfenced cliffs, and can be dangerous in wet and/or windy weather. High tides can temporarily block the way at either end of White Park Bay; check tide times in advance.

After testing your nerve on the **1 Carrick-a-Rede Rope Bridge** (p609), take the path from its **2 Larrybane car park** along a clifftop with views of Sheep Island, then cut inland. At **3 Ballintoy church**, turn right and follow the road down to **4 Ballintoy Harbour**.

Continue along the shoreline past a series of conical sea stacks and arches, and scramble around the foot of a limestone crag to reach the 2km-long sandy sweep of **5 White Park Bay**. The going here is easiest at low tide, when you can walk on the firm sand. At the far end of the bay, scramble over rocks and boulders at the bottom of a high limestone cliff for 250m (slippery in places) to **6 Portbradden**.

Beyond Portbradden, white limestone gives way to black basalt, and the path threads through a natural tunnel in the rocks before weaving around several rocky coves. At tiny **7 Dunseverick Harbour** you follow a minor road for 200m before descending steps on the right. The path then wanders along the grassy foreshore, rounds a headland and crosses a footbridge above a waterfall before reaching **8 Dunseverick Castle**.

From here the often-narrow, clifftop path climbs steadily, passing an **9 old salmon fishery** (the little rusty-roofed cottage on the shore far below). Near Benbane Head, the walk's highest and most northerly point, a wooden bench marks the viewpoint known as **10 Hamilton's Seat** (after 18th-century clergyman and amateur geologist William Hamilton). Soak up the spectacular panorama of 100m-high sea cliffs, stacks and pinnacles stretching away to the west, before you set off on the final stretch. Descend the **11 Shepherd's Steps** (signposted), about 1km before the Giant's Causeway Visitor Experience to reach **12 Giant's Causeway**.

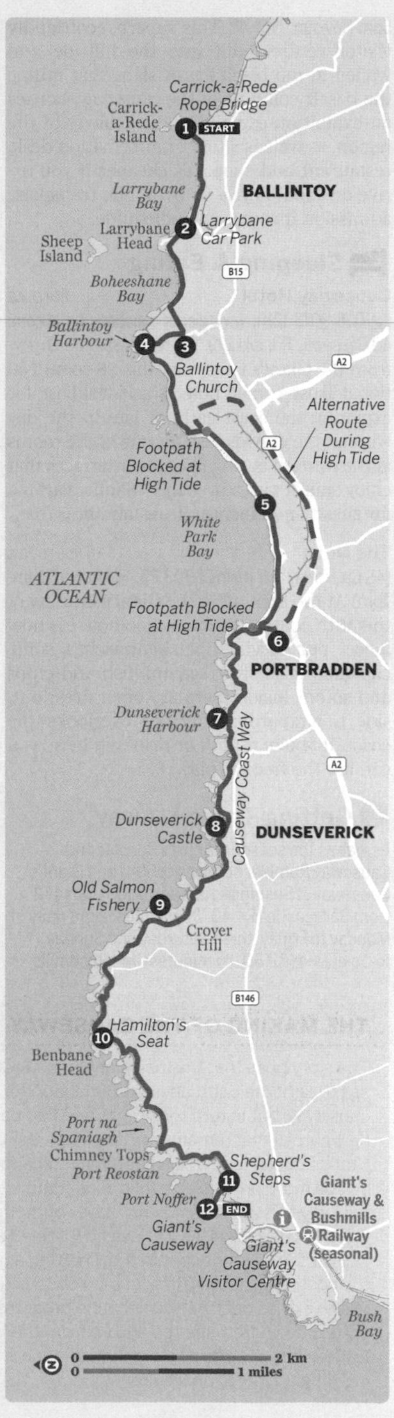

5pm Nov-Jan;) This superb, ecofriendly visitor centre, built into the hillside and walled in tall black basalt slabs that mimic the basalt columns of the causeway, houses an exhibition explaining the geology of the region, as well as a tourist information desk, restaurant and shop. It's cheaper if you arrive on foot, bicycle or by public transport; admission includes an audioguide.

Sleeping & Eating

Causeway Hotel HOTEL ££
(028-9073 1210; www.giants-causeway-hotel.com; 40 Causeway Rd; s/d £79/99;) A stone's throw from the Giant's Causeway, this 28-room National Trust–owned hotel is an ideal base for exploring the coast early or late in the day without the crowds. Ask for one of the rooms at the western end, with outdoor terraces that enjoy sunset views over the Atlantic. Parking for guests and diners at its restaurant is free.

The Nook PUB FOOD £
(48 Causeway Rd; mains £9-12.25; kitchen 11am-7pm) At the turn-off to the Giant's Causeway, this 18th-century former schoolhouse is now a cosy pub serving open sandwiches, soup, chowder, Irish stew, scampi, fish and chips and so on. Inside there are open fires; outside a wraparound terrace overlooks the coast. If you're dining or drinking here, you can use the free car park.

Getting There & Away

As well as the seasonal Antrim Coaster and Causeway Rambler services (p604) and Giant's Causeway & Bushmills Railway (p605), bus 172 from Ballycastle (£4.40, 30 minutes, eight daily Monday to Friday, three Saturday and Sunday) to Coleraine (£2.80, 25 minutes) and Bushmills (£2.30, five minutes) stops here year-round. From Coleraine, trains run to Belfast or Derry.

Getting Around

It's an easy 1km-walk from the Giant's Causeway Visitor Experience car park down to the causeway but **minibuses** (one-way/return £1/2) ply the route every 15 minutes.The buses are wheelchair accessible.

Giant's Causeway to Ballycastle

The Causeway Coast is at its most scenic between the Giant's Causeway and Ballycastle, with sea cliffs of contrasting black basalt and white chalk, rocky islands, picturesque little harbours and broad sweeps of sandy beach.

Sights & Activities

The main attractions can be reached by car or bus, but the 16.5km stretch between the Carrick-a-Rede car park and the Giant's Causeway is best enjoyed on a walk (p607) following the waymarked **Causeway Coast Way** (www.walkni.com).

About 9.5km east of the Giant's Causeway is the tiny seaside hamlet of **Portbradden**, with half a dozen harbourside houses. Visible from Portbradden and accessible via the next junction off the A2 is the spectacular **White Park Bay**, with its wide sandy beach.

Some 3km further east is **Ballintoy** (Baile an Tuaighe). This pretty village tumbles down the hillside to a picture-postcard harbour, better known to *Game of Thrones* fans as the Iron Islands' Lordsport Harbour (among other scenes filmed here). The re-

THE MAKING OF THE CAUSEWAY

The story goes that the Irish giant Finn McCool built the causeway so he could cross the sea to fight the Scottish giant Benandonner. Benandonner pursued Finn back across the causeway, but in turn took fright and fled back to Scotland, ripping up the causeway as he went. All that remains are its ends – the Giant's Causeway in Ireland, and the island of Staffa in Scotland (which has similar rock formations).

The more prosaic scientific explanation is that the causeway rocks were formed 60 million years ago, when a thick layer of molten basaltic lava flowed along a valley in the existing chalk beds. As the lava flow cooled and hardened – from the top and bottom surfaces inward – it contracted, creating a pattern of hexagonal cracks at right angles to the cooling surfaces (think of mud contracting and cracking in a hexagonal pattern as a lakebed dries out). As solidification progressed towards the centre of the flow, the cracks spread down from the top and up from the bottom, until the lava was completely solid. Erosion has cut into the lava flow, and the basalt has split along the contraction cracks, creating the hexagonal columns.

stored limekiln on the quayside once made quicklime using stone from the chalk cliffs and coal from Ballymoney.

★ Carrick-a-Rede Rope Bridge BRIDGE
(www.nationaltrust.org.uk; Ballintoy; adult/child £5.90/3; ⏲9.30am-7.30pm Apr-Aug, to 6pm late Feb–late Mar & Sep–late Oct, to 3.30pm late Oct–late Feb) This 20m-long, 1m-wide bridge of wire rope spans the chasm between the sea cliffs and the little island of Carrick-a-Rede, swaying 30m above the rock-strewn water. Crossing the bridge is perfectly safe, but frightening if you don't have a head for heights, especially if it's breezy (in high winds the bridge is closed). From the island, views take in Rathlin Island and Fair Head to the east.

There's a small National Trust information centre and cafe at the car park.

Carrick-a-Rede has sustained a salmon fishery for centuries; fishermen stretch their nets out from the tip of the island to intercept the passage of salmon migrating along the coast to their home rivers. The fishermen put the bridge up every spring.

Kinbane Castle CASTLE
(Whitepark Rd) FREE On a limestone headland jutting out from the basalt cliffs, with stupendous views of Rathlin Island and Scotland, this ruined castle was first built in 1547 by Colla MacDonnell (son of Alexander MacDonnell, Lord of Islay and Kintyre, and Catherine, daughter of the Lord of Ardnamurchan), and rebuilt in 1555 following an English siege. It was inhabited until the 17th century, when it was abandoned. From the car park, 140 steep steps lead down to the castle.

Sleeping & Eating

Sheep Island View Hostel HOSTEL £
(☎028-2076 9391; www.sheepislandview.com; 42a Main St; dm/d/tr/f £18/40/60/80; @📶) This excellent independent hostel offers dorm beds in its camping barn and basic rooms with private bathroom. There's a kitchen and laundry and a village store nearby. It's on the main coast road near the turn-off to Ballintoy Harbour, with a bus stop at the door, and makes a handy overnight stop if you're hiking between Bushmills and Ballycastle.

Whitepark Bay Hostel HOSTEL £
(☎028-2073 1745; www.hini.org.uk; 157 White Park Rd, Ballintoy; dm/tw from £18/42; ⏲mid-Mar–Oct; 📶) Near the west end of White Park Bay, this modern, purpose-built hostel has mostly four-bed dorms, plus twin rooms with TV, all with private bathroom. The common room is warmed by a fireplace and positioned to soak up the view, and the beach is just a few minutes' walk through the dunes.

★ Kinbane Farmhouse B&B ££
(☎028-2076 9947; www.kinbane.com; 85 Whitepark Rd; s/d £35/60; 📶) Just by Kinbane Castle, this wonderfully welcoming working farmstead has three pine-furnished guest rooms (all have private bathroom, but one's outside the room), a toasty turf fire, and binoculars for zooming in on Rathlin Island and Scotland beyond.

Whitepark House B&B £££
(☎028-2073 1482; www.whiteparkhouse.com; 150 White Park Rd, Ballintoy; s/d £80/120; 📶) A beautifully restored 18th-century house overlooking White Park Bay, this B&B has traditional features such as antique furniture and a peat fire complemented by Asian artefacts gathered during the welcoming owners' travels. There are three rooms – ask for one with a sea view.

Roark's Kitchen CAFE £
(Ballintoy Harbour; mains £4-8; ⏲11am-7pm Jun-Aug, Sat & Sun only May & Sep, closed rest of year) On the quayside at Ballintoy Harbour, this cute little chalk-built tea room serves teas, coffees, ice cream, home-baked apple, cherry and rhubarb tart, and lunch dishes such as Irish stew or chicken and ham pie.

Red Door Cottage CAFE £
(☎028-2076 9048; 14a Harbour Rd, Ballintoy; dishes £3.75-9; ⏲11am-4pm Mon-Fri, 10am-4pm Sat & Sun Mar-Sep, 11am-4pm Sat & Sun Oct-Dec, closed Jan & Feb) Fronted by a fire-engine-red door, this little cottage sits 200m off the main coast road along the side road to Ballintoy. Everything is homemade: soups, chowders, burgers, Irish stew, and cakes (including strawberry shortcake). The garden's picnic tables are idyllic in the sunshine; when it's chilly there's a turf fire indoors. It's worth booking ahead in peak holiday seasons.

Getting There & Away

Bus 172 between Ballycastle, Bushmills and Coleraine (eight daily Monday to Friday, three daily Saturday and Sunday) is the main, year-round service along this coast, stopping at the Giant's Causeway, Ballintoy and Carrick-a-Rede. The Antrim Coaster and Causeway Rambler buses (p604) cover the route in season.

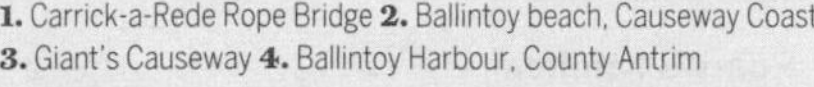

1. Carrick-a-Rede Rope Bridge **2.** Ballintoy beach, Causeway Coast
3. Giant's Causeway **4.** Ballintoy Harbour, County Antrim

DESIGN PICS/THE IRISH IMAGE COLLECTION/GETTY IMAGES ©

Counties Londonderry & Antrim: The Causeway Coast

The north coast of County Antrim from Ballycastle west to Portrush is known as the Causeway Coast, one of the most impressively scenic stretches of coastline in all of Ireland. Whether you drive, cycle or walk its length, it's not to be missed.

Giant's Causeway

The grand geological centrepiece of the Antrim coast is the Giant's Causeway, a spectacular rock formation composed of countless hexagonal basalt columns. A Unesco World Heritage site, it is the north coast's most popular tourist attraction.

Causeway Coast

The Causeway Coast isn't just about the scenery. There are picturesque villages at Ballintoy and Portbradden, historic ruined fortresses at Dunluce and Dunseverick castles, and the chance to savour a dram of Irish whiskey at Old Bushmills Distillery.

Carrick-a-Rede Rope Bridge

Originally rigged and used by local salmon fishermen, the famous Carrick-a-Rede Rope Bridge is now a popular test of nerve for Causeway Coast visitors, swaying gently 30m above the rocks and the sea.

Antrim Coast

Although famous for its dramatic sea-cliff scenery, the Antrim coast also has some excellent sandy beaches. As well as the family-friendly strand at Ballycastle, there's the harder-to-reach but twice-as-beautiful White Park Bay.

Ballycastle

POP 4000

The harbour town and holiday resort of Ballycastle (Baile an Chaisil) marks the eastern end of the Causeway Coast. It's a pretty town with a good bucket-and-spade beach. Apart from that, there's not a lot to see. Ferries to Rathlin Island depart from here.

Sights & Activities

Ballycastle has a family-friendly **promenade**, with a giant sandpit for kids overlooking the marina. A footbridge leads east across the mouth of the River Glenshesk to a good sandy **beach**.

Marconi Memorial MONUMENT

In the harbour car park, a plaque at the foot of a rock pinnacle commemorates the day in 1898 when Guglielmo Marconi's assistants contacted Rathlin Island by radio from Ballycastle to prove to Lloyd's of London that wireless communication was a viable proposition. The idea was to send notice to London or Liverpool of ships arriving safely after a transatlantic crossing – most vessels on this route would have to pass through the channel north of Rathlin.

Festivals & Events

Ould Lammas Fair CULTURE

Ballycastle's Ould Lammas Fair dates back to 1606. Thousands of people descend on the town for the market stalls and fairground rides, and to sample 'yellowman' (a hard chewy toffee-like honeycomb) and dulse (dried edible seaweed). Held on the last Monday and Tuesday of August.

Sleeping

Ballycastle Backpackers HOSTEL £

(028-2076 3612; www.ballycastlebackpackers.net; 4 North St; dm/tw from £15/35, cottage £80;) Overlooking the harbour, this small, homey terrace house has one six-bed dorm, a family room and a couple of twin and double rooms. There's also a cosy self-catering cottage in the backyard, containing two twin rooms and a private bathroom (minimum two nights).

Watertop Open Farm CAMPGROUND £

(028-2076 2576; www.watertopfarm.co.uk; 188 Cushendall Rd; tent sites for two people £15, per additional person £5, caravan sites from £24; Easter–Oct;) About 10km east of Ballycastle on the road to Cushendun, family favourite Watertop is based at a working farm and **activity centre** (open 11am to 5.30pm; per activity adult/child £3/2), offering pony trekking, sheep shearing and farm tours.

An Caislean Guesthouse GUESTHOUSE ££

(028-2076 2845; www.ancaislean.co.uk; 42 Quay Rd; dm/s/d/f from £20/40/80/110;) Originally two guesthouses, now linked by a covered walkway, An Caislean has a luxurious lounge, a summer tea room and restaurant, and a warm and welcoming family atmosphere. Rooms are spacious and comfortable, if a bit creaky in the floorboard department, but the trump card is the location, just a few minutes' walk from the beach.

Eating

★**Morton's Fish & Chips** FISH & CHIPS £

(The Harbour, Bayview Rd; fish £1.90-5.40, chips £1.20-2.40; 3-8pm Mon-Thu, noon-9pm Fri & Sat, 1-8pm Sun) Fish and chips don't come fresher: local boats unload their daily catch right alongside this little harbourside hut. The cod, haddock, sea bass, scallops, scampi et al, as well as chips made from locally farmed potatoes, see huge queues in summer (expect to wait). Gluten-free options, cooked in separate oil, are also available.

Thyme & Co CAFE £

(www.thymeandco.co.uk; 5 Quay Rd; dishes £3.50-7; 8.30am-4.30pm Tue-Fri, 8.30am-10pm Sat, 10am-3.30pm Sun;) Lush salads, shepherd's pie, and salmon and egg crumble are among the homemade dishes prepared using local produce at this welcoming cafe. Many of its cakes and bakes are gluten-free; there's excellent coffee, too. Saturday nights offer various specials, such as pizza.

Cellar Restaurant IRISH ££

(028-2076 3037; www.cellarballycastle.com; 11b The Diamond; mains £13-25; noon-10pm daily Jun-Aug, 5-9.30pm Sun-Fri, noon-10pm Sat Sep-May) Down a flight of steps from the street, this cosy little basement restaurant with intimate wooden booths and a big slate fireplace is a good place to sample Ulster produce like locally caught crab claws grilled, Carrick-a-Rede salmon and Rathlin Island lobster, along with Irish beef and lamb.

Drinking & Nightlife

O'Connor's PUB

(http://oconnorsbar.ie; 5-7 Ann; 11.30am-1am) Just off the Diamond, O'Connor's is Ballycastle's best pub for music, with trad Thursday nights year-round. From Easter to

September, there's also trad on Wednesday, folk and singalongs on Friday, bands in the bar and DJs in the beer garden on Saturday, and jam sessions on Sunday. Hearty food is served non-stop until 9pm.

Information

Ballycastle Visitor Centre (028-2076 2024; www.heartofthecausewaycoastandglens.com; 14 Bayview Rd; 9.30am-7pm Mon-Fri, 10am-5pm Sat & Sun Jul & Aug, 9.30am-5pm Mon-Fri, 10am-4pm Sat Sep-Jun) is on the road leading to the Rathlin Island ferry.

Getting There & Away

The bus station is on Station Rd, just east of the Diamond. Bus 217 links Ballycastle with Ballymena (£6.70, 50 minutes, hourly Monday to Friday, five Saturday) where you can connect to Belfast.

Bus 172 goes along the coast to Coleraine (£6.70, one hour, eight daily Monday to Friday, three Saturday and Sunday) via Ballintoy, the Giant's Causeway and Bushmills.

The seasonal Antrim Coaster (p604) also stops here.

Kintyre Express (01586 555895; www.kintyreexpress.com) runs high-speed passenger ferries link Ballycastle with Campbeltown, Scotland (one way/return £35/60, 1½ hours, one daily May to September).

A separate one-hour service runs to Port Ellen on Islay, Scotland (one way/return £55/95, one hour, one daily Friday to Monday June to August).

WORTH A TRIP

KINGSROAD

Planted by the Stuart family in the 18th century as the formal entrance to their property, the shadowy, gnarled, entwined beech trees of **Dark Hedges** (Bregagh Rd, Ballymoney) are now among Northern Ireland's most photographed sights after doubling as the Kingsroad in *Game of Thrones*. Getting a photo without cars (and crowds) isn't easy: do your fellow fans a favour and park at either end of the tree-covered road and walk up. The Dark Hedges are 14km southwest of Ballycastle via the A44 and Ballykenver Rd.

The most atmospheric time to visit is at sunset.

Rathlin Island

POP 110

Rugged Rathlin Island sits 6km offshore from Ballycastle. An L-shaped island just 6.5km long and 4km wide, Rathlin is home to hundreds of seals and thousands of nesting seabirds in spring and summer.

Scottish hero Robert the Bruce spent time here in 1306 while hiding out after being defeated by the English king. Watching a spider's resoluteness in repeatedly trying to spin a web gave him the courage to have another go at the English, whom he subsequently defeated at Bannockburn. The cave where he is said to have stayed is beneath the East Lighthouse, at the northeastern tip of the island.

Sights & Activities

Rathlin is famous for the coastal scenery and birdlife at **Kebble National Nature Reserve** at the island's western end.

If you don't have time to visit the Kebble Nature Reserve, the best short walk on the island is through the National Trust's **Ballyconagan Nature Reserve** to the Old Coastguard Lookout on the north coast, with great views along the sea cliffs and across to the Scottish islands of Islay and Jura.

The island is surrounded by some 40 shipwrecks, including the HMS *Drake* (which can be dived with Aquaholics; p602).

RSPB Rathlin Seabird Centre WILDLIFE RESERVE
(www.rspb.org.uk; 10am-4pm Apr-Aug) FREE At the refurbished Rathlin West Lighthouse, this Royal Society for the Protection of Birds (RSPB) centre provides stunning views of the neighbouring sea stacks, thick with guillemots, kittiwakes, razorbills and puffins. Binoculars and telescopes are free to use; there's a cafe and gift shop here.

Boathouse Visitor Centre VISITOR CENTRE
(07708 869605; www.rathlincommunity.org; 9.30am-12.30pm & 1-5pm Apr-Sep) South of the harbour, this combined visitor centre/museum details the history, culture and ecology of the island, and can give advice on walks and wildlife.

Paul Quinn WALKING TOUR
(07745 566924; www.rathlinwalkingtours.com; per person from £4) Insightful guide Paul Quinn offers entertaining walking tours of the island.

Sleeping & Eating

The island has a pub, a shop and a handful of sleeping and eating options (much of it seasonal); it's essential to book accommodation in advance.

Rathlin Island Hostel HOSTEL £
(☎ 028-2076 0070; dm £18; 👪) Just a five-minute walk south of the harbour, this hostel opened in 2014. The five simple but bright rooms have four to 12 beds, with the option to book each as a private room (£67 to £200). All share bathrooms (including one for visitors with limited mobility). There's a self-catering kitchen and fantastic ocean-view terrace. Cash only.

Kinramer Camping Barn HOSTEL £
(☎ 028-2076 3948; Kinramer; dm £12) Kinramer is a basic bunkhouse located on an organic farm, 5km (a one-hour walk) west from the harbour. You'll need to bring your own food and bedding.

Coolnagrock B&B B&B ££
(☎ 028-2076 3983; Coolnagrock; s/d from £35/70; ⏱ closed Dec; 📶) Views stretch across the sea to Kintyre from this well-appointed guesthouse in the eastern part of the island. It's a 15-minute walk from the ferry, but you can arrange for the owner to pick you up.

Emma's Chip Ahoy FISH & CHIPS £
(www.emmaschipahoy.com; The Harbour; dishes £3-5.60; ⏱ 1-6pm May-Sep, 1-6pm Tue, Fri & Sat Oct-Apr; 👪) By the harbour in a small cottage, Emma's cooks up daily caught fish as well as crab burgers (and double-cheese burgers, and veggie burgers), pan-fried mackerel, scampi, chicken goujons and battered sausages.

Drinking & Nightlife

McCuaig's Bar PUB
(☎ 028-2076 0011; The Harbour; ⏱ 11am-midnight; 📶) Rathlin Island's pub and beer garden overlooks the harbour, with wooden picnic tables providing an idyllic spot for a pint. Inside, historic black-and-white photos of Rathlin line the walls. There's an ATM here.

Getting There & Around

Only residents can take their car to Rathlin (except for disabled drivers), but nowhere on the island is more than 6km (about 1½ hours' walk) from the ferry pier.

Rathlin Island Ferry (☎ 028-2076 9299; www.rathlinballycastleferry.com; adult/child/bicycle return £12/6/3.30) operates daily services from Ballycastle; advance booking is essential. From April to mid-September there are up to 10 crossings a day, half of which are fast catamaran services (20 minutes), the rest via a slower car ferry (45 minutes). In winter the service is reduced.

McGinn's (☎ 028-2076 3451; per adult/child £5/3) shuttles visitors between the ferry and Kebble Nature Reserve from April to August; contact the company for other transport requests.

Glens of Antrim

The northeastern corner of Antrim is a high plateau of black basalt lava overlying beds of white chalk. Along the coast, between Cushendun and Glenarm, the plateau has been dissected by a series of scenic, glacier-gouged valleys known as the Glens of Antrim.

Two waymarked footpaths traverse the region: the **Ulster Way** sticks close to the sea, passing through all the coastal villages, while the 32km **Moyle Way** runs inland across the high plateau from Glenariff Forest Park to Ballycastle.

Torr Head Scenic Road

A few kilometres east of Ballycastle, a minor road signposted 'Scenic Route' branches north off the A2. This alternative route to Cushendun is not for the faint-hearted driver (nor for caravans), as it clings, precarious and narrow, to steep slopes high above the sea. Side roads lead off to the main points of interest. On a clear day, there are superb views across the sea to Scotland, from the Mull of Kintyre to the peaks of Arran.

The first turn-off ends at the National Trust car park at Coolanlough, the starting point for a waymarked 5km return hike to **Fair Head**. The second turn-off leads steeply down to **Murlough Bay**. From the parking area at the end of this road, you can walk north along the shoreline to some ruined miners' cottages (10 minutes); coal and chalk were once mined in the cliffs above, and burned in a limekiln (south of the car park) to make quicklime.

The third turn-off leads you past some ruined coastguard houses to the rocky headland of **Torr Head**, crowned with a 19th-century coastguard station (abandoned in the 1920s). This is Ireland's closest point to Scotland – the Mull of Kintyre is a mere 19km away across the North Channel. In late spring and summer, a fixed-net salmon fishery operates here. The ancient icehouse beside the approach road was once used to store the catch.

Cushendun

POP 350

The pretty seaside village of Cushendun is famous for its distinctive Cornish-style cottages, now owned by the National Trust. Built between 1912 and 1925 at the behest of the local landowner, Lord Cushendun, they were designed by Clough Williams-Ellis, the architect of Portmeirion in north Wales.

Sights & Activities

Cushendun has a sandy **beach**, various short **coastal walks** (outlined on an information board beside the car park), and some impressive **caves** – a *Game of Thrones* filming location – cut into the overhanging conglomerate sea cliffs south of the village (follow the trail around the far end of the holiday apartments south of the river mouth).

Some 6km north of the village on the A2 road to Ballycastle is **Loughareema**, also known as the Vanishing Lake. Three streams flow in but none flow out. The lough fills up to a respectable size (400m long and 6m deep) after heavy rain, but the water gradually drains away through fissures in the underlying limestone, leaving a dry lakebed.

Sleeping & Eating

The kitchen at Mary McBride's pub keeps unreliable hours; Cushendall is the nearest place where you can be sure of finding an evening meal.

★Villa Farmhouse B&B ££
(☎028-2176 1252; www.thevillafarmhouse.com; 185 Torr Rd; s/d from £35/60; 📶) This lovely old whitewashed farmhouse is set on a hillside, 1km north of Cushendun, with great views over the bay and the warm atmosphere of a family home, decorated with photos of children and grandchildren. The owner is an expert chef and breakfast will be a highlight of your stay – best scrambled eggs in Northern Ireland?

Cloneymore House B&B ££
(☎028-2176 1443; ann.cloneymore@btinternet.com; 103 Knocknacarry Rd; s/d £50/60; 📶 👪) A traditional family B&B on the B92 road 500m southwest of Cushendun, Cloneymore has three spacious and spotless rooms named after Irish and Scottish islands – Aran is the biggest. There are wheelchair ramps and a stairlift, and rooms are equipped for visitors with limited mobility.

Drinking

Randal's PUB
(10 Strand View Park; ⏲11.30am-11.30pm) By the bridge, Randal's occupies a pair of vintage rooms in what was the Cushendun Hotel. There are just two choices on tap – Guinness and Harp – but also a great selection of whiskeys. On sunny days, the best seats are on the pavement overlooking the River Dun.

Getting There & Away

Bus 150 runs from Ballymena (£6.70, one hour, six daily Monday to Friday, four Saturday) to Cushendun via Glenariff Forest Park (£6.20, 40 minutes) and Cushendall (£6.30, 50 minutes).

The seasonal Antrim Coaster (p604) also stops here.

Cushendall

POP 1250

Despite its small, shingly beach, Cushendall is a holiday centre (and traffic bottleneck) at the foot of Glenballyeamon, overlooked by the prominent flat-topped hill of Lurigethan.

Sights

Curfew Tower HISTORIC BUILDING
The unusual red sandstone Curfew Tower at the central crossroads was built in 1817, based on a building the landowner had seen in China. It was originally a prison 'for the confinement of idlers and rioters'.

Layd Old Church RUINS
From the car park beside the beach (follow the golf club signs), a coastal path leads 1km north to the picturesque ruins of Layd Old Church, with views across to Ailsa Craig (a prominent conical island also known as 'Paddy's Milestone') and the Scottish coast. Founded by the Franciscans, it was used as a parish church from the early 14th century until 1790. The graveyard contains several grand MacDonnell memorials.

Sleeping & Eating

Village B&B B&B ££
(☎028-2177 2366; www.thevillagebandb.com; 18 Mill St; s/d/f from £40/65/95; 📶 👪) Right in the middle of town, the Village offers three spotless rooms with private bathrooms and fireplaces, and huge hearty breakfasts (including a vegetarian option).

Cullentra House B&B ££
(☎028-2177 1762; www.cullentrahouse.com; 16 Cloughs Rd; s/d from £35/54; 📶) This modern

bungalow sits high above the village, offering good views of the craggy Antrim coast. The three rooms are spacious and comfy, and the breakfasts (accompanied by home-baked bread) are as hearty as the owners' hospitality.

Harry's Restaurant BISTRO ££
(☎028-2177 2022; http://harryscushendall.com; 10 Mill St; mains lunch £8-13, dinner £10-19; ⊙noon-10pm Easter–Sep, to 9pm Oct–Easter; 📶) With its cosy lounge-bar atmosphere and friendly welcome, Harry's is a local institution, serving pub grub staples from noon to 6pm plus an à la carte evening menu that ranges from steak to lobster.

Drinking

McCollam's PUB
(Johnny Joe's; www.mccollamsbar.com; 23 Mill St; ⊙noon-11.30pm) Locally known as Johnny Joe's, this rhubarb-coloured pub is the town's liveliest. Trad music plays every Friday year-round, plus every Tuesday, Saturday and Sunday from Easter to September. Its restaurant (called Upstairs at Joe's, or just Upstairs) serves pub classics like battered scampi and steak-and-Guinness pie.

Information

The **Tourist Office** (☎028-2177 1180; 24 Mill St; ⊙10am-1pm Mon-Sat Apr-Sep, 10am-1pm Tue-Sat Oct-Mar) is run by the Glens of Antrim Historical Society.

Getting There & Away

Bus 150 links Cushendall with Cushendun (£2.70, 40 minutes, eight daily Monday to Friday, four Saturday) and Glenariff Forest Park (£3, 45 minutes).

It's also on the seasonal Antrim Coaster (p604) route.

Glenariff

About 2km south of Cushendall is the village of **Waterfoot**, with a 2km-long sandy beach, the best on Antrim's east coast. From here the A43 Ballymena road runs inland along Glenariff, the loveliest of Antrim's glens. Views of the valley led the writer Thackeray to exclaim that it was a 'Switzerland in miniature' (a claim that makes you wonder if he'd ever been to Switzerland).

Sights & Activities

Glenariff Forest Park FOREST
(www.nidirect.gov.uk; car/motorcycle/pedestrian £5/2.50/2; ⊙10am-dusk) At the head of the Glenariff Valley is Glenariff Forest Park, where the main attraction is **Ess-na-Larach Waterfall**, an 800m walk from the visitor centre. You can also walk to the waterfall from Laragh Lodge, 600m downstream. Wonderful hikes in the park include a 10km circular trail. There are plans to build a caravan park here.

Sleeping & Eating

Ballyeamon Barn HOSTEL £
(☎028-2175 8451; www.ballyeamonbarn.com; 127 Ballyeamon Rd; dm £15; 📶) Run by professional storyteller Liz Weir, this whitewashed barn has hostel accommodation for hikers and hosts regular sessions of traditional Irish music, poetry, dance and storytelling. It's 8km southwest of Cushendall on the B14 (1km north of its junction with the A43), close to the Moyle Way and about 1.5km walk from the main entrance to the forest park.

Laragh Lodge PUB FOOD ££
(☎028-2175 8221; 120 Glen Rd; mains £8-12, 4-course Sun lunch £18; ⊙11am-9pm daily Mar-Oct, 11am-9pm Fri-Sun Nov-Feb) A renovated Victorian tourist lodge with assorted bric-a-brac dangling from the rafters, the Laragh dates from 1890 and serves hearty meals such as cottage pie, steak sandwiches and fish and chips, as well as a traditional roast lunch on Sunday. It's on a side road off the A43, 3km northeast of the main park entrance.

Getting There & Away

You can reach Glenariff Forest Park on bus 150 from Cushendun (£4.20, 20 minutes, eight daily Monday to Friday, four Saturday) and Ballymena (£6.70, 30 minutes).

The seasonal Antrim Coaster (p604) stops at Waterfoot.

Glenarm

POP 600

Delightful little Glenarm (Gleann Arma) is the oldest village in the glens.

Sights & Activities

Take a stroll into the old village of neat Georgian houses (off the main road, immediately south of the river). Where the street opens into the broad expanse of Altmore St, look right to see the **Barbican Gate** (1682), the entrance to Glenarm Castle grounds.

Up steep Vennel St, turn left after the last house along the Layde Path to the **viewpoint**, which has a grand view of the village and the coast.

Glenarm Castle & Walled Garden CASTLE
(www.glenarmcastle.com; walled garden adult/child £5/2.50; ⌚garden 10am-5pm Mon-Sat, 11am-5pm Sun May-Sep) Since 1750 Glenarm has been the family seat of the MacDonnell family; the present 14th Earl of Antrim lives in Glenarm Castle, hidden behind an impressive wall. The castle itself is closed to the public, except during the **Tulip Festival** on the May bank holiday weekend, and for two days in July when a **Highland Games** competition takes place, but you can visit the lovely **walled garden**.

Steensons GALLERY
(www.thesteensons.com; Toberwine St; ⌚9am-5pm Mon-Sat) Watch craftspeople at work at Steensons, the designer-jewellery workshop that produces the jewellery worn in the *Game of Thrones*. (You can't buy copyrighted *Game of Thrones* pieces, but you can buy similarly inspired designs.)

ℹ Information

The **Tourist Office** (☎028-2884 1087; www.glenarmtourism.org; 2 The Bridge; ⌚9.30am-5pm Mon-Fri, 2-6pm Sun) is beside the bridge on the main road.

ℹ Getting There & Away

The seasonal Antrim Coaster (p604) stops in the village.

Larne & Around

POP 17,600

As a major port for ferries from Scotland, Larne (Lutharna) is one of Northern Ireland's main gateways. However, with its concrete overpasses and the huge chimneys of Ballylumford power station opposite the harbour, poor old Larne is a little lacking in the charm department. After a visit to the excellent tourist office, there's no real reason to linger.

Larne Harbour train station is in the ferry terminal. It's a short bus ride or a 15-minute walk from here to the town centre – turn right on Fleet St and right again on Curran Rd, then left on Circular Rd. At the big roundabout, Larne Town train station is to your left, the tourist office is to the right, and the bus station is ahead (beneath the road bridge).

Sleeping & Eating

★**Billy Andy's** IRISH ££
(☎028-2827 0648; www.billyandys.com; 66 Browndod Rd, Gloe; mains lunch £9.50-10.50, dinner 12-21.50; ⌚5-8.30pm Wed-Fri, noon-9pm Sat, noon-7.30pm Sun) Situated 7km southwest of Larne, this 19th-century country pub–with open log and peat fires, low ceilings, and live traditional music on Saturday afternoons–rewards a detour, not least for its gastropub fare: scallops with black-pudding mousse, venison with blackberry purée, lamb shanks with truffled mash, and sticky toffee pudding with spiced rum butterscotch. Book ahead.

Upstairs, cosy double/family rooms start from £60/75.

ℹ Information

The **Tourist Office** (☎028-2826 0088; www.midandeastantrim.gov.uk; Narrow Gauge Rd; ⌚9am-5pm Mon-Fri, 10am-4pm Sat, 11am-3pm Sun Jun-Sep, 9am-5pm Mon-Fri, 10am-4pm Sat Oct-May) has extensive information on all of Northern Ireland, and an exhibition on local history and wildlife.

ℹ Getting There & Away

Bus 156 provides a direct service to Belfast (£5.20, one hour, hourly Monday to Saturday, three Sunday). Larne is also the terminus of the seasonal Antrim Coaster (p604).

P&O Ferries (www.poferries.com) links Larne with Cairnyan and Troon, both in Scotland.

Larne has two **train** stations, Larne Town and Larne Harbour. Trains run from Larne Town to Belfast Central (£7.20, one hour, hourly Monday to Saturday, every two hours Sunday); those from the harbour are timed to connect with ferries.

Carrickfergus

POP 28,000

Northern Ireland's most impressive medieval fortress commands the entrance to Belfast Lough from the rocky promontory of Carrickfergus (Carraig Fhearghais), just 18km northeast of Belfast. The old town centre opposite the castle has some attractive 18th-century houses and you can still trace a good part of the 17th-century city walls.

Sights

Carrickfergus Castle CASTLE
(Marine Hwy; adult/child £5/3; ⌚10am-5pm Easter–Sep, to 4pm Oct–Easter) The central keep of Ireland's first and finest Norman fortress was built by John de Courcy soon after his 1177 invasion of Ulster. The massive walls of the outer ward were completed in 1242, while the red-brick gun ports were added in the 16th century. The keep houses a **museum** and the site is dotted with life-size figures illustrating the castle's history.

The castle overlooks the harbour where William of Orange landed on 14 June 1690, on his way to the Battle of the Boyne. A blue plaque on the old harbour wall marks the site where he stepped ashore, and a bronze statue of 'King Billy' stands on the shore nearby.

Carrickfergus Museum MUSEUM
(11 Antrim St; ⌚10am-6pm Mon-Fri, 10am-4pm Sat Apr-Sep, 10am-5pm Mon-Fri, 10am-4pm Sat Oct-Mar) FREE The glass-fronted **Museum and Civic Centre** on Antrim St houses the local museum's small collection of artefacts relating to the town's history, and a pleasant cafe.

Andrew Jackson Centre HISTORIC SITE
(2 Boneybefore; ⌚by appt 11am-3pm Thu-Sat, 1-4pm Sun May-Oct, 11am-3pm Fri & Sat Nov-Apr) FREE The seventh US president's parents left Carrickfergus in the 18th century. His ancestral home was demolished in 1860, but a replica thatched cottage now houses this memorial 2km north of Carrickfergus Castle. Displays include the Jackson family in Ulster, and Ulster's US connections.

Next door, the **US Rangers Centre** commemorates the first US rangers, who trained during WWII in Carrickfergus before heading for Europe.

Contact Carrickfergus' tourist office in advance to arrange your visit.

Sleeping & Eating

Dobbin's Inn Hotel HOTEL ££
(☎028-9335 1905; www.dobbinsinn.co.uk; 6-8 High St; s/d/f from £55/70/85;) In the centre of the old town, Dobbin's is a friendly and informal place with 15 small and creaky-floored but comfortable rooms. The building has been around for over three centuries, and has a priest's hole and an original 16th-century fireplace to prove it.

Sozo CAFE ££
(☎028-9332 6060; www.eatsozo.com; 2 North St; mains lunch £7.50-14.50, dinner £12-18; ⌚8am-5.30pm Mon-Thu, to 9.30pm Fri & Sat;) Local favourite Sozo is an unpretentious spot with friendly service and a comfort-food menu of sandwiches and salads through to lasagne, steaks and barbecue ribs. It's tiny, so book ahead for dinner.

Drinking

Ownies PUB
(http://owniesbarbistro.co.uk; 16-18 Joymount; ⌚10am-11pm Sun-Wed, to 1am Thu-Sat) Carrickfergus' most traditional bar – formerly the Joymount Arms, dating from 1846 – is complete with snugs, fireplaces, a beer garden and upstairs bistro overlooking the castle.

Windrose BAR
(☎028-9335 1164; www.thewindrose.co.uk; Rodgers Quay; ⌚10am-midnight Sun-Thu, to 1am Fri & Sat) This modern bar-bistro has dining on two levels but the real reason to drop by is for a drink on the sundrenched timber-decked terrace overlooking the yacht masts in the marina.

Information

The **Tourist Office** (☎028-9335 8049; www.carrickfergus.org/tourism; 11 Antrim St, Heritage Plaza; ⌚10am-5pm Mon-Fri & 10am-4pm Sat year-round, to 6pm Mon-Fri Apr-Sep;) is in the Museum and Civic Centre complex (p618).

Getting There & Away

Trains link Carrickfergus with Belfast Central (£4.30, 30 minutes, hourly Monday to Saturday, every two hours Sunday).

Inland County Antrim

To the west of the high moorland plateau above the Glens of Antrim, the hills slope down to the agricultural lowlands of Lough Neagh and the broad valley of the River Bann. This region is rarely visited by tourists, who either take the coast road or speed through on the way from Belfast to Derry, but there are a few places worth seeking out if you have time to spare.

Antrim Town

POP 19,800

The county town of Antrim (Aontroim) straddles the River Sixmilewater, close to the shores of Lough Neagh. During the 1798 Rising, the United Irishmen fought a pitched battle along the length of the town's High St.

Sights & Activities

Pick up a free, self-guided heritage trail booklet from the tourist office, housed in the beautifully restored **Old Courthouse** (1762), a gem of Georgian architecture.

A walking and cycling trail leads west along the river from Antrim's castle gardens to **Antrim Lough Shore Park**, where the vast size of Lough Neagh is apparent. There are picnic tables and lakeside walking trails.

Antrim Castle Gardens GARDENS
(⌚9.30am-7pm, or dusk if earlier) FREE Pass through the **Barbican Gate** (1818), a por-

tion of the old castle walls, and the underpass beyond to reach Antrim Castle Gardens. The castle burned down many years ago, but the grounds remain as one of the few surviving examples of a 17th-century ornamental garden.

Round Tower HISTORIC BUILDING
(Steeple Rd) Antrim's 10th-century round tower, on the northeast edge of town, is 28m tall, and one of the finest examples of these monastic towers in Ireland. The tower itself is closed to the public but you're free to explore the surrounding site.

WALK: SLEMISH

The distinctive craggy peak of Slemish (438m) hill is one of many sites in the North associated with **St Patrick**, who is said to have tended goats on its slopes. On St Patrick's Day, thousands make a pilgrimage to its summit; the rest of the year it's a pleasant climb, though steep and slippery in wet weather, rewarded with a fine view (allow one hour return from the parking area).

Eating

Nanabelles CAFE £
(24b Railway St; dishes £1.80-3.50; 9.30am-4.30pm Mon-Sat) Find this 12-seat cafe hidden up the back of a charming gift/homewares shop. Tea is served on vintage china, along with heavenly home-baked scones, biscuits, banana bread, walnut and date bread and cakes such as carrot or chocolate-apple.

Information

The **Tourist Office** (028-9442 8331; www.antrimandnewtownabbey.gov.uk; Market Sq; 9am-5.30pm Mon-Fri, 10am-3pm Sat Jul & Aug, 9am-5pm Mon-Wed, 9am-5.30pm Thu & Fri, 10am-1pm Sat May-Jun & Sep, closed Oct-Apr) is located inside the Old Courthouse.

Getting There & Away

Buses 218 and 219 from Belfast to Ballymena stop in Antrim (£4.40, 40 minutes, hourly Monday to Friday, seven on Saturday).

Trains link Belfast Central with Antrim (£5.70, 30 minutes, hourly), continuing to Derry (£12, 1¾ hours).

Ballymena & Around

POP 29,467

Ballymena (An Baile Meánach) is a bustling market town with good shopping, making it a handy place to stock up if you're heading for remoter pastures. Sights are few but there are some superb places to sleep, eat and drink in and around the town.

Sleeping & Eating

★**Galgorm Resort & Spa** HOTEL ££
(028-2588 1001; www.galgorm.com; 136 Fenaghy Rd, Galgorm; d/cottage from £145/90;) About 6km west of Ballymena, a 19th-century manor house by the River Main has been redeveloped and extended to create one of Ireland's top country-house hotels. Cottages, with private bathroom and kitchenette, sleep two to eight people. Treatments at the state-of-the-art spa start from £50; there are several excellent restaurants and bars, including one in the former stables.

★**Blackstone** IRISH ££
(028-2564 8566; www.blackstonebar.co.uk; 15-17 Hill St; mains lunch £8.50-15, dinner £10-20; noon-2.30pm & 5-9pm Mon-Thu, noon-9pm Fri & Sat, noon-7.30pm Sun) Just off Ballymena's main street, this gastropub is an exceptional find for seriously good cooking. All of the breads and condiments are made on the premises, including exquisite pea-and-mint purée accompanying fresh fish and hand-cut chips. Other standouts include succulent Portavogie scampi; pan-fried pigeon with beetroot, gingerbread, and pomegranate dressing; and lamb with roast cauliflower and goat's-cheese bonbons.

Drinking

★**Crosskeys Inn** PUB
(40 Grange Rd, Toomebridge; 11.30am-1am Mon-Sat, noon-11pm Sun) Dating from 1654, Ireland's oldest thatched pub is an absolute treasure, with tiny, antique-filled rooms, a crackling turf fire, the best Guinness for miles around, and fabulous craic. Live traditional music plays every Saturday, with impromptu sessions on Wednesday, Friday and Sunday. It's 13km southwest of Ballymena.

Getting There & Away

Bus 217 links Ballymena with Ballycastle (£6.70, 50 minutes, hourly Monday to Friday, five Saturday). Buses 218 and 219 serve Belfast's Europa BusCentre (£12, 40 minutes, hourly Monday to Saturday).

Trains link Ballymena with Belfast Central (£8.30, 50 minutes, hourly); some continue from Ballymena to Derry (£11.50, 1½, every two hours).

Counties Fermanagh & Tyrone

Includes ➡

Best Places to Eat

➡ Cafe Merlot (p625)

➡ Brewer's House (p636)

➡ Kitchen Restaurant (p636)

➡ Jolly Sandwich Bar (p625)

➡ Thatch Coffee Shop (p631)

Best Places to Stay

➡ Westville Hotel (p624)

➡ Tullylagan Country House (p636)

➡ MullaghmoreHouse(p634)

➡ Lusty Beg Island (p631)

➡ Watermill Lodge (p629)

Why Go?

The ancient landscape of Fermanagh is shaped by ice and water, with rugged hills rising above quilted plains of half-drowned drumlins (rounded hills formed by retreating glaciers) and shimmering, reed-fringed lakes. A glance at the map shows the county is around one-third water – as the locals will tell you, the lakes are in Fermanagh for six months of the year; for the other six, Fermanagh is in the lakes. This watery maze is a natural playground for boaters, kayakers and anglers. The surrounding landscape is laced with good walks.

County Tyrone – from Tír Eoghain (Land of Owen, a legendary chieftain) – is dominated by the tweed-tinted moorlands of the Sperrin Mountains, whose southern flanks are dotted with prehistoric sites. Apart from hiking these heather-clad hills, visitors can enjoy several excellent sites that celebrate the county's heritage, including the historic ties to the USA.

When to Go

➡ May marks the start of the mayfly season, the most exciting time for trout fishing on Lough Erne, while June is the ideal month for cruising the lakes.

➡ If hiking is more to your taste, July is ideal for hill walking in the Sperrins. You can join a mass pilgrimage to the summit of Mullaghcarn, above Gortin, on Cairn Sunday, the last Sunday in the month.

➡ The tail end of summer is enlivened by the Ulster American Folk Park's annual Appalachian and Bluegrass Music Festival.

COUNTY FERMANAGH

POP 61,810 / AREA 1691 SQ KM

Enniskillen & Around

POP 13,800

Perched amid the web of waterways that link Upper and Lower Lough Erne, Enniskillen (Inis Ceithleann, meaning Ceithleann's Island, after a legendary female warrior) is an appealing town with a mile-long main street that rides the roller-coaster spine of an island drumlin. Its attractive waterside setting, bustling with boats in summer, plus a range of lively pubs and restaurants, make Enniskillen a good base for exploring Upper and Lower Lough Erne, Florence Court and the Marble Arch Caves.

Though neither was born here, both Oscar Wilde and Samuel Beckett were pupils at Enniskillen's Portora Royal School (Wilde from 1864 to 1871, Beckett from 1919 to 1923); it was here that Beckett first studied French, a language he would later write in. The town's name is also prominent in the history of the Troubles – on Poppy Day (11 November) in 1987 an IRA bomb killed 11 people during a service at Enniskillen's war memorial.

Sights & Activities

★Enniskillen Castle MUSEUM

(☎028-6632 5000; www.enniskillencastle.co.uk; Castle Barracks; adult/child £4/3; ⏰2-5pm Mon, 10am-5pm Tue-Fri year-round, 2-5pm Sat May-Sep, 2-5pm Sun Jul & Aug) Enniskillen Castle, a former stronghold of the 16th-century Maguire chieftains, guards the western end of the town's central island, its twin-turreted **Watergate** looming over passing fleets of cabin cruisers. Within the walls you'll find the **Fermanagh County Museum**, which has displays on the county's history, archaeology, landscape and wildlife.

The 15th-century keep contains the **Royal Inniskilling Fusiliers Regimental Museum**, full of guns, uniforms and medals, including eight Victoria Crosses awarded in WWI; it's dedicated to the regiment that was raised at the castle in 1689 to support the army of William I. Much of this facility was refurbished in 2015.

St Michael's Church CHURCH

(☎028-6632 2075; www.saintmichaels-parish.com; 4 Darling St; ⏰8am-5pm) Dominating the centre, this soaring church dates from only 1875, having replaced an early church that was collapsing. There's lavish artwork and ornamentation, including paintings by Charles Russell.

★Castle Coole HISTORIC BUILDING

(☎028-6632 2690; www.nationaltrust.org.uk; off A4; house tour adult/child £5/2, grounds £2.50/1.50; ⏰house 11am-5pm daily Jul & Aug, Fri-Wed Jun, Sat, Sun & public holidays mid-Mar–May & Sep, grounds 10am-7pm Mar-Oct, to 4pm Nov-Feb) The 600 hectares of landscaped **grounds** contain a lake that is home to the UK's only nonmigratory colony of greylag geese. You can also join a tour of the grand 18th-century **house**.

The estate is 2.5km southeast of Enniskillen. You can easily walk there from Enniskillen town centre in 30 minutes – beyond Dunnes Stores, fork left on Tempo Rd and keep going straight along Castlecoole Rd.

When King George IV visited Ireland in 1821, the second Earl of Belmore had a state bedroom specially prepared at Castle Coole in anticipation of the monarch's visit. The king, however, was more interested in dallying with his mistress at Slane Castle and never turned up. The bedroom, draped in red silk and decorated with paintings depicting *A Rake's Progress* (the earl's sniffy riposte to the king's extramarital shenanigans), is one of the highlights of the one-hour guided tour.

Designed by James Wyatt, this Palladian mansion was built between 1789 and 1795 for Armar Lowry-Corry, the first Earl of Belmore, and is probably the purest expression of late-18th-century neoclassical architecture in Ireland.

It's said that if the geese ever leave, the earls of Belmore will lose Castle Coole.

Sheelin Antique Irish Lace Shop SHOP

(☎028-6634 8052; www.antiqueirishlace.co.uk; off A509, Bellanaleck; ⏰10am-6pm Mon-Sat) This shop also houses a small collection of Irish lace dating from 1850 to 1900. Lace-making was an important cottage industry in the region both before and after the Famine – prior to WWI there were at least 10 lace schools in County Fermanagh. The shop is just over 6km southwest of Enniskillen.

Kingfisher Trail CYCLING

(www.cycleni.com) The Kingfisher Trail is a waymarked, long-distance cycling trail that starts in Enniskillen and wends its way through the back roads of Counties Fermanagh, Leitrim, Cavan and Monaghan. You can get a trail map from the Enniskillen tourist office or online.

The full route is around 370km long, but a shorter loop, starting and finishing in

Counties Fermanagh & Tyrone Highlights

❶ Pondering the meaning of the strange stone figures on **White Island** (p630) and **Boa Island** (p630).

❷ Making amazing underground discoveries at the **Marble Arch Caves** (p633).

❸ Hiring a canoe or kayak and exploring the reed-fringed backwaters of **Lough Erne** (p628).

❹ Revelling in the historical links between Ireland and the USA at the **Ulster American Folk Park** (p634).

❺ Seeing how the Irish aristocracy enjoyed the high life in the elegant country house of **Castle Coole** (p628).

❻ Exploring the Celtic monastic settlement on **Devenish Island** (p629), and climbing to the top of its ancient round tower.

❼ Feeling the pounding beat of an authentic old linen mill at **Wellbrook Beetling Mill** (p635).

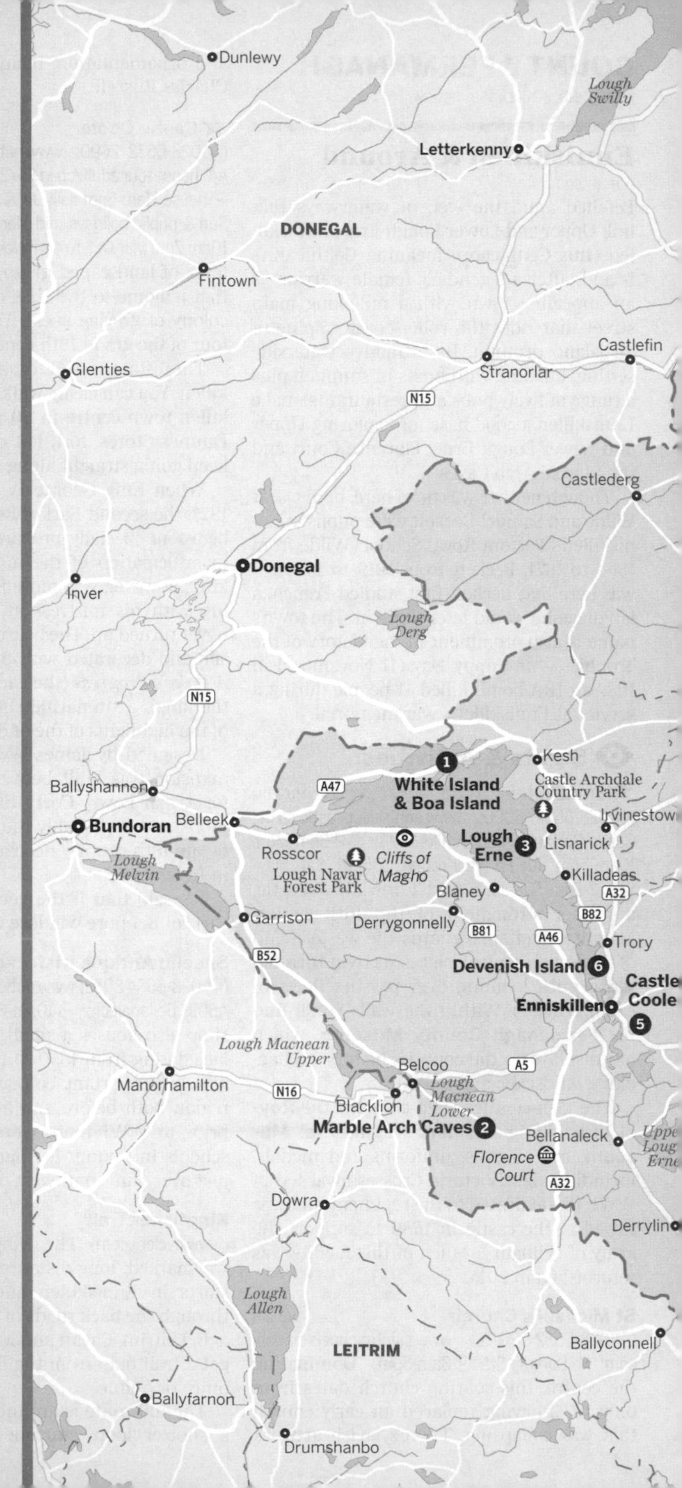

Derry
ANTRIM
Ulster Way
LONDONDERRY
River Foyle
Dungiven
A6
Claudy
A5
Dunnamanagh
Maghera
A6
Lifford
Strabane
Sperrin Mountains
Sperrin
Cranagh
Plumbridge
B47
A5
B48
Gortin Lakes
Beaghmore Stone Circles
Davagh Forest Park
B162
Gortin
Newtownstewart
Gortin Glen Forest Park
Wellbrook Beetling Mill
Ulster American Folk Park
4
Mullaghcarn (542m)
An Creagán
7
Coagh
Creggan
Kildress
Cookstown
Ardboe High Cross
A505
TYRONE
Lough Neagh
Omagh
River Camowen
Pomeroy
A45
A29
B43
Coalisland
River Drumragh
Donaghmore
Dungannon
Castlecaulfield
Dromore
A5
Fintona
A4
Moygashel
M1
Argory
Ballygawley
Grant Ancestral Homestead
Moy
Portadown
N2
Benburb
Augher
Aughnacloy
A4
A28
Tempo
Fivemiletown
Emyvale
Caledon
Armagh
A4
A28
Lisbellaw
Markethill
FERMANAGH
B514
Monaghan
ARMAGH
Lisnaskea
A34
N2
Newtownhamilton
MONAGHAN
B127
Newtownbutler
Clones
Crom Estate
A509
Ballybay
Castleblayney
N2
Cootehill
Butlersbridge
0
20 km
0
10 miles
N

Enniskillen

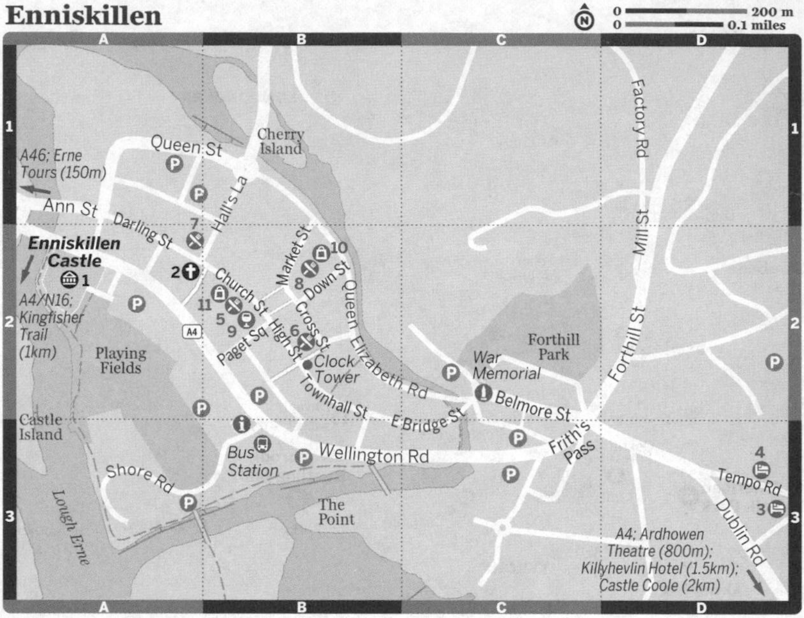

Enniskillen

Top Sights
1 Enniskillen Castle........A2

Sights
2 St Michael's Church........A2

Sleeping
3 Belmore Court & Motel........D3
4 Westville Hotel........D3

Eating
5 Cafe Merlot........B2
6 Dollakis........B2
7 Jolly Sandwich Bar........A2
8 Rebecca's Coffee Shop........B2

Drinking & Nightlife
9 Blakes of the Hollow........B2

Shopping
10 Buttermarket........B2
11 Home, Field & Stream........B2

Enniskillen, and travelling via Kesh, Belleek, Garrison, Belcoo and Florencecourt, is 115km – easily done in two days with an overnight stay at Belleek.

Erne Angling FISHING
(☎ 07884 472121; www.erneangling.com; 2 anglers half-/full-day £80/130) Hook the pike of your dreams on the Upper Lough Erne with these experienced guides.

Tours

Erne Tours BOAT TOUR
(☎ 028-6632 2882; www.ernetoursltd.com; Brook Park, Round 'O' Jetty; adult/child £10/6, dinner cruise £25/15; ⏱ 4 daily Jul & Aug, 2 daily Jun, 2 on Tue, Sat & Sun May & Sep) Operates 1¾-hour cruises on Lower Lough Erne aboard the 56-seat waterbus MV *Kestrel,* calling at Devenish Island (April to September) along the way. It departs from the Round 'O' Quay, just west of the town centre on the A46 to Belleek. There are also Saturday-evening cruises (May to September) that include dinner at the Killyhevlin Hotel, departing from the hotel jetty.

Sleeping

★ **Westville Hotel** HOTEL ££
(☎ 028-6632 0333; www.westvillehotel.co.uk; 14-20 Tempo Rd; s/d from £65/70; @ 📶 👪) The Westville adds a dash of four-star comfort to Enniskillen's rather staid accommodation scene with designer fabrics, cool colour combinations and good food. The family suite offers great value, sleeping four in two adjoining rooms.

Belmore Court & Motel HOTEL ££
(☎028-6632 6633; www.motel.co.uk; Tempo Rd; r from £65;) Set in a centrally located original row of terrace houses linked to a large modern extension, the Belmore offers stylish and spacious 'superior' rooms in the new building and family 'miniapartments' with small kitchens in the old section. Some motel-style rooms sleep up to four.

Greenwood Lodge B&B ££
(☎028-6632 5636; www.greenwoodlodge.co.uk; 17 Killyvilly Ct, Tempo Rd; s/d from £40/50) This spacious and modern house is set on a quiet side street 3km northeast of town off the B80. The three comfy bedrooms have private bathrooms, there's an airy lounge and it has secure storage available for bikes.

Killyhevlin Hotel HOTEL £££
(☎028-6632 3481; www.killyhevlin.com; off A4, Killyhevlin; s/d from £95/160; @) Enniskillen's top hotel is 1.5km south of town on the Maguiresbridge road, in an idyllic setting overlooking Upper Lough Erne. Many of its 70 elegant rooms enjoy stunning views over landscaped gardens to the lough. It has a lavish spa and health club.

Eating

★Jolly Sandwich Bar CAFE £
(☎028-6632 2277; www.thejollysandwichbar.co.uk; 3 Darling St; mains from £4; ⏲8am-4pm Mon-Fri, 8.30am-4pm Sat) Find happiness between the buns at this cheap and cheery cafe, which has a wide range of sandwiches to eat in or take away. Ingredients include seasonal and local produce. The baked goods are divine.

Rebecca's Coffee Shop CAFE £
(☎028-6632 9376; Buttermarket; snacks €2-5; ⏲9am-5.30pm Mon-Sat) A traditional cafe, Rebecca's serves good sandwiches, salads, scones and pastries. People rave about its cottage pie. There are airy courtyard tables in summer.

★Cafe Merlot BISTRO ££
(☎028-6632 2143; www.blakesofthehollow.com/cafe-merlot; 6 Church St; mains lunch £6-10, dinner £13-17; ⏲noon-2pm, 6-9pm) French flair comes to this beautiful space located under vaulted brick ceilings. There are seasonal specials in addition to the regular menu, which features meat and seafood. The wine list is the best in town. It's below Blakes of the Hollow pub.

Dollakis MEDITERRANEAN £££
(☎028-6634 2616; www.dollakis.com; 2 Cross St; mains lunch £7-11, dinner £14-26; ⏲10am-10pm Tue-Sat) As well as serving lunch, cakes and snacks through the day, this chic little cafe transforms into an upscale Greek-Mediterranean restaurant in the evening (from 6pm). The dinner menu includes classic Greek fare plus an array of small plates *(meze)* and seasonal specials.

Drinking & Nightlife

★Blakes of the Hollow PUB
(William Blake; ☎028-6632 2143; 6 Church St; ⏲noon-late) Ulster's best pint of Guinness awaits in this traditional Victorian pub, almost unchanged since 1887. It comes complete with marble-topped bar, four huge sherry casks, antique silver lamp holders, an open fire and ancient wood panelling kippered by a century of cigarette smoke. There's traditional music from 9pm on Fridays.

Entertainment

Ardhowen Theatre THEATRE
(☎028-6632 5440; www.ardhowentheatre.com; 97 Dublin Rd; ⏲box office 9.30am-4.30pm Mon-Fri, to 7pm before a performance, 11am-1pm, 2-5pm & 6-7pm Sat) The program here includes concerts, local amateur and professional drama and musical productions, pantomimes and films. The theatre is about 1km southeast of the town centre on the A4, in an impressive glass-fronted building overlooking a lake. It has a good cafe.

Shopping

Buttermarket CRAFTS
(Down St; ⏲9am-5pm Mon-Sat) The restored buildings in the old marketplace house an appealing variety of craft shops and studios selling paintings, ceramics, jewellery and even fishing tackle.

Home, Field & Stream OUTDOOR EQUIPMENT
(☎028-6632 2114; www.hfs-online.com; 18-20 Church St; ⏲9am-5.30pm Mon-Sat) Has a wide range of fishing tackle and also sells fishing licences and permits.

Information

Near the bus station, this very helpful **Tourist Office** (☎028-6632 3110; www.fermanaghlakelands.com; Wellington Rd; ⏲9am-5.30pm Mon-Fri year-round, 10am-6pm Sat, 11am-5pm Sun Easter–Sep;) has plenty of parking.

2

CHRIS HILL/GETTY IMAGES ©

1. Lough Erne (p628)
There is no shortage of accommodation around the lake, from camping grounds to golf resorts.

2. Janus Stone (p630)
This two-faced pagan figure on Boa Island is approximately 2000 years old.

3. Castle Coole (p621)
This mansion is a perfect example of late-18th-century neoclassical architecture in Ireland.

CHRIS HILL/GETTY IMAGES ©

Getting There & Away

The main street changes name half a dozen times between the bridges at either end; the prominent clock tower marks the town centre. The other principal street is Wellington Rd, south of and parallel to the main street, where you'll find the bus station, tourist office and car parking. If you're driving, try to avoid rush hour – the bridge at the west end is a traffic bottleneck.

The bus station is central. Ulsterbus and Bus Éireann services run to/from Belfast (£12, 2¼ hours, hourly Monday to Saturday, two on Sunday), Omagh (£8, one hour, one daily Monday to Saturday), Dublin (€20, 2½ hours, eight daily), plus a run to Donegal (€15, one hour, four daily Monday to Saturday, two on Sunday) and on to Sligo (€17, 1½ hours).

Lough Erne

About 80km long, Lough Erne is made up of two sections: the Upper Lough to the south of Enniskillen, and the Lower Lough to the north. The two are connected by the River Erne, which begins its journey in County Cavan and meets the sea at Donegal Bay west of Ballyshannon. This is a great region for exploring with your own wheels, having picnics at will and enjoying no end of water sports and other aquatic activities.

ULSTER WAY

The Ulster Way **long-distance walking trail** makes a circuit around the six counties of Northern Ireland and Donegal. In total the route covers just over 900km, so walking all of it might take four to five weeks. However, much of the way is on minor roads rather than footpaths, a criticism that has been taken on board by the Northern Ireland Tourist Board. The board has divided the route into two categories: 'Quality Sections' – good, scenic, off-road walking – separated by 'Link Sections', which can be covered by public transport. Check the website of **WalkNI** (www.walkni.com) for details.

Short sections of the Ulster Way that make good day walks include **Cuilcagh Mountain Park** (www.cuilcaghmountainpark.com) and the **Causeway Coast Way** (p607).

Activities

The Enniskillen tourist office (p625) can help you find where to rent canoes and boats, plus it has full details on angling.

It's easy to hire **day boats** at Enniskillen, Killadeas and Castle Archdale Country Park. Rates range from about £10 to £15 per hour for an open rowing boat with outboard motor, to £60/90 per half-/full day for a six-seater with cabin and engine.

The **Lough Erne Canoe Trail** (www.canoeni.com) highlights the attractions along the 50km of lough and river between Belleek and Belturbet. The wide open expanses of the Lower Lough can build up big waves in a strong breeze and are best left to experts, but the sheltered backwaters of the Upper Lough are ideal for beginners and families.

You can download maps and info from the website.

Share Canoe Hire CANOEING
(☎028-6772 2122; www.sharevillage.org; off Newbridge Rd, Share Discovery Village; canoe rental per hour/day £12/35; ⏲Jun-Aug) Has kayaks, canoes and gear for rent.

Upper Lough Erne

Upper Lough Erne is not so much a lake as a watery maze of more than 150 islands, inlets, reedy bays and meandering backwaters. Birdlife is abundant: flocks of whooper swan and goldeneye overwinter here; great crested grebes nest in the spring; and you'll find Ireland's biggest heronry in a 400-year-old oak grove on the island of Inishfendra, just south of Crom Estate.

No-nonsense **Lisnaskea** is the main town, with shops and pubs.

Sights & Activities

Crom PARK
(☎028-6773 8118; www.nationaltrust.org.uk; Crom Rd, Newtownbutler; adult/child £5/2; ⏲grounds 10am-7pm Jun-Aug, to 6pm mid-Mar–May, Sep & Oct, visitor centre 11am-5pm daily Easter–Sep, Sat & Sun only Oct) Home to the largest area of natural woodland in Northern Ireland, the National Trust's beautiful Crom Estate is a haven for pine martens, rare bats and many species of bird. You can walk from the visitor centre to the ruins of old **Crom Castle**, with its ancient **walled garden**, abandoned bowling green and gnarled yew trees, and views over the reed-fringed lough to an island folly.

The estate is on the eastern shore of the Upper Lough, 5km west of Newtownbutler.

Check the website for details on wildlife watching and other events. Rent a rowboat (per hour £7.50) or a powerboat (per day £75).

Inishcruiser BOAT TOUR

(☎028-6772 2122; www.sharevillage.org/inishcruiser; off Newbridge Rd, Share Discovery Village; adult/child £10/6; ⏰10.30am Sun Easter–Sep, also 2pm Sun Jul & Aug) The *Inishcruiser* offers 1½- to two-hour cruises on the lough, leaving from 5km southwest of Lisnaskea.

Sleeping & Eating

★**Watermill Lodge** B&B ££

(☎028-6772 4369; www.watermillrestaurantfermanagh.com; Kilmore Quay, Lisnaskea; s/d from £60/95) A secluded lakeside setting makes for a peaceful night's rest in one of the seven lake-view guest rooms here. The luxurious rooms are next to the plush, thatch-roofed **Watermill Restaurant** (3-course dinner from £26; ⏰5-9.30pm Wed-Fri, noon-10pm Sat, noon-8pm Sun), where the seasonal menu leans French.

Kissin Crust CAFE £

(☎028-6772 2678; 152 Main St, Lisnaskea; mains £3-7; ⏰8.30am-5pm Mon-Sat) Popular with locals, this coffee shop is stacked with home-baked pies, quiches and scones, and serves up a lunch menu of homemade soup, sandwiches and hot dishes. It's good for picnic-shopping. Note its slogan: 'Thank goodness there are places like this for people's enjoyment even in the modern world.'

Getting Around

From Enniskillen, Ulsterbus service 95 runs along the east side of the lough to Lisnaskea (£4, 30 minutes, six daily Monday to Friday and five on Saturday). Bus 58 goes down the west side to Derrylin (£4, 40 minutes, five daily Monday to Friday, two on Saturday), and continues to Belturbet in County Cavan.

Lower Lough Erne

Lower Lough Erne is a more open expanse of water than the Upper Lough, with its 90-odd islands clustered mainly in the southern reaches. In early Christian times, when overland travel was difficult, Lough Erne was an important highway between the Donegal coast and inland Leitrim, and there are many ancient religious sites and other antiquities dotted around its shores. In medieval times the lough was part of an important pilgrimage route.

Getting Around

On the eastern side of the lough, **Ulsterbus** runs from Enniskillen to Pettigo via Irvinestown (three to five Monday to Saturday) and stops near Castle Archdale Country Park (35 minutes) and Kesh (one hour). **Bus Eireann's** Dublin to Donegal service links Enniskillen and Belleek (€8, 35 minutes, eight daily).

Devenish Island

Devenish Island, from Daimh Inis, meaning Ox Island, is the biggest of several 'holy islands' in Lough Erne. The remains of an **Augustinian monastery**, founded here in the 6th century by St Molaise, include a superb 12th-century **round tower** in near-perfect condition, the ruins of St Molaise's Church and St Mary's Abbey, an unusual 15th-century high cross and many fascinating old gravestones. Climb to the top of the round tower for a cramped view.

A small **ferry** (☎07702 052873; Trory Point Landing; adult/child return £3/2; ⏰daily Jul & Aug, times vary, less often May-Jun) crosses to Devenish Island from Trory Point landing. From Enniskillen, take the A32 north towards Irvinestown and after 5km look for the sign on the left, just after a service station and immediately before the junction where the B82 and A32 part company.

You can also visit as part of a cruise with Erne Tours (p624) in Enniskillen.

Castle Archdale Country Park

This park has pleasant woodland and lakeshore walks and cycle tracks in the former estate of 18th-century Archdale Manor. The island-filled bay was used in WWII as a base for Catalina flying boats.

Activities

Vendors at the park offer pony trekking (£15 per hour), as well as short rides (£10) for beginners. There are also boats for hire and you can rent fishing rods.

Ultimate Watersports WATER SPORTS

(☎07808 736818; www.ultimatewatersports.co.uk; Castle Archdale County Park; kayaks from £13 per hour; ⏰10am-6pm daily Jul & Aug, Sat & Sun Apr-Jun & Sep-Oct) Working out of Castle Archdale marina and Lusty Beg island, this company offers equipment hire and instruction in water-skiing, wakeboarding, jet-skiing, canoeing and dinghy sailing.

Sleeping

Castle Archdale Caravan Park CAMPGROUND £
(☎028-6862 1333; www.castlearchdale.com; off B82, Rossmore; tent sites £10-30, caravan sites £25-30; ⏰Easter–Oct; 👪) This tree-sheltered site in the park is dominated by on-site caravans, but has good facilities, including a shop, launderette, playground and pub.

Information

Castle Archdale Country Park Visitor Centre (☎028-6862 1588; off B82, Rossmore; ⏰park 9am-7pm Easter–Sep, to 9pm Jul & Aug, visitor centre 10am-5pm daily Jun-Aug, 1-5pm Sat & Sun May & Sep) The park's history is explained in the visitor centre's small museum.

Getting There & Away

The park is 16km northwest of Enniskillen, near Lisnarick.

White Island

White Island, in the bay to the north of Castle Archdale Country Park, is the most haunting of Lough Erne's monastic sites.

Sights

Church Ruins HISTORIC SITE
(White Island) At the eastern tip of the island are the ruins of a small 12th-century church with a beautiful Romanesque door on its southern side. Inside are six extraordinary **Celtic stone figures**, thought to date from the 9th century, lined up along the wall like miniature Easter Island statues.

This line-up is a modern arrangement; most of the figures were discovered buried in the walls of the church in the 19th century, where the medieval masons had used them as ordinary building stones. The six main figures, all created by the same hand, are flanked on the left by a **sheila-na-gig** (carved female figure with exaggerated genitalia), which is probably contemporary with the church, and flanked on the right by a scowling stone face. The age and interpretation of these figures has been the subject of much debate; it has been suggested that the two central pairs, of equal height, were pillars that once supported a pulpit, and that they represent either saints or aspects of the life of Christ.

Getting There & Away

White Island Ferry (☎028-6862 1892; off B82, Castle Archdale Marina; per person £4; ⏰10.30am-4.30pm daily Jul-Aug, also Sat & Sun Easter & May, call to confirm times) crosses to the island from the marina in Castle Archdale Country Park; buy your ticket from the Castle Archdale boat-hire office. The crossing takes 15 minutes, and allows you around half an hour on the island.

Boa Island

Boa Island, at the northern end of Lower Lough Erne, is connected to the mainland at both ends – the main A47 road runs along its length. Spooky, moss-grown Caldragh graveyard, towards the western end of the island, contains the famous **Janus Stone**. Perhaps 2000 years old, this pagan figure is carved with two grotesque human heads, back to back. Nearby is a smaller figure called the

FISHING ON LOUGH ERNE

The lakes of Fermanagh are renowned for both coarse and game fishing. The Lough Erne trout-fishing season runs from the beginning of March to the end of September. Salmon fishing begins in June and also continues to the end of September. The mayfly season usually lasts a month from the second week in May.

You'll need a combined licence and a permit, which costs £9.50 for three days. See www.nidirect.gov.uk/angling for full details. In addition, Enniskillen's tourist office provides a free guide to angling in Fermanagh and South Tyrone, which has full details of lakes and rivers, fish species, seasons and permit requirements.

Licences and permits can be purchased from the **Enniskillen tourist office** (p625), **Home, Field & Stream** (p625) plus from the marina in **Castle Archdale Country Park** (p630), which also hires out fishing rods.

The **Belleek Angling Centre** in the **Thatch Coffee Shop** in Belleek sells fishing tackle and can arrange boat hire for anglers. Hire an experienced guide with **Erne Angling** (p624).

Lusty Man, brought here from Lusty More island. Their origin and meaning have been lost to the mists of time.

There's a small sign indicating the graveyard about 1.5km from the bridge at the western tip of the island.

Sleeping & Eating

★**Lusty Beg Island** RESORT £££
(☎028-6863 3300; www.lustybegisland.com; Boa Island; s/d B&B from £100/120, cabins from £175, minimum 2 nights; ⊙restaurant 12.30-9pm; @ ≋) This lush private island retreat, reached by ferry (on demand from 8.30am to 11pm, use a telephone at the dock) from a jetty halfway along Boa Island, has self-catering cabins and chalets that sleep two to six people as well as B&B rooms in its rustic 40-room motel. There's a tennis court, nature trail and canoeing on the lough for guests.

Lusty Beg's informal **restaurant** is open to all. It serves a wide range of comfort food, from burgers to steaks and seafood.

Finn Lough RESORT £££
(☎028-6838 0360; www.finnlough.com; 41 Letter Rd, off B136; r from £125, cottages from £260; @) On the mainland shore overlooking Boa Island, this posh resort has a big range of accommodation. Three rooms in the main house are suites, decorated in white with bold colour accents. Cottages sleep from six to eight people, all are very large and some have great water views. The **cafe** has fresh, locally sourced fare served through the day.

Activities at the lush complex include water sports, kayaking, tennis and cycling.

Belleek

POP 550

Belleek's (Beal Leice) village street of colourful, flower-bedecked houses slopes up from a bridge across the River Erne where it flows out of the Lower Lough towards Ballyshannon and the sea. The village is right on the border – the road south across the bridge passes through a finger of the Republic's territory for about 200m before leaving again – and shops accept both euros and pounds sterling.

Pick up a copy of the engrossing *Town Trail* brochure.

Sleeping

Fiddlestone Bar & B&B B&B £
(☎028-6865 8008; 15-17 Main St; s/d from £40/70; ⊙pub noon-11pm;) This classic village-centre pub has six basic rooms that are just right after a long day touring followed by hours spent enjoying the trad-music sessions downstairs.

CRUISING HOLIDAYS ON LOUGH ERNE

If you fancy exploring Lough Erne as captain of your own motor cruiser, well, you can – and without any previous experience or qualification. Several companies in Fermanagh hire out self-drive, live-aboard cabin cruisers by the week, offering a crash course (not literally, you hope) in boat-handling and navigation at the start of your holiday. Weekly rates in the high season (July and August) range from about £900 for a two-berth to £1500 for a four-berth and £1900 for an eight-berth boat. Low- and mid-season rates are around 75% of the high-season rates.

Check www.fermanaghlakelands.com for details on holidays and boat-hire companies.

Eating & Drinking

★**Thatch Coffee Shop** CAFE £
(☎028-6865 8181; 20 Main St; mains £4-8; ⊙9am-5pm Mon-Sat) This cute little thatched cottage may be Belleek's oldest building (late 18th century), but it serves excellent coffee, delicious soups and sandwiches, plus superb homemade cakes and scones. The trad breakfasts are a treat.

Black Cat Cove PUB
(☎028-6865 8942; 28 Main St; mains €7-10; ⊙kitchen noon-9pm) This family-run pub with antique furniture and an open fire serves good bar meals. It also has live music most nights in summer, and at weekends in winter.

Shopping

★**Belleek Pottery Visitor Centre** POTTERY
(☎028-6865 8501; www.belleekpottery.ie; 3 Main St; tours adult/child £4/free; ⊙9am-6pm Mon-Fri, 10am-6pm Sat, noon-5.30pm Sun Jul-Sep, shorter hours Oct-Jun, closed Sat & Sun Jan-Feb) The imposing Georgian-style building beside Belleek's main bridge houses the world-famous Belleek Pottery, founded in 1857 to provide local employment in the wake of the Potato Famine. It has been producing fine

OFF THE BEATEN TRACK

WALK: CUILCAGH MOUNTAIN VIA THE LEGNABROCKY TRAIL

Rising above Marble Arch and Florence Court, Cuilcagh (*cull*-kay) Mountain (666m) is the highest point in Counties Fermanagh and Cavan, its summit right on the border between Northern Ireland and the Republic.

The mountain is a geological layer cake, with a cave-riddled limestone base, shale and sandstone flanks draped with a shaggy tweed skirt of blanket bog, and a high gritstone plateau ringed by steep, craggy slopes, all part of the Marble Arch Caves.

Hidden among the sphagnum moss, bog cotton and heather of the blanket bog, you can find the sticky-fingered sundew, an insect-eating plant, while the crags echo to the 'krok-krok-krok' of ravens and the mewing of peregrine falcons. The otherworldly summit plateau is a breeding ground for golden plover and is rich in rare plants such as alpine clubmoss.

The **hike** to the summit is a 15km round trip (allow five or six hours); the first part is on an easy gravel track, but you'll need good boots to negotiate the boggy ground and steep slopes further on. Start at the Cuilcagh Mountain Park car park, 300m west of the entrance to Marble Arch Caves visitor centre (grid reference 121335; you'll need the Ordnance Survey 1:50,000 Discovery series map, sheet 26). Right next to the car park is the **Monastir sinkhole**, a deep depression ringed by limestone cliffs where the River Aghinrawn disappears underground for its journey through the Marble Arch Caves system.

Climb the stile beside the gate and set out along the **Legnabrocky Trail**, a well-groomed track (extensive improvements were made in 2015) that winds through rich green limestone meadows before climbing across the blanket bog on a 'floating' bed of gravel and geotextiles – boardwalks off to one side offer a closer look at bog-regeneration areas. The gravel track comes to an end at a gate about 4.5km from the start. From here you follow a line of waymarked wooden posts, making your way across bog (don't stray from the route – there are deep bog holes where you can get stuck) before climbing steeply to the summit ridge, with great views west to the crags above little Lough Atona. The waymarkers come to an end here, so you're on your own for the final kilometre across the plateau, aiming for the prominent cairn on the summit (a map and compass are essential in poor visibility).

The **summit cairn** is actually a Neolithic burial chamber; about 100m south of the summit you will find two rings of boulders, the foundations of prehistoric huts. On a clear day the view extends from the Blue Stack Mountains of Donegal to Croagh Patrick, and from the Atlantic Ocean to the Irish Sea. Return the way you came.

For **downloadable maps** of other walks in the area, see www.fermanaghlakelands.com/walking-A229.

Parian china ever since, and is especially noted for its delicate basket-ware.

There's a small museum, showroom and cafe. **Guided tours** run every half-hour from 9.30am to 12.15pm and 1.45pm to 4pm (till 3pm on Friday) weekdays year-round, plus summer weekends.

Lough Navar Forest Park

This free Forest Service park lies at the western end of Lower Lough Erne, where the **Cliffs of Magho** – a 250m-high and 9km-long limestone escarpment – rise above a fringe of native woodland on the south shore.

Sights & Activities

An 11km **scenic drive** through the park leads to the **Magho Viewpoint** – the panorama from the clifftop here is one of the finest in Ireland, especially before sunset. The view looks out over the shimmering expanse of lough and river to the Blue Stack Mountains, the sparkling waters of Donegal Bay and the sea cliffs of Slieve League.

Getting There & Away

The entrance to Lough Navar Forest Park is on the minor Glennasheevar road between Garrison and Derrygonnelly, 20km southeast of Belleek (take the B52 towards Garrison, and fork left after 2.5km). It's open 10am to dusk.

West of Lough Erne

Florence Court HISTORIC BUILDING

(☎ 028-6634 8249; www.nationaltrust.org.uk; Swanlinbar Rd; house tour only adult/child £4/2, whole property £6/3; ⏰ house 11am-5pm daily Jul & Aug, Wed-Mon May & Jun, Sat-Thu Sep, Sat & Sun Apr & Oct, grounds 10am-7pm Mar-Oct, to 4pm Nov-Feb) Set in lovely wooded grounds in the shadow of Cuilcagh Mountain, Florence Court is famous for its rococo plasterwork and antique Irish furniture, which you can see on a one-hour **tour**. In the **grounds** you can explore the walled garden and, on the edge of Cottage Wood, southeast of the house, admire an ancient Irish yew tree. It's said that every Irish yew around the world is descended from this one.

Florence Court is 12km southwest of Enniskillen, off the A32. Don't confuse Florence Court with the nearby, single-worded village of Florencecourt.

Part of the first Earl of Belmore's motivation for building Castle Coole (near Enniskillen) was keeping up with the Joneses – in the 1770s his aristocratic neighbour William Willoughby Cole, the first Earl of Enniskillen, oversaw the addition of grand Palladian wings to this beautiful, baroque country house.

It was badly damaged by fire in 1955 and much of what you see on the tour is the result of meticulous restoration, but the magnificent plasterwork on the ceiling of the dining room is original.

Marble Arch Caves CAVE

(☎ 028-6634 8855; www.marblearchcaves.net; 43 Marlbank Rd, Legnabrocky; adult/child £9/6; ⏰ 10am-5pm Jul & Aug, to 4pm late Mar–Jun & Sep-Oct; 📶) To the south of Lower Lough Erne lies a limestone plateau, where Fermanagh's abundant rainwater has carved out a network of subterranean caverns. The largest of these are the Marble Arch Caves. The popular 1¼-hour tours feature spectacular chambers and underwater rivers. (The listed closing time is the last tour's starting time.)

The caves are 16km southwest of Enniskillen, and some 4km west of Florence Court (an hour's walk), reached via the A4 and the A32. Book tours ahead in summer.

Tours begin with a short boat trip along the peaty, foam-flecked waters of the underground River Cladagh to **Junction Jetty**, where three subterranean streams meet up. You then continue on foot past the Grand Gallery and Pool Chamber, regaled all the time with food-related jokes from your guide. An artificial tunnel leads into the **New Chamber**, from which the route follows the underground River Owenbrean through the **Moses Walk** (a walled pathway sunk waist-deep into the river) to the **Calcite Cradle**, where the most picturesque formations are to be found. The caves are very popular, so it's wise to phone ahead and book a tour, especially if you're in a group of four or more.

Unexpected serious flooding of the caves in the 1990s was found to have been caused by mechanised peat-cutting in the blanket bog on the slopes of Cuilcagh Mountain, whose rivers feed the caves. **Cuilcagh Mountain Park** was established to restore and preserve the bog environment, and in 2001 the entire area was designated a Unesco Geopark. The park's geology and ecology are explained in the caves' visitor centre.

The caves take their name from a natural **limestone arch** that spans the River Cladagh where it emerges from the caves; you can reach it via a short walk along a signposted footpath from the visitor centre. They were first explored by the French caving pioneer Édouard Martel in 1895.

Loughs Melvin & Macnean

Lough Melvin and Lough Macnean are situated along the border with the Republic, on the B52 road from Belcoo to Belleek. Lough Melvin is famous for its salmon and trout fishing, and is home to two unusual trout species that are unique to the lough – the sonaghan, with its distinctive black spots, and the crimson-spotted gillaroo – as well as brown trout, ferox trout and char.

COUNTY TYRONE

POP 177,990 / AREA 3263 SQ KM

Omagh

POP 21,300

Situated at the confluence of the Rivers Camowen and Drumragh, which join to form the River Strule, Omagh (An Ógh-magh) is a busy market town with a handful of historic Georgian buildings.

A new district is emerging in the centre along the banks of the river. The focus is a £4.3 million pedestrian bridge with a controversial cutting-edge design that opened in 2015.

Sights

Memorial Obelisk MEMORIAL

(www.omaghbombmemorial.com; Market St) For a long time to come, Omagh will be remembered for the devastating 1998 car bomb that killed 29 people and injured 200. Planted by the breakaway group Real IRA, the bomb was the worst single atrocity in the 30-year history of the Troubles.

An impressive 4.5m-high glass obelisk marks the spot of the explosion. It's part of a project that includes a **memorial garden** 300m north across the river on Drumragh Ave.

Sleeping & Eating

★ **Mullaghmore House** B&B ££

(☎07710 539449; www.mullaghmorehouse.com; Old Mountfield Rd; s/d from £45/80;) Offering affordable country-house luxury, this beautifully restored Georgian villa boasts a mahogany-panelled library. The bedrooms have period cast-iron fireplaces and antique furniture (some share bathrooms). The owners run courses on antique restoration and traditional crafts. It's 1.5km northeast of the town centre.

Philly's Phinest FAST FOOD £

(Bridge St; mains £4-6; ⏲11am-5pm Mon-Sat;) This tiny fast-food joint, a popular hang-out for local students, serves up some of the tastiest food in town, inspired by the USA's Philly cheesesteak (fried steak, onion and cheese in a soft bun).

Weir Cafe CAFE £

(Bridge St, Strule Arts Centre; snacks from £2; ⏲10am-4pm Mon-Sat;) A pleasant spot for coffee and cake within the arts centre. It has comfy sofas, books to browse and huge picture windows overlooking the river and bridge.

Bogan's Bar PUB FOOD £

(☎028-8224 2183; 26 Market St; mains from £6; ⏲noon-late) Hugely popular, this pub has a small beer garden on a terrace overlooking the river, regular barbecues, decent burgers, comedy nights and a lot more.

Information

Omagh Tourist Office (☎028-8224 7831; www.visitomagh.co.uk; Bridge St, Strule Arts Centre; ⏲10am-5.30pm Mon-Sat;) is located in the arts centre.

Getting There & Away

The bus station is on Mountjoy Rd, just north of the town centre along Bridge St.

Translink Goldline (www.translink.co.uk) bus 273 goes from Belfast to Omagh (£12, 1¾ hours, hourly Monday to Saturday, six on Sunday) via Dungannon and on to Derry (£8, 1¼ hours). Bus 94 goes to Enniskillen (£8, one hour, six or seven Monday to Friday, three on Saturday, one on Sunday).

Ulster American Folk Park

In the 18th and 19th centuries thousands of Ulster people left their homes to forge a new life across the Atlantic; 200,000 emigrated in the 18th century alone. Their story is told at **Ulster American Folk Park** (☎028-8224 3292; www.nmni.com/uafp; 2 Mellon Rd; adult/child £9/5.50; ⏲10am-5pm Tue-Sun Mar-Sep, 10am-4pm Tue-Fri, 11am-4pm Sat & Sun Oct-Feb), one of Ireland's best museums, which features a sprawling **outdoor history park**, where exhibits are split into Old World and New World areas and come alive through re-enactments.

The two parts of the park are cleverly linked by passing through a mock-up of an emigrant ship. Original buildings from various parts of Ulster have been dismantled and re-erected here, including a blacksmith's forge, a weaver's thatched cottage, a Presbyterian meeting house and a schoolhouse. In the American section of the park you can visit a genuine 18th-century settler's stone cottage and a log house, both shipped across the Atlantic from Pennsylvania, plus many more original buildings.

The **Exhibition Hall** explains the close connections between Ulster and the USA – the American Declaration of Independence was signed by several Ulstermen – and includes an original Calistoga wagon.

Costumed guides and artisans are on hand to explain the arts of spinning, weaving, candle-making and so on. **Special events** are held throughout the year, including re-enactments of American Civil War battles, a festival of traditional Irish music in May, American Independence Day celebrations in July, and the Appalachian and Bluegrass Music Festival in late August/September. At least half a day is needed to do the place justice.

The park is 8km northwest of Omagh off the A5. Last admission is 1½ hours before closing.

Translink Goldline bus 273 from Belfast to Derry (hourly Monday to Saturday, six on Sunday) stops in Omagh, and will stop on request at the park gates.

Sperrin Mountains

When representatives of the London guilds visited Ulster in 1609, the Lord Deputy of Ireland made sure they were kept well away from the Sperrin Mountains, fearing that the sight of these bleak, moorland hills would put them off the idea of planting settlers here. However on a sunny spring day, when the russet bogs and yellow gorse stand out against a clear blue sky, the Sperrins can offer some grand walking. The area is also dotted with thousands of standing stones and prehistoric tombs.

Getting Around

Ulsterbus service 403, the *Sperrin Rambler*, runs twice daily Monday to Saturday between Omagh and Magherafelt, stopping at Gortin.

Gortin

The village of Gortin, about 15km north of Omagh, lies at the foot of Mullaghcarn (542m), the southernmost of the Sperrin summits (unfortunately capped by two prominent radio masts). Hundreds of hikers converge for a mass ascent of the hill on **Cairn Sunday** (the last Sunday in July), a revival of an ancient pilgrimage. There are several good walks around the village, and a scenic drive to **Gortin Lakes**, with views north to the main Sperrin ridge.

Creggan

Enjoy an exhibition covering the ecology of the surrounding bogs and the archaeology of the region at museum and nature centre, **An Creagán** (028-8076 1112; www.an-creagan.com; A505, Creggan; bike rental ½-day £7, admission free; 11am-5pm). Informative **nature trails** range from 400m to 5.5km. There are 44 prehistoric monuments within 8km of the centre, including the **Beaghmore Stone Circles**. It's about halfway between Omagh and Cookstown (20km east of Omagh). There's a simple **cafe**.

What the ancient stone circles lack in stature – the stones are all less than 1m tall – they make up in complexity, with seven stone circles (one filled with smaller stones, nicknamed 'dragon's teeth') and a dozen or so alignments and cairns. The sites are signposted about 8km east of Creggan, and 4km north of the A505.

OFF THE BEATEN TRACK

DAVAGH FOREST PARK TRAILS

Remote Davagh Forest Park provides some of the best **mountain biking** in all of Ireland, ranging from family-friendly green and blue trails along a wooded stream to 16km of red trails leading to the top of Beleevenamore Mountain, with several challenging rock slabs and drop-offs on the descents.

Walking gives visitors time to enjoy this landscape of rolling hills and sweeping forests. A 3km loop trail takes in the forests and red-hued stream.

The trailhead is on a minor road, 10km northwest of Cookstown, signposted from the A505 Cookstown to Omagh road at Dunnamore. For details see www.mountainbikeni.com and www.walkni.com.

East Tyrone

The market towns of Cookstown and Dungannon are the main settlements in the eastern part of County Tyrone, but the main sights here are in the surrounding countryside.

Sights

★**Wellbrook Beetling Mill** HISTORIC BUILDING
(028-8674 8210; www.nationaltrust.org.uk; 20 Wellbrook Rd, Corkhill; adult/child £5/free; 2-5pm Sat, Sun & public holidays mid-Mar–late Sep) Beetling, the final stage of linen-making, involves pounding the cloth with wooden hammers, or beetles, to give it a smooth sheen. This 18th-century mill still has its original machinery and stages loud demonstrations of the linen-making process led by guides in period costume. The whitewashed mill is on a pretty stretch of the River Ballinderry, 7km west of Cookstown, just off the A505.

Ardboe High Cross HISTORIC SITE
(off B73) This 6th-century monastic site overlooking Lough Neagh is home to one of Ireland's best-preserved and most elaborately decorated Celtic stone crosses. The

10th-century Ardboe high cross stands 5.5m tall, with 22 carved panels depicting biblical scenes. It's an evocative place 16km east of Cookstown, with distant views and a nearby cemetery. Take the B73 through Coagh and watch for the signs for Ardboe High Cross, which leads along a narrow country road.

The western side of the cross (facing the road) has New Testament scenes including the Adoration of the Magi and Christ's entry into Jerusalem; the more weathered eastern face (towards the lough) shows Old Testament scenes.

Argory HISTORIC BUILDING
(028-8778 4753; www.nationaltrust.org.uk; 144 Derrycaw Rd; grounds adult/child £3/1.50, house tour £5/2.30; noon-5pm Thu-Sun Mar-Jun, daily Jul & Aug, to 4pm Wed-Sun Sep;) This 1824 grand mansion could as well be preserved in amber as it has changed little since the early 1900s. Electricity was never installed and you can wander around as if living the life of a character in a BBC costume drama. It has a new playground for visitors who may find the thrills otherwise elusive.

Argory is just on the border with County Armagh, 5km northwest of Moy off the B106.

Grant Ancestral Homestead HISTORIC SITE
(028-8555 7133; 45 Dergenagh Rd, Ballygawley; 9am-5pm) FREE Ulysses Simpson Grant (1822–85) led Union forces to victory in the American Civil War and later served as the USA's 18th president for two terms, from 1869 to 1877. His maternal grandfather, John Simpson, emigrated from County Tyrone to Pennsylvania in 1760, but the farm he left behind at Dergina has been restored in the style of a typical Ulster smallholding, as it would have been during the time of Grant's presidency.

The site is 20km west of Dungannon, signposted south of the A4.

Sleeping & Eating

★Tullylagan Country House HOTEL ££
(028-8676 5100; www.tullylaganhotel.com; 40b Tullylagan Rd, Cookstown; r £75-135, mains £11-18; restaurant 7am-9pm Mon-Sat, to 4pm Sun;) Set amid beautiful riverside gardens, the ivy-clad Tullylagan has a Victorian country-manor feel, with gilt-framed mirrors, polished wooden floors and marble-effect bathrooms. The hotel's excellent **Kitchen Restaurant** specialises in locally sourced seafood, game and beef. It's 4km south of Cookstown (just off the A29).

Grange Lodge B&B ££
(028-8778 4212; www.grangelodgecountryhouse.com; 7 Grange Rd, Dungannon; s/d from £75/85, set dinner from £40; dinner 7.30pm, book 48hr in advance;) The five-room Grange is a period gem set in its own 8-hectare grounds. Parts of the house, which is packed with antiques, date from 1698, though most are Georgian with Victorian additions. The proprietor is an award-winning chef and the Grange runs cookery courses. It's 5km southeast of Dungannon, signposted off the A29.

Deli on the Green MODERN IRISH £
(028-8775 1775; www.delionthegreen.com; 30 Linen Green, Moygashel; mains £6-10; deli 8.30am-5.30pm Mon-Sat, bistro to 3pm Mon-Thu, to 6pm Fri & Sat) Take a break from the Linen Green shops at this stylish little deli-bistro. Fresh local and seasonal fare makes for great picnics from the deli, while you'll find creative takes on sandwiches, salads and hot meals in the bistro.

★Brewer's House MODERN IRISH ££
(028-8776 1932; www.thebrewershouse.com; 73 Castlecaulfield Rd, Donaghmore; mains £10-24; kitchen noon-9pm;) This much-loved (and awarded) old village pub does exceptional food, with meat, seafood, burgers, and fish and chips prepared creatively. The beer and wine lists are tops. There are tables outside. It's 7km northwest of Dungannon.

Shopping

Linen Green Designer Village SHOPPING CENTRE
(028-8775 3761; www.thelinengreen.co.uk; off A29, Moygashel; 10am-5pm Mon-Sat) Housed in the former Moygashel Linen Mills, this stylish complex includes a range of designer shops and factory outlets, plus a **visitor centre** with an exhibition covering the history of the local linen industry. It's a good place to shop for men's and women's fashion, shoes, accessories and linen goods. It's southeast of Dungannon.

Information

Tourist information for County Tyrone can be found at **Ranfurly House Arts & Visitor Centre** (028-8772 8600; www.dungannon.info; 26 Market Sq, Dungannon; 9am-5pm Mon-Sat year-round, 1-4pm Sun Apr-Sep;), with an exhibition on the Flight of the Earls in 1607, when Hugh O'Neill and 90 other Ulster chiefs fled the country, leaving Ulster open to English rule.

Understand Ireland

Ireland Today

The Republic of Ireland has travelled a long way since the dawn of the new millennium. It has yo-yoed out of recession and back before once again emerging from the economic gloom of the global financial crisis. As the nation continues to shed its conservative skin, it is growing increasingly comfortable with its multicultural, more socially liberated identity and its progressive presence on the global stage.

Best in Print

Dubliners (James Joyce, 1914) A collection of short stories still as poignant and relevant today as when they were written.

Room (Emma Donoghue, 2010) A harrowing but beautiful account of a boy and his mother being held prisoner, told from the boy's perspective.

The Secret Scripture (Sebastian Barry, 2008) The story of a 100-year-old patient of a mental hospital who writes her autobiography; now a 2015 film directed by Jim Sheridan.

The Gathering (Anne Enright, 2007) Powerful account of alcoholism and domestic abuse in an Irish family.

Best on Film

Bloody Sunday (Paul Greengrass, 2002) Unmissable account of events in Derry in 1972.

The Dead (John Huston, 1987) Huston brings James Joyce's story to life in his last film, with powerful performances by Donal McCann and Anjelica Huston.

'71 (Yann Demange, 2014) About a British soldier separated from his unit during a Belfast riot in 1971.

What Richard Did (Lenny Abrahamson, 2012) A privileged youth assaults a romantic rival who dies of his injuries; loosely based on real events that occurred in 2000.

A Social Revolution

On 22 May, 2015, the Republic of Ireland became the first country to legalise gay marriage by popular vote. The margin of victory (62%) was noteworthy given that homosexual activity had only been decriminalised in 1993, and showed just how far Ireland had come in the intervening years. It was, for supporters of same-sex marriage at least, an extraordinary result: on the night of the announcement, Dublin (where the referendum was passed with more than a 70% majority) celebrated with wild abandon. For once in a long time, the reasoning went, Ireland was making headlines for all the right reasons (that night, Hillary Clinton tweeted 'Well done, Ireland!').

Most observers agreed that the result had a deeper significance than just reflecting the majority attitude toward LGBT rights. The Catholic bishops, once the last word on all matters related to morality and social affairs, had maintained a dignified opposition to the motion, but their muted objections were a tacit recognition that the Church's conservative voice no longer carries like it once did, especially for those under 30. The referendum had galvanised huge numbers of Generation Y that had become chronically apathetic in the face of a political system that had – in their experience – delivered nothing but incompetence, disappointment and hard times. The times they are a-changing, a lot of the Irish have chimed, and it's about bloody time.

Back in the Black

The other bit of good news was that in late 2013 the Republic finally exited the restrictive austerity program imposed on it in 2010 by its international creditors in exchange for a €78 billion bailout that saved the country from bankruptcy. But the country could barely crack a smile in response: the cost of austerity was prohibitively high for many Irish, especially those on the vulnerable margins. Key social services were slashed or eliminated altogether in a deep-cutting cost-saving effort; wages fell by an average of 15% across the board; and a slew of new indirect taxes put additional burdens on households already put to the pin of their collars.

In 2015, key economic statistics showed that the country had definitely turned a corner. Unemployment, which had risen above 15% during the worst of the recession, fell to below 10%, even if government critics put that down to skyrocketing emigration – but even that fell by 20% in 2015 and instead there was a rise in the number of returning Irish, eager it seems to take advantage of Europe's fastest-growing economy, with growth rates of over 3.5% (almost triple the European average).

A Vote of Confidence?

Needless to say, the government – a coalition of right-leaning Fine Gael and left-of-centre Labour which came to power in 2011 with the promise of repairing the damage of the financial crisis – are taking full credit for the recovery, which couldn't come at a better time. The pending election will determine whether the electorate buys the government's 'we did it for your own good' message or punishes them for every cut and extra charge they've had to endure over the previous five years.

Waiting in the wings is Sinn Féin, the old political wing of the IRA. Still led by the old war horse Gerry Adams, the party has reinvented itself dramatically. In Northern Ireland they're coalition partners in government with their bitterest rivals the Democratic Unionist Party, while in the Republic they're now – according to some polls – the most popular party due to a compelling (many say populist) rhetoric of anti-austerity that has a broad appeal.

Easter Rising Centenary

Whatever happens, the election will take place against the backdrop of the most significant anniversary for decades: the centenary of the Easter Rising of 1916, when republican nationalists declared a republic before being captured and executed by British forces. Every party wants to use the occasion to make political hay, but Fine Gael's own historical ideology as a conservative party staunchly opposed to violent rebellion makes it a tougher fit; not so for Sinn Féin, which sees itself as the natural heir of the heroes of 1916.

POPULATION: **4.83 MILLION / 1.81 MILLION (REPUBLIC/NORTHERN IRELAND)**

AREA: **84,421 SQ KM / 13,843 SQ KM (R/NI)**

INFLATION: **-0.7% / 0% (R/NI)**

UNEMPLOYMENT: **9.8% / 6.2% (R/NI)**

belief systems
Republic of Ireland
(% of population)

belief systems
Northern Ireland
(% of population)

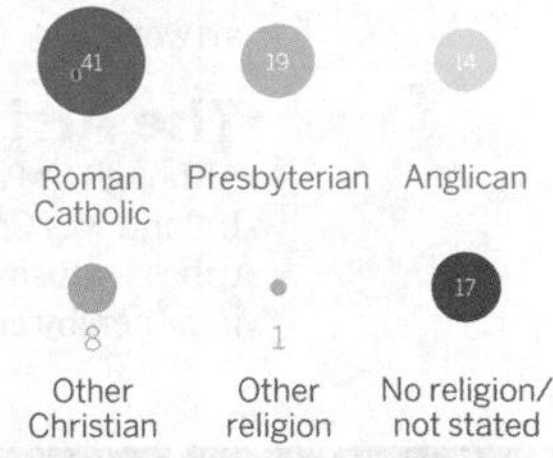

population per sq km

History

From pre-Celts to Celtic cubs, Ireland's history has been a search for identity, which would have been a little more straightforward if this small island hadn't been of such interest to a host of foreign parties – Celtic tribes, Viking marauders, Norman invaders and the English. Indeed, it is Ireland's fractious relationship with its nearest neighbour that has occupied much of the last thousand years, and it is through the prism of that relationship that a huge part of the Irish identity is reflected – but what emerges isn't nearly as clear-cut as you might expect.

For a concise, 10-minute read on who the Celts were, see www.ibiblio.org/gaelic/celts.html.

The Native Irish

It took the various Celtic tribes roughly 500 years to settle in Ireland, beginning in the 8th century BC. The last of the tribes, commonly known as the Gaels (which in the local language came to mean 'foreigner'), came ashore in the 3rd century BC and proceeded to divide the island into five provinces – Leinster, Meath, Connaught, Ulster and Munster (Meath later merged with Leinster) – that were subdivided into territories controlled by as many as one hundred minor kings and chieftains, all of whom nominally paid allegiance to a high king who sat at Tara, in County Meath.

The Celts set about creating the basics of what we now term 'Irish' culture: they devised a sophisticated code of law called the Brehon Law, which remained in use until the early 17th century; and their swirling, mazelike design style, evident on artefacts nearly 2000 years old, is considered the epitome of Irish design. Some excellent ancient Celtic designs survive in the Broighter Hoard in the National Museum in Dublin. The Turoe Stone in County Galway is another fine representative of Celtic artwork.

The Arrival of Christianity

Although St Patrick gets all the credit, between the 3rd and 5th centuries Ireland was Christianised by a host of missionaries, who converted pagan tribes by fusing their local Druidic rituals with the new Christian teaching, thereby creating a hybrid known as Celtic or Insular Christianity.

TIMELINE

10,000–8000 BC

After the last ice age ends, humans arrive in Ireland during the Mesolithic era, originally crossing a land bridge between Scotland and Ireland. Few archaeological traces remain of this group.

4500 BC

The first Neolithic farmers arrive in Ireland by boat from as far afield as the Iberian peninsula, bringing cattle, sheep and crops, marking the beginnings of a settled agricultural economy.

700–300 BC

Iron technology gradually replaces bronze. The Celtic culture and language arrive, ushering in a thousand years of cultural and political dominance and leaving a legacy still visible today.

Irish Christian scholars excelled in the study of Latin and Greek philosophy and Christian theology in the monasteries that flourished at, among other places, Clonmacnoise in County Offaly, Glendalough in County Wicklow and Lismore in County Waterford. It was the Golden Age, and the arts of manuscript illumination, metalworking and sculpture flourished, producing such treasures as the *Book of Kells,* ornate jewellery and the many carved stone crosses that dot the 'island of saints and scholars'.

Top Monastic Sites

Cashel *County Tipperary*

Clonmacnoise *County Offaly*

Glendalough *County Wicklow*

The Vikings Are Coming!

The next group to try their luck were the Vikings, who first showed up in AD 795 and began plundering the prosperous monasteries. In self-defence, the monks built round towers, which served as lookout posts and places of refuge during attacks; you can see surviving examples throughout the country including some fine examples at Glendalough, Kells and Steeple, near Antrim.

Despite the monks' best efforts, the Vikings had their way, mostly due to superior weaponry but also thanks to elements of the local population, who sided with the marauders for profit or protection. By the 10th century the Norsemen were well established in Ireland, having founded towns such as Wicklow, Waterford, Wexford and their capital Dyfflin,

ST PATRICK

Ireland's patron saint is remembered all around the world on 17 March, when people of all ethnicities drink Guinness and wear green clothing. But behind the hoopla was a real man with a serious mission. For it was Patrick (389–461) who introduced Christianity to Ireland.

The plain truth of it is that he wasn't Irish. This symbol of Irish pride hailed from what is now Wales, which at the time of his birth was under Roman rule.

Patrick's arrival in Ireland was made possible by Irish raiders who kidnapped him when he was 16, and took him across the channel to work as a slave. He found religion, escaped from captivity and returned to Britain. But he vowed to make it his life's work to make Christians out of the Irish. He was ordained, then appointed Bishop of Ireland. Back he went over the channel.

He based himself in Armagh, where St Patrick's Church of Ireland Cathedral stands on the site of his old church. Patrick quickly converted peasants and noblemen in great numbers. Within 30 years, much of Ireland had been baptised and the country was divided into Catholic dioceses and parishes. He also established monasteries throughout Ireland, which would be the foundations of Irish scholarship for many centuries.

So next St Paddy's Day, as you're swilling Guinness and champing down corned beef and cabbage, think of who the man really was.

AD 431–2

Pope Celestine I sends Bishop Palladius to Ireland to minister to those 'already believing in Christ'; St Patrick arrives the following year to continue the mission.

550–800

The flowering of early monasticism in Ireland. The great monastic teachers begin exporting their knowledge across Europe, ushering in Ireland's 'Golden Age'.

795–841

Vikings plunder Irish monasteries; their raping and pillaging urges sated, they establish settlements throughout the country, including Dublin, and soon turn it into a centre of economic power.

1014

The Battle of Clontarf takes place on Good Friday between the forces of the high king, Brian Ború, and the forces led by the king of Leinster, Máelmorda mac Murchada.

which later became Dublin. The Vikings were defeated at the Battle of Clontarf in 1014 by Brian Ború, king of Munster, but Ború was killed and the Vikings, much like the Celts before them, eventually settled, giving up the rape-rob-and-run policy in favour of integration and assimilation: by intermarrying with the Celtic tribes, they introduced red hair and freckles to the Irish gene pool.

The Course of Irish History by TW Moody and FX Martin is a hefty volume by two Trinity College professors who trace much of Ireland's history back to its land and its proximity to England.

The English Invade

The '800 years' of English rule in Ireland nominally began with the Norman invasion of 1169, which was really more of an invitation as the barons, led by Richard Fitz Gilbert de Clare, earl of Pembroke (1130–76; aka Strongbow), had been asked to assist the king of Leinster in a territorial squabble. Two years later, King Henry II of England came ashore with a substantial army and a request from Pope Adrian IV to bring the rebel Christian missionaries to heel.

Despite the king's overall authority, the Anglo-Norman barons carved Ireland up between them and over the next 300 years set about consolidating their feudal power. Once again the effects of assimilation were in play, as the Anglo-Normans and their hirelings became, in the oft-quoted phrase, *Hiberniores Hibernis ipsis* ('more Irish than the Irish themselves'). They dotted the country with castles, but their real legacy is in the cities they built, such as magnificent Kilkenny, which today retains much of its medieval character. The Anglo-Normans may have pledged allegiance to the English king, but in truth they were loyal only to themselves: by the turn of the 16th century, the Crown's direct rule didn't extend any further than a cordon surrounding Dublin known as the Pale. But you can only ignore an English king for so long...

The expression 'beyond the Pale' came into use when the Pale was the Anglo-Norman-controlled part of Ireland. To them, the rest of Ireland was an uncivilised territory populated by barbarians.

Ireland & the Tudors

When Henry VIII declared himself head of the Church in England in 1534, following his split with the papacy over his divorce from Catherine of Aragon, the Anglo-Normans cried foul and some took arms against the crown. Worried that an Irish rising would be of help to Spain or France, Henry responded firmly, quashing the rebellion, confiscating the rebels' lands and (as in England) dissolving all Irish monasteries. He then had himself declared King of Ireland.

Elizabeth I (1533–1603) came to the throne in 1558 with the same uncompromising attitude to Ireland as her father. Ulster was the most hostile to her, with the Irish fighting doggedly under the command of Hugh O'Neill, earl of Tyrone, but they too were finally defeated in 1603. O'Neill, though, achieved something of a pyrrhic victory when he refused to surrender until after he heard of Elizabeth's death. He and his fellow earls then fled the country in what become known as the Flight of the Earls. It

1169

Henry II's Welsh and Norman barons land in Wexford and capture Waterford and Wexford with MacMurrough's help. It is the beginning of an 800-year occupation by Britain.

1171

King Henry II invades Ireland, forcing the Cambro-Norman warlords and some of the Gaelic Irish kings to accept him as their overlord.

1350–1530

The Anglo-Norman barons establish power bases independent of the English Crown. Over the following two centuries, English control gradually recedes to an area around Dublin known as 'the Pale'.

1366

The English Crown enacts the Statutes of Kilkenny, outlawing intermarriage, the Irish language and other Irish customs to stop the Anglo-Normans from assimilating too much with the Irish. It doesn't work.

left Ulster open to English rule and to the policy of Plantation, which involved confiscating the lands of the flown earls and redistributing them to subjects loyal to the crown. Although the confiscations happened all over the country, they were most thorough in Ulster.

Oliver Cromwell Invades Ireland

At the outset of the English Civil War in 1642, the Irish threw their support behind Charles I against the very Protestant parliamentarians in the hope that victory for the king would lead to the restoration of Catholic power in Ireland. When Oliver Cromwell and his Roundheads defeated the Royalists and took Charles' head off in 1649, Cromwell turned his attention to the disloyal Irish. His nine-month campaign was effective and brutal (Drogheda was particularly mistreated); yet more lands were confiscated – Cromwell's famous utterance that the Irish could 'go to hell or to Connaught' seems odd given the province's beauty, but there wasn't much arable land out there – and Catholic rights restricted even more.

A History of Ulster by Jonathan Bardon is a serious and far-reaching attempt to come to grips with Northern Ireland's saga.

The Boyne & Penal Laws

Catholic Ireland's next major setback came in 1690. Yet again the Irish had backed the wrong horse, this time supporting James II after his deposition in the Glorious Revolution by the Dutch Protestant King William of Orange (who was married to James' daughter Mary!). After James had unsuccessfully laid siege to Derry for 105 days (the Loyalist cry of 'No surrender!', in use to this day, dates from the siege), in July he fought William's armies by the banks of the Boyne in County Louth and was roundly defeated.

The final ignominy for Catholics came in 1695 with the passing of the Penal Laws, which prohibited them from owning land or entering any higher profession. Irish culture, music and education were banned in the hope that Catholicism would be eradicated. Most Catholics continued to worship at secret locations, but some prosperous Irish converted to Protestantism to preserve their careers and wealth. Land was steadily transferred to Protestant owners, and a significant majority of the Catholic population became tenants living in wretched conditions. By the late 18th century, Catholics owned barely 5% of the land.

Cromwell: An Honourable Enemy by Tom Reilly advances the unpopular view that perhaps the destruction of Cromwell's campaign is grossly exaggerated. You're no doubt familiar with the common view; here's the contrary position. (Yes, Reilly is Irish.)

Revolt Against British Rule

Beginning towards the end of the 18th century, the main thrust of opposition to Irish inequalities resulting from the Penal Laws came from an unlikely source. A handful of liberal Protestants, versed in the ideologies of the Enlightenment and inspired by the revolutions in France and the newly established United States of America, began organising direct opposition to British rule.

1536–41

Henry VIII orders the dissolution of the monasteries and confiscation of church property. In 1541 he arranges for the Irish Parliament to declare him King of Ireland.

1585

Potatoes from South America are introduced to Ireland, where they eventually become a staple on nearly every table in the country.

1594

Hugh O'Neill, earl of Tyrone, orders lead from England to reroof his castle, but instead uses it for bullets – instigating the start of the Nine Years' War.

1601

The Battle of Kinsale is fought between Queen Elizabeth I's armies and the combined rebel forces led by Hugh O'Neill. O'Neill surrenders and the back of the Irish rebellion against the Crown is broken.

The best known was Theobald Wolfe Tone (1763–98), a young Dublin lawyer who led a group called the United Irishmen in their attempts to reform and reduce British power in Ireland (Loyalist Protestants prepared for the possibility of conflict by forming the Protestant Orange Society, later known as the Orange Order). Wolfe Tone attempted to enlist French help in his uprising, but the French failure to land an army of succour in 1796 left the organisation exposed to retribution and the men met their bloody end in the Battle of Vinegar Hill in 1798. Three years later, the British sought to put an end to Irish agitation with the Act of Union, but the Nationalist genie was already out of the bottle.

For the Cause of Liberty: A Thousand Years of Ireland's Heroes by Terry Golway vividly describes the struggles of Irish nationalism.

The Famine, O'Connell & Parnell

The 19th century was marked by repeated efforts to wrest some kind of control from Britain. There were the radical Republicans, who advocated use of force to found a secular, egalitarian republic that tried – and failed – in 1848 and 1867. And there were the moderates, who advocated nonviolent and legal action to force the government into concession.

The Great Liberator

Dominating the moderate landscape for nearly three decades was Kerry-born Daniel O'Connell (1775–1847), who tirelessly devoted himself to the cause of Catholic emancipation. In 1828 he was elected to the British Parliament but, being a Catholic, he couldn't actually take his seat: to avoid the possibility of an uprising, the government was forced to pass the 1829 Act of Catholic Emancipation, allowing some well-off Catholics voting rights and the right to be elected as Members of Parliament.

O'Connell continued to fight for Irish self-determination and became known as a powerful speaker, not only on behalf of Ireland but against all kinds of injustice, including slavery: the abolitionist leader Frederick Douglass was one of his greatest admirers (their relationship was specifically referred to by President Obama during his 2011 visit). O'Connell, known as 'the Liberator', was adored by the Irish, who turned out in their tens of thousands to hear him speak, but his unwillingness to step outside the law was to prove his undoing: when the government banned one of his rallies from going ahead, O'Connell stood down – ostensibly to avoid the prospect of violence and bloodshed. But Ireland was in the midst of the Potato Famine, and his failure to defy the British was seen as capitulation; he was imprisoned for a time and died a broken man in 1847.

Ireland Since the Famine by FSL Lyons is a standard text for all students of modern Irish history.

The Uncrowned King of Ireland

Charles Stewart Parnell (1846–91) was the other great 19th-century statesman. Like O'Connell, he too was a powerful orator, but the primary

1607	1649–53	1688–90	1695
O'Neill and 90 other Ulster chiefs sail to Europe, leaving Ireland forever. Known as the Flight of the Earls, it leaves Ulster open to English rule and the policy of Plantation.	Cromwell lays waste to Ireland after the Irish support Charles I in the English Civil War; this includes the mass slaughter of Catholic Irish and the confiscation of two million hectares of land.	Following the deposition of King James II, James' Catholic army fights the Protestant forces of his successor, King William, resulting in William's victory at the Battle of the Boyne, 12 July 1690.	The Penal Laws (aka the 'popery code') prohibit Catholics from owning a horse, marrying outside their religion, building churches out of anything but wood, and from buying or inheriting property.

focus of his artful attentions was land reform, particularly the reduction of rents and the improvement of working conditions (conveniently referred to as the 'Three Fs': fair rent, free sale and fixity of tenure). Parnell championed the activities of the Land League, which instigated the strategy of 'boycotting' (named after one particularly unpleasant agent called Charles Boycott) tenants, agents and landlords who didn't adhere to the Land League's aims: these people were treated like lepers by the local population. In 1881 they won an important victory with the passing of the Land Act, which granted most of the League's demands.

The Great Hunger by Cecil Woodham-Smith is the classic study of the Great Famine of 1845–51.

Parnell's other great struggle was for a limited form of autonomy for Ireland. Despite the nominal support of the Liberal leader William Gladstone, Home Rule bills introduced in 1886 and 1892 were uniformly rejected by Parliament. Like O'Connell before him, Parnell's star plummeted dramatically: in 1890 he was embroiled in a divorce proceeding that scandalised puritanical Ireland. The 'uncrowned king of Ireland' was forced to resign and died less than a year later.

THE GREAT FAMINE

As a result of the Great Famine of 1845–51, it's estimated that a staggering one million people died and some two million were forced to emigrate from Ireland. This great tragedy is all the more inconceivable given that the scale of suffering was attributable to selfishness as much as to natural causes. Potatoes were the staple food of a rapidly growing, desperately poor population and, when a blight hit the crops, prices soared. The repressive Penal Laws ensured that farmers, already crippled with high rents, could ill afford the few subsistence potatoes provided. Inevitably, most tenants fell into arrears with little or no concession given by the mostly indifferent landlords and were evicted or sent to the dire conditions of the workhouses.

Shamefully, during this time there were abundant harvests of wheat and dairy produce – the country was producing more than enough grain to feed the entire population and it's said that more cattle were sold abroad than there were people on the island. But while millions of its citizens were starving, Ireland was forced to export its food to Britain and overseas.

The Poor Laws, in place at the height of the Famine, deemed landlords responsible for the maintenance of their poor and encouraged many to 'remove' tenants from their estates by paying their way to America. Many Irish were sent unwittingly to their deaths on board the notoriously scourged 'coffin ships'. British prime minister Sir Robert Peel made well-intentioned but inadequate gestures at famine relief, and some – but far too few – landlords did their best for their tenants.

Mass emigration continued to reduce the population during the next one hundred years and huge numbers of Irish emigrants who found their way abroad, particularly to the USA, carried with them a lasting bitterness.

1795

Concerned at the attempts of the Society of United Irishmen to secure equal rights for non-establishment Protestants and Catholics, a group of Protestants create the Orange Order.

1798

The flogging and killing of potential rebels sparks a rising led by the United Irishmen and their leader, Wolfe Tone. Wolfe Tone is captured and taken to Dublin, where he commits suicide.

1801

The Act of Union comes into effect, uniting Ireland politically with Britain. Irish Parliament votes itself out of existence following a campaign of bribery. Around 100 Members of Parliament move to the House of Commons in London.

1828–29

Daniel O'Connell exploits a loophole in the law to win a seat in Parliament but is unable to take it because he is Catholic. The prime minister passes the Catholic Emancipation Act, giving limited rights to Catholics.

Fomenting Revolution

Ireland's struggle for some kind of autonomy picked up pace in the second decade of the 20th century. The radicalism that had always been at the fringes of Irish Nationalist aspirations was once again beginning to assert itself, partly in response to a hardening of attitudes in Ulster. Mass opposition to any kind of Irish independence had resulted in the formation of the Ulster Volunteer Force (UVF), a Loyalist vigilante group whose 100,000-plus members swore to resist any attempt to impose Home Rule on Ireland. Nationalists responded by creating the Irish Volunteer Force (IVF) and a showdown seemed inevitable.

The Irish in America by Michael Coffey takes up the history of the Famine where many histories leave off: the turbulent experiences of Irish immigrants in the USA.

Home Rule was finally passed in 1914, but the outbreak of WWI meant that its enactment was shelved for the duration. For most Irish, the suspension was disappointing but hardly unreasonable, and the majority of the volunteers enlisted to help fight the Germans.

The Easter Rising

A few, however, did not heed the call. Two small groups – a section of the Irish Volunteers under Pádraig Pearse and the Irish Citizens' Army led by James Connolly – conspired in a rebellion that took the country by surprise. A depleted Volunteer group marched into Dublin on Easter Monday 1916 and took over a number of key positions in the city, claiming the General Post Office on O'Connell St as its headquarters. From its steps, Pearse read out to passers-by a declaration that Ireland was now a republic and that his band was the provisional government. Less than a week of fighting ensued before the rebels surrendered to the superior British forces. The rebels weren't popular and had to be protected from angry Dubliners as they were marched to jail.

The Easter Rising would probably have had little impact on the Irish situation had the British not made martyrs of the rebel leaders. Of the 77 given death sentences, 15 were executed, including the injured Connolly, who was shot while strapped to a chair. This brought about a sea change in public attitudes, and support for the Republicans rose dramatically.

For articles exploring the whole gamut of Irish history, check out the National Library's historical blog at www.nli.ie/blog.

War with Britain

By the end of WWI, Home Rule was far too little, far too late. In the 1918 general election, the Republicans stood under the banner of Sinn Féin and won a large majority of the Irish seats. Ignoring London's Parliament, where technically they were supposed to sit, the newly elected Sinn Féin deputies – many of them veterans of the 1916 Easter Rising – declared Ireland independent and formed the first Dáil Éireann (Irish assembly or lower house), which sat in Dublin's Mansion House under the leadership of Eamon de Valera (1882–1975). The Irish Volunteers

1845–51

A mould ravages the potato harvest. The British government adopts a laissez-faire attitude, resulting in the deaths of between 500,000 and one million, and the emigration of up to two million others.

1879–82

The Land War, led by the Land League, sees tenant farmers defying their landlords en masse to force the passing of the Land Act in 1881, which allows for fair rent, fixity of tenure and free sale.

1884

The Gaelic Athletic Association (GAA) is founded in Hayes Hotel, Thurles, County Tipperary. Its aim is to promote Gaelic games and culture; today hurling and Gaelic football are immensely popular.

1890s

The Gaelic Revival, championed by poet WB Yeats, sees a focused interest in the Irish language and Irish culture, including folklore, sport, music and the arts.

became the Irish Republican Army (IRA) and the Dáil authorised it to wage war on British troops in Ireland.

As wars go, the War of Independence was pretty small fry. It lasted two and a half years and cost around 1200 casualties. But it was a pretty nasty affair, as the IRA fought a guerrilla-style, hit-and-run campaign against the British, whose numbers were swelled by returning veterans of WWI known as Black and Tans (on account of their uniforms, a mix of army khaki and police black), most of whom were so traumatised by their wartime experiences that they were prone to all kinds of brutality.

Brendan O'Brien's popular *Pocket History of the IRA* summarises a lot of complex history in a mere 150 pages; it's a good introduction.

A Kind of Freedom

A truce in July 1921 led to intense negotiations between the two sides. The resulting treaty, signed on 6 December 1921, created the Irish Free State, made up of 26 of 32 Irish counties. The remaining six – all in Ulster – remained part of the UK. The treaty was an imperfect document: not only did it cement the geographic divisions on the island that 50 years later would explode into the Troubles, it also caused a split among Nationalists – between those who believed the treaty to be a necessary stepping stone towards full independence, and those who saw it as capitulation to the British and a betrayal of Republican ideals. This division was to determine the course of Irish political affairs for virtually the remainder of the century.

Civil War

The treaty was ratified after a bitter debate and the June 1922 elections resulted in a victory for the pro-treaty side. But the anti-treaty forces rallied behind de Valera, who, though president of the Dáil, had not been a member of the treaty negotiating team (affording him, in the eyes of his critics and opponents, maximum deniability should the negotiations go pear-shaped) and objected to some of the treaty's provisions, most notably the oath of allegiance to the British monarch.

Within two weeks of the elections, civil war broke out between comrades who, a year previously, had fought alongside each other. The most prominent casualty of this particularly bitter conflict was Michael Collins (1890–1922), mastermind of the IRA's campaign during the War of Independence and a chief negotiator of the Anglo-Irish Treaty – shot in an ambush in his native Cork. Collins himself had presaged the bitterness that would result from the treaty: upon signing it, he is said to have declared, 'I tell you, I have signed my own death warrant.'

Neil Jordan's movie *Michael Collins*, starring Liam Neeson as the revolutionary, depicts the Easter Rising, the founding of the Free State and Collins' violent demise.

1904

16 June is the day in which all of the events of James Joyce's *Ulysses* takes place – chosen because it was the date Joyce first went out with his wife, Nora.

1916

The Easter Rising: a group of Republicans takes Dublin's General Post Office and announces the formation of an Irish republic. After less than a week of fighting, the rebels surrender to the superior British forces.

1919–21

Irish War of Independence, aka the Black and Tan War on account of British irregulars wearing mixed police (black) and army (khaki) uniforms, begins in January 1919.

1921

Two years and 1200 casualties later, the war ends in a truce on 11 July 1921 that leads to peace talks. After negotiations in London, the Irish delegation signs the Anglo-Irish Treaty on 6 December.

The Making of a Republic

The Civil War ground to an exhausted halt in 1923 with the victory of the pro-treaty side, who governed the new state until 1932. Defeated but unbowed, de Valera founded a new party in 1926 called Fianna Fáil (Soldiers of Ireland) and won a majority in the 1932 elections – they would remain in charge until 1948. In the meantime, de Valera created a new constitution in 1937 that did away with the hated oath of allegiance, reaffirmed the special position of the Catholic Church and once again laid claim to the six counties of Northern Ireland. In 1948 Ireland officially left the Commonwealth and became a republic but, as historical irony would have it, it was Fine Gael, as the old pro-treaty party was now known, that declared it – Fianna Fáil had surprisingly lost the election that year. After 800 years, Ireland – or at least a substantial chunk of it – was independent.

Growing Pains & Roaring Tigers

Unquestionably the most significant figure since independence, Eamon de Valera made an immense contribution to an independent Ireland but, as the 1950s stretched into the 1960s, his vision for the country was mired in a conservative and traditional orthodoxy that was at odds with the reality of a country in desperate economic straits, where chronic unemployment and emigration were but the more visible effects of inadequate policy. De Valera's successor as Taoiseach (Republic of Ireland prime minister) was Sean Lemass, whose tenure began in 1959 with the dictum 'a rising tide lifts all boats'. By the mid-1960s his economic policies had halved emigration and ushered in a new prosperity that was to be mirrored 30 years later by the Celtic Tiger.

The events leading up to the Anglo-Irish War and their effect on ordinary people are movingly and powerfully related in JG Farrell's novel *Troubles*, first published in 1970.

Partners in Europe

In 1972 the Republic (along with Northern Ireland) became a member of the European Economic Community (EEC). This brought an increased measure of prosperity thanks to the benefits of the Common Agricultural Policy, which set fixed prices and guaranteed quotas for Irish farming produce. Nevertheless, the broader global depression, provoked by the oil crisis of 1973, forced the country into yet another slump and emigration figures rose again, reaching a peak in the mid-1980s.

The Celtic Tiger

In the early 1990s, European funds helped kick-start economic growth. Huge sums of money were invested in education and physical infrastructure, while the policy of low corporate tax rates coupled with incentives made Ireland very attractive to high-tech businesses looking for a door into EU markets. In less than a decade, Ireland went from being one of

1921–22

The Anglo-Irish treaty gives 26 counties of Ireland independence and allows six largely Protestant Ulster counties the choice of opting out. The Irish Free State is founded in 1922.

1922–23

Unwilling to accept the terms of the treaty, forces led by Eamon de Valera take up arms against their former comrades, led by Michael Collins. A brief but bloody civil war ensues, resulting in the death of Collins.

1932

After 10 years in the political wilderness, de Valera leads his Fianna Fáil party into government and goes about weakening the ties between the Free State and Britain.

1948

Fianna Fáil loses the 1948 general election to Fine Gael in coalition with the new Republican Clann an Poblachta. The new government declares the Free State to be a republic at last.

the poorest countries in Europe to one of the wealthiest: unemployment fell from 18% to 3.5%, the average industrial wage somersaulted to the top of the European league, and the dramatic rise in GDP meant that the country laid claim to an economic model of success that was the envy of the entire world. Ireland became synonymous with the term 'Celtic Tiger'.

In 1870, after the Great Famine and ongoing emigration, more than a third of all native-born Irish lived outside Ireland.

Recession Looms

From 2002 the Irish economy was kept buoyant by a gigantic construction boom that was completely out of step with any measure of responsible growth forecasting. The out-of-control international derivatives market flooded Irish banks with cheap money, and they lent it freely.

Then Lehman Brothers and the credit crunch happened. The Irish banks nearly went to the wall, but were bailed out at the last minute, and before Ireland could draw breath, the International Monetary Fund (IMF) and the EU held the chits of the country's mid-term economic future. Ireland found itself yet again confronting the familiar demons of high unemployment and emigration, but a deep-cutting program of austerity saw the corner turned by the end of 2014.

It's (Not So) Grim Up North

Since 8 May 2007, Northern Ireland has been governed in relative harmony by a constituent assembly, currently led by First Minister Peter Robinson of the Democratic Unionist Party (DUP) and Deputy First Minister Martin McGuinness of Sinn Féin (SF). Even if you'd only kept a lazy eye on Irish affairs these last four decades, you'd know that the presence of a one-time Loyalist firebrand like Robinson – who made his career on his vocal enmity towards all forms of Irish nationalism – and an ex-IRA commander like McGuinness in the same cabinet is a minor political miracle.

But it isn't really. It's the painstaking result of a process of dialogue and negotiation that has sought to untie a Gordian knot of historical resentment, mistrust, violence and engrained prejudice that began with the Plantations of Ireland in the 16th century.

Ireland Divided

Following the Anglo-Irish Treaty, a new Northern Ireland Parliament was constituted on 22 June 1922, with James Craig as the first prime minister. His Ulster Unionist Party (UUP) was to rule the new state until 1972, with the minority Catholic population (roughly 40%) stripped of any real power or representative strength by a Parliament that favoured the Unionists through economic subsidy, bias in housing allocations and gerrymandering: Derry's electoral boundaries were redrawn so as

1969

Marches by the Northern Ireland Civil Rights Association are disrupted by Loyalist attacks and police action, resulting in rioting and culminating in the Battle of the Bogside. The Troubles begin.

1972

The Republic (and Northern Ireland) become members of the EEC. On Bloody Sunday, 13 civilians are killed by British troops; Westminster suspends the Stormont government and introduces direct rule.

1973–74

The Sunningdale Agreement results in a new Northern Ireland Assembly. Unionists oppose the agreement and the Ulster Workers' Council calls a strike that paralyses the province and brings an end to the Assembly.

1981

Ten Republican prisoners die from a hunger strike. The first to die, Bobby Sands, had three weeks earlier been elected to Parliament. Over 100,000 people attend Sands' funeral.

to guarantee a Protestant council, even though the city was two-thirds Catholic. The overwhelmingly Protestant Royal Ulster Constabulary (RUC) and their paramilitary force, the B-Specials, made little effort to mask their sectarian bias. To all intents and purposes, Northern Ireland was an apartheid state.

We Shall Overcome

The first challenge to the Unionist hegemony came with the long-dormant IRA's border campaign in the 1950s, but it was quickly quashed and its leaders imprisoned. A decade later, however, the authorities met with a far more defiant foe in the shape of the Civil Rights Association, founded in 1967 and heavily influenced by its US counterpart as it sought to redress the blatant sectarianism in Derry. In October 1968 a mainly Catholic march in Derry was violently broken up by the RUC amid rumours that the IRA had provided 'security' for the marchers. Nobody knew it at the time, but the Troubles had begun.

In January 1969 another civil rights movement, called People's Democracy, organised a march from Belfast to Derry. As the marchers neared their destination, they were attacked by a group of Protestants. The police first stood to one side and then swept through the predominantly Catholic Bogside district. Further marches, protests and violence followed, with many Republicans arguing that the police only added to the problem. In August British troops went to Derry and then Belfast to maintain law and order. The British army was initially welcomed in some Catholic quarters, but soon it too came to be seen as a tool of the Protestant majority. Overreaction by the army actually fuelled recruitment into the long-dormant IRA, whose numbers especially increased after Bloody Sunday (30 January 1972), when British troops killed 13 civilians in Derry.

Books on the Troubles

- *Lost Lives*, David McKittrick
- *Ten Men Dead*, David Beresford
- *The Faithful Tribe: An Intimate Portrait of the Loyal Institutions*, Ruth Dudley Edwards

The Troubles

Following Bloody Sunday, the IRA more or less declared war on Britain. While continuing to target people in Northern Ireland, it moved its campaign of bombing to the British mainland, targeting innocents and earning the condemnation of citizens and parties from both sides of the sectarian divide. Meanwhile, Loyalist paramilitaries began a sectarian campaign against Catholics. Passions reached fever pitch in 1981 when Republican prisoners in the North went on a hunger strike, demanding the right to be recognised as political prisoners. Ten of them fasted to death, the best known being an elected MP, Bobby Sands.

The waters were further muddied by an incredible variety of parties splintering into subgroups with different agendas. The IRA had split into 'official' and 'provisional' wings, from which sprang more extreme Republican organisations such as the Irish National Liberation Army

1993
Downing Street Declaration is signed by British prime minister, John Major, and Irish prime minister, Albert Reynolds. It states that Britain has no 'selfish, strategic or economic interest in Northern Ireland'.

mid-1990s
Low corporate tax, restraint in government spending, transfer payments from the EU and a low-cost labour market result in the 'Celtic Tiger' boom, transforming Ireland into one of Europe's wealthiest countries.

1994
Sinn Féin leader Gerry Adams announces a 'cessation of violence' on behalf of the IRA on 31 August. In October the Combined Loyalist Military Command also announces a ceasefire.

1998
On 10 April negotiations culminate in the Good Friday Agreement, under which the new Northern Ireland Assembly is given full legislative and executive authority.

(INLA). Myriad Protestant, Loyalist paramilitary organisations sprang up in opposition to the IRA, and violence was typically met with violence.

Overtures of Peace

By the early 1990s, it was clear to Republicans that armed struggle was a bankrupted policy. Northern Ireland was a transformed society – most of the injustices that had sparked the conflict in the late 1960s had long since been rectified and most ordinary citizens were desperate for an end to hostilities. A series of negotiated statements between the Unionists, Nationalists and the British and Irish governments – brokered in part by George Mitchell, Bill Clinton's special envoy to Northern Ireland – eventually resulted in the historic Good Friday Agreement of 1998.

The agreement called for the devolution of legislative power from Westminster (where it had been since 1972) to a new Northern Ireland Assembly, but posturing, disagreement, sectarianism and downright obstinance on both sides made slow work of progress, and the Assembly was suspended four times – the last from October 2002 until May 2007.

During this period, the politics of Northern Ireland polarised dramatically, resulting in the falling away of the more moderate UUP and the emergence of the hardline Democratic Unionist Party (DUP), led by Ian Paisley; and, on the Nationalist side, the emergence of the IRA's political wing, Sinn Féin, as the main torch-bearer of Nationalist aspirations, under the leadership of Gerry Adams and Martin McGuinness.

Many films depict events related to the Troubles, including *Bloody Sunday* (2002), *The Boxer* (1997; starring Daniel Day-Lewis) and *In the Name of the Father* (1994; also starring Day-Lewis).

AMERICAN CONNECTIONS

Today more than 40 million Americans have Irish ancestry – a legacy of successive waves of emigration, spurred by events from the Potato Famine of the 1840s to the Depression of the 1930s. Many of the legendary figures of American history, from Davy Crockett to John Steinbeck, and 18 out of the 44 US presidents to date are of Irish descent – including Barack Obama, whose mother's family includes an emigrant called Falmouth Kearney, from Moneygall, County Offaly.

Here's a list of places that have links to past US presidents or deal with the experience of Irish emigrants to the USA:

- **Andrew Jackson Centre** (p618), County Antrim
- **Dunbrody Famine Ship** (p169), County Wexford
- **Grant Ancestral Homestead** (p636), County Tyrone
- **Kennedy Homestead** (p170), County Wexford
- **Cobh, The Queenstown Story** (p223), County Cork
- **Ulster American Folk Park** (p634), County Tyrone

1998

The 'Real IRA' detonates a bomb in Omagh, killing 29 people and injuring 200. It's the worst single atrocity in the history of the Troubles; public outrage and swift action by politicians prevent a Loyalist backlash.

2005

The IRA orders its units not to engage in 'any other activities' apart from assisting 'the development of purely political and democratic programmes through exclusively peaceful means'.

2007

The Northern Ireland Assembly resumes after a five-year break when talks between Unionists and Republicans remain in stalemate. They resolve their primary issues.

2008

The Irish banking system is declared virtually bankrupt following the collapse of Lehman Brothers; Ireland is on the brink of economic disaster as the extent of the crisis is revealed.

A New Northern Ireland

Eager to avoid being seen to surrender any ground, the DUP and Sinn Féin dug their heels in on key issues, with the main sticking points being decommissioning of IRA weapons and the identity and composition of the new police force ushered in to replace the RUC. Paisley and the Unionists made increasing demands of the decommissioning bodies (photographic evidence, Unionist witnesses etc) as they refused to accept anything less than an open and complete surrender of the IRA. Sinn Féin refused to join the police board that monitored the affairs of the Police Service of Northern Ireland (PSNI), effectively making no change to their policy of total noncooperation with the security forces.

A History of Ireland by Mike Cronin summarises all of Ireland's history in less than 300 pages. It's an easy read, but doesn't offer much in the way of analysis.

But the IRA did finally decommission all of its weapons, and Sinn Féin eventually agreed to join the police board. The DUP abandoned its intransigence towards its former Republican enemies and the two sides got down to the business of governing a province whose pressing needs had long since been shunted aside by sectarianism. Proof that Northern Ireland had finally achieved some kind of normality came with the 2011 Assembly elections, which returned the DUP and Sinn Féin as the two largest parties, mandating them to keep going.

But old enmities die hard. The murder of a young PSNI officer called Ronan Kerr in April 2011 was a bitter reminder of the province's violent history, but even in tragedy there was a sense that something fundamental had shifted: Kerr was a Catholic member of a police force that has gone to great lengths to disavow its traditionally pro-Protestant bias and his murder was condemned with equal strength by both sides of the divide. Perhaps most tellingly, First Minister Peter Robinson's presence at the funeral was the first time Robinson had ever been to a Catholic requiem mass.

2010
Ireland receives €85 billion bailout package from the IMF and the EU, which alleviates the banking crisis but leaves the country in strict financial shackles.

2011
Queen Elizabeth II is the first British monarch to visit the Republic of Ireland; the visit is heralded as a resounding affirmation of the close ties between the two nations.

2013
Ireland becomes the first stricken eurozone country to successfully exit the terms of the bailout.

2015
Ireland becomes the first country in the world to introduce marriage equality for same-sex couples by plebiscite.

The Irish Way of Life

The Irish reputation for being affable is largely well-deserved, but it only hints at a more profound character, one that is more complex and contradictory than the image of the silver-tongued master of blarney might suggest. This dichotomy is best summarised by a quote usually ascribed to the poet William Butler Yeats: 'Being Irish, he had an abiding sense of tragedy, which sustained him through temporary periods of joy.'

The Irish Pulse

The Irish are famous for being warm and friendly, which is just another way of saying that the Irish love a bit of a chat, whether it be with friends or strangers. They will entertain you with their humour, alarm you with their willingness to get stuck into a good debate and cut you down with their razor-sharp wit. Slagging – the Irish version of teasing – is an art form, which may seem caustic to unfamiliar ears, but is quickly revealed as an intrinsic element of how the Irish relate to one another. It is commonly assumed that the mettle of friendship is proven by how well you can take a joke rather than by the payment of a cheap compliment.

According to the 2011 census, the average number of children per family has fallen to 1.38, the lowest in Irish history.

Yet beneath all of the garrulous sociability and self-deprecating twaddle lurks a dark secret, which is that at heart the Irish have traditionally been low on self esteem. Which is partly why they're so suspicious of easy compliments, but the last three decades have seen a paradigm shift in the Irish character.

Prosperity and its related growth in expectations has gone a long way towards transforming the Irish from a people who wallowed in false modesty like a sport to a nation eager to reap the rewards of its achievements and successes. Inevitably, this personality shift has been largely driven by the appetites and demands of the younger generations, but there's no doubt that many older Irish, for too long muted by a fear of appearing unseemly or boastful, have wholeheartedly embraced the change.

The harsh realities of postcrash Ireland, which resulted in the country taking the biggest bailout in its history, prompted something of a backlash. Many blamed a tawdry and materialistic culture of exaggerated excess for Ireland's woes, an attitude memorably summarised by a minister who sheepishly declared on TV that 'we all partied!'.

The mea culpa was a vestige of an older, more puritanical country that had absorbed poverty and struggle into the very fabric of its DNA, but contemporary Ireland is having none of it. The younger generation, raised on the boundless possibilities of the Celtic Tiger, confidently declare that while the last few years have been tough, austerity is just a temporary measure rather than the fulfilment of their destiny. They'll do what's necessary to get along, but they're doing it in the certain knowledge that things will inevitably get better.

Nurse & Curse of the People

Ireland has a fractious relationship with alcohol. The country regularly tops the list of the world's biggest binge drinkers, and while there is an increasing awareness of, and alarm at, the devastation caused by alcohol to Irish society (especially to young people), drinking remains the country's most popular social pastime, with no sign of letting up; spend a weekend night walking around any town in the country and you'll get a firsthand feel of the influence and effect of the booze.

Some experts put Ireland's binge-drinking antics down to the dramatic rise in the country's economic fortunes, but statistics have long revealed that Ireland has had an unhealthy fondness for 'taking the cure', although the acceptability of public drunkenness is a far more recent phenomenon: the older generation are never done reminding the youngsters that they would *never* have been seen staggering in public.

Lifestyle

In 2014, 37.8% of the population lived in rural areas.

The Irish may like to grumble – about work, the weather, the government and those *feckin' eejits* on reality TV shows – but if pressed will tell you that they live in the best country on earth. There's loads *wrong* with the place, but isn't it the same way everywhere else?

Traditional Ireland – of the large family, closely linked to church and community – is quickly disappearing, as the increased urbanisation of Ireland continues to break up the social fabric of community interdependence that was a necessary element of relative poverty. Contemporary Ireland is therefore not altogether different from any other European country, and you have to travel further to the margins of the country – the islands and the isolated rural communities – to find an older version of society.

Gay-Friendly Ireland

The passing of the Marriage Equality referendum in May 2015 was a major watershed for not just the LGBT community in Ireland, but for the global LGBT movement as a whole, as Ireland was the first country in the world to adopt same-sex marriage by universal plebiscite.

The margin of victory – 62.4% – testified to a profound shift in attitudes to homosexuality: same-sex sexual activity was only decriminalised in 1993, and then only after a long and often lonely campaign by Joycean scholar and gay rights activist David Norris. All but one constituency in Ireland voted in favour, demonstrating that attitudes had changed everywhere and not just in big cities such as Dublin, where the LGBT community has been out and proud for many years and Dublin Pride is one of the biggest and most boisterous festivals on the calendar.

The pronounced change in rural attitudes was exemplified when in 2009 Cork hurler Donal ÓG Cusack became the first Gaelic Athletics Association (GAA) player (and elite Irish sportsperson) to come out as gay – the generally positive reaction he received (he's currently president of the Gaelic Players Association) from peers and supporters prove that traditional Ireland has come a long way towards accepting homosexuality. Which isn't to say that the inhabitants of a small rural community would necessarily be comfortable with a pride march through their village or the opening of a gay bar on the main street: for many, the new attitudes have simply evolved from an older notion that people are entitled to do as they please so long as they keep it in the private sphere, and that includes same-sex marriage. The old trope that young gay men and women needing to move to larger urban centres in order to find greater acceptance is still true.

Multiculturalism

Ireland has long been a pretty homogenous country, but the arrival of thousands of immigrants from all over the world – 17% of the population is foreign-born – has challenged the mores of racial tolerance and integration. To a large extent it has been successful, although if you scratch beneath the surface, racial tensions can be exposed.

Polish people have overtaken UK nationals as the largest non-Irish group living in Ireland.

The tanking of the economy has exacerbated these tensions and the 'Irish jobs for Irish people' opinion is being stated with greater vehemence and authority – even though its supporters remain very much a minority for now. Irrespectively, the flow of emigrants from Eastern Europe has slowed up dramatically as many believe their prospects to be better at home.

Religion

About 3.8 million residents in the Republic (or 84.2%) call themselves Roman Catholic, followed by 2.8% Protestant, 0.5% Muslim and the rest an assortment of other beliefs including none at all. In the North, the breakdown is about 53% Protestant and 44% Catholic (with about 3% other or no religion). Most Irish Protestants are members of the Church of Ireland, an offshoot of the Church of England, and the Presbyterian and Methodist churches.

Attendance at Catholic mass has fallen from 91% of the population in the early 1970s to 30% in 2011.

But while Catholicism remains a powerful cultural identifier, many Irish (especially the younger generation) have distanced themselves from the Church, whose teachings appear out of step with the major social issues of the day, including divorce, contraception, abortion, homosexuality and cohabitation. The Church has also been roundly condemned for its role in the clerical abuse scandal and its untidy efforts to avoid responsibility, provoking an acute sense of betrayal in many older believers that has made them question a lifetime's devotion to their local parishes.

TV & Radio

There are four terrestrial TV channels in Ireland, three operated by the national broadcaster, Raidió Teilifís Éireann (RTE), the other a privately owned commercial station. RTE's strengths are its widespread sports coverage and news and current affairs programming. TV3 has a lightweight programming philosophy, with second-string US fluff to complement its diet of reality TV shows and celebrity profiles. The Irish-language station TG4 shows movies and dramas, mostly *as gaeilge* (in Irish with English subtitles). The main British TV stations – BBC, ITV and Channel 4 – are also available in most Irish homes, through satellite or cable; in Northern Ireland they're the main players.

The Irish are avid radio listeners – up to 85% of the population tunes in on any given day. The majority tend to stick with RTE, the dominant player with three stations: Radio 1 (88.2–90FM; mostly news and discussion), Radio 2 (90.4–92.2FM; lifestyle and music) and Lyric FM (96–99FM; classical music). Telecommunications impresario Denis O'Brien owns a number of radio stations including talk radio Newstalk (106–108FM; news, current affairs and lifestyle) and Today FM (100–102FM; music, chat and news). The rest of the radio landscape is filled out by the 25 or so local radio stations that represent local issues and tastes: the northwest's Highland Radio – heard in Donegal, Sligo, Tyrone and Fermanagh – is Europe's most successful local radio station, with an 84% market share. In Northern Ireland, the BBC rules supreme, with BBC Radio Ulster flying the local flag in addition to the four main BBC stations.

Top of the list for most popular baby names in 2015 were Liam and Emma.

Music

Ireland's literary tradition may have the critics nodding sagely, but it's the country's ability to render music to the ear that will remain with you long after your Irish day is done. There's music for every occasion and every mood, from celebration to sorrow. The Irish do popular music as well as anyone, but it is its traditional forms that make Ireland a special place to hear live music.

Traditional & Folk

Top Trad-Music Venues

- *Hughes' Bar, Dublin*
- *Crane Bar, Galway*
- *De Barra's Folk Club, Clonakilty (Cork)*
- *MacDiarmada's, Doolin (Clare)*
- *Leo's Tavern, Crolly (Donegal)*

Irish music (known in Ireland as traditional music, or just trad) has retained a vibrancy not found in other traditional European forms, which have lost out to the overbearing influence of pop music. Although Irish music has kept many of its traditional aspects, it has itself influenced many forms of music, most notably US country and western – a fusion of Mississippi Delta blues and Irish traditional tunes that, combined with other influences like gospel, is at the root of rock and roll.

The music was never written down, it was passed on from one player to another and so endured and evolved – regional 'styles' only developed because local musicians sought to play just like the one who seemed to play better than everybody else. The blind itinerant harpist Turlough O'Carolan (1670–1738) 'wrote' more than 200 tunes – it's difficult to know how many versions their repeated learning has spawned. This characteristic of fluidity is key to an appreciation of traditional music, and explains why it is such a resilient form today.

Nevertheless, in the 1960s composer Seán Ó Riada (1931–71) tried to impose a kind of structure on the music. His ensemble group, Ceoltóirí Chualann, were the first to reach a wider audience, and from it were born the Chieftains, arguably the most important traditional group of them all. They started recording in 1963 – any one of their nearly 40 albums are worth a listen, but you won't go wrong with their 10-album eponymous series.

The other big success of the 1960s were the Dubliners. More folksy than traditional, they made a career out of bawdy drinking songs that got everybody singing along. Other popular bands include the Fureys, com-

THE NUTS & BOLTS OF TRADITIONAL MUSIC

Despite popular perception, the harp isn't widely used in traditional music (it *is* the national emblem, but that probably has more to do with the country traditionally being run by people pulling strings). The bodhrán (*bow*-rawn) goat-skin drum is much more prevalent, although it makes for a lousy symbol. The uillean pipes, played by squeezing bellows under the elbow, provide another distinctive sound, although you're not likely to see them in a pub. The fiddle isn't unique to Ireland but it is one of the main instruments in the country's indigenous music, along with the flute, tin whistle, accordion and bouzouki (a version of the mandolin). Music fits into five main categories (jigs, reels, hornpipes, polkas and slow airs), while the old style of singing unaccompanied versions of traditional ballads and airs is called *sean-nós*.

prising four brothers originally from the travelling community (no, not like the Wilburys) along with guitarist Davey Arthur. And if it's rousing renditions of Irish rebel songs you're after, you can't go past the Wolfe Tones.

Since the 1970s, various bands have tried to blend traditional with more progressive genres, with mixed success. The Bothy Band were formed in 1975 and were a kind of trad supergroup – bouzouki player Dónal Lunny, uillean piper Paddy Keenan, flute and whistle player Matt Molloy (later a member of the Chieftains), fiddler Paddy Glackin and accordion player Tony MacMahon were all superb instrumentalists and their recordings are still as electrifying today as they were four decades ago.

Musicians tend to come together in collaborative projects. A contemporary group worth checking out are The Gloaming, who've taken traditional reels and given them a contemporary sound – their eponymous debut album (2011) is sensational. A key member of the group, fiddler Caoimhín Ó Raghallaigh, is also worth checking out in his own right; his latest album, *Laghdú*, displays both his beautiful fiddle playing and his superb understanding of loops and electronic texturing.

And if you want to check out a group that melds rock, folk and traditional music, you won't go far wrong with The Spook of the Thirteenth Lock, who've released a couple of albums since 2008 – their second album is *The Brutal Here And Now* (2012).

And no discussion of traditional music would be complete without a mention of *Riverdance*, which made Irish dancing sexy and became a worldwide phenomenon, despite the fact that most aficionados of traditional music are seriously underwhelmed by its musical worth. Good stage show, crap music.

Trad Playlist

- *The Quiet Glen (Tommy Peoples)*
- *Paddy Keenan (Paddy Keenan)*
- *Compendium: The Best of Patrick Street (Various)*
- *The Chieftains 6: Bonaparte's Retreat (The Chieftains)*
- *Old Hag You Have Killed Me (The Bothy Band)*

Popular Music

From the 1960s onward, Ireland produced its fair share of great rock musicians, including Van Morrison, Thin Lizzy, Celtic rockers Horslips, punk poppers the Undertones and Belfast's own Stiff Little Fingers (SLF), Ireland's answer to the Clash. And then there were Bob Geldof's Boomtown Rats, who didn't like Mondays or much else either.

But they all paled in comparison to the supernova that is U2, formed in 1976 in North Dublin and as of the late 1980s one of the world's most successful rock bands. What else can we say about them that hasn't already been said? After 13 studio albums, 22 Grammy awards and 150 million album sales they have nothing to prove to anyone – and not even their minor faux pas in 2014, when Apple 'gave' copies of their latest release, *Songs of Innocence*, to iTunes subscribers whether they wanted it or not, has managed to dampen their popularity. Their iNNOCENCE + eXPERIENCE tour (note the typographic ode to Apple), which ran until the end of 2015, was a massive success.

Of all the Irish acts that followed in U2's wake during the 1980s and early 1990s, a few managed to comfortably avoid being tarred with 'the next U2' burden. The Pogues' mix of punk and Irish folk kept everyone going for a while, but the real story there was the empathetic songwriting of Shane MacGowan, whose genius has been overshadowed by his chronic drinking – but he still managed to pen Ireland's favourite song, 'A Fairytale of New York', sung with emotional fervour by everyone around Christmas. Sinéad O'Connor thrived by acting like a U2 antidote – whatever they were into she was not – and by having a damn fine voice; the raw emotion on *The Lion and the Cobra* (1987) makes it a great offering. And then there were My Bloody Valentine, the pioneers of late 1980s guitar-distorted shoegazer rock: *Loveless* (1991) is one of the best Irish albums of all time.

Best Irish Rock Albums

The Joshua Tree (U2)

The End of History (Fionn Regan)

Loveless (My Bloody Valentine)

Live & Dangerous (Thin Lizzy)

I Do Not Want What I Haven't Got (Sinéad O'Connor)

Hot Press (www.hotpress.com) is a fortnightly magazine featuring local and international music interviews and listings.

The 1990s were largely dominated by DJs, dance music and a whole new spin on an old notion, the boy band. Behind Ireland's most successful groups (Boyzone and Westlife) is the Svengali of Saccharine, impresario Louis Walsh, whose musical sensibilities seem mired in '60s showband schmaltz. In the last decade, Walsh, who then became a judge on *X Factor* in the UK, unleashed Jedward on the world – identical twins who couldn't sing a note but endeared themselves to everyone with their wacky antics.

The Contemporary Scene

If Boyzone and Westlife were big, their success pales in comparison to that of One Direction, another product of the X Factory. We mention them here because one of their members, Niall Horan, is from Mullingar, County Westmeath – which inevitably means that their Irish fan base (young teens and pre-teens) have earnestly adopted the band as at least part-Irish.

One Direction's success means that they'll rarely play in Ireland, and when they do, they'll play the giant stadiums rather than the myriad small and midsize venues that can be found in virtually every Irish town and city. These are the purview of virtually every other Irish performer, from the experimental ex-DJ working a laptop to the singer-songwriter with a guitar.

The Irish love their sensitive souls, and there's no shortage of the feelings-out-front singer-songwriter. The established crop include Damien Rice, who came out of self-imposed seclusion in 2014 with a new album called *My Favourite Faded Fantasy*; Belfast-born Duke Special, whose vaudeville and music-hall-inspired performances have earned him huge critical acclaim and a big fan base. His newest album is *Look Out Machines* (2015). Although he spends a lot of his time in New York these days, Glen Hansard (of *Once* fame) is still a major presence in Ireland, and occasionally goes on the road with his old band, The Frames. But in 2015 not even he could compete with the success of Bray-born Hozier, who went global in 2014 with his hit 'Take Me to Church' from his eponymous debut album.

As the DJ lost his/her preeminent status amongst music fans in the early noughties, so the rock band returned in full force. Besides U2, Ireland's most successful rock band are Snow Patrol. The Northern Irish quintet announced that they would release their eighth studio album in 2015; in the meantime, singer Gary Lightbody returned to his native Belfast where he's been a key figure in the city's thriving music scene, helping to promote local artists.

In a similar vein, Dublin trio The Script pack out the stadiums and sell millions of records (the latest is *No Sound Without Silence*, released in 2014) with their melodic pop-rock, which has also found its way onto a host of TV programs from from *90210* to *Made in Chelsea*. They mightn't sell nearly as many records, but Villagers, fronted by Conor O'Brien, have earned kudos from every Irish critic for their brand of indie-folk rock – their third album, *Darling Arithmetic*, was released in 2015. And if you like your rock tinged with electronica, then look no further than Jape – the hypnotic sound of their 2015 album *This Chemical Sea* was very well received.

But nobody can quite hold a candle to the phenomenon that is Enya, who is the best-selling solo artist in Irish history and one of the best-selling female artists in the world. The Donegal-born composer and instrumentalist was raised in Irish traditional music, but in the early 1980s she and her siblings in the group Clannad created Celtic New Age music, based around synthesizers and heavy, looping effects. Enya broke out on her own and 75 million record sales later, she stands alone atop the New Age music pyramid, even though she hasn't recorded a new album since 2008.

Literary Ireland

Of all their national traits, characteristics and cultural expressions, it's perhaps the way the Irish speak and write that best distinguishes them. Their love of language and their great oral tradition have contributed to Ireland's legacy of world-renowned writers and storytellers. And all this in a language imposed on them by a foreign invader. The Irish responded to this act of cultural piracy by mastering a magnificent hybrid – English in every respect but flavoured and enriched by the rhythms, pronunciation patterns and grammatical peculiarities of Irish.

The Mythic Cycle

Before there was anything like modern literature there was the Ulaid (Ulster) Cycle – Ireland's version of the Homeric epic – written down from oral tradition between the 8th and 12th centuries. The chief story is the Táin Bó Cúailnge (Cattle Raid of Cooley), about a battle between Queen Maeve of Connaught and Cúchulainn, the principal hero of Irish mythology. Cúchulainn appears in the work of Irish writers right up to the present day, from Samuel Beckett to Frank McCourt.

Listowel Writers' Week takes place over the last weekend in May in Listowel, County Kerry, and is one of the most popular of all literary festivals – mostly because it gives readers a chance to meet their favourite writers in person.

Modern Literature

Zip forward 1000 years, past the genius of Jonathan Swift (1667–1745) and his *Gulliver's Travels;* stopping to acknowledge acclaimed dramatist Oscar Wilde (1854–1900); and *Dracula* creator Bram Stoker (1847–1912) – some have claimed that the name of the count may have come from the Irish *droch fhola* (bad blood) – to the literary giant that was James Joyce (1882–1941), whose name and books elicit enormous pride in Ireland.

The majority of Joyce's literary output came when he had left Ireland for the artistic hotbed that was Paris, which was also true for another great experimenter of language and style, Samuel Beckett (1906–89). Beckett's work centres on fundamental existential questions about the human condition and the nature of self. He is probably best known for his play *Waiting for Godot,* but his unassailable reputation is based on a series of stark novels and plays.

Of the dozens of 20th-century Irish authors to have achieved published renown, some names to look out for include playwright and novelist Brendan Behan (1923–64), who wove tragedy, wit and a turbulent life into his best works including *Borstal Boy, The Quare Fellow* and *The Hostage* before dying young of alcoholism.

THE GAELIC REVIVAL

While Home Rule was being debated and shunted, something of a revolution was taking place in Irish arts, literature and identity. The poet William Butler Yeats (p422; 1865–1939) and his coterie of literary friends (including Lady Gregory, Douglas Hyde, John Millington Synge and George Russell) championed the Anglo-Irish literary revival, unearthing old Celtic tales and writing with fresh enthusiasm about a romantic Ireland of epic battles and warrior queens. For a country that had suffered centuries of invasion and deprivation, these images presented a much more attractive version of history.

Belfast-born CS Lewis (1898–1963) died a year earlier, but he left us *The Chronicles of Narnia,* a series of allegorical children's stories, three of which have been made into films. Other Northern writers have, not surprisingly, featured the Troubles in their work: Bernard MacLaverty's *Cal* (also made into a film) and his more recent *The Anatomy School* are both wonderful.

Contemporary Scene

Yes, the stalwarts are still great, but ask your average Irish person who their favourite home-grown writer is and they'll most likely mention someone who's still alive.

They might mention Roddy Doyle (1958–), whose mega-successful Barrytown quartet – *The Commitments, The Snapper, The Van* and *Paddy Clarke, Ha Ha Ha* – have all been made into films; his latest book, *The Guts* (2013), saw the return of *The Commitments* protagonist, Jimmy Rabbitte – older, wiser and battling illness.

Sebastian Barry (1955–) has been shortlisted twice for the Man Booker Prize, for his WWI drama *A Long Long Way* and the compelling *The Secret Scripture* (2008), about a 100-year-old inmate of a mental hospital called Roseanne who decides to write an autobiography. His latest novel, *The Temporary Gentleman* (2014), tells the story of Roseanne's brother-in-law, Jack McNulty, an ex–British Army officer posted to Africa during WWII but unable to return home to Ireland because of personal and professional guilt.

One of the most successful Irish authors is Eoin Colfer, creator of the *Artemis Fowl* series, eight fantasy novels following the adventures of Artemis Fowl II as he grows from criminal antihero to saviour of the fairies.

Anne Enright (1962–) did nab the Booker for *The Gathering* (2007), a zeitgeist tale of alcoholism and abuse – she described it as 'the intellectual equivalent of a Hollywood weepie' – her latest novel, *The Green Road* (2015), continues to mine the murky waters of the Irish family. Another Booker Prize winner is heavyweight John Banville (1945–), who won it for *The Sea* (2005); we also recommend either *The Book of Evidence* (1989) or the masterful roman-à-clef *The Untouchable* (1997), based loosely on the secret-agent life of art historian Anthony Blunt. Banville's literary alter-ego is Benjamin Black, author of a series of seven hard-boiled detective thrillers set in the 1950s starring a troubled pathologist called Quirke – the latest book is *Even the Dead* (2015). Another big hitter is Wexford-born Colm Tóibín (1955–), author of nine novels including *Brooklyn* (2009; made into a film in 2015 starring Saoirse Ronan) and, most recently, *Nora Webster* (2014), a powerful study of widowhood.

Emma Donoghue (1969–) followed the award-winning *Room* (2010) with *Frog Music* (2014), about the real-life shooting of cross-dressing gamine

TOP IRISH READS

Angela's Ashes (1996) The Pulitzer Prize–winning novel by Frank McCourt tells the relentlessly bleak autobiographical story of the author's poverty-stricken Limerick childhood in the Depression of the 1930s.

Amongst Women (1990) John McGahern's simple, economical piece centres on a west-of-Ireland family in the social aftermath of the War of Independence.

Reading in the Dark (1996) Seamus Deane (the Guardian Fiction Prize winner) recounts a young boy's struggles to unravel the truth of his own history growing up during the Troubles of Belfast.

The Sea (2005) The Booker Prize–winning novel by John Banville is an engrossing meditation on mortality, grief, death, childhood and memory; it was made into a film in 2013.

Strumpet City (1969) James Plunkett brings Dublin to life around the time of the 1913 Lockout in what is considered to be a masterpiece of 20th-century Irish literature.

The Butcher Boy (1992) Patrick McCabe's novel is a brilliant, gruesome, tragicomedy about an orphaned Monaghan boy's descent into madness. It was later made into a successful film by Neil Jordan.

LIVING POET'S SOCIETY

Ireland's greatest modern bard was Derry-born Nobel laureate Seamus Heaney (1939–2013), whose enormous personal warmth and wry humour flows through each of his evocative works. He was, unquestionably, the successor to Yeats and one of the most important contemporary poets of the English language. After winning the Nobel Prize in 1995 he compared the ensuing attention to someone mentioning sex in front of their mammy. *Opened Ground – Poems 1966–1996* (1998) is our favourite of his books.

Dubliner Paul Durcan (1944–) is one of the most reliable chroniclers of changing Dublin. He won the prestigious Whitbread Prize for Poetry in 1990 for *Daddy, Daddy* and is a funny, engaging, tender and savage writer. Poet, playwright and Kerryman Brendan Kennelly (1936–) is an immensely popular character around town. He lectures at Trinity College and writes a unique brand of poetry that is marked by its playfulness, as well as historical and intellectual impact. Eavan Boland (1944–) is a prolific and much-admired writer, best known for her poetry, who combines Irish politics with outspoken feminism; *In a Time of Violence* (1994) and *The Lost Land* (1998) are two of her most celebrated collections.

Jenny Bonnet in late-19th-century San Francisco. John Boyne (1971–) made his name with Holocaust novel *The Boy in the Striped Pyjamas* (2006; the film version came out in 2008); his latest novel, *A History of Loneliness* (2014), explores the thorny issue of child abuse and the Catholic Church.

Colum McCann (1965–) left Ireland in 1986, eventually settling in New York, where his sixth novel, the post–September 11 *Let the Great World Spin* (2009), won him the National Book Award for fiction as well as the International IMPAC Dublin Literary Award. His next novel, *TransAtlantic* (2013) weaves three separate stories together: the flight of Alcock and Brown, the visit of Frederick Douglass to Ireland in 1845 and the story of the Northern Irish peace process of the late 1990s.

The Troubles have been a rich and powerful subject for Northern Irish writers. Derry native Sean O'Reilly's (1969–) novels are populated by characters freed from sectarianism but irreparably damaged by it: his last novel was *Watermark* (2005), about a young woman on the edge of desire and reason in an unnamed Irish town. Eoin McNamee (1961–) has written a series that explores the conflict directly, teasing out the effects of religion and history on the lives of individuals. His novel *Blue is the Night* (2014) is the last in a trilogy that includes *The Blue Tango* (2001) and *Orchid Blue* (2010).

Paul Murray's (1975–) second novel, *Skippy Dies* (2010), about a group of privileged students at an all-boys secondary school, won him lots of critical praise (and an upcoming movie version directed by Neil Jordan) but his follow-up, *The Mark and the Void* (2015), which is set against the backdrop of the financial crisis, met with far more lukewarm praise. Not so Shane Hegarty (1976–), who published the first volume of *Darkmouth* in 2015, a Young Adult novel set in a fictional Irish town (Darkmouth) where young Finn is learning about girls and fighting monsters.

Contemporary Fiction

- *Brooklyn* (Colm Tóibín)
- *The Thrill of It All* (Joseph O'Connor)
- *Skippy Dies* (Paul Murray)
- *The Green Road* (Anne Enright)
- *The Gamal* (Ciarán Collins)

Chick Lit

Authors hate the label and publishers profess to disregard it, but chick lit is big business, and few have mastered it as well as the Irish. Doyenne of them all is Maeve Binchy (1940–2012), whose mastery of the style saw her outsell most of the literary greats – her last novel before she died was *A Week in Winter* (2012). Marian Keyes (1963–) is another author with a long line of best-sellers, including her latest, *The Woman Who Stole My Life* (2014). She's a terrific storyteller with a rare ability to tackle sensitive issues such as alcoholism and depression, issues that she herself has suffered from and is admiringly honest about. Former agony aunt Cathy Kelly turns out novels at the rate of one a year: a recent book is *It Started With Paris* (2014), where a young man proposes beneath the Eiffel Tower before trouble begins...

Irish Landscapes

Irish literature, song and painting makes it pretty clear that the landscape – spread across 486km north to south and only 275km from east to west – exerts a powerful sway on the people who have lived in it. This is especially true for those who have left, for whom the aul' sod is still a land worth pining for, and for many visitors the vibrant greenness of gentle hills and the fearsome violence of jagged coasts are an integral part of experiencing Ireland.

In 1821 the body of an Iron Age man was found in a bog in Galway with his cape, shoes and beard still intact.

Cliffs & Stones

Massive rocky outcrops, such as the Burren in County Clare, are for the most part inhospitable to grass, and although even there the green stuff does sprout up in enough patches for sheep and goats to graze on, these vast, otherworldly landscapes are mostly grey and bleak. Nearby, the dramatic Cliffs of Moher are a sheer drop into the thundering surf below. Similarly, there is no preparing for the extraordinary hexagonal stone columns of the Giant's Causeway in County Antrim or the rugged drop of County Donegal's Slieve League, Europe's highest sea cliffs. Sand dunes buffer many of the more gentle stretches of coast. Smaller islands dot the shores of Ireland, many of them barren rock piles supporting unique ecosystems – Skellig Michael is a breathtakingly jagged example just off the Kerry coast.

Look for *Reading the Irish Landscape* by Frank Mitchell and Michael Ryan for info on Ireland's geology, archaeology, urban growth, agriculture and afforestation.

The rural farms of the west coast have a rugged, hard-earned look to them, due mostly to the rock that lies so close to the surface. Much of this rock has been dug up to create tillable soil and converted into stone walls that divide tiny paddocks. The Aran Islands stand out for their spectacular networks of stone walls.

Mountains & Forests

The west of Ireland is a bulwark of cliffs, hills and mountains and is the country's most mountainous area. The highest mountains are in the southwest; the tallest mountain in Ireland is Carrauntoohil (1040m) in County Kerry's Macgillycuddy's Reeks.

The Irish frequently lament the loss of their woodlands, much of which were cleared by the British (during the reign of Elizabeth I) to build ships for the Royal Navy. Little of the island's once plentiful oak forests survive today, and much of what you'll see is the result of relatively recent planting. Instead, the countryside largely comprises green fields divided by hedgerows and stone walls. Use of this land is divided between cultivated fields and pasture for cattle and sheep.

Plants

Although Ireland is sparsely wooded, the range of surviving plant species is larger here than in many other European countries, thanks in part to the comparatively late arrival of agriculture.

There are remnants of the original oak forest in Killarney National Park and in southern Wicklow near Shillelagh. Far more common are pine plantations, which are growing steadily. Hedgerows, planted to divide fields and delineate land boundaries throughout Ireland, actually host many of the native plant species that once thrived in the oak forests – it's an intriguing example of nature adapting and reasserting itself. The Burren in County Clare is home to a remarkable mixture of Mediterranean, alpine and Arctic species.

The bogs of Ireland are home to a unique flora adapted to wet, acidic, nutrient-poor conditions, whose survival is threatened by the depletion of bogs for energy use. Sphagnum moss is the key bog plant and is joined by other species such as bog rosemary, bog cotton, black-beaked sedge (whose spindly stem grows up to 30cm in height) and various types of heather and lichen. Carnivorous plants also thrive, such as the sundew, whose sticky tentacles trap insects, and bladderwort, whose tiny explosive bladders trap aquatic animals in bog pools.

For information on parks, gardens, monuments and inland waterways, see www.heritageireland.ie.

Mammals

Apart from the fox and badger, which tend to shy away from humans and are rarely seen, the wild mammals of Ireland are mostly of the ankle-high 'critter' category, such as rabbits, hedgehogs and shrews. Hikers often spot the Irish hare, or at least glimpse the blazing-fast blur of one running away. Red deer roam the hillsides in many of the wilder parts of the country, particularly the Wicklow Mountains and in Killarney National Park, which holds the country's largest herd.

For most visitors, the most commonly sighted mammals are those inhabiting the sea and waterways. The otter, rarely seen elsewhere in Europe, is thriving in Ireland. Seals are a common sight in rivers and along the shore, as are dolphins, which follow the warm waters of the Gulf Stream towards Ireland. Some colonise the coast of Ireland year-round, frequently swimming into the bays and inlets off the western coast.

The illustrated pocket guide *Animals of Ireland* by Gordon D'Arcy is a handy, inexpensive introduction to Ireland's varied fauna.

Birdlife

Many travellers visit Ireland specifically for the birding. Ireland's westerly location on the fringe of Europe makes it an ideal stopover point for birds migrating from North America and the Arctic. In autumn, the southern counties become a temporary home to the American waders (mainly sandpipers and plovers) and warblers. Migrants from Africa, such as shearwaters, petrels and auks, begin to arrive in spring in the southwestern counties.

The reasonably rare corncrake, which migrates from Africa, can be found in the western counties, in Donegal and around the Shannon Callows, and on islands such as Inishbofin in Galway. In late spring and early summer, the rugged coastlines, particularly cliff areas and islands, become a haven for breeding seabirds, mainly gannet, kittiwake, Manx shearwater, fulmar, cormorant and heron. Puffins, resembling penguins with their tuxedo colour scheme, nest in large colonies on coastal cliffs.

The lakes and low-lying wetlands attract large numbers of Arctic and northern European waterfowl and waders such as whooper swans, lapwing, barnacle geese, white-fronted geese and golden plovers. The important Wexford Wildfowl Reserve holds half the world's population of

THE BOG

The boglands, which once covered one-fifth of the island, are more of a whiskey hue than green – that's the brown of heather and sphagnum moss, which cover uncut bogs. Visitors will likely encounter a bog in County Kildare's Bog of Allen or while driving through the western counties – much of the Mayo coast is covered by bog, and huge swaths also cover Donegal.

Greenland white-fronted geese, and little tern breed on the beach there, protected by the dunes. Also found during the winter are teal, redshank and curlew. The main migration periods are April to May and September to October.

Irish Birds by David Cabot is a pocket guide describing birds and their habitats, which outlines the best places for serious birdwatching.

The magnificent peregrine falcon has been making something of a recovery and can be found nesting on cliffs in Wicklow and elsewhere. In 2001, 46 golden eagle chicks from Scotland were released into Glenveagh National Park in Donegal in an effort to reintroduce the species. The project has been afflicted by adverse weather and, sadly, by unknowns poisoning and shooting the birds, but as of 2013 it has managed to survive courtesy of two separate nests that have produced a handful of surviving chicks between them. More recent reintroductions include the white-tailed sea eagle, with a pair called Saoirse and Caimin successfully breeding a chick in 2014 – the first native-born sea eagle in 110 years. For more information (and live cam action), check out www.goldeneagle.ie.

Environmental Issues

Ireland does not rate among the world's biggest offenders when it comes to polluting the environment, but the country's recent economic growth has led to an increase in industry and consumerism, which in turn generate more pollution and waste. While the population density is among Europe's lowest, the population is rising. The last 20 years have seen a massive expansion of suburban developments around all of Ireland's major towns and cities; the biggest by far is, inevitably, around Dublin, especially in the broadening commuter belt of Counties Meath and Kildare. The collapse of the construction bubble in 2008 has put an end to much of this development, but the rows of semidetached houses still remain. As more people drive cars and fly in planes, Ireland grows more dependent on nonrenewable sources of energy. The amount of waste has risen substantially since the early 1990s.

Needless to say, concern for the environment is growing and the government has taken some measures to offset the damage that thriving economy can cause. Since 2007 the Sustainable Energy Authority of Ireland has been charged with promoting and assisting the development of renewable energy resources, including solar, wind, hydropower, geothermal and biomass resources. As it stands, the country is only tapping a fraction of these: in 2013, 7.8% of the country's energy requirements (heat, electricity and transport) were being met by renewables.

The European Renewables Directive set Ireland a target of sourcing 16% of all energy requirements by 2020, which seems unlikely to be met in time: Ireland's recent economic woes mean that there just isn't the

FRACKING

The Irish government is currently debating whether to allow fracking – hydraulic fracturing – in the shale-rich areas of the northwest, known as the Northwest Ireland Carboniferous Basin, roughly covering parts of Counties Leitrim, Roscommon, Sligo, Cavan, Donegal and Fermanagh. Australian exploration company Tamboran has estimated that Fermanagh alone has the potential to yield up to 2.2 trillion cubic feet of shale gas, which could satisfy Northern Ireland's electricity needs for up to 50 years, but in late 2014 the Northern Ireland Executive put a stop to the drilling for environmental reasons, including concerns about air pollution and the contamination of underground water reserves. Tamboran appealed the decision in 2015. In the Republic, the government commissioned the Environmental Protection Agency (EPA) to study the issue: their report will be finalised in 2016.

NATIONAL NATURE RESERVES

There are 66 state-owned and 10 privately owned National Nature Reserves (NNRs) in the Republic, represented by the **National Parks & Wildlife Service** (www.npws.ie), which are defined as areas of importance for their special flora, fauna or geology. Northern Ireland has more than 45 NNRs which are leased or owned by the Department of the Environment. These include the Giant's Causeway and Glenariff in Antrim, and North Strangford Lough in County Down. More information is available from the **Northern Ireland Environment Agency** (www.ni-environment.gov.uk).

funding for major infrastructure investments in renewable technology such as wind farms or the manufacture of solar panels.

On a more practical level, a number of recycling programs have been very successful, especially the 'plastax' – a €0.24 levy on all plastic bags used within the retail sector, which has seen their use reduced by a whopping 90%.

While this is a positive sign, it doesn't really put Ireland at the vanguard of the environmental movement. Polls seem to indicate the Irish are slightly less concerned about the environment than are the citizens of most other European countries, and the country is a long way from meeting its Kyoto Protocol requirement for reduced emissions. The government isn't pushing the environmental agenda much beyond ratifying EU agreements, although it must be said that these have established fairly ambitious goals for reduced air pollution and tighter management of water quality.

Ireland's National Parks

- Burren
- Connemara
- Glenveagh
- Killarney
- Wicklow Mountains
- Ballycroy

Sustainable Tourism

The annual number of tourists in Ireland far exceeds the number of residents (by a ratio of about 1.5 to one), so visitors can have a huge impact on the local environment. Tourism is frequently cited as potentially beneficial to the environment – that is, responsible visitor spending can help stimulate ecofriendly sectors of the economy. Ecotourism is not really burgeoning in a formalised way, although EcoTourism Ireland is charged with maintaining standards for ecotourism on the island and promotes tour companies that comply with these standards. The rising popularity of outdoor activities such as diving, surfing and fishing creates economic incentives for maintaining the cleanliness of Ireland's coasts and inland waters, but increased activity in these environments can be harmful if not managed carefully.

Ireland's comprehensive and efficient bus network makes it easy to avoid the use of a car, and the country is well suited to cycling and walking holidays. Many hotels, guesthouses and hostels tout green credentials, and organic ingredients are frequently promoted on restaurant menus. It's not difficult for visitors to minimise their environmental footprint while in Ireland.

Sporting Ireland

For many Irish, sport is akin to religion. For some it's all about faith through good works such as jogging, cycling and organised team sports. For everybody else, observance is enough, especially from the living room couch or the pub stool, where the mixed fortunes of their favourite teams are followed with elevated hope and vocalised despair.

Gaelic Football & Hurling

Every county capital has a stadium where counties play representative Gaelic football and hurling matches. The league and championship seasons run roughly from February to late September and tickets for all but the biggest matches (usually at Dublin's Croke Park) are easy to get; see www.gaa.ie for schedules.

Gaelic games are at the core of Irishness; they are enmeshed in the fabric of Irish life and hold a unique place in the heart of its culture. Their resurgence towards the end of the 19th century was entwined with the whole Gaelic revival and the march towards Irish independence. The beating heart of Gaelic sports is the **Gaelic Athletic Association** (GAA; www.gaa.ie), set up in 1884 'for the preservation and cultivation of National pastimes'. The GAA is still responsible for fostering these amateur games. It warms our hearts to see that after all this time – and amid the onslaught of globalisation and the general commercialisation of sport – they are still far and away the most popular sports in Ireland.

Gaelic games are fast, furious and not for the faint-hearted. Challenges are fierce, and contact between players is extremely aggressive. Both sports are county-based games. The dream of every club player is to represent his county, with the hope of perhaps playing in an All-Ireland final in September at Croke Park in Dublin, the climax of a knockout championship that is played first at a provincial and then interprovincial level.

Football

There is huge support in Ireland for the 'world game', although fans are much more enthusiastic about the likes of Manchester United, Liverpool and the two Glasgow clubs (Rangers and Celtic) than the struggling pros and part-timers who make up the National League (www.fai.ie) in the Republic and the Irish League (www.irishfa.com) in Northern Ireland. It's just too difficult for domestic teams to compete with the multimillionaire glitz and glamour of the English Premiership, which has always drawn off the cream of Irish talent.

At an international level, the Republic and Northern Ireland field separate teams but both struggle to qualify for major tournaments. It's all a far cry from their respective moments of glory – the 1980s for Northern Ireland and 1988 to 2002 for the Republic.

YOU SAY SOCCER, I SAY FOOTBALL

To distinguish it from Gaelic football, you'll often hear football referred to as 'soccer' – especially in Gaelic strongholds whereby doing so implies scorn on so-called 'garrison sports' – which will allay American confusion but only irritate the Brits. But Irish fans of Association Football (the official name of the sport) will always call it football and the other, Gaelic football or, in Dublin, 'gah' – which is just the pronunciation of the letters GAA (Gaelic Athletic Association).

RULES OF THE GAMES

Both Gaelic football and hurling are played by two teams of 15 players whose aim is to get the ball through what resembles a rugby goal: two long vertical posts joined by a horizontal bar, below which is a soccer-style goal, protected by a goalkeeper. Goals (below the crossbar) are worth three points, whereas a ball placed over the bar between the posts is worth one point. Scores are shown thus: 1-12, meaning one goal and 12 points, giving a total of 15 points.

Gaelic football is played with a round, soccer-size ball, and players are allowed to kick it or hand-pass it, like Australian Rules. Hurling, which is considered by far the more beautiful game, is played with a flat stick or bat known as a hurley or *camán*. The small leather ball, called a *slíothar,* is hit or carried on the hurley; handpassing is also allowed. Both games are played over 70 action-filled minutes.

In order to avoid competing (and losing) with the more popular English Premier League, whose season runs from mid-August to mid-May, the League of Ireland runs its season from April to November, the only European league to do so. Northern Ireland's Irish League still follows the British winter timetable.

Rugby

Although traditionally the preserve of Ireland's middle classes, rugby captures the mood of the whole island in February and March during the annual Six Nations Championships, because the Irish team is drawn from both sides of the border and is supported by both Nationalists and Unionists. In recognition of this, the Irish national anthem is no longer played at internationals, and is replaced by the thoroughly inoffensive '*Ireland's Call*', a song written especially for the purpose. In recent years, Ireland has been very successful, winning the championship in 2015 for the second year in a row. In 2014 the Irish women's rugby team also won the championship, the first time Ireland ever did the double.

At a provincial level, Leinster and Munster are major players on the European stage, having won the Heineken Cup (renamed the European Champions Cup in 2014) three times and twice respectively; Ulster are just a step behind with one win.

Most counties are good at one Gaelic sport and not the other. Kilkenny, Waterford, Clare and Tipperary are traditionally hurling counties; Kerry, Meath, Mayo and all nine Ulster counties are better at football. Cork, Galway, Offaly, Wexford and Dublin have the privilege of being good at both sports.

Golf

Scotland may be the home of golf, but Ireland is where golf goes on holiday. The Scots have some fine courses, it's true – but Ireland has its own names that can hold their own with the very best in the world.

With over 400 courses to choose from, there's no shortage of choice when it comes to teeing it up. These include a host of parkland (or inland) courses – worth checking out are the wonderful, American-style resort courses built over the last couple of decades, with immaculate, lawnlike fairways, white sand bunkers and strategically placed water features ready to swallow the chunkily hit ball.

But the essence of Irish golf is to be found on seaside links, dotted in a spectacular string of scenery along virtually the entire coastline. Here, nature provides the perfect raw material, and the very best of them are not quite built into the landscape as found within it, much like Michelangelo 'found' his figures hiding in the blocks of marble.

Finally, a word about the Irish golfer. Clubhouse snobs and high-handicap etiquette junkies aside, the real Irish golfer is the man or woman who puts their shoes on in the car park and can't wait to tee it up on the first; they know all the safe spots to land the ball and see it as their duty to share local knowledge. If you land up in the club on your own and they're doing a little putting practice before heading out, they're the ones who will offer a twosome because it's just not right to play on your own. The Irish golfer is friendly, easygoing and always recognises that you will never win at golf, and that today's bad round is just for today and tomorrow will turn up something different. And they know that golf is played over 19 holes – sure what's the point of playing unless you can laugh about it all over a drink when the round is done?

Horse Racing & Greyhound Racing

A passion for horse racing is deeply entrenched in Irish life and comes without the snobbery of its English counterpart. If you fancy a flutter on the gee-gees you can watch racing from around Ireland and England on the TV in bookmakers shops every day. No money ever seems to change hands in the betting, however, and every Irish punter will tell you they 'broke even'.

Ireland has a reputation for producing world-class horses for racing and other equestrian events such as showjumping, also very popular albeit in a much less egalitarian kind of way. Major annual races include the Irish Grand National (Fairyhouse, April), Irish Derby (the Curragh, June) and Irish Leger (the Curragh, September). For more information on events, contact Horse Racing Ireland (www.hri.ie).

Traditionally the poor-man's punt, greyhound racing (colloquially, 'the dogs'), has been smartened up in recent years and partly turned into a corporate outing. It offers a cheaper, more accessible and more local alternative to horse racing. There are 20 tracks across the country, administered by the Irish Greyhound Board (www.igb.ie).

Road Bowling

Irish academic Dr Fintan Lane's book *Long Bullets: A History of Road Bowling in Ireland* traces the sport to the 17th century.

The object of this sport is to throw a cast-iron ball weighing approximately 800g along a public road (normally one with little traffic) for a designated distance, usually 1km or 2km, with speed, control and accuracy. The person who does it in the least number of throws is the winner. Participants traditionally bet during the game.

The ball is known as a bowl or bullet. A shot is a throw and a kitterpaw is a left-handed thrower. If you hear someone talking about their butt, they are referring to the throwing mark on the road. Breaking butt means someone has stepped over the mark before releasing the ball. *Faugh an Bheallach* is a traditional Irish battle cry and means you should get out of the way. A sop is a tuft of grass placed where the bowl should first strike the road and a score is a match.

The main centre for road bowling is Cork, which has 200 clubs, and, to a lesser extent, Armagh. Competitions take place throughout the year, attracting considerable crowds. The sport has been taken up in various countries around the world, including the US, UK, Germany and the Netherlands, and a world championship competition has been set up (see www.irishroadbowling.ie). In Ireland the sport is governed by the Irish Road Bowling Association.

Survival Guide

Directory A–Z

Accommodation

Accommodation options range from bare and basic to pricey and palatial. The spine of the Irish hospitality business is the ubiquitous B&B, in recent years challenged by a plethora of midrange hotels and guesthouses. Beyond Expedia, Booking.com, Trivago and other hotel price comparison sites, Ireland-specific online resources for accommodation include the following:

www.daft.ie Online classified paper for short- and long-term rentals.

www.elegant.ie Specialises in self-catering castles, period houses and unique properties.

www.familyhomes.ie Lists family-run guesthouses and self-catering properties.

www.imagineireland.com Modern cottage rentals throughout the whole island, including Northern Ireland.

www.irishlandmark.com Not-for-profit conservation group that rents self-catering properties of historical and cultural significance, such as castles, tower houses, gate lodges, schoolhouses and lighthouses.

www.stayinireland.com Lists guesthouses and self-catering options.

B&Bs & Guesthouses

Bed and breakfasts are small, family-run houses, farmhouses and period country houses with fewer than five bedrooms. Standards vary enormously, but most have some bedrooms with private bathroom at a cost of roughly €35 to €40 (£25 to £30) per person per night. In luxurious B&Bs, expect to pay €55 (£40) or more per person. Off-season rates – usually October through to March – are usually lower, as are midweek prices.

Guesthouses are like upmarket B&Bs, but bigger – the Irish equivalent of a boutique hotel. Facilities are usually better and sometimes include a restaurant.

Other tips:

- Facilities in B&Bs range from basic (bed, bathroom, kettle, TV) to beatific (whirlpool baths, rainforest showers) as you go up in price. Wi-fi is standard and most have parking (but check).
- Most B&Bs take credit cards, but the occasional rural one might not have facilities; check when you book.
- Advance reservations are strongly recommended, especially in peak season (June to September).
- Some B&Bs and guesthouses in more remote regions only operate from Easter to September or other months.
- If full, B&B owners may recommend another house in the area (possibly a private house taking occasional guests, not in tourist listings).
- To make prices more competitive at some B&Bs, breakfast may be optional.

Camping, Caravan Parks & Canals

Camping and caravan parks aren't as common in Ireland as they are elsewhere in Europe. Some hostels have camping space for tents and also offer house facilities, which makes them better value than the main camping grounds. At commercial parks the cost is typically somewhere between €12 and €20 (£8 to £14) for a tent and two people. Prices given for campsites are for two people unless stated otherwise. Caravan sites cost around €15 to €25 (£10 to

BOOK YOUR STAY ONLINE

For more accommodation reviews by Lonely Planet authors, check out lonelyplanet.com/hotels. You'll find independent reviews, as well as recommendations on the best places to stay. Best of all, you can book online.

£18). Most parks are open only from Easter to the end of September or October.

An alternative to normal caravanning is to hire a horse-drawn caravan with which to wander the countryside. In high season you can hire one for around €800 a week. Search Fáilte Ireland's www.discoverireland.ie for a list of operators, or see www.irishhorsedrawncaravans.com.

Another unhurried and pleasurable way to see the countryside (with slightly less maintenance) is by barge on one of the country's canal systems. Contact Fáilte Ireland for a list of rental companies.

Yet another option is to hire a boat, which you can live aboard while cruising Ireland's inland waterways. One company offering boats for hire on the Shannon–Erne Waterway is **Emerald Star** (071-962 0234; www.emeraldstar.ie).

Hostels

Prices quoted for hostel accommodation apply to those aged over 18. A high season dorm bed generally costs €10 to €25 (£7 to £18). Many hostels now have family and double rooms.

Relevant hostel associations include the following:

An Óige (www.anoige.ie) Hostelling International (HI) – associated national organisation with 26 hostels scattered around the Republic.

HINI (www.hini.org.uk) HI-associated organisation with five hostels in Northern Ireland.

Independent Holiday Hostels of Ireland (IHH; www.hostels-ireland.com) Fifty-five tourist-board approved hostels throughout all of Ireland.

Independent Hostel Owners of Ireland (IHO; www.independenthostelsireland.com) Independent hostelling association.

Hotels

Hotels range from the local pub to medieval castles. In most cases, you'll get a better rate than the one published if you book online or negotiate directly with the hotel, especially out of season. The explosion of bland midrange chain hotels (many Irish-owned) has proven to be a major challenge to the traditional B&Bs and guesthouses: they might not have the same personalised service, but their rooms are clean and their facilities generally quite good (although there may be a charge for wi-fi).

House Swapping

House swapping can be a popular and affordable way to visit a country and enjoy a real home away from home. There are several agencies in Ireland that, for an annual fee, facilitate international swaps. The fee pays for access to a website and a book giving house descriptions, photographs and the owner's details. After that, it's up to you to make arrangements. Use of the family car is sometimes included.

Homelink International House Exchange (www.homelink.ie) Home exchange service running for over 60 years.

Intervac International Holiday Service (www.intervac-homeexchange.com) Long-established, with agents in 45 nations worldwide.

Rental Accommodation

Self-catering accommodation is often rented on a weekly basis and usually means an apartment, house or cottage where you look after yourself. The rates vary from one region and season to another. **Fáilte Ireland** (Republic 1850 230 330, the UK 0800 039 7000; www.discoverireland.ie) publishes a guide for registered self-catering accommodation; you can check listings at its website.

Children

Families travelling the Emerald Isle should note the following:

- Children are not allowed in pubs after 9pm (10pm May to September).
- Car seats (around €50/£35 per week) are

A 'STANDARD' HOTEL RATE?

There is no such thing. Prices vary according to demand – or have different rates for online, phone or walk-in bookings. B&B rates are more consistent, but virtually every other accommodation will charge wildly different rates depending on the time of year, day, festival schedule and even your ability to do a little negotiating. The following price ranges have been used in our reviews of places to stay. Prices are all based on a double room with private bathroom in high season.

BUDGET	REPUBLIC	NORTHERN IRELAND
Budget (€/£)	<€80	<£50
Midrange (€€/££)	€80–180	£50–120
Top end (€€€/£££)	>€180	>£120

mandatory in rental cars for children aged nine months to four years.

➡ Baby-changing facilities can be found only in larger cities, and then only in large shopping centres.

Online Resources

For further general information check out the following:

www.lonelyplanet.com/family-travel Useful and extensive resource on travelling with children.

www.eumom.ie For pregnant women and parents with young children.

www.babygoes2.com Travel site with family-friendly accommodation worldwide.

Customs Regulations

Both the Republic of Ireland and Northern Ireland have a two-tier customs system: one for goods bought duty-free outside the European Union (EU), the other for goods bought in another EU country where tax and duty is paid. There is technically no limit to the amount of goods transportable within the EU, but customs will use certain guidelines to distinguish personal use from commercial purpose. Allowances are as follows:

Duty free For duty-free goods from outside the EU, limits include 200 cigarettes, 1L of spirits or 2L of wine, 60mL of perfume and 250mL of eau de toilette.

Tax and duty paid Amounts that officially constitute personal use include 3200 cigarettes (or 400 cigarillos, 200 cigars or 3kg of tobacco) and either 10L of spirits, 20L of fortified wine, 60L of sparkling wine, 90L of still wine or 110L of beer.

Climate

Belfast

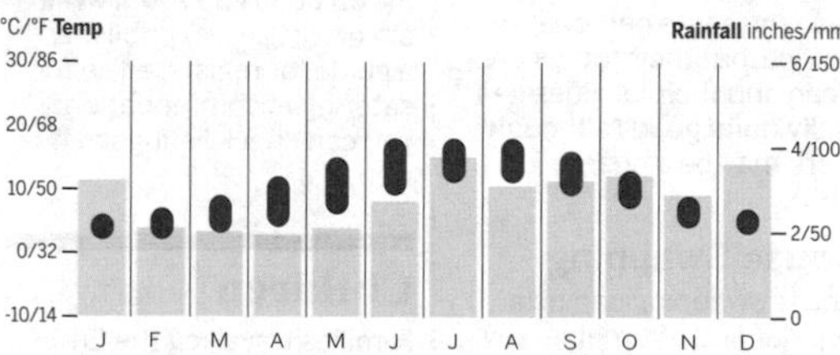

Dublin

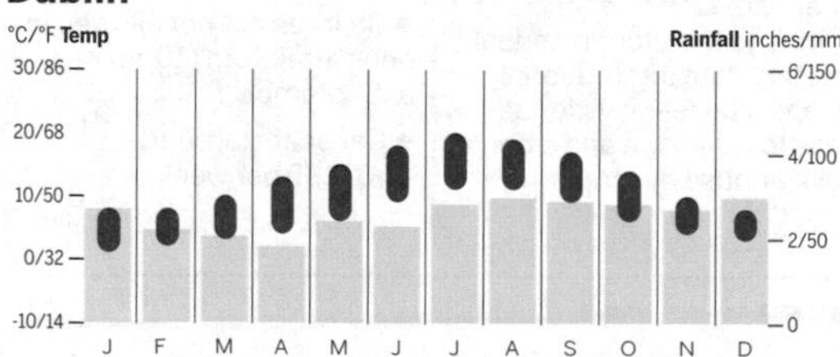

Galway

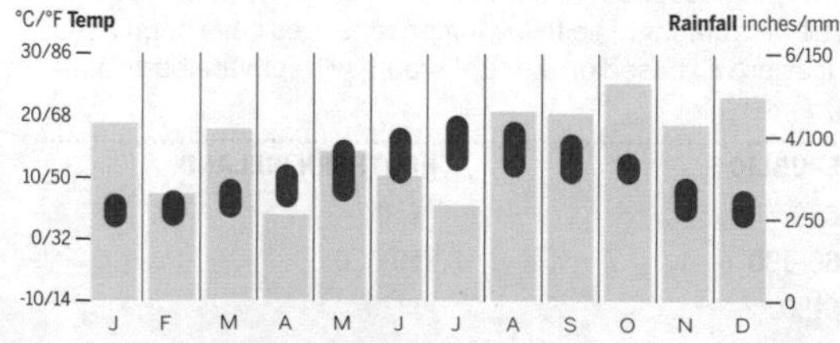

Cats & Dogs

Cats and dogs from anywhere outside Ireland and the UK are subject to strict quarantine laws. The EU Pet Travel Scheme, whereby animals are fitted with a micro chip, vaccinated against rabies and blood-tested six months *prior* to entry, is in force in the UK and the Republic of Ireland. No preparation or documentation is necessary for the movement of pets directly between the UK and the Republic. Contact the **Department of Agriculture, Food & Rural Development** (☎01-607 2000; www.agriculture.gov.ie) in Dublin for further details.

Electricity

Embassies & Consulates

This is a selection of embassies in Dublin and consular offices in Belfast. For a complete list, see the website of the **Department of Foreign Affairs** (www.dfa.ie), which also lists Ireland's diplomatic missions overseas.

Australian Embassy (☎01-664 5300; www.ireland.embassy.gov.au; 7th fl, Fitzwilton House, Wilton Tce, Dublin 2)

Canadian Embassy (☎01-234 4000; www.canada.ie; 7-8 Wilton Tce, Dublin 2)

Dutch Embassy (☎01-269 3444; www.netherlandsembassy.ie; 160 Merrion Rd, Ballsbridge, Dublin 4) Also a consulate (☎028-9077 9088; 14-16 West Bank Rd, c/o All-Route Shipping Ltd, Belfast) in Belfast.

French Embassy (☎01-277 5000; www.ambafrance-ie.org; 66 Fitzwilliam Ln, Dublin 2)

German Embassy (☎01-269 3011; www.dublin.diplo.de; 31 Trimleston Ave, Booterstown, Blackrock, County Dublin) Also a consulate (☎028-9024 4113; 22 Great Victoria St, Chamber of Commerce House, Belfast) in Belfast.

Italian Embassy (☎01-660 1744; www.ambdublino.esteri.it/Ambasciata_Dublino; 63-65 Northumberland Rd, Ballsbridge, Dublin 4)

UK Embassy (☎01-205 3700; www.gov.uk/government/world/organisations/british-embassy-dublin; 29 Merrion Rd, Ballsbridge, Dublin 4)

US Embassy (☎01-630 6200; http://dublin.usembassy.gov; 42 Elgin Rd, Ballsbridge, Dublin) Also a consulate (☎028-9038 6100; http://belfast.usconsulate.gov/embassy-info.html; Danesfort House, 223 Stranmillis Rd, Belfast) in Belfast.

Food

Our cafe and restaurant listings appear in budget order, with the cheapest budget range first. Within the ranges, listings are given in preference order.

Gay & Lesbian Travellers

Ireland is a pretty tolerant place for gays and lesbians. Bigger cities such as Dublin, Galway and Cork have well-established gay scenes, as does Belfast and Derry in Northern Ireland. In 2015, Ireland overwhelmingly backed same-sex marriage in a historic referendum. Nonetheless, you'll still find pockets of homophobia throughout the island, particularly in smaller towns and rural areas. Resources include the following:

Gaire (www.gaire.com) Message board and info for a host of gay-related issues.

Gay & Lesbian Youth Northern Ireland (www.cara-friend.org.uk/projects/glyni) Voluntary counseling, information, health and social space organisation for the gay community.

Gay Men's Health Project (☎01-660 2189; http://hse.ie/go/GMHS) Practical advice on men's health issues.

National Lesbian & Gay Federation (NLGF; ☎01-671 9076; http://nxf.ie) Publishes the monthly *Gay Community News* (http://theoutmost.com).

Northern Ireland Gay Rights Association (Nigra; ☎9066 5257; http://nigra.org.uk)

Outhouse (☎01-873 4932; www.outhouse.ie; 105 Capel St, Dublin; 🚌all city centre) Top gay, lesbian and bisexual resource centre. Great stop-off point to see what's on, check noticeboards and meet people. It publishes the free Ireland's *Pink Pages*, a directory of gay-centric services, which is also accessible on the website.

The Outmost (www.theoutmost.com) Excellent and resourceful for gay news, entertainment, lifestyle and opinion.

Health

No jabs are required to travel to Ireland. Excellent health care is readily available. For minor, self-limiting illnesses, pharmacists can give valuable advice and sell over-the-counter medication. They can also advise when more specialised help is required and point you in the right direction.

EU citizens equipped with a European Health Insurance Card (EHIC), available from health centres or, in the UK, post offices, will be covered for most medical care – but not nonemergencies or emergency repatriation. While other countries, such as Australia, also have reciprocal agreements with Ireland and Britain, many do not.

In Northern Ireland, everyone receives free emergency treatment at accident and emergency (A&E) departments of state-run NHS hospitals, irrespective of nationality.

Insurance

Insurance is important: it covers you for everything from medical expenses and luggage loss to cancellations

EATING PRICE RANGES

BUDGET	REPUBLIC	NORTHERN IRELAND
Budget (€/£)	<€12	<£12
Midrange (€€/££)	€12-25	£12-20
Top end (€€€/£££)	>€25	>£20

PRACTICALITIES

Currency Republic of Ireland: Euro (€); Northern Ireland: Pound Sterling (£).

Newspapers *Irish Independent* (www.independent.ie), *Irish Times* (www.irishtimes.com), *Irish Examiner* (www.examiner.ie), *Belfast Telegraph* (www.belfasttelegraph.co.uk).

Radio RTE Radio 1 (88-90 MHz), Today FM (100–103 MHz), Newstalk 106-108 (106-108 MHz), BBC Ulster (92–95 MHz; Northern Ireland only).

Weights & Measures Metric units; exception is for liquid measures of alcohol, where pints are used.

or delays in your travel arrangements, depending on your policy.

While EU citizens have most medical care covered with an EHIC card, an additional insurance policy for all other issues is recommended.

Worldwide travel insurance is available at www.lonelyplanet.com/travel-insurance. You can buy, extend and claim online at any time – even if you're already on the road.

All cars on public roads must be insured. If you are bringing your own vehicle, check that your insurance will cover you in Ireland.

Internet Access

If using a laptop, tablet, phablet or smartphone to get online, the vast majority of hotels, B&Bs, hostels, bars and restaurants offer wi-fi access, usually for free (though there may be a charge in a minority of hotels).

Internet cafes are increasingly disappearing. The survivors generally charge up to €6/£5 per hour.

Legal Matters

Illegal drugs are widely available, especially in clubs. The possession of small quantities of marijuana attracts a fine or warning, but harder drugs are treated more seriously. Public drunkenness is illegal but commonplace – the police will usually ignore it unless you're causing trouble.

Contact the following for assistance:

Legal Aid Board (☎066-947 1000; www.legalaidboard.ie) Has a network of local law centres.

Legal Services Agency Northern Ireland (☎028-9076 3000; www.dojni.gov.uk/legalservices) Administers the statutory legal aid scheme for Northern Ireland, but cannot offer legal advice.

Maps

Michelin's 1:400,000-scale Ireland map (No 923) is a decent single sheet map, with clear cartography and most of the island's scenic roads marked. The four maps – North, South, East and West – that make up the Ordnance Survey Holiday map series at 1:250,000 scale are useful for more detail.

The Ordnance Survey Discovery series covers the whole island in 89 maps at a scale of 1:50,000, also available as digital versions. These are all available through **Ordnance Survey Ireland** (www.osi.ie) and many bookshops around Ireland.

Collins also publishes a range of maps covering Ireland, also available at bookshops.

Money

The currency in the Republic of Ireland is the euro (€). The island's peculiar political history means that the six Ulster counties that make up Northern Ireland use the pound sterling (£). Although notes issued by Northern Irish banks are legal tender throughout the UK, many businesses outside of Northern Ireland refuse to accept them and you'll have to swap them in British banks.

ATMs

Usually called 'cash machines', ATMs are easy to find in cities and all but the smallest of towns. Watch out for ATMs that have been tampered with; card-reader scams (skimming) have become a real problem.

Credit & Debit Cards

Visa and MasterCard credit and debit cards are widely accepted in Ireland. American Express is only accepted by the major chains, and very few places accept Diners or JCB. Smaller businesses, such as pubs and some B&Bs, prefer debit cards (and will charge a fee for credit cards), and a small number of rural B&Bs only take cash.

Taxes & Refunds

Non-EU residents can claim Value Added Tax (VAT, a sales tax of 21% added to the purchase price of luxury goods – excluding books, children's clothing and educational items) back on their purchases, so long as the store operates either the Cashback or Taxback refund program (they should display a sticker). You'll get a voucher with your purchase that must be stamped at the *last point of exit* from the EU. If you're travelling on to Britain or mainland Europe from Ireland, hold on to your voucher until you pass through your final customs stop in the EU; it can then be stamped and you can post it back for a refund of duty paid.

VAT in Northern Ireland is 20%; shops participating in the Tax-Free Shopping refund scheme will give you a form or invoice on request to be presented to customs when you leave. After customs have certified the form, it will be returned to the shop for a refund and the cheque sent to you at home.

Tipping

You're not obliged to tip if the service or food was unsatisfactory (even if it's been automatically added to your bill as a 'service charge').

Hotels Only for bellhops who carry luggage, then €1/£1 per bag.

Pubs Not expected unless table service is provided, then €1/£1 for a round of drinks.

Restaurants 10% for decent service, up to 15% in more expensive places.

Taxis 10% or rounded up to the nearest euro/pound.

Toilet attendants €0.50/50p.

Opening Hours

Hours in both the Republic and Northern Ireland are roughly the same.

Banks 10am to 4pm Monday to Friday (to 5pm Thursday).

Offices 9am to 5pm Monday to Friday.

Post offices Northern Ireland 9am to 5.30pm Monday to Friday, 9am to 12.30pm Saturday; Republic 9am to 6pm Monday to Friday, 9am to 1pm Saturday. Smaller post offices may close at lunch and one day per week.

Pubs Northern Ireland 11.30am to 11pm Monday to Saturday, 12.30pm to 10pm Sunday. Pubs with late licences open until 1am Monday to Saturday and midnight Sunday; Republic 10.30am to 11.30pm Monday to Thursday, 10.30am to 12.30am Friday and Saturday, noon to 11pm Sunday (30 minutes of 'drinking up' time allowed). Pubs with bar extensions open to 2.30am Thursday to Saturday. All pubs close Christmas Day and Good Friday.

Restaurants Noon to 10.30pm in Dublin, till 9pm outside (aim to be seated by 8pm at the latest); many close one day of the week.

Shops 9am to 5.30pm or 6pm Monday to Saturday (until 8pm on Thursday & sometimes Friday), noon to 6pm Sunday (in bigger towns only). Shops in rural towns may close at lunch and one day per week.

Tourist offices 9am to 5pm Monday to Friday, 9am to 1pm Saturday. Many extend their hours in summer and open fewer hours/days or close from October to April.

Tourist sights Some sights only open from Easter through to September or October.

Photography

➡ Natural light can be very dull, so use higher ISO speeds than usual, such as 400 for daylight shots.

➡ In Northern Ireland, get permission before taking photos of fortified police stations, army posts or other military or quasi-military paraphernalia.

➡ Don't take photos of people in Protestant or Catholic strongholds of West Belfast without permission; always ask and be prepared to accept a refusal.

Public Holidays

Public holidays can cause road chaos as everyone tries to get somewhere else for the break. It's wise to book accommodation in advance for these times.

The following are public holidays in both the Republic and Northern Ireland:

New Year's Day 1 January

St Patrick's Day 17 March

Easter (Good Friday to Easter Monday inclusive) March/April

May Holiday 1st Monday in May

Christmas Day 25 December

St Stephen's Day (Boxing Day) 26 December

St Patrick's Day and St Stephen's Day holidays are taken on the following Monday when they fall on a weekend. In the Republic, nearly everywhere closes on Good Friday even though it isn't an official public holiday. In the North, most shops open on Good Friday, but close the following Tuesday.

Northern Ireland

Spring Bank Holiday Last Monday in May

Orangemen's Day 12 July

August Holiday Last Monday in August

Republic

June Holiday 1st Monday in June

August Holiday 1st Monday in August

October Holiday Last Monday in October

Safe Travel

Ireland is safer than most countries in Europe, but normal precautions should be observed.

Northern Ireland is as safe as anywhere else, but there are areas where the sectarian divide is bitterly pronounced, most notably in parts of Belfast. It's probably best to ensure your visit to Northern Ireland doesn't coincide with the climax of the Orange marching season on 12 July; sectarian passions are usually inflamed and even many Northerners leave the province at this time.

Telephone

Area codes in the Republic have three digits and begin with a 0, eg ☎021 for Cork, ☎091 for Galway and ☎061 for Limerick. The only exception is Dublin, which has a two-digit code (☎01). Always use the area code if calling from a mobile phone, but you don't need it if calling from a fixed-line number within the area code.

In Northern Ireland, the area code for all fixed-line numbers is ☎028, but you only need to use it if calling from a mobile phone or from outside Northern Ireland. To call Northern Ireland from the Republic, use ☎048 instead of ☎028, without the international dialling code.

Other codes:

- ☎1550 or ☎1580 – premium rate
- ☎1890 or ☎1850 – local or shared rate
- ☎0818 – calls at local rate, wherever you're dialling from within the Republic
- ☎1800 – free calls

Free-call and low-call numbers are not accessible from outside the Republic. Other tips:

- Prices are lower during evenings after 6pm and weekends.
- If you can find a public phone that works, local calls in the Republic cost €0.30 for around three minutes (around €0.60 to a mobile), regardless of when you call. From Northern Ireland local calls cost about 40p, or 60p to a mobile, although this varies somewhat.
- Prepaid phonecards can be purchased at both news agencies and post offices, and work from all payphones for both domestic and international calls.

Directory Enquiries

For directory enquiries, a number of agencies compete for your business.

- In the Republic, dial ☎11811 or 11850; for international enquiries it's ☎11818.
- In the North, call ☎118 118, 118 192, 118 500 or 118 811.
- Expect to pay at least €1/£1 from a land line and up to €2/£2 from a mobile phone.

International Calls

To call out from Ireland dial ☎00, then the country code (1 for USA, 61 Australia etc), the area code (you usually drop the initial zero) then the number. Ireland's international dialling code is ☎353, Northern Ireland's is ☎44.

Mobile Phone

- Ensure your mobile phone is unlocked for use in Ireland.
- Pay-as-you-go mobile phone packages with any of the main providers start at around €40 and usually include a basic handset and credit of around €10.
- SIM-only packages are also available, but make sure your phone is compatible with the local provider.

Time

In winter, Ireland is on Greenwich Mean Time (GMT), also known as Universal Time Coordinated (UTC), the same as Britain. In summer, the clock shifts to GMT plus one hour, so when it's noon in Dublin and London, it's 4am in Los Angeles and Vancouver, 7am in New York and Toronto, 1pm in Paris, 7pm in Singapore, and 9pm in Sydney.

Tourist Information

In both the Republic and the North there's a tourist office or information point in almost every big town; most offer a variety of services, including accommodation and attraction reservations, currency-changing services, map and guidebook sales, and free publications.

In the Republic, the tourism purview falls to **Fáilte Ireland** (☎Republic 1850 230 330, the UK 0800 039 7000; www.discoverireland.ie); in Northern Ireland, it's the **Northern Irish Tourist Board** (NITB; ☎head office 028-9023 1221; www.discovernorthernireland.com). Outside Ireland, Fáilte Ireland and the NITB unite under the banner **Tourism Ireland** (www.tourismireland.com).

See the individual destinations for the location of major tourist offices in Dublin, Cork, Donegal, Galway, Mullingar, Sligo and other towns.

Travellers with Disabilities

All new buildings have wheelchair access, and many hotels have installed lifts, ramps and other facilities. Others, especially B&Bs, have not adapted as successfully so you'll have far less choice. Fáilte Ireland's and NITB's accommodation guides indicate which places are wheelchair accessible.

In big cities, most buses have low-floor access and priority space on board, but the number of kneeling buses on regional routes is still relatively small.

Trains are accessible with help. In theory, if you call ahead, an employee of Irish Rail (Iarnród Éireann) will arrange to accompany you to the train. Newer trains have audio and visual information systems for visually impaired and hearing-impaired passengers.

The **Citizens' Information Board** (☎0761 079 000; www.citizensinformationboard.ie) in the Republic and **Disability Action** (☎028-9066 1252; www.disabilityaction.org) in Northern Ireland can give some advice to travellers with disabilities.

Visas

European Economic Area (EEA) nationals don't need a visa to visit (or work in) either the Republic or Northern Ireland. Citizens of Australia, Canada, New Zealand, South Africa and the US can visit the Republic for up to three months, and Northern Ireland for up to six months but are not allowed to work unless sponsored by an employer.

Full visa requirements for visiting the Republic are available online at www.dfa.ie; for Northern Ireland's visa requirements see www.gov.uk/government/organisations/uk-visas-and-immigration.

To stay longer in the Republic, contact the local *garda* (police) station or the **Garda National Immigration Bureau** (☎01-666 9100; www.garda.ie; 13-14 Burgh Quay, Dublin). To stay longer in Northern Ireland, contact the **Home Office** (UK Border Agency; www.gov.uk/government/organisations/uk-visas-and-immigration).

Women Travellers

Ireland should pose no problems for women travellers. Finding contraception is not the problem it once was, although anyone on the pill should bring adequate supplies.

Rape Crisis Network Ireland (☎091-563 676; www.rcni.ie) In the Republic. App available.

Nexus NI (☎028-9032 6803; Belfast; www.nexusni.org; ⏲8.30am-5pm Mon & Thu, 8.30am-8pm Tue & Wed, 9am-4pm Fri) Offers counselling and support to survivors of sexual abuse and victims of sexual violence and sexual assault. Offices in Belfast, Derry, Portadown and Enniskillen.

Work

EEA citizens are entitled to work legally in the Republic of Ireland and Northern Ireland. Non-EEA citizens with an Irish parent or grandparent are eligible for dual citizenship (and the right to work), although this procedure can be quite lengthy – enquire at an Irish embassy or consulate in your own country.

Full-time US students aged 18 and over can get a four-month work permit for Ireland, plus insurance and support information, through **Work & Travel Ireland** (☎01-602 1788; www.workandtravelireland.org).

Most Commonwealth citizens with a UK-born parent are entitled to work in the North (and the rest of the UK) through the 'Right of Abode'. Most Commonwealth citizens under 31 are eligible for a Working Holidaymaker Visa – valid for two years, it allows you to work for a total of 12 months and must be obtained in advance. Check with the **UK Border Agency** (UK Border Agency; www.gov.uk/government/organisations/uk-visas-and-immigration) for more info.

Transport

GETTING THERE & AWAY

Entering the Country

Dublin is the primary point of entry for most visitors to Ireland, although some do choose Shannon and Belfast.

➡ The overwhelming majority of airlines fly into Dublin.

➡ Dublin is home to two seaports that serve as the main points of sea transport with Britain; ferries from France arrive in the southern ports of Rosslare and Cork.

➡ Dublin is the nation's rail hub.

Flights, tours and rail transfers can be booked online at www.lonelyplanet.com/bookings.

Air

Airports

The main airports are:

Cork Airport (ORK; www.corkairport.com) Airlines servicing the airport include Aer Lingus and Ryanair.

Dublin Airport (DUB; www.dublinairport.com) Ireland's major international gateway airport, with direct flights from the UK, Europe, North America and the Middle East.

Shannon Airport (SNN; www.shannonairport.com) Has a few direct flights from the UK, Europe and North America.

Belfast International Airport (BFS; www.belfastairport.com) Has direct flights from the UK, Europe and North America.

Land

Eurolines (www.eurolines.com) has a daily coach and ferry service from London's Victoria Station to Dublin Busáras.

Sea

The main ferry routes between Ireland and the UK and mainland Europe:

➡ Belfast to Liverpool (England; eight hours)

➡ Belfast to Cairnryan (Scotland; 1¾ hours)

➡ Cork to Roscoff (France; 14 hours; April to October only)

➡ Dublin to Liverpool (England; fast/slow four/8½ hours)

➡ Dublin & Dun Laoghaire to Holyhead (Wales; fast/slow two hours/3½ hours)

➡ Larne to Cairnryan (Scotland; two hours)

➡ Larne to Troon (Scotland; two hours; March to October only)

➡ Larne to Fleetwood (England; six hours)

➡ Rosslare to Cherbourg/Roscoff (France; 18/20½ hours)

CLIMATE CHANGE & TRAVEL

Every form of transport that relies on carbon-based fuel generates CO_2, the main cause of human-induced climate change. Modern travel is dependent on aeroplanes, which might use less fuel per kilometre per person than most cars but travel much greater distances. The altitude at which aircraft emit gases (including CO_2) and particles also contributes to their climate change impact. Many websites offer 'carbon calculators' that allow people to estimate the carbon emissions generated by their journey and, for those who wish to do so, to offset the impact of the greenhouse gases emitted with contributions to portfolios of climate-friendly initiatives throughout the world. Lonely Planet offsets the carbon footprint of all staff and author travel.

Ferry Fast Boat Routes

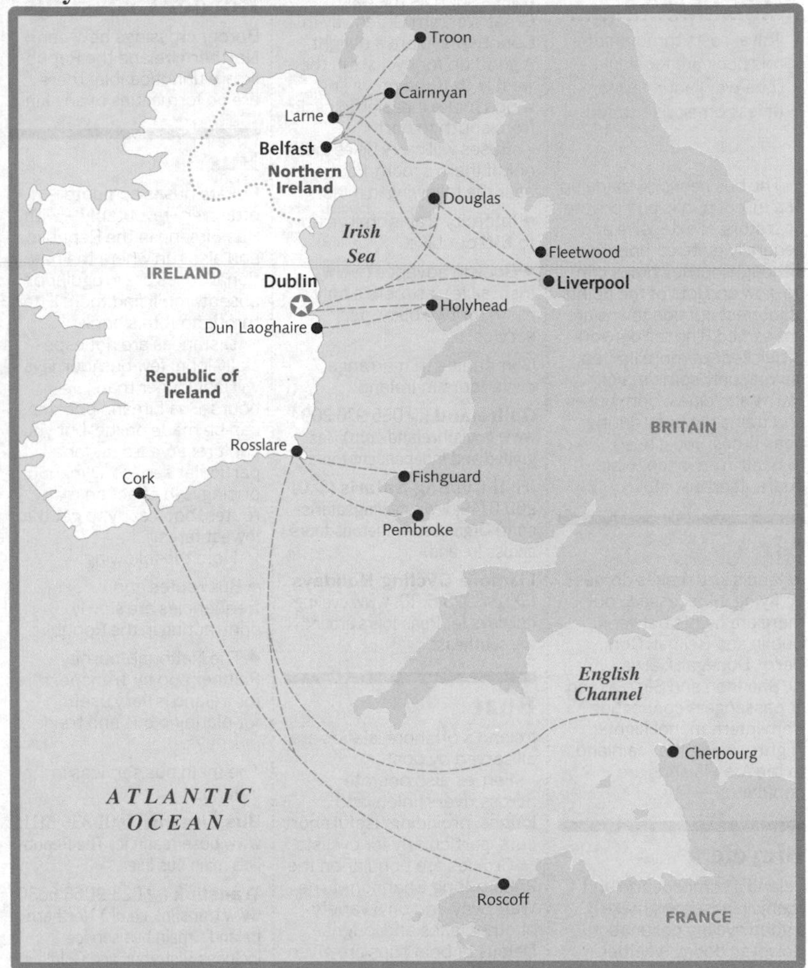

➡ Rosslare to Fishguard & Pembroke (Wales; 3½ hours)

Competition from budget airlines has forced ferry operators to discount heavily and offer flexible fares.

A useful website is www.ferrybooker.com, which covers all sea-ferry routes and operators to Ireland.

Main operators include the following:

Brittany Ferries (www.brittanyferries.com) Cork to Roscoff; April to October.

Irish Ferries (www.irishferries.com) It has Dublin–Holyhead ferries (up to four per day year-round); and France to Rosslare (three times per week).

P&O Ferries (www.poferries.com) Daily sailings year-round from Dublin to Liverpool, and Larne to Cairnryan. Larne to Troon runs March to October only.

Stena Line (www.stenaline.com) Daily sailings from Holyhead to Dublin Port, from Belfast to Liverpool and Cairnryan, and from Rosslare to Fishguard.

GETTING AROUND

The big decision in getting around Ireland is to go by car or use public transport. Your own car will make the best use of your time and help you reach even the most remote of places. It's usually easy to get very cheap rentals – €10 per day or less is common – and if two or more are travelling together, the fee for rental and petrol can be cheaper than bus fares.

FARE DETAILS

Travel costs throughout this book are for single (one-way) adult fares, unless otherwise stated.

The bus network, made up of a mix of public and private operators, is extensive and generally quite competitive – although journey times can be slow and lots of the points of interest outside towns are not served. The rail network is quicker but more limited, serving only some major towns and cities. Both buses and trains get busy during peak times; you'll need to book in advance to be guaranteed a seat.

Air

Ireland's size makes domestic flying unnecessary, but there are flights between Dublin and Belfast, Cork, Derry, Donegal, Galway, Kerry, Shannon and Sligo aimed at passengers connecting from international flights. Flights linking the mainland to the Aran Islands are popular.

Bicycle

Ireland's compact size and scenic landscapes make it a good cycling destination. However, dodgy weather, many very narrow roads and some very fast drivers are major concerns. Special tracks such as the 42km Great Western Greenway in County Mayo are a delight. A good tip for cyclists in the west is that the prevailing winds make it easier to cycle from south to north.

Buses will carry bikes, but only if there's room. For trains, bear the following in mind:

- Intercity trains charge up to €10 per bike.
- Book in advance (www.irishrail.ie), as there's only room for two bikes per service.

Companies that arrange cycle tours in Ireland:

Go Ireland (☎066-976 2094; www.govisitireland.com) Has guided and independent tours.

Irish Cycling Safaris (☎01-260 0749; www.cyclingsafaris.com) Organises numerous tours across Ireland.

Lismore Cycling Holidays (☎087-935 6610; www.cycling-holidays.ie) Runs tours around the southeast.

Boat

Ireland's offshore islands are all served by boat.

Ferries also operate across rivers, inlets and loughs, providing useful short cuts, particularly for cyclists.

Cruises are popular on the 258km-long Shannon–Erne Waterway and on a variety of other lakes and loughs. Details of boat trips are given under the relevant sections throughout this book.

BUS/TRAIN & FERRY COMBOS

It's possible to combine bus, ferry and train tickets from major UK centres to most Irish towns. This might not be as quick as flying on a budget airline but leaves less of a carbon footprint. The journey between London and Dublin takes about 12 hours by bus, eight hours by train; the London–Belfast trip takes 13 to 16 hours by bus. Both can be had for as little as £30 one-way. **Eurolines** (www.eurolines.com) has bus-ferry combos while **Virgin Trains** (www.virgintrains.co.uk) has combos that include London to Dublin. For more options, look for SailRail fares.

Border Crossings

Border crossings between Northern Ireland the Republic are unnoticeable; there are no formalities of any kind.

Bus

Private buses compete – often very favourably – with Bus Éireann in the Republic and also run where the national buses are irregular or absent. You'll find them listed throughout this book.

Distances are not especially long: few bus journeys will last longer than five hours. Bus Éireann bookings can be made online, but you can't reserve a seat for a particular service. Dynamic pricing is in effect on many routes: book early to get the lowest fares.

Note the following:

- Bus routes and frequencies are slowly contracting in the Republic.
- The National Journey Planner app by Transport for Ireland is very useful for planning bus and train journeys.

The main bus services in Ireland:

Bus Éireann (☎01-836 6111; www.buseireann.ie) The Republic's main bus line.

Translink (☎028-9066 6630; www.translink.co.uk) Northern Ireland's main bus service; includes Ulsterbus and Goldline.

Car & Motorcycle

Travelling by car or motorbike means greater flexibility and independence. The road system is extensive, and the network of motorways has cut driving times considerably. But also note that many secondary roads are very narrow and at times rather perilous.

Hire

Compared with many countries, hire rates are cheap in Ireland; you should find rates in advance for €10 to €20 per

ROAD DISTANCES (KM)

	Athlone	Belfast	Cork	Derry	Donegal	Dublin	Galway	Kilkenny	Killarney	Limerick	Rosslare Harbour	Shannon Airport	Sligo	Waterford
Belfast	242													
Cork	219	424												
Derry	209	117	428											
Donegal	183	180	402	69										
Dublin	127	167	256	237	233									
Galway	93	306	209	272	204	212								
Kilkenny	116	284	148	335	309	129	172							
Killarney	232	436	87	441	407	304	193	198						
Limerick	363	323	105	328	287	202	98	113	111					
Rosslare Harbour	201	330	208	397	391	153	274	98	275	211				
Shannon Airport	133	346	128	351	282	218	93	135	135	25	234			
Sligo	117	206	336	135	66	214	138	245	343	227	325	218		
Waterford	164	333	126	383	357	163	220	48	193	129	82	152	293	
Wexford	184	309	187	378	372	135	253	80	254	190	19	213	307	61

day for a small car (unlimited mileage). Shop around and use price comparison sites as well as company sites (which often have deals not available on booking sites).

Other tips:

➡ Most cars are manual; automatic cars are available, but they're much more expensive to hire.

➡ If you're travelling from the Republic into Northern Ireland, it's important to be sure that your insurance covers journeys to the North.

➡ The majority of hire companies won't rent you a car if you're under 23 and haven't had a valid driving license for at least a year.

Parking

All big towns and cities have covered and open short-stay car parks that are conveniently signposted.

➡ On-street parking is usually by 'pay and display' tickets available from on-street machines or disc parking (discs, which rotate to display the time you park your car, are usually provided by rental agencies). Costs range from €1.50 to €5 per hour; all-day parking in a car park will cost around €24.

➡ Yellow lines (single or double) along the edge of the road indicate restrictions. Double yellow lines mean no parking at any time. Always look for the nearby sign that spells out when you can and cannot park.

Roads & Rules

Ireland may be one of the few countries where the posted speed limits are often much faster than you'll find possible.

➡ Motorways (marked by M+number on a blue background): modern, divided highways.

➡ Primary roads (N+number on a green background in the Republic, A+number in Northern Ireland): usually well-engineered two-lane roads.

➡ Secondary and tertiary roads (marked as R+number in the Republic, B+number in Northern Ireland): Can be *very* narrow and winding.

➡ Tolls are charged on many motorways, usually by machine at a plaza. On the M50, pay the automated tolls between junctions 6 and 7 at www.eflow.ie.

➡ Directional signs are often not in evidence.

➡ GPS navigation via your smartphone or device is very helpful.

➡ EU licences are treated like Irish licences.

➡ Non-EU licences are valid in Ireland for up to 12 months.

➡ If you plan to bring a car from Europe, it's illegal to drive without at least third-party insurance.

The basic rules of the road:

➡ Drive on the left; overtake to the right.

➡ Safety belts must be worn by the driver and all passengers.

MOTORING ORGANISATIONS

The two main motoring organisations:

Automobile Association (AA; ☎NI breakdown 00 800 8877 6655, Republic breakdown 1800 66 77 88; www.theaa.ie)

Royal Automobile Club (RAC; ☎NI breakdown 0333 200 0999, Republic breakdown 0800 015 6000; www.rac.ie)

➡ Children aged under 12 aren't allowed to sit in the front passenger seat.

➡ When entering a roundabout, give way to the right.

➡ In the Republic, speed-limit and distance signs are in kilometres; in the North, speed-limit and distance signs are often in miles.

Speed limits:

Republic 120km/h on motorways, 100km/h on national roads, 80km/h on regional and local roads, and 50km/h or as signposted in towns.

Northern Ireland 70mph (112km/h) on motorways, 60mph (96km/h) on main roads, 30mph (48km/h) in built-up areas.

Drinking and driving is taken very seriously; in both the Republic and Northern Ireland you're allowed a maximum blood-alcohol level of 50mg/100mL (0.05%) in the Republic and 35mg/100mL (0.035%) in Northern Ireland.

Hitching

Hitching is becoming less popular in Ireland. Travellers who decide to hitch should understand that they are taking a small but potentially serious risk, and we don't recommend it. It's illegal to hitch on motorways.

Local Transport

Dublin and Belfast have comprehensive local bus networks, as do some other larger towns.

➡ The Dublin Area Rapid Transport (DART) rail line runs roughly the length of Dublin's coastline, while the Luas tram system has two popular lines.

➡ Taxis tend to be expensive: flagfall is daytime/nighttime €3.60/4 plus €1.10/1.40 per km after the first 500m.

➡ Uber is in Dublin and is expected to spread elsewhere.

Tours

Organised tours are a convenient way of exploring the country's main highlights if your time is limited. Tours can be booked through travel agencies, tourist offices, or through the tour companies. Some of the most reputable operators:

Bus Éireann (☎01-836 6111; www.buseireann.ie) Offers day trips from Dublin and Cork to popular destinations.

CIE Tours International (www.cietours.ie) Runs multiday bus tours of the Republic and the North.

Paddywagon Tours (☎01-823 0822; www.paddywagontours.com) Activity-filled tours all over Ireland.

Railtours Ireland (☎01-856 0045; www.railtoursireland.com) For train enthusiasts.

Taxi Tours Ireland (☎085-276 5991; www.taxitoursireland.ie) One- to 14-day custom tours with your own vehicle and driver.

Train

Given Ireland's relatively small size, train travel can be quick and advance-purchase fares are competitive with buses.

➡ Many of the Republic's most beautiful areas, such as whole swaths of the Wild Atlantic Way are not served by rail.

➡ Most lines radiate out from Dublin, with limited ways of interconnecting between lines, which can complicate touring.

➡ There are four routes from Belfast in Northern Ireland, one links with the system in

BUS & RAIL PASSES

There are a few bus-, rail- and bus-and-rail passes worth considering:

Irish Explorer Offers customers five days unlimited Irish Rail travel out of 15 consecutive days (adult/child €160/80).

Open Road Pass Three days travel out of six consecutive days (€60) on Bus Éireann; extra days cost €16.50.

Sunday Day Tracker One day's unlimited travel (adult/child £9/4.50) on Translink buses and trains in Northern Ireland, Sunday only.

Trekker Four Day Four consecutive days of unlimited travel (€110) on Irish Rail.

Note that Eurail one-country pass for Ireland is a bad deal in any of its permutations.

Train Routes

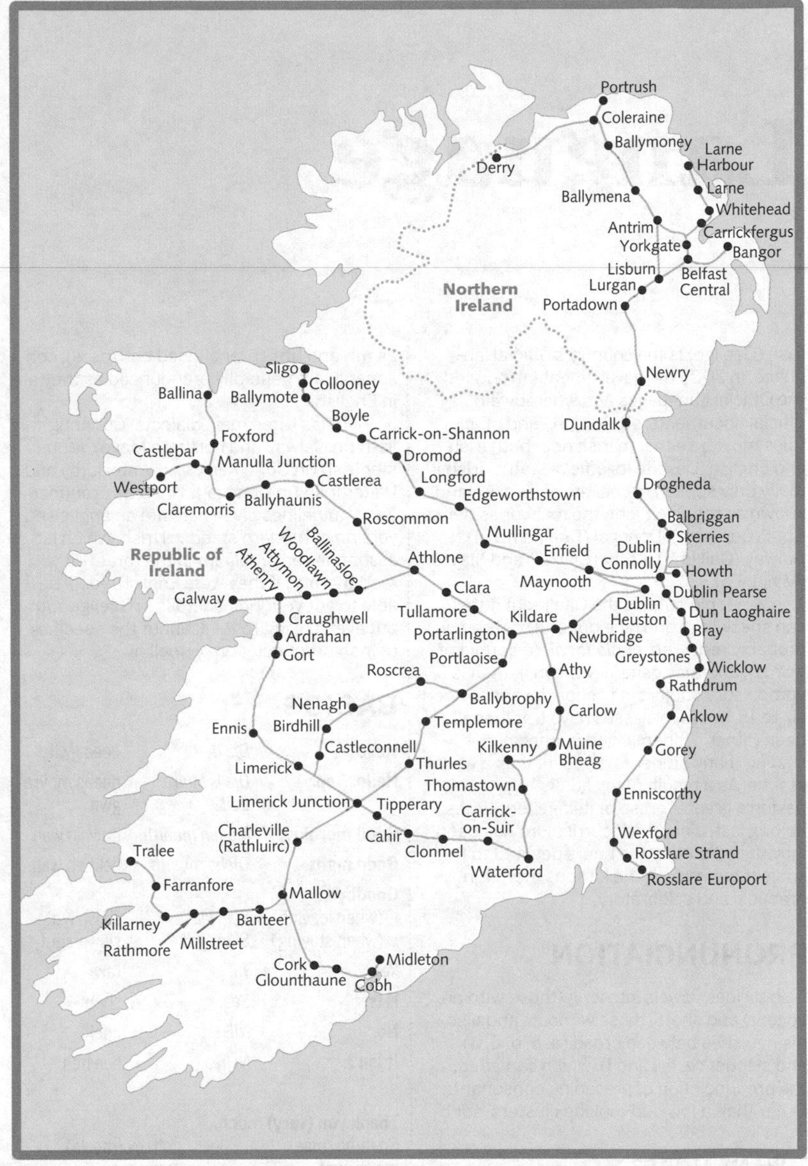

the Republic via Newry to Dublin.

➡ True 1st-class only exists on the Dublin–Cork and Dublin–Belfast lines. On all other trains, seats are the same size as in standard class, despite any marketing come-ons such as 'Premier' class.

Irish Rail (Iarnród Éireann; ☎1850 366 222; www.irishrail.ie) Operates trains in the Republic.

Translink NI Railways (☎028-9066 6630; www.translink.co.uk) Operates trains in Northern Ireland.

Language

Irish (Gaeilge) is the country's official language. In 2003 the government introduced the Official Languages Act, whereby all official documents, street signs and official titles must be either in Irish or in both Irish and English. Despite its official status, Irish is really only spoken in pockets of rural Ireland known as the Gaeltacht, the main ones being Cork (Corcaigh), Donegal (Dún na nGall), Galway (Gaillimh), Kerry (Ciarraí) and Mayo (Maigh Eo).

Ask people outside the Gaeltacht if they can speak Irish and nine out of 10 of them will probably reply, *'ah, cupla focal'* (a couple of words), and they generally mean it. Irish is a compulsory subject in schools for those aged six to 15, but Irish classes have traditionally been rather academic and unimaginative, leading many students to resent it as a waste of time. As a result, many adults regret not having a greater grasp of it. In recent times, at long last, a new Irish curriculum has been introduced cutting the hours devoted to the subject but making the lessons more fun, practical and celebratory.

PRONUNCIATION

Irish divides vowels into long (those with an accent) and short (those without) and also disinguishes between broad (**a**, **á**, **o**, **ó**, **u**) and slender (**e**, **é**, **i** and **í**), which can affect the pronunciation of preceding consonants. Other than a few odd-looking clusters, such as **mh** and **bhf** (pronounced both as w), consonants are generally pronounced as they are in English.

Irish has three main dialects: Connaught Irish (in Galway and northern Mayo), Munster Irish (in Cork, Kerry and Waterford) and Ulster Irish (in Donegal). The blue pronunciation guidelines given here are an anglicised version of modern standard Irish, which is essentially an amalgam of the three – if you read them as if they were English, you'll be able to get your point across in Gaeilge without even having to think about the specifics of Irish pronunciation or spelling.

WANT MORE?

For in-depth language information and handy phrases, check out Lonely Planet's *Irish Language & Culture*. You'll find it at **shop.lonelyplanet.com**, or you can buy Lonely Planet's iPhone phrasebooks at the Apple App Store.

BASICS

Hello.	*Dia duit.*	deea gwit
Hello. (reply)	*Dia is Muire duit.*	deeas moyra gwit
Good morning.	*Maidin mhaith.*	mawjin wah
Good night.	*Oíche mhaith.*	eekheh wah
Goodbye.		
(when leaving)	*Slán leat.*	slawn lyat
(when staying)	*Slán agat.*	slawn agut
Yes.	*Tá.*	taw
It is.	*Sea.*	sheh
No.	*Níl.*	neel
It isn't.	*Ní hea.*	nee heh

Thank you (very) much.
Go raibh (míle) maith agat. — goh rev (meela) mah agut

Excuse me.
Gabh mo leithscéal. — gamoh lesh scale

I'm sorry.
Tá brón orm. — taw brohn oruhm

I don't understand.
Ní thuigim. — nee higgim

Do you speak Irish?	
An bhfuil Gaeilge agat?	on wil gaylge oguht
What is this?	
Cad é seo?	kod ay shoh
What is that?	
Cad é sin?	kod ay shin
I'd like to go to...	
Ba mhaith liom dul go dtí...	baw wah lohm dull go dee...
I'd like to buy...	
Ba mhaith liom... a cheannach.	bah wah lohm... a kyanukh

another/ one more	*ceann eile*	kyawn ella
nice	*go deas*	goh dyass

MAKING CONVERSATION

Welcome.	
Ceád míle fáilte. (lit: 100,000 welcomes)	kade meela fawlcha
How are you?	
Conas a tá tú?	kunas aw taw too
..., (if you) please.	
...más é do thoil é.	...maws ay do hall ay
What's your name?	
Cad is ainm duit?	kod is anim dwit
My name is (Sean Frayne).	
(Sean Frayne) is ainm dom.	(shawn frain) is anim dohm

DAYS OF THE WEEK

Monday	*Dé Luaín*	day loon
Tuesday	*Dé Máirt*	day maart
Wednesday	*Dé Ceádaoin*	day kaydeen
Thursday	*Déardaoin*	daredeen
Friday	*Dé hAoine*	day heeneh
Saturday	*Dé Sathairn*	day sahern
Sunday	*Dé Domhnaigh*	day downick

Signs

Fir	fear	Men
Gardaí	gardee	Police
Leithreas	lehrass	Toilet
Mna	mnaw	Women
Oifig An Phoist	iffig ohn fwisht	Post office

CUPLA FOCAL

Here are a few phrases *os Gaeilge* (in Irish) to help you impress the locals:

Tóg é gobogé.
Take it easy.
tohg ay gobogay

Ní féidir é!
Impossible!
nee faydir ay

Ráiméis!
Nonsense!
rawmaysh

Go huafásach!
That's terrible!
guh hoofawsokh

Ní ólfaidh mé go brách arís!
I'm never ever drinking again!
knee ohlhee mey gu brawkh ureeshch

Slainte!
Your health!/Cheers!
slawncha

Táim go maith.
I'm fine.
thawm go mah

Nollaig shona!
Happy Christmas!
nuhlig hona

Cáisc shona!
Happy Easter!
kawshk hona

Go n-éirí an bóthar leat!
Bon voyage!
go nairee on bohhar lat

NUMBERS

1	*haon*	hayin
2	*dó*	doe
3	*trí*	tree
4	*ceathaír*	kahirr
5	*cúig*	kooig
6	*sé*	shay
7	*seacht*	shocked
8	*hocht*	hukt
9	*naoi*	nay
10	*deich*	jeh
11	*haon déag*	hayin jague
12	*dó dhéag*	doe yague
20	*fiche*	feekhe

GLOSSARY

12 July – the day the *Orange Order* marches to celebrate Protestant King William III's victory over the Catholic King James II at the Battle of the Boyne in 1690

An Óige – literally 'the Youth'; Republic of Ireland Youth Hostel Association
Anglo-Norman – Norman, English and Welsh peoples who invaded Ireland in the 12th century
Apprentice Boys – *Loyalist* organisation founded in 1814 to commemorate the Great Siege of Derry in August every year
ard – literally 'high'; Irish place name
Ascendancy – refers to the Protestant aristocracy descended from the Anglo-Normans and those who were installed here during the *Plantation*

bailey – outer wall of a castle
bawn – area surrounded by walls outside the main castle, acting as a defence and as a place to keep cattle in times of trouble
beehive hut – see *clochán*
Black & Tans – British recruits to the Royal Irish Constabulary shortly after WWI, noted for their brutality
Blarney Stone – sacred stone perched on top of Blarney Castle; bending over backwards to kiss the stone is said to bestow the gift of gab
bodhrán – hand-held goatskin drum
Bronze Age – earliest metalusing period, around 2500 BC to 300 BC in Ireland; after the Stone Age and before the *Iron Age*
B-Specials – Northern Irish auxiliary police force, disbanded in 1971
bullaun – stone with a depression, probably used as a mortar for grinding medicine or food, often found at monastic sites

caher – circular area enclosed by stone walls
cairn – mound of stones over a prehistoric grave
cashel – stone-walled *ring fort*; see also *ráth*
céilidh – session of traditional music and dancing; also called 'ceili'
Celtic Tiger – nickname of the Irish economy during the growth years from 1990 to about 2002
Celts – *Iron Age* warrior tribes that arrived in Ireland around 300 BC and controlled the country for 1000 years
chancel – eastern end of a church, where the altar is situated, reserved for the clergy and choir
chipper – slang term for fish-and-chips fast-food restaurant
cill – literally 'church'; Irish place name; also 'kill'
Claddagh ring – ring worn in much of *Connaught* since the mid-18th century, with a crowned heart nestling between two hands; if the heart points towards the hand then the wearer is partnered or married, if towards the fingertip he or she is looking for a mate
clochán – circular stone building, shaped like an oldfashioned beehive, from the early Christian period
Connaught – one of the four ancient provinces of Ireland, made up of Counties Galway, Leitrim, Mayo, Roscommon and Sligo; sometimes spelled 'Connacht'; see also *Leinster, Munster* and *Ulster*
craic – conversation, gossip, fun, good times; also known as 'crack'
crannóg – artificial island made in a lake to provide habitation in a good defensive position
currach – rowing boat made of a framework of laths covered with tarred canvas; also known as 'cúrach'

Dáil – lower house of the parliament of the Republic of Ireland; see also *Oireachtas* and *Seanad*
DART – Dublin Area Rapid Transport train line
demesne – landed property close to a house or castle
diamond – town square
dolmen – tomb chamber or portal tomb made of vertical stones topped by a huge capstone; from around 2000 BC
drumlin – rounded hill formed by retreating glaciers
Dúchas – government department in charge of parks, monuments and gardens in the Republic; formerly known as the Office of Public Works
dún – fort, usually constructed of stone
DUP – Democratic Unionist Party; founded principally by Ian Paisley in 1971 in hardline opposition to *Unionist* policies held by the *UUP*

Éire – Irish name for the Republic of Ireland
esker – raised ridge formed by glaciers

Fáilte Ireland – 'Welcome Board'; Irish Tourist Board
Fianna – mythical band of warriors who feature in many tales of ancient Ireland
Fianna Fáil – literally 'Warriors of Ireland'; a major political party in the Republic, originating from the *Sinn Féin* faction opposed to the 1921 treaty with Britain
Fine Gael – literally 'Tribe of the Gael'; a major political party in the Republic, originating from the *Sinn Féin* faction that favoured the 1921 treaty with Britain; formed the first government of independent Ireland
fir – men (singular 'fear'); sign on men's toilets; see also *leithreas* and *mná*
fleadh – festival

GAA – Gaelic Athletic Association; promotes Gaelic football and hurling, among other Irish games
Gaeltacht – Irish-speaking

gallóglí – mercenary soldiers of the 14th to 15th century; anglicised to 'gallowglasses'
garda – Irish Republic police; plural 'gardaí'
ghillie – fishing or hunting guide; also known as 'ghilly'
gort – literally 'field'; Irish place name

hill fort – a hilltop fortified with ramparts and ditches, usually dating from the *Iron Age*
HINI – Hostelling International of Northern Ireland
Hunger, the – colloquial name for the Great Famine of 1845–51
hurling – Irish sport similar to hockey

Iarnród Éireann – Republic of Ireland Railways
INLA – Irish National Liberation Association; formed in 1975 as an *IRA* splinter group; it has maintained a ceasefire since 1998
IRA – Irish Republican Army; the largest Republican paramilitary organisation, founded 80 years ago with the aim to fight for a united Ireland; in 1969 the IRA split into the Official IRA and the Provisional IRA; the Official IRA is no longer active and the PIRA has become the IRA
Iron Age – metal-using period that lasted from the end of the *Bronze Age,* around 300 BC (the arrival of the Celts), to the arrival of Christianity, around the 5th century AD

jarvey – driver of a *jaunting car*
jaunting car – Killarney's traditional horse-drawn transport; see also *jarvey*

Leinster – one of the four ancient provinces of Ireland, made up of Counties Carlow, Dublin, Kildare, Kilkenny, Laois, Longford, Louth, Meath, Offaly, West Meath, Wexford and Wicklow; see also *Connaught, Munster* and *Ulster*
leithreas – toilets; see also *mná* and *fir*
leprechaun – mischievous elf or sprite from Irish folklore
lough – lake, or long narrow bay or arm of the sea
Loyalist – person, usually a Northern Irish Protestant, insisting on the continuation of Northern Ireland's links with Britain
Luas – light-rail transit system in Dublin; Irish for 'speed'

marching season – *Orange Order* parades, which take place from Easter and throughout summer to celebrate the victory by Protestant King William III of Orange over Catholic James II in the Battle of the Boyne on 12 July 1690, and the union with Britain
Mesolithic – also known as the Middle Stone Age; time of the first human settlers in Ireland, about 8000 BC to 4000 BC; see also *Neolithic*
mná – women; sign on women's toilets; see also *fir* and *leithreas*
motte – early Norman fortification consisting of a raised, flattened mound with a keep on top; when attached to a *bailey* it is known as a motte-and-bailey fort, many of which were built in Ireland until the early 13th century
Munster – one of the four ancient provinces of Ireland, made up of Counties Clare, Cork, Kerry, Limerick, Tipperary and Waterford; see also *Connaught, Leinster* and *Ulster*

nationalism – belief in a reunited Ireland
Nationalist – proponent of a united Ireland
Neolithic – also known as the New Stone Age; a period characterised by settled agriculture lasting from around 4000 BC to 2500 BC in Ireland; followed by the *Bronze Age;* see also *Mesolithic*
NIR – Northern Ireland Railways
NITB – Northern Ireland Tourist Board
NNR – National Nature Reserves
North, the – political entity of Northern Ireland, not the northernmost geographic part of Ireland
NUI – National University of Ireland; made up of branches in Dublin, Cork, Galway and Limerick

Ogham stone – a stone etched with Ogham characters, the earliest form of writing in Ireland, with a variety of notched strokes
Oireachtas – Parliament of the Republic of Ireland, consisting of the *Dáil,* the lower house, and the *Seanad,* the upper house
Orange Order – the largest Protestant organisation in Northern Ireland, founded in 1795, with a membership of up to 100,000; name commemorates the victory of King William of Orange in the Battle of the Boyne
óstán – hotel

Palladian – style of architecture developed by Andrea Palladio (1508–80), based on ancient Roman architecture
paramilitaries – armed illegal organisations, either *Loyalist* or *Republican,* usually associated with the use of violence and crime for political and economic gain
partition – division of Ireland in 1921
passage grave – Celtic tomb with a chamber reached by a narrow passage, typically buried in a mound
penal laws – laws passed in the 18th century forbidding Catholics from buying land and holding public office
Plantation – settlement of Protestant immigrants (known as Planters) in Ireland in the 17th century
poitín – illegally brewed whiskey, also spelled 'poteen'
provisionals – Provisional IRA, formed after a break with the official *IRA* (who are now largely inconsequential); named after the provisional government declared in 1916, they have been the main force combating the British army in *the North;* also known as 'provos'
PSNI – Police Service of Northern Ireland

ráth – *ring fort* with earthen banks around a timber wall; see also *cashel*

Real IRA – splinter movement of the *IRA*; opposed to *Sinn Féin's* support of the Good Friday Agreement; responsible for the Omagh bombing in 1998 in which 29 people died; subsequently called a ceasefire but has been responsible for bombs in Britain and other acts of violence

Republic of Ireland – the 26 counties of *the South*

Republican – supporter of a united Ireland

republicanism – belief in a united Ireland, sometimes referred to as militant nationalism

ring fort – circular habitation area surrounded by banks and ditches, used from the *Bronze Age* right through to the Middle Ages, particularly in the early Christian period

RTE – Radio Telifís Éireann; the national broadcasting service of the Republic of Ireland, with two TV and four radio stations

RUC – Royal Ulster Constabulary, the former name for the armed Police Service of Northern Ireland *(PSNI)*

Seanad – upper house of the parliament of the Republic of Ireland; see also *Oireachtas* and *Dáil*

shamrock – three-leafed plant said to have been used by St Patrick to illustrate the Holy Trinity

shebeen – from the Irish 'síbín'; illicit drinking place or speakeasy

sheila-na-gig – literally 'Sheila of the teats'; female figure with exaggerated genitalia, carved in stone on the exteriors of some churches and castles; explanations include male clerics warning against the perils of sex to the idea that they represent Celtic war goddesses

Sinn Féin – literally 'We Ourselves'; a *Republican* party with the aim of a united Ireland; seen as the political wing of the *IRA* but it maintains that both organisations are completely separate

slí – hiking trail or way

snug – partitioned-off drinking area in a pub

souterrain – underground chamber usually associated with *ring* and *hill forts;* probably provided a hiding place or escape route in times of trouble and/or storage space for goods

South, the – Republic of Ireland

standing stone – upright stone set in the ground, common across Ireland and dating from a variety of periods; some are burial markers

Taoiseach – Republic of Ireland prime minister

teampall – church

trá – beach or strand

Treaty – Anglo-Irish Treaty of 1921, which divided Ireland and gave relative independence to the South; cause of the 1922–23 Civil War

tricolour – green, white and orange Irish flag symbolising the hoped-for union of the 'green' Catholic Southern Irish with the 'orange' Protestant Northern Irish

turlough – a small lake that often disappears in dry summers; from the Irish 'turlach'

UDA – Ulster Defence Association; the largest *Loyalist* paramilitary group; it has observed a ceasefire since 1994

uillean pipes – Irish bagpipes with a bellow strapped to the arm; 'uillean' is Irish for 'elbow'

Ulster – one of the four ancient provinces of Ireland; sometimes used to describe the six counties of *the North,* despite the fact that Ulster also includes Counties Cavan, Monaghan and Donegal (all in the Republic); see also *Connaught, Leinster* and *Munster*

Unionist – person who wants to retain Northern Ireland's links with Britain

United Irishmen – organisation founded in 1791 aiming to reduce British power in Ireland; it led a series of unsuccessful risings and invasions

UUP – Ulster Unionist Party; the largest *Unionist* party in Northern Ireland and the majority party in the Assembly; founded in 1905 and led by *Unionist* hero Edward Carson from 1910 to 1921; from 1921 to 1972 the sole *Unionist* organisation but is now under threat from the *DUP*

UVF – Ulster Volunteer Force; an illegal *Loyalist* Northern Irish paramilitary organisation

Volunteers – offshoot of the IRB that came to be known as the *IRA*

Behind the Scenes

SEND US YOUR FEEDBACK

We love to hear from travellers – your comments keep us on our toes and help make our books better. Our well-travelled team reads every word on what you loved or loathed about this book. Although we cannot reply individually to your submissions, we always guarantee that your feedback goes straight to the appropriate authors, in time for the next edition. Each person who sends us information is thanked in the next edition – the most useful submissions are rewarded with a selection of digital PDF chapters.

Visit **lonelyplanet.com/contact** to submit your updates and suggestions or to ask for help. Our award-winning website also features inspirational travel stories, news and discussions.

Note: We may edit, reproduce and incorporate your comments in Lonely Planet products such as guidebooks, websites and digital products, so let us know if you don't want your comments reproduced or your name acknowledged. For a copy of our privacy policy visit lonelyplanet.com/privacy.

OUR READERS

Many thanks to the travellers who used the last edition and wrote to us with helpful hints, useful advice and interesting anecdotes:

A Andrzej Januszewski, Annelise Bak **C** Chris Keegan, Colin Saunderson, Courtney Shucker **D** Denis O'Sullivan **J** Jack Clancy, Jacob Harris, Jane Barrett, Joe O'Brien, John Devitt, Joyce Taylor, Juliette Tirard-Collet **K** Karen Boss, Katrin Riegelnegg **L** Laura Teece, Lavin Graviss, Luc Tétreault **M** Marguerite Harber, Marilyn Helterline, Martin Coyle, Mic Porter, Michael Kischner, Michelle Coen, Miranda Keating **O** Orla Dolan **P** Paul Grayhurst **R** Robyn Spurdle, Ruth Yanor **S** Sam Dieterle, Samantha Corrigan **W** Wayne Harber

AUTHOR THANKS

Fionn Davenport

Thanks to my editor at Lonely Planet and all those who worked on the guide. A huge thanks to Laura, who's the best support team any guidebook author could hope for.

Damian Harper

Big thanks to Declan in Limerick, Gerard Madden, the reception staff at Rockwell College, Anthony Sheehy, Mike at the Hunt Museum, Steve Whitfield, Stevie Winder, Ann in Galway, the anonymous farmer who pointed the way to Knockgraffon Motte and all the truly delightful people I met on the road who brought sunshine to the wettest of Irish days. Thanks also, as always, to Daisy, Tim and Emma.

Catherine Le Nevez

Sláinte first and foremost to Julian, and to all of the locals, fellow travellers and tourism professionals en route for insights, information and great craic. Thanks especially to Victoria Moore at Translink, Gerry, Tricia, Inez and family in County Antrim, and Laura, Peter and all in Belfast. Huge thanks also to DE James Smart, Neil Wilson for Northern Ireland tips and everyone at LP. As ever, *merci encore* to my parents, brother, *belle-sœur* and *neveu*.

Ryan Ver Berkmoes

Like a conversation over nothing in particular in an Irish pub, thanks to those who helped me on this book threaten to go on and on and on... But a few: Charley Adley was a friend and muse as always; Angela Cullen introduced me to all things Donegal and turned me on to obscure author Mike Hunt; and golden thanks to my big plum in the Big Apple, Alexis.

Neil Wilson

Thanks to the friendly and helpful tourist office staff in Cork, Waterford, Wexford, Kilkenny and Killarney; to Sean at Glengarriff and to Moira and Hillary at Fleming's White Bridge in Killarney; to Cathal and Damian at Lough Hyne; and, as ever, to Carol Downie. Thanks also to James and the editorial team at Lonely Planet.

ACKNOWLEDGEMENTS

Climate map data adapted from Peel MC, Finlayson BL & McMahon TA (2007) 'Updated World Map of the Köppen-Geiger Climate Classification', *Hydrology and Earth System Sciences*, 11, 1633–44.

Illustrations pp68-9, pp142-3 by Javier Zarracina; pp312-13 by Michael Weldon.

Cover photograph: Carrick-a-Rede Rope Bridge, Causeway Coast Chris Hill/Alamy.

THIS BOOK

This 12th edition of Lonely Planet's *Ireland* guidebook was researched and written by Fionn Davenport, Damian Harper, Catherine Le Nevez, Ryan Ver Berkmoes and Neil Wilson. This guidebook was produced by the following:

Destination Editor James Smart **Product Editors** Kate Chapman, Bruce Evans **Regional Senior Cartographer** Mark Griffiths **Book Designer** Wendy Wright **Assisting Editors** Carolyn Bain, Imogen Bannister, Bridget Blair, Kate Evans, Sam Forge, Helen Koehne, Kellie Langdon, Rosie Nicholson, Erin Richards

Assisting Cartographer Rachel Imeson **Assisting Book Designer** Virginia Moreno **Cover Researcher** Naomi Parker **Thanks to** Gemma Graham, Andi Jones, Elizabeth Jones, Kate Kiely, Claire Naylor, Karyn Noble, Alison Ridgway, Kathryn Rowan, Vicky Smith, Lauren Wellicome, Tony Wheeler, Tracy Whitmey

Index

C

Map Pages **000**
Photo Pages **000**

Map Pages **000**
Photo Pages **000**

G

H

Map Pages **000**
Photo Pages **000**

N

O

P

Map Pages **000**
Photo Pages **000**

Q

R

Map Pages **000**
Photo Pages **000**

Map Legend

Sights
- Beach
- Bird Sanctuary
- Buddhist
- Castle/Palace
- Christian
- Confucian
- Hindu
- Islamic
- Jain
- Jewish
- Monument
- Museum/Gallery/Historic Building
- Ruin
- Shinto
- Sikh
- Taoist
- Winery/Vineyard
- Zoo/Wildlife Sanctuary
- Other Sight

Activities, Courses & Tours
- Bodysurfing
- Diving
- Canoeing/Kayaking
- Course/Tour
- Sento Hot Baths/Onsen
- Skiing
- Snorkelling
- Surfing
- Swimming/Pool
- Walking
- Windsurfing
- Other Activity

Sleeping
- Sleeping
- Camping

Eating
- Eating

Drinking & Nightlife
- Drinking & Nightlife
- Cafe

Entertainment
- Entertainment

Shopping
- Shopping

Information
- Bank
- Embassy/Consulate
- Hospital/Medical
- Internet
- Police
- Post Office
- Telephone
- Toilet
- Tourist Information
- Other Information

Geographic
- Beach
- Gate
- Hut/Shelter
- Lighthouse
- Lookout
- Mountain/Volcano
- Oasis
- Park
- Pass
- Picnic Area
- Waterfall

Population
- Capital (National)
- Capital (State/Province)
- City/Large Town
- Town/Village

Transport
- Airport
- Border crossing
- Bus
- Cable car/Funicular
- Cycling
- Ferry
- Metro station
- Monorail
- Parking
- Petrol station
- S-Bahn/Subway station
- Taxi
- T-bane/Tunnelbana station
- Train station/Railway
- Tram
- Tube station
- U-Bahn/Underground station
- Other Transport

Note: Not all symbols displayed above appear on the maps in this book

Routes
- Tollway
- Freeway
- Primary
- Secondary
- Tertiary
- Lane
- Unsealed road
- Road under construction
- Plaza/Mall
- Steps
- Tunnel
- Pedestrian overpass
- Walking Tour
- Walking Tour detour
- Path/Walking Trail

Boundaries
- International
- State/Province
- Disputed
- Regional/Suburb
- Marine Park
- Cliff
- Wall

Hydrography
- River, Creek
- Intermittent River
- Canal
- Water
- Dry/Salt/Intermittent Lake
- Reef

Areas
- Airport/Runway
- Beach/Desert
- Cemetery (Christian)
- Cemetery (Other)
- Glacier
- Mudflat
- Park/Forest
- Sight (Building)
- Sportsground
- Swamp/Mangrove

Neil Wilson

Counties Wexford, Waterford, Carlow & Kilkenny; County Cork; County Kerry

Neil's first visit to Ireland was on a sailing trip to Kinsale in 1990. Since then he has travelled most of the Republic and all of Northern Ireland, often while researching for Lonely Planet guidebooks. Working on this edition allowed him to hike the main ridge of MacGillicuddy's Reeks, cycle to the top of Priest's Leap, and eat far too much farmhouse cheese in West Cork (mmm, Gubbeen...). Neil is a full-time travel writer based in Scotland, and has written more than 70 guidebooks for half a dozen publishers. Neil also wrote the Great Outdoors chapter.

OUR STORY

A beat-up old car, a few dollars in the pocket and a sense of adventure. In 1972 that's all Tony and Maureen Wheeler needed for the trip of a lifetime – across Europe and Asia overland to Australia. It took several months, and at the end – broke but inspired – they sat at their kitchen table writing and stapling together their first travel guide, *Across Asia on the Cheap*. Within a week they'd sold 1500 copies. Lonely Planet was born.

Today, Lonely Planet has offices in Franklin, London, Melbourne, Oakland, Beijing and Delhi, with more than 600 staff and writers. We share Tony's belief that 'a great guidebook should do three things: inform, educate and amuse'.

OUR WRITERS

Fionn Davenport
Dublin; Counties Wicklow & Kildare Irish-born and raised, Fionn has been writing about his native country for close to two decades and is constantly surprised by its ability to surprise him. From his home in Dublin he's struck out to find the best new attractions and distractions, restaurants, cafes and hotels. It's a dirty job but he's happy to do it. You'll also find his work in the travel section of the *Irish Times*. Fionn also wrote the Welcome to, Ireland's Top 21, Need to Know, First Time, What's New, If You Like, Month by Month, Itineraries, Eat & Drink Like a Local, The Wild Atlantic Way, Regions at a Glance, and the Understand chapters.

Damian Harper
Counties Limerick & Tipperary; County Clare; County Galway A Lonely Planet author for almost two decades, Damian first visited Ireland when he worked for a year in Dublin as a bookseller at Waterstones' first international branch on Dawson St. With two university degrees, Damian has contributed to a host of Lonely Planet titles from *London* to *Shanghai*, *Vietnam* and *England*, and seized the opportunity to explore the astonishingly beautiful west coast of Ireland. Damian also wrote the Directory chapter.

Catherine Le Nevez
Counties Meath, Louth, Cavan & Monaghan; Belfast; Counties Down & Armagh; Counties Londonderry & Antrim Catherine's wanderlust kicked in when she road-tripped across Europe aged four and she's been hitting the road at every opportunity since, completing her Doctorate of Creative Arts in Writing, Masters in Professional Writing, and post-grad qualifications in Editing and Publishing along the way. Catherine's Celtic connections include Irish and Breton heritage, and a love of Guinness. She's travelled throughout every county in the Emerald Isle, and has covered the vast majority for Lonely Planet, including numerous editions of this guide.

Ryan Ver Berkmoes
Counties Mayo & Sligo; County Donegal; The Midlands; Counties Fermanagh & Tyrone From Malin Head to Durrow, with plenty of pleasures in between, Ryan Ver Berkmoes has delighted in great swaths of Ireland. He first visited Galway in 1985 when he remembers a grey place where the locals wandered the muddy tidal flats for fun and frolic. How things change! From lost rural pubs to lost memory, he's revelled in a place where his first name brings a smile and his surname brings a 'huh?' Ryan also wrote the Transport chapter.
Follow him at ryanverberkmoes.com; @ryanvb

OVER PAGE MORE WRITERS

Published by Lonely Planet Publications Pty Ltd
ABN 36 005 607 983
12th edition – March 2016
ISBN 978 1 74321 686 6

10 9 8 7 6 5 4 3
Printed in China